£35

1 MONTH OF FREE READING

at

www.ForgottenBooks.com

By purchasing this book you are eligible for one month membership to ForgottenBooks.com, giving you unlimited access to our entire collection of over 1,000,000 titles via our web site and mobile apps.

To claim your free month visit: www.forgottenbooks.com/free911750

* Offer is valid for 45 days from date of purchase. Terms and conditions apply.

ISBN 978-0-266-93218-5
PIBN 10911750

This book is a reproduction of an important historical work. Forgotten Books uses state-of-the-art technology to digitally reconstruct the work, preserving the original format whilst repairing imperfections present in the aged copy. In rare cases, an imperfection in the original, such as a blemish or missing page, may be replicated in our edition. We do, however, repair the vast majority of imperfections successfully; any imperfections that remain are intentionally left to preserve the state of such historical works.

Forgotten Books is a registered trademark of FB &c Ltd.
Copyright © 2018 FB &c Ltd.
FB &c Ltd, Dalton House, 60 Windsor Avenue, London, SW19 2RR.
Company number 08720141. Registered in England and Wales.

For support please visit www.forgottenbooks.com

NO-FAULT MOTOR VEHICLE INSURANCE

HEARINGS
BEFORE THE
SUBCOMMITTEE ON CONSUMER PROTECTION AND FINANCE
OF THE
COMMITTEE ON INTERSTATE AND FOREIGN COMMERCE HOUSE OF REPRESENTATIVES
NINETY-FOURTH CONGRESS

FIRST SESSION

ON

H.R. 285, H.R. 1272, H.R. 1900, H.R. 7985, and H.R. 8441

BILLS TO REQUIRE NO-FAULT MOTOR VEHICLE INSURANCE AS A CONDITION PRECEDENT TO USING A MOTOR VEHICLE ON THE PUBLIC ROADWAYS

JUNE 17, 19; JULY 8, 14, 17, 22, 23, 24, 25, 1975

Serial No. 94-42

Printed for the use of the
Committee on Interstate and Foreign Commerce

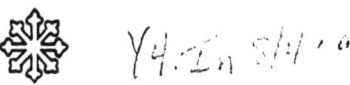

COMMITTEE ON INTERSTATE AND FOREIGN COMMERCE

HARLEY O. STAGGERS, West Virginia, *Chairman*

TORBERT H. MACDONALD, Massachusetts
JOHN E. MOSS, California
JOHN D. DINGELL, Michigan
PAUL G. ROGERS, Florida
LIONEL VAN DEERLIN, California
FRED B. ROONEY, Pennsylvania
JOHN M. MURPHY, New York
DAVID E. SATTERFIELD III, Virginia
BROCK ADAMS, Washington
W. S. (BILL) STUCKEY, JR., Georgia
BOB ECKHARDT, Texas
RICHARDSON PREYER, North Carolina
JAMES W. SYMINGTON, Missouri
CHARLES J. CARNEY, Ohio
RALPH H. METCALFE, Illinois
GOODLOE E. BYRON, Maryland
JAMES H. SCHEUER, New York
RICHARD L. OTTINGER, New York
HENRY A. WAXMAN, California
ROBERT (BOB) KRUEGER, Texas
TIMOTHY E. WIRTH, Colorado
PHILIP R. SHARP, Indiana
WILLIAM M. BRODHEAD, Michigan
W. G. (BILL) HEFNER, North Carolina
JAMES J. FLORIO, New Jersey
ANTHONY TOBY MOFFETT, Connecticut
JIM SANTINI, Nevada
ANDREW MAGUIRE, New Jersey

SAMUEL L. DEVINE, Ohio
JAMES T. BROYHILL, North Carolina
TIM LEE CARTER, Kentucky
CLARENCE J. BROWN, Ohio
JOE SKUBITZ, Kansas
JAMES F. HASTINGS, New York
JAMES M. COLLINS, Texas
LOUIS FREY, JR., Florida
JOHN Y. McCOLLISTER, Nebraska
NORMAN F. LENT, New York
H. JOHN HEINZ III, Pennsylvania
EDWARD R. MADIGAN, Illinois
CARLOS J. MOORHEAD, California
MATTHEW J. RINALDO, New Jersey

W. E. WILLIAMSON, *Clerk*
KENNETH J. PAINTER, *Assistant Clerk*

Professional Staff

ROBERT F. GUTHRIE
CHARLES B. CURTIS
LEE S. HYDE
ELIZABETH HARRISON
JEFFREY H. SCHWARTZ

JAMES M. MENGER, Jr.
WILLIAM P. ADAMS
ROBERT R. NORDHAUS
BRIAN R. MOIR
WILLIAM G. PHILLIPS

KAREN NELSON

SUBCOMMITTEE ON CONSUMER PROTECTION AND FINANCE

LIONEL VAN DEERLIN, California, *Chairman*

W. S. (BILL) STUCKEY, JR., Georgia
BOB ECKHARDT, Texas
RALPH H. METCALFE, Illinois
WILLIAM M. BRODHEAD, Michigan
JAMES H. SCHEUER, New York
HARLEY O. STAGGERS, West Virginia
  (ex officio)

JOHN Y. McCOLLISTER, Nebraska
MATTHEW J. RINALDO, New Jersey
SAMUEL L. DEVINE, Ohio
  (ex officio)

SIEGMUND W. SMITH, *Staff Administrator*
PETER KINZLER, *Counsel*

(II)

CONTENTS

	Page
Hearings held on—	
June 17, 1975	1
June 19, 1975	283
July 8, 1975	321
July 14, 1975	455
July 17, 1975	551
July 22, 1975	575
July 23, 1975	653
July 24, 1975	713
July 25, 1975	757
Text of—	
H.R. 285	2
H.R. 1272	2
H.R. 1900	30
H.R. 7985	103
H.R. 8441	169
Report of—	
Justice Department on H.R. 285, H.R. 1272, and H.R. 1900	235
Justice Department on H.R. 8441	240
Statement of—	
Albovias, Jose, M.D., Ormond Beach, Fla	489
Allen, Lyle W., Special Committee on Automobile Insurance Legislation, American Bar Association	757
Bailey, Robert, staff actuary, National Association of Insurance Commissioners	618
Blume, Paul, vice president and general counsel, National Association of Independent Insurers	600
Brock, Paul W., president, Defense Research Institute, Inc	846
Calabresi, Guido, professor of law, Yale University School of Law	561
Carpenter, H. Paul, vice president and general counsel, Meridian Mutual Insurance Co	647
Chidness, Patrick, vice chairman, Florida Bar No-Fault Insurance Committee	492, 500
Cohen, William, professor of law, Stanford Law School, Stanford, Calif	306
Coleman, Hon. William T., Secretary, Department of Transportation	241
Cook, John G., president, National Association of Mutual Insurance Agents	575
Cronk, Shanler D., staff attorney, American Bar Association	757
Downs, Thomas, Esq., chairman, Committee of the National Conference of Commissioners on Uniform State Laws	265
Dunning, David F., Washington office legislative representative, National Retired Teachers Association and American Association of Retired Persons	537, 744
Frink, Gary, executive director, National Committee for Effective No-Fault	740
Granger, Carl V., M.D., president-elect, American Academy of Physical Medicine and Rehabilitation, and member, American Congress of Rehabilitation Medicine	713
Griswold, Erwin N., on behalf of State Farm Mutual Automobile Insurance Co. and the American Insurance Association	551
Gross, Harold, chairman, Florida Bar No-Fault Insurance Committee	492
Hemmings, Richard, counsel, National Association of Insurance Commissioners	618
Huff, William H., III, insurance commissioner, State of Iowa, and president, National Association of Insurance Commissioners	618

(III)

Statement of—Continued	Page
Hutto, Jack, president, Georgia Trial Lawyers Association	528
Hyatt, Charles H., chairman, No-fault Automobile Reparation Committee, State Bar of Georgia	528
Ives, Alden A., chairman, National Association of Mutual Insurance Companies	642
Jeffers, Leroy, past president, State Bar of Texas, and chairman, Coordinating Committee of State Bar Presidents	790
Jones, T. Lawrence, president, American Insurance Association	584
Keeton, Robert E., Langdell professor of law, Harvard Law School	666
Kircher, John J., professor of law, Marquette University School of Law, and research director and counsel, Defense Research Institute, Inc	846
Kremer, Edward J., chairman, Federal Affairs Committee, National Association of Insurance Agents	638
LaRaia, Henry, National Retired Teachers Association and the American Association of Retired Persons	537
McCue, William G., Jr., director, division of insurance company regulation, office of treasurer, State of Florida	455
McHugh, Donald P., vice president and general counsel, State Farm Mutual Automobile Insurance Co	321
Mackay, John R., immediate past president, Illinois State Bar Association	811
Maisonpierre, André, vice president, American Mutual Insurance Alliance	344
Martin, John B., legislative consultant, Federal legislation, National Retired Teachers Association and American Association of Retired Persons	744
Matthews, F. Lawrence, Florida Bar Association	492, 494
Mitchell, Prentiss R., associate director, Florida Association of Life and Casualty Insurers, Inc	472
O'Reilly, Kathleen F., legislative director, Consumer Federation of America	338
Perin, Donald W., Jr., director of research, National Association of Insurance Agents	638
Rogers, Samuel B., Florida Association of Insurance Agents	483
Rottman, Dick I., insurance commissioner, State of Nevada	375
Scott, James W., program supervisor, workmen's compensation and no-fault insurance programs, division of vocational rehabilitation, National Rehabilitation Association	750
Sedberry, Leland S., Jr., New Mexico State Bar Association	837
Shield, Theodore P., past president, International Association of Insurance Counsel, and member, Defense Research Institute, Inc	846
Sicula, Hon. Paul E., member, House of Representatives, State of Wisconsin, on behalf of the Conference on Insurance Legislators and the National Conference of State Legislators	653
Skandamis, John Paul, Daytona Beach, Fla	546
Spangenberg, Craig, Esq., Cleveland, Ohio	283, 666, 683
Spolyar, Robert J., vice president, legislative services, and counsel, National Association of Mutual Insurance Companies	642
Stoup, Arthur H., president, the Missouri Bar	821
Tammen, Fred R., legislative analyst, National Rehabilitation Association	750
Traub, Harold W., president-elect, National Association of Mutual Insurance Agents	575
Verville, Richard E., counsel, American Academy of Physical Medicine and Rehabilitation and American Congress of Rehabilitation Medicine	713
Walsh, Richard F., Deputy Director for Policy and Plan Development, Office of the Secretary, Department of Transportation	241
Additional material submitted for the record by—	
Allstate Insurance Co., responses to questions of Chairman Van Deerlin contained in his letter of July 31, 1975	438
American Academy of Physical Medicine and Rehabilitation, New York University Medical Center study on spinal cord injury rehabilitation	713

Additional material submitted for the record by—Continued

American Automobile Association, letter dated September 11, 1975, with attachments, from John de Lorenzi, managing director, Public Policy Division, to Chairman Van Deerlin_____ Page 893

American Congress of Rehabilitation Medicine, New York University Medical Center study on spinal cord injury rehabilitation_____ 713

American Mutual Insurance Alliance, letter dated August 12, 1975, from André Maisonpierre, vice president, to Chairman Van Deerlin, in response to request to supply no-fault studies done by the alliance_____ 372

American Trucking Associations, Inc., letter dated August 27, 1975, from W. A. Bresnahan, president, to Chairman Van Deerlin_____ 897

Blue Cross Association and National Association of Blue Shield Plans, letter dated September 8, 1975, from Walter J. McNerny and Ned F. Parish, presidents, to Chairman Van Deerlin_____ 897

Car and Truck Renting and Leasing Association (CATRALA), statement_____ 857

Combined Insurance Company of America, statement_____ 859

Continental Association of Funeral and Memorial Societies, Inc., statement_____ 863

Dorsen, Norman, professor of law, New York University School of Law, letter dated August 7, 1975, to Peter Kinzler, counsel, Subcommittee on Consumer Protection and Finance_____ 901

Farm Bureau Mutual Insurance Co. of Michigan and Community Service Insurance Co., Robert E. J. Wiseman, executive vice president, statement_____ 864

Farmers Insurance Group, Inc., Herbert R. Wells, chief product research specialist_____ 866

Florida Association of Life and Casualty Insurers, Inc., letter dated August 6, 1975, from Prentiss R. Mitchell, associate director, to Chairman Van Deerlin, in response to request for data on the average claim payout under tort versus no-fault_____ 476

Florida Bar Association:
  Article entitled "A Technical Look at Federal No-Fault Insurance" by F. Lawrence Matthews, from Florida Bar Journal, November 1974_____ 521
  Letter dated June 30, 1975, from F. Lawrence Matthews, to Chairman Van Deerlin, presenting views of committee on no-fault insurance_____ 516
  Resolution opposing Federal no-fault insurance_____ 526

Illinois State Bar Association:
  Extract from proceedings of Illinois State Bar Association assembly—Auto accident reparations_____ 817
  Telegram dated July 28, 1972, from Lyle W. Allen, president, Illinois State Bar Association, to Hon. Charles H. Percy, a U.S. Senator from the State of Illinois_____ 818

Interstate and Foreign Commerce Committee:
  Letter dated June 20, 1975, from Daniel J. Demlow, commissioner of insurance, State of Michigan, to Chairman Magnuson, Senate Commerce Committee, concerning cost and availability of reinsurance for auto insurance providing unlimited medical and rehabilitation benefits_____ 411
  Letter dated July 31, 1975, from Chairman Van Deerlin, to Donald P. McHugh, vice president and general counsel, State Farm Mutual Automobile Insurance Co., posing questions on cost estimates for H.R. 1900 and S. 354_____ 430
  Letter dated July 31, 1975, from Chairman Van Deerlin, to Donald Shaffer, vice president and general counsel, Allstate Insurance Co., posing questions on cost estimates for H.R. 1900 and S. 394__ 437
  Letter dated August 26, 1975, from Chairman Van Deerlin, to Secretary of Transportation Coleman, requesting further information with respect to the DOT Study on Motor Vehicle Crash Losses and Their Compensation in the United States___ 264

Kaiser Foundation Health Plan, Inc., letter dated August 7, 1975, from Arthur H. Bernstein, counsel, to Chairman Van Deerlin_____ 900

Additional material submitted for the record by—Continued
  Keeton, Robert E., Langdell professor of law, Harvard Law School, supplementary statement: The impact of no-fault on insurance costs_____ Page 675
  LaRaia, Henry, National Retired Teachers Association and American Association of Retired Persons, article from Wall Street Journal dated February 25, 1975, entitled "Silver Lining"_____ 543
  McCue, William G., Jr., director, division of insurance company regulation, office of treasurer, State of Florida, letter dated September 10, 1975, responding to request for backup data to statement that without no-fault, Florida auto insurance rates would be 50 percent higher_____ 460
  Memorial Society of Metropolitan Washington, statement_____ 876
  MFA Mutual Insurance Co., A. D. Sappington, president, statement__ 878
  National Association of Casualty and Surety Agents, Edward W. Sunder, Jr., president, statement_____ 880
  National Association of Mutual Insurance Agents:
    Primacy_____ 579
    Response to question on unlimited medical expenses_____ 581
  Reinsurance Association of America, statement_____ 883
  State Farm Mutual Automobile Insurance Co.:
    Breakdown of operating expenses_____ 385
    Letter dated August 18, 1975, from Donald P. McHugh, vice president and general counsel, responding to questions posed in letter of July 31, 1975, on cost estimates_____ 431
    Loss and expense ratios—Automobile insurance_____ 402
  Transportation Association of America, letter dated June 18, 1975, from Paul J. Tierney, president, to Chairman Van Deerlin_____ 901
  Transportation, Department of:
    Estimated percentage of motor vehicle accidents in which an out-of-State registered vehicle was involved_____ 256
    Impact of no-fault on company legal expenses_____ 251
    Letter dated September 2, 1975, from Irwin P. Halpern, Acting Assistant Secretary for Policy, Plans and International Affairs, to Chairman Van Deerlin, responding to questions posed in letter of August 26, 1975, regarding DOT study on motor vehicle crash losses and their compensation in the United States_____ 264
    Reinsurance costs_____ 263
  United Methodist Church, statement of board of church and society__ 887
  United Transportation Union, James R. Snyder, national legislative director, statement_____ 888
  Webb, Bernard L., professor of actuarial science and insurance, Georgia State University, statement_____ 889

ORGANIZATIONS REPRESENTED AT THE HEARINGS

American Academy of Physical Medicine and Rehabilitation:
  Granger, Carl V., M.D., president-elect.
  Verville, Richard E., counsel.
American Association of Retired Persons:
  Dunning, David F., Washington office legislative representative.
  LaRaia, Henry.
  Martin, John B., legislative consultant, Federal legislation.
American Bar Association:
  Allen, Lyle W., Special Committee on Automobile Insurance Legislation.
  Cronk, Shanler D., staff attorney.
American Congress of Rehabilitation Medicine:
  Granger, Carl V., M.D., member.
  Verville, Richard E., counsel.
American Insurance Association:
  Griswold, Erwin N., Esq.
  Jones, T. Lawrence, president.
American Mutual Insurance Alliance, André Maisonpierre, vice president.
Conference on Insurance Legislators, Hon. Paul E. Sicula, member, House of Representatives, State of Wisconsin.
Consumer Federation of America, Kathleen F. O'Reilly, legislative director.
Coordinating Committee of State Bar Presidents, Leroy Jeffers, chairman.

ORGANIZATIONS REPRESENTED AT THE HEARINGS—Continued

Defense Research Institute, Inc.:
  Brock, Paul W., president.
  Kircher, John J., research director and counsel.
  Shield, Theodore P., member.
Florida Association of Insurance Agents, Samuel B. Rogers.
Florida Association of Life and Casualty Insurers, Inc., Prentiss R. Mitchell, associate director.
Florida Bar Association:
  Chidnese, Patrick, vice chairman, No-Fault Insurance Committee.
  Gross, Harold, chairman, No-Fault Insurance Committee.
  Matthews, F. Lawrence.
Florida, State of, William G. McCue, Jr., director, Division of Insurance Company Regulation, Office of Treasurer.
Georgia, State Bar of, Charles H. Hyatt, chairman, No-Fault Automobile Reparations Committee.
Georgia Trial Lawyers Association, Jack Hutto, president.
Illinois State Bar Association, John R. Mackay, immediate past president.
Meridian Mutual Insurance Co., H. Paul Carpenter, vice president and general counse.
Missouri Bar, Arthur H. Stoup, president.
National Association of Independent Insurers, Paul Blume, vice president and general counsel.
National Association of Insurance Agents:
  Kremer, Edward J., chairman, Federal Affairs Committee.
  Perin, Donald W., Jr., director of research.
National Association of Insurance Commissioners:
  Bailey, Robert, staff actuary.
  Hemmings, Richard, counsel.
  Huff, William H., III, insurance commissioner, State of Iowa, president.
National Association of Mutual Insurance Agents:
  Cook, John G., president.
  Traub, Harold W., president-elect.
National Association of Mutual Insurance Companies:
  Ives, Alden A., chairman.
  Spolyar, Robert J., vice president, legislative services, and counsel.
National Committee for Effective No-Fault, Gary Fink, executive director.
National Conference of Commissioners on Uniform State Laws, Thomas Downs, Esq., committee chairman.
National Conference of State Legislators, Hon. Paul E. Sicula, member, House of Representatives, State of Wisconsin.
National Rehabilitation Association:
  Scott, James W., program supervisor, workmen's compensation and no-fault insurance programs, Division of Vocational Rehabilitation.
  Tannen, Fred R., legislative analyst.
National Retired Teachers Association:
  Dunning, David E., Washington office legislative representative.
  LaRaia, Henry.
  Martin, John B., legislative consultant, Federal legislation.
Nevada, State of, Dick I. Rottman, Insurance Commissioner.
New Mexico State Bar Association, Leland S. Sedberry, Jr.
State Farm Mutual Automobile Insurance Co.:
  Griswold, Erwin N., Esq.
  McHugh, Donald P., vice president and general counsel.
Texas, State Bar of, Leroy Jeffers, past president.
Transportation, Department of:
  Coleman, Hon. William T., Secretary.
  Walsh, Richard F., Deputy Director for Policy and Plan Development, Office of the Secretary.

NO-FAULT MOTOR VEHICLE INSURANCE

TUESDAY, JUNE 17, 1975

House of Representatives,
Subcommittee on Consumer Protection and Finance,
Committee on Interstate and Foreign Commerce,
Washington, D.C.

The subcommittee met at 2 p.m., pursuant to notice, in room 2123, Rayburn House Office Building, Hon. Lionel Van Deerlin, chairman, presiding.

Mr. Van Deerlin. The subcommittee will come to order. This afternoon we start down what many of us anticipate will be a very long road leading toward resolution of the important question of policy, whether or not no-fault automobile insurance should be a subject for Federal legislation or whether it is a subject better left to the States.

We have before us for consideration, although our discussion will by no means be limited to them, H.R. 1272 by Mr. Eckhardt, and several others, and H.R. 1900 introduced by Mr. Matsunaga of Hawaii.

[The text of H.R. 285, H.R. 1272, H.R. 1900, H.R. 7985, and H.R. 8441, together with departmental reports thereon, follow:]

[H.R. 285, 94th Cong., 1st sess., introduced by Mr. Carney on January 14, 1975, and H.R. 1272, 94th Cong., 1st sess., introduced by Mr. Eckhardt (for himself, Mr. Dingell, Ms. Abzug, Mr. Drinan, Mr. Mitchell of Maryland, Mr. Scheuer, Mr. Charles H. Wilson of California, Mr. Helstoski, Mr. Van Deerlin, Mr. Stark, Mr. Ashley, Mr. Carney, and Mr Edwards of California) on January 14, 1975, are identical as follows:]

A BILL

To require no-fault motor vehicle insurance as a condition precedent to using the public streets, roads, and highways in order to promote and regulate interstate commerce.

1 *Be it enacted by the Senate and House of Representa-*
2 *tives of the United States of America in Congress assembled,*
3 That this Act may be cited as the "National No-Fault Motor
4 Vehicle Insurance Act".

5 DEFINITIONS

6 SEC. 2. As used in this Act—
7 (1) The term "motor vehicle" means any vehicle
8 driven or drawn by electrical or mechanical power which is

1 manufactured primarily for use on the public streets, roads,
2 or highways, except any vehicle operated exclusively on a
3 rail or rails.

4 (2) The term "insured motor vehicle" means a motor
5 vehicle (A) which is insured under a qualifying no-fault
6 policy, or (B) the owner of which is a self-insurer with
7 respect to such vehicle.

8 (3) The term "uninsured motor vehicle" means a motor
9 vehicle which is not an insured motor vehicle.

10 (4) The term "qualifying no-fault policy" means an
11 insurance policy which meets the requirements of section 5
12 (a) and (b) (but such term does not refer to additional
13 coverage or benefit referred to in section 5(e)).

14 (5) The term "owner" means a person who holds the
15 legal title to a motor vehicle; except that in the case of a
16 motor vehicle which is the subject of a security agreement
17 or lease with option to purchase with the debtor or lessee
18 having the right to possession, such term means the debtor
19 or lessee.

20 (6) The term "insurer" means any person or govern-
21 mental entity engaged in the business of issuing or delivering
22 motor vehicle insurance policies and where not otherwise
23 stated means the first party insurer.

24 (7) The term "first party insurer" means the insurer

who has issued a no-fault policy to the insured person in question.

(8) The term "self-insurer" with respect to any motor vehicle means a person who has satisfied the requirements of section 4 (a) in the manner provided by section 4 (a) (2).

(9) The term "operation, maintenance, or use" when used with respect to a motor vehicle includes loading or unloading the vehicle, but does not include conduct within the course of a business of repairing, servicing, or otherwise maintaining vehicles unless the conduct occurs outside the premises of such business.

(10) The term "motor vehicle accident" means an accident arising out of the operation, maintenance, or use of a motor vehicle.

(11) The term "accidental harm" means bodily injury, death, sickness, or disease caused by a motor vehicle accident while in or upon or entering into or alighting from, or through being struck by a motor vehicle or object drawn or propelled by a motor vehicle.

(12) The term "death" (except as used in this paragraph and paragraphs (11) and 13)) means accidental harm resulting at any time in death.

(13) The term "injury" means accidental harm not resulting in death.

(14) The term "economic loss" with respect to any injury or death means—

(A) all appropriate and reasonable expenses necessarily incurred for medical, hospital, surgical, professional nursing, dental, ambulance, prosthetic services, and any federally recognized religious remedial care and treatment;

(B) all appropriate and reasonable expenses necessarily incurred for psychiatric, physical, and occupational therapy and rehabilitation;

(C) an amount equal to the lesser of—

(i) $1,000 per month, or

(ii) the monthly earnings for the period during which the injury or death results in the inability to engage in available and appropriate gainful activity, or

(D) a monthly amount equal to the amount (if any) by which (i) a person's monthly earnings (as defined in paragraph (15)) or $1,000, whichever is less, exceeds (ii) any lesser monthly earnings of such person at such time as he resumes gainful activity.

(E) all appropriate and reasonable expenses necessarily incurred as a result of such injury or death, including, but not limited to, (i) expenses incurred in obtaining services in substitution of those that the injured or deceased person would have performed for the benefit of himself or his family, (ii) funeral expenses, and (iii) attorneys' fees and costs to the extent provided in section 9.

(15) The term "monthly earnings" means—

(A) in the case of a regularly employed person, one-twelfth of the average annual compensation after income taxes at the time of injury or death;

(B) in the case of a person regularly self-employed, one-twelfth of the average annual earnings after income taxes at the time of injury or death;

(C) in the case of an unemployed person or a person not regularly employed or self-employed, one-twelfth of the anticipated annual compensation after income taxes of such person paid from the time such person would reasonably have been expected to be regularly employed:

Provided, however, That such sums are to be periodically increased in a manner corresponding to annual compensation increases that would predictably result but for the injury or death. The Secretary is authorized to promulgate rules consistent with this paragraph defining further the term "monthly earnings."

(16) The term "net economic loss" means, in the case of injury or death; economic loss reduced (but not below

zero) by the amount of any benefit or payment received (or legally entitled to be received and actually available to the claimant) for losses resulting from such injury or death from any of the following sources—

    (A) any public health insurance or plan;

    (B) any private insurance or plan containing explicit provisions making its benefits primary to any benefits under a qualifying no-fault policy.

(17) The term "property damage" means injury to or destruction of property (including loss of use thereof) caused by a motor vehicle accident.

(18) The term "damage other than economic loss" means in the case of injury or death the difference between economic loss and the total loss sustained measured by the State tort law which would have been applicable but for section 3, including, where recoverable under State tort law, damage characterized as pain and suffering and general damage.

(19) The term "motor vehicle in use" means a motor vehicle being operated on any public street or roadway or in any other public place; it does not mean a motor vehicle legally parked to the side of any public street or roadway or in any public place.

(20) The term "without regard to fault" means irrespective of fault as a cause of injury or death, and without

application of the principle of liability based on negligence.

(21) The term "criminal conduct" means the commission of an offense punishable by imprisonment for one year or more, or operation or use of a motor vehicle with the specific intent of causing injury or damage, or operation or use of a motor vehicle as a converter without a good faith belief that the operator or user is legally entitled to operate or use such vehicle.

(22) The term "Secretary" means the Secretary of Transportation.

(23) The term "State" means any State, the District of Columbia, the Commonwealth of Puerto Rico, the Virgin Islands, Guam, American Samoa, or the Canal Zone.

TORT EXEMPTION

SEC. 3. No person who is—

(a) the owner, operator, or user of an insured motor vehicle, or

(b) the operator or user of an uninsured motor vehicle who operates or uses such vehicle without any reason to believe that such vehicle is an uninsured motor vehicle,

shall be liable for tort damages of any nature arising out of the ownership, maintenance, operation, or use of such vehicle unless that person is engaging in criminal conduct (as defined in section 2(21)) which causes such damage in which case he shall be liable to the extent provided by State law for all damages other than economic loss.

CONDITIONS OF OPERATION AND REGISTRATION

SEC. 4. (a) (1) No person may register any motor vehicle in a State or operate or use a motor vehicle upon any public street, road, or highway of any State at any time unless such motor vehicle is insured under a qualifying no-fault policy (as defined in section 2 (4)), pursuant to such regulations (including those determining the manner and term of proof of such insurance) as the Secretary shall prescribe.

(2) The requirements of this subsection may be satisfied by any owner of a motor vehicle if—

> (A) such owner provides a surety bond, proof of qualifications as a self-insurer, or other securities affording security substantially equivalent to that afforded under a qualifying no-fault policy, as determined and approved by the Secretary under regulations, and

> (B) the Secretary is satisfied that, in case of injury or death or property damage, any claimant would have the same rights against such owner under applicable State law as the claimant would have had under such law had a qualifying no-fault policy been applicable to such vehicle.

(b) No State may require the purchase or acquisition

of insurance or other security as a condition to the ownership, registration, operation, or use of any motor vehicle upon the public streets, roads, or highways of such State that is inconsistent with a qualifying no-fault policy.

(c) Any person who knowingly violates the provisions of subsection (a) of this section shall be punished by a fine not to exceed $1,000 or imprisonment for a period of not to exceed six months, or both. The Attorney General and United States Attorneys are authorized to bring suits to enforce this provision in an appropriate Federal district court or in any State court of competent jurisdiction. Such State official or agency having authority and responsibility under State law to enforce this provision shall have concurrent authority to bring such actions in State courts of competent jurisdiction.

INSURANCE REQUIREMENTS

SEC. 5. (a) In order to be a qualifying no-fault policy, an insurance policy covering a motor vehicle shall provide benefits for injury or death (as defined in section 2, paragraphs (12) and (13)) as follows:

(1) Except as otherwise provided in paragraph (2)—

(A) in the case of injury to any person (including the owner, operator, or user of the insured motor vehicle), the insurer shall pay, without regard to fault, to such person an amount equal to the net economic loss (as defined in section 2(16)) sustained by such person as a result of such injury; or

(B) in the case of death of any person (including the owner, operator, or user of the insured motor vehicle), the insurer shall pay, without regard to fault, to the legal representative of such person, for the benefit of the surviving spouse and any dependent (as defined in section 152 of the Internal Revenue Code of 1954) of such person, an amount equal to the net economic loss sustained by such spouse and dependent as a result of the death of such person.

(2) No payment may be made for net economic loss sustained by—

(A) the occupants of a motor vehicle other than the insured motor vehicle; or

(B) the operater or user of a motor vehicle engaging in criminal conduct (as defined in section 2(21)) which causes any such loss.

(3) Payments for net economic loss shall be made as such loss is incurred except that in the case of death, payment for such loss may, at the option of the beneficiary, be made immediately in a lump sum payment appropriately discounted in accordance with regulations of the Secretary. Amounts of net economic loss unpaid thirty days after the

insurer has received reasonable proof of the fact and amount of loss realized, and demand for payment thereof shall (after the expiration of such thirty days) bear interest at the rate of 2 per centum per month.

(4) A claim for net economic loss based upon injury to or death of a person who is not an occupant of any motor vehicle involved in an accident may be made against the insurer of any involved vehicle. The insurer against whom the claim is asserted shall process and pay the claim as if wholly responsible, but such insurer shall thereafter be entitled to recover from the insurers of all other involved vehicles porportionate contribution for the benefits paid and the costs of processing the claim.

(5) No part of loss benefits paid under a qualifying no-fault policy (except those paid by provisions required in subsection 5(b)(1) of this section) shall be applied in any manner as attorney's fees in the case of injury or death for which such benefits are paid. Any contract in violation of this provision shall be illegal and unenforceable, and it shall constitute an unlawful act for any attorney to solicit, enter into, or knowingly accept benefits under any such contract.

(b) In order to be a qualifying no-fault policy, an insurance policy covering a motor vehicle shall provide the following benefits in addition to those enumerated in subsection (a) of this section—

(1) in the case of injury or death to any person the insurer shall pay, without regard to fault, to such person compensation for damages other than economic loss sustained by such person as the result of such injury or death;

(2) in the case of property damage to a motor vehicle in use arising out of a motor vehicle accident, the insurer shall pay, without regard to fault, to any person whose property is so damaged compensation for such damages less such deductibles as are provided in the insurance policy covering such persons; and insurer shall offer policies containing such deductibles as the insured elects;

(3) in the case of damage to any property other than a motor vehicle in use arising out of a motor vehicle accident, insurers of any motor vehicles involved in the motor vehicle accident shall pay on a proportionate basis to the owner of such property an amount equal to the loss occasioned by the damage.

(c) (1) A person may not proceed to trial, and no judgment may be rendered (other than a judgment to which all of the parties to the suit consent), in a suit which includes a claim for damage other than economic loss unless one or more of the following conditions exist:

(A) all claims of such person for net economic losses have been satisfied,

(B) there exists a claim for a net economic loss (i) which is arguably the result of the accidental harm for which the claim for damage other than economic loss is made, and (ii) which has not been paid within thirty days after the insurer has received reasonable notice of the fact and amount of loss realized and demand for payment thereof,

(C) three years have elapsed since the date of the event upon which the claim is based, or

(D) one year has elapsed since the date of the event upon which the claim is based and all claims of such person which are attributable to economic losses described in subparagraphs (C) and (D) of section 2 (14) of this Act have been satisfied.

(2) A contract for settlement of any claim or future claim for damage other than economic loss in consideration for the payment of any economic loss which is arguably the result of the accidental harm for which the claim is made shall be unenforceable. The fact that any purported contract for settlement of any claim or future claim for damage other than economic loss was made during the time between the date of the accident and the time that a person may proceed

to trial under paragraph (1) of this subsection creates a presumption that such contract was made upon the consideration of payment of economic loss. Such presumption may be rebutted by a showing:

    (A) that payment of economic loss was not in fact a part of the consideration for settlement of the non-economic loss claim; and

    (B) that the insurer, in dealing with the injured person, satisfied that standard of fair and equitable dealing required of a fiduciary.

(3) Contingent fee arrangements for the prosecution of claims under a policy for compensation for damages other than economic loss shall be made in accordance with section 8(b) of this Act.

(d) Notwithstanding any provision of State law to the contrary, the statute of limitation for bringing suit under provisions providing compensation for damages other than economic loss shall be—

    (1) four years from the date of the motor vehicle accident upon which the claim is based, or

    (2) one year after the last payment for economic loss recoverable under paragraph (1) of this subsection is paid,

whichever be the lesser length of time.

(e) (1) Any policy of insurance described in this section may contain—

    (A) additional coverages and benefits with respect to any injury, death, or any other loss from motor vehicle accidents or loss from operation of a motor vehicle; and

    (B) terms, conditions, exclusions, and deductible clauses;

Provided, That such are consistent with the required provisions of such policy and approved by the Secretary, who shall only approve terms, conditions, exclusions, deductible clauses, coverages, and benefits which—

    (i) are fair and equitable,

    (ii) limit the variety of coverage available so as to give buyers of insurance reasonable opportunity to compare the cost of insuring with various insurers; and

    (iii) do not reduce coverage below that provided for in this Act.

(2) Any policy of insurance described in this section shall contain a provision, in accordance with regulations of the Secretary, specifying the periods within which claims may be filed and actions against the insurer may be brought.

(f) Any policy of insurance described in this section must offer different standardized categories of premium reductions reflecting benefits available to the policyholder and members of his family as a result of public or private insurance or plans or other benefit sources described in section 2(16) of this Act, as being primary to benefits under a qualified no-fault policy.

(g) (1) No insurer may issue or offer to issue any policy which he represents is a qualifying no-fault policy unless such policy meets the requirements of subsections (a) and (b), is consistent with the requirements of subsection (e), and includes all applicable standard uniform policy provisions under section 6(d).

(2) Any insurer who violates paragraph (1) shall be assessed a civil penalty of not to exceed $5,000 for each policy which the insurer issues or offers to issue in violation of such paragraph and, if such violation is willful, he may in addition be imprisoned for not more than one year.

(h) (1) Subject to paragraph (2)—

(A) An application for a qualifying no-fault policy covering a motor vehicle in a State may not be rejected by an insurer authorized to issue such a policy in such State unless—

(i) the principal operator of such vehicle does not have a license which permits him to operate such vehicle, or

(ii) the application is not accompanied by a

reasonable portion of the premium (as determined under regulations of the Secretary),

(B) A qualifying no-fault policy once issued may not be canceled or refused renewal by an insurer except for—

(i) suspension or revocation of the license of the principal operator to operate a motor vehicle, or

(ii) failure to pay the premium for such policy after reasonable demand therefor.

In any case of cancellation or refusal to renew under clause (ii), written notice shall be given to the insured.

(2) An insurer may reject or refuse to accept additional applications for, or refuse to renew qualifying no-fault policies (A) if the domiciliary State insurance supervisory authority of such insurer deems in writing that the financial soundness of such insurer would be impaired by the writing of additional policies of such insurance, or (B) such insurer ceases to write any new policies of insurance of any kind in the jurisdiction of the rejected applicant.

(3) Whoever knowingly violates, or conspires to violate, the provisions of paragraph (1) or (2) of this subsection shall be assessed a civil penalty of not to exceed $1,000 for each separate violation. Each violation of paragraph (A) of this subsection with respect to any policy-

holder or applicant for insurance shall constitute a separate violation.

UNIFORM STATISTICAL PLAN AND PRICE INFORMATION

SEC. 6. (a) The Secretary shall, after consultation with insurers and State insurance supervisory authorities, promulgate a common, uniform statistical plan for the allocation and compilation of claims and loss experience data for each coverage under section 5 of this Act, and upon promulgation, such plan shall be followed by every insurer writing qualifying no-fault policies, and by every rating or advisory organization or statistical agent used by any such insurer to gather, compile, or report claims and loss experience data.

(b) Such statistical plan shall contain data pertaining to the claims and loss experience for the classes of risk in each rating territory within each coverage under section 5 of this Act. Such statistical plan shall not contain data pertaining to expenses for adjusting losses, underwriting expenses, general administration expenses, or any other expense experience for any class of risk in each rating territory within the coverages under section 5 of this Act. In carrying out the provisions of this section, no insurer, rating, or advisory organization, or statistical agent, or any other association of insurers, may pool, or in any manner combine, any such expenses or expense experience, or otherwise act in concert with respect thereto.

(c) Every insurer writing policies of insurance which meet the requirements of section 5 of this Act, and every rating or advisory organization or statistical agent used by such insurer to gather or compile claims and loss experience data, shall report such data in accordance with the provisions of the statistical plan required by this section at such times and in such manner as the Secretary shall by regulations prescribe.

(d) The Secretary shall prescribe regulations which shall require a minimal number of standard uniform—

  (1) policy provisions for each coverage under section 5 of this Act; and

  (2) classes of risk and rating territories for each coverage under section 5 of this Act;

in order to accomplish the purposes of the statistical plan required by this section.

(e) Every insurer writing qualifying no-fault policies shall provide the Secretary with the actual rate or premium being charged for each class of risk in each rating territory within each coverage under section 5 of this Act at such times and in such manner as the Secretary shall by rules and regulations prescribe.

(f) The Secretary may, after consultation with the insurers and State insurance supervisory authorities, appoint a statistical agent or agents, to receive, gather, compile, report, and analyze the claims and loss experience data, and actual rates or premiums, specified in subsections (c) and (e) of this section.

(g) From time to time, but not less often than semi-annually, the Secretary shall analyze and freely and fully make available to the State insurance supervisory authorities and to the general public, with respect to every insurer writing qualifying no-fault policies, a comparison of such insurer's indicated rate based solely upon the claims and loss experience data for each class of risk in each rating territory within each coverage under section 5 with the actual rate or premiums being charged by the insurer for such class of risk in each rating territory within such coverage. The claims and loss experience data, and actual rates or premiums specified in subsections (c) and (e) of this section shall be made available to the general public at such times and in such manner as the Secretary shall by regulation prescribe.

(h) Any insurer writing qualifying no-fault policies, or any rating or advisory organization or statistical agent used by any such insurer to gather, compile, or report claims and loss experience data with respect to policies meeting the requirements of section 5, who fails to:

    (1) follow the statistical plan promulgated in accordance with subsections (a) and (b) of this section, or

(2) observe the prohibition in subsection (b) of this section against pooling, or in any manner combining expense experience, or

(3) report to the Secretary, or his statistical agent or agents, the claims and loss experience data as required in subsections (c) and (f) of this section, or

(4) follow the standard uniform classes of risk and rating territories prescribed by the Secretary as required in subsection (d) of this section, or

(5) provide the Secretary, or his statistical agent or agents, with the actual rate or premium being charged for each class of risk in each rating territory within such coverage as required in subsections (e) and (f) of this section,

shall be assessed a civil penalty of not to exceed $5,000 for each violation.

ASSIGNED CLAIMS PLAN

SEC. 7. (a) (1) The Secretary shall, after consultation with insurers and State insurance supervisory authorities, organize an assigned claims bureau and assigned claims plan in each State. Upon organization, each such bureau and plan shall be maintained, subject to regulation by the applicable State insurance supervisory authority, by the insurers writing qualifying no-fault policies in such State if (and for so long as) the Secretary is satisfied that all such insurers are required under State law to participate and that no such insurer may withdraw without the consent of the State.

(2) In any case in which an assigned claims bureau and assigned claims plan in any State is not maintained in a manner considered by the Secretary to be consistent with the provisions of this Act, the Secretary shall maintain such bureau and plan.

(3) The Secretary shall prescribe regulations which shall set forth the extent to which, for purposes of this section—

   (A) a self-insurer shall be treated as an insurer, and
   (B) benefits which a self-insurer is obligated to pay shall be treated as insurance benefits under a qualifying no-fault policy.

(b) The costs incurred in the operation of each assigned claims bureau and assigned claims plan shall be assessed against insurers in each State by the applicable State insurance supervisory authority (or by the Secretary during any period during which such bureau and plan are maintained by him under subsection (a) (2)) according to regulations of such State authority (or of the Secretary if the bureau and plan are maintained by him) that as sure fair allocations among such insurers writing qualifying policies in the State, on a basis reasonably related to the volume of insurance written under qualifying no-fault policies.

(c) (1) No insurer may write any qualifying no-fault policy unless the insurer participates in the assigned claims bureau and assigned claims plan in each State in which such insurer writes such policies.

(2) An insurer who violates paragraph (1) of this subsection shall be assessed a civil penalty of $5,000 for each policy he issues in violation of such paragraph.

(d) Except as provided in subsection (e) of this section, each person sustaining injury or death (or his legal representative) may obtain the insurance benefits described in sections 5 (a) and (b) of this Act through the assigned claims bureau and assigned claims plan in the State in which such person resides if—

 (1) no insurance benefits under qualifying no-fault policies are applicable to the injury or death; or

 (2) no such insurance benefits applicable to the injury or death can be identified; or

 (3) the only identifiable insurance benefits under qualifying no-fault policies applicable to the injury or death will not be paid in full because of financial inability of one or more insurers to fulfill their obligations.

(e) A person shall be disqualified from receiving benefits through any assigned claims bureau and assigned claims plan established pursuant to this section if—

 (1) such person is disqualified under section 5 (a)

(2) (B) of this Act from receiving the insurance benefits under section 5 (a) of this Act,

(2) such person was—

(A) the owner or registrant of an uninsured motor vehicle at the time of its involvement in the accident out of which such person's injury arose, or

(B) the operator of such a vehicle at such time with reason to believe that such vehicle was an uninsured motor vehicle.

(f) A claim or claims arising from injury or death to one person sustained in one accident and brought through the applicable assigned claims plan shall be assigned to one insurer, or to the applicable assigned claims bureau, which after such assignment shall have the same rights and obligations as it would have had had it issued a qualifying no-fault policy (or such form as the Secretary by regulation prescribes) applicable to such injury or death.

(g) The assignment of claims shall be made according to regulations of the State supervisory authority (or the Secretary if the bureau and plan are maintained by him under subsection (a) (2)) that assure fair allocation of the burden of assigned claims among insurers doing business in the particular State on a basis reasonably related to the volume of insurance written under sections 5 (a) and (b) of this Act.

(h) A person or his legal representative claiming through an assigned claims plan shall notify the applicable bureau of his claim within the period prescribed under section 5 (c) (2) for filing a claim for insurance benefits under section 5 (a) or (b). The bureau shall promptly assign the claim and notify the claimant of the identity and address of the insurer to which the claim is assigned, or of the bureau if the claim is assigned to it. No action by the claimant against the insurer to which his claim is assigned, or against the bureau if the claim is assigned to it, shall be commenced later than sixty days after receipt of notice of the assignment or after the expiration of the period prescribed in section 5 (c) (2) for commencing an action against an insurer, whichever is later.

(i) All reasonable and necessary costs incurred in the handling and disposition of assigned claims, including amount paid pursuant to assessments under subsection (b) of this section, may be considered in making or regulating rates for the insurance under sections 5 (a) and (b) of this Act, but if such costs are considered in the rates or premiums for such insurance, the pure loss portion of such costs shall be reported separately under the uniform statistical plan provided for by section 6 of this Act, and that portion of the actual rate or premium being charged for such insurance attributable to the entire amount of such costs incurred in the handling and disposition of assigned claims shall be reported separately under subsection (e) of section 6 of this Act.

(j) An insurer who makes an assigned claims payment shall be subrogated to any rights the person to whom the payment was made may have had against the owner or operator of any uninsured motor vehicle involved in the accident out of which the claim arose.

CLAIMANT'S ATTORNEY'S FEES

SEC. 8. (a) A person making a claim under a qualifying no-fault policy may be allowed an award of a reasonable sum for attorney's fee (based upon actual time expended) and all reasonable costs of suit in any case in which the insurer denies all or part of a claim for benefits under such policy unless the court determines that the claim was fraudulent, excessive, or frivolous.

(b) A person making claim under policy provisions meeting the requirements of section 5(b) may enter into a contingent fee arrangement with an attorney but in no event may the fee exceed 25 per centum of any award the claimant receives, and may be further limited at the discretion of the court.

FRAUDULENT CLAIMS

SEC. 9. Within the discretion of the court, an insurer or self-insurer may be allowed an award of a reasonable sum as attorney's fee (based upon actual time expended) and all reasonable costs of suit for its defense against a person making claim against such insurer or self-insurer where such claim was fraudulent, and such attorney's fee and all such reasonable costs of suit so awarded may be treated as an offset against any benefits due or to become due to such person.

ADMINISTRATION

SEC. 10. In order to carry out the provisions and fulfill the purpose of this Act the Secretary shall—

>   (1) consult with representatives of State agencies charged with the regulation of the business of insurance, representatives of the private insurance business, and such other persons, organizations, and agencies of the Federal, State, or local governments as he deems necessary; and

>   (2) make, promulgate, amend, and repeal such regulations as he deems necessary.

JURISDICTION

SEC. 11. (a) No district court of the United States may entertain an action for breach of any contractual or other obligation assumed by an insurer or self-insurer under a policy of insurance containing provisions in accordance with section 5 of this Act unless a person bringing such action meets the jurisdictional requirements of section 1332 of title 28 of the United States Code.

(b) Any person may bring suit for breach of any contractual obligation assumed by an insurer under a policy of insurance containing such mandatory or optional provisions in any State court of competent jurisdiction.

EFFECTIVE DATE

SEC. 12. (a) Except as provided in subsection (b), this Act shall take effect one year after its enactment.

(b) Sections 4, 5(g), and 7(d) shall take effect on the first day of the eighteenth calendar month which begins after the date of enactment of this Act. Section 3 shall apply with respect to accidents occurring on or after the first day of such eighteenth calendar month.

94TH CONGRESS
1ST SESSION
H. R. 1900

IN THE HOUSE OF REPRESENTATIVES

JANUARY 23, 1975

Mr. MATSUNAGA introduced the following bill; which was referred to the Committee on Interstate and Foreign Commerce

A BILL

To regulate commerce by establishing a nationwide system to restore motor vehicle accident victims and by requiring no-fault motor vehicle insurance as a condition precedent to using a motor vehicle on public roadways.

1   *Be it enacted by the Senate and House of Representa-*
2   *tives of the United States of America in Congress assembled,*
3   TITLE I—GENERAL PROVISIONS
4   FORMAL PROVISIONS
5   SEC. 101. (a) SHORT TITLE.—This Act may be cited
6   as the "National No-Fault Motor Vehicle Insurance Act".

2

(b) TABLE OF CONTENTS.—

TITLE I—GENERAL PROVISIONS

Sec. 101. Formal provisions.
    (a) Short title.
    (b) Table of contents.
Sec. 102. Declaration of policy.
    (a) Findings.
    (b) Purposes.
Sec. 103. Definitions.
Sec. 104. Required motor vehicle insurance.
    (a) Security covering a motor vehicle.
    (b) Self-insurance.
    (c) Obligated government.
    (d) Obligations upon termination of security.
Sec. 105. Availability of insurance.
    (a) Plan.
    (b) Cancellation, refusal to renew, or other termination of insurance.
Sec. 106. Payment of claims for no-fault benefits.
    (a) In general.
    (b) Release or settlement of claim.
    (c) Time limitations on actions to recover benefits.
    (d) Assignment of benefits.
    (e) Deduction and setoff.
    (f) Exemption of benefits.
Sec. 107. Attorney's fees and costs.
    (a) Fees of claimant's attorney.
    (b) Fees of restoration obligor's attorney.
Sec. 108. Assigned claims.
    (a) General.
    (b) Assigned claims plan.
    (c) Time for presenting claims under assigned claims plan.
Sec. 109. State regulation.
    (a) Rates and rating.
    (b) Public information.
    (c) Accountability program.
    (d) Availability of services.
Sec. 110. Motor vehicles in interstate travel.
    (a) General.
    (b) Conforming coverage.
    (c) Applicable law.
Sec. 111. Rights and duties of restoration obligors.
    (a) Reimbursement and subrogation.
    (b) Duty to pay basic restoration benefits.
    (c) Indemnity.
    (d) Referral for rehabilitation services.
Sec. 112. Jurisdiction of Federal courts.
Sec. 113. Federal motor vehicle.
    (a) General.
    (b) Procedures.
    (c) Definitions.
Sec. 114. Separability.

TITLE II—NATIONAL STANDARDS FOR STATE NO-FAULT MOTOR VEHICLE INSURANCE PLAN

Sec. 201. State no-fault plan in accordance with this title.
    (a) Preemption.
    (b) State plan.
    (c) Determination by Secretary.
    (d) Periodic review.
    (e) Alternative State plan.
    (f) Procedure.
    (g) Exceptions.
    (h) Reporting requirements.
    (i) Financial assistance to States.
    (j) Authorization for appropriations.
Sec. 202. National standards.
    (a) General.
    (b) Criteria.
Sec. 203. Right to basic restoration benefits.
    (a) Accident within a State.
    (b) Accident outside any State.
Sec. 204. Limitations on benefits.
Sec. 205. Source of basic restoration benefits.
    (a) Applicable security.
    (b) Multiple sources of equal priority.
Sec. 206. Restrictions on tort liability.
    (a) Partial abolition.
    (b) Nonreimbursable tort fine.
Sec. 207. Work loss.
    (a) Regularly employed.
    (b) Seasonally employed.
    (c) Not employed.
    (d) Changes in benefits.
    (e) Definitions.
Sec. 208. Net loss.
    (a) General.
    (b) Tax deduction.
    (c) Allowable expense deduction option.
Sec. 209. Added restoration benefits.
    (a) Optional offering.
    (b) Mandatory offering.
    (c) Territorial applicability.
Sec. 210. Ineligible claimants.
    (a) Converter.
    (b) Intentional injuries.
Sec. 211. Other provisions.
    (a) Included coverage.
    (b) Approval of terms and forms.

TITLE III—ALTERNATIVE STATE NO-FAULT MOTOR VEHICLE INSURANCE PLAN

Sec. 301. Provisions.
Sec. 302. Limitations on basic restoration benefits.
Sec. 303. Restrictions on tort liability.
    (a) Partial abolition.
    (b) Nonreimbursable tort fine.
Sec. 304. Added restoration benefits.
    (a) Optional offering.
    (b) Mandatory offering.
    (c) Territorial applicability.

DECLARATION OF POLICY

SEC. 102. (a) FINDINGS.—The Congress hereby finds and declares that—

(1) motor vehicles are the primary instrumentality for the interstate transportation of individuals;

(2) the intrastate transportation of individuals by motor vehicle over Federal-aid highways and other highways significantly affects interstate commerce, particularly in metropolitan areas encompassing more than one State;

(3) the maximum feasible restoration of all individuals injured and compensation of the economic losses of the survivors of all individuals killed in motor vehicle accidents on Federal-aid highways, in interstate commerce, and in activity affecting interstate commerce is essential to the humane and purposeful functioning of commerce;

(4) to avoid any undue burden on commerce during the interstate or intrastate transportation of individuals, it is necessary and proper to have a nationwide low-cost, comprehensive, and fair system of compensating and restoring motor vehicle accident victims and the survivors of deceased victims;

(5) exhaustive studies by the United States Department of Transportation, the Congress, and some

States have determined that the present basic system of motor vehicle accident and insurance law, which makes compensation and restoration contingent upon—

    (A) every victim first showing that someone else was at fault;

    (B) every victim first showing that he was without fault; and

    (C) the person at fault having sufficient liability insurance and other available financial resources to pay for all the losses,

is not such a low-cost, comprehensive, and fair system;

(6) careful studies, intensive hearings, and some State experiments have demonstrated that a basic system of motor vehicle accident and insurance law which—

    (A) assures every victim payment of all his medical and rehabilitation costs, and recovery of almost all his work loss plus a reasonable amount of replacement services and survivor's loss; and

    (B) eliminates the need to determine fault except when a victim is very seriously injured,

is such a low-cost, comprehensive, and fair system;

(7) nationwide adoption of the system described in paragraph (6) in place of the system described in paragraph (5) would remove an undue burden on commerce;

(8) pursuant to the power vested in it "to regulate Commerce . . . among the several States", the Government of the United States is authorized to require a nationwide low-cost, comprehensive, and fair system of compensating and restoring motor vehicle accident victims and the survivors of the deceased victims;

(9) in all the States there should be uniformity as to the essential elements of the system of motor vehicle accident and insurance law to avoid confusion, complexity, uncertainty, and chaos which would be engendered by a multiplicity of noncomplementary State systems, but the need for a nationwide basic system does not require that the Federal Government itself directly administer, operate, or direct the administration or operation of such system; and

(10) a nationwide low-cost, comprehensive, and fair system of compensating and restoring motor vehicle accident victims can—

 (A) recognize, respect, and avoid interfering with the historical role of the States in regulating and exercising legislative authority over the business of insurance; and

 (B) save and restore the lives of countless victims by providing and paying the cost of services so that every victim has the opportunity to—

(i) receive prompt and comprehensive professional treatment, and

(ii) be rehabilitated to the point where he can return as a useful member of society and a self-respecting and self-supporting citizen.

(b) PURPOSES.—Therefore, it is hereby declared to be the policy of the Congress to establish—

(1) at reasonable cost to the purchaser of insurance, a nationwide system of prompt and adequate restoration benefits for motor vehicle accident victims and the survivors of deceased victims; and

(2) minimum standards which each State must meet or exceed so as to assure a nationwide low-cost, comprehensive, and fair system of motor vehicle accident and insurance law and which enables each State to participate legislatively, to administer without interference, and to continue regulating the business of insurance.

DEFINITIONS

SEC. 103. As used in this Act—

(1) "Added restoration benefits" means benefits provided by added restoration insurance in accordance with section 209 or section 304 of this Act.

(2) "Allowable expense" means reasonable charges incurred for, or the reasonable value of (where no charges are

incurred), reasonably needed and used products, services, and accommodations for—

    (A) professional medical treatment and care;

    (B) emergency medical services;

    (C) medical and vocational rehabilitation services; and

    (D) expenses directly related to the funeral, burial, cremation, or other form of disposition of the remains of a deceased victim, not to exceed $1,000.

The term does not include—

    (i) that portion of a charge for a room in a hospital, clinic, convalescent, or nursing home, or any other institution engaged in providing nursing care and related services, in excess of a reasonable and customary charge for semiprivate accommodations, unless more intensive care is medically required; or

    (ii) any amount includable in work loss, replacement services loss, or survivor's loss.

(3) "Basic restoration benefits" means benefits provided in accordance with this Act for the net loss sustained by a victim, subject to any applicable limitations, exclusions, deductibles, waiting periods, disqualifications, or other terms and conditions provided or authorized in accordance with this Act. Basic restoration benefits do not include benefits for damage to property.

(4) "Commissioner" means the commissioner of insurance or the head of the department, commission, board, or other agency of a State which is charged by the law of that State with the supervision and regulation of the business of insurance.

(5) "Department" means the department of motor vehicles or the department, commission, board, or other agency of a State which is charged by the law of that State with the administration of laws and regulations regarding registration of motor vehicles.

(6) "Emergency medical services" means services necessary to mitigate injury to any victim during the period immediately and proximately following an accident (including, but not limited to, communications, transportation, and treatment by medical and paramedical personnel through an emergency medical services system), which are supplied or provided in accordance with applicable State law.

(7) "Emergency medical services system" means a system which provides for the arrangement of personnel, facilities, and equipment for the effective and coordinated delivery in an appropriate geographical area of health care services under emergency conditions, which is administered by a public or nonprofit private entity which has the authority and the resources to provide effective administration, and which

meet the requirements of section 1206(b)(4) of the Public Health Service Act.

(8) "Government" means the government of the United States, any State, any political subdivision of a State, any instrumentality of two or more States, or any agency, subdivision, or department of any such government, including any corporation or other association organized by a government for the execution of a government program and subject to control by a government, or any corporation or agency established under an interstate compact or international treaty.

(9) "Injury" means accidentally sustained bodily harm to an individual and that individual's illness, disease, or death resulting therefrom.

(10) "Insurance" means a contract, self-insurance, or any other legally binding obligation to pay or provide no-fault benefits or any required tort liability.

(11) "Insured" means—

    (A) an individual identified by name as an insured in a contract of basic restoration insurance complying with this Act; and

    (B) a spouse or other relative of a named insured, a minor in the custody of a named insured, and a minor in the custody of a relative of a named insured if—

        (i) not identified by name as an insured in any

other contract of basic restoration insurance complying with this Act, and

   (ii) in residence in the same household with a named insured.

An individual is in residence in the same household if he usually makes his home in the same family unit, even though he temporarily lives elsewhere.

(12) "Insurer" means a legally constituted entity, other than a self-insurer or an obligated government, which is authorized under State law to provide security covering a motor vehicle in such State.

(13) "Loss" means accrued economic detriment resulting from injury arising out of the maintenance or use of a motor vehicle consisting of, and limited to, allowable expense, work loss, replacement services loss, and survivor's loss.

(14) "Loss of income" means gross income actually lost by a victim or that would have been lost but for any income continuation plan, reduced by—

   (A) ninety per centum of any income which such individual earns from substitute work;

   (B) income which such individual would have earned in available substitute work he was capable of performing but unreasonably failed to undertake; or

   (C) any income which such individual would have

earned by hiring an available substitute to perform self-employment services but unreasonably failed to do.

(15) "Maintenance or use of a motor vehicle" means maintenance or use of a motor vehicle as a vehicle, including, incident to its maintenance or use as a vehicle, occupying, entering into, or alighting from it. Maintenance or use of a motor vehicle does not include—

(A) conduct within the course of a business of repairing, servicing, or otherwise maintaining motor vehicles unless the conduct occurs off the business premises; or

(B) conduct in the course of loading or unloading a motor vehicle unless the conduct occurs while occupying, entering into, or alighting from it.

(16) "Medical and vocational rehabilitation services" means services necessary to reduce disability and to restore the physical, psychological, social, and vocational functioning of a victim. Such services may include, but are not limited to, medical care, diagnostic and evaluation procedures, physical and occupational therapy, other medically necessary therapies, speech pathology and audiology, nursing care under the supervision of a registered nurse, medical social services, vocational rehabilitation and training services, occupational licenses and tools, and transportation where necessary to secure medical and vocational rehabilitation services.

A restoration obligor is not obligated to provide basic restoration benefits for allowable expense for medical and vocational rehabilitation services unless the facility in which or through which such services are provided has been accredited by the department of health, the equivalent government agency responsible for health programs, or the accrediting designee of such department or agency of the State in which such services are provided, as being in accordance with applicable requirements and regulations.

(17) "Motor vehicle" means a vehicle of a kind required to be registered under the laws relating to motor vehicles of the State in which such vehicle is located except that a vehicle having less than four wheels may be specially treated, at the option of a State establishing a no-fault plan for motor vehicle insurance in accordance with title II of this Act, with respect to the requirements and benefits of such plan.

(18) "Net loss" means loss less benefits or advantages required to be subtracted from loss in calculating net loss pursuant to section 208 of this Act.

(19) "Noneconomic detriment" means pain, suffering, inconvenience, physical impairment, and other nonpecuniary damage recoverable under the tort law applicable to injury arising out of the maintenance or use of a motor vehicle. The term does not include punitive or exemplary damages.

(20) "No-fault benefits" means basic restoration benefits, added restoration benefits, or both.

(21) "No-fault insurance" means basic restoration insurance, added restoration insurance, or both.

(22) "Owner" means an individual, government, corporation, company, association, firm, partnership, joint stock company, foundation, institution, society, union, club, church, or any other group of persons organized for any purpose, other than a lienholder or secured party, that owns or has title to a motor vehicle or is entitled to the use and possession of a motor vehicle subject to a security interest held by another. The term includes a lessee of a motor vehicle having the right to possession under a lease with option to purchase.

(23) "Restoration obligor' means an insurer, self-insurer, or obligated government providing no-fault benefits in accordance with this Act.

(24) "Replacement services loss" means expenses reasonably incurred in obtaining ordinary and necessary services in lieu of those the victim would have performed, not for income, but for the benefit of himself or his family, if he had not been injured.

(25) "Secretary" means the Secretary of Transportation.

(26) "Secured vehicle" means a motor vehicle for

which security is provided in accordance with section 104 of this Act.

(27) "Security covering a motor vehicle", "security covering the vehicle", and "security" mean the security which is provided in accordance with section 104 of this Act.

(28) "Self-insurer" means an owner or any person providing security pursuant to subsections (b) or (c) of section 104 of this Act.

(29) "State" means a State of the United States, the District of Columbia, Guam, and the Virgin Islands.

(30) "State vocational rehabilitation agency" means the agency in the State which administers the State plan for vocational rehabilitation services under the Vocational Rehabilitation Act (29 U.S.C. 35).

(31) "Survivor" means an individual identified in the wrongful death statute of the State of domicile of a deceased victim as one entitled to receive benefits by reason of the death of another individual.

(32) "Survivor's loss" means the—

 (A) loss of income of a deceased victim which would probably have been contributed to a survivor or survivors, if such victim had not sustained the fatal injury; and

 (B) expenses reasonably incurred by a survivor or survivors, after a victim's death resulting from

injury, in obtaining ordinary and necessary services in lieu of those which the victim would have performed, not for income, but for their benefit, if he had not sustained the fatal injury,
reduced by expenses which the survivor or survivors would probably have incurred but avoided by reason of the victim's death resulting from injury.

(33) "Victim" means an individual who suffers injury arising out of the maintenance or use of a motor vehicle; "deceased victim" means a victim suffering death resulting from injury.

(34) "Without regard to fault" means irrespective of fault as a cause of injury.

(35) "Work loss" means—

(A) loss of gross income of a victim, as calculated pursuant to the provisions of section 207 of this Act; and

(B) reasonable expenses of a victim for hiring a substitute to perform self-employment services, thereby mitigating loss of income, or for hiring special help, thereby enabling a victim to work and mitigate loss of income.

REQUIRED MOTOR VEHICLE INSURANCE

SEC. 104. (a) SECURITY COVERING A MOTOR VEHICLE.—Every owner of a motor vehicle which is registered in a State in which a State no-fault plan for motor vehicle insurance in accordance with title II or title III of this Act is in effect, or which is operated in such State by the owner or with his permission, shall continuously provide security covering such motor vehicle while such vehicle is either present or registered in such State. Security shall be provided for the payment of basic restoration benefits, and at the option of a State establishing a plan in accordance with title II of this Act, for the payment of other benefits or tort liability. The owner or any other person may provide security covering a motor vehicle by a contract of insurance with an insurer or by qualifying as a self-insurer or as an obligated government.

(b) SELF-INSURANCE.—Self-insurance, subject to approval of the commissioner or department, is effected by filing with the department in satisfactory form—

> (1) a continuing undertaking by the owner or other appropriate person to pay basic restoration benefits and any tort liability required by State law in amounts not less than those required by such State law, to perform all obligations imposed in accordance with this Act, and to elect to pay such added restoration benefits as are specified in the undertaking;

> (2) evidence that appropriate provision exists for prompt and efficient administration of all claims, benefits,

nd obligations provided in accordance with this Act; and

(3) evidence that reliable financial arrangements deposits, resources, or commitments exist providing assurance substantially equivalent to that afforded by a contract of insurance complying with this Act for payment of no-fault benefits, any required tort liability, and performance of all other obligations imposed in accordance with this Act.

(c) OBLIGATED GOVERNMENT.—A government may provide security with respect to any motor vehicle owned or operated by it by lawfully obligating itself to pay basic restoration benefits in accordance with this Act, and such added restoration benefits as are specified in the undertaking.

(d) OBLIGATION UPON TERMINATION OF SECURITY.—An owner of a motor vehicle who ceases to maintain the security required in accordance with this Act shall immediately surrender the registration certificate and license plates for the vehicle to the department and may not operate or permit operation of the vehicle in any State until security has again been furnished as required in accordance with this Act. A person other than the owner who ceases to maintain such security shall immediately notify the owner and the department, who may not operate or permit operation of the vehicle until security has again been furnished. An insurer who has issued a contract of insurance and knows or has reason to believe the contract is for the purpose of providing security shall immediately give notice to the department of the termination of the insurance. If the commissioner or department withdraws approval of security provided by a self-insurer or knows that the conditions for self-insurance have ceased to exist, he shall immediately give notice thereof to the department. These requirements may be modified or waived by the department.

AVAILABILITY OF INSURANCE

SEC. 105. (a) PLAN.—(1) The commissioner shall establish and implement or approve and supervise a plan assuring that any required no-fault benefits and tort liability coverages for motor vehicles will be conveniently and expeditiously available, subject only to payment or provisions for payment of the premium, to each individual who cannot conveniently obtain insurance through ordinary methods at rates not in excess of those applicable to similarly situated individuals under the plan. The plan may provide reasonable means for the transfer of individuals insured thereunder into the ordinary market, at the same or lower rates, pursuant to regulations established by the commissioner. The plan may be implemented by assignment of applicants among insurers, pooling, any joint insuring or reinsuring arrangement, or any other method, including a State fund, that results in all applicants being conveniently afforded the insurance coverages on reasonable and not unfairly discriminatory terms.

(2) The plan shall make available added restoration benefits and tort liability coverage together with other contract provisions which the commissioner determines are reasonably needed by applicants and are commonly afforded in voluntary markets. The plan must also assure that there is available through the private sector or otherwise to all applicants adequate premium financing or provision for the installment payment of premiums subject to customary terms and conditions.

(3) All insurers writing no-fault benefits and tort liability coverages in a State shall participate in the plan in such State. The plan shall provide for equitable apportionment, among all participating insurers writing any insurance coverage required under the plan, of the financial burdens of insurance provided to applicants under the plan and the costs of operation of the plan.

(4) Subject to the supervision and approval of the commissioner, insurers may consult and agree with each other and with other appropriate persons as to the organization, administration, and operation of the plan and as to rates and rate modifications for insurance coverages provided under the plan. Rates and rate modifications adopted or

charged for insurance coverages provided under the plan shall—

   (A) be first adopted or approved by the commissioner; and

   (B) be reasonable and not unfairly discriminatory among similarly situated applicants for insurance pursuant to regulations established by the commissioner.

(5) Subject to the supervision and approval of the commissioner, the plan shall afford required coverages for motor vehicles to any economically disadvantaged individual, at rates as determined by the State, which shall not be so great as to deny such individual access to insurance which it is necessary for him to have in order to earn income and to be or remain gainfully employed.

(6) To carry out the objectives of this subsection, the commissioner may adopt rules, make orders, enter into agreements with other governmental and private entities and individuals, and form and operate or authorize the formation and operation of bureaus and other legal entities.

(b) CANCELLATION, REFUSAL TO RENEW, OR OTHER TERMINATION OF INSURANCE.—(1) Every contract of insurance providing security covering a motor vehicle which is not one of five or more motor vehicles under common ownership insured under a single insuring agreement, except as provided by paragraphs (2) and (5) of this subsection, may not be canceled, modified, or otherwise terminated by the insurer nor may the insurer fail to renew except at specified dates or intervals which may not be less than six months after the inception of coverage or thereafter less than six months apart.

(2) An insurer may terminate insurance if written notice of termination, including the reasons therefor, is mailed or delivered to the insured at least thirty days before the effective date of termination—

    (A) by cancellation at any time within seventy-five days after the inception of initial coverage;

    (B) by cancellation for nonpayment of—

        (i) premium when due, or

        (ii) any premium installment when due for which reasonable and separate notice has been given; or

    (C) by exclusion of an insured whose license to operate a motor vehicle has been revoked, following a hearing and pursuant to State law.

(3) Except as permitted in paragraph (2) of this subsection, any termination of insurance by an insurer which is permitted by the insurance contract and not prohibited by paragraph (1) of this subsection, including any refusal by the insurer to renew the insurance at the expiration of its term and any modification by the insurer of the terms and condi-

tions of the insurance unfavorable to the insured, is nevertheless ineffective, unless written notice of intention to modify, not to renew, or otherwise to terminate the insurance has been mailed or delivered to the insured at least thirty days before the effective date of the modification, expiration, or other termination of the insurance.

(4) For purposes of this subsection a cancellation or refusal to renew by or at the direction of any person acting pursuant to any power or authority under any premium finance plan, agreement, or arrangement, whether or not with power of attorney or assignment from the insured, constitutes a cancellation or refusal to renew by the insurer.

(5) This subsection does not limit or apply to any termination, modification, or cancellation of the insurance, or to any suspension of insurance coverage, by or at the written request of the insured or upon the sale or other transfer of the secured vehicle to an individual who is not an insured under the same contract of insurance.

(6) This subsection does not affect any right an insurer has under other law to rescind or otherwise terminate insurance because of fraud or other willful misconduct of the insured at the inception of the insuring transaction or the right of either party to reform the contract on the basis of mutual mistake of fact.

(7) An insurer, his authorized agents and employees,

and any person furnishing information upon which he has relied, are not liable in any action or proceeding brought because of any statement made in good faith pursuant to paragraph (2) of this subsection.

PAYMENT OF CLAIMS FOR NO-FAULT BENEFITS

SEC. 106. (a) IN GENERAL.—(1) No-fault benefits are payable monthly as loss accrues. Loss accrues not when injury occurs, but as allowable expense, work loss, replacement services loss, or survivor's loss is sustained.

(2) No-fault benefits are overdue if not paid within thirty days after the receipt by the restoration obligor of each submission of reasonable proof of the fact and amount of loss sustained, unless the restoration obligor designates, upon receipt of an initial claim for no-fault benefits, periods not to exceed thirty-one days each for accumulating all such claims received within each such period, in which case such benefits are overdue if not paid within fifteen days after the close of each such period. If reasonable proof is supplied as to only part of a claim, but the part amounts to $100 or more, benefits for such part are overdue if not paid within the time mandated by this paragraph. An obligation for basic restoration benefits for an item of allowable expense may be discharged by the restoration obligor by reimbursing the victim or by making direct payment to the supplier or provider of products, services, or accommodations within the time man-

dated by this paragraph. Overdue payments bear interest at the rate of eighteen per centum per annum.

(3) A claim for no-fault benefits shall be paid without deduction for the benefits or advantages which are to be subtracted from loss in calculating net loss in accordance with section 208 (a) of this Act, if such benefits or advantages have not been paid or provided to such claimant prior to the date the no-fault benefits are overdue or the no-fault benefits claim is paid. The restoration obligor is thereupon entitled to recover reimbursement from the person obligated to pay or provide such benefits or advantages or from the claimant who actually receives them.

(4) A restoration obligor may bring an action to recover reimbursement for no-fault benefits which are paid upon the basis of an intentional misrepresentation of a material fact by a claimant or a supplier or provider of an item of allowable expense, if such restoration obligor reasonably relied upon such misrepresentation. The action may be brought only against such supplier or provider, unless the claimant has intentionally misrepresented the facts or knew of the misrepresentation. A restoration obligor may offset amounts he is entitled to recover from the claimant under this paragraph against any no-fault benefits otherwise due.

(5) A restoration obligor who rejects a claim for basic restoration benefits shall give to the claimant written notice

of the rejection promptly, but in no event more than thirty days after the receipt of reasonable proof of the loss. Such notice shall specify the reason for such rejection and inform the claimant of the terms and conditions of his right to obtain an attorney. If a claim is rejected for a reason other than that the person is not entitled to basic restoration benefits claimed, the written notice shall inform the claimant that he may file his claim with the assigned claims bureau and shall give the name and address of the bureau.

(b) RELEASE OR SETTLEMENT OF CLAIM.—(1) Except as otherwise provided in this subsection, no-fault benefits shall not be denied or terminated because the victim executed a release or other settlement agreement. A claim for no-fault benefits may be discharged by a settlement agreement for an agreed amount payable in installments or in a lump sum, if the reasonably anticipated net loss does not exceed $2,500. In all other cases, a claim may be discharged by a settlement to the extent authorized by State law and upon a finding, by a court of competent jurisdiction, that the settlement is in the best interest of the claimant and any beneficiaries of the settlement, and that the claimant understands and consents to such settlement, and upon payment by the restoration obligor of the costs of such proceeding including a reasonable attorney's fee (based upon actual time expended) to the attorney selected by or appointed for the claimant. Such costs may not be charged to or deducted from the proceeds of the settlement. Upon approval of the settlement, the court may make appropriate orders concerning the safeguarding and disposing of the proceeds of the settlement and may direct as a condition of the settlement agreement, that the restoration obligor pay the reasonable cost of appropriate future medical and vocational rehabilitation services.

(2) A settlement agreement for an amount payable in installments shall be modified as to amounts to be paid in the future, if it is shown that a material and substantial change of circumstances has occurred or that there is newly-discovered evidence concerning the claimant's physcian condition, loss, or rehabilitation which could not have been known previously or discovered in the exercise of reasonable diligence.

(3) A settlement agreement may be set aside if it is procured by fraud or if its terms are unconscionable.

(c) TIME LIMITATIONS ON ACTIONS TO RECOVER BENEFITS.—(1) If no-fault benefits have not been paid for loss arising otherwise than from death, an action therefor may be commenced not later than two years after the victim suffers the loss and either knows, or in the exercise of reasonable diligence should have known, that the loss was caused by the accident, or not later than four years after the accident, whichever is earlier. If no-fault benefits have been paid for loss arising otherwise than from death, an action for further

28

benefits, other than survivor's benefits, by either the same or another claimant, may be commenced not later than two years after the last payment of benefits.

(2) If no-fault benefits have not been paid to the deceased victim or his survivor or survivors, an action for survivor's benefits may be commenced not later than one year after the death or four years after the accident from which death results, whichever is earlier. If survivor's benefits have been paid to any survivor, an action for further survivor's benefits by either the same or another claimant may be commenced not later than two years after the last payment of benefits. If no-fault benefits have been paid for loss suffered by a victim before his death resulting from the injury, an action for survivor's benefits may be commenced not later than one year after the death or six years after the last payment of benefits, whichever is earlier.

(3) If timely action for basic restoration benefits is commenced against a restoration obligor and benefits are denied because of a determination that the restoration obligor's coverage is not applicable to the claimant under the provisions of section 205 of this Act, an action against the applicable restoration obligor or the restoration obligor to whom a claim is assigned under an assigned claims plan may be commenced not later than sixty days after the determination becomes final

or the last date on which the action could otherwise have been commenced, whichever is later.

(4) Except as paragraph (1), (2), or (3) prescribes a longer period, an action by a claimant on an assigned claim which has been timely presented in accordance with the provisions of section 108(c) of this Act may not be commenced more than sixty days after the claimant receives written notice of rejection of the claim by the restoration obligor to which it was assigned.

(5) If a person entitled to no-fault benefits is under a legal disability when the right to bring an action for the benefits first accrues, the period of his disability is not a part of the time limited for commencement of the action.

(d) ASSIGNMENT OF BENEFITS.—An assignment of or an agreement to assign any right in accordance with this Act for loss accruing in the future is unenforceable except as to benefits for—

   (1) work loss to secure payment of alimony, maintenance, or child support; or

   (2) allowable expense to the extent the benefits are for the cost of products, services, or accommodations provided or to be provided by the assignee.

(e) DEDUCTION AND SETOFF.—Except as otherwise

provided in this Act, basic restoration benefits shall be paid without deduction or setoff.

(f) EXEMPTION OF BENEFITS.—(1) No-fault benefits for allowable expense are exempt from garnishment, attachment, execution, and any other process or claim, except upon the claim of a creditor who has provided products, services, or accommodations to the extent benefits are for allowable expense for those products, services, or accommodations.

(2) Basic restoration benefits other than those for allowable expense are exempt from garnishment, attachment, execution, and any other process or claim for benefits attributable to loss sustained within the first sixty days following the accident resulting in injury. Other basic restoration benefits (except for items of allowable expense) are exempt to the extent that wages or earnings are exempt under any applicable law exempting wages or earnings from such process or claims.

ATTORNEY'S FEES AND COSTS

SEC. 107. (a) FEES OF CLAIMANT'S ATTORNEY.— (1) If any overdue no-fault benefits are paid by the restoration obligor after receipt of notice of representation of a claimant in connection with a claim or action for no-fault the court determines that the claim (or any significant part thereof is fraudulent or so excessive as to have no reasonable foundation), a reasonable attorney's fee (based upon actual time expended) shall be paid by the restoration obligor to such attorney. No part of the attorney's fee for representing the claimant in connection with a claim or action for no-fault benefits may be charged or deducted from benefits otherwise due to such claimant and no part of such benefits may be applied to such fee.

(2) In any such action brought against the claimant by the restoration obligor, the court may award the claimant's attorney a reasonable attorney's fee for defending such action, which shall be paid by the restoration obligor.

(b) FEES OF RESTORATION OBLIGOR'S ATTORNEY.— A restoration obligor shall be allowed a reasonable attorney's fee for defending a claim if the court determines that the claim or any significant part thereof is fraudulent or so excessive as to have no reasonable foundation. The fee may be treated as an offset against any benefits due or to become due to the claimant.

ASSIGNED CLAIMS

SEC. 108. (a) GENERAL.—(1) If a State no-fault plan for motor vehicle insurance in accordance with title II or title III of this Act is in effect on the date when the accident resulting in injury occurs, a victim or the survivor or survivors of a deceased victim may obtain basic restoration benefits through the assigned claims plan established, pursuant to subsection (b) of this section, in the State of domicile, if any, of the victim or deceased victim, or if none, in the State, in which the accident resulting in injury occurs, if basic restoration insurance—

    (A) is not applicable to the injury for a reason other than those specified in the provisions on ineligible claimants;

    (B) is not applicable to the injury because the victim converted a motor vehicle while he was under fifteen years of age;

    (C) applicable to the injury cannot be identified;

    (D) applicable to the injury is inadequate to provide the contracted-for benefits because of financial inability of a restoration obligor to fulfill its obligations; or

    (E) benefits are refused by a restoration obligor for a reason other than that the individual is not entitled in accordance with this Act to the basic restoration benefits claimed.

(2) If a claim qualifies for assignment under paragraph (1) (C), (D), or (E) of this subsection, the assigned claims bureau or any insurer to whom the claim is assigned is subrogated to all rights of the claimant against the restoration obligor legally obligated to provide basic restoration benefits to the claimant, or against any successor in interest to or substitute for such obligor for such benefits as are provided by the assignee.

(3) If an individual receives basic restoration benefits through the assigned claims plan for any reason other than because of the financial inability of a restoration obligor to fulfill its obligation, all benefits or advantages that such individual receives or is entitled to receive as a result of such injury, other than life insurance benefits or benefits by way of succession at death or in discharge of familial obligations of support, shall be subtracted from loss in calculating net loss.

(4) An assigned claim of an individual who does not comply with the requirement of providing security for the payment of basic restoration benefits, or of an individual as to whom the security is invalidated because of his fraud or willful misconduct, is subject to—

>   (A) all the maximum optional deductibles and exclusions required to be offered; and

>   (B) a deduction in the amount of $500 for each year or part thereof of the period of his continuous failure to provide security, applicable to any benefits otherwise payable except basic restoration benefits for allowable expense.

(b) ASSIGNED CLAIMS PLAN.—(1) Restoration obligors providing basic restoration insurance in a State may organize and maintain, subject to approval and regulation by the commissioner, an assigned claims bureau and an assigned claims plan and adopt rules for their operation and for assessment of costs on a fair and equitable basis consistent with this Act. If such bureau and plan are not organized and maintained in a manner considered by the commissioner to be consistent with this Act and with State law, he shall organize and maintain an assigned claims bureau and an assigned claims plan. Each restoration obligor insurer providing basic restoration insurance in a State shall participate in the assigned claims bureau and the assigned claims plan in that State. Costs incurred shall be allocated fairly and equitably among the restoration obligors.

(2) The assigned claims bureau shall promptly—

    (A) assign each claim for no-fault benefits to an assignee who shall be a participating insurer; and

    (B) notify the chairman of the identity and address of such assignee.

Claims shall be assigned so as to minimize inconvenience to claimants. The assignee thereafter has rights and obligations as if he had issued a policy of basic restoration insurance complying with this Act applicable to the injury or, in a case involving the financial inability of a restoration obligor to perform its obligations, as if the assignee had written the applicable basic restoration insurance, undertaken the self-insurance, or lawfully obligated itself to pay basic restoration benefits.

(c) TIME FOR PRESENTING CLAIMS UNDER ASSIGNED CLAIMS PLAN.—(1) Except as provided in paragraph (2) of this subsection, an individual authorized to obtain basic restoration benefits through the assigned claims plan shall notify the assigned claims bureau of his claim within the time that would have been allowed pursuant to section 106(c) of this Act for commencing an action for basic restoration benefits against any restoration obligor, other than an assigned claims bureau, in any case in which identifiable no-fault insurance coverage was in effect and applicable to the claim.

(2) If timely action for basic restoration benefits is commenced against a restoration obligor who is unable to fulfill his obligations because of financial inability, an individual authorized to obtain basic restoration benefits through the assigned claims plan shall notify the bureau of his claim within six months after his discovery of such financial inability.

STATE REGULATION

SEC. 109. (a) RATES AND RATING.—The commissioner, in accordance with applicable State law, shall regulate restoration obligors providing security covering a motor vehicle in his State. The rates charged for security shall be established, determined, and modified in each State only in accordance with the provisions of the applicable rating law of such State.

(b) PUBLIC INFORMATION.—The commissioner shall provide the means to inform purchasers of insurance, in a manner adequate to permit them to compare prices, about rates being charged by insurers for no-fault benefits and tort liability coverage.

(c) ACCOUNTABILITY PROGRAM.—(1) The commissioner, through the State vocational rehabilitation agency, shall establish and maintain a program for the regular and periodic evaluation of medical and vocational rehabilitation services for which reimbursement or payment is sought from a restoration obligor as an item of allowable expense to assure that—

>   (A) the services are medical and vocational rehabilitation services, as defined in section 103(16) of this Act;

>   (B) the recipient of the services is making progress toward a greater level of independent functioning and the services are necessary to such progress and continued progress; and

>   (C) the charges for the services for which reimbursement or payment is sought are fair and reasonable.

Progress reports shall be made periodically in writing on each case for which reimbursement or payment is sought under security for the payment of basic restoration benefits. Such reports shall be prepared by the supervising physician or

1 rehabilitation counselor and submitted to the State vocational
2 rehabilitation agency. The State vocational rehabilitation
3 agency shall file reports with the applicable restoration obligor
4 or obligors. Pursuant to this program, there shall be provision
5 for determinations to be made in writing of the rehabilitation
6 goals and needs of the victim and for the periodic assessment
7 of progress at reasonable time intervals by the supervising
8 physician or rehabilitation counselor.

9 (2) The commissioner is authorized to establish and
10 maintain a program for the regular and periodic evaluation
11 of his State's no-fault plan for motor vehicle insurance.

12 (d) AVAILABILITY OF SERVICES.—The commissioner
13 is authorized to coordinate with appropriate government
14 agencies in the creation and maintenance of an emergency
15 medical services system or systems, and to take all steps
16 necessary to assure that emergency medical services are
17 available for each victim suffering injury in the State. The
18 commissioner is authorized to take all steps necessary to as-
19 sure that medical and vocational rehabilitation services are
20 available for each victim resident in the State. Such steps
21 may include, but are not limited to, guarantees of loans or
22 other obligations of suppliers or providers of such services,
23 and support for training programs for personnel in programs
24 and facilities offering such services.

38

MOTOR VEHICLES IN INTERSTATE TRAVEL

SEC. 110. (a) GENERAL.—An owner of a motor vehicle who has complied with the requirements of security covering a motor vehicle in the State of registration of such vehicle shall be deemed to have complied with the requirements for such security in any State in which such vehicle is operating.

(b) CONFORMING COVERAGE.—(1) A restoration obligor providing security for the payment of basic restoration benefits shall be obligated to provide, and each contract of insurance for the payment of basic restoration benefits shall be construed to contain, coverage sufficient to satisfy the requirements for security covering a motor vehicle in any State in which any victim who is a claimant or whose survivors are claimants is domiciled or is injured.

(2) A restoration obligor providing security for the payment of basic restoration benefits shall be obligated to provide, and each contract of insurance for the payment of basic restoration benefits shall be construed to contain, coverage of $50,000 to protect the owner or operator of a motor vehicle from tort liability to which he is exposed through application of the law of the State of domicile of a victim (or in the State in which the accident resulting in injury or harm to property occurs if a victim is not domiciled in any State), but to which he would not have been exposed

through application of the law of the State of registration of the motor vehicle.

(c) APPLICABLE LAW.—(1) The basic restoration benefits available to any victim or to any survivor of a deceased victim shall be determined pursuant to the provisions of the State no-fault plan for motor vehicle insurance in accordance with title II or title III of this Act which is in effect in the State of domicile of the victim on the date when the motor vehicle accident resulting in injury occurs. If there is no such State no-fault plan in effect or if the victim is not domiciled in any State, then basic restoration benefits available to any victim shall be determined pursuant to the provisions of the State no-fault plan for motor vehicle insurance, if any, in effect in the State in which the accident resulting in injury occurs.

(2) The right of a victim or of a survivor of a deceased victim to sue in tort shall be determined by the law of the State of domicile of such victim. If a victim is not domiciled in a State, such right to sue shall be determined by the law of the State in which the accident resulting in injury or damage to property occurs.

RIGHTS AND DUTIES OF RESTORATION OBLIGORS

SEC. 111. (a) REIMBURSEMENT AND SUBROGATION.—
(1) Except as provided in paragraphs (2), (3), and (4) of this subsection, a restoration obligor—

(A) does not have and may not contract, directly or indirectly, in whole or in part, for a right of reimbursement from or subrogation to the proceeds of a victim's claim for relief or to a victim's cause of action for noneconomic detriment; and

(B) may not directly or indirectly contract for, or be granted by a State, any right of reimbursement from any other restoration obligor not acting as a reinsurer for no-fault benefits which it has paid or is obligated to pay as a result of injury to a victim.

(2) Whenever an individual who receives or is entitled to receive no-fault benefits for an injury has a claim or cause of action against any other person for breach of an obligation or duty causing the injury or for breach of express or implied warranty, the restoration obligor is subrogated to the rights of the claimant and has a claim for relief or a cause of action, separate from that of the claimant, to the extent that:

(A) elements of damage compensated for by security for the payment of no-fault benefits are recoverable; and

(B) the restoration obligor has paid or become obligated to pay accrued or future no-fault benefits.

(3) Notwithstanding the provisions of paragraph (1)(B) of this subsection, a State may grant a right of reimbursement among and between restoration obligors based

upon a determination of fault, where such restoration obligors have paid or are obligated to pay benefits for loss arising out of an accident resulting in injury in which one or more of the motor vehicles is of a type other than a private passenger motor vehicle and by designation the State has determined that the owner of such type would receive an unreasonable economic advantage or suffer an unreasonable economic disadvantage in the absence of the grant of such right of reimbursement: *Provided,* That in such event such right of reimbursement may be granted only with respect to benefits paid for loss in excess of $5,000.

(4) Nothing in this subsection shall preclude any person supplying or providing products, services, or accommodations from contracting or otherwise providing for a right of reimbursement to any basic restoration benefits for allowable expense.

(b) DUTY TO PAY BASIC RESTORATION BENEFITS.— A restoration obligor providing security for the payment of basic restoration benefits shall pay or otherwise provide such benefits without regard to fault to each individual entitled thereto, pursuant to the terms and conditions of the State no-fault plan for motor vehicle insurance applicable thereto.

(c) INDEMNITY.—A restoration obligor has a right of indemnity against an individual who has converted a motor vehicle involved in an accident, or against an individual who

42

has intentionally injured himself or another individual, for no-fault benefits paid for—

 (1) the loss caused by the conduct of that individual;

 (2) the cost of processing the claims for such benefits; and

 (3) the cost of enforcing this right of indemnity, including reasonable attorney's fees.

(d) REFERRAL FOR REHABILITATION SERVICES.—The restoration obligor shall promptly refer each victim to whom basic restoration benefits are expected to be payable for more than two months to the State vocational rehabilitation agency.

JURISDICTION OF FEDERAL COURTS

SEC. 112. No district court of the United States may entertain an action for no-fault benefits unless the United States is a party to the action.

FEDERAL MOTOR VEHICLE

SEC. 113. (a) (1) GENERAL.—Notwithstanding any other provision of law, a claim against the United States as a restoration obligor for injury arising out of the maintenance or use of a Federal motor vehicle which is a secured vehicle shall be governed by this Act. A Federal motor vehicle is a secured vehicle, for purposes of this Act, whenever it is located or operated in the territorial area of any State, Puerto Rico, Canada, or Mexico.

(2) The level of basic restoration benefits which the United States shall pay or provide shall be controlled by the no-fault plan for motor vehicle insurance in effect in the State of domicile of the victim, if any, or if none, in the State in which the accident resulting in injury occurs.

(b) PROCEDURES.—The Secretary, in cooperation with the Administrator of General Services, shall promulgate, and may from time to time revise, regulations with respect to security covering a Federal motor vehicle and administrative procedures to be followed in claims against the United States for no-fault benefits.

(c) DEFINITIONS.—As used in this section—

(1) "Federal agency" means any branch, department, commission, administration, authority, board, or bureau of, or any corporation owned or controlled by, the Government of the United States.

(2) "Federal motor vehicle" means a motor vehicle owned or leased by a Federal agency and operated with its express or implied permission.

SEPARABILITY

SEC. 114. If any provision of this Act or any application thereof to any individual or circumstance is held invalid, the invalidity shall not affect any provision or application of the Act which can be given effect without the involved provision or application, and to this end the provisions of this Act are separable: *Provided*, That if any provision in paragraph (5) of subsection (a) of section 206 of this Act, or any application thereof to any individual or circumstance, is held invalid, this Act shall be interpreted as if such paragraph (5) had never been enacted.

TITLE II—NATIONAL STANDARDS FOR STATE NO-FAULT MOTOR VEHICLE INSURANCE PLAN

STATE NO-FAULT PLAN IN ACCORDANCE WITH THIS TITLE

SEC. 201. (a) PREEMPTION.—Any provision of any State law which would prevent the establishment or administration in such a State of a no-fault plan for motor vehicle insurance in accordance with this title or title III of this Act is preempted.

(b) STATE PLAN.—By the completion of the first general session of the State legislature which commences after the date of enactment of this Act, a State may establish a no-fault plan for motor vehicle insurance in accordance with this title. Upon the establishment of such a plan, the commissioner shall promptly submit to the Secretary a certified copy of such plan, together with all relevant information which is requested by the Secretary.

(c) DETERMINATION BY SECRETARY.—Within ninety days after the Secretary receives a copy of a State no-fault plan established under subsection (b) or (e) of this section, the Secretary shall make a determination whether such State has established a no-fault plan for motor vehicle insurance in accordance with this title. Unless the Secretary determines, pursuant to this section, that a State no-fault plan is not in accordance with this title, the plan shall go into effect in such State on the date designated in the plan. In no event shall such State plan go into effect less than nine months or more than twelve months after the date of its establishment.

(d) PERIODIC REVIEW.—The Secretary shall periodically, but not less than once every three years, review each State no-fault plan for motor vehicle insurance, which has been approved under subsection (c) of this section and for which there is experience, to determine whether such plan is still in accordance with this title and to evaluate the success of such plan in terms of the policy set forth and declared in section 102 of this Act. To facilitate such review, the commissioner in each such State shall submit to the Secretary periodically all relevant information which is requested by the Secretary. The Secretary shall report to the President and Congress simultaneously on July 1 each year on the results of such reviews, including any recommendations for legislation.

(e) ALTERNATIVE STATE PLAN.—(1) The alternative State no-fault plan for motor vehicle insurance (the State no-fault plan in accordance with title III of this Act) shall become applicable following the completion of the first general session of the State legislature which commences after the date of enactment of this Act unless, prior to such date, the Secretary has made a determination that such State has established a no-fault plan for motor vehicle insurance in accordance with this title. The alternative State no-fault plan shall go into effect in a State on the first day of the ninth month after such plan becomes applicable or on a date designated by the Secretary, whichever is earlier.

(2) If, after the alternative State no-fault plan is applicable or in effect in a State, the Secretary, upon petition, makes a determination, pursuant to subsection (c) of this section, that such State has established a no-fault plan in accordance with this title, such State no-fault plan shall go into effect and the alternative State no-fault plan shall cease to be applicable or in effect on a date to be designated by the Secretary.

(3) If, after a State no-fault plan in accordance with this title is in effect in a State, the Secretary makes a determination, pursuant to subsection (d) of this section, that such State no-fault plan is no longer in accordance with this title, then the plan which is no longer in accordance with this title shall cease to be in effect on a date to be designated by the

Secretary, and on that date the alternative State no-fault plan shall go into effect in such State.

(f) PROCEDURE.—(1) Before making any determination under this section, the Secretary shall publish a notice in the Federal Register and afford the State and all interested parties a reasonable opportunity to present their views by oral and written submission.

(2) The Secretary shall notify in writing the Governor of the affected State of any determinations made under this section and shall publish these determinations with reasons therefor in the Federal Register.

(3) Any determinations made by the Secretary under this section shall be subject to judicial review in accordance with chapter 7 of title 5, United States Code, in the United States court of appeals for the circuit in which is located the State whose plan is the subject of such determination or in the United States Court of Appeals for the District of Columbia Circuit. Any such review shall be instituted within sixty days from the date on which the determination made by the Secretary is published in the Federal Register.

(g) EXCEPTIONS.—(1) The provisions of this section are inapplicable to the extent inconsistent with this subsection.

(2) Any State which is a no-fault State, as defined in paragraph (4) of this subsection, may establish a no-fault plan for motor vehicle insurance in accordance with this title by the fourth anniversary of the date of enactment of this Act.

(3) The alternative State no-fault plan for motor vehicle insurance (the State no-fault plan in accordance with title III of this Act) shall become applicable in any State which is a no-fault State, as defined in paragraph (4) of this subsection on the fourth anniversary of the date of enactment of this Act unless, prior to such date, the Secretary has made a determination that such State has established a no-fault plan for motor vehicle insurance in accordance with this title.

(4) As used in this subsection, a "no-fault State" means a State which has enacted into law and put into effect a motor vehicle insurance law not later than September 1, 1975, which provides, at a minimum, for compulsory motor vehicle insurance; payment of benefits without regard to fault on a first-party basis where the value of such available benefits is not less than $2,000; and restrictions on the bringing of lawsuits in tort by victims for noneconomic detriment, in the form of a prohibition of such suits unless the victim suffers a certain quantum of loss or in the form

of a relevant change in the evidentiary rules of practice and proof with respect to such lawsuits.

(h) REPORTING REQUIREMENTS.—The Secretary, in cooperation with the commissioners, shall annually review the operation of State no-fault plans for motor vehicle insurance established in accordance with this Act and report on—

>   (1) the cost-savings resulting from the institution of any such plan which meets or exceeds the national standards set forth in this Act and any subsequent savings resulting from the continuing operation of such plans;

>   (2) appropriate methods for refunding to members of the motoring public any cost-savings realized from the institution and operation of such no-fault insurance plans;

>   (3) the impact of no-fault insurance on senior citizens; those who live in farming and rural areas; those who are economically disadvantaged, and those who live in inner cities;

>   (4) the impact of no-fault insurance on the problem of duplication of benefits when an individual has other insurance coverage which provides for compensation or reimbursement for lost wages or for health and accident (including hospitalization) benefits;

>   (5) the effect of no-fault insurance on court con-

gestion and delay resulting from backlogs in State and Federal courts;

(6) the impact of no-fault insurance, reduced speed limits, and other factors on automobile insurance rates; and

(7) the impact of no-fault insurance on competition within the insurance industry, particularly with respect to the competitive position of small insurance companies. The Secretary shall report to the President and Congress simultaneously on July 1 each year on the results of such review and determination together with his recommendations thereon.

(i) FINANCIAL ASSISTANCE TO STATES.—The Secretary is authorized to provide grants to any State for the purpose of reimbursing such State for any governmental cost increases resulting from the implementation or administration of a no-fault plan for motor vehicle insurance in accordance with this Act. The Secretary shall, by regulation, establish procedures for awarding such grants on a fair and equitable basis among the States.

(j) AUTHORIZATION FOR APPROPRIATIONS.—There is authorized to be appropriated to the Secretary to carry out his responsibilities under this Act such sums as are necessary, not to exceed $10,000,000, such sums to remain available until expended.

NATIONAL STANDARDS

SEC. 202. (a) GENERAL.—A State establishing a no-fault plan for motor vehicle insurance in accordance with this title shall enact a law which incorporates, at a minimum, title I of this Act, except sections 101, 102, 112, and 113, and this title except this section and section 201. The provisions of these sections, taken together, shall be known as the "national standards" for State no-fault motor vehicle insurance.

(b) CRITERIA.—A State no-fault plan for motor vehicle insurance is in accordance with this title if it meets or exceeds all of the national standards. A provision in a State plan "meets" a provision in the national standards if the substance of the State plan provision is the same as or the equivalent of the corresponding provision in the national standards. A provision in a State plan "exceeds" a provision in the national standards if the substance of the State plan provision is more favorable or beneficial to an insured or a claimant or more restrictive of tort liability than the corresponding provision in the national standards. Any provision in a State plan as to which there is no corresponding provision in the national standards shall not be evaluated in determining whether such plan meets or exceeds national standards provided such provision is not inconsistent with the national standards or the policy set forth and declared in section 102 of this Act.

RIGHT TO BASIC RESTORATION BENEFITS

SEC. 203. (a) ACCIDENT WITHIN A STATE.—If the accident resulting in injury occurs in a State in which a no-fault plan for motor vehicle insurance in accordance with this title or title III of this Act is in effect, any victim or any survivor of a deceased victim is entitled to receive basic restoration benefits.

(b) ACCIDENT OUTSIDE ANY STATE.—If the accident resulting in injury occurs outside a State in which a no-fault plan is in effect, but in any other State, Puerto Rico, Canada, or Mexico, a victim or a survivor of a deceased victim is entitled to receive basic restoration benefits if such victim is or was—

    (1) an insured; or

    (2) the driver or other occupant of a secured vehicle.

LIMITATIONS ON BENEFITS

SEC. 204. A State establishing a no-fault plan for motor vehicle insurance in accordance with this title—

    (a) may not limit basic restoration benefits for allowable expense, as defined in section 103(2) of this Act;

(b) may limit basic restoration benefits for work loss to—

   (1) a monthly amount equal to the lesser of the following—

      (A) $1,000 multiplied by a fraction whose numerator is the average per capita income in the State and whose denominator is the average per capita income in the United States, according to the latest available United States Department of Commerce figures; or

      (B) the disclosed amount, in the case of a named insured who, prior to the accident resulting in injury, voluntarily discloses his actual monthly earned income to his restoration obligor and agrees in writing with such obligor that such sum shall measure work loss; and

   (2) a total amount equal to— .

      (A) $25,000 multiplied by a fraction whose numerator is the average per capita income in the State and whose denominator is the average per capita income in the United States, according to the latest available United States Department of Commerce figures; or

      (B) such total amount as may be deter-

54

1 mined by the State but in no event less than
2 $15,000;
3 (c) may provide reasonable exclusions from or
4 monthly or total limitations on basic restoration benefits
5 for replacement services loss;
6 (d) may provide reasonable exclusions from or
7 monthly or total limitations on basic restoration benefits
8 for survivor's loss;
9 (e) may provide that any contract of insurance for
10 no-fault benefits allow an insurer to offer—
11 (1) a deductible not to exceed $100 for each
12 individual;
13 (2) a deductible not to exceed an amount
14 deemed reasonable by the insurance commissioner
15 of such State for each individual if he sustains injury
16 while he is operating a motor vehicle having less
17 than four wheels, is a passenger on such a vehicle,
18 or both; or
19 (3) a waiting period not to exceed one week.
20 Deductibles and waiting periods shall be applicable only
21 to claims of insureds and, in the case of the death of an
22 insured, to the claims of his survivors; and
23 (f) shall permit any legally constituted entity,
24 which is providing benefits other than no-fault bene-
25 fits on account of an injury, to coordinate such bene-

fits with benefits payable by any restoration obligor on account of the same injury. In order for such coordination to occur, there must be an equitable reduction or savings in the direct or indirect cost to the purchasers of benefits other than no-fault benefits. If benefits other than no-fault benefits are provided to an individual through a program, group, contract, or other arrangement for which some other person pays in whole or in part, then reduction or savings in the direct or indirect cost to such person of such benefits resulting from coordination shall be returned to such individual or utilized for his benefit.

SOURCE OF BASIC RESTORATION BENEFITS

SEC. 205. (a) APPLICABLE SECURITY.—The security for the payment of basic restoration benefits applicable to an injury to—

(1) an employee, or to the spouse or other relative of an employee residing in the same household as the employee, if the accident resulting in injury occurs while the victim or deceased victim is driving or occupying a motor vehicle furnished by such employee's employer, is the security for the payment of basic restoration benefits covering such motor vehicle or, if none, any other security applicable to such victim;

56

1   (2) an insured is the security under which the victim
2   or deceased victim is an insured;

3   (3) the driver or other occupant of a motor vehicle
4   involved in an accident resulting in injury who is not
5   an insured is the security covering such vehicle;

6   (4) an individual who is not an insured or the
7   driver or other occupant of a motor vehicle involved
8   in an accident resulting in injury is the security covering
9   any motor vehicle involved in such accident. For pur-
10   poses of this paragraph, a parked and unoccupied motor
11   vehicle is not a motor vehicle involved in an accident,
12 . unless it was parked so as to cause unreasonable risk
13   of injury; and

14   (5) any other individual is the applicable assigned
15   claims plan.

16   (b) MULTIPLE SOURCES OF EQUAL PRIORITY.—If
17 two or more obligations to pay basic restoration benefits
18 apply equally to an injury under the priorities set forth in
19 subsection (a) of this section, the restoration obligor against
20 whom a claim is asserted first shall process and pay the claim
21 as if wholly responsible. Such obligor is thereafter entitled
22 to recover contribution pro rata from any other such obligor
23 for the basic restoration benefits paid and for the costs of
24 processing the claim. If contribution is sought among restora-
25 tion obligors responsible under paragraph (4) of subsection

(a) of this section proration shall be based on the number of involved motor vehicles.

RESTRICTIONS ON TORT LIABILITY

SEC. 206. (a) PARTIAL ABOLITION.—Tort liability is abolished with respect to any injury that takes place in a State in which a no-fault plan for motor vehicle insurance in accordance with this title is in effect prior to such injury, if such injury arises out of the maintenance or use of a motor vehicle, except that—

(1) An owner of a motor vehicle involved in an accident remains liable if, at the time of the accident, the vehicle was not a secured vehicle.

(2) A person in the business of designing, manufacturing, repairing, servicing, or otherwise maintaining motor vehicles remains liable for injury arising out of a defect in such motor vehicle which is caused or not corrected by an act or omission in the course of such business, other than a defect in a motor vehicle which is operated by such business.

(3) An individual remains liable for injuring another individual, either intentionally or as a consequence of intending to injure himself.

(4) A person remains liable for loss which is not compensated because of any limitation in accordance with section 204 (b) (2), (c), or (d) of this Act.

58

A person is not liable for loss which is not compensated because of limitations in accordance with subsection (b) (1) or (e) of section 204 of this Act.

(5) A person remains liable for damages for non-economic detriment if the accident results in—

>(A) death, serious and permanent disfigurement, or other serious and permanent injury; or

>(B) more than ninety continuous days of total disability. As used in this subparagraph, "total disability" means medically determinable physical or mental impairment which prevents the victim from performing all or substantially all of the material acts and duties which constitute his usual and customary daily activities.

(6) A person or government remains liable if such injury was caused or not corrected by an act or omission not connected with the maintenance or use of a motor vehicle.

(b) NONREIMBURSABLE TORT FINE.—Nothing in this section shall be construed to immunize an individual from liability to pay a fine on the basis of fault in any proceeding based upon any act or omission arising out of the maintenance or use of a motor vehicle: *Provided*, That such fine may not be paid or reimbursed by an insurer or other restoration obligor.

WORK LOSS

SEC. 207. (a) REGULARLY EMPLOYED.—The work loss of a victim whose income prior to the injury was realized in regular increments shall be calculated by—

(1) determining his probable weekly income by dividing his probable annual income by fifty-two; and

(2) multiplying that quantity by the number of work weeks, or fraction thereof, the victim sustains loss of income during the accrual period.

(b) SEASONALLY EMPLOYED.—The work loss of a victim whose income is realized in irregular increments shall be calculated by—

(1) determining his probable weekly income by dividing his probable annual income by the number of weeks he normally works; and

(2) multiplying that quantity by the number of work weeks, or fraction thereof, the victim was unable to perform and would have performed work during the accrual period but for the injury.

(c) NOT EMPLOYED.—The work loss of a victim who is not employed when the accident resulting in injury occurs shall be calculated by—

(1) determining his probable weekly income by dividing his probable annual income by 52; and

(2) multiplying that quantity by the number of

work weeks, or fraction thereof, if any, the victim would reasonably have been expected to realize income during the accrual period.

(d) CHANGES IN BENEFITS.—(1) Sums for work loss shall be periodically increased in a manner corresponding to annual compensation increases that would predictably have resulted but for the injury.

(2) Beginning in 1978, and at five-year intervals thereafter, whenever a dollar figure limits benefits for work loss, that figure shall be multiplied by a number whose numerator is the average weekly earnings of production or nonsupervisory workers in the private nonfarm economy for that year and whose denominator is the average weekly earnings of this group of workers in the base year 1973, according to the latest available figures published by the Bureau of Labor Statistics of the United States Department of Labor.

(e) DEFINITIONS.—As used in this section—

(1) "Probable annual income" means, absent a showing that it is or would be some other amount, the following—

(A) twelve times the monthly gross income earned by the victim from work in the month preceding the month in which the accident resulting in injury occurs, or the average annual income earned by the victim from work during the years, not to exceed three, preceding the year in which the accident resulting in injury occurs, whichever is greater, for a victim regularly employed at the time of the accident;

(B) the average annual gross income earned by the victim from work during the years in which he was employed, not to exceed three, preceding the year in which the accident resulting in injury occurs, for a victim seasonally employed or not employed at the time of the accident; or

(C) the average annual gross income of a production or nonsupervisory worker in the private nonfarm economy in the State in which the victim is domiciled for the year in which the accident resulting in injury occurs, for a victim who has not previously earned income from work.

(2) "Work week" means the number of days an individual normally works in a seven-day period; "weekly income" means income earned during a work week.

NET LOSS

SEC. 208. (a) GENERAL.—Except as provided in paragraph (3) of subsection (a) of section 108 of this Act, all benefits or advantages (less reasonably incurred collection costs) that an individual receives or is entitled to receive from social security (except those benefits provided under title XIX of the Social Security Act), workmen's compensation, any State-required temporary, nonoccupational disability insurance, and all other benefits (except the proceeds of life insurance) received by or available to an individual because of the injury from any government, unless the law authorizing or providing for such benefits or advantages makes them excess or secondary to the benefits in accordance with this Act, shall be subtracted from loss in calculating net loss.

(b) TAX DEDUCTION.—If a benefit or advantage received to compensate for loss of income because of injury, whether from no-fault benefits or from any source of benefits or advantages subtracted under subsection (a) of this section, is not taxable income, the income tax saving that is attributable to such loss of income because of injury is subtracted in calculating net loss for work loss. Subtraction may not exceed fifteen per centum of the loss of income and shall be in such lesser amount as the insurer reasonably determines is appropriate based on a lower value of the income tax advantage.

(c) ALLOWABLE EXPENSE DEDUCTION OPTION.—A State no-fault plan for motor vehicle insurance established in accordance with title II of this Act shall include the substantive provisions of this subsection, unless such State finds and reasonably determines, in the course of establishing such plan under section 201 (b) of this title, that the inclusion of such provisions in the plan would affect adversely or discriminate against the interests of persons required to provide security covering motor vehicles in such State: Benefits or advantages that an individual receives or is entitled to receive for allowable expense from a source other than no-fault insurance shall be subtracted from loss in calculating net loss for allowable expense where—

(1) such source other than no-fault insurance provides or is obligated to provide such benefits or advantages for allowable expense, as defined in section 103 (2) of this Act, without any limitation as to the total amount of such benefits or advantages obligated to be provided;

(2) such benefits or advantages are provided by such source other than no-fault insurance on terms and conditions which comply wholly with the provisions of sections 103 (6), (7), and (16), 109 (c) and (d), and 111 (d) of this Act and subject to all authority set forth therein;

(3) such source other than no-fault insurance is required by the applicable State no-fault plan for motor vehicle insurance in accordance with this Act to share, on an equitable basis, in the financial burdens and costs of operation of plans established pursuant to sections 105 and 108 of this Act;

(4) such benefits or advantages are provided by

1   such source other than no-fault insurance through group
2   insurance where the individuals who are likely to be the
3   beneficiaries under such group insurance have received
4   notice that there will be such subtraction; and

5   (5) the commissioner finds that such subtraction
6   will result in economic benefits greater than those which
7   would result from coordination pursuant to section 204
8   (f) of this Act, on the basis of a hearing in which in-
9   terested parties present competent evidence, and such
10   finding is reviewed in a similar procedure by the com-
11   missioner not less than once every three years.
12   The commissioner shall promulgate rules to assure that the
13   economic benefits found under paragraph (5) of this sub-
14   section are realized. As used in this subsection, (A) "group
15   insurance" means any plan of insurance offered or provided
16   to members of a group not organized solely for the purpose
17   of obtaining insurance, under the terms of a master policy or
18   operating agreement between an insurer and the group
19   sponsor, and incorporating group average rating, guaran-
20   teed issue with or without minimum eligibility requirements,
21   group experience rating, employer contributions, and any
22   other benefit to the members as insureds that they may be
23   unable to obtain in the ordinary channels of insurance mar-
24   keting on an individual basis; and (B) "group sponsor"
25   means the employer or other representative entity of an

65

employment-based group. Sections 103 (10), (11), and (12) of this Act are inapplicable with respect to such definitions.

ADDED RESTORATION BENEFITS

SEC. 209. (a) OPTIONAL OFFERING.—Restoration obligors providing security for the payment of basic restoration benefits may offer or obligate themselves to provide added restoration benefits for injury or damage arising out of the ownership, maintenance, or use of a motor vehicle, including—

    (1) loss excluded from basic restoration benefits by limits on allowable expense, work loss, replacement services loss, and survivor's loss;

    (2) benefits for damage to property;

    (3) benefits for loss of use of a motor vehicle; and

    (4) benefits for expense for remedial religious treatment and care.

Subject to the approval of terms and forms by the commissioner, restoration obligors may offer or obligate themselves to provide other added restoration coverages.

(b) MANDATORY OFFERING.—(1) Insurers providing basic restoration insurance shall offer the following added restoration coverage:

    (A) for physical damage to a motor vehicle, a coverage for all collision and upset damage, subject to an optional deductible of not to exceed $100;

(B) for the payment of tort liability, if a State determines that security for the payment of tort liability is not required motor vehicle insurance;

(C) for economic detriment, a coverage for work loss sustained by a victim in excess of limitations on basic restoration benefits for work loss; and

(D) for basic restoration benefits, if a State determines that a vehicle having less than four wheels is not a motor vehicle.

(2) The commissioner may adopt rules requiring that insurers providing basic restoration insurance offer, in accordance with State law, any other specified added restoration coverages.

(c) TERRITORIAL APPLICABILITY.—All added restoration coverages are applicable in any State, Puerto Rico, or Canada.

INELIGIBLE CLAIMANTS

SEC. 210. (a) CONVERTER.—(1) Except as provided for assigned claims, a converter of a motor vehicle is ineligible to receive no-fault benefits, including benefits otherwise due him as a survivor, from any source other than a contract of insurance under which he is an insured, for any injury arising out of the maintenance or use of the converted vehicle.

If a converter dies from such injuries, his survivor or survivors are not entitled to no-fault benefits for survivor's loss from any source other than a contract of insurance under which the converter is an insured.

(2) For purposes of this subsection and subsection (c) of section 111 of this Act, an individual is not a converter of a motor vehicle if he used it in the good faith belief that he was legally entitled to do so.

(b) INTENTIONAL INJURIES.—(1) An individual who intentionally injures himself or another individual is ineligible to receive no-fault benefits for injury arising out of his acts, including benefits otherwise due him as a survivor. If an individual dies as a result of intentionally injuring himself, his survivor or survivors are not entitled to no-fault benefits for survivor's loss. An individual intentionally injures himself or another individual if he acts or fails to act for the purpose of causing such injury or with knowledge that such injury is substantially certain to follow. An individual does not intentionally injure himself or another individual—

(A) merely because his act or failure to act is intentional or done with his realization that it creates a grave risk of causing injury; or

(B) if the act or omission causing the injury is for the purpose of averting bodily harm to himself or another individual.

(2) For purposes of subsection (c) of section 111 and paragraph (3) of subsection (a) of section 206 of this Act, an individual does not intentionally injure himself or another individual merely because his act or failure to act is intentional or done with his realization that it creates a grave risk of harm.

OTHER PROVISIONS

SEC. 211. (a) INCLUDED COVERAGE.—A contract of insurance covering liability arising out of the ownership, maintenance, or use of a motor vehicle registered in a State includes basic restoration benefits and any other benefit coverages required by the no-fault plan for motor vehicle insurance in effect in such State unless such contract—

   (1) provides tort liability coverages only in excess of any of those required by such State no-fault plan; or

   (2) is a contract which the commissioner determines by regulation provides motor vehicle liability coverages only as incidental to some other basic coverage.

(b) APPROVAL OF TERMS AND FORMS.—Terms and conditions (including forms used by insurers) of any contract, certificate, or other evidence of insurance sold or issued pursuant to a State no-fault plan for motor vehicle insurance in accordance with this title or title III of this Act and providing no-fault benefits or any required tort liability are subject to approval and regulation by the commissioner in such State. The commissioner shall approve only terms and conditions which are consistent with the purposes of this Act and fair and equitable to all persons whose interests may be affected. The commissioner may limit by rule the variety of coverage available in order to give purchasers of insurance a reasonable opportunity to compare the cost of insuring with various insurers.

TITLE III—ALTERNATIVE STATE NO-FAULT MOTOR VEHICLE INSURANCE PLAN

PROVISIONS

SEC. 301. The alternative State no-fault plan for motor vehicle insurance (the State no-fault plan in accordance with this title), which becomes applicable and goes into effect in a State pursuant to subsection (e) of section 201 of this Act, is composed of title I of this Act, except sections 101, 102, 112, and 113; sections 201 (d), 203, 204 (e) and (f), 205, 207, 208, 210, and 211 of title II of this Act; and this title, except this section. A State may establish additional requirements provided that they are not inconsistent with the provisions of the alternative State no-fault plan for motor vehicle insurance or the policy set forth and declared in section 102 of this Act.

LIMITATIONS ON BASIC RESTORATION BENEFITS

SEC. 302. Basic restoration benefits payable to a victim or the survivor or survivors of a deceased victim for—

(a) allowable expense, as defined in section 103 (2) of this Act, may not be limited;

(b) work loss may not exceed a monthly amount equal to $1,000 multiplied by a fraction whose numerator is the average per capita income in the State and whose denominator is the average per capita income in the United States, according to the latest available United States Department of Commerce figures; and

(c) replacement services loss and survivor's loss may not exceed $200 for the calendar week during which the accident resulting in injury occurs and for each calendar week thereafter.

RESTRICTIONS ON TORT LIABILITY

SEC. 303. (a) PARTIAL ABOLITION.—Tort liability is abolished with respect to any injury that takes place in a State in which the alternative State no-fault plan for motor vehicle insurance is in effect, if such injury arises out of the maintenance or use of a motor vehicle, except that—

(1) An owner of a motor vehicle involved in an accident remains liable if, at the time of the accident, the vehicle was not a secured vehicle;

(2) A person in the business of designing, manufacturing, repairing, servicing, or otherwise maintaining motor vehicles remains liable for injury arising out of a

defect in such motor vehicle which is caused or not corrected by an act or omission in the course of such business, other than a defect in a motor vehicle which is operated by such business; and

(3) An individual remains liable for intentionally injuring himself or another individual.

(b) NONREIMBURSABLE TORT FINE.—Nothing in this section shall be construed to immunize an individual from liability to pay a fine on the basis of fault in any proceeding based upon any act or omission arising out of the maintenance or use of a motor vehicle: *Provided*, That such fine may not be paid or reimbursed by an insurer or other restoration obligor.

ADDED RESTORATION BENEFITS

SEC. 304. (a) OPTIONAL OFFERING.—Restoration obligors providing security for the payment of basic restoration benefits may offer or obligate themselves to provide added restoration benefits for injury or damage arising out of the ownership, maintenance, or use of a motor vehicle, including:

(1) loss excluded from basic restoration benefits by limits on allowable expense, work loss, replacement services loss, and survivor's loss;

(2) benefits for damage to property;

(3) benefits for loss of use of a motor vehicle; and

(4) benefits for expense for remedial religious treatment and care.

Subject to the approval of terms and forms by the commissioner, restoration obligors may offer or obligate themselves to provide other added restoration coverages.

(b) MANDATORY OFFERING.— (1) Insurers providing basic restoration insurance shall offer the following added restoration coverages:

>(A) for physical damage to a motor vehicle, a coverage for all collision and upset damage, subject to an optional deductible of not to exceed $100;

>(B) for physical damage to a motor vehicle, a coverage for all collision and upset damage to the extent that the insured has a valid claim in tort against another identified person; and

>(C) for noneconomic detriment to a victim, a coverage in such amounts and upon such conditions as the commissioner directs and the insured selects.

(2) The commissioner may adopt rules requiring that insurers providing basic restoration insurance offer, in accordance with State law, any other specified added restoration coverages.

(c) TERRITORIAL APPLICABILITY.—All added restoration coverages are applicable in any State, Puerto Rico, or Canada.

94TH CONGRESS 1st SESSION **H. R. 7985**

IN THE HOUSE OF REPRESENTATIVES

JUNE 17, 1975

Mr. RINALDO introduced the following bill; which was referred to the Committee on Interstate and Foreign Commerce

A BILL

To regulate commerce by establishing a nationwide system to restore motor vehicle accident victims and by requiring no-fault motor vehicle insurance as a condition precedent to using a motor vehicle on public roadways.

1 *Be it enacted by the Senate and House of Representa-*
2 *tives of the United States of America in Congress assembled,*
3   TITLE I—GENERAL PROVISIONS
4   FORMAL PROVISIONS
5   SEC. 101. (a) SHORT TITLE.—This Act may be cited
6 as the "National No-Fault Motor Vehicle Insurance Act".

(b) TABLE OF CONTENTS.—

TITLE I—GENERAL PROVISIONS

Sec. 101. Formal provisions.
    (a) Short title.
    (b) Table of contents.
Sec. 102. Declaration of policy.
    (a) Findings.
    (b) Purposes.
Sec. 103. Definitions.
Sec. 104. Required motor vehicle insurance.
    (a) Security covering a motor vehicle.
    (b) Self-insurance.
    (c) Obligated government.
    (d) Obligations upon termination of security.
Sec. 105. Availability of insurance.
    (a) Plan.
    (b) Cancellation, refusal to renew, or other termination of insurance.
Sec. 106. Payment of claims for no-fault benefits.
    (a) In general.
    (b) Release or settlement of claim.
    (c) Time limitations on actions to recover benefits.
    (d) Assignment of benefits.
    (e) Deduction and setoff.
    (f) Exemption of benefits.
Sec. 107. Attorney's fees and costs.
    (a) Fees of claimant's attorney.
    (b) Fees of restoration obligor's attorney.
Sec. 108. Assigned claims.
    (a) General.
    (b) Assigned claims plan.
    (c) Time for presenting claims under assigned claims plan.
Sec. 109. State regulation.
    (a) Rates and rating.
    (b) Public information.
    (b) Accountability program.
    (d) Availability of services.
Sec. 110. Motor vehicles in interstate travel.
    (a) General.
    (b) Conforming coverage.
    (c) Applicable law.
Sec. 111. Rights and duties of restoration obligors.
    (a) Reimbursement and subrogation.
    (b) Duty to pay basic restoration benefits.
    (c) Indemnity.
    (d) Referral for rehabilitation services.
Sec. 112. Jurisdiction of Federal courts.
Sec. 113. Federal motor vehicle.
    (a) General.
    (b) Procedures.
    (c) Definitions.
Sec. 114. Separability.

TITLE II—NATIONAL STANDARDS FOR STATE NO-FAULT MOTOR VEHICLE INSURANCE PLAN

Sec. 201. State no-fault plan in accordance with this title.
    (a) Preemption.
    (b) State plan.
    (c) Determination by Secretary.
    (d) Periodic review.
    (e) Alternative State plan.
    (f) Procedure.
    (g) Exceptions.
    (h) Reporting requirements.
    (i) Financial assistance to States.
    (j) Authorization for appropriations.
Sec. 202. National standards.
    (a) General.
    (b) Criteria.
Sec. 203. Right to basic restoration benefits.
    (a) Accident within a State.
    (b) Accident outside any State.
Sec. 204. Limitations on benefits.
Sec. 205. Source of basic restoration benefits.
    (a) Applicable security.
    (b) Multiple sources of equal priority.
Sec. 206. Restrictions on tort liability.
    (a) Partial abolition.
    (b) Nonreimbursable tort fine.
Sec. 207. Work loss.
    (a) Regularly employed.
    (b) Seasonally employed.
    (c) Not employed.
    (d) Definitions.
Sec. 208. Net loss.
    (a) General.
    (b) Tax deduction.
    (c) No-fault benefits primary.
Sec. 209. Added restoration benefits.
    (a) Optional offering.
    (b) Mandatory offering.
    (c) Territorial applicability.
Sec. 210. Ineligible claimants.
    (a) Converter.
    (b) Intentional injuries.
Sec. 211. Other provisions.
    (a) Included coverage.
    (b) Approval of terms and forms.

TITLE III—ALTERNATIVE STATE NO-FAULT MOTOR VEHICLE INSURANCE PLAN

Sec. 301. Provisions.

DECLARATION OF POLICY

SEC. 102. (a) FINDINGS.—The Congress hereby finds and declares that—

(1) motor vehicles are the primary instrumentality for the interstate transportation of individuals;

(2) the intrastate transportation of individuals by motor vehicle over Federal-aid highways and other highways significantly affects interstate commerce, particularly in metropolitan areas encompassing more than one State;

(3) the maximum feasible restoration of all individuals injured and compensation of the economic losses of the survivors of all individuals killed in motor vehicle accidents on Federal-aid highways, in interstate commerce, and in activity affecting interstate commerce is essential to the humane and purposeful functioning of commerce;

(4) to avoid any undue burden on commerce during the interstate or intrastate transportation of individuals, it is necessary and proper to have a nationwide low-cost, comprehensive, and fair system of compensating and restoring motor vehicle accident victims and the survivors of deceased victims;

(5) exhaustive studies by the United States Department of Transportation, the Congress, and some

States have determined that the present basic system of motor vehicle accident and insurance law, which makes compensation and restoration contingent upon—

 (A) every victim first showing that someone else was at fault;

 (B) every victim first showing that he was without fault; and

 (C) the person at fault having sufficient liability insurance and other available financial resources to pay for all the losses,

is not such a low-cost, comprehensive, and fair system;

(6) careful studies, intensive hearings, and some State experiments have demonstrated that a basic system of motor vehicle accident and insurance law which—

 (A) assures every victim payment of all his medical and rehabilitation costs, and recovery of almost all his work loss plus a reasonable amount of replacement services; and

 (B) eliminates the need to determine fault except when a victim is very seriously injured,

is such a low-cost, comprehensive, and fair system;

(7) nationwide adoption of the system described in paragraph (6) in place of the system described in paragraph (5) would remove an undue burden on commerce;

(8) pursuant to the power vested in it "to regulate Commerce . . . among the several States", the Government of the United States is authorized to require a nationwide low-cost, comprehensive, and fair system of compensating and restoring motor vehicle accident victims and the survivors of the deceased victims;

(9) in all the States there should be uniformity as to the essential elements of the system of motor vehicle accident and insurance law to avoid confusion, complexity, uncertainty, and chaos which would be engendered by a multiplicity of noncomplementary State systems, but the need for a nationwide basic system does not require that the Federal Government itself directly administer, operate, or direct the administration or operation of such system; and

(10) a nationwide low-cost, comprehensive, and fair system of compensating and restoring motor vehicle accident victims can—

(A) recognize, respect, and avoid interfering with the historical role of the States in regulating and exercising legislative authority over the business of insurance; and

(B) save and restore the lives of countless victims by providing and paying the cost of services so that every victim has the opportunity to—

(i) receive prompt and comprehensive professional treatment, and

(ii) be rehabilitated to the point where he can return as a useful member of society and a self-respecting and self-supporting citizen.

(b) PURPOSES.—Therefore, it is hereby declared to be the policy of the Congress to establish—

(1) at reasonable cost to the purchaser of insurance, a nationwide system of prompt and adequate restoration benefits for motor vehicle accident victims and the survivors of deceased victims; and

(2) minimum standards which each State must meet or exceed so as to assure a nationwide low-cost, comprehensive, and fair system of motor vehicle accident and insurance law and which enables each State to participate legislatively, to administer without interference, and to continue regulating the business of insurance.

DEFINITIONS

SEC. 103. As used in this Act—

(1) "Added restoration benefits" means benefits provided by added restoration insurance in accordance with section 209 or section 304 of this Act.

(2) "Allowable expense" means reasonable charges incurred for, or the reasonable value of (where no charges are

incurred), reasonably needed and used products, services, and accommodations for—

    (A) professional medical treatment and care;

    (B) emergency medical services; and

    (C) medical and vocational rehabilitation services.

The term does not include—

    (i) that portion of a charge for a room in a hospital, clinic, convalescent, or nursing home, or any other institution engaged in providing nursing care and related services, in excess of a reasonable and customary charge for semiprivate accommodations, unless more intensive care is medically required;

    (ii) any amount includable in work loss, replacement services loss, or survivor's loss; or

    (iii) expenses directly related to the funeral, burial, cremation, or other form of disposition of the remains of a deceased victim.

(3) "Basic restoration benefits" means benefits provided in accordance with this Act for the net loss sustained by a victim, subject to any applicable limitations, exclusions, deductibles, waiting periods, disqualifications, or other terms and conditions provided or authorized in accordance with this Act. Basic restoration benefits do not include benefits for damage to property.

(4) "Commissioner" means the commissioner of insur-

ance or the head of the department, commission, board, or other agency of a State which is charged by the law of that State with the supervision and regulation of the business of insurance.

(5) "Department" means the department of motor vehicles or the department, commission, board, or other agency of a State which is charged by the law of that State with the administration of laws and regulations regarding registration of motor vehicles.

(6) "Emergency medical services" means services necessary to mitigate injury to any victim during the period immediately and proximately following an accident (including, but not limited to, communications, transportation, and treatment by medical and paramedical personnel through an emergency medical services system), which are supplied or provided in accordance with applicable State law.

(7) "Emergency medical services system" means a system which provides for the arrangement of personnel, facilities, and equipment for the effective and coordinated delivery in an appropriate geographical area of health care services under emergency conditions, which is administered by a public or nonprofit private entity which has the authority and the resources to provide effective administration, and which meets the requirements of section 1206(b)(4) of the Public Health Service Act.

(8) "Government" means the government of the United States, any State, any political subdivision of a State, any instrumentality of two or more States, or any agency, subdivision, or department of any such government, including any corporation or other association organized by a government for the execution of a government program and subject to control by a government, or any corporation or agency established under an interstate compact or international treaty.

(9) "Injury" means accidentally sustained bodily harm to an individual and that individual's illness, disease, or death resulting therefrom.

(10) "Insurance" means a contract, self-insurance, or any other legally binding obligation to pay or provide no-fault benefits or any required tort liability.

(11) "Insured" means—

(A) an individual identified by name as an insured in a contract of basic restoration insurance complying with this Act; and

(B) a spouse or other relative of a named insured, a minor in the custody of a named insured, and a minor in the custody of a relative of a named insured if—

(i) not identified by name as an insured in any other contract of basic restoration insurance complying with this Act, and

(ii) in residence in the same household with a named insured.

An individual is in residence in the same household if he usually makes his home in the same family unit, even though he temporarily lives elsewhere.

(12) "Insurer" means a legally constituted entity, other than a self-insurer or an obligated government, which is authorized under State law to provide security covering a motor vehicle in such State.

(13) "Loss" means accrued economic detriment resulting from injury arising out of the maintenance or use of a motor vehicle consisting of, and limited to, allowable expense, work loss, replacement services loss, and survivor's loss.

(14) "Loss of income" means gross income actually lost by a victim or that would have been lost but for any income continuation plan, reduced by—

(A) ninety per centum of any income which such individual earns from substitute work;

(B) income which such individual would have earned in available substitute work he was capable of performing but unreasonably failed to undertake; or

(C) any income which such individual would have earned by hiring an available substitute to perform self-employment services but reasonably failed to do.

(15) "Maintenance or use of a motor vehicle" means maintenance or use of a motor vehicle as a vehicle, including, incident to its maintenance or use as a vehicle, occupying, entering into or alighting from it. Maintenance or use of a motor vehicle does not include—

 (A) conduct within the course of a business of repairing servicing, or otherwise maintaining motor vehicles unless the conduct occurs off the business premises; or

 (B) conduct in the course of loading or unloading a motor vehicle unless the conduct occurs while occupying, entering into, or alighting from it.

(16) "Medical and vocational rehabilitation services" means services necessary to reduce disability and to restore the physical, psychological, social, and vocational functioning of a victim. Such services may include, but are not limited to, medical care, diagnostic and evaluation procedures, physical and occupational therapy, other medically necessary therapies, speech pathology and audiology, nursing care under the supervision of a registered nurse, medical social services, vocational rehabilitation and training services, occupational licenses and tools and transportation where necessary to secure medical and vocational rehabilitation services. A restoration obligor is not obligated to provide basic restoration benefits for allowable expense for medical and voca-

tional rehabilitation services unless the facility in which or through which such services are provided has been accredited by the department of health, the equivalent government agency responsible for health programs, or the accrediting designee of such department or agency of the State in which such services are provided, as being in accordance with applicable requirements and regulations.

(17) "Motor vehicle" means a vehicle of a kind required to be registered under the laws relating to motor vehicles of the State in which such vehicle is located except that a vehicle having less than four wheels may be specially treated, at the option of a State establishing a no-fault plan for motor vehicle insurance in accordance with title II of this Act, with respect to the requirements and benefits of such plan.

(18) "Net loss" means loss less benefits or advantages required to be subtracted from loss in calculating net loss pursuant to section 208 of this Act.

(19) "Noneconomic detriment" means pain, suffering, inconvenience, physical impairment, and other nonpecuniary damage recoverable under the tort law applicable to injury arising out of the maintenance or use of a motor vehicle. The term does not include punitive or exemplary damages.

(20) "No-fault benefits" means basic restoration benefits, added restoration benefits, or both.

(21) "No-fault insurance" means basic restoration insurance, added restoration insurance, or both.

(22) "Owner" means an individual, government, corporation, company, association, firm, partnership, joint stock company, foundation, institution, society, union, club, church, or any other group of persons organized for any purpose, other than a lienholder or secured party, that owns or has title to a motor vehicle or is entitled to the use and possession of a motor vehicle subject to a security interest held by another. The term includes a lessee of a motor vehicle having the right to possession under a lease with option to purchase.

(23) "Restoration obligor" means an insurer, self-insurer, or obligated government providing no-fault benefits in accordance with this Act.

(24) "Replacement services loss" means expenses reasonably incurred in obtaining ordinary and necessary services in lieu of those the victim would have performed, not for income, but for the benefit of himself or his family, if he had not been injured.

(25) "Secretary" means the Secretary of Transportation.

(26) "Secured vehicle" means a motor vehicle for which security is provided in accordance with section 104 of this Act.

(27) "Security covering a motor vehicle", "security covering the vehicle", and "security" means the security which is provided in accordance with section 104 of this Act.

(28) "Self-insurer" means an owner or any person providing security pursuant to subsection (b) or (c) of section 104 of this Act.

(29) "State" means a State of the United States, the District of Columbia, Guam, and the Virgin Islands.

(30) "State vocational rehabilitation agency" means the agency in the State which administers the State plan for vocational rehabilitation services under the Vocational Rehabilitation Act (29 U.S.C. 35).

(31) "Survivor" means an individual identified in the wrongful death statute or Constitution of the State of domicile of a deceased victim as one entitled to receive benefits by reason of the death of another individual.

(32) "Victim" means an individual who suffers injury arising out of the maintenance or use of a motor vehicle; "deceased victim" means a victim suffering death resulting from injury.

(33) "Without regard to fault' means irrespective of fault as a cause of injury.

(34) "Work loss" means—

 (A) loss of gross income of a victim, as calculated pursuant to the provisions of section 207 of this Act; and

(B) reasonable expenses of a victim for hiring a substitute to perform self-employment services, thereby mitigating loss of income, or for hiring special help, thereby enabling a victim to work and mitigate loss of income.

REQUIRED MOTOR VEHICLE INSURANCE

SEC. 104. (a) SECURITY COVERING A MOTOR VEHICLE.—(1) Every owner of a motor vehicle which is registered in a State in which a State no-fault plan for motor vehicle insurance in accordance with title II or title III of this Act is in effect, or which is operated in such State by the owner or with his permission, shall continuously provide security covering such motor vehicle while such vehicle is either present or registered in such State. Security shall be provided for the payment of basic restoration benefits in accordance with paragraph (2) of this subsection, and at the option of a State establishing a plan in accordance with title II of this Act, for the payment of other benefits or tort liability. The owner or any other person may provide security covering a motor vehicle by a contract of insurance with an insurer or by qualifying as a self-insurer or as an obligated government.

(2) A State no-fault plan for motor vehicle insurance under this Act may entitle a victim to payment of $10,000, or such higher amount as determined pursuant to State law,

in basic restoration benefits. If the total amount of a victim's allowable expense, work loss, and replacement services loss exceeds $10,000, or such higher amount as determined pursuant to State law, the victim shall be entitled to determine the manner in which such basic restoration benefits shall be allocated among the victim's allowable expense, work loss, and replacement services loss.

(3) A State no-fault plan for motor vehicle insurance under this Act shall include payment of $1,000, or such higher amount as may be required pursuant to State law, for expenses directly related to the funeral, burial, cremation, or other form of disposition of the remains of a deceased victim.

(b) SELF-INSURANCE.—Self-insurance, subject to approval of the commissioner or department, is effected by filing with the department in satisfactory form—

    (1) a continuing undertaking by the owner or other appropriate person to pay basic restoration benefits and any tort liability required by State law in amounts not less than those required by such State law, to perform all obligations imposed in accordance with this Act, and to elect to pay such added restoration benefits as are specified in the undertaking;

    (2) evidence that appropriate provision exists for

prompt and efficient administration of all claims, benefits, and obligations provided in accordance with this Act; and

(3) evidence that reliable financial arrangements deposits, resources, or commitments exist providing assurance substantially equivalent to that afforded by a contract of insurance complying with this Act for payment of no-fault benefits, any required tort liability, and performance of all other obligations imposed in accordance with this Act.

(c) OBLIGATED GOVERNMENT.—A government may provide security with respect to any motor vehicle owned or operated by it by lawfully obligating itself to pay basic restoration benefits in accordance with this Act, and such added restoration benefits as are specified in the undertaking.

(d) OBLIGATION UPON TERMINATION OF SECURITY.—An owner of a motor vehicle who ceases to maintain the security required in accordance with this Act shall immediately surrender the registration certificate and license plates for the vehicle to the department and may not operate or permit operation of the vehicle in any State until security has again been furnished as required in accordance with this Act. A person other than the owner who ceases to maintain such security shall immediately notify the owner and the department, who may not operate or permit operation of the vehicle until security has again been furnished. An insurer who has issued a contract of insurance and knows or has reason to believe the contract is for the purpose of providing security shall immediately give notice to the department of the termination of the insurance. If the commissioner or department withdraws approval of security provided by a self-insurer or knows that the conditions for self-insurance have ceased to exist, he shall immediately give notice thereof to the department. These requirements may be modified or waived by the department.

AVAILABILITY OF INSURANCE

SEC. 105. (a) PLAN.—(1) The commissioner shall establish and implement or approve and supervise a plan assuring that any required no-fault benefits and tort liability coverages for motor vehicles will be conveniently and expeditiously available, subject only to payment or provisions for payment of the premium, to each individual who cannot conveniently obtain insurance through ordinary methods at rates not in excess of those applicable to similarly situated individuals under the plan. The plan may provide reasonable means for the transfer of individuals insured thereunder into the ordinary market, at the same or lower rates, pursuant to regulations established by the commissioner. The plan may be implemented by assignment of applicants among insurers, pooling, any joint insuring or reinsuring arrangement, or any other method, including a State fund, that results in all applicants being conveniently afforded the insurance coverages on reasonable and not unfairly discriminatory terms.

(2) The plan shall make available added restoration benefits and tort liability coverage together with other contract provisions which the commissioner determines are reasonably needed by applicants and are commonly afforded in voluntary markets. The plan must also assure that there is available through the private sector or otherwise to all applicants adequate premium financing or provision for the installment payment of premiums subject to customary terms and conditions.

(3) All insurers writing no-fault benefits and tort liability coverages in a State shall participate in the plan in such State. The plan shall provide for equitable apportionment, among all participating insurers writing any insurance coverage required under the plan, of the financial burdens of insurance provided to applicants under the plan and the costs of operation of the plan.

(4) Subject to the supervision and approval of the commissioner, insurers may consult and agree with each other and with other appropriate persons as to the organization, administration, and operation of the plan and as to rates and rate modifications for insurance coverages provided

21

under the plan. Rates and rate modifications adopted or charged for insurance coverages provided under the plan shall—

    (A) be first adopted or approved by the commissioner;

    (B) be reasonable and not unfairly discriminatory among similarly situated applicants for insurance pursuant to regulations established by the commissioner; and

    (C) reflect the propensities of different motor vehicles with respect to the probability and severity of injuries.

(5) To carry out the objectives of this subsection, the commissioner may adopt rules, make orders, enter into agreements with other governmental and private entities and individuals, and form and operate or authorize the formation and operation of bureaus and other legal entities.

(b) CANCELLATION, REFUSAL TO RENEW, OR OTHER TERMINATION OF INSURANCE.—(1) Every contract of insurance providing security covering a motor vehicle which is not one of five or more motor vehicles under common ownership insured under a single insuring agreement, except as provided by paragraphs (2) and (5) of this subsection, may not be canceled, modified, or otherwise terminated by the insurer nor may the insurer fail to renew except at specified dates or intervals which may not be less than six months after the inception of coverage or thereafter less than six months apart.

(2) An insurer may terminate insurance if written notice of termination, including the reasons therefor, is mailed or delivered to the insured at least thirty days before the effective date of termination—

(A) by cancellation at any time within seventy-five days after the inception of initial coverage;

(B) by cancellation for nonpayment of—

(i) premium when due, or

(ii) any premium installment when due for which reasonable and separate notice has been given; or

(C) by exclusion of an insured whose license to operate a motor vehicle has been revoked, following a hearing and pursuant to State law.

(3) Except as permitted in paragraph (2) of this subsection, any termination of insurance by an insurer which is permitted by the insurance contract and not prohibited by paragraph (1) of this subsection, including any refusal by the insurer to renew the insurance at the expiration of its term and any modification by the insurer of the terms and conditions of the insurance unfavorable to the insured, is nevertheless ineffective, unless written notice of intention to modify,

not to renew, or otherwise to terminate the insurance has been mailed or delivered to the insured at least thirty days before the effective date of the modification, expiration, or other termination of the insurance.

(4) For purposes of this subsection a cancellation or refusal to renew by or at the direction of any person acting pursuant to any power or authority under any premium finance plan, agreement, or arrangement, whether or not with power of attorney or assignment from the insured, constitutes a cancellation or refusal to renew by the insurer.

(5) This subsection does not limit or apply to any termination, modification, or cancellation of the insurance, or to any suspension of insurance coverage, by or at the written request of the insured or upon the sale or other transfer of the secured vehicle to an individual who is not an insured under the same contract of insurance.

(6) This subsection does not affect any right an insurer has under other law to rescind or otherwise terminate insurance because of fraud or other willful misconduct of the insured at the inception of the insuring transaction or the right of either party to reform the contract on the basis of mutual mistake of fact.

(7) An insurer, his authorized agents and employees, and any person furnishing information upon which he has relied, are not liable in any action or proceeding brought

because of any statement made in good faith pursuant to paragraph (2) of this subsection

PAYMENT OF CLAIMS FOR NO-FAULT BENEFITS

SEC. 106. (a) IN GENERAL.—(1) No-fault benefits are payable monthly as loss accrues. Loss accrues not when injury occurs, but as allowable expense, work loss, replacement services loss, or survivor's loss is sustained.

(2) No-fault benefits are overdue if not paid within thirty days after the receipt by the restoration obligor of each submission of reasonable proof of the fact and amount of loss sustained, unless the restoration obligor designates, upon receipt of an initial claim for no-fault benefits, periods not to exceed thirty-one days each for accumulating all such claims received within each such period, in which case such benefits are overdue if not paid within fifteen days after the close of each such period. If reasonable proof is supplied as to only part of a claim, but the part amounts to $100 or more, benefits for such part are overdue if not paid within the time mandated by this paragraph. An obligation for basic restoration benefits for an item of allowable expense may be discharged by the restoration obligor by reimbursing the victim or by making direct payment to the supplier or provider of products, services, or accommodations within the time mandated by this paragraph. Overdue payments bear interest at the rate of 18 per centum per annum.

25

(3) A claim for no-fault benefits shall be paid without deduction for the benefits or advantages which are to be subtracted from loss in calculating net loss in accordance with section 208(a) of this Act, if such benefits or advantages have not been paid or provided to such claimant prior to the date the no-fault benefits are overdue or the no-fault benefits claim is paid. The restoration obligor is thereupon entitled to recover reimbursement from the person obligated to pay or provide such benefits or advantages or from the claimant who actually receives them.

(4) A restoration obligor may bring an action to recover reimbursement for no-fault benefits which are paid upon the basis of an intentional misrepresentation of a material fact by a claimant or a supplier or provider of an item of allowable expense, if such restoration obligor reasonably relied upon such misrepresentation. The action may be brought only against such supplier or provider, unless the claimant has intentionally misrepresented the facts or knew of the misrepresentation. A restoration obligor may offset amounts he is entitled to recover from the claimant under this paragraph against any no-fault benefits otherwise due.

(5) A restoration obligor who rejects a claim for basic restoration benefits shall give to the claimant written notice of the rejection promptly, but in no event more than thirty

days after the receipt of reasonable proof of the loss. Such notice shall specify the reason for such rejection and inform the claimant of the terms and conditions of his right to obtain an attorney. If a claim is rejected for a reason other than that the person is not entitled to basic restoration benefits claimed, the written notice shall inform the claimant that he may file his claim with the assigned claims bureau and shall give the name and address of the bureau.

(b) RELEASE OR SETTLEMENT OF CLAIM.—(1) Except as otherwise provided in this subsection, no-fault benefits shall not be denied or terminated because the victim executed a release or other settlement agreement. A claim for no-fault benefits may be discharged by a settlement agreement for an agreed amount payable in installments or in a lump sum, if the reasonably anticipated net loss does not exceed $2,500. In all other cases, a claim may be discharged by a settlement to the extent authorized by State law and upon a finding, by a court of competent jurisdiction, that the settlement is in the best interest of the claimant and any beneficiaries of the settlement, and that the claimant understands and consents to such settlement, and upon payment by the restoration obligor of the costs of such proceeding including a reasonable attorney's fee (based upon actual time expended) to the attorney selected by or appointed for the claimant. Such costs may not be charged to or deducted from the proceeds of the settlement. Upon approval of the settlement the court may make appropriate orders concerning the safeguarding and disposing of the proceeds of the settlement and may direct as a condition of the settlement agreement, that the restoration obligor pay the reasonable cost of appropriate future medical and vocational rehabilitation services.

(2) A settlement agreement for an amount payable in installments shall be modified as to amounts to be paid in the future, if it is shown that a material and substantial change of circumstances has occurred or that there is newly discovered evidence concerning the claimant's physical condition, loss, or rehabilitation which could not have been known previously or discovered in the exercise of reasonable diligence.

(3) A settlement agreement may be set aside if it is procured by fraud or if its terms are unconscionable.

(c) TIME LIMITATIONS ON ACTIONS TO RECOVER BENEFITS.—(1) If no-fault benefits have not been paid for loss arising otherwise than from death, an action therefor may be commenced not later than two years after the victim suffers the loss and either knows, or in the exercise of reasonable diligence should have known, that the loss was caused by the accident, or not later than four years after the accident, whichever is earlier. If no-fault benefits have been paid for loss arising otherwise than from death, an action for further benefits, other than survivor's benefits, by either the same or another claimant, may be commenced not later than two years after the last payment of benefits.

(2) If no-fault benefits have not been paid to the deceased victim or his survivor or survivors, an action for survivor's benefits may be commenced not later than one year after the death or four years after the accident from which death results, whichever is earlier. If survivor's benefits have been paid to any survivor, an action for further survivor's benefits by either the same or another claimant may be commenced not later than two years after the last payment of benefits. If no-fault benefits have been paid for loss suffered by a victim before his death resulting from the injury, an action for survivor's benefits may be commenced not later than one year after the death or six years after the last payment of benefits, whichever is earlier.

(3) If timely action for basic restoration benefits is commenced against a restoration obligor and benefits are denied because of a determination that the restoration obligor's coverage is not applicable to the claimant under the provisions of section 205 of this Act, an action against the applicable restoration obligor or the restoration obligor to whom a claim is assigned under an assigned claims plan may be commenced not later than sixty days after the determination becomes final or the last date on which the action could otherwise have been commenced, whichever is later.

(4) Except as paragraph (1), (2), or (3) prescribes a longer period, an action by a claimant on an assigned claim which has been timely presented in accordance with the provisions of section 108(c) of this Act may not be commenced more than sixty days after the claimant receives written notice of rejection of the claim by the restoration obligor to which it was assigned.

(5) If a person entitled to no-fault benefits is under a legal disability when the right to bring an action for the benefits first accrues, the period of his disability is not a part of the time limited for commencement of the action.

(d) ASSIGNMENT OF BENEFITS.—An assignment of or an agreement to assign any right in accordance with this Act for loss accruing in the future is unenforceable except as to benefits for—

    (1) work loss to secure payment of alimony, maintenance, or child support; or

    (2) allowable expense to the extent the benefits are for the cost of products, services, or accommodations provided or to be provided by the assignee.

(e) DEDUCTION AND SETOFF.—Except as otherwise provided in this Act, basic restoration benefits shall be paid without deduction or setoff.

(f) EXEMPTION OF BENEFITS.—(1) No-fault benefits for allowable expense are exempt from garnishment, attachment, execution, and any other process or claim, except upon the claim of a creditor who has provided products, services, or accommodations to the extent benefits are for allowable expense for those products, services, or accommodations.

(2) Basic restoration benefits other than those for allowable expense are exempt from garnishment, attachment, execution, and any other process or claim for benefits attributable to loss sustained within the first sixty days following the accident resulting in injury. Other basic restoration benefits (except for items of allowable expense) are exempt to the extent that wages or earnings are exempt under any applicable law exempting wages or earnings from such process or claims.

ATTORNEY'S FEES AND COSTS

SEC. 107. (a) FEES OF CLAIMANT'S ATTORNEY.—
(1) If any overdue no-fault benefits are paid by the restoration obligor after receipt of notice of representation of a claimant by an attorney or if an action is maintained (unless the court determines that the claim or any significant part thereof is fraudulent or so excessive as to have no reasonable foundation), a reasonable attorney's fee (based upon actual time expended) shall be paid by the restoration obligor to such attorney. No part of the attorney's fee for representing the claimant in connection with a claim or action for no-fault benefits may be charged or deducted from benefits otherwise

due to such claimant and no part of such benefits may be applied to such fee.

(2) In any such action brought against the claimant by the restoration obligor, the court may award the claimant's attorney a reasonable attorney's fee for defending such action, which shall be paid by the restoration obligor.

(b) FEES OF RESTORATION OBLIGOR'S ATTORNEY.—A restoration obligor shall be allowed a reasonable attorney's fee for defending a claim if the court determines that the claim or any significant part thereof is fraudulent or so excessive as to have no reasonable foundation. The fee may be treated as an offset against any benefits due or to become due to the claimant.

ASSIGNED CLAIMS

SEC. 108 (a) GENERAL.—(1) If a State no-fault plan for motor vehicle insurance in accordance with title II or title III of this Act is in effect on the date when the accident resulting in injury occurs, a victim or the survivor or survivors of a deceased victim may obtain basic restoration benefits through the assigned claims plan established, pursuant to subsection (b) of this section, in the State of domicile, if any, of the victim or deceased victim, or if none, in the State, in which the accident resulting in injury occurs, if basic restoration insurance—

(A) is not applicable to the injury for a reason

other than those specified in the provisions on ineligible claimants;

(B) is not applicable to the injury because the victim converted a motor vehicle while he was under fifteen years of age;

(C) applicable to the injury cannot be identified;

(D) applicable to the injury is inadequate to provide the contracted-for benefits because of financial inability of a restoration obligor to fulfill its obligations; or

(E) benefits are refused by a restoration obligor for a reason other than that the individual is not entitled in accordance with this Act to the basic restoration benefits claimed.

(2) If a claim qualifies for assignment under paragraph (1) (C), (D), or (E) of this subsection, the assigned claims bureau or any insurer to whom the claim is assigned is subrogated to all rights of the claimant against the restoration obligor legally obligated to provide basic restoration benefits to the claimant, or against any successor in interest to or substitute for such obligor for such benefits as are provided by the assignee.

(3) If an individual receives basic restoration benefits through the assigned claims plan for any reason other than because of the financial inability of a restoration obligor to fulfill its obligation, all benefits or advantages that such indi-

vidual receives or is entitled to receive as a result of such injury, other than life insurance benefits or benefits by way of succession at death or in discharge of familial obligations of support, shall be subtracted from loss in calculating net loss.

(4) An assigned claim of an individual who does not comply with the requirement of providing security for the payment of basic restoration benefits, or of an individual as to whom the security is invalidated because of his fraud or willful misconduct, is subject to—

    (A) all the maximum optional deductibles and exclusions required to be offered; and

    (B) a deduction in the amount of $500 for each year or part thereof of the period of his continuous failure to provide security, applicable to any benefits otherwise payable except basic restoration benefits for allowable expense.

(b) ASSIGNED CLAIMS PLAN.—(1) Restoration obligors providing basic restoration insurance in a State may organize and maintain, subject to approval and regulation by the commissioner, an assigned claims bureau and an assigned claims plan and adopt rules for their operation and for assessment of costs on a fair and equitable basis consistent with this Act. If such bureau and plan are not organized and maintained in a manner considered by the commissioner to be consistent with this Act and with State law, he shall organize and maintain an assigned claims bureau and an assigned claims plan. Each restoration obligor insurer providing basic restoration insurance in a State shall participate in the assigned claims bureau and the assigned claims plan in that State. Costs incurred shall be allocated fairly and equitably among the restoration obligors.

(2) The assigned claims bureau shall promptly—

(A) assign each claim for no-fault benefits to an assignee who shall be a participating insurer; and

(B) notify the claimant of the identity and address of such assignee.

Claim shall be assigned so as to minimize inconvenience to claimants. The assignee thereafter has rights and obligations as if he had issued a policy of basic restoration insurance complying with this Act applicable to the injury or, in a case involving the financial inability of a restoration obligor to perform its obligations, as if the assignee had written the applicable basic restoration insurance, undertaken the self-insurance, or lawfully obligated itself to pay basic restoration benefits.

(c) TIME FOR PRESENTING CLAIMS UNDER ASSIGNED CLAIMS PLAN.—(1) Except as provided in paragraph (2) of this subsection, an individual authorized to obtain basic restoration benefits through the assigned claims plan shall notify the assigned claims bureau of his claim within the time that would have been allowed pursuant to section 106(c) of this Act for commencing an action for basic restoration benefits against any restoration obligor, other than an assigned claims bureau, in any case in which identifiable no-fault insurance coverage was in effect and applicable to the claim.

(2) If timely action for basic restoration benefits is commenced against a restoration obligor who is unable to fulfill his obligations because of financial inability, an individual authorized to obtain basic restoration benefits through the assigned claims plan shall notify the bureau of his claim within six months after his discovery of such financial inability.

STATE REGULATION

SEC. 109. (a) RATES AND RATING.—The commissioner, in accordance with applicable State law, shall regulate restoration obligors providing security covering a motor vehicle in his State. The rates charged for security shall be established, determined, and modified in each State only in accordance with the provisions of the applicable rating law of such State and shall reflect the propensities of different motor vehicles with respect to the probability and severity of injuries.

(b) PUBLIC INFORMATION.—The commissioner shall

provide the means to inform purchasers of insurance, in a manner adequate to permit them to compare prices, about rates being charged by insurers for no-fault benefits and tort liability coverage.

(c) ACCOUNTABILITY PROGRAM.—(1) The commissioner, through the State vocational rehabilitation agency, shall establish and maintain a program for the regular and periodic evaluation of medical and vocational rehabilitation services for which reimbursement or payment is sought from a restoration obligor as an item of allowable expense to assure that—

(A) the services are medical and vocational rehabilitation services, as defined in section 103 (16) of this Act;

(B) the recipient of the services is making progress toward a greater level of independent functioning and the services are necessary to such progress and continued progress; and

(C) the charges for the services for which reimbursement or payment is sought are fair and reasonable.

Progress reports shall be made periodically in writing on each case for which reimbursement or payment is sought under security for the payment of basic restoration benefits. Such reports shall be prepared by the supervising physician or

rehabilitation counselor and submitted to the State vocational rehabilitation agency. The State vocational rehabilitation agency shall file reports with applicable restoration obligor or obligors. Pursuant to this program, there shall be provision for determinations to be made in writing of the rehabilitation goals and needs of the victim and for the periodic assessment of progress at reasonable time intervals by the supervising physician or rehabilitation counselor.

(2) The commissioner is authorized to establish and maintain a program for the regular and periodic evaluation of his State's no-fault plan for motor vehicle insurance.

(d) AVAILABILITY OF SERVICES.—The commissioner is authorized to coordinate with appropriate government agencies in the creation and maintenance of an emergency medical services system or systems, and to take all steps necessary to assure that emergency medical services are available for each victim suffering injury in the State. The commissioner is authorized to take all steps necessary to assure that medical and vocational rehabilitation services are available for each victim resident in the State. Such steps may include, but are not limited to, guarantees of loans or other obligations of suppliers or providers of such services, and support for training programs for personnel in programs and facilities offering such services.

MOTOR VEHICLES IN INTERSTATE TRAVEL

SEC. 110. (a) GENERAL.—An owner of a motor vehicle who has complied with the requirements of security covering a motor vehicle in the State of registration of such vehicle shall be deemed to have complied with the requirements for such security in any State in which such vehicle is operating.

(b) CONFORMING COVERAGE.—(1) A restoration obligor providing security for the payment of basic restoration benefits shall be obligated to provide, and each contract of insurance for the payment of basic restoration benefits shall be construed to contain, coverage sufficient to satisfy the requirements for security covering a motor vehicle in any State in which any victim who is a claimant or whose survivors are claimants is domiciled or is injured.

(2) A restoration obligor providing security for the payment of basic restoration benefits shall be obligated to provide, and each contract of insurance for the payment of basic restoration benefits shall be construed to contain, coverage of $50,000 to protect the owner or operator of a motor vehicle from tort liability to which he is exposed through application of the law of the State of domicile of a victim (or in the State in which the accident resulting in injury or harm to property occurs if a victim is not domiciled in

any State), but to which he would not have been exposed through application of the law of the State of registration of the motor vehicle.

(c) APPLICABLE LAW.—(1) The basic restoration benefits available to any victim or to any survivor of a deceased victim shall be determined pursuant to the provisions of the State no-fault plan for motor vehicle insurance in accordance with title II or title III of this Act which is in effect in the State of domicile of the victim on the date when the motor vehicle accident resulting in injury occurs. If there is no such State no-fault plan in effect or if the victim is not domiciled in any State, then basic restoration benefits available to any victim shall be determined pursuant to the provisions of the State no-fault plan for motor vehicle insurance, if any, in effect in the State in which the accident resulting in injury occurs.

(2) The right of a victim or of a survivor of a deceased victim to sue in tort shall be determined by the law of the State of domicile of such victim. If a victim is not domiciled in a State, such right to sue shall be determined by the law of the State in which the accident resulting in injury or damage to property occurs.

RIGHTS AND DUTIES OF RESTORATION OBLIGORS

SEC. 111. (a) REIMBURSEMENT AND SUBROGATION.—
(1) Except as provided in paragraphs (2), (3), and (4) of this subsection, a restoration obligor—

(A) does not have and may not contract, directly or indirectly, in whole or in part, for a right of reimbursement from or subrogation to the proceeds of a victim's claim for relief or to a victim's cause of action for noneconomic detriment; and

(B) may not directly or indirectly contract for, or be granted by a State, any right of reimbursement from any other restoration obligor not acting as a reinsurer for no-fault benefits which it has paid or is obligated to pay as a result of injury to a victim, except that a restoration obligor may seek reimbursement from any other restoration obligor in an arbitration proceeding based upon a determination of fault, for no-fault benefits exceeding $2,000 which it has paid or is obligated to pay as a result of injury to a victim involving one or more private passenger motor vehicles. The arbitration hearing shall be conducted in accordance with procedures established by the commissioner.

(2) Whenever an individual who receives or is entitled to receive no-fault benefits for an injury has a claim or cause of action against any other person for breach of an obligation

or duty causing the injury or for breach of express or implied warranty, the restoration obligor is subrogated to the rights of the claimant and has a claim for relief or a cause of action, separate from that of the claimant, to the extent that:

    (A) elements of damage compensated for by security for the payment of no-fault benefits are recoverable; and

    (B) the restoration obligor has paid or become obligated to pay accrued or future no-fault benefits.

(3) Notwithstanding the provisions of paragraph (1) (B) of this subsection, a State may grant a right of reimbursement among and between restoration obligors based upon a determination of fault, where such restoration obligors have paid or are obligated to pay benefits for loss arising out of an accident resulting in injury in which one or more of the motor vehicles is of a type other than a private passenger motor vehicle and by designation the State has determined that the owner of such type would receive an unreasonable economic advantage or suffer an unreasonable economic disadvantage in the absence of the grant of such right of reimbursement: *Provided*, That in such event such right of reimbursement may be granted only with respect to benefits paid for loss in excess of $5,000.

(4) Nothing in this subsection shall preclude any person supplying or providing products, services, or accommoda-

tions from contracting or otherwise providing for a right of reimbursement to any basic restoration benefits for allowable expense.

(b) DUTY TO PAY BASIC RESTORATION BENEFITS.—A restoration obligor providing security for the payment of basic restoration benefits shall pay or otherwise provide such benefits without regard to fault to each individual entitled thereto, pursuant to the terms and conditions of the State no-fault plan for motor vehicle insurance applicable thereto.

(c) INDEMNITY.—A restoration obligor has a right of indemnity against an individual who has converted a motor vehicle involved in an accident, or against an individual who has intentionally injured himself or another individual, for no-fault benefits paid for—

(1) the loss caused by the conduct of that individual;

(2) the cost of processing the claims for such benefits; and

(3) the cost of enforcing this right of indemnity, including reasonable attorney's fees.

(d) REFERRAL FOR REHABILITATION SERVICES.—The restoration obligor shall promptly refer each victim to whom basic restoration benefits are expected to be payable for more than two months to the State vocational rehabilitation agency.

43

JURISDICTION OF FEDERAL COURTS

SEC. 112. No district court of the United States may entertain an action for no-fault benefits unless the United States is a party to the action.

FEDERAL MOTOR VEHICLE

SEC. 113. (a) (1) GENERAL.—Notwithstanding any other provision of law, a claim against the United States as a restoration obligor for injury arising out of the maintenance or use of a Federal motor vehicle which is a secured vehicle shall be governed by this Act. A Federal motor vehicle is a secured vehicle, for purposes of this Act, whenever it is located or operated in the territorial area of any State, Puerto Rico, Canada, or Mexico.

(2) the level of basic restoration benefits which the United States shall pay or provide shall be controlled by the no-fault plan for motor vehicle insurance in effect in the State of domicile of the victim, if any, or if none, in the State in which the accident resulting in injury occurs.

(b) PROCEDURES.—The Secretary, in cooperation with the Administrator of General Services, shall promulgate, and may from time to time revise, regulations with respect to security covering a Federal motor vehicle and administrative procedures to be followed in claims against the United States for no-fault benefits.

(c) DEFINITIONS.—As used in this section—

(1) "Federal agency" means any branch, department, commission, administration, authority, board, or bureau of, or any corporation owned or controlled by, the Government of the United States.

(2) "Federal motor vehicle" means a motor vehicle owned or leased by a Federal agency and operated with its express or implied permission.

SEPARABILITY

SEC. 114. If any provision of this Act or any application thereof to any individual or circumstance is held invalid, the invalidity shall not affect any provision or application of the Act which can be given effect without the involved provision or application, and to this end the provisions of this Act are separable.

TITLE II—NATIONAL STANDARDS FOR STATE NO-FAULT MOTOR VEHICLE INSURANCE PLAN

STATE NO-FAULT PLAN IN ACCORDANCE WITH THIS TITLE

SEC. 201. (a) PREEMPTION.—Any provision of any State law which would prevent the establishment or administration in such a State of a no-fault plan for motor vehicle insurance in accordance with this title or title III of this Act is preempted.

(b) STATE PLAN.—By the completion of the first general session of the State legislature which commences after the date of enactment of this Act, a State may establish

45

a no-fault plan for motor vehicle insurance in accordance with this title. Upon the establishment of such a plan, the commissioner shall promptly submit to the Secretary a certified copy of such plan, together with all relevant information which is requested by the Secretary.

(c) DETERMINATION BY SECRETARY.—Within ninety days after the Secretary receives a copy of a State no-fault plan established under subsection (b) or (e) of this section, the Secretary shall make a determination whether such State has established a no-fault plan for motor vehicle insurance in accordance with this title. Unless the Secretary determines, pursuant to this section, that a State no-fault plan is not in accordance with this title, the plan shall go into effect in such State on the date designated in the plan. In no event shall such State plan go into effect less than nine months or more than twelve months after the date of its establishment.

(d) PERIODIC REVIEW.—The Secretary shall periodically, but not less than once every three years, review each State no-fault plan for motor vehicle insurance, which has been approved under subsection (c) of this section and for which there is experience, to determine whether such plan is still in accordance with this title and to evaluate the success of such plan in terms of the policy set forth and declared in section 102 of this Act. To facilitate such review, the commissioner in each such State shall submit to the Secretary periodically all relevant information which is requested by the Secretary. The Secretary shall report to the President and Congress simultaneously on July 1 each year on the results of such reviews, including any recommendations for legislation.

(e) ALTERNATIVE STATE PLAN.—(1) The alternative State no-fault plan for motor vehicle insurance (the State no-fault plan in accordance with title III of this Act) shall become applicable upon the expiration of the eighteen-month period following the completion of the first general session of the State legislature which commences after the date of enactment of this Act unless, prior to such date, the Secretary has made a determination that such State has established a no-fault plan for motor vehicle insurance in accordance with this title. The alternative State no-fault plan shall go into effect in a State on the first day of the ninth month after such plan becomes applicable or on a date designated by the Secretary, whichever is earlier.

(2) If, after the alternative State no-fault plan is applicable or in effect in a State, the Secretary, upon petition, makes a determination, pursuant to subsection (c) of this section, that such State has established a no-fault plan in accordance with this title, such State no-fault plan shall go into effect and the alternative State no-fault plan shall cease

to be applicable or in effect on a date to be designated by the Secretary.

(3) If, after a State no-fault plan in accordance with this title is in effect in a State, the Secretary makes a determination, pursuant to subsection (d) of this section, that such State no-fault plan is no longer in accordance with this title, then the plan which is no longer in accordance with this title shall cease to be in effect on a date to be designated by the Secretary, and on that date the alternative State no-fault plan shall go into effect in such State.

(f) PROCEDURE.—(1) Before making any determination under this section, the Secretary shall publish a notice in the Federal Register and afford the State and all interested parties a reasonable opportunity to present their views by oral and written submission.

(2) The Secretary shall notify in writing the Governor of the affected State of any determinations made under this section and shall publish these determinations with reasons therefor in the Federal Register.

(3) Any determinations made by the Secretary under this section shall be subject to judicial review in accordance with chapter 7 of title 5, United States Code, in the United States court of appeals for the circuit in which is located the State whose plan is the subject of such determination or

in the United States Court of Appeals for the District of Columbia Circuit. Any such review shall be instituted within sixty days from the date on which the determination made by the Secretary is published in the Federal Register.

(4) The Secretary shall establish such advisory boards as he determines necessary to assist in making determinations under subsections (c) and (d) of this section and any such advisory board shall be representative of the different geographic areas of the United States.

(g) EXCEPTIONS.—(1) The provisions of this section are inapplicable to the extent inconsistent with this subsection.

(2) Any State which is a no-fault State, as defined in paragraph (4) of this subsection, may establish a no-fault plan for motor vehicle insurance in accordance with this title by the fourth anniversary of the date of enactment of this Act.

(3) The alternative State no-fault plan for motor vehicle insurance (the State no-fault plan in accordance with title III of this Act) shall become applicable in any State which is a no-fault State, as defined in paragraph (4) of this subsection on the fourth anniversary of the date of enactment of this Act unless, prior to such date, the Secretary has made a determination that such State has established a no-

fault plan for motor vehicle insurance in accordance with this title.

(4) As used in this subsection, a "no-fault State" means a State which has enacted into law and put into effect a motor vehicle insurance law not later than September 1, 1975, which provides, at a minimum, for compulsory motor vehicle insurance; payment of benefits without regard to fault on a first-party basis where the value of such available benefits is not less than $2,000; and restrictions on the bringing of lawsuits in tort by victims for noneconomic detriment, in the form of a prohibition of such suits unless the victim suffers a certain quantum of loss or in the form of a relevant change in the evidentiary rules of practice and proof with respect to such lawsuits.

(h) REPORTING REQUIREMENTS.—The Secretary, in cooperation with the commissioners, shall annually review the operation of State no-fault plans for motor vehicle insurance established in accordance with this Act and report on—

    (1) the cost-savings resulting from the institution of any such plan which meets or exceeds the national standards set forth in this Act and any subsequent savings resulting from the continuing operation of such plans;

    (2) appropriate methods for refunding to members of the motoring public any cost-savings realized

from the institution and operation of such no-fault insurance plans;

(3) the impact of no-fault insurance on senior citizens; those who live in farming and rural areas; those who are economically disadvantaged, and those who live in inner cities;

(4) the impact of no-fault insurance on the problem of duplication of benefits when an individual has other insurance coverage which provides for compensation or reimbursement for lost wages or for health and accident (including hospitalization) benefits;

(5) the effect of no-fault insurance on court congestion and delay resulting from backlogs in State and Federal courts;

(6) the impact of no-fault insurance, reduced speed limits, and other factors on automobile insurance rates; and

(7) the impact of no-fault insurance on competition within the insurance industry, particularly with respect to the competitive position of small insurance companies. The Secretary shall report to the President and Congress simultaneously on July 1 each year on the results of such review and determination together with his recommendations thereon.

(i) FINANCIAL ASSISTANCE TO STATES.—The Secretary is authorized to provide grants to any State for the purpose of reimbursing such State for any governmental cost increases resulting from the implementation or administration of a no-fault plan for motor vehicle insurance in accordance with this Act, The Secretary shall, by regulation, establish procedures for awarding such grants on a fair and equitable basis among the States.

(j) AUTHORIZATION FOR APPROPRIATIONS.—There is authorized to be appropriated to the Secretary to carry out his responsibilities under this Act such sums as are necessary, not to exceed $10,000,000, such sums to remain available until expended.

NATIONAL STANDARDS

SEC. 202. (a) GENERAL.—A State establishing a no-fault plan for motor vehicle insurance in accordance with this title shall enact a law which incorporates, at a minimum, title I of this Act, except sections 101, 102, 112, and 113, and this title except this section and section 201. The provisions of these sections, taken together, shall be known as the "national standards" for State no-fault motor vehicle insurance.

(b) CRITERIA.—A State no-fault plan for motor vehicle insurance is in accordance with this title if it meets or exceeds all of the national standards. A provision in a State plan "meets" a provision in the national standards if the substance of the State plan provision is the same as or the equivalent of the corresponding provision in the national standards. A provision in a State plan "exceeds" a provision in the national standards if the substance of the State plan provision is more favorable or beneficial to an insured or a claimant or more restrictive of tort liability than the corresponding provision in the national standards. Any provision in a State plan as to which there is no corresponding provision in the national standards shall not be evaluated in determining whether such plan meets or exceeds national standards provided such provision is not inconsistent with the national standards or the policy set forth and declared in section 102 of this Act.

RIGHT TO BASIC RESTORATION BENEFITS

SEC. 203. (a) ACCIDENT WITHIN A STATE.—If the accident resulting in injury occurs in a State in which a no-fault plan for motor vehicle insurance in accordance with this title or title III of this Act is in effect, any victim or any survivor of a deceased victim is entitled to receive basic restoration benefits.

(b) ACCIDENT OUTSIDE ANY STATE.—If the accident resulting in injury occurs outside a State in which a no-fault plan is in effect, but in any other State, Puerto Rico, Canada, or Mexico, a victim or a survivor of a deceased victim is entitled to receive basic restoration benefits if such victim is or was—

(1) an insured; or

(2) the driver or other occupant of a secured vehicle.

LIMITATIONS ON BENEFITS

SEC. 204. A State establishing a no-fault plan for motor vehicle insurance in accordance with this title—

(a) may limit basic restoration benefits for allowable expense, work loss, and replacement services loss, to $10,000, or such higher amount as determined pursuant to State law, in accordance with section 104(a)(2) of this Act·

(b) may limit basic restoration benefits for work loss to a monthly amount equal to the lesser of the following—

(1) $1,000; or

(2) 85 per centum of the actual monthly earned income of the victim; and may provide a reasonable total limitation on restoration benefits for work loss and may also provide reasonable exclusions from basic restoration benefits for work loss;

(c) may provide reasonable exclusions from, or

monthly or total limitations on, basic restoration benefits for replacement services loss; and

(d) may provide that any contract of insurance for no-fault benefits allow an insurer to offer—

(1) a deductible not to exceed $100 for each individual; and

(2) a deductible not to exceed an amount deemed reasonable by the commissioner of each State for each individual if he sustains injury while he is operating in a motor vehicle having less than four wheels, or is a passenger on such a vehicle.

SOURCE OF BASIC RESTORATION BENEFITS

SEC. 205. (a) APPLICABLE SECURITY.—The security for the payment of basic restoration benefits applicable to an injury to—

(1) an employee, or to the spouse or other relative of an employee residing in the same household as the employee, if the accident resulting in injury occurs while the victim or deceased victim is driving or occupying a motor vehicle furnished by such employee's employer, is the security for the payment of basic restoration benefits covering such motor vehicle or, if none, any other security applicable to such victim;

(2) an insured is the security under which the victim or deceased victim is an insured;

(3) the driver or other occupant of a motor vehicle involved in an accident resulting in injury who is not an insured is the security covering such vehicle;

(4) an individual who is not an insured or the driver or other occupant of a motor vehicle involved in an accident resulting in injury is the security covering any motor vehicle involved in such accident. For purposes of this paragraph, a parked and unoccupied motor vehicle is not a motor vehicle involved in an accident, unless it was parked so as to cause unreasonable risk of injury; and

(5) any other individual is the applicable assigned claims plan.

(b) MULTIPLE SOURCES OF EQUAL PRIORITY.—If two or more obligations to pay basic restoration benefits apply equally to an injury under the priorities set forth in subsection (a) of this section, the restoration obligor against whom a claim is asserted first shall process and pay the claim as if wholly responsible. Such obligor is thereafter entitled to recover contribution pro rata from any other such obligor for the basic restoration benefits paid and for the costs of processing the claim. If contribution is sought among restoration obligors responsible under paragraph (4) of subsection (a) of this section proration shall be based on the number of involved motor vehicles.

RESTRICTIONS ON TORT LIABILITY

SEC. 206. (a) PARTIAL ABOLITION.—Tort liability is abolished with respect to any injury that takes place in a State in which a no-fault plan for motor vehicle insurance in accordance with this title is in effect prior to such injury, if such injury arises out of the maintenance or use of a motor vehicle, except that—

(1) An owner of a motor vehicle involved in an accident remains liable if, at the time of the accident, the vehicle was not a secured vehicle.

(2) A person in the business of designing, manufacturing, repairing, servicing, or otherwise maintaining motor vehicles remains liable for injury arising out of a defect in such motor vehicle which is caused or not corrected by an act or omission in the course of such business, other than a defect in a motor vehicle which is operated by such business.

(3) An individual remains liable for injuring another individual, either intentionally or as a consequence of intending to injure himself.

(4) A person remains liable for loss which is not compensated because of any limitation in accordance with section 104 or 204 of this Act, except that no action may be maintained for any damages (other than damages for noneconomic detriment) if any such damages

are less than the amount specified in section 104 (a) (2) of this Act.

(5) A person remains liable for damages for noneconomic detriment, except that the victim, or his survivor, is precluded from pleading or introducing into evidence in an action for noneconomic detriment any amounts paid by the restoration obligor for basic or added restoration benefits.

(6) A person or government remains liable if such injury was caused or not corrected by an act or omission not connected with the maintenance or use of a motor vehicle.

(b) NONREIMBURSABLE TORT FINE.—Nothing in this section shall be construed to immunize an individual from liability to pay a fine on the basis of fault in any proceeding based upon any act or omission arising out of the maintenance or use of a motor vehicle: *Provided*, That such fine may not be paid or reimbursed by an insurer or other restoration obligor.

WORK LOSS

SEC. 207. (a) REGULARLY EMPLOYED.—The work loss of a victim whose income prior to the injury was realized in regular increments shall be calculated by—

(1) determining his probable weekly income by dividing his probable annual income by fifty-two; and

(2) multiplying that quantity by the number of work weeks, or fraction thereof, the victim sustains loss of income during the accrual period.

(b) SEASONALLY EMPLOYED.—The work loss of a victim whose income is realized in irregular increments shall be calculated by—

(1) determining his probable weekly income by dividing his probable annual income by the number of weeks he normally works; and

(2) multiplying that quantity by the number of work weeks, or fraction thereof, the victim was unable to perform and would have performed work during the accrual period but for the injury.

(c) NOT EMPLOYED.—The work loss of a victim who is not employed when the accident resulting in injury occurs shall be calculated by—

(1) determining his probable weekly income by dividing his probable annual income by 52; and

(2) multiplying that quantity by the number of work weeks, or fraction thereof, if any, the victim would reasonably have been expected to realize income during the accrual period.

(d) DEFINITIONS.—As used in this section—

(1) "Probable annual income" means, absent a showing that it is or would be some other amount, the following—

(A) twelve times the monthly gross income earned by the victim from work in the month preceding the month in which the accident resulting in injury occurs, or the average annual income earned by the victim from work during the years, not to exceed three, preceding the year in which the accident resulting in injury occurs, whichever is greater, for a victim regularly employed at the time of the accident;

(B) the average annual gross income earned by the victim from work during the years in which he was employed, not to exceed three, preceding the year in which the accident resulting in injury occurs, for a victim seasonally employed or not employed at the time of the accident; or

(C) the average annual gross income of a production or nonsupervisory worker in the private nonfarm economy in the State in which the victim is domiciled for the year in which the accident resulting in injury occurs, for a victim who has not previously earned income from work.

(2) "Work week" means the number of days an individual normally works in a seven-day period; "weekly income" means income earned during a work week.

NET LOSS

SEC. 208. (a) GENERAL.—Except as provided in paragraph (3) of subsection (a) of section 108 of this Act, all benefits or advantages (less reasonably incurred collection costs) that an individual receives or is entitled to receive from social security (except those benefits provided under title XIX of the Social Security Act) workmen's compensation, any State-required temporary, nonoccupational disability insurance, and all other benefits (except the proceeds of life insurance) received by or available to an individual because of the injury from any government, unless the law authorizing or providing for such benefits or advantages makes them excess or secondary to the benefits in accordance with this Act, shall be subtracted from loss in calculating net loss.

(b) TAX DEDUCTION.—If a benefit or advantage received to compensate for loss of income because of injury, whether from no-fault benefits or from any source of benefits or advantages subtracted under subsection (a) of this section, is not taxable income, the income tax saving that is attributable to such loss of income because of injury is subtracted in calculating net loss for work loss. Subtraction may not exceed fifteen per centum of the loss of income and shall be in such lesser amount as the insurer reasonably determines is appropriate based on a lower value of the income tax advantage.

(c) NO-FAULT BENEFITS PRIMARY.—If any individual is entitled to receive benefits or advantages from a source other than no-fault insurance, he may receive such benefits or advantages (other than benefits or advantages from social security (except those benefits provided under title XIX of the Social Security Act), workmen's compensation, any State-required temporary, nonoccupational disability insurance, and all other benefits (except the proceeds of life insurance) received by or available to an individual because of the injury from any government) only to the extent that basic restoration advantages exceed $10,000, or whatever higher amount a State may prescribe under section 104(a) (2), whichever is greater.

ADDED RESTORATION BENEFITS

SEC. 209. (a) OPTIONAL OFFERING.—Restoration obligors providing security for the payment of basic restoration benefits may offer or obligate themselves to provide added restoration benefits for injury or damage arising out of the ownership, maintenance, or use of a motor vehicle, including—

 (1) loss excluded from basic restoration benefits by limits on allowable expense, work loss, replacement services loss, and survivor's loss;

 (2) benefits for damage to property;

 (3) benefits for loss of use of a motor vehicle; and

(4) benefits for expense for remedial religious treatment and care.

Subject to the approval of terms and forms by the commissioner, restoration obligors may offer or obligate themselves to provide other added restoration coverages.

(b) MANDATORY OFFERING.—(1) Insurers providing basic restoration insurance shall offer the following added restoration coverage:

(A) for physical damage to a motor vehicle, a coverage for all collision and upset damage, subject to an optional deductible of not to exceed $100;

(B) for the payment of tort liability, if a State determines that security for the payment of tort liability is not required motor vehicle insurance;

(C) for economic detriment, a coverage for work loss sustained by a victim in excess of limitations on basic restoration benefits for work loss; and

(D) for basic restoration benefits, if a State determines that a vehicle having less than four wheels is not a motor vehicle.

(2) The commissioner may adopt rules requiring that insurers providing basic restoration insurance offer, in accordance with State law, any other specified added restoration coverages.

(c) TERRITORIAL APPLICABILITY.—All added restoration coverages are applicable in any State, Puerto Rico, or Canada.

INELIGIBLE CLAIMANTS

SEC. 210. (a) CONVERTER.—(1) Except as provided for assigned claims, a converter of a motor vehicle is ineligible to receive no-fault benefits, including benefits otherwise due him as a survivor, from any source other than a contract of insurance under which he is an insured, for an injury arising out of the maintenance or use of the converted vehicle. If a converter dies from such injuries, his survivor or survivors are not entitled to no-fault benefits for survivor's loss from any source other than a contract of insurance under which the converter is an insured.

(2) For purposes of this subsection and subsection (c) of section 111 of this Act, an individual is not a converter of a motor vehicle if he used it in the good faith belief that he was legally entitled to do so.

(b) INTENTIONAL INJURIES.—(1) An individual who intentionally injures himself or another individual is ineligible to receive no-fault benefits for injury arising out of his acts, including benefits otherwise due him as a survivor. If an individual dies as a result of intentionally injuring himself, his survivor or survivors are not entitled to no-fault benefits for survivor's loss. An individual intentionally injures himself or another individual if he acts or fails to act for the purpose of causing such injury or with knowledge that such injury is substantially certain to follow. An individual does not intentionally injure himself or another individual—

>   (A) merely because his act or failure to act is intentional or done with his realization that it creates a grave risk of causing injury; or

>   (B) if the act or omission causing the injury is for the purpose of averting bodily harm to himself or another individual.

(2) For purposes of subsection (c) of section 111 and paragraph (3) of subsection (a) of section 206 of this Act, an individual does not intentionally injure himself or another individual merely because his act or failure to act is intentional or done with his realization that it creates a grave risk of harm.

OTHER PROVISIONS

SEC. 211. (a) INCLUDED COVERAGE.—A contract of insurance covering liability arising out of the ownership, maintenance, or use of a motor vehicle registered in a State includes basic restoration benefits and any other benefit coverages required by the no-fault plan for motor vehicle insurance in effect in such State unless such contract—

>   (1) provides tort liability coverages only in excess of any of those required by such State no-fault plan; or

>   (2) is a contract which the commissioner determines

1 by regulation provides motor vehicle liability coverages
2 only as incidental to some other basic coverage.

3 (b) APPROVAL OF TERMS AND FORMS.—Terms and
4 conditions (including forms used by insurers) of any con-
5 tract, certificate, or other evidence of insurance sold or issued
6 pursuant to a State no-fault plan for motor vehicle insurance
7 in accordance with this title or title III of this Act and pro-
8 viding no-fault benefits or any required tort liability are
9 subject to approval and regulation by the commissioner in
10 such State. The commissioner shall approve only terms and
11 conditions which are consistent with the purposes of this Act
12 and fair and equitable to all persons whose interests may be
13 affected. The commissioner may limit by rule the variety of
14 coverage available in order to give purchasers of insurance a
15 reasonable opportunity to compare the cost of insuring with
16 various insurers.

17 TITLE III—ALTERNATIVE STATE NO-FAULT
18 MOTOR VEHICLE INSURANCE PLAN
19 PROVISIONS

20 SEC. 301. The alternative State no-fault plan for motor
21 vehicle insurance (the State no-fault plan in accordance
22 with this title), which becomes applicable and goes into
23 effect in a State pursuant to subsection (e) of section 201 of
24 this Act, is composed of title I of this Act, except sections
25 101, 102, 112, and 113; title II of this Act, except sections

66

201 and 202; and this title. A State may establish additional requirements provided that they are not inconsistent with the provisions of the alternative State no-fault plan for motor vehicle insurance or the policy set forth and declared in section 102 of this Act.

94TH CONGRESS
1ST SESSION
H. R. 8441

IN THE HOUSE OF REPRESENTATIVES

JULY 8, 1975

Mr. RINALDO introduced the following bill; which was referred to the Committee on Interstate and Foreign Commerce

A BILL

To regulate commerce by establishing a nationwide system to restore motor vehicle accident victims and by requiring no-fault motor vehicle insurance as a condition precedent to using a motor vehicle on public roadways.

1 *Be it enacted by the Senate and House of Representa-*
2 *tives of the United States of America in Congress assembled,*
3   TITLE I—GENERAL PROVISIONS
4   FORMAL PROVISIONS
5   SEC. 101. (a) SHORT TITLE.—This Act may be cited
6 as the "National No-Fault Motor Vehicle Insurance Act".

(b) TABLE OF CONTENTS.—

TITLE I—GENERAL PROVISIONS

Sec. 101. Formal provisions.
    (a) Short title.
    (b) Table of contents.
Sec. 102. Declaration of policy.
    (a) Findings.
    (b) Purposes.
Sec. 103. Definitions.
Sec. 104. Required motor vehicle insurance.
    (a) Security covering a motor vehicle.
    (b) Self-insurance.
    (c) Obligated government.
    (d) Obligations upon termination of security.
Sec. 105. Availability of insurance.
    (a) Plan.
    (b) Cancellation, refusal to renew, or other termination of insurance.
Sec. 106. Payment of claims for no-fault benefits.
    (a) In general.
    (b) Release or settlement of claim.
    (c) Time limitations on actions to recover benefits.
    (d) Assignment of benefits.
    (e) Deduction and setoff.
    (f) Exemption of benefits.
Sec. 107. Attorney's fees and costs.
    (a) Fees of claimant's attorney.
    (b) Fees of restoration obligor's attorney.
Sec. 108. Assigned claims.
    (a) General.
    (b) Assigned claims plan.
    (c) Time for presenting claims under assigned claims plan.
Sec. 109. State regulation.
    (a) Rates and rating.
    (b) Public information.
    (b) Accountability program.
    (d) Availability of services.
Sec. 110. Motor vehicles in interstate travel.
    (a) General.
    (b) Conforming coverage.
    (c) Applicable law.
Sec. 111. Rights and duties of restoration obligors.
    (a) Reimbursement and subrogation.
    (b) Duty to pay basic restoration benefits.
    (c) Indemnity.
    (d) Referral for rehabilitation services.
Sec. 112. Jurisdiction of Federal courts.
Sec. 113. Federal motor vehicle.
    (a) General.
    (b) Procedures.
    (c) Definitions.
Sec. 114. Separability.

TITLE II—NATIONAL STANDARDS FOR STATE NO-FAULT MOTOR VEHICLE INSURANCE PLAN

Sec. 201. State no-fault plan in accordance with this title.
    (a) Preemption.
    (b) State plan.
    (c) Determination by Secretary.
    (d) Periodic review.
    (e) Alternative State plan.
    (f) Procedure.
    (g) Exceptions.
    (h) Reporting requirements.
    (i) Financial assistance to States.
    (j) Authorization for appropriations.
Sec. 202. National standards.
    (a) General.
    (b) Criteria.
Sec. 203. Right to basic restoration benefits.
    (a) Accident within a State.
    (b) Accident outside any State.
Sec. 204. Limitations on benefits.
Sec. 205. Source of basic restoration benefits.
    (a) Applicable security.
    (b) Multiple sources of equal priority.
Sec. 206. Restrictions on tort liability.
    (a) Partial abolition.
    (b) Nonreimbursable tort fine.
Sec. 207. Work loss.
    (a) Regularly employed.
    (b) Seasonally employed.
    (c) Not employed.
    (d) Definitions.
Sec. 208. Net loss.
    (a) General.
    (b) Tax deduction.
    (c) No-fault benefits primary.
Sec. 209. Added restoration benefits.
    (a) Optional offering.
    (b) Mandatory offering.
    (c) Territorial applicability.
Sec. 210. Ineligible claimants.
    (a) Converter.
    (b) Intentional injuries.
Sec. 211. Other provisions.
    (a) Included coverage.
    (b) Approval of terms and forms.

TITLE III—ALTERNATIVE STATE NO-FAULT MOTOR VEHICLE INSURANCE PLAN

Sec. 301. Provisions.

DECLARATION OF POLICY

SEC. 102. (a) FINDINGS.—The Congress hereby finds and declares that—

(1) motor vehicles are the primary instrumentality for the interstate transportation of individuals;

(2) the intrastate transportation of individuals by motor vehicle over Federal-aid highways and other highways significantly affects interstate commerce, particularly in metropolitan areas encompassing more than one State;

(3) the maximum feasible restoration of all individuals injured and compensation of the economic losses of the survivors of all individuals killed in motor vehicle accidents on Federal-aid highways, in interstate commerce, and in activity affecting interstate commerce is essential to the humane and purposeful functioning of commerce;

(4) to avoid any undue burden on commerce during the interstate or intrastate transportation of individuals, it is necessary and proper to have a nationwide low-cost, comprehensive, and fair system of compensating and restoring motor vehicle accident victims and the survivors of deceased victims;

(5) exhaustive studies by the United States Department of Transportation, the Congress, and some

States have determined that the present basic system of motor vehicle accident and insurance law, which makes compensation and restoration contingent upon—

(A) every victim first showing that someone else was at fault;

(B) every victim first showing that he was without fault; and

(C) the person at fault having sufficient liability insurance and other available financial resources to pay for all the losses,

is not such a low-cost, comprehensive, and fair system;

(6) careful studies, intensive hearings, and some State experiments have demonstrated that a basic system of motor vehicle accident and insurance law which—

(A) assures every victim payment of all his medical and rehabilitation costs, and recovery of almost all his work loss plus a reasonable amount of replacement services; and

(B) eliminates the need to determine fault except when a victim is very seriously injured,

is such a low-cost, comprehensive, and fair system;

(7) nationwide adoption of the system described in paragraph (6) in place of the system described in paragraph (5) would remove an undue burden on commerce;

(8) pursuant to the power vested in it "to regulate Commerce . . . among the several States", the Government of the United States is authorized to require a nationwide low-cost, comprehensive, and fair system of compensating and restoring motor vehicle accident victims and the survivors of the deceased victims;

(9) in all the States there should be uniformity as to the essential elements of the system of motor vehicle accident and insurance law to avoid confusion, complexity, uncertainty, and chaos which would be engendered by a multiplicity of noncomplementary State systems, but the need for a nationwide basic system does not require that the Federal Government itself directly administer, operate, or direct the administration or operation of such system; **and**

(10) a nationwide low-cost, comprehensive, and fair system of compensating and restoring motor vehicle accident victims can—

    (A) recognize, respect, and avoid interfering with the historical role of the States in regulating and exercising legislative authority over the business of insurance; and

    (B) save and restore the lives of countless victims by providing and paying the cost of services so that every victim has the opportunity to—

(i) receive prompt and comprehensive professional treatment, and

(ii) be rehabilitated to the point where he can return as a useful member of society and a self-respecting and self-supporting citizen.

(b) PURPOSES.—Therefore, it is hereby declared to be the policy of the Congress to establish—

(1) at reasonable cost to the purchaser of insurance, a nationwide system of prompt and adequate restoration benefits for motor vehicle accident victims and the survivors of deceased victims; and

(2) minimum standards which each State must meet or exceed so as to assure a nationwide low-cost, comprehensive, and fair system of motor vehicle accident and insurance law and which enables each State to participate legislatively, to administer without interference, and to continue regulating the business of insurance.

DEFINITIONS

SEC. 103. As used in this Act—

(1) "Added restoration benefits" means benefits provided by added restoration insurance in accordance with section 209 or section 304 of this Act.

(2) "Allowable expense" means reasonable charges incurred for, or the reasonable value of (where no charges are

incurred), reasonably needed and used products, services, and accommodations for—

   (A) professional medical treatment and care;
   (B) emergency medical services; and
   (C) medical and vocational rehabilitation services.

The term does not include—

   (i) that portion of a charge for a room in a hospital, clinic, convalescent, or nursing home, or any other institution engaged in providing nursing care and related services, in excess of a reasonable and customary charge for semiprivate accommodations, unless more intensive care is medically required;
   (ii) any amount includable in work loss, replacement services loss, or survivor's loss; or
   (iii) expenses directly related to the funeral, burial, cremation, or other form of disposition of the remains of a deceased victim.

(3) "Basic restoration benefits" means benefits provided in accordance with this Act for the net loss sustained by a victim, subject to any applicable limitations, exclusions, deductibles, waiting periods, disqualifications, or other terms and conditions provided or authorized in accordance with this Act. Basic restoration benefits do not include benefits for damage to property.

(4) "Commissioner" means the commissioner of insur-

ance or the head of the department, commission board, or other agency of a State which is charged by the law of that State with the supervision and regulation of the business of insurance.

(5) "Department" means the department of motor vehicles or the department, commission, board, or other agency of a State which is charged by the law of that State with the administration of laws and regulations regarding registration of motor vehicles.

(6) "Emergency medical services" means services necessary to mitigate injury to any victim during the period immediately and proximately following an accident (including, but not limited to, communications, transportation, and treatment by medical and paramedical personnel through an emergency medical services system), which are supplied or provided in accordance with applicable State law.

(7) "Emergency medical services system" means a system which provides for the arrangement of personnel, facilities, and equipment for the effective and coordinated delivery in an appropriate geographical area of health care services under emergency conditions, which is administered by a public or nonprofit private entity which has the authority and the resources to provide effective administration, and which meets the requirements of section 1206(b)(4) of the Public Health Service Act.

(8) "Government" means the government of the United States, any State, any political subdivision of a State, any instrumentality of two or more States, or any agency, subdivision, or department of any such government, including any corporation or other association organized by a government for the execution of a government program and subject to control by a government, or any corporation or agency established under an interstate compact or international treaty.

(9) "Injury" means accidentally sustained bodily harm to an individual and that individual's illness, disease, or death resulting therefrom.

(10) "Insurance" means a contract, self-insurance, or any other legally binding obligation to pay or provide no-fault benefits or any required tort liability.

(11) "Insured" means—

(A) an individual identified by name as an insured in a contract of basic restoration insurance complying with this Act; and

(B) a spouse or other relative of a named insured, a minor in the custody of a named insured, and a minor in the custody of a relative of a named insured if—

(i) not identified by name as an insured in any other contract of basic restoration insurance complying with this Act, and

11

(ii) in residence in the same household with a named insured.

An individual is in residence in the same household if he usually makes his home in the same family unit, even though he temporarily lives elsewhere.

(12) "Insurer" means a legally constituted entity, other than a self-insurer or an obligated government, which is authorized under State law to provide security covering a motor vehicle in such State.

(13) "Loss" means accrued economic detriment resulting from injury arising out of the maintenance or use of a motor vehicle consisting of, and limited to, allowable expense, work loss, replacement services loss, and survivor's loss.

(14) "Loss of income" means gross income actually lost by a victim or that would have been lost but for any income continuation plan, reduced by—

(A) ninety per centum of any income which such individual earns from substitute work;

(B) income which such individual would have earned in available substitute work he was capable of performing but unreasonably failed to undertake; or

(C) any income which such individual would have earned by hiring an available substitute to perform self-employment services but reasonably failed to do.

(15) "Maintenance or use of a motor vehicle" means maintenance or use of a motor vehicle as a vehicle, including, incident to its maintenance or use as a vehicle, occupying, entering into or alighting from it. Maintenance or use of a motor vehicle does not include—

    (A) conduct within the course of a business of repairing servicing, or otherwise maintaining motor vehicles unless the conduct occurs off the business premises; or

    (B) conduct in the course of loading or unloading a motor vehicle unless the conduct occurs while occupying, entering into, or alighting from it.

(16) "Medical and vocational rehabilitation services" means services necessary to reduce disability and to restore the physical, psychological, social, and vocational functioning of a victim. Such services may include, but are not limited to, medical care, diagnostic and evaluation procedures, physical and occupational therapy, other medically necessary therapies, speech pathology and audiology, nursing care under the supervision of a registered nurse, medical social services, vocational rehabilitation and training services, occupational licenses and tools and transportation where necessary to secure medical and vocational rehabilitation services. A restoration obligor is not obligated to provide basic restoration benefits for allowable expense for medical and voca-

tional rehabilitation services unless the facility in which or through which such services are provided has been accredited by the department of health, the equivalent government agency responsible for health programs, or the accrediting designee of such department or agency of the State in which such services are provided, as being in accordance with applicable requirements and regulations.

(17) "Motor vehicle" means a vehicle of a kind required to be registered under the laws relating to motor vehicles of the State in which such vehicle is located except that a vehicle having less than four wheels may be specially treated, at the option of a State establishing a no-fault plan for motor vehicle insurance in accordance with title II of this Act, with respect to the requirements and benefits of such plan.

(18) "Net loss" means loss less benefits or advantages required to be subtracted from loss in calculating net loss pursuant to section 208 of this Act.

(19) "Noneconomic detriment" means pain, suffering, inconvenience, physical impairment, and other nonpecuniary damage recoverable under the tort law applicable to injury arising out of the maintenance or use of a motor vehicle. The term does not include punitive or exemplary damages.

(20) "No-fault benefits" means basic restoration benefits, added restoration benefits, or both.

(21) "No-fault insurance" means basic restoration insurance, added restoration insurance, or both.

(22) "Owner" means an individual, government, corporation, company, association, firm, partnership, joint stock company, foundation, institution, society, union, club, church, or any other group of persons organized for any purpose, other than a lienholder or secured party, that owns or has title to a motor vehicle or is entitled to the use and possession of a motor vehicle subject to a security interest held by another. The term includes a lessee of a motor vehicle having the right to possession under a lease with option to purchase.

(23) "Restoration obligor" means an insurer, self-insurer, or obligated government providing no-fault benefits in accordance with this Act.

(24) "Replacement services loss" means expenses reasonably incurred in obtaining ordinary and necessary services in lieu of those the victim would have performed, not for income, but for the benefit of himself or his family, if he had not been injured.

(25) "Secretary" means the Secretary of Transportation.

(26) "Secured vehicle" means a motor vehicle for which security is provided in accordance with section 104 of this Act.

(27) "Security covering a motor vehicle", "security covering the vehicle", and "security" means the security which is provided in accordance with section 104 of this Act.

(28) "Self-insurer" means an owner or any person providing security pursuant to subsection (b) or (c) of section 104 of this Act.

(29) "State" means a State of the United States, the District of Columbia, Guam, and the Virgin Islands.

(30) "State vocational rehabilitation agency" means the agency in the State which administers the State plan for vocational rehabilitation services under the Vocational Rehabilitation Act (29 U.S.C. 35).

(31) "Survivor" means an individual identified in the wrongful death statute or Constitution of the State of domicile of a deceased victim as one entitled to receive benefits by reason of the death of another individual.

(32) "Victim' means an individual who suffers injury arising out of the maintenance or use of a motor vehicle; "deceased victim" means a victim suffering death resulting from injury.

(33) "Without regard to fault" means irrespective of fault as a cause of injury.

(34) "Work loss" means—

(A) loss of gross income of a victim, as calculated pursuant to the provisions of section 207 of this Act; and

(B) reasonable expenses of a victim for hiring a substitute to perform self-employment services, thereby mitigating loss of income, or for hiring special help, thereby enabling a victim to work and mitigate loss of income.

REQUIRED MOTOR VEHICLE INSURANCE

SEC. 104. (a) SECURITY COVERING A MOTOR VEHICLE.—(1) Every owner of a motor vehicle which is registered in a State in which a State no-fault plan for motor vehicle insurance in accordance with title II or title III of this Act is in effect, or which is operated in such State by the owner or with his permission, shall continuously provide security covering such motor vehicle while such vehicle is either present or registered in such State. Security shall be provided for the payment of basic restoration benefits in accordance with paragraph (2) of this subsection, and at the option of a State establishing a plan in accordance with title II of this Act, for the payment of other benefits or tort liability. The owner or any other person may provide security covering a motor vehicle by a contract of insurance with an insurer or by qualifying as a self-insurer or as an obligated government.

(2) A State no-fault plan for motor vehicle insurance under this Act may entitle a victim to payment of $50,000 or such higher amount as determined pursuant to State law,

in basic restoration benefits. If the total amount of a victim's allowable expense, work loss, and replacement services loss exceeds $50,000 or such higher amount as determined pursuant to State law, the victim shall be entitled to determine the manner in which such basic restoration benefits shall be allocated among the victim's allowable expense, work loss, and replacement services loss.

(3) A State no-fault plan for motor vehicle insurance under this Act shall include payment of $1,000, or such higher amount as may be required pursuant to State law, for expenses directly related to the funeral, burial, cremation, or other form of disposition of the remains of a deceased victim.

(b) SELF-INSURANCE.—Self-insurance, subject to approval of the commissioner or department, is effected by filing with the department in satisfactory form—

(1) a continuing undertaking by the owner or other appropriate person to pay basic restoration benefits and any tort liability required by State law in amounts not less than those required by such State law, to perform all obligations imposed in accordance with this Act, and to elect to pay such added restoration benefits as are specified in the undertaking;

(2) evidence that appropriate provision exists for

prompt and efficient administration of all claims, benefits, and obligations provided in accordance with this Act; and

(3) evidence that reliable financial arrangements deposits, resources, or commitments exist providing assurance substantially equivalent to that afforded by a contract of insurance complying with this Act for payment of no-fault benefits, any required tort liability, and performance of all other obligations imposed in accordance with this Act.

(c) OBLIGATED GOVERNMENT.—A government may provide security with respect to any motor vehicle owned or operated by it by lawfully obligating itself to pay basic restoration benefits in accordance with this Act, and such added restoration benefits as are specified in the undertaking.

(d) OBLIGATION UPON TERMINATION OF SECURITY.—An owner of a motor vehicle who ceases to maintain the security required in accordance with this Act shall immediately surrender the registration certificate and license plates for the vehicle to the department and may not operate or permit operation of the vehicle in any State until security has again been furnished as required in accordance with this Act. A person other than the owner who ceases to maintain such security shall immediately notify the owner and the department, who may not operate or permit operation of the vehicle until security has again been furnished. An insurer who has issued a contract of insurance and knows or has reason to believe the contract is for the purpose of providing security shall immediately give notice to the department of the termination of the insurance. If the commissioner or department withdraws approval of security provided by a self-insurer or knows that the conditions for self-insurance have ceased to exist, he shall immediately give notice thereof to the department. These requirements may be modified or waived by the department.

AVAILABILITY OF INSURANCE

SEC. 105. (a) PLAN.—(1) The commissioner shall establish and implement or approve and supervise a plan assuring that any required no-fault benefits and tort liability coverages for motor vehicles will be conveniently and expeditiously available, subject only to payment or provisions for payment of the premium, to each individual who cannot conveniently obtain insurance through ordinary methods at rates not in excess of those applicable to similarly situated individuals under the plan. The plan may provide reasonable means for the transfer of individuals insured thereunder into the ordinary market, at the same or lower rates, pursuant to regulations established by the commissioner. The plan may be implemented by assignment of applicants among insurers, pooling, any joint insuring or reinsuring arrangement, or any other method, including a State fund, that results in all applicants being conveniently afforded the insurance coverages on reasonable and not unfairly discriminatory terms.

(2) The plan shall make available added restoration benefits and tort liability coverage together with other contract provisions which the commissioner determines are reasonably needed by applicants and are commonly afforded in voluntary markets. The plan must also assure that there is available through the private sector or otherwise to all applicants adequate premium financing or provision for the installment payment of premiums subject to customary terms and conditions.

(3) All insurers writing no-fault benefits and tort liability coverages in a State shall participate in the plan in such State. The plan shall provide for equitable apportionment, among all participating insurers writing any insurance coverage required under the plan, of the financial burdens of insurance provided to applicants under the plan and the costs of operation of the plan.

(4) Subject to the supervision and approval of the commissioner, insurers may consult and agree with each other and with other appropriate persons as to the organization, administration, and operation of the plan and as to rates and rate modifications for insurance coverages provided

under the plan. Rates and rate modifications adopted or charged for insurance coverages provided under the plan shall—

 (A) be first adopted or approved by the commissioner;

 (B) be reasonable and not unfairly discriminatory among similarly situated applicants for insurance pursuant to regulations established by the commissioner; and

 (C) reflect the propensities of different motor vehicles with respect to the probability and severity of injuries.

(5) To carry out the objectives of this subsection, the commissioner may adopt rules, make orders, enter into agreements with other governmental and private entities and individuals, and form and operate or authorize the formation and operation of bureaus and other legal entities.

(b) CANCELLATION, REFUSAL TO RENEW, OR OTHER TERMINATION OF INSURANCE.—(1) Every contract of insurance providing security covering a motor vehicle which is not one of five or more motor vehicles under common ownership insured under a single insuring agreement, except as provided by paragraphs (2) and (5) of this subsection, may not be canceled, modified, or otherwise terminated by the insurer nor may the insurer fail to renew except at specified dates or intervals which may not be less than six months after the inception of coverage or thereafter less than six months apart.

(2) An insurer may terminate insurance if written notice of termination, including the reasons therefor, is mailed or delivered to the insured at least thirty days before the effective date of termination—

    (A) by cancellation at any time within seventy-five days after the inception of initial coverage;

    (B) by cancellation for nonpayment of—

        (i) premium when due, or

        (ii) any premium installment when due for which reasonable and separate notice has been given; or

    (C) by exclusion of an insured whose license to operate a motor vehicle has been revoked, following a hearing and pursuant to State law.

(3) Except as permitted in paragraph (2) of this subsection, any termination of insurance by an insurer which is permitted by the insurance contract and not prohibited by paragraph (1) of this subsection, including any refusal by the insurer to renew the insurance at the expiration of its term and any modification by the insurer of the terms and conditions of the insurance unfavorable to the insured, is nevertheless ineffective, unless written notice of intention to modify,

not to renew, or otherwise to terminate the insurance has been mailed or delivered to the insured at least thirty days before the effective date of the modification, expiration, or other termination of the insurance.

(4) For purposes of this subsection a cancellation or refusal to renew by or at the direction of any person acting pursuant to any power or authority under any premium finance plan, agreement, or arrangement, whether or not with power of attorney or assignment from the insured, constitutes a cancellation or refusal to renew by the insurer.

(5) This subsection does not limit or apply to any termination, modification, or cancellation of the insurance, or to any suspension of insurance coverage, by or at the written request of the insured or upon the sale or other transfer of the secured vehicle to an individual who is not an insured under the same contract of insurance.

(6) This subsection does not affect any right an insurer has under other law to rescind or otherwise terminate insurance because of fraud or other willful misconduct of the insured at the inception of the insuring transaction or the right of either party to reform the contract on the basis of mutual mistake of fact.

(7) An insurer, his authorized agents and employees, and any person furnishing information upon which he has relied, are not liable in any action or proceeding brought

because of any statement made in good faith pursuant to paragraph (2) of this subsection.

PAYMENT OF CLAIMS FOR NO-FAULT BENEFITS

SEC. 106. (a) IN GENERAL.—(1) No-fault benefits are payable monthly as loss accrues. Loss accrues not when injury occurs, but as allowable expense, work loss, replacement services loss, or survivor's loss is sustained.

(2) No-fault benefits are overdue if not paid within thirty days after the receipt by the restoration obligor of each submission of reasonable proof of the fact and amount of loss sustained, unless the restoration obligor designates, upon receipt of an initial claim for no-fault benefits, periods not to exceed thirty-one days each for accumulating all such claims received within each such period, in which case such benefits are overdue if not paid within fifteen days after the close of each such period. If reasonable proof is supplied as to only part of a claim, but the part amounts to $100 or more, benefits for such part are overdue if not paid within the time mandated by this paragraph. An obligation for basic restoration benefits for an item of allowable expense may be discharged by the restoration obligor by reimbursing the victim or by making direct payment to the supplier or provider of products, services, or accommodations within the time mandated by this paragraph. Overdue payments bear interest at the rate of 18 per centum per annum.

(3) A claim for no-fault benefits shall be paid without deduction for the benefits or advantages which are to be subtracted from loss in calculating net loss in accordance with section 208 (a) of this Act, if such benefits or advantages have not been paid or provided to such claimant prior to the date the no-fault benefits are overdue or the no-fault benefits claim is paid. The restoration obligor is thereupon entitled to recover reimbursement from the person obligated to pay or provide such benefits or advantages or from the claimant who actually receives them.

(4) A restoration obligor may bring an action to recover reimbursement for no-fault benefits which are paid upon the basis of an intentional misrepresentation of a material fact by a claimant or a supplier or provider of an item of allowable expense, if such restoration obligor reasonably relied upon such misrepresentation. The action may be brought only against such supplier or provider, unless the claimant has intentionally misrepresented the facts or knew of the misrepresentation. A restoration obligor may offset amounts he is entitled to recover from the claimant under this paragraph against any no-fault benefits otherwise due.

(5) A restoration obligor who rejects a claim for basic restoration benefits shall give to the claimant written notice of the rejection promptly, but in no event more than thirty

days after the receipt of reasonable proof of the loss. Such notice shall specify the reason for such rejection and inform the claimant of the terms and conditions of his right to obtain an attorney. If a claim is rejected for a reason other than that the person is not entitled to basic restoration benefits claimed, the written notice shall inform the claimant that he may file his claim with the assigned claims bureau and shall give the name and address of the bureau.

(b) RELEASE OR SETTLEMENT OF CLAIM.—(1) Except as otherwise provided in this subsection, no-fault benefits shall not be denied or terminated because the victim executed a release or other settlement agreement. A claim for no-fault benefits may be discharged by a settlement agreement for an agreed amount payable in installments or in a lump sum, if the reasonably anticipated net loss does not exceed $2,500. In all other cases, a claim may be discharged by a settlement to the extent authorized by State law and upon a finding, by a court of competent jurisdiction, that the settlement is in the best interest of the claimant and any beneficiaries of the settlement, and that the claimant understands and consents to such settlement, and upon payment by the restoration obligor of the costs of such proceeding including a reasonable attorney's fee (based upon actual time expended) to the attorney selected by or appointed for the claimant. Such costs may not be charged to or deducted from the

27

proceeds of the settlement. Upon approval of the settlement, the court may make appropriate orders concerning the safeguarding and disposing of the proceeds of the settlement and may direct as a condition of the settlement agreement, that the restoration obligor pay the reasonable cost of appropriate future medical and vocational rehabilitation services.

(2) A settlement agreement for an amount payable in installments shall be modified as to amounts to be paid in the future, if it is shown that a material and substantial change of circumstances has occurred or that there is newly discovered evidence concerning the claimant's physical condition, loss, or rehabilitation which could not have been known previously or discovered in the exercise of reasonable diligence.

(3) A settlement agreement may be set aside if it is procured by fraud or if its terms are unconscionable.

(c) TIME LIMITATIONS ON ACTIONS TO RECOVER BENEFITS.—(1) If no-fault benefits have not been paid for loss arising otherwise than from death, an action therefor may be commenced not later than two years after the victim suffers the loss and either knows, or in the exercise of reasonable diligence should have known, that the loss was caused by the accident, or not later than four years after the accident, whichever is earlier. If no-fault benefits have been paid for loss arising otherwise than from death, an action for further benefits, other than survivor's benefits, by either the same or another claimant, may be commenced not later than two years after the last payment of benefits.

(2) If no-fault benefits have not been paid to the deceased victim or his survivor or survivors, an action for survivor's benefits may be commenced not later than one year after the death or four years after the accident from which death results, whichever is earlier. If survivor's benefits have been paid to any survivor, an action for further survivor's benefits by either the same or another claimant may be commenced not later than two years after the last payment of benefits. If no-fault benefits have been paid for loss suffered by a victim before his death resulting from the injury, an action for survivor's benefits may be commenced not later than one year after the death or six years after the last payment of benefits, whichever is earlier.

(3) If timely action for basic restoration benefits is commenced against a restoration obligor and benefits are denied because of a determination that the restoration obligor's coverage is not applicable to the claimant under the provisions of section 205 of this Act, an action against the applicable restoration obligor or the restoration obligor to whom a claim is assigned under an assigned claims plan may be commenced not later than sixty days after the determination becomes final or the last date on which the action could otherwise have been commenced, whichever is later.

(4) Except as paragraph (1), (2), or (3) prescribes a longer period, an action by a claimant on an assigned claim which has been timely presented in accordance with the provisions of section 108(c) of this Act may not be commenced more than sixty days after the claimant receives written notice of rejection of the claim by the restoration obligor to which it was assigned.

(5) If a person entitled to no-fault benefits is under a legal disability when the right to bring an action for the benefits first accrues, the period of his disability is not a part of the time limited for commencement of the action.

(d) ASSIGNMENT OF BENEFITS.—An assignment of or an agreement to assign any right in accordance with this Act for loss accruing in the future is unenforceable except as to benefits for—

 (1) work loss to secure payment of alimony, maintenance, or child support; or

 (2) allowable expense to the extent the benefits are for the cost of products, services, or accommodations provided or to be provided by the assignee.

(e) DEDUCTION AND SETOFF.—Except as otherwise provided in this Act, basic restoration benefits shall be paid without deduction or setoff.

(f) EXEMPTION OF BENEFITS.—(1) No-fault benefits for allowable expense are exempt from garnishment, attachment, execution, and any other process or claim, except upon the claim of a creditor who has provided products, services, or accommodations to the extent benefits are for allowable expense for those products, services, or accommodations.

(2) Basic restoration benefits other than those for allowable expense are exempt from garnishment, attachment, execution, and any other process or claim for benefits attributable to loss sustained within the first sixty days following the accident resulting in injury. Other basic restoration benefits (except for items of allowable expense) are exempt to the extent that wages or earnings are exempt under any applicable law exempting wages or earnings from such process or claims.

ATTORNEY'S FEES AND COSTS

SEC. 107. (a) FEES OF CLAIMANT'S ATTORNEY.—(1) If any overdue no-fault benefits are paid by the restoration obligor after receipt of notice of representation of a claimant by an attorney or if an action is maintained (unless the court determines that the claim or any significant part thereof is fraudulent or so excessive as to have no reasonable foundation), a reasonable attorney's fee (based upon actual time expended) shall be paid by the restoration obligor to such attorney. No part of the attorney's fee for representing the claimant in connection with a claim or action for no-fault benefits may be charged or deducted from benefits otherwise due to such claimant and no part of such benefits may be applied to such fee.

(2) In any such action brought against the claimant by the restoration obligor, the court may award the claimant's attorney a reasonable attorney's fee for defending such action, which shall be paid by the restoration obligor.

(b) FEES OF RESTORATION OBLIGOR'S ATTORNEY.—A restoration obligor shall be allowed a reasonable attorney's fee for defending a claim if the court determines that the claim or any significant part thereof is fraudulent or so excessive as to have no reasonable foundation. The fee may be treated as an offset against any benefits due or to become due to the claimant.

ASSIGNED CLAIMS

SEC. 108 (a) GENERAL.—(1) If a State no-fault plan for motor vehicle insurance in accordance with title II or title III of this Act is in effect on the date when the accident resulting in injury occurs, a victim or the survivor or survivors of a deceased victim may obtain basic restoration benefits through the assigned claims plan established, pursuant to subsection (b) of this section, in the State of domicile, if any, of the victim or deceased victim, or if none, in the State, in which the accident resulting in injury occurs, if basic restoration insurance—

(A) is not applicable to the injury for a reason

other than those specified in the provisions on ineligible claimants;

(B) is not applicable to the injury because the victim converted a motor vehicle while he was under fifteen years of age;

(C) applicable to the injury cannot be identified;

(D) applicable to the injury is inadequate to provide the contracted-for benefits because of financial inability of a restoration obligor to fulfill its obligations; or

(E) benefits are refused by a restoration obligor for a reason other than that the individual is not entitled in accordance with this Act to the basic restoration benefits claimed.

(2) If a claim qualifies for assignment under paragraph (1) (C), (D), or (E) of this subsection, the assigned claims bureau or any insurer to whom the claim is assigned is subrogated to all rights of the claimant against the restoration obligor legally obligated to provide basic restoration benefits to the claimant, or against any successor in interest to or substitute for such obligor for such benefits as are provided by the assignee.

(3) If an individual receives basic restoration benefits through the assigned claims plan for any reason other than because of the financial inability of a restoration obligor to fulfill its obligation, all benefits or advantages that such indi-

vidual receives or is entitled to receive as a result of such injury, other than life insurance benefits or benefits by way of succession at death or in discharge of familial obligations of support, shall be subtracted from loss in calculating net loss.

(4) An assigned claim of an individual who does not comply with the requirement of providing security for the payment of basic restoration benefits, or of an individual as to whom the security is invalidated because of his fraud or willful misconduct, is subject to—

> (A) all the maximum optional deductibles and exclusions required to be offered; and
>
> (B) a deduction in the amount of $500 for each year or part thereof of the period of his continuous failure to provide security, applicable to any benefits otherwise payable except basic restoration benefits for allowable expense.

(b) ASSIGNED CLAIMS PLAN.—(1) Restoration obligors providing basic restoration insurance in a State may organize and maintain, subject to approval and regulation by the commissioner, an assigned claims bureau and an assigned claims plan and adopt rules for their operation and for assessment of costs on a fair and equitable basis consistent with this Act. If such bureau and plan are not organized and maintained in a manner considered by the commissioner to be consistent with this Act and with State law, he shall organize and maintain an assigned claims bureau and an assigned claims plan. Each restoration obligor insurer providing basic restoration insurance in a State shall participate in the assigned claims bureau and the assigned claims plan in that State. Costs incurred shall be allocated fairly and equitably among the restoration obligors.

(2) The assigned claims bureau shall promptly—

 (A) assign each claim for no-fault benefits to an assignee who shall be a participating insurer; and

 (B) notify the claimant of the identity and address of such assignee.

Claim shall be assigned so as to minimize inconvenience to claimants. The assignee thereafter has rights and obligations as if he had issued a policy of basic restoration insurance complying with this Act applicable to the injury or, in a case involving the financial inability of a restoration obligor to perform its obligations, as if the assignee had written the applicable basic restoration insurance, undertaken the self-insurance, or lawfully obligated itself to pay basic restoration benefits.

(c) TIME FOR PRESENTING CLAIMS UNDER ASSIGNED CLAIMS PLAN.—(1) Except as provided in paragraph (2) of this subsection, an individual authorized to obtain basic restoration benefits through the assigned claims plan shall notify the assigned claims bureau of his claim within the time that would have been allowed pursuant to section 106(c) of this Act for commencing an action for basic restoration benefits against any restoration obligor, other than an assigned claims bureau, in any case in which identifiable no-fault insurance coverage was in effect and applicable to the claim.

(2) If timely action for basic restoration benefits is commenced against a restoration obligor who is unable to fulfill his obligations because of financial inability, an individual authorized to obtain basic restoration benefits through the assigned claims plan shall notify the bureau of his claim within six months after his discovery of such financial inability.

STATE REGULATION

SEC. 109. (a) RATES AND RATING.—The commissioner, in accordance with applicable State law, shall regulate restoration obligors providing security covering a motor vehicle in his State. The rates charged for security shall be established, determined, and modified in each State only in accordance with the provisions of the applicable rating law of such State and shall reflect the propensities of different motor vehicles with respect to the probability and severity of injuries.

(b) PUBLIC INFORMATION.—The commissioner shall

provide the means to inform purchasers of insurance, in a manner adequate to permit them to compare prices, about rates being charged by insurers for no-fault benefits and tort liability coverage.

(c) ACCOUNTABILITY PROGRAM.—(1) The commissioner, through the State vocational rehabilitation agency, shall establish and maintain a program for the regular and periodic evaluation of medical and vocational rehabilitation services for which reimbursement or payment is sought from a restoration obligor as an item of allowable expense to assure that—

    (A) the services are medical and vocational rehabilitation services, as defined in section 103 (16) of this Act;

    (B) the recipient of the services is making progress toward a greater level of independent functioning and the services are necessary to such progress and continued progress; and

    (C) the charges for the services for which reimbursement or payment is sought are fair and reasonable.

Progress reports shall be made periodically in writing on each case for which reimbursement or payment is sought under security for the payment of basic restoration benefits. Such reports shall be prepared by the supervising physician or

rehabilitation counselor and submitted to the State vocational rehabilitation agency. The State vocational rehabilitation agency shall file reports with applicable restoration obligor or obligors. Pursuant to this program, there shall be provision for determinations to be made in writing of the rehabilitation goals and needs of the victim and for the periodic assessment of progress at reasonable time intervals by the supervising physician or rehabilitation counselor.

(2) The commissioner is authorized to establish and maintain a program for the regular and periodic evaluation of his State's no-fault plan for motor vehicle insurance.

(d) AVAILABILITY OF SERVICES.—The commissioner is authorized to coordinate with appropriate government agencies in the creation and maintenance of an emergency medical services system or systems, and to take all steps necessary to assure that emergency medical services are available for each victim suffering injury in the State. The commissioner is authorized to take all steps necessary to assure that medical and vocational rehabilitation services are available for each victim resident in the State. Such steps may include, but are not limited to, guarantees of loans or other obligations of suppliers or providers of such services, and support for training programs for personnel in programs and facilities offering such services.

MOTOR VEHICLES IN INTERSTATE TRAVEL

SEC. 110. (a) GENERAL.—An owner of a motor vehicle who has complied with the requirements of security covering a motor vehicle in the State of registration of such vehicle shall be deemed to have complied with the requirements for such security in any State in which such vehicle is operating.

(b) CONFORMING COVERAGE.—(1) A restoration obligor providing security for the payment of basic restoration benefits shall be obligated to provide, and each contract of insurance for the payment of basic restoration benefits shall be construed to contain, coverage sufficient to satisfy the requirements for security covering a motor vehicle in any State in which any victim who is a claimant or whose survivors are claimants is domiciled or is injured.

(2) A restoration obligor providing security for the payment of basic restoration benefits shall be obligated to provide, and each contract of insurance for the payment of basic restoration benefits shall be construed to contain, coverage of $50,000 to protect the owner or operator of a motor vehicle from tort liability to which he is exposed through application of the law of the State of domicile of a victim (or in the State in which the accident resulting in injury or harm to property occurs if a victim is not domiciled in

any State), but to which he would not have been exposed through application of the law of the State of registration of the motor vehicle.

(c) APPLICABLE LAW.—(1) The basic restoration benefits available to any victim or to any survivor of a deceased victim shall be determined pursuant to the provisions of the State no-fault plan for motor vehicle insurance in accordance with title II or title III of this Act which is in effect in the State of domicile of the victim on the date when the motor vehicle accident resulting in injury occurs. If there is no such State no-fault plan in effect or if the victim is not domiciled in any State, then basic restoration benefits available to any victim shall be determined pursuant to the provisions of the State no-fault plan for motor vehicle insurance, if any, in effect in the State in which the accident resulting in injury occurs.

(2) The right of a victim or of a survivor of a deceased victim to sue in tort shall be determined by the law of the State of domicile of such victim. If a victim is not domiciled in a State, such right to sue shall be determined by the law of the State in which the accident resulting in injury or damage to property occurs.

RIGHTS AND DUTIES OF RESTORATION OBLIGORS

SEC. 111. (a) REIMBURSEMENT AND SUBROGATION.—
(1) Except as provided in paragraphs (2), (3), and (4) of this subsection, a restoration obligor—

    (A) does not have and may not contract, directly or indirectly, in whole or in part, for a right of reimbursement from or subrogation to the proceeds of a victim's claim for relief or to a victim's cause of action for noneconomic detriment; and

    (B) may not directly or indirectly contract for, or be granted by a State, any right of reimbursement from any other restoration obligor not acting as a reinsurer for no-fault benefits which it has paid or is obligated to pay as a result of injury to a victim, except that a restoration obligor may seek reimbursement from any other restoration obligor in an arbitration proceeding based upon a determination of fault, for no-fault benefits exceeding $2,000 which it has paid or is obligated to pay as a result of injury to a victim involving one or more private passenger motor vehicles. The arbitration hearing shall be conducted in accordance with procedures established by the commissioner.

(2) Whenever an individual who receives or is entitled to receive no-fault benefits for an injury has a claim or cause of action against any other person for breach of an obligation

or duty causing the injury or for breach of express or implied warranty, the restoration obligor is subrogated to the rights of the claimant and has a claim for relief or a cause of action, separate from that of the claimant, to the extent that:

    (A) elements of damage compensated for by security for the payment of no-fault benefits are recoverable; and

    (B) the restoration obligor has paid or become obligated to pay accrued or future no-fault benefits.

(3) Notwithstanding the provisions of paragraph (1)(B) of this subsection, a State may grant a right of reimbursement among and between restoration obligors based upon a determination of fault, where such restoration obligors have paid or are obligated to pay benefits for loss arising out of an accident resulting in injury in which one or more of the motor vehicles is of a type other than a private passenger motor vehicle and by designation the State has determined that the owner of such type would receive an unreasonable economic advantage or suffer an unreasonable economic disadvantage in the absence of the grant of such right of reimbursement: *Provided*, That in such event such right of reimbursement may be granted only with respect to benefits paid for loss in excess of $5,000.

(4) Nothing in this subsection shall preclude any person supplying or providing products, services, or accommoda-

tions from contracting or otherwise providing for a right of reimbursement to any basic restoration benefits for allowable expense.

(b) DUTY TO PAY BASIC RESTORATION BENEFITS.—A restoration obligor providing security for the payment of basic restoration benefits shall pay or otherwise provide such benefits without regard to fault to each individual entitled thereto, pursuant to the terms and conditions of the State no-fault plan for motor vehicle insurance applicable thereto.

(c) INDEMNITY.—A restoration obligor has a right of indemnity against an individual who has converted a motor vehicle involved in an accident, or against an individual who has intentionally injured himself or another individual, for no-fault benefits paid for—

(1) the loss caused by the conduct of that individual;

(2) the cost of processing the claims for such benefits; and

(3) the cost of enforcing this right of indemnity, including reasonable attorney's fees.

(d) REFERRAL FOR REHABILITATION SERVICES.—The restoration obligor shall promptly refer each victim to whom basic restoration benefits are expected to be payable for more than two months to the State vocational rehabilitation agency.

43

JURISDICTION OF FEDERAL COURTS

SEC. 112. No district court of the United States may entertain an action for no-fault benefits unless the United States is a party to the action.

FEDERAL MOTOR VEHICLE

SEC. 113. (a) (1) GENERAL.—Notwithstanding any other provision of law, a claim against the United States as a restoration obligor for injury arising out of the maintenance or use of a Federal motor vehicle which is a secured vehicle shall be governed by this Act. A Federal motor vehicle is a secured vehicle, for purposes of this Act, whenever it is located or operated in the territorial area of any State, Puerto Rico, Canada, or Mexico.

(2) the level of basic restoration benefits which the United States shall pay or provide shall be controlled by the no-fault plan for motor vehicle insurance in effect in the State of domicile of the victim, if any, or if none, in the State in which the accident resulting in injury occurs.

(b) PROCEDURES.—The Secretary, in cooperation with the Administrator of General Services, shall promulgate, and may from time to time revise, regulations with respect to security covering a Federal motor vehicle and administrative procedures to be followed in claims against the United States for no-fault benefits.

(c) DEFINITIONS.—As used in this section—

44

(1) "Federal agency" means any branch, department, commission, administration, authority, board, or bureau of, or any corporation owned or controlled by, the Government of the United States.

(2) "Federal motor vehicle" means a motor vehicle owned or leased by a Federal agency and operated with its express or implied permission.

SEPARABILITY

SEC. 114. If any provision of this Act or any application thereof to any individual or circumstance is held invalid, the invalidity shall not affect any provision or application of the Act which can be given effect without the involved provision or application, and to this end the provisions of this Act are separable.

TITLE II—NATIONAL STANDARDS FOR STATE NO-FAULT MOTOR VEHICLE INSURANCE PLAN

STATE NO-FAULT PLAN IN ACCORDANCE WITH THIS TITLE

SEC. 201. (a) PREEMPTION.—Any provision of any State law which would prevent the establishment or administration in such a State of a no-fault plan for motor vehicle insurance in accordance with this title or title III of this Act is preempted.

(b) STATE PLAN.—By the completion of the first general session of the State legislature which commences after the date of enactment of this Act, a State may establish a no-fault plan for motor vehicle insurance in accordance with this title. Upon the establishment of such a plan, the commissioner shall promptly submit to the Secretary a certified copy of such plan, together with all relevant information which is requested by the Secretary.

(c) DETERMINATION BY SECRETARY.—Within ninety days after the Secretary receives a copy of a State no-fault plan established under subsection (b) or (e) of this section, the Secretary shall make a determination whether such State has established a no-fault plan for motor vehicle insurance in accordance with this title. Unless the Secretary determines, pursuant to this section, that a State no-fault plan is not in accordance with this title, the plan shall go into effect in such State on the date designated in the plan. In no event shall such State plan go into effect less than nine months or more than twelve months after the date of its establishment.

(d) PERIODIC REVIEW.—The Secretary shall periodically, but not less than once every three years, review each State no-fault plan for motor vehicle insurance, which has been approved under subsection (c) of this section and for which there is experience, to determine whether such plan is still in accordance with this title and to evaluate the success of such plan in terms of the policy set forth and declared in section 102 of this Act. To facilitate such review, the commissioner in each such State shall submit to the Secretary periodically all relevant information which is requested by the Secretary. The Secretary shall report to the President and Congress simultaneously on July 1 each year on the results of such reviews, including any recommendations for legislation.

(e) ALTERNATIVE STATE PLAN.—(1) The alternative State no-fault plan for motor vehicle insurance (the State no-fault plan in accordance with title III of this Act) shall become applicable upon the expiration of the eighteen-month period following the completion of the first general session of the State legislature which commences after the date of enactment of this Act unless, prior to such date, the Secretary has made a determination that such State has established a no-fault plan for motor vehicle insurance in accordance with this title. The alternative State no-fault plan shall go into effect in a State on the first day of the ninth month after such plan becomes applicable or on a date designated by the Secretary, whichever is earlier.

(2) If, after the alternative State no-fault plan is applicable or in effect in a State, the Secretary, upon petition, makes a determination, pursuant to subsection (c) of this section, that such State has established a no-fault plan in accordance with this title, such State no-fault plan shall go into effect and the alternative State no-fault plan shall cease

to be applicable or in effect on a date to be designated by the Secretary.

(3) If, after a State no-fault plan in accordance with this title is in effect in a State, the Secretary makes a determination, pursuant to subsection (d) of this section, that such State no-fault plan is no longer in accordance with this title, then the plan which is no longer in accordance with this title shall cease to be in effect on a date to be designated by the Secretary, and on that date the alternative State no-fault plan shall go into effect in such State.

(f) PROCEDURE.—(1) Before making any determination under this section, the Secretary shall publish a notice in the Federal Register and afford the State and all interested parties a reasonable opportunity to present their views by oral and written submission.

(2) The Secretary shall notify in writing the Governor of the affected State of any determinations made under this section and shall publish these determinations with reasons therefor in the Federal Register.

(3) Any determinations made by the Secretary under this section shall be subject to judicial review in accordance with chapter 7 of title 5, United States Code, in the United States court of appeals for the circuit in which is located the State whose plan is the subject of such determination or

216

48

in the United States Court of Appeals for the District of Columbia Circuit. Any such review shall be instituted within sixty days from the date on which the determination made by the Secretary is published in the Federal Register.

(4) The Secretary shall establish such advisory boards as he determines necessary to assist in making determinations under subsections (c) and (d) of this section and any such advisory board shall be representative of the different geographic areas of the United States.

(g) EXCEPTIONS.—(1) The provisions of this section are inapplicable to the extent inconsistent with this subsection.

(2) Any State which is a no-fault State, as defined in paragraph (4) of this subsection, may establish a no-fault plan for motor vehicle insurance in accordance with this title by the fourth anniversary of the date of enactment of this Act.

(3) The alternative State no-fault plan for motor vehicle insurance (the State no-fault plan in accordance with title III of this Act) shall become applicable in any State which is a no-fault State, as defined in paragraph (4) of this subsection on the fourth anniversary of the date of enactment of this Act unless, prior to such date, the Secretary has made a determination that such State has established a no-

fault plan for motor vehicle insurance in accordance with this title.

(4) As used in this subsection, a "no-fault State" means a State which has enacted into law and put into effect a motor vehicle insurance law not later than September 1, 1975, which provides, at a minimum, for compulsory motor vehicle insurance; payment of benefits without regard to fault on a first-party basis where the value of such available benefits is not less than $2,000; and restrictions on the bringing of lawsuits in tort by victims for noneconomic detriment, in the form of a prohibition of such suits unless the victim suffers a certain quantum of loss or in the form of a relevant change in the evidentiary rules of practice and proof with respect to such lawsuits.

(h) REPORTING REQUIREMENTS.—The Secretary, in cooperation with the commissioners, shall annually review the operation of State no-fault plans for motor vehicle insurance established in accordance with this Act and report on—

(1) the cost-savings resulting from the institution of any such plan which meets or exceeds the national standards set forth in this Act and any subsequent savings resulting from the continuing operation of such plans;

(2) appropriate methods for refunding to members of the motoring public any cost-savings realized

from the institution and operation of such no-fault insurance plans;

(3) the impact of no-fault insurance on senior citizens; those who live in farming and rural areas; those who are economically disadvantaged, and those who live in inner cities;

(4) the impact of no-fault insurance on the problem of duplication of benefits when an individual has other insurance coverage which provides for compensation or reimbursement for lost wages or for health and accident (including hospitalization) benefits;

(5) the effect of no-fault insurance on court congestion and delay resulting from backlogs in State and Federal courts;

(6) the impact of no-fault insurance, reduced speed limits, and other factors on automobile insurance rates; and

(7) the impact of no-fault insurance on competition within the insurance industry, particularly with respect to the competitive position of small insurance companies.

The Secretary shall report to the President and Congress simultaneously on July 1 each year on the results of such review and determination together with his recommendations thereon.

(i) FINANCIAL ASSISTANCE TO STATES.—The Secretary is authorized to provide grants to any State for the purpose of reimbursing such State for any governmental cost increases resulting from the implementation or administration of a no-fault plan for motor vehicle insurance in accordance with this Act, The Secretary shall, by regulation, establish procedures for awarding such grants on a fair and equitable basis among the States.

(j) AUTHORIZATION FOR APPROPRIATIONS.—There is authorized to be appropriated to the Secretary to carry out his responsibilities under this Act such sums as are necessary, not to exceed $10,000,000, such sums to remain available until expended.

NATIONAL STANDARDS

SEC. 202. (a) GENERAL.—A State establishing a no-fault plan for motor vehicle insurance in accordance with this title shall enact a law which incorporates, at a minimum, title I of this Act, except sections 101, 102, 112, and 113, and this title except this section and section 201. The provisions of these sections, taken together, shall be known as the "national standards" for State no-fault motor vehicle insurance.

(b) CRITERIA.—A State no-fault plan for motor vehicle insurance is in accordance with this title if it meets or exceeds all of the national standards. A provision in a State plan "meets" a provision in the national standards if the substance of the State plan provision is the same as or the equivalent of the corresponding provision in the national standards. A provision in a State plan "exceeds" a provision in the national standards if the substance of the State plan provision is more favorable or beneficial to an insured or a claimant or more restrictive of tort liability than the corresponding provision in the national standards. Any provision in a State plan as to which there is no corresponding provision in the national standards shall not be evaluated in determining whether such plan meets or exceeds national standards provided such provision is not inconsistent with the national standards or the policy set forth and declared in section 102 of this Act.

RIGHT TO BASIC RESTORATION BENEFITS

SEC. 203. (a) ACCIDENT WITHIN A STATE.—If the accident resulting in injury occurs in a State in which a no-fault plan for motor vehicle insurance in accordance with this title or title III of this Act is in effect, any victim or any survivor of a deceased victim is entitled to receive basic restoration benefits.

(b) ACCIDENT OUTSIDE ANY STATE.—If the accident resulting in injury occurs outside a State in which a no-fault plan is in effect, but in any other State, Puerto Rico, Canada, or Mexico, a victim or a survivor of a deceased victim is entitled to receive basic restoration benefits if such victim is or was—

    (1) an insured; or

    (2) the driver or other occupant of a secured vehicle.

LIMITATIONS ON BENEFITS

SEC. 204. A State establishing a no-fault plan for motor vehicle insurance in accordance with this title—

    (a) may limit basic restoration benefits for allowable expense, work loss, and replacement services loss, to $50,000 or such higher amount as determined pursuant to State law, in accordance with section 104 (a) (2) of this Act;

    (b) may limit basic restoration benefits for work loss to a monthly amount equal to the lesser of the following—

        (1) $1,000; or

        (2) 85 per centum of the actual monthly earned income of the victim; and may provide a reasonable total limitation on restoration benefits for work loss and may also provide reasonable exclusions from basic restoration benefits for work loss;

    (c) may provide reasonable exclusions from, or

monthly or total limitations on, basic restoration benefits for replacement services loss; and

(d) may provide that any contract of insurance for no-fault benefits allow an insurer to offer—

(1) a deductible not to exceed $100 for each individual; and

(2) a deductible not to exceed an amount deemed reasonable by the commissioner of each State for each individual if he sustains injury while he is operating in a motor vehicle having less than four wheels, or is a passenger on such a vehicle.

SOURCE OF BASIC RESTORATION BENEFITS

SEC. 205. (a) APPLICABLE SECURITY.—The security for the payment of basic restoration benefits applicable to an injury to—

(1) an employee, or to the spouse or other relative of an employee residing in the same household as the employee, if the accident resulting in injury occurs while the victim or deceased victim is driving or occupying a motor vehicle furnished by such employee's employer, is the security for the payment of basic restoration benefits covering such motor vehicle or, if none, any other security applicable to such victim;

(2) an insured is the security under which the victim or deceased victim is an insured;

55

(3) the driver or other occupant of a motor vehicle involved in an accident resulting in injury who is not an insured is the security covering such vehicle;

(4) an individual who is not an insured or the driver or other occupant of a motor vehicle involved in an accident resulting in injury is the security covering any motor vehicle involved in such accident. For purposes of this paragraph, a parked and unoccupied motor vehicle is not a motor vehicle involved in an accident, unless it was parked so as to cause unreasonable risk of injury; and

(5) any other individual is the applicable assigned claims plan.

(b) MULTIPLE SOURCES OF EQUAL PRIORITY.—If two or more obligations to pay basic restoration benefits apply equally to an injury under the priorities set forth in subsection (a) of this section, the restoration obligor against whom a claim is asserted first shall process and pay the claim as if wholly responsible. Such obligor is thereafter entitled to recover contribution pro rata from any other such obligor for the basic restoration benefits paid and for the costs of processing the claim. If contribution is sought among restoration obligors responsible under paragraph (4) of subsection (a) of this section proration shall be based on the number of involved motor vehicles.

RESTRICTIONS ON TORT LIABILITY

SEC. 206. (a) PARTIAL ABOLITION.—Tort liability is abolished with respect to any injury that takes place in a State in which a no-fault plan for motor vehicle insurance in accordance with this title is in effect prior to such injury, if such injury arises out of the maintenance or use of a motor vehicle, except that—

(1) An owner of a motor vehicle involved in an accident remains liable if, at the time of the accident, the vehicle was not a secured vehicle.

(2) A person in the business of designing, manufacturing, repairing, servicing, or otherwise maintaining motor vehicles remains liable for injury arising out of a defect in such motor vehicle which is caused or not corrected by an act or omission in the course of such business, other than a defect in a motor vehicle which is operated by such business.

(3) An individual remains liable for injuring another individual, either intentionally or as a consequence of intending to injure himself.

(4) Noneconomic detriment such as pain, suffering, and inconvenience may be recovered on traditional tort grounds if either the incurred medical and hospital expenses exceed $2,000 (subject to the definition of incurred medical and hospital expenses) regardless of

whether the expenses have been paid or reimbursed by the obligor; or the motor vehicle collision results in death, permanent maiming or serious disfigurement of a body member, permanent injury within reasonable medical probability or total disability for ninety days. (The definition of total disability for the purposes of this Act is the medically determined inability to perform substantial amount of one's customary activities.)

(5) A person remains liable for damages for noneconomic detriment, except that the victim, or his survivor, is precluded from pleading or introducing into evidence in an action for noneconomic detriment any amounts paid by the restoration obligor for basic or added restoration benefits.

(6) A person or government remains liable if such injury was caused or not corrected by an act or omission not connected with the maintenance or use of a motor vehicle.

(b) NONREIMBURSABLE TORT FINE.—Nothing in this section shall be construed to immunize an individual from liability to pay a fine on the basis of fault in any proceeding based upon any act or omission arising out of the maintenance or use of a motor vehicle: *Provided,* That such fine may not be paid or reimbursed by an insurer or other restoration obligor.

WORK LOSS

SEC. 207. (a) REGULARLY EMPLOYED.—The work loss of a victim whose income prior to the injury was realized in regular increments shall be calculated by—

(1) determining his probable weekly income by dividing his probable annual income by fifty-two; and

(2) multiplying that quantity by the number of work weeks, or fraction thereof, the victim sustains loss of income during the accrual period.

(b) SEASONALLY EMPLOYED.—The work loss of a victim whose income is realized in irregular increments shall be calculated by—

(1) determining his probable weekly income by dividing his probable annual income by the number of weeks he normally works; and

(2) multiplying that quantity by the number of work weeks, or fraction thereof, the victim was unable to perform and would have performed work during the accrual period but for the injury.

(c) NOT EMPLOYED.—The work loss of a victim who is not employed when the accident resulting in injury occurs shall be calculated by—

(1) determining his probable weekly income by dividing his probable annual income by 52; and

(2) multiplying that quantity by the number of work weeks, or fraction thereof, if any, the victim would

reasonably have been expected to realize income during the accrual period.

(d) DEFINITIONS.—As used in this section—

(1) "Probable annual income" means, absent a showing that it is or would be some other amount, the following—

(A) twelve times the monthly gross income earned by the victim from work in the month preceding the month in which the accident resulting in injury occurs, or the average annual income earned by the victim from work during the years, not to exceed three, preceding the year in which the accident resulting in injury occurs, whichever is greater, for a victim regularly employed at the time of the accident;

(B) the average annual gross income earned by the victim from work during the years in which he was employed, not to exceed three, preceding the year in which the accident resulting in injury occurs, for a victim seasonally employed or not employed at the time of the accident; or

(C) the average annual gross income of a production or nonsupervisory worker in the private nonfarm economy in the State in which the victim is domiciled for the year in which the accident resulting in injury occurs, for a victim who has not previously earned income from work.

(2) "Work week" means the number of days an individual normally works in a seven-day period; "weekly income" means income earned during a work week.

NET LOSS

SEC. 208. (a) GENERAL.—Except as provided in paragraph (3) of subsection (a) of section 108 of this Act, all benefits or advantages (less reasonably incurred collection costs) that an individual receives or is entitled to receive from social security (except those benefits provided under title XIX of the Social Security Act) workmen's compensation, any State-required temporary, nonoccupational disability insurance, and all other benefits (except the proceeds of life insurance) received by or available to an individual because of the injury from any government, unless the law authorizing or providing for such benefits or advantages makes them excess or secondary to the benefits in accordance with this Act, shall be subtracted from loss in calculating net loss.

(b) TAX DEDUCTION.—If a benefit or advantage received to compensate for loss of income because of injury, whether from no-fault benefits or from any source of benefits or advantages subtracted under subsection (a) of this section, is not taxable income, the income tax saving that is attributable to such loss of income because of injury is subtracted in calculating net loss for work loss. Subtraction may not exceed fifteen per centum of the loss of income and shall be in such lesser amount as the insurer reasonably determines is appropriate based on a lower value of the income tax advantage.

(c) NO-FAULT BENEFITS PRIMARY.—If any individual is entitled to receive benefits or advantages from a source other than no-fault insurance, he may receive such benefits or advantages (other than benefits or advantages from social security (except those benefits provided under title XIX of the Social Security Act), workmen's compensation, any State-required temporary, nonoccupational disability insurance, and all other benefits (except the proceeds of life insurance) received by or available to an individual because of the injury from any government) only to the extent that basic restoration advantages exceed $10,000, or whatever higher amount a State may prescribe under section 104(a)(2), whichever is greater.

ADDED RESTORATION BENEFITS

SEC. 209. (a) OPTIONAL OFFERING.—Restoration obligors providing security for the payment of basic restoration benefits may offer or obligate themselves to provide added restoration benefits for injury or damage arising out of the ownership, maintenance, or use of a motor vehicle, including—

(1) loss excluded from basic restoration benefits by limits on allowable expense, work loss, replacement services loss, and survivor's loss;

(2) benefits for damage to property;

(3) benefits for loss of use of a motor vehicle; and

(4) benefits for expense for remedial religious treatment and care.

Subject to the approval of terms and forms by the commissioner, restoration obligors may offer or obligate themselves to provide other added restoration coverages.

(b) MANDATORY OFFERING.—(1) Insurers providing basic restoration insurance shall offer the following added restoration coverage:

(A) for physical damage to a motor vehicle, a coverage for all collision and upset damage, subject to an optional deductible of not to exceed $100;

(B) for the payment of tort liability, if a State determines that security for the payment of tort liability is not required motor vehicle insurance;

(C) for economic detriment, a coverage for work loss sustained by a victim in excess of limitations on basic restoration benefits for work loss; and

(D) for basic restoration benefits, if a State determines that a vehicle having less than four wheels is not a motor vehicle.

(2) The commissioner may adopt rules requiring that insurers providing basic restoration insurance offer, in accordance with State law, any other specified added restoration coverages.

(c) TERRITORIAL APPLICABILITY.—All added res-

INELIGIBLE CLAIMANTS

SEC. 210. (a) CONVERTER.—(1) Except as provided for assigned claims, a converter of a motor vehicle is ineligible to receive no-fault benefits, including benefits otherwise due him as a survivor, from any source other than a contract of insurance under which he is an insured, for an injury arising out of the maintenance or use of the converted vehicle. If a converter dies from such injuries, his survivor or survivors are not entitled to no-fault benefits for survivor's loss from any source other than a contract of insurance under which the converter is an insured.

(2) For purposes of this subsection and subsection (c) of section 111 of this Act, an individual is not a converter of a motor vehicle if he used it in the good faith belief that he was legally entitled to do so.

(b) INTENTIONAL INJURIES.—(1) An individual who intentionally injures himself or another individual is ineligible to receive no-fault benefits for injury arising out of his acts, including benefits otherwise due him as a survivor. If an individual dies as a result of intentionally injuring himself, his survivor or survivors are not entitled to no-fault benefits for survivor's loss. An individual intentionally injures himself or another individual if he acts or fails to act for the purpose of causing such injury or with knowledge that such injury is substantially certain to follow. An individual does not intentionally injure himself or another individual—

 (A) merely because his act or failure to act is intentional or done with his realization that it creates a grave risk of causing injury; or

 (B) if the act or omission causing the injury is for the purpose of averting bodily harm to himself or another individual.

(2) For purposes of subsection (c) of section 111 and paragraph (3) of subsection (a) of section 206 of this Act, an individual does not intentionally injure himself or another individual merely because his act or failure to act is intentional or done with his realization that it creates a grave risk of harm.

OTHER PROVISIONS

SEC. 211. (a) INCLUDED COVERAGE.—A contract of insurance covering liability arising out of the ownership, maintenance, or use of a motor vehicle registered in a State includes basic restoration benefits and any other benefit coverages required by the no-fault plan for motor vehicle insurance in effect in such State unless such contract—

 (1) provides tort liability coverages only in excess of any of those required by such State no-fault plan; or

 (2) is a contract which the commissioner determines

by regulation provides motor vehicle liability coverages only as incidental to some other basic coverage.

(b) APPROVAL OF TERMS AND FORMS.—Terms and conditions (including forms used by insurers) of any contract, certificate, or other evidence of insurance sold or issued pursuant to a State no-fault plan for motor vehicle insurance in accordance with this title or title III of this Act and providing no-fault benefits or any required tort liability are subject to approval and regulation by the commissioner in such State. The commissioner shall approve only terms and conditions which are consistent with the purposes of this Act and fair and equitable to all persons whose interests may be affected. The commissioner may limit by rule the variety of coverage available in order to give purchasers of insurance a reasonable opportunity to compare the cost of insuring with various insurers.

TITLE III—ALTERNATIVE STATE NO-FAULT MOTOR VEHICLE INSURANCE PLAN

PROVISIONS

SEC. 301. The alternative State no-fault plan for motor vehicle insurance (the State no-fault plan in accordance with this title), which becomes applicable and goes into effect in a State pursuant to subsection (e) of section 201 of this Act, is composed of title I of this Act, except sections 101, 102, 112, and 113; title II of this Act, except sections

201 and 202; and this title. A State may establish additional requirements provided that they are not inconsistent with the provisions of the alternative State no-fault plan for motor vehicle insurance or the policy set forth and declared in section 102 of this Act.

DEPARTMENT OF JUSTICE,
Washington, D.C., August 19, 1975.

Hon. HARLEY O. STAGGERS,
*Chairman, Committee on Interstate and Foreign Commerce,
House of Representatives, Washington, D.C.*

DEAR MR. CHAIRMAN: This is in response to your request for the views of the Department on H.R. 285 and H.R. 1272, identical bills to be cited as the National No-Fault Vehicle Insurance Act. The Department's views on H.R. 1900 are identical to those expressed by the Attorney General in his testimony of June 5, 1975, on S. 354, a copy of which is attached. The bills would require no-fault motor vehicle insurance as a condition precedent to using the public streets, roads, and highways in order to promote and regulate interstate commerce.

The bills would establish a mandatory nationwide no-fault insurance law, replacing all existing State compensation systems, whether based upon the principle of fault or upon a no-fault rationale, with a federally-defined system of strict liability based upon ownership of motor vehicles. The Federal system would supersede present State compensation and insurance systems.

There is little doubt that Congress may enact an appropriate national system of compensation for automobile injuries under the powers conferred by the Commerce Clause of the Constitution, Art. I, § 8. See *United States v. South Eastern Underwriters Association*, 322 U.S. 533 (1944). It is also clear that it may constitutionally enact an automobile reparations system which encourages States to adopt conforming legislation. Encouragement may consist in the availability of conditional grants-in-aid or the imposition of a superseding Federal program. See *Steward Machine Co. v. Davis*, 301 U.S. 548 (1936).

While the proposed scheme would provide national uniformity through complete federal preemption, it would not allow any state options, as would for example H.R. 1900, a bill pending before the Committee. The level of benefits prescribed in the instant bills would be both mandatory and exclusive (§ 4(b)). The several States, with widely varying patterns of motor vehicle accidents and injury, would not have the ability to provide additional benefits in excess of the economic loss provisions of § 2(14), as they could under H.R. 1900. This rigidity will prevent further experimentation by the States with alternative compensation programs tailored to local needs. As you may be aware, the Attorney General recently testified in opposition to a similar bill in the Senate (S. 354, a companion bill to H.R. 1900, which is presently before the Committee). Two of the three chief questions raised as to that measure are equally applicable to the instant bills. A copy of the Attorney General's statement is appended for the Committee's convenience.

Those objections, in brief, were that (1) the Senate measure raised serious constitutional questions by requiring the States to act as arms of the federal government; (2) the measure seriously contravened the basic tenets of Federalism by injecting the federal government into an area that has traditionally been reserved to the States; and (3) the probable economic impact of a federal no-fault program is insufficiently clear to justify departing from accepted principles of Federalism and overriding the clearly expressed preferences of the States.

The instant bills seek to avoid the constitutional problem by greatly expanding the role of the federal government in a no-fault program. But as the Attorney General noted with respect to S. 354, they would inject the federal government deeply into the operation and regulation of the insurance industry, as to which it has very little regulatory experience, and which has been traditionally an area of particular state interest. They would wholly oust the States from any real nfluence over the local field of motor vehicle insurance.

This system would seriously disrupt settled patterns of insurance regulation, and would necessitate the practical forfeiture of all that expertise in regulation and administration of automobile insurance which the States have accumulated over a long period. The issue of Federalism is not a frivolous one. Federalism is a basic ingredient in the fostering of diversity, creativity, and freedom within our constitutional system. The importance of protecting and promoting these values should be a compelling consideration in determining whether a federal uniform automobile insurance law is desirable, and particularly whether such a law is to be enforced in ways which would wholly oust the States from their historic role as experimental laboratories in our system of government.

A respect for Federalism requires respect for State decisions that balance competing interests, and toleration of a variety of efforts to solve complex social and economic issues. The States are already experimenting with a variety of innovative approaches to the problem of compensation for victims of automobile accidents, as you are aware. Some twenty-four States have already enacted one form or another of no-fault compensation, tailored to local needs. Several of those plans continue the injured victim's right to sue on traditional negligence grounds. That feature represents a reasoned choice by the States, which is worthy of consideration in the Committee's deliberations. Wide state experimentation in the area of no-fault motor vehicle insurance is especially important in order to provide experience in how various methods will work in practice. The policy issues raised by such schemes are complex, and their costs and benefits now can be only dimly perceived.

The numerous studies and articles on the subject of no-fault display wide disagreement on such matters as the anticipated reduction in insurance premiums and increase in benefits per premium dollar. A study funded by the Department of Transportation estimated that S. 354 would save consumers $2 billion annually on insurance premiums, but it noted that the estimate was highly uncertain. There is respectable evidence that no-fault programs would not decrease the premiums of all individuals.

Fifteen states have recently enacted varying types of no-fault legislation, ten since 1973. Experience under these laws must be described as inconclusive.

In sum, in the Department's view, the probable economic impact of H.R. 1272 and 285 is insufficiently clear to justify departing from accepted principles of Federalism and overriding the clearly expressed preference of many States.

The Department has also noticed a number of omissions in the instant bills which raise substantial questions. Most of these relate to the role of the federal government as a party under a no-fault system. The bills do not expressly include the Federal government as a "person" subject to their coverage (§§ 3, 4(a)(2)). It is thus uncertain whether the federal government would be required to act as a self-insurer under § 4(a)(2) or whether it would continue to be subject to tort liability.

A number of existing statutes govern the liability of the United States for tort claims arising from motor vehicle accidents. The instant bills neither expressly continue nor repeal those statutes, and the resulting ambiguity could on the one hand expose the Federal government to multiply liability (if there were no implied repeal) and on the other might deny it the benefit of revenue-producing indemnity and subrogation statutes (if the bills were held to repeal other systems of compensation). The Federal Tort Claims Act (28 U.S.C. §§ 1346(b), 2671–80), the Military Claims Act (10 U.S.C. § 2733), the Federal Employees Compensation Act (5 U.S.C. § 116(c)), the National Guard Claims Act (32 U.S.C. § 715), and the Medical Care Recovery Act (42 U.S.C. § 2651–3) are examples of statutes whose coverage might be affected by enactment of the proposed legislation. Accordingly, the Department recommends that, in any event, the Committee should consider the adoption of an amendment specifically repealing only those provisions of existing statutes which it desires to supersede and continuing all others in force.

Assuming that the federal government is subject to the bills, the bills would extend the present two-year statute of limitations on tort suits against the federal government, to a four year period. They also would confer jurisdiction to entertain suits against the United States (now in contract rather than in tort) on the state courts as compared to the present statute, 28 U.S.C. § 1346(b), which gives Federal district courts exclusive jurisdiction of motor vehicle tort claims against the federal government. These two provisions would substantially increase the uncertainty and cost of litigation and would raise the likelihood of subjecting the United States to the risk of contradictory findings and rules of liability in different States.

On the same assumption, the bills would further greatly increase the cost and burden to the United States in the administration of claims. Whereas present practice is to provide for a single lump sum payment in settlement of a claim, the proposed legislation would require processing and investigating a monthly claim on each injury, with punitive interest due for payment more than 30 days after submission of the claim. With the great volume of claims which are annually filed against the United States, such delays and interest costs could be very large in amount.

Since State regulation is superseded with respect to the concerted action by insurers contemplated by Section 6 of H.R. 1272, the Sherman Act would apply to activities such as concerted efforts to combine expense experience and arrive at uniform rates. Accordingly, a separate penalty provision is not required for such conduct. Therefore we recommend deleting the penalty provision in section 6 (h)(2).

In view of the serious concerns discussed above as to the impact of the bills on the principles of Federalism, their uncertain and speculative economic effect at a time when the States are actively experimenting with many alternative compensation systems, and the many questions concerning the liability of the United States, the Department of Justice must recommend against enactment of this legislation.

As to the specifics of the provisions dealing with the responsibilities of the Secretary of Transportation in regulating and administering the no-fault program, the Department of Justice defers to the opinion of the Department of Transportation.

The Office of Management and Budget has advised that there is no objection to the submission of this report from the standpoint of the Administration's program.

Sincerely,

MICHAEL M. UHLMANN,
Assistant Attorney General.

TESTIMONY OF EDWARD H. LEVI, ATTORNEY GENERAL, BEFORE THE COMMITTEE ON COMMERCE, U.S. SENATE, CONCERNING S. 354—NATIONAL STANDARDS NO-FAULT MOTOR VEHICLE INSURANCE ACT, JUNE 5, 1975

Mr. Chairman and Members of the Committee: The invitation of this Committee gives me an opportunity of expressing the Department of Justice views on the constitutionality of S. 354 and its Federalism implications. The views of the Department as of April, 1974 were set forth in a letter to Senator Eastland, Chairman, Committee on the Judiciary, by Robert Dixon, Jr., Assistant Attorney General, Office of Legal Counsel. Mr. Dixon's letter stated that "as a matter of constitutional law, it would appear that Congress, acting under the Commerce Clause of the Constitution, can enact a national, Federally *directed and administered* system of compensation for automobile injuries without constitutional impediment." S. 354 would not, however, establish a system which is both Federally directed and administered. Instead, it requires affirmative State actions to implement the no-fault system. As to this point, Mr. Dixon's letter of opinion concludes, "We believe the bill raises constitutional issues which strike at the traditional balance of our federal system. These novel and substantial constitutional questions cannot be overlooked." This view remains valid today.

I realize this Committee is throughly knowledgeable about the structure of S. 354. Nevertheless, to put the Department's views in some perspective, I would like to say a word about that structure.

Basically the bill provides for three levels of approaches. The first approach recognizes a temporary category of no-fault States which have adopted no-fault plans with minimum standards by September 1, 1975. The minimum standards for States in this category require no-fault benefits of not less than $2,000 and restrictions on traditional law suits which allow recovery for pain and suffering.

The second level of approach of this bill establishes higher standards for acceptable State plans. Under these standards there must be compensation for all reasonable medical, rehabilitation, and related costs, and in addition a coverage of a minimum of $15,000 for basic restoration benefits for work loss. Tort liability for injury arising out of the maintenance or use of a motor vehicle would be abolished by virtue of the Federal legislation, with certain important exceptions.

The third level of approach of the bill would impose upon the States which have failed to enact an acceptable State plan an alternative State no-fault motor vehicle insurance plan. This alternative would further reduce the traditional tort remedies which could remain available under the second approach of an acceptable State plan. Thus tort liability would no longer be allowed, as it would under the second approach, where the accident resulted in death, serious and permanent disfiguration, or other serious and permanent injury, or more than 90 continuous days of total disability. The alternative also would provide fewer dollar limitations on the benefits which could be paid to an insured individual or to a claimant.

In general I suppose it can be said that the first approach is intended to induce States to begin experimenting with no-fault plans even though these plans may not meet the full Federal standards. The inducement is to grant States in this category a grace period of four years from the date of enactment of S. 354 in which to raise their standards to the bill's requirements. The third level, imposing the highest standards where the State has failed to enact or promulgate an acceptable State plan, appears to be an additional encouragement for State action.

It is my understanding that 16 States have adopted compulsory no-fault plans which probably meet the standards of the temporary category of a "no-fault State," but only one of the 16—Michigan—has adopted a plan which meets the higher national standards for an acceptable State plan. In addition to these 16 States, eight other States, while having enacted a form of no-fault insurance, do not qualify under any of the bill's approaches, because the plans fail to restrict the victim's right to sue on traditional negligence grounds.

In his letter to Senator Eastland, Mr. Dixon emphasized the importance of certain provisions of S. 354 which required affirmative State actions. It was "these features of the bill and their practical effect upon the fundamental tenets of federalism that give rise to issues concerning the bill's constitutionality," he wrote "The specific question," he said, "involves the authority of Congress to employ a regulatory scheme that requires the states to devote their funds and personnel, and to create agencies and facilities to administer a federal law, regardless of local feeling."

In reviewing this matter, let me once again set forth what these provisions are. Section 104 generally would require each State to insure that the owners of any motor vehicles registered or present in that State obtain no-fault insurance. Section 105 would require a State to establish and administer an assigned risk plan; compel the State insurance commissioner to approve, among other arrangements, certain insurance company agreements relating to assigned risks; and establish favorable insurance rates for the economically disadvantaged. Section 108 would require a State to establish an assigned risk claims fund and an assigned claims bureau. Section 109 would require the State insurance commissioner to establish and maintain a program for the regular evaluation of medical and rehabilitation services. Section 111(d) can be interpreted to require a State to create a vocational rehabilitation agency if it lacks one.

The constitutional or Federalism problem which S. 354 raises is not whether, under the Commerce Clause, Congress has authority to enact a national system of no-fault insurance to be administered and enforced by the Federal government. Nor is it whether Congress can constitutionally enact legislation which would encourage States to adopt Federally prescribed no-fault auto insurance standards. Instead, the issue is whether it is permissible or appropriate for the Congress to intrude upon such State sovereignty as is left by requiring State agencies and employees to perform as though they were Federal instruments or employees, or as though the Federal Congress were the state legislature and possessor of the State's sovereignty. I realize, of course, that different views have been expressed about this matter, and Supreme Court cases have been cited which, it is argued support this intrusion.

Dean Griswold in the opinion which he gave as to the complete constitutionality of S. 354 referred to the question of the power of Congress to impose mandatory duties on the States as an "important legal question fully worthy of consideration" but one which might not be of great relevance as far as S. 354 is concerned. This was because "all but a minimal amount of implementation could be done through action in the courts which would not require state administrative or state legislative action," I take note, however, that having said as much, the next section of Dean Griswold's opinion goes on to recognize that at least a minimal amount of State administrative or State legislative action is required, action of such significance that the section is devoted to the issue of whether, in the absence of the State action, an appropriate remedy—mandamus, mandatory injunction, or otherwise—can be enforced in the courts against the relevant State officials or legislature. I note also that previously in the opinion Dean Griswold was concerned about the absence of alternative Federal administrative machinery to act in the event that a State should withdraw from automobile insurance regulation. As to this, Dean Griswold writes that no State is likely to withdraw from the field, and if this in fact did occur, Congress could then act to fill the gap. The argument there being made, if I understand it, is not that the State's governmental agencies are not being used by the Federal government, but rather that they can be so used because this can be a condition exacted as long as the State continues in a field which can be preempted by the Federal government. But it is not the ability to preempt which is involved, but the way of preemption.

On this, Professor Kurland has written, "Never, to my knowledge, have the courts justified the substitution of the national legislature for recalcitrant legislatures, to enact laws that purport to be state laws, for the purported benefit of the local citizenry." As Professor Dorsen has written, "The No-Fault Act's coercive use of state officials to organize and manage a comprehensive regulatory program is not typical of congressional legislation."

I am of course aware, as is the Committee, of the various Supreme Court decisions which are sometimes urged as removing the constitutional doubt from S. 354. My belief is that all of these cases are distinguishable, involving either remedial steps imposed upon the States to rectify prior constitutional deficiencies, or cases where the claims advanced by private parties would be in the nature of rights which State courts had jurisdiction to handle, or cases where the State mechanism was regarded as similar to that of any private employer or entrepreneur. As to this last category, the case of *Maryland* v. *Wirtz* is, I suppose, the cornerstone. There the court upheld the constitutionality of minimum wage and overtime provisions of the Fair Labor Standards Act as applied to employees of State-operated schools and hospitals. But I think it is worthy of comment that the Supreme Court has recently set down for reargument the case of *National League of Cities* v. *Brennan*, which directly raises the scope of this type of intrusion into State sovereignty.

Dean Griswold mentions the Clean Air Act of 1970 with amendments as perhaps the most striking example of conferral by Congress of additional affirmative powers and duties on State agencies and officials. It is indeed a notable exception. Under that Act, the Environmental Protection Agency has authority to reject part or all of a State plan as inadequate, and, as the Act has been construed, to compel a State to implement an EPA-devised plan instead. In *Commonwealth of Pennsylvania* v. *EPA*, decided one year ago in the Third Circuit, the constitutionality of an EPA regulation requiring Pennsylvania to insure that in the Philadelphia region all pre-1968 automobiles were equipped with a certain pollution-reducing device was upheld, over the objections of Pennsylvania that this requirement to implement the Federal program was an infringement upon the State's sovereignty. I must confess that the brief for the Environmental Protection Agency, submitted by the Department of Justice, reads in part as though it were a defense of the constitutionality of S. 354. The brief argues that the Clean Air Act leaves to the Commonwealth control over traditional state areas and is substantively far less of an enroachment than would be a Federal takeover of these traditional State functions.

In upholding the enforcement of the regulation, the Court said that it was true that: "compliance with the plan will require the Commonwealth to exercise its legislative and administrative powers, for that is the means by which a state regulates its transportation system . . . In enacting the Clean Air Amendments of 1970, Congress created an interlocking governmental structure in which the Federal Government and the states would cooperate to reach the primary goal of the Act—the attainment of national ambient air quality standards. Under its provisions, state and local governments retain responsibility for the basic design and implementation of air pollution strategies, subject to approval and if necessary, enforcement by the Administrator. We believe that this approach represents a valid adaptation of federalist principles to the need for increased federal involvement. The only alternative implementation would be for the Federal Government to assume some of the functions of traffic control and vehicle registration and directly enforce the programs contained in the various transportation plans."

As to this the Court said, "We fail to see how this would represent less of an intrusion upon state sovereignty." The Court did go on to say: "We recognize that there may remain a legitimate concern for possible intrusions upon the proper functioning of our federalist system as a result of future developments in the implementation of the Clean Air Act and this Court will remain ready to protect that concern in any appropriate case."

There are obviously similiarities and differences between the Clean Air Act and the proposed compulsory national no-fault insurance program that would be State-administered. I do not know whether the existence of this Third Circuit case should give particular comfort to anyone concerned about principles of Federalism. Perhaps it indicates that one must be zealous in attempting to safeguard these principles, or that the need to impose responsibilities in some exceptional cases should be counter-balanced by special case in others.

As a constitutional matter, the *Pennsylvania* case does not remove the substantial doubt which arises from the method of the Federal intrusion in the proposed no-fault legislation. Only a few days ago, in the Supreme Court's opinion in *Fry* v. *United States*, where the Court upheld the enjoining of the payment of wage and salary increases to State employees above the amount authorized by the Federal Pay Board, the Court through Justice Marshall referred to the Tenth Amendment as expressly declaring "the constitutional policy that Congress may not exercise power in a fashion that impairs the States' integrity or the ability to function effectively in a federal system." The Court did not regard the Tenth Amendment as a mere truism without significance. Moreover, I would suggest that anyone seriously concerned about the constitutional issue should read Mr. Justice Rehnquist's dissent in *Fry*. The issue is most certainly not a frivolous one.

The reference to the Tenth Amendment in *Fry*, the strong dissent in *Fry* and the Supreme Court's action in setting down for reargument the *National League of Cities* case and staying the operation of the recent amendments to the statute which raise the question in that case all indicate that the issue involved here is a serious one, located at the margin of constitutionality. The essence of the sovereignty of the States that remains is that State employees are not just Federal employees in disguise.

Nor is the issue of constitutional Federalism a frivolous one. It is close to the protection of diversity, creativity and freedom within our system. The importance of protecting and promoting these values should be a compelling consideration in determining whether a Federal uniform automobile insurance law is desirable and particularly whether requiring State agencies to implement such a law is appropriate.

I do want to take note of Senator Stevens Amendment No. 497. The Amendment suggests a way whereby the States could exercise the option of refusing to implement or administer the Federally imposed alternate State no-fault motor vehicle insurance plan. But that amendment only applies to accomplish this if a judicial determination bars a State from implementing or administering the alternative Federal plan or allows the State the option of declining. I do not know why the exercise of choice or discretion inherent in State sovereignty should be dependent upon permission of a court. I would think a more efficacious amendment would permit the State to act through its constituted authorities.

There are today many difficult and important questions concerning the balance of power among the branches of government and between the Federal and the State governments. Unbalancing, I suppose, almost always occurs in what is regarded as a good cause. I suppose one can only ask is the cause good enough to justify the impairment which accomplishing it in a particular way causes to the intricate structure of our Federal system. If the failure of a uniform law to win acceptance among the States within three years is to be regarded as a reason for national enactment, I would suggest that the Commissioners on Uniform State Laws ought to go out of business right now. The whole basis of their endeavor was to win acceptance through reason, the example of experience, the possibility of diversity and change. Since 1972, when the National Conference of Commissioners voted approval of the Uniform Motor Vehicle Accident Reparations Act, fourteen States have adopted no-fault statutes, and four additional States have added no-fault features to existing statutes. To be sure there is great diversity among them.

It has also been sometimes suggested that the normal course of the political processes of the States is not to be trusted in this area. I think such an argument places a heavy burden upon the one who makes it. I also think that if the predictions which have been lately made about the economic advantages which will appear in no-fault plans already adopted come true, then the example of experience will have a powerful effect. If they turn out not to be that way, we should learn from that also.

I do believe this committee has accomplished a great work. It has brought to the fore a movement which had deep roots in academic thought—with, I must say, much difference of view among academies—and it has provided a great deal in terms of a searchlight on what is wrong with our present systems. I do not think the success of this Committee's endeavor, if I may be so bold to say so, should be judged by the enactment of S. 354. I rather think the judgment of history may be the other way. The greater success of the committee could be in its long-term effect upon genuine State legislation. These are, of course, legislative questions. But in its present form, in my judgment, S. 354 does raise serious constitutional questions and does involve an impairment of constitutional Federalism.

DEPARTMENT OF JUSTICE,
Washington, D.C., September 10, 1975.

Hon. HARLEY O. STAGGERS,
Chairman, Committee on Interstate and Foreign Commerce, House of Representatives, Washington, D.C.

DEAR MR. CHAIRMAN. This is in response to your request for the views of the Department on H.R. 8441, a bill "To regulate commerce by establishing a nationwide system to restore motor vehicle accident victims and by requiring no-fault motor vehicle insurance as a condition precedent to using such a vehicle on the public roadways." This bill is similar to H.R. 1900 and S. 354, the latter being the subject of testimony delivered by the Attorney General on June 5, 1975.

While there are differences between the above bills and H.R. 8441, none would alter or otherwise change our position as stated both in the Attorney General's testimony referenced above and my letter to you on August 19, 1975, reciting the Department's views on H.R. 285, H.R. 1272 and H.R. 1900.

The Office of Management and Budget has advised that there is no objection to the submission of this report from the standpoint of the Administration's program.

Sincerely,

MICHAEL M. UHLMANN,
Assistant Attorney General.

Mr. VAN DEERLIN. We will be hearing in the coming weeks from a great many authoritative and distinguished witnesses, none, I imagine, more distinguished than our leadoff witness today, the Secretary of Transportation, William T. Coleman, Jr.

Mr. Coleman, you are very welcome before this subcommittee and we would like you to proceed as the leadoff witness.

STATEMENT OF HON. WILLIAM T. COLEMAN, SECRETARY, DEPARTMENT OF TRANSPORTATION; ACCOMPANIED BY RICHARD F. WALSH, DEPUTY DIRECTOR FOR POLICY AND PLAN DEVELOPMENT, OFFICE OF THE SECRETARY, DOT

Secretary COLEMAN. Thank you very much, Mr. Chairman and members of this committee. I certainly welcome this opportunity to be here today to present the administration's views for H.R. 1272, H.R. 1900, and other bills proposing the enactment of a Federal no-fault standards law to deal with personal injuries in automobile accidents.

This subcommittee will, I understand, be reviewing a number of different pieces of auto insurance reform legislation, as well as the performance of certain existing State plans. With respect to the latter I think you are particularly wise, as I understand this committee is in almost all of its endeavors, in deciding to conduct field hearings and obtain firsthand the views of those who have actually been living with no-fault because there is no other subject which touches as many people and as many families as does the automobile.

The various Federal bills you will be considering fall generally into two categories. One category is called a Federal no-fault standards bill; namely, a bill which would establish minimum standards which State no-fault plans must meet but which they can also exceed or vary from in certain aspects. If that minimum standard is met, then the State's law is the law which is completely effective. If not, the State is forced to apply the standards of a Federal law. I believe that H.R. 1900 fits into this category. The Senate counterpart is S. 354.

As I understand it, H.R. 1900 would essentially require the States to adopt the standards proposed by the Uniform Motor Vehicle Reparations Act, an act which I will talk about later. If the States do not adopt such a standard, then a different set of standards would be imposed, but the plan would still be administered by the State.

The other category comprises those bills which would preempt some or all auto insurance matters dealing with automobiles and place them under Federal jurisdiction, including in some cases various insurance regulatory functions currently vested in the States. H.R. 1272 is a bill which is in this category. This bill would involve the

Secretary in promulgating regulations regarding the operation of the insurance plan and the Attorney General would be called upon to enforce the statute. An interesting feature of this bill is that the no-fault policy would also cover noneconomic damages.

The administration opposes both types of bills. In fact, at this time, it opposes any Federal legislation in this area. The reasons for this opposition are both practical and philosophical. We believe there is much to be gained from allowing the States to continue experimenting with different plans and approaches. At least as important, however, is the fact that President Ford and this administration is strongly committed to the principles of federalism—to keeping the decisions of Government and the administration of Government's functions as close to the people as possible. This philosophy, which as I understand it, is the basis for the Federal Constitution, results in political decisions to take away from the States only those functions which are either, one: essentially national or international in character or, two: matters in which the State's failure to resolve the problem is clear, undisputable, and beyond doubt and delayed too long after there is recognition that the basic change must be made.

Some have argued and will continue to argue that the State actions in accepting no-fault has been too slow or misdirected. In each of the last 4 years, however, several States have enacted new no-fault laws. In all, 17 States have adopted new no-fault statutes. Progress is being made and experience gained, but I for one—and I am pretty sure I can speak for Secretary Brinegar and also Secretary Volpe—would have hoped for more State action. This, however, is really not the point. Either we believe in a Federal system or we don't. We will not have a Federal system if the Federal Government interferes with the State activity every time we in the Federal sector disagree either with the pace or the direction of the State activity.

The State governments and legislatures can provide invaluable experimentation, innovation and wisdom in the development of social policy. Mr. Justice Brandeis, in a series of brilliant decisions, pointed out that in the Federal system the States should be the laboratories to test various economic and social theories. I wish to make it clear that as far as the Department of Transportation is concerned, we think that no-fault is the way that automobile insurance should be handled and we in the Federal sector have developed a model bill we think is the answer. If we immediately attempt to impose it upon the States without giving the States reasonable time to investigate and make their own determinations, we will stifle the resources of the States with excessive Federal intervention. If I were a State legislator and knew that the difficult economic problem I was working on would ultimately be decided by a Federal law, then why should I work on it and risk failure or disapproval. Let the Federal Government face the political knocks and bumps. This is what we must avoid. Having said that, I want to underscore that we do agree with much of the substantive reform processes contained in these various pieces of legislation. It is very wrong to categorize the administration's position in any way as opposition to no-fault. We support the principle but we seek the adoption through actions of the individual States.

I think the administration position is more clearly understood if I for the moment describe to you the involvement of the Department of Transportation in the automobile liability area and involvement which in large part constitutes both the predicate and the context for the administration's position on the various relevant issues today.

The starting point for this involvement is May 22, 1968, when the Congress passed Public Law 90-313, a joint resolution directing the Secretary of Transportation to conduct a comprehensive study and investigation of the existing compensation system for automobile losses. To finance and staff this study, the legislation authorized the expenditure of $2 million. A special staff was duly assembled. Under the direction of Secretary Alan Boyd and later Secretary John Volpe, this study effort produced over the 1968-70 period some 25 volumes of research findings.

Two other Federal agencies, the Federal Trade Commission and the Federal Judicial Center, played major roles in the conduct of the study. The insurance study, the organized bar, State insurance regulators and interested consumer groups advised on the conduct of the study, and in many cases actively assisted or participated in various aspects of the research program.

On March 26, 1971, then Secretary Volpe presented the Administration's policy findings and conclusions to the Congress in the study's final report. This study is entitled "Motor Vehicle Crash Losses and Their Compensation in the United States."

Before this, however, two important events occurred. First, after several years of debate, the Commonwealth of Massachusetts passed in August 1970 the Nation's first no-fault law. Second, without waiting for the administration's policy conclusions and recommendations, no-fault bills were introduced in both Houses of the Congress.

Summarizing the study's principal conclusions, Secretary Volpe reported:

> The existing system ill serves the accident victim, the insuring public and society. It is inefficient, overly costly, incomplete and slow. It allocates benefits poorly, discourages rehabilitation and overburdens the courts and the legal system. Both on the record of its performance and on the logic of its operation, it does little if anything to minimize crash losses.

The principal recommendations of the report were:

First. That the existing system of insured tort liability should be supplanted by one based on first party, no-fault insurance, and that tort lawsuits and the adversary process should be eliminated for the mass of accidents.

Second. That this change should be made, if at all possible, at the State level, and that the States should be given a reasonable time to do the job.

I think it is quite significant that Secretary Volpe was the one who developed this report. This is subject to check, but as I understand it, when Secretary Volpe was Governor of Massachusetts he was against no-fault laws, but after the study and seeing the empirical evidence, he, like many other political leaders, had the ability to say that he was wrong and to change his mind. So ever since that date, first with Secretary Volpe, then with Secretary Brinegar and now with myself, the Department of Transportation believes that the way to handle the automobile accident problem is through no-fault legislation.

The essence of this position was incorporated in an administration proposed concurrent resolution which would have expressed Congress will in favor of State adoption of no-fault laws and would have directed the Secretary of Transportation to monitor the actions of the States and report back to the Congress after 25 months as to what additional Federal action would be necessary to achieve meaningful no-fault legislation.

Unfortunately, the Congress never acted on that proposal but instead pursued its consideration of the various Federal no-fault bills.

The administration's involvement in the auto insurance no-fault area did not stop with the completion of the study. In late spring 1971, the Department joined with the Ford Foundation to finance at a cost of $200,000 the drafting of a model State no-fault bill by the National Conference of Commissioners on Uniform State Laws.

This model statute was to reflect the principles set down in the Department's final report and the administration's proposed concurrent resolution. The National Conference completed the model statute in August 1972 and voted to recommend its adoption by the States.

In the fall of 1972, the Department again joined with the Ford Foundation to finance at a cost of $150,000 a project of the National Association of Insurance Commissioners—NAIC—to develop a computer model and data base to explore the cost and price implications of different approaches to no-fault.

NAIC subcontracted the development of the model to a firm of consulting actuaries, Milliman & Robertson. No-fault proposals had been foundering in many State legislatures and in the Congress for that matter because of widely differing claims by actuaries from the different factions of the insurance industry.

The costing model was first employed in late spring of 1973 and had been used by a number of States and the District of Columbia and by both the House and Senate Commerce Committees.

During the past 4 years, all States have considered some form of no-fault plan and some 17 States or territories have actually enacted no-fault laws. While these plans are all different, and vary significantly in terms of coverage, adequacy, and cost savings features, their basic thrust and design do accord with the administration's reform goals.

Another 8 or 10 States have enacted changes in their auto insurance laws which, while sometimes called no-fault, are either irrelevant to the administration's principles, or positively antithetical.

The Department's investigation of automobile insurance under the tort liability system showed it to have serious but correctable shortcomings. It should be noted that these disabilities had all been identified and described by previous investigators. What the Department's study did was to validate and document these findings and generalize them from the experience of a nationwide study.

One major shortcoming of the traditional compensation system stems not from the way it performs, but rather from its intended scope of operation. In most cases, only those who can prove others were at fault while they were without fault in an accident have a legal right to recover their losses from liability insurance.

With only 45 percent of those killed or seriously injured in auto accidents benefiting in any way from that system and only 1 out of every 10 of such victims receiving anything from any reparations source, it is clear that the coverage of the traditional compensation mechanism is seriously deficient.

Another major shortcoming of insured tort liability is the very uneven way it allocates benefits among the limited number of victims that it purports to serve. The victim with large economic losses, who generally also suffers more severe intangible losses, has a far poorer chance of being fully compensated for his economic losses, much less for any intangible losses, than does the victim with only minor injuries.

Indeed, only about half of the total compensable economic losses of seriously or fatally injured victims were compensated from any reparations system. For those whose economic losses were more than $25,000, only one-third was usually recovered. By contrast, those with relatively small economic losses fared much better. Thus, victims with losses less than $500 who recovered from tort received on the average 4½ times their actual economic loss.

Still another shortcoming of the auto accident liability reparations system has to do with its cost efficiency. This system would appear to possess the highly dubious distinction of being the least cost effective major compensation system in our society. The DOT study showed that for every dollar of net benefits that the system provides the victims, it consumes another dollar. As it presently operates, the system absorbs vast amounts of resources, primarily in performing the functions of marketing insurance policies and of settling claims. The costs of these two functions alone approach in general magnitude all net benefits received by auto accident victims through the tort liability system.

Yet another problem with the insured tort liability system is that it tends to deliver benefits without regard to the victim's need, in some cases paying too late, in other cases too soon, frequently underpaying and sometimes overpaying. The system pays most slowly in cases where the need for timely payment appears to be the greatest, that is, in case of permanent impairment or disfigurement.

Moreover, it can often operate to discourage early rehabilitation efforts and places a premium on their deferment beyond the time when they could be most effective. It is important to keep these facts about the insured tort liability system clearly in mind when examining the merits and defects of various reform proposals. All too often such reform proposals are compared against some idealized conception of how the insured tort liability system should work in theory.

Against such an unreal criterion, one should not be surprised that the no-fault proposals appear to be less than perfect solutions. But the use of this standard is simply wrong. Compared to how the insured tort liability system should work, no serious alternative comes off as poorly as the existing tort system does in actual practice.

For example, when it is proposed to curb, and in some cases, eliminate payments for pain and suffering, what you will hear from no-fault's opponents are the great injustices that would occur in some hypothetical case involving permanent injury or disfigurement.

The fact is that most liability claims for personal injury do not involve such serious kinds of intangible loss—only about 7.6 percent of the total according to one of the Department's surveys. Moreover, as insured tort liability works in the real world, even innocent victims with any tangible losses do not on the average come even close to recovering their economic losses from liability insurance, much less any intangible losses.

For example, one survey found that while the average economic loss for permanent and totally disabled tort victims was $78,000, their liability insurance paid on average only $12,566. Moreover, most of the commonly advanced plans as well as the administration's no-fault principles would retain the right of the truly seriously injured victim to recover his intangible losses under tort rules. The curb on intangible damage recovery would, under these plans, apply only to the less than seriously or permanently injured victim, victims who under the present system are often grossly overcompensated with respect to their measurable economic losses.

The administration's goals or principles for the auto accident reparations system are spelled out in detail in the report entitled Motor Vehicle Crash Losses and Their Compensation in the United States and in the draft concurrent resolution originally proposed in March 1971. Among the most important of these goals are the following:

> Basic benefits should be forthcoming to the injured person on a first-party contractual basis to the end that such person would be receiving benefits from the insurer with whom he has contracted and to whom he had paid his premiums * * *
>
> Basic benefits under the reparations system should be payable to all accident victims without regard to fault, excluding, of course, those who willfully injure themselves.
>
> Such benefits should provide compensation for all economic loss, subject to reasonable deductibles and limits, and the tort lawsuit should be eliminated, at least to the extent first-party benefits apply, avoiding the adversary process for the mass of accidents.

Nothing has occurred over the past 4 years that does anything other than strengthen our belief that these are sound principles which could be beneficially applied in the auto accident reparations plans across the country.

Over the past several years, a wealth of survey experience with the public's feelings toward automobile insurance has shown beyond doubt the average motorist's great sensitivity to the size of his insurance premium. It is not surprising then that the matter of costs has figured prominently in the no-fault debate at both national and State levels.

Specifically with respect to the cost and price implications of the no-fault plans called for by the various bills before this subcommittee, the Department of Transportation does not currently have the technical, analytical capability to make confident quantitative assessments as noted earlier.

Two years ago, at the request of the National Association of Insurance Commissioners, the Department did help finance the development of a no-fault costing model. During the last Congress, the House Subcommittee on Banking and Finance used this model and you should have those results. The Department, lacking the ability to validate independently the work of these experts, neither endorses nor rejects their findings. Suffice it to say that no-fault costing is an area in which expert views diverge widely, and, as you have already learned, truly disinterested experts such as those who developed the NAIC's model are few and far between.

There are some observations about no-fault costs that we do want to make, however. First, from the perspective of the public policymaker, cost savings, while admittedly important, should not, and in my view do not, constitute the primary purpose of no-fault reform. Much more important, for example, are the adequacy of victim's benefits, the certainty and universality of their insurance coverage, and the elimination of the adversary process from the benefit decision. Happily, there are very large opportunities for cost savings in the shift from insured tort liability to no-fault. Much of these savings should be used to finance no-fault's higher benefit levels and the economic losses of the additional beneficiaries that no-fault will cover. These, I suggest, should be the priority uses of these savings. In many, perhaps in most cases, however, the savings will be sufficiently large so that there can be a reduction in the average motorists' premium relative to what it would have been under insured tort liability.

A second point about no-fault costs has to do with comparisons. In the welter of claims and counter-claims about whether no-fault will cost more or less and by how much, it is easy to see how even the informed observer can become confused. Frequently, the problem is that the wrong comparison is made—that is, the cost of no-fault next year is compared to the cost of insured tort liability this year. The result is that the real difference in cost, if any, is usually obscured if not overwhelmed by the effects of inflation and the effect of year-to-year changes in the frequency and severity of accident losses.

The only fair comparison, and one that is incomplete at that, is to compare the costs of each system for the same period. Even here, however, it must be borne in mind that what are being compared are very different things, In the auto insurance context, the only meaningful comparison is the one that addresses both the costs and the benefits of different systems. For truly, the important advantages of no-fault over insured tort liability lie principally in the much greater benefits it delivers to victims rather than in whatever premium reduction it may permit. Thus, in comparing different no-fault plans, our focus should be principally on the benefits they provide, for only here do we see how much more valuable no-fault is to the consumer.

H.R. 1900 has drawn heavily, both in concept and in language, from the Uniform Motor Vehicle Accident Reparations Act which was designed to reflect the administration's principles. If this legislation were before one of the several States, we would enthusiastically be urging its passage and we will continue to monitor State action in this area and its adequacy. But I think that the issue now before the Congress is whether once it has been demonstrated through the studies by DOT and others that no-fault is the way to handle this problem, should the Federal Government step in at this time and pass a nationwide statute or should this be left to the States?

It is the administration's position that at this time the matter should be left to the States. In summary and before I present myself for questioning—and I hope you do have questions—the administration's position is:

One, the no-fault principle is the appropriate way to handle injuries which result from automobile accidents.

Two, the administration has in the past and will continue in the future, to make available the evidence on which to decide the important question of public policy.

The issue of automobile insurance and automobile accident claims have traditionally been held in the State's jurisdiction and the State should be given reasonable time to see the problem, propose a solution and then adopt it.

Sufficient time has not yet elapsed in the process to justify intervention in the State by the Federal Government and the administration does not feel that the current proposed Federal no-fault bills should be enacted at this time by the Congress.

Mr. Chairman, that concludes my prepared statement. I would be pleased to respond to any questions that you or your colleagues might have.

Mr. VAN DEERLIN. Thank you, Mr. Secretary. I would imagine that there will be questions abounding.

You say that if H.R. 1900 were before a State legislature and you were asked for advice, you would enthusiastically recommend its adoption by the State?

Secretary COLEMAN. Yes.

Mr. VAN DEERLIN. Suppose a bill embodying most of these principles were placed on the desk of the President of the United States and he asked you for a recommendation on signing it. What kind of advice would you give him?

Secretary COLEMAN. Mr. Chairman, I hope that this is an issue I would not have to come to. I think my answer would have a lot to do with my concept of federalism and I do not claim the expertise in this area. I hope I have in some other field. At this time, frankly, I really don't know what I would do. I could not in good conscience give you an answer as to whether I would advise the President to veto the bill or to sign it.

Mr. VAN DEERLIN. I very much appreciate your taking that position. Then you don't get yourself locked in anywhere. Perhaps we can all manage to keep an open opinion on it.

Secretary COLEMAN. I think that is the problem. There should be full debate and discussion, Mr. Chairman, and we each should try to come to what I think would be the correct solution and I don't think at this time anybody should be taking hard and fast positions.

Mr. VAN DEERLIN. One of the recent developments in the study of no-fault has, of course, been the announced determination by the Attorney General that in his view the Federal standards approach of H.R. 1900 and S. 354 would be unconstitutional. I suppose that you might say that is his department, not yours. But we all know, of course, that Mr. Levi is not the only constitutional authority in the Cabinet. The Secretary of Transportation is a pretty good constitutional lawyer himself. Could you address yourself to the question of the constitutionality as you see it?

Secretary COLEMAN. Well, as you pointed out, Mr. Chairman, in the Cabinet and the Government, the primary officer responsible for law and constitutional matters is the Attorney General of the United States. Mr. Levi has said in his judgment the bill in the present form is probably unconstitutional. I would say that that would be the administration's position because it was given by the Attorney General of the United States unless he was instructed otherwise by the President of the United States.

Mr. VAN DEERLIN. So I am not going to be successful in extracting an independent opinion on that element?

Secretary COLEMAN. Well sir, if you address a question to me, I am here to answer as if I am under oath all of your questions, sir. I am not refusing to answer.

Mr. VAN DEERLIN. May I ask you to tell the committee whether you personally think that Federal no-fault legislation would be constitutional?

Secretary COLEMAN. Well, to the extent that I have studied the problem, and to the extent that I have had previous experience, it would be my feeling that the no-fault standard, the Federal no-fault standards bill as proposed in S. 354 and H.R. 1900 would probably be declared constitutional by the U.S. Supreme Court if and when that issue got to the Supreme Court. It has been a long time since the Supreme Court of the United States declared unconstitutional a statute which deals mainly with economic matters.

Second, as I understand the constitutional argument, and it is a serious argument, there is some doubt as to whether the Federal Government can impose duties on a State officer unless as part of that imposition the Federal Government provides the money. I know that is the position of the Attorney General of the United States and in testimony before the Senate committee, I think he presented that position quite clearly. I feel that *Testa* v. *Katz*—which was an OPA case where the Federal statute said that the State court has to enforce the penalty provision of the OPA law and the Supreme Court said that it was constitutional—would be precedent on the other side, however.

I also think that *Aaron* v. *Cooper*, which is the Little Rock case where the court went out of the way to say that every State officer took an oath to uphold the Federal Constitution and the Federal statutes would also be held to be precedent. But it is not an open and clear case. I do think that you ought to pay very close attention to Attorney General Levi's presentation in the Senate and I am pretty sure that he will be called before you to say it better than I do. I was very impressed with his testimony dealing with the issue of federalism.

If you leave aside the constitutional question, I still want to emphasize that this is a Federal Government, that there are certain things left to the States, that traditionally insurance matters have been left to the States and that there is not sufficient evidence yet why that should be taken away from the State. I still think that the statute would be constitutional. But as Justice Holmes once said, that a statute is constitutional is the least you can say about it. It merely says it is not so bad that it turns my stomach. So I think the insurance issue before this committee has to be broader than whether the statute would be constitutional.

Mr. VAN DEERLIN. Except, of course, if we were persuaded that it was going to be held unconstitutional then we would be disinclined to give these long afternoon hours to its consideration.

Mr. METCALFE. Mr. Chairman, I would like to ask the Secretary—first let me express my pleasure in having you appear before this committee today, but I want to make certain that in regard to this, did you say in your opinion that this no-fault bill would or would not be constitutional?

Secretary COLEMAN. As I looked at it, and I certainly am not the chief law officer of the United States; I have a different job from the Attorney General of the United States—but from my point of view, I would say that if presented to the Supreme Court of the United States, the Supreme Court would probably uphold the constitutionality of the statute.

Mr. METCALFE. Thank you.

Mr. VAN DEERLIN. If the Chairman is to be successful in enforcing some semblance of the 5-minute rule on questioning, he has to start by enforcing it against himself. Therefore, I recognize Mr. McCollister.

Mr. MCCOLLISTER. I very much appreciate your statement. I appreciate your candor in answering the question on the constitutionality that I suspect you confronted with some reluctance because it is the Attorney General's duty, but I appreciate your candor, sir.

I have several questions on your statement itself. First, on page 3, you say that 17 States have adopted true no-fault statutes and then I think you referred to 8 or 10 States that were enacting some sort of no-fault which in your opinion weren't true no-fault plans. Can you tell me what the distinction is? Wherein did 8 or 10 States fail to address the no-fault issue?

Secretary COLEMAN. Well, I think the basic difference, sir, is that in these 8 or 10 States, there is no limitation whatsoever on lawsuits, and that you have the best of both worlds where you can proceed pretty much under the no-fault principle or you can proceed under the general tort liability principle.

Mr. MCCOLLISTER. Isn't it a little remarkable that with the threat of Federal action hanging over the heads of these 17 States that they have acted. It is not an easy thing to confront. There has been a fight in every one of those States. It would have been easy for each of those 17 to defer action on the issue saying, the Federal Government will do it. I think it is remarkable that 17 States have acted. Evidently you do too; is that correct?

Secretary COLEMAN. Yes, I have never had the guts myself to run for public office, but I must often admire those who do. They show courage on a lot of issues and I think this shows the advantage of a democratic system where people do have to submit themselves to the voters. It is clear from all of the statistics I have seen that in most places where the question is asked, the voting public does favor a no-fault law. Therefore, those who are involved in the political process take that into consideration.

I would hasten to add that there are two States now, one Illinois and the other California, and you would think this political process ought to work but no-fault is at pretty much of a standstill. I think it is highly plausible to argue that it is at a standstill because the States are waiting for the Federal Government to act, of course there may be other reasons. It is hard enough where I work to figure out why Congress does something. I hope you never put the burden upon me of trying to figure out why Congress doesn't do something. The same is true of State legislation.

Mr. McCOLLISTER. On page 10 of your statement, you say the DOT study showed that for every dollar of net benefits that the system provides the victims, it consumes another dollar and then you say the system absorbs vast amounts of resources, primarily performing the functions of marketing insurance policies and settling claims.

No-fault will have no effect on the costs of marketing, will it?

Secretary COLEMAN. Well, my understanding is that no-fault would be a condition precedent to getting the insurance, to being able to drive. Two, that the benefits would essentially be uniform. It seems to me that the policy becomes pretty fungible.

Mr. McCOLLISTER. Under a general standards bill, wouldn't there be differences in policy?

Secretary COLEMAN. Some, but I think there would be a tendency toward greater standardization.

Mr. McCOLLISTER. More about that in a moment. But is it not so that most of the costs of marketing relate to whether company A gets the business before company B gets the business? I can't see how that would advance the proposition that no-fault is going to be able to effect much savings in the marketing area.

Secretary COLEMAN. Well, Mr. Congressman, I think I am not going to stay here and defend that statement because you are tending to convince me that I should revise and qualify that statement.

Mr. McCOLLISTER. Let's take the other costs, the nonbenefit costs, the overhead costs and that of claims. Does anybody have any information which shows to what extent the legal expenses companies incur would be eliminated by the advent of no-fault? It seems to me that either 2 or 4 years ago when we were deciding the same issue——

Secretary COLEMAN. Congressman, I will supply that for the record for you. I don't have that figure right at hand. I will supply it for you by the end of the month for the record.

[The following information was received for the record.]

IMPACT OF NO-FAULT ON COMPANY LEGAL EXPENSES

The impact of no-fault insurance on loss adjustment expenses is difficult to predict and will vary depending on the no-fault coverages adopted.

Loss adjustment expenses under the present tort system average approximately 14 percent of premium for stock companies and 19 percent of premium for direct writing companies. In analyzing S. 354 last year, the American Insurance Association estimated that the loss adjustment expenses of their members would fall approximately 50 percent.

Mr. McCOLLISTER. Thank you, Mr. Chairman.

Mr. VAN DEERLIN. Mr. Eckhardt?

Mr. ECKHARDT. Mr. Secretary, as I see it, the constitutional question is, Can the Federal Government constitutionally compel a State to administer a program whose general framework is federally devised for paying a man? Do you feel that that is the general constitutional question?

Secretary COLEMAN. Well, I think that it is a very important constitutional question and if you are looking for cases which say yea or nay on that proposition, I don't think you can find many cases.

Mr. ECKHARDT. I can't think of any case in which the Federal Government has widely and sweepingly removed State authority to engage in a typically State field. That is the whole field of tort law in the area of automobile reparation.

If a State does not administer a federally designed plan, of course I have stated in terms of what this law actually does, but in general terms I can't think of an analogous situation in our law. Can you think of anything that would be analogous to that?

Secretary COLEMAN. Well, I am pretty sure that at the time before the Federal Liability Act was enacted, whenever there was an accident involving an employee of a railroad, that it was covered by State law—it was then covered by the Federal law.

Mr. ECKHARDT. Frequently it is going the other way. Frequently the Federal—for instance in a Federal enclave such as a military base—has adopted State law for use, say criminal law to enforce as Federal law. But I don't know of any instances in which a State is called upon to adopt a federally devised plan.

Secretary COLEMAN. I think that is the case in the Clean Air Act, sir, which the third circuit upheld. I assume the State law prior to the adoption of the Federal Clean Air Act was that if you dirty up the air too much, it would be a common law nuisance.

Now as I understand the Federal Clean Air Act, the Federal Government has set up certain standards and they pretty much supersede what would otherwise be the State standard, and I think there are a lot of laws, the whole area of the regulation of securities for example, prior to the time in 1933 and 1934 when you had the Securities Act there was a lot of common law in the States which deal with that problem.

Mr. ECKHARDT. I don't think that there is any question but that in the securities field or other fields the Federal Government can devise its standards and put them into effect as law and with respect to those transactions which are in interstate commerce, it may preempt the State's field and I have no question but that the Federal Government may adopt policy in connection with the Clean Air Act that may establish minimum standards within the States and in the meantime permit the States to proceed.

But the analogous situation was something that you closely approach with respect to wiping out, for instance, the States nuisance law. Of course, those are rather narrow compared to the total area of tort liability with respect to auto accidents. But I don't know that State nuisance laws are wiped out by the Clean Air Act. I may be wrong about that. I am struggling for an example.

Secretary COLEMAN. My understanding from what they tell me is the Clean Air Act is a close analogy to what the Federal standards law purports to be as any that one can find. I am pretty sure there are other instances where the Federal Government has set up a standard and has imposed that on the States.

Mr. ECKHARDT. Of course in the Clean Air Act what the Federal Government is actually doing is setting standards for State control and permitting the State to control, but it is within a relatively narrow and specific area in which, were it not for these standards in most instances there would not be any law at all except a very restricted nuisance law.

Secretary COLEMAN. The nuisance law is restricted, sir, only because the bright and able young lawyers haven't gotten around to it yet. But it seems to me that as you move into an organized society and you get a lot of scientific evidence that dirty air can affect the health of human beings, that the common law of the State has the same vitality that has taken us through a thousand years of civilization, and that the law would begin to develop. That you don't have as many cases in this area doesn't hold much water because I think as these able young lawyers begin to develop the rules to help to cover us as we get more and more people, that that would have been a natural development.

Mr. ECKHARDT. But I think both you and I are not quite sure that the nuisance law is applied by the Federal Government.

Secretary COLEMAN. I think it is, but I haven't reread the case with that exactly in mind yet.

Mr. ECKHARDT. I notice on page 3 of your statement you say either we have a Federal system or we do not. Of course in the case of the air and water law, I think we pretty clearly have a Federal system but I do join you in saying that this does fall short of either being a Federal system or a State system. I merely state that if the States are within certain brackets and those brackets are not compelled, they retain a considerable breadth. Then the State exercising its duties with respect to rate setting, enforcement procedures, and so forth, may move statewide, but within federally defined brackets.

I find that something far different than either established Federal standards with the authority to make rates and set rates or State activity which as you pointed out would ordinarily have a very wide scope for experimentation and adaptation to that State's problem and that concerns me aside from the constitutional question.

Secretary COLEMAN. It concerns me and it concerns the administration. I think that this matter should be talked about and studied more before you rush in with a Federal law. This is a matter of judgment, but I just don't think that 4 years in the life of this type of issue is a long time.

As I understand it, certain legislatures, for example, now meet every year, but some of them in the odd year can only deal with revenue laws and that they can't deal with the general agenda. If that is so, it just means that the State has had it. Those States are going to need two opportunities and though no-fault is a very important thing. I think in the life of most States, if you follow what the Governors have spent more time trying to figure out, whether they are going to go to an income tax or other method of handling this problem, and no-fault is a problem which just hasn't had that high a place on the agenda. If you really believe that the States ought to have an adequate opportunity and that is the basis on which you are reaching a decision, I don't think 4 years is a sufficient time before you can say they haven't acted soon enough, and that we will now have to step in and take Federal action.

Mr. ECKHARDT. I think I agree with what seems to me to be a constitutional conclusion that this may well be constitutional, but that it does raise very serious policy questions.

Secretary COLEMAN. Yes, sir, and I think really that is what President Ford's position is on that matter, a really serious policy question and we welcome the opportunity for the full debate and taking a look at this, testing these ideas and also keep pointing out the situation to the States that if they don't take a look at this problem that the Congress may act.

I think that certainly is the Department's point of view and I think it is the President's point of view.

Mr. METCALFE. Mr. Secretary, on page 3, lines 14 and 15 of your testimony, are you saying that you hope that by now there would be more State action in the area of no-fault insurance?

Secretary COLEMAN. Yes, sir, I would have hoped, and I think reading the testimony of previous Secretaries indicates that they thought that by now more States would have adopted the uniform no-fault bill.

Mr. METCALFE. To what do you attribute the fact that just 17 States have adopted it?

Secretary COLEMAN. Well, I think that no-fault in principle is a relatively new idea. I think, second, that the States have had a lot of other problems which in the agenda of the leadership of the State have a higher priority. Third, I think it may be because some States felt the Federal Government was going to act and therefore they felt they wouldn't have to do it. Fourth, even though the Department feels that this is the way to go and there is no other way, in life you find that different people have different ideas and therefore there is not a hundred percent consensus.

Mr. METCALFE. Thank you, Mr. Secretary. I refer you to page 17 of your statement in No. 4. In summary of the administration's position you state that "Sufficient time has not yet elapsed in the process to justify intervention in the State by the Federal Government and the administration does not feel that the current proposed Federal no-fault bills should be enacted at this time by the Congress."

On March 26, 1971, according to your testimony, Secretary Volpe presented the administration's conclusions to the Congress and again according to your testimony on page 6, "this change should be made if at all possible, at the State level". That was 4 years ago. How much time do you think we should give the States before we would be willing to have the Federal Government become involved?

Secretary COLEMAN. Congressman Metcalfe, I was hoping that somebody wouldn't ask me that question, but from the moment you started I knew you were going to zero in on that problem.

Well, as you know, with Ambassador Volpe, the suggestion was that there be a concurrent resolution where Congress would tell the States we are going to take another look at this in 25 months. That never happened. I would say that if I was asked to give a figure and figures are always arbitrary, that it would be somewhere between 6 and 10 years. I think with an issue of this type and with the public debate, that somewhere between 2 and 5 years more is the period of time that I would suggest before we move. But I do think it would be very helpful if the Congress would adopt a joint resolution to indicate that we have collected all this data, that the Department of Transportation has made all these studies and that there seems to be a general consensus that no-fault is the way to go.

We urge this upon the States and if they haven't acted within the next 2 to 4 years we are going to take another look.

Mr. METCALFE. There is quite a bit of difference between what former Secretary Volpe proposed, which is just in excess of 2 years and your statement of between 6 and 10 years.

Secretary COLEMAN. From now. We are starting from now. When I said 6 to 10 years, I was adding on the 4 and then I cut down to 2 to 5 additional years. What I am saying is 4 years have already gone by but the Congress has never passed the joint resolution, so I would say that from here on out, 2 or 5 additional years would be the time and that is why I did the change in arithmetic.

Mr. METCALFE. Thank you very much. I yield back the balance of my time.

Mr. VAN DEERLIN. I am going to follow on the line of your questioning.

Mr. McCOLLISTER. Could I interrupt for a moment? Mr. Secretary, are you not making it all the more possible for State legislators to say, "Don't do anything because the Federal Government will take over in 2 or 4 years." Why should we expose ourselves to all that political flak when the Secretary of Transportation says the Federal Government will do it in 2 or 4 years?

Secretary COLEMAN. Obviously this is a political matter and you have more expertise on that than I do. I do think that this matter has been subject to debate in the legislature, the State legislature and I think you need something to shove it over the line and I think that a recognition by the Congress that this is an important problem will do that.

By the same token, as you know, traditionally one of the things which have caused this Congress to act is when it receives resolutions from the States about something which they feel is important. I think that when the Federal Congress indicates that something is of importance that that would cause the leadership in the States to pay more attention to it, but it is a matter of judgment.

Mr. VAN DEERLIN. I would like to inquire what the track record of the State is thus far in your opinion. I guess every State legislature has considered no-fault and 17 of them have adopted what you might call true no-fault laws. How many of these 17 measure up to the standards set forth in the DOT study of 1973?

Secretary COLEMAN. Well, I would say that of the number about 9 of them are pretty close to the DOT standards, 9 of the 17. I would also say that the State track record is nowhere near as good as the track record that Congressman Metcalfe has. On the other hand, I would say it is much better than mine.

Mr. VAN DEERLIN. We are mixing tracks.

Secretary COLEMAN. That is right, but I would say that when you look at it, my understanding is, for example, that if California would enact the no-fault law, then something like over 50 percent of the people in the United States would be covered by some form of State no-fault law. The Commonwealth of Pennsylvania, Michigan, and New York—these are very populous States—and they have adopted no-fault. I think that when you look at the political facts that this track record over a period of 4 years is not a bad track record.

Mr. VAN DEERLIN. If 33 States have considered and rejected "true" no-fault laws and, by your testimony, 9 have adopted laws which measure up to the DOT standards, then that means that 41 have not.

Secretary COLEMAN. Well, 41 have not, but there are some of those that don't measure up to the DOT standards. Some of the rest have still fairly good no-fault laws. If you make an analogy, for example,

I don't think there is any more uniform law than the Uniform Commercial Code. But the fact is that a lot of States adopted it, but they did have amendments and some States did not adopt it and there is certainly much more rationale to say that when you are dealing with the Uniform Commercial Code, the bills of lading and negotiable instruments and contracts and that kind of thing, that once you had a good Uniform Commercial Code that every State should adopt it just like that and nobody should have an amendment—but the facts of legislative life have always been that everybody in that legislature thinks that he or she should add something which makes it just a little better. Those are the facts that you live with.

Mr. VAN DEERLIN. We are a highly mobile society. What about the fellow who is protected in the State of New York, but when he gets into the Lincoln Tunnel and crosses over into New Jersey, his protection falls off considerably. What do your records show about where we do most of our getting killed and getting injured?

Secretary COLEMAN. We have these figures which we can put in the record.

[The following material was received for the record:]

Estimated percentage of motor vehicle accidents in which an out-of-State registered vehicle was involved

	Percentage		Percentage
Alabama	23.1	Nebraska	29.3
Alaska	12.0	Nevada	61.7
Arizona	37.9	New Hampshire	(¹)
Arkansas	31.5	New Jersey	29.6
California	9.6	New Mexico	41.9
Colorado	32.1	New York	15.6
Connecticut	(¹)	North Carolina	24.1
Delaware	46.6	North Dakota	23.1
District of Columbia	(¹)	Ohio	16.1
Florida	21.0	Oklahoma	30.1
Georgia	30.1	Oregon	22.2
Hawaii	0.0	Pennsylvania	21.2
Idaho	36.0	Puerto Rico	0.0
Illinois	16.8	Rhode Island	23.6
Indiana	20.8	South Carolina	31.3
Iowa	20.6	South Dakota	40.6
Kansas	30.1	Tennessee	29.6
Kentucky	32.3	Texas	14.6
Louisiana	21.7	Utah	25.0
Maine	20.6	Vermont	39.7
Maryland	34.1	Virginia	33.9
Massachusetts	22.9	Washington	13.7
Michigan	10.0	West Virginia	35.4
Minnesota	17.0	Wisconsin	19.1
Mississippi	34.4	Wyoming	61.0
Missouri	31.0		
Montana	31.3	Total	22.4

¹ These estimates have been developed from statistical counts of motor vehicle registration by States for calendar year 1973. State fatalities were compiled from State accident reports as summarized in the National Highway Traffic Safety Administration's Fatal Accident File. For purposes of developing estimates, it was assumed that all accidents involved two motor vehicles.

Mr. COLEMAN. We have a very mobile society and it is a fact that people do get injured or get killed outside of the State in which they are driving.

Mr. VAN DEERLIN. Just as a lack of adequate clean air laws in one State might very well destroy the ambient air quality of an adjoining

State, couldn't a person who is moving in interstate traffic be very greatly handicapped by a Balkanization of his protection?

Secretary COLEMAN. Yes, but Mr. Chairman, you have gone to the heart of the Federal system. There is no doubt that if you have 50 separate solvent and independent States, which is the basis of the Constitution, that this is going to happen in every field of law and I am willing to bet you that with respect to contract disputes, you have the same problem. With respect to a lot of common law you have the same problem, I am sure. Anyway, you probably place as many telephone calls outside of Washington as you do within Washington, but this is part of being in a Federal system. You name it.

Mr. VAN DEERLIN. I would say your allusion to telephone calls is not well chosen. How do various State laws impede us or in any way inconvenience us or threaten our well-being?

Secretary COLEMAN. What I am saying is that I take it ofttimes when one places a telephone call, he may well say something which is libelous, and therefore you have the legal problem. Do you measure the liability by the law of the District of Columbia or by Montana if someone is speaking to Montana. All I am saying is that in the Federal system this is a problem that we live with everyday and the fact that to a great extent people outside the State are involved is no reason to say you bring into play the Federal law.

Mr. VAN DEERLIN. Wouldn't it lead us in the direction of some Federal standards?

Secretary COLEMAN. No, sir; not unless you are going to scrap the Constitution and say that we are going to do away with the States. This happens everyday. Every morning I get a Philadelphia Enquirer and I read it in Virginia and then in the District of Columbia and therefore whoever publishes that newspaper brings into play this same conflict of laws. But this is the society we live in and because an accident happened and you have this interstate shifting, is not sufficient reason to say you have to have a Federal law. What you are suggesting is a repeal by statute of all of the common law of all of the States or at least implying that in each instance there has to be a final Federal law. We just haven't gone that far and I don't think it would benefit the country if we did go that far.

Mr. ECKHARDT. If the matter involved liability, it would be governed by the law of the States, but if it involved an antiracketeering law or an antitrust or any matter of Federal law, the Federal law would govern.

Mr. VAN DEERLIN. Mr. McCollister?

Mr. MCCOLLISTER. Thank you, Mr. Chairman. Mr. Secretary, what effect would the national proposal have on existing State no-fault laws?

Secretary COLEMAN. Sir, my understanding, and this is subject to check—if H.R. 1900 is enacted I would imagine that every statute other than the Michigan statute would have to be amended. That is the only statute that I know of, State statute, which may comply with the standards set up in H.R. 1900.

Mr. MCCOLLISTER. Let's talk a little but more about the constitutional question. Assume we do enact a Federal law and it were found unconstitutional, what would be the effect of that upon people whose policies were written under that Federal statute? Would they still be covered or would they be uninsured?

Secretary COLEMAN. Well, sir, I see there would be a lot of problems.
Mr. McCOLLISTER. Which is what we are trying to do away with.
Secretary COLEMAN. As you know, the general common law is that whenever a statute is clearly unconstitutional, it is unconstitutional ab initio, from the very beginning, and therefore anything happening in the meantime is the malady. But you also know that the Supreme Court and other places have struggled with that problem and ofttimes they said that law is constitutional, but only prospectively.
I know there is a dissent by Justice Douglas in an antitrust case dealing with, I think, section 3 of the Clayton Act and he said the same thing, that this practice is constitutional, but we think this should be applied prospectively and not retroactively.
Mr. McCOLLISTER. I would imagine that there would be many things that would have to be revised and other insurance established and that it would seem to me to present some difficulty to the people.
Secretary COLEMAN. There is no doubt of it, there would be a serious problem and it is one reason why the constitutional question is close there. As a legislator, you may decide not to enact a law even though your colleagues and advisers say you will win in the Supreme Court 5 to 4. That is more reason to say see what the States will do.
Mr. McCOLLISTER. Mr. Secretary, in addition to this committee, I have the good fortune to serve on the Small Business Committee. In that committee we are concerned about the impact of Federal regulations disproportionately affecting small business.
In Nebraska and in the Midwest there are a number of small insurance companies. Some of them have expressed to me the concern that were Federal no-fault standards enacted, that they would have to be relicensed and make all sorts of new arrangements, which for many, would make it very difficult to continue in business. Do you have any comment on the effects of Federal no-fault standards on the smaller companies?
Secretary COLEMAN. That would be a problem because the small company would have an unlimited exposure with respe
payments. I think that the problem is handled by reinsurance. I think the small companies have lived with their problem and I really don't think it is a real major problem.
Mr. VAN DEERLIN. Does this concern address itself only to a Federal no-fault plan?
Mr. McCOLLISTER. Yes, there are widely varying circumstances in the States. What is good for Boston or Michigan or Florida or any city or State might not apply elsewhere. In fact, I remember, 2 years ago when people from Michigan came here to testify on behalf of the Federal bill, but when asked if they would accept the Massachusetts plan, were strongly opposed to it and the people from Massachusetts felt the same way about it. I am thinking that in Pennsylvania and in some of the widespread open areas the risks are different. There we should develop a little different way to do it because it does give you an opportunity under the State initiatives to tailor it to the circumstances which apply in that State.
Secretary COLEMAN. Mr. Chairman, I think the Congressman raises a very good point and it is something that you ought to consider.
Mr. VAN DEERLIN. Although I suppose that if the side of your car is bashed in, it doesn't make much difference whether it is in Boston or Omaha.

Mr. McCollister. In Boston they would leave you alone on the road while in Omaha they would pick you up and help you put it back together again.

Two years ago we addressed the whole question of the extra cost that would come to the elderly and economically disadvantaged covered by medicaid and the fact that your hospital bills would be paid for under medicare or medicaid and yet they would be required to pay a premium that would include a certain risk compensation for a certain risk of injury in hospitals and the whole question of whether health insurance covers that. Do you have any comment about if that would be helpful on how we lay out those risks?

Secretary Coleman. Well, that is a problem that might have to be considered. I do suggest, however, that the premium dollar is based upon a lot of different risks and I don't see any evidence that as a person gets much older, the chance of accident goes up. In an overall public policy you don't want to deny the older person the opportunity to drive before it is absolutely necessary.

Mr. McCollister. We had some testimony from the National Council of Senior Citizens and the American Association of Retired Teachers which suggest maybe the contrary is true.

Secretary Coleman. Yes, that is what I say, there is argument. I didn't say evidence. I have heard argument both ways and I have never seen a study which says that a person, say 60, or since I am getting there myself I had better say 75, is a greater risk in driving. I am just saying that in the overall policy determination that there may be a trade off and I don't think you can shave it so closely.

Mr. McCollister. Different States have different mixes of population and age groups.

Thank you very much.

—Mr. Van Deerlin. Mr. Eckhardt?

Mr. Eckhardt. I have one other question. The discussion we had about constitutionality is all going to the question of whether you may impose upon a State a duty as the cost of its being deprived of processing its own law. None of this has anything to do with H.R. 1272. There is no such constitutional question involved there at all. The reparation system on its own, the questions that have been raised by the Attorney General with respect to imposing would not be there.

Secretary Coleman. I think that is correct. Certainly the regulation doesn't apply when there is a Federal law saying this is what the law is, or I guess the only conceivable issue would be whether the Congress has the constitutional power to pass that type of statute. If it is sufficiently connected with interstate commerce and the use of highways which are federally aided, then there would be a constitutional power to pass that type of statute. I do think that on the policy question that statute, if anything, should be enforced the other way.

Mr. Eckhardt. In what way?

Secretary Coleman. I just think that the States basically ought to be left with the responsibility of handling the whole question of accident claims.

Mr. Eckhardt. Well, I guess that is a policy question upon which reasonable men may differ and differ differently at different times, because for instance Mr. Metcalfe's question was if only 17 States have now adopted the plan, why don't we do something about it? I think that was the implication of his question.

Secretary COLEMAN. I think the Federal standards law would be a better way to handle the problem than, with all due respect, your bill.

Mr. ECKHARDT. What about this: Suppose in setting up a Federal standards law in an area of reparation—of course when you are dealing with an area of fines for pollution or something like that, you might have some flexibility, but in the area of reparation if one State accepts an absolute minimum standard and another State sets an absolute maximum, what we may be establishing federally is we may be setting a requirement that results in good law in one State and bad law in another.

It seems to me that if in one State economic damages, for instance, are limited to a figure and another State permits economic damages to exceed that figure by some 20 percent, it seems that it is a serious question in my mind as to whether as a matter of policy, not a matter of constitutionality, that affords really equal protection of law.

Secretary COLEMAN. I think, sir, that with all due respect, I think the argument cuts just the other way and that is the basis of the whole question of federalism. I think that some of the Federal statutes now that we have, have problems because we try to legislate nationally one standard or one sum of money for 210 million or 215 million people, with diverse backgrounds living in diverse places. You get these problems and therefore you might have a Federal statute for Illinois which is completely inadequate in another State like Pennsylvania and for other reasons it may be completely adequate. I think this is one of the problems that we have.

Mr. ECKHARDT. I don't think I altogether disagree with you. I believe in a Federal system too, and I think one of its advantages is its flexibility and its position of experimentation, but I think we ought to either have a Federal law or we shouldn't have a Federal law. That is, if the Federal law is going to enter the field, it ought to make the decision. It seems to me the law falls between two chairs when it purports to tell a State that no law will go into effect unless they are adopted within the standards, but it is not prepared to say that the laws should for instance cover a person for certain general injuries that affect that person's ability to work without pain for the rest of his life. It seems to me we ought to either settle that one way or another federally or turn it over to the States to decide.

Secretary COLEMAN. I understand the argument you are making, sir, but I think that as we try to deal with this society in a refined way, some of us at least without being anti any of the Federal statutes realize that they have created great problems.

I understand that the Federal standards for aid to dependent children may be too low all over the country. A standard for the city of New York where the cost of living may be higher than some other cities in the Midwest or Far West States. If you set the standards for what is right nationally by what you can get from a consensus of the Congress, where you have Congressmen and Senators from different places, then that standard may be one which is too low for a place like New York.

I think this is a problem that we ought to begin to face up to and maybe one of the reasons for some of the dissatisfaction that we have in laws now is that in theory everything is great and they can't understand why some of the recipients are unhappy. We are dealing with diverse people and you should permit the States to have different standards.

Mr. ECKHARDT. I can see that the amount it takes to support a dependent child in New York might be more than it would be in Alabama, but I cannot see why there is any difference between a person hurt in Alabama or New York with respect to whether or not he should receive some money with respect to general damages concerning his ability to work because of pain while he is doing his job. It seems to me a person in New York is just like a person in Alabama in this respect.

Secretary COLEMAN. When you talk about Federal standards, that is for every place throughout the country, and the situation may be different.

Mr. ECKHARDT. The question of how much one recovers for his injury depends on how much is expended in that State, so we may set the States' standards, but the application of those standards in Alabama and New York may be different because medical bills and hospital bills may be different, though I doubt there is so much difference today.

Secretary COLEMAN. The other argument, sir, is that I just don't think at this time the Federal Government should go into the business of being a regulator of the whole automobile insurance activities. This is a whole new department, a whole new question of fixing rates and a lot of considerations where I just see no reason why the Federal Government has to go into this field.

Mr. ECKHARDT. Nobody is asking that.

Secretary COLEMAN. That is the effect of saying there is a Federal law which begins to set Federal standards. You then get involved with the insurance companies that are running the business and I would certainly say you will need much more Federal regulation of those insurance companies.

Mr. ECKHARDT. I am not saying that we should or we shouldn't, but I am saying we ought to make the decision.

Secretary COLEMAN. I agree and that is why I think this discussion is very helpful and I hope we will have adequate time and people will realize the seriousness of the problem and not get wedded to any one solution too soon.

Mr. ECKHARDT. Thank you.

Mr. VAN DEERLIN. Mr. Metcalfe, do you have further questions?

Mr. METCALFE. No.

Mr. VAN DEERLIN. Could you give us about 10 minutes to go over and vote, and stick around because we would like the counsel on both sides to have any cleanup questions they have. They are known as the designated hitters on this team. If you stick around, we would surely appreciate it; it won't be more than 10 minutes.

[Brief recess.]

Mr. VAN DEERLIN. The hearing will resume. The majority counsel, Mr. Kinzler.

Mr. KINZLER. Mr. Secretary, at page 9 of your testimony you say that one major shortcoming of the traditional compensation system stems from its intended scope of operation and you go on to state no-fault system?

Secretary COLEMAN. I would say no. I would say that under the adopted system that everybody should be recompensed with the exception of the people that willfully cause the accident and then they can make an exception if the willfulness was due to a person's being mentally deficient, but deficient to the extent that they didn't know right from wrong.

Mr. KINZLER. You would also have the problem that this person's family might be perfectly innocent.

Secretary COLEMAN. Yes; but I don't remember that much tort law, but I think that in most States the negligence of the mother would not be imputed to the child.

Mr. KINZLER. Even in such States, if there is one child in the car and there are four more at home, the child in the car might be able to recover, but the four kids at home wouldn't have any money forthcoming from the tort system, would they?

Secretary COLEMAN. That is true. That is the reason why we suggested that the appropriate way would be by a no-fault system.

Mr. KINZLER. OK, because I suspect what it boils down to is that if we are dealing with people who can't conform their behavior to the reasonable man standard, maybe that standard doesn't make very much sense. Are you suggesting here that we would be better off simply protecting the driver in an inherently dangerous environment?

Secretary COLEMAN. I don't think there is any relationship between whether you have a no-fault system and whether a person would drive negligently. I think that argument is a lot like the argument that if you gave more money to a mother who is on welfare that she will have another child to get more money. I think that is a phony argument. I don't think anybody says "because I will be paid whether I am negligent or not, I will go out and have an accident"; or on the other hand say "I will have to drive a little more carefully in order to get paid if I have an accident." I don't think that is the way the people react.

Mr. KINZLER. You also have an insurance system at the moment which might vitiate any deterrent effect as well, might it not?

Secretary COLEMAN. Yes.

Mr. KINZLER. Thank you.

Ms. NORD. Mr. Secretary, I would like to follow up on the question that Mr. McCollister asked. You stated in response to his question about how a national no-fault plan would affect car companies, that these companies could go out and get reinsurance. Do you have any feel for what has been happening to the costs of reinsurance? Have they been going up in the States that have no-fault plans in operation?

Secretary COLEMAN. I have no knowledge on that. If you want me to try to find out, if you will give me a week, I will try to find out.

Ms. NORD [minority counsel]. Thank you. That would be helpful.

[The following information was supplied for the record:]

REINSURANCE COSTS

Michigan and New Jersey have adopted no-fault legislation which provides unlimited medical, hospital and rehabilitation benefits. The insurance departments of both States deny that there is any serious problem in small companies' obtaining reinsurance. New Jersey is considering the establishment of a State-operated reinsurance fund.

Workmen's compensation insurance and accident and health insurance in several States provide unlimited medical benefits. Insurance companies of all sizes have been writing and reinsuring these coverages for many years.

Ms. NORD. One other question, Mr. Secretary. I believe that both of the bills state that a victim is to collect under social security or medicare or some alternative to no-fault first. Do you have any thoughts on the wisdom of this kind of a policy?

Secretary COLEMAN. As far as I know, I have no knowledge of that provision. I take it the rates under medicare and social security are fixed to the risks for everybody for every type of injury and if you have an injury from an automobile accident to the extent that there is already in place a system of insurance that reimburses the person, I see no reason why you can't continue that system.

The only provision would be that as we at least from time to time— I believe that the social security funding is less than adequate and we might determine that to the extent that we can believe it by substituting the insurance, that might make sense. But that is not my bailiwick and my initial reaction is that I think the provision is good. Although I could see that with the great ability of Secretary Weinberger he might come up and have some different ideas, but as far as I am concerned, I think that provision of the bill is all right.

Ms. NORD. Thank you.

Mr. VAN DEERLIN. Mr. Secretary, I apologize for having detained you so long for such short questioning by counsel, but I do thank you again for staying.

Secretary COLEMAN. Thank you, Mr. Chairman. I appreciate being here and I just say that I think this is one of the parts of working for the Government which makes it pleasant; namely, that you can come up and exchange ideas, some of which you know the people on the other side of the table feel differently on, but they do it with understanding and courtesy and all I can say is that my department will make itself available and we will try to provide you with any information you wish and will try to do whatever we can to try to help you reach the proper conclusion because I am convinced that your committee wants to do so.

Mr. VAN DEERLIN. Thank you and I hope you retain your kind thoughts far into your term of service.

Secretary COLEMAN. Thank you, sir.

[The following exchange of correspondence was received for the record:]

Chairman, Subcommittee on Consumer Protection and Finance.

OFFICE OF THE SECRETARY OF TRANSPORTATION,
Washington, D.C., September 2, 1975.

Hon. LIONEL VAN DEERLIN,
Chairman, Subcommittee on Consumer Protection and Finance, Committee on Interstate and Foreign Commerce, House of Representatives, Washington, D.C.

DEAR MR. VAN DEERLIN: Secretary Coleman has asked me to respond to your request for answers to two questions regarding the Department's *Study on Motor Vehicle Crash Losses and Their Compensation in the United States.* The questions and our replies to them are attached.

If I can be of any further assistance to you in this regard, please let me know.

Sincerely,

IRWIN P. HALPERN,
Acting Assistant Secretary,
Policy, Plans and International Affairs.

Attachment.

Question 1. Table 9 on page 36 of the final report indicates that people with economic losses of $25,000 or more recover only 30 percent of their loss, regardless of whether they have a tort suit or not. Would you please explain how it is possible that people with tort suits recover no more than people without tort suits?

Answer. Table 9 in the Final Report is a summary tabulation of detailed data found on pages 250, 251 and 272 of *Economic Consequences of Automobile Accident Injuries.* These data show that among those having total economic losses of $25,000 or more *and having tort recovery,* the average loss was $82,665, the average tort recovery (excluding legal costs) was $9,507, recovery from other sources averaged $13,019 and total recovery averaged $22,526. For those who had total economic losses over $25,000 *but who had no tort recovery,* the average loss was $72,917 and total recovery averaged $24,112. In both cases, the recovery ratio was 0.3.

These figures, despite their seeming precision, are, of course, simply rough approximations made on the basis of the cases sampled by the study. All are subject to a range of error, but that error is not so large as to impair their usefulness in making public policy judgments about the performance of the existing auto accident reparations system.

In interpreting these figures, it is important to remember that they are averages and as such hide much of the underlying variability of the data. For example, in the $25,000 plus loss category referred to above, fatality cases accounted for about two-thirds of the group without tort recovery and only about on-half of the group that received some tort recovery. Thus, one could surmise that life insurance made a much larger total contribution to the no-tort recovery category than it did to the tort recovery category. This is not to say that this factor alone accounts for the somewhat higher average total recovery for those not receiving tort but only that there are many subtle factors which help determine the averages.

Question 2. The Automobile Personal Injury Claims Study breaks down benefit recovery figures into economic and general damages. Is it possible that the economic loss portion is understated and the general damages portion is overstated because the figures reflect only losses to the date of settlement, i.e., that the settlements actually include some money for anticipated economic loss which the victim would have suffered after the date of settlement?

Answer. As discussed in some detail on pages 27 and 28 of *Automobile Personal Injury Claims* (and elsewhere in the report as well), the economic losses "to date of settlement" measured in this study do exclude a major element of total economic loss arising from auto accidents, i.e., future lost earnings. As a practical matter, in the vast bulk of the cases examined in this study—i.e., where there was no death, permanent disfigurement or permanent disability (92.4% of the cases)—it was usually quite clear from the facts that there were no future economic losses beyond the date of settlement. Conversely, in many of the most serious cases, it was plain from the facts that the losses were going to be far greater than the insurance company's obligation to cover, with the company settling quickly at the policy limits. In those cases involving death or permanent total disability, it was possible to estimate future lost earnings by using the same technique employed in the *Economic Consequences* Study. This was done and the results are discussed on pages 28, 53, 56 and 57 of *Automobile Personal Injury Claims.*

In summary, while it is true that some payments in excess of economic loss to date of settlement may have been intended for future economic losses, it does not seem likely that the undetected amount was large or that it jeopardizes the validity of the Study's findings and conclusions.

Mr. VAN DEERLIN. Our next witness is Mr. Thomas Downs of Downs & Edwards.

Mr. Brodhead wants very much to present you to the subcommittee and we are going to see if we can get our hands on him for that purpose, otherwise you will have to take his blessing in absentia, I guess. But if you will just wait a minute, we will see if he can be reached.

[Brief recess.]

Mr. VAN DEERLIN. I regret that Mr. Brodhead is on the Floor in the House where perhaps he belongs and we will have to dispense with the introduction he wanted to give you. But I bid you welcome and ask you to present your testimony.

STATEMENT OF THOMAS DOWNS, ESQ., CHAIRMAN, COMMITTEE OF THE NATIONAL CONFERENCE OF COMMISSIONERS ON UNIFORM STATE LAWS

Mr. DOWNS. Thank you very much, Mr. Chairman. It is a pleasure to appear before you. I have filed a statement with your committee.

Mr. Chairman, if it is agreeable with the committee, rather than read this statement, I would like to make a visual presentation, which I will also assure the committee will take less time than reading the filed statement. If that is agreeable, I would like to proceed.

Mr. VAN DEERLIN. I think I can speak for the subcommittee in saying it would be most agreeable.

Mr. Downs. I believe, Mr. Chairman, in getting any sort of legislation passed, those of us that advocate the thing have three responsibilities: one is to show what the evil is; second, to show what our remedy is; and third, to show that our cure or remedy is not worse than the disease. I would like here to put in very simple terms how the tort system works.

This red circle represents all the economic losses: The medical costs, the wage loss, replacement services, survivors' benefits. Under the tort system, this white represents the actual benefits paid. You will notice right away that half of this circle represents those under the fault system who cannot prove they were not at fault where there was negligence by both parties. So, to begin with, in the fault system, we have half the people receiving nothing. So we say at least the other half gets something. What about that? I believe the white shows what was demonstrated statistically by the speaker before me. Some get overpaid and some get underpaid, but nobody gets his exact economic loss taken care of by no-fault, and I think this is a very serious weakness of the present tort system.

First, half get nothing. Those who are compensated are either overpaid or underpaid. The studies made show the tendency is for the small claim to be overpaid and the large one underpaid, and the low-income or poor person usually gets less compensation because he is under the economic gun to make a settlement.

The next chart I would like to use shows that under tort, nobody gets paid when his losses occur, and I think I can show that on this chart perhaps. I will show this, Mr. Chairman, in a time sequence. Here is the date of the accident. The tort settlement by its very definition is sometimes forward in time; maybe months, and it could be years.

At this point when the settlement is made, tort can be accurate for the person's economic losses. That is for that period of time we can determine what the wage loss was, what the hospital and medical bills were; but if tort is accurate, it is late and this is extremely important. If tort is accurate in amount, it is late in payment. Then when claims adjusters or a jury try to determine the award for future benefits, they must look into a crystal ball. A labor economist will predict what the average wage would be, another economist will talk about inflation, doctors will talk about what they think the duration of the medical problem will be, and the jury or claims adjuster, no matter how sophisticated they are, make a guess so that if tort pays on time, it is inaccurate in amount.

Remember we are dealing, Mr. Chairman, with individual cases, and not being an actuary, I can speak rather freely on statistics. Our actuary friends can say if there are 10,000 people with a broken arm, on the average it will take so long for them to go back to work, so much medical bills. But you ask then about any one person, and they will say no, they cannot make the decision because they only work on what they call the law of large numbers.

The analogy is if you flip a coin 10,000 times, you get about the same number of heads and tails, but if someone says what will the 10,001 flip be, nobody can say with accuracy what that will be. It is a little bit like trying to predict the future. It is like the fellow who couldn't swim, and he drowned in the river that was on an average of

2 feet deep because he stepped in a sinkhole. So what I am saying is, the nature of tort, if it is accurate in amount, it is late in time. If it is timely, it is inaccurate in amount.

Now, I think that has a terrible effect on the people involved because it means, Mr. Chairman, that the individual involved gets concerned more about his tort claim than he does about getting back into society.

I will just read two sentences from the statement I have filed. This is a statement by Dr. John Nemiah, M.D., in the March/April 1971 issue of Trial magazine, and I will just read these two sentences:

> It should be appreciated by all concerned that the adversary nature of a tort or compensation action subsequent to injury heightens the patient's sense of grievance, entitlement to redress and revenge—which tends to foster his aggressive drives and to shift his attention away from goals of rehabilitation and eventual regained independence.
>
> Finally, it should be recognized that the delays so frequently encountered in ettling personal injury litigation tend to keep the patent trapped for months, even years, in a limbo of indecision and idleness in which dependency needs are fostered. During this time, it frequently becomes so pointless to try to work toward rehabilitation that, practically the patient remains an invalid until legal elements emanating from his injury are resolved.

I had a friend who was in a rather serious auto accident, and I said, "It must have hurt a lot, Tom." But he said, "I was on the job where my paychecks kept coming, my salary was paid, my health insurance took care of the medical costs, and I didn't hurt near so bad." I think this is one of the very clear things in our tort system. It is inherent that it is the delay in settlement that gets the injured people more concerned about what that legal settlement will be than getting him back in the rehabilitation area.

Now, Mr. Chairman, having shown this summary on tort, I will make a chart which I think will show the difference with no-fault.

Here you will see on no-fault, we have the yellow or mustard being the medical cost taken care of, and the wage, survivors' benefits, replacement services, medical, and rehab. Here in the true no-fault system all persons would get benefits on an economic basis. The red indicates those outside the system. This is the criminal, the bank robber, the person who has not bought into the system; the intentional injuries, though, theoretically could be covered.

The medical: Most of the plans provide that only a double bedroom is provided. That would be the added cost over a single bed. On the wages, the matter of how much a month is paid some uninsured.

Now, I submit to your committee, Mr. Chairman, that in any legislative process, the inherent compromises will make little differerences with the red, the yellow, and the blue, and all I ask this committee as I have other committees I have appeared before, is to compare this to this.

We are not comparing no-fault in a bill to a perfect system. Compared to a perfect system, it doesn't measure up. Compared to the evils of tort, it stands up pretty good, and I use the analogy I have in other committees.

For example, when social security was passed, there were great inequities on those employed in shops of eight or more who were covered, and the person in a smaller place was not only unprotected, but had to pay for the benefits of the others.

I did make one presentation in which this whole white part fell down, and I told the committee that that was to show the committee that the individual lost the appeal that he had in his original claim. So I think this does show that a no-fault system has an inherent logic to it, fairness, and the benefits are paid as they are incurred.

This means, for example, that if a person is in an accident, he is getting some medical. There is no dispute about the injury or the regular hospital bill. There may be a dispute on an outpatient service or an X-ray of $25, $50, or $100, but you don't hold up the whole claim in settling that one dispute. What is agreed upon is paid as it occurs, and the balance can usually be worked out.

This is another evil of tort, that if there is any dispute, it is all solved at once so the person with a good big claim may sacrifice the minor one to get the larger amount of money that he needs because the tort has been delayed.

I would like to speak just briefly on the matter of Federal standards versus State action. The bill is before you, and I am not an authority in detail, but none of these that I know of prevents a State from going ahead now or in the future.

I do think that unless this Congress acts, the prodding necessary to help the States get on about their business will be lacking. I feel that this is almost a partnership or a system where the Congress by setting minimum standards encourages the States to act. I see no inconsistency.

We are now celebrating the Bicentennial, and remember we are one Nation when we do work together. In other words, my emphasis, Mr. Chairman, is this is not Federal or State action. Let's have both of them solve the problem as it comes about. I think that with the idea of a Federal standard, each State can then experiment to make whatever improvements it wishes.

Mr. Chairman, I have tried to give the high points. If there are any questions, I will be pleased to try to respond to them.

[Mr. Downs' prepared statement follows:]

STATEMENT OF TOM DOWNS OF LANSING, MICH.

The Honorable L. Van Deerlin, chairman of the Subcommittee on Consumer Protection and Finance, and members of the committee:

I

It is a privilege to appear before your Subcommittee. I hope the statement I have filed with you with the informal comments I make and any questions from your committee will be of assistance in the important deliberations you are making on the subject of no-fault automobile insurance.

To identify myself, I am Tom Downs, an attorney from Lansing, Michigan of the firm of Downs and Edwards.

I am presently Chairman of the Committee of the National Conference of Commissioners on Uniform State Laws dealing with no-fault automobile insurance, more commonly called UMVARA (Uniform Motor Vehicle Accident Reparations Act). I am also attorney for League General Insurance Company of Michigan and have been and am representing that organization in litigation currently in Michigan on the constitutionality of Michigan's no-fault law. I am also retained by the Michigan UAW-CAP, the arm of the UAW that is concerned with Community Action Programs. I am also retained by Aetna Life & Casualty Insurance Company in the capacity of legislative consultant in the state of Michigan.

I call these affiliations to your attention and have so advised the various clients I am appearing before your committee today. However, in speaking before your committee, I am giving these ideas solely as an individual citizen that is interested in no-fault insurance and hope that these comments will be of assistance to you.

The comments I am making are not necessarily those of any client mentioned, but are designed to be of whatever assistance they can be to your committee.

I do speak, however, as a strong advocate of the principles of no-fault automobile insurance.

II

Those of us who advocate legislation have three questions that we are rightfully asked and must reasonable satisfy. These three questions are:
1. What is the evil?
2. What is our proposed cure?
3. Are we reasonably sure that the cure is not worse than the disease?

With your permission, I would like to ask and answer these three questions regarding no-fault automobile insurance, dividing into the two major parts: that is, (1) bodily injury; and (2) property damage.

Bodily Injury and No-Fault Auto Insurance

A. EVILS OF TORT

Many evils existed in the pre-no-fault tort system as far as bodily injury damages were concerned. These included but were not limited to the following:

1. More than half the people who were injured received no benefits

The tort system was one in which individuals were able to collect only if they were injured because of the negligence of others and they were not guilty of contributory negligence. Thus, old-fashioned tort was based on the concept of fault. If you could prove someone else was at fault and you weren't, then you could recover. Otherwise, you couldn't.

Since in any accident involving two automobiles only one car could be blameless, then only one could recover. In many cases both were at fault, such as when each car passed the yellow line. In many single car accidents, such as the case of an individual running off the road into a tree or bridge abutment, no one was at fault so no one could recover.

Thus, statistically, less than half the people could recover in tort.

2. Those who recovered under tort were either overpaid or underpaid for their actual economic damages, and never paid on time

The tort or fault system provided that the injured person was paid, with a very few exceptions, in one lump sum. If a person had been injured and was out of work for several months and would be out of work for several more months because of the injury, the past economic loss, the wage loss and medical expenses could be determined accurately. However, the payment for these damages would be late in time.

When the lump sum payment was made, there would be a guess as to what the economic damages would be in the future; that is, both the wage loss and medical expenses. No matter how good a crystal ball a jury had or claims adjusters or lawyers for both sides, it would be impossible to predict these amounts accurately.

Thus, some persons would be overpaid for their future losses and others would be underpaid, but none would be paid as the loss occurred.

Much has been said about the awards for pain and suffering in tort. Every statistical study of any reliability has shown that tort tended to overpay the small claims, underpay the large claims, and discriminate against the poor.

Pain and suffering awards often amounted only to enough to pay legal and other costs in determining fault to get an award.

3. Tort discriminates against the poor

An individual who is severely injured with overdue bills and is unable to return to work would have the greatest economic pressure to settle a claim for less than it was worth. A high income person with economic resources could wait indefinitely for a settlement. Thus, the tort or fault system discriminates against the poor who need money immediately to provide for the needs of their families.

4. Rehabilitation was discouraged through the fault system

One of the terrible evils of the tort system is that the injured person, while waiting for the settlement of the claim, would be so absorbed in possible litigation that the person was not able to go ahead with a positive attitude of getting back to work or retrained for a new job. Injured individuals, awaiting settlements, would be pre-occupied with newspaper stories of million dollar awards for damages they knew were less than theirs—never reading of those who collected nothing under tort!

Tort would hold out false hopes of large awards for injured workers awaiting settlement of their claims, rather than encouraging rehabilitation for the seriously injured.

The importance of fast payments bears very heavily on the whole matter of rehabilitation. The following quotations are important from the viewpoint of time lag, tort system, and rehabilitation:

2. UTILIZATION OF REHABILITATION TECHNIQUES

It has been observed that "[s]ince the basic purpose of present day automobile liability insurance is protection of the policyholder, and since the basic principle of rehabilitation is service to the injured person, it is only that very special situation and that very special claimant in which the goals of rehabilitation and liability insurance coincide." [8]

* * * * * * *

"The size of the attorney's fee is directly dependent on the size of the settlement, thus heightening the adversary nature of the settlement environment. Thus, considerable time, energy and expense must be devoted to controversy just when rehabilitation measures might most benefit the victim. The disabled person will usually be the focus of conflicting efforts toward the financial settlement of his "case," and here questions of fault and degree of disability press for immediate answer." [9]

U.S. Department of Transportation, *Motor Vehicle Crash Losses and Their Compensation in the United States*, March, 1971, pp. 58–59.

. . . A close and cooperative working relationship between claims representatives and claimants is perhaps the most effective but least often employed type of insurance-supported rehabilitation under the present tort liability system. This may be due, in part, to the pressures on adjusters for speedy closings of claims files. But even where insurance companies have sought to apply rehabilitation techniques to the settlement of third-party bodily injury claims, numerous obstacles remain, not the least lf which is the credibility of the liability insurer's motives in the eyes of its third-party claimant.

—DOT, cited above, p. 60.

The fault insurance system, however, does not promote rehabilitation. It hinders rehabilitation.[53]

* * * * * * *

Rehabilitation programs must be planned and often take a long time, thus requiring certainty that money be available for payment over an extended period. The fault insurance system is, as we have seen unreliable and unpredictable as to whether and, if so, how much it will pay.[56] Moreover, it makes its payments all at once, in a lump sum, which means that any allowance for future rehabilitation expenses can only be estimated and that there can be no assurance that the money awarded for rehabilitation will still be available when it is needed.[57]

—*Automobile Insurance . . . For Whose Benefit?* State of New York Insurance Dept., 1970, pp. 32–33.

---

[8] John Henle, *Rehabilitation of Auto Accident Victims* (1970) for the U.S. Department of Transportation, pp. 18–19.
[9] *Ibid.*, p. 13.
[53] Professor Alfred Conard, co-author of a leading empirical study of automobile accident victims, *Automobile Accidents and Payments* (*see* note 25 *supra*), has testified:

"The first objective of any reparation system should be to rehabilitate injury victims, using 'rehabilitation' in a broad sense to embrace comprehensive care from first aid through occupational retraining (if needed). Rehabilitation not only relieves the individual's own misery, but enables him to carry his weight in society. The tort liability system is a failure in this connection, because its payments come too uncertainly and too late; even when the victim is certain of payment, he has to make an agonizing choice between money and treatment."

Hearings on H.J. Res. 968 Before the Subcomm. on Commerce and Finance of the House Comm. on Interstate and Foreign Commerce, 90th Cong., 2d Sess., ser. 90–30, at 85 (1968). *See also* J. APONTE & H. DENENBERG, *supra* note 6, at 37; N.A.I.C. REPORT, *supra* note 44, at 108.
[56] *See* pp. 22–24, *supra*.
[57] New York University Center for Rehabilitation Services, *supra* note 54, at 12, 49–50.

Turning from medical care to vocational rehabilitation, it appears that there is very little tendency for any of the prevailing types of reparation for automobile injuries to bring about rehabilitation. In industrial accidents, the laws of a few states provide for employers' liability for rehabilitation costs, and some insurance companies publicize their rehabilitation programs. Although tort law theoretically would provide the costs of rehabilitation, its actual effect is probably to disfavor it. Pending the settlement, the injury victim's impulse to be rehabilitated conflicts with his desire to prove the highest possible degree of disability. After the settlement, there is no mechanism for channeling the proceeds toward a rehabilitation program, rather than toward paying debts, buying a car, or other purposes which press more strongly on the victim's consciousness.[9]

—Conrad, Alfred F. et al, *Automobile Accident Costs and Payments* (Univ. of Mich. 1964) p 81.

The following quote from *Trial Magazine*, March/April, 1971, in an article by John C. Nemiah, M.D., states this problem:

. . . It should be appreciated by all concerned that the adversary nature of a tort or compensation action subsequent to injury heightens the patient's sense of grievance, entitlement to redress, and revenge—which tends to foster his aggressive drives and to shift his attention away from goals of rehabilitation and eventual regained independence.

Finally, it should be recognized that the delays so frequently encountered in settling personal injury litigation tend to keep the patient trapped for months, even years, in a limbo of indecision and idleness in which dependency needs are fostered. During this time it frequently becomes so pointless to try to work toward rehabilitation that, practically the patient remains an invalid until legal elements emanating from his injury are resolved.
—7 *Trial* 2:61, 62.

B. THE CURE—NO-FAULT INSURANCE FOR BODILY INJURY

These five weaknesses in the conventional tort system are solved by no-fault in the following manner:

1. Almost every victim of an automobile accident is covered by no-fault

Theoretically, no-fault can protect *all* victims of automobile accidents. As a practical matter, most proposals eliminate a small percentage such as those engaged in criminal activities, or those who have deliberately not paid their insurance premiums. Some proposals provide that those who don't pay premiums, instead of being completely excluded from the system, suffer a high first-dollar economic penalty on recovery. Thus, the tort system which permits injured persons to collect *only* if they have proved the negligence of others and were *not* guilty of contributory negligence is replaced by a system that considers the economic needs of the injured victim and his dependents rather than the moralistic aspect of fault. Thus, under no-fault the dependents of the victim are not penalized economically because of the fault of the breadwinner, as in the case of tort.

2. The victim is paid on time as losses occur and the economic loss replaced is accurate in amount, neither being overpaid nor underpaid

One of the basic principles of the no-fault system is that the economic loss of the victim is paid as that loss is incurred. If part of the loss is in dispute, the undisputed portion is paid when it occurs. For example, if there is no question about the wage loss of a victim of an automobile accident to be replaced, and no question about the medical and hospital bill except for perhaps an out-patient call of $25; all would be paid but the $25 in dispute.

It is easy to see that the result would be that even the disputed amounts can readily be compromised in most cases. The payment as loss occurs gives the individual a security that is far superior to the "rolling of the dice" of the tort system. The attached chart graphically shows the contrast between tort and no-faultin payments.

3. No-fault benefits the rich and poor alike

Since the economic loss is paid as it occurs, the rich and poor are equally compensated. The real advantage to low income persons is that they are made economically whole as though they were working and do not have the terrible problem of arranging credit or sacrificing a legitimate tort claim because they immediately need rent or grocery money.

---
[9] Compare Cheit, Injury and Recovery in the Course of Employment, p. 299.

4. Rehabilitation is encouraged

No-fault systems provide not only for medical benefits but also for both medical and economic rehabilitation. The individual who was living in hopes of a tort settlement and psychologically blocked from economic rehabilitation, is now encouraged to take the medical and training steps necessary for economic rehabilitation, knowing that he will benefit and in no way be penalized by his emphasis on the positive re-entry into the labor market and working force. The victim can concentrate on rehabilitation instead of worrying about unsettled tort claims.

5. A higher percentage of the insurance premium dollar goes to the victims of accidents than prior to no-fault

As the costs of tort settlement and delays inherent therein are eliminated, it is obvious that a higher percentage of the premium dollar can go to compensate the victim. Another advantage of no-fault timely benefits of economic loss is that the pain and suffering of accident victims *is* less because they have economic security for themselves and their families rather than the uncertainty of delays in the ultimate settlement of the case.

Property Damage and No-Fault Automobile Insurance

A mandatory first-party system is needed for bodily injury to assure that individuals do not suffer the catastrophe of extended periods of unemployment and medical expense due to automobile injuries.

The situation is different for property damage, particularly vehicular property damage. While it is socially desirable and necessary to have bodily injury mandatory on a first-party basis, it is socially desirable for the individual to have a free choice as to whether or not his vehicular property should be covered on a first-party basis. An individual can freely and voluntarily make the choice as to whether or not he can afford the finite limits of the damage to his own car being totalled, whereas no individual can absorb the risk of a catastrophic accident to himself as wage earner and the medical expenses that are not only catastrophic but are not finite. Experience shows that most individuals will cover their automobiles on a first-party damage basis, having deductibles varying with the wishes of the individual.

There are many advantages to first-party voluntary property insurance for vehicular damage including the consistency of the system.

A very real advantage is that the low income person can buy insurance based on the value of his car and not have the premium established higher on the chance he might hit an expensive car, such as a $10,000 or $20,000 automobile, and be responsible for the total property damage to that car.

In these days when driving is a practical necessity for so many persons, the ability to insure a person's car based on the economic value of that particular automobile is of tremendous help to low and middle income persons. From a social viewpoint, those who can afford a $25,000 luxury car are also in a position to afford the more expensive first-party insurance on the car if they so desire.

III

No-Fault Automobile Insurance Cures More Problems Than It Creates

No system of legislation is perfect. If no-fault is compared to an ideal system, there will always be lint-picking and theoretical difficulties often called the "horrible hypotheticals."

However, if the realists—and Congressmen and state legislators in the United States are realists or they don't stay in office very long—analyze the problem, it is obvious that no-fault is a tremendous step forward over the past tort system. I do think it is important for your committee, as you doubtless already are, to be aware of the fact that any new social legislation does have critics that can legitimately find weaknesses in the system. However, the solution is not that of "throwing out the baby with the bath," but rather of adopting a realistic improvement and then making further improvements as the years go on.

I would like to call your committee's attention to two areas of social legislation that have long been accepted as so vital to our present economy. The first is unemployment compensation and the second is workman's compensation. We have a system of unemployment compensation that has been improved throughout the years, yet there are still unemployed workers who are not covered by this act. This means that often those who are in the lowest income group are not covered and when they buy products, they must help pay for the cost of unemployment insurance for other persons that is built into the purchase price of what they buy, yet they themselves are not covered. The answer to this problem is not to eliminate unemployment compensation, but to do as the Congress and the states have done over the years; namely, to expand the coverage.

I would like to cite what has happened in my own state of Michigan for medical benefits in workmen's compensation.

When Michigan's workmen's compensation law was first passed in September 1912, it provided for medical benefits and hospital care for the magnificent duration of three weeks after injury! Seven years later, in 1919, medical care was extended to the total of 90 days after injury. In 1943, twenty-four years after this extension to 90 days, medical care was provided as a matter of right to the first six months and one additional six-month period at the discretion of the department. We will not bore you will all the details of the expansion, but tell you that in 1935, thirty-six years after the passage of Michigan's original workmen's compensation law, medical benefits were for the first six months and indefinite six-month periods of extension at the discretion of the department. In 1965, forty-three years after the original passage of the original workmen's compensation law, provisions for unlimited medical and hospital benefits and vocational rehabilitation became law.

The solution to the inadequacy of medical benefits of Michigan's 1912 workmen's compensation law was to make constant legislative improvements, not eliminate the entire law because of its limitations.

You as legislators constantly face the problem of picking a specific figure that on the surface may seem arbitrary. Should there be a cap on duration or amount of benefits—medical, rehabilitation, survivor's wage loss, or replacement services? If so, what figure? If there is a maximum on monthly wage loss benefits protected by no-fault, should the maximum be $900 a month, $1,000 a month, $1,100 a month, or what? You as legislators know there is no such thing as a "free lunch" and are in the constant dilemma of balancing between the needs of a satisfactory system and trying to hold costs down to a reasonable level.

The need in legislative process to strike a line that seems arbitrary but is not is well-stated in the following quote of Justice Holmes in his minority opinion:

> When a legal distinction is determined, as no one doubts that it may be, between night and day, childhood and maturity, or any other extremes, a point has to be fixed or a line has to be drawn, or gradually picked out by successive decisions, to mark where the change takes place. Looked at by —itself without regard to the necessity behind it the line or point seems arbitrary. It might as well or nearly as well be a little more to one side or the other. But when it is seen that a line or point there must be, and that there is no mathematical or logical way of fixing it precisely, the decision of the legislature must be accepted unless we can say that it is very wide of any reasonable mark.
> *Louisville Gas Co.* v. *Coleman*, 277 U.S. 32, 41 (1928).

See also the unanimous opinion of the Michigan Supreme Court in 1968 in *Jones* v. *Bouza*:

> An important piece of legislation enacted by elected representatives of the people is seldom philosophically cohesive. The give and take of the legislative process and the divergent views of legislators dictate that almost every statute which reaches the governor's desk is brimming with compromise.
>
> It is difficult for judges to determine which words of a statute are intended by the legislature to effectuate the broad philosophy of the proponents of the measure and which words are deliberately inserted by the legislature as intended compromise of the broader purpose.
>
> That being so, judges are better advised to read it like it is—and give effect to the plain words that the legislature has used.
> —*Jones* v *Bouza*, 381 Mich 299, 302 (1968).

:V:

State action or Federal action???

Most people, I believe, including state legislators as well as members of the Congress, would prefer that the states took positive action in the field of no-fault automobile insurance, thereby eliminating any need for federal action. If the states fail to act, state minimum standards should be adopted by the Congress, with the third alternative a single, uniform federal system adopted by the Congress of the United States and administered through a federal agency.

The question of where to put the emphasis—that is, on state or federal action—often depends upon the degree of optimism of the individuals involved and not upon their ultimate objective of no-fault legislation for all fifty states.

I am aware that my good friend Harold E. Read, President of the National Conference of Commissioners on Uniform State Laws—whom I respect as a friend, an attorney, and a most dedicated president of that organization—on November 20, 1974, wrote the Honorable John E. Moss, Chairman of the Subcommittee on No-Fault Motor Vehicle Insurance, supporting UMVARA in the hope and belief that the states would act positively in this field, and indicated that federal legislation is not needed. He, as President of the NCCUSL, speaks for that organization, not I.

At one time, I believe I would as an individual have shared Mr. Read's optimism in having this matter resolved *solely* by state action. Perhaps the conviction that we need federal standards as well as state action results more from my impatience than from a sound qualitative analysis of the problem. However, with the lag in state action, I am of the personal opinion there is a legitimate necessity for the Congress to do some prodding through federal legislation to encourage and ensure that the states take more affirmative action. I am glad that Michigan, the state in which I reside, has adopted one of the, if not the, outstanding state laws in the field of no-fault. I believe those of us who have followed this subject matter are in agreement that as the states adopt various laws and learn from them, there will be constant improvement resulting from that experience. However, at this point of history, I do feel that federal standards are needed to assure more positive action by the states. Your committee and the Congress have a particular responsibility to provide no-fault to federally owned or operated vehicles that are beyond the direct control of the states.

v

Conclusion

The facts show that about half the victims of automobile accidents are not compensated at all under the conventional tort system. Even when they are compensated, they receive too little or too much to make them economically whole, and are never paid on time. Adequate no-fault systems do solve this economic problem of making persons who are victims of automobile accidents economically whole and the experience to date of states such as Michigan has shown that this is a substantial improvement over the conventional tort system; although, admittedly, additional improvements will come as experience develops.

Although I have read both H.R. 1272, introduced January 14 by Congressman Eckhardt and others, and H.R. 1900, introduced January 23, 1974 by Congressman Matsunaga, I have not made detailed comments on these bills, both because I have not studied them that thoroughly and more important because I thought it would be more helpful to your committee for me to outline some of the principles of no-fault.

I do feel that to the extent your committee keeps these basic principles in mind, you will come up with a result that will benefit all the citizens of the United States and not only protect those who are victims of automobile accidents, but also give others who are not injured the security of knowing there is a sound system available to them.

I appreciate the chance of appearing before your committee and will attempt to answer any questions you have.

BENEFITS UNDER TORT

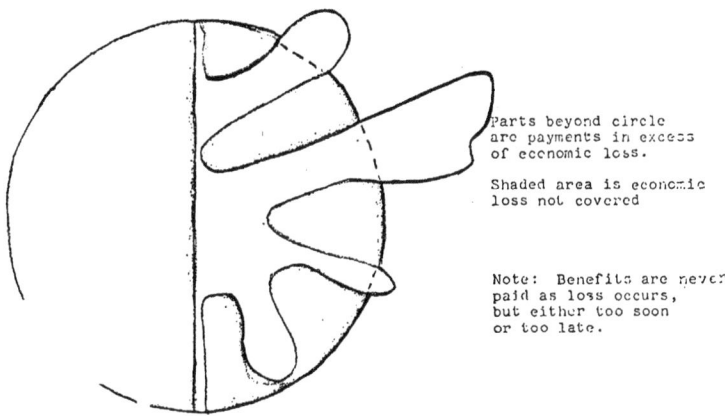

Parts beyond circle are payments in excess of economic loss.

Shaded area is economic loss not covered

Note: Benefits are never paid as loss occurs, but either too soon or too late.

BENEFITS UNDER NO-FAULT

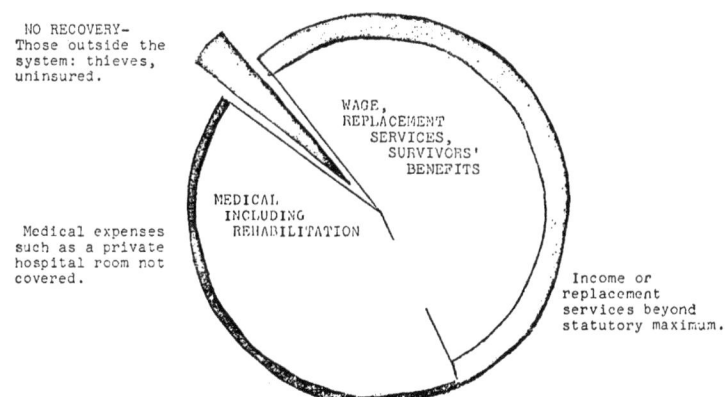

NO RECOVERY—Those outside the system: thieves, uninsured.

WAGE, REPLACEMENT SERVICES, SURVIVORS' BENEFITS

MEDICAL INCLUDING REHABILITATION

Medical expenses such as a private hospital room not covered.

Income or replacement services beyond statutory maximum.

Mr. VAN DEERLIN. You come from a State which more closely than any other has no-fault legislation which matches the standards that were set forth in the DOT study of 4 years ago. Did you play a part in bringing this law about?

Mr. DOWNS. Well, there are a lot of people who played a part. I think as you may know, this is in litigation. In fact, I am going to be one of the attorneys arguing this this Friday in our court of appeals. I am going to use the same chart and I hope it is as favorably received by our appellate court.

I will say that the Michigan House has passed—there were a lot of people participating. There were a lot of people participating. There were a lot of promises made in the process. But I think that the net result—we had about an 8-week trial on this. We had our Michigan constitution which provides that the legislature can refer constitutional questions to the Supreme Court. Three aspects the Supreme Court found were constitutional and left other questions up to the regular judicial process.

I think one of the main things that came out in the trial and the evidence, Mr. Chairman, is the fact that payments are made timely. While the law had not been in effect a long time, the witnesses from insurance companies and carriers were making payments timely and again it showed that those started the first payment within a matter of days after an injury was reported. I feel that that timeliness of payment is one of the best things and it does help the victim. It helps him psychologically and if you ask me the one significant advantage, probably I would say that was it.

Mr. Van Deerlin. Would it be too complicated an area to ask on what constitutional baisis the law is being challenged?

Mr. Downs. Well, I would say that those who are fully against it are challenging it on every constitutional basis that they can conceive, which is part of the adversary process. Others are challenging the part for vehicular damage put not the personal injury. The trial court that held this found the bodily injury part constitutional, but not the vehicular damage.

We had litigation. We had one of our trial courts, I believe there were five judges en banc. We had a very technical question that a pedestrian in one case might be in a different position from the pedestrian in another and that court unanimously held that such a classification was reasonable and constitutional.

There are very real problems in classification whenever you set up any kind of legislation. Now, that also will probably be appealed, but the act is in effect and this is very important, Mr. Chairman, that while this litigation is going on, it is in effect and any question as to the constitutionality or lack of it has been stayed until there will probably be a final decision by our State supreme court.

Mr. Van Deerlin. Could you provide an informed estimate of how soon we might have a final determination on that?

Mr. Downs. That one I hesitate to. Whenever I predict what courts will do, I seem to guess wrong, Mr. Chairman. I can say that the briefs are all in the court of appeals and it is about 3 feet or a good bushel basket. Oral arguments will be this Friday and then on this complex a question my guess is that the court of appeals, which is a three-man court in our State, will take time to review it and in all probability it would then be an appeal to the State supreme court which would take additional time.

There are also individual cases, such as the one I mentioned decided en banc which may also go up to the Supreme Court and there may ultimately be some kind of consolidation. I certainly can't speak for the court or the parties on it, but in the meantime, the act is functional.

Mr. Van Deerlin. Mr. McCollister?

Mr. McCollister. You are a very effective witness and I congratulate you not only on the brevity, but the incisiveness of your testimony. How I wish that even a small percentage of the witnesses who appear before us as well as you did.

Mr. DOWNS. Thank you.

Mr. MCCOLLISTER. You have some considerable experience not only in Michigan but as a result of your being Chairman of the National Conference of Commissioners on Uniform State Laws. How did you happen to set a tort threshold on general damages of $5,000 or how did Michigan?

Mr. DOWNS. Michigan, and I think I can quote it, is "death, permanent injury or serious impairment of bodily functions" and probably the key language is "serious impairment of bodily functions."

The point was made in some parts of Michigan the medical expenses are greater than in other parts and finally the person who had as much as anybody to do with it was the Speaker of the House who said what the real problem is and the parties pretty much said, well, we don't want these small claims in that really cost a lot, but we don't want to preclude the serious situations and out of these and other conversations came the idea of serious impairment of bodily functions.

Mr. MCCOLLISTER. There are some quite wide differences, are there not, in how other States have set that threshold?

Mr. DOWNS. Yes, there is a considerable difference. Some of them have used an amount of medical expenses. One proposal was to take so many days off work from your regular occupation. I think this was one of the questions our State supreme court addressed itself to.

Mr. MCCOLLISTER. My point, Mr. Downs, is that although perhaps Michigan is well satisfied with that $5,000 threshold for noneconomic damages, other States have resolved it differently and it seems to me this argues convincingly for non-Federal action to allow the States time to enact their own laws and to generate their own experience and to develop the body of experience on this whole question. You evidently feel differently.

Mr. DOWNS. The UMVARA set a much higher threshold. I think the lower threshold, the more tort claims will be paid out and the higher the cost and this gets down to a legislative policy decision.

My own feeling is that in order to hold the cost down and the benefits up for the economic loss—and Professor Keeton testified in our court and said the more we hold down the tort, the greater can be the economic benefits without increasing costs.

Mr. MCCOLLISTER. Doesn't that argue for letting States develop their own initiatives on this?

Mr. DOWNS. The argument here is how much initiative do you want from the States and how much standards and I think that as time goes on, my own feeling is that if there is a minimum standard then the States will accept up to and beyond that and I guess what I would not want to see is for us to quibble over should it be $1,000 a month wage loss, $1,100, $900, or $1,200 and get so bound up with the minutiae we forget we are trying to solve the basic problem and so forth.

Mr. MCCOLLISTER. Except that $1,000 a month in New York City has one meaning and $1,000 a month in Nebraska has a different meaning; doesn't it?

Mr. DOWNS. Well, I think there is where the concept of a minimum and if New York State wants to go above that, that is a decision for them to make. What the reasonable minimum is, is basically, I believe, a legislative matter.

Mr. McCollister. I know it is, but the question is, is it a federally legislated matter or is it a State legislated matter?

Mr. Downs. If you leave the benefits solely up to the States I am agreed we would not have effective no-fault legislation. I think we need some kind of standard and I think there is a tendency to confuse the standards of living with the costs of living. While it is true some items cost more in urban areas, it is also true that there are some items that cost less in rural areas.

Mr. McCollister. Are you familiar with the Massachusetts law?

Mr. Downs. Let's say I have discussed it. I do not claim to be an authority on it.

Mr. McCollister. Have you discussed it or do you know enough about it to know whether or not it could be applicable in Michigan?

Mr. Downs. I would say they have many appropriate parts. I would say if the Michigan legislature adopts the law we have and if this does not quite come up to the Federal standards of some of the bills, I would think that Michigan could catch up to any Federal standards that were set.

Mr. McCollister. On the subject of unlimited reparation of medical damages, doesn't this place a considerable drain on insurance companies to be able to cost it out?

Mr. Downs. I couldn't agree with you more. In fact, I remember one of the UMVARA meetings of several years ago. Then medical costs were about $40 or $50 a day and one of the persons said the day will come when hospital costs will be $100 a day.

Then if we get into the catastrophic, if you put a maximum on it, how is that to be picked up, by social security, welfare, some other system? I think we agree at least in the United States we don't want people to die for lack of medical care.

Mr. McCollister. Is the retained tort liability for noninsured vehicles meant as an incentive for motorists to self-insure?

Mr. Downs. Are you talking about the Minnesota law?

Mr. McCollister. Yes.

Mr. Downs. If the person tried to beat the system and not insure, that is considered one of the incentives. I am not sure if it is a very good incentive. My own philosophy is the punitive approach isn't particularly productive. In UMVARA, as I recall, we had a system whereby there would be some kind of penalty and I think that refers to the red part of the chart. How much of a penalty do you want to put on the person that is not in the system.

Mr. McCollister. Finally, in previous Congresses, on the subject of commercial vehicle coverage, it was felt that under a no-fault system this would be a windfall to those people insured on a commercial vehicle in that there is such a greater risk. How would you react to that?

Mr. Downs. I would react to it several ways. I think in one sense the function—what type of vehicles do you mean?

Mr. McCollister. Taxicabs, trucks, any commercial vehicle that is on the street a lot.

Mr. Downs. I would say particularly the large truck rates would probably go down. You can argue that the Public Service Commission or ICC should then reduce their rates. The other process Professor

Keeton had was to put in a rate factor for the propensity to damage which would mean the car that had all the safety devices and air bags and bumpers and things like that would have a lower basic rate than say, the Mack truck, for example.

Now that too is a legislative matter. Some of these things can get sophisticated so it is more practical to use a broad brush. Michigan did not make these exceptions for the truck or the vehicle like that and I think it is the kind of thing the legislature might look at to take additional action on.

Mr. McCOLLISTER. Thank you, Mr. Downs.

Mr. VAN DEERLIN. Counsel?

Mr. KINZLER. Mr. Downs, Mr. McCollister has raised a rather obvious and basic question here. Should there be a Federal plan or Federal standards plan or should we follow a State approach. You have said you support Federal standards.

I was wondering if you would talk a little more specifically as to the question of why you would pick the Federal standards approach. Are the standards in H.R. 1900 minimum or maximum standards, that is, are they really minimums for Nebraska as well as New York?

Mr. DOWNS. Yes. I think one thing we tend to confuse is the whole rating system which is a complex problem whether it is no-fault or fault.

For example, the argument is made that in some areas the medical costs are less because the protection is less. Now, if that is true, the rating in turn should provide lower premiums. I think as far as the wage part goes, if we pick some ceiling, then the rating should relate to that. For example, the question was asked about the retiree, the person who is on a pension or social security that has no wage loss at risk should pay a lower rate than the person making $1,000 a month or more.

So I think rating, once set at, say, $1,000, then rating will take care of that and if you are in a State where there is a high number of people on social security and pensions who do not have any wages at risk, they would pay a lower rate. If you are in an area where there is a very young population all in comparatively high-wage jobs, then they would pay a higher rate, because there is a bigger risk.

Mr. KINZLER. That could also relate to the question of whether the present system discriminates against the poor. You have argued in your statement that it does. Would this also be the case with respect to the premiums because of the risks that you have to insure against under the tort system?

Mr. DOWNS. I would say categorically one of the terrible things that any attorney that is trying to settle a case; to give the example, you tell a client here is a good $100,000 claim. You can get $60,000 today or if we take it through court you mey get $100,000 2 or 3 years from now and if that victim is under economic pressure as many are, he is forced to settle for a smaller amount. So I think that is one of the real evils for the poor.

I think on the first party property coverage we didn't come into, I think there too, the person who has a $500 car to get to work, if he only needs to have the risk of that $500 car it is much fairer than the tort system where he as a practical matter needed insurance on the chance he might hit a $5,000, $10,000, or $15,000 car.

So I would say that basically with a good rating system one of the real advantages of no-fault is to assist the low-income group but it does not solve all the problems of poverty and should not be expected to.

Mr. KINZLER. I must say you anticipated my next question but let me pursue it a little bit further. One of the arguments raised with respect to having compulsory first party insurance for bodily injury but not for property damage is that you lose out on those small claims. The man who does not carry collision insurance and suffers a very small economic loss may have a claim that is not worth pursuing, certainly through litigation, absent a decent small claims courts.

You are suggesting here that what might happen is, for example, if a man is paying $50 for collision insurance on a car that is worth $500, he is insuring to protect himself against the possibility of hitting a $10,000 or $12,000 car whereas if we go to a no-fault system, he would only have to protect himself to the extent of the $500 and this might reduce his premium by some significant amount.

Mr. DOWNS. If it is a first party system the person either takes the risk or insures the value of his own car. As a practical matter, in most cases he will have it. He is buying the car on credit from a bank or credit union or some financial institution that requires him to have the insurance on that.

But the car is worth, say, $500 or $1,000. Obviously, the premium is less than if it is $10,000 or $15,000. We have had in Michigan, let's call it the uninsured motorist where the person pays into a State fund $50 and then he has insurance but in reality he doesn't.

Mr. KINZLER. You have described in your testimony the difficulties with the single car accident for which there is no recovery and you have talked about innocent parties in a single car accident. I wonder if you could expand on that a little bit.

Mr. DOWNS. I think as we look at the conception here, we are trying to make the person economically whole and let's use the horrible example: I haven't heard anything about drinking. That usually crops up. But here a wage-earner, man or woman, drinks too much, the car goes off the road; there is no way to collect because you can't say there was a bad architectural design of the road. The person can't collect under a tort system. The ones who are really suffering are the family and children and that, to my way of thinking, is not any sense of economic justice.

If we were to say the person should have his drivers license taken away or restricted, that is another matter, but the conception of no-fault is to make the person and his or her dependents economically whole, not to act in a judgmental or punitive fashion.

Mr. VAN DEERLIN. Ms. Nord?

Ms. NORD. Mr. Chairman. Mr. Downs, Mr. McCollister has some concern about how a national no-fault plan will impact on the smaller insurance companies. Could you tell us what the experience in Michigan has been?

Mr. DOWNS. Yes. I represent, one of my clients is one of the small insurance companies I am representing in this case. I would be pleasantly surprised if we do 3 or 4 percent of the business in the State—not that much; and we have been strong supporters, the president has, of no-fault.

I think the problem that was touched upon is the larger ceilings must be insured by small companies, why can't some of that risk be reinsured by larger companies, and I think the social policy is do you set something to meet the needs of people or the needs of the people that are trying to serve the people.

I think on that social question, we have to come out and say the catastrophic needs of people are greater than the convenience of particular companies. So really Michigan will probably need more experience before we can categorically answer and I think that is something that needs to be raised.

I think we should have good insurance laws to see that if an insurance company needs to reinsure, that there is regulation to see that that reinsurance rate is fair and reasonable. So I think that some of these problems can be solved equitably through our whole insurance regulation system.

Ms. NORD. Is any data available to determine what has been happening to reinsurance costs in Michigan?

Mr. DOWNS. In Michigan, I don't have any facts. It may be that the Insurance Commissioner would have that and you should, I am sure, direct the question to him or I would be glad to call you.

Ms. NORD. You have been very much involved in the State no-fault plans. Why do you think the States have been so very slow in moving in this area?

Mr. DOWNS. Oh, there are a lot of factors. I suppose one thing actually is change. My guess is that if we had had a no-fault system where we would get moralistic and punish those wrongdoing and shift over to that, many of the people who don't want to shift from fault to no-fault would now want to shift from no-fault to fault.

That is purely conjecture. I think as some have said, the State legislatures have very serious problems on unemployment, inflation, education, and many other matters and I suppose don't trouble trouble if trouble troubles you. Each thinks someone else may have an accident and he won't and why not take care of other things. So I think there are a lot of factors. I think we are getting into the psychology of legislators and I think the Congress is much better able to answer than than I am.

Ms. NORD. Do I understand you correctly in saying that you think a national plan is necessary because the States have been so slow to move, or do you think we should have a national uniform system such as that envisioned by Mr. Eckhardt's bill?

Mr. DOWNS. I would like to say a national Federal standard. Certainly it would be possible theoretically to have a single national system administered from Washington, but I think there is some value in our Federal/State system to have the Federal standards and then have the States administer them.

I think our whole point, therefore, is State regulation of insurance and the premiums and speaking for our own system, I believe many States have had various satisfactory insurance departments, so I would say at this point in time I think a few years ago I might have said let's just leave it up to the States. But I think with the slowness of the States, the Federal standards would be the next desirable step.

Mr. VAN DEERLIN. Thank you, Mr. Downs. We appreciate your testimony and that concludes the hearing for today. I am hopeful that despite the convening of the full committee tomorrow afternoon that it will be possible to hold our subcommittee hearing as planned. On that pious hope, I will adjourn the first day's hearing.

Mr. DOWNS. Thank you, Mr. Chairman.

[Whereupon, at 4:45 p.m., the subcommittee adjourned, to reconvene at 2:30 p.m., Wednesday, June 18, 1975.]

NO-FAULT MOTOR VEHICLE INSURANCE

THURSDAY, JUNE 19, 1975

House of Representatives,
Subcommittee on Consumer Protection and Finance,
Committee on Interstate and Foreign Commerce,
Washington, D.C.

The subcommittee met at 2:30 p.m., pursuant to notice, in room 2322, Rayburn House Office Building, Hon. Lionel Van Deerlin, chairman, presiding.

Mr. Van Deerlin. Our first witness on H.R. 1272 by Mr. Eckhardt and H.R. 1900 by Mr. Matsunaga is Mr. Craig Spangenberg, of Cleveland, Ohio.

Mr. Spangenberg is one of the most widely listened to authorities on one side of this subject and we are very happy to welcome him before the subcommittee.

Mr. Spangenberg, I understand you have no prepared statement.

STATEMENT OF CRAIG SPANGENBERG, ESQ., CLEVELAND, OHIO

Mr. Spangenberg. Chairman Van Deerlin, I am delighted to be here and meet with your committee and to receive the opportunity from you to discuss background concepts that will guide your thinking. I would not wish to appear as a proponent or opponent of anything today. I am simply an advocate of the proposition that whatever you do, you ought to do for the right reason, and if you are going to do it for the right reason you have to know what the background factors are and what the reasons are.

My competence in the general field of automobile reparations is that I have served since 1967 as the chairman of the Auto Reparations Committee for the Association of Trial Lawyers of America. I served throughout the term of the Department of Transportation's study on automobile accidents and their consequences as a member of the Legal Advisory Committee.

I served also on the Legal Advisory Committee of the Commission on Uniform State Laws, a special committee on automobile accident reparations commonly known, because the other title is so long, as UMVARA.

My background is as a trial lawyer. I have been that for 37 years. I have served as dean of the International Academy of Trial Lawyers and president of the International Society of Barristers.

As it happens, I have participated in one international conference on no-fault. I wish I could transfer to you automatically all I know and go home. My task would be over.

Let us start with a history of the tort action and what tort is because that word, itself, is not generally understood. I suppose a simple explanation of tort is that it consists of a wrongful invasion of another's rights. Slander is a tort. Assault is a tort. Negligent driving of an automobile is a tort. The term is very general. Its history goes back over the centuries.

The beginning thought in English jurisprudence was that there was absolute liability on any actor for the consequence of what he did. If he acted and the result was unfavorable to another he was liable simply by reason of acting.

In the early 1600's that rule was modified with some language in an opinion saying that he would be liable for acting unless the result was utterly unavoidable. The example given was that if the soldier discharged his firearm because someone else reached over his hand and closed his finger he would not be liable. But it took that kind of completely unavoidable result in order to escape liability.

A couple of centuries later the definition had softened. He was liable unless the result was unavoidable without negligence on his part, which changed gradually in the pleading rule that he was liable if caused by negligence and the plaintiff had to prove that. Then the modification came in the 1800's, the actor was liable for negligence unless the claimant was also negligent.

In this century we see a modification of that, a growing trend that there will be a liability for negligence but the damages will be apportioned by a comparison of the negligence of the actor and the victim. The no-fault trend is a complete reversal, as I see it, of our history.

Instead of absolute liability it moves to absolute nonliability. No actor is liable for anything he does. His victim must insure himself against the consequences. That kind of proposition has not yet been tested on a mass scale to the point where we can believe that the people have really changed their fundamental natures.

The reason for liability may be of interest to you. Going back perhaps too far, the Magna Charta said that no free man could be deprived of his rights except by the judgment of his peers, which gave us jury trial and the rule of "per legem terrae," by the law of the land.

Within a century or so that had been translated to due process of law and Coke's translation of that in the 1600's was due process of the common law.

Coke defined in his writings the fundamental rights of Englishmen which were said to be the natural rights of man derived not from human institution or societal institution but just by the nature of man, the fact that he was born as a man.

I suppose John Locke should be given the most credit for the concept of natural law. But certainly a great deal of our modern jurisprudence derives from that notion that there is a natural law, that there are natural and fundamental rights.

Ten Broek, another famous writer, said the primary duty of government, indeed the reason for government, is to protect men in their natural rights by law, saying that their natural and fundamental rights cannot be stripped away without due process of law and must be accorded equal and nondiscriminatory protection.

Mr. SCHEUER. Will my colleague yield?

I suppose if you will look at the history of this Congress in the last generation there are a thousand ways in which we have amended and enlarged and in some cases narrowed common law rights of action. Are you going to suggest that the Congress does not have the right to amend common law rights of action?

Mr. SPANGENBERG. Certainly not. I will be there in 5 minutes and tell you the ways in which you can do it.

Mr. SCHEUER. Do you remember the expression, "the forms of action"?

Mr. SPANGENBERG. There is no vested interest——

Mr. SCHEUER. "The forms of action are long dead but they rule us from the grave."

Mr. SPANGENBERG. I remember that.

Mr. SCHEUER. I don't think we are going to get hung up on any implications of the common law. The question is, is there a need in this country for shortcircuiting the incredibly expensive and cumbersome and brutally unfair workings of American tort law which is clogging up the courts in solving the business of accident cases?

Excuse me, Mr. Chairman.

Mr. SPANGENBERG. I think within a few minutes I will be at your point and will answer the questions implicit in your statement.

I was not speaking of common law rights as such. I was speaking rather of what I call fundamental rights or the natural rights of man defined by Blackstone as those absolute rights which are vested in him by the immutable laws of nature, Blackstone's view and that of the founding fathers of this country being that the fundamental and principal aim of society is to protect individuals in the enjoyment of those natural and absolute rights, and I would suggest to you a test for any legislative action is whether you have enlarged or diminished fundamental and natural rights.

If your program gives more fundamental rights you will be applauded. If it is less you run counter to everything that America stands for. Blackstone, defining those rights, said they may be reduced to three primary articles, the right of personal security, the right of personal liberty, and the right of private property.

He drew no distinction between the co-equality of those three fundamental rights. The right of personal security consists of a person's legal and uninterrupted enjoyment of his life, his limbs, his body, his health, and his reputation. This is a quotation from Blackstone's commentaries. "His person," he said, "is entitled by the same natural right to security from corporal insults or menaces, assaults, beating, and wounding."

If that be so, and I submit it is, it makes no difference whether the beating or wounding comes from a stick or gun or automobile or being trampled by a horse. The fundamental right is that your body is secure.

In the line of natural rights I think there are two authors who stated them perhaps in a stilted and old fashioned way but still in a very delightful way—I would like to take a short quote from each of them— one is Puffendorf, the author of the Laws of Nature. From book three he said, "In the series of absolute duties, or such as oblige all men antecedently to any human institution, this seems with justice to challenge the first and noblest place, that no man hurt another." He is not saying because Congress said so. His view is that you are born with this fundamental right. "And in case of any hurt or damage done by him, he fail not to make reparation. This duty is the widest of all in its extent." I suspect all Americans really believe in that, that they do have a right not to be injured by another.

Rutherforth in his "Institutes of Natural Law' said it a little differently but this is the basic argument for a tort reparation system.

As the law of nature forbids us to hurt any man, it cannot allow any act of ours, whereby another is hurt, to stand good, or to obtain any effect. But the law, if it does not allow the act to stand good, or to obtain any effect, must, after we have done it, require us to undo it again. The only way of undoing it again, or of preventing the effect of it, that is, the only way of satisfying the law, is to * * * make reparation for the damages which such person has sustained. The same law, therefore, which guards a man from being hurt, by requiring others not to hurt him, gives him a demand upon them when they have done him any hurt to undo it again, or gives him a right to demand reparation of damages.

Pausing there, indeed it is true that legislatures have changed some of the common law rights. The field of workman's compensation is cited as a major example. The committee should be aware that the State which passed upon a workman's compensation law in the first instance had it declared unconstitutional. Ohio has one because the Constitution of Ohio was amended. New York has one because the Constitution of New York was amended. This is the history throughout the United States except for the States that walked around it by saying it can be done in a voluntary way in those States.

When the workman is employed he signs a form of contract that he elects to be bound by the workman's compensation law. It is not a simple matter of saying that legislatures can change rights. The constitutional cases on that point are that there is no vested interest in any rule of the common law but the law, itself, as a rule of conduct may be changed at the will of the legislature unless prevented by constitutional limitation.

So, in *New York Central* v. *White*, in which it was determined that a workman's compensation law made constitutional by the amendment of the State Constitution would not offend the Federal Constitution the court said that negligence is merely the disregard of some duty imposed by law and the nature and extent of the duty may be modified by legislation with according change in the test of negligence.

Note they didn't say you can take away a cause of action for negligence. They said you may change the duty and between employer and employee the duty was changed by the Workman's Compensation Act.

Now, if that test be followed it is simple to have a completely constitutional no-fault. Simply abolish the traffic code. If it is lawful to drive on the wrong side of the road then the head-on collision cannot be negligent. If it is unlawful to crash a red light then crashing it is not negligence.

But that concept of changing the duty is not what the present no-fault statutes are all about. They allow the duty to remain. They simply arrange the reparation for one who violates his duty which raises other problems.

Truax v. *Corrigan*, a U.S. Supreme Court constitutional case on this subject, said that:

> The broad decision between one's right to protection against a direct injury to one's fundamental property right by another who has no special relation to him as contrasted with the relationship to another with whom he establishes a voluntary relation under a statute is manifest upon its face.

Saying that White did-not control Truax. White was a voluntary relation between a special class but not the relation between strangers.

"We venture to say," said the court in *Truax*:

> That not in any of the cases in this court has classification of persons of sound mind and full responsibility having no special relation to each other in respect

of remedial procedure for an admitted tort been sustained. The classification must be reasonable.

Now, that brings us to the point of equal protection, or fair and reasonable exchanges in which *White* held that all duties may be modified but said further that the new remedies for new duties, if the statute takes that constitutional approach, must be a fair and reasonable exchange for the old duties and the old remedies.

On that point I hear much testimony by those who say, well, of course it is fair to take away remedies. You take away the man's right to sue but you give him in exchange an immunity from being sued. Since he cannot be sued and cannot be liable this is a fair exchange for being liable.

It sounds good on its face. If that argument should be made to you by a later witness I trust one of you will say, who is liable in the automobile field? It is only the driver. What about the half of the population that never drives? What about the children? What would they ever be liable for? What have you given them in return for taking away their right to sue? What do you give the older people who no longer drive for taking away this right to recover? What do you take away from middle age nondrivers? There is no exchange there. I don't think that a flat statement that you take away the right to recover but you give them immunity from being sued would ever pass an equal protection test. It is too equal for some and does not exist for others.

In the tort system, and here I can be brief, I think you all realize what the rule of recovery is. I will state it broadly without the refinements of comparative negligence—if the victim is innocent and he is injured by reason of breach of duty or fault or negligence of another he is entitled to full reparation.

The whole theory of the natural right was full reparation. Not half, not a quarter, but you must make him whole. Tort was really not designed as a punishment, another argument I hear. It was designed simply to make whole the innocent victim. It had no concern with the guilty victim. They did not really think of punishing him or fining him or the other propositions you hear. He was liable simply because of the need to compensate in full the innocent victim.

Now, in the modern world very few of those who are liable do compensate the innocent victim directly. They buy insurance instead. For the last half century at least most recoveries have come from insurers of the guilty drivers, though by no means all. I would say that the major cases I have had were against uninsured defenders, like General Motors and others, so big that they are bigger than any insurance company and are simply self insurers.

But for the routine driver certainly the insurance mechanism is the method used to protect himself against his liabilities.

So far as the victim is concerned, however, he by no means relies upon the tort system. A great deal of debate about no-fault centers upon the plight of the uncompensated victim as though somehow the tort system was supposed to compensate everyone.

From the background it must be obvious that it was designed only to compensate innocent victims. So that in the whole class of single-car accidents the single-car driver would not expect that somehow the tree he hits would be insured and would pay him or the underpass whose abutment he wraps his car around would somehow owe him recovery.

Single-car victims are not only not in the tort system, they are to a large extent uncounted in statistics. Nobody knows how many they are. What is known is that they are much higher in severity than the normal run of double-car collisions.

I can give you one surprising statistic. This is a solid one on deaths on the interstate highways. Fifty-four percent of all deaths on the interstate are from single car, off-the-road collisions, rollovers, and impacts with off-highway devices.

Mr. VAN DEERLIN. Noncollisions.

Mr. SPANGENBERG. Noncollisions. More than half the deaths on the Interstate System. It is probably a little less than that on the secondary systems. But death cases are a large part of the loss. So when you bring into a no-fault system the necessity for paying for all the single-car accidents you don't simply say we will bring in 30 or 40 percent more victims and therefore pay 30 or 40 percent more dollars. It is more likely to be 30 or 40 percent more victims and perhaps 50 percent more dollars because these are very, very serious injuries and deaths that are in that field.

In the two-car collision situations there is one DOT study, "Price Variability" was the beginning of the title, on what kind of collision it is that produces the serious injury. That was done by studying files of the insurance company reserved for more than $20,000. I have studied those statistics and can run them off briefly. Exactly half of them were head-on collisions on the wrong side of the road, passing on a double yellow line, passing at high speed in a fog, passing trucks on the hill, and so forth.

You would expect that, that the head-on collision between the two moving cars is the most violent. The driver on the wrong side of the road does not come into the tort system. He is one of the uncompensated victims. His injuries are likely to be very serious also. If you adopt a system in which you pay the driver of the head-on collision for his losses and do it by deducting from the normal tort recovery of the driver on the right side of the road, it hardly seems to me that you can call that system fair. That innocent victim subsidizes the cost of the driver on the wrong side. If, on the other hand, you say there is such a need to compensate everyone, that we will require everyone to insure himself, then you will do no violence to any of the constitutional principles. That is, simply requiring a first-party insurance system in which everyone must carry some level of insurance to pay his own losses is not forbidden by common law, by the Constitution, or so far as I can find by any principle ever announced by the writers on the natural law.

It follows that I have never opposed and I think most people do not oppose no-fault insurance if you define it as a system of first-party insurance similar to fire insurance, life insurance, and all the other insurances we carry.

The difficulty comes when it is said that any system which does not take away rights from the innocent victim is a phony system and a system which does pay innocent victims their full losses is unfair, to quote a favorite word of no-fault proponents.

Let me discuss that feature, first-party insurance.

It would be a mistake for any of you to believe that the tort system is the only source of recovery for the accident victim or indeed the primary source. The DOT study on Economic Consequences gives some figures that were surprising to me and I suspect will be startling to you, that all automobile accident victims in fact recover very substantially more from other first-party systems that now exist in our multisystem society than they recover from the whole tort system. The ratio is 43 percent from tort and 57 percent from other systems.

Now, that is a very substantial swing. If the witness says "the uncompensated victim," the question should be do you mean uncompensated by tort liability or totally uncompensated? How many uncompensated victims are there? Rather few. Ninety percent of everyone in the United States is covered by hospital insurance and 80 percent by some form of medical insurance and 80 percent of all employed workmen under union benefit fringe contracts which covers most of the work force or Government systems which covers another major section, 80 percent have wage continuation protection now.

It is a double system because many—well, it is a triple system, many of them also carry medical payments insurance on their own automobile. About 80 percent of all drivers who buy liability insurance buy medical payment insurance. They collect both from that and the other system.

To require no-fault insurance is to require another source of coverage and the question is whether you really need to require it and if you do require it what do you make primary and what secondary?

If time permits, I would discuss that briefly. But on the main track be advised that the majority of the recovery made today is already made from the other systems which compete in the marketplace. The public wants them, the public feels they need that much. The public decides what they will pay. The public buys it. It is not mandated except for one of the sources, social security which, of course, is mandatory. Social security now takes care of the permanently disabled victim. If the person is disabled more than 6 months he is entitled to social security disability benefits.

Mr. SCHEUER. May I ask a question?

Mr. SPANGENBERG. Certainly.

Mr. SCHEUER. Would you care to comment on the effects as you see them in no-fault insurance in those jurisdictions where it exists where it has had a track record of some years.

Mr. SPANGENBERG. I am anxious to do that. I have prepared a detailed study of statistical results. Might I ask your indulgence to defer that? I am supposed to testify later as an active proponent or opponent of bills on detailed provisions of bills in which that kind of material will be most important, but I can give you a quick answer and document it later, that the track record of no-fault in the States that have it is that it does not reduce premiums but increases cost.

It does not reduce severity. It does reduce the frequency of claim. The frequency of claim reduction, however, is matched by an increase in the average severity of the remaining claims. That should be obvious.

If you knock out half the claims but knock out the small half there is a very small reduction in total dollars because you increase the severity index.

Mr. VAN DEERLIN. How do you account for the reduction in claims?

Mr. SPANGENBERG. That is simple. If you give people first party benefits—bear in mind, over half of all claims in the tort system are settled for less than $500, for everything, economic loss, wage loss, pain, and suffering. On those cases if you just give the people their economic loss it is totally uneconomic to press further to get something for pain and suffering.

If they are paid promptly they do not make claims. Oregon is the best example of that. They passed a good benefit law with no threshold at all. They have had a 25-percent track record, proven real world experience in reduced claims.

Mr. VAN DEERLIN. Claims against the other party?

Mr. SPANGENBERG. Yes, tort lawsuits, claims against the other party.

Mr. VAN DEERLIN. Not claims against insurance companies?

Mr. SPANGENBERG. No, you are quite right. I have to be careful in spelling out things. There has been a 25-percent reduction in the number of claims under tort made in Oregon as a result of a no-threshold bill.

Let me be very general on this and document it later, please. The cost is reduced by comparing frequency, the number of claims by a policyholder after no-fault times severity, the amount of the average claim. When you knock out claims you tend to knock out small claims. The remaining claims are the large ones. Therefore the severity index goes up.

Mr. VAN DEERLIN. The ones that were not decided voluntarily?

Mr. SPANGENBERG. Yes, the frequency goes down, severity goes up. As a result the index of changes, multiplying frequency times severity, that is, suppose the number of claims went down to 50 percent, frequency index 0.5, but the average severity of the remaining claims went up and was doubled, 0.5 times 2 would be the result. There would be no change.

On that kind of index, New York with a $500 threshold resulted in a 0.9 resulting index. That is the amount you had to pay out under residual tort was reduced to 90 percent of what had been paid out under the old pure fault tort, with a $500 threshold. New Jersey got the same results with a $200 threshold. Oregon got the same result with no threshold. Florida went to a thousand dollar threshold. Their resulting index went up to 1.15. It cost 15 percent more for residual claims than it cost under the old tort system.

I would really like to elaborate upon that later. It takes a little time to explain why it comes out that way. But there is going to be no great magic in no-fault that somehow is going to just reduce premiums.

Let me touch on some of the other problems you will have when you deal with no-fault. Particularly the problem of the uncompensated victim as he is called.

The result of the DOT studies was that 98 percent of all victims had total medical expense of less than $2,000, ranging from $1 to $1,999. Only 2 percent of all victims, whether under tort system or not, ever achieved a medical expense of more than $2,000. However, these 2 percent did achieve some very high medical expenses.

I had one kid with crushed kidneys in a car accident. One crushed kidney and one damaged. The crushed one died. The damaged one failed. He had two kidney transplants, both of which were rejected and he wound up on a dialysis machine, $65,000 worth at the time the claim was settled. You can get very large medical expenses. Not for long because there are not enough dialysis machines. He was told he would be taken off and would die. That was one of the reasons for settlement, so he could buy his own machine, which we achieved for him. You can have major medical expense in rare cases, but most people do not.

Let me give you a quick summary of the general levels of economic loss. Of all victims of all automobile accidents, 96 percent suffer total loss, medical, wage, lost service, survivors benefits, everything of less than $2,500. Ninety-seven percent, less than $5,000. Ninety-eight percent, less than $10,000. The actual figure for over $10,000 is 1.8 percent. But be careful in your thinking.

I am talking numbers of victims, not amount of loss. No one really knows the amount of loss. The DOT Economic Consequences Study gave estimates. I quote these numbers because they are the only numbers I know. I know there is some deficiency in the numbers, but the numbers say that. Sixty-six percent of all losses would be in the class of losses over $10,000. Only 34 percent are in the class of losses under $10,000. Some 57 percent of all losses are sustained by those whose losses average $75,000, and that class is only a 1 percent class of all victims.

Now, the earlier promise of no-fault was that we would take care of all this loss, all losses of all victims would be paid. That was a 1968 study. The result of the study has shown that the cost would be horrendous. The handful of victims with losses of a quarter of a million dollars so destroy your cost factor that they cannot be compensated. Therefore, I don't know of any system now seriously proposed anywhere which says we will pay the losses of all victims. It says we will pay the losses in part. Eighty percent up to 1 year, up to 2 years, up to 3 years, up to $800, up to $1,000 a month up to total cap.

Every bill before you will say the same thing. Caps, limitations, percentages, prorations, trying to get the cost down. The sad result is that what is left pays for the losses already being perfectly adequately handled by the existing systems in which you require duplicate coverage, but you leave unattended the seriously injured uncompensated victim as all systems do because it costs too much to compensate him. So does social security. It pays the victim to be sure but it does not pay him what he really lost.

It gives him a fixed monthly payment, and leaves the rest of the loss uncompensated. Medical expenses are a problem, to be sure, but my own feeling is you should decide where you go on national health before you decide on auto health. Auto health is less than 5 percent of the total medical cost. Now, you are not going to do anything with the health problem by dealing with 4½ percent of it. You are not going to do much for the health insurance premium if you make the auto primary and then ask them to reduce their fee. They can't find the 4½ percent in the fee by the time they get through investigating it.

If you have a national health plan that comprehends a total problem you will then know what to do with auto legislation.

It ought to be at the catastrophic end. Most of us don't need help with the small bills.

If so, you solve the auto health problem by doing that. Bear in mind that most losses are small. One or 2 percent of the victims have great losses. You can't afford to pay the great losses anyway so you won't. There is no point in claiming how fair the no-fault system will be. It will be partly fair, but I don't think it will be nearly as fair as tort which says what we at least give the victim a right to be made whole.

On one other question, or an implicit question, that arises is whether we have to do something to unclog the courts. I know the numbers in the DOT study on litigation, but the director of the study said the system was efficient, not cost wasting but efficient. His study showed that only 1 out of 300 automobile accident victims ever got a verdict in an injury trial. The percentages reflect claims settled without a lawyer, which are about 75 percent of them; claims settled with a lawyer on a letter; then claims with suit filed and settled during preparing; claims settled when called for trial, and it finally winds up that 1 case in 300 goes to verdict which uses the court and jury system.

It is an important part, though, because the reason it is efficient is that the verdict is a standard setter. You will spend thousands of dollars for a platinum, I think it is, yardstick that you keep in an argon atmosphere in the Bureau of Standards. That is the standard. You can buy a yardstick in the hardware store for 10 cents because you have the standard.

The rare trial tells everyone what injuries in cases are worth, what the juries are doing this year. Everyone looks at it, everything else gets settled. So you wind up 299 claims by trying one. The director of the study considered that efficient and I suggest to you that it is.

If you think eliminating automobile accidents will unclog the courts, I doubt that you know the percentage of cases today that are in the courts that relate to automobiles. Surely less than 10 percent all over the country. If you eliminate half the criminal cases by a no-fault law on dope pushing, mugging, and car theft, you would do more to unclog the courts.

Mr. VAN DEERLIN. We will have some statistics on that, I am sure.

Mr. McCOLLISTER. Mr. Chairman, I suggest we go vote.

Mr. VAN DEERLIN. We will ask your indulgence for a few minutes. Thank you.

[Brief recess.]

Mr. SPANGENBERG. I will conclude briefly to allow time for questioning.

During the intermission I received a question which perhaps ought to be answered in my more formal statement to you about what is the right under the commerce power to cut across fundamental rights. Under the commerce clause if there is a compelling State interest, that is if you can show a burden on commerce you may invade fundamental rights to protect the overall right, provided it is done with a reasonable substitution of new rights for the old rights and done without arbitrary classifications.

If so, you must do as little as needs to be done. There are many cases along that line. So that you immediately raise the question, is there a compelling necessity to do anything on the national level. This goes to the heart of the question, should there be a national bill or do you let the States handle it under their State constitutional provisions, whatever they are, under their equal protection and due process clauses.

If you find a national compelling interest should you really find it, or can you invent some words that pretend it? Does that satisfy your duty to uphold the Constitution? That is a moral question, of course. Then, is the classification reasonable and nonarbitrary?

So, cases are coming down from different courts on that, New York at the trial court stage has just relied on due process and legal protection, holding it is ridiculous to say that a $500 medical expense really defines injury.

Florida had a bizarre threshold, a $1,000 medical expense plus a verbal threshold for a fracture of a weight-bearing bone. Is a skull a weight-bearing bone? Is there some difference between the skull which is nonweight bearing and your little finger which carries packages and is weight bearing? That was held unconstitutional for absurdity. The legal phrase is "arbitrary and whimsical".

There are other States now where you may recover only if you have a comminuted or compound fracture. So a splintered finger is a worse injury than a simple fracture of the surgical neck of the femur which may cripple you for life.

Although you might come under the medical threshold with a broken hip, still you might get a broken hip nailed in some localities for less than some of the medical expense thresholds I hear proposed.

So, the definitions that delve into the medical terms generally reflect legislative ignorance of what medicine is all about and what these injuries are like and the real seriousness of some soft tissue injuries, as compared to such things as comminuted or compound fractures of weightbearing bones.

But reasonableness is something you have to deal with when you get into the specifics of a particular bill. One of the things said to justify the requirement of compelling State interest are the burden on commerce. The queer thing about that is that I haven't seen anyone who can give me one instance of one fellow who didn't drive from Ohio to Pennsylvania because of something in the driving laws.

The State traffic laws are different, State tort laws are different, State death laws are different. It does not deter anybody from driving. You drive. You don't expect to be in an accident. I don't think people will drive more, or less, because you do or do not do anything about a no-fault compensation system.

Indeed, so far as compelling interest is concerned, all the insurance companies on a voluntary basis now say whatever your own State law is goes with you. I got that in the mail from my carrier with a letter saying you haven't asked for it, but here it is free. Your liability policy in Ohio, which has not yet adopted any no-fault law, now gives you the no-fault benefit of Michigan when you drive to Michigan for no additional cost. The no additional cost means that the cost impact of any loss I might have in Michigan must be so small that it is not worth calculating.

Most companies are now doing that as a voluntary measure. I don't think you have to worry about the conflicts between different State laws as a burden on commerce. Maybe you worry about whether one

State is treating its own citizens as well as another State treats its citizens, but I view that as a State matter really rather than as a national concern.

Another suggestion just made is the courts are congested but aside from New York City, which already has a no-fault law—or did until it was declared unconstitutional—and a few other major metropolitan centers court congestion simply does not exist as a result of automobile cases. No studies suggest that it has. The studies that did suggest it also said it is not a problem of the automobile, it is a problem of the urban society. The criminal docket is more than 60 percent of the court docket anyway. In the urban centers it gets to be more than that.

So that a no-fault compensation system can't be really based upon court congestion as a pretended compelling interest.

Before I conclude and go to questions, let me deal with one specific finding that I have seen in S. 354 in which the Senate at least was asked to find, and in your bill you would be asked to find that the tort liability system is a high cost, inefficient system, and you should substitute for it a low-cost and efficient system such as a particular no-fault scheme.

Now, on that I would like to let the committee members know and their staffs know that there is published every year in the United States a book called "Best's Aggregates and Averages." Every insurance company in the United States in the casualty and liability and property insurance business reports in detail its total operating expense, subclassified, its acquisition expense, its brokerage, its taxes, its underwriting profit and loss, premiums, premium earned, premiums unearned, losses incurred, and adjustment expense. Best's collates and prints that complete performance report for every company in the United States, subcategorized as to stocks, municipals, reciprocals. It gives the detail line by line: Fire, allied lines, accident and health group, accident and health nongroup, private auto liability, commercial auto liability, and so forth. It is all there.

So far as cost is concerned and efficiency is concerned, let me say that in some areas perhaps I say things that the insurance companies don't agree with, but on this one I know they will agree with me enthusiastically. Automobile liability insurance is the most efficient form of insurance in the U.S. market today for any individual buyer of any type of insurance. It is not the least efficient. It is the most. It is not the most wasteful; it is the least wasteful. Now, that is something I will document for you.

Mr. VAN DEERLIN. I was hoping you would.

Mr. SPANGENBERG. I view efficiency, as a consumer of a product, as what will I get for the price I pay. You will find that by looking at the loss incurred ratio, for the losses incurred for any line of insurance. Loss incurred means the losses they pay out.

Now the general rule of thumb for most insurance is that operating the company takes about half the premiums. Operating the company and adjusting expenses takes about half the premium. The other half goes to pay the claimants.

Let me give you the loss incurred ratio for substantially all the lines of insurance listed in Best's Aggregates and Averages. Let me say further: The rule of thumb, as many of you know who know insurance, is that a dollar of premium generates a dollar of reserve.

The insurance companies' income comes from investing the reserves and that invested income is not considered as income in insurance company reporting and is not dealt with in Best. They deal only with the statutory figure for underwriting profit and loss. The insurance company can adjust reserves, decreasing them slightly in bad years so they don't show their stockholders too small a profit or increasing them in good years so that they don't show the insurance commissioners too high a profit. There can be tailoring particularly of the "loss incurred but not reported" reserve.

So, in order to be sure of my figures, knowing that these things balance out, I have run through Best for the last 11 years and I will give you the average for the last 11 years with the assurance that they change very little from year to year.

Loss incurred ratio for automobile liability insurance, 64.1 percent. For auto physical damage, auto collision insurance, which is strictly no-fault, 59.2 percent. So they pay out more for fault liability insurance than they pay out in no-fault collision insurance. Ocean marine, 67.9.

Mr. VAN DEERLIN. Is this take-home money for the beneficiary?

Mr. SPANGENBERG. I will come to that and deal with it as a question if I can run through the list.

Ocean marine, 67.9. This is paid to the claimant; yes, it is take-home money to the claimant.

Mr. VAN DEERLIN. Does he take it home past his attorney's office?

Mr. SPANGENBERG. He may or may not. That is a separate question. I assure you I will answer it in a minute. Let us go through the list, if I may.

Most of us don't buy ocean marine, so I don't call it the most efficient you can buy because you don't buy it.

Inland marine for your outboard motor, 55.5 percent. Homeowner's multiple peril, 59.6; commercial multiple peril, 50.3 percent. Fire, 54.8. Allied lines 53.8. Miscellaneous, 51. Glass, 50.4. Nongroup accident and health 49.5. That is not group. All the individual accident and health, 49.5. Fidelity, 48.7. Burglary and theft, 47.8. Boiler and machinery, 36.2. Surety, 29.2.

In the insurance field group accident and health is a good buy because you put most of the cost on the group sponsors. 84 percent. Workmen's Compensation is group insurance in which the employer does a lot of the work. That pays 65 percent. Note that workmen's compensation pays very little more of the premium than does auto liability.

Now to your question, sir. Is this take-home pay? Tell me about the claimant. The insurance companies will tell you that you are making a lot of settlement of full policy limits with the claimant within weeks after injury when the injury is severe and liability is clear. Those claimants pay nothing to the lawyer. In order to answer your question you will have to tell me whether the claimant is one who hires a lawyer or one who does not.

There are approximately 75 percent who do not hire a lawyer but rely on availability of one as part of their threatening power, for which lawyers don't get paid. Those 75 percent take it all home. Those who do hire a lawyer do so only because if they didn't they could not get the settlement they wanted.

There is a DOT study on that which makes you proud to be a lawyer. I find I earn my keep. Their national study was that those who hire a lawyer do a little better, not much but a little better, net, after paying the lawyer's fee than those who do not hire a lawyer. But they hire a lawyer because they want to. No part of the premium is paid to the lawyer. I am never paid anything by the insurance company when I represent a client. The client pays me. He does not come to me until he has been offered a settlement and has decided to reject it. On that my own track record is good. My clients get more than they are offered. If I don't think they will, I don't take the case.

From the consumer's standpoint the ability to get a lawyer is an important part of his bargaining power. It is the only one he has. What he has left after paying a lawyer is a little more on the average than he would have had without the lawyer. He might choose to take a lower settlement and keep all of it without paying a lawyer, and without the time and trouble and effort of going to a lawyer setting up a claim.

Mr. VAN DEERLIN. Did the DOT study give us any statistics on what percentage of the total payoff did go in the plaintiff's legal fees?

Mr. SPANGENBERG. Not on any national basis. They did some estimating. Unfortunately they included the worse States in the country so the estimates are skewed.

Mr. VAN DEERLIN. Worst from what standpoint?

Mr. SPANGENBERG. Massachusetts, for example, had a crazy system in which they didn't have compulsory PD insurance but had compulsory liability insurance. After 30 years, the population got trained. If someone hit you, don't say your fender was dented, say your neck hurts. That was to get the fender paid for.

So, the Massachusetts statistics showed that Massachusetts residents have five times as many injuries per mile driven as Ohio residents. They are not really that much more fragile than Ohio residents. They were using bodily injury as a device to get fenders paid for. They showed for a hundred million miles driven, 687 injuries. Ohio showed 150-some. Sixty-seven percent of the claimants hired a lawyer. They just enjoyed their war, I guess. That is not the way we live in Ohio.

Massachusetts passed a no-fault fill and said we are going to reduce bodily injury premiums. They did, 15 percent. They increased the property damage liability premiums 38 percent which is just what you would expect if you now start paying for fenders with fender money instead of with whiplash money. The overall premium was a little higher when they were all done tailoring the rates. If you put Massachusetts statistics into how many people hire lawyers you are going to get a disturbing result. The same is true in New York in which more than 60 percent of claimants hired lawyers. If you look at the Northeast quadrant, the people are litigious. Maybe they enjoy it. It is part of this life style.

Mr. MCCOLLISTER. We think it is that way here, too.

Mr. SPANGENBERG. It is not the life style in Kansas, Utah, most other places. I don't get hired by many claimants for automobile cases. I think we have a happy system and we would like to keep it that way. We don't want to encourage setting up a system which encourages people to hire lawyers. I can't really tell you what a modern statistic is on it.

Now that Massachusetts, New York, New Jersey, and Connecticut have gone to the no-fault route I assume they have their representation by lawyers way down and perhaps pretty close to the rest of the country.

Certainly you are going to have insurance company people testifying here, State Farm, Allstate people. Tell them to run their computers through all their claims that are settled and tell you how many are settled directly by the claim adjuster and how many are settled with a lawyer. I don't want to say I will eat my hat because I don't wear one. I will do something absurd, I will roll peanuts across the room with my nose if more than 25 percent of claims are presented by lawyers in the majority of States.

Lawyers tend to be hired in the larger claims. Bear in mind all your no-fault bills provide for residual tort for the seriously injured victims. Now, those are the people who hire lawyers. They are still going to hire lawyers. They had better if they want a good recovery.

Look at your Florida figures and see how many tort claimants now hire lawyers. Their residual in Florida is 35 percent, 35 percent of the tort claims are left but the severity index is 3.3. Most of those claimants have lawyers.

So that when you talk take-home pay may I ask you, please to talk take-home pay about residual no-fault, too, and the residual damage benefits that get paid out of no-fault.

There are lawyers that are going to be there after no-fault as they were before when people needed them, just as there are lawyers in workmen's compensation cases now, and in homeowners' liability cases and in all these other insurance areas.

Lawyers come in when people need them. Any system that takes the right to have the lawyer away is a bad system for the consumer. A system that compels a consumer to hire a lawyer would be a bad system and I would be against that, too. The consumer can tell when he does and when he does not need a lawyer.

Mr. VAN DEERLIN. Mr. McCollister.

Mr. McCOLLISTER. Mr. Spangenberg, I have enjoyed your presentation very much.

Mr. SPANGENBERG. Thank you.

Mr. McCOLLISTER. The Secretary of Transportation was here the day before yesterday. He testified that the tort system is inefficient, particularly in the area of marketing and settling claims. Do you have any comment on the general cost of administering a no-fault system compared with the tort system?

Mr. SPANGENBERG. I do.

Mr. McCOLLISTER. As it relates to marketing and settling claims?

Mr. SPANGENBERG. I do. Best & Co. gives the operating expenses of all the companies and these figues I have derived from Best in anticipation of that type of question and in particular reference to the Milliman & Robertson actuarial study. This is the figure for all stocks, all mutuals, and all reciprocals in the United States private passenger and commercial auto liability.

The operating expenses classified as commissions, other acquisitions, general administrative and tax expense under the tort system averages 26 percent.

Milliman & Robertson's assumption, 24 in their list of 25 assumptions states that under the no-fault system the operating expenses of the insurance industry as a percentage of the premium dollar will remain the same.

Assumption 25 says we hope that is so, in a little different words, saying there are factors which might make it cost more and we hope the industry will resist cost increasing factors that are inherent in no-fault. So, 24 says they will cost as much and 25 says we hope so.

Mr. McCollister. How does that 26 percent operating expense of the tort system compare with no-fault?

Mr. Spangenberg. It is the same.

Mr. McCollister. They are both the same?

Mr. Spangenberg. They are both the same. Milliman & Robertson says they will be the same. The operating expense figure will be the same. The assumption is that under no-fault operating expense will be the same percentage as it is under tort and assumption 25 is that we hope that will be true, it may be more.

The next figure is loss adjusting expense. What does it cost to adjust the losses? In the Milliman & Robertson report it says residual tort should cost 25 percent of the benefits, not of the premiums. The no-fault portion of the benefits will cost 13 percent to adjust, and death cases would cost 10 percent. I really think death cases are going to cost more than that. But they have a three-way figure, three different numbers for the three classes.

The only way I can determine what the average number will be is to go through Milliman & Robertson's State-by-State analysis and tabulations which were given to the House last year and the Senate last year on what will happen after the Federal no-fault bill and see what the loss adjusting expense postulated for each State is as a percentage of the benefits. That average figure for the whole United States is 15 percent of the benefits compared to their assumption that in tort it will be 19 percent of the benefits.

Translating that to percentage of the premium dollar, however, if no-fault pays out as much of the premium dollar as tort does the cost of adjusting no-fault claims predicted will be 9½ percent of the premium.

The actual proven cost of all adjustment under the tort system is 12 percent. So, the maximum saving that can be expected if all the predictions come true will be that 2½ percent premium that might be saved if adjustment costs are reduced.

If I may, I would like to leave for the next time analysis of what has happened in the States that have proven real would experience which will show that this prediction has not worked out, that the expense remains about the same.

Mr. Van Deerlin. We have to take 10. The big issue to be resolved is whether the House comes in at 10 o'clock in the morning.

[Brief recess.]

Mr. Van Deerlin. Mr. Rinaldo has joined us, Mr. Spangenberg. He was a member of the New Jersey legislature at the time the no-fault was passed. He is a very valuable member of the subcommittee.

Mr. Spangenberg. Mr. McCollister, you asked me about administrative and marketing expenses. One of your staff has dug out for me the Milliman & Robertson study submitted to the House on H.R. 10. The assumption is the same as in the Senate committee. Assumption 24: "Administrative and marketing expenses will remain constant as a proportion of total premiums." Assumption 25: "The bill provisions tending to increase insurance company operating expenses or claim payments will not be administered so liberally as to cause appreciable premium increases."

Mr. McCOLLISTER. How will all of this affect the premium costs for consumer?

Mr. SPANGENBERG. I think it will cost more but I will come back and testify on that with some charts and documents that I think will prove it to your satisfaction. I can give you a quick example for Ohio with which I am intensely familiar.

They predicted that per 100,000 injuries fault in Ohio cost $83 million, but under no-fault it would cost $104 million.

Now, if there is just a small saving in adjustment expenses and if operating expenses are the same then the insurance company is either going to lose a lot of money or they are going to have to raise premiums. There are mathematical gimmicks that hide the increased cost.

One is that they charge as part of tort, all the medical payment coverage for the Ohio motorist. They assume every one has it, they assume it is a cost of the tort system to pay for a first party medical payment benefit system. I submit it is bad statistical reporting to include in the fault system the cost of that partial no-fault system.

Then they assume that more drivers will buy the compulsory insurance. In Ohio they assume that we had 81 percent insured and they assume there will be 94 percent insured. They assume the cost will be spread through the 13 percent additional insured so they reduce the average cost by that greater percentage of insurance buyers.

One thing I will talk about next time, and the insurance company people who testify will confirm this, I guarantee, that when you set up a compulsory system and bring in an additional 10 percent of the drivers, who do not now have insurance, you are bringing in the worse drivers on the American road, the absolute dregs of the market.

The real world experience of losses from these few drivers brought in by the compulsory program is that their loss ratios, their actual ratios, the severity ratios are worse than the assigned risk pool and they are not cost reducing but cost increasing.

Mr. McCOLLISTER. One more question and then I will yield the floor.

The bills we are considering assume that compensation for medical and work loss will occur through existing means first. How many people have health and accident insurance, social security, medicare and so forth?

Mr. SPANGENBERG. Eighty-four percent of the population over 65 has medicare and social security coverage and they are primary. However, although the bill says they are primary, bear in mind that the bill also says, in its present form at least, that for everyone else except for those covered by social security and workman's compensation the auto insurance carrier is primary. That is the bulk of it.

Mr. McCOLLISTER. Are not medical costs resulting from automobile accidents something less than 5 percent of the total?

Mr. SPANGENBERG. That includes the social security and medicare cost, too. You have a bill now in which you have a division between primary and excess but it requires the auto insurance to be primary for all except social security and workman's compensation.

Mr. McCollister. Then in comparison with the present tort system that would be a windfall for hospital savings and medical insurance companies, would it not?

Mr. Spangenberg. No. The people who have medicare benefits——

Mr. McCollister. I am referring to those with private hospital insurance.

Mr. Spangenberg. Yes, sure. It is part of the cost inducing factor which is part of a later presentation and part of the difference between Allstate figures and State Farm figures.

Let me just touch on it because you may have other witnesses you may want to ask about it. It is well known that if you set up a system of benefits that were not available before, people will use them, particularly if they are free. If you are going to have free benefits or essentially free, you can't predict the cost of those benefits by comparing them to market costs. That is why medicare costs went up three times over the estimate. They were comparing what people were buying and thinking that is what they would use.

Once it is there and they apy the premium for it through the social security cost they use it. That is one factor that tends to create more expense in medical.

The second is this. If they have a system in which you compel a man to buy medical insurance on his car but he already has Blue Cross for his family and he is in a job where he gets his medical as a fringe benefit and he gets injured, then every time he goes to the doctor and and gets a $10 bill he makes $20, he makes $30. He has already paid for all the benefits.

So, it becomes a financial gain to him to get more treatment because he is being paid double or triple. Whenever you set up that kind of system you find more utilization than probably is necessary.

Now, add to it a threshold factor which explains the horrendous Florida figures. You have to spend $1,000 in medical to have a tort suit. "But we will give you the $1,000 to spend and you can collect $1,000 from your Blue Cross" the victim is going to spend it and you will have not only a higher than anticipated number of people passing the threshold but you will have a lot more medical cost which you are feeding out to get him up to the threshold.

Mr. McCollister. Is this why the low threshold States that you referred to have had a number of court contested claims much like in our traditional system?

Mr. Spangenberg. Yes. What I said was that New Jersey which had a $2,000 threshold had reduced claims by 40 percent. Florida has reduced claims by 65 percent. But the residual claims in Florida have cost more than tort used to cost and residual claims in New Jersey cost less than tort used to cost.

So that New Jersey with a lower threshold got a better result. It is a better result because of psychological factors that are built into the human being that you can't legislate against, I don't think.

Mr. McCollister. Thank you, Mr. Chairman.
Mr. Van Deerlin. Mr. Rinaldo.
Mr. Rinaldo. I have no questions.
Mr. Van Deerlin. Majority counsel, Mr. Kinzler.
Mr. Kinzler. Mr. Spangenberg, can you give us some figures on how many people are covered by medicare, medicaid, social security?

Mr. SPANGENBERG. Yes.

Mr. KINZLER. With all of these other systems also in the marketplace, do you have any idea of exactly how much they contribute to recovery in serious accidents or nonserious accidents for that matter?

Mr. SPANGENBERG. I don't know of any statistics that really break it out that finely.

Mr. KINZLER. Let me suggest one table, table III in the Department of Transportation study.

Mr. SPANGENBERG. I am familiar with it but it is based on 1967 and I don't think it has much validity any more.

Mr. KINZLER. The table lists net reparations received and future benefits expected by dependents of deceased persons and seriously injured persons. "Seriously injured," of course, is defined as more than $500 economic damage.

Mr. SPANGENBERG. Or 3 weeks' loss of work.

Mr. KINZLER. Hospital and medical insurance pay 11 percent of benefits and social security disability pays 1 percent. If you do it for nonserious accidents nondeath, hospital and medical insurance provides 4 percent of the benefits. You don't even have social security disability there, obviously.

So they don't cover very much. Although they cover a lot of people they don't cover very much in terms of losses at the moment do they?

Mr. SPANGENBERG. That table is a percentage of the total benefits from other sources going to all automobile accident figures; is that right?

Mr. KINZLER. Right.

Mr. SPANGENBERG. Yes. The percentage from social security is a small percentage of the total although the table does not tell you what the gross dollars are but I would expect it to be a small percentage of the total because the amount of payment from social security for permanent disability is a quite modest figure as you know.

Mr. KINZLER. In fact, under medicare and medicaid there are various deductibles. It depends on how wealthy you are. There are no rehabilitation services covered by medicare nor replacement services, survivor benefits or death benefits?

Mr. SPANGENBERG. Right.

Mr. KINZLER. Let me go back for a moment to the cost figures. You indicated, or I assume we are talking about Mr. Keeton's figures, that the high return for plaintiffs' attorneys' fees based on rather litigious States.

Mr. SPANGENBERG. Mr. Keeton really didn't say what people say he said.

Mr. KINZLER. Mr. Keeton's book indicates that approximately 16 percent of the premium dollar went to plaintiffs' attorneys' fees. The same figures that in fact were found by the Senate Antitrust Committee at the time.

Mr. SPANGENBERG. They did not find it. They quoted Professor Keeton's paper delivered to the Massachusetts Legislature based on an actuarial study that I think went back to about 1961.

As I understand it it dealt chiefly with that area which he was then concerned with. I don't think it is a valid figure for the rest of the country. I don't think it is a valid figure today. But you can certainly ask the major insurers who appear before you what today's figures are.

Mr. KINZLER. Those figures also, however, included approximately 8 percent for such things as defense attorneys' fees. When you add all these figures up, they come to about 30 percent; 30 percent of those benefits are not dollar bills going to the claimant. So, they are insurance company pay-out, but they are not consumer paid-in.

Mr. SPANGENBERG. They are not consumer retention. My only argument was that if the consumer didn't have the attorney he would not get the benefits.

Mr. KINZLER. Right. Now, when the consumer with the attorney, going back again to the Department of Transportation study, suffers catastrophic losses, of $25,000 or more, that consumer receives only 30 percent of his economic loss, putting aside all noneconomic loss. How much help is that attorney to him? Thirty percent with tort, 30 percent without tort.

Mr. SPANGENBERG. That is an average figure.

Mr. KINZLER. That is correct, exactly. With some people recovering 100 or 400 percent of the loss, doesn't that bring the figure way down for the rest of the people?

Mr. SPANGENBERG. It may be. I certainly hope you don't think my clients only recover 30 percent.

Mr. KINZLER. I'm sure your clients recover a great deal more.

Mr. SPANGENBERG. It depends on who hit you. The basic problem is if you get a serious disabling horrendous injury you had better pray to God it came from an insured tractor trailer outfit on an interstate run that had a million dollar umbrella behind it. Now then you will get compensated. If you are hit by someone who has the $10,000/$20,000 minimum policy, you will get $10,000. If they predict your loss was $500,000, you will get a percentage of 2 percent of your loss which is a reflection on our insurance limits, which are a scandal if you compare them with the rest of the world. I learned that on the international conference as to what insurance limits are in the rest of the world, a hundred thousand and unlimited.

Mr. KINZLER. If we were to raise minimum insurance coverage from $10,000/$20,000, to say $100,000/$300,000, that would cost the consumers. It would cost innocent drivers as well as "negligent" drivers under the system.

Mr. SPANGENBERG. May I give a sales pitch for another idea?

If you don't have much exposure to financial loss, to wage loss, and if you have medical coverage, you probably don't need any more. But if you are exposed to substantial income loss, then you do have a high exposure. However, then you can afford more coverage.

Now, the kind of insurance I would like to see mandated as being made available is uninsured motorist coverage. I am sure you are familiar with the fact that for most States for $2 or $3 you can buy a policy that insures the uninsured motorist who hits you.

Mr. KINZLER. Up to a rather low limit.

Mr. SPANGENBERG. Up to the State minimum limit. That is all I can buy in Ohio. Three or four States in the United States have said the carrier must sell to every driver as much uninsured motorist as he carries liability. So that in my case if I carried a $300,000/$500,000 base and a $1 million umbrella I can buy another $1 million uninsured motorist coverage. It would probably cost me $10 or $15 a year and it would be a tremendous buy.

I am sure the actuaries can cost it and I am sure the companies can sell it. All I ask is that they sell it to me and post a rate where they can make a profit. But the easy way to solve that problem, for the men who might have a high loss is to let him buy uninsured motorist coverage in addition to his other first party coverage.

Mr. KINZLER. He could also solve it by a no-fault system or an add-on system.

Mr. SPANGENBERG. In the no-fault system I haven't seen one that will give me unlimited benefits and unlimited wage loss for life and you don't have a bill in front of you that will do it.

Mr. KINZLER. We do have a bill before us, in fact, H.R. 1272, Mr. Eckhardt's bill.

Mr. SPANGENBERG. Excuse me. I am still thinking S. 354.

Mr. KINZLER. Let me go through one more basic thing.

Mr. SPANGENBERG. Next time I will have cost estimates for unlimited for life.

Mr. KINZLER. Much of your discussion seems to be premised upon the guilt of certain drivers you talk about or their negligence. You talk about drivers going off the road, you talk about drivers crossing the double line.

Mr. SPANGENBERG. Yes.

Mr. KINZLER. Let us take a situation. Take a driver who runs off the road. Say he does so because he is a father who is not very used to handling two kids. He is driving on a weekend. He turns around to the back seat to quiet the kids because they are making a lot of noise. I run off the road and I hit a tree. Under the tort system I have no recovery; is that correct?

Mr. SPANGENBERG. You would not expect one, would you?

Mr. KINZLER. I just wonder what social gain there is from depriving me and those children who were doing nothing, very innocently jumping up and down in the back seat. What social benefit is gained by depriving me and those children of recovery?

Mr. SPANGENBERG. What social gain is made by making me pay for it if that is the way you drive the car?

Mr. KINZLER. You pay for it through welfare, you pay for it through social security disability.

Mr. SPANGENBERG. I am willing to do it but I did not pay it for you. Most of us carry our own insurance to insure ourselves against losses due to our own carelessness. You may justify it, but you were careless.

Mr. KINZLER. Let me give you another situation.

Mr. SPANGENBERG. I am sure you have first party coverage which you paid for. I think you had better consider the cost implications of bringing everyone under the system saying everyone who runs off the road will get paid and if he does not buy insurance he will get benefits anyhow.

Mr. KINZLER. What if you veer to the left instead of to the right and you hit another car?

Mr. SPANGENBERG. If you cross the median and hit me I would think you were a pretty careless driver.

Mr. KINZLER. What if all of a sudden I saw a child run out in the street and I crossed the median line?

Mr. SPANGENBERG. You would not be liable under tort.

Mr. KINZLER. What if I am injured? What if I hit a car under the circumstances where I swerve because of the child?

Mr. SPANGENBERG. Then you are not at fault.

Mr. KINZLER. I have $25,000 worth of injuries.

Mr. SPANGENBERG. I hope you have $25,000 worth of coverage. May I ask you, do you?

Mr. KINZLER. A lot more than that.

Mr. SPANGENBERG. Fine, then there is no problem, is there. I hear a lot of examples given. But are these real people in the real world? No.

Mr. KINZLER. Real people in the real world have $10,000/$20,000 minimum.

Mr. SPANGENBERG. Two thirds of them have more than that. Less than a third carry only the minimum. Those that carry the minimum carry it because that is about all they can afford on liability. They have lots of other sources for first party which is what we are talking about. I am saying that the tort system is designed for a very limited function and that is to give the innocent injured victim a right to full compensation for his disability, his loss of enjoyment of life, his real injury. It is a concept centuries old. It is a fundamental and natural concept. It is a concept that represents what America is all about.

You can have the third system going, and the first party system going side by side and accomplish all your social needs and still maintain a fair and just system. I do not argue against any first party system.

I have supported many first party bills. I have testified in favor of them many times, and in many places, and do here. I thoroughly believe in it. My only objection is financing the cost of it by taking away rights from innocent victims so that they get less. There I think you become unfair. If it is a good system, impose it and let the marketplace decide how much coverage people want to buy or should buy.

Mr. KINZLER. Let us take the innocent driver. Say it is 1971. I am driving on the road and a car comes across the median line, hits me, but I am about 10 percent negligent. He is 90 percent negligent. I have 10 percent contributory negligence. In 1971, in 37 States I recover nothing.

Mr. SPANGENBERG. That is right.

Mr. KINZLER. What is fair about that?

Mr. SPANGENBERG. Nothing. I am in favor of comparative insurance. I have written on it. It is a growing trend.

Mr. KINZLER. Today 32 States have comparative negligence. Comparative negligence has been around a long time.

Mr. SPANGENBERG. Is comparative negligence in any of your minimum standards under your Federal no-fault bill?

Mr. KINZLER. No.

Mr. SPANGENBERG. Why not? If you want a better system why should it not be better for residual tort liability too?

Mr. KINZLER. By my examples here I am trying to determine whether the reasonable standard really bears much relationship to reality. Should someone be penalized for what is not vicious conduct, not intentional conduct, but conduct, say, caused by inexperience, caused by a wandering mind, by things that happen to people all the time. Should we have a system that does not permit these people to recover?

Mr. SPANGENBERG. No, I don't think he should be penalized. I don't now any system that penalizes, except the criminal law systems, the drunken driving and reckless driving. That is a penalty, the criminal law. So far as the tort system is concerned, it is not thought of really as a system to penalize the other driver. It is a system only to preserve the rights of the innocent driver to give him reparation, not as a penalty but because he is entitled to it. He was innocent. He has been injured by the wrongful act of another. It is his fundamental right to get reparations.

He looks to the insurance company to get it. If the other driver carries insurance the other driver will pay higher rates for several years after his act of careless driving. So there is some financial penalty to him, but that is built into the system, and I don't question it.

Now you say is there some way to keep him from getting other benefits? I don't know of a system that keeps him from getting other benefits. If he is drunk and wraps his car around a bridge abutment, doesn't his family get the insurance? Yes, he gets Blue Cross. He gets wage continuation benefits.

Mr. KINZLER. All those first party benefits still add up to only 30 percent for catastrophic losses.

Mr. SPANGENBERG. Maybe people should have more. Who is going to pay for them is my question. When you talk about these quarter-million, and half-million dollar losses, I think in a social way I would like to see them all paid provided someone has to pay for it.

If you decide we should all pay for it, I would like to see us all pay for it equally, and not have a system that deprives the badly injured innocent man of a part of his recovery in order to subsidize it. We should all pay for it, if this is good, on a pro rata basis.

Mr. KINZLER. The present system pays 450 percent of economic losses for injuries under $500. It pays 30 percent over $25,000. If proponents of no-fault are correct, for the same amount of dollars or even less you can pay 100 percent of economic losses up to $25,000 and approximately 90 percent over that. Now we will debate the cost later, but those are the claims. We are talking about the same dollar. We are talking about eliminating the extra 350 percent at the bottom, talking about eliminating half of the plaintiff's attorney's fees, and half of the defendant's attorney's fees.

Mr. SPANGENBERG. I don't mind if you eliminate half the plaintiff's fees. I don't mind if you eliminate half the defense's fees. I know how little they are in the overall cost. I know that the operating cost, adjustment expenses includes all defense attorneys' fees. I know it will not change much after no fault.

When you talk about the savings that will come from eliminating the supposed overpayment of claims under $500 we both know from DOT studies that it is only 7 to 8 percent of the total payout of the whole industry.

Mr. KINZLER. Which is many billion dollars.

Mr. SPANGENBERG. Seven percent of the payout?

Mr. KINZLER. No; the total system is several billion dollars of payout. You are talking about 7 to 8 percent.

Mr. SPANGENBERG. Not of bodily injury liability insurance. You are too high. Let's look it up and discuss it next time.

Mr. VAN DEERLIN. We do have another witness who is waiting very patiently. We have enjoyed your testimony, Mr. Spangenberg.

Mr. SPANGENBERG. Mr. Chairman, I am sorry I have taken this time. I might say I have been rather anxious to fold up and leave and come back, myself, but I did not feel I should leave while you still had questions.

I am very thankful for the opportunity to see you. I hope I have not offended anyone here. I will be glad to come back and back up any numbers I have given you because I know they are based on sound evidentiary figures.

Thank you.

Mr. VAN DEERLIN. Our second witness will be Prof. William Cohen, from the Stanford Law School in the great State of California.

STATEMENT OF WILLIAM COHEN, PROFESSOR OF LAW, STANFORD LAW SCHOOL, STANFORD, CALIF.

Mr. COHEN. Mr. Chairman, I am not sure my credentials are as impressive as Mr. Spangenberg. I have taught tort law for 16 years at UCLA and Stanford, as well as constitutional law during that period. In the mid-1960's, I was a member of the personal injury committee of the California State Bar, which wrote a pioneering report on automobile compensation. For several years, I was coreporter draftsman for the Commissioners on Uniform State Laws, and participated in the drafting of the Uniform Motor Vehicle Accident Reparations Act.

I think I would like to start at the same point Mr. Spangenberg did, which is to remind you that whatever you do, do it for the right reasons.

I think the question is: What are the reasons that so many legislatures, including the National Legislature, have been grappling with the problem of automobile compensation? I doubt that it is because the system is working well. I suggest that if the system were working well, none of us would be here today.

Mr. Spangenberg suggested that the idea of the tort system was that innocent victims recover as a matter of right, Mr. Spangenberg called it natural right, full compensation for their injuries.

Without getting into no-fault and no-fault reforms, the system has never worked in that manner. The tort system, as Mr. Spangenberg pointed out, is primarily a 19th century development, which suggested that not all innocent victims recover full compensation for their injuries, but that innocent victims recover full compensation from other people who are at fault and cause accidents.

Why is that? Looking simply at tort liability, it is becoming increasingly clear that innocent victims, particularly the most seriously injured innocent victims, are not recovering anything like full compensation from the tort system.

What are the gaps that create that situation? There are in the tort system two kinds of gaps as the system works today. One is the solvency gap. National figures indicate that somewhere between one-fifth and one-fourth of all drivers on the road are uninsured. An abstract right to recover in tort full compensation means nothing against an insolvent and uninsured defendant.

If the ideal of the tort system itself is going to be met, we have to take steps, and this is irrespective of no-fault, we have to take steps to see that a larger percentage of those who drive will be insured.

But there is a second solvency gap which may be more serious, particularly for the seriously injured victim, which is the underinsured motorist. Even in States which have made giant strides in the percentage of insured drivers, the limit of required insurance are quite low, it may mean for the single victim the policy limits are $10,000 to $15,000, which in these days of inflation will not go very far in paying any percentage of a very serious loss.

A second series of gaps are what might be called liability gaps, some of which might be closed again with reform of the tort system. In about half of our States, there are guest statutes, which means if you are an innocent victim, injured by the negligence of your host-driver, you recover nothing because these statutes bar recovery.

Another liability gap has been the rule of contributory negligence. It provides if you are the least bit at fault, you recover nothing, even against someone who has been much more at fault.

Now, that rule has shown a remarkable tendency to change in the last few years. All of a sudden we have discovered that over half of our States have some form of comparative negligence.

Finally, and we don't know the percentages here because no one keeps statistics, there are innocent victims who are injured through no one's fault. It has never been the function of the tort system to compensate innocent victims if there are no tort feasors.

Now, no reform will compensate for those innocent victims because the whole concept of the tort system has always been that it is the responsibility not of an insurance system but of a negligent or in some way at-fault tort feasor to pay those damages.

What would happen if they made those reforms just in the tort system itself, it we really enforced compulsory insurance laws so that 98 percent of the drivers on the road had insurance, if we increased the compulsory limits, if we eliminated the guest statutes.

Mr. VAN DEERLIN. Which statute?

Mr. COHEN. The guest statutes. Those are the statutes under which you cannot sue the driver of your own car. Under the guest statutes in effect in about half the States, you recover nothing.

If we traded in the rule of contributory negligence for the rule of comparative negligence in most States, I always tell my tort classes that there is only one rule you need to remember in torts, there is no such thing as a free lunch.

It is quite clear that if you compensated everyone who is now being compensated by the system, took away none of their rights, and added on top of it compensation for persons not now being compensated, it is going to cost more.

Mr. McCOLLISTER. Except you are insuring 20 percent more motorists.

Mr. COHEN. Mr. Spangenberg pointed out that if we add that last 10 percent, and again that is the experience in the States which have compulsory insurance which does produce something like 98 percent coverage, you don't really make that last 10 percent pay the full cost of insuring themselves. There is a good chance that a compulsory insurance law even without an increase in limits will result in a general increase in cost for the other 90 percent of motorists as well.

Certainly, higher limits could have produced an increase in cost for those persons now buying a minimum policy. Eliminating the guest statute is going to provide an increment in the liability. Going to comparative negligence it is predicted will result in an increase in the premium because many persons now who set a little lower figure for fear they might get nothing at all will have a claim with a higher settlement value.

You don't need statistics to know that adding people to the rolls is going to increase total cost. It is not going to increase total cost simply for wrongdoers.

The point has been that for 75 years automobile liability insurance has been the crucial feature of the system. It has been the crucial feature not reflected specifically in any rule. Persons who have not had an accident in 50 years are paying part of the cost, and will continue to pay part of the cost of accidents caused by "faulty" drivers.

Tort benefits don't come free. In a system in which most people are insured, tort benefits are paid for by all persons who drive automobiles. At that point it seems to me that automobile insurance, particularly if you have a really efficient compulsory insurance system, begins to look very much like a tax for the privilege of driving.

Mr. McCollister. Mr. Cohen, that "tax" varies with your driving record to some extent.

Mr. Cohen. Again, having spent a year and a half drafting an automobile compensation bill I know just how complex the issue is. That would continue to be true under most no-fault plans I have seen.

In fact, the question of how premiums are computed for individual drivers, what rates substandard or premium drivers pay is an issue that is entirely separate from the issue of whether the system is a fault system or no-fault system.

One of the things I have discovered is that the system of rating drivers can be nearly identical, and the factors that go to making up the surcharges can be nearly identical whether the underlying system is tort or some form of no-fault.

I think that is an issue that is entirely distinct from the issue of whether the basic system for reparation of claims ought to be the tort system or system of first party insurance. The system by which individual drivers pay particular premiums can be quite similar.

To the extent they are different I have seen a lot of issues on which a rating system under no fault might indeed be fairer. I think some of the premium ratings that certain drivers pay now are based not so much on their accident records but on how they are likely to perform in lawsuits. Part of the surcharge for younger drivers is not just their accident records but the fact that in a lawsuit a younger driver who has been involved in injury in which an older driver has been injured is not likely to provide the kind of witness who is going to be believed.

All the studies have shown that an incredibly high percentage of drivers in two car accidents think it was the other guy who was at fault. The percentages, if all witnesses were believed, would indicate there are an enormous number of two car accidents in which both drivers were at fault, or no drivers were at fault.

I think that people who come from minority groups, and live in minority group areas pay higher premiums, which are based not only on their accident rates but how they are likely to perform as a defendant in a tort suit. To some extent the premium ratings under no fault could be a fairer approximation of how safe the driver is. The issue is entirely distinct from the issue of what the basic rule of liability ought to be.

Mr. McCollister. Thank you.

Mr. Cohen. There are two kinds of figures in this maze of figures that surround no fault that are crucial, I think. The basic figures are contained in the Department of Transportation studies. They have been confirmed by other studies.

The most startling figure is to compare people's economic loss, their out-of-pocket hard losses, with what they recover not only from the tort system but from all systems. The figures show this uncanny situation in which those with the least injury receive four and five times their economic loss. Those with the most serious injury receive the smallest percentage of their economic loss.

I don't believe that that is because as injuries increase in severity people tend to be more at fault themselves. I don't know of any figure that would indicate that.

I don't know of any set of suppositions which would match that pattern of payments, and match it with who is at fault.

It is particularly impressive when you look at the percentage of recoveries from all sources. The tort source is dependent on fault. The percentage or economic loss recovered by injured victims drops drastically as the size of injury increases.

Mr. Spangenberg suggests when you think of national health insurance that what you ought to keep foremost in your mind is the plight of those with serious catastrophic injury. I suggest the same thing is true when you start to think about automobile insurance. You have to keep foremost in mind the plight of the person who suffers catastrophic injury.

Not only our tort system but all the systems of compensation, which have grown quite complex, do a very poor job of providing full recovery simply for economic loss as the size of catastrophic injury increases. That is very bad insurance.

You wouldn't think of going out and insuring your house against fire in a way that would cover only the first third of your loss and leave the really catastrophic losses to bear yourself. If you are sensible you will come up with a system where you will bear the first $100 of loss yourself, or the first $500, or the first $1,000, depending on your financial situation, and rely on insurance to prevent you against catastrophe.

Mr. McCollister. It is more easily measured against what your maximum loss will be when your house burns down.

Mr. Cohen. That is true. There are cost problems in drafting any modification of the present tort system. That includes not only no fault but modifications in the fault system itself. I am not an actuary. I don't speak the same language. I guess I have a lawyer's arrogance to accuse the actuaries of speaking in jargon—not we lawyers, however.

The question of cost, you are right, is crucial. To a large extent the push for reforms in the system interestingly has not come from the plight of the injured victim. The group of persons who are injured in automobile accidents, the group most seriously injured, don't present any kind of visible group that we can see. The studies about them have to begin with finding them, which has in many cases proved to be not at all easy. There was no pressure from that group for legislation.

The fact is that the pressure for legislative reform has come, in terms of the cost-benefit analysis, from the cost side. The concern over rising insurance rates has initially produced the push for reform of the system. It seems to me that politically, and maybe for a number of other reasons, we can't hope to solve the problems of what is a terrible compensation system by leaving the present system with its present cost in place, and then simply piling additional cost on to take care of the other kinds of losses which are not now being compensated.

Many laws which qualify as no fault laws by the strictest definitions have been most concerned with cutting costs. The Massachusetts law does really nothing for the seriously injured victim. The compensation under Massachusetts law was $2,000 the last time I looked. The Massachusetts law was concerned with simply reducing premiums.

Mr. McCollister. Has it done that?

Mr. Cohen. It has. Premium comparisons are treacherous. First you have to ask what are you comparing on both sides, pre-inflation figure on one side with a post-inflation figure on the other side. If you are comparing no fault and tort, what kind of tort system with what kind of benefits, and with what kind of liability, and with what kind of no fault system. There are an infinite number of possibilities.

It seems to me that any reform ought to try to accomplish two things. It seems to me that there are two things that ought to be accomplished. I think any reform of the automobile compensation system ought to begin by focusing on seriously injured victims.

The cost involved in injuries to seriously injured victims does not go away. If we fail to provide adequate compensation in many cases we will provide inadequate compensation through a welfare system which is not financed by automobile premiums but is a governmental cost.

In many cases the victim bears his own catastrophic loss. He may be unable to pay for medical rehabilitative treatment which could make him an asset to society again, and his family suffers. I don't think we know the exact magnitude of the tragedy involved with the number of uncompensated people involved in the automobile compensation system today. I think that is the plight we ought to focus on.

It is clear that providing adequate compensation through automobile premium dollars for these people will cost money. The question is where does it come from? It can come from general tax revenues. I would guess that it can come from increases in the present premiums paid by people who drive automobiles, or it can come from cutting costs.

Mr. Van Deerlin. Do you reject out of hand Mr. Spangenberg's contention that the consumer gets more for his money under the tort system than he would under any other proposal?

Mr. Cohen. Mr. Spangenberg is an expert in statistics. I would like to step back from statistics for a moment. It seems clear to me that if a large number of claims that are now being administered under the fault system with people haggling about who is at fault in the accident, that is going to cost money on both sides, both on plaintiff's and defendant's side to investigate and determine who is at fault in those accidents. If there is a system where we can determine the compensation payout for large numbers of these people without trying to reconstruct what happened in that split second, months or years ago——

Mr. McCOLLISTER. Don't the figures he quoted, Best, I believe, show a very small difference?

Mr. COHEN. Again, his figures still include payout which includes the plaintiff's attorney's fees. From the insurance companies standpoint the amount they pay out is the amount of judgment in settlements.

Mr. McCOLLISTER. Except that the insurance company just pays it out to the victim.

Mr. COHEN. That is right. That is a cost of running the system. An insurance company has to compare what victims are getting for their injuries as against how many dollars of premiums are being spent.

Every study I have seen indicates that somewhere between 50 and 60 percent, my own guess is that if we get more up-to-date figures we will find it running closer to 60 percent in those States which have not enacted any no-fault reform, that out of every dollar paid for insurance premiums only about 40 percent will find itself in the pockets of injured victims.

I can't accept an explanation that the amount of money which goes to pay attorney's fees is not a cost, because that is paid by the client and not by the insurance company.

Mr. McCOLLISTER. How do you deal with this in no-fault where you have a threshold of $200 or $2,000, and where most of the big claims are those where you have an attorney?

Mr. COHEN. We will not unless you go to a pure no-fault system. There is no tort recovery at all. Eliminate attorneys. Under a pure tort system people would be well advised to have attorneys.

Mr. SCHEUER. From the point of view of society there might be a great deal to be said for that proposition. I say that as an attorney.

Mr. COHEN. As one who trains attorneys I have not come to accept yet that the first thing we ought to do is kill off the lawyers.

Mr. SCHEUER. I did not say kill them. We could rehabilitate them.

Mr. COHEN. We could train them to do something socially useful.

It is clear to me that a large chunk of attorneys' fees which are actually collected by attorneys, which represent a cost to the system, does come from attorney fees in the smaller cases. It is not true that the bulk of attorneys' income in this area comes from the large cases. The reduction in attorneys' income in Massachusetts which I have heard about have been substantial. The Massachusetts no-fault system knocks out really only the tiniest of cases, but the reduction in attorneys' income in Massachusetts has been subtantial.

Now Massachusetts is not the world, but my best guess has been that a thoroughgoing no-fault reform may result in something like a two-thirds drop in plaintiff's attorney's fees from automobile accidents. I would guess that the plaintiff's lawyers would not care as much about this issue if that were not true, or something like it were not true.

Mr. McCollister. We are not considering a complete abolition——

Mr. Cohen. I am not suggesting that. If, for example, for 97 percent of personal injury claims the issue of who was at fault in the accident can be removed, the cost of administering the system has to go down, because under the present system even for the $100 or $200 claim there has to be some preliminary investigation on the defense side as to who is likely to be at fault in the accident. That costs something. As the size of the claim goes up, even before it reaches the catastrophic levels, I suggest a significant amount of money is spent on both sides paying attention to who is at fault in a particular accident.

A simple traffic accident can be quite complex in deciding on the basis of conflicting testimony who is at fault. It costs money. There are some savings that can be achieved there. The magnitude will vary from State to State depending on how litigious the State is.

You don't need statistics to know in a large number of cases they are no longer spending expensive professional time to engage in a particular activity. It is going to result in a cost saving.

Mr. McCollister. Would you define large as a percentage of the total number of cases? I think Mr. Spangenberg said 75 percent of them were settled without any litigation.

Mr. Cohen. Mr. Spangenberg I do not recall gave us the source of that statistic, and I don't have the counter-statistic. I think you are right though, that simply eliminating any particular part of the administrative cost of the system, I assume you are going to be arguing several days as how large or how small or how trivial it is.

No one has suggested that that alone will provide the cost savings to do what has to be done to handle the plight of the seriously injured victims. If we could, by some magic way, reduce plaintiff's attorney's cost by two-thirds, and defendant's attorney's cost by two-thirds, that would not provide a large enough pool of dollars in themselves to provide compensation for those persons seriously injured. Unless we talk higher premiums, we can't pay that cost.

There is only one other place for it to come from, and that is to do what Mr. Spangenberg thinks violates Magna Carta, which is looking at the pattern of compensation, those persons with the most trivial injury are receiving four, five times their economic loss because even the smallest suit has nuisance value.

Not only that, but the percentage of people recovering in tort is higher, which suggests for a very small claim it may be easy to get some compensation well above your economic loss even if you were the one who was at fault in the accident because the cost of defending such suits exceeds the cost of payout even on an aggregate basis.

What you can do, and this probably represents the largest source of money for injured victims is to limit recovery to persons with the smaller injury to their economic loss. The money expended in paying for pain, suffering, and inconvenience for this group of people is, I think, the major source of money that could be used to pay people who have suffered the most serious loss.

I don't know where else the money is going to come from. In terms of fairness I think you have to make this comparison. What is fair? The large numbers, indeed more than a majority of those persons hurt in accidents having the least injury, recover their economic losses over, and over, and over again. Or that we try to provide some basis for compensating the most seriously injured people in automobile accidents.

Even though I have taught torts for 16 years, and spent most of my activity teaching the substantive rules of the system, I have come more and more to conclude that the system is inefficient, and it is tragically skewed in terms of where the total dollars go.

Mr. Chairman, that completes my statement.

If there are any other questions, I will be glad to try to answer them.

Mr. VAN DEERLIN. Everyone seems to agree that any no-fault system is going to offer very little saving in premiums. The benefits to be derived, of course, are in the speed of settlement.

Mr. COHEN. Mr. Chairman, you could have a system that is designed primarily for the reduction of premiums. Any system that is built on the pattern of Massachusetts is more, as I see it, a system of reducing premiums than a system for taking care of the compensation of very serious injuries. The Massachusetts system provided very little in the way of compulsory benefits.

You could design a so-called no-fault system whose major function is to reduce premiums that people who drive automobiles pay out. I think that would be the wrong way to go.

I think there is an enormous identity between the people who pay premiums and the people who are injured. I don't think the way to go about it is to look at the percentage of the population who has a driver's license. The amount of money that I pay for auto insurance is a family expense, an expense that affects my entire family including the people who do and don't drive. I think the only difference in the two groups is those people who come from auto-owning families and those people who do not.

In my part of the country there is 100 percent in one group and zero percent in the other. My guess is that except for a few areas, metropolitan areas of the country, the two groups are nearly identical. As someone who pays insurance premiums and as a potential victim, I would like to buy insurance that protects me against serious injury rather than protecting other persons for their trivial injuries.

I would like my insurance dollar and every insurance dollar of everyone else who drives to be better spent.

Mr. VAN DEERLIN. Can't you do that?

Mr. COHEN. I can do that at a substantial increase in cost. I can protect myself as an innocent victim against underinsured and uninsured motorists, against the failing memory of witnesses, and against a number of other uncertainties in the negligence case by having generous third-party coverage. I have it. A lot of people do not.

One of the unique things about the tort system is how it discriminates against the poor. The poor are the least likely to have these collateral sources or savings on which they can stand the least catastrophe in an automobile accident. In fact, these people under the tort system, have the least leverage for settlement, somebody whose car is destroyed who has immediate medical bills calling for attention.

Mr. VAN DEERLIN. He will be under pressure to settle.

Mr. COHEN. Yes.

One advantage of no-fault for those persons for whom tort recoveries are retained is that they get some immediate financial first aid even under the least generous of the bills to tide them over that period.

Mr. McCollister. Mr. Cohen, I have appreciated your testimony. I think the question before us is not whether we adopt no-fault or stay with tort. As far as I am concerned, the basic question is should there be Federal mandate for one or the other.

I think that the testimony I have heard on the variety of circumstances and the different opinions that there are on whether premium savings should be emphasized or better coverage should be emphasized, all argue in favor of allowing the States to continue their process of designing a system which they think best and letting those systems compete with one another in the attitudes of people, and argues in favor of no Federal intervention in this area.

Mr. Cohen. Mr. McCollister, I did not come prepared to discuss the issue of Federalism, but I happen to teach constitutional law. I have thought a lot about the issue of Federalism. I have also been a firm believer in the Brandeis philosophy of the States as laboratories. I think we have let the laboratory operate long enough.

Mr. McCollister. Are those 3 or 4 years really long enough?

Mr. Cohen. It is more than 4 years. It is something closer to 75. The problem did not begin 3 years ago. The problem began when the first automobile had the first automobile accident.

The tort system has operated for 75 years. The problems of the tort system have been apparent at least for 42 years. The Columbia report, which was the first attempt to think about reform of the compensation system was done in the early 1930's. So to talk about the States having had only 2 or 3 years to work on this problem I think is a misstatement.

The theory of federalism, leaving these issues to the States, has always been based on the notion of conforming local laws to local conditions. The thing that strikes me about the variety of laws that have been passed in the several States is how little they have to do with local conditions. The variations from State to State which I see, variations from California, which still operates with a 19th century tort system, to New York, cannot be explained on any local difference between those States that I know of. The variances from State to State have largely been the result of lobbying pressures by groups vitally interested in the outcome.

My preference for State legislation in the field of torts, I think, has been overcome by looking at what the results have been. The results have been that at the most only two or three States have passed laws which deal with what I consider the heart of the problem, which is the plight of the seriously injured accident victim.

My own feeling is that the laboratories have operated long enough, and have operated very poorly.

Mr. Scheuer. Would you describe the elements in that poor operation? What are the elements?

Mr. Cohen. The major element as I see it is that in only two or three States has anything been done about the plight of the seriously injured victim in automobile accidents. The Department of Transportation statistics as to what happens to those victims indicate that in a way that cannot be explained on the basis of fault or any sound insurance principle, a lot of the most tragically injured people are receiving the least dollars. That, I think, is the major problem with the present system.

Mr. SCHEUER. What percentage of all cases would these be? Would it be approximately 2 percent?

Mr. COHEN. Approximately 2 percent on the basis of the Department of Transportation statistics. They do suffer a great share of the economic loss.

Mr. SCHEUER. What percentage of the economic loss would they represent?

Mr. COHEN. I don't have that figure at my fingertips. Maybe committee counsel does.

Mr. SCHEUER. These are not fatalities. These are seriously injured.

Mr. COHEN. That is my understanding. If you put fatalities in on top of the seriously injured you have the same discrepancy.

Mr. SCHEUER. How does the tort system work vis-a-vis their estate?

Mr. COHEN. The same pattern that shows up in the other statistics. A lot of the death cases are by definition cases where there is serious economic loss, family loss of the breadwinner. To the extent that is true the percentage of compensation is still drastically below the economic loss suffered by the family.

Mr. SCHEUER. If you took the total number of injured people that come in the system, 300,000 to 400,000 a year?

Mr. COHEN. I don't have the statistics.

Mr. KINZLER. There are 450,000 seriously injured people a year.

Mr. SCHEUER. If you take that 450,000 as a basis, and take 2 percent of that, which is 9,000 or 10,000 seriously injured, and you add the 50,000 fatalities where there were gross unfairness and inequity in the remedy that these estates would enjoy, then you are talking about 65,000, you are talking about 15 percent of the population, obviously the most seriously injured 15 percent. You go from 2 to 15, it puts it in a different context.

Mr. COHEN. I agree. I think any sensible system of compensation ought to worry about those people who suffer losses that are so large that no individual can hope to provide his own protection for them in advance, particularly the poorest victim.

Mr. SCHEUER. If it is a $1,500 guy I might not like it, you might not be moved to turn heaven and earth to remedy it, but when you are talking about serious injury or death, and when you are talking about really disrupting people's lives, destroying the fabric of families, then it becomes a much more serious matter. It is a quantum jump in terms of what you are really talking about.

Mr. COHEN. The statistic that is the most disturbing is the quantum jump down in the percentage of losses covered by all sources as the losses approach the catastrophic level. That, I think, is the major problem.

I suggested to Mr. McCollister I think the States with only a few exceptions have not come close to even beginning to meet that problem. A number of States which have laws which are called no-fault laws, have benefits at such a low level that nothing is being done for the most seriously injured among them.

Mr. SCHEUER. How about Massachusetts? That is probably the granddaddy of all.

Mr. COHEN. Again, the Massachusetts system is a system of premium reduction by throwing out the pain and suffering and recoveries of the least seriously injured, giving as a tradeoff, again for the least seriously injured, some compulsory first-party benefits.

The original Massachusetts legislation, which I don't think has been made substantially more generous, provides benefits up to a maximum of $2,000. So that for the seriously injured they are still thrown back on the tort system and other systems of compensation as they are in other States.

I suppose I prefer the Massachusetts system to a pure tort system because it does provide some efficiencies which does result in premium saving to motorists, but I don't think the Massachusetts system has even addressed what I consider the most serious problem, which is the plight of the seriously injured.

Mr. SCHEUER. Is that a factor of time as well as dollars? In other words, the delay where you have a seriously injured person with all kinds of enormous hospital expenses and loss of work, and so forth. Is the time that it takes to put the case through the judicial system a serious or considerable part of the problem as well as the amount by which the ultimate recovery is less than the financial loss suffered?

Mr. COHEN. It is a serious problem. Again to the extent that people have the fewest resources the problem is the greatest. Even for someone with significant resources the fact that you have lump-sum judgments under the tort system paid out once and, predicting what the future will be, creates various kinds of discrepancies. There is a tendency not to get well. There is a tendency sometimes not to take full advantage of rehabilitation mechanisms until after the settlement is made.

Mr. MCCOLLISTER. Doesn't that same situation occur any time you have a threshold?

Mr. COHEN. The question is what kind of treshold do you use. Mr. Spangenberg suggested a number of tresholds that have been used are silly and stupid. I couldn't agree more.

During the drafting of the Uniform Motor Vehicle Accident Reparation Act we had some interesting obscene discussions in the halls as to what was a weight-bearing bone. That is silly, but that does does not make the case against no-fault.

I think the most dangerous threshold of all is the one that appears in most State bills which is the low medical threshold. Of all the thresholds that ought to be avoided in any soundly drafted bill, the one that allows you to recover or get your full ticket in the negligence lottery once there has been somewhere between $200 and $300, or $500 medical expenses or even $1,000, is terribly dangerous.

What happened in those States is that there is a tendency to inflate medical bills to get the full ticket in the negligence lottery. For that reason the Uniform Act avoided any medical payment threshold of any kind. They are attractive because unlike other thresholds which speak in judgmental terms, here you have something in firm dollars figures.

Mr. MCCOLLISTER. Can you use a treshold?

Mr. COHEN. All the other threholds are judgmental. If you start getting specific they get silly. Double comminuted fracture.

Mr. McCollister. A threshold approach may be a fatal defect for a no-fault plan.

Mr. Cohen. No; I don't think so. I think it is possible first to have a judgmental threshold, such as serious injury. True they are judgmental. I think they ought to be accompanied by another device which was contained in the Uniform Act which was to have not only a threshold which might be met, such as requiring that before you get any pain and suffering recovery you have to show serious disfigurement or serious injury. For that reason I think they ought to be accompanied by another provision which makes the first $2,000 to $5,000 of pain and suffering not compensable at all whether there is a threshold or not.

That knocks out those claims for somebody who has lost a front tooth and who claims that is serious disfigurement. He has to get over two hurdles. One is that it is serious disfigurement. He also has to convince you he has an arguable case for over $5,000 in pain and suffering. I think the first party system ought to pick up all the economic loss.

The other argument will be over pain and suffering. I think the two together do provide a viable approach to cost reduction and keeping a lot of marginal claims from invoking settlement cost under the system. No bill has been enacted that I know of that combines the two devices.

Mr. Van Deerlin. Could you help provide some language?

Mr. Cohen. The language is in the Uniform Motor Vehicle Accident Reparation Act which couples the two devices together. It was done deliberately because there is a dilemma. The thresholds that are specific are either dangerous, as the medical threshold is, or silly. The thresholds that try to describe serious injury in general terms are judgmental. They provide a basis for argument for a lost tooth.

The combination of the two in my own judgment provides a way of making it more certain that you are going to be eliminating the claims for inconvenience, pain, and suffering in the "really trivial cases," but retaining the tort system for the dignitary loss that people suffer for the loss of an arm or leg, et cetera.

I think the combination of the two is a way out of the dilemma. I wish more States had paid attention to the combination. I don't know any State no-fault bill which has done it.

The Michigan bill has thresholds which are quite similar to those in the Uniform Act, but does not have that initial $5,000 deductible that the Uniform Act does. None of the bills before you have that feature. I commend that to you as a possible way out of the problem.

Mr. Kinzler. Mr. Spangenberg suggested in his testimony that there was really no difficulty using no-fault laws when you get into other States because your State coverage would follow you everywhere. Is that what happens, or what does happen?

Mr. Cohen. Mr. Kinzler, no one knows what happens. The no-fault concept is relatively new. I know of no reported appellate decisions that deal with conflict of laws problems. I used to teach conflict of laws, and I received some correspondence from somebody who is now writing about this problem prodding me to think about it even further. The more I thought about it the more I decided that I am glad that I am teaching torts instead of conflict of laws.

You can imagine a situation in which you have a two-car accident. The two drivers of the two cars both come from no-fault States, but different no-fault States. The accident happens in a State where there is no no-fault system at all. Because you don't know where people are going to go, and what the laws in the other States are, there is a tendency to provide your own State no-fault benefits wherever you go. In other words, there is a tendency to provide, if I am a New York resident, that New York no-fault benefits follow me even in accidents outside of New York. I don't know if New York law provides that, but a number of no-fault bills do. They treat it somewhat as medical payments insurance where you get coverage nationwide for medical payments.

There is also a tendency for States with no-fault laws to insist that no-fault laws apply to all accidents that happen in their State even to out-of-staters because that is the tradeoff for eliminating the tort recovery. I confess I do not know how to solve the problem.

I have tried to think it through in terms of how sensibly you work out a structure where you can dovetail not only the tort system but the no-fault systems of the 50 different States. It is simply insoluble.

That is one problem that can only be solved on a national level. You can decide yourself whether it is important enough that it ought to be, but there is no other solution.

Two things have to be done. First, the enormous discrepancies between State laws have to be reduced. There is no way you can reconcile the policies of a State which has a straight old-fashioned 19th century tort system, and a State like New York, which has a very generous no-fault system as well as a retained tort system.

The problem is this. The State with a no-fault system wants to insist that its citizens not be liable in tort any more.

Mr. SCHEUER. The State which has a fault system insists that its citizens recover from other drivers only on the basis of fault.

Mr. COHEN. Now, if you have a State which relies mostly on no-fault for most of the compensation and a State which relies almost entirely on the tort system, there is no way to reconcile the policies of those two States.

Mr. SCHEUER. This is not a case where the Federal Government could have some kind of national program and States that are providing a little bit more assistance.

Mr. COHEN. Because no-fault is not only a system of benefits, it is a system of elimination of tort liability as well. What makes it complex is that you have to have the system dovetail, a tort system and a no-fault system.

Mr. VAN DEERLIN. And the fact that a substantial percentage of accidents, I think 20 percent of the fatalities and 17 percent of all accidents, take place in a State other than the State in which the driver is registered, suggests that in a significant number of cases this problem would arise.

Mr. COHEN. Not only that, but the problem will get more and more serious if States continue to go the way of getting more and more divergent in what their laws provide. The experience in the 3 or 4 years since pressure has been put on States to do something about no-fault has been that the laws get more and more divergent as more and more States enter the ranks. The divergences have to be reduced a great deal if there is any hope of solving the problem.

If there were no-fault laws in every State, even if the State had some room for movement in how much of the tort system should be retained, the discrepancies would get small enough you could start dealing with them by saying, OK, let us decide in advance how to handle this.

The current Senate bill which I had some part in drafting a few years ago does do a sensible thing by deciding that once you have reduced discrepancies between State laws you can come up in advance with a uniform rule of conflict of laws which is that each victim recovers compensation according to the law of the State where he lives, which would mean that a Californian hit by a taxicab in New York City would recover compensation on the basis of California law. Now the discrepancy between California and New York law is narrowed to the point where policies are not irreconcilably in conflict, both New York and California could live with that.

Mr. KINZLER. What about Mr. Spangenberg's contention that you can get some kind of binder so that when you drive from Ohio to Indiana you would be covered. Is that a low-cost item?

Mr. COHEN. I think it depends on where you live. I have a hunch if you live on the eastern seaboard the cost involved in adjoining States, which are very close, and very close driving distance, is going to be very significant. I would guess if you lived in Hawaii it would be a trivial cost.

Mr. KINZLER. Wouldn't there have to be some built-in cost that everybody shares in case you get in an accident in a tort State?

Mr. COHEN. Certainly. Assuming you have no-fault benefits it is not uncommon to provide that no-fault benefits follow you in the other States. So you might have a situation where you have no-fault benefits which have been designed primarily with the notion in mind that you would not have a tort remedy. Then you have an accident in a State which has a full tort remedy, there is no way to dovetail those systems.

Mr. SCHEUER. You are telling us that without the intervention of the Federal Government there is no way that these divergent State plans are ever going to be harmonious? In fact, you are suggesting that the divergences will grow larger.

Mr. COHEN. They seem to be.

Mr. SCHEUER. Are you telling us that there is no way even under a Federal system to harmonize a basically tort system with a basically no-fault system between the States?

Mr. COHEN. That is right.

Mr. SCHEUER. And that the Federal Government has practically no choice but to intervene and virtually eliminate, if not totally eliminate, the tort system except perhaps for the very highest reach of the accident.

Mr. COHEN. I think there are a number of choices that are still open. The various drafts of Federal bills I have seen, most of them allow a great variety of choice, but the choice no longer becomes so fundamental as the choice between an add-on plan with a $1,000 benefit, a no-fault plan like Massachusetts' which still relies on the tort system to compensate major injured parties, and New York's law which provides very generous benefits.

The divergence would be smaller than that. If the divergence is small enough you can say in advance which State law will apply. There is no way on a State-by-State basis to insure a uniform rule on conflict of laws.

I was involved in drafting a uniform act. Even in drafting a uniform act we did not start with the assumption that we would have 50 States immediately enacting the law. As a result we had to provide that a State that passed such a law would provide protection for its citizens everywhere else.

Assume a State passed the uniform act—no State has—and its citizen is injured somewhere else, he would have generous no-fault benefits under his own policy. He would also have the right to sue in tort in the State in which he had the accident if it was a tort State.

We did not know of any way in which State "A" could change the tort system of State "B". It seemed unlikely to us we would ever convince the States to come up with a reciprocal uniform approach just to handle the tort problem.

Even in cases where they don't reach the appellate courts because the law is clear, I think they are going to produce in some cases odd patterns of overcompensation and odd patterns of undercompensation, depending on how the laws of the two States fit together.

Mr. VAN DEERLIN. There has been much discussion of thresholds today. We have reached a threshold on your catching a plane at 6:30.

Mr. COHEN. I think you have passed it.

Mr. VAN DEERLIN. I see your suitcase in the back. In that case we sure do thank you. We won't hold you a bit longer. You have been most helpful. I am sorry we messed up your week so much.

Mr. COHEN. Thank you, Mr. Chairman.

Mr. VAN DEERLIN. The hearing will recess subject to the call of the Chair.

[Whereupon, at 5:57 p.m., the subcommittee adjourned to reconvene subject to the call of the Chair.]

NO-FAULT MOTOR VEHICLE INSURANCE

TUESDAY, JULY 8, 1975

House of Representatives,
Subcommittee on Consumer Protection and Finance,
Committee on Interstate and Foreign Commerce,
Washington, D.C.

The subcommittee met at 10 a.m., pursuant to notice, in room 2322, Rayburn House Office Building, Hon. Lionel Van Deerlin, chairman, presiding.

Mr. Van Deerlin. Good morning. The hearings will resume today on legislation designed to develop a Federal national no-fault insurance system, and we have this morning a panel of four witnesses of, so I am told, divergent views. They include Mr. Donald P. McHugh of State Farm Mutual Auto Insurance Company in Illinois; Ms. Kathleen O'Reilly of Consumer Federation of America; Mr. André Maisonpierre, American Mutual Insurance Alliance; and Mr. Dick L. Tottman, Nevada's Commissioner of Insurance.

I think we will take them each in order for statements of up to about 10 minutes and then we will let them bat the shuttlecock back and forth, with questions from up here If you, Mr. McHugh, will proceed we will be very pleased to hear your testimony.

STATEMENTS OF A PANEL CONSISTING OF DONALD P. McHUGH, VICE PRESIDENT AND GENERAL COUNSEL, STATE FARM MUTUAL AUTOMOBILE INSURANCE CO.; KATHLEEN F. O'REILLY, LEGISLATIVE DIRECTOR, CONSUMER FEDERATION OF AMERICA; ANDRE MAISONPIERRE, VICE PRESIDENT, AMERICAN MUTUAL INSURANCE ALLIANCE; AND DICK L. ROTTMAN, INSURANCE COMMISSIONER, STATE OF NEVADA

Mr. McHugh. Thank you, Mr. Chairman. I have a fairly lengthy statement, which I will not read. I would like to refer to portions of this and summarize it.

Mr. Van Deerlin. You have my consent and your entire statement will be included in the record and we will be glad to hear you paraphrase it for us.

Mr. McHugh. Thank you, sir.

On behalf of the State Farm Insurance Co. I would like to thank this subcommittee for the opportu ity to participate in an important and, I hope, useful discussion of no-fault auto accident reparations.

I am here today to express our strong support of Federal no-fault standards legislation, along the lines of H.R. 1900, which contains the provisions of S. 354, the bill passed by the Senate in the previous Congress and now under active consideration by the Senate after approval by the Senate Commerce Committee.

Since 1942, State Farm has been the Nation's largest automobile insurer, insuring at the present time more than 15 million automobiles and over 11 percent of the total automobile insurance market.

I think maybe I can best contribute to this panel by focusing broadly on the basic issues. The matter of Federal action on no-fault can be made to seem complex and even impenetrable. It need not be so. As I see it the problem can readily be broken down into five basic questions. These questions are:

1. Why no-fault? What are the reasons which have produced such wide and strong support for no-fault reform?

2. Why Federal no-fault? Why is Federal action required to put no-fault into effect?

3. Why a Federal standards law? That is, why should Federal legislation take the form of minimum standards for the States to follow rather than a full-scale Federal automobile insurance system?

4. Why this particular bill, H.R. 1900? Why are the concepts and formulations in that bill the best vehicles for a nationwide no-fault program?

5. Finally, how much will it cost? What is the cost impact of legislation like H.R. 1900 likely be be?

I will briefly examine each of these issues.

1. THE VALUE OF NO-FAULT REFORM

Why does State Farm want no-fault? It is the way we can give our customers, the American motoring public, what they quite legitimately demand—the best possible value for their insurance dollar. Our customers want comprehensive protection against auto accident bodily injury losses for the best possible price. We want to deliver that product.

But we can't do it without your help. While the insurance industry bears some of the responsibility for the present reparations system, our role is, in fact, merely to provide coverage for the needs imposed on the public by the legal system.

We cannot cut the waste, the delay and the simple injustice and personal tragedy without changes in the governing law.

No-fault, as contemplated under H.R. 1900, effectively plugs those compensation gaps in the fault system. It simply provides that tort suits for economic losses, and pain, and suffering be limited to cases of serious harm. For relatively less serious injuries, tort liability is abolished. In exchange, immediate and comprehensive compensation for economic losses is made mandatory for all victims.

In what we consider to be the best type of no-fault legislation, such as H.R. 1900, the concept of economic loss is expanded to include emergency medical service and rehabilitation so that their insurance coverage will help victims be restored as functioning members of society.

Our experience with no-fault plans has shown us that a no-fault plan which meets the Federal standards under H.R. 1900 will give consumers the greater value for their premium dollar they rightfully demand. We estimate that, under such a no-fault program, at least 60 percent more persons—on an average, 75 percent—will be paid compared to a pure fault system.

Claimants will receive more total benefits under such no-fault laws and about 55 percent more benefits to compensate persons for economic losses. Not only will there be more benefit payments to more claimants but payments will be received more rapidly and with considerably less friction between claimants and insurers.

All these elements add greater value to the bodily injury premium dollar.

2. WHY IS FEDERAL ACTION NEEDED ON NO-FAULT?

Like most of the insurance industry, State Farm has always sought first to achieve State action on insurance-related matters. In the case of no-fault we labored as a company long and unsuccessfully at the State level and now strongly support Federal no-fault standards for the States to follow. We have made this agonizing decision only with reluctance and only because bitter experience has convinced us that the States have not done and will not do the job which must be done.

We view it as our job to get the best products to the customer. We don't believe the States are passing the kind of laws that permit us to do it. In our judgment there is no other way to go other than to support the kind of strong Federal standards bill we are talking about here today.

When we testified before this subcommittee a little less than 1 year ago 14 States had adopted laws restricting tort liability to any degree at all. As will be noted later virtually all these laws are, in our judgment, quite inadequate. Since that time only two more States have managed to put no-fault on the books.

Indeed the very troubling reality is that no-fault activity at the State level—which, in our judgment, never proceeded at the rapid pace which many of us originally expected—has actually been slowing down. I think this is something to think about. It is rather alarming to think we were once expecting the possibility of fairly effective State action and it seems to have gone the opposite way and the pace at which States are moving is even slower than it was.

It took 37 years—from 1911 to 1948—to obtain workers' compensation statutes in all the States and many of those laws are very dissimilar. In our view it makes no sense to force Americans to wait 37 years for a program such as no-fault auto insurance, which for clear economic and humanitarian reasons is justified and needed now.

There is no reason to expect that, without Federal action, the future history of no-fault auto reparations will be any more favorable than the past history of workers' compensation. Current legislative prospects are discouraging in even such populous States, for example, as California and Illinois, where State Farm has its largest volume of business.

You might be interested in the Illinois experience. In Illinois, supporters of no-fault were dealt two crushing blows by the Illinois Legislature within the past 2 weeks. With press stories confidently predicting acceptance of a modest no-fault law, the Illinois Legislature seemed on the brink of enacting such a law.

The more substantial reform incorporated in earlier drafts had been modified and a compromise no-fault law seemed a real possibility. Then, on two separate occasions, the Illinois House emasculated these no-fault bills—one of which had passed the Senate—by completely deleting the tort threshold and substituting instead a bill that would require purchase of no-fault benefits without touching the tort system in any way. The legislature adjourned with no action on no-fault, and even this bill did not pass. The legislature met again and that bill got hung up and, despite numerous references to the favorable vote by the U.S. Senate Commerce Committee on S. 354—which occurred on the same date the Illinois House was debating no-fault—the legislature took no action on this bill at all.

Ohio is apparently following the same course. California again is deadlocked.

In short, it is no longer realistic for one to profess support for no-fault but to oppose Federal action to achieve no-fault. That position was originally our own. In 1975 it is tantamount to being for no-fault in principle but against it in practice.

3. WHY FEDERAL STANDARDS RATHER THAN A FULL-SCALE FEDERAL AUTOMOBILE INSURANCE SYSTEM?

During the past few years of generally adverse experience at the State level great improvements were made in the Federal approach to no-fault insurance by the Senate Commerce Committee. Their product, S. 354/H.R. 1900—is, in our judgment, a generally well-conceived and well-drafted Federal no-fault standards bill.

State Farm strongly supports this Federal standards approach. By preserving intact the traditional State responsibility for regulation of insurance, Federal no-fault standards promote the decentralist values inherent in our Federal system of Government while, at the same time, achieving areawide reform. This approach emphasizes the real genius of our Federal system—a cooperative working partnership between the Federal Government and the States.

In that context, Mr. Chairman, State Farm feels strongly that the scheme of the McCarran Act for continuing State regulation is preserved to the letter and intent of the bill you are considering before you today. The McCarran Act clearly contemplated Congress could, in fact, exercise general power over interstate commerce and legislate in the insurance industry and it could nullify and set aside State insurance regulatory acts if it specifically made those Federal acts applicable to insurance.

That is what H.R. 1900 does. It prescribes a system of first party no-fault reparations benefits. Therefore it is specifically an act of the law referring to the business of insurance.

But, if you will notice, throughout the balance of the bill it seems to us it is very carefully drawn in such a way as to preserve the essential reliance upon the States for the regulation of the business.

I am impressed with the most recent developments which occurred before the Senate Commerce Committee on the question of whether or not this represents an improper intrusion of the Federal Government into the State regulatory bill. The committee has been responsive to almost all of those suggestions and has gone out of its way, as it had done in the redraft, to accommodate those concerns and give the States the broadest possible latitude in enforcing whatever regulation is called for under this bill.

4. WHY H.R. 1900? FULL INSURANCE PROTECTION AND A SUBSTANTIAL RESTRICTION ON TORT LIABILITY

To endorse Federal no-fault standards is, of course, merely to beg the important question: What ought the standards be? The basic answers to this question are not, in our judgment, complex. They emerge naturally from the findings of the DOT study. I won't enumerate them but they are contained on page 15 of the statement.

But, to solve these problems, no-fault legislation has to meet two fundamental tests. First there must be meaningful benefit levels. To us this requirement means comprehensive coverage of medical and rehabilitation costs and substantial coverage of lost income.

Second, no-fault laws must restrict traditional tort liability to cases of truly serious injury—"serious and permanent injury" in the formulation used by H.R. 1900 and S. 354—or a substantial period of continuous disability.

Without a meaningful tort threshold, full no-fault protection for the serious injured victim cannot be financed—unless insurance premium levels are raised for everyone.

When measured against these standards the performance of the States is far more disappointing even than it would appear from a simple head count of the number of States which have passed some form of no-fault legislation. With only a small number of exceptions, in our judgment, State no-fault laws now on the books are sadly inadequate, incorporating minimal benefit levels and providing porous or very limited tort exemptions.

We proceed to describe the State statutes at some length, indicating limits in which we find them deficient.

I suppose the most telling criticism of the DOT report concerning our present system is the abject failure of the present system to compensate the seriously injured persons. You had before you recently Prof. William Cohen of Stanford, who testified to this committee that any reform of the automobile compensation system ought to begin by focusing on seriously injured victims. Professor Cohen observed that, in only two or three States has anything been done about the plight of the seriously injured victim.

5. THE COSTS OF FEDERAL NO-FAULT STANDARDS

The final question is: What will be the likely impact on insurance costs if a Federal standards bill such as S. 354 is enacted?

Reformers are sometimes alleged to dwell on the benefits of proposed social change while neglecting the price that will have to be paid for those benefits. As businessmen, we in the auto insurance industry do not have this luxury. We cannot afford reforms which cannot be financed. Our customers will blame us if no-fault imposes new insurance costs on them which are out of line with the benefits they receive.

We have recently completed a review of the probable cost impact on the average cost of bodily injury insurance for private passenger automobiles of H.R. 1900 on each State meeting the Federal no-fault standards established by the bill. Mr. Chairman, attached as exhibit I is a summary of the results and a discussion of our methodology. I won't go into those now but will be able to respond to any questions that members of the committee may like to ask.

But, in presenting these cost estimates, I think I should emphasize that it would be false and misleading for us to state or imply that several years from now States having no-fault laws meeting Federal standards will be receiving rate cuts equivalent to the cost reductions indicated in these tables.

Several important considerations should be kept clearly in mind. These cost estimates are based on the comparative cost of bodily-injury-type coverage. These costs are only approximately 40 percent of the total insurance cost of a typical full package of automobile insurance coverage, including property damage liability coverage, collision, and comprehensive coverage.

In addition, these cost estimates isolate only one factor that can influence cost—a change to a no-fault law which meets the Federal standards.

There are now and there will continue to be other factors which will have a substantial impact on the cost of automobile insurance under any system. These include the severe impact of inflation, particularly on crash parts prices, labor costs, medical costs, income replacement costs as wage levels rise, as well as other factors—enforcement of speed limits, availability and cost of gasoline and the size and safety features of motor vehicles and highways, all of which have a bearing upon what the price of insurance will be.

The cost savings features of no-fault can easily be offset by adverse experience resulting from these other factors or a combination of them. So it would be wrong to use this as a prediction of what the actual costs for automobile insurance will be in the future.

But we continue to regard as structurally sound the cost analysis of S. 354 by the independent actuarial firm of Milliman & Robertson. This firm was chosen by the National Association of Insurance Commissioners to devise a model for costing no-fault plans.

We agree substantially with the methodology employed. Our own estimates, although not always precisely the same as Milliman & Robertson's conclusions for various types of no-fault programs, are in most cases very close.

Some specific comments on our cost analysis might prove helpful. The Milliman & Robertson model combined insurance costs for private passenger automobiles and commercial vehicles. Our figures relate solely to private passenger motor vehicles.

We believe that H.R. 1900 as now written contains a feature which excessively benefits commercial vehicle policyholders at the expense of private passenger policyholders. This is the $5,000 deductible in section 111(a)(3) on subrogation in accidents between private passenger cars and other types of motor vehicles.

I won't dwell on the subrogation issue other than to note that at the request of the Senate committee the revised draft eliminated the $5,000 deductible and reduced it to a $100 deductible. In terms of costing the effect of this on for private passenger vehicles, our general conclusion was that, as the bill had been drafted with the $5,000 deductible—which, in substance, meant no subrogation between private passenger and commercial vehicles—this would have produced a nationwide average savings for private passenger vehicles of about 5 percent.

With the elimination of the $5,000 or reducing it to $100—which is what the committee did—that, then, produced a cost savings which doubled our estimates; it moved this nationwide average savings of 5 percent to 10 percent; and, for this reason, we very strongly urge your committee to consider taking similar action so that the principal benefits of no-fault can be passed on to private passenger vehicle owners.

At the end of our statement we detail a number of major changes which occurred in the bill dealing with the federalism issue and I won't attempt to go into them any further at this point. I will be glad to respond to questions on these changes. In general, I will say we are sympathetic to the new changes the Senate has adopted to accommodate itself to the concern about unnecessary intrusion of the Federal Government into the State regulatory process and we would commend these changes for your consideration.

In conclusion, we are firmly convinced that the time has come for enactment of a Federal no-fault standards bill. Our experience at the State level has demonstrated that Federal standards are necessary to assure that the States enact well-conceived no-fault laws. We would urge your subcommittee to act promptly in reporting favorably on such a Federal standards bill. Thank you, Mr. Chairman.

[Mr. McHugh's prepared statement follows:]

STATEMENT ON BEHALF OF STATE FARM MUTUAL AUTOMOBILE INSURANCE CO., BLOOMINGTON, ILL., BY DONALD P. MCHUGH, VICE PRESIDENT AND GENERAL COUNSEL

On behalf of the State Farm Insurance Companies, I would like to thank this Subcommittee for the opportunity to participate in an important and, I hope, useful discussion of no-fault auto accident reparations. I am here today to express our strong support for federal no-fault standards legislation, along the lines of H.R. 1900, which contains the provisions of S. 354, the bill passed by the Senate in the previous Congress and now under active consideration by the Senate after approval by the Senate Commerce Committee.

Since 1942, State Farm has been the nation's largest automobile insurer, insuring at the present time more than fifteen million automobiles and over eleven percent of the total automobile insurance market.

State Farm has vigorously worked with consumer, industry and labor groups, to achieve enactment of meaningful state no-fault laws across the country. Along with a substantial, and growing portion of our industry, State Farm has also, more recently, determined to give its full support at the national level for congressional adoption of federal no-fault standards. It is my understanding that all members of the present panel, who may represent differing views on the question of federal action, are nevertheless unanimous in their recognition of the value of the basic no-fault concept.

What I would like to share with you today, are the reasons why State Farm has come to support the particular type of no-fault embodied in H.R. 1900. In summary, it is our appraisal that, unless Congress moves to enact federal no-fault standards legislation like H.R. 1900, no-fault will prove to be an idea whose time has come—and gone—with only a fraction of its potential realized for the public whom all of us here are trying to serve.

I believe I can best contribute to this panel by focusing broadly on the basic issues. The matter of federal action on no-fault can be made to seem complex and even impenetrable. It need not be so. As I see it, the problem can readily be broken down into five basic questions. These questions are:

(1) Why no-fault? What are the reasons which have produced such wide and strong support for no-fault reform?

(2) Why federal no-fault? Why is federal action required to put no-fault into effect?

(3) Why a federal standards law? That is, why should federal legislation take the form of minimum standards for the states to follow, rather than a full-scale federal automobile insurance system?

(4) Why this particular bill, H.R. 1900? Why are the comcepts and formulations in that bill the best vehicles for a nationwide no-fault program?

(5) Finally, how much will it cost? What is the cost impact of legislation like H.R. 1900 likely to be?

I will briefly examine each of these issues.

1. THE VALUE OF NO-FAULT REFORM

Why does State Farm want no-fault? It is the way we can give our customers—the American motoring public—what they quite legitimately demand—the best possible value for their insurance dollar. Our customers want comprehensive protection against auto accident bodily injury losses for the best possible price. We want to deliver that product. But we can't do it without your help. While the insurance industry bears some of the responsibility for the present reparations system, our role is in fact merely to provide coverage for the needs imposed on the public by the legal system. We cannot cut the waste, the delay, and the simple injustice and personal tragedy, without changes in the governing law.

As the members of this Subcommittee know, national and state no-fault proposals have been actively considered for the past ten years. In early 1971, the Department of Transportation published the results of its massive, $2 million study of the auto reparations system, implemented under special legislation. That study concluded:

"In summary, the existing system ill serves the accident victim, the insuring public and society. It is inefficient, overly costly, incomplete and slow. It allocates benefits poorly, discourages rehabilitation and overburdens the courts and the legal system. Both on the record of its performance and on the logic of its operation, it does little if anything to minimize crash losses." [1]

DOT's study clearly demonstrated that under the fault system accident victims with inconsequential injuries were being seriously overpaid—more than twice the amount of economic loss was the average recovery for claimants with $500 or less in actual economic losses. It showed that seriously injured victims generally received far *less* than their losses—30 percent of economic loss was the average recovery for victims with $25,000 or more in such losses.

The root cause for these glaring injustices in the distribution of insurance dollars to accident victims was, according to the study, the tremendous expense, delay, and uncertainty incident to auto accident litigation. The potential cost of litigation gives leverage to the small "nuisance" claimant to get more than his due. The DOT study noted that the seriously injured victim, especially one with an uncertain legal case, is under pressure to accept less than he or she requires to cope with medical bills and income losses.

Even more tragic is the sometimes desperate situation faced by the accident victim with no one to sue—where no one was at fault, or where the driver who was at fault was uninsured and judgment-proof.

No-fault, as contemplated under H.R. 1900, effectively plugs those compensation gaps in the fault system. It simply provides that tort suits for economic losses and pain and suffering be limited to cases of serious harm. For relatively less serious injuries, tort liability is abolished. In exchange, immediate and comprehensive compensation for economic losses is made mandatory for all victims. In what we consider to be the best type of no-fault legislation, such as H.R. 1900, the concept of economic loss is expanded to include emergency medical service and rehabilitation, so that their insurance coverage will help victims be restored as functioning members of society.

Our experience with no-fault plans has shown us that a no-fault plan which meets the federal standards under H.R. 1900 will give consumers the greater value for their premium dollar they rightfully demand. We estimate that under such a no-fault program at least 60 percent more persons (on an average, 75 percent) will be paid compared to a pure fault system. Claimants will receive more total benefits under such no-fault laws and about 55 percent more benefits to compensate persons for economic losses. Not only will there be more benefit payments to more claimants, but payments will be received more rapidly and with considerably less friction between claimants and insurers.

All these elements add greater value to the bodily injury premium dollar.

---

[1] Motor Vehicle Crash Losses and Their Compensation in the United States, Report of the Department of Transportation, March 1971, page 100.

2. WHY IS FEDERAL ACTION NEEDED ON NO-FAULT?

Like most of the insurance industry, State Farm has always sought first to achieve state action on insurance related matters. In the case of no-fault we labored long and unsuccessfully at the state level, and now strongly support federal no-fault standards for the states to follow. We have made this agonizing decision only with reluctance, and only because bitter experience has convinced us that the states have not, and will not do the job which must be done.

When we testified before this Subcommittee a little less than one year ago, fourteen states had adopted laws restricting tort liability, to any degree at all. As will be noted later, virtually all these laws are in our judgment quite inadequate. Since that time, only two more states have managed to put no-fault on the books.

Indeed, the very troubling reality is that, no-fault activity at the state level, which never proceeded at the rapid pace which many of us originally expected, has actually been slowing down. After Massachusetts and Florida adopted rather limited no-fault laws in 1970 and 1971, three states (Connecticut, Michigan, and New Jersey) followed suit in 1972 and six in 1973 (Colorado, Hawaii, Kansas, Nevada, New York and Utah). However, in 1974, only four states moved ahead (Georgia, Minnesota, Pennsylvania, and Kentucky) and this year only North Dakota has been added to the no-fault list.[2]

We are discouraged about the prospects for no-fault in the states this year, and see little hope for the future.

It took 37 years—from 1911 to 1948—to obtain Worker's Compensation statutes in all the states, and many of those laws are very dissimilar. In our view it makes no sense to force Americans to wait 37 years for a program such as no-fault auto insurance which, for clear economic and humanitarian reasons, is justified and needed now.

There is no reason to expect that, without federal action, the future history of no-fault auto reparations will be any more favorable than the past history of Worker's Compensation. Current legislative prospects are discouraging in even such populous states, for example, as California and Illinois, where State Farm has its largest volume of business.

In Illinois, supporters of no-fault were dealt two crushing blows by the Illinois legislature within the past two weeks. With press stories confidently predicting acceptance of a modest no-fault law, the Illinois legislature seemed on the brink of enacting such a law. The more substantial reform incorporated in earlier drafts had been modified and a compromise no-fault law seemed a real possibility. Then, on two separate occasions, the Illinois House emasculated these no-fault bills, one of which had passed the Senate, by completely deleting the tort threshold and substituting instead a bill that would require purchase of no-fault benefits without touching the tort system in any way. The legislature adjourned with no action on no-fault again despite numerous references to the favorable vote by the U.S. Senate Commerce Committee on S. 354, which occurred on the same date the Illinois House was debating no-fault.

Ohio is apparently following the same course. California again is deadlocked.

In short, it is no longer realistic for one to profess support for no-fault, but to oppose federal action to achieve no-fault. That position was orginally our own. In 1975, it is tantamount to being for no-fault in principle, but against it in practice.

3. WHY FEDERAL STANDARDS RATHER THAN A FULL-SCALE FEDERAL AUTOMOBILE INSURANCE SYSTEM?

During the past few years of generally adverse experience at the state level, great improvements were made in the federal approach to no-fault insurance by the Senate Commerce Committee. Their product, S. 354 (H.R. 1900), is, we believe, a generally well-conceived and well-drafted federal no-fault standards bill. It is a substantial improvement over S. 354 as first introduced; it is a dramatic im-

---

[2] The disappointing trend of no-fault progress at the state level can be seen from the following:
1970 : Mass.
1971 : Fla.
1972 : Conn. ; Mich. ; N.J.
1973 : Colo. ; Hawaii ; Kans. ; Nev. ; N.Y. ; Utah.
1974 : Ga. ; Minn. ; Pa. ; Ky.
1975 : N. Dak.

provement over its immediate predecessor, S. 945, introduced in 1971. S. 945 was not a federal standards bill; it called for a complete federal no-fault plan. S. 945 would have created, not flexible minimum standards, but rigid uniform requirements. This inflexibility would result in substantial cost increases for a great number of automobile insurance policy owners, particularly those who live in rural areas.

This full-scale federal preemption offered no opportunity to tailor solutions to local conditions. Furthermore, under that approach, authority to regulate important insurance aspects of the program would be vested in the Secretary of Transportation rather than state insurance regulatory officials. Changes in the current structure of insurance regulation are neither essential nor germane to needed modifications of tort law as applicable to automobile accidents. Furthermore, threats to traditional regulation of insurance by the states will endanger the passage of any no-fault law.

The standards approach of S. 354 allows states to lower total payments for wage losses to as low as $15,000. It also permits states to place reasonable limitations on survivors benefits and other expenses. This flexibility is essential because of important demograbic differences among the various states—e.g., different mixes betweed urban and rural population, differences in average wages, and differences in medical costs. This flexibility in first party benefits will permit the adoption by each state of no-fault programs which can be in cost balance with tort restrictions meeting the minimum standards, or even provide for the possibility of cost savings.

The structure of S. 354—H.R. 1900 demonstrates that these important reforms can be achieved, without displacing state insurance departments in their responsibility for administering the regulation of insurance. As the Senate Judiciary Committee concluded, after hearing extensive testimony on this point:

"The role prescribed by S. 354 for State insurance commissioners, under either Title II or Title III, is simply to continue performing the same supervisory functions which they have traditionally performed under the requirements of State law. The major changes mandated by the bill—the curtailment of tort liability in auto accident cases and the provision of no-fault insurance policies meeting Federal minimum standards—directly affect only State court systems and writers of casualty insurance. These changes will alter the environment in which insurance departments operate, but they will not require insurance regulators to respond with any basic changes in their *modus operandi*."

Secretary Coleman, in his recent testimony before the Senate Commerce Committee agreed that, except in relatively "peripheral areas" the provisions of S. 354 generally "appear simply to confirm the existing authorities of regulators or to require them to regulate auto no-fault insurance as they now regulate auto liability insurance."

State Farm strongly supports this federal standards approach. By preserving intact the traditional state responsibility for regulation of insurance, federal no-fault standards promote the decentralist values inherent in our federal system of government while, at the same time, achieving nationwide reform. This approach emphasizes the real genius of our federal system—a cooperative working partnership between the federal government and states.

4. WHY H.R. 1900? FULL INSURANCE PROTECTION AND A SUBSTANTIAL RESTRICTION ON TORT LIABILITY

To endorse federal no-fault standards is, of course, merely to beg the important question—what ought the standards be. The basic answers to this question are not, in our judgment, complex. They emerge naturally from the findings of the DOT study.

Minimum federal standards should be designed specifically to rectify the identified vices of the fault system. As we review the DOT study and the general experience of insurers and consumers, we see four main problems:

First, the high costs imposed by the litigation, or threatened litigation, of small nuisance claims;

Second, the abysmal failure of the system to provide adequate protection for the seriously injured victim, even where a suable defendant can be found;

Third, the failure of the fault system to provice any protection for the many accident victims who for a variety of reasons, cannot find a suitable defendant to sue; and

Fourth, the misuse of the judicial system in establishing general damage claims.

To solve these problems, no-fault legislation has to meet two fundamental tests. First, there must be meaningful benefit levels. To us, this requirement means comprehensive coverage of medical and rehabilitation costs, and substantial coverage of lost income. Second, no-fault laws must restrict traditional tort liability to cases of truly serious injury—"serious and permanent injury" in the formulation used by H.R. 1900 and S. 354, or a substantial period of continuous disability. Without a meaningful tort threshold, full no-fault protection for the seriously injured victim cannot be financed—unless insurance premium levels are raised for everyone.

When measured against these standards, the performance of the states is far more disappointing even than it would appear from a simple head-count of the number of states which have passed some form of no-fault legislation. With only a small number of exceptions, state no-fault laws now on the books are sadly inadequate—incorporating minimal benefit levels and providing porous or very limited tort exemptions.

Of the 16 no-fault states, only one provides for limitations on pain and suffering recovery through a definition of serious injuries which qualify for payment (Michigan). Two states have enacted medical thresholds in excess of $1,000 (Hawaii and Minnesota), two a $1,000 threshold (Florida and North Dakota), one $1,000 on an "optional" basis (Kentucky), two with a $750 threshold (Nevada and Pennsylvania), six a $500 threshold (Massachusetts, Colorado, Kansas, New York, Utah and Georgia), and two states have provided for a thseshold of less than $500 (Connecticut and New Jersey). Medical thresholds are easily susceptible to abuse through the exaggeration of medical bills; they promote overutilization of medical facilities and are subject to constant erosion by inflation.

With regard to benefit levels, of the twenty-four states which either require insurers to offer, or consumers to purchase first party benefits, half have benefit levels below a total of $10,000 for medical expenses and wage losses (South Carolina, Massachusetts, Florida, South Dakota, Virginia, Connecticut, Maryland, Arkansas, Texas, Oregon, Utah and Georgia); only twelve require coverages of $10,000 or more to meet these basic expenses (New Jersey, Michigan, New York, Nevada, Colorado, Hawaii, Kansas, Delaware, Kentucky, Pennsylvania and Minnesota). Although coverage in lesser amounts such as $2,000 or $2,500 will meet the needs of a majority of the accident victims, these limits fall woefully short of providing the coverage needed for those seriously injured in automobile accidents.

Probably the most telling criticism in the DOT report on the auto accident reparations system is the failure adequately to compensate the severely injured person. Very recently (on June 19, 1975), Professor William Cohen of Stanford testified to this Committee that "[A]ny reform of the automobile compensation system ought to begin by focusing on seriously injured victims." Professor Cohen observed that, "In only two or three states has anything been done about the plight of the seriously injured victim." We concur that, for a no-fault law to be truly effective, it must provide medical and rehabilitation benefits sufficient to meet the needs of the severely injured.

In sum, left to themselves, the states have not done the job which must be done.

The two features noted above—meaningful benefit levels and substantial tort exemption—are the basic criteria by which no-fault standards legislation should be evaluated. There are, of course, other necessary aspects of no-fault plans. We have continued to alert Congress to our concerns with some of the secondary issues in H.R. 1900 and S. 354. But on the main points, H.R. 1900 and S. 354 are in our judgment excellent pieces of reform legislation.

In this regard, I would like to add one final point, of particular importance to a major auto insurance writer which will have to administer any no-fault plan Congress determines to adopt. We support S. 354 because of its high technical quality. As the Subcommittee know, the bill now before you is the culmination of several years of study and research by DOT, the sifting of many concepts and proposals reflected in prior federal bills, and, most recently, the best provisions of the model act adopted in August 1972 by the National Conference of Commissioners on Uniform State Laws—the Uniform Motor Vehicle Reparations Act (UMVARA).

5. THE COSTS OF FEDERAL NO-FAULT STANDARDS

The final question is what will be the likely impact on insurance costs if a federal standards bill such as S. 354 is enacted.

Reformers are sometimes alleged to dwell on the benefits of proposed social change, while neglecting the price that will have to be paid for those benefits. As businessmen, we in the auto insurance industry do not have this luxury. We cannot afford reforms which cannot be financed. Our customers will blame us, if no-fault imposes new insurance costs on them which are out of line with the benefits they receive.

We believe the importance of cost projections has been overemphasized. Although cost projections are necessary as general background so as to give decision-makers information to determine whether they are creating a reparations system beyond reasonably affordable cost for consumers, by far the most important test, as we previously stated, is one of value. Fortunately, in our judgment, we believe, conversion to no-fault programs meeting the standards established by a S. 354 type law would generally introduce a cost-reducing element into the total rate making picture. No-fault can assure coverage of economic losses, compensating far more people at much higher levels than the tort system, without creating upward pressure on costs, because of the elimination of needless costs incident to the tort system.

We have recently completed a review of the probable cost impact on the average cost of bodily injury insurance for private passenger automobiles of H.R. 1900 on each state meeting the federal no-fault standards established by the bill. Attached as Exhibit I is a summary of the results and a discussion of our methodology.

In presenting these cost estimates, it would be false and misleading for us to state or imply that several years from now states having no-fault laws meeting federal standards will be receiving rate cuts equivalent to the cost reductions indicated in these tables. Several important considerations should be kept clearly in mind. These cost estimates are based on the comparative cost of bodily injury type coverage. These costs are only approximately 40% of the total insurance cost of a typical full package of automobile insurance coverage (including property damage liability coverage, collison and comprehensive coverage). In addition, these costs estimates isolate only one factor that can influence cost—a change to a no-fault law which meets the federal standards.

There are now and there will continue to be other factors which will have a substantial impact on the cost of automobile insurance under any system. These include the severe impact of inflation, particularly on crash parts prices, labor costs, medical costs, income replacement costs (as wage levels rise), as well as other factors—enforcement of speed limits, availability and cost of gasoline, and the size and safety features of motor vehicles and highways. The cost-savings features of no-fault can easily be offset by adverse experience resulting from these other factors. Therefore, it would be erroneous to cite our figures—or any no-fault cost estimates—as indications of what the actual cost for automobile insurance will be in the future.

There has been considerable controversy over actuarial estimates as to the cost impact of S. 354. Actuarial costing of no-fault bills is not an exact science and differing assumptions can produce dramatically different results. From the very beginning of the no-fault debate, a number of insurance companies and insurance trade associations have presented cost estimates on no-fault programs which differ dramatically—from large decreases to large increases. We have, on occasion, been requested to critique cost estimates made by others. Attached as Exhibit II is a letter we sent on June 4, 1975 to the Senate Commerce Committee, in response to the Committee's request for analysis of cost projections recently made of S. 354 by another insurance company. On June 17, 1975, in response to a request from Senators Warren Magnuson and Frank Moss, we provided cost data on the staff working draft of S. 354 dated June 13. The data in this response is basically the same as the data in Exhibit I.

We continue to regard as structurally sound the cost analysis of S. 354 by the independent actuarial firm of Milliman and Robertson. This firm was chosen by the National Association of Insurance Commissioners to devise a model for costing no-fault plans. We agree substantially with the methodology employed. Our own estimates, although not always precisely the same as Milliman and Robertson's conclusions for various types of no-fault programs, are in most cases very close.

We believe it is appropriate to place much reliance on the cost analysis done by Milliman and Robertson. As for cost estimates of insurance companies, including State Farm, the forces of competition will modify the prices indicated by actuarial estimates.

Some specific comments on our cost analysis would, we believe, prove helpful. The Milliman and Robertson model combined insurance costs for private passenger automobiles and commercial vehicles. Our figures relate solely to private passenger motor vehicles. We believe that H.R. 1900 as now written contains a feature which excessively benefits commercial vehicle policyholders at the expense of private passenger policyholders. This is the $5,000 deductible in Section 111(a)(3) on subrogation in accidents between private passenger cars and other types of motor vehicles. In such accidents, because of the difference in weight between commercial vehicles and private passenger automobiles, commercial vehicles cause a disproportionate amount of bodily injury. We believe that full subrogation without a deductible is the preferred way to rectify this inequity. The new version of S. 354 just reported out by the Senate Commerce Committee reduces the deductible from $5,000 to $100. Column 2 of our Exhibit I indicates the cost impact of this proposed change in S. 354. As Exhibit I shows, reducing the deductible from $5,000 to $100 will double the indicated nationwide average savings for private passenger automobile insurance rates, from 5 percent to 10 percent.

With a $100 deductible on subrogation, this bill will produce indicated cost savings in 45 states plus the District of Columbia, with no indicated change in one state. Four states will show indicated increases. The reason that these four states show indicated increases is that they already have no-fault laws, but with relatively modest benefit packages. H.R. 1900 will require substantially more comprehensive no-fault benefits than these states now have, the cost of which will not be completely offset by the somewhat higher tort limitation of H.R. 1900. For example, Massachusetts under H.R. 1900 would have to increase its no-fault benefits from its current $2,000 minimum on all no-fault benefits to unlimited medical type coverage, $15,000 for wage loss and $5,000 for survivor losses. This substantial increase in no-fault benefits for Massachusetts motorists is not offset by the more restrictive tort liability provisions of H.R. 1900—an increase from a $500 medical threshold to a three month disability threshold.

Changes in S. 354 as Reported by The Senate Commerce Committee

Since the Senate Commerce Committee as recently reported out a new version of S. 354, we would be remiss in not commenting on the major differences between this bill and H.R. 1900, which tracks S. 354 as originally introduced in the Senate in the 94th Congress.

Apart from technical "fine-tuning" improvements, we would identify three significant modifications made by the Senate Commerce Committee. The first of these changes, involving Section 111(a)(3), reduces the deductible limit on subrogation in accidents involving commercial vehicles from $5,000 to $100. As noted above, we strongly endorse this amendment and urge this Subcommittee to incorporate it in H.R. 1900.

The second major change in S. 354 completely revamps Sections 201 and 202 of the bill. The new provisions incorporate suggestions offered by former critics of the original Senate version regarding questions or state-federal relations. Under the new version, the Secretary of Transportation will no longer review the adequacy of state no-fault plans under the national standards of Title II of the bill. The review function is vested in a five-person "No-fault Insurance Plan Review Board," consisting of the Secretary, two persons appointed by the President from a list provided by the National Association of Insurance Commissioners, and two persons appointed by the President from a list operated by the National Governors Conference.

Another aspect of the changes made in Sections 201 and 202 was drafted by Attorney General Levi at the request of the Senate Commerce Committee. This amendment provides, in effect, an option for states subject to Title III of the bill to permit assumption by the federal Department of Transportation of administrative functions incident to implementing that Title. This amendment assures that, in the last analysis, state administration of the bill is a purely voluntary matter. Thus it eliminates any basis there may have previously been for a charge leveled by some critics that the bill invaded state sovereignty in a manner that was possibly unconstitutional.

These "federalism" amendments will ease the concerns of some who saw in the earlier bill certain troublesome problems in terms of federal-state relations. We are in sympathy with the purposes of these changes.

However, we oppose a third major change in the bill. This involves the elimination of Sections 204(f) and 208(c) in original S. 354 (and current H.R. 1900), and their replacement by a new Section 209. Under the Senate Commerce Committee's new Section 209, states are required to institute a program for "coordination of benefits" among providers of no-fault insurance and providers of other overlapping coverages. Section 209 does not, however, set specific guidelines, restrictions, or criteria for the states to follow. We are concerned that, without any such boundaries, the play of political pressures within some states may lead to excessive bifurcation among different types of insurers of the responsibility for financing auto accident costs. Such a balkanization of compensation responsibility will raise administrative costs, complicate the accident victim's search for swift and comprehensive service, and blunt incentives to promote long-run cost reduction measures; such measures include safe vehicle and highway design, and improved emergency medical and rehabilitation treatment for victims.

Under S. 354 as originally introduced this year, and H.R. 1900 in its current form, it was contemplated that no-fault insurance would ordinarily play the primary compensating role. Non-governmental providers of certain overlapping health coverages were permitted to substitute for no-fault insurance only if such insurers offered the full range of benefits and shared in the burdens required of no-fault insurers, and if it was affirmatively demonstrated that placing a health insurer in this primary role would produce comparatively greater cost savings.

Although we opposed the inclusion of this latter provision in a federal standards no-fault bill, it at least had the virtue of assuring the consumer that automobile insurance could be placed in a secondary role for the medical portion of no-fault benefits, only in specific cases in which the consumer would derive greater benefits from such an arrangement. We believe that it can be demonstrated that the consumer will derive greater benefits if no-fault automobile insurance remains the primary source of recovery.

As is shown by experience in those few states which have adopted a program for minimizing duplication, coordination with no-fault auto insurance in the primary compensating role has produced greater cost savings. In New York and New Jersey, community rated Blue Cross and Blue Shield programs are by regulation required to make themselves secondary to automobile no-fault coverages, and to reduce their premiums by 2-½% and 3% respectively, for an average of approximately $18 per year.[3] In Michigan and Pennsylvania, no-fault auto insurers are required to offer to their policyholders the option of placing their no-fault coverage in a position secondary to the duplicative coverages they may carry. Where the consumer opts to coordinate health coverages, the no-fault auto insurers are providing an average of approximately $8 premium reduction.

The basic reason why cost-savings are maximized by assigning no-fault insurance the primary role in coordinating overlapping coverages was succintly stated by Transportation Secretary William T. Coleman in his recent testimony before the Senate Commerce Committee. He explained:

"It . . . seems logical to us [the Department of Transportation] that the mandatory system of benefits, especially one providing high limits, universal coverage for a class of victims or a class of losses such as the type of no-fault system we advocate, should be primary in relation to a voluntary system, and especially when the latter system has significant gaps in coverage or provides only limited benefits."

The Secretary's point was that it is cheaper for a "secondary" health insurer to coordinate against a relatively uniform, mandatory system, than for a secondary no-fault insurer to coordinate against a patchwork of health coverages offering many different types of policies, with significant gaps in coverage, and in which a particular individual's policy may lapse at any time. Where the mandatory system is primary, the secondary insurer may speedily and confidently calculate the amount by which his exposure is reduced; where the voluntary health "system" is mandatory, this calculation becomes cumbersome, expensive, and uncertain.

In sum, compensation of auto accident injuries from a single source—no-fault insurance—maximizes cost-savings for the premium payer, assures comprehensive service in the most convenient fashion for the victim, and promotes cost-reduction measures to reform the reparations system. We believe that these important objectives of no-fault reform are better served by Sections 204(f) and 208(c) of H.R. 1900 than by Section 209 of the new version of the Senate bill.

[3] See State of New York Insurance Department, In the Matter of a Proposed Fourth Amendment to Regulation No. 62. Opinion and Decision August 16, 1974; State of New Jersey Department of Insurance, Official News Release, November 21, 1972.

In the event that a decision is made to change these provisions, we would hope that the Subcommittee does not simply copy the action taken by the Senate. We would suggest that, in any new provisions dealing with coordination of benefits, guidelines be incorporated to reflect more specifically than Section 209 of the Senate bill the fact that the objectives of the bill are generally best served by primary reliance on single-source reparations for auto accident costs.

CONCLUSION

We are firmly convinced that the time has come for enactment of a federal no-fault standards bill. Our experience at the state level has demonstrated, that federal standards are necessary to assure that the states enact well conceived no-fault laws. We would urge your Subcommittee to act promptly in reporting favorably on such a federal standards bill.

EXHIBIT I
COST IMPACT OF H.R. 1900—ESTIMATED AVERAGE EFFECT ON PRIVATE PASSENGER VEHICLES
[In percent]

	As now drafted (with a $5,000 deductible on subrogation)	As proposed in Senate staff working draft of S. 354 (with $100 deductible on subrogation)		As now drafted (with a $5,000 deductible on subrogation)	As proposed in Senate staff working draft of S 354 (with $100 deductible on subrogation)
Alabama	−14	−19	Nebraska	−6	−11
Alaska	−2	−7	Nevada	+5	−1
Arizona	−13	−18	New Hampshire	+4	−2
Arkansas	−3	−9	New Jersey	+9	+3
California	−9	−14	New Mexico	−5	−10
Colorado	+3	−3	New York	+10	+4
Connecticut	+5	−1	North Carolina	+6	+0
Delaware	−8	−13	North Dakota	+1	−5
District of Columbia	−16	−21	Ohio	−8	−13
Florida	+14	+8	Oklahoma	−8	−13
Georgia	−6	−11	Oregon	−9	−14
Hawaii	−5	−10	Pennsylvania	−6	−11
Idaho	−4	−9	Rhode Island	−4	−9
Illinois	−6	−11	South Carolina	−1	−6
Indiana	−7	−12	South Dakota	+5	−1
Iowa	−2	−7	Tennessee	+3	−3
Kansas	+3	−3	Texas	−22	−26
Kentucky	−6	−11	Utah	+4	−2
Louisiana	−13	−18	Vermont	−5	−10
Maine	−7	−12	Virginia	+3	−3
Maryland	−12	−17	Washington	−10	−15
Massachusetts	+22	+15	West Virginia	−3	−8
Michigan	−2	−7	Wisconsin	+1	−5
Minnesota	−7	−12	Wyoming	−4	−9
Mississippi	−2	−7			
Missouri	−1	−6	CW average	−5	−10
Montana	−6	−11			

Note: These estimates are based on the minimum benefit plan provided by H R. 1900, including unlimited medical expense benefits, $15,000 of wage loss, and $5,000 survivor's benefit. The percentage changes are relative to State Farm's current average rates (Dec. 31, 1974) in each State for a typical policyholder for bodily injury liability, uninsured motorist and medical payments coverages (and basic personal injury protection coverage in those States already under a no-fault plan.)

STATEMENT CONCERNING STATE FARM'S COST ESTIMATES

1. Relative costs are expressed in terms of the present statewide average rates used by State Farm Mutual. Accordingly, they are not necessarily representative of the industry as a whole, and certainly do not reflect what would happen to a specific policyholder in a given class or rating territory. Unlike Milliman and Robertson's cost-analysis, our analysis compares actual average rates charged, including the actual rates currently charged in no-fault and add-on rates with projected rates under S. 354. Milliman and Robertson compared projected rates under S. 354, with a hypothetical pure tort system in each state, even if the state had an add-on or no-fault law in effect. This difference reflects no basic disagreements in principle, but merely alternative methods of calculating costs.

2. The indicated variations by state, for the most part, are due to known differences in fatality rates and in the relative importance of single car crashes. Differences inherent in the existing tort systems are also reflected.

3. In determining these cost estimates, a number of important, yet hopefully realistic assumptions are made; notably:

(a) The Closed Claim Survey conducted in 1969 by the insurance industry for the Department of Transportation represented an accurate cross-section of the economic losses sustained by injured persons recovering through tort and the reparations they received. This survey covered 19 states and, where necessary, reasonable extrapolations concerning general damages, etc., are made for the other states.

(b) There will be a significant increase in the number of injured persons receiving economic loss benefits as compared to the number recovering through tort, ranging from 60% up to 110% depending largely on the relative proportion of single car accidents. Further, these new claimants will sustain somewhat higher (+10%) economic losses on average—resulting partially from the addition of single car accidents, which are generally more serious, and partially from a disproportionate increase in the number of injured drivers, who tend to have greater economic loss potential.

(c) In the area of loss adjustment expenses, the relative cost for administering the residual tort claims will be about the same as under a tort system, and the cost of handling the 1st Party benefits will be similar to existing 1st Party coverages (Medical Payments, Collision, Comprehensive).

4. Because of these assumptions, it should be recognized that any cost estimates derived therefrom are just that—*estimates*. In particular, they are subject to considerable differences of opinion. In addition, they are probably accurate to within only 5%. For example, to state that the expected cost of a particular plan is 110% of present coverage is somewhat misleading. A much safer, but of course less useful, response is "somewhere between 105 and 115% of present coverage". The attached table presents a comparison of these estimates with the actual experience being developed by several of the No-Fault plans already in effect.

5. One important factor not explicitly recognized in these cost estimates is "How will the game be played—either by the public, by the attorneys, or by the companies?" At the present time there is no way of knowing whether the extent to which the various sides take advantage of each other will be more or less than that under the present tort liability systems.

6. Nor do these estimates reflect some of the longer range implications of No-Fault on the rates for individual risks. For instance, there will be a tendency for the rating differentials between the adult and youthful principal operator classifications to diminish—partly because of differences in relative economic loss potential. In general, claim severity will become more important as a determining factor on individual rates. For example, the importance of family size and income on expected economic losses may result in new classifications. The type of insured vehicle may become a rating factor on the personal injury coverages as well as the vehicle damage coverages.

EXHIBIT I

COMPARISON OF STATE FARM'S ACTUAL NO-FAULT EXPERIENCE WITH ESTIMATED COSTS

[Average cost per insured car [1]]

State (effective date)	Actual experience for the year prior to no-fault	Estimated effect of inflation, etc. (percent) [2]	Expected cost in following year	Estimated effect of no-fault (percent)	Expected cost	Actual cost	Difference (percent)
Delaware (1972)	$22.35	+6	$23.69	+22	$28.90	$32.82	[3] +14
Florida (1972)	53.08	+6	56.26	−9	51.20	52.86	+3
Kansas (1974)	17.37	-------	17.37	−5	16.50	16.71	+1
Maryland (1973)	42.61	+6	45.17	+21	54.66	56.19	+3
Michigan (October 1973)	36.05	-------	36.05	+5	37.85	35.63	−6
New Jersey (1973)	53.66	+6	56.88	+7	60.86	59.97	−1
New York (February 1974)	62.74	-------	62.74	−12	55.21	53.21	−4
Oregon (1972)	26.52	+6	28.11	+10	30.92	29.63	−4
Utah (1974)	22.67	-------	22.67	-------	22.67	23.85	+5

[1] Incurred losses for the bodily injury liability, uninsured motorist, medical payments, and personal injury protection coverages divided by the number of insured cars. Losses have been evaluated on the latest available data. The average cost per insured car represents the pure loss cost (pure premium) portion of the insurance rate, and does not include provision for acquisition or other operating expenses.

[2] Estimated effect of inflation on claim costs in 1972 and 1973 was plus 6 percent per year; in 1974, the decline in accident frequency (arising from the oil embargo and reduced travel) just about offset the increase in claim costs.

[3] This large difference is partially due to the small volume of business in Delaware; in 1973, the average cost per car dropped back to $28.95.

EXHIBIT II

STATE FARM MUTUAL AUTOMOBILE INSURANCE CO.,
Bloomington, Ill., June 4, 1975.

S. LYNN SUTCLIFFE, Esq.,
Senate Commerce Committee,
128 Russell Senate Office Building,
Washington, D.C.

DEAR MR. SUTCLIFFE: You have asked us for our reaction to the testimony Allstate Insurance Company has given on S. 354 before the Senate Commerce Committee. In that testimony, Allstate presented cost projection figures for state no-fault laws that would meet the requirements of S. 354. Their figures indicated, in general, substantial cost increases in almost all states.

As you are aware, the cost estimates that were supplied by Allstate are just that, estimates. I would assume that the actual price that they would charge in each of the states would be influenced to a great degree by the cost that competitors would be charging for similar coverages. Also, as I am sure you are aware, actuarial cost estimates on no-fault assume that all other factors remain constant. Traffic safety programs, inflation, lack of availability of gasoline, etc., could all have a significant impact on cost.

Keeping these very important caveats in mind, we have arrived at significantly different cost estimates from Allstate. Our cost estimates are approximately on a countrywide average 30 percent lower than Allstate's. Where they project a countrywide average increase on private passenger automobiles of approximately 25 percent, we would project a countrywide savings of 5 percent for private passenger automobiles under S. 354. If the $5,000 deductible on subrogation between vehicles of different sizes were eliminated, this 5 percent savings would be increased to a savings of 10 percent.

Although Allstate's testimony does not indicate the exact weight given to various assumptions used in arriving at their estimates, after reviewing the testimony Allstate presented before the Senate Commerce Committee and the House Subcommittee on Commerce and Finance in July of 1974, we believe our sifferences are due to three main factors:

1. Allstate has assumed the limitation of payment on survivor's benefits to be $15,000 rather than the $5,000 as was costed by Milliman and Robertson. Clearly under S. 354 as written, a state could limit survivor's benefits to $5,000 or an amount lower than that if desired. This difference in assumption, our actuaries tell us, accounts for an additional average increase of 10 percent. Also, the cost of increasing the amount of survivor's benefits varies dramatically between urban and rural states. In rural areas, there is a higher proportion of one car accidents and fatal accidents. The range of increase that this one assumption alone would produce as between urban states and rural states is between 5 and 30 percent, with 10 percent being the average. This accounts to a great extent for the reason why under Allstate's figures some of the rural states have rate indications so significantly higher than the present system.

2. Allstate has apparently, according to our actuaries, costed the "allowabl expense" portion of S. 354 15 percent higher than we have. We have a difference of opinion as to the cost of unlimited "allowable expenses" and in particular, the use of an increased cost factor that Allstate has added because of expected over-utilization. Allstate has apparently used this over-utilization factor because such a factor has been used in costing national health plans. We believe this is an incorrect analogy. Over-utilization of health plans primarily comes about from persons who contract an illness or sickness of a minor nature and decide to use available medical resources covered by their program which, without such a program, they may well treat themselves. This is not generally the case for automobile accidents where medical-type expenses arise out of the trauma of an automobile accident. Obviously, persons are not going to become involved in automobile accidents in order to utilize the medical portion of their no-fault coverages. It is true that there are some minor auto accident injuries which may not truly necessitate medical care but which persons may nevertheless utilize the rather extensive coverages contained under the provisions of S. 354. However, we do not believe that this is going to be a very serious problem. Our experience with voluntarily purchased medical payment coverages now sold with automobile insurance policies indicates to us that S. 354 will not create the problem Allstate apparently anticipates.

Mr. VAN DEERLIN. Thank you, Mr. McHugh. Ms. O'Reilly.

STATEMENT OF KATHLEEN F. O'REILLY

Ms. O'REILLY. Thank you, Mr. Chairman. I appreciate the opportunity to testify before this subcommittee on behalf of Consumer Federation of America, the Nation's largest consumer organization. CFA is composed of over 200 national, State and local non-profit organizations that have joined together to espouse the consumer viewpoint.

This statement on behalf of CFA is fully endorsed by the National Committee for Effective No-Fault, to which CFA belongs. The National Committee for Effective No-Fault is a coalition of consumer, labor, automotive, and insurance groups whose goal is the enactment of Federal legislation which would: (1) assure all auto accident victims of prompt and complete payment of their economic losses without regard to fault; (2) lower the high cost of auto insurance; and (3) end the abuses of the prevailing fault system of auto accident reparations. Among the members and affiliates of the National Committee are the following organizations, whose millions of members have a vital interest in reform of the automobile accident reparations system:

The AFL-CIO, the American Association of Retired Persons and the National Retired Teachers Association, the American Insurance Association, the Car and Truck Rental and Leasing Association, the State Farm Mutual Automobile Insurance Company, the American Congress of Rehabilitation Medicine and the American Academy of Physical Medicine and Rehabilitation, the International Brotherhood of Teamsters, the United Auto Workers of America, the United Steelworkers of America, the Communications Workers of America, the International Brotherhood of Electrical Workers, the American Federation of Government Employees, the Aetna Life and Casualty Company, and the CNA Financial Corporation.

Clearly, there is citizen support for federal no-fault legislation. The current system of auto reparations is not a sacred, rigid American tradition, but is, in fact, a relatively recent legal concept and one that is not serving the consumers well. It is inhuman, inadequate, inefficient, and unpredictable. The time has come for the law once again to adapt to changing times and return to the principle of focusing on victims of auto accidents.

Why is the present "fault" system a failure? Because of the complexity which surrounds today's driving situation, an accident is often not the singular "fault" of any one driver. An automobile mishap may result from a mechanical failure of an intricate automobile, a malfunctioning of or absence of adequate highway safety devices, weather or road conditions beyond the control of the driver, the cumulative negligence of all the principals in the accidents, or a combination of these factors. In any event, the often tragic result is that as a practical matter, victims are too often precluded from any recovery, either because of the above-described factors, the principle of contributory negligence or because the responsible party is a hit and run driver, uninsured, inadequately insured or is otherwise judgment proof.

While the legal "fault" system has been failing consumers, the auto insurance policy has simultaneously proven to be a very poor consumer investment. Whereas 67 cents of the workmen's compensation premium dollar is returned to claimants and in excess of 90 cents per group accident and health premium dollar is received in benefits, a mere 45 cents of the automobile injury liability premium dollar is received by claimants. A full $31.80 out of every $100 of bodily injury liability insurance premiums is being consumed by the overhead inherent in the "fault" system. Such an inefficient and inadequate system must be abandoned.

Consumers are also distressed because the present system results in an undercompensation of the most seriously injured victims and an overcompensation of those with smaller claims. The Department of Transportation study states, "Those with small economic losses recover, on the average, nearly twice their loss, but those with high economic losses recover only one-fifth."

Even when payment is made, consumers are being "punished" with delays. The DOT study revealed that seriously injured victims must wait an average of 16 months for compensation of their losses; those with total economic losses exceeding $2,500 face an average delay of 19 months.

Although consumers have supported Federal no-fault legislation for several years, the current economic crisis has dramatized the cost issue. Today's consumers are faced with increasing job insecurity and rising food, utility, and health care costs, all of which have sensitized them to wasteful policies that diminish the value of the consumer dollar. Today's consumer simply cannot afford the tedious delays inherent in the "fault" system. The DOT study showed the 30 percent of those seriously injured must withdraw from their savings accounts or sell property in order to survive and that 12 percent miss debt payments. A full 45 percent of the seriously injured receive no compensation from auto liability insurance.

Delay also means postponement of necessary medical treatment. As a practical reality, plaintiffs who look the worst to the jury often recover the most and are consequently encouraged to wait until the jury verdict is in before making arrangements for cosmetic surgery or rehabilitation. This practice exacts a double price from the seriously injured consumer: Increased medical costs because treatment was not initiated immediately and the anxiety of waiting for months or years for a jury verdict which may prove unfavorable.

The "fault" concept is clearly unfair, inefficient, expensive, unpredictable, and inadequate. Why then after 8 years of debate must consumers still press for national reform? The arguments used by opponents to national no-fault have grown increasingly stale and tedious.

In terms of legal issues involved, the thorough and persuasive report prepared last year by the Senate Judiciary Committee demonstrates that the national no-fault legislation embodied in S. 354 and H.R. 1900: (1) is constitutionally sound; (2) is consistent with the McCarran-Ferguson Act; and (3) preserves the traditional predominant role of State regulation in the field of insurance.

In terms of cost, the results of the widely acclaimed Milliman & Robertson study have been confirmed by the recently released cost estimates of State Farm Insurance. Both studies emphasized that cost estimates are not conclusive because cost is influenced by a host of factors such as inflation, highway safety, effectiveness, the quality of the automobile mechanism, driver attitudes, et cetera. Yet, with that caveat in mind, the State Farm figures do anticipate a nationwide premium savings of 10 percent for private passenger car owners, an amount equivalent to almost $1 billion a year in consumer savings for current policyholders.

It cannot be overemphasized, however, that cost savings is not the paramount consideration which leads to consumer endorsement of S. 354 and H.R. 1900. If no-fault reform results in immediate and quality medical treatment, prompt payment to all who are injured, increased insurance company commitment to accident prevention, and a return to policyholders of a larger percentage of their premium dollars—all at a cost equal to or even slightly more than present premium levels—consumers will be better served. Assurance of lower premiums is an added extra, not the cornerstone of consumer support for national no-fault.

Finally, with respect to the argument that no-fault insurance should be delegated exclusively to the States—despite strong public sentiment in favor of reform, a vast majority of the States have failed to create effective no-fault legislation. The slow pace of State responsiveness has strengthened CFA's commitment to the development of national standards. Only on the Federal level can legislation effectively minimize the insurance difficulties of interstate travel and help eliminate much of the unnecessary administrative cost and confusion resulting from the wide disparity of State no-fault laws.

Even with Federal minimum standards, State law will still determine the regulations of insurance, litigation procedures, rates, taxation, motor vehicle registration, and claims investigation. This sound and reasonable structure recognizes the historic need for each State to provide a flexible response to the varying needs of its citizens.

Because of the ineffectiveness of the "fault" system, CFA and other members of the NACENT coalition support H.R. 1900 because of its focus on the victims of automobile accidents.

Without detracting from our strong support of H.R. 1900, we wish to take this opportunity to recommend three changes which would enhance the effectiveness of the legislation as drafted:

1. The disability threshold in section 206(a)(5)(B) should be increased to 180 days. This would result in a 3-cent-per-premium dollar savings to policyholders.

2. Section III(a)(3) must be modified so as to establish an equitable portion of no-fault cost savings to the private passenger vehicle owner. We are pleased that $5,000 deductible originally included in S. 354 was lowered to $100 when the bill was reported by the Commerce Committee. We urge a similar reduction in H.R. 1900.

3. Finally, it is imperative that section 208(c) be replaced by a provision permitting consumers to buy, and requiring insurers to sell auto insurance coverage at prices reflecting the availability of adequate benefits for auto accident medical and hospital costs and loss of wages from reliable sources outside the auto insurance system.

Indicative of the cost saving to the consumer that should result from from such a modification is Michigan's Coordinated Coverage Statute. As explained by Rovert E. Vanderbeek, in April of 1975, this provision has resulted in an approximate consumer saving of $60 million in the State of Michigan. Such requirements have resulted in minimum savings or premium reductions of 40 to 50 percent of the no-fault personal injury protection portion of the premium. This reduction may mean a 10 to 25 percent reduction in the overall cost of auto insurance.

Clearly then, S. 354 and H.R. 1900 are in the best interests| of those who are most affected by the present system—namely consumers both in their role as policyholders and in their role as potential victims.

Thank you.

[Ms. O'Reilly's prepared statement follows:]

STATEMENT OF KATHLEEN F. O'REILLY, LEGISLATIVE DIRECTOR, CONSUMER FEDERATION OF AMERICA

Mr. Chairman and members of the Committee, I appreciate the opportunity to testify before this Subcommittee on behalf of Consumer Federation of America, the nation's largest consumer organization. CFA is composed of over 200 national, state and local non-profit organizations that have joined together to espouse the consumer viewpoint. Among our members are Consumers Union, publishers of Consumer Reports, 17 cooperatives and credit union leagues, 45 state and local consumer organizations, 66 rural electric cooperatives, 27 national and regional organizations ranging from Nationwide Insurance to the National Board of the YWCA to the National Education Association, and 16 national labor unions.

This statement on behalf of CFA is fully endorsed by the National Committee for Effective No-Fault, to which CFA belongs. The National Committee for Effective No-Fault is a coalition of consumer, labor, automotive and insurance groups whose goal is the enactment of federal legislation which would: (1) assure all auto accident victims of prompt and complete payment of their economic losses without regard to fault; (2) lower the high cost of auto insurance; and (3) end the abuses of the prevailing fault system of auto accident reparations. Among the members and affiliates of the National Committee are the following organizations, whose millions of members have a vital interest in reform of the automobile accident reparations system:

The *AFL–CIO*, whose affiliated unions represent 13.4 million working men and women, most of whom own cars;

The *American Association of Retired Persons* and the *National Retired Teachers Association*, many of whose 6.7 million members live on fixed incomes and would benefit most from the lower auto insurance costs and prompt and adequate payments that no-fault will bring;

The *American Insurance Association*, whose 127 member companies have more than 20 million auto insurance policyholders and have backed no-fault reform since 1968;

The *Car and Truck Rental and Leasing Association* (CATRALA), whose 2500 members see lower customer costs in an improved auto insurance system;

The *State Farm Mutual Automobile Insurance Company*, whose 14 million auto insurance policyholders see in no-fault a better product for their premium dollars;

The *American Congress of Rehabilitation Medicine* and the *American Academy of Physical Medicine and Rehabilitation*, whose members see benefits for seriously injured accident victims in a system that pays for prompt and complete rehabilitation without regard to fault;

The *International Brotherhood of Teamsters*, most of whose 2 million members drive to make their living;

The *United Auto Workers of America,* whose 1.4 million members make the cars most Americans drive;
The *United Steelworkers of America,* with 1.4 million members;
The *Communications Workers of America,* with over 575,000 members;
The *Internationa Brotherhood of Electrical Workers,* with more than one million members;
The *American Federation of Government Employees,* with 650,000 federal employees in exclusive recognition units;
The *Aetna Life and Casualty Company,* the nation's largest multiline insurance company;
The *CNA Financial Corporation,* a Chicago-based company with a substantial share of the auto insurance market.

The law had historically focused on victims by discouraging dangerous activities which could result in injury until the 19th century fascination with the Industrial Revolution necessitated a reappraisal of earlier policies. The legal system's response was an attempt to strike an equitable balance between the plight of victims and the evolving, socially desirable goal of engouraging technological advancement. Demonstrating an adaptability to changing times the courts developed the current "fault" system, an inducement to use technology by an assurance to drivers that they would be held legally liable to another only if the victim could demonstrate that the driver had been negligent.

In growing numbers, consumers invested in auto insurance as a cushion against the cost and risks contained in the fault system. Insurance was to be their source of compensation, devoid of the "punishment" implications of the legal "fault" system.

More than a century later it is apparent that we have come full circle. Once again it is technology coupled with socially desirable goals which force us to reappraise our present system. It is apparent that once again the law must adapt to changing times. For however appropriate the "fault" system may have been when it was first instituted, it has not served consumers well. It must be immediately abandoned in favor of a return to a humane system which will focus on the victim.

Why is the present "fault" system a failure? Because of the complexity which surrounds today's driving situation, an accident is often not the singular "fault" of any one driver. An automobile mishap may result from a mechanical failure of an intricate automobile, a malfunctioning of or absence of adequate highway safety devices, weather or road conditions beyond the control of the driver, the cumulative negligence of all the principals in the accident, or a combination of these factors. In any event, the often tragic result is that as a practical matter, victims are too often precluded from any recovery, either because of the above-described factors, the principle of contributory negligence or because the responsible party is a hit and run driver, uninsured, inadequately insured or is otherwise judgment-proof.

While the legal "fault" system has been failing consumers, the auto insurance policy has simultaneously proven to be a very poor consumer investment. Whereas 67¢ of the workmen's compensation premium dollar is returned to claimants and in excess of 90¢ per group accident and health premium dollar is received in benefits, a mere 45¢ of the automobile bodily injury liability premium dollar is received by claimants. A full $31.80 out of every $100 of bodily injury liability insurance premiums is being consumed by the overhead inherent in the "fault" system. Such an inefficient and inadequate system must be abandoned.

As documented by the Department of Transportation study, the present system has likewise resulted in an undercompensation of the most seriously injured victims and an overcompensation of those with smaller claims. "Those with small economic losses recover, on the average, nearly twice their loss, but those with high economic losses recover only one-fifth."

Even when payment is made, consumers are being "punished". The DOT study revealed that seriously injured victims must wait an average of 16 months for compensation of their losses; those with total economic losses exceeding $2500 face an average delay of 19 months.

These are but a few of the reasons which led CFA's membership at its annual meeting in February of this year to give overwhelming support to a resolution which recognized that because the single most crucial issue before the insurance consumer today is the present automobile insurance system, prompt enactment of legislation emboying the substance of S. 354 is imperative. H.R. 1900 is substantially in accord with CFA's goal.

The current economic crisis has dramatized the cost issue which has been a recurring theme of no-fault discussions for the past eight years. Today's consumers are faced with increasing job insecurity and rising food, utility and health care cost, all of which have sensitized them to wasteful government and industry policies that diminish the value of the consumer dollar.

The conditions of today's economy emphasize the urgent need for an automobile insurance system which would give the consumer more for his or her premium dollar and would provide prompt payment of all accident claims. Today more than ever, consumers simply cannot afford the tedious delays inherent in the "fault" system. The DOT study showed that 30% of those seriously injured must withdraw from their savings accounts or sell property in order to survive and that 12% miss debt payments. A full 45% of the seriously injured receive no compensation from auto liability insurance.

Delay also means postponement of necessary medical treatment. As a practical reality, plaintiffs who look the worst to the jury often recover the most and are consequently encouraged to wait until the jury verdict is in before making arrangements for cosmetic surgery or rehabilitation. This practice exacts a double price from the seriously injured consumer: increased medical costs because treatment was not initiated immediately and the anxiety of waiting for months or years for a jury verdict which may prove unfavorable.

The "fault" concept is clearly unfair, inefficient, expensive, unpredictable, and inadequate. Why then after eight years of debate must consumers still press for national reform? The arguments used by opponents to national no-fault have grown increasingly stale and tedious.

Those who cry that the negligence concept as applied to the automotive accident is somehow a sacred American institution have either not done their history and legal homework or are the servants of that segment of the personal injury bar whose self-serving interests are the obvious basis for such arguments. The very thorough and persuasive report of the Senate Judiciary Committee dated March 27, 1974 demonstrates that the national no-fault legislation embodied in S. 354 and H.R. 1900: (1) is constitutionally sound; (2) is consistent with the McCarran-Ferguson Act; and (3) preserves the traditional predominant role of state regulation in the field of insurance.

In terms of cost, the results of the widely acclaimed Milliman and Robertson study have been confirmed by the recently released cost estimates of State Farm Insurance. Both studies emphasized that cost estimates are not conclusive because cost is influenced by a host of factors such as inflation, highway attitudes, etc. Yet, with that caveat in mind, the State Farm figures do predict a nationwide premium savings of 10% for private passenger car owners—an amount equivalent to almost one billion dollars a year in consumer savings for current policyholders.

It cannot be overemphasized, however, that cost savings is not the paramount consideration which leads to consumer endorsement of S. 354 and H.R. 1900. If no-fault reform results in immediate and quality medical treatment, prompt payment to all who are injured, increased insurance company commitment to accident prevention, and a return to policyholders of a larger percentage of their premium dollars—all at a cost equal to or even slightly more than present premium levels, consumers will be better served. Assurance of lower premiums is an added extra, not the cornerstone of consumer support for national no-fault.

Opponents still cling to the argument that no-fault insurance should be delegated exclusively to the states. Despite strong public sentiment in favor of reform, a vast majority of the states have failed to create effective no-fault legislation. The slow pace of state responsiveness has strengthened CFA's commitment to the development of national standards. Only on the federal level can legislation effectively minimize the insurance difficulties of interstate travel and help eliminate much of the unnecessary administrative cost and confusion resulting from the wide disparity of state no-fault laws.

Under the language of this legislation, the determination of whether a state no-fault plan is in accord with the national standards is the only operational responsibility of the Federal government. State law will still determine the regulations of insurance, litigation procedures, rates, taxation, motor vehicle registration, and claims investigation. This sound and reasonable structure recognizes the historic need for each state to provide a flexible response to the varying needs of its citizens.

Because of the ineffectiveness of the "fault" system, CFA and other members of the NASCENT coalition support H.R. 1900 because of its focus on the victims of automobile accidents. It would assure prompt, adequate and reliable compensation for all accident victims. No longer would a victim have to rely on the costly and often unpredictable route of litigation which pits victims against policyholders. No longer would victims have to risk having their injuries aggravated because at the outset they hesitated to obtain good and thorough medical care, not knowing if they could afford to undertake that expense until the settlement negotiations or litigation had been resolved.

Without detracting from our strong support of H.R. 1900, we wish to take this opportunity to recommend three changes which would enhance the effectiveness of the legislation as drafted:

1. The disability threshold in Section 206(a)(5)(B) should be increased to 108 days. This would result in a three cent per premium dollar savings to policyholders.

2. Section III(a)(3) must be modified so as to establish an equitable portion of no-fault cost savings to the private passenger vehicle owner. We are pleased that $5,000 deductible originally included in S. 354 was lowered to $100 when the bill was reported by the Commerce committee. We urge a similar reduction in H.R. 1900.

3. Finally, it is imperative that Section 208(c) be replaced by a provision permitting consumer to buy, and requiring insurers to sell auto insurance coverage at prices reflecting the availability of adqeuate benefits for auto accident medical and hospital costs and loss of wages from reliable sources outside the auto insurance system.

Indicative of the cost saving to the consumer that should result from such a modification is Michigan's Coordinated Coverage Statute. As explained by Robert E. Vanderbeek, in April of 1975, this provision has resulted in an approximate consumer saving of $60 million in the state of Michigan. Such requirements have resulted in minimum savings or premium reductions of 40 to 50 per cent of the no-fault personal injury protection portion of the premium. This reduction may mean a 10 to 25 percent reduction in the over-all cost of auto insurance.

Clearly then, S. 354 and H.R. 1900 are in the best interests of those who are most affected by the present system—namely consumers both in their role as policyholders and in their role as potential victims.

Mr. VAN DEERLIN. Thank you, Ms. O'Reilly.
Our next witness is Mr. Maisonpierre.

STATEMENT OF ANDRE MAISONPIERRE

Mr. MAISONPIERRE. Thank you, Mr. Chairman. The American Mutual Insurance Alliance appreciates the opportunity of appearing today before the subcommittee. We have two statements that we prepared in advance and one was prepared for the hearing which was postponed on June 19 and a supplemental statement was prepared for these hearings, which discusses the action taken by the Senate Commerce Committee. Both of those statements are rather voluminous and I would appreciate their being introduced into the record and I will briefly summarize some of the major points we believe to be pertinent to this discussion at this time.

Mr. VAN DEERLIN. Fine. Without objection they will both be included.

Mr. MAISONPIERRE. Thank you very much, sir.

The discussion today is State or Federal no-fault automobile insurance reform?

In these few minutes we will argue the case for State action by emphasizing four important areas.

One, constitutionality and federalism. There are two important issues here to consider. On the one hand, there are those provisions in the Federal standards bill which would transform State agencies and employees into Federal instrumentalities. Constitutional obstacles created by these provisions can be overcome as is being done by the Senate Commerce Committee. But the cure involves the establishment of a Federal bureaucracy to administer no-fault reparations, insurance regulation, and the registration of motor vehicles, an essential element to implement the compulsory automobile insurance.

The second issue cannot be overcome. It is the matter of federalism. Simply put, the question is whether it is appropriate or desirable for Congress to impose its will on the States in matters which are basically of local concern.

One of the important advantages of our Federal system is that it permits two levels of government, the States and the Federal Government, to share in the policy decision process. If every time Congress becomes frustrated with State action or inaction it decides to take over an area which has traditionally been handled by State legislatures it will soon have little or no time available to act in those areas in which it and it alone can act—energy, defense, foreign affairs, et cetera.

Let there be no mistake about it. If Congress enacts no-fault insurance reform legislation, it must be prepared to assume a long-term, time-consuming commitment. No-fault is an area which can only be invaded by Congress as a matter of last resort. We do not believe that the State activities to date warrant Federal involvement.

Two, Federal Regulation and Administration: H.R. 1272 forthrightly provides for Federal administration while the Federal standards bills maintain a facade of State administration and regulation. But as the Senate Commerce Committee has recognized, to overcome the constitutional obstacles this bill will need to establish also direct Federal administration in noncomplying States.

No one has really asked: How can the Federal Government administer these laws? The legislation merely provides that DOT do so. One should question the ability of the Federal bureaucracy to implement the detailed regulatory responsibility demanded by Federal no-fault legislation. Take compulsory insurance, for example. States that have compulsory automobile insurance laws have found the only way those can be implemented is to relate their enforcement to registration of automobiles. When an individual registers his car he is asked to furnish evidence of insurance. If he cancels his insurance coverage after his car has been registered, local or State police forces are enlisted to pick up the registration tags unless proof is shown of renewed insurance.

Is the Federal Government prepared to establish a Federal motor vehicle registry and who will substitute for the local police in enforcing the system?

There will be need to enlarge the existing Federal enforcement agencies or a new Federal police force will have to be created for this purpose. It may be said it is not realistic to expect the States to give up control over motor vehicle registration, et cetera. But the States may find substantial incentive to turn the administrative functions over to the Federal Government. It costs New York State, for instance, millions of dollars a year to enforce compulsory auto insurance. Would it not make sense for New York to turn over the function to the Federal Government, thus releasing substantial funds for administration of other State programs?

This is precisely the States' attitude toward the administration of the Occupational Safety and Health Act. Federal laws authorize and in fact encourage, through substantial subsidies, State administration, yet more and more States are rejecting the opportunity to administer OSHA, turning the function over to the Federal Government. In turn the Department of Labor just projected a need for 8,000 inspectors to administer OSHA.

How many new employees would be required here to administer and enforce a Federal auto insurance program with millions of individual units instead of OSHA's thousands?

Frankly, we believe that the enactment of Federal automobile insurance, no-fault, will ultimately lead to complete federalization of the regulation of automobile insurance. This is inescapable and inevitable. The federalization of automobile insurance will in turn lead to a total restructuring of the competitive forces within the insurance business. This business is a highly competitive one, composed of hundreds of companies, both very large and very small. The Federal regulation will lead to an attrition of the smaller companies, with a much greater concentration of pricing power in the hands of a few giants. We do not believe this is in the public interest.

Three, diversity among reparation systems and not uniformity is in the public interest. It is argued that uniformity among State no-fault laws is good per se. Supporters of uniformity never explain why they believe uniformity of auto insurance systems is more important, for instance, than uniformity in the rules of the road. A June 17, 1975, Wall Street Journal article describes the hazards one incurs driving in Massachusetts. It blames in part the State's extremely high accident frequency on the fact that its driving laws are obsolete and fail to conform with similar laws in other States. It would seem, as a matter of obvious priority, that the establishment of a uniform standard for operating motor vehicles on public highways should take precedence over creation of a uniform system to compensate individuals after they have been involved in accidents. The priority should be to reduce accidents. Those that argue for uniformity of no-fault laws seem to be strangely affected by the lack of symmetry between State no-fault systems, but it is precisely this lack of symmetry which allows for response to local needs. Federal legislation is geared to overcome the worst problems which have been identified in a few urban centers and while the proposed solutions may resolve some of these problems they will result in substantial overkill everywhere else creating new problems of their own.

Four, the need to experiment: When DOT issued its report and recommendations, it stated that the States should experiment with reform. Today, 24 States are experimenting. The question is often asked: How long should we experiment? The question reveals both frustration and impatience with State activities. It also reflects a failure to appreciate the difference in timespan required to achieve credible results in experimenting with changes in social policy as against scientific experimentation.

As Eric Hoffer recently stated, we live in an instantaneous age. We demand instant tea and instant coffee, and although we would like to have instant no-fault experimentation result, this is just impossible. We are only now beginning to get adequate feedback in a few States on their no-fault operations, and what we are getting demonstrates serious flaws in our theoretical expectations. A clear demonstration of the need for additional experimentation is the extremely confusing cost story. You must be bewildered, just as we are, at the many conflicting cost projections being presented to Congress. The variations are a direct manifestation of the inability of experts, actuaries, and others to forecast with any degree of accuracy how no-fault would really work in any one State. Actuarial assumptions cannot predict the cost impact of changes resulting from the behavior of people in new legal environments.

What has happened to the theoretical cost assumption in the real world? The story cuts both ways. As for Massachusetts, no one expected its no-fault law to reduce costs as dramatically as has been the case. On the other hand, Connecticut and Florida no-fault laws are leading to substantial increases in the cost of automobile insurance in those States. While cost reduction may not be the sole criteria or objective of no-fault legislation, it is clear that Federal no-fault is being sold to both Congress and the American public as an important cost reducer. Both Congress and our customers have a right to know that Federal action may well lead to substantial automobile insurance cost increases on a countrywide basis. Anyone who categorically claims that the pending Federal bills will decrease cost has to be blind to the real world indications eminating from many States that have enacted no-fault.

When the Senate originally considered standards legislation, we were told that the pending bill was the best system that could be devised. The bill to be considered by the Senate now bears very little resemblance to its initial version, yet it, too, is being touted as the best. Frankly, there are no best no-fault systems. Each State must evaluate how best to balance the often contradictory needs of accident victims and the financial burden on policyholders as it reforms its automobile accident reparations system.

Thank you very much, sir.

[Mr. Maisonpierre's prepared and supplementary statements follow:]

STATEMENT OF THE AMERICAN MUTUAL INSURANCE ALLIANCE

AUTO INSURANCE REFORM—STATE VERSUS FEDERAL ACTION

I. INTRODUCTION

My name is Andre Maisonpierre and I am a vice president of the American Mutual Insurance Alliance. We are the major association of mutual property and casualty insurance companies. Our member companies write automobile and other property/casualty insurance coverages in all 50 states and the District of Columbia.

We appreciate the opportunity to present our views at this time. We are opposed both to the bills pending before this subcommittee and to any federal legislation on the subject of automobile reparations. Our position, which we have maintained consistently for more than seven years both before Congress and also before the various state legislatures, is one in support of sound auto accident reparations reforms *at the state level.*

In our view, federal legislation on this subject, whether in the form of "minimum standards" disclaiming federal control or a complete federal system, would result in a federalization of automobile insurance *regulation* as well as reparations. Federalization would create regulatory confusion, present constitutional hazards, prevent needed experimentation, reduce competition and increase costs—all to the detriment of the consumer. This is the primary basis for our opposition to federal action.

Our state action program for responsible auto insurance reform attempts to achieve a reasonable balance among five different and often contradictory objectives:

(1) To provide crash victims with prompt and fair compensation. Payment of no-fault benefits to auto accident victims to insure that 90% of auto accident victims be reimbursed for over 95% of their medical expenses; payment for substantial wage losses, survival losses, funeral and household expenses for victims and their families; restriction of the traditional tort recovery system to the more serious claims involving permanent injuries or death.

(2) To encourage driver accountability. Automobile accident reparation plans should meet the accident victim's sense of justice as well as his economic needs. Accordingly, any auto reparations reform plan must hold careless drivers accountable for losses they cause innocent victims.

(3) To lower costs. The benefits paid automobile accident victims must aim at a reduction in the total automobile insurance losses paid for bodily injury from losses which would be paid under the traditional tort reparations system. Hence, in order to offset the cost of paying most auto accident victims most of their economic losses, we have endorsed some restrictions on the tort systems.

(4) To equitably allocate costs. The present method of distributing automobile accident losses on the basis of causation must be retained. Good drivers should not subsidize careless ones. Innocent accident victims should not pay a greater share of the automobile accident losses, than those who cause such losses. Neither should private passenger automobile owners subsidize the cost of insurance for commercial vehicles.

To achieve this proper allocation of losses, we have supported a subrogation system of compulsory inter-company arbitration which allows for the equitable allocation of losses on the basis of causation. The system works both fairly and efficiently.

Equitable allocation of losses further requires that all losses arising out of automobile accidents—medical losses, wage losses,—be allocated to the automobile insurance system. This internalization of costs allows for the determination of the true costs of automobile operations. Without such internalization, there would be no way to identify the actual losses caused by auto accidents and it would be impossible to implement programs such as Title II of the Motor Vehicle Information & Cost Savings Act, a law which had its genesis in this subcommittee in 1972.

(5) To reduce court congestion. We support improved judicial administration to eliminate such court congestion which exists due to inefficient management. Our courts would be congested even if they did not have to handle a single auto accident case. Nevertheless, we seek by all means possible the facilitation of the handling of claim disputes so as to minimize recourse to the courts.

Our program and record demonstrate that we share with the sponsors of the several bills pending before this subcommittee a desire for reform of the auto reparation system. Our dispute is not with the need for reform, but rather as to how such reform should best be accomplished.

We have actively worked for the enactment of state no-fault automobile insurance plans which implement the objectives stated above. Our reform program both embodies no-fault benefits and tort restrictions. The level of no-fault benefits and the nature of the tort restrictions which we have supported, have varied from state to state, depending on the local conditions and the nature of the problems that had developed with the traditional automobile reparation system in a particular state.

II. STATE ACTION

All 50 state legislatures have been deeply involved in automobile accident reparation reform over the past six years. State action can be classified under three headings—(1) states which have enacted no-fault auto insurance reform meeting the basic objectives described above—(2) states which have enacted no-fault reform programs which *they* believe to be appropriate to meet their needs and interest but which we feel to be inadequate and (3) states which are still in the process of considering the type of reform which would be best suited to meet their problems.

Every state has considered no-fault legislation. The fact that a state has not enacted a plan does not indicate rejection of the principle of reform.

Twenty-four states have enacted no-fault automobile benefit laws. (See Exhibit 1). As a result, 53.2% of our nation's population resides in a jurisdiction governed by a no-fault benefit law. This accomplishment speaks for itself. Of the 24 states which have adopted no-fault benefit laws, 16 states have enacted legislation which would limit recovery under the tort system. We believe that these states have, for the most part, met the objectives for reform which we have described above.

No doubt, there are some who will discount the level of state activities. But, the dire predictions which were repeatedly made in the past—that state legislatures would not or could not act—can no longer be supported. Although differences exist among the states in the enacted programs, these differences tend to reflect conscientious efforts by state legislatures to meet their particular local problems. Reform tailored to the needs of local communities is being achieved, carefully balancing the total needs of accident victims as against the cost of insurance to road users. That certain reform plans fail to meet *our* objectives or do not conform with the expectations of theorists is beside the point. What matters is that these reform programs work in the interests of the citizens of the states involved. Let me give you an example:

Oregon was one of the first states to enact automobile insurance reform. We opposed the reform plan ultimately enacted by the Oregon legislature. The Oregon reform program provides for substantial first-party, no-fault benefits but does not limit the tort system. Our concern was that such a plan would substantially increase the cost of auto insurance in regon. So far, we have been proven wrong. The average private passenger automobile rates in that state have remained stable, despite a substantial additional increase in their level of no-fault benefits.

III. WHAT'S WRONG WITH FEDERAL LEGISLATION?

A. UNIFORMITY

Supporters of federal legislation maintain that the differences among state no-fault plans would give rise to such a hodge-podge of benefit structures and legal requirements as to create chaos in interstate driving. They claim this alone demonstrates the need for federal legislation.

It is interesting to note that those who argue in support of a uniform no-fault program have done little if anything to achieve uniformity of those laws which govern the rules of the road. Greater uniformity among our states' automobile traffic laws and ordinances should lead to a reduction in accidents. Thus, as a matter of priority, if uniformity is thought to be important, shouldn't the emphasis be placed on legislation which would result in the control of accident losses first rather than on the compensation system designed to pay for those losses?

Even if we assume that uniformity is desirable, federal minimum standards would not bring it about. The proponents of standard legislation, while claiming that such uniformity is an essential element of reform, demonstrate an obvious inconsistency in their thinking. The Senate Committee on Commerce Report on S. 354, for instance, states "each state is given wide latitude to choose its own no-fault plan while adhering to the basic national standards."

By contrast, we believe that uniformity in auto insurance reform, is not a virtue but a handicap. For example, most states forming the eastern seaboard corridor have adopted differing forms of no-fault automobile benefit reparation. The predicted chaos has not occurred. In fact, state insurance commissioners and our member companies have reported that they have received no complaints, or evidence of confusion on the part of those involved in interstate travel.

Perhaps one reason why no confusion has arisen is the preventive and voluntary action taken by insurance companies to insure the proper meshing among different state programs. The insurance industry voluntarily moved to provide its customers with automatic policy endorsements extending policy coverage to include the full legal requirements on the owner or driver wherever the automobile is driven in the United States or Canada. For instance, a California driver (coming from his none no-fault state) injured in Michigan (a no-fault state) will automatically be covered under his own automobile policy for the economic losses he sustains just as though he were a Michigan resident meeting the compulsory legal requirements of that state. This "worry-free" insurance endorsement (Exhibit 2) has been filed in all jurisdictions by the Insurance Services Office on behalf of its members and subscribing companies. These companies write about 40% of the total private passenger automobile insurance in the United States; the balance of the industry has followed suit.

Diversity, not uniformity, is in the public interest. The auto insurance reform solutions required vary so much from state to state that it is impossible for Congress to structure one reform package compatible for all 50 states and the District of Columbia. Those who argue there is something wrong per se about differences in laws among the various states are quarreling with the whole concept of federalism and the sovereignty of individual states. The problems that have developed from our traditional auto reparation system vary extensively among the states.

For example, urban communities generate more tort claims per capita than rural areas. On the other hand, single car accidents are much more prevalent in rural communities. Predictably, these different problems respond best to different solutions. Each individual state knows better than the federal government how its public policy should bear on the responsibilities of the insurance carrier, the automobile owner, the doctor, the hospital, and the attorney in their relationships with automobile accident victims. No federal bill will allow adequate diversity. We will discuss this in more detail as we analyze some elements of the pending bills.

B. CONSTITUTIONAL PROBLEMS

Our legal and constitutional arguments are limited to the "standards" bill. We do not, and have never questioned the legality of Congress enacting a uniform Federal reparation system for the states with the administration of the system under Federal control.

As to the "standards" bills, we submit that their unique and coercive use of state officials to administer a Federal law violates the requirements of our system of Federalism set forth in the Tenth Amendment to the U.S. Constitution.

The provisions of Title III of S. 354 and of H.R. 1900 would become the Federal law in those states failing to enact legislation in compliance with Titles I and II standards. These provisions would preempt, in the affected states, all existing conflicting state laws. Among the laws to be preempted would be not only those laws dealing with the automobile reparation system but also many parts of the states insurance code dealing with automobile insurance regulation. Since Title III does not provide for a Federal regulatory apparatus to administer the Federal law imposed on those states, and since the regulatory laws of those states will have been preempted, a regulatory vacuum will have been created.

The sponsors of S. 354 and H.R. 1900 take the position that state officials would administer the Federal law as they had administered state laws previously. It is this coercive use of state officials—including the appropriation and disbursement of state revenues to administer federal law—which we believe raises a serious constitutional question.

If the administrative system contemplated by Title III is constitutional, there would be no reason, for instance, why the Federal government could not forcefully require state officials to administer the Internal Revenue Code in all of the states. If the Federal Government has the power to require state administrators to administer Federal laws and to compel state legislators to appropriate state funds for the administration of federal law, then what has become of states' sovereignty? As the Attorney General recently stated in testimony before the Senate Commerce Committee on S. 354, the issue of constitutional federalism is not a frivolous one. "It is close to the protection of diversity, creativity and freedom within our system. The importance of protecting and promoting these values should be a compelling consideration in determining whether a Federal uniform automobile insurance law is desirable and particularly whether requiring State agencies to implement such a law is appropriate."

The Attorney General has categorically stated that S. 354 raises important constitutional questions. As a matter of policy, it would be contrary to the public interest for Congress to enact legislation which would give rise to substantial constitutional arguments and which would tie the fate of automobile accident reform and the administration of reform and automobile insurance in the courts for years to come.

C. FEDERAL REGULATION OF AUTOMOBILE INSURANCE

Present national policy relating to insurance regulation is governed by the McCarran-Ferguson Act which leaves regulation to the states. Every bill pending before this subcommittee would alter this policy by bringing about a substantial element of federal regulation.

In the past 30 years, since enacting McCarran-Ferguson, Congress has held a number of extensive investigations of the relationship between it, states, and the insurance industry. On balance, Congress has concluded that the regulation of the insurance business should be left to the states. We believe that any decision to change this policy should be confronted squarely by Congress rather than being changed without overall policy consideration in the course of automobile reparation reform.

Insurance is one of the most diverse businesses in the nation. In most respects, it is a local business serving local needs. The Alliance believes the regulation of insurance must recognize and respond to this diversity.

An intrusion of federal regulation would be justified only if the states utterly failed in their job and there was a reasonable expectation that federal regulation would be immune from serious failings. We see no credible evidence that either of these conditions prevail. The states have moved and continue to move, to protect the public in innumerable areas relating to automobile insurance, including laws governing the prevention of cancellation, insolvency, residual market programs and consumer complaint systems. Conversely, there is nothing in the history of the federal regulatory system to instill confidence that federal regulation of insurance would be, on the whole, more efficient than the present state system. The shortcomings of federal regulation are frequently pointed out by public interest advocates.

Testimony received in late 1974 by the House Commerce and Interstate Committee as well as by the Senate Commerce Committee, was replate with criticisms of federal regulatory agencies for their dilatory procedures, inflexibility, lack of independence and incompetence. As a consequence, both the public and the affected industries have suffered.

Federal regulation has almost universally been held to be a failure if consumer protection is supposed to be its objective. Indeed, a report evaluating the responsiveness of 15 government agencies to the individual consumer, which was recently prepared for the Office of Consumer Affairs, is sharply critical of most of these agencies' awareness of problems in the marketplace and its consumer complaint-handling procedures.

By contrast, we believe that state regulation of insurance is acting in the public interest. Although often viewed as "big business," most automobile insurnace companies are relatively small. A handful of large companies are balanced by hundreds of medium size and small companies. The state regulatory mechanism has provided for a balancing of the needed protection of the smaller companies from possible anti-competitive activities of the larger ones while also allowing the competitive nature of the business to keep cost at a minimum and service at a high level. These desirable features could not be achieved under federal regulation.

Without question, federal regulation would allow the larger companies with extensive financial resources to be in a better position to plead their cases with the federal regulator while the smaller companies would find access to him very difficult. It would not take long for the thrust of regulation to be oriented against the needs of the smaller companies. The result would be, in a relatively short time, for the smaller companies to either merge, dissolve or disappear altogether. Therefore, federal regulation will create great economic concentration in the automobile insurance business with lessened rate competition and reduced market availability. Is it any wonder that, for the most part, companies which have expressed support for federal no fault legislation are the larger companies?

Today, the public is served by 51 insurance regulators strategically located in geographical centers which are readily available to all consumers for complaints, inquiries and any other asistance. These regulators are in a position to respond to consumer problems with solutions applicable to local situations. This local flexibility would not exist under a federal regulatory mechanism.

D. THE NEED FOR EXPERIMENTATION

Even though no-fault has now been in force in a number of states for several years, questions as to its operations remain unanswered.

First, there are questions as to constitutionality under both state and Federal constitutions being raised. For example, while the Senate Commerce Committee was considering S. 354 during the past Congress, the Florida Supreme Court held that the abolition of the tort system in property damage cases violated both the Federal and Florida constitutions. Apparently, in response to this decision, the Committee quietly struck from S. 354 a standard which would have required all states to abolish the tort system in property damage claims. But, imagine the national confusion which would have resulted from this court decision had the original S. 354 been enacted.

Consider also the lower court decision in Michigan which found a number of sections of the Michigan no-fault law to be in violation of both Michigan and Federal constitutions. The court came to the same conclusion as the Florida court as to property damage and, in addition, held invalid a provision requiring that no-fault benefits be in excess to other government mandated benefits. Significantly, this same provision is contained in S. 354 and H.R. 1900 and, in a somewhat modified form, in H.R. 1272. Incidentally, the constitutionality of the Michigan no-fault law has been reviewed by a number of additional lower courts in that state. Some have held the total Act to be unconstitutional and some, on the other hand, have held the Act to be constitutional. It will be some time yet for the appeals process to follow its course.

A New York state lower court has also held that states no-fault law to be in violation of both state and Federal constitutions. That decision has also now been appealed but, again, it will be some time before the highest court in the state renders a decision. A number of other constitutional cases are pending in other jurisdictions. Decisions in these cases will shed additional light on constitutional issues, both state and Federal.

Further, considerable question remains as to the extent of changes in the tort system desired by the public. The public has been led to believe that no-fault insurance will save them a lot of money. Newspaper editorials supporting federal no-fault legislation have all been bottomed on the theory that no-fault will pay out more benefits and will cost less than the traditional tort system—an obvious incongruity in itself. Most of the arguments advanced in support of S. 354 continue to be centered around the fact that passage of the bill will substantially reduce automobile insurance premiums on a countrywide basis. But, it has become quite obvious that no-fault auto insurance holds very little, if any promise of reducing automobile insurance premiums for personal passenger automobile owners. Real world experience is showing increasing evidence that no-fault may very well substantially increase automobile insurance costs, although it clearly does spread out benefits to more automobile accident victims.

The only company which has, to date, released no-fault operational results testified at length before the Senate Commerce Committee. In the state of Florida, for example, this large company reported that the reduction in benefit payouts resulting from the decrease in the number of tort liability claims due to the no-fault threshold has been more than absorbed by the high cost of tort claim judgments due to the unexpected increase in jury awards. The Florida no-fault law has been operational long enough to permit its results to be examined with a good deal of credibility.

Connecticut is another state whose no-fault law has been operative for some time. This company reported the same type of results in the operation of no-fault in Connecticut as it described for Florida. We believe that these laws have had sufficient opportunity to mature to provide us with some indication of how they are likely to operate in the future.

The New York no-fault law has been operative for only about a year and, accordingly, its results cannot be considered conclusive. However, the same tendencies exhibited in the operations of the Connecticut and Florida laws are clearly developing in New York.

What does this all mean? Clearly, consumers have been and are being misled by assertions that no-fault auto insurance can automatically be equated with lower automobile insurance costs. The fact is that automobile insurance premiums for bodily injury liabilities, including no-fault insurance are increasing today after having been held constant for the past two or three years. Admittedly, the increase in premium is due in part to the natural affect of inflation. But, more and more in an increasing number of states, rate increases can be traced directly to the operation of no-fault.

Supporters of federal legislation have urged the passage of S. 354 and H.R. 1900 on the basis of the Michigan no-fault experience. It is said that the Michigan no-fault law—a law which comes closest to S. 354 and H.R. 1900—is working well. Frankly, those who argue that all is well in Michigan are playing the ostrich game. We know that a large backlog of potential claims is being held back pending the determination of the constitutional issues as well as a court interpretation of the significance of the Michigan threshold which some maintain to be a very tight threshold while some others maintained it to be very loose. Hence, urging the adoption of Federal legislation based on a totally incomplete Michigan experience does not make good "sense".

Some additional light as to the extent of changes desired by the public may be shed as a result of the experience to be drawn from the operation of the Kentucky no-fault law. Kentucky recently enacted legislation allowing private passenger automobile owners to elect whether they would be compensated under a no-fault system or whether they would prefer the traditional tort remedy. The law requires that anyone electing a no-fault remedy receive a 10% automobile insurance premium discount. Although we might expect that this premium discount will act as a substantial inducement to automobile owners to select no-fault, the test will be the market place.

We forecast that as more data becomes available from each of the 24 states that have enacted no-fault laws, we will find that the most desirable may well be a nonsystem. We may have to accept that a no-fault plan which works well in one state may bring disastrous consequences in another. Continued experimentation will provide to policymakers the necessary facts to determine whether a uniform no-fault law is desirable and, if it is desirable, the best plan to adopt.

Certainly, there remains many unanswered questions relative to the costs and operation of no-fault automobile insurance. It is one thing to recognize the need and direction of reform. It is quite another to know the exact nature which the reform should take. We are confident that future no-fault laws will benefit from answers obtained from this needed field experimentation.

IV. OBSERVATION ON AUTO INSURANCE REFORM COSTS

Sooner or later, any discussion of automobile reparation reform leads to consideration of the cost of auto insurance. Although we agree that automobile reparation reform should not be promoted on the basis of cost reduction alone, we cannot accept a reform system which will increase the cost of automobile insurance to private passenger car owners.

Contrary to what the supporters of S. 354 and H.R. 1900 claim, the no-fault programs will increase insurance costs for private passenger automobile owners in almost every state. Proponents of these bills have relied entirely on the actuarial cost study performed by Milliman and Robertson at the joint request of the Department of Transportation and the National Association of Insurance Commissioners. However, the Milliman and Robertson study does not claim to measure the cost impact of alternative no-fault programs on private passenger automobile owners. All that the study does is to attempt to predict the impact of no-fault proposals on average and total premiums within a state. We submit that consumers, the press and others have been grossly misled by allegations that the "averages" published by Milliman and Robertson provide any clue as to what private passenger automobile owners would be required to pay for automobile insurance if S. 354 or H.R. 1900 were to become law. We are not here to argue the merits of the model developed by Milliman and Robertson. We do urge, however, that its report be placed in its proper perspective.

We have no quarrel with the format used by Milliman and Robertson. It is not with Milliman and Robertson that we are quarreling. Its report clearly warns of its limitation. Yet, proponents of these bills continue to disregard these warnings. State insurance regulators, speaking through the National Association of Insurance Commissioners have expressed their grave concern at the misleading use of the report. (See Exhibit 3.)

The Milliman and Robertson study does not—nor does it claim to—distinguish between the effects of cost on private passenger automobile owners and commercial vehicle owners. Since S. 354 and H.R. 1900 would transfer most of the cost of accidents caused by commercial vehicle owners on to private automobile owners, the "averages" cited by Milliman and Robertson are meaningless as to private automobile owners. If the Milliman and Robertson cost study is carried one step further by breaking out from the "averages" the impact on private passenger or commercial automobile insurance rates, the evidence demonstrates overwhelmingly that S. 354 and H.R. 1900 will increase cost to private automobile insurers in just about every state.

The American Mutual Insurance Alliance actuaries have taken the Milliman and Robertson Cost study this additional step forward. They have taken Milliman and Robertson's state by state "averages" and have applied to those "averages" two factors in order to measure the cost impact of alternative no-fault plans on private passenger car owners.

The first factor involves a correction needed to compensate for the inability to subrogate under the pending bills. In prior testimonies before this, and other Congressional Committees, we have discussed the Alliance's ongoing subrogation study which we undertook in the State of Massachusetts. That study involves an analysis of 1971 accident year claims, to analyze the potential impact which would ensue on personal lines and commercial line automobile insurance rates were the Massachusetts no-fault law prohibit subrogation. A total of $2,344,000 in no-fault first party benefit losses were examined. This is a credible sample. The study tells us that without subrogation no-fault first party benefit auto insurance premiums would need to be increased by 9% for private passenger car owners but decreased by 57% for commercial owners.

There is every indication that this modification would be generally applicable countrywide since the rate of subrogation in Massachusetts does not vary significantly from the rest of the nation. Hence we have applied this subrogation modification to the Milliman and Robertson "averages" as one of the factors in order to reach the theoritical impact of cost on private passenger owners under S. 354 and H.R. 1900.

The other factor which we have used relates to the primacy of workmen's compensation benefits. Please note that Milliman and Robertson have reduced medical expenses—wage loss costs in each state by 5% to reflect the fact that workmen's compensation benefits are made primary under the federal bills. However, this reduction clearly does not affect those losses generated by noncommercial vehicle owners. Hence, in order to differentiate between private passenger and commercial automobile insurance "averages", we have limited the impact of the affect of the primacy of workmen's compensation benefits to commercial lines only.

We have calculated what the average automobile insurance cost increase or reduction would be, on a state by state basis, for both personal lines and commercial lines, using Milliman and Robertson two alternatives—High Benefits and Tight Threshold and High Benefit and Loose Threshold. (See Exhibit 4). We have also accounted for the mandated rate decreases legislated in a number of states where no-fault laws were enacted.

As for High Benefit and Tight Threshold, 44 states show an increase in private passenger automobile insurance costs. The increases range all the way to 65.9% for Massachusetts. Seven jurisdictions show a decrease, with California showing the largest decrease—11.6%. All 51 jurisdictions show a substantial decrease for commercial insurance cost—a decrease in excess of 60% in most states.

As for the High Benefit and Loose Threshold alternative, every single state shows an increase in the cost of private passenger automobile insurance rates and, every single jurisdiction shows substantial decrease in the cost of commercial automobile insurance.

Although these figures do provide us with a better insight on how individual policyholders will be affected by differing no-fault alternatives, they do not reflect variations within the states as between rural and urban centers. One should anticipate that no-fault will bring about important cost shifts between urban and rural areas within a state. This is based on actual experience. For instance, while the average annual cost of compulsory bodily insurance for private passenger cars in Massachusetts was significantly reduced following enactment of no-fault insurance in that state, this "average" reflected both substantial reductions in Boston and increases for residents of small towns and rural areas.

However, Exhibit 4 does give us some insight as to what is likely to happen to the direction of the cost of private passenger automobile owners in each state under alternative no-fault plans. It is certainly a more accurate tool than the "averages" provided by Milliman and Robertson. It does not, in any way, contradict Milliman and Robertson. It merely carries the Milliman and Robertson's "averages" one step further.

One might well question the apparent universal preoccupation with Milliman and Robertson since it may well have become an irrelevant tool in costing S. 354 and H.R. 1900. The benefit package alternatives priced by Milliman and Robertson are quite different from those contained in the pending legislation. Section 206(a) was amended on the floor of the Senate by eliminating that provision which required any allowable tort liability recovery for non-economic losses to be reduced by $2,500. Our actuaries warn us that this amendment will produce at least a 5% increase swing in the Milliman and Robertson figures. For example, a state showing a 1% decrease would now indicate a 4% increase. There is no doubt that with these amendments, the benefit package contained in the pending bills comes close to the High Benefit-Loose Threshold alternative.

If costs were looked upon as an important consideration when the Senate acted in 1973 an S. 354, it must be looked upon today as the essential consideration in view of the combined inflationary and recessionary pressures converging on the nation. Accordingly, every effort should be made to assess the potential cost of S. 354 and H.R. 1900 with the best actuarial tools that can be devised. Let us remember that Milliman and Robertson worked from a theoretical model. Real life experience does not always parallel theoretical expectations. No-fault is no exception to this general rule.

We are beginning to get enough hard data in some no-fault states to allow a better insight into the operation of no-fault. We have found, for instance, that our cost expectations in Massachusetts were conservative. The cost effectiveness of no-fault in Massachusetts went considerably beyond our theoretical projections. Conversely, we have been disappointed at the operations of no-fault in Florida. There, contrary to our Massachusetts expericnee, the real experience fell far short of our theories. As a result, the companies have had to substantially increase automobile premiums in that state.

It has always been very difficult to predict human behavior under changing insurance situations. A classic example is the very low projections that had been made as to the utilization of Medicare and Medicaid. We are experiencing the same difficulty in predicting behavior under no-fault.

The Milliman and Robertson cost analysis was developed from a highly theoretical model. Since no-fault is now operational in may states, should it not be evident that actual experience should be used to project the cost implication of federal no-fault legislation rather than theories? Extensive evidence was produced to the Senate Commerce Committee that S. 354 will increase cost of insurance for owners of private automobiles in just about every jurisdiction.

There has not been any attempt to cost Title III of S. 354 and H.R. 1900. Our studies indicate that Title III benefits would increase Milliman and Robertson's cost projections by at least 55% over their highest estimates. Although it may be the hope and expectation of the bills supporters that all states will enact Title I and Title II federal requirements, this should not be taken for granted. Would not it be prudent to require testimony on the possible cost of title III before enacting a program which could very substantially increase the cost of automobile insurance to most motorists? Title III benefits would cost anywhere from 44% to 59% more than present auto insurance costs, depending on which state the federal reparation system would be imposed.

We have made no attempt to cost H.R. 1272. Since the bills benefit package would provide for the payment of non economic losses in all cases, regardless of fault, we earnestly believe that it will have a very serious escalation impact on automobile insurance rates.

V. SPECIFIC OBJECTIONS TO PENDING FEDERAL LEGISLATION

We have examined the pending federal legislation in light of some of the basic concepts which we have already expressed. We cannot support any of the pending bills for the following reasons:

A. ALL OF THE BILLS WOULD FEDERALIZE THE REGULATION OF AUTOMOBILE INSURANCE IN CONFLICT WITH NATIONAL POLICY

In enactment of the McCarran-Ferguson Act, Congress established national policy with regard to the regulation of the insurance industry. The Act provides, "Congress declares that the continued regulation and taxation by the several states of the business of insurance is in the public interest, and that silence on the part of Congress shall not be construed to impose any barrier to the regulation or taxation of such business by the several states." (empahsis added).

Further, the Act states, "The business of insurance, and every person engaged therein, shall be subject to the laws of the several states which relate to the regulation or taxation of such business."

We have already argued against the federalization of the automobile insurance business. H.R. 1272 is a complete federal system. By contrast, S. 354 and H.R. 1900 appear to recognize the desirability of state regulation of automobile insurance. Both bills clearly state the need to "recognize, respect and avoid interfering with the historical role of the states in regulating and exercising legislative authority over the business of insurance."

However, in spite of these clear and unambiguous statements, the substantive provisions of S. 354 and H.R. 1900, are in direct confrontation and conflict with state automobile insurance laws and regulations. The areas of confrontation and conflict can be divided into three:

    1. Requirements which would exceed existing authority of state insurance regulators.

    2. Requirements which overlap existing state automobile insurance laws and regulations which would require substantial state legislative action to conform with the specifics of S. 354 and H.R. 1900.

    3. Regulations which are in direct conflict with existing state automobile insurance regulatory laws.

Let us describe each of these in some detail.

1. Areas wherein the State Insurance Regulator would require Additional Authority

State insurance regulators, like any other state or federal administrators, derive their authority from those appropriate state or federal lwas which create their respective offices and which assign responsibilities to them. Unless they can trace their actions to such authority, they are powerless.

The bills would require the state insurance commissioner to assume certain responsibilities and to discharge certain obligations which are beyond the scope of state laws. Here are some examples. For purposes of simplicity, herafter, we will refer to the section numbers of S. 354.

Section 109(c) would require the insurance commissioner to establish and maintain, for automobile accident victims, medical and vocational rehabilitation programs.

This would include the establishment of procedures to evaluate treatment rendered, charges for services and the rendering of periodic reports. No state insurance commissioner has such authority today. To the extent that such authority does exist in the states it is being exercised by state vocational rehabilitation agencies. For the state insurance commissioner to involve himself as required would necessitate specific state legislative action. It is questionable whether the states would respond to this federal mandate, since it is poor management to detach responsibility for the rehabilitaion of automobile accident victims from another state agency which has the expertise in rehabilitation.

Section 109(d) "authorizes" the state insurance commissioner to coordinate with other appropriate government agencies "in the creation and maintenance of an emergency health services system."

First of all, no state insurance commissioner has such authorization; other state officials have this responsibility. Again, the desirability of establishing an emergency care system for automobile accident victims alone is questionable. However, apart from this, it is wrong to assume that federal legislation is either required to permit the states to grant this authority to their insurance commissioners or that federal legislation can, by itself, provide this increased authority to the state insurance commissioners. This "authorization" is illustrative of the basic fallacy in which these bills view state-federal relations.

Section 108(b) would require state insurance commissioners to establish assigned claims plans.

Few state insurance commissioners have this power today, and their authority to establish such plans must come from state laws and not from Congress.

Section 109(b) requires commissioners to establish a consumer information system whereas purchasers of automobile insurance would be able to compare prices, rates, etc.

Although state insurance commissioners may have sufficient authorization to allow them to establish such consumer information services, most of them have questioned such programs as misleading insurance buying information. In any event, the establishment of such programs would require the gathering of statistical data at costs often beyond that permitted by the budgets of some state insurance departments. Thus, this particular provision would require, at the very least, substantial increases in those budgets.

2. Interference with the Administration of State Automobile Insurance Laws

Again, referring to their Declaration of Policy, S. 354 and H.R. 1900 assert that "The Federal Government itself (should not) directly administer, operate or direct the administration of operation of such system (a motor vehicle accident and insurance law)."

We support this declaration of intent.

However, we believe that the substantive provisions of these bills fail to carry it out.

State automobile insurance regulatory laws not only generally require the state administrators to act in certain general areas, but also establish standards which the administrators must use in the implementation of their responsibilities. S. 354 and H.R. 1900 would require performance of specific administrative acts in areas already covered by state insurance law. However, the standards describing what an insurance commissioner would be expected to do, or not to do, may be at variance with many existing state requirements. Here are some examples:

Section 104(b) details how "self-insurance" shall be regulated.

Today, every state insurance law requires the state insurance commissioner to regulate self-insurance. But, the methods of regulations vary as the need for regulations vary among the states. The fact that the states do regulate self-insurance today is beside the point. No longer would a state official be able to carry on with his administration of self-insurance under his state insurance law.

Section 105(a) would require each state insurance commissioner to establish and implement an insurance system through which any required no-fault benefits and tort liability coverages will be conveniently and expeditiously available.

Today, each state has a Plan through which any licensed automobile insurance driver can secure insurance. But, as should be expected, because of local situations, these Plans vary substantially among the states. However, Section 105 sets forth specific standards for the operations of these Plans. For instance, commissioners would be required to insure that these Plans provide coverage at a subsidy to the economically disadvantaged in need of their automobiles for work-related purposes. Not only is this particular requirement absent from any existing state Plan, but on its face it is discriminatory, and flies against the basic foundation of every state rating law, which, without exception, are predicated on the requirements that rates shall not be excessive, inadequate, or discriminatory.

Section 201(d) would require the state insurance commissioner to submit to the federal Department of Transportation "periodically all relevant information which is requested by the Secretary" for the purpose of evaluating whether the state automobile insurance reparation plan is in accordance with federal requirements.

This would require the state insurance commissioner to collect, on a periodic or routine basis, data requested by a federal agency may be of little or no value in assisting him in discharging his obligations. The collection of data and information is a costly undertaking. Insurance commissioners do collect a considerable amount of data today to assist them in implementing their responsibilities. However, in order to avoid conflicting data collection systems, existing statistical gathering programs would have to be abandoned if they are different from federal requirements. Thus, the quality of state insurance regulations may very well suffer because of an inadequacy of information which state insurance commissioners may feel are needed for proper implementation of state laws.

Section 211(b) limits the powers of the state insurance commissioners to approve the terms and conditions of any contracts, certificates, or other evidence of insurance to those which "are consistent with the purposes of this Act and fair and equitable to all persons whose interests may be affected."

Thus, very clearly, if "the purposes of this Act" vary from the purposes of a specific state law, that insurance commissioner would be powerless to approve those terms and conditions of insurance contracts which attempt to implement state insurance requirements.

3. Conflict with State Insurance Laws

Both the legislative purpose clauses of S. 354 and H.R. 1900 and the Report filed in support of S. 354 by the Senate Commerce Committee go to great lengths in attempting to persuade that these bills do not conflict with state automobile insurance laws or regulations. Again, the substantive provisions are directly to the contrary. For example:

Section 105(b) deals with cancellation, refusal to renew, or termination of the automobile insurance contract.

Every state insurance law does restrict substantially the right to cancel automobile insurance contracts. But, not one state follows the detailed and often unrealistic provisions contained in this section.

Section 108(a)(D) would require that in case of an insolvent insurer, the insured shall collect his basic restoration insurance benefits from the Assigned Claims Plan.

This provision is in direct conflict with laws existing in 47 states and the District of Columbia for the payment of benefits and the reimbursement for unearned premiums to victims of insolvent property and casualty insurance companies. In fact, the states would be required to dismantle the apparatus which was created in a period of a little less than two years following extensive studies by the Senate Anti-Trust and Monopoly Subcommittee and the Senate Commerce Committee on the problems created by automobile insurance company insolvencies. As an aftermath of those investigations, the same sponsors and supporters of S. 354 introduced legislation to establish a federal insolvency program since "hearings had demonstrated that a major consumer problem existed and in no way could the states take appropriate action in timely fashion." The fact is that the states "surprised" the supporters of federal legislation when they took action in a highly commendable time frame.

Section 108(a)(D) perhaps should be characterized as a "Freudian slip" clearly revealing a general intent and purpose to federalize the automobile insurance regulatory system in spite of the laudable purposes expressed in the Declaration of Policy of S. 354 and H.R. 1900. Significantly, the federal insolvency program which would be imposed by this section and which would vacate existing state plans falls far short of the protection which consumers presently enjoy. State plans reimburse policyholders of insolvent companies for unearned premiums whereas Section 108(a)(D) contains no such protection.

Interestingly enough, the Senate Commerce Committee, when studying the automobile insurance insolvency question was very critical of then existing state plans because of their failure to provide reimbursement to policyholders for unearned premiums. Accordingly, all existing state insolvency plans were amended to provide for such consumer protection and no plan enacted thereafter failed to so provide. Yet, ironically, Section 108(a)(D) would deny existing automobile insurance policy holders the type of protection provided by the states at the urging of Congress itself.

Section 209 requires that insurers make available certain automobile insurance coverages over and above "basic restoration benefits."

For example, (b) requires the mandatory offering of physical damage insurance, subject to an optional deductible not to exceed $100; or a coverage for work loss which exceeds limitations on basic restoration benefits. These and other mandatory offerings are in direct conflict with provisions of existing state insurance law. Thus, once again, the federal insurance law and regulations would preempt and replace existing state insurance codes.

This has not been an exhaustive presentation of the substantive provisions of S. 354 and H.R. 1900 which not only conflict, contradict and interfere with existing state automobile insurance laws and regulations but also fly in the face of the avowed purposes of these bills.

In addition, these examples demonstrate that these bills conflict with national policy as reflected in the McCarran-Ferguson Act.

In interpreting McCarran-Ferguson, the courts have held that the primary legislative purpose of the Act was to reaffirm the states' power to regulate insurance, subject to constitutional limitation, and insure that state regulatory plans would not be impaired and overriden except by specific and explicit Congressional enactments.

These bills are in direct conflict with this public policy. They direct that the ultimate judgment as to whether the automobile insurance business is being regulated to a requisite standard be made not by the states, not by Congress, but by a federal administrative agency—the Department of Transportation. For instance, the Department would decide whether:

The law of the state complies with Title II.

A state insurance commissioner has established and maintained a medical and vocational rehabilitation program.

A state insurance commissioner has established an assigned claims plan.

A state insurance commissioner has established a consumer information system.

A state insurance commissioner has regulated "self-insurance."

A state insurance commissioner has established an insurance system through which required no-fault benefits and tort liability coverages will be offered to the consumer.

The automobile insurance rates of a state are "reasonable and not fairly discriminatory among similarly situated applicants."

A state insurance commissioner has submitted data to the Department of Transportation.

Terms and conditions of insurance contracts approved by the state insurance commissioner are "consistent with the purposes of this Act, and fair and equitable to all persons whose interest may be affected."

It is self-evident that requiring the Department of Transportation to judge whether state law complies with all the above stated provisions cannot be reconciled with the existing public policy to leave regulation of the insurance business to the states.

If this leaves any doubt as to the pervasive role of the Secretary of Transportation in the regulation of automobile insurance business, they should be dispelled upon analysis of Section 201(h). This section would require the Secretary to

review annually the operation of state no-fault plans and report and make recommendations based on his findings as to:
  cost savings;
  appropriate methods for refunding any cost savings realized from the institution and operation of no-fault insurance;
  the impact of no-fault insurance on senior citizens, rural residents, farmers, the economically disadvantaged, and those who live in the inner city;
  the impact of no-fault insurance on the problem of duplication of benefits;
  the effect of no-fault insurance on court congestion;
  the impact of no-fault insurance, reduced speed limits and other factors on automobile insurance rates; and
  the impact of no-fault insurance on competition within the insurance industry particularly with respect to the competitive position of small insurance companies.

Further, S. 354 and H.R. 1900 would not necessarily replace state regulation of automobile insurance. They would, however, add another and higher administrative layer. Issuance of regulations at the state level would be only an intermediate step since any fundamental regulatory changes would require approval of the Secretary of Transportation. This would create substantial conflict and delay. Even if regulations did not create such problems at the federal level, doubt, and uncertainty would be injected into regulation at the state level because nothing could be final until reviewed by the Secretary. Additionally, since the review by the Secretary is continual, the possibility arises that at any future time current regulations could suddenly become unacceptable to the Secretary. For example, he might conclude that since the majority of states had one type of regulation, in the interest of uniformity, all non-comforming states should change.

H.R. 1272 is explicit in its stated objectives to transfer the regulation of the automobile insurance business to the Secretary of Transportation. Consequently, the bill would do serious damage to existing state regulatory bodies and to the orderly process of the automobile insurance business. The bill provides for federal preemption of much regulation of the automobile insurance business presently performed by the states. However, it fails to provide for some regulatory functions relating to the business, such as the licensing and examination of companies, handling of consumer complaints. The result would be dual regulation of automobile insurance and a corresponding increase cost and confusion to both the industry and the consuming public.

Additionally, the bill does not address the intricacies of automobile insurance regulation. No consideration is given to how the Secretary of Transportation would implement the following necessary regulatory responsibilities:
  The administration of self insurance.
  The approval of form and terms of insurance contracts.
  The evaluation, approval and establishment of an assigned claims bureau.
  The establishment and implementation of a plan to assure that insurance will be conveniently and expeditiously available at proper rates to all applicants for insurance who cannot conveniently obtain insurance through ordinary methods.
  The supervision of individual insurance contracts, including terminationl non-renewal, etc. The allocation of financial burden of losses among reparations obligors based upon the propensities of different vehicles.
  The enforcement of "compulsory insurance."

B. THE BENEFIT PACKAGES ARE EITHER UNFAIR OR TOO COSTLY

Except for H.R. 1272, pending federal bills fail to provide a proper balance between the economic and non-economic loss recoveries. S. 354 and H.R. 1900 cut much too deeply into the right to recover for non-economic losses of innocent automobile accident victims. The criteria established to determine the accessability to the tort system for non-economic losses are unfair because they discriminate against large population groups.

For example, the elderly victim will receive limited no-fault benefits, since frequently he will incur no loss of wages and since Medicare will cover a substantia, portion of his medical bills.

Further, many elderly persons do not own automobiles and yet continue to be subject to automobile accidents. Clearly, they would not benefit from any possible automobile insurance premium reduction resulting from no-fault.

working population.

Contrary to the assertion of its supporters, S. 354 and H.R. 1900 do not allow innocent automobile accident victims the right to recover for economic losses exceeding no-fault benefits under any circumstances. Since, the bills would set an average monthly limit of 1000 in wage replacement, those earning in excess of $12,000 per year would be unable to collect benefits for their full economic losses even if their injuries were clearly caused by another person's negligence. There is little justice to this and the inequities resulting will be difficult to accept by consumers adversely affected.

As to H.R. 1272, we believe that the benefit package proposed will be so costly as to be completely impractical. Compensation for all accident victims for all of their losses, economic and non-economic, may be a desirable social objective. However, the higher cost of such a program appears inconsistent with the goal of achieving a reduction in the cost of auto insurance.

We also question the desirability of requiring that unlimited medical benefits be provided in the reparation package. The impact of this provision on the cost of automobile insurance cannot be measured. No one knows today what the cost of medical care will be 1, 5, 10 years hence. This cost not only relates to the procedures and care of today but also will reflect the application of new procedures yet to be developed. New medical techniques will prolong life at very high costs. When cost projections are made of the impact of new benefit structures on premium rates, it is generally assumed that the level of use of medical care will remain constant. This assumption may be valid if the medical care costs being contemplated are provided within a relatively short time from the day of the calculations. But, if the care is to be given over a period which could cover decades, the assumptions becomes totally invalid. Our concern is that in time unlimited medical care may drive the cost of automobile insurance out of reach of the average automobile owner. This is particularly true if the medical care benefits are totally unrestricted, without co-insurance, inside limits, insurer participation or control.

A California workmen's compensation medical study demonstrates that the rate of inflation of the more costly medical techniques is considerably greater than routine medical care. The study reveals that over the past 10 years the percentage of medical losses paid under the California workmen's compensation law of over $25,000 has almost doubled compared to the total medical losses paid.

Further, unlimited medical care benefits will create severe problems, particularly for small automobile insurers. The Reinsurance Association of America, is now urging that a cap on medical benefits be established in all no-fault legislation. The problems of providing unlimited medical benefits reinsurance to automobile insurance companies is becoming increasingly evident as a result of the experience developing in those states which provide for unlimited medical benefits.

This should come as no surprise. In a letter to Senator Hart dated February 13, 1974, Mr. Harold J. Hudson, Chairman of the Board, General Reinsurance Corporation, answering questions from Senator Hart as to the impact of unlimited medical benefits on smaller insurers, warned:

"Unlimited medical, hospital and rehabilitation payments would cause difficulty to the small companies, since they would have to purchase reinsurance for high limits on a small premium basis. Large companies could distribute the cost of high limit reinsurance for the relatively rare jumbo claim over a much larger premium volume." Mr. Hudson further stated that "there is no question that this (unlimited medical care) presents a substantial problem to the small company which would have to purchase reinsurance on a restricted premium basis." A number of chief executives of small companies, in testimony before the Senate Judiciary Committee in 1974, expressed fear that this provision alone might force them out of business.

Perhaps this cost impact and its threat to small companies led Senator Magnuson to write to Senator Burdick on February 20, 1974, that the Senate Commerce Committee "would welcome an amendment to S. 354 proposing a minimum limit of $100,000 for medical and rehabilitation expense."

C. NONE OF THE BILLS WOULD PERMIT FULL SUBROGATION

Accountability, which we believe to be an essential element of any automobile reparation reform plan, can only be reflected in no-fault automobile insurance systems through subrogation. Automobile drivers expect and demand accountability in the use of the road by other drivers. Yet, none of the pending federal no-fault bills permit subrogation. Is it equitable for government to protect careless drivers to the financial detriment of their innocent victims? Further, as for the allocation of costs, in the absence of subrogation, there is an implied insistence that the private passenger automobile owners subsidize the losses caused by commercial vehicles. We believe the owners of commercial vehicles are in a better position to absorb the cost of highway losses which they cause. Why should the primary incentive for careful use of the road—the impact of carelessness on insurance rates—be eliminated as to commercial owners?

We believe that the Senate recognized the validity of these arguments when it voted in 1974 to add to S. 354 an amendment which would allow a state law to provide for subrogation of claims as between private passenger motor vehicles and commercial vehicles. However, while recognizing the need for equity on the one hand, the Senate rendered this amendment totally ineffective by limiting its application to losses exceeding $5,000. The DOT automobile reparation study revealed that only 15% of all economic losses resulting from motor vehicle accidents exceed $5,000. Thus, 85% of the losses would escape loss transfer as a result of the limiting clause of Section 111 (a) (3).

The elimination of subrogation as between commercial and private passenger vehicles will result, as we have shown, in a substantial subsidy of commercial automobile insurance premiums by private passenger automobile owners. Remember that, if the subrogation provisions under the Massachusetts no-fault system were removed, commercial automobile insurance premiums would be reduced 57% while passenger car premiums would increase by 9%.

In the February 24, 1975, issue of *Business Insurance* Chairman Magnuson was quoted as stating that "at the rate we are going, 'saving to the taxpayer'—should be changed to 'reduction of the federal budget deficit'." It is a fact that the federal government is the largest owner and operator of motor vehicles in the United States and it would therefore save a considerable amount of money from what it now pays as a self insurer of all those postal service, military and other motor vehicles.

We agree with Senator Magnuson that S. 354 is likely to reduce the cost of automobile insurance to the federal government, but, the reduction comes about as a result of the federal government being the owner of commercial vehicles and no longer accountable for the costs of the highway losses it generates. No doubt, the federal government would reap substantial benefits from the inequitable subsidy of commercial automobile insurance rates by private passenger owners if the limitations to Section 111(a)(3) were to be enacted by Congress.

D. PENDING FEDERAL BILLS WOULD MAKE HEALTH INSURANCE BENEFITS PRIMARY

The Senate Commerce Committee's (1973) report on S. 354 clearly recognized that the cost of all vehicle accidents should be borne by motorists and should not be subsidized by the entire population through their health insurance policies. This was reflected in Section 204(f) which allowed the states to permit other benefit providers, i.e., health insurers, to coordinate their benefits with no-fault coverages in order to avoid payment of duplicate benefits.

Section 208(c) of S. 354 and H.R. 1900 reverses this decision for all practical purposes. It would require a health insurance policy to pay for all medical losses arising from automobile accidents unless a state would find that such provisions "would affect adversely or discriminate against the interests of persons required to provide security covering motoring vehicles in such state."

It is to be assumed, of course, that Section 208(c) contemplates that if a motorist carries health insurance coverage, his automobile insurance premium shall be reduced, since the automobile insurance benefits would be excess to the benefits to be paid under his health insurance policy. No consideration was given on the floor of the Senate when S. 354 was amended as to the potential impacts of this and in violation of the law.

Additionally, this section places costly new and unnecessary administrative burdens on automobile insurance carriers—ultimately reflected in higher insurance costs. One of the alleged benefits of S. 354 is to reduce the administrative cost of automobile insurance, but Section 208(c) will substantially increase these costs.

Perhaps the most undesirable effect of Section 208(c) is that it will deny automobile accident victims the benefit of those techniques developed by casualty insurers in the management of trauma cases. Already, those techniques which were developed by workers' compensation insurers are being applied to automobile no-fault coverages. Consider, for instance, the case of a 22 year-old school-teacher, paralyzed from the waist down, when a sudden tire blow-out rammed her car into a bridge abutment in May 1973. Hers was one of the first catastrophic injury cases to be reported under New Jersey's no-fault benefits auto insurance law. Although it was obvious from the nature of her injuries that she would be permanently paralyzed below the waist, a blending of the efforts of the individual and her family, the medical specialists and the trained staff of the casualty insurer allowed for a maximum level of recovery, including her return to a rewarding professional career as home economics teacher.

The automobile insurer did much more than just sign the checks for the $22,000 in costs associated with her accident. Since the insurer was able to coordinate basic medical expenses with a variety of other benefits—including wage loss payments—there were strong financial incentives to provide the injured with the very best in medical care, encouraging the fullest degree of rehabilitation in the shortest time period possible. It is this coordinated package of care that is the real strength of the casualty insurance system.

Splitting the claims between the casualty insurer on the one hand and the health plans on the other, would result in an expensive duplication of effort in the investigation of these claims. Payment to the injured would be delayed and the overall cost to the consumer would probably increase.

Of course, most auto crash victims do not require the extensive wage benefits and long term medical care and rehabilitative services now available under no-fault coverages in many states. But in every accident case, the policyholder expects prompt and efficient handling of his claim—even where the only consequence is damage to his car.

In cases where more than one car is involved in the crash, the policy holder wants assurances that he will be protected against legal liability. Although no-fault laws do place limits on the drivers liability, it is not abolished entirely. In a serious accident, one where several people may be injured, the driver will need the services of trained investigators and attorneys—services which will be provided by his auto insurer.

This is the great advantage of casualty insurance—the only system which gives the accident victim a single, reliable source responding to his total needs.

That this is recognized by individual consumers can readily be ascertained by taking a look at what is going on today in the State of Michigan. The Michigan no-fault law provides that an automobile insurance carrier *must* offer its policyholders a 20% reduction in his no-fault automobile insurance coverage if he elects to make health insurance primary. Less than 5% of policy holders have opted for this 20% reduction in no-fault insurance premium. In other words, in excess of 95% of Michigan's private passenger automobile owners· have rejected an insurance coverage similar to that which would be imposed upon them by Section 208 (c).

Today, anti-duplicative provisions have been incorporated in three state no-fault systems.

They are in the states of Colorado, New York and New Jersey. All three require that automobile insurance shall be primary. The advantages of making casualty insurance primary over health have been recognized by consumers themselves, state legislators and regulators. It is difficult to understand why Congress would want to reverse these carefully considered decisions.

E. PRACTICAL EFFECTS OF CONSTITUTIONAL PROBLEMS

We have already discussed the constitutional issues which would arise as a result of the state-federal confrontations under S. 354 and H.R. 1900. However, we call attention to practical considerations of the highest importance which will have to be dealt with if the courts were to find unconstitutional the state-federal scheme contemplated under this bill.

The practical consideration and application of this displacement of state automobile insurance law should be of particular concern to this Committee since it is likely to create utter chaos for years to come.

Most of the testimony before this Committee has emphasized the changes which state legislatures would have to enact in their automobile reparation system to meet federal requirements. However, to achieve conformance with the federal standards, states will also have to amend their automobile regulatory insurance laws. As we have seen, existing state laws dealing with insurance contracts, assigned risk plans, insolvency payments, rating, self-insurance, cancellation, etc., will have to be brought into federal conformity. Additional powers will have to be legislated for state insurance departments. These additional powers and responsibilities will require substantially greater budgets which may not be of any material benefit to the states.

What must be emphasized is that failure to take legislative action in any one of these many areas will automatically disqualify a state. We submit it is unlikely that any number of states will legislate the multiple legislative changes contemplated in the bills in the limited time constraints allowed. The large number of state officials who testified before the Senate Judiciary Committee in opposition to national standards demonstrates that full state "compliance" cannot be assumed. If states do not comply, what is likely to result?

Clearly, Title III would apply. The question is—who would then administer the new federal automobile insurance regulatory auto reparation systems?

As we have already stated, we question whether the federal government can constitutionally require a state insurance commissioner to administer federal insurance laws or to force a state legislator to appropriate state funds to administer federal insurance laws. If these contentions are correct—and many unimpeachable constitutional authorities have raised these same constitutional doubts—a regulatory vacuum will exist. Yet, S. 354 and H.R. 1900 are not self-executing. They, specifically prohibit "self-regulation" of the system. The bills mandate the approval of the terms and conditions of policy forms before they can be used by automobile insurers. Insurers would be required to include new provisions in their policy contracts—but since many of these provisions would be in direct conflict with state insurance codes, these policies could not then be approved by state insurance commissioners. It is easy to appreciate the dilemma which would result if a state insurance commissioner finds that he cannot legally approve a new insurance contract. Insurance companies would then be barred from issuing policies in the state and, in turn, since Title III requires that insurance be compulsory, automobile owners would not be able to drive their automobiles legally. Hence, it must be recognized that enactment of S. 354 and H.R. 1900 in their present form may very well lead to the establishment of a new, vast federal bureaucracy, empowered to administer Title III and to regulate the business of insurance as well in those states failing to take all appropriate actions required under the bills.

The bills can best be described as a very daring gamble, in that they assume that state legislators are prepared to junk their existing automobile reparation programs and automobile insurance regulation systems, whether or not they believe the federal substitute to be in the interest of their constituents. We question whether the gamble can succeed. The odds are insurmountable.

F. S. 354, H.R. 1900, AND H.R. 1272 WOULD BAR THE OPPORTUNITY FOR FURTHER EXPERIMENTATION

Finally, we want to comment on the need for additional time for experimentation. The different provisions of benefits, the extent of no-fault, the constitutional limitations, are all areas which remain to be resolved. Also, the real impact in the market place of the costs of reform continues to be unknown. For these reasons, experimentation through different state approaches is in the public interest.

Yet, such experimentation will come to an abrupt halt should federal no fault legislation be acted upon by Congress.

Sponsors of S. 354 and H.R. 1900 claim that state experimentations could be carried out under the federal standards since the standards required are "minimum standards." We believe that the standards called for under the bill are maximum and not minimum. In support of this, we cite the fact that even though 24 jurisdictions have enacted some form of no-fault legislation, not one of these laws would meet the standards set forth in the bill. If the federal standards were as flexible as claimed, should we not expect that at least one of these laws would meet them? Exhibit 5 summarizes this lack of flexibility.

VI. Action Program—Past, Present and Future

States have produced an impressive legislation record on automobile reparation reform since attention was focused on the problem. The first serious attempt to identify public reaction to no-fault automobile reparation was undertaken just seven years ago when the Alliance launched its Guaranteed Benefits Experiment. The results of this experiment were of immense importance in structuring reform programs.

Moreover, only a little more than four years ago, the Department of Transportation published its study of Motor Vehicle Crash Losses and Their Compensation in the United States. In that brief interval—especially when considering the gestation time involved in our legislative progress—24 states have enacted some type no-fault law. As a result, over 53.2% of the nation's population is covered by no-fault.

The momentum for state action continues and the question no longer is whether the states will act, but rather when and in what manner they shall act.

Those who have expressed impatience with the speed at which reform is taking place at the state level fail to appreciate the normal time involved in any legislative process—state or federal.

However, no-fault auto reparation reform does not stop once the legislature has taken action and the governor has signed a bill into law. In numerous instances, legislatures have amended their original no-fault law either to correct inconsistencies, such as in Hawaii, or to solve certain constitutional problems, such as in Kansas, or to generally make it more efficient, as in New Jersey. Automobile reparation reform requires constant legislative oversight if its objectives are to be accomplished.

Also, implementation and administration of no-fault law require careful consideration by all involved interests. Consequently, in states that have enacted no-fault programs, insurance commissioners held a series of meetings for the purpose of establishing claims guidelines, developing simplified medical reporting procedures to speed up the payment of claims, and developing improved hospital admission and payment procedures. Additionally, the insurance companies and agents have launched extensive public education campaigns to inform all automobile owners of their rights and opportunities under the new reform plans.

VII. Conclusion

We reiterate our strong support for automobile reparation reform. For the reasons stated, we believe this reform should take place at the state level. As the record demonstrates, impressive state action has already been obtained and the momentum for reform continues.

We oppose any federal legislative action which, we submit, would inevitably bring federalization of the automobile insurance system. Federal legislation will create regulatory confusion, present constitutional hazards, prevent needed experimentation, reduce competition and increase costs—all to the detriment of the consumer.

We urge the committee to reject the proposals before it and permit state **reform** efforts to continue.

EXHIBIT 1

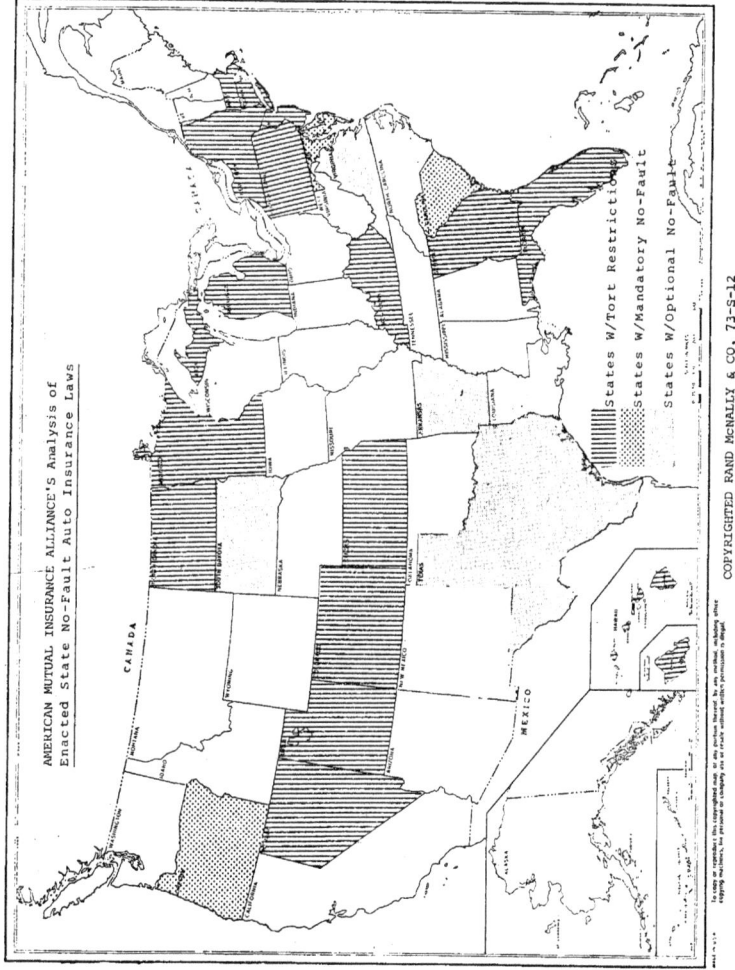

Exhibit 1

STATE No-FAULT LAWS

Percentage of Nation's population covered

Optional:	Percent	With tort restrictions:	Percent
South Dakota	0.3	Massachusetts	2.8
Virginia	2.3	Florida	3.3
Arkansas	.9	Connecticut	1.5
Texas	5.5	New Jersey	3.5
		Michigan	4.4
4 States	[1] 9.0	New York	9.0
		Utah	.5
Mandatory:		Nevada	.2
Oregon	1.0	Kansas	1.1
Delaware	.3	Hawaii	.4
Maryland	1.9	Colorado	1.1
South Carolina	1.3	Georgia	2.3
		Minnesota	1.9
4 States	[2] 4.5	Kentucky	1.6
		Pennsylvania	5.8
		North Dakota	.3
		16 States	[3] 39.7
		24 States	[4] 53.2

[1] 19,000,000 people.
[2] 9,000,000 people.
[3] 84,000,000 people.
[4] 24 States with some form of no-fault auto insurance covering 53.2 percent of the Nation's total population, some 112,000,000 people.

[Exhibit 2]

AUTOMOBILE OUT-OF-STATE INSURANCE ENDORSEMENT

It is agreed that, subject to all the provisions of the policy except where modified herein, the following provision is added:

If, under the provisions of the motor vehicle financial responsibility law or the motor vehicle compulsory insurance law or any similar law of any state or province, a non-resident is required to maintain insurance with respect to the operation or use of a motor vehicle in such state or province and such insurance requirements are greater than the insurance provided by the policy, the limits of the company's liability and the kinds of coverage afforded by the policy shall be as set forth in such law, in lieu of the insurance otherwise provided by the policy, but only to the extent required by such law and only with respect to the operation or use of a motor vehicle in such state or province; provided that the insurance under this provision shall be reduced to the extent that there is other valid and collectible insurance under this or any other motor vehicle insurance policy. In no event shall any person be entitled to receive duplicate payments for the same elements of loss.

INSTRUCTION

This endorsement must be attached to—or its provisions made a part of (by overprinting upon or incorporation into)—all Policies which afford Motor Vehicle Liability Insurance.

INSURANCE SERVICES OFFICES.

[Exhibit 3]

NATIONAL ASSOCIATION OF INSURANCE COMMISSIONERS—PROPERTY AND LIABILITY (D) COMMITTEE ATTACHMENT TWO

Whereas, the NAIC has consistently supported the development and implementation of no-fault automobile insurance plans by the individual states;

Whereas, the NAIC by resolution has recommended and encouraged experimentation at the state level as the best method of ultimately achieving a no-fault automobile insurance system that would best serve the interests of the consumers in the respective states;

Whereas, the NAIC recognizes there are many diverse approaches to the development of a no-fault automobile insurance program which embody varying concepts as to benefit levels, tort restrictions, contractual provisions and other factors.

Whereas the NAIC also recognizes that the cost implications of any no-fault automobile insurance system are of utmost concern to the public, insurance regulators, legislators and others;

Whereas, to develop information in furtherance of state experimentation, an independent study conducted by Milliman and Robertson (M&R), consulting actuaries, to (a) obtain actual cost figures from early state no-fault laws and (b) to prepare estimates based upon a methodology developed by M&R where actual figures were not available;

Whereas, in devising this methodology and in the absence of actual experience over an adequate period of time with a significant number of no-fault laws, many significant actuarial assumptions were necessary which placed limitations on the accuracy of such estimates;

Whereas, in recognition of these assumptions and consequent accuracy limitations, M&R attached to its reports a series of important caveats and cautionary notes discouraging the placing of undue reliance on the estimates produced;

Whereas, in some instances it appears these caveats and cautionary notes have not received adequate consideration;

Whereas, notwithstanding the limitations on the estimates produced by M&R, such estimates have been useful as initial guides to the cost implications of no-fault proposals in various states and have been of assistance particularly as respects state legislative deliberations in furthering experimentation by individual states;

Whereas, twenty-one states representing 45% of the nation's population have now enacted no-fault laws of varying kinds which provide a firm foundation for testing the acceptability and propriety of various benefit structures, levels, restrictions, and costs;

Whereas, the operation of these programs over an adequate period of time would enable all states to evaluate the advantages and disadvantages of the various components and plans as well as the public's acceptance;

Whereas, the usual practice of collecting experience and other data on a scientific basis provides the means by which such plans can be evaulated on the basis of actual knowledge as opposed to estimates;

Whereas, flexibility and the consequent ability to effect changes promptly and efficiently as warranted by emerging data and public attitudes transcends any need for uniformity in the present embryonic stage of no-fault automobile insurance;

Whereas, S. 354 does not simply provide minimum standards but, rather, would impose a rigid and unyielding automobile insurance system with significant federal regulatory demands on all citizens while at the same time placing severe limitations on the ability of the individual states to accommodate localized needs as well as their ability to regulate the business of automobile insurance in the best interests of the citizens within their borders;

Whereas, the passage of S. 354 by the U.S. Senate was premature because the systematic experimentation and data gathering activities now in progress at the state level has not had sufficient time to produce credible results; and

Whereas, the continuation and expansion of the state-by-state experimentation process is the only viable means by which different no-fault concepts, structures, cost-benefit relationships and public acceptance can be adequately tested: Now, therefore, be it

Resolved That:

1. The NAIC reaffirms its conviction that the respective states should continue and increase their efforts to enact and experiment with no-fault programs compatible with the needs and desires of their respective citizens;

2. The NAIC reaffirms its opposition to the enactment of S. 354 or other similar federal no-fault automobile insurance plans,

3. The NAIC emphasizes the caution which must be exercised in placing reliance on cost estimates including those prepared by M&R and stresses the reduced reliability which can be attached to such estimates as a basis for enacting a single national program, and

4. A copy of this resolution be transmitted by the NAIC to all members of the U.S. Senate and House of Representatives.

EXHIBIT 4

FEDERAL NO-FAULT AUTO INSURANCE COST BASED ON MILLIMAN AND ROBERTSON ESTIMATES—PRIVATE PASSENGERS AND COMMERCIAL[1]

	I. High benefits–Tight threshold		II. High benefits–Loose threshold [2]	
	Private	Commercial	Private	Commercial
Alabama	−1.5	−66.6	+9.7	−62.8
Alaska	+13.1	−61.6	+25.4	−57.5
Arizona	+.7	−65.8	+11.9	−62.0
Arkansas	+.7	−65.8	+10.8	−62.4
California	−11.6	−70.0	+.4	−65.8
Colorado	+13.1	−61.6	+24.3	−57.8
Connecticut	+7.0	−63.7	+20.7	−59.1
Delaware	+11.9	−62.0	+24.3	−57.8
District of Columbia	−4.9	−67.7	+9.7	−62.8
Florida [3]	+19.9	−59.3	+33.1	−54.8
Georgia [3]	+26.5	−57.1	+39.6	−52.6
Hawaii [3]	+9.3	−62.9	+23.8	−58.0
Idaho	+11.9	−62.0	+23.1	−58.2
Illinois	+5.2	−64.3	+17.5	−60.1
Indiana	+11.9	−62.0	+24.3	−57.8
Iowa	+13.1	−61.6	+25.4	−57.5
Kansas	+8.6	−63.2	+19.8	−59.4
Kentucky [3]	+21.9	−58.7	+35.6	−54.0
Louisiana	−1.5	−66.6	+11.9	−62.0
Maine	+18.7	−59.7	+29.8	−55.9
Maryland	+10.8	−62.4	+24.3	−57.8
Massachusetts [3]	+65.9	−43.8	+89.8	−35.5
Michigan	+16.4	−60.5	+28.7	−56.3
Minnesota [3]	+53.6	−47.9	+71.1	−42.0
Mississippi	+.7	−65.8	+11.9	−62.0
Missouri	−.4	−66.2	+11.9	−62.0
Montana	+15.3	−60.9	+25.4	−57.5
Nebraska	+17.5	−60.1	+29.8	−55.9
Nevada [3]	+14.6	−62.2	+27.8	−56.7
New Hampshire	+9.7	−62.8	+22.0	−58.6
New Jersey [3]	+2.7	−65.2	+17.2	−60.2
New Mexico	+5.2	−64.3	+17.5	−60.1
New York [3]	+20.2	−59.3	+35.4	−54.1
North Carolina	+17.5	−60.1	+29.8	−55.9
North Dakota	+22.0	−58.6	+33.2	−54.8
Ohio	+3.0	−65.1	+15.3	−60.9
Oklahoma	+4.1	−64.7	+18.7	−59.7
Oregon	+13.1	−61.6	+25.4	−57.5
Pennsylvania [3]	+17.2	−60.2	+33.1	−54.8
Rhode Island	+1.9	−65.4	+15.4	−60.9
South Carolina	+22.0	−58.6	+34.3	−54.4
South Dakota	+14.2	−61.3	+25.4	−57.5
Tennessee	+1.9	−65.4	+14.2	−61.3
Texas	−3.7	−67.3	+8.6	−63.2
Utah	+3.0	−65.1	+15.3	−60.9
Vermont	+19.8	−59.4	+32.1	−55.2
Virginia	+18.7	−59.7	+31.7	−55.6
Washington	+6.3	−63.9	+17.5	−60.1
West Virginia	−.4	−66.2	+10.8	−62.4
Wisconsin	+15.3	−60.9	+27.6	−56.7
Wyoming	+16.4	−60.5	+26.5	−57.1

[1] AMIA evaluation of Millman and Robertson's "State averages."
[2] Approximates title II, S. 354 benefits.
[3] Reflects legislative rate decreases in these no-fault States

EXHIBIT 5

Compatibility of existing no-fault laws with proposed national standards

Existing no-fault laws	(1) Work loss benefits up to $35,000	(2) Unlimited medical benefits	(3) Unlimited emergency health services	(4) Unlimited rehabilitation services	(5) Tort limitation	(6) Price Comparison	(7) Assigned claims plan	(8) Prohibits subrogation	(9) Subsidy for disadvantaged
Puerto Rico	No	Yes	No	Yes	No	No	No	Yes	No.
Massachusetts	No	No	No	No	No	No	Yes	No	No.
Minnesota	No	No	No	No	No	No	Yes	Yes	No.
South Dakota	No	No	No	No	No	No	No	No	No.
Florida	No	No	No	No	No	No	No	No	No.
Delaware	No	No	No	No	No	No	No	No	No.
Oregon	No	No	No	No	No	No	No	No	No.
Maryland	No	No	No	No	No	No	No	Yes	No.
Connecticut	No	No	No	No	No	No	Yes	No	No.
Virginia	No	No	No	No	No	No	No	No	No.
New Jersey	No	Yes	No	Yes	No	No	No	No	No.
Michigan	Yes	Yes	No	Yes	No	No	Yes	Yes	No.
New York	Yes	Yes	No	No	No	No	No	No	No.
Arkansas	No	No	No	No	No	No	No	Yes	No.
Utah	No	No	No	No	No	No	No	No	No.
Kansas	No	No	No	No	No	No	Yes	No	No.
Texas	No	No	No	No	No	No	No	Yes	No.
Hawaii	No	No	No	No	No	No	Yes	No	Yes.
Nevada	No	No	No	No	No	No	Yes	No	No.
Colorado	No	No	No	No	No	No	No	No	No.
Georgia	No	No	No	No	No	No	No	No	No.
Kentucky	No	No	No	No	No	No	Yes	No	No.
South Carolina	No	No	No	No	No	No	Yes	Yes	No.
Pennsylvania	No	Yes	Yes	Yes	No	No	Yes	Yes	No.
North Dakota	No	No	No	No	No	No	Yes	No	No.

SUPPLEMENTARY STATEMENT OF THE AMERICAN MUTUAL INSURANCE ALLIANCE

This supplements the American Mutual Insurance Alliance statement of June 19, 1975. Discussion is limited to the effect of four major amendments to S. 354 adopted by the Senate Commerce Committee on June 27, 1975.

I. THE AUTHORITY OF THE SECRETARY OF TRANSPORTATION

S. 354 sets forth a number of continuing federal requirements, both as to automobile insurance regulation and automobile accident reparation, which each state must adopt to implement a state program.

The bill, as introduced, would have required the Secretary of Transportation to examine each state plan to determine whether it was in accordance with national standards before any approval. Additionally, the Secretary was required to periodically review and evaluate each approved state plan, and to make any needed recommendations to Congress.

The bill, as reported, now provides that a state plan become operative upon certification by a state's chief executive officer to a newly created No-Fault Insurance Plan Review Board, a new agency of the Department of Transportation. The state's chief executive officer would also be required to report periodically to the No-Fault Insurance Plan Review Board on the operation of no-fault in the state and, the Review Board would then make appropriate recommendations to Congress.

While this amendment creates an impression of reduced federal interference with state regulation, in fact, there has been no change in the essential federal functions previously required of the Secretary. A staff report to the Senate Commerce Committee specifically states that the amendment "authorizes this Review Board to exercise the essential functions previously granted to the Secretary."

This amendment is totally inconsistent with the basic principles of McCarran-Ferguson. Moreover, it creates two new problems.

First there is a matter of good government and management. The amendment disturbs the balanced relationship between a state's executive branch and its legislature by giving the governor in effect an absolute veto over legislative action in this area. Consider the following:

good government.

Second is a matter of realistic future legislative needs. State experience has taught us that any state no-fault law enacted in one session of a legislature will need to be amended in the very next session. No-fault auto reform affects thousands of people, many with conflicting interests. Both the legislative and executive branches of government must remain responsive and flexible to meet the problems which arise out of no-fault reform. The procedures contemplated by the S. 354 for needed changes are cumbersome, narrow and inflexible. They give state governments very little maneuverability to correct defects in the operation of their laws.

Furthermore, what might prove to be a disastarous requirement for one state may not create any undue problem in another. For instance, one state court might interpret a standard one way and another state court might interpret the same standard an entirely different way. There is no way to correct for these different applications of federal standards under the system contemplated by S. 354. It is an awkward system likely to create substantial hardships.

II. THE ADMINISTRATION OF A TITLE III

Our basic statement discusses the constitutional problems with Title III of the original bill (Pages 8–10 and 54–57). Title III required state agencies to administer federal law and state legislatures to fund its administration. This, we believe, raises grave constitutional questions. The Attorney General, in his testimony before the Senate Commerce Committee, supported our contentions. The Senate Commerce Committee has recognized these constitutional handicaps. It has amended S. 354 by requiring that Title III be administered by the Secretary of Transportation in all applicable states unless a state governor certifies that his state has enacted appropriate legislation authorizing its administratirs to implement Title III. In our June 19, 1975, statement, we said that there was no way to avoid the establishment of a new federal bureaucracy to regulate insurance in the states if S. 354 were to become law. The Senate Commerce Committee's action concedes our point. Title III shall be "implemented, administered, operated, and maintained exclusively by the Secretary."

Even though there is a provision allowing states to assume these functions, there will have to be at least a standby federal bureaucracy. It may be said that it is not realistic to expect the states to give up control and withdraw from the administration of insurance regulation, motor vehicle registration, etc. But the states may find substantial incentives to turn these administrative functions over to the federal government. It costs New York State, for instance, millions of dollars a year to enforce compulsory auto insurance. Would it not make sense for New York to turn over this function to the federal government, thus releasing substantial state funds for the administration of other programs? This is precisely the states' attitude toward the administration of the Occupational Safety and Health Act. That federal law authorizes and, in fact, encourages through substantial subsidies, state administration. Yet, more and more states are rejecting the opportunity to administer the law, turning the job over to the federal government.

It is clear that the Senate Commerce Committee amendment is necessary to overcome the constitutional barriers which we have already discussed. To overcome this barrier, we are being led to a complete federalization of the regulation of automobile insurance. This is inescapable and inevitable. As we have discussed in our basic statement, this federalization will bring about a restructuring of the competitive forces within the insurance business, with a much greater concentration of pricing power in the hands of a few giant companies.

Aside from that, no one has really asked how can the federal government practically administer these laws. The Senate Commerce Committee merely states that the Secretary shall do so. One should question the ability of the federal bureaucracy to implement the detailed regulatory and administrative responsibilities demanded by federal no-fault legislation. Take compulsory insurance, for example. States that have had compulsory automobile insurance laws have found that the only way these statues can be implemented is to relate their enforcement to the registration of automobiles. Once an individual registers his automobile he is asked to furnish evidence of insurance. If the insurance coverage is canceled after the car has been registered, local or state police forces are enlisted to pick up the registration tags. Is the federal government prepared to establish a federal motor vehicle registry? Who will substitute for the local police in the very difficult job of enforcing the system? Will there be a need to enlarge existing federal enforcement agencies or should there be a new federal police force created just for this purpose?

If Congress enacts no-fault insurance reform legislation it must be prepared to provide, finance and support the very broad federal bureaucracy which will be required to implement the law. We question whether this bureaucracy, regardless of how well financed, will be capable of responding to the needs of millions of automobile owners and automobile accident victims in every small locality in the United States.

III. COST

The Senate Commerce Committee has accepted an amendment to S. 354 which will allow states to subrogate losses as between classes of insureds. Our basic statement argues for this type of subrogation. Without it, individual consumers would be required to subsidize the cost of commercial automobile insurance. Subrogation will, of course, reduce private passenger automobile insurance costs.

However, we continue to be very much concerned at the impact of the S. 354 on the cost of insurance, particularly in the rural states. To pay for the increased number of persons receiving benefits from a no-fault system, there must be an elimination of the smaller, often nuisance claims of the traditional tort system. To the extent that there is extreme claims consciousness in any territory or state, experience has shown that there has been a large number of small, nuisance claims. In those territories, it is possible to pay more people benefits without raising the cost of insurance, if these nuisance claims are eliminated. But in areas where there is little or no claims consciousness and where there have been considerably fewer nuisance claims filed, no-fault is likely to increase cost. Traditionally, the more rural states have been much less claim conscious. Therefore, much fewer nuisance claims have been filed and paid in those states.

In this regard, State Farm Insurance Companies stated to the Senate Commerce Committee, "there will be a significant increase in the number of injured persons receiving economic loss benefits as compared to the number recovering through tort, ranging from 60% to 110% depending largely on the relative proportion of single care accidents, Further, these new claimants will sustain somewhat higher (+10%) economic losses on average—resulting partially from the addition of single car accidents, which are generally more serious, and partially from a disproportionate increase in the number of injured drivers, who tend to have a greater economic loss potential."

Since single car accidents occur more frequently in the more rural states, one should expect that perhaps twice as many people will be paid benefits under no-fault in these areas. The question is, where will those benefits come from, except higher automobile insurance premium? As previously stated, restricting tort remedy in those states will not have the cost saving impact expected in the more urban centers.

Another cost concern which we continue to have is the impact of unlimited medical benefits. The Reinsurance Insurance Association of America, in a letter dated June 16, 1975, to Chairman Warren G. Magnuson of the Senate Commerce Committee stated that "the seriousness and frequency of injuries requiring extensive medical expenses in excess of $50,000 have been greater than anticipated." The "open ended financial liability" on automobile insurers proposed by sections 103 and 204 of S. 354 will substantially inflate the cost of automobile insurance in the years to come.

IV. THE COORDINATION OF BENEFITS BETWEEN HEALTH INSURANCE AUTOMOBILE INSURANCE

As introduced, S. 354 required health insurance policies to pay for all medical losses arising from automobile accidents unless a state would find that such provisions "would affect adversely or discriminate against the interest of persons required to provide security covering motor vehicle in such states." Our basic statement argues that this provision is against public interest (pages 49–54). The bill, as reported, now provides that each state be allowed to elect how to eliminate duplicate benefits.

Although from an efficiency standpoint it can be argued that duplicate benefits should be eliminated, policyholders have indicated that they do not consider such elimination in their interests.

In a recent extensive policyholder survey conducted by Louis Harris and Associates, under the direction and supervision of the Wharton School of the University of Pennsylvania, a number of questions were asked consumers to test support for coordination between automobile and health insurance benefits. Specifically, the following questions were asked:

As it is now, if a person is injured in an automobile accident and he has auto and health-accident insurance policies that cover the same claim, he can collect on both his automobile and health—accident insurance. Would you be willing or not to give up this right to collect on both auto and health insurance if it meant that you could obtain a reduction in the auto insurance you pay?

Only 35% of those asked were in favor of the proposition while 49% were opposed. Of those expressing an opinion, 42% were in favor and 58% against.

This consumer attitude is clearly reflected in the very small percentage of policyholders now opting for coordination of benefits where such coordination is made optional. As our statement shows, in Michigan, where automobile insurance carriers must offer a policy holder a 20% reduction in his no-fault automobile cost if he elects to make health insurance primary, less than 5% of the policyholders have opted for this 20% reduction in no-fault insurance premiums.

Over the years we have found that insurance policy exclusions are often misunderstood by policyholders. Insurance regulators as well as company executives have sought to eliminate as many of these exclusions as possible. We question whether federal legislation should impose such exclusions upon the states. The matter of coordinating benefits between insurance programs should be a policy left to the discretion of each state legislature.

V. CONCLUSION

The American Mutual Insurance Alliance opposed S. 354 when it was introduced in Congress. We have carefully reviewed the amendments made by the Senate Commerce Committee and we do not see any basis for a change in our opposition to the bill. To the contrary, we believe that a number of these amendments, while correcting some of the technical deficiencies of the legislation, will establish programs which will lead to total federal regulation of automobile insurance. For reasons stated in our statements, we believe this to be against public interest.

[The following letter, with attachments, was received for the record:]

AMERICAN MUTUAL INSURANCE ALLIANCE,
Washington, D.C., August 12, 1975.

Hon. LIONEL VAN DEERLIN,
Chairman, Subcommittee on Consumer Protection and Finance, Rayburn House Office Building, Washington, D.C.

DEAR MR. VAN DEERLIN: Your letter of July 31, 1975, asks that we supply your Subcommittee with no-fault cost studies done by the American Mutual Insurance Alliance on S. 945, in the 92nd Congress and on S. 354 in the 93rd and 94th Congress.

As we testified in answer to a question from Subcommittee Counsel, Mr. Peter Kinzler, the American Mutual Insurance Alliance has never performed any specific cost studies on S. 945 or S. 354. We did make certain observations as regard the cost impact of S. 945, Committee Print Number 1, 2, and 3 and we did perform a cost analysis of UMVARA, a proposal somewhat similar to S. 945.

As for the cost observations of the three prints of S. 945, I have attached to this letter a copy of the statements which we distributed to the Senate Commerce Committee. It is to be emphasized that since the pending federal legislation (S. 354 and H.R. 1900) is so dissimilar from any of the versions of S. 945 that the observations made as regard S. 945 bear little, if any relevance to those bills pending before your Subcommittee.

Additionally, the Senate Commerce Committee invited actuaries from the three national insurance trade associations, including the American Mutual Insurance Alliance, to discuss the cost of S. 945 on May 17, 1972. At that time, the Committee was interested in the cost impact of S. 945 on an actual existing insurance coverage package. This is, of course, quite different from the present costing approach which attempts to price the total automobile insurance premium which will be paid by all policyholders in a state under a no-fault system as against the total insurance premium for automobile insurance being paid today.

In the course of those hearings, the Alliance specifically stated that it had not made any attempt to cost S. 945 but, drawing on its UMVARA study, S. 945 would have very little cost impact on the assumed benefit package—perhaps a 2% reduction.

In addition to the above, we have made some studies on the impact of subrogation or the lack of subrogation on cost. These were detailed in our statement to your Subcommittee of June 19, 1975, specifically pages 21 and 22. Also, we have attempted to relate Title III to the Milliman and Robertson study, and as we stated to the Subcommittee, we expect that Title III will increase Milliman and Robertson's cost projections by about 55%.

We hope that this information will be of use to the Subcommittee.

Sincerely,

ANDRE MAISONPIERRE, *Vice President.*

COMMITTEE PRINT NO. 1—S. 945

COST

The American Mutual Insurance Alliance has estimated the cost of the Compulsory Economic Coverage to be *37% greater* than current bodily injury liability cost.

The American Insurance Association, in turn, has estimated the cost of this same coverage to be *27% lower* than current bodily injury liability cost.

WHICH IS CORRECT?

The Department of Transportation estimates the annual compensable economic loss resulting from automobile accidents (1967) to be $5.7 billion (excluding property damage).[1]

Since S. 945's Compulsory Economic Coverage does not pay all such losses, an adjustment must accordingly be made to reflect only the benefits to be paid under that coverage. We estimate these benefits to be $5.2 billion (1967).

However, total annual Bodily Injury Liability insurance premium (including Medical Pay) is only $4.5 billion (1967).[2]

The facts speak for themselves. One cannot pay the $5.2 billion benefits from the full $4.5 billion premium collected—much less reduce the $4.5 billion by 27%. It just cannot be done.

Considering the fact that even the most efficient administration system adds to the cost of paying the losses, the American Mutual Insurance Alliance's estimate of a 37% cost increase is obviously a very conservative projection.

THE COSTS OF COMMITTEE PRINT NO. 2—S. 945

The fact that Committee Print No. 2 of S. 945 will substantially increase the cost of automobile insurance is irrefutable.

A. *The D.O.T. Report verifies this.*—Pure losses paid under Committee Print 2 would amount to $5 billion, as based on D.O.T.'s 1967 figures. Insurance premiums

---

[1] Motor vehicle crash losses and their compensation in the United States—Department of Transportation—table 2, p. 6.
[2] Best's aggregates and averages.

paid by all policyholders to cover bodily injury and medical payments (1967) were $4.5 billion.

It is just impossible to pay $5 billion in pure losses with total premiums of $4.5 billion.

B. *Actuaries tell us* that for every $100 spent today for auto bodily injury insurance, consumers will pay about $135 for the *minimum* compulsory coverages required by Committee Print 2 of S. 945. This is a 35% *increase.*

A consumer desiring and able to afford full insurance protection under Committee Print 2 will pay about $255 for every $100 he now spends for bodily injury insurance protection. This is a 155% *increase.*

Consumers expect auto insurance reform to lower the cost of insurance protection— not to increase it.

COMMITTEE PRINT No. 3—S. 945

COST

A comparison of insurance cost as between existing minimum system coverage and comparable coverage under print 3 reveals the following:

The federal standard requirements would, on the average, increase the existing minimum coverage cost by 28.3%.

The federal requirements would increase on the average present minimum coverage cost by 27.3%.

These calculations assume that the policyholder would elect coverage to pay for damage to his vehicle, *only* if the damage is the fault of a thrid party. This is the coverage the policyholder now has and without which he would have to totally self insure his vehicle losses.

These cost estimates for Print #3 *do not* include premium cost to cover:
1. Tort Liability arising from excess tangible loss.
2. No-fault intangible loss benefits to be paid to an injured who is not an owner of a motor vehicle or to an injured member of a household of a non-vehicle owner. This could be considerable since members of non-car owning families represent about 25% of the total population.

Additionally, these costs *do not* reflect any other optional coverages which a policyholder must be offered, such as the no-fault intangible loss benefit coverage which itself would increase the existing bodily injury and uninsured motorist cost by one hundred twenty percent.

FEDERAL STANDARDS —TITLE II

	Present system	Pt. 3
10/20 B1—Personal injury protection and bodily injury liability	$72	$102
10/20 UM—Uninsured motorists	4	
5 PD—Property damage liability	33	33
	109	135

1. Assuming policyholder elects coverage to pay for damage to his vehicle only if the damage is the fault of a third party. This is, the coverage he now has and without such coverage he would totally self insure his vehicle losses.
2. Does not include premium cost for tort liability arising from excess tangible damage.

This represents an average cost increase of 28.3%.

FEDERAL NO-FAULT INSURANCE TITLE III

	Present system	Pt. 3
10/20 B1—Personal injury protection bodily injury liability	$72	$101
10/20 UM—Uninsured motorist	4	
5 PD—Property damage liability	33	33
	109	134

1. Does not include cost for no-fault intangible damage loss sustained by a person not an owner of a motor vehicle or a member of the household of such owner. This could be considerable since this group represents 20% of the total population.

2. Assuming policyholder elects coverage to pay for damage to his vehicle, *only* if the damage is the fault of a third party. This is the coverage he now has and without such coverage he would totally self insure his vehicle losses.

This represents an average cost increase of 27.3%.

Mr. VAN DEERLIN. The final witness is Mr. Dick Rottman, Commissioner of Insurance in Nevada.

STATEMENT OF DICK L. ROTTMAN

Mr. ROTTMAN. Mr. Chairman and members of the committee, I appreciate the opportunity to appear before you today, and perhaps I should use the microphone.

In addition to being Insurance Commissioner, I am also vice president and chairman of the executive committee of the National Association of Insurance Commissioners. I appreciate this opportunity to offer my views on Federal no-fault legislation. I would like to emphasize at the outset that, as an insurance regulator, I do not represent the industry, the legal profession, or any other special interest group. I work for the people of Nevada.

The long debate on S. 354 and its equivalent, H.R. 1900, has uncovered a multitude of flaws. Many, including the NAIC, have expressed deep misgivings over the arrogation of State regulatory powers by the Federal branch in most of the bills that have been proposed. Notwithstanding the continual pretense by some of its proponents that S. 354 leaves State regulation untouched, the Federal Government, under the bill, would have authority to investigate, challenge, modify, or reverse State actions, or it could assume, at least in one of the cases, a very direct and absolute role in the State regulation or, rather, in the regulation of insurance.

Generally, they could demand unlimited amounts of information and accountability. The amended version of S. 354, for example, creates a wholly new regulatory scheme if the States don't act according to the dictates of the Federal Government.

I think it is ironic and certainly disturbing that these proposals to confer new powers on the Department of Transportation and the review board in at least the one case come at a time when the effectiveness and the cost of Federal regulatory agencies are under intense scrutiny. The President and others have called into question much of the regulating presently undertaken by the Federal branch. It is difficult for me to see why these powers in these areas need to be expanded now basically at the expense for the added bureaucracy that is imposed or that would be imposed on the consumers of the Nation.

Overall, the bill that we have before us today is a blueprint for Federal takeover. How it can be interpreted by anyone as being other than that is difficult to imagine.

Equally hard to fathom is the desire to force a sweeping, practically irreversible system on the Nation when cautious experimentation is needed at this time. No-fault remains as a very practical matter largely theoretical. It deals with a complex cluster of legal, economic and behavioral problems. The State experience to date has demonstrated that no one can accurately predict how no-fault will work or where it will need adjusting. For example, the experience in Florida has indicated that there has been a definite over utilization or excessive utilization of no-fault benefits much the same as you found under medicare and it has driven up the price of medicare. I have noticed some tendency for this same thing in the Southern Nevada area. Furthermore, the recent amendments to S. 354 at least are tacit admissions in my judgment that too little is known about the Federal no-fault impact. The bill's supporters seem to be suggesting that it is acceptable to set up a system involving about 200 million consumers and literally billions of dollars and then find out afterwards whether the system in fact actually does work.

The Federal no-fault or Federal standards, in my judgment, makes even less sense when you consider that 24 States and over 50 percent of the population are already covered under some form of no-fault today. This is something that the critics generally fail to point out.

The various jurisdictions do have special insurance needs and conditions and, contrary to what some would have us believe, this won't change the facts. Take the matter of rates, for example. As a regulator, the rates are perhaps the best barometer of the insurance environment, for in these rates are reflected the strength of the competition, the health of the market, financial responsibility of the public, driving habits, highway safety standards, propensity to sue and a host of other factors that you find. At the present time you will find a wide variety of or a wide divergence of rates among States that reflect a wide divergence of needs among States.

As a matter of fact, in some just general figures that my actuaries have furnished to me you will find that some of the lower rated States you come up with a premium, say, for B of $30 or $35 and some of the higher States you come up with anywhere from $110 to $135 or $130 and I think that in and of itself reflects some vast differences.

The State no-fault laws that have been passed to date, I think, represent or reflect the variances, at least to some degree. I think that the work that has been started should be permitted to continue. That is at least until we know what is really happening under the no-fault laws that have been enacted. To enact a Federal standards bill at this time would really ignore this work that has been done in many of the States and as an official of a State with a no-fault law I can't imagine how much action by the Federal Government would create anything but strong resentment to State legislators and others who worked diligently to try to put no-fault laws on the books of their respective States and I would include in that a number of Governors who worked diligently to get these laws on the books, also.

Another aspect of the Federal no-fault bill which concerns me vitally as a regulator is to some degree, and perhaps, on the one hand, it is fairly small, but I think it is fairly significant, is that its anticompetitive effect. The public is best served by a variety of available sources of insurance by the competition among these sources in price and product and by the progress and innovations engendered by competition. Safeguarding variety and its attendant competition is a principal goal of the consumer-oriented regulation.

Yet these bills would thwart the regulator's efforts in one major respect. The bill's mandate for unlimited medical and rehabilitation benefits, while laudatory in one respect, would present many companies, particularly smaller ones, with unmanageable increases in reinsurance costs. These costs added to the financial burdens of recession and the inflation could tip the balance against survival in some cases. In that event the capacity of the market to provide coverage to the public could seriously diminish and competition for the consumer's dollar would actually be reduced. The hard-to-insure, or the substandard market, would probably be the hardest hit and it is the one that I am most concerned about, for it is oftentimes that the smaller company that picks up this substandard risk, or hard-to-insure risk, is the one that all of us as regulators really need in the marketplace in order to do a good job for the people and as a practical matter it is these companies, the ones that are dealing in the substandard market, that have been hit hardest under our no-fault insurance law in the State of Nevada in terms of the need for rate increases.

As important as the foregoing arguments and others may be, there is one which, in my opinion, is more convincing than all of the rest. This has to do with just what I touched on there, that is, the cost. It seems to me that cost is one of the real cutting issues in the whole no-fault argument. Proponents of the bill have spoken at length about what the public wants.

I would like to dwell just for a moment on what I think the public is willing to pay for and perhaps can pay for in these times of economic recession and inflation, which we are experiencing simultaneously. Our knowledge of the costs of the Federal bill, H.R. 1900 and S. 354, can be described as dubious at best. The much disputed actuarial studies have projected both decreases and increases in rates. The 1973 study by the firm of Milliman & Robertson predicted decreases across the board. Those decreases were presented over on the Senate side on a big billboard the last time I was over there to testify and, by and large, as I indicated over there, I think they were really false and misleading. The firm of M. & R. warned that the predictions were highly uncertain inasmuch as they didn't take into account the difference for rates for various types of vehicles, various types of drivers, variance between geographical areas, any inadequacies in the present rates, and a whole host of caveats that appear in that M. & R. study.

As a practical matter, the costing of what was then S. 354 or a version of S. 354 is completely obsolete and I think it is a dire mistake for anybody to rely on those cost estimates. I was on the board of directors of NAIC and I have been on there continuously since when the bill was commissioned and have a good idea of what we requested and what we actually got there. Other actuaries predict sizable rate increases for consumers and claim to have corrected oversights and imperfections of the M. & R. study. I think to some degree they have. They stress that they studied the amended version of the bill and so that their work has some relevancy that is perhaps missing in the M. & R. study, but differences of the experts in this regard are not trifling. The M. & R. study forecasts a savings of some, I think, 3 to 25 or 30 percent, while on the other hand, all State figures that were presented forecast an increase ranging up to something in excess of 80 or 90 percent in a few States and some increase in most all States.

I am really not here to defend or disparage either of these studies. They both appear to be sound as far as methodology itself goes. The dispute arises over which bill is under discussion and over the underlying assumptions used by the actuaries and ultimately the study stands or falls depending on how credible we believe the assumptions are that you put into the model and how important we believe the amendments are to a particular bill that is under consideration.

This morning, for example, as one of the witnesses indicated, a rate prediction of, I was not sure whether he was talking about rate prediction for H.R. 1900 or S. 354 and in the material I had received from him earlier it was S. 354 and in his testimony I was led to believe it is H.R. 1900, just as an example of how careful you have to be about which bill you are talking about and what assumptions you are going to use.

Mr. VAN DEERLIN. Would you like Mr. McHugh to indicate right now it was H.R. 1900?

Mr. MCHUGH. Yes. We did submit costing to you earlier, Mr. Rottman, based upon material we had furnished to the Senate committee which was considering the cost impact of S. 354, but then in response to this committee's interest, we costed H.R. 1900, and the exhibit that is attached to our statement shows our State-by-State cost of H.R. 1900.

Mr. ROTTMAN. I appreciate, or could I have a copy of it so in our discussion later on we might want to refer to that.

Mr. MCHUGH. Yes.

Mr. ROTTMAN. For all of our disagreement cn the specifics, the experts seem to concur indirectly at least on one point and that is the decisive factor of what is at stake in this cost issue. Really, the actuaries seem to be telling us there is probably no middle ground. It is either, possibly you have a lot of savings or you have a lot of increased costs. Practically speaking, nobody seems to know for sure. It depends on which actuary you talk to on which day. The total effect of these has been really to blur the cost picture and to show, or throw into focus the high degree of risk involved by the passage of a Federal standards bill.

I think in light of these considerations and some that others have been mentioning here this morning I find it very hard to believe how the U.S. Congress can give serious consideration to passing a bill that may mandate a heavy rate increase on all American motorists.

Thank you.

[Mr. Rottman's prepared statement follows:]

STATEMENT OF DICK L. ROTTMAN, OF THE STATE OF NEVADA

Mr. Chairman and members of the committee, I am Dick Rottman, insurance commissioner of the state of Nevada and vice president and chairman of the executive committee of the National Association of Insurance Commissioners. I appreciate this opportunity to offer my views on federal no-fault legislation. I would like to emphasize at the outset that, as an insurance regulator, I do not represent the industry, the legal profession or any other special interest group. I work for the people of Nevada.

The long debate on S. 354 and its equivalent HR 1900 has uncovered a multitude of flaws. Many, including the NAIC, have expressed deep misgivings over the arrogation of state regulatory powers by the federal branch. Notwithstanding the continual pretense by some of its proponents that S. 354 leaves state regulation untouched, the federal government, under the bill, would have authority to investigate, challenge, modify or reverse state actions. It could demand unlimited amounts of information and accountability. It would require state officials to act as agents of the federal branch. Sen. Percy's amendment alone creates a wholly new layer of federal review of state insurance departments, and even reaches beyond no-fault by requiring reports on the effect shortages on insurance rates.

It is ironic and disturbing that these proposals to confer new powers on the Department of Transportation come at a time when the effectiveness and cost of federal regulatory agencies are under intense scrutiny. The President and others have called into question much of the regulating presently undertaken by the federal branch. Why expand those powers now and impose added expense and bureaucracy on the consumer?

Over-all, the bill is a blueprint for federal takeover. How it can be interpreted as affirming the state regulatory role defies understanding.

Equally hard to fathom is the desire to force a sweeping, practically irreversible system on the nation when cautious experimentation is needed. No-fault remains largely theoretical. It deals with a complex cluster of legal, economic and behavioral problems. State experience has demonstrated that no one can accurately predict how no-fault will work or where it will need adjusting.

For instance, experience emerging in Florida indicates a pattern of overutilization of no-fault benefits, a situation not unlike the overutilization that now burdens Medicare and drives up that system's cost.

Furthermore, the Percy amendment itself is a tacit admission that too little is known about federal no-fault's impact. The bill's supporters seem to be suggesting that it is acceptable to set up a system involving more than 200,000,000 consumers and billions of dollars, and *then* find out if it works.

Federal no-fault makes even less sense in view of the fact that 24 states comprising 53 per cent of the public have enacted no-fault reforms that those sovereign powers believe are best suited to their special needs and conditions.

The various jurisdictions *do* have special insurance needs and conditions and, rhetoric to the contrary, or a sloughing-off of this problem, will not change the facts. Take the matter of rates, for example. To the regulator, rates are perhaps the best barometer of the insurance environment, for in them are reflected the strength of competition, the health of the market, the financial responsibility of the public, driving habits, highway safety standards, the propensity to sue and many other factors.

At present, there are large disparities in the rate levels of the states—clear proof of the wide differences in those insurance climates.

State no-fault laws recognize these variances. No-fault work in the laboratory of the states should be continued, not pre-empted by federal action the risks and ramifications of which are unknown. Enactment of federal no-fault standards would ignore this work and invalidate it. As an official of a state with a no-fault law, I cannot imagine how such action by the federal government could create anything but bitter resentment in the state legislators and other who fought for no-fault. In my judgment, the same resentment would be felt by all state officials pressed into duty as federal servants.

Another aspect of S. 354 which concerns me vitally as a regulator is its anticompetitive effect. The public is best served by a variety of available sources of insurance, by the competition among those sources in price and product and by the progress and innovation engendered by competition. Safeguarding variety and its attendant competition is a principal goal of consumer-oriented regulation.

Yet S. 354 would thwart the regulators' efforts. The bill's mandate for unlimited medical and rehabilitation benefits would present many companies, particularly smaller ones, with unmanageable increases in their reinsurance costs. Those costs, added to the financial burdens of recession, could tip the balance against survival. In that event, the capacity of the market to provide coverage to the public would be seriously diminished and competition for the consumer's dollar would be reduced. The hard-to-insure, or substandard market, would probably be hardest hit, for it is the smaller company that frequently picks up the substandard risk. S. 354 would simply thrust higher costs on these companies and the markets they serve.

As important as the foregoing arguments and others may be, there is one other which, in my opinion, is more convincing than all the rest.

To the consumer, and to regulators like myself whose duty it is to protect the insurance-buying public, the cutting edge of the no-fault issue is cost. Proponents of the bill have spoken at length about what the public wants. I would like to take a few moments to speak about the public—in the middle of this recession—can, or is willing to pay for.

Our knowledge of the costs of S. 354 can be described as dubious at best. Much-disputed actuarial studies have projected both decreases and increases in rates. A 1973 study by the firm of Milliman and Robertson predicted decreases across the board. The firm warned however, that its predictions were highly uncertain, inasmuch as they did not take into account differences in rates for various types of drivers and vehicles, the variances between geographical areas, any inadequacy in present rates and many changing economic conditions. In any case, Milliman and Robertson reported on S. 354 before it was drastically amended. The study is therefore obsolete.

Other actuaries predict sizeable rate increases for the consumer. They claim to have corrected the oversights and imperfections of Milliman and Robertson and to have based their studies on a more realistic picture of the insurance market. They stress that they studied the amended version of the bill, so that their work has a relevancy that is missing in Milliman and Robertson study.

The differences of the experts in this regard are not trifling. Milliman and Robertson forecasted a saving of 3 to 28 per cent under the old S. 354. Using the amended version, industry actuaries forecasted increases ranging as high as 97 per cent, and a total nationwide rate boost of more than $1 billion a year for the public.

I am not here to defend or disparage either of these studies. They both appear to be sound as far as methodology is concerned. The dispute arises over which bill is under discussion and over the underlying assumptions used by the actuaries; and ultimately, the study stands or falls depending on how credible we believe the assumptions are and how important we believe the amendments are.

For all their disagreement on specifics, the experts do seem to concur indirectly on one point and this, to me, is the decisive factor regarding the cost issue. The actuaries seem to be telling us that there is no middle ground here; it is all or nothing; a consumer's paradise or a disaster.

The total effect of these studies has been to blur the cost picture, while throwing into sharp focus the very high degree of risk involved. Without a clear indication of the cost, I respectfully suggest that the risk is too high.

In light of all these considerations, I am absolutely amazed that the Congress would even consider a program that may raise costs for most American motorists.

Mr. VAN DEERLIN. Thank you, Mr. Rottman.

There are 24 States that have passed bills and have laws now. I suppose one side says, "Only 24 States have done this," and another viewpoint could be, "At least half of the States have done this already, it is on the way."

Now, isn't it possible one of the reasons for the recent slowdown in State enactments has been the expectation there was going to be Federal legislation?

There has been a turnaround in some of the important opposition to Federal standards or a turnaround at least in some of the organized opposition to no-fault itself. They are taking the position now that: "Well, no-fault itself may be inevitable, but it should be left to the States." What is your feeling, Mr. Maisonpierre?

Mr. MAISONPIERRE. Mr. Chairman, I think the slowdown in the State activities is due in large part to the preoccupation of State legislatures in areas which they believe may be perhaps of more importance, the economy of the States, the unemployment situations in the States. After all, we have just gone through and are still going through a period of very uncomfortable economic conditions, recession, and State budgets have been substantially reduced. The demands, or the need, rather, for allocating the State resources is calling for entirely new views and reviews of State programs and activities and this is taking one heck of a lot of time away from what has been the traditional concern of State legislatures. Now this has been, we feel, a handicap, frankly, in the pursuit.

Mr. VAN DEERLIN. Yes, but of course not all committees of State legislatures are involved in the attack on recession. And there has been no letup in general or consumer-oriented legislation. If anything, the fact that many people of moderate income are hurting has prompted a setup in consumer-related legislation.

Mr. MAISONPIERRE. But, here, again, one of the important elements is a matter of cost and the uncertainty as to what no-fault will do as far as its cost.

Let me read to you some excerpts here from a statement which was presented in November 1974, to the Virginia Legislature by State Farm. It describes some efforts that were made to cost no-fault in the past and this was in regard to the consideration of no-fault in Virginia. It says:

> This all adds up to a situation wherein we have a mass of data relevant to probable cost of a no-fault system for compensating accident victims but lacking vital links of information from which a projection of cost can be made that carries a high degree of confidence in the results.

Then it goes on to say:

> Several jurisdictions have already legislated some form of no-fault program. While this approach tends to postpone the time of massive acquiring of data for estimating costs becomes available, it has the virtue of making available to the buying public a variety of schemes. As time goes on, it should be possible to ascertain a scope of program and level of benefits that is most sensible to the public. In the interim period of 3 to 5 years before credible data becomes available generally and public preference levels of benefit seems to emerge, it will be necessary to cont nue to estimate probable no-fault cost from the type of data presently available. i

Then it goes on to talk about the possible effect on specific individuals. It is this uncertainty, this cost uncertainty, in light of today's economic situation, which has made a number of State legislatures step back and say, "Is this the thing to do at this time."

Mr. VAN DEERLIN. Since he quoted your company, Mr. McHugh, would you like to respond to that?

Mr. McHUGH. I would be pleased to respond. I am not sure of the days of the testimony Mr. Maisonpierre is referring to. What was the date?

Mr. MAISONPIERRE. November 1974.

Mr. McHUGH. I can say that it does reflect the fact that in State Farm's consideration of the no-fault situation, that we did approach the whole question of "how much no-fault was good" very cautiously. We actively supported State experimentation on the ground that we believed we didn't know enough to be able to embrace a system that we thought was what the public would accept. We were, I think, rightfully leery about some of the cost projections that were being made about no-fault. In the whole history of the debate over no-fault, State Farm has been very careful not to hold out any promises to the public that this was a system which would substantially reduce their premiums.

In plain point of fact we never believed that it would have this consequence. We have come to a conclusion, however, that there is a broad outline of a no-fault program contained in H.R. 1900 which we think now makes sense and we are now no longer at that indecisive state where we say, "We cannot support a specific program." We think the experimentation has been sufficient to tell us what kind of no fault program will do an effective job and essentially it is the kind of program that we have in this bill.

Now I would be very greatly concerned that the comments expressed by both Commissioner Rottman and Mr. Maisonpierre would lead this committee to believe that it can go on deferring a decision on this whole issue because of the uncertainties of the cost.

First of all, I would urge you strongly not to overemphasize the cost issue. We, as the largest provider of automobile insurance, I suppose, have as large a stake in this as anybody, and we feel very strongly that we would do a great injustice to the issue when we overemphasize cost as the factor on which we make a decision as to whether or not we should move to no-fault insurance.

Mr. McCollister. Will you yield?

Mr. Van Deerlin. Yes.

Mr. McCollister. Hasn't the benefit of no-fault been sold to the American public largely on the basis of its cost savings?

Mr. McHugh. I would hope not, Congressman. I think some have done this. As I pointed out, we have cautioned against that because we believe it is a mistake.

Mr. McCollister. Mr. McHugh, my mail tells me that is almost the only benefit that people think they are going to get, and how long have we been talking about it, four and a half years now. Cost has been the benefit that was earlier alluded to in the 92d Congress, in the 93d Congress, and there was the most careful attention given to that.

Mr. McHugh. I have no doubt that many of the proponents have attempted to sell the bill on that basis but I would suggest to you that the most comprehensive scholarly analysis of the problem is contained in the Department of Transportation study and it very carefully sets forth what ought to be the major advantages and the major features of a no-fault program.

Mr. Van Deerlin. Prompt settlement.

Mr. McHugh. Yes, prompt settlement. The fact that we get rid of the overpayment of a small claim. This is a terrible curse upon the present system. We ought to get rid of it. We don't pay the people seriously injured adequately. We don't pay enough of them. These are the things that we really ought to be talking about. I was quite interested to hear a person speaking on behalf of consumers stating that even if it cost a little bit more, in view of what is gained, what you are getting in the trade-off in terms of better protection for far more people, far more comprehensive treatment, is worth the price. These ought to be the major considerations on which we base our decision.

With reference to these conflicting actuarial estimates on impact of cost, it must be a baffling job for legislators to hear experts come in and project costs that conflict so substantially with each other and yet you have to make a legislative judgment upon the basis of this kind of information.

Well, I would suggest to you if you really look at the differences that are reflected in those cost estimates, essentially what we are saying we believe is a correct one, that it really ought not be to a critical factor. It has been overemphasized.

Now, you take a look at the State Farm costing on a nationwide figure setting aside State-by-State estimates. We are projecting for private passenger vehicles a 10 percent reduction if you move to elimination of the deductible and permit subrogation as against a commercial vehicle.

On the other hand, Allstate, whose criticisms of the Milliman & Robertson costing is probably at the other extreme, on the high side, suggests a nationwide average increase of about 17 percent. Mr. Rottman noted in some States it comes out as high as 90 or 95 percent and that is true. But we can only talk about average.

Mr. McCollister. Not to constituents that write to me.

Mr. McHugh. I understand that, but for our purposes we have to make some judgments upon which we can logically decide the issue and we have to take what the national average comes out with. In Allstate's case, they predict a 17 percent increase. If you take the average case of a person paying, say, $160 for his insurance premium, you have to realize that only $60 out of that $160 is what we are talking about here, because $100, roughly, covers property damage, collision, comprehensive, physical damage, liability insurance. So we are really only talking about $60 of that $160 average premium. If you take State Farm's judgment that this will produce a 10 percent reduction, you are talking about a $6.00 savings. If you take Allstate's judgment, it is, roughly, about a $10.00 increase or less than $1.00 a month. I suggest to you if that is the differences between us as to cost you should balance that against what no-fault really does in terms of paying countless more people, in terms of getting prompt payment to them, in terms of really taking care of the people who are seriously injured in auto accidents, who all of the studies show are woefully underpaid for even their actual economic loss. These are the kinds of judgments, it seems to me, as legislators you will be confronted with.

I would ask you to seriously examine whether or not you can afford to continue further delay upon the basis of these conflicting cost statements. The tenor of the comments here this morning is that cost issues have not been resolved and we need far more experimentation. That simply means to us more and more delay which defeats the purpose of getting some action now.

Mr. Van Deerlin. Mr. McCollister.

Mr. McCollister. Mr. McHugh, you referred to those people whose claims are not adequately compensated through the tort system. Are they not compensated through various other forms of coverage that they have, their health and accident insurance or Blue Cross-Blue Shield?

Mr. McHugh. Some are, Congressman, but there are great gaps in those coverages which the Department of Transportation study showed. There are vast numbers of seriously injured people who get no compensation in many cases, so, because of the fact there are available alternative sources of recovery does not give any assurance that those people are being properly and fully compensated.

Mr. McCollister. Could you be more specific when you say "vast numbers?" Can you tell me more exactly what you mean?

Mr. McHugh. Well, I would have to refer you again to some of the figures in the Department of Transportation study with reference to major injuries and I don't have those precisely in mind but I think we could furnish them to you very easily. They do describe the amount of economic losses recovered for injuries where the damage is in excess of $25,000 and it is a small percentage of the total.

Mr. Van Deerlin. Mr. Rottman.

Mr. Rottman. Yes, sir. Mr. Chairman, to respond fairly directly to your question about what is going on in the States and why haven't the States moved faster, one thing I think you ought to recognize is that some of firms like State Farm and the American Insurance Association and some of the insurance industry are not actively even supporting no-fault changes at the State level any more. As a matter of fact, in Nevada in 1973 when we enacted the law out there, State Farm gave us practically no support and the American Insurance Association, the best I could get from them was not to oppose a bill. So I don't think they are being totally fair when they give the impression they have been working diligently at the State level to try to get changes.

Mr. VAN DEERLIN. I believe Mr. McHugh made the point rather emphatically they have had a rather recent conversion on this subject.

Mr. McHUGH. May I make perfectly clear our decision to support Federal no-fault, which was based largely on the failure of the States, has not been accompanied by a determination not to support State no-fault plans, and we have actively worked to push State no-fault plans. We have done that and continued to do that in every State, and I would like more specifics from Commissioner Rottman on the failure of State Farm to support the Nevada bill because I can only tell you I was in close contact with the official on my staff who had responsibility for Nevada, and he was actively joining in the efforts of the people who were trying to get a no-fault bill passed. There were unquestionably disagreements between us and Mr. Rottman concerning what was the ideal form of the bill and what should be included in the bill. I hope that was not interpreted to mean we are in opposition to the bill. We have and continue to actively support State no-fault efforts.

Mr. ROTTMAN. They didn't do it as a practical matter in the State of Nevada, and also I think it should be revealed to you what happens when they predict a rate increase.

Mr. VAN DEERLIN. When who predicts a rate increase?

Mr. ROTTMAN. State Farm, for example. They went along, we had a mandate of 15 percent or based on the judgment of the Commissioner on what it would be, we had that kind of caveat in our bill. State Farm went along with that and said, "Fine." But previously they were paying dividends to policyholders, but immediately after the enactment, they gave a token decrease but they cut out dividends, so any effect of an alleged decrease was about a "wash," so I question seriously when people tell me they are going to give large decreases in rates or even any decreases, that these decreases will in fact come to light or won't show up again, say, 6 to 12 months down the line in a substantial request for a rate increase.

Very specifically, Travelers, when called in on a hearing, had this in mind. They gave the Nevada people a slight decrease going in, but they had programed immediately that they would come right back 6 months later and ask for a substantial increase in costs. I think this is deceiving.

Mr. McHUGH. I suggest to you that Commissioner Rottman has not listened to what I said. State Farm did not predict no-fault would reduce premiums in his State. We did not do that anyplace.

Mr. McCOLLISTER. In page 21 of your testimony, Mr. McHugh, you say, top of page, "We believe conversion to no-fault programs meeting the standard established by the S. 354 law would generally introduce a cost reducing element into the total ratemaking picture."

Mr. McHugh. That is absolutely correct. We continue to believe that. I point out there is a big difference between whether or not you have cost-reducing factors in the picture, and clearly the important cost-reducing factor that you have, Congressman, is the substantial elimination of the tort system and with that all of the accompanying high expenses in connection with determining and administering the fault issue. We have a substantial claim force that we employ to determine the very complicated, difficult issues of "who is at fault." We have to retain a vast network of counsel all over the country which we have to pay for, and in turn the people pressing claims against us have to pay for counsel who are representing them. We say that most of those costs can be eliminated by moving to a no-fault system.

Mr. McCollister. What percentage of your total costs do those factors account for now under the present tort system?

Mr. McHugh. I would have to ask our actuaries because they have actually broken out the specifics of our total premium dollar, what amount is represented by these costs. I could get it for you.

Mr. McCollister. What are your administrative costs, not counting those legal costs, the acquisition cost of your total premium dollar, what does it, as a percentage, cost?

Mr. McHugh. Total administrative costs are in the neighborhood of 30 or 32 percent.

Mr. McCollister. Does it include the legal expenses in connection with determining who is at fault?

Mr. McHugh. Yes.

Mr. McCollister. Does that figure also include acquisition costs?

Mr. McHugh. It would include the acquisition costs, too.

Mr. McCollister. Can you be more specific as to what each of those administrative costs would be?

Mr. McHugh. Yes. If you would, I would like to submit that to you specifically, and we have, I think, attempted to break out what portion of the premium dollar is represented by the administrative costs, acquisition costs, and would also include servicing of the fault system. We can furnish it.

Mr. McCollister. I ask unanimous consent, Mr. Chairman, that the record be held open to receive that information.

Mr. Van Deerlin. At this point in the testimony, yes, without objection.

[The following material was received for the record:]

Breakdown of Operating Expenses

Based on State Farm Mutual's 1974 Experience, the following is the breakdown of operating expenses for Auto BI, expressed as percentages of the premium dollar:

Acquisition costs:	Percent
Agents compensation	10.0
State premium tax	2.3
Claims adjustment, including adjustors salaries and legal defense costs	15.9
General expense, including underwriting data processing, administrative overhead	9.7
Total	37.9

For the 1st Party Coverages and for PD Liability the overall expense ratio is 30.8%, with the difference due to a Claims Adjustment ratio of 8.8% rather than 15.9%. For all coverages combined, the ratio is 33.3%.

Mr. McCollister. My time is about up, I have a number of questions, Mr. Chairman, but I think I would prefer to defer, so that others might have a chance to ask questions yet this morning.

Mr. Van Deerlin. First, Mr. Rottman is champing at the bit.

Mr. Rottman. One of the things I think we ought to make clear so that you understand this, is that oftentimes, what we usually talk about average rates, either, you know, it goes up an average five or down an average five, something like that, but as most of the bills have been written that do not permit or would not permit a State to have a subrogation provision among private passenger automobiles, what you will have is a dramatic shifting of cost within a couple of years. You will have the cost for what is considered now the safe type driver, the middle-aged individual who is married with some kids, his costs are going to go up rather substantially because he is the one that is going to start receiving the benefits without this subrogation provision and the so-called high risk driver now that most people say ought to bear the major portion of the costs, his rates are going to go down. As a regulator, I will find I am pretty hard pressed to tell my people in Nevada why their rates for the so-called good drivers are going to go up rather dramatically. I think you ought to to be aware of that kind of potential backlash if you decide to pass a bill.

Mr. McCollister. Would it not be likely that the high risk driver, the person who has frequent accidents and who has many claims, first-party claims, would be still charged more premiums just as he is now?

Mr. Rottman. I don't see how you can set your rating system up that way if you don't have a subrogation provision in your policy because the companies won't keep their data that way. We are having a tough enough time right now in getting data they have.

Mr. McCollister. What about that, Mr. McHugh?

Mr. McHugh. Moving to a no-fault system will have a different effect on costing of our product on different classes of insured.

Mr. McCollister. Will the high risk driver receive a lower premium cost?

Mr. McHugh. No. I am confident that the high risk driver who is involved in a higher number of accidents in the rating of his insurance will in fact be receiving insurance premiums that reflect his higher involvement in accidents. This can be done. There is no reason why, because you move to a no-fault system, that we are going to abandon the system of measuring claim frequency as a factor determining how we rate.

Mr. McCollister. Mr. Maisonpierre.

Mr. Maisonpierre. Let me give you an example of some things that will occur.

Experience has shown unquestionably that young, and by "young" I mean 25 years old or less, 17 to 25 year old drivers.

Mr. McCollister. I have one of those.

Mr. Van Deerlin. Male and unmarried?

Mr. Maisonpierre. Male and unmarried and we have to include female as well. You know sexism has crept into this, too. We find that females and males are getting to be about as reckless, one as the other.

Mr. Van Deerlin. That is the spirit of the times.

Mr. MAISONPIERRE. Right. They have many more accidents than the balance of the population, but they are young and they recover much more quickly from injuries which they themselves are likely to incur in accidents.

Since the company, the insurance company, will be measuring the premium on the losses that it pays to these people, and since these people are recovering a lot quicker than an elderly person who may, as a result of a very simple accident, be crippled for life, the young people will receive substantial premium reductions and the people that are more likely to be injured for long durations and draw benefits from the system are likely to pay more for their insurance premiums. I think this is inescapable under a system of this nature, particularly when the bill prohibits subrogation. All of the Federal bills specifically prohibit subrogation, except between classes of insured, that is commercial versus private passengers. So I don't really see how a mechanism can be brought to bear within the insurance system, a mechanism through which we could charge those people that have caused accidents more than others.

Mr. McCOLLISTER. Mr. McHugh, on this earlier question raised by Commissioner Rottman on rating, State Farm now does this on comprehensive, does it not?

Mr. McHUGH. Yes, certainly.

Mr. McCOLLISTER. My bills for my own and my wife's and my son's is on my desk now and there is a substantial difference and I know of the accident my son has had that makes his premium about five times what it is for his mother.

Mr. McHUGH. Yes.

Mr. McCOLLISTER. That is basically the comprehensive, not the bodily injury, right?

Mr. McHUGH. No. It is true in bodily injury, too. This is certainly the case in the younger driver because they are likely to have more accidents and cause more accidents and will pay more for bodily injury liability coverage, too. I would suggest moving to a no-fault is likely to have some effect upon premium structure, but I would simply disagree with the other witnesses here today as to what the extent of that would be. Yes, it is true, as Mr. Maisonpierre says, when you are paying for the youthful driver upon the basis of the injuries which he suffered, since his income at this point is probably limited and he is not as likely to have as long a confinement in the hospital, that means his loss is likely to be reduced, and he does not have any or as many dependents and, therefore, the amount of pay-out by the insurance company is likely to be less. Those will be reflected in his premiums. This is not to suggest that the young are very careless and have bad driving record that this also won't have a bearing and won't be used by insurance companies in determining rates.

Mr. McCOLLISTER. Thank you, Mr. Chairman.

Mr. VAN DEERLIN. Mr. Eckhardt, have you been around here long enough to get into this?

Mr. ECKHARDT. I think so, sir. I am trying to dig into it. I heard two estimates of the number of States that have no-fault systems and I gather that the difference between 16 and 24 is the key, or the key to that is on page 17 of Mr. McHugh's statement in which he says, "twenty-four States which either require insurers to offer or consumers to purchase first-party benefits,' I would assume that 16 require consumers to purchase and 24 either require insurers to offer or consumers to purchase, and would that be the situation?

Mr. McHugh. No. Sixteen have limited tort in some form or other. Twenty-four have required consumers to purchase add-on coverages and only some have eliminated tort in some form.

Mr. Eckhardt. Well, I thought you said on page 17 that "24 either require insurers to offer and consumers to purchase" and I think there is a difference. For instance, in Texas, insurers are required to offer but consumers are not required to purchase.

Mr. McHugh. Well, I think this may be true. What we are trying to show here is that of the 24 States, all of those 24 States contain some sort of a sale of add-on no-fault insurance benefits. In some cases they are required to buy and in other cases the insurer is required to offer.

But all of those contain that feature of a requirement that there be first-party no-fault benefits available. The critical difference, I think, between us is that among those 24 States, 16 of them will also have modified the tort system in some way.

Mr. Eckhardt. Yes. Of course, to call it a true no-fault law, that is a necessary ingredient.

Mr. McHugh. That is our judgment. I think this is what makes the difference.

Mr. Eckhardt. And you make a rather eloquent presentation here that even of those 16, most of them are seriously lacking in elements of what we consider no-fault provisions that would essentially increase the efficiency of the insurance system.

Mr. McHugh. This is correct. It is hard for us to take seriously, Congressman, bills which restrict or limit tort by establishing a medical threshold of something under $500.

Mr. Eckhardt. One thing that troubles me a bit, though, is that if these States have, when acting on their own, such a very poor record of establishing a no-fault system, what makes you think that if we set standards within somewhat flexible brackets that the States would do any better?

In the first place, they might accept the bottom of the bracket, and, in the second place, they might administer the system in such a way as not to afford very adequate coverage and what makes you think they will do so much better if we tell them what the standards ought to be within brackets?

Mr. McHugh. Well, I think we have come to the conclusion that the reasons for the failure of State action and the decline in the movement of States to no-fault has been the result of very sophisticated, very effective opposition that has been coming from the personal injury bar. I think they have discovered the most effective ways in which they can slow down the passage of no-fault legislation.

Now, why would we think that with the passage of a Federal standards bill the States are likely to pass bills that comply with these higher Federal standards and why would the substantial opposition of the personal injury bar decline? I think that is because of the threat that is represented in title III, if title III comes into being there is a complete elimination of the tort system. So the personal injury bar that may not like a system which eliminates tort in the way that must be done in order to comply with the standards set up in title III are likely in our judgment, to embrace that approach very readily when they know that the failure to do that will mean they will be confronted with the consequences of title III which is the complete elimination of the tort system with no room left for tort for the seriously injured.

Mr. ECKHARDT. If I should establish a "lexicon of demonology," which I do not do, I would include in it not only the bar but also in some instances the insurance companies who would, I would assume, exercise pressure on the administration of the system within a State in the direction of reducing the payout and keeping the premium payments relatively high. Might there not be such an influence upon States purportedly operating under Federal standards?

Mr. McHUGH. I think it is possible. However, I would have to say that in our judgment the elements of the insurance industry that might be joining forces to block the enforcement of no-fault would be very largely concentrating their efforts upon the prospects of a Federal no-fault bill and what that means to them as they view the whole federalism scheme and what ought to be the role of the Federal Government versus the States. But once confronted with the fait accompli of a Federal standards bill and the prospect then of living either with a title III or what we would consider to be a much more moderate standards bill embraced in title III, most of those companies would accept that type of bill.

Mr. ECKHARDT. I imagine they would. But if there is any lesson in recent history, it is that an administrator at odds with a policymaker will not effectively administer a law. Now, what we are doing here is acting as a policymaker, we are setting up standards, and we have a certain limited reach for investigation and we are calling on the States, then, to administer that which we have set out policywise. In the first place, we have denied ourselves of the power to deal with rates at a Federal level through the McCarran Act.

In the second place, we will have acted only to set the standards initially. We will then permit the States without Federal interference to operate within those brackets in whatever manner they desire without necessarily balancing their alterations within the brackets. Now, I think that when we say that this will result in a good end, we are assuming that the States will come to the same policy conclusions we have and will energetically and fairly administer their laws within those brackets. But we will continue to have an influence on those States to decrease the amount of payout, to keep the premium payments high, and we will have pressures on those States presumably from the bar to maintain the widest range of residual tort. We will have influence on those States to create a result by which you pay a premium for no-fault insurance and also some kind of a premium for that which falls over into the area of tort. We will have all of those pressures existing and what makes you think that we will come out with a more efficient system by merely setting goals at one level of government and administering them in another?

Mr. McHUGH. Well, I think it is very wrong to suggest or to hope that by the passage of a Federal standards no-fault bill we have automatically solved all of the problems in the auto accident reparations area. It seems to us you have to make some choices between what you currently have and what you could have. It seems to us what we have is very bad. What we could have is a considerable improvement over it.

Now, I think it is probably true there will be some resistence at the State regulatory level if the Federal standards bill were to be enacted. But what are the choices that are left to those State regulators? It is hard for me to think they will consciously decline to assume the responsibilities that they have pursuant to their State law to seize all of the power they can in administering this system, because if they do not, if they decline, and if they thrust this responsibility back upon the Federal Government, clearly that will push the Federal Government into the business of creating a Federal bureaucracy for the regulation of insurance. I should think that is the last thing in the world that the State regulator wants.

Mr. ECKHARDT. Why is it a Federal bureaucracy but not a State bureaucracy when the same thing is done at two different levels of Government?

Mr. McHUGH. There is indeed a State bureaucracy.

Mr. ECKHARDT. Why is the Federal bureaucracy bad but the State bureaucracy at least acceptable? I have seen some State bureaucracies that were awful. For instance, the bureaucracy that administered the Blue Sky law in Texas for a long term was far worse than SEC and I suspect it is not up to the SEC today.

Mr. McHUGH. I suppose, Congressman, on this point as a company, our difference, if any, with you on this point, on the federalism issue, goes to some of the practical judgments about "whether or not we are going to get any kind of bill at all" and I think we have come to the conclusion if we are to get any bill at all, we had better do it pursuant to as much dependence upon the State regulatory machinery as we can.

Mr. ECKHARDT. I recognize the practical need for that approach but I am wondering if your gradual and soul-seeking movement from the position of favoring State "no-fault" to favoring Federal standards State "no-fault" may be repeated 2 years from now as you gradually move to the acceptance of the fact that, if we are to have "no-fault," we are going to have to simply draft a bill that we think will work and put it into effect federally.

Mr. McHUGH. Well, at this point in time, I can only say to you that we are confident that, as you look at the business of insurance regulations and whatever its imperfections, we are confident that the States are doing a good job, will continue to do a good job and we would like to see as much of their authority continued intact.

We would hope that under this bill, if enacted, the States will in fact continue the kind of regulation which they have and if anything, it will be improved.

Mr. ECKHARDT. Thank you. I do have a question for Mr. Rottman, if I may.

Mr. VAN DEERLIN. I think the intention is to come back at 1:30 if the panel is agreeable.

Ms. O'REILLY. I am to appear at 1:30 before the Consumer Affairs Subcommittee of the Banking and Currency Committee, but I will try to make arrangements to be the last witness.

Mr. VAN DEERLIN. Mr. Brodhead.

Mr. BRODHEAD. I must say I was struck by the statement Mr. McHugh made. It seems to me it cuts to the heart of the issue, and it seems to me the issue is "What is the most effective way and fairest way to compensate people who have suffered injuries in all accidents?"

As a person who has had good deal of experience in respresenting both plaintiffs and defendants in these cases—and I must say that the current system leaves a great deal to be desired—I found Mr. McHugh's statement and Ms. O'Reilly's statement most persuasive, and I felt keenly the lack in Mr. Rottman's testimony and Mr. Maisonpierre's testimony of some comment with respect to that issue.

It seems to me indisputable that, as the Department of Transportation 1971 study showed, a great number of people who are injured in automobile accidents are overcompensated. I find this to be quite true from my own experience and that equally perhaps a greater number of people who are seriously injured in automobile accidents are inadequately compensated or not compensated at all.

It seems to me the no-fault system at least offers hope or promise of being able to do something about this. As I attempt to work out a position on this proposed legislation, it would be most helpful to me in making up my mind if I could have some comment from either Mr. Maisonpierre, or Mr. Rottman on that specific point.

Mr. Maisonpierre.

Mr. MAISONPIERRE. Congressman, the reason I did not touch on the matter of fault or no-fault is that I was under the assumption that all of the witnesses today were supportive of a no-fault program. The difference between the four of us is whether we should have Federal no-fault or State no-fault.

We have supported State "no fault." We have supported the concept of no-fault going back now to about 1966 or 1967 with experimenting in a number of States.

The primary reason that we oppose Federal legislation at this time is that we do not know yet and we will not know for some time yet, what is the balance between the fault and no-fault benefits that can bring about an acceptable level of insurance premium, an acceptable level of benefits to first-party and third-party injured, and how the different types of no-fault approaches will work.

Mr. Rottman indicated that in the southern portion of his State and Allstate, in its testimony before the Senate Commerce Committee stated that a number of serious abuses were developing in the implementation of no-fault programs. That does not mean that no-fault is bad per se. It means that we have got to know a little bit more about how these programs operate before we can go in with a Federal approach which will create a nationwide program which would be very difficult to correct or to backtrack from.

We also think that in order to get the proper balancing between the cost to policyholders and benefits to injured victims whether they be first-party or third-party victims, that we will need to have major differences among the States in their no-fault systems.

After all, the problems with the fault system today vary considerably. The problems in New York City are quite different from the problems in Iowa and Nebraska. So why would we think a solution which was applicable to New York City is the solution that would be applicable in those areas. We do not think they are. We think each State should look at its systems and its problems and correct the problems but we do believe that no-fault is the answer, no question about it.

Mr. BRODHEAD. Mr. Rottman.

Mr. ROTTMAN. Yes, sir. I certainly would not want to leave the impression I am against the no-fault concept.

As a matter of fact, I can show you a few scars I received from trial lawyers in Nevada and a few insurance companies as a result of pushing hard to get the bill through during the first session we tried to get a bill through.

But I think Andre has summed it up probably pretty good in terms of the differences you have among your States. For example, if you go back and look at really why the no-fault concept came into being or became very popular, one of the aspects was the court congestion that existed in some of the major metropolitan areas. We do not have that degree of court congestion in a lot of our smaller States.

Also, if you, or I suppose—and I may be talking a little bit counter here but—if you go back and look at a couple of other reasons, it was the heavy risk of almost yearly cost increases in most States during the sixties that prompted a search for new and better systems. If you can go back and look at the literature during that period of time, you will find that is a heavy motivating force during that time.

That largely abated, that particular reason, during the 1970's now so I think there is a little less pressure. But nevertheless, I think the concept is good and it provides fast benefits and it provides much more equitable benefits. There is no question at all in my mind.

Take a look at the Oregon situation, which several years ago I would have said, you know, the people up there and the Commissions used to tell me "My system is working good" and my response was "I just did not believe it, I guess" but as a practical matter you go up and find those people pretty happy with the add-on system up there. Why it works as to alleviate some of their problems, I do not know. I cannot tell you but apparently it relieves some of the court congestion and their caseload is down there and it provides prompt payment and somewhat more equitable payment I think.

Mr. BRODHEAD. Thank you, sir.

Mr. VAN DEERLIN. It being now 5 minutes into the House session, perhaps we should abandon ship at this point and come back at 1:30. The hearing will resume at 1:30 this afternoon.

[Whereupon, at 12:05 p.m., the subcommittee recessed to reconvene at 1:30 p.m. the same day.]

AFTER RECESS

[The subcommittee reconvened at 1:30 p.m., Hon. Lionel Van Deerlin presiding.]

Mr. VAN DEERLIN. The hearing will resume and Mr. McCollister is recognized.

Mr. MCCOLLISTER. Thank you, Mr. Chairman.

Pursuing a question that Mr. Eckhardt asked about on this difference in the number of States that have no-fault legislation, I think it developed from that question and answers to it that there is a wide difference in no-fault proposals in the various States, some of which it has been suggested should not be called no-fault.

I was wondering if the panel could tell me if there is consensus among you on what States, other than Michigan perhaps, have in your opinion, a real no-fault insurance law.

Mr. McHugh, would you like to start?

Mr. McHugh. I think we have said that, of the States that have passed no-fault laws, the Michigan bill is the best. We have had some reservations about the tort limitations in the Michigan bill as to whether or not it will be quite as strong as it is thought to be. It appears to be working well.

Beyond that, I would suppose the Minnesota bill probably would come next to being a reasonably strong no-fault bill.

There the package of benefits is reasonably high and the limitation on tort is among the strongest limitations that has been adopted.

Mr. McCollister. Could you tell me what those short limitations are.

Mr. McHugh. My recollection of the Minnesota bill is that, and I think I have a list in here—I believe it is a $1,500 medical threshold.

Mr. Van Deerlin. How long has this bill been enacted in Minnesota?

Mr. McHugh. I guess it is now 2 years.

Andre, you may have more precise information on that.

Mr. Maisonpierre. It was enacted 2 years ago but I think in Minnesota it actually became effective 1 year ago. There was a year lapse between enactment and date of effectiveness.

Mr. McHugh. It is a $2,000 medical threshold or disability exceeding 60 days. The benefit package is $20,000 for medical expense and $10,000 for other benefits. It has a $15 a day benefit for replacement services for the 7-day waiting period and survivors' benefits go up to $200 a week. I believe that is for 1 year.

Mr. McCollister. Of the 24 States, you would classify only Minnesota and Michigan or do I read more into your comments there than I should?

Mr. McHugh. Yes, I think that is probably right. We would view that most of the other 16 States that have passed no-fault laws, in which they have modifications of the tort system, as inadequate.

On the other hand, I think, Congressman, maybe it is too much of an overgeneralization from that to conclude that all of those laws should be junked and to start from scratch.

The important thing to recognize is that the legislature in those States did take the one major step which was to recognize that, if we are going to get at the evils of the auto accidents reparations system, we ought to do something about limiting the tort system. They did it. We may view those as not a strong enough action to really produce effective no-fault but it was the major decision that had to be made. So, in State Farm's judgment from that point on in those States we do not really think the burden is that great to move them toward a little stronger emphasis upon tort limitation.

Mr. McCollister. That is an interesting comment as it relates to what your testimony conveys, to me at least, which is the utter hopelessness of depending on the States to react in any—using your definition—responsible fashion.

Mr. McHugh. Well, I think my comments are aimed essentially at what attitude of the States which have no no-fault laws would be if no Federal bill passed.

Now, absent a Federal bill, I think we do not see much hope for meaningful effort even if they pass some type of bill.

Mr. McCollister. Well, let me come back and ask Ms. O'Reilly.

Ms. O'REILLY. Briefly, Consumer Federation of America has neither endorsed nor opposed any particular State no-fault bill but to the extent Michigan no-fault legislation is consistent with the consumer benefit package contained in S. 354 and H.R. 1900, we would undoubtedly endorse it.

I would also like to point out that our consumer representatives in the State of Michigan who are members of CFA have had a favorable response to this legislation.

In terms of its cost, there are at least two aspects of the Michigan situation which should be considered when criticism is given that there is not yet sufficient evidence of the cost benefit to consumers.

Until October 1976, Michigan insurers will have to pay under the old tort system for claims which arose before the date of enactment as well as under the new no-fault legislation. Logically insurance companies in Michigan have to establish larger reserves to reflect that dual payment schedule.

Also as the constitutionality of Michigan's no-fault legislation is still being litigated, it is leading the insurance companies within Michigan to keep very secure reserves so they are not faced with the dilemma which confronted the Illinois Insurance companies when that State's no-fault law was declared unconstitutional Because they were then forced to pay out under both systems, it had disastrous effects on their economy.

Therefore, it is premature to pass on the cost impact in Michigan. But it is reasonable to assume that the reserves will be reduced in the near future with a resultant cost saving to policy holders.

Mr. McCOLLISTER. All of this is preliminary to another question I want to get to. Thank you.

Mr. Maisonpierre.

Mr. MAISONPIERRE. We feel all of the States that have limited the tort recovery to some extent, have enacted acceptable no-fault laws. It does not mean we think those laws are necessarily going to work. We think that New York probably will have to raise its low threshold.

On the other hand, we have to admit even though we opposed the Oregon law all along, we have to admit it works, to the extent that it has eliminated whatever problems existed in automobile insurance in Oregon. We cannot argue with success. As to Michigan, we are very concerned about the Michigan law. No. 1, of course is the constitutionality issue, but more important, the threshold under the Michigan law says that the tort system is abolished except for a number of specific types of injuries and injuries creating serious impairments.

The courts have not passed on the meaning of "serious impairment. If I sprain my little finger at the time of the accident, it is a "serious impairment." It does not have to be permanent impairment. So we do not know what Michigan has done and we will not know what Michigan has done until the court interprets that phrase "serious impairment."

Basically, as long as the State has enacted a tort threshold, we think that, if the law works with the level or threshold that has been enacted, fine, but we do not know as yet how the laws work on all of the States that have enacted no-fault. This is why we think there is need for experimentation.

Mr. McCOLLISTER. Mr. Rottman.

Mr. ROTTMAN. Sir, I have to take a broader definition of that. I would include the States even that have not limited the tort liability as falling into the no-fault category.

I do not think, if you look back to the literature and talk to those people involved in this thing for 10 or 12 years, that they have a common-path definition that they have set forth.

I guess I would just have to say that whatever works in this and whatever proves the tort liability system where it exists today, I think is beneficial under those circumstances.

That is one reason we at NAIC have taken the position that of the State-by-State approach to deal with the specific problems in that given State and to try to help the people there as much as possible.

Mr. MCCOLLISTER. With the wide variety of State programs that there are, assuming that this subcommittee and then the full committee and then Congress will approve some sort of Federal standard, mandating the States to do something within those brackets, is it not likely that those State legislators are going to be unwilling to pass legislation where they bear the burden of telling the insurance purchaser, the consumer, that he is going to have to pay higher premiums— are they not likely to react against this Federal mandate and to not do anything. Is it not likely to cause more difficulty than it is to actually solve problems?

Mr. MAISONPIERRE. Mr. McCollister, exhibit 5 in our statement shows how each of these State no-fault laws comply with the standards of S. 354. These are the standards before S. 354 was amended and this new bill does not contain that much of a change. It demonstrates very few areas of compatibility.

My feeling is this and I think Mr. McHugh has given me support in this feeling in a statement he made this morning, I do not think the States are going to react favorably to Federal standards, hence, I think we need to examine the impact of title III, S. 354. I do not think the States will react favorably for a number of reasons.

No. 1, a very practical reason and as legislators, I am sure you are very much aware of your relationship with your constituents. So are State legislators aware of their relationships with constituents and they are not going to want to accept the direct brunt of exposing their constituents to automobile insurance cost increases. They will leave that burden on you in Washington.

Mr. VAN DEERLIN. If I may interrupt, you are not in doubt, are you, that the idea of no-fault is a popular one with the poeple?

Mr. MAISONPIERRE. The idea of cost increase is not a popular one with the people.

Mr. VAN DEERLIN. We must assume they understand somewhat, because it has been kicked about for a good many years now, and there are impressive majorities in favor of no-fault insurance systems.

Whether it is at the State or Federal level, they like the idea.

Mr. MAISONPIERRE. Mr. Chairman, the polls have indicated time and time again when asked, "Why do you like no-fault," they say "Because it is going to reduce costs."

If the promise does not follow through, there will be a backlash. I do not think that anybody can say that there is going to be a cost reduction. I think that particular issue there is wide open, unless there is a mandated cost reduction, which is probably the reason why, a very difficult—well, we question whether the smaller companies will be able to operate under title III.

Mr. McHugh, this morning, started out by saying that the day that Senate Commerce Committee reported out S. 354, in fact, when it reported out S. 354, this was reported to the Illinois Legislative Committee which was considering no-fault at the time. It made no impression whatever and the Illinois committee rejected State no-fault.

I think that the answer is that Federal action, that if Congress does enact a standard bill of the S. 354 nature, that the State legislatures are going to say, we leave it up to Congress.

Mr. Van Deerlin. It was the intent of this panel that you feel free to interrupt one another with crossfire at any time, if you wish.

Mr. McHugh. I just want to say, Mr. Chairman, I completely disagree with the underlying assumption of Mr. Maisonpierre's statement.

We feel quite certain that, while State legislatures may not be entirely happy or comfortable with what they are confronted with if a Federal bill is passed, they are practical men, they will be dealing with the fact that the Federal Government has now established a Federal no-fault auto accident reparations system.

Mr. McCollister. Let me interrupt you to say that recently the courts ruled that in fact the Corps of Engineers has jurisdiction over navigable waters which definition extends the reach of the Corps of Engineers very broadly.

And there has been a reaction around my State and a number of other States among State legislators that are quite concerned about the jurisdiction passing from State law, in our case the Platte River, which is about a mile wide and an inch deep. It is in no way navigable. There has been a reaction, not only in Nebraska but many other States on this Federal question of Federal preemption and I think you can help us here in determining how our State legislators are going to react on this question of State no-fault.

I think they are going to say, "OK you guys created a problem, you go ahead and enact a Federal no-fault law not on a standards basis but on a complete preemption basis as required in title III."

Mr. McHugh. To me that is not the way I would see the States responding. You have heard the very strong and almost anguished cries of criticism about this bill because of the alleged unnecessary intrusion of the Federal Government brought about by this. What you are suggesting is that the States are prepared to abandon the whole auto accident reparations system, including regulation of automobile insurance. After being in the business for 13 years I find extremely hard to believe.

I do not believe the legislators will do it and, while they may not like the notion of a Federal law suggesting the kind of State laws to be passed, the net objective is to induce the States to meet those standards. But I believe, Congressman, we ought to get back to the underlying question which suggests States will not be willing to move toward the passage of no-fault laws because of the fact it will increase costs.

We disagree with that judgment. Our judgment of the cost is it will not increase costs. We caution against trying to oversell no-fault on the grounds it is going to produce tremendous cost savings because we do not believe it will, but our own cost estimate is it will produce reductions in 46 of the 50 States.

Mr. ROTTMAN. Does it include the rate filing you have, for an average 18-percent increase of bodily injury?

Mr. McHUGH. In each case on that table the reduction we suggest is over the ending 1974 State Farm rate for combined bodily injury coverages.

Mr. ROTTMAN. You propose to raise rates in Arizona by 18 percent and then come back and give a reduction of 18 percent according to your table.

Mr. McHUGH. Again, Mr. Rottman, we have not suggested we will cut premiums by that amount.

Mr. ROTTMAN. That is what the projection is here.

Mr. McHUGH. It is a projection what the cost impact of that bill will be.

What I am suggesting to you is in answer to your questions: "How will State legislators feel if they have to pass a no-fault bill?" and "What will be the consequences to them if it is going to vote to increase rates?"

Our judgment is it will not have that effect, the cost impact will not be to increase premiums as the Allstate costing would suggest.

Now, look at what happened in most of the State no-fault bills, the legislatures there in most cases have assumed that it will automatically produce decreases and mandated rate decreases.

We think that is a mistake for the legislatures to have done it.

Mr. McCOLLISTER. It does not prescribe a form of no-fault that fits the standards we talk about.

Mr. McHUGH. But they are no-fault bills predicated upon the assumption that State legislators do believe that no-fault will produce cost savings and have written these reductions into the statute.

Ms. O'REILLY. Before I leave I wish to make this point.

When we talk about cost as the consumer views it, it can have a very different meaning depending on the context. The cost of auto insurance is not just the bare figure of policy premiums but the cost in terms of what they get for what they pay—the value. It also means what the system costs the consumer in terms of anxiety, lives lost, injuries, treatment and rehabilitation postponed overall inefficiency.

Mr. McCOLLISTER. Nobody that buys insurance ever expects to have an accident.

Ms. O'REILLY. Realistically, I think they do or they would not take out insurance. It is anxiety and anguish about what is going to happen to them when they do have an accident that is leading more and more consumers to endorse the concept of national no-fault as opposed to State no-fault.

There has been a number of polls set forth in the Congressional Record that show, for example, in Chairman Brooks' district, two and a half times as many constituents favor a national no-fault approach as opposed to a State no-fault approach.

I would like to read for the record other constituent positions.

Congressman Abruzo's constituency, 66 favored national no-fault and 25.2 did not.

Congressman John Ashbrook's (R.-Ohio), 59.6 percent in favor of national and 35.5 percent against.

Congressman Frelinghuysen (N.J.), 33 percent in favor and 17 percent against.

Congressman Bob Wilson of California, 67 percent in favor and 23 percent opposed.

The poll taken in the late Congressman Pettis of California's district in 1972, 72 percent in favor and 28 percent against.

Senator Harry F. Byrd of Virginia, 51 percent in favor and 30 percent against.

Mr. McCollister. Before you take that brief leave of absence, do those polls also sample why those constituents want them?

Ms. O'Reilly. The poll responses do not elaborate on that issue but in terms of "why," once again we must return to the definition of "cost." Consumers want to know what they get for their dollar and they see in the present "fault" system a tremendous amount of waste.

To see so much of their premium dollar absorbed by litigation as opposed to being returned to policyholders' pockets; to experience needless delay; the frustration of not knowing whether they are going to have a successful jury verdict—these are the factors and issues many consumers reject in today's situation. It is leading them to an urgent desire for no-fault on a national level.

Mr. Rottman. Have you talked to people on the street about how they feel? I get calls almost daily.

Ms. O'Reilly. The most intense anxieties to consumers are delay, and inadequate return for their investment, as opposed to cost.

Mr. McCollister. You actually talked to these people?

Ms. O'Reilly. Yes, I have; and CFA's constituency of 208 organizations including local and national consumer groups reflect that concern.

Mr. McCollister. Your insurance companies tell you they are in favor of it, too?

Ms. O'Reilly. To the best of my knowledge, only one insurance company belongs to CFA. They have but one vote whereas our CFA consumer groups have votes which vary in size according to their membership. In no way does Nationwide Insurance dominate CFA.

Mr. Maisonpierre. Back to this issue of waste, efficiency, and so on, and what it is that the public, consumers, and policyholders think they are getting. I do not frankly think that the policyholders, that many policyholders really understand and appreciate what they are getting in no-fault.

Let me give you some reasons.

I recall that some 18 months or so ago when Mr. Morrell of State Farm testified, I think it was before the Senate Commerce Committee, as to his company's experience in Florida. He stated that approximately one-third of the no-fault claimants were retaining attorneys to get their first-party benefits.

That just means that one-third of the people who had been injured in accidents really did not understand what benefits they were entitled to under no-fault, because otherwise why should they have hired an attorney?

State Farm indicates today that about 25 percent of their claimants in Florida, no-fault claimants, have obtained attorneys to secure no-fault benefits when this is something that is payable right off the bat. So, that shows people really do not understand what they are getting.

Mr. ECKHARDT. Will the chairman yield?

It is payable right off the bat? There are penalties, of course, attached but the question is, are these attorneys just called in to do nothing or have they been active in demanding payment by insurance companies that would not pay off the bat?

Mr. ROTTMAN. I can give you first hand experience on that.

By and large the companies have done a pretty fair job in making fairly rapid payments in most of the States, including Nevada, and oftentimes what happens is there is some misunderstanding or, you know, lack of understanding of how things work and they have some contact with an attorney and sometimes that attorney never gets fully employed. In other words, he just serves as somewhat of an adviser and sometimes they get in and go ahead and do the suing also if the injuries are serious.

Mr. McHUGH. I would say this.

Mr. McCOLLISTER. Maybe I could wind up this a bit because I have abused my colleague's time.

Mr. McHugh, if I am right, and you are wrong, on what happened to State legislators as they are faced with this bill and you are faced then with a somewhat different situation, what would your attitude be on this legislation if State Farm and insurance companies generally would then find themselves having to deal with some sort of Federal specifications?

Mr. McHUGH. Is your question directed to how we would respond to the type of no-fault program that is contained in the title III issue?

Mr. McCOLLISTER. Yes.

Mr. McHUGH. Or how we respond to regulation that is involved.

Mr. McCOLLISTER. No; the title III aspect of no-fault.

Mr. McHUGH. We have now from the beginning expressed some reservations to the committee about the length to which the Senate was prepared to go in title III. We had never thought it necessary to provide for a complete abolition of the tort remedy.

I think that, given our preference we would have preferred some residual tort liability under title III and we continue to express those reservations to the committee.

The possibility that, confronted with a title III, you may have more of a role for the Department of Transportation in the area is one which is not wholly to our liking.

But very frankly, unlike the gentlemen here who are prepared to position their fundamental statement on who regulates them, State Farm's major position is "What is the best deal for your customer?"

Then we will worry secondly about who is going to have the job of regulating us. We are convinced the best job for our customer is not the present system. I understand that.

Mr. ROTTMAN. I wish the gentleman from State Farm would instruct his claims people in my State to be that generous. The attitude he conveys here we would be happier with.

Mr. MCHUGH. They receive the same instructions as our claims men do in all other States.

Mr. ROTTMAN. May I respond to the popularity thing very briefly?

Our experience was that for a while, just a couple of years ago it was a popular issue but once we got the bill passed and implemented, the popularity of no-fault seemed to be down considerably. Maybe it was because you got a bill and it is actually working; maybe it is not as high standards as Don would like, but nevertheless it is working.

I do not think that is their overwhelming push across the Nation as I see it for enactment of the Federal standards bill, also, that cost issue regardless of how we try to play it down, is grabbing. A week ago Saturday morning, or a week ago Saturday, both Las Vegas papers made a broad headline that the Senate bill will put pleasure back into driving and the article went on: "State Farm is suggesting there is a $2 billion rate savings across the Nation."

I think it is inescapable that this kind of publicity continues to interest people that say, "Sure we want no-fault." I think some no-fault is good, no doubt about it.

Mr. MCHUGH. I want to point out I never said that, and we caution again it is a great mistake to oversell on the basis of cost. Other people used our statistics to jump to this conclusion but we did not say that.

Mr. MAISONPIERRE. The Washington Star had a strong editorial for endorsing no-fault and what was the reason? It was "This will save consumers billions of dollars."

Mr. VAN DEERLIN. It did not say "in premiums," however, did it?

Mr. MAISONPIERRE. I believe it did.

Mr. VAN DEERLIN. My guess is it did not, because I was well aware at the time there was unlikely to be savings of premiums and I think it would have jumped out and hit me. However, we can check it out.

Mr. MCCOLLISTER. Nevertheless, Mr. Chairman, the point is the very close correlation when you say "no-fault" with "savings" and I think most people do interpret it as it will cost them less out of their pockets in terms of premiums. At least my mail reflects that.

Thank you.

Mr. ROTTMAN. A point that was brought up I think by Kathleen earlier this morning, the one I talked to Senator Cannon about last week was the aspect of uniformity and he was sort of expressing the idea generally, paraphrasing it, "One of the reasons he perhaps would like to see a Federal standards bill, if you would vote for it, is there would be uniformity among States and traveling from State to State there would be no question about which benefits you would get" and so forth.

First, you are not going to get that kind of uniformity unless or because some States fail to act and you will have a hodgepodge of different plans across the States.

Second, I think, under the system we have now were some States have acted and some have not acted, for our residents in Nevada traveling any place else, they have Nevada benefits and for anybody else coming into Nevada they have Nevada benefits. And you would have diversity 5 years down the pike with just a State-by-State enactment. There is still, I think, a reasonable degree of certainty about what you get because usually your benefits will follow you wherever you are unless some other State has a higher level of benefits.

Mr. VAN DEERLIN. Mr. Eckhardt.

Mr. ECKHARDT. For a number of years I have been asking of witnesses that have come before this committee to give me, to the best of their ability, the ratio of payout to premiums. I notice Mrs. Reilly refers to that as a measure of efficiency of the program.

It may be that we have some figures on that but if we have received figures on that from no-fault States, I do not recall what those figures were and I do not recall anyone giving me figures to that effect.

Now, we have in the reports to our committee with respect to the average payout against premiums, the premium paid in—something like a 40-percent ratio in the past, maybe 44 percent, in that neighborhood.

Mr. MCCOLLISTER. State Farm is 65 they say.

Mr. ECKHARDT. I am talking about national figures. I think those were the ones made around 1969 or 1970 and I think it is about correct but as I recall some 20 percent of litigation costs, attorney costs, and so forth, for the plaintiffs and for an insurance company's costs with respect to their investigations, attorneys' fees and so forth, I think it was something around 15 percent, as I recall.

Mr. McHUGH. I would think it is closer to 7 or 8 percent.

Mr. ECKHARDT. In addition there was acquisition costs which constituted an additional figure and all in all, the overhead cost, the insurance was nearly 60 percent as I recall those figures.

Now, do we have any figures with respect to Michigan? It has had a no-fault system put into effect in 1972. Do we have any comparable ratios with respect to the State of Michigan?

Mr. McHUGH. You really have only 1 year of experience in Michigan.

Mr. ECKHARDT. Well, do we have it with respect to Massachusetts?

Mr. McHUGH. I believe there is, although State Farm does have little business in Massachusetts. I would suspect some of the companies that Mr. Maisonpierre's association represents might do more business there.

Mr. MAISONPIERRE. I could provide you, Congressman, with some figures as to the amount of premium collected and losses paid. I would probably not have the amount of money that went to lawyers in fees, because this is not something we are privy to and they require special outside research, because we, of course, do not know what is paid.

Mr. ECKHARDT. I am not asking for that because I understand it is difficult but you have to make assumptions with respect to that but it should not be difficult to draw a ratio between payouts and premiums.

Mr. McHUGH. I can tell you this. What it will show unquestionably is, we limit ourselves to the last year, that is the last 6 months of 1974 and first 6 months of the year 1975 to the extent it is available, we are going to find a very high amount of payout as related to premium collection because rates have been inadequate, countrywide. Insurance companies have been losing their shirts. I will be glad, if the record can be kept open, Mr. Chairman, to provide you with some figures on this point.

Mr. Van Deerlin. It will be held open.
[The following material was received for the record:]

LOSS AND EXPENSE RATIOS—AUTOMOBILE INSURANCE

	U.S. totals	
	Industry	State Farm
1971:		
Earned premiums (in millions)	$15,892	$1,792
Incurred loss ratio (percent)	59.0	54.9
Operating expense ratio	36.8	31.7
Combined	95.8	86.6
1972:		
Earned premiums (in millions)	$17,282	$1,965
Incurred loss ratio (percent)	59.3	58.3
Operating expense ratio	37.1	33.3
Combined	96.4	91.6
1973:		
Earned premiums (in millions)	$18,241	$2,096
Incurred loss ratio (percent)	63.1	64.0
Operating expense ratio	37.1	32.8
Combined	100.2	96.8
1974:		
Earned premiums (in millions)	$18,725	$2,198
Incurred loss ratio (percent)	65.5	65.4
Operating expense ratio	[1] 38.1	34.0
Combined	103.6	99.4
1st quarter 1975: Combined ratio	[1] 112.0	103.7

[1] Estimated.

Note: Loss ratio is losses incurred to premiums earned, adjusted for policyholder dividends and excluding loss adjustment expenses. Operating expense ratio is the sum of the ratio of loss adjustment expense to premiums earned and the ratio of other expenses to premiums written.

Source: Annual statement data, as compiled by A. M. Best Co.

Mr. Eckhardt. Mr. Rottman, do you have the figures for the State of Nevada for the year 1974?

Mr. Rottman. Yes, sir, we have them. I tell you what and I think this gets to the heart of the measure, we have had a number of requests for rate increases and within this we have to get the figures in terms of what they did collect and what they have actually paid out, but the biggest figure in there and the reason that things are almost meaningless is the biggest figure is IBNR, incurred but not reported, reserve and you do not know how much water is in that figure. Practically speaking, I can submit what we have but the credibility is extremely low there I think.

Mr. Eckhardt. Well, you would be able, though, to determine in the year 1974, how much was paid out to injured motorists and how much was paid in in premium, would you not?

Mr. Rottman. Yes, sir. That figure in and of itself is very low but what you have, you have losses that have been incurred but have not yet been paid, to look at it just on the basis for one single year of what has been taken in versus what has been paid out is totally misleading.

Mr. Eckhardt. Well, could you compare that to what happened say in 1972, the errors would be of the same magnitude; should they not?

Mr. Rottman. We tried that and we got some wild variations, frankly.

Mr. Eckhardt. Now, the thing that troubles me about this whole question, of course, if you tell people that you are going to reduce costs of premiums and extend liabilities that might have been guilty of contributory negligence, of course they are going to say they want such a program and of course you can reduce costs and it just depends on what percentage of the total injury is paid out. If you suddenly decide you are going to pay people half as much as they previously got and pass a law to that effect, you have a reduction in premium costs but it is not going to be to the advantage of the insured and in the long run not to the insurer.

But it just passes my understanding why there are not presently some figures that show this ratio of payouts to premiums.

Mr. ROTTMAN. Sir, if I may, I think what you would find from my experienced judgment, let us put it this way, what you would find is your payout ratio is going to be about the same.

Mr. ECKHARDT. Well, then, I suppose what you are saying is that the program has simply saved for the injured person the attorney fees?

Mr. ROTTMAN. And it shifted and paid some of those that did not get recovery before and it also saved the premium payment on the small losses that have been overpaid usually in the past.

Mr. ECKHARDT. There is one other question I have of Mr. McHugh and that is I noted you stated "One of the major purposes of any program of this type was to pay the seriously injured person because of the abysmal failure of the system to provide adequate protection for the seriously injured victims even where a suable defendant can be found."

Yet you recommend to us, it seems to me, for that kind of person, that we not use the no-fault system but that rather we do use the tort system.

Why, if the no-fault system is a good system, why do you not utilize it for one of the main critical areas you describe with respect to the present system?

Mr. MCHUGH. The no-fault system would apply to those people to pay for their economic loss but what we are suggesting is that we ought to also provide the very seriously injured recovery for their pain and suffering so that in addition to the first-party benefit compensating them for economic loss, the seriously injured then will be able to receive what is generally recognized to be full compensation in those cases.

Mr. ECKHARDT. You would hope both to collect a premium with respect to the no-fault section of coverage and also a premium with respect to the tort section?

Mr. MCHUGH. No, but we would expect the amount of their recovery in tort to be reduced by the benefits they received on first-party benefits.

Mr. ECKHARDT. And they would have to hire an attorney then for their actions in their third-party tort case.

Mr. MCHUGH. Yes.

Mr. ECKHARDT. At any rate, they would have to investigate any serious injury, they would have to go to a lawyer to have him do that and you would also have to use your counsel for investigating those matters.

Mr. MCHUGH. That is correct.

Mr. ECKHARDT. So that part of the attorney overhead is not eliminated?

Mr. MCHUGH. No, it is not.

portation.

Mr. ECKHARDT. Your investigators pay off the claim because they think there is too much risk not to pay it off, so they consider there is some merit to the claim?

Mr. McHUGH. It is correct that the claims are paid but it is because it is too expensive to defend those cases.

Mr. ECKHARDT. This is not in response to my question. Of course I agree under our present system, every claim is worth some gambling figure and it is that gambling figure that tends to increase the total overhead improperly, but the question I am asking is this: If it is a good system to pay the economic losses of a person having relatively moderate injury from which he totally recovers, why is it not also a good system to utilize the same no-fault basis for paying the person who has permanent general damage?

Mr. McHUGH. Well, I suppose it is really a comparative judgment you make—a relative judgment that you make.

We would assume that for the person with a very small injury, we ought not to be paying for the costs to recover excessive amounts which are included in the pain and suffering awards for the purpose of getting that case settled, whereas in fact a very seriously-injured person, a paraplegic person, for example, who will have a lifetime of misery ahead, we can appropriately say in that case that merely paying all of his economic loss is really not treating that person fairly. He does have other losses.

Mr. ECKHARDT. Why not pay all of his losses through a no-fault system?

"Third, the failure of the tort system to provide any protection for the many accident victims who, for a variety of reasons, cannot find a suitable defendant to sue."

Now the paraplegic may well not find a suitable defendant to sue to take care of his very extensive permanent injuries. And if you leave that to the tort system, he is not going to get anything above the limitation that has been placed on your no-fault system, is that not so?

Mr. McHUGH. Yes.

Mr. ECKHARDT. So, if he is so unluckily cast to not find a suitable defendant to sue under a proposal which triggers in tort with respect to serious and extensive injuries, you still have the problem of a person who is permanently injured, a terrible expense to his family or to the Government or to someone, and you have not solved that problem under this system of triggering in the torts, have you?

Mr. McHUGH. Well, left to the tort system, we do not but if you move to this type of system which we are suggesting here, where we are prepared to provide no-fault first-party benefits, that takes care of the economic loss of the seriously-injured and that is being done irrespective of fault.

Mr. ECKHARDT. What is this maximum that he can recover? Say a person is injured so that from thenceforward, he has to have somebody take care of him and take care of his ordinary needs; what is the maximum he can receive without going into the tort system?

Mr. McHUGH. Under this bill?

Mr. ECKHARDT. Yes.

Mr. McHUGH. He can receive unlimited medical expenses including all of his rehabilitation, vocational or medical rehabilitation expenses. He can receive wage losses and survivors' benefits up to the minimum.

Mr. ECKHARDT. A maximum, you mean?

Mr. McHUGH. Well, it can be, under the law no less than $15,000. The State law meeting the Federal requirements will have to provide at least $15,000.

Mr. ECKHARDT. So he has his medical and rehabilitation and at the point where he has been rehabilitated as much as he can be, that, of course, would stop and he could get as little as $15,000 for wage loss under this provision.

Mr. McHUGH. Yes, of course, the inducement built into the law is designed to try to persuade the States to enact more beneficial recovery for the wage loss and the lost income but it cannot be less than $15,000.

Mr. ECKHARDT. It can be as low as that and still qualify.

Mr. McHUGH. Yes.

Mr. ECKHARDT. Of course, he would presumably be able to establish the threshold for tort under conditions of the type I mentioned, but at that point, he is under the same dangers of not having a solvent defendant as he would be under the present system.

Mr. McHUGH. That is right but at least he has gotten a substantial portion of his actual economic loss taken care of.

Mr. ECKHARDT. I would not say $15,000 is a substantial portion of economic loss in serious accidents.

Mr. McHUGH. Well, certainly the bulk of it, I would guess over 50 percent of his actual economic loss will be represented by his medical bills, his hospital bills and the expenses he has in connection with the medical portion of it.

Mr. ECKHARDT. He does not get unlimited loss of earnings.

Mr. McHUGH. No, he certainly does not.

Mr. ECKHARDT. Say he is a lawyer or engineer or architect; he gets $15,000 maximum under the weakest of the bills permitted under this proposal.

Mr. McHUGH. That is correct.

Mr. ROTTMAN. For quadraplegic or paraplegics, you got a serious problem and that is totally inadequate.

Mr. MAISONPIERRE. I might point out, under no circumstance can the individuals whom you cited, the engineer and lawyer, ever make up for the noncompensated economic losses which run above the monthly limit, $1,000 per month.

He is prohibited and even if he has a perfect tort case from recovering those excess economic losses at any time.

Mr. ECKHARDT. Well, is that not so only for the period in which he is paid economic loss?

Mr. MAISONPIERRE. While he is paid economic loss. If he earned $3,000 or $4,000 a month during the period of economic loss payment, he would not be able to collect anymore than the basic monthly limit that is legislated by the State.

Mr. ECKHARDT. That is right but when he runs through his economic losses claimed under the act he could receive a recovery under tort for that period beyond the period covered by this but your point is that this bill not only limits him in amount of economic recovery but also limits him with respect to tort recovery during the period covered by the economic loss, is that correct?

Mr. MAISONPIERRE. Yes.

Mr. McHUGH. What you talk about here is a feature of the bill in which maybe those people in society who are a little bit better off do not get quite as good a deal under the bill and I think the theory of the bill is that for people in that financial category, they would be able to purchase the optional coverages that the bill suggests you ought to get to properly protect yourself.

Mr. ECKHARDT. It does not strike me that a person has to be a particularly privileged person to make more than $15,000 in economic recovery for the rest of his life.

I mean this is not just for the rich. This $15,000 is a limitation on recovery for wage loss from now on and that is not a big figure. That could include a household servant, could it not?

Mr. McHUGH. Yes it could.

Mr. MAISONPIERRE. I think we have to recognize that any reparations system including no-fault is a compromise, a compromise based on the nature and amount of benefits that can be paid to accident victims as against what individual policyholders are willing or capable of paying in insurance premiums. Now, a no-fault system, and again I repeat that we are in support of no-fault, we are bringing about some inequities in that compromise that is in the no-fault system.

Let me give you a good example. Under no-fault you give up your right to recover a certain amount of money for pain and suffering against the certainty of collecting for your certain economic losses.

Well, we know that, among the elderly in our society, there are a large number of those who do not drive or own automobiles. Many of those get injured either as just passengers or as pedestrians. Once there elderly people are injured, what do they get?

Well, they are eligible for no-fault benefits but they are on social security, hence they are not eligible for economic losses because they have no loss of wages, and Medicare is paying for their medical benefits.

But they have given up their opportunity of collecting for pain and suffering and they do have pain and suffering, probably much more than younger people. That is unless their disability exceeds the threshhold.

Now, sure, maybe you would say: Now, these people may pay less for their automobile insurance premium but they do not pay anything anyway because they do not own cars. So they have really taken a rather raw deal through this type of no-fault.

There are people who I will say, some other people, that will benefit.

Mr. ECKHARDT. Mr. Maisonpierre, it seems to me, when we strike these compromises, when we decide that one value of certainty is more important than the value of equal justice, it strikes me that we should strike that balance at one place, we should either strike it at the Federal level, we should decide that balance in Congress or permit it to be struck at some other place. It seems to me that, when we set standards here, but we do not set rates, we do not ultimately decide between a $15,000 limit on economic damages or $150,000, it seems to me we simply renege on our duty to draw these balances of this type of insurance.

Mr. MAISONPIERRE. I think this is a strong case in point for State legislation because a State can look at its population parameters. Florida has a different type of population than New York and Nebraska and Iowa and California and it can look at its population structure and see what its population needs are and what is the best compromise that can be struck for the population in that State.

Mr. ECKHARDT. May I say I disagree with you as is where the balance should be struck but I do think it is necessary to strike it some place and it seems to me that we do not do it in the bill, H.R. 1900.

Thank you, Mr. Chairman.

Mr. VAN DEERLIN. Mr. Metcalfe, any questions?

Mr. METCALFE. I have no questions.

Mr. VAN DEERLIN. Mr. Brodhead, any questions?

Mr. BRODHEAD. Yes; Mr. Chairman.

I have been listening with some interest to this discussion of premium costs under no-fault versus the current system. I am wondering whether there will be a reduction in the premium in no-fault or some type of no-fault program going into effect. I am thinking back years ago, to where there was a great deal of concern about the tremendous increases in premium. In Michigan, we have not experienced tremendous premium reductions, yet we have not had increases. I am wondering whether our discussion of premium cost is really adequate without some sort of discussion of what increases we might expect under the tort system in any case?

Would you care to comment on that, Mr. McHugh, or Mr. Maisonpierre?

Mr. MCHUGH. I think it is very important, as we think about this element of cost, that we relate that to the premium level and whether or not the premium level we are talking about is adequate or inadequate.

I think what we are all finding out is that under the present tort system and under a no-fault system costs are going up at a tremendous rate and inflation is probably the most significant factor that we have to deal with in adjusting our rates at what should be to the appropriate level today.

Mr. BRODHEAD. Exactly. I guess what I am suggesting is, isn't the increasing costs of medical care and the increasing costs of repairing automobiles a lot more significant factor in what the premiums are going to be rather than whether or not it is no fault?

Mr. MCHUGH. Far more significant. The cost of living has been going up at an annual rate of between 8 and 10 percent or something in that order.

What State Farm is suggesting here is you might have a reduction annually in your cost of about 10 percent if you go to a no-fault system. Well, that is eaten up in 1 year alone by the normal increase in inflation and we are looking at these laws coming into being within the next 3 to 4 years. So assuming that the rate of inflation drops down to 6 percent by the end of that period you have still experienced something in the neighborhood of a 25-percent increase in inflation.

Mr. BRODHEAD. Of course, in the field of medical care, you have the cost increasing much faster than the average rate of inflation, don't you?

Mr. MCHUGH. Yes, indeed you do.

Mr. BRODHEAD. Thus if you reduce the administrative cost with a no-fault system and reduce the cost of litigation, you may find that you are not able to reduce the premium because of a tremendous increase in the cost of medical care.

Mr. MCHUGH. This is very likely to be the case.

Mr. BRODHEAD. It is the kind of thing that would take place anyway regardless of what kind of system you use, right?

Mr. MAISONPIERRE. I think, when we look at the cost of automobile insurance, we should really segregate the cost of automobile insurance for bodily injuries, "BI" versus cost of automobile insurance to repair a car because no-fault, certainly S. 354 or H.R. 1900, does not affect, in any way, the cost increase that is bound to come as a result of inflation, and the costs of repair. In the "BI" area you have mentioned and I agree with you 100 percent, that we are headed into a very frightening spiraling inflation due to the cost of medical care. Both S. 354 and H.R. 1900 provide there shall be paid unlimited medical benefits. The industry and the smaller companies particularly, have found it extremely difficult to be able to cost out automobile insurance with unlimited medical benefits because of this frightening spiraling inflation of medical cost. If we have a paraplegic today, in the State of Michigan or in New Jersey, and as I understand the committee will be receiving testimony from the reinsurance association and will go into some detail on this but if we have a paraplegic in the States of Michigan or New Jersey with unlimited medical benefits, we have to set aside a reserve on that case to pay for the lifetime medical benefits on that case. What kind of reserve are we to put on the case? Who is to know what is going to be the cost of medical care 10 or 15 years from now?

But yet today is when we have to price that case. So that today is when the cost impact of medical inflation must be reflected in the automobile insurance premium that people will be paying in Michigan and New Jersey.

Mr. BRODHEAD. But aren't these same arguments made to juries in court cases and aren't juries being asked to take these same factors into account and aren't jury verdicts going up tremendously as a result of the same problem? As there are increasing needs, you set aside increasing reserves and jury verdicts go up.

Mr. MAISONPIERRE. That is a different matter because it is a jury verdict, the case is disposed of, either settled or tried and a verdict is rendered within a reasonable period of time.

Mr. BRODHEAD. But if jury verdicts in State X are up 20 percent this year over last year, surely you have to take into account when you set your reserves.

Mr. MAISONPIERRE. But we know, Mr. Brodhead, what the loss is going to be relatively soon after the incident has occurred—what the total amount of the loss will be. But with unlimited medical benefits both as to amount and duration, we just do not have the knowledge as to what this loss is going to cost.

Dick had mentioned the fact that we have what is known as IBNR, incurred but not reported.

We do not know what these losses are going to be in the long-time future in a period of spiraling inflation.

Mr. BRODHEAD. Except you do know, at least from the standpoint of the consumer, the person receiving the benefits, that the amount of money that the person is going to be receiving is going to be, with respect to medical benefits, is no more and no less than the exact amount of the loss that has been incurred, whereas in the jury verdict you are really throwing dice.

Mr. MAISONPIERRE. But you were asking about the impact on automobile insurance premiums and the impact is going to be a very frightening impact. We have to recognize the fact that we are seeing many more very high shock losses, medical losses, in New Jersey and Michigan, than was anticipated. These will have to reflect the long-range impact on the high cost of medical care and will affect adversely the cost of automobile insurance.

Mr. McHUGH. I can only say with reference to Michigan undoubtedly we have a very substantial exposure. We are the second largest writer in the State. The unlimited medical, with its unlimited rehabilitation expenses, poses a very great liability for us, in fact, we have a number of very serious cases in which we are paying lifetime rehabilitation expenses.

As Mr. Maisonpierre indicated it has been difficult to adequately reserve for those types of cases.

While, maybe you cannot, I do not intend to generalize from the basis of the rather limited Michigan experience which we have today but the plain fact is State Farm is doing reasonably well in Michigan as against most of the country today. We have a very high benefit package.

Mr. BRODHEAD. Doing better than you were before the advent of no-fault?

Mr. McHUGH. Doing better. Let me put it this way. We are doing comparatively better than in most other States in the country. How it compares with the experience before, I do not know. It may roughly be about the same.

Mr. BRODHEAD. Let me ask this because I think this is the most important question. Is it your conviction your policyholders are doing better, are they getting better protection?

Mr. McHUGH. We could cite you an example. One of the cases State Farm has been involved in in Michigan, where, as a result of the accident, we practically rebuilt a person's first floor so as to accommodate the use of a wheelchair. We also made a decision to purchase for that person an automobile with special hand controls at the recommendation of the rehabilitation expert that the automobile is necessary to get that person back into the work force.

We had never been paying such benefits before and obviously, in the case of that person, this law must be a Godsend.

Mr. BRODHEAD. I think it is important to point out, too, that in the workmen's compensation system, that we have been providing unlimited medical benefits for a long time.

It is the same kind of problem. It is not a question of setting a premium but setting aside reserves for that type of thing.

Mr. MAISONPIERRE. I think there are important differences between workmen's compensation and automobile insurance. We believe strongly in unlimited medical benefits in workmen's compensation. We do have, No. 1, in workmen's compensation, a somewhat homogeneous population, working people generally between the ages of 20 to 65.

No. 2, the workmen's compensation laws allow for a tremendous legitimate amount of control over medical costs as well as the type of medical treatment to be rendered to the workmen's compensation insurance carrier and to the industrial commissions. Under no-fault today really the insurance carrier has very little control over health care costs. The individual goes, gets his care and submits his bill. Under workmen's compensation, the individual does not pay his medical expenses. It is the insurance carrier or the employer who is responsible for the payment of the bill and there is a very large degree of control over health care costs by workmen's compensation carriers which is not existent in any no-fault bill.

This worries me very substantially. I think it is unfortunate that no-fault systems do not provide for that type of control mechanisms because, in workmen's compensation we have been able to control the spiraling costs of health care much better than under any health care system.

Mr. RINALDO. Will you yield?

Mr. BRODHEAD. Yes.

Mr. RINALDO. I just cannot agree with the last statement you made because I happen to come from a no-fault State, New Jersey, and I would say that there is certainly far more control over the no-fault insurance medical payments that there is over workmen's compensation.

The workmen's compensation system in our State is noted for its flagrant abuses and for the fact that a worker who suffers an injury as a result of an accident arising out of and in the course of his employment can go on ad infinitum running up medical bills. I sat in those workmen's compensation courts time and time again in a room larger than this full of attorneys settling case after case which in many instances took less than a few minutes to decide. Certainly you know and I understand both sides of this argument very well, but I would say that at least with respect to the State of New Jersey, I could never allow that statement to remain on the record unchallenged.

Mr. MAISONPIERRE. I agree with you, Mr. Rinaldo, New Jersey is probably the worst problem State in workmen's compensation. As you may know, there have been a number of Governor's commissions and legislative commissions trying to straighten up the New Jersey Workmen's Compensation mess but it always fails at the last minute and it has been very much of a thorn in the side of the workmen's compensation system. Even there, in serious cases, you do have substantial control over cost of medical care in New Jersey and there are opportunities of controlling the cost of medical care in New Jersey.

There are no opportunities for controlling the cost of medical care in no-fault.

Mr. RINALDO. I do not want to take any more of his time, but there is some opportunity to control the cost of extremely serious industrial accidents. However, when you compare the small opportunity that you have now in that type of accident with the flagrant abuses that take place in the so-called nuisance claims, I would say by no means does it even out with the insurance carrier. While, on the other hand, from all of the evidence I have obtained it appears to me that the no-fault system, while it has some defects it is working out fairly well in the State of New Jersey.

Mr. BRODHEAD. Mr. Chairman.

Mr. RINALDO. Thank you.

Mr. BRODHEAD. If I might conclude here, I have a letter from the Michigan Commissioner of Insurance, Daniel J. Demlow, dated June 20, 1975, addressed to the Honorable Warren Magnuson, chairman of the Senate Commerce Committee and I want to quote one sentence and ask permission to have the entire letter inserted in the record. He concludes:

To summarize, in Michigan we have not been aware of any problems of either availability or costs for unlimited no-fault benefits during our experience with such benefits beginning October 1, 1973, the same time these benefits have been of great value to the State of Michigan.

I ask unanimous consent, Mr. Chairman, to have it inserted in the body of the record.

[The letter referred to follows:]

STATE OF MICHIGAN,
DEPARTMENT OF COMMERCE,
INSURANCE BUREAU,
Lansing, Mich., June 20, 1975.

Hon. WARREN G. MAGNUSON,
*Chairman, Senate Commerce Committee, Senate Office Building,
Washington, D.C.*

DEAR CHAIRMAN MAGNUSON: We understand that during the course of hearings on Senate Bill 354 there has been some concern expressed regarding cost and availability of reinsurance for auto insurance providing unlimited medical and rehabilitation benefits. Our Michigan No-Fault auto insurance has provided unlimited medical and rehabilitation benefits since October 1, 1973. Although some apprehension was expressed on behalf of some of the smaller insurers during the months before the Act became effective it is our understanding that all auto insurers in the state have satisfactorily reinsured for the unlimited benefits. In fact on several occasions I and members of my staff have invited representatives of the insurance industry at public meetings to come to us with any problems they encounter in meeting their reinsurance requirements. I am aware that several of our domestic auto insurers both large and small are reinsured with some of the most highly regarded reinsuring companies.

I feel that some of the apprehension concerning unlimited benefits comes from insurers who in the past have devoted themselves to auto insurance where fixed liability limits had been customary. Other insurers familiar with Workers Compensation coverage in Michigan and a number of other states have for a number of years been accustomed to providing unlimited medical and rehabilitation benefits for injured workers. Reinsurers, of course, are familiar with unlimited workers compensation benefits and presumably transfer their experience in this field to the provision of reinsurance for unlimited No-Fault auto benefits.

The unlimited medical and rehabilitation benefits fo Michigan's No-Fault law have worked exceptionally well. Prior to no-fault in Michigan rehabilitation was almost non-existent; benefits provided were invariably in lump sums. Now extensive rehabilitation is taking place. There is a very real incentive for an insurance company to restore an injured policyholder to health, for the sooner that occurs, the sooner the company is no longer obligated. This incentive has been of inestimable value to Michigan citizens injured in auto accidents.

To summarize, in Michigan we have not been aware of any problems of either availability or cost for unlimited auto No-Fault benefits during our experience with such benefits beginning October 1, 1973. At the same time those benefits have been of great value to the citizens of Michigan. If I can be of any other assistance in your deliberations please do not hesitate to contact me.

Very truly yours,

DANIEL J. DEMLOW,
Commissioner of Insurance.

Mr. VAN DEERLIN. Without objection.

Mr. McHUGH. If I may make a comment which is with reference to Mr. Maisonpierre's comment, I find it rather strange that he expresses this concern about the failure of the no-fault system to build in controls over the payment of medical bills and yet he apparently is very concerned and very much opposed to the one effort of the Federal bills, H.R. 1900 and S. 354, to build in some controls over the abuses of vocational and medical rehabilitation. The bills do provide for standards for determining whether or not the rehabilitation costs are proper and are reasonable and yet I understand that he continues to express strong opposition to those features of the law which are in fact designed to permit insurers to have better control over those costs.

Mr. MAISONPIERRE. Mr. Chairman, we oppose every section of the law, not any individual section.

Mr. VAN DEERLIN. Off the record.

[Discussion off the record.]

Mr. VAN DEERLIN. Mr. Maisonpierre.

Mr. MAISONPIERRE. In a letter by the Reinsurance Association to Chairman Magnuson of the Senate Commerce Committee, the following is stated:

> Experience under the New Jersey and Michigan laws has already shown that the analogy to unlimited medical benefits under workmen's compensation status is not completely appropriate because we are seeing more serious head and spinal cord injuries suffered by younger individuals with greater life expectancy.
>
> Second, the primary premiums attributable to such no-fault coverages have not been adequate. Simply stated, the serious injuries and the frequency of injuries requiring extensive medical expenses in excess of $50,000 had been greater than anticipated. This has resulted in some primary company experience in significant increases in their reimbursement costs.
>
> Another troublesome factor in these cases requiring long-term medical care is ability to forecast accurately the cost of medical expenses 25 years from now for some one injured today. We believe that a minimum standards bill should recognize these problems and provide for some reasonable limitation on the medical benefits and rehabilitation expenses now in section 204.

I think it is extremely important to recognize for a company like State Farm, it can well absorb a number of large unlimited medical losses because of its very size, but as I stated before, the insurance business is composed of hundreds of companies, some very large like State Farm and some very very small.

A single accident involving unlimited medical benefits without adequate reinsurance and there is very great difficulty in defining "unlimited medical benefits" in reinsurance, a single accident, a serious case may very well put this company in insolvency.

Mr. McHUGH. Mr. Chairman, I would only suggest that the letter of the Reinsurance Association of America is not very definitive about just where the limits ought to be. I think they are calling to your attention and to everybody's attention the fact that there may be problems in connection with the unlimited medical, which suggests different treatment from that accorded in Workmen's Compensation. I think it would be very interesting if they are to appear before your committee, as I understand they are, if they can give us some clue as to just how serious the reinsurance problems which are created by the unlimited medical are for small companies and what kinds of limitation if any they are talking about.

Mr. VAN DEERLIN. We will surely be getting that testimony.

Mr. Rinaldo.

Mr. RINALDO. Thank you very much, Mr. Chairman.

Mr. Maisonpierre, in your statement on page 18 you state that a: "no-fault plan which works well in one State may bring disastrous consequences in another." Can you give me a specific example of what you mean?

Mr. MAISONPIERRE. Yes, as I said before, this morning, we oppose no fault plans that are so-called addons, where you have no cost reduction. We opposed the Oregon bill because we felt the Oregon bill would just add on benefits and would ultimately increase the cost of insurance in the State of Oregon.

It has worked well in the State of Oregon, without any question. We would be scared to death, Mr. Rinaldo, to see that type of law enacted in the State of California because we believe in the State of California it would be disastrous on the pocket of policyholders.

Mr. RINALDO. What about the plans that work well in one State?

Mr. MAISONPIERRE. Oregon, there is one State it works well.

Mr. RINALDO. All right. You go on to list six specific objections to pending no-fault legislation.

If there was a bill drafted which nullified those objections, would you then be inclined to favor a no-fault bill similar to the one which I recently introduced which permits subrogation and makes no fault insurance primary? Would this change your opposition?

Mr. MAISONPIERRE. It would not, Mr. Rinaldo, because at this time we do not really know, as we have explained in our statement, what type of no fault program should be imposed countrywide—nationwide. We do not think that we have the experience as yet to be able to forecast how national standards for no-fault will work, how no-fault plans will work; as I said before, I think the State of Florida, for instance, has a no-fault program which is fairly similar in many respects to your bill.

As Allstate testified before the Senate Commerce Committee and some of our companies are beginning to report, there are some pretty substantial difficulties with the operation of no-fault in Florida.

We see a buildup of no-fault benefits in order to get over the threshold, medical benefits in order to get over the threshold.

Allstate testified that the frequency of tort claims had gone down to some degree but the severity of tort claims has increased to an extent that all of the cost savings resulting from the decreased frequency of claims has been absorbed in higher severity of these claims and when they compare the increased severity in Florida with increased severity in other States that one might expect from inflation, it is much greater in Florida.

One of the attitudes which I think we might be considering or certainly is worth watching in the operation of some no-fault programs is whether, once an individual is able to get over the threshold, whether the jury itself thinks of the individual as being pretty badly injured and certainly warranting very substantial judgment just because he has been able to get over the threshold.

So, it this is a jury attitude, then, again, we have to research it to see whether or not the type of balancing program we have between tort and first-party benefits is a good program, whether it should not be restructured or changed in some way.

I think we have to get this information first before we can launch into a Federal standards program. This is the reason why at this time we are not prepared to support your bill.

Mr. RINALDO. Aren't you contradicting your statement when you say: "There is not enough information?" You have just given a rather lucid description of the data from the various State laws that are in effect which I think, if examined properly, would enable this committee to put together the type of bill that would be agreeable to most of us.

You know, we have spoken, we have spoken to many witnesses here, but one thing that appears to me in these hearings is that we neglect to consider the citizens, themselves, the constituents that we are supposed to be representing. The people in my Congressional District are probably 90 percent or more completely satisfied with the no-fault system in New Jersey.

While we certainly have a duty and obligation to listen to your views and we certainly respect them on the other hand, we also have, I think, a primary responsibility and an obligation to listen to our constituents.

The question is, what is right for most of the people in the country. There are different types of legislation that have been presented. I think perhaps it would be better to elaborate on those features of the no-fault plan that you think would be most desirable if national no-fault were to be passed.

Mr. MAISONPIERRE. Mr. Rinaldo, I think the subcommittee should be congratulated for going into the field because this is the only way you are going to get a true feeling from the people as to how the system is working today. But in addition to looking, to get the feeling as to how the system is operating today and how your constituents are reacting to the present operation of the system, it is also important to see what are the problems which are developing.

Now, the State of Florida is the one which I cited, because the State of Florida no-fault law has been in existence for a long enough period of time that today data are beinning to flow back as to its operation.

We cannot tell what is happening in New York which has been operating, I think since February 1974 because just not enough time has elapsed for a true feedback as to its real operation. It takes a little bit of time for people to appreciate the new legal environment in which they find themselves and so it takes time.

As I said before, we are not going to get instantaneous results from no-fault. It is not because the law becomes effective that we will have results tomorrow but it takes time for the results to pour in.

But the information that we are getting from these no-fault laws should be available to you, to the State legislators, because, out of those results, we are going to be able to fashion what should be the most adequate compromise, because it has to be a compromise, for your constituents.

Mr. RINALDO. In other words, you are saying the time has not yet come because we do not have enough experience but would I be correct in also stating that you feel that eventually we will need a Federal no-fault law?

Mr. MAISONPIERRE. No, I am not saying this. I am saying, you were not here this morning, but I said there that we do not know enough to even appreciate whether a national system would ever work.

Mr. RINALDO. I am trying hard, though.

Mr. MAISONPIERRE. But this is the concluding statement I made this morning. It was that experience will tell us whether a national standards program might be best or whether or not perhaps a non-Federal system, each State going its own way might be best. We do not know that as yet. Certainly right now, we seem to think that a State-by-State approach may be desirable. But we are not saying that we may not change our mind. That is once we see the results of the experience in the States, we will be in a better position to do this.

Mr. VAN DEERLIN. If I may intrude, was there a promise of reduced premiums when the New Jersey legislature was enacting its no-fault insurance?

Mr. RINALDO. I believe there was at that time.

Mr. VAN DEERLIN. Have any reductions occurred?

Mr. RINALDO. If I remember correctly, there was an immediate reduction.

Mr. MCHUGH. By statute.

Mr. MAISONPIERRE. 15-percent reduction in premiums.

Mr. RINALDO. Most of it has been eaten away as a result of inflation.

Mr. MAISONPIERRE. There has been a filing for 30-percent increase.

Mr. RINALDO. It is not, of course, in effect.

Mr. MAISONPIERRE. Yes, a lot of that is due to inflation.

Mr. RINALDO. Because inflation has been tremendous?

Mr. MAISONPIERRE. Yes, this is a difficult thing to be able to differentiate, what is due to no-fault and what is due to inflation.

Mr. RINALDO. I agree with you. At least you have come part way down the road by your last statement where you indicated you have somewhat of an open mind.

Mr. MAISONPIERRE. We always have an open mind.

Mr. RINALDO. Do I still have any time left Mr. Chairman?

Mr. VAN DEERLIN. Absolutely, if your larynx is holding up.

Mr. RINALDO. Mr. McHugh, do you think that subrogation rights ought to be rescinded?

Mr. MCHUGH. We have supported the elimination of the $5,000 deductible in H.R. 1900, so that you can have subrogation between private passengers and the commerical vehicles.

We believe that is the best way to achieve the greatest cost savings per private passenger vehicles and would urge the committee to permit subrogation on this basis.

Mr. RINALDO. How about medical benefits; do you favor limited or unlimited medical benefits?

Mr. MCHUGH. We have supported the bill with the inclusion of unlimited medical benefits. We have taken the position that to really make an auto accident reparations system the most effective system, we should be sure we are paying out all of the medical expenses of the seriously-injured.

Unlimited medical is the best way to achieve that. Now, it is true that the State Farm's position, because of our size, is considerably different from that of many small companies. We are not in the position of a small company which is exposed to the consequences of the luck of the draw for unlimited medical. We would say, however, we have seen no demonstrative evidence yet, that the consequences that Mr. Maisonpierre refers to, that it can cause the collapse of some of those companies, has in fact occurred. I would be very much interested in the testimony of the American Reinsurance Association as to how much reinsurance costs have gone up for the small companies.

Now, whether or not you go to unlimited medical or an extremely high medical benefit level, I think you have to balance against insurance concerns other factors. Even though from the insurers point of view there is great uncertainty about unlimited medical. I think it is part of the insurance man's thinking that he can operate his business better if he knows precisely what his total liability will be at any one point in time.

But then as against that, you have to take into account the concerns which Commissioner Demlow has pointed out, what will be the impact in terms of a more efficient auto accident system if we can guarantee that all of these tremendous rehabilitation costs are in fact being paid.

This is an issue I think on which legislators and insurers will differ. The one thing that we would feel absolutely certain about is even if some limit is ultimately put on, it ought to be a very high limit. From our point of view, we would just as soon have unlimited medical.

Mr. RINALDO. Your company is very active in the State of New Jersey. What is your opinion of the way the New Jersey law has worked out to date?

Mr. MCHUGH. Well, we are not one of the largest writers in New Jersey, but we do write a substantial volume of business there. I think to some extent it has taught us something in the course of this laboratory that we have gone through as to how no-fault works or how it does not work and it has played a part in shaping the decision of State Farm that a no-fault system cannot really meet the needs of the motoring public, particularly in the big industrial States such as New Jersey, unless it has a very substantial limitation on tort and the kind of tort limitation we have in New Jersey in our judgment is totally inadequate.

Mr. RINALDO. Let me ask Mr. Rottman one question.

This follows from what you said, Mr. McHugh. What is the law in the State of Nevada on tort liability and what is your analysis of it?

Mr. ROTTMAN. We have a $750 medical threshold that is primary and also one for breaking of a major bone or a few things such as that as you normally find.

Mr. RINALDO. Disfigurement?

Mr. ROTTMAN. No, sir. Permanent disfigurement about the same thing you have in the Federal bill that is under consideration along with the $750 medical threshold. We found that is pretty good. Personally, I would like to have seen that a little higher, but I am not sure that, well, I am not sure we would be serving the interests of a great number of our citizens by increasing it too much. I do not think we really bring down the cost measurably quite frankly by doing this. I would, if I may, comment on this aspect of subrogation.

We have subrogation in our bill among private passenger vehicles and primary so as to maintain the rating base, for those people who still cause accidents, if you can define them, to have them pay the highest premiums and that is one thing I would recommend in any bill you have, that you do have subrogation so you have some sort of retention of the rating base so that it is not a matter of not shifting a major burden of the cost to those who receive the benefits.

Mr. VAN DEERLIN. Majority counsel, Mr. Kinzler.

Mr. KINZLER. Mr. Maisonpierre, there are certain dangers is using averages and perhaps equal danger in using individual cases.

A few minutes ago we heard that $15,000 of wage loss benefits was not very much protection. Do you recall from the Department of Transportation study what people with economic losses of $25,000 or over recovered, either with tort or without tort?

Mr. MAISONPIERRE. I do not recall the figure but are you referring here to the analysis on the "Economic Consequence of Automobile Accident Injuries"?

Mr. KINZLER. Right.

Mr. MAISONPIERRE. I think we have to use that study with extreme care and caution. In statements which we made before the preceding House Subcommittee on Commerce and Finance in 1971, we critiqued and analyzed the DOT "Economic Consequence of Automobile accident Injuries' and we were very critical of the conclusions drawn by DOT in the study, particularly since the researchers themselves, the people that had been contracted to do the study, warned against its use the way DOT used it. After all, I believe that the study contemplated approximately 1,300 accident victims, that those were broken down into about 15 different categories, and so that the cells themselves were extremely limited in numbers. There was an attempt by DOT to expand those small cells to cover the total population. This was something which, from a statistical standpoint, just did not hold water. In addition, in that study itself, some real inaccuracies in the data were noted. For instance, I believe the study indicated that 65 percent of the respondents were covered by medical and hospital insurance and that 51.4 of the seriously injured collected some more medical insurance, but the health insurance people are telling us that 85 percent of the population are protected by health insurance. So that there were some real inaccuracies. I can go down this list.

Mr. KINZLER. Mr. Maisonpierre, from our standpoint, and I am sure we would all appreciate reading your critique, I think as a practical matter we are left with the DOT study. I am not aware that anybody else has criticicized it and I, for tne record, would like to read in the exact statistics of the study. Those statistics indicate that people with a $25,000 economic loss through injuries, recovered only 30 percent of their economic loss whether or not they had a tort case. So we are talking about a $7,500 recovery, which makes $15,000 look a lot better by comparison. That is without even calculating medical loss recovery.

In addition, perhaps, if one were concerned about individuals protecting their own rights, would it not be feasible to limit tort recovery in title II for wage loss of above $15,000 and replace it with a mandatory offering to individuals of a wage loss protection up to the limit of their annual income so they could make a choice as to how much protection they wish to have?

Mr. MAISONPIERRE. In the first place, again, I want to emphasize the fact that we support no-fault—no-fault benefits. We do not have a quarrel there. But I think that we have to balance out what it is that people want and should be paying for and should be paid for.

The question is as to what are the losses that should be compensated. Now, on the average, again, generally speaking, people say we can give priority to compensating for economic losses and it is difficult to argue against that until you start dealing with the individual who has sustained the loss. And he says, "Well", but I have, or my inability to do something to perform certain acts"——

Mr. KINZLER. But we have to make judgments, this Congress has to make judgments based upon averages, not based upon an individual case and of course you cannot devise a system to cope with every possible case.

You can tell us chamber of horror stories, but it does us no good with respect to legislating. If these figures are accurate, we are not comparing it to a perfect system that pays people 100 percent of losses but comparing it with a system that pays 30 percent of their losses and we cannot escape this.

Mr. MAISONPIERRE. Yes, and I am not arguing against no-fault. I am saying that no-fault is a good system but I am arguing against Federal action at this time.

Mr. KINZLER. All right.

Mr. MAISONPIERRE. Because we are not prepared as yet to say how No Fault Systems will operate.

Mr. KINZLER. Let us come back to that in a second, but we heard today of two cost studies in addition to Milliman & Robertson. We heard about Allstate's cost study and State Farm's cost study.

Has the American Mutual Insurance Alliance ever done any cost studies on the old S. 945 or more recently?

S. 945 the original bill, was of course, a much more extensive bill with much greater coverage.

Mr. MAISONPIERRE. No, we have not. What we have done and have done it fairly recently and this is appended to our statement of June 19, we did take the Milliman & Robertson analysis and we carried it one or two steps further to break out the cost impact on private passengers versus commercial, the original S. 354 as originally introduced.

But we have not performed any independent cost studies.

Mr. KINZLER. Was there a national average that you concluded as to increase or decrease in premium costs?

Mr. MAISONPIERRE. It was a substantial increase in costs in most of the States for private passengers and substantial decrease in cost in most States——

Mr. KINZLER. Wasn't there an average figure for private passenger cars?

Mr. MAISONPIERRE. No, we do not have an average figure. They range all the way from, as to which benefit level you are costing out in Milliman & Robertson but the increase ran, I would say, looking at the figures here, about 15 or 20 percent on the average.

Mr. KINZLER. Oh, now if you take the Senate amendment with respect to subrogation of commercial vehicles, would you assume that would be not more than 5 or 6 percent in most States.

Mr. MAISONPIERRE. Yes.

Mr. KINZLER. If I understand you correctly, your study has a $15,000 survivors' benefit level. If that were reduced to $5,000, what would that do to your figures?

Mr. MAISONPIERRE. This study was of Milliman & Robertson, obviously $5,000 would have substantial effect.

Mr. KINZLER. But $5,000 would be a permissible level of survivors' benefits under H.R. 1900. My only point is if you change those two figures, you are down to State Farm's range, are you not?

Mr. MAISONPIERRE. I am not sure of what level of benefits would be considered reasonable under H.R. 1900 or S. 354. Survivors, if you recall, the first-party, survivors' benefits have to be reasonable and what a State legislator or Governor will consider reasonable is difficult to assess.

Most States, if not all States, no-fault laws that have been enacted provide the same benefit level for survivors' benefits as are provided for wage loss replacement.

Mr. KINZLER. But there is no reasonable statement attached to the wage loss as there is to survivors' benefits which might indicate it means a different level.

Mr. MAISONPIERRE. But they indicate what a State legislature may consider to be reasonable. For this matter, "reasonable" may be just $1.

Mr. KINZLER. Mr. Rottman, under Nevada's law, if you have insurance protection coverage in another State and you drive into Nevada I understand the Nevada law applies, is that correct?

Mr. ROTTMAN. Yes.

Mr. KINZLER. What happens if you come from the State of California and decide to go gambling or get a divorce or both in the State of Nevada and you happen——

Mr. VAN DEERLIN. One takes a little longer.

Mr. ROTTMAN. Not much, Mr. Chairman.

Mr. KINZLER. You happen to be uninsured, as 20 percent of the American population is, are you covered in Nevada or not?

Mr. ROTTMAN. No, sir, if you are uninsured, you are not.

Mr. KINZLER. Do you have tort recovery if you are uninsured?

Mr. ROTTMAN. Yes, sir.

Mr. KINZLER. You would have full limits in tort recovery?

Mr. ROTTMAN. No, not full limits. Not full limits in the tort recovery, you have or you go to, in effect, jump your basic threshold. There is a little bit of it I suppose that is unclear.

Mr. KINZLER. $750 threshold?

Mr. ROTTMAN. Yes.

Mr. KINZLER. Some people or some uninsured motorists would be worse off in Nevada?

Mr. ROTTMAN. Yes, sir.

Mr. ECKHARDT. Will you yield a moment, Mr. Chairman?

Mr. VAN DEERLIN. Yes.

Mr. ECKHARDT. Do you mean, if you are from outside of the State, you would not benefit or you could not bring a tort action for a claim in which you did not reach the threshhold for tort liability and still you would not have this other coverage?

Mr. ROTTMAN. If you do not have insurance, yes. There is a requirement in the law; yes, sir.

Mr. ECKHARDT. That strikes me as a failure of full faith and credit within the State of Nevada with respect to a traveler there.

Mr. ROTTMAN. I do not think so.

Mr. ECKHARDT. How can you discriminate against a person outside of Nevada who did not have the opportunity to buy no-fault insurance in Nevada and take away from him a right that he would ordinary have? It seems to me you treat him differently than a citizen of Nevada and can you do it under State law?

Mr. ROTTMAN. A citizen of California—well, I am not sure we can. That is the interpretation of the bill, but you do have a right in any State in the Nation, I believe, to say, you have a right, I mean, you have an opportunity to buy insurance.

Mr. ECKHARDT. Yes; but I am not going to buy insurance in Nevada because I might be passing through it.

Mr. ROTTMAN. No; but if you are covered in another State, no; and you come into Nevada, you would have the full force of the no-fault benefits in Nevada.

Mr. MAISONPIERRE. If I may say something. The insurance industry has developed an endorsement, if you are a citizen of California, if you go to Nevada today, your automobile insurance policy that you had in California would provide you with the legal requirements of Nevada.

Mr. ECKHARDT. I understand all of that. That is a contract right. Now, that is a contract right, that by contract, you either extend or you do not extend.

But what I am talking about is a personal right, it seems to me what we keep forgetting here is we are not just dealing with a contract insurance right but also dealing with a question of a personal tort right that has nothing to do with paying one thin nickel for coverage, and it seems to me utterly wrong for a State to deprive a person altogether of his tort rights and at the same time not afford some means by which he is protected by something that is in place of it.

That is one thing that worries me about a statewide approach to no-fault excluding tort liability, but I will not belabor it; it is a difficult question.

Mr. ROTTMAN. May I answer.

I do not think we are discriminating because we give the same opportunity to Nevada citizens that choose to remain uninsured, in effect, have to bear the first dollar of their medical cost, so we are not discriminating between California or any other citizen in the country in that respect.

Mr. ECKHARDT. I certainly disagree with you.

Mr. ROTTMAN. The law says you are supposed to buy insurance in Nevada, but California has not such a law that makes mandatory your insurance, but the individual does have the opportunity, and I suppose that is an incentive, to be insured, if you will.

Mr. ECKHARDT. It would be an incentive for me to stay out of Nevada.

Mr. ROTTMAN. We would certainly like to have your business, sir, any time. May I make one statement and I have to leave to catch a plane in a little bit, if I may.

Mr. VAN DEERLIN. Yes, sir.

Mr. ROTTMAN. In devising one of the things we kind of got off on, I guess this is one of my key areas, perhaps—it seems to me to be extremely difficult to devise a Federal-type no-fault bill that does not have its own consequences of the serious encroachment upon the State regulation of insurance. I think that, in my judgment, it ought to make a determination whether you really want to do it.

If you really want to do it then, you know, you could certainly do it. But I think it would be a serious mistake for the citizens of the respective States, because with the State regulation of insurance, I think you do have a responsive viable mechanism that is at the reach of the average citizen and he can go some place and get help but which I do not think you have in some of the agencies in the Federal Government who, even though they have branch offices out in the field, it is sometimes months before you get any kind of decent response, so that issue ought to be focused on fairly clearly.

Mr. McCollister. Mr. Chairman, if the gentleman from Nevada is indicating a philosophy, he must have acquired it during his early days in Nebraska.

Mr. Rottman. Yes, sir.

Mr. Van Deerlin. That is very interesting.

Mr. Rottman. Most of this approaches that one way or another, and even though it was the amendment, S. 354, and more recent amendment to S. 354, however, you cut it, the alternative still is a regulation probably by DOT or one of the Federal agencies for at least part of the States for automobile insurance.

Mr. McHugh. I would take strong exception to that, Mr. Chairman, and I would suggest here that the Senate gave very strong consideration to that issue at all times. The issue, it seems to me, was uppermost in their minds. A reading of the Senate report would make clear both the Judiciary and Commerce Committees were absolutely satisfied that this represented a minimal intrusion of the Federal Government into the State regulatory scheme.

Mr. Rottman seems to suggest that we are making a choice here between whether or not the Federal Government or States are going to regulate insurance.

I think the choice has been made. The Senate Commerce Committee makes perfectly clear it intends it to be regulation at the State level, and to the extent that some kind of Federal "look-see" would be involved, in the version that passed the Senate last year, it only involved the Department of Transportation approving the State enacted "no-fault" laws.

Now, as you know, even that provision has been amended. The Department of Transportation has been taken out of it entirely, and a no-fault review board appointed by the President consisting of two members recommended by the National Association of Insurance Commissioners and two representatives of the National Governors Conference and the Secretary of DOT makes the decisions on whether State no-fault laws quality. All of these are efforts designed to accommodate the concern that the Federal Government might be attempting to exercise too much regulation over State regulation of insurance.

Mr. McCollister. Mr. Chairman, in the AMIA report here, there are quite a few pages on the question of impact on State regulatory agencies, and I wonder if Mr. Maisonpierre would like to comment further on what Mr. McHugh just said is a very minimal intrusion into the question of State versus Federal regulation.

Mr. Rottman. I have to leave to catch a limousine to Dulles.

Mr. Van Deerlin. You may be excused. We appreciate your coming.

Mr. Maisonpierre. Mr. McCollister, as you say, our statement details the extent to which the Federal Government will oversight and will restructure State regulations.

Mr. McCollister. I would like some argument from Mr. McHugh contrary, if you will, and I really do not think I need to encourage you.

Mr. Maisonpierre. The Federal requirements as contained in titles I, II, and III not only will alter existing State regulations but at times they are contrary to existing State regulations and at times they create new regulations.

Now Mr. McHugh indicates that the DOT is not going to have any oversight in these areas that is the law to regulate the insurance industry will be set by the standards and the State will go ahead without any DOT supervision.

But a staff working paper developed by the staff of the Senate Commerce Committee specifically indicates there is no contemplation in the recent amendment to S. 354 that there will be any change in function of DOT and that the responsibilities of DOT will remain the same as initially planned in S. 354.

So that which we said in our statement of June 19, which is detailed in about 20 pages of our statement as to what the impact of this is, or the confrontation between State and Federal regulation still stands.

Mr. McHugh. I am not sure of what comment he refers to in the staff paper but I will say that in the bill originally passed by the Senate, the so-called Percy amendment, did require a good deal of reporting by the States to the Department of Transportation which would have exercised oversight responsibility with reference to a whole variety of those areas including rates, the operation of no-fault plans, effects of speed limits, and such issues. That has now been completely deleted from the bill and reports concerning the performance of the State no-fault laws are now made, not to the Department of Transportation but to the National Review Board.

So I would suggest on its face there already is some modification of the responsibilities which the Department of Transportation may have had in one of the original drafts.

Mr. McCollister. On page 38 of Mr. Maisonpierre's statement he says these words "For instance the Department of Transportation would decide whether the law of the State complies with title II a State Insurance Commissioner has established and maintained a medical and vocational rehabilitation program, a State——

Mr. McHugh. Excuse me, with reference to the medical and vocational rehabilitation programs the bill in its original form did require the State insurance commissioner to establish such a program. That has been deleted. They are now authorized to do it. They are not required to do it and it is only pursuant to standards in the Federal bill without any specificity as to who is to do it or how it is to be done.

Mr. McCollister. What about an assigned claims plan?

Mr. McHugh. That is a very interesting question. Almost all of the State no-fault plans that have been enacted have in fact contained an assigned claims plan so that if States move to no-fault in all cases for constitutional reasons, if no other, they must include an assigned claims plan.

We would take the position that States currently all have authority under existing law to establish assigned claim plans.

Mr. McCollister. But the Department of Transportation was to decide whether or not they had this.

Mr. McHugh. Yes, whether or not, the plans existed. When the Department of Transportation had the responsibility of deciding when the title II plans complied, they in fact made the judgment as to whether, in fact, they did exist.

Now, it is moved out of the Department of Transportation to a no-fault review board in which four of the representatives are nominally representing State positions.

Mr. McCollister. What would you have to say Mr. Maisonpierre?

Mr. Maisonpierre. In the first place, there is no question about the fact that there is authority on the part of the State legislature, not the State commissioner to legislate an assigned claims plan today.

But we have had very few assigned claims plans in fact established in the States. Hence, States would be required to enact programs which they have not felt desirable to put in operation.

Again, I go back to the staff statement as to the functions of the review board. The review board should—the review board will be an administration within DOT and it is quite clear that it will be responsible to DOT. The position and responsibilities of DOT have not changed one iota as regards the total overall responsibility and oversight of a State plan.

Mr. McCollister. Mr. McHugh looks troubled by that statement.

Mr. McHugh. I am to this extent, that the Commerce Committee apparently was sufficiently concerned with the role of the DOT being charged with deciding whether or not State no-fault plans complied and that this contained with it the inherent possibility that here is another Federal bureaucracy coming into being, including staffing, for the purpose of regulating the business of insurance. It decided not to utilize any of the existing well-staffed Federal regulatory agencies to do that. It now proposes to create a new Federal review board, which I have no notion about what, if any, kind of staffing is contemplated. It is that agency, not the Department of Transportation, that is charged with the responsibility of deciding whether or not those State no-fault plans do comply.

Mr. McCollister. Is that agency independent of the Department of Transportation?

Mr. McHugh. I do not think it is clear. I am not sure about that. I believe it is. Yes, it is. All we know is that it is appointed by the President and the Secretary of Transportation is only one of the five members.

Mr. Maisonpierre. Isn't it a fact that the review board is a part of the Department of Transportation?

Mr. McHugh. I do not know that to be a fact. It is appointed by the President and I would have been led to believe that this was intended to be an independent review board.

Mr. Maisonpierre. The chairman of the review board will be the Secretary of Transportation in order to take advantage of the expertise which the Department of Transportation has developed in this field. It seems to me from that it shall be quite clearly.

Mr. McHugh. It may be a combination.

Mr. Maisonpierre. It certainly contemplates a considerable impact by the Department of Transportation.

Mr. McHugh. I would think these are appropriate issues if this committee decides to pursue that avenue, to go into it in greater depth. I think, Mr. Chairman, this is a rather recent development that has occurred and it may be that there are aspects of this which at this time have not been really run into a corner yet.

Mr. McCollister. No further questions.

Mr. Van Deerlin. Minority counsel, Ms. Nord.

Ms. Nord. Thank you, Mr. Chairman.

State Farm favors a primary single source recovery system?

Mr. McHugh. Yes.

Ms. Nord. Would you support a bill that made not only social security and workmen's compensation primary but also made health insurance primary?

Mr. McHugh. No, we would prefer to have a single source such as automobile insurance to be the primary source of benefits for people involved in auto accidents.

Ms. Nord. How does it impact? Why is it you favor that?

Mr. McHugh. Because we think it is the best way to treat the policyholder. When we create a system in which we have a required system of first-party benefits that is designed to be sure that everybody gets their economic loss when they are involved in an automobile accident, the people who are injured will look to the source that is providing the restoration benefits of this new legislatively created system. Therefore, we say the logical thing is to look to the people who are required to pay out under that system as that being the primary source of benefit.

You ought not to have a policyholder, when involved in an auto accident, wondering if he will get paid from two or three different sources, one which is required by law and others which he may or may not have.

Mr. McCollister. Did you do or did you say you do not want medicare and Blue Shield and Blue Cross to be primary?

Mr. McHugh. I understood her to be talking about other primary private health insurance which would be Blue Cross and the health insurance system.

Ms. Nord. Right, and I also included medicare.

Mr. McHugh. I think, to the extent that the bill currently provides that any existing national health insurance system has been primary, this would not be our preference. But we would hope that in adopting new laws, by Congress creating an automobile accident insurance system, you should look to such a system for as much of the benefits as can be paid by the source that is required under that act to pay automobile accident victims.

It may be that we cannot stand back from medicare at this point but, in turn, we would hope at such time as the national health insurance system comes into being, if it does, we would then be able to say that we have a very effective automobile insurance system that provides for these benefits and no national health insurance system need provide them or duplicate them.

Mr. Eckhardt. May we get an answer from other members of the panel as to whether or not they would also favor a national or any national health program as being primary or secondary to auto reparations insurance?

Mr. Maisonpierre. If I may address this question, we support national health insurance but we strongly support national health insurance with automobile insurance benefits as being primary.

Mr. ECKHARDT. What you said a minute ago about these extensive medical recovery programs might break a small company, why not let the national health insurance bear that unlimited liability?

Mr. MAISONPIERRE. Because of a number of reasons, Mr. Eckhardt. No. 1, we think it is important that the cost of automobile insurance be internalized. More importantly, the automobile insurance carrier, the first-party benefit carrier, has responsibilities considerably beyond the payment of medical benefits. He is paying medical benefits and he is paying wage losses and he may be paying for rehabilitation.

Now, if we are going to have one system to pay one type of benefit and another to pay for another type of benefit, we are tearing the individual apart. He should not be made to look to different sources for his total benefit payments.

Mr. ECKHARDT. What difference does it make, if he is going to be assured of national health insurance? Otherwise, he may have to argue with you as to whether or not his slipped disc occurred prior to the accident and it was a disability which he had long before the accident or whether it occurred during the accident so he really has more trouble in establishing liability there with you than he would have in simply going and getting health insurance.

Mr. MCCOLLISTER. If the gentleman would yield, Would he, if he has his medical treatment paid for by, let us say, someone of national health insurance and his wage-loss benefit paid for by the insurance company, might there not be a point of argument develop that the treatment being followed under the terms of the national health insurance was not such to take care of, to rehabilitate him so he could be back to work.

Mr. MAISONPIERRE. Yes.

Mr. MCCOLLISTER. And the insurance company is obligated to keep paying the wage loss.

Mr. ECKHARDT. If I were the injured person, I would rather have the ability to make a claim and be assured I would be paid for the injury by someone.

Mr. MCCOLLISTER. The point being that the national health coverage only bankrupting the Treasury of the United States is a more certain payment than the insurance company which might be bankrupted.

Mr. ECKHARDT. Well, I think that you might be able to work out means by which tax contributions, because of driving an automobile, would be a portion of the base upon which the governmental expense occurred but I think we are really framing our questions in a majority of ways and it is not very prudent.

Mr. MAISONPIERRE. I think Mr. McCollister's point is well taken. If you concentrate all of the benefit payment responsibilities in the auto carriers, you are increasing the incentive to the auto insurance carrier to provide good adequate rehabilitation so that the sooner the individual is rehabilitated, the sooner it can terminate all benefit payments.

Now, if health insurance pays medical and rehabilitation care, there is no way for the auto carrier who is paying wage benefits to really assist in the rehabilitation of the person and, as Mr. McHugh has indicated, we do provide substantial rehabilitation of injured automobile accident victims in no-fault States.

Mr. ECKHARDT. Maybe then they could pay more of his wage losses than $15,000.

Mr. MAISONPIERRE. There is another point. The matter, well, we were talking this morning about the efficiency and the waste of administration. If health insurance pays and auto insurance pays, we are then duplicating the administrative expenses and this, in itself, is a waste. We do not see any reason why there should be this duplication.

Another reason is this: Again, we were talking this morning and this afternoon about the reasons for enacting no-fault. One such reason is because so many people are not getting their medical expense paid by the auto insurance system.

If you make health insurance primary, you do not need no-fault any more.

Mr. ECKHARDT. Let me ask you, would you be willing under no-fault, the automobile reparations plan, to simply pay all disability if it were triggered by the accident without looking into the question of whether or not there was a prior existing malfunctioning or disability?

Mr. MAISONPIERRE. No, I think Mr. Eckhardt, in all fairness, that the disability and the medical that are paid for should be related to the accident.

Mr. ECKHARDT. They would be related, it would be triggered, it would be caused by it ultimately. But would you be willing to simply overlook the question of some contributory situation that pre-existed the accident or would you argue that with them?

Mr. MAISONPIERRE. I can assure you the courts will hold if the automobile accident was a contributory factor, the automobile insurance policy will have to pay.

Mr. ECKHARDT. All of it?

Mr. MAISONPIERRE. All of it until the individual is back to pre-accident status, whatever that is.

Mr. ECKHARDT. Then you would not have any objection to putting that into the act?

Mr. MAISONPIERRE. This is the way the Workmen's Compensation system handled the issue. We would object to putting it in Federal law, since we oppose a Federal law, whatever the law may be.

Mr. MCCOLLISTER. If you would yield, would it not become necessary for everybody to take a physical examination to learn what pre-existent disabilities may have existed in which case the cost of that medical examination is there?

Mr. ECKHARDT. That is why I raised the medical disability as being primary.

Mr. MAISONPIERRE. We raised the point in prior testimony, not before this committee but in the Senate, that people with physical handicaps will find themselves in some difficulty getting no-fault insurance. Then they will be the high risks in the no-fault system.

Mr. ECKHARDT. You are again arguing my position for the primary responsibility of public insurance.

Mr. MAISONPIERRE. I do not think so, Mr. Eckhardt. I think these individuals still will be paid by the auto insurance system but if under a health insurance system, they would also be likely to be charged higher rates unless they fall within a group and there is no reason why we cannot have group auto insurance. Today, these people are being surcharged for health insurance coverage.

Ms. O'REILLY. I wish an opportunity to briefly answer the question.

CFA favors the inclusion of a provision similar to section 209 in S.354 which would require the State to provide some type of coordination of benefits program. This would avoid any duplication of coverage and thereby hopefully reduce costs.

Mr. MAISONPIERRE. One comment about this section. We think it is very inappropriate for congressional legislation to provide competitive advantages to one form of insurance, health insurance, over another form of insurance, casualty insurance.

As you read through S.354, there are very substantial controls put on casualty insurance companies. They must participate in assigned risk plans, assigned claims plans, they must do all sorts of things, and they must be responsible for the total medical expenses.

Then we find that health insurance companies can come in and provide these benefits but none of the impediments which we find applicable to casualty insurance would be applicable to health insurance or the Blues. It seems to me—well, we question very much whether Congress here should impose antiduplication programs on the States, but if it should do it, it should put everyone on an equal footing and all competing companies and systems should be subject to the same handicaps.

Mr. McHUGH. I find myself in agreement with Mr. Maisonpierre on this point.

Mr. VAN DEERLIN. We waited long enough.

Mr. McHUGH. And I should suggest here that we have also concluded that where automobile insurance is made primary, and other group benefits are made secondary, the policyholder can achieve greater savings than where his automobile insurance is made secondary.

Mr. ECKHARDT. Mr. Chairman, I have just one comment.

Mr. VAN DEERLIN. Sure.

Mr. ECKHARDT. I had not said that one type of private insurance should be primary over another. I had merely suggested that when there was public insurance, which I think most of our experience indicates has had a higher ratio of payout to premium cost than the 60-40 ratio with respect to auto insurance and even perhaps an improved ratio which may exist now, but concerning which I have not been able to get any statistics, but I was merely suggesting that when the competition is between public insurance and private insurance, the public insurance should be primary and I believe Ms. O'Reilly was not stating that any private insurance should be favored over another but that there be a means by which it can be assured that a person was not insuring at two places.

Ms. O'REILLY. That is correct.

Mr. ECKHARDT. For only one set of benefits.

Ms. O'REILLY. Coordination should be among not just the no-fault system of benefits but between other systems which provide benefits to the victims so that there is not a duplication of coverage.

Mr. ECKHARDT. That is all I understood you to say and I would agree with that. Of course, there are two questions involved here. One, as to whether or not public insurance should be primary above private, and I understand that the gentlemen think otherwise but with respect to the question of whether or not there should be coordination of the insurance programs, I would assume the gentlemen are agreed that there should be coordination so there never will be a duplication of premium payments for the same benefits.

Mr. McHugh. I think it is very difficult to say there can never be duplication.

Mr. Eckhardt. At least we should do the best we can in the bill or in any bill whether it is State or Federal, to provide that this shall not be done or that notice be given with respect to the nature of the coverage by each of the insurers.

Mr. McHugh. Well, I think in the amendment adopted by the Senate Commerce Committee, which we did not support, the emphasis is upon minimizing overlapping coverages.

We have found in polls taken of our customers, customers are perfectly willing to pay for and receive duplicate benefits in some circumstances.

I do think as a matter of public policy, it is wise and advisable to try to minimize duplication and to keep it as low as possible.

Mr. Eckhardt. Don't you think there are cases in which a person may believe that he can get benefits from both of his insurance policies when, in fact, he cannot?

Mr. McHugh. No; but there are certainly some instances when he can, in fact, recover from both sources.

Mr. Eckardt. That is right but certainly there should be every effort made and the law should make it mandatory that every precaution be taken to let the insured know whether he is purchasing dual coverage or whether in fact his purchase of the second coverage will not avail him anything.

Mr. McHugh. I have no problem with that at all. Our concerns are in the instances where the policyholder was aware he was buying duplicate coverage and was paying for that and was willing to do so with the expectation he was going to get paid under both coverages.

Mr. Eckhardt. I would think that raises considerable damages because it seems to me it lends confusion in the consumer market and it might be better if we simply did not encourage that kind of double insurance.

Mr. McHugh. I think the thrust of the Senate action is to try to minimize the overlap of it. With reference to your concern and the distinction you made with reference to public programs, national health insurance, I think I was conscious of the distinction you were making there in answer to the question as to whether or not public health programs should be primary or the auto insurance, we have felt that the automobile insurance industry is going to be in a very difficult position in arguing that it ought to be primary as against a national health insurance system, unless it can improve the payout under the present system and that that is one of the reasons we feel it is mandatory that we move toward a really effective no-fault program where we can show we have in fact paid out a much higher percentage of the premium dollar than we are currently doing if we expect to win the fight when national health insurance comes into play by proving we can do a better job than the national health insurance system.

Mr. McCollister. But you will never be able to reduce your acquisition cost to compete with the Federal Government acquisition cost on national health insurance.

Mr. McHugh. It all depends on what we understand to be the Government costs which strike me at that time needs a lot of careful examination.

Mr. McCollister. We will get the answer.

Mr. Maisonpierre. Mr. Eckhardt, you made a statement that bothers me a little when you talk about efficiency of a public program. You said on a payin-payout relationship, it is much greater and the efficiency of the public program is greater. I do not think that it is necessary, in fact I am convinced that this is a wrong basis for measuring efficiency of a system. If your public program is merely a payin-payout system, it just pays out the bills, doesn't control the loss; doesn't control rehabilitation, doesn't expend any dollars in the control of medical costs, it is a wasteful system.

If the private program, in turn, involves expenses in hiring nurses, in hiring medical technicians, that can assist in the control of the medical care, this reduces the amount of payout that is available but it also reduces the total amount of losses which society sustained and this is the true measure of efficiency.

Mr. Eckhardt. I do not quarrel with you on that proposition. I was merely assuming if you did have a public program, that would pay the bill upon some basis, then you have a public program that is either wasteful or it is not wasteful, the money is ultimately going to be paid out and that it simply seemed to me better to pay it out by that party which does not have to argue over whether or not it is liable and also I felt it was better to pay it out by a party that may not have as heavy an overhead load and that payout partially of course because of its lack of any acquisition cost.

Mr. Maisonpierre. Well, I think we have some evidence that the public programs, even though there might not be controversies associated with it, does involve substantial delay in payment and I am sure your information reveals that social security beneficiaries are not paid as promptly as they think they should be paid and there are substantial delays in payment of some of their benefits.

Mr. Eckhardt. They are paid a little quicker than persons claiming against third-party insurance.

Mr. Maisonpierre. They are not paid quicker than people claiming health insurance benefits or even no-fault benefits in States that have enacted these laws.

Mr. Eckhardt. First party.

Ms. O'Reilly. Before this is concluded I would like to emphasize that CFA's support for coordination of benefits is not limited to public health aspects. We would be distressed for example, if the present Michigan coordination statute were precluded by national legislation. The coordination that exists in Michigan has been estimated to save consumers in Michigan some $60 million. Competition is healthy and there is a demonstrated cost savings to consumers by such coordination.

Mr. Eckhardt. Yes, thank you.

Mr. Van Deerlin. Any further participation?

Thank you, all of you and that concludes today's hearings.

Mr. McCollister. A very interesting panel, Mr. Chairman, and I am grateful to them.

Mr. Van Deerlin. Yes, I think they contributed greatly to our stimulation. We will resume tomorrow on another subject, toxic substances, and again take up no-fault insurance on the balmy shores of Daytona Beach next Monday.

The hearing is adjourned.

[The following correspondence was received for the record:]

[Whereupon at 4 p.m., the hearing was adjourned, to reconvene at 9 a.m., July 14, 1975, at Daytona Beach, Fla.]

U.S. HOUSE OF REPRESENTATIVES,
COMMITTEE ON INTERSTATE AND FOREIGN COMMERCE,
Washington, D.C., July 31, 1975.

Mr. DONALD P. MCHUGH,
*State Farm Mutual Auto Insurance Co.,
State Farm Plaza, Bloomington, Ill.*

DEAR MR. MCHUGH: You will find attached a list of questions to which we would appreciate your answers. They relate to questions which were raised with respect to cost estimates of H.R. 1900 and S. 354 subsequent to the time of your testimony before the Subcommittee on Consumer Protection and Finance.

We would appreciate your answers to the questions by August 14, 1975.

Sincerely,

LIONEL VAN DEERLIN,
Chairman, Subcommittee on Consumer Protection and Finance.

Enclosure.

1. Would you please supply the Subcommittee with the absolute dollar figure you used in each state as the basis for determining the effect S. 354 would have on premiums? Could you please breakout the portion of the premium that would go for medical coverage and wage loss coverage under S. 354? Could you tell the Subcommittee what the difference in premium cost is between $50,000 of medical benefits and unlimited medical benefits?

2. During the Subcommittee's hearings, a challenge was made to State Farm's finding that S. 354 would result in a nationwide average decrease in premiums of 10%. Instead, it was contended that if one adds up the State Farm projections for all 50 states and simply divides by 50, one would come out with a nationwide average decrease of only 8%. Do you accept this approach? If not, would you please indicate why not?

3. Enclosed are two charts prepared by Allstate Insurance Company. Would you please prepare similar charts based upon your experience in the named states and supply the Subcommittee with the charts and your explanation of their significance?

4. Could you please supply the Subcommittee with information on your experience in no-fault and "add-on" states with respect to utilization of medical insurance benefits?

5. The Subcommittee is interested in learning the actual impact of no-fault laws on how much money the insured is able to retain. Could you please supply the Subcommittee with your experience in both no-fault and add-on states, before and after adoption of the new laws, with respect to the following items: insurance company loss ratio and insurance company expense ratio; accident frequency and severity; insurance company selling expenses, profit and overhead, taxes and fees, claim adjusting expenses, claimant's attorneys' fees, litigation costs, economic loss not otherwise compensated, non-economic loss and duplicate recovery for economic loss already compensated. To the extent that these figures are not available, could you advise us as to whether there is any feasible way of estimating them and supply us with the results of those estimates? What assumptions do you use in your no-fault costing model for consumer retention of benefits?

NO-FAULT THRESHOLD EFFECT ON BODILY INJURY FREQUENCY AND SEVERITY

State	Threshold	Bodily injury (relative to tort system)		
		Incurred frequency	Incurred severity	Combined
Florida	$1,000	0.35	3.30	1.15
New York	500	.60	1.50	.90
New Jersey	200	.60	1.50	.90
Connecticut	400	.30	3.50	1.05
Oregon	None	.75	1.20	.90
Maryland	None	.80	1.50	1.20
Michigan	(¹)	.15	5.00	.75

¹ Serious injury.

NO-FAULT EFFECT ON CLOSED CLAIM SEVERITY (ALL REPORT YEARS EVALUATED AT 24 MOS. DEVELOPMENT)
NUMBER OF CLOSED CLAIM COURTS

Claim interval	Florida		New Jersey	
	Report year 1971	Report year 1973	Report year 1972	Report year 1973
0 to $5,000	7,057	1,671	7,804	3,932
$5,000 to $10,000	369	391	180	176
$10,000 to $20,000	137	191	83	108
Over $20,000	47	94	37	62
Total counts	7,610	2,347	8,104	4,278
Total dollars	$12,850,000	$13,629,000	$9,789,000	$9,175,000

STATE FARM MUTUAL AUTOMOBILE INSURANCE CO.,
Bloomington, Ill., August 18, 1975.

Hon. LIONEL VAN DEERLIN,
House of Representatives,
Rayburn House Office Building, Washington, D.C.

DEAR CONGRESSMAN VAN DEERLIN: Following are our responses to the questions you submitted to us in your letter of July 31, 1975:

1. Exhibit I shows the underlying average rates used in each state to determine the effects of S. 354. Also included are estimates of the Medical and Wage Loss (including Replacement Services and Survivor's Loss) portions of the indicated rates for S. 354.

For the purposes of these estimates, we have assumed that the cost difference between $50,000 of medical benefits and unlimited benefits is negligible. This does not mean that there won't be any claims above $50,000, but rather that their expected cost per insured will be quite small (i.e., substantially less than 50¢). As a matter of interest, in New Jersey for 1973, out of 3200 Medical claims settled 7 involved payment in excess of $25,000. The average on these was less than $40,000, with the largest being $51,000. In Michigan, out of some 25,000 claims reported to date 10 involve potential costs in excess of $100,000. Thus far, the maximum paid on any one of these is $46,500. It will, of course, take a number of years before the ultimate cost of these serious cases can be determined with any precision.

2. We do not view the estimate of 8% as being significantly different than our 10% estimate. However, we believe the method of calculating the nationwide average in your question to be incorrect. We arrived at our average rate by using a substantially different method. In particular, the 10% represents the average reduction for State Farm Mutual policyholders, and takes into account the differing premium rates and volume of business by state. Referring to Exhibit I, the 10% average reduction was determined by relating the countrywide indicated average premium ($55) to the countrywide present average premium ($61). Both of these, in turn were calculated as weighted averages of the respective state premiums with their corresponding number of insured cars. Under a simple averaging, equal weight would be given to the average rate in the state of Alaska where we have about 20,000 policyholders and California where we have about 1,600,000 policyholders.

3. The attached Exhibit II provides a comparison of Threshold Effects similar to the first chart prepared by Allstate. You will note that we have adjusted the relationships to eliminate the effects of inflation and the oil embargo—both being necessary to develop a meaningful and valid comparison. You will also note that in the Add-On states (Delaware, Maryland, Oregon) the No-Fault provisions have had essentially no impact on tort activity. (Delaware is a small state, and you can expect considerable variation from year to year, which probably accounts for the increase.) In the "true" No-Fault states, savings have accrued in all cases, although perhaps not as much as might be expected. Generally, the figures indicate that the tighter the threshold, the greater the savings. It should be noted that any effective tort threshold will have the effect of greatly increasing the incurred severity. By eliminating from the tort system recovery for many small cases, the average recovery will be substantially increased. This translates into higher severity ratios. Although we believe we have adequate experience to make valid judgments on the effects of state No-Fault laws, it will take several more years of experience to see exactly how the pattern will settle. Also, other factors—such as tort propensity—influence the effectiveness of a given threshold in a given state.

(Because of State Farm's small amount of business in Connecticut—only 9300 cars insured—the results are now shown on the exhibit. However, the available numbers indicate a savings in that state as well: a frequency reduction of 70% together with a cost increase of 90%, or a combined relationship of .57.)

State Farm does not regularly compile data on a basis similar to Allstate's second chart, on claims by size. However, we do have information relative to the dollar amount of incurred claims in excess of $10,000. This shows results similar to Allstate's. For example, in 1971 in Florida, the aggregate amount of such "excess" loss was $1,380,000; in 1973, $2,200,000, or an increase of 60%. In New Jersey, the amount was $650,000 in 1972 and $2,870,000 in 1974, or an increase of 340%. This is not a phenomenon unique to No-Fault states—California, for example, shows increases of 49% and 95% over the same two periods. In fact, No-Fault probably contributes to it only to the extent that the more serious claims can be handled faster, now that the small claims are out of the system, and hence accelerates the development of these losses. Actually, we feel the large increases stem from three other factors:

(i) An increase in exposure, with more insureds carrying higher limits. In 1971, State Farm insured 6.2 million cars with BI limits in excess of $20,000; in 1974, that figure had increased to 9.0 million.

(ii) The impact of inflation is to increase the number of claims exceeding any given dollar amount, and this increase becomes greater the higher the cut-off amount.

(iii) The increased claims consciousness of the public. This is particularly pronounced in the medical malpractice arena, but the effect is apparent in all liability lines.

4. Exhibit III summarizes the medical claims experience during 1974 in the several states which have auto reparation laws. While the figures reflect considerable differences from the "expected", the degree of such variation is not unusually large for data of this nature. In particular, there is no evidence of the high frequency which could be expected if there were any appreciable amount of overutilization. In fact, if anything, the frequencies may be lower than expected.

5. Exhibit IV sets forth the assumptions on benefit/cost ratios and expense savings implicit in our costing of S. 354. The ratio of Claim Payments to Premium (the portion we pay out) is expected to increase slightly. But the portion of the premium dollar being returned to claimants in the form of Direct Benefits (the amount claimants receive after payment of any legal fees to their attorneys), and more particularly Economic Loss Benefits, is expected to be increased markedly.

The actual experience being incurred in the No-Fault states generally reflects these expectations, although the effects are distorted by the adverse impact of inflation on claim costs and expenses and by the mandated rate reductions which were imposed along with No-Fault. For these reasons, we would caution against attributing the changes in loss and expense ratios in the individual states solely, or even in some cases primarily, to the introduction of automobile reparations laws. Also, conditions vary considerably from state to state. Therefore, it would be erroneous to assume that the effect on claims cost and expenses that the enactment of a reparation law had in a particular state would be exactly duplicated if enacted in another state.

Exhibit V shows the loss ratios for all the personal injury coverages (Bodily Injury Liability, Uninsured Motorist, Medical Payments—about 90% of our policyholders carry this voluntary coverage—and Personal Injury Protection coverage) in several No-Fault and add on states for the last full (accident) year prior to the effective dates of the reparation laws and for the two subsequent years (if available). Of course, loss ratios alone are not ture indicators of a greater percentage of the premium dollars actually retained by claimants. Therefore, we have also included estimates of the portion of the premium utlimately received by the claimant (Direct Benefits) and the portion relating to actual out-of-the-pocket expenses (Economic Loss Benefits). Also, it should be noted that high loss ratios can be, and often are indications, that companies are losing money rather than indications of greater "efficiency."

In this exhibit, no attempt has been made to estimate the extent of "economic loss not otherwise compensated" or "duplicate recovery." We are not aware of any source for such information—barring, of course, a survey of claimants.

Exhibit VI provides data on expense and profit ratios for the same group of states and for the same periods of time. These data are on a calendar year basis and for all automobile coverages combined. This is because the bulk of the administrative expenses are actually accured on a calendar year, total operations basis an cannot be allocated by coverage or accident year other than by formula.

It should also be recognized that since nearly all of the claims adjustment and general administrative expenses are salaries, the actual expense savings expected under No-Fault will only materialize over a period of time and in conjunction with reallocation and attrition of our manpower resources.

Exhibit VII shows some bsaic information on the claim severity and frequency for the coverages affected by No-Fault.

We have been informed that the National Association of Insurance Commissioners is creating a task force to monitor the results of No-Fault laws. I would imagine that the task force will be gathering much of the same type of information you are requesting. It will probably take some time to gather industry figures. However, I am sure the NAIC will make the figures available when they are gathered.

Sincerely,

DONALD P. McHUGH,
Vice President and General Counsel.

COMPARISON OF PRESENT SYSTEM WITH NATIONAL STANDARDS PLAN

	Number of cars insured at Dec. 31, 1974 (in thousands)	Present	Percent change	S. 354 indicated	Medical	Wage loss
Alabama	363	$44	—19	$36	$14	$12
Alaska	20	74	—7	69	28	23
Arizona	177	69	—18	57	22	19
Arkansas	149	47	—9	43	17	15
California	1,559	79	—14	68	27	22
Colorado	271	58	—3	56	23	19
Connecticut	9	58	—1	57	23	19
Delaware	63	39	—13	34	13	11
District of Columbia	12	106	—21	84	32	26
Florida	641	64	+8	69	28	23
Georgia	371	54	—11	48	19	16
Hawaii	42	82	—10	74	29	24
Idaho	74	36	—9	33	13	12
Illinois	929	75	—11	67	26	22
Indiana	481	44	—12	39	15	13
Iowa	250	32	—7	30	12	10
Kansas	296	39	—3	38	15	13
Kentucky	243	45	—11	40	16	14
Louisiana	268	81	—18	66	26	22
Maine	18	43	—12	38	15	13
Maryland	286	83	—17	69	28	23
Massachusetts	12	68	+15	78	32	26
Michigan	656	67	—7	62	25	21
Minnesota	437	65	—12	57	22	19
Mississippi	194	47	—7	44	17	15
Missouri	478	53	—6	50	20	17
Montana	87	30	—11	27	11	10
Nebraska	205	30	—11	27	10	9
Nevada	71	73	—1	72	28	24
New Hampshire	22	75	—2	74	30	25
New Jersey	239	77	+3	79	32	26
New Mexico	111	42	—10	38	15	13
New York	354	90	+4	94	38	31
North Carolina	232	49	+0	49	21	17
North Dakota	47	29	—5	28	11	10
Ohio	500	53	—13	46	19	15
Oklahoma	188	46	—13	40	16	13
Oregon	188	56	—14	48	20	16
Pennsylvania	699	63	—11	56	23	19
Rhode Island		55	—9	50	20	17
South Carolina	233	51	—6	48	19	17
South Dakota	60	29	—1	29	12	11
Tennessee	380	59	—3	57	23	20
Texas	720	58	—26	43	17	14
Utah	147	51	—2	50	20	17
Vermont	8	40	—10	36	14	13
Virginia	423	63	—3	61	25	21
Washington	225	58	—15	49	20	17
West Virginia	217	39	—8	36	14	13
Wisconsin	237	61	—5	58	23	20
Wyoming	63	28	—9	25	10	9
Countrywide average	13,955	61	—10	55	22	18

Note: These estimates are based on the minimum benefit plan provided by S. 354, including unlimited medical expense benefits, $15,000 of wage loss, and $5,000 survivor's benefit. The present costs are State Farm's current average rates (Dec. 31, 1974) in each State for a typical policyholder for bodily injury liability, uninsured motorist, and medical payments coverages (and basic personal injury protection coverage in those States already under a no-fault plan).

EXHIBIT II

NO-FAULT THRESHOLD EFFECT ON BODILY INJURY LIABILITY FREQUENCY AND SEVERITY

State	Threshold	Relative to tort system		
		Incurred frequency	Incurred severity	Combined
Delaware	None	0.82	1.40	1.15
Florida	$1,000	.32	2.34	.75
Kansas	500	.33	1.90	.63
Maryland	None	.84	1.19	1.00
Michigan	(¹)	.11	3.85	.42
New Jersey	200	.45	1.68	.76
New York	500	.31	1.40	.43
Oregon	None	.91	1.08	.98
Utah	500	.56	1.22	.68

¹ Serious injury.

Note: The comparison is based on the loss experience for the year just prior to no-fault and the 1st year under the plan, with the losses evaluated on the latest available data. For this comparison, the severity effects have been reduced by 6 percent (10 percent in 1974) to eliminate the expected impact of inflation on claim costs, and the 1974 frequencies were increased 10 percent to eliminate the effect of the oil embargo and reduced travel.

MEDICAL EXPERIENCE IN SEVERAL AUTOMOBILE REPARATION LAW STATES

State	Benefit limit	1974	
		Average paid claim cost	Claim frequency (per 1,000 insured cars)
Delaware	$10,000	$456	20.5
Florida	5,000	511	20.0
Kansas	2,000	447	14.6
Maryland	2,500	633	21.3
Michigan	Unlimited	516	22.5
New Jersey	Unlimited	499	27.9
New York	50,000	615	28.7
Oregon	5,000	498	20.6
Utah	2,000	400	16.8

Note: Based on the 1969 DOT study, the expected costs per claim (at 1974 price levels) are: $2,000 limit—$400; $5,000 limit—$475; $10,000 limit—$525; unlimited—$550. The combined frequencies for residual liability and personal injury protection coverage were expected to be 60 percent to 110 percent higher than the frequency for the pre no-fault liability coverage. (Cf. exhibit IV).

EXHIBIT IV

IMPACT OF NO-FAULT ON BENEFIT/COST RATIOS

Item	Present system			S. 354 (estimated)			Change in total (percent)
	Liability	Medical payments	Total	PIP	Reserve liability	Total	
1. Gross premium cost	$53	$8	$61	$41	$14	$55	—10
2. General expenses, acquisition, and profit	12	2	14	10	3	13	—10
3. Claims adjustment	8	1	9	4	2	6	—33
4. Total claim payments (=1—2—3)	33	5	38	27	9	36	—5
5. Palintiff attorney fees	8	0	8	0	3	3	—60
6. Direct benefits (=4—5)	25	5	30	27	6	33	+10
7. General damages	12	0	12	0	5	5	—60
8. Economic loss benefits (=6—7)	13	5	18	27	1	28	+56
Benefit/cost ratios (percent):							
Claim payments (=4/1)	62	63	62	66	64	65	
Direct benefits (=6/1)	47	63	49	66	43	60	
Economic loss (=8/1)	25	63	30	66	7	51	

LOSS RATIOS, PERSONAL INJURY COVERAGES COMBINED [1]

[In percent]

State and accident year	Total incurred losses	Direct benefits	Economic loss benefits
Delaware:			
1971	46.7	37.1	22.6
1972 [1]	68.9	58.8	43.7
1973	64.2	56.7	45.4
Florida:			
1971	68.6	55.6	36.0
1972 [1]	79.4	68.0	50.7
1973	83.7	71.2	52.3
Kansas:			
1973	49.0	40.4	27.6
1974 [2]	56.3	49.7	39.7
Maryland:			
1972	53.4	41.6	23.9
1973 [3]	64.4	52.7	35.2
1974	69.6	57.7	39.8
Michigan: [3]			
1972	62.0	49.6	31.0
1973	62.6	51.1	33.9
1974	65.2	59.8	51.6
New Jersey:			
1972	55.3	44.8	25.8
1973 [3]	86.1	72.8	52.9
1974	91.9	78.5	58.4
New York:			
1973	62.6	49.1	28.9
1974 [2]	58.3	51.7	41.8
Oregon:			
1971	49.8	40.5	26.7
1972 [2]	59.9	44.0	30.6
1973	54.7	45.7	32.1
Utah:			
1973	51.0	40.8	25.4
1974 [3]	58.5	50.3	38.0

[1] Bodily injury liability coverages, uninsured motorist coverages, medical payments coverages (prior to reparation law), and personal injury coverages under reparation law.
[2] 1st year under reparation law.
[3] No-fault was effective Oct. 1, 1973.

Note: Ratios are to premiums earned, with losses evaluated on the basis of the latest available data.

EXHIBIT VI

EXPENSE AND PROFIT RATIOS—ALL AUTOMOBILE COVERAGES COMBINED

[In percent]

State and year	General administration	Claims adjustment	Total expense ratio	Underwriting profit (before Federal taxes)
Deleware:				
1971	9.1	13.2	34.8	7.1
1972 [1]	9.2	14.6	36.3	−.2
1973	8.6	15.5	36.6	−18.4
Florida:				
1971	9.0	11.3	32.8	6.1
1972 [1]	8.8	9.9	31.2	6.7
1973	7.9	13.0	33.4	−11.8
Kansas:				
1973	8.3	8.9	29.7	9.0
1974 [1]	9.6	9.0	31.1	4.2
Maryland:				
1972	7.7	9.3	29.5	9.7
1973 [1]	6.8	10.9	30.3	−2.0
1974	8.8	11.9	33.2	.1
Michigan: [2]				
1972	7.8	12.1	32.4	2.9
1973	8.5	11.9	32.9	2.1
1974	9.1	10.0	31.6	7.4
New Jersey:				
1972	8.5	12.7	33.7	13.6
1973 [1]	9.4	11.9	33.9	4.2
1974	13.9	14.7	41.1	−16.5
New York:				
1973	8.6	12.1	33.2	3.4
1974 [1]	8.7	10.3	31.5	3.1
Oregon:				
1971	9.0	12.6	34.1	5.3
1972 [1]	9.9	12.9	35.3	2.6
1973	10.3	12.3	35.2	3.6
Utah:				
1973	10.1	10.5	33.1	3.5
1974 [1]	11.3	11.7	35.5	3.6

[1] 1st year under reparation law.
[2] No-fault was effective Oct. 1, 1973.

Note: Ratios are to premiums earned. Total expense ratio includes 12.5 percent for agents compensation and premium taxes.

EXHIBIT VII

AUTO REPARATION CLAIM EXPERIENCE

State and year	Bodily injury liability C	F	Uninsured motorist C	F	Medical payments C	F	Personal injury protection C	F
Delaware:								
1971	$3,143	18.5	$2,505	1.5	$218	11.6		
1972 [1]	2,421	16.6	1,665	.7			$625	19.0
1973	3,087	17.2	2,775	.8			860	22.8
Florida:								
1971	2,007	28.9	1,995	4.8	339	17.6		
1972 [1]	3,593	11.4	3,338	1.7	403	2.9	737	24.4
1973	5,268	7.2	4,241	1.5	591	1.8	691	25.3
Kansas:								
1973	1,835	13.0	2,174	1.0	441	11.4		
1974 [1]	3,794	3.8	6,307	.3			570	14.6
Maryland:								
1972	2,200	30.5	4,399	.3	392	12.4		
1973 [2]	2,408	30.2	2,988	.4			1,167	18.9
1974	2,871	25.4	1,567	.9			1,045	21.3
Michigan: [2]								
1972	2,042	25.3	2,000	2.8	308	16.3		
1973	2,466	18.9	2,780	2.2	342	12.4	644	23.3
1974	5,433	3.8	4,235	.8			952	22.5
New Jersey:								
1972	1,508	40.2	1,407	3.4	273	15.4		
1973 [1]	3,004	14.6	1,667	1.6			639	29.5
1974	3,182	12.9	1,974	1.0			671	27.9
New York:								
1973	2,313	37.0	2,921	1.4	389	22.3		
1974 [1]	3,010	11.3	3,949	.6			1,180	28.7
Oregon:								
1971	1,677	22.9	1,394	2.5	326	19.5		
1972 [1]	1,731	22.4	1,493	2.4			514	21.7
1973	1,897	19.6	1,214	2.4			586	23.6
Utah:								
1973	1,878	17.9	1,709	1.4	346	14.2		
1974 [1]	2,117	13.7	2,461	.6			943	16.8

[1] 1st year under reparation law.
[2] No-fault was effective Oct. 1, 1973.

Note: C = Average paid claim cost; F = Number of claims reported per 1,000 insured.

U.S. HOUSE OF REPRESENTATIVES,
COMMITTEE ON INTERSTATE AND FOREIGN COMMERCE,
Washington, D.C., July 31, 1975.

Mr. DONALD SCHAFFER,
*Vice President and General Counsel, Allstate Insurance Co.,
Allstate Plaza, Northbrook, Ill.*

DEAR MR. SCHAFFER: You will find attached a list of questions to which we would appreciate your answers. These are questions which were raised with respect to Allstate's cost estimates for H.R. 1900 and S. 354 during the hearings before the Subcommittee on Consumer Protection and Finance.

We would appreciate a response to these questions by August 14, 1975. Thank you for your cooperation.

Sincerely,

LIONEL VAN DEERLIN,
Chairman, Subcommittee on Consumer Protection and Finance.

LVD/DCB
Enclosure

1. Would you please supply the Subcommittee with the absolute dollar figure you used in each state as the basis for determining the effect S. 354 would have on premiums? Could you please breakout the portion of the premium that would go for medical coverage and wage loss coverage under S. 354? Could you tell the Subcommittee what the difference in premium cost is between $50,000 of medical benefits and unlimited medical benefits?

2. In Allstate's testimony statement before the Senate Commerce Committte on April 30, 1975, there is a chart entitled "Allstate Costing Model Reconciliation" which has model indication and first year experience indication for adequate rates for the affected coverage for the states of Florida, Connecticut, New Jersey, Maryland, and Oregon. The statement also refers to Allstate's actual costs in these states before no-fault went into effect. Would you please supply for the record what these actual costs were and whether you considered them adequate at the time? If you did not consider them adequate, please indicate what an adequate pre-no-fault rate would have been. Would you also please indicate what your actual rate experience has been in the states since that time and how that experience compares with what you consider an adequate rate?

3. Could you please supply the Subcommittee with information on your experience in no-fault and "add-on" states with respect to utilization of medical insurance benefits?

4. The Subcommittee is interested in learning the actual impact of no-fault laws on how much money the insured is able to retain. Could you please supply the Subcommittee with your experience in both no-fault and add-on states, before and after adoption of the new laws, with respect to the following items: insurance company loss ratio and insurance company expense ratio; accident frequency and severity; insurance company selling expenses, profit and overhead, taxes and fees, claim adjusting expenses, claimant's attorneys' fees, litigation costs, economic loss not otherwise compensated, non-economic loss and duplicate recovery for economic loss already compensated. To the extent that these figures are not available, could you advise us as to whether there is any feasible way of estimating them and supply us with the results of those estimates? What assumptions do you use in your no-fault costing model for consumer retention of benefits?

EXHIBIT 1

RESPONSES TO QUESTIONS OF CHAIRMAN VAN DEERLIN CONTAINED IN HIS LETTER OF JULY 31, 1975

(1) A. Your first question requests the dollar figure used in each state as the basis for determining the effect S. 354 would have on premiums. The absolute dollar figures requested produce no real meaningful data which would be helpful to the committee. The reason is that our model assumes that the rate base from which the projection is made is "adequate" in accordance with accepted rate making practices. However, in many instances the base rate from which the projection is made is, in fact, inadequate and, thus, the dollar change in going from a fault to a no-fault system could be substantially higher than the percentage change we indicate. Furthermore, some of the base rates used in our projections are now out of date since we have recently taken rate increases in several states. These recent rate changes do not affect, to any extent, our cost projections in terms of percentage increases or decreases, but they would produce dollar figures, both total and per benefit component, which would not represent either actual current or actual projected premiums and would thus serve only to confuse the subcommittee.

In our opinion, the subcommittee should view somewhat skeptically cost predictions stated in terms of dollars, since the dollar price projected will probably not reflect the actual price charged the policyholder if a Title II plan were to be implemented in a given state. Furthermore, as we have noted before, such dollar projections do not even attempt to account for factors such as inflation which will continue to place cost pressures on the system in the future. Consumers should not be led to believe that they will be charged a specific price for a national standards no-fault product when such price does not reflect what they will in fact be asked to pay. This is particularly true in view of the fact that any cost projection attempts to measure only the *average* change in cost in a given state. Thus, costs will vary widely within that state by rate classification and territory, and it would be impossible to identify the exact increase or decrease for any individual.

Accordingly, in our opinion, a percentage comparison reflects the only appropriate method of measuring the cost impact of going from a fault to a no-fault system such as that contemplated by S. 354, and even percentage estimates suffer from the infirmities applicable to all average cost estimates.

B. In the second portion of your first question, you ask for information with respect to the difference in cost between an unlimited medical benefit and a $50,000 medical benefit. The cost of the unlimited medical benefit feature is very difficult to identify. However, we are now beginning to acquire evidence which reveals that the cost of this benefit is much higher than we originally anticipated. The Department of Transportation Study indicated the difference in cost to be only approximately 0.1%, although one of the generally accepted serious data deficiencies of that Study was in the area of large losses. Notwithstanding those deficiencies we were forced to rely on the DOT Study data in costing the unlimited medical benefit because it was the only base available. We did make some slight upward adjustment in the DOT data, but the conservative nature of those adjustments is now becoming quite clear.

Experience is beginning to demonstrate that the DOT figure and our cost projections substantially understate the cost of the unlimited medical benefit component. Early experience from New Jersey and Michigan indicates that the very large losses are not as infrequent as originally anticipated. Accordingly, our judgment now is that the difference in price between an unlimited medical benefit and a $50,000 medical benefit could range from 5% to 10%. This cost impact would also obviously differ from state to state.

This estimate would appear to be verified by reinsurance cost experience in at least one state currently administering such benefits.

We have been advised that in Michigan the costs of reinsuring that portion of the medical benefit in excess of $50,000 have now reached approximately 6% of the first party premium and are continuing to trend upward. It is not unreasonable to assume that this upward trend could reach 10% in the not too distant future. Accordingly, in our opinion, the subcommittee should realistically view the unlimited medical benefit as causing a potential 10% increase in costs over a $50,000 medical benefit.

If this data is realistic, and we believe that it is, the committee should be aware of the fact that the Allstate costing is essentially too low and that prices will increase even more than we now predict. (As soon as the data on the unlimited medical benefit has developed for an adequate period of time, an appropriate change will be made in the Allstate costing model.)

(2) A. Again, the first part of your second question requests information which is essentially irrelevant to the subcommittee's inquiry into the cost impact of national no-fault proposals. Whether our pre-no-fault rate in a given state was adequate or not is unimportant because, as we indicated in our response to question 1, our model assumes the pre-existing rate to be adequate. To repeat, this is done to assure that our projections measure *only* the cost changes involved in going from a fault to a no-fault system and that such cost projections are not distorted by the adequacy or nonadequacy of the rate base in any given state. Accordingly, if we assume that our post national no-fault rates will be adequate, the percentage increase of the price actually charged the customer will in many states be much higher than the percentage increases contained in our costing because of present rate inadequacies.

B. In the second half of your second question you seek information with respect to our actual rate experience in certain no-fault states. We have displayed the requested data in the attached exhibit. You will note, for example, that in Florida Allstate's average bodily injury liability premiums have increased by 159% and that our rates for the first party benefits there have increased by 28%. If our most recent rate filing is approved in New Jersey, our bodily injury rates will have increased 60% and our first party rates there will have increased by 74%. Whether these rates are now adequate will not be known until we are able to analyze sufficiently developed data.

No-fault will not save money and indeed will cost substantially more unless substantial sums of money are saved on the bodily injury (tort system) component of the coverage. The attached exhibit clearly demonstrates that attempts to accomplish that end have not yet been successful.

The subcommittee should not cavalierly assume that it has the answer without awaiting and studying carefully the real world results of the variety of tort preclusion mechanisms now in effect in various states which attempt to reduce the cost of the bodily injury coverage.

(3) Your third question seeks information with respect to the utilization of medical benefits. While it would be possible to provide raw data with respect to the frequency and security of first party claims in no-fault states, such would not be of assistance to the committee unless related to some other benefit component in such a manner as to offer a reasonable means of comparison.

Accordingly, we have compared the frequency of utilization of the no-fault medical benefits under medical payments coverage which we sell in all states and which 75-80% of our policyholders purchase. We have compared the two benefit components on a "per 100 cars insured" basis to eliminate any distortion which might result from the fact that different percentages of policyholders carry mandated no-fault medical benefit coverages and voluntary medical payments coverage.

Accordingly, the following chart indicates the percentage increase or decrease in the number of incurred PIP claims [1] in the first year of no-fault as compared with the number of incurred claims under the medical payments coverage in the year immediately preceding implementation of no-fault insurance in the state in question.

State:	Percent increase or decrease
Colorado	+60
Connecticut	+54
Delaware	+0
Florida	+16
Hawaii	+108
Kansas	+30
Maryland	+40
Michigan	+21
Nevada	+0
New Jersey	+25
New York	+5
Oregon	−11
Utah	+33

The above data reveals that first party benefits in no-fault states with tort thresholds are being used more frequently than the benefits previously available under the similar medical payments coverage. In those states with "add-on" plans the frequency of first party PIP claims does not substantially exceed the frequency of "med pay" claims in the previous year, and in one instance the frequencies have actually decreased. However, in this context it is important to note that in the "add-on" states the first party benefits represent essentially an extension of medical payments benefits, and because they are not a part of a completely reformed system substantial changes in frequencies would not be anticipated. However, once a system has been completely reformed, such as S. 354 would require, and citizens are made aware of its operation, substantial increases in utilization can be expected.

While no-fault clearly creates an increase demand for first party medical benefits, increased utilization is not in and of itself a bad result. To the contrary, it is desirable, but the committee must bear in mind that such utilization comes at a substantial price.

That considerable price is increased even further when the element of "overutilization" is introduced. It is impossible to quantify the nature and extent of overutilization. Such determinations require an individual review of each claim file and a subjective judgment with respect to whether or not the medical benefits were in fact overused or abused. We have made such a review in Florida and have concluded that as many as 50% of all medical claimants overused the available benefits. We are in the process of conducting a similar review in New Jersey, and early indications are that the results will be as bad or worse there.

The danger of overutilization of an unlimited medical benefit, such as that provided in S. 354, is substantial. A claimant knows there is absolutely no limit on the amount of benefits available to him, and thus has no psychological incentive to use the benefits with care. The claimant's doctor has no reason to discourage his overutilization, and indeed has a direct financial incentive to encourage frequent medical visits or tests. This fact holds true for the entire health care industry. Similarly, the victim's lawyer has a financial interest in the victim's utilization of medical benefits, because such can be used to exceed a dollar threshold or to prove disability for the period of time required under the no-fault statute. Furthermore, if a statute allows tort actions in the event of "serious injury", chronic medical care and testing represent substantial evidence in the eyes of a jury making the requisite determination of seriousness.

(4) Your fourth question requests a variety of information with respect to various company expenses and also with respect to the economic benefits paid or payable to accident victims from all sources.

---

[1] We do not segregate data into each first party benefit component. However, we have been able to observe from experience that we process only a *de minimis* number of PIP claims that do not seek compensation for medical losses.

Some of the information you request we are unable to produce either because we simply do not have access to the data or because we do not maintain data in the manner which would be necessary to fully answer your questions.

You indicate that these questions are designed to assist the subcommittee in learning the actual impact of no-fault laws on how much money the insured is able to retain.

At the outset, we would like to refer you to a submission made to the subcommittee on Commerce and Finance by the National Association of Independent Insurers on August 1, 1974. As a part of that submission, which we helped to prepare, is an exhibit entitled Cost Benefit Ratios. This material was prepared in response to several questions raised by Congressman Eckhardt during no-fault hearings last year with respect to benefits to be retained by claimants. While the data contained in that exhibit is now completely out of date, we believe the accompanying explanatory statement would still be helpful in an analysis of cost/benefit ratios.

Turning again to your specific questions, we must emphasize that we made no assumption in our model with respect to consumer retention of benefits. Benefit retention, as you describe it, is a *result* of a system change and not an input. The answer you seek can be found only after a studied evaluation of the results of no-fault plans in actual operation.

Generally, however, it would appear that the consumer will benefit from an S. 354 type of no-fault system to the same extent that he benefits today.

Our overall operating expense is about 23.8% of premiums with approximately 8% going for agents' commissions and 3.6% for state premium taxes, licenses, and fees. The remaining 11.3% is used for the operation of the company—a very low amount in comparison to most other industries. Since we are budgeted for a 5.0% pre-tax profit in most states, this leaves 71.2 cents out of every premium dollar for the benefits of the claimant.

Since the materials that follow demonstrate that no substantial change is anticipated in our loss adjustment expenses, the claimant's ability to retain more benefits in cash is dependent on the amount of money a claimant pays to his lawyer.

Accordingly, it would appear that a reduction in the total amounts payable under the bodily injury liability portion of the coverage is essential if the total population of claimants is to receive more in the form of cash payments under the no-fault system.

As our testimony before the Senate Commerce Committee, our response to your second question and the materials that follow indicate, no no-fault plan currently in operation has measurably reduced total bodily injury liability payments. Thus, no clear path is now available to reach the goal you seek, more benefits, per premium dollar, for the policyholder.

Turning to your specific requests for data, we have attached loss ratio information for fourteen no-fault states. The data demonstrates loss ratios for the coverages affected by no-fault in the year preceding implementation of no-fault and for all subsequent years. The data would not, however, appear t be of much assistance to the committee in terms of formulating policy on national no-fault auto insurance. The data does demonstrate, however, that results differ substantially from state to state, and that the citizens of the various states react differently to auto insurance reform plans. This is particularly true in regard to the problem of the uninsured motorist. This would tend to verify the frequently argued point that a national solution is simply not appropriate when the problems at which it is aimed differ so radically from state to state.

With respect to your request for expense data, we have attached three exhibits. The first displays our acquisition and general expenses, our expenses for taxes, licenses, and fees, and our profit and contingency allowance.

The second represents an analysis of our allocated loss adjustment expenses. We have displayed data for the States of Florida and New Jersey and have also displayed countrywide data to offer a basis of comparison. For example, you will note that while our allocated legal expenses have declined in New Jersey and Florida, they have also declined to essentially the same extent countrywide. Consequently, the only firm conclusion which can be reached is that no-fault does not seem to have a major impact on this element of expense.

The third exhibit displays an analysis of our allocated and total loss adjustment expense.[2] You will note that while total loss adjustment expense as a percentage of the total incurred loss has decreased slightly in Florida and New Jersey, such

---

[2] The data displayed relates to all lines offered by Allstate Insurance Company. However, such should not affect the analysis, since automobile insurance coverages represent the vast bulk of our total book of business.

has also decreased countrywide. Again, no-fault does not appear to have any major impact on the loss adjustment expense factor.

We have also attached the requested data with respect to the frequency and severity of claims.

In our opinion, the important information to be learned from this data is that no-fault is not reducing total bodily injury liability payments. While frequencies have declined in those states with reform plans, severities have increased so substantially as to result in liability payments at least equal to, and in most instances greater than, those which prevailed under the old tort system.

With respect to your question regarding claimants' attorneys fees, we simply do not have access to the requested data. We merely pay the claimant a total sum, and he in turn compensates his attorney in accordance with whatever agreement they may have. Neither do we have any company data with respect to "economic loss not otherwise compensated" or the nature and extent of duplicate recoveries which result from benefits payable by other compensation sources.

The process of settling a bodily injury claim essentially precludes the acquisition of any specific data in this area. The process is essentially one of negotiation and lacks the kind of precision which would be necessary to provide adequate responses to your questions. Individuals who have attempted quantitative analysis in this area have been forced to work backward from a closed claim file in an attempt to break down the total payment into components reflecting various loss categories. Obviously, this is a difficult process, and because of the substantial amount of judgment involved the results produced are far from precise.

We are also without precise data in the area of "non-economic loss" payments. This is also attributable to the fact that a bodily injury settlement or judgment is not broken down into each category or component of loss. It is a well known fact that the level of non-economic loss benefits is relatable to the proven special damages or actual economic loss. However, some elements of economic loss may not have accrued by the date of settlement or may not have been included in the accounting of special damages. Thus, out of a total settlement or judgment, it is impossible to determine the exact amount of compensation for non-economic loss. Even after an exhaustive study identifying every element of actual economic loss, both past and future, it would be necessary to substract from the remaining sum the precise dollar figure representing compensation by a claimant to his lawyer.

DEVELOPMENT OF EXPECTED LOSS AND LOSS ADJUSTMENT RATIO
[In percent]

	Provision in premium		
	Liability	Collision	Compensation
Commission and brokerage	8.9	8.9	8.9
Other acquisition expense	7.3	7.3	7.3
General expense	4.0	4.0	4.0
Taxes, licenses, and fees [1]	3.6	3.5	3.5
Underwriting profit and contingencies	5.0	5.0	5.0
Subtotal			
Loss and loss adjustment			
Total	100.0	100.0	100.0

[1] State taxes—Does not include Federal income tax.

ALLOCATED EXPENSE ANALYSIS
[In percent]

	Florida		New Jersey		Countrywide	
	1971	1974	1971	1974	1971	1974
Investigative adjustment	0.1	0.2	0.3	0.1	0.4	0.5
Legal	74.0	65.0	57.0	53.0	69.0	62.0
Medical	.3	.6	10.0	12.0	.5	.6
Photo survey appraisal	0	.1	.2	.2	.1	.2
Depositions	.9	10.0	.4	.5	.6	.7
Court reporting	.1	.1	.2	.3	.1	.2
Witnesses	.5	.4	.3	.3	.2	.2
Jury fees/court cost	.2	.2	.6	.4	.4	.5
Confidential investigation	.1	.2	.3	.1	.2	.2
Other	.3	.7	10.0	16.0	.5	.7
Total	100.0	100.0	100.0	100.0	100.0	100.0

ANALYSIS OF LOSS ADJUSTMENT EXPENSE

	Allocated LAE	Total LAE	Pg. 14 earned premium	Percent Allocation	LAE	Pg. 14 incurred loss	Percent Allocation	LAE
Countrywide:								
1971	34,964,447	168,933,958	1,750,087,882	2.0	9.7	1,114,090,609	3.1	15.2
1974	35,048,705	208,370,980	2,286,299,327	1.5	9.1	1,534,774,993	2.3	13.6
Florida:								
1971	2,700,902	9,282,191	94,939,487	2.8	9.8	65,242,823	4.1	14.2
1974	2,796,015	12,213,070	137,837,838	2.0	8.9	101,492,477	2.8	12.0
New Jersey:								
1971	2,258,525	11,890,846	129,754,462	1.7	9.2	87,233,344	2.6	13.6
1974	2,424,253	15,500,062	154,760,106	1.6	10.0	123,139,705	2.0	12.6

RATE ACTIVITY SUMMARY—VOLUNTARY RATE CHANGES

	BI	PD	PIP	VM	MOD	Collision	Compensation	Total
Florida:								
November 1973	+33	+33	+15	+57	−60	+05	−15	+15
January 1975	+38	+17	+11	+15	−15	+10	−11	+18
August 1975	+41	+03	0	+19	−05	+14	+31	+20
Connecticut:								
February 1975	+10	+15	0	+0	0	+18	+25	+12.5
Filed	+10	+05	+05	+38	0	+10	+05	+08
New Jersey:								
November 1974	+16	+12	+16	0	0	0	0	09.5
Filed	+38	0	+50	50	0	+28	+03	+25
Maryland: April 1975	+29	+20	0	0	0	−06	−13	+11
Oregon: April 1975	+03	+16	+30	0	0	+30	−10	+12

FREQUENCY AND SEVERITY DATA
COLORADO
VOLUNTARY PRIVATE PASSENGER AUTO, NO-FAULT EXPERIENCE

	Paid at— 15 mo.	Paid at— 27 mo.	Incurred at 15 mo.	Incurred at 27 mo.	Paid at (percent) 15 mo.	Paid at (percent) 27 mo.	Incurred at (percent) 15 mo.	Incurred at (percent) 27 mo.
BI:								
1973	$838	$1,613	$2,993	$3,049	0.7	0.8	1.0	1.0
1974	1,389		6,566		.3		.4	
PIP: 1974	759		978		1.3		1.6	
MED:								
1973	522	518	552	529	.8	.9	1.0	.9
1974	518		551		.3		.3	
UM:								
1973	1,486	2,085	2,402	2,505	.1	.1	.1	.1
1974	1,283		1,848		.1		.1	
XPIP: 1974	0		2,232		0		.4	

Note: All losses adjusted to include unallocated loss adjustment expenses.

CONNECTICUT

	Paid at— 15 mo	Paid at— 27 mo	Paid at— 39 mo	Incurred at— 15 mo	Incurred at— 27 mo	Incurred at— 39 mo	Paid at (percent)— 15 mo	Paid at (percent)— 27 mo	Paid at (percent)— 39 mo	Incurred at (percent) 15 mo	Incurred at (percent) 27 mo	Incurred at (percent) 39 mo
BI:												
1972	$459	$1,084	$1,570	$2,324	$2,498	$2,475	1.3	1.6	1.7	1.9	2.0	2.0
1973	1,500	3,787		8,471	8,050		.2	.3		.5	.6	
1974	1,889			9,311			.2			.5		
PIP:												
1973	522	540		604	573		1.8	2.0		2.0	2.0	
1974	698			743			1.6			1.9		
MED:												
1972	404	475	498	451	498	506	1.1	1.3	1.3	1.3	1.3	1.3
1973												
1974												
UM:												
1972	783	1,489	1,924	1,781	2,367	2,221	.1	.1	.1	.2	.2	.2
1973	2,500	3,075		2,920	4,558		.02	.04		.04	.04	
1974	3,585			6,529			.01			.04		
XPIP:												
1973	0	0		0	16,436		0	0		0	.04	
1974	2,565			5,860			.02			.04		

ALLSTATE INSURANCE CO. NO FAULT EXPERIENCE—VOLUNTARY PRIVATE PASSENGER AUTOMOBILE

DELAWARE, EFFECTIVE JANUARY 1972

Calendar accounting year	Paid severity				Incurred severity				Paid frequency				Incurred frequency			
	15 mo	27 mo	39 mo	51 mo	15 mo	27 mo	39 mo	51 mo	15 mo	27 mo	39 mo	51 mo	15 mo	27 mo	39 mo	51 mo
BI:																
1971	527	845	1,694	2,208	1,859	2,486	2,347	2,428	1.1	1.2	1.3	1.4	1.4	1.4	1.4	1.4
1972	495	898	2,151		3,208	3,521	3,283		.8	.9	1.0		1.1	1.1	1.1	
1973	253	1,869			3,142	3,188			.6	.7			.9	.9		
1974	278				2,554				.5				.8			
PIP:																
1971																
1972	716	557	499		1,021	606	553		.8	1.0	1.0		1.1	1.0	1.0	
1973	867	758			1,229	886			.9	1.0			1.1	1.1		
1974	1,094				1,226				.7				1.0			
MED:																
1971	387	399	404	401	416	422	420	401	.7	.9	.9	.9	1.0	.9	.9	.9
1972	251	272	706		354	352	727		.1	.1	.1		.2	.2	.2	
1973	225	494			345	494			.0	.1			.2	.1		
1974	1,289				1,289				.0				.0			
UM:																
1971	870	897	1,178	1,355	1,386	1,389	1,194	1,355	.1	.1	.1	.1	.1	.1	.1	.1
1972	838	1,020	1,062		1,637	1,344	1,062		.1	.1	.1		.1	.1	.1	
1973	820	729			790	729			.1	.1			.1	.1		
1974	289				1,506				.0				.1			
BI:																
1971	1,137	1,992	2,349	2,574	2,385	2,644	2,693	2,713	1.4	1.8	1.9	1.9	2.0	1.9	1.9	2.0
1972	2,347	4,487	5,728		6,487	6,352	6,553		.3	.5	.6		.7	.7	.7	
1973	2,732	5,934			8,156	8,190			.3	.6			.7	.7		
1974	3,683				8,704				.3				.6			
PIP:																
1971	0	0	0	0	0	0	0	0	.0	.0	.0	0	.0	.0	.0	0
1972	726	684	672		832	720	680		1.7	2.1	2.1		2.2	2.1	2.1	
1973	812	803			942	836			1.7	2.1			2.1	2.1		
1974	942				977				1.5				1.9			
MED:																
1971	548	589	595	597	546	599	598	598	1.5	1.9	1.9	1.9	1.9	1.9	1.9	1.9
1972	1,099	1,123	1,125		1,014	1,129	1,127		.1	.1	.1		.1	.2	.2	
1973	1,542	1,465			1,351	1,460			.1	.1			.1	.2		
1974	1,718				1,441				.1				.1			
UM:																
1971	1,331	2,118	2,286	2,361	2,525	2,468	2,388	2,393	.3	.4	.4	.4	.4	.4	.4	.4
1972	1,715	2,823	3,548		3,615	3,809	3,819		.1	.2	.2		.2	.2	.2	
1973	2,059	4,484			4,780	6,284			.1	.2			.2	.2		
1974	4,057				7,706				.1				.2			

444

BI: 1971				3,470	4,793	3,660	3,517	1.1	1.3	1.5	1.6	1.6
1972	997	1,882	2,780	6,046	4,538	4,247		.7	1.0	1.1	1.2	1.2	1.6
1973	1,066	2,254	3,131	4,378	4,128			.7	1.2		1.3	1.4
1974	873	2,490	2,978	5,161							.9		
PIP: 1971	1,456												
1972													
1973													
1974				1,283				1.6			2.5		
MED: 1971	921												1.3
1972	475	471	481	486	478	485	500	.1	1.3	1.3	1.4	1.3	1.3
1973	339	376	396	445	380	396		.8	1.1		1.2	1.1	1.1
1974	346	425	494	444	439			.9	1.1		1.2		
UM: 1971	539			583				0.5			.6		.2
1972	1,217	1,838	1,987	2,558	2,436	2,299	2,209	.2	.2	.2	.2	.2	.2
1973	468	1,161	1,593	2,832	2,250	2,259		.2	.2	.2	.2	.2
1974	1,019	1,871		2,876	2,022			.2	.2		.2		
	2,263			2,668				.1			.1		
BI: 1971													
1972	700	1,171		2,871	2,072			1.0	1.1		1.2	1.2	
1973	1,364			5,561				.3			.5		
1974													
PIP: 1971													
1972													
1973				653				1.1			1.3		
1974	573												
MED: 1971													
1972	470	489		493	495			.9	1.0		1.0	1.0	
1973	1,078			951				.1			.1		
1974													
UM: 1971													
1972													
1973	1,235	1,412		1,793	1,435			.1	.1		.1	.1	
1974	326			5,314				0			0		

MARYLAND, EFFECTIVE JANUARY 1973

BI: 1971											
1972	931	1,490		2,294	2,213	2,211		1.8	2.1	2.2	2.2	2.2
1973	966	1,587	1,828	2,889	2,579			1.6	1.9	2.2	2.1	2.1	2.3
1974	978			3,263				1.4			1.8		

ALLSTATE INSURANCE CO. NO FAULT EXPERIENCE—VOLUMTARY PRIVATE PASSENGER AUTOMOBILE

Calendar accounting year	Paid severity 15 mo	27 mo	39 mo	51 mo	Incurred severity 15 mo	27 mo	39 mo	51 mo	Paid frequency 15 mo	27 mo	39 mo	51 mo	Incurred frequency 15 mo	27 mo	39 mo	51 mo

MARYLAND EFFECTIVE JANUARY 1973—Continued

PIP:
1971																
1972																
1973	891	903			1,087	923			.9	1.4			1.4	1.4		
1974	840				1,093				.1				1.3			

MED:
1971																
1972	455	528	544		467	532	549		.8	1.2	1.2		.9	1.2	1.2	
1973	589	658			593	660			.1	.9			.1	.9		
1974	2,312				2,136											

UM:
1971																
1972	606	1,695	1,805		2,805	3,073	2,461		0	0	0		0	0	0	
1973	649	1,537			1,801	2,220			.0	.1			.1	.1		
1974	1,402				2,408				.1				.1			

MICHIGAN, EFFECTIVE OCTOBER 1973

BI:
1971	955	1,591	2,035	2,355	2,356	2,803	2,908	2,903	1.1	1.4	1.5		1.7	1.7	1.7	
1972	878	1,613	2,098		3,003	2,966	3,064		.8	.9			1.2	1.2		
1973	1,153	1,820			3,682	3,706			.1				1.2			
1974	3,669				18,163											

PIP:
1971																
1972																
1973	0	0			0	0			0	0			0	0		
1974	935				1,329				1.4				1.7			

MED:
1971	413	457	485	492	450	491	506	508	1.	1.2	1.2	1.2	1.4	1.3	1.3	
1972	391	449	470		481	495	498		.8	.9			1.0	1.0		
1973	499	553			566	586										
1974	957				1,041											

UM:
1971	1,254	2,087	2,802	2,910	3,207	3,083	2,980	3,090	.1	.2	.2	.2	.2	.3	.3	
1972	841	1,839	2,492		2,586	3,238	3,101		.1	.1			.2	.2		
1973	949	2,089			3,199	3,657			.0				0			
1974	1,436				3,383											

NEVADA
VOLUNTARY PRIVATE PASSENGER AUTO, NO FAULT EXPERIENCE

	Severity				Paid at (percent)—		Incurred at (percent)—	
	Paid at—		Incurred					
	15 mo	27 mo	15 mo	27 mo	15 mo	27 mo	15 mo	27 mo
BI:								
1973	$1,366	$2,171	$3,769	$3,094	1.0	1.3	1.4	1.4
1974	2,374		5,357		.4		.7	
PIP: 1974	1,504		1,415		1.2		1.7	
MED:								
1973	656	681	672	687	1.4	1.7	1.8	1.7
1974	611		670		.3		.3	
UM:								
1973	1,010	1,420	1,841	1,783	.3	.3	.4	.4
1974	2,266		4,275		0		.1	
XPIP: 1974	12,034		9,111		.1		.2	

Note: All losses loaded for unallocated loss adjustment expenses.

NEW JERSEY
VOLUNTARY PRIVATE PASSENGER AUTO NO FAULT EXPERIENCE

	Severity											
	Paid at—			Incurred at—			Paid at (percent—			Incurred at (percent)		
	15 mo	27 mo	39 mo	15 m	27 mo	39 mo	15 mo	27 mo	39 mo	15 mo	27 mo	39 mo
BI:												
1972	$517	$1,270	$2,162	$2,617	$2,806	$2,828	1.5	1.9	2.2	2.3	2.4	2.4
1973	465	1,807		3,822	4,052		.8	1.2		1.4	1.5	
1974	751			4,767			.7			1.2		
PIP:												
1973	761	814		890	945		1.7	2.2		2.5	2.3	
1974	834			1,094			1.6			2.2		
MED:												
1972	406	480	500	486	519	509	1.5	1.9	1.9	2.0	1.9	2.0
1973												
1974												
UM:												
1972	818	1,540	1,922	1,852	2,172	2,129	.1	.2	.2	.2	.2	.2
1973	862	1,991		2,031	2,761		.05	.1		.1	.1	
1974	811			2,345			.1			.1		
XPIP:												
1973	2,963	2,532		3,110	6,909		.2	.3		.5	.4	
1974	1,393			3,472			.3			.6		

Note: Losses include all loss adjustment expenses.

NEW YORK
VOLUNTARY PRIVATE PASSENGER AUTO NO FAULT EXPERIENCE

	Severity				Paid at (percent)—		Incurred at (percent)—	
	Paid at—		Incurred					
	15 mo	27 mo	15 mo	27 mo	15 mo	27 mo	15 mo	27 mo
BI:								
1973	$453	$996	$2,675	$2,784	1.6	2.1	2.7	2.8
1974	419		4,087		.9		1.5	
PIP:								
1973								
1974	962		1,163		1.5		2.2	
MED:								
1973	435	478	526	533	1.5	1.9	2.1	2.0
1974	633		720		.2		.2	
UM:								
1973	907	1,866	2,203	2,447	0	.1	.1	.1
1974	761		2,601		0		0	
XPIP:								
1973								
1974	1,762		1,964		.1		.2	

Note: Losses include all loss adjustment expenses.

ALLSTATE INSURANCE CO., NO FAULT EXPERIENCE, VOLUNTARY PRIVATE PASSENGER AUTOMOBILE

OREGON, EFFECTIVE JANUARY 1972

Calendar accounting year	Paid severity				Incurred severity				Paid frequency				Incurred frequency			
	15 mo	27 mo	39 mo	51 mo	15 mo	27 mo	39 mo	51 mo	15 mo	27 mo	39 mo	51 mo	15 mo	27 mo	39 mo	51 mo
BI:																
1971	657	1,301	1,749	1,897	2,193	1,946	1,912	2,008	1.2	1.4	1.4	1.4	1.5	1.5	1.5	1.5
1972	984	1,731	2,046		2,151	2,227	2,268		1.1	1.3	1.3		1.3	1.3	1.3	
1973	792	1,433			2,093	2,057			1.0	1.2			1.2	1.3		
1974	1,127				2,623				.8				1.1			
PIP:																
1971	678	605	571		700	623	571		1.2	1.5	1.5		1.6	1.5	1.5	
1972	741	618			769	642			1.1	1.4			1.5	1.4		
1973									1.0				1.4			
1974	1,038				1,031											
MED:																
1971	526	498	503	504	528	501	503	504	1.4	1.8	1.8	1.8	1.8	1.8	1.8	1.8
1972	470	460	462		498	462	462		1.6	1.7	1.7		1.7	1.7	1.7	
1973	2,499	2,558			1,604	2,558			0	0			0	0		
1974	361				386				0				0			
UM:																
1971	680	1,262	1,438	1,427	1,646	1,469	1,476	1,427	.1	.1	.2	.2	.1	.2	.2	.2
1972	1,044	1,477	1,520		1,775	1,491	1,565		.1	.2	.2		.2	.2	.2	
1973	878	1,124			1,411	1,191			.1	.2			.2			
1974	589				1,179				.1				.2			
BI:																
1971	1,106	1,536	1,720	1,809	1,720	1,870	1,844	1,838	0.8	0.9			0.9	1.0		
1972	825	1,754	2,054		3,033	2,758	2,586		.4				.4			
1973	1,185	1,769			2,384	2,652										
1974	1,023				5,310											
PIP:																
1971																
1972																
1973																
1974	721				1,001				1.0				1.2			
MED:																
1971	400	440	449	454	410	442	449	454	.8	.9			.9			
1972	370	443	447		399	446	447		.1				.1			
1973	500	526			515	529										
1974	263				340											
UM:																
1971	526	860	1,312	1,274	1,016	1,397	1,312	1,274	0	.1	.1		.1	.1		
1972	1,230	2,351	3,219		2,966	2,934	3,303		0				0			
1973	533	716			968	716										
1974	381				1,521											

LOSS RATIO DATA

COLORADO VOLUNTARY PRIVATE PASSENGER AUTO NO-FAULT EXPERIENCE

Accident year	Earned premium	Loss ratios at (percent) 15 mo	27 mo
BI:			
1973	$4,200,259	67.7	68.4
1974	3,193,329	90.7	
PIP: 1974	2,011,591	60.4	
MED:			
1973	729,519	58.7	52.9
1974	222,397	36.4	
UM:			
1973	381,166	75.6	77.5
1974	340,361	57.0	
XPIP: 1974	3,587	62.2	
Total:			
1973	5,310,944	67.0	66.9
1974	5,771,265	76.0	

Note: All losses adjusted to include unallocated loss adjustment expenses.

CONNECTICUT VOLUNTARY PRIVATE PASSENGER AUTO NO FAULT EXPERIENCE

Accident year	Earned premium	Loss ratios at (percent) 15 months	27 months	39 months
BI:				
1972	$9,726,084	52.8	58.5	59.7
1973	7,923,471	69.8	72.0	
1974	8,174,646	68.6		
PIP:				
1973	2,615,289	57.6	54.2	
1974	2,703,794	67.6		
MED:				
1972	1,188,110	46.4	50.0	50.9
1973				
1974				
UM:				
1972	503,485	63.3	84.6	83.4
1973	331,423	41.4	75.6	
1974	342,982	89.5		
XPIP:				
1973	33,766	0	48.7	
1974	60,938	19.2		
Total:				
1972	11,417,679	52.6	58.8	59.8
1973	10,903,949	65.8	67.8	
1974	11,282,360	68.8		

Note: Losses include all loss adjustment expenses.

ALLSTATE INSURANCE CO., NO FAULT EXPERIENCE VOLUNTARY PRIVATE PASSENGER AUTOMOBILE DELAWARE EFFECTIVE JANUARY 1972

Calendar/accident year	Earned premium at 12 mos	15 mo	27 mo	39 mo	51 mo,
BI:					
1971	723,347	73.9	97.6	94.1	97.7
1972	802,927	96.3	104.8	99.4	
1973	845,690	75.1	76.2		
1974	912,282	57.4			
PIP:					
1971					
1972	256,519	88.0	50.3	45.9	
1973	267,663	116.1	82.4		
1974	279,689	107.9			
MED:					
1971	132,095	58.0	54.3	53.5	51.0
1972	93,654	11.7	12.0	24.8	
1973	55,381	7.5	9.8		
1974	36,299	21.3			
JM:					
1971	75,350	47.8	47.9	41.2	45.0
1972	67,651	43.5	37.8	29.8	
1973	47,080	33.6	34.1		
1974	26,880	84.0			
Total:					
1971	930,792	69.5	87.4	84.0	86.8
1972	1,220,751	85.1	82.5	78.6	
1973	1,215,814	79.4	72.9		
1974	1,265,150	68.5			

FLORIDA, EFFECTIVE JANUARY 1972

BI:					
1971	24,756,628	73.3	80.7	82.3	83.0
1972	18,477,372	102.5	103.7	108.0	
1973	19,519,185	137.2	140.3		
1974	22,162,808	120.4			
PIP:					
1971	0	0	0	0	0
1972	9,506,686	82.4	70.5	66.6	
1973	10,461,490	91.7	81.7		
1974	11,430,783	81.1			
MED:					
1971	4,420,939	80.7	86.5	86.1	86.4
1972	3,886,598	15.5	16.8	16.6	
1973	4,237,853	19.4	21.7		
1974	3,276,239	26.8			
JM:					
1971	2,575,996	144.6	142.3	138.2	139 2
1972	2,069,044	131.2	142.3	149.0	
1973	2,358,643	163.9	232.6		
1974	5,130,497	125.7			
Total:					
1971	31,753,536	80.1	86.5	87.4	88.1
1972	33,939,664	88.7	86.8	88.5	
1973	36,577,152	112.3	115.7		
1974	42,000,288	103.0			

HAWAII, EFFECTIVE SEPTEMBER 1974

BI:					
1971	2,045,259	77.2	107.6	82.9	79.3
1972	2,578,978	95.2	70.6	66.5	
1973	3,241,476	65.9	62.3		
1974	2,884,188	61.2			
PIP:					
1971					
1972					
1973					
1974	630 520	70.2			
MED:					
1971	309,284	54.5	51.1	51.8	53.3
1972	372,442	44.3	33.9	35.6	
1973	362,744	48.7	42.8		
1974	239,907	40.6			

HAWAII, EFFECTIVE SEPTEMBER 1974—Continued

Calendar/accident year	Earned premium at 12 mos	15 mo	27 mo	39 mo	51 mo
UM:					
1971	104,306	159.4	154.1	147.7	141.9
1972	126,081	177.4	141.0	141.5	
1973	158,280	156.3	108.6		
1974	158,774	70.6			
Total:					
1971	2,458,849	77.8	102.4	81.7	78.7
1972	3,077,501	92.4	69.0	65.9	
1973	3,762,500	68.0	62.3		
1974	3,913,389	61.8			

KANSAS, EFFECTIVE JANUARY 1974

BI:					
1971					
1972					
1973	1,996,530	84.7	61.6		
1974	1,485,397	98.5			
PIP:					
1971					
1972					
1973					
1974	620,257	72.5			
MED:					
1971					
1972					
1973	390,295	52.7	53.2		
1974	89,727	67.8			
UM:					
1971					
1972					
1973	99,856	102.4	81.9		
1974	53,787	148.2			
Total:					
1971					
1972					
1973	2,486,681	80.4	61.1		
1974	2,249,168	91.3			

MARYLAND, EFFECTIVE JANUARY 1973

BI:					
1971					
1972	9,977,335	76.5	74.6	75.0	
1973	10,418,708	90.0	81.7		
1974	10,618,113	91.0			
PIP:					
1971					
1972					
1973	2,081,613	60.1	52.7		
1974	4,001,715	60.1			
MED:					
1971					
1972	1,283,666	50.3	64.8	68.2	
1973	727,370	53.4	64.1		
1974	171,581	31.1			
UM:					
1971					
1972	277,922	37.3	45.3	37.2	
1973	445,110	38.0	54.4		
1974	600,010	70.2			
Total:					
1971					
1972	11,538,923	72.7	72.8	73.3	
1973	13,672,801	81.8	75.5		
1974	15,391,419	81.5			

MASSACHUSETTS VOLUNTARY PRIVATE PASSENGER AUTO NO-FAULT EXPERIENCE

Accident year	Earned premium	Loss ratios at (percent)—				
		15 mo	27 mo	39 mo	51 mo	61 mo
BI+PIP:						
1970	$6,342,302	69.7	82.3	83.1	76.0	75.4
1971	6,052,887	42.6	54.1	49.1	47.7	
1972	5,820,222	75.3	59.1	56.5		
1973	6,556,120	71.4	64.2			
1974	7,832,599	76.5				
MED:						
1970	507,224	70.1	78.5	81.1	82.0	81.8
1971	454,814	17.7	26.0	27.3	27.5	
1972	365,323	19.1	29.6	28.9		
1973	300,995	31.1	43.1			
1974	293,956	70.6				
UM:						
1970	132,162	41.2	61.8	65.2	67.0	64.1
1971	236,411	14.7	12.3	14.9	16.4	
1972	1,192,046	22.1	24.0	21.0		
1973	195,556	42.9	89.4			
1974	184,352	44.4				
Total:						
1970	6,981,688	69.2	81.6	82.6	76.3	75.7
1971	6,744,112	39.9	50.7	46.4	45.2	
1972	6,377,591	70.5	56.4	53.9		
1973	7,052,671	68.9	64.0			
1974	8,310,907	75.6				

Note: All losses loaded for unallocated loss adjustment expenses.

ALLSTATE INSURANCE CO., NO FAULT EXPERIENCE, VOLUNTARY PRIVATE PASSENGER AUTOMOBILE MICHIGAN, EFFECTIVE OCTOBER 1973

Calendar/accident year	Earned premium at 12 mo	Loss ratios			
		15 mo	27 mo	39 mo	51 mo
BI:					
1971					
1972	18,903,337	86.1	85.9	88.6	
1973	18,432,942	77.4	75.6		
1974	12,666,571	93.8			
PIP:					
1971					
1972					
1973	3,862,110	0			
1974	16,822,533	45.5			
MED:					
1971					
1972	2,680,777	62.9	60.3	60.1	
1973	2,161,530	53.4	51.8		
1974	0	0			
UM:					
1971					
1972	1,664,751	120.2	155.0	154.2	
1973	1,766,031	100.5	117.0		
1974	985,325	51.2			
Total:					
1971					
1972	23,248,832	85.9	87.9	90.0	
1973	26,222,560	65.6	65.3		
1974	30,474,400	65.8			

NEVADA VOLUNTARY PRIVATE PASSENGER AUTO NO FAULT EXPERIENCE

Accident year	Earned premium	Loss ratios at (percent) 15 mos	27 mos
BI:			
1973	$1,649,658	93.4	76.3
1974	1,418,362	91.0	
PIP: 1974	895,762	83.7	
MED:			
1973	387,802	70.9	70.3
1974	59,348	53.0	
UM:			
1973	157,372	124.0	119.0
1974	96,761	141.4	
XPIP: 1974	9,402	193.8	
Total:			
1973	2,194,832	91.6	78.8
1974	2,479,635	89.8	

Note: All losses loaded for unallocated loss adjustment expense.

NEW JERSEY VOLUNTARY PRIVATE PASSENGER AUTO NO FAULT EXPERIENCE

Accident year	Earned premium	Loss ratios at (percent) 15 mo	27 mo	39 mo
BI:				
1972	$41,957,600	76.0	83.1	84.1
1973	31,863,395	96.3	105.1	
1974	33,308,888	98.7		
PIP:				
1973	9,681,447	127.3	124.9	
1974	9,874,864	140.6		
MED:				
1972	6,364,801	66.8	68.4	67.8
1973				
1974				
UM:				
1972	2,566,258	67.5	85.6	84.4
1973	1,100,231	81.6	119.5	
1974	1,146,303	100.4		
XPIP:				
1973	164,416	90.8	163.9	
1974	242,510	117.4		
Total:				
1972	50,888,659	74.4	81.4	82.1
1973	42,809,489	102.9	110.2	
1974	44,572,565	108.1		

Note: Losses include all loss adjustment expenses.

NEW YORK VOLUNTARY PRIVATE PASSENGER AUTO NO-FAULT EXPERIENCE

Accident year	Earned premium	Loss ratios at (percent) 15 mos	27 mo
BI:			
1973	$87,202,480	69.0	74.9
1974	55,903,364	92.3	
PIP:			
1973			
1974	25,115,738	81.1	
MED:			
1973	7,137,881	88.2	86.1
1974	1,547,156	54.8	
UM:			
1973	3,376,409	48.8	57.6
1974	2,600,877	63.4	
XPIP:			
1973			
1974	1,670,252	54.0	
Total:			
1973	97,716,770	69.7	75.1
1974	86,837,387	86.0	

Note: Losses include all loss adjustment expenses.

ALLSTATE INSURANCE CO., NO FAULT EXPERIENCE, VOLUNTARY PRIVATE PASSENGER AUTOMOBILE
OREGON, EFFECTIVE JANUARY 1972

Calendar/accident year	Earned premium at 12 mo	Loss ratios			
		15 mo	27 mo	39 mo	51 mo
BI:					
1971	4,594,685	74.6	66.0	64.5	67.6
1972	4,945,491	64.4	66.9	68.0	
1973	5,280,249	58.4	57.9		
1974	5,454,859	64.0			
PIP:					
1971					
1972	736,999	92.9	78.0	71.3	
1973	1,448,530	93.7	74.4		
1974	1,820,008	96.8			
MED:					
1971	1,152,823	75.3	69.6	70.2	70.3
1972	596,616	62.7	57.4	57.3	
1973	0	0	0		
1974	0	0			
UM:					
1971	389,563	66.8	61.5	62.1	59.7
1972	409,742	79.3	66.6	70.3	
1973	432,719	63.2	53.7		
1974	448,309	55.7			
Total:					
1971	6,137,071	74.2	66.4	65.4	67.6
1972	6,688,848	68.3	67.3	67.6	
1973	7,161,498	65.9	61.0		
1974	7,723,176	71.3			

UTAH, EFFECTIVE JANUARY 1974

BI:					
1971					
1972					
1973	1,485,175	56.7	64.1		
1974	1,365,040	66.1			
PIP:					
1971					
1972					
1973					
1974	693,627	63.7			
MED:					
1971					
1972					
1973	251,309	58.2	59.5		
1974	36,917	11.1			
UM:					
1971					
1972					
1973	97,438	20.9	16.2		
1974	85,062	12.5			
Total:					
1971					
1972					
1973	1,833,922	55.0	60.9		
1974	2,180,646	65.5			

NO-FAULT MOTOR VEHICLE INSURANCE

MONDAY, JULY 14, 1975

House of Representatives,
Subcommittee on Consumer Protection and Finance,
Committee on Interstate and Foreign Commerce,
Daytona Beach, Fla.

The subcommittee met at 9 a.m., pursuant to notice, in the Quality Inn Reef Motel, Daytona Beach, Fla., Hon. Lionel Van Deerlin, chairman, presiding.

Mr. Van Deerlin. The hearing will come to order.

This is a continuation of hearings begun recently in Washington on several bills dealing with no-fault automobile insurance. Because Florida was one of the earliest States to enact a no-fault auto law, the committee has come into the field to see how that law has been working and to get the views of both public and private citizens in this State as to the desirability of no-fault insurance.

On the panel is our ranking minority member, Mr. McCollister of Nebraska, who disappoints us only in that he seeks to go into the U.S. Senate next year, giving up his happy life in the House; Ms. Nord, minority counsel, and Congressman Metcalfe from Illinois, a very able legislator whom we all first saw in 1932 when he was the No. 1 sprinter on America's Olympic track team out of Los Angeles. On his right is Congressman Jim Scheuer from New York who represents a Long Island district.

Mr. Scheuer. New York City, I am a New York City harmonica champion.

Mr. Van Deerlin. Also next to me is Mr. Kinzler, our subcommittee counsel.

Our first witness this morning is Mr. William G. McCue, Jr., director, division of insurance company regulation, office of treasurer, State of Florida.

You may proceed, Mr. McCue.

STATEMENT OF WILLIAM G. McCUE, JR., DIRECTOR, DIVISION OF INSURANCE COMPANY REGULATION, OFFICE OF TREASURER, STATE OF FLORIDA

Mr. McCue. Mr. Chairman and members of the committee, it is a pleasure to be here today representing Insurance Commissioner Phil Ashler. The purpose of my statement this morning is to provide the Florida Insurance Department's views on the effectiveness of the no-fault law in Florida, its deficiencies and suggested remedies to correct deficiencies.

EFFECTIVENESS

What have been the results of no-fault in the State of Florida up until now? Let's look at some of the reports. Dr. Joseph Little, law professor at the University of Florida, reports in the September 1973, edition of the American Bar Association Journal, the following information, and I quote:

> The indications of a study in Florida of that State's no-fault automobile accident reparations statute, while fragmentary and tentative, are that the system is fulfilling some of its advocates' predictions and promises. But the hard cases and the important interpretative decisions are yet to be made. Whether true reform has occurred must be determined later.
>
> Among the expected social gains are quicker payments and settlements of personal injury claims, more equitable distribution of benefits according to actual losses sustained, and lower costs of insurance because of simplified claims processing and the elimination of noneconomic losses from recoveries. Small claimants should be paid quickly in the exact amount of verified losses with no compensation for pain and suffering allowed, while more severely injured claimants, being sustained by P.I.P. payments, should be better able to resist hasty settlement and thereby gain a total recovery more closely approximating actual losses. A secondary expected benefit is the freeing up of court dockets for other litigation.
>
> One expected consequence of no-fault would be a redistribution of the types of claims filed. The number of tort claims should drop, and the number of first party claims—P.I.P. under no-fault—should increase.
>
> What do the data show to be happening? Statistics in table 1 suggest that the anticipated redistribution has occurred in the exhaustive sample as of the end of 1972.

TABLE 1

Claims distributions, exhaustive cases sample

Type claim:	
Tort:	
1971 (percent)	46.5
1972 (percent)	5
Medical payments:	
1971 (percent)	53.5
1972 (percent)	-----
P.I.P.:	
1971 (percent)	-----
1972 (percent)	95
Number of cases:	
1971	185
1972	148

Dr. Little further reports and, again, I quote:

> Turning now to more readily measurable parameters, it can be reported that no-fault is apparently haveng some of the desired effects on claims processing. For example, the time delay between the crash and the initial receipt of a benefit payment has been shortened in P.I.P. claims as compared to tort claims and medical payments claims.

TABLE 5.—AMOUNT OF TIME TAKEN TO RECEIVE 1ST PAYMENT AND TO SETTLE CLAIMS
MAJOR CLAIMS SAMPLE

	1971 tort	1971 medical payments	1972 tort	1972 PIP
Time to 1st payment (days)	93 (119/90)	47 (75/75)	-----	32 (44/52)
Time to settle (days)	119 (139/95)	83 (119/94)	-----	78 (105/78)

Dr. Little summarizes his report as follows:

In summary, the hard data that are now available suggest that no-fault is producing some of the promised results, but it is too early to pass final judgement. For one thing, it remains to be seen how easy it will be to work the system to clear claims over the tort exemption thresholds. If lawyers and claimants inflate a large proportion of claims to get over the $1,000 threshold, then the system might prove counterproductive. Not only would exceeding the tort threshold reopen non-economic losses, but it also might represent a misuse of medical resources. American Bar Association Journal, Volume 59, September, 1973, "How No Fault Is Working In Florida," Pages 1020-1023.

I would like to point out that the statistics on file with the Florida Insurance Department also indicate that there has been a clear redistribution of claims under no-fault.

What has the average citizen's reaction to no-fault been?

The Florida Association of Insurance Agents conducted a survey of 1,108 members. The results of this survey were contained in Bulletin No. 17, volume XXII, Tuesday p.m., February 20, 1973:

(1) Which system:
Better serves public? No-fault 662 (96 percent); old system 26 (4 percent).
Does public prefer: No-fault 570 (91 percent); old system 54 (9 percent).
Do companies perform better under? No-fault 584 (92 percent); old system 50 (8 percent).
(2) Has no-fault altered public attitude toward insurance? No 207 (33 percent); yes 425 (67 percent).
If so, how: Favorably 381 (93 percent); unfavorably 28 (7 percent).
(4) Are your policyholders satisfied with:
Speed of payments: Yes 553 (80 percent); no 137 (20 percent).
Benefit levels: Yes 635 (95 percent); no 35 (5 percent).

I would also like to point out that through the Insurance Department's 21 service offices located in key areas throughout the State of Florida, reports indicate that the average man on the street has been pleased with the workings of no-fault since its inception.

RATE REDUCTIONS

Florida's no-fault law went into effect January 1, 1972, with a mandatory 15-percent rate reduction on basic liability limits of 10/20/5—$10,000 bodily injury for any one person injured, $20,000 bodily injury per occurrence, and $5,000 for property damage. The following month companies were directed to submit quarterly and annual reports on claim frequency and average cost per claim paid under the various no-fault coverages.

Effective January 31, 1973, an additional 11-percent rate reduction was ordered for companies writing 90 percent of the automobile insurance market in Florida. Since the no-fault law went into effect, it has been estimated that Florida motorists have benefited in premium savings of approximately $100 million.

It should be stressed here that actuarial indications developed from all insurance companies reporting to the Florida Insurance Department as required by statutes show that, as of December 1974, private passenger automobile rates for limits of 10/20/5 would have been 50 percent higher under the old pre-no-fault system as compared to the actual rates in effect at that time. In other words, due to the workings of the Florida no-fault law, insurance premiums are lower even though there have been numerous rate increases since its inception. Such rate increases would have been 50 percent more had it not been for the workings of the law involving limitations of liability, thresholds, et cetera.

It should also be pointed out that a portion of the premium increase in Florida is directly attributable to legislative mandate as follows:

A. The increase in minimum financial responsibility limits from 10/20/5 to 15/30/5.

B. The mandated availability of increased limits of uninsured motorists and underinsured motorists.

DEFICIENCIES

What are the deficiencies of Florida's no-fault law?

Let us first take a look at two decisions of the Florida Supreme Court.

1. The court declared the property damage of the no-fault law unconstitutional. In a four to three majority decision in the case of *Kluger v. White*, 281 So. 2d 1, July 1973, the court held that the restriction of an individual's tort right for damages to an owned vehicle when such damages were under the $550 threshold was unconstitutional. The court said that the common law and statutory right of action for redress had been denied without there being provided an adequate alternative.

2. In a five to two decision, *Lasky v. State Farm*, 296 So. 2d 9, May 28, 1974, the Florida Supreme Court upheld the constitutionality of the bodily injury portions of the no-fault law, but amended the tort threshold. The only change required by this court decision was the deletion of provisions relating to a defined fracture.

Another deficiency is the overutilization of medical services intended to breach the $1,000 medical threshold.

In 1973, the Insurance Commissioner conducted an investigation and held a public hearing on apparent efforts of certain members of the medical and law professions to inflate auto accident medical expenses above threshold levels of the no-fault law.

The Fraud Committee found pairings of doctors and lawyers with others in what appeared to be an effort to increase medical expenses.

Still another is the exclusion of commercial vehicles. Florida's no-fault law applies only to private passenger-type vehicles.

Finally, there is the overutilization of equitable distribution. Statistics indicate that insurance companies are recovering on a statewide average only 20 percent of the no-fault dollar paid from the individual recipient. The original concept of the law was to provide for 100-percent reimbursement, less attorneys' fees.

SUGGESTED REMEDIES

The Insurance Department feels that the Florida no-fault law, if amended, would become broader in scope and more effectively bring about better reform in the automobile reparations act.

A first suggested remedy would be to increase thresholds.

Due to inflation and higher doctor and hospital bills, higher repair and labor bills, it is felt that thresholds should be increased to compensate for these increased costs. A proposal was introduced in the 1975 session of the Legislature to increase the threshold from $1,000 to $3,500 and the benefits package from $5,000 to $10,000, but it failed to pass.

Another suggested remedy would be to include commercial vehicles under no-fault. This would result in a fairer distribution of losses and would lend needed strength to the enforcement tools available.

A third remedy would be to remove the growth provision relating to equitable distribution and to provide for either intercompany subrogation or 100 percent reimbursement.

SUMMARY

These are the deficiencies and remedies to Florida's no-fault law which the Department feels the legislature, in time, will consider favorably.

Meanwhile, it is the Department's viewpoint that Florida's no-fault law is working and fulfilling predictions and promises.

There have been quicker payments and settlements of personal injury claims, more equitable distribution of benefits according to actual losses sustained, lower costs of insurance because of simplified claims processing, elimination of noneconomic losses from recoveries, and a redistribution of types of claims filed.

More importantly, the constitutionality of the law generally has been upheld by the Florida Supreme Court, and in one instance strengthened.

That is all, Mr. Chairman.

Mr. SCHEUER. Mr. Chairman, may I ask a question at this point?

Mr. VAN DEERLIN. Certainly.

Mr. SCHEUER. What were the particular reasons for not including commercial vehicles?

Mr. MCCUE. At the outset of passage of our law in 1971, Mr. Congressman, it was felt the major social problem, if you will, involving automobiles in the State of Florida did involve only the private passenger percentage of the market within the State of Florida. The market availability, if you will, of private passenger automobile insurance in the State of Florida was a prime factor in considering limiting it to the private passenger automobiles. The market availability, those problems the individual insuring public in the State of Florida were facing with the availability on the insurance market because of the continued rise in costs. This goes back to the laws that were effective at this time dealing with open competition rating laws, special sessions of our legislature dealing with rating treatment, and the prime problem was in the area of private passenger automobiles.

The overall viewpoint of the Florida Insurance Department and Commissioner Ashler, through our network of service officers in the State of Florida, is that the no-fault law in Florida is working, and working well.

We have experienced some difficulties which most of our sister States have experienced in their passage of no-fault. Mr. Chairman, that concludes my prepared statement, and if you desire I will be glad to answer questions.

Mr. VAN DEERLIN. Thank you. It was an excellent prepared statement.

We have been joined by two additional members of the subcommittee, Mr. Rinaldo of New Jersey, who was a member of the New Jersey Legislature when that State passed its no-fault law, and Mr. Stuckey of Georgia.

general damages.

This was a factor put in by all of the companies to relate to the Florida Insurance Department as required by law and taking those claims that would have been settled, the 46 percent under the old tort basis and with certainly the increased factor of economic conditions from the inflationary growth, and these were added in, and it was done mathematically through an actuarial basis.

I am not an actuary, and cannot explain in detail the act's formula. Then they talk about the line of lease factors, and the trend factors, and they lose me.

I can only testify as to what the actuarial information was given to me by our Department actuary, which was taking all of those areas into consideration, going back to the old era of the true pain and suffering, the first dollars, if you will, of general damages versus limiting it to true medical expenses.

Mr. VAN DEERLIN. If there are available statistics to support that contention, we will be interested in them.

Mr. McCUE. I will be glad to make them available.

[The following letter was received for the record:]

OFFICE OF TREASURER,
INSURANCE COMMISSIONER,
Tallahassee, Fla., September 10, 1975.

Hon. LIONEL VAN DEERLIN,
Chairman, Subcommittee on Consumer Protection and Finance, Congress of the United States, House of Representatives, Rayburn House Office Building, Washington, D.C.

DEAR CONGRESSMAN VAN DEERLIN: I had the opportunity to talk to a member of the staff of the Subcommittee on Consumer Protection and Finance. It was pointed out that in my prepared remarks in testimony before your Committee on July 14, 1975, I made the following statement:

"It should be stressed here that actuarial indications developed from all insurance companies reporting to the Florida Insurance Department as required by Statutes show that as of December 1974 private passenger automobile rates for limits of 10/20/5 would have been 50 per cent higher under the old pre-No-Fault system as compared to the actual rates in effect at that time."

It was requested by a member of the Committee that any written information in support of this statement be forwarded and made a part of the official transcript.

Congressman Van Deerlin, the actuarial information furnished by all carriers would be of a volume that would be virtually impossible to readily compile and summarize. The simple mathematical computations and the statutory requirements that would justify the percentage figure used would be as follows:

1. All carriers were required to reduce the rates for bodily injury and property damage liability by 15% at the inception of the Law. The majority of these rates were 1970 rates and were reduced statutorily effective January 1, 1972.

2. The Legislature placed a moratorium on any rate increases during the entire year of 1972.

3. An additional 11% reduction was mandated in January of 1973 for bodily injury only. This was as a result of the experience gained during the first six months of 1972.

4. There were no major rate increases filed with this Department during the first ten months of 1973.

Congressman Van Deerlin, let me point out that since my testimony on July 14, this Department has received numerous rate increases from major carriers in the State of Florida. Some examples would be as follows:

State Farm Insurance Company—Statewide average increase for bodily injury and property damage liability and no-fault benefits—+27%

Allstate Insurance Company—Statewide average increase for bodily injury and property damage liability and no-fault benefits—+20%

Liberty Mutual Insurance Company—Statewide average increase for bodily injury and property damage liability and no-fault benefits—+14.7%

Aetna Casualty and Surety Insurance Company—Statewide average increase for bodily injury and property damage liability and no-fault benefits—+40%

Therefore, while the percentage of 50% was indeed accurate at the time of my presentation, these latest rate increases which are effective during the months of August, September and October would certainly tend to decrease the 50% figure.

Hopefully this is the information you require. If I may be of further assistance, please do not hesitate to contact me.

Sincerely,

PHILIP F. ASHLER,
Insurance Commissioner and Treasurer.
WILLIAM G. McCUE, Jr.,
Director, Division of Insurance Company Regulation.

Mr. VAN DEERLIN. I understand that the $1,000 medical threshold may be a deficiency in the new law, particularly in Dade County. I'm told that medical bills are being inflated artificially to get claimants beyond the $1,000 threshold so they can sue. Rather than a gap in the law, perhaps this might be viewed as a gap in the ethics of certain doctors and lawyers who have thus, as you suggested, connived.

You talk about pairings between doctors and lawyers. Do you mean that certain doctors and certain lawyers have passed patients along?

Mr. McCUE. Quite frequently, from the results of the study done by the Florida Insurance Department and investigation and in conjunction with the State office in 1973, and this was found in many instances, and we did not, due to our lack of knowledge in the medical area, try to pass any judgments on where the legitimate medical expense is, certainly we were not, from the department's standpoint, equipped and knowledgeable enough to say, "This indeed was a legitimate medical injury', or if indeed the treatments were necessary.

The only area we could look at which brought to our attention some possibility was the area that a given attorney would represent a given doctor, and vice versa on a large majority if not—well, in some situations almost 100 percent of all of his cases, and this was brought to the public's attention for the validity of those figures for whatever it may have brought about. That was in 1973.

The Insurance Crime Prevention Institute, at a later date, was instrumental in bringing some criminal actions, several indictments, when I heard it was the Post Office.

Mr. VAN DEERLIN. If they are going to commit fraud they should hand deliver it.

Mr. McCUE. Yes, sir.

Mr. VAN DEERLIN. Mr. McCollister.

Mr. McCOLLISTER. Mr. McCue, I have two questions. The first relates to the fact that commercial vehicles do not have no-fault coverage. What happens when a private vehicle causes an accident to a commercial vehicle, how does the commercial vehicle recover?

Mr. McCUE. All right, sir, if indeed the operator of the private passenger vehicle were at fault in the State, and I have to say at fault and taking into consideration the fact we are now faced with comparative rather than contributory negligence, a different ballgame. If the operator of the private passenger vehicle is negligent, the owner of the commercial vehicle has first dollar tort rights, and you go back to the old pre-no-fault tort system, he is not limited in any action he can bring against the owner or operator of the private passenger vehicle. The injured occupant of the private passenger vehicle has a right to recover from his own insurer the personal protection benefit, but that is the old sue and be sued.

Mr. McCOLLISTER. Doesn't that build into the private vehicles insurance costs a liability factor?

Mr. McCUE. Certainly.

Mr. McCOLLISTER. That inflates the premium?

Mr. McCUE. Yes. sir. If you keep in mind Florida's law is what is referred to as a limited no-fault law in the area of bodily injury and no property damage although originally it was.

In the area of bodily injury in the limited tort system law, there are restrictions, certain of them on the area of tort, but commercial vehicles, no, sir.

Mr. McCOLLISTER. The real question I think the committee is concerned with is not whether no-fault is a good idea. What this committee, at least this member has as his primary concern is, should there be a Federal law or should States be allowed to find their way as their circumstances dictate? I personally favor the latter.

I am going to ask Ms. Nord to recite what would happen to the Florida law in the event that H.R. 1900 were passed, and to get some comment from you as to the desirability of that. Ms. Nord, would you tell Mr. McCue the effect of the Federal law on the State of Florida?

Ms. NORD. Yes, Mr. McCollister.

Mr. McCue, if H.R. 1900 were put into effect it would mean substantial changes for the Flordia law. For example, H.R. 1900 has mandated work loss benefits of up to $15,000 and unlimited medical benefits. It calls for an assigned claims plan, and it does prohibit subrogation. It has a number of subsidies, if you will, for the disadvantaged or low-income people.

Mr. McCUE. From the Florida insurance department's standpoint, I was instructed by the commissioner to review the effects on the Florida law, if you will, if the Federal law were passed, or if the Federal bill was passed, the total bill, were to be passed, and what effect would it have on the State, and immediately, as you pointed out, all of the benefits contained there would certainly have to be increased, corresponding increase for first-party benefits on premiums.

I would have to rely on the Milliman & Robertson study done at the direction of NAIC, as far as the total effect on the current premium structure in Florida as to increasing benefit levels. In looking at the Milliman & Robertson study, not being an actuary, I found first it was a difficult problem for me to interpret what it was saying. In looking at it, it had numerous possibilities, high threshold low benefits, low threshold and high benefits. They had a total. It took me 2 days to figure out the total. In looking at it it appeared to me what they indicated was a possibility of roughly an 8-percent increase by taking those benefits and applying them to Florida's law as it appears now.

Certainly, if you are increasing the first party benefits without further restriction on the tort rights, then the 8-percent figure is erroneous. You cannot give additional administration of completely unlimited Federal $15,000 wage loss when we have a package of $5,000 unless you restrict the availability of tort, which again the Federal proposal does, restrict the availability of tort, thus the small increase, if you will, of let's say plus 8 percent.

Florida, in responding to the second portion of the Congressman's question as to Florida's viewpoint on the Federal proposal, the Commissioner has appeared on numerous occasions before various committees throughout the country, various national associations, the National Association of Insurance Commissioners, and his basic philosophy fresh out of the Department is there is need for some type of minimum Federal standards for uniformity within the benefits package at a very minimal level. Hopefully, what his concern is it should be implemented and regulated State by State.

Mr. RINALDO. In other words, can I interpret that as meaning you would prefer a bill that would establish minimum standards which each State must meet or exceed, which would enable each State to participate legislatively, to administer the plan without interferance from the Federal Government, and to continue regulating the business of insurance as opposed to a plan, such as the bill that was just mentioned, which would cause your system to be changed as a result of conflicting Federal standards?

Mr. McCUE. Yes, sir, you certainly can, sir. That is exactly what I was trying to express to the committee.

Mr. RINALDO. Thank you.

is pretty hard to do.

Mr. Chairman, I yield.

Mr. VAN DEERLIN. Mr. Stuckey.

Mr. STUCKEY. Thank you, Mr. Chairman.

Mr. McCue, would you briefly explain the difference between Florida's no-fault plan and an add-on type of no-fault, let's say, like the State of Georgia has?

Mr. McCUE. Yes, sir. Both of them accomplish one common purpose, Mr. Congressman, that is the first party benefits for the injured occupant of a private passenger vehicle or commercial vehicle in the case of Georgia.

That is the common goal. In other words, the individual can look to his own insurance company to receive first party benefits for his medical expenses and lost wages.

The difference between, of course, the add-on benefits and the Florida law is we have a limitation or modification of a person's tort right, and in a complete add-on State, there is no such limitation, if you will.

You take the current tort system. You tell the individual if he is at fault in an accident certainly he is going to be entitled to collect from his own company. However, there would be not tort exemption that he might incur out of that accident and if there is bodily injury or property liability the insurer would respond immediately to payment for the injured party not at fault. Some of our sister States certainly add-on plans. They feel that they are working and working well. Again, that I think is one of the problems that you would experience from a national level if it were just complete add-on.

I am not so sure that the populace of a given State would have the same reaction to an add-on plan as, let's say, the citizens of Dade County, both from a socioeconomic and standard of living standpoint, availability to certain medical standards, it may not be the same in another State. The common goal would be to make available first party benefits and the difference on add-on there would be no limitation on tort rights where in Florida we have a limitation on tort rights.

Mr. STUCKEY. Did you have opportunity to compare the cost of Florida's no-fault versus Georgia's or a State with add-on?

Mr. McCUE. No, sir.

Mr. STUCKEY. Do you have any idea which would be the higher cost to the individual?

Mr. McCUE. Well, Mr. Congressman, as I pointed out we have had indications from other States that have an add-on plan. One

State that crosses my mind immediately after 6 months of their law being enforced, there was certain rate reductions that came about. Again, to me this was not what we would have expected to experience in Florida, from the standpoint that if we increased the benefits package in Florida with a limited tort ratio we have seen some experience in that area of a people utilizing both the tort system by exceedng the threshold of $1,000 as well as those increased medical expenses.

In Florida I think it would be most difficult to experience any reduction from this because we have purely an add-on benefit.

Mr. STUCKEY. You are saying Florida has rejected the add-on approach because of the cost?

Mr. MCCUE. Well, sir, you know, again, I cannot speak for the legislature in its wisdom in Florida, but there has been no bill presented to the legislature in Florida by any industry association, the Florida Bar Association, or any other interested group to even consider an add-on benefit in the State of Florida, to my knowledge.

Mr. STUCKEY. Has there been thought given to raising the threshold say from $1,000 to $2,500 and do you think it would have additional benefits?

Mr. MCCUE. Yes, sir. In the 1974 session of the Florida Legislature, there was a bill introduced at the department's request that would have increased it from $1,000 to $3,500 and at the same time it increased the benefits package from $5,000 to $10,000.

Mr. STUCKEY. Thank you.

Mr. VAN DEERLIN. Mr. Metcalfe.

Mr. METCALFE. Thank you, Mr. Chairman.

Mr. McCue, does Florida have a compulsory insurance provision for automobile insurers or all automobile owners?

Mr. MCCUE. Yes, sir, Mr. Congressman, they do. It is a twofold compulsory provision and let me point out what I mean by twofold. If you are an owner of a private passenger vehicle as defined by no-fault laws, then you are required by State statute to provide at least minimum limits of liability which as of July 1 are 15, 30, and 5, plus no-fault benefits.

Prior to receiving a valid inspection sticker for your private passenger vehicle in the State of Florida you must present evidence of insurance at the time of inspection. You present the evidence if your vehicle further qualifies as meeting the safety standards and you would receive a valid inspection sticker and without evidence of insurance you would not receive an inspection sticker.

In the area of commercial vehicle it is also compulsory the owners of commercial vehicles carry minimum limits of liability only, not no-fault benefits, and they have to present a policy at the time of inspection or an identification card or other method certifying that they have insurance for at least 15–30.

Mr. METCALFE. I am concerned about the time factor. This is a hypothetical case. A person goes into an automobile agency, purchases an automobile, at what point is he required to have that car inspected and therefore indicate he has proper insurance?

Mr. MCCUE. Mr. Congressman, that is one of, if you will, the deficiencies of using an automobile inspection station system. Due to the fact that licensed automobile dealers in the State of Florida can qualify as self-inspectors. They would inspect that vehicle when they owned it and they would be required to carry what is referred to in the insurance language as open lot coverage or dealers' coverage, blanket coverage on automobiles sold by the dealership. Theyg use their insurance.

The day they sell it to the individual consumer purchasing the vehicle, he is not required to present evidence so there could be a 1-year factor that man may go in without any insurance. The latest figures ending fiscal year June 30, 1975, indicated that 86.6 percent of those people that were involved in accidents in the State of Florida had insurance at the time of the accident, even though it is a 100-percent compulsory State. These are some of the problems you run into.

Mr. METCALFE. If an individual purchases a car I am concerned as to whether or not he would know there is such a thing as a no-fault insurance law in the State of Florida? How does he know that? What about the difference between the 86 percent and the 100 percent, what about those people? Why is it they do not have no-fault insurance?

Mr. McCUE. Mr. Congressman, in Florida, as well as other States that have compulsory insurance laws, we can relate it back to the State of New York, which has had a law for a number of years, and the State of North Carolina had a compulsory insurance law, and every State would probably give you the same answer, that there is approximately 5 percent of those people insuring, I mean the motoring public within the State that are just not going to purchase insurance. Even under the fear of jail sentences they won't purchase insurance. There are all kinds of ways to circumvent it.

Mr. METCALFE. They know they are required to do that, that is what I want to find out, do they all know it, 100 percent of the automobile purchasers know they are expected to have no-fault insurance?

Mr. McCUE. We certainly have done everything from the Florida Insurance Department that we can to notify the people. On the passage of the no-fault law, there was quite an extensive public relations campaign through all of our service officers, through the local news media, and we hope they are, sir. At the time of the inspection they are notified then they must have it.

Mr. METCALFE. So that a year can elapse between that particular time. What I am trying to elicit from you is whether or not you, when you purchase a car, are told at that point? Are you told at that point that you must have or should have no-fault insurance?

Mr. McCUE. There is no requirement that the automobile dealership notify the person. I can't tell you, Mr. Congressman, whether they do or don't.

Mr. METCALFE. Would you not think that would be a desirable procedure to follow?

Mr. McCUE. Yes, sir.

Mr. METCALFE. So as to make certain?

Mr. McCUE. Certainly.

Mr. METCALFE. I am concerned about the person who is not very astute and does not know the proper benefits as far as carrying proper insurance.

Mr. McCUE. I can answer to this degree. If the vehicle that is purchased is subject to any kind of lien, there is going to be a requirement from the person selling it or the lending institution financing it that physical damage coverage is carried, and that is common not only in Florida but every State. At the time the person purchases physical damage coverage, he is notified then he is required to carry bodily injury and property damage because there is a stamp that under the rules of the Florida Insurance Department this policy does not provide the required coverage to meet the financial stability law in the State of Florida.

Mr. METCALFE. Must he provide the coverage before he can actually take possession of the car even though there is a lien on it in the form of payment over a period of 12 or 24 months?

Mr. McCUE. Normally, yes, sir, due to the fact that that institution providing the financing on that vehicle is not going to let him have possession until such time as their interest is protected.

Mr. METCALFE. What county are we in?

Mr. McCUE. At the present time, Volusia.

Mr. METCALFE. It is not in Dade County?

Mr. McCUE, No, sir.

Mr. METCALFE. I notice in Dade County they were sort of out of step with the rest of the parts of Florida in coverage, is that right?

Mr. McCUE. Yes, sir, that is an accurate statement.

Mr. METCALFE. I think you touched upon this in your presentation. Would you go over it again, please, and tell me why Dade County is perhaps different and why are they different than other counties?

Mr. McCUE. Mr. Congressman, I wish I could give you a simple answer as to why Dade is so much different than other counties. Dade County consists mainly of one large metropolitan area, Miami and Miami Beach. The makeup of those citizens within that area and their social standards and socioeconomic status within the State of Florida, in some areas it ranges from affluent to in certain areas of Dade County very, very low economic standards. The situation in that area, I think we are dealing with an area that is not a rural area within the State of Florida.

Florida has basically two metropolitan areas within the State, the Dade County area and the Pinellas County area over on the west coast of Florida. I think we are dealing with the only metropolitan area within the State as compared to all other semirural areas within the State, and you run into differences within the State of Florida, socioeconomic situations within that area that cause some of the problems.

The rates within Dade County are tremendously high. I think that the populace in that area, because of their experience. their loss experience, the companies presenting the information as required by the statute of the Florida Insurance Department justify those rates within that area.

Many, many factors go into it, Mr. Congressman. I wish I could give you as I said a simple answer to why we experience problems in Dade County which we don't in other areas of the State.

Mr. METCALFE. May I go off the record?

Mr. VAN DEERLIN. Mr. Metcalfe is off the record.

[Discussion off the record.]

Mr. METCALFE. Mr. Chairman, I will go back on the record. Thank you, Mr. McCue, for your statements. I have no further statements and give back the balance of time I have.

Mr. VAN DEERLIN. Mr. Rinaldo.

Mr. RINALDO. Thank you, Mr. Chairman.

with that bill?

Mr. McCue. No, sir.

Mr. Rinaldo. I might ask one further question. How does the Florida system handle a situation where there are multiple sources of insurance of equal priorities? For example, an insured husband driving his wife's insured car?

Mr. McCue. All right, sir. In the Florida law the owner of the private passenger vehicle is entitled to collect benefits from his insurance company regardless of whose vehicle he is occupying at the time of the accident. If the wife owned the vehicle and the husband did not own a vehicle he was operating his wife's vehicle he would be entitled to collect from the wife's private passenger automobile insurance company.

If he himself owned a vehicle, he was occupying his wife's vehicle involved in an accident, he would be entitled to collect from his insurance company that was providing him coverage on his own vehicle.

Mr. Rinaldo. Thank you. I have no further questions.

Mr. Van Deerlin. Mr. Scheuer.

Mr. Scheuer. No questions, Mr. Chairman.

Mr. Van Deerlin. The majority counsel, Mr. Kinzler.

Mr. Kinzler. Mr. McCue, do you think the Florida law is adequately protecting the seriously injured?

Let me give you a reference point. The Department of Transportation's final study indicated that in 1967 approximately 1 percent of the people in the United States nationwide suffered injuries of $10,000, but that these people accounted for 77 percent of the total economic loss in the country.

Mr. McCue. Well, Mr. Kinzler, I can point this out, that with a limitation of $5,000 on the total package which includes both medical expenses and loss of wages, if that coincides with the DOT study you talk about, depending upon what the average loss is, if you will, for those seriously injured individuals, then certainly we can fall short with a relatively small package amount of $5,000.

Mr. Kinzler. The reason I asked is that I think part of the premise of Federal legislation is that unlimited medical benefits are essential, or at least a very high threshold of medical benefits are essential, to pick up the people suffering the worst losses and that one of the ways of shaping such legislation, as is done in S. 534 and H.R. 1900, would be to have unlimited medical and leave the question of wage protection more to the States, with a $15,000 minimum. I am wondering if you would comment on the philosophy of that?

Mr. McCue. Well, sir, as I pointed out, I think in the area of unlimited medical expenses, if you are going to bring that in, there are a number of factors you have to consider there such as primacy of coverage. What is going to be the prime, if you will, insurance mechanism to provide those unlimited medical expenses? Will it be automatically the private passenger automobile insurance? Will it be workmen's compensation in case the individual is involved in an accident while performing his duties as an employee? Will it be the benefits that a person may be entitled to under some Federal program such as medicare or medicaid, one of the Federal programs or will it be, if you will, providing of health care such as in Blue Shield, and in looking at it I think you have to take into consideration in looking at the total cost of the overall insurance package an individual is going to be required to carry to protect himself.

You have to look at what is going to be the primacy of coverage? If you feel it is going to be the automobile insurance mechanism that will be the primacy of coverage, without some restrictions on that person's tort availability, then it has to, in my opinion, and from what I have been told with unlimited medical, it has to increase the cost of his automobile insurance.

Mr. Kinzler. As you know, the Federal bill also restricts the tort threshold severely.

Mr. McCue. Yes, sir. With those restrictions in there, again I can only go back to the actuarial study that was done indicating approximately 8 percent increase in Florida to provide the unlimited medical portion of it.

Mr. Kinzler. Right. That 8 percent increase for the total package of benefits and restrictions under H.R. 1900 and S. 354 has been carried through in updates of that study by Allstate and State Farm. Those more recent studies were in fact based on late 1974 figures before the recent increases in Florida by the Florida insurance companies. How would you feel? Would you feel the people of Florida would be better protected by a package that increased their benefits as much as H.R. 1900 and S. 354 would for 8 percent more on the average premium or by the Florida law?

Mr. McCue. Again I can only speak from the standpoint of the official position of the commissioner of the State of Florida. His position is that a given package of benefits, and he did not address himself to an unlimited amount, but a minimum package of benefits that each State can modify as to how it affects the individual citizens within its State and what they would benefit from, certainly with certain areas in the State of Florida I think unlimited medical benefits would be necessary in those situations, with certain groups of the State of Florida I think it may be necessary, but from the overall reactions to it, I can go back to the relationship that the State of Florida feels, from the insurance department's standpoint, that minimum guidelines shoud be set and left to the individual States to regulate those minimum guidelines.

Mr. Kinzler. How is Florida handling the conflict of law problems that invariably exist under this patchwork system?

Mr. McCue. We, to the best of my knowledge, Mr. Kinzler, from the insurance department's standpoint, I was making this observation two weeks ago appearing before a group that, to the best of my knowledge, there have been no conflicts from that standpoint once they have a compulsory no-fault insurance law providing their citizens with certain coverages. Well, in the Florida law, the companies providing coverage, we do have some nonresident provisions contained in our law.

We have benefits available to the Florida resident when traveling in another State if he is occupying his own vehicle. We have had no direct conflict, to my knowledge, and certainly someone from the legal profession that may be before you today may be aware of certain conflicts involving a resident of the State where they have compulsory insurance laws, compulsory no-fault laws versus ours. I am not aware of conflicts that have been written or any case law on it. Certainly conflict possibilities are there.

Mr. KINZLER. Doesn't the fact that a large number of States retain the tort system cause additional costs to the Florida driver, in that his premium not only has to cover losses in the State but the potential that will be liable in tort in other States?

Mr. McCUE. Probably more so in Florida than many of our sister States due to the fact a large percentage of our income in the State of Florida is developed from the tourist industry and we have a number of nonresidents coming in and out of the State, a tremendous number. With the good benefits we have to offer those people coming into the State of Florida, the sunshine State and retirement, yes, sir, we have potential and it is a factor in the bodily injury and liability ratemaker, certainly, those accidents involving Florida and nonresidents going in there.

Mr. KINZLER. That is part of the reason the Commissioner favors some form of no-fault legislation in every State?

Mr. McCUE. That is one of the reasons, yes.

Mr. KINZLER. Thank you.

Mr. VAN DEERLIN. Thank you, Mr. McCue.

Mr. SCHEUER. Mr. Chairman, may I ask a question?

Mr. VAN DEERLIN. Of course.

Mr. SCHEUER. I am reading through the letter under the letterhead of Cramer & Matthews, a letter I believe signed by Mr. Matthews, Lawrence Matthews, on no-fault.

They start out by saying "We hope our experience in Florida will help your committee and congress as a whole in resolving the ongoing controversy concerning automobile no-fault." They say, "Our sole discussion will be directed to the different State plans emphasizing Florida's and their relative effectiveness."

Then time after time in the ensuing 8 or 10 pages, they say as they said on page 4, "Instead of the Congress making mandatory standards to be followed by all 50 States, based on theoretical projections of an actuarial survey, we suggest that the States which have no-fault plans be allowed to continue them for several years as actual laboratories determining which plans and which features are effective in obtaining the social goal of victim compensation at the most reasonable cost to the consumer."

That general approach is repeated here. Nowhere in this letter is there any broad gauge opposition to the concept of no-fault insurance, but they seem to oppose at this time a Federal response.

Now, do you think the state of the art is such considering the experience Florida has had and the experience other States have had that on the major questions facing you, you can come up with some answers? You obviously have, because you recommended to the legislature that the $1,000 limit be raised to $3,500, and the $5,000 be raised to $10,000.

Can you look across the board at the open questions and say, "Yes, with almost 50 States having had some experience we can come up with some anwers to these open question, and it would be reasonable for Congress to act now or as per contract"?

Do you think it would be a reasonable position to say, "Look, the various States are each in their own way considering these matters, the States are passing new laws and are building on the experience of the States, or the early State laws, and probably it might be worthwhile for Congress to wait a year, or two, or three"?

Do you feel that the proper approach is, "Yes we believe no-fault is OK, but this is not the time for the Federal Government to act"?

Do you believe that is a corollary of the rhyme we all learned, "Mother, may I go and swim"? "Yes, my darling daughter. Hang your clothes on yonder limb, but don't go near the water."

Is it that kind of approach you support, or do you believe we have the necessary information now to bite the bullet and to pass the law?

Mr. McCue. Mr. Congressman, I believe that, from the Florida standpoint, the position that the insurance department will have to take in that situation would be that we certainly, even though we were the second State to pass a no-fault law, in our current situation if we had the perfect no-fault law, one of the favorable facts of the no-fault law in its inception was Massachusetts had the perfect plan, and that Massachusetts increased it from $500 to $1,000, and $5,000 to $25,000, and in some other areas that Massachusetts had problems in that brought about legal action in Massachusetts from the insurer's standpoint, we tried to modify the Massachusetts law, and we were told at that time it looks like we have the greatest law.

We have gained experience with our law since January 1, 1972, which has led us to believe there are certain modifications that need to be made further in our law.

I think each State passing such a law, certainly in a newer State than us and Massachusetts, have run into certain problems. The only fear that the Florida Insurance Department would have is that, if it is a Federal program, setting forth certain guidelines, that drawing from the wisdom of the States that have enacted a law, that it may be felt in the Congress' wisdom this is again a perfect type law.

I am not so sure we are going to develop, in my lifetime, the perfect answer to the private passenger automobile problem within this country.

The Congress by enacting this will apply uniformly in all States, and if it is a large benefit level, and if there are certain restrictions, go back to what is referred to as the Keeton-O'Connell plan, I think it will be difficult to change those on the national basis.

While I don't agree there should be prolonged waiting in Florida to react to those problems that we are encountering in Florida, I do believe that a period of time to develop statistics from all States having no-fault laws should be there prior to the Federal Congress taking some action on it.

I hope I answered the question. I beat around the bush, but I hope I answered the question.

Mr. SCHEUER. Thank you very much.
Mr. VAN DEERLIN. Thank you.
Our next witness is Prentiss Mitchell, representing the Florida Association of Life and Casualty Insurers.
Welcome to the subcommittee, Mr. Mitchell.

STATEMENT OF PRENTISS R. MITCHELL, ASSOCIATE DIRECTOR, FLORIDA ASSOCIATION OF LIFE AND CASUALTY INSURERS, INC.

Mr. MITCHELL. Thank you, Mr. Chairman.
Mr. Chairman, members of the committee. My name is Prentiss R. Mitchell, and I am the associate director of the Florida Association of Life and Casualty Insurers, Inc. I might add our association represents 158 life, casualty, health, and title insurers that write business in the State of Florida. We represent both domestic and foreign insurers and, therefore, I believe that the views that we will express here today are representative of not only the large national writers of insurance, but of those insurers that write exclusively within the State of Florida.

As Mr. McCue pointed out, Florida was the second State to pass and to implement a no-fault law after Massachusetts, and, therefore, the experience that we have gleaned from no-fault is second only to the State of Massachusetts.

With that background, certainly we would like to express our gratitude to this committee for conducting these hearings in Florida to get some idea of how our law works and how it would compare with Senate bill 354.

At the outset, I think it would be well to state our general proposition as it relates to no-fault, and that is, gentlemen, a firm belief that only through State action and implementation can a no-fault law and the concepts that are embodied within such a law be properly framed. We believe this to be true because we have seen within our own law the necessity to adjust and fine-tune our law in order that it can more properly achieve the original objectives of the legislation.

While Mr. McCue has indicated background to you as to what the benefit levels are within the law and his statement we certainly concur with in that we believe that at the outset when we passed this law that we had the absolute model because we thought we had utopia, and much to our dismay at this point, representing the industry in Florida, we do find that we have some problems with it, and as you have noted in my statement there, that the inherent problems that we have now deal pretty much with the Dade County area, the Miami area.

I was asked by this committee to expound somewhat on the area of fraud as it exists in Dade County, which we certainly will do.

As Mr. McCue pointed out, the investigations are taking place at this time in Dade County by the U.S. Postal authorities. We have been in touch with them and are working with them and plan a meeting tomorrow with the U.S. Postal authorities and with the U.S. Attorney's Office, and other members of the industry to deal with the subject.

The problem, I might add, is while many times in the insurance industry we tend to generalize and say that all attorneys and all doctors are leading to the demise of our law, I might add this is not true. We have had excellent cooperation from the Florida Bar, from the Academy of Trial Lawyers, and from the Florida Medical Association.

But the problems that we have in Dade County deal probably with 1 or 2 percent of the attorney's fees and doctors in that city. So from that standpoint, and with that background, I might say that the problems that we see are those that dealt initially with inadequate rates.

That thing that actually brought about a no-fault law in Florida at the outset was that many of you will recall when the State of Massachusetts passed their no-fault law they mandated a 15-percent reduction. The feeling at that time in Florida was this appeared to be a way to, if you will, just to calm the irate policyholders that existed in the State at that time.

The companies came in with a round of rate increases after a long history of inadequate rates in Florida. They took the increases, and perhaps politically it was not the smart thing to do because elections were coming up and they took the rate increase and had two sessions of the Florida Legislature at this point. The idea was to go with a no-fault law which the State did.

A year later the insurance department mandated an 11-percent reduction. Bearing in mind that Florida has ranked historically 37th among all of the States in the price of insurance, that is to say, that in 36 States automobile insurance costs more than it does in the State of Florida, however, this is of little consequence really to the number of retirees who are on the fixed incomes which we have in this State.

Therefore, the legislature in their wisdom decided "let's go with the no-fault law, let's mandate the 15-percent reduction and subsequently an 11-percent reduction."

Now, then, if you asked the insurance companies in Florida how do you think the no-fault law is working from a pure profit standpoint, they will say it is a dismal failure because from an underwriting standpoint, they are losing money in record proportions in this State.

Again, it has nothing to do really with the law itself. The problem was of rate inadequacy going in and a continuing inadequacy at this time.

However, all is not lost. We see light again at the end of the tunnel from the industry standpoint and that is that the rate increases have been granted. Two have been granted to most of the stipends in the 15 or 18 months and perhaps there will be additional increases as we go.

As Mr. McCue pointed out, another of the problems that we have in addition to the fraud activities, is in the area of equitable distribution. While I cannot add a great deal to what Mr. McCue has already told you, I can only say that the problem really deals with the interpretation of the law by the judiciary of the State. We were told when the law was passed, and we are certainly of the understanding that we would get 100-percent recovery as a company when we paid first-party benefits, but in some jurisdictions you get back 10 percent, so the law is not being interpreted as passed.

Let me conclude my comments by just again reemphasizing that we believe that at the State level we should be permitted, as a number of other States have been, to enact a no-fault law and to experiment with it. We think this should be the laboratory as someone pointed out and we do not believe that Senate bill 354 is going to answer the problems you are going to try to solve. Again, we thought we had passed a Utopia and you perhaps, or the authors of this bill believe it will be Utopia. We do not.

We would urge the committee to permit us as an industry to continue to operate within the framework of the State Legislatures and State Insurance Departments where, when we see problems, and the problems I mentioned here, we can in turn take action at the State level, because, gentlemen, we have a great fear of trying to change anything in Washington from an industry standpoint. We believe we can do it at the State level, and we certainly urge you to permit us to continue this experiment.

Thank you, Mr. Chairman.

[Mr. Mitchell's prepared statement follows:]

STATEMENT OF PRENTISS R. MITCHELL, ASSOCIATE DIRECTOR, FLORIDA ASSOCIATION OF LIFE AND CASUALTY INSURERS, INC.

Mr. Chairman, members of the committee. . . . my name is Prentiss R. Mitchell and I am the associate director of the Florida Association of Life and Casualty Insurers, Inc. Our association represents 158 life, casualty, health and title insurers that write business in the State of Florida. We represent both domestic and foreign insurers and, therefore, I believe that the views that we will express here today are representative of not only the large national writers of insurance, but of those insurers that write exclusively within the State of Florida. As you are no doubt aware, Florida was the second state to pass and to implement a no-fault law and, therefore, the experience that we have gleaned from no-fault is second only to the State of Massachusetts. With that background, and with our thanks for conducting these regional congressional hearings in the State of Florida, I will attempt to provide your committee with both a synopsis of the manner in which the Florida no-fault law has been working and express our views on the bill that the U.S. Congress is now considering and on which the U.S. Senate has already completed its hearings; to wit, SB-354.

At the outset, I think it would be well to state our general proposition as it relates to no-fault and that is, gentlemen, a firm belief that only through State action and implementation can a no-fault law and the concepts that are embodied within such a law be properly framed. We believe this to be true because we have seen within our own law the necessity to adjust and fine-tune our law in order that it can more properly achieve the original objectives of the legislation. The Florida no-fault law is one that contains a $1,000 threshold and a benefit level of $5,000. When this bill was passed, it was lauded both by the industry, the legislature and, in many instances, the public as "The Model" no-fault law that other States should copy and implement. We, in Florida, looked with a great deal of pride upon our law for we felt it would not only provide compensation on a no-fault basis to over 95% of all individuals injured in automobile accidents, but would remove from the tort system those cases which are generally considered to be of a non-serious nature. We felt then much like many of those at the Federal level do now, that we had the answer—that the Florida no-fault was perfection. We now find or, at least, we now sense the same type of philosophy coming from Washington where we are told that the provisions of SB-354 are, in fact, the ultimate answer to the problems that may beset the casualty insurance mechanism. The Federal Government, by virtue of SB-354, has taken the same approach that we, in Florida, did when we felt that every State should examine our bill since it had no equal nor inherent problems. Well, that was in 1972 and now, gentlemen, we must admit to you as we have to the insurance department, to the legislature, to our member companies, and to the consuming public that the Florida no-fault bill is not the panacea, not the utopia, that we, in 1972, thought it was. Rather, we have found that because of the differences in both population, in the tort environment that exists in parts of our State and in the actual legislation that the model that we desired to be copied by all States was, in fact, not perfect. Yet, on the academic drawing board, this bill should have worked precisely like the proponents of no-fault had suggested it would. We are fortunate here in Florida because we have a legislature, and an insurance department which are not only aware of the deficiencies that we have experienced under no-fault, but more importantly, have realized that we must change portions of the law in order that we can adapt it to respond more consistently and equally in its application to the desires of the insuring public.

What are the problems and what corrections are needed?

Florida has historically ranked in the lower one-third percentile for auto insurance premiums charged. The most recent survey indicates that 37 States charge higher auto insurance premiums than those now charged in Florida. While this is a fact of life, it is of little consequence for many of our retired citizens on fixed incomes.

In late 1970, after two years of no rate increases, the companies began filing for increases under the open-competitive rating law in existence at that time. The public's response was less than enthusiastic, as it is when the price of any product is increased. This is particularly true of insurance since the average person has little understanding of how insurance companies price their products. This round of rate increases in turn provoked legislative action. Their belief was that a no-fault system would control the costs, thus, eliminate the continuing need for price increases. A rate freeze was invoked on the companies by the legislature.

During the 1971 legislative session, the current no-fault law was enacted to be effective January 2, 1972. This act mandated a 15% rate reduction from existing rates for $10,000/$20,000 limits (the compulsory coverage). In February 1973, the insurance commissioner, by department order, reduced rates by another 11%. These reductions were mandated during one of the highest inflationary periods in our Nation's history. The inadequacy of these rates has resulted in companies withdrawing from Florida, restricting the writing of new business or, in some cases, declaring bankruptcy.

The adequacy of rates is important because when the question is asked of insurance company executives as to how no-fault is working, they answer negatively. If pressed, they qualify their answer by stating that the law would work if the rates were adequate. Thus, we must state that the Florida law has accrued to the advantage of the consumer, but not for the companies from a profit standpoint.

The simple fact is that rates were inadequate going into no-fault and they are still inadequate. Primarily because of inflation and the insurers are still paying out the same benefits as they were during the pre-no-fault time. The only difference is they are paying to their own insureds.

The insurance department is now more prone to permit rate increases since Florida has the poorest loss ratios in the Nation. Therefore, companies will eventually reach a break-even point or make a modest profit. Thus, the rate crisis is slowly being eliminated.

Our law addresses itself to equitable distribution, however, the Judiciary is interpreting this question with uncertainty. The rule of equitable distribution should require 100% recovery of personal injury protection benefits to the insurer once a jury verdict has been awarded. There are many instances where a PIP insurer has paid $5,000 in benefits to his own insured and only recovered 10% when a jury verdict was over $50,000. There are many cases depending upon the judge, where 100% recovery is given. We believe that the Florida Legislature will address itself to this inequity and permit 100% recovery in all jurisdictions. Certainly, our law should not permit double recovery.

Another area of concern involves fraud. This is currently concentrated in South Florida, however, the cancer is spreading. The legislature, judiciary and the industry are investigating this problem now. The major problem in South Florida is where there is an obvious build-up of a minor injury to achieve the magic threshold of $1,000 in medical expenses.

In many cases, the companies would rather pay the demand than attempt litigation for two reasons:
 1. The defense cost could exceed the demand, and
 2. The fear of a jury awarding an extremely high judgment.

There are instances where claimants are placed in hospitals two weeks after an accident for soft tissue injuries. The medical specials are always slightly over $1,000. The plaintiff attorney enters and suit is filed.

We have theorized on many solutions within the industry. Would a higher or lower threshold soften the blow? We believe that regardless of the threshold some attorneys would find a way to abort the system.

An alternate method seeking a tort remedy involves that section of the law dealing with permanency. The law reads: "Permanent disfigurement, a fracture to a weight bearing bone, a compound, comminuted, displaced, or compressed fracture, loss of a body member, permanent injury within reasonable medical probability, permanent loss of a bodily function, or death." This broad language does little to discourage litigation. We believe that the legislature should address itself to this section of the law. A clearer definition of permanency would help. Many claimants are given 5% disability rating by a physician, which automatically permits the filing of a suit against the third party.

At the present time, the U.S. Attorney's Office, in conjunction with the U.S. Postal Authorities, are conducting an investigation into what appears to be obvious build-up of medical specials to reach the threshold. All attempts by the industry and the Florida Insurance Department to secure indictments by local grand juries have met with failure.

As an example of how the build-up works, let us examine a typical case. A school bus, occupied by 17 children, is struck in the rear by a 1971 Chevrolet. Metal damage to the automobile is $79. There was no damage to the school bus. Exactly 14 days later all 17 children were admitted to a Miami osteopathic hospital.

According to the medical reports, they were given anesthetics for the purpose of performing manipulative therapy. Their confinement times varied by child, however, each one exceeded the $1,000 threshold by amounts ranging from $10 to $100. Of interest in this case, the insurance company investigating the accident learned from the attendance records of the school, that one of the occupants of the bus did not attend school on the date of the accident. However, the child was given treatment as though he were an occupant.

While we have dealt with the problems, the consumer has found that dealing with his own company is pleasant, fair and efficient. The medical bills, wages and services are paid without the claimant's direct involvement. We have not found excessive malingering primarily because the threshold is at a level to provide sufficient funds for recovery from minor injuries. In the more serious injury cases, the benefits are paid by the first party carrier with the third party carrier intervening after the initial benefits are exhausted.

Gentlemen, we appreciate the opportunity of appearing before you this day and only ask that you re-examine the whole concept of no-fault as it relates to a state's inherent interest in this subject and recognize that a federal bill would not only throw the business of insurance into chaos affecting many of our small, but nevertheless excellent domestic insurers, but more importantly deny the residents of states like Florida the ability to demand of their state officials, whether they be appointed or elected, meaningful state action in insurance matters.

Thank you.

Mr. VAN DEERLIN. Mr. Mitchell, do you have any records that might help concerning the relative payout to the customer, the consumer, under your no-fault law as compared with the tort system, the percentage of premium dollar that returns to the insured?

Mr. MITCHELL. Mr. Chairman, I don't have those figures with me. Those are readily available from the Florida Insurance Department because we make filings, annual statements of, or filings with the Department each year which indicates to you the benefits paid to the citizens of this State versus the pre-no-fault time.

Mr. VAN DEERLIN. I think that would be quite useful to us to have that information since that is the proof of the pudding.

Mr. MITCHELL. Right. I am sure we can get that information for you and your committee.

Mr. VAN DEERLIN. We would appreciate having it, and we will accept it for the record if you make it available.

[The following letter was received for the record:]

FLORIDA ASSOCIATION OF LIFE AND CASUALTY INSURERS, INC.,
Tallahassee, Fla., August 6, 1975.

Hon. LIONEL VAN DEERLIN,
Chairman, Subcommittee on Consumer Protection and Finance,
Committee on Interstate and Foreign Commerce, Washington, D.C.

DEAR CONGRESSMAN VAN DEERLIN: My sincere thanks to you and your committee for the courtesies extended to me during your recent visit to Florida. It was our desire to give you all of the information needed to make a sound decision on a Federal No-Fault bill.

During my testimony, you requested data reflecting the average claim payout under *tort versus no-fault*. A review of your request with the Florida Insurance Department did not generate the exact information you desired.

According to the Department's Actuary, you have basically the same percentage of the claim dollar allocated to the claimant. Under the tort system, if Driver "A" struck Driver "B", "A's" insurance company paid 100% of the loss to "B" with "A" recovering nothing. The no-fault concept would require that Driver "A", if injured, would collect from his own company, with "B" collecting from his company. If "B's" medical and other expenses exceed the thresholds, then "A" would pay the additional expenses.

During the original debate of the Florida Law, it was stated that the no-fault concept would free up more money for the claimant. However, expenses and loss adjustment expenses have continued to escalate. The loss adjustment expense was the portion of the claim dollar that was to be reduced theoretically. This was not the case since claim investigators and attorneys' expenses remain necessary expense items under this law.

In conclusion, we must assume that there has been no substantial shift in the allocation of the claim dollar.

Congressman Van Deerlin, if you need additional input from us, please let us know.

Sincerely,

PRENTISS R. MITCHELL,
Associate Director.

Mr. Stuckey.

Mr. STUCKEY. No questions.

Mr. VAN DEERLIN. Mr. Metcalfe.

Mr. METCALFE. I have one question, Mr. Chairman.

Traditionally, as people become more financially competent they take on additional insurance to make certain they have adequate insurance in the event of death or illness, and I notice in your statement that you said that the Florida law should not permit double recovery. Would you elaborate on that and tell us why you think it should not have double recovery?

Mr. MITCHELL. Yes, sir.

I am glad you asked this question because it does need clarifying. The problem that we see that perhaps you might like to address yourself to at some future date, is by virtue of the fact Florida has a tremendous number of retirees, these people on medicare and medicaid, and those types of victims, auto accident victims are recovering from the insurance companies and getting the same benefits through medicare. So while we believe that if someone cares to carry two or three policies, if they are willing to pay the premium they are entitled to recover benefits and we have no objection to that. But I think perhaps where many of us as taxpayers may be paying the price on medicare, that perhaps you might want to look at that aspect and that is what I had reference to in double recovery. We just don't believe that someone should actually make a profit as a result of being an accident victim.

Mr. METCALFE. Thank you very much.

Mr. VAN DEERLIN. Mr. Scheuer.

Mr. SCHEUER. Thank you for your very interesting testimony. On your last page you oppose Federal intervention and you give one reason and say, "More importantly because it denies the residents of States like Florida the ability to demand of State officials, whether appointed or elective, meaningful State action in insurance matters."

Don't you believe citizens of States like Florida have a right also to demand of their Federal officials, appointed and elected, meaningful Federal action in insurance matters?

Mr. MITCHELL. Certainly. Obviously, that is why you are here to examine this.

Mr. SCHEUER. Right. So if we can set aside that more important of your two objections to Federal intervention in here, what precisely is your problem with a Federal bill that takes into account and reflects the experience that various States have had and the answers that a number of States have come up with that throws insight and considerable analysis into the experience of these States?

Take States like your own State, why they had successful experience and where their experience indicate that certain adjustments be made, certain recastings and adjustments of the original legislation be made. What are your reasons for opposing a Federal statute that takes into account all of the experience and all of the analysis and all of the reappraisals that have taken place on the State level?

Mr. MITCHELL. Mr. Congressman, I think the inherent fear here is, as I pointed out a minute ago, is that it is much easier for us at the State level, if we run into difficulties with the Federal bill, with S. 354 we begin to come up with the problems we pointed out here we have in this law, I am not so sure it would not take us forever to have those changes made in the law and before you can react to it you probably are going to be bankrupting some companies. That is our basic fear.

Mr. SCHEUER. Well, you already bankrupted some of your companies at the State level with inadequate structures.

Mr. MITCHELL. That is right.

Mr. SCHEUER. What makes you think the Federal Government would have a worse record in that regard?

Mr. MITCHELL. I am not so sure that some of those companies that went bankrupt had a great deal to do with the law. Some of that is just pure mismanagement more than anything else.

Mr. SCHEUER. You can't blame that on the Federal Government.

Mr. MITCHELL. No, you can't. But again I think our concern is we would have some difficulty in getting any amendments passed on your bill once it gets to that level.

Mr. SCHEUER. At the Federal level?

Mr. MITCHELL. Yes, sir.

Mr. SCHEUER. My goodness, if that is your only objection, we can show you experience with laws by the dozens and hundreds where after original passage of the law, Congress, through subcommittees like this, had conducted oversight, has conducted continuous scrutiny and has come in year after year with perfecting amendments to the original statute and we have passed those perfecting amendments just as the State legislature has done and as they are trying to do now with your no-fault.

Mr. MITCHELL. I am not so sure as to the people of Wyoming, for example, whose driving habits might be different from those of Florida.

Mr. SCHEUER. Do you have evidence for that?

Mr. MITCHELL. I have no evidence other than to tell you if you have a highly congested area such as Miami and you have many, many multicar pileups on expressways where it is so difficult to determine who originated the accident as opposed to not having that many multicar accidents as you probably would come up with in a small town in Wyoming and I say if you use those two analogies, you can't legislate from a Federal level a law that would encompass all of this.

Mr. SCHEUER. My goodness, we have been doing it for 199 years.

Mr. MITCHELL. I know, but in our estimation it just will not work and we just don't believe a Federal bill, or you can write a Federal bill that will encompass every eventuality as we can't do in Florida.

Mr. SCHEUER. No, no. Look, that is not good enough. I would like to come up with specific conditions, some specifics that a Federal bill could not contemplate, that a Federal bill could not rationalize. We have a big country here, but we have been passing laws for 199 years which seem to meet the varying and pluralistic population groups in our society, we have done it very well.

What makes you think on this one particular piece of legislation we could not pass a bill that would reflect both the needs of Washington and Wyoming if they are driving the same kinds of cars under the same federally mandated highway standards and this is a very homogeneous country when it comes to the internal combustion machine. We have, as I say, intelligent highway standards and cars are not produced for one State for use in that State, but they are produced in Detroit for use nationally.

Can you give me a single condition that would be beyond our means to treat with a single piece of national legislation? Give us some specifics.

Mr. MITCHELL. I would only suggest to you, Mr. Congressman, that we have only been involved in this no-fault question since Massachusetts passed their law in about 1970 or 1971. It would seem to me that, and I can't give you any specific specifics at this point, but it would seem to me if you wanted to pass a Federal bill that you should at least have the opportunity of having the expertise and the product of a number of other States. We only have the law right now in some eight or nine States in the country.

Mr. SCHEUER. Eighteen.

Mr. MITCHELL. Eighteen.

Mr. SCHEUER. We have come here to get your expertise. We have been to New York to get theirs, as I expect we will go to California for theirs and a few other States. We have gotten intelligent testimony from your State commissioner where he indicated experience showed a few adjustments ought to be made. Why do you believe it wouldn't be possible for us to canvas your experience and others of the 18 States and put together a package?

Mr. MITCHELL. That is what I am suggesting, if you will do that.

Mr. SCHEUER. That is what we have an intention of doing and that is why we are here this morning.

Mr. MITCHELL. I have no objections. I think that is good.

Mr. SCHEUER. Well, what is wrong with that process or a process that produces at the end of that pipeline a piece of legislation that seems to fit the needs of this State?

And that is why we are here, to find out what your needs are, as well as the other 18 States, and come up with a formula that seems to meet the national needs.

Mr. MITCHELL. When we talk about the fact we have 18 to 20 States that currently have a no-fault law, the laws have only been in effect a very short period of time. Unfortunately, it takes a lot of time to generate credible statistics. I am only suggesting to you, and I agree you could perhaps come up with a sound package in Washington, but I would only suggest to you that, perhaps because you are now in the posture, as I understand it, to be considering Senate bill 354 when it comes before your committee very soon, we would like this situation.

Mr. SCHEUER. This is a subcommittee of the House of Representatives and we may consider that or write our own bill based on our experience and listening to you and other expert witnesses like you and we are not bound to the Senate bill.

Mr. MITCHELL. We would urge you, Mr. Congressman, before whatever action you may take, that you have this committee look at statistics that have been matured, that are mature statistics from all of these States that have adopted these plans and then I think you would come up with a much better bill as opposed to trying to draft one at this point. That is our contention. It may be that down the road you will have one.

Mr. SCHEUER. We are not drafting a bill now, but having hearings now.

Mr. MITCHELL. You are, sure, and that is my suggestion.

Mr. SCHEUER. We are trying to distill the experience of all States that have had experience and to listen to informed local experts like yourself and out of all of this to distill out of that a bill that meets the national need and this is the process we are going through. This is a hearing. We are not writing a bill now. We are having hearings now and distilling information.

After having hearings here and in other States, we will sit down and try to collate all of this expert testimony, impressive testimony from people like yourself, and put together a bill that meets the national needs. Do you think it is possible?

Mr. MITCHELL. Yes; and I commend you for it. I think that is the way to go.

Mr. SCHEUER. Thank you.

Mr. VAN DEERLIN. Mr. McCollister.

Mr. MCCOLLISTER. Carrying on with Mr. Scheuer's line of questioning, isn't there some evidence that there are differing circumstances indicated by the fact that of the 24 States, or 18, if you ignore add-on States, that have come up with widely varying answers to that question in their own State, that is some evidence at least that the State-by-State approach is working? Had we legislated in 1971 on the basis of the Massachusetts model, I am sure that Michigan and a great many other States would have objected to it.

But more than that I think the fact that we do not have a single traffic law and that each State and each community has the jurisdiction as it relates to traffic, that is of some consequence in the argument as the compelling need for a national Federal no-fault law.

I have no other questions or comments, Mr. Chairman, in the interest of saving time.

Mr. VAN DEERLIN. I was waiting for the question.

Mr. Rinaldo.

Mr. RINALDO. Thank you, Mr. Chairman. I tend to agree with what you have just said in response to Mr. Scheuer but, on the other hand, I have to say that I also agree with Congressman Scheuer and Congressman McCollister in this respect, that while I think there is a great, almost insurmountable, difficulty in passing a bill that is going to be administered by each of the States, that is going to be compatible with all State plans; but, on the other hand, I think it would be relatively easy for Congress to dispose of this question by establishing minimum standards which each State must meet or exceed so that we do have some Federal jurisdiction over the matter and a law which will enable each State to participate legislatively, to administer their own plans without what I consider undue Federal interference, without what I consider the type of Federal interference that would create problems with existing plans, and would still allow each individual State to continue regulating the business of insurance.

Now, if we had a bill like this, would you have any objections to that type of legislation?

Mr. MITCHELL. Well, the basic premise is good and I don't think we would have any strong objections to it. It would work out. I would have a feeling it would sort of work a great deal better, Mr. Congressman, if, for example, in your State of New Jersey, if we took a look at the experience that is being generated by your State or by Congressman Stuckey's State, then we would have no particular qualms about taking a portion of your bill to make it compatible or maybe you do have the answer in New Jersey or maybe Georgia has the answer, but we think that we can do it that way, from an industry standpoint.

We are terribly displeased in Florida with the definition of permanency that I pointed out in my statement. We believe that perhaps in a State such as Michigan they have much more definitive language in their bill concerning permanency and we think this is the way we can go with it, because, believe me, the industry is not going to sit by idly and watch their business corrode simply because of law.

I am not sure that, as we suggest, minimum standards from the Federal Congress is the answer, that the industry would be—I think would like very much to continue the experiment by taking portions of other laws to come up with a model bill and I think they can do it.

Mr. RINALDO. Well, now, you confuse me. A little while ago you seemed to say that you were opposed to any type of Federal law in response to a question by Congressman Scheuer. Now you are saying minimum standards are not the answer but taking sections of different laws and trying to put together a model should be the approach?

Mr. MITCHELL. I just believe that is the experiment we should continue to try, Mr. Congressman, and then down the road somewhere if we find it is not working, I think you will probably see the industry come to you and say, let's have minimum standards. I think at this point of time because of the units of this concept, that it would be wise for Congress to let us continue to try this approach of taking a portion of your law and not give us minimum standards at this time, but we may be back later and say we wish we had not set it.

Mr. RINALDO. Do you favor a so-called model Federal law or Federal law with minimum standards?

Mr. MITCHELL. Well, if we had our choice we would probably take the limited standards.

Mr. MCCOLLISTER. You prefer not to take any?

Mr. MITCHELL. That is correct, we prefer not to take any.

Mr. RINALDO. I have no more questions.

Mr. VAN DEERLIN. Mr. Kinzler.

Mr. KINZLER. Mr. Mitchell, do you represent all of the casualty insurance companies in Florida?

Mr. MITCHELL. No, sir. We do not represent all of them.

Mr. KINZLER. Do you represent State Farm?

Mr. MITCHELL. Yes, sir.
Mr. KINZLER. Do you represent Aetna Life and Casualty?
Mr. MITCHELL. Yes.
Mr. KINZLER. Do they favor H.R. 1900 and S. 354?
Mr. MITCHELL. I believe they do.
Mr. KINZLER. So, could you give me a little feeling when you are here as a representative of this group who are you representing exactly?
Mr. MITCHELL. Right. The way we have to approach this subject with our member companies is generally based on what their input is to us. We go to the majority of the companies and ask them what their preference is.
Mr. KINZLER. Is the majority determined by permitting each company one vote or do the bigger companies have more votes?
Mr. MITCHELL. Not really. We try to poll all of the companies to get their feelings on it and we know we have conflicts within our own companies.
Mr. KINZLER. Do you have an approximate breakdown as to how many companies favor your approach and how many would favor the Federal standards approach?
Mr. MITCHELL. I don't have it available right now.
Mr. KINZLER. If I understood you correctly before, you talked about possibility of, not a uniform Federal law but a uniform State law for a model State code. There is a uniform State law in existence, is there not, a code called UMVARA. By the standards of UMVARA, which came out in 1972, can you give me an estimate of how many State laws would comply?
Mr. MITCHELL. No.
Mr. KINZLER. Let me suggest to you the number is one now—Michigan.
In response to Mr. Scheuer, you talked about certain things that you didn't think could be reconciled between States. Let me deal with the question of serious accidents. Is a serious accident different in Nebraska than it is in New York? Than it is in Michigan?
Mr. MITCHELL. Is a serious accident?
Mr. KINZLER. Yes.
Mr. MITCHELL. No it is not different.
Mr. KINZLER. In other words if we drafted a Federal bill or a uniform State code, wouldn't we want to try, if economically feasible, to cover most of the medical losses because they wouldn't vary from State to State?
Mr. MITCHELL. The only difference you would see in that type of situation, if you were, and this is in certain instances that have created the unconstitutional part of the law, is where you have an accident victim seriously injured in a small town and where you have a major metropolitan center, as we have in Florida, and because of the lesser cost of medical services in that particular town versus a major metropolitan center, you run into constitutional problems and that is the difference, as I see it.
For example, in a very small town, a person with a broken leg and confinement in a hospital, the room charge will be maybe $20 or $30 a day and the doctor makes a charge of $150 for a broken leg, but you take the same accident victim with the same broken leg in a city like Miami the room charge may be $100. He will reach that threshold so much quicker and this is a constitutional question that is raised.

Mr. KINZLER. This is a problem with dollar thresholds, be it a $1,000 threshold or a $200 threshold. Nobody has suggested any type of constitutional problems with the Senate type of verbal threshold, have they?

Mr. MITCHELL. Right.

Mr. KINZLER. Now, do you have in your control a profile of recovery of victims in Florida under the tort system as opposed to the no-fault system? Now, I don't mean the payout the chairman talked about, but the question of who was recovering how much in the $100 to $500 bracket, all the way up to $25,000 and over bracket?

Mr. MITCHELL. No. I think again that information is readily available because I saw it generated on our medical malpractice matters in Florida and I think it should be gotten from the Florida department, if you would like it?

Mr. KINZLER. If you could supply it for us, it would be of tremendous help. Let me state the reason I asked for it. If you have a system that covers up to $5,000 worth of benefits, again going back to the Department of Transportation study as a nationwide average and not necessarily Florida, of course, the recovery under the old tort system for those 44 percent of the people who had tort recovery was 160 percent of the economic loss, so you really have not helped them any, but, in fact, have taken something from them.

On the other hand, the other 56 percent would only recover 60 percent, so you see it will be useful to see a profile.

Mr. VAN DEERLIN. Ms. Nord.

Ms. NORD. One question. As you know, H.R. 1900 provides unlimited medical and concern has been expressed to the subcommittee as to the impact of such a provision on smaller insurance companies. Can you give us your opinion as to what the impact would be on the small Florida companies?

Mr. MITCHELL. I certainly can. The only problem or real problem we see with unlimited medical is that you have virtually no control from a time standpoint as to how long you may treat the patient. As soft tissue injury, whiplash, if you will, in this State could mean that that victim could be treated for an idefinite period of time and a company, from a pure reserving standpoint for that claim, would have almost no idea of the ultimate payout in certain instances.

So the unlimited medical from a small and even from a large company's standpoint, would we believe be absolutely chaotic.

Ms. NORD. Thank you.

Mr. VAN DEERLIN. Thank you, sir, for your very helpful testimony.

Mr. MITCHELL. Thank you, Mr. Chairman.

Mr. VAN DEERLIN. The next witness is Mr. Sam Rogers representing the Florida Association of Insurance Agents.

Good morning, Mr. Rogers.

STATEMENT OF SAMUEL B. ROGERS, FLORIDA ASSOCIATION OF INSURANCE AGENTS

Mr. ROGERS. Good morning, Mr. Chairman. My name is Samuel B. Rogers. I represent the Florida Association of Insurance Agents.

I have also a prepared statement that is before the committee, Mr. Chairman, and for the record I will also briefly summarize it, if I might. Primarily that is because our position is fundamentally the same as that of the Florida Insurance Department and there is some duplication in our testimony.

I would say that we appreciate the opportunity of appearing here before you on the subject of vital importance to insurance agents in this State because our members write a significant majority of the $400 million in no-fault automobile insurance premiums.

At the outset, I think it is important for the subcommittee to understand the membership of the association has long been among the strongest advocates of no-fault from the beginning of legislative study and debate nearly 4 years ago. After 3½ years experience, we remain convinced the law is in the public interest both as to injured accident victims and auto insurance consumers. We believe that no-fault automobile insurance is here to stay subject only to future expansion and improvement.

Our association and its members originally came out in support of no-fault after months of careful study and after years of endless problems caused by rising insurance rates, restrictive underwriting practices and bankrupt insurance companies in this State.

We believe that something had to give because the public was mad and it was frustrated with the whole what could be described as a sorry mess in the State of Florida.

Mr. McCue has already mentioned the fact we conducted a survey and the overwhelming support of the members was in favor of a no-fault approach. I can tell you from daily contact with our members that insurance agents remain enthusiastic in their acceptance of the law and the public benefits for citizens of Florida.

The injured accident victims are paid promptly by their own insurance companies and the right of the seriously injured person to recover in tort has not been impaired in any way. There is a strong competitive market in the State except in the lower east coast area of the State for automobile insurance.

The insurance consumer is paying less today than he would have had we remained under the tort system.

As Mr. McCue has said, without no-fault rates in Florida today it could well have been 50 to 60 percent higher than it otherwise would be. From the very beginning, the no-fault law, as it is in Florida today, was never represented as the perfect answer to all problems that beset Florida consumers and accident victims, but it was believed to be a careful first step subject to constant review and to subject improvements.

Now, with the experience of some 3½ years, we believe that it is time for revision and expansion in this State. We believe that the law should be modified as follows:

First, expansion to all vehicles, as Mr. McCue has pointed out. Second, keep personal injury protection benefits as they presently are at the $5,000 minimum, but enact legislation which would authorize the policyholder to buy limits up to $25,000 of first party benefits. By doing this, we believe that the increased benefits could be coordinated with the other types of insurance that the policyholder purchases.

We would also recommend an increase in the so-called lawsuit exemption or tort threshold from the current $1,000 up to $3,500, as has the Department. We believe that this would go a long way towards stopping some of the problems that exist in collusion when some doctors and some lawyers and some claimants in the lower east coast of

Florida today. Besides, the economics of inflation dictate some change in the last 3 or 4 years in the threshold is necessary.

We would also support legislation which would amend Florida law to provide for an assigned claims fund similar to what S. 354 has because there are some people in the State of Florida who are not able to collect no-fault benefits and primarly these are pedestrians hit by uninsured motorists.

We would also support enactment of a property damage provision which would enable the policyholder to collect from his own insurance company for property damage losses without the necessity of having to prove fault. As the bill was first passed in Florida, the Florida law contained such a provision which was subsequently ruled unconstitutional by the Florida Supreme Court, in I believe, *Kluger* v. *White*. We believe that such a provision can be reenacted in a manner consistent with the court decision in *Kluger* under which a policyholder would have a right to elect whether he wanted to sue in tort or collect from his own insurance company with a form of limited collision coverage.

On the subject of Federal versus State legislation, to us the best approach seems to be State legislation. We believe that the State legislatures are more responsive to the varying needs and can usually respond somewhat quicker than Congress can in the totality of the picture.

For example, on another somewhat related subject, about 6 months ago we woke up in Florida one morning with a medical malpractice crisis on our hands. Six thousand Florida doctors and 200 hospitals were faced with imminent loss of malpractice insurance and many doctors were threatening to quit work and indeed some did. Two legislative committees got started on the problem in March and by mid-April Governor Askew had signed into law the Medical Malpractice Reform Act of 1975 which carried with it the guarantee of insurance availability for medical malpractice insurance.

It was a crisis in 1971 that caused the Florida State legislature to enact no-fault in the first place, largely unplowed ground at that time. Yet, today the Congress is still debating the issue.

I would add that that is not intended as criticism of the Congress. Differences between Tallahassee and Miami can be resolved we believe much quicker than differences between Los Angeles and Macon, Ga., for example. Nonetheless we recognize that the public interest may well necessitate some form of Federal legislation and, if it is to come, we would prefer legislation which sets forth minimum standards, I believe, which is somewhat the legislation embodied in S. 354.

First, we believe that the legislation should set forth minimum standards as to benefits and coverage.

Second, permit maximum flexibility on a State-by-State basis to recognize the varying needs and circumstances.

Third, to vest regulatory control in State insurance commissioners and not in the Federal Government.

Fourth, to allow each State a reasonable period of time in which to comply.

Now, I will just close by saying we believe we made great progress in Florida in solving our own problems not only in the area of reparations but traffic safety, competitive insurance market availability, protection of the public from broke insurance companies and it would be our earnest hope that a Federal bill, if enacted, would not impair or interfere with the progress we believe we have made here in the sunshine State.

That pretty much concludes my remarks, sir.

[Mr. Rogers prepared statement follows:]

STATEMENT OF SAMUEL B. ROGERS, FLORIDA ASSOCIATION OF INSURANCE AGENTS

Mr. Chairman and members of the Committee—for the record—I am Sam Rogers, and I represent the Florida Association of Insurance Agents before the Florida Legislature and other instruments of government which regulate our business. Our membership consists of 1,260 Florida independent insurance agencies that employ some 6,000 local businessmen and women who earn their living from the sale and service of all forms of property and casualty insurance. Our members write a significant majority of the $400 million in auto insurance premium subject to Florida's No-Fault Law.

Mr. Smith requested that my remarks be addressed generally to Florida's No-Fault Auto Insurance Law (Florida Automobile Reparations Reform Act) from the perspective of the local insurance agent—and, specifically, to our views on the law's effectiveness, its deficiencies including needed improvements, and to the issue of state versus federal no-fault legislation.

At the outset, I believe it is important for the Committee to understand the membership of this Association have been among the strongest advocates of no-fault from the beginning of legislative study and debate nearly four years ago. After three years experience, we remain convinced the law is in the public interest both as to injured accident victims and auto insurance consumers. We are convinced no-fault automobile insurance is here to stay subject only to future expansion and improvement.

To understand the reason for our position requires some understanding of the plight of the insurance agent in attempting to provide for the automobile insurance needs of his policyholders during the period from 1967–71 immediately prior to enactment. Florida motorists were justifiably angry and frustrated, both with the insurance industry and with public officials over what could best be described as a "sorry mess" in the auto insurance business.

The motorist was being whip-sawed between rising auto insurance rates on the one hand, and a reluctance on the part of insurance companies to even write auto insurance on the other. It was estimated in 1969–70 that one-third of all Florida motorists were forced to buy auto insurance through the Assigned Risk Plan or, high-risk/high-rate companies. Public complaints of cancellations and arbitrary underwriting practices were rampant.

At least a half dozen insurance companies writing automobile insurance were in bankruptcy leaving thousands of policyholders without insurance and claimants unpaid. Five legislative investigating committees and two special sessions of the Legislature attempted to deal with the problem.

A major source of the problem—we believe—was the tort system of reparations.

The motorist was forced by law to buy an insurance policy for the protection of someone else. Then, when he had a claim, he was forced to look to the other fellow's insurance company and could collect only after proving himself totally blameless. Even then, he sometimes had a hassle in getting a proper claim settlement because the adversary nature of the tort system made a release of liability the primary object of settlement with equity of secondary concern.

In the summer of 1972, we completed a comprehensive survey of our membership seeking the result of, and their opinions on, Florida's new law after it had been in operation about three months. 706 of our member insurance agencies (65% of the total membership) participated in the survey. We believe it presents a fully credible, accurate representation of insurance agent attitude toward no-fault, both then and now. The results are summarized as follows:

1. Which system serves the public better? No-Fault—662 (94%); Old System—26 (3.6%).
2. Which system does the public prefer? No-Fault—570 (81%); Old System—54 (8.0%).
3. Under which system do companies perform better? No-Fault—587 (84%); Old System—50 (7.0%).
4. Has no-fault altered public attitude toward insurance? Yes—425; No—207. Favorably—381; Unfavorably—28.

5. Do your clients with claims appear to be satisfied with speed of payment: Yes—553 (78%); No—137 (19%). Benefit levels: Yes—635 (90%); No—35 (5%).

6. How are adjusters performing on no-fault claims (fairness, promptness, accuracy)? Excellent—153; Adequate—485; Inadequate—79.

7. How do you appraise your agency's current insurance market availability? Excellent—242; Adequate—397; Inadequate—50; None—23.

8. How do you rate your agency's standard auto insurance market availability now compared to pre no-fault? Better—412 (63%); Same—206 (31%); Poorer—35 (5%).

That is a brief summary of the more important responses to the questionnaire to give you an overview of insurance agent reaction to no-fault during its first year of operation. I can tell you, from daily contact with our membership, that insurance agents remain enthusiastic in their acceptance of the law.

Injured accident victims are paid promptly by their own insurance company on a first-party basis. The right of the seriously injured to recover in tort has not been impaired. With the exception of the lower East Coast of Florida, there is a strong competitive market available for the auto insurance needs of Florida motorists. It is my understanding that others are prepared to discuss the claims and market problems of South Florida.

The insurance consumer is paying less today for his automobile insurance as the result of no-fault. In the first two years after enactment, rate reductions of approximately 26% were implemented by most all insurance companies for the required coverages. While it is true that most companies have increased their automobile insurance rates in the past year, those increases were necessitated by the back-breaking effect of inflation on medical expenses and auto repair costs. Indeed, without no-fault, auto insurance rates in Florida today would probably be 50-60% higher than they presently are.

The current Florida Law was recognized as a careful first step in correcting some serious problems and in improving the system of delivering insurance benefits to injured persons. With over three years of experience now, we believe it is time to seriously consider expansion and improvement of the law. This Association will support amendments to existing law as follows:

1. Expansion to all vehicles except federally-owned vehicles. Present law covers only private passenger type vehicles.

2. Increase the availability of first-party, personal injury protection benefits to a maximum of up to $25,000 per person at the option of the policyholder. Minimum PIP benefits should be retained at the current $5,000. This would enable policyholders to coordinate no-fault benefits with other forms of insurance such as group hospitalization, accidental death and disability, and income protection benefits.

3. Increase the tort or law-suit exemption from the current $1,000 to $3,500. This change would go a long way toward correcting problems of collusion between claimants, doctors and lawyers on the lower East Coast of Florida.

4. Establish an assigned claims fund. There are some persons in Florida who have no way to receive no-fault benefits. Primarily, these are persons who do not own an automobile and are struck by an uninsured motorist.

5. Re-enact a property damage provision which enables a policyholder to collect from his own insurance company for damage to his automobile regardless of fault. As originally enacted, the Florida Law did contain a property damage provision which was ruled unconstitutional by the Florida Supreme Court. We believe such a provision can be re-enacted in a manner consistent with the Court ruling which would give the policyholder the right to elect whether to recover in tort or from his own insurance company.

In the past five years, it is my understanding that nearly every state legislature has considered no-fault automobile insurance and only about half have actually enacted such laws. If one is to conclude, generally, that the public benefits of no-fault far outweigh those of the tort system, Congress then has an understandable interest in making certain those benefits are available to all citizens.

Obviously, the best approach is state legislation. The state legislature is more responsive to the varying needs of states and generally can respond to those needs much quicker than Congress. For example, less than six months ago we in Florida woke up one morning to a crisis of major proportion in the field of medical malpractice insurance. Six thousand Florida doctors and about 200 hospitals were faced with the imminent loss of vitally needed medical malpractice insurance. Many doctors were threatening to quit work and indeed, some did. Early in March, two legislative committees began work and, by the end of April, Governor

Askew had signed into law the Florida Medical Malpractice Reform Act which carries with it an immediate statutory guarantee of a malpractice insurance market.

In 1970, it was a crisis in Florida that caused the Florida Legislature to enact the No-Fault Automobile Insurance Law. Yet, Congress is still debating. And that is not intended as criticism of Congress. Differences between Tallahassee and Miami can be reconciled much quicker than differences between Los Angeles and Macon, Georgia.

Nonetheless, we recognize that the public interest may well call for some form of federal legislation assuring the benefits of no-fault to all citizens in every state. If federal legislation becomes necessary, we would prefer a bill which:

1. Sets forth minimum standards with respect to benefits and coverage requirements.
2. Permits maximum flexibility on a state-by-state basis so as to recognize variances in need and circumstances between individual states.
3. Vests regulatory control in the state's supervisory authority and not the Federal Government.
4. Gives each state a reasonable period of time to comply.

In summary, we believe the states should be given the greatest possible latitude in developing no-fault legislation, both as to substance and time frame. Florida has made great progress in solving its own problems relating to the automobile, not only in terms of reparations, but traffic safety, competitive insurance market availability and protection of the public from the consequences of bankrupt insurance companies. It would be our earnest hope that federal legislation would not interfere with or impede the progress we are to achieve here in the Sunshine State.

Mr. VAN DEERLIN. Thank you, Mr. Rogers.

I must say in both of the areas you cited, Florida—whether or not we can call it a sunshine State this afternoon—has moved more swiftly than my own State of California.

Mr. McCollister.

Mr. MCCOLLISTER. I want to thank Mr. Rogers for his testimony and I have no questions.

Mr. VAN DEERLIN. Mr. Stuckey.

Mr. STUCKEY. Thank you, Mr. Chairman.

I have no questions other than to comment that you commented on Congressmen moving slowly and I think in many instances the American people ought to be very thankful that they move as slowly as they do.

Mr. ROGERS. We agree with that.

Mr. VAN DEERLIN. Mr. Rinaldo.

Mr. RINALDO. No questions.

Mr. VAN DEERLIN. Mr. Metcalfe.

Mr. METCALFE. Thank you very much, Mr. Chairman. I have no questions other than to make an observation that Mr. Rogers has given us a lot of thought as to some provisions that may very well be considered when we go into the markup for the bill and I think it can be translated in terms of national and Federal legislation emanating out of Washington.

I notice he did not take a very hard line against Federal legislation, which is encouraging. Thank you very much.

Mr. VAN DEERLIN. Mr. Scheuer.

Mr. SCHEUER. I want to thank the witness for his extremely interesting testimony. I take it that subject to the strictures on page 4, the four requirements you state, that you do favor a Federal bill?

Mr. ROGERS. No, sir, we do not necessarily favor a Federal bill. We would prefer it if the States could enact their own legislation. But we understand that the Congress has an interest in seeing that benefits of no-fault will be available to all citizens and in that context, if we have to have it, we prefer a minimum standards bill. I don't necessarily refer to S. 354 as the bill to do that job either.

Mr. SCHEUER. Thank you very much.

Mr. VAN DEERLIN. Mr. Kinzler.

Mr. KINZLER. I have just one question. Do you have any figures as to the cost experience of insurance companies in the State of Florida since the inception of the law? I know Florida started off with a 15-percent reduction built into law and followed with an 11 percent in 1973. Do you know what the experience of the insurance companies has been in terms of rates since that time?

Mr. ROGERS. In terms of rate increases?

Mr. KINZLER. Rate increases, yes.

Mr. ROGERS. No, sir. I think that probably rates very probably, in the last 2½ years, in total, have increased about 25 percent. They are probably back at the level they were on the date that no-fault was enacted.

Mr. KINZLER. Three and a half years ago.

Mr. ROGERS. Yes, sir.

Mr. KINZLER. I think that is accurate with respect to Allstate, which has had increases of 15 and 19.1 percent, which is about a washout.

Mr. ROGERS. That is correct.

Mr. KINZLER. Thank you.

Mr. VAN DEERLIN. Ms. Nord.

Ms. NORD. No questions.

Mr. VAN DEERLIN. Thank you, Mr. Rogers.

Mr. ROGERS. Thank you, sir.

Mr. VAN DEERLIN. Mr. McCollister notes when hearings are conducted in Omaha they take a 5-minute break for coffee and suggests that that happy practice be observed.

Mr. MCCOLLISTER. Not just the committee, but the audience also. [Brief recess.]

Mr. VAN DEERLIN. The hearing will resume.

One of the purposes in coming into the field in the manner that the subcommittee has done is to hear evidence from persons who have had individual experiences under the law.

Our next witness, therefore, will be Dr. Jose Albovias from Ormond Beach who is going to describe his own experience as an accident victim under the Florida law.

Dr. Albovias, will you sit down and simply proceed at your own desired pace.

STATEMENT OF JOSE ALBOVIAS, M.D., ORMOND BEACH, FLA.

Dr. ALBOVIAS. Thank you.

The accident happened around October 30, 1974. There was nobody involved except myself. I was confined in the hospital for over a month and then I was confined again December 29, 1974, for about 7 days.

Mr. VAN DEERLIN. What was the nature of the accident, doctor? Was it a collision?

Dr. ALBOVIAS. It was a collision. I hit a tree.

Mr. VAN DEERLIN. You hit a tree?

Dr. ALBOVIAS. Yes, sir.

Mr. Van Deerlin. I believe that is not referred to technically as a collision?

Dr. Albovias. No, sir.

Mr. Van Deerlin. A collision is between two moving vehicles.

Mr. Scheuer. That tree might have moved right out of that place and moved into the road to hit him.

Mr. Van Deerlin. Don't let the committee upset you.

Mr. Stuckey. Do you know the colloquialism of the South, Mr. Chairman, that is known as straightening out a curve.

Dr. Albovias. I was driving and it was early morning and I hit a tree. What really happened I don't have any idea except I hit a tree and I was contacted by letter stating I sustained a fractured left leg, several ribs, and several vertebrae for which I stayed in the hospital from October 30th until I think December 3d and then I went back on December 29th until January 11th. Up to this time I am still under treatment for followup.

Mr. Van Deerlin. What occurred under your insurance?

Dr. Albovias. The insurance, the insurance paid me on the loss of income and the hospitalization and medical expenses.

Mr. McCollister. When did you receive your payment from your insurance company?

Dr. Albovias. I received it I think around December when I was in the hospital.

Mr. McCollister. Did it cover all of your hospital costs and all of your loss of income?

Dr. Albovias. No.

Mr. McCollister. Do I recall right that it was a $5,000 limit?

Dr. Albovias. The way I understood it the first $5,000 for loss of income and medical expenses. Part of it I receive as loss of income and part of it as medical expenses. After that I received again the extra $1,000 for medical expenses.

I believe the loss of income was about, over $3,100 of the first $5,000.

Mr. Van Deerlin. Are you a medical doctor?

Dr. Albovias. Yes, sir.

Mr. Van Deerlin. So that loss of income might have been rather substantial, am I correct, doctors being among our better paid practitioners?

Dr. Albovias. For the first 2 or 3 months for me that is not enough for my expenses.

Mr. Van Deerlin. I didn't understand that doctor.

Dr. Albovias. The reason I say for the first 3 months I qualified because I am covered also with other insurance, but from the time of the accident up to this time, the only thing I got is around $3,100.

Mr. Van Deerlin. I see. Are you generally satisfied with the manner in which you were treated?

Dr. Albovias. Yes, in a way, yes. The reason I say in a way is that I received what I am supposed to receive under the law and I think probably it should have been a little bit more.

Mr. Van Deerlin. You received it quickly?

Dr. Albovias. Yes.

Mr. Van Deerlin. And you say you think it should have been a little bit more?

Dr. ALBOVIAS. Well, in a way, because it is supposed to be your loss of income, and I am not trying to say I should be paid for everything, but in my condition it was not enough.

Mr. VAN DEERLIN. Had you ever, before the no-fault law, been in an accident where you had dealt with your insurance company, so that you have some way of comparing the manner in which you were taken care of under this law as you might have been without the law?

Dr. ALBOVIAS. Yes. Sometime I think around 1971 I was hit from the back in Ohio, that was a collision, this is the collision part of the insurance where I had to pay deductible, although it was not my fault I still had to pay deductible because the other party did not have insurance, State insurance. There was no State insurance.

Mr. VAN DEERLIN. Would any members like to question the doctor?

Mr. Scheuer.

Mr. SCHEUER. Doctor, there must have been a reason why you consented to appear before us today. There must have been something you want to tell us. Is there something you have not been asked that you really feel would help us in our insight, in our understanding of how this bill affects the consumer, the driver, the passenger who is involved in an accident?

Dr. ALBOVIAS. Well, the only thing, of course, you see, my appearance was mainly voluntary.

Mr. SCHEUER. Yes.

Dr. ALBOVIAS. I wanted to see, you know, what experience other people have, or whatever they think, may affect the community. What I am trying to say actually, it seems like no-fault insurance, under this present provision, might not be enough.

Mr. SCHEUER. What do you think additionally would be needed?

Dr. ALBOVIAS. Well, probably contingent benefits somehow.

Mr. STUCKEY. I wonder if someone can answer a question for me. Does Florida have provisions for the purchase of additional insurance?

Mr. McCUE. No.

Mr. STUCKEY. I wonder if this has come up? That should not be a problem to enact into law.

Mr. McCUE. Yes.

Mr. STUCKEY. I think this would answer your question, doctor, for people in your position who are highly specialized and where result of injury or loss of your work would be substantial.

Mr. McCUE. If I can make a statement, in May of this year there were filed with the Department voluntary increases up to $25,000 in P.I.P. benefits that the individual can purchase, it is strictly up to them and not compulsory, but there are provisions from a company standpoint that they are providing.

Mr. STUCKEY. We seem to have a great disagreement.

Mr. MATTHEWS. We are on next.

Mr. STUCKEY. Thank you.

I think in this situation, if it does exist, those in a specialized field could take advantage of this.

Mr. SCHEUER. Is there anything else you would like to tell us that you think would enrich our understanding of the needs of the driving public?

Dr. ALBOVIAS. No.

Mr. SCHEUER. Anything as to how we could write a law benefiting the people in cars and walking on the streets?

Dr. ALBOVIAS. To me, what I am thinking about is really the increasing of the benefit portion that you can get out of your insurance.

Mr. SCHEUER. Mostly to cover your loss in earnings?

Dr. ALBOVIAS. Loss in earnings and hospitalization or medical expenses.

Mr. SCHEUER. Thank you.

Mr. VAN DEERLIN. Mr. Metcalfe.

Mr. METCALFE. Doctor, you indicated you received how much in benefits as a result of no-fault insurance all together?

Dr. ALBOVIAS. $7,000.

Mr. METCALFE. Now you indicated that was not enough to take care of your medical as well as your loss of income. How much do you estimate that the medical plus your loss of income was?

Dr. ALBOVIAS. I am trying to figure it out. The income actually the loss of income, I am basing it on 3 months, should be at least double what I received.

Mr. METCALFE. Well, we have to differentiate because part of that money you received was for loss of income and the other was medical and I am trying to keep them together because it is still expenses that you had to consider. So you were paid $7,000 for medical benefits as well as for loss of income?

Dr. ALBOVIAS. That is what I was paid for.

Mr. METCALFE. Yes. Now what I am trying to find out is how much more money do you think you required when you say $7,000 is not enough?

Dr. ALBOVIAS. I can't, I don't have the exact figure on what your question was.

Mr. METCALFE. Let me pose this question in another way. You said you had other medical benefits. In receiving those benefits, did that compensate you for your medical bills, your loss of income, minus what you were reimbursed in the amount of $7,000, in other benefits?

Dr. ALBOVIAS. Yes, sir.

Mr. METCALFE. I have no other questions.

Mr. VAN DEERLIN. Any further questions for the witness?

Thank you very much, doctor, for sharing your experience with us.

Our next witness will be F. Lawrence Matthews, representing the Florida Bar Association, who will be accompanied by Harold Gross and Patrick Chidnese.

STATEMENT OF HAROLD GROSS, CHAIRMAN, FLORIDA BAR NO-FAULT INSURANCE COMMITTEE; ACCOMPANIED BY F. LAWRENCE MATTHEWS, FLORIDA BAR ASSOCIATION; AND PATRICK CHIDNESE, VICE CHAIRMAN, FLORIDA BAR NO-FAULT INSURANCE COMMITTEE

Mr. GROSS. I am Harold Gross, chairman of the Florida Bar No-Fault Insurance Committee and on my right is Mr. Matthews and to my left Patrick Chidnese, vice chairman.

We came in force because each of us handled many areas in no-fault throughout the State in the course of the year and we contributed articles and lectured throughout the State for the Florida

Bar, and Larry Matthews wrote articles nationally, and Pat Chidnese, to my left, does a great deal of defense work representing major insurance carriers in the State of Florida, Larry and I both do plaintiff work and I did defense for 5 years, but have not for a number of years.

I have no prepared statement at this point other than to say that the Florida Bar is absolutely not opposed to no-fault legislation as it exists today in the State of Florida. We are opposed to a national no-fault at this time. That is not the same as saying we might not be opposed sometime in the future. What we would like to do is see exactly how our plan would work after at least a period of 5 years, see how the other States would work after a period of 5 years sort of as some type of laboratory to see if we need a Federal plan.

I rarely comment at a trial on other people's comments, but there were some comments made a few minutes ago about threshold. As far as I am concerned, in my personal opinion, based upon trying lawsuits since this law has been enacted in Florida, I think there should be no threshold requirement at this point. That is not to say I would not change my position after seeing more study from other States. This is based on my personal observations.

It is extremely difficult to see somebody come into the office and say they have $900 in medical bills and $950 in medical expenses and no broken bones and they don't come within the exceptions, since we have a $1,000 threshold in Florida and I say to them: "I'm sorry, you don't have a third party claim. You have not reached the threshold requirement. All you are entitled to is the set benefits." They can't seem to understand.

I say, "I'm sorry, that is the way it is.' Well we will see about it, and the next thing you know they wind up with another lawyer and another doctor and all of a sudden they have $1,000 in medical bills and file a lawsuit. I can't see that $1,500, $2,500 or $3,500 is going to make any difference. You are just fostering theft, that is exactly what you do between lawyers, doctors, and clients, or whatever. There is no necessity for it.

Mr. VAN DEERLIN. You mean if you can get to the $1,000, you can get to $3,500?

Mr. GROSS. They go into a hospital 7 days a+ $90 or $95 a day and then you have X-rays and tests. Your general practitioner calls in the neurological man and the orthopedic man to check your liver or spleen or this and that and then you have the EKG man and the radiologist and before you leave the hospital you have $3,500 in bills from the hospital review.

Mr. VAN DEERLIN. Would peer review help?

Mr. GROSS. Well, peer review would probably help, assuming the hospital has sufficient financial means not to need the money. There are many hospitals, they have no peer review at all, none whatsoever. They will keep you in there as long as you want to stay. There is just no necessity for it.

My personal opinion, based upon 10 years of practicing law, is if you have a man that comes into your office and let's say he has $300 or $400 in medical bills, it is easier to resolve the claim for $1,500 or $1,700 or $1,800 than to see the man to go another doctor or another lawyer and come up with $1,000 in medical bills and cost the insurance carrier $5,000 or $7,500 or $10,000 to resolve that claim. If you have a man with maybe a $300 or $400 bill if the insurance carriers would get their adjusters off their rear ends working in the field they would be able to speak with these people and say: Listen, we have first party benefits here. You are going to receive your loss of wages and medical expenses and we will be glad to resolve any pain and suffering. They won't need a lawyer and I wouldn't be opposed to that. Not at all.

That is just the brief remarks I had.

Larry Matthews and Pat Chidnese have individual remarks and we would like to answer your questions because we feel we have answers to questions you asked and I know Mr. Scheuer had some questions and we don't think they were properly answered in some respects and we think we can give you some of the answers.

Mr. STUCKEY. Do you have more crooks than in Miami or is that where everybody goes?

Mr. GROSS. Unfortunately, no, we sat in the back and heard everybody relate to Miami. Pat works in Broward County and we try lawsuits all over the State. You know, fortunately as people are human I imagine it can happen anywhere in the country where there is money involved and it is hard to say to a man, "You are not hurt." He says, "Listen, I have not slept with my wife for two days and she's mad at me," and he can't go to work.

It is difficult to explain to that man his $300 hospital bill does not qualify him to allow him to file a lawsuit.

Mr. VAN DEERLIN. You may have gone over that a little too fast for me.

Mr. GROSS. You know when a man brings his wife into the office and she sits and says my husband has not been with me for 2 days, he just is not the same man, he is hurt, he is in pain, I have been married to him 25 years and I have never seen him like this before, and I say to her, "He has only $600 in medical expenses, there is nothing we can do."

Mr. STUCKEY. I want to know how you handle a situation like that?

Mr. RINALDO. How about pain and suffering?

Mr. VAN DEERLIN. There are some that might want a test of more than 2 days.

Mr. GROSS. If I may, I would like Larry Matthews to make his statement, please.

Mr. VAN DEERLIN. Mr. Matthews.

STATEMENT OF F. LAWRENCE MATTHEWS

Mr. MATTHEWS. Mr. Chairman, we must confess a bias, all of the witnesses that appeared before you have some sort of bias in one direction or another.

Our bias as attorneys who are practicing in the personal injury area is in favor of benefits to injured people. We represent plaintiffs and we represent defendants. To us, the question of the cost of the premium is secondary because our day-to-day work is involved with people who have been unfortunate enough to be involved in automobile accidents. Assuming this, and we know the committee is very interested in the costs of different types of insurance plans and particularly the cost of different insurance plans which have brought our arguments here today and the arguments we have been making within the Florida Bar for the last 2½ years.

Our basic position is not in opposition to no-fault insurance and not even in opposition to Federal no-fault insurance. We are not making a presentation strongly for States' rights and "Save your Confederate money, boys, the South shall rise again."

Mr. STUCKEY. Why do people always refer to the South when they think of States' rights?

Mr. MATTHEWS. When State laws came into effect one State after another enacted plans and modified the plans based on the previous State's experience. We are afraid if Congress enacts a plan at this point which sets out specific guidelines that that will stop experimentation. There will be no further development in the law.

Now it is absolutely true that because Congress has been inquiring into this area since 1972, that has stimulated many of the 24 States which have some sort of no-fault insurance to enact a plan to beat Congress to the punch.

Mr. McCOLLISTER. May I interrupt you at that point, Mr. Matthews. There are some who say that the effect of the Congress consideration of this issue has indeed inhibited States from acting, that their attitude is why should we go through all of this when it is likely the Congress will pass some sort of law that will make all of our efforts useless.

Mr. MATTHEWS. I think that might be an argument that is being put forward in some States that strongly resisted no-fault.

Mr. McCOLLISTER. You don't think it is real?

Mr. MATTHEWS. I don't think it is valid. Where we go from 1971 to 1975 and in 4 years have almost half of the States enacting some sort of no-fault insurance plan, I think it is very definitely because of congressional pressure and interest in the area.

As the plans have been developed, they have been changed and modified in definitions, in the types of relief, in the threshold relief, in the different types of coverage. In the report we submitted we detailed some of them which go beyond just the question of premium or threshold, whether it should be $1,000 or death or permanent or serious disability, to other questions.

I would like to go beyond the report and mention some other examples. The beneficial effect of no-fault insurance has been to bring in compulsory insurance in all of the States which have threshold plans, we have gone from three States now to 24 States which have some sort of compulsory insurance. From one working in the field, I think this is a definite benefit. I am opposed and I have a good friend who spends his career helping migrant farmworkers in the South and around Homestead and his clients cannot afford automobile insurance and is afraid compulsory insurance will drive his clients, who are presently working in agriculture as migrant farmworkers commuting from job to job and place to place in uninsured vehicles, off the roads and force them on to welfare. For that reason, he is opposed.

Mr. STUCKEY. Will you yield?

That is one of the reasons you need some type of compulsory insurance. For example, in the District of Columbia, over 40 percent of the drivers of automobiles have no auto insurance. I think that is ridiculous. You know, that is what you have an uninsured pool for.

Mr. MATTHEWS. I agree.

Mr. STUCKEY. Does Florida not have such a pool?

Mr. MATTHEWS. It has a pool and the rates run from two to three times what the standard rates would be. Going just to the type of development here.

Mr. SCHEUER. In dollars, how much per month would drive a man off a gainful occupation on to welfare?

Mr. MATTHEWS. Your minimum premium could be as high as $400 to $600 a year, depending upon where he lives, how many people there are in the family.

Mr. MCCOLLISTER. How much, $400 to $600 a year?

Mr. MATTHEWS. It is dependent upon the number of people in his family. If you have a large family with three or four drivers and heaven help us, if any of those drivers under the age of 25, your assured risk premium will be several hundred dollars a year for minimum limits.

Mr. VAN DEERLIN. Mr. Kinzler has a question.

Mr. KINZLER. There is a provision in H.R. 1900 and S. 354 to take care of exactly the situation you are talking about. It is a provision which says in essence, if the premium would prevent a person from being able to work, in effect, there is a subsidy for that. Isn't that more effective than the Florida approach?

Mr. MATTHEWS. Absolutely. This is the kind of thinking which is going into developing no-fault plans, that here is an area, Florida, being the second State, where we have more experience, but there have been developments since then such as this, providing a mechanism for relief when the premium level is too high.

Mr. KINZLER. What further advancement could you possibly see under this?

Mr. MATTHEWS. I will give you examples of types of advancements. Florida and Massachusetts and many of the States who passed laws originally and S. 354 and the House bills under consideration all talk about paying reasonable medical expenses, and reasonable is nowhere defined. Certainly the insurance companies and doctors often disagree.

Mr. KINZLER. Let's stay away from reasonable medical expense. You can go back, but let's stay to the specific point you raised. Can you see any advance beyond what the Federal legislation would do? If not, it seems to me that problem is taken away and then you can go back to talk about other things.

Mr. MATTHEWS. I believe the Pennsylvania act not yet in effect has a provision identical to the Federal one and the Pennsylvania act, which is the most recent comprehensive no-fault act, incorporates all of the developments from States that were early in the field like Massachusetts and Florida, and bring it to the state of the art as it is now, including such provisions as this.

It is too soon and it has not gone into effect so we can tell how effective it will be in delivering not only the social benefits of reparations to victims, but also the practical benefit of better equalization of costs and equaling of premiums.

What I say, S. 354, and H.R. 1900, Congressman Eckhardt's bill, to totally abolish automobile tort suits and all of these other things are the state of the art as they are now. There are numerous experiments going on in the States. These experiments we think should continue.

Now, I think that Congress can provide a valuable service at this time either by continuing to investigate the area, to continue the Federal pressure, or if Congress wishes to, to pass a law just mandating all States pass some type of Federal no-fault insurance and after a period of time the information being developed from the 50 States, through the Department of Transportation, if at that point on empirical data it appears that a Federal solution is required for all States that would mandate certain minimum requirements, then I think it would be warranted.

But to overturn the automobile casualty industry, which is the insurance industry, now being the largest individual industry in the country, based on theoretical projections and what we think would be best at the current time, I think that is unwarranted.

Mr. RINALDO. Excuse me. Your point intrigued me, when you said Congress should pass some kind of law mandating all States to have Federal no-fault. I think it is almost an impossibility for Congress to pass a law saying you should have some kind of no-fault. There has to be something in that Federal legislation.

I assume, despite the fact you said there should be minimum standards, you are saying there has to be some minimum standards in that Federal law, because otherwise you won't provide guidelines of any substance and with sufficient direction to the various States.

Mr. VAN DEERLIN. What he is saying is you can't demand a bill entitled no-fault legislation without describing what you mean by it, Mr. Matthews.

Mr. SCHEUER. Mr. Chairman, didn't Mr. Rogers, on page 6 of his testimony, state pretty much what this gentleman is talking about. He says the public interest may well call for some form of Federal legislation and the first would be minimum standards with respect to benefits and coverage. Second, maximum flexibility on a State-by-State basis to recognize the variances in need and circumstances.

Third, vest regulatory control in the State's supervisory authority and not the Federal Government.

Fourth, give each State a reasonable period to comply.

This would continue the experimentation you talk about in sort of an eclectic collection of data, but it would provide for some kind of program and it seems to me that is one possible approach.

Mr. MATTHEWS. Yes. If you require the States to enact compulsory liability insurance and compulsory first person benefits, you will have every State then having some sort of no-fault act. If you require $1,000 or $2,000 as some States have, or $5,000 personal, or rather first person benefits, we think the door should be left open on questions of threshold and of exemptions and subrogation and insurers' rights.

Mr. STUCKEY. What is the problem with subrogation?

Mr. MATTHEWS. The question of subrogation is whether or not it is beneficial in the long run at all. Subrogation is a suit between one insurance company and another insurance company.

Mr. STUCKEY. Have you looked at the actual figures, though?

Mr. MATTHEWS. The actual figures, I read the testimony put forth by the Insurance Co. of North America which has been a strong proponent of abolishing it and at least in their State of Pennsylvania, they have been successful in abolishing it.

Mr. STUCKEY. I am not talking about that but what the figures actually show?

Mr. MATTHEWS. Their figures show, to the best of my recollection, that about 30 to 35 percent of the benefits are lost to attorneys' fees and costs in the system.

Mr. STUCKEY. Also at the end of the year, do the figures show they would have come out just about the same without this swapping of dollars?

Mr. MATTHEWS. That is their whole position. That, in the course of a year, a company is going to pay out as much in subrogation claims as it gets back in, and the only ones to benefit from the system are attorneys handling cases and it has the second detrimental effect on the system of increasing docket pressure and the docket load. We don't have that problem in Florida because we have a common docket or we have common dockets and are able to obtain trials within 6 to 9 months or shorter, where some Northern States may wait 3 to 5 years.

Mr. SCHEUER. Isn't it largely because you have a no-fault system here?

Mr. MATTHEWS. No. It is mostly because we have a bunch of judges pushing very hard and we have a constitutional provision or did have until 2 years ago which automatically increased the number of judges with the population without requiring legislative act, which kept us with a judiciary which was satisfactory to handle the cases and has been extremely hardnosed in pushing the case through to conclusion.

So we have short docket times here. We don't have problems of a major urban center like things in the Northeast or the Midwest where the judiciary has been far down on the list of appropriations in the State House. That is because there just was not enough interest in it and docket times have just expanded and expanded.

Down here we have very short docket times which has enabled us I think to gain more experience in no-fault because you have more cases that have been tried and appealed.

To get back to subrogation, we go from one end, Pennsylvania, which abolished it completely, to the other end, to Michigan, which gives a complete indemnity to the insurance company. If an injured person does have a third party claim, and has $5,000 worth of no-fault benefits paid and makes a third party claim and collects $5,000, his insurance company gets $5,000 and the injured person gets $10,000. Florida has attempted equitable distribution which was roundly castigated by a witness earlier in which a company gets a proportion of the recovery, but the individual judge handling it has discretion to adjust it on a case-by-case basis, based on the equities of the situation wherein the term equitable distribution comes in.

It is still too soon to tell which of these types of remedies are going to be successful in accomplishing the dual goal of compensation of accident victims and reducing the social cost of automobile accidents.

The Senate bill, S. 354, which I mentioned because it has the most publicity, gives the insurance company a complete payback, complete subrogation right. I think it would be wrong to cut off experimentation in this field.

Another field that is undergoing development, and I mentioned it briefly before, was reasonable medical expenses. Now, the States that went into it in the beginning, like Massachusetts and Florida, said reasonable medical expenses without any definition.

The Uniform Act and the legislation originally presented to Congress several years ago which has just been talked about and talked about with some minor modifications, also retains that clause of reasonable medical expenses.

Experience has shown that doctors and insurance companies and injured people usually have wildly different definitions of what is reasonable. Now, later States, and I am thinking particularly of Utah, which has just put in a plan to define "reasonable" and it sets out in its statute how the Department of Insurance is to determine what is reasonable and provide a schedule.

Another part of that plan also would provide for an impartial board of three doctors to arbitrate the question between the company and the doctor over what is reasonable. This is experimentation which can be helpful to Congress which would be cut off if Congress passes a uniform act with guidelines for the States at this time.

We can go directly through practically every part of the act. We can talk about thresholds. We have a variety of thresholds from Michigan's which is identical to Senate bill 354 because they both came from the basic source to Hawaii which sets up a flexible threshold that the Department of Insurance would adjust every year so as to include 90 percent of all suits the dollar amounts from $200 in New Jersey for soft tissue injuries, only to $2,000 in North Dakota, which has just been enacted to the Delaware type plans which have no threshold, which we personally like, but you will not know, when you make your decision, what type of law would be best for the entire country, which is actually the best, unless this period of experimentation is allowed to continue until at least several years. And by "several years" I mean if an accident occurs, you have to wait until a substantial period, say the statute of limitations has run, and a little period beyond, that to close all of the claims we evaluate, even the first accident years that is the basis of it.

You asked the doctor to testify about payment, and he said he was paid rapidly. Florida's no-fault plan has an excellent provision which puts the burden on the insurance company to establish in 30 days whether or not they will pay the person and to pay him. The burden is on the insurance company rather than the injured person to accumulate the information and to begin the payment.

Other States in the proposed Federal solutions are silent on this point, which would generally result in insurance companies saying: Okay, when you can completely document all of your medical care and lost wages, we will begin payments within 30 days.

We think the Florida provision that mandates they must aggressively go out and establish coverage or noncoverage and begin payments within 30 days is a benefit because it gets the payments to injured people as rapidly as possible.

This is essentially the conclusion of my remarks in support of the report I submitted to you and it is all generally saying the same thing, we are not against no-fault insurance. I mean we are not even against the idea of some sort of nationwide plan, when there is hard empirical data to support it. There is not now. But Congress has been pushing and it has been effective in getting the States to pass plans and we would wish Congress would continue this process of prodding the States until a point is reached until every State has a no-fault plan and information can be developed.

That may require the passage of some sort of act to require mandatory first person benefits and mandatory compulsory insurance.

Mr. RINALDO. I would suggest you take a look at your convenience at H.R. 7985 which I introduced as a late starter, and therefore has not received some of the tremendous publicity that the other bills have received. But I would like you to take a look at that bill and for the record forward your comments to the committee.

Mr. MATTHEWS. Yes.

Mr. RINALDO. I think it is more in line.

Mr. MCCOLLISTER. Do you have a copy?

Mr. RINALDO. Yes.

Mr. GROSS. Does anybody have an extra copy and within a few weeks we will send you a response.

Mr. RINALDO. Yes. I think that falls more in line with what you are interested in because quite frankly I could foresee a considerable number of problems of great dimension if we enacted the type of legislation that we have discussed this morning.

Mr. GROSS. Mr. Chairman, if you wouldn't mind, Pat Chidnese has a short statement and the reason I say this is he does defense work representing major carriers in the State and he may be able to develop thoughts in that area.

Mr. VAN DEERLIN. Fine.

STATEMENT OF PATRICK CHIDNESE

Mr. CHIDNESE. Basically, I would like to limit my remarks to practical experience. What we talked about is experimentation and a lot of the experimentation has not worked and some has. I can tell you I was under the impression when no-fault was first enacted in this State at least its purpose was to reduce rates to assure prompt payment to accident victims, to assure fair and equal treatment to accident victims, and also have the collateral benefit of reducing the court caseload.

Well, so far in the State it appears as though no-fault is going to substantially increase the rates. One major carrier right now is looking for a substantial increase.

Mr. VAN DEERLIN. You mean no-fault is going to increase rates or the insurance companies are going to increase rates despite no-fault?

Mr. CHIDNESE. It looked like it increased rates when you totaled them. It may have reduced the liability rate. What we have not heard this morning and the statistics we can't seem to get from the State, is the fact when you total them up the no-fault costs with liability costs with collision costs with uninsured motorists costs, we then have a premium which is substantially in excess of what was charged when no-fault was first passed.

You have to add it up and it is the bottom line and not take just liability and say we have been able to reduce liability 15 percent and you hit the bottom line and you see the total premium is 20 percent in excess of what the person paid the previous year.

Mr. MCCOLLISTER. If I might interrupt, isn't the major reason for the increase in the other coverages because it costs more to repair a fender and the automobiles are more expensive and the general costs of general inflation on everything? Is it your point that no-fault by itself has done this?

Mr. CHIDNESE. I can only tell you the first year that no-fault was enacted we were supposed to get 15 percent increase in premium and it never occurred. As a matter of fact many premiums went up because they added a little box on the daily, the cover sheet saying this is your charge for P.I.P. They reduced liability in some cases more than 15 percent but added an additional cost.

Since then all of the costs across the board for uninsured motorists and collision and so on have gone up, some of it I am sure because of increased costs and one of the increased costs is now the insurance company has an additional department called the no-fault department. I know a company in Broward that employs 26 people to handle no-fault claims, employees they didn't have prior to January 1, 1972.

Mr. RINALDO. I agree with what Mr. McCollister said. If you take the increase in costs and subtract from that the inflation factor, I think then you really get to the bottom line, but you know we are not doing it. We are talking about the cost of the increase.

The experience in New Jersey as reported in yesterday's paper was that lower premiums do result from no-fault, and certainly there is enough empirical evidence already that premiums would have been substantially higher without no-fault.

Mr. CHIDNESE. Larry, you said you wanted to say something.

Mr. MATTHEWS. I can answer. I don't know if your committee received it for the record but on April 30, 1975, Allstate Insurance Co. presented a study to the Senate Commerce Committee which shows the no-fault benefits, just the first person benefits, not only had increased the amount of payout and the amount of premiums in the different States which they had personal experience with, but had increased it more than they had anticipated. Now they put several different factors on why there was this increase but I think the third factor they mentioned has been, I think, perhaps understated, that they assumed when no-fault came in that their liability payouts would be reduced and instead of being reduced the liability payouts have been increased.

I think the basic reason is this, that the insurance companies, under the standard tort scene, were able to get settlements of many cases merely through economic pressure, that the injured person was out of work, that he had a lot of doctor bills and while his claim may have been worth $25,000 he had to settle for $5,000 or $6,000 just to pay his creditors and to continue to exist.

When you have mandatory first person benefits, they turn around and they laugh at the adjuster and he says, OK, I will settle your claim for $5,000.

There is no more incentive to settle at a bargain price a substantial liability claim because the man's medical expenses are paid, his work loss is paid, and he will insist upon full value for his claims. This has increased the liability payouts.

Now it may be, and I am violently opposed to it, but it may be that on complete proof, that the tort system will have to be greatly reduced or even eliminated, as some have suggested because of the expenses of maintaining a liability in a medical payments type of program. I am professionally and personally violently opposed to it on philosophical grounds as well as practical grounds from seeing and handling cases for injured people. But that may be.

All I am saying now is the question is still open and should not be closed now. This is one of the things that would be developed if the States are allowed to continue to experiment.

Mr. RINALDO. While you three lawyers are here, has any part of the Florida plan been challenged in the courts?

Mr. GROSS. All of it.

Mr. CHIDNESE. I would like to get on with what I have been saying. Again, my statement is limited.

Mr. RINALDO. I would like the answer to the question afterwards.

Mr. CHIDNESE. It has been challenged and upset, *Laskey* v. *State Farm*, no-fault, and has been declared unconstitutional as to property damage in the *White* case as to automobile property damage because of a fault they found in arbitrarily saying $500 for property damage you could collect and $499 you can't and they found ways to distinguish the *Kluger* v. *White* decision and *Laskey* v. *State Farm* decision based on some esoteric grounds, but they did it. Anyhow the decisions may warrant your reading, if you are interested.

Mr. RINALDO. They are very interesting cases.

Mr. CHIDNESE. They are, these two cases, and we can provide you with copies, if you desire.

Mr. RINALDO. Please.

Mr. CHIDNESE. We will be glad to. My experience is not based upon statewide statistics or anything else, but on the fact I handled maybe 900 to 1,200 cases since no-fault and I have represented both claimants and defendants and people coming into my office with complaints or insurance companies that have had complaints.

I can tell you, to get back to what I said before, reasons against certain plans, it has not reduced rates. That has not been the experience that I have had on a personal level with my clients, both sides. It has not increased or assured payment of claims. As a matter of fact, every one that goes by the number of claims being filed in our circuit court in Broward County for first party benefits increasing by hundreds of percent. It is not just one or two or three per week, like the first week there were two or four and now this week we are up to 10,000 cases in Broward County which we never had before in this point of time.

To add to that, thresholds result in anything but fair and equal treatment. You have an honest man who is a wage earner with a $600 medical bill and he comes to your office and he says, "I can go back to work, but my docotor wants me to have treatment and I think I can go back to work." I can't do that because you have only $600 of bills and no doctor will sign a disability rate. There is only three cases in this State you can get it, that is based on the fact the driver of the vehicle is not in a commercial vehicle or is not a nondefined vehicle and nonresident. If you have medical bills in excess of $1,000 and permanent injury within reasonable medical probability and/or you die. Those are the only three ways in Florida that you can make recovery against somebody running into the rear end of your car. That is it.

Now, as far as decreasing the caseload——

Mr. SCHEUER. Excuse me. What is wrong with the situation where the fellow thinks he can go back to work and has not been hurt badly, what is wrong with the situation?

Mr. CHIDNESE. Because many of them say I want to get that guy for making me miss 6 weeks and making it miserable around the work and who is going to take care of my headaches if I have to go to the doctor and get an unnecessary 6 weeks treatment to get a disability rating or additional medical bills, well, then I am going to do it. What it does, that threshold then benefits the malingerer or the phony and it penalizes the honest man. Many people are vindictive, believe it or not, many of my clients and claimants against me have a vindictive attitude against somebody that causes them bodily harm through their negligence and can't understand why they shouldn't go to jail.

If someone runs a red light, and at 40 miles an hour, and puts you in the hospital 3 or 4 days and causes you misery for 4 or 5 years——

Mr. SCHEUER. Excuse me. That is a fact of life having to do with personal injury. What I say is if we have a system that compensates the guy who is not seriously hurt, who admits he is not seriously hurt and it takes care of his problems, making it unnecessary to go to court, what is wrong?

Mr. CHIDNESE. What are you compensating him for, his wages and medical bills. He says, "What about my inconvenience and pain and suffering and the fact I don't enjoy being with my family, I have had aggravation and nervousness and I am fighting with the wife and now she wants a divorce." These are the practical problems I get every day.

The fact I no longer have any patience or boss is angry with me because I don't do the job as well as I used to, those are the practical problems you get every day, the kind you have no answers to. You are asking me now for answers. You should hear me trying to explain it to people with no working knowledge of the law and trying to say I am sorry, there is nothing you can do. I can't tell you fraudulently to go back to your doctor and I won't send you to another doctor who will assign you a disability rating because he likes the color of your hair.

That is what thresholds have led to. That is exactly the kind of problem we have. I used to be able to settle cases for $1,700 or $3,000 and I have not seen a $2,500 settlement in a year where the liability was clear.

In questionable liability cases, we used to get reasonable settlements. Now in comparable negligence, it created additional consideration, however, as long as you have a target the malingerer is going to hit it and the honest guy is penalized and that is what it comes down to.

Mr. SCHEUER. Congressman Stuckey just said that has existed for 5,000 years and will continue.

Mr. CHIDNESE. It is pretty hard to convince an individual of that and it is a pretty cynical world where you have to convince an individual that being honest does not pay.

Mr. SCHEUER. You can't write a law that will solve the problem of the malingerer, otherwise we won't have national health insurance or any program. You can put protections in the law to reduce the ripoffs but won't eliminate them entirely. You have to start out with that as a necessity and do the best you can.

Mr. MATTHEWS. What you describe is the Delaware plan.

Mr. CHIDNESE. I will get to that, Larry, please. That is next. That has been my experience and thresholds do seem to profit a malingerer, but penalize an innocent or honest man and I don't think it is necessary.

The next thing is the caseloads, and I mentioned that. Our caseloads have not gone down. Larry meant it was a good 6 to 9 months in Dade County and in Broward up to a year and a half ago we used to be able to get a case filed and tried in 4 to 6 months and I wait almost a year now. That is per case to get to trial. As a matter of fact, one judge set me a year and 2 months ahead.

Now, the solution. I don't know if it is a solution, however, I honestly don't think this is biased based on the history of Delaware and other States that enacted similar plans and these I would suggest may be minimum standards, that is provide first party benefits.

Mr. SCHEUER. Are you saying the Federal Government?

Mr. CHIDNESE. I think maybe that is going to be the only place you would have anything like this.

Mr. SCHEUER. What you are saying is the Federal Government should require the following general framework and you are going to lay out the framework?

Mr. CHIDNESE. No, sir. I am saying if the Federal Government does act, if it does, it should follow some sort of idea along this line. I have no idea whether you gentlemen want to act or not.

Mr. SCHEUER. That is what we are here for.

Mr. CHIDNESE. All right. We don't need Federal intervention because we seem to be solving our problems step by step. It is slow. There are problems with court interpretation and legislative enactment, but we are getting there.

The fear of everybody is the Federal Government will act and base their actions on the history of New York, Pennsylvania, Ohio, maybe California, some of the larger States, and some of the smaller States are going to have problems.

Mr. SCHEUER. But we are here, aren't we, to learn from you?

Mr. CHIDNESE. Yes, sir, and again insurance rates are based on a small locality such as a county and we feel, my personal feeling is that the closer to home you remain in an area such as that is purely geographical or personal or rate territory, whatever you want to call it in insurance the better off you are.

Mr. SCHEUER. What would your formula be for Federal intervention here?

Mr. CHIDNESE. Well, I don't know if it is Federal intervention. However, the best plan I seem to have knowledge of is requiring first party benefits for property damage, for wages, for medical expenses with no deductibles, and additional multiples optional, to provide for and allow that.

The next thing I would like to see happen with any type of national standard would be to eliminate subrogation. Do you want to clear the court caseload and eliminate the necessity for a lot of judicial labor or the unnecessity is a better word, eliminate subrogation.

I would like to see elimination of the collateral source rule, which allows for a person to collect multiple benefits for the same medical bill, to collect multiple benefits for the same lost wages. However, in conjunction with that you must penalize insurance companies that insist on collecting additional and double premiums for the same benefits. That is what the industry, or why they have not come up and said, let's eliminate that collateral source rule because every policy you see has the other insurance clause, well, you know, you have other insurance, they are primary.

It takes a court decision to say they contribute pro rata. That is not a good example because while they contribute pro rata that is sometimes less than half but they still pay a full premium.

Mr. SCHEUER. What is the rest of your program?

Mr. CHIDNESE. Basically, that is it as far as I can see. First party benefits, eliminate subrogation and collateral source rule and I think with that interpretation, you will be able to achieve some of the purposes. You may reduce rates. You may reduce the court caseload. You may have some fair and equitable treatment if the companies are fair.

Again, that is up to the individual company and the individual local and also the particular adjuster that happens to process the case. There is no guarantee of any of this. But based on what I have seen in my cases, if you wanted to achieve some of the purposes you would give some idea along these lines.

My experience has been that there are a tremendous number of problems with no-fault that nobody anticipated and by eliminating experimentation and not having any further experimentation on the State level while the problems may surface there probably is not going to be anything done about it.

Mr. RINALDO. It sounds like what you are saying is what we should do at the Federal level to eliminate some of the problems at the Florida level and that is not our intention.

Mr. CHIDNESE. No, sir. I think our State is basically moving closer and closer every day to something like this. All I say is if there is Federal intervention it should be minimal and in these areas without saying, you know, a man has to have a serious and significant permanent injury which is 80 percent of the body as a whole before he can sue or some definition like that defining what is it. I think you have to have as much leeway in each State as possible with some assurance to the consuming public they will have benefits and that the rates wouldn't skyrocket. That seems to be, or that seems to be the public, at least my clients' primary fear. Basically, also mine.

Mr. GROSS. Let me tell you this. We have given you two cases that Florida has had, *Laskey* and *Kluger*. There has been an awful lot of interpretation of the present laws, equitable distribution, and the question of constitutionality which will go all the way up. The rumor in the State legislature and you have rumors, it was that threshold will be raised either to $4,500 or $3,500. It did not materialize. The present rumor is that a major carrier in Florida is going to move ahead to knock out the threshold requirements completely in Florida because they are of the opinion now, based upon their studies, without a threshold they would be better off than they were with the threshold.

The only thing I can say to you is, as I said originally, we are not going to know until we experiment a little and see what happens.

Mr. SCHEUER. If you knock out the threshold and therefore have no restrictions as to tort and there are increases in benefits, isn't this ultimately going to increase premiums?

Mr. GROSS. I don't think so. I tell you why.

Mr. SCHEUER. I mean where is the cost savings?

Mr. GROSS. I will tell you where the saving is, you have your first party benefits no question about it.

Mr. SCHEUER. Let me say as I understand the Delaware cost savings is only because the insurance commissioner arbitrarily refused to let premiums go up.

Mr. GROSS. We are not going to know that in Florida until we see it and go through it.

Mr. SCHEUER. In a case where you eliminate a threshold and have complete availability of your tort remedy and collections go up, you are not going to be able indefinitely to set on premiums, the way they tried to do in Delaware.

Mr. GROSS. No question about it.

Mr. SCHEUER. It seems to me your costs will go up.

Mr. GROSS. Except for the following. You have had $10,000 payout; now where you force the man to get over $1,000 of medical expenses as opposed to $1,500 payout, with a man of $300 or $400 of medical bills you talk about close to $8,000 or $8,500 back into the coffers of the insurance carrier which normally reduces the premium and if it does not the thing to do is say to the president of the company, you don't need 40 assistants but only one, and your salary ought to be reduced.

Mr. SCHEUER. Would either of you, Larry, is it all right if I call you Larry, they all are, would either of you gentlemen like to add to the third gentleman's thumbnail description of the possible elements of the Federal approach?

Mr. MATTHEWS. Yes. Pat covered I think the most important ones. There are other things added to it. I would like to go back about 20 years when Massachusetts became the first State in the country to have compulsory insurance. At that time they mandated a reduction in the insurance agents' commission on the theory that now, with everybody being required to buy insurance, the agents did not have to work so hard to get business and people have to come to them.

All of the States now that have put in no-fault plans with compulsory insurance have not included this mandatory reduction of the agents' commission and this is one area which could be explored and experimented in to reduce the agents' commission, and therefore reduce costs.

Mr. SCHEUER. In other words, there has been no competition you would say as between agents, knowing that the consumer is a captive market, in reducing their commissions and therefore coming up with a cheaper price?

Mr. MATTHEWS. Not that I know of.

Not only in Delaware plans, they eliminate the collateral source rule but they had one other thing which prevents, say if you have a third party claim you can introduce to the jury the cost of any benefits you recovered under any insurance or recovered anything for that. So this takes away the motivation to have someone build up a $2,000 medical bill because it will impress the jury with how much money is needed to pay the man.

He can't introduce this at all. You are left then with liability suits to a judge and jury on just a question of liability and a question of pain and suffering.

I think that the courts and our judicial system is the best way of eliminating a malingerer, which we mentioned. If all of these doctor visits and the built-up pyramiding of expenses bring him no benefit in his liability claim it mitigates against his undergoing that type of expense.

Many of the States are now having optional arbitration in small claims where, if you have a small claim and you have not been hurt and it does not warrant a lawsuit.

Mr. SCHEUER. The kind of case that Pat was talking about?

Mr. MATTHEWS. Right.

Mr. SCHEUER. Where the guy admittedly didn't have to go to the hospital.

Mr. MATTHEWS. That is right.

Mr. CHIDNESE. I have hundreds of those I defend.

Mr. MATTHEWS. It saves costs, it saves the company attorney's fees and costs and it is an experiment which some States are undertaking now and should be continued.

The more and more you look at no-fault insurance, the more complex it becomes. It is not just a simple question.

We can sit down now, the three of us here, based on our experience and lay out for you what we would think would be an ideal no-fault plan in the state of art as it is right now.

Mr. SCHEUER. Mr. Chairman, can I ask unanimous consent that the gentlemen do just that and that their recommendations be included as part of the record of this hearing?

Mr. VAN DEERLIN. Certainly, without objection it is so ordered.

[At the time the hearings were printed the material had not been received.]

Mr. SCHEUER. I didn't mean to close you off but I eagerly looked forward to such a recommendation and let me say I think this panel has been terrific and highly professional and extremely helpful to the committee.

Mr. STUCKEY. I agree they have done a fine job.

Mr. MCCOLLISTER. Of all of the witnesses we had, they are the best.

Mr. CHIDNESE. If anybody wants to look at my files, defendants or plaintiffs, of my clients, with their consent, you can have a look and see how it works in a vacuum.

Mr. SCHEUER. Would you be willing to consider the possibility of a partnership.

Mr. GROSS. That is what Mr. Stuckey should say with his sense of humor.

Mr. CHIDNESE. Are you licensed in Florida?

Mr. VAN DEERLIN. I would suppose the views of the association have changed somewhat since the original enactment of no-fault in Florida?

Mr. CHIDNESE. Yes; about every week.

Mr. VAN DEERLIN. Your original stance was not one of unbridled enthusiasm for a State law, I must assume.

Mr. MATTHEWS. As I said before, we deal with people injured, plaintiffs or defendants and are down in the pits worrying about that problem. We have seen with no-fault from personal experience what personal benefits it is providing as far as social goals, and the Bar Association as a whole when it went into no-fault, had a great deal of doubts, but we are seeing benefits and we just don't want to see it cut off now.

Mr. VAN DEERLIN. And you have not seen your colleagues put out of work in droves, which must have been one of the original fears.

Mr. GROSS. The marginal lawyer thought he would be out on the street doing commercial litigation and a lot of the marginal attorneys' practices have been cut down and that is their problem and we can't worry about promoting work for them. It is not our problem.

Mr. CHIDNESE. Because of the complexities, in my experience the lawyer with 5 or 10 or 15 personal injury cases a year is no longer academically or professionally qualified to perform so he therefore must refer the cases to an expert. There are those cases that do not achieve a threshold, you simply close your file. There are those that go over the threshold.

Mr. SCHEUER. On this type of arbitration proceeding, you would not have to close your file on that case.

Mr. MATTHEWS. The person would never come to you. They would be told by the adjuster you can arbitrate it.

Mr. SCHEUER. Without a lawyer?

Mr. MATTHEWS. Right. The same way when we talk about, we are trying to give you a straight picture of how it is working and our opinion is not based on self interest. When we come out and say we are against subrogation suits that is for the system as a whole. An awful lot of lawyers are making a good living handling nothing but subrogation suits.

Mr. SCHEUER. You asked us to make decisions and you thought maybe we ought to have a little more time in experimentation and are you sure you want Congress to make as many firm decisions as indicated?

Mr. CHIDNESE. I thought I indicated what in my opinion was ideal in the way of minimum standards.

Mr. SCHEUER. And you feel there has been enough time to make some of those?

Mr. CHIDNESE. Not on a national level.

Mr. SCHEUER. We can only pass national legislation and not Florida legislation.

Mr. CHIDNESE. I understand that. You see in back of my mind I still have the fear and that is exactly what it is that Congress will act without sufficient experimentation, therefore I express my views based on my experience to date. I changed my opinion at least 20 times in the last couple of years as to what would be right and wrong.

We are getting experience in the State of Florida now that was completely unexpected. We have insurance companies going bankrupt that we didn't anticipate. Again that may completely change my philosophy as to what you should provide in first party benefits if any should be provided in these areas.

We may be better off going back to the old system. I don't know, if the companies cannot financially handle it or project their costs and their outlay and their reserves so as to stay alive then maybe we are fooling around with something we should not be fooling around with. I don't know. Again I may change my opinion in two or three months if a couple of major carriers have trouble.

Mr. METCALFE. Will you yield?

Mr. SCHEUER. Yes, but let me first say I was sort of throwing this at you, a formula that would have minimum standards and maximum flexibility in the States and leave the jurisdiction in the States to insurance commissions with a reasonable time to comply and that would mean rather minimum decisionmaking on our part, on this side of the table at this time, respecting your desire for continued State experimentation. Under this kind of approach we would probably have some kind of annual review of all of the experiences of the States and after a period of perhaps 5 years or something like that, then we might be in a better position to make some of the hard decisions you referred to.

We might have fewer hard decisions than you are actually recommending.

Mr. CHIDNESE. Again, don't take them as recommendations. Again, take them as simple areas you should consider.

Mr. SCHEUER. Yes. I am sure all of us will look forward to the report you will submit and let me again express my admiration for your extremely thoughtful and professional testimony and my gratitude for your coming here today.

Mr. VAN DEERLIN. Mr. Metcalfe.

Mr. METCALFE. I simple wanted my colleague to yield to ask one question, and I will refrain from asking many of the questions I had wanted to ask, but, Mr. Chidnese, you indicated it will require some time before you can actually come up with a definitive program and it seems to me that all of the witnesses, and I, too, want to compliment the panel on the expert testimony, but all of the witnesses talked in vague terms about needing more time. I would hope that you could pin it down to some time certain or more than the vagueness which has been a part of all of the testimony.

Mr. CHIDNESE. Sir, since law is supposed to be a dynamic growing thing, I really could not give you a definite time. I can say this. That this year there are major substantial revisions either requested or made in our existing law. I am sure the same will occur next year. I think that in the next 3 to 5 years the companies themselves will have a sufficient rate history from whence we can know whether or not there is going to be benefit to the consumer.

I think that we didn't have enough States, enough cross-sections of the States at least, a major metropolitan State, industrial State, a southern State, an agricultural State, upon which to base any kind of intelligent decision. I think as more and more States pass no-fault laws, that they feel are tailored to or suit their particular needs, you will have a better foundation from which to make a decision.

As it stands right now, I think in Florida, perhaps in 3 years you will have that kind of history for the State of Florida. I think in a State like Pennsylvania where they just passed no-fault legislation, and I don't know if it is in effect now and Larry knows at the national level, but perhaps it is going to take them 3 to 5 years or a little longer because of the size of their State, in which to have some sort of empirical data available for you gentlemen to make a logical sensible decision based on needs of the American public and the particular industries with which you are involved.

Mr. METCALFE. It may be we are running into a problem because if we do not come up with some form of legislation at this particular time, while there are 24 States it seems to me which either have or are contemplating enacting no-fault insurance we still have 26 left, so what would be the incentive for those States to pass a no-fault insurance law because right now there does not seem to be a great inclination on the part of many States to address themselves to it. I think we need to give some stimulus to those other 26 States.

Mr. GROSS. I think it is a question of pressure. We don't have Federal legislation now but we have 24 States that have passed it.

Mr. METCALFE. The 24 are not going to influence the 26, though. As an example, I mean there are only what, there are four States that have not passed ERA and they may not pass it and the remaining States have not passed it.

Mr. GROSS. As with Senate Bill 354, in Florida we thought it would be a reality until Watergate came around and they shelved it temporarily. More and more States have passed the law now and I have a funny feeling that between this time this year and this time next year there will be more than 24 States so long as the threat of no-fault remains.

Mr. CHIDNESE. I know how Florida got a lot of support. The word was that if Florida didn't pass a no-fault law that Congress would and you would be surprised as to how fast it changed the law.

Mr. GROSS. I think it will happen in many other States and that is the purpose for States passing it today.

Mr. MATTHEWS. The ABA on a regular basis sends out a report of the status of no-fault legislation in different States and in virtually every one of the 26 States where there is not now a no-fault plan, there are plans which have been worked up and passed and only in one house and not the other and we are going to have another 10 or 15 States in another year, including Congressman Van Deerlin's State of California which started in one direction of the threshold plan but now appears to pass a Delaware type plan without any kind of threshold within 6 months.

Mr. VAN DEERLIN. When in doubt, pass nothing.

Mr. STUCKEY. You suggest the committee go into the States that have not adopted a plan and just scare the devil out of them?

Mr. MATTHEWS. That is one way. Either scaring the devil out of them or passing some type of law that would force them to conduct these experiments.

Mr. STUCKEY. That scares me, though, when you say pass some type of law that would make them do that because once you get into that area everybody has a different concept on what that law should be and I have a great fear of that.

Mr. GROSS. I think from fear itself that Congress has pushed other States into legislation, the recent ABA survey showed there must have been 15 or more that put legislation through their house, but it died there and in committee. But I don't think it will die too often.

Mr. VAN DEERLIN. I must say that earlier witnesses led us to believe there was a situation in Florida which had prompted widespread public dissatisfaction with the conventional auto insurance system. I find it difficult to believe really that it was this untoward fear of Federal action that solely prompted the Florida legislature to enact that pioneer no-fault law.

Mr. GROSS. That was not the sole reason. One of the reasons also was the question of rates. You say rates in every editorial throughout the State of Florida, "Your rates would decrease." Now my rates have increased.

Mr. VAN DEERLIN. Well, I suppose if they even held reasonably steady, it would be a decrease in light of all of the other rises in the cost of living.

Mr. CHIDNESE. My personal rates went up over 300 percent and I had no accidents or tickets.

Mr. MATTHEWS. You are a lawyer.

Mr. CHIDNESE. I don't know it has anything to do with it.

Mr. VAN DEERLIN. Any more questions?

Mr. METCALFE. I have one question I would like to ask Mr. Gross. In your initial presentation you made reference to the fact that you go into a hospital and you have the doctor calling in different consultants, which seems to be a national policy, and this is a hard question but isn't that one of our major problems in these increased rates, that the medical costs and the fact that the medical profession now has the need to call in consultants and keep you in the hospital much longer?

Mr. GROSS: It is the buddy system.

Mr. METCALFE. It is the buddy system. What do we do about it? Don't we have to address it?

Mr. GROSS. I would. We keep reading about lawyers increasing rates in malpractice. It is the lawyers' fault, malpractice, lawyers did this when I had a guy that came to my office that they took the left arm off instead of the right arm, I didn't have anything to do with. Every editorial you read it is the lawyer.

One of the recent editorials in the local paper was who is policing the doctor. I don't know who is because I am not in the medical profession, but somebody should be policing the doctor. They talk about lawyers and ethics and you should have hearings open to the public on disbarments. I don't ever hear it about the medical profession. If you try to get involved in a philosophical conversation with a doctor he looks down upon you as the lawyer like you are an ambulance chaser but if he has a secretary add $30 on to a bill for medicare, that is fine, that is just terrific.

There is nothing wrong with it. I agree with you, Congressman, unfortunately I don't know what to do about that.

Mr. METCALFE. Maybe you need a good lobbyist.

Mr. CHIDNESE. How would you feel on a first visit to an orthopedic surgeon in any county, six X-rays, physical examination and heat treatments or whatever physical therapy he prescribes, that is $420, that is for one visit. That is the kind of thing which is being foisted on insurance companies.

Mr. STUCKEY. Perhaps we have to go back to med school.

Mr. VAN DEERLIN. Perhaps the peer review committees of both associations could be more active.

Mr. GROSS. Florida is extremely active, very active.

Mr. VAN DEERLIN. What part?

Mr. GROSS. The bar.

Mr. STUCKEY. We are talking about a peer review group for doctors.

Mr. GROSS. That is what we talked about and they get uptight pretty good upon that. They will look down upon you pretty fast.

Mr. VAN DEERLIN. Mr. Kinzler.

Mr. KINZLER. Mr. Chidnese, earlier you spoke eloquently about the poor person who misses two days with his wife and various and assorted pain and suffering situations, but let's say you had a choice between two systems.

Mr. SCHEUER. That is after 25 years of marriage. You forgot that element.

Mr. KINZLER. That is an important element.

Mr. SCHEUER. I would like to add, for the record, if in this State after 25 years, 2 days of this problem in marriage constitutes deprivation, there must be some sort of theory about the salt air here which you ought to exploit.

Mr. VAN DEERLIN. Mr. Kinzler is recognized.

Mr. KINZLER. If you were offered a choice between the system that paid people with less than $500 worth of economic damages, an average of 450 percent of their economic loss and people with $25,000 in economic loss 30 percent of their economic losses; and another system which, for the same dollar—and that is my premise—paid people with losses up to $500, 100 percent of their economic loss and people with $25,000, 100 percent of their economic losses, which system would you prefer?

Mr. CHIDNESE. Can I ask you a question?

Mr. KINZLER. My question comes first.

Mr. CHIDNESE. I can't answer you until you tell me what you are doing. Really, are you equating the dollar out-of-pocket economic expense with pain and suffering then, if that is the case, I will tell you the cheapest medical expense there is to lose an arm or leg. Your medical bills run about $700 or $800 for an amputation.

Mr. KINZLER. We are talking about a complete system, where 77 percent of their economic losses in automobile accidents are suffered by only 1 percent of the accident victims.

There are going to be, of course, inequitable situations on a single case basis but look at the people who now have the right to sue for pain and suffering—they are getting only 30 percent recovery when their economic loss runs over $25,000.

Mr. CHIDNESE. Why do you say they are only getting 30 percent?

Mr. KINZLER. Because of the Department of Transportation, which spent $2 million studying this problem.

Mr. MATTHEWS. Mr. Kinzler, you have identified the basic problem which has motivated Congress and the States to try no-fault insurance, because we have overcompensation of people with minor injuries and undercompensation of people with major injuries and all we can do is stumble ahead because even the Milliman & Robertson actuarial study based on S. 354 said their estimate was weakest in the large loss area.

Now the best thing, while we have not been able to answer the problem, either us or any of the States or the Congress on how to equalize it, I think the provision that is in some of the Federal plans, in some of the State plans, of unlimited medical expense will come closer because we all run into the case of the person that is completely destroyed. There is no amount of money for pain and suffering that can compensate him.

What we try to do in representing a plaintiff is maximize the pain and suffering amount so we can get some custodial care and we can absorb the future medical expenses. If it can be absorbed in a system that the insurance compnay has been mandated to pay that, this is a tremendous benefit.

Mr. KINZLER. The only system we have seen that has been developed and devised that would meet exactly what you are talking about is the system in S. 354 which would permit tort suits for death, disability, et cetera. If your threshold is not that high, you still have those costs in there, the nuisance value to the insurance companies of the small claims.

Mr. MATTHEWS. Yes, and we may eventually have to get to that point. We are still reaching out.

Mr. KINZLER. But here with a system as in Florida with a $5,000 limit you are not reaching the people with 77 percent of the economic losses.

Mr. CHIDNESE. May I say something?

Mr. MATTHEWS. Let me say one more thing. DOT figures also show a $5,000 limit which is going to cover something like 95 or 96 percent of all losses.

Mr. KINZLER. No. Ninety-five percent of all victims, not losses, and not the most significant losses because a very small percentage of the victims actually suffer 77 percent of the losses.

Mr. MATTHEWS. These people with catastrophic losses are a severe problem and we may have to pay the price of sacrificing the minor cases. Philosophically, I am opposed to it because the courts are our Government system of resolving problems and conflicts. When we start closing courthouse doors to some people for this, for efficiency or economics, there is no question where it can end, but it may be necessary, it may not.

This is what the States are experimenting with and playing with, whether it be a very limited threshold approach like Michigan which is similar to S. 354 or a broad approach like Delaware and Maryland, or a broad approach like in Texas.

All we are saying is, we don't have the answer now. But hopefully if California passes a Delaware type plan, a comparison over the years of two or three years of California experience, a major popular State with a Delaware plan, Michigan with a plan like 354 and New York and Massachusetts, major industrial and Northeastern States with a basic threshold plan plus all other States and their experiences, then perhaps in three years we can come back and tell you in our opinion we think this plan with all of these features would be the best answer.

Mr. KINZLER. That is an excellent answer, Mr. Matthews, but when you buy fire insurance or health insurance, do you insure the first third of your house and leave the rest for yourself or do you take some kind of deductible to keep your premium down and make sure you are covered for the catastrophic loss?

Mr. MATTHEWS. I am more personally concerned with the catastrophic loss and tend to overinsure but you mention here when you talk to fire insurance and health insurance to the point that gets to the public.

When you insure your house you are paying one-twelfth of the premium each month in your mortgage payment and when you pay health insurance most people are insured on a growth plan that a portion is taken out of the paycheck and the employer is paying a part of it and it is not the same as being hit with a bill for $400 or $600 or $800 at one time when you have not had an accident, so the extraction of premiums is less painful.

Mr. KINZLER. If that is the only real problem preventing people from protecting themselves from catastrophic injuries, we can separate the payments into 12 parts easily.

Mr. MATTHEWS. I believe that the same type of study, I believe it was Senator Baker in his minority report to the Senate Committee when S. 354 went through the second time, their figures were based on an offering of deductibles, which are another feature which we have not mentioned at all today.

Mr. KINZLER. Yes, Senator Baker indicated that but I don't think that is accurate. The Milliman & Robertson figures were not based on assumption of people taking deductibles. The deductibles are in there as a way to reduce premiums, but the Milliman & Robertson study was not based upon people electing deductibles.

Mr. MATTHEWS. Practical experience indicates if people can take a deductible or take a minimum limit, that is what most of the poeple are going to do because of premium pressure or they feel the accident will happen to the other guy. If you are prudent you don't take it.

We have a new law called uninsured motorist protection in which you can elect to take not in $10,000 limits but $100,000, whatever the limits of your automobile policy are. If your liability is $100,000, you can get $100,000 worth of uninsured motorist coverage.

I signed up and am willing to pay the premium, but most people aren't. And you have, when you try to sit down and elect something for all of theypeople and you are trying to achieve a social goal that they are not willing themselves to accept, there has to be some element of coercion to force them to do it or they will not protect themselves.

It is the same with automobile insurance as it is with property insurance. If people did not have to have fire insurance on their houses because the mortgage company required it, there would be an awful lot lower insurance on the fire policy and a lot more houses uninsured.

Mr. KINZLER. Yes. We are making that kind of judgment when we look at this kind of legislation.

Mr. MATTHEWS. Absolutely.

Mr. CHIDNESE. Your concern then I believe is with the catastrophic loss and a fact of a disparity in benefits received.

Mr. KINZLER. A huge disparity.

Mr. CHIDNESE. The biggest is a simple and absolute one, the fact that you are, in conjunction with this no-fault, then going to require liability limits of a minimum of $250,000 on the no-fault vehicle because if you don't the catastrophic losses won't be compensated?

Mr. KINZLER. When you have first party, it is compensated and has nothing to do with 100 or 200.

Mr. CHIDNESE. You will compensate them for lost wages.

Mr. KINZLER. A State would have to require minimum coverage of at least $15,000 for lost wages.

Mr. CHIDNESE. And it is catastrophic and you wind up with a $10,000 or $15,000 policy on the other car, you left the man with no future pain and suffering.

Mr. KINZLER. Wait a minute, You have the potential problem today. No State requires liability coverage of more than 15-30 so you still have the problem. The problem you don't have with no-fault is unlimited medical. Let me go back.

Mr. CHIDNESE. We are speaking reform, so if you are going to reform we should do the whole area if you are concerned with catastrophic loss.

Mr. KINZLER. Let's go back and spell out the reform we are talking about. According to the Department of Transportation, if a person has $25,000 in economic loss, he receives 30 percent—30 percent of $25,000 is $7,500. If that person were injured under the S. 354 or the H.R. 1900 approach, he would receive $15,000 in wage protection and since in an accident of that magnitude, the medical and wage loss are about the same—that person would also receive $15,000 in medical benefits, since he has unlimited medical. Thus, he receives $30,000. I should say if economic loss was $30,000, as opposed to $25,000, 30 percent of $30,000 is $9,000, so the victim would get $30,000 under this plan, compared to $9,000 in your existing practice.

We are talking about reform, not the perfect 100 percent system which no one has devised yet. If you move to a $100,000/$200,000 liability requirement under the existing system, your cost goes through the ceiling and if you eliminate the guest statute, it goes through the ceiling.

Mr. CHIDNESE. We have done all of that.

Mr. KINZLER. And it is going to increase your premiums.

Mr. CHIDNESE. It has not.

Mr. KINZLER. It has to because more people will recover.

Mr. CHIDNESE. It has not had time anyhow.

Mr. KINZLER. We are not talking about a 100 percent perfect system, but a system that up to $25,000 pays 100 percent of the losses.

Mr. CHIDNESE. All I say is if your concern is with catastrophic losses and those are the cases under S. 354 that can proceed with a tort remedy, you are giving them something illusory unless you provide a viable means of recovering which you are not talking about and again the rates will skyrocket.

Mr. KINZLER. We are talking about $25,000 of benefits and that is a viable recovery and viable alternative, is it not, for $25,000 worth of loss?

Mr. CHIDNESE. Out-of-pocket. What about his future loss of earnings?

Mr. KINZLER. If the State chooses to go higher, he can go higher. If a guy hits a tree in a single car accident, he gets no recovery in tort, so what are you talking about?

Mr. SCHEUER. He may have a recovery in tort against a manufacturer.

Mr. KINZLER. If he is very lucky.

Mr. CHIDNESE. Or against a phantom vehicle and I have defended on those.

Mr. KINZLER. What's the difference if he is recovering only 30 percent, with or without tort?

Mr. CHIDNESE. A case came up last week like the doctor's, and he said nobody knows or he said somebody forced him off the road and nobody saw it. He brought an uninsured motorist's claim and we gave him the $10,000.

Mr. MATTHEWS. Mr. Kinzler, you will not find lawyers who are going to oppose increasing benefits. When you talk about catastrophic cases, increasing benefits, we are against a reduction of benefits in other areas and a reduction of rights, but are in favor of increasing benefits. In terms of increasing benefits, we are unalterably in favor of it and the political question is how much is it going to cost and where, if we are going to protect this 1 percent, is it going to cost too much to be politically acceptable in any State or in the Nation as a whole?

To protect this 1 percent, do we then exclude 40 percent of the people with small claims, so that the dollars remain the same? This is the essential political question on costs.

Hopefully it will not be necessary to exclude people from recovery in order to finance at least the first person benefits for the catastrophic losses. It might be. The question is still up in the air on whether or not it is either going to be necessary to exclude many people from any recovery to finance the few catastrophic losses or whether it is politically unacceptable to exclude 40 percent of the people just to benefit that 1 percent and give them something which they don't have in the existing system.

Mr. KINZLER. One percent is 45,000 people; 45,000 suffer 77 percent of the losses. I think that a system which pays most of its money to people with minor losses is a perversion of a premium system.

Mr. MATTHEWS. Absolutely. We don't argue with that at all.

Mr. VAN DEERLIN. Any further questions for the panel?

If not, we are again most grateful for your appearance. It has been very helpful and, as you may have noticed, provocative.

Mr. MATTHEWS. One thing, I would like to give to Mr. Metcalfe the ABA report dated June 30 which gives the status of the different States, the status of proposed legislation.

Mr. VAN DEERLIN. Thank you.

Mr. GROSS. The Florida Bar thanks you kindly.

Mr. VAN DEERLIN. Thank you for being with us.

Mr. MITCHELL. May I ask these people if they represent the position of the Florida Bar?

Mr. GROSS. No-Fault Insurance Committee, Florida Bar, and if you read that as representing the Florida Bar, you would be speaking the truth but the Florida Bar did not set out a pattern for us today except to come here as we did in the last year, that is to speak as we want to speak. They have not told us anything about what we would say.

Mr. MATTHEWS. They just hold their breath.

[The following letter and attachments were received for the record:]

CRAMER & MATTHEWS,
ATTORNEYS AT LAW,
Miami, Fla., June 30, 1975.

Hon. LIONEL VAN DEERLIN,
Chairman, Subcommittee on Consumer Protection and Finance, Committee on Interstate and Foreign Commerce, 333 Rayburn Office Building, Washington, D.C.

DEAR CONGRESSMAN VAN DEERLIN: This letter presents the view of the Florida Bar's Committee on No Fault Insurance. It is submitted to you in preparation for your hearings concerning the effectiveness of state no-fault insurance plans, to be held on July 14, 1975, in Daytona Beach, Florida. I am preparing this report at the request of Howard Gross, Committee Chairman.

Presently pending before the Congress are several bills seeking to establish a federal system of automobile no-fault insurance. Different approaches, from the complete abolition of common law tort remedies to optional additional first person benefits are being suggested. The most well-known plan is that contained in Senate Bill 354. The different suggested plans, and the basic question of whether there should be a federal system of no-fault insurance, have caused widespread controversy, discussion, and argument among responsible persons in the Congress, the media, the Bar, the insurance industry, and consumer protection groups. The severe differences of opinion that exist between individuals knowledgable about the subject matter of automobile insurance indicates that this area is not one in which clear choices between different alternatives exist. In this regard, the Florida Bar is able to perform what we think is a valuable service to the United States Congress. Florida was the second state in the Union to adopt a no-fault insurance plan. It is also a state in which, traditionally, there has always been a great deal of litigation. Our state and federal courts have been able to maintain short calendar times, so many no-fault insurance cases have been tried, concluded, and appealed in the three years that we have had no-fault insurance. Many other states, as you are well aware, have encountered much greater docket congestion with delays between the filing of suit and ultimate conclusion, which can reach three to five years. Obviously, those states, and the lawyers practicing in those states, have not had the opportunity to consider as many of the legal ramifications of no-fault insurance as we have here in Florida. We hope that our experience in Florida will help your committee, and the Congress as a whole, in resolving the ongoing controversy concerning automobile no-fault insurance.

The Board of Governors of the Florida Bar have twice, by unanimous vote, opposed the passage of Senate Bill 354, In addition, I prepared an article, which was published in last November's *Florida Bar Journal*, discussing the technical aspects of Senate Bill 354. Copies of those resolutions and the article are attached to this letter. As your current hearings are concerned solely with the operation and effectiveness of state no-fault insurance plans, we will not discuss the different proposed federal approaches further in this report. Our sole discussion will be directed to the different state plans, emphasizing Florida's and their relative effectiveness.

No-fault insurance is a new concept. The insurance industry is the largest industry in the country, and automobile insurance reflects that part of the industry which affects almost every family in the country. The premiums for automobile insurance are an individual's largest single exposure to the cost of insurance since automobile insurance premiums are usually due in yearly or twice yearly payments, payable in a lump sum. Other types of insurance, like homeowner's property insurance, or group accident and health insurance, or even life insurance, do not raise the consumer's indignation like automobile insurance premiums charges, since they ae invariably spread out into many monthly payments, partially hidden in mortgage payments, or partially paid by the individual's employer. Whatever other social pressures are involved, the general demand for some relief from high automobile insurance premiums provides the fuel for the campaign in favor of no-fault insurance. Whatever the motives, and whatever the social goals being sought, the various supporters and proponents of federal no-fault insurance are attempting to convince the Congress and the country that nationwide no-fault insurance will result in lower automobile insurance premiums. Any legislation passed which does not have that effect, especially when the country has been led to expect it, will only complicate the more important question of a proper system to compensate the victims of automobile accidents.

President Fellers of the American Bar Association stated in an article in the July, 1975 issue of the *American Bar Association Journal* that the primary purpose of no-fault automobile legislation was to obtain a more equitable and just system for compensating the victims of automobile accidents than the customary common law tort system. To him, premium reduction is a secondary objective. He concludes that the proposed Senate Bill 354 would cause a premium increase. All persons involved in the automobile operations system are anxious to reform and improve the system and achieve the social goal of compensation of automobile accident victims. With this as a basic axiom, your committee is now considering various alternatives to achieve your goal at a hopefully reduced cost to the individual citizen. Our position is the same as that of Allstate Insurance Company, as presented in its testimony before the Senate Committee on Commerce on April 30, 1975. In that testimony, Donald Schaffer, Vice-President, Secretary-in-General Counsel of the company, concluded:

"We are not here today to oppose meaningful reform. We are here to oppose an untried and untested system which will increase the cost of automobile insurance. These increased costs will be borne by the individual consumer or, during an interim period, by the insurance companies. Neither can afford them.

"We must deliver to our customer and service the product ultimately required by either state or Federal law. To meet the customer's expectations it must cost less, perform better, and operate as advertised. The product envisioned by Senate Bill 354 can meet none of these tests."

Automobile insurance and its costs are a vital issue. The solution we urge, is based on the developing experience of Florida and other states. There have been economic projections that federal no-fault insurance will both increase and decrease the cost of automobile insurance. The country and the Congress have a unique opportunity presented to them at this time. Almost 50 states now have some form of no-fault insurance. It appears that California will soon pass a Delaware-type of plan calling for mandatory first-person benefits, but with no restrictions on the common law right to sue. Should that occur, we will then have three of the most populous states in the country, New York, Michigan, and California, with radically different no-fault insurance plans. New York has a standard threshold plan, while the Michigan act is very similar to the proposed Senate Bill 354. The other 20 states with no-fault insurance plans vary, in some degree, from these three basic prototypes.

Instead of the Congress making mandatory standards to be followed by all 50 States, based on theoretical projections of an actuarial survey, we suggest that the states which have no-fault plans be allowed to continue them for several years as actual laboratories, determining which plans and which features are effective in obtaining the social goal of victim compensation at the most reasonable cost to the consumer.

You are most often presented summaries of the different plans, grouping them into the three predominant types. Such groupings, however, do you a great disservice. They overlook the state-by-state variations in the plans and ignore the developing legislative skill of the states in drawing such plans. The several states which have passed plans in the recent past, have drawn upon the errors and omissions of the first states to legislate in this area. As each state draws a no-fault plan, the draftsmanship of the plan improves as additional factors are considered. In addition, some of the states are attempting experiments, modifying the basic concept, which deserve a chance to either prove or disprove themselves. Imposition of natiional standards at this time would terminate the creative process of developing adequate legislation in this very complex area. There is no simple answer to the questions posed by no-fault insurance. The ultimate answer may be the complete abolition of tort liability, as proposed by Mr. Eckhardt, or the complete retention of tort liability, as shown in the Delaware-type plans. It may also be that the answer is somewhere between these two extremes. Some of the different experiments, not embodied in any of the proposed federal plans, should be allowed to develop and possibly prove their worth.

The Massachusetts plan, the first state no-fault insurance plan, provided no monetary limit, but set a time limit in benefits at two years after the accident. Florida's plan, the second in the country, has a $5,000 monetary limit. Other states have varying limits and varying thresholds. It is still too soon to tell, with any finality, which of the various limitations, if any, strikes the magic balance between victim compensation and reasonable cost. Some different approaches are taken by different states to limit the amount of automobile tort litigation that exists. Several states, for example, Colorado, have mandatory arbitration of claims between two insurance companies. Others, like Hawaii, have voluntary arbitration of all claims for no-fault benefits. Finally, some states, like Minnesota, have mandatory arbitration of small, third-party claims.

Another issue which deeply divides the insurance industry is the question of subrogation. Subrogation is when an insurance carrier pays benefits and then pursues its own remedy against the alleged wrongdoer to recover the expenses which it has paid out. Traditionally, insurance companies have maintained that allowing them to pursue subrogation remedies and recover payments from tort feasors reduces their overall cost and therefore keeps premiums lower than they might otherwise be. This traditional thinking has been challenged by some of the major companies, more significantly, Insurance Company of North America, with a contrary argument that if a company is large enough and has generally sound underwriting practices, the amount recovered through subrogation suits will approximate the amount paid out by the same company in defending such suits brought against its insureds. In this line of thinking, a net dollar amount is lost each year in the costs and expenses of prosecuting and defending subrogation suits with no benefit obtained for the entire system. Supporters of this belief conclude that the only group which benefits from subrogation suits are the attorneys which handle them. Elimination of such suits would reduce court congestion and may result in a significant net savings to the insuror, which would be considered in their rate base. Only those companies which consistently have poor underwriting or insure substantially sub-standard risks would lose as their net losses would have to be wholly absorbed by them rather than spread out over the entire system. I cannot see that this would be a bad result as it would confine the insurance costs of sub-standard risks to that group of risks more completely than exists under the current system.

The question of subrogation in no-fault insurance acts is being handled in several different ways. In Delaware, it is abolished. In Minnesota, the insuror has a right of complete indemnity, and in Hawaii, it has a proportional right of subrogation. Florida takes a unique approach under the general doctrine of equitable distribution. Florida apportions the amount the company can recover as a function of the total amount recovered in any third-party claim and gives the trial court judge discretion to adjust the figures on a case-by-case basis, considering the equities involved in each unique fact pattern. The proposed federal legislation would cut short these different experiments in the field of subrogation and in the name of reform, mandate the traditional view that the insuror is entitled to recover 100 percent of its payments from the tort feasor. We believe the experiment should continue until an empirical data base is established determining whether the existing subrogation system should be changed.

Another thorny problem with no-fault insurance which is undergoing experimentation concerns the vehicles to be included within the act. The initial states which enacted no-fault plans, such as Massachusetts and Florida, limited them to private passenger automobiles. Some of the more recent acts, such as Michigan's and Minnesota's included commercial vehicles as well. Proposed Senate Bill 354 and other proposed federal solutions include commercial vehicles. As pointed out in the Allstate Insurance Company study mentioned before, as well as the wave of criticism against the Milliman and Robertson actuarial study, the inclusion of commercial vehicles in a no-fault insurance plan substantially alters the premium computation. A reduction in total insurance premiums gained by inclusion of commercial vehicles hides an increase in premiums for private passenger vehicles. If commercial vehicles are brought within the act, those businesses and their insurors receive the benefit of the tort immunity conferred in a limited no-fault insurance plan. This reduces the liability exposure of the commercial operator and therefore ultimately reduces his liability insurance premium. As most occupants of commercial vehicles will be covered by workmen's compensation statutes, whose benefits are uniformly primary before automobile insurance, there is no corresponding increase in the first-person insurance premium needed. We believe that such an advantage given to commercial operators and their insurors is unwise and deceitful. The commercial operator is allowed to deduct from his gross income the amounts paid for insurance coverage before computing his income tax. The ordinary individual is allowed no such deduction. High insurance costs do not weigh as heavily against those businesses as it does against the individual because of those tax benefits. Including a reduced commercial automobile insurance premium into an average, concealing increases for the private passenger cars, leads to confusion and distrust when the individual reads in the media that average insurance premiums may decrease, but he finds that his personal premium increases.

The whole question of thresholds runs throughout the no-fault insurance controversy. Beyond the basic question of whether there should be any limitation on the common law right to pursue a negligence remedy, there is the question of the extent to which the tort remedy should be limited. The threshold concept is a compromise between the extremes of no limitation and complete abolition. It appears that each state has approached the threshold compromise in a slightly different fashion. As time passes, and experience is gained, the very definition of the threshold and other exemptions from tort immunity are improved. Different amounts from $200 to $2,000 are used. The most minimal plan is that of New Jersey where the threshold applies to soft tissue injury, while all other types of suits can proceed to the Michigan plan, similar to Senate Bill 354, which has no threshold amount, but only certain limited exemptions to tort immunity. Probably the most interesting experiment in the question of thresholds is that being conducted by Hawaii, which has a flexible threshold to be adjusted yearly so as to exclude 90 percent of all tort claims from suit.

As the Allstate study shows, practical experience, to date, has been different from the projected expense with threshold plans. Rather than make a permanent decision at this time based on theoretical estimates, we believe that further experimentation by the states in this area is necessary to determine what, if any, thresholds or exemptions are desirable.

Involved in any controversy where more than one insurance company is involved is a dispute over which benefits are primary. In automobile no-fault insurance, this dispute continues on two levels. The first is when an injured person is counted as an insured under more than one insurance policy. While the proposed federal plans put no limitation on the amount of medical expense to be paid, most state plans do have some limitation, which can range from $2,000 to $25,000. It is extremely possible, and, in fact regularly occurs, that the medical expense can exceed one insurance policy. A question then arises whether the insured is allowed to "tack" different insurance coverages to increase the maximum amount recoverable and a subsidy question of whether the two insurance companies involved must both participate in the payment of a claim which is less than the total amounts of both policies. The cases and the statutes can best be described as being hopeless confusion, but the present trend is in favor of allowing coverages to be combined.

Often an individual will have courage from different types of insurance policies for injuries suffered in an automobile accident. There may be workmen's compensation, personal medical insurance, disability income insurance, life insurance, social security, and medicare. In this complex thicket of conflicting insurance coverages, different approaches are being attempted. Generally, workmen's compensation comes before automobile coverage. Proposed Senate Bill 354 is an example of the extremes which can be reached in this controversy in an attempt to hide the true costs of automobile accidents. Not only would workmen's compensation come before automobile insurance, but so also would social security, medicare, medicaid, and any private health insurance which does not contain an excess escape clause. Most group health insurance plans, the most common type of health and accident insurance, do not contain excess escape clauses. This is a major change from the standard automobile insurance policy existing today, which declares it to be primary over everything except workmen's compensation.

Also pending before the Congress are different plans for national health insurance. One of the disputes in that area is whether this national health insurance is to be primary coverage. If so, then most automobile insurance exposure would be eliminated and individuals will have lost some or all of their tort remedies with nothing to show for it. Particularly in Florida, which contains a high percentage of retired persons, dependent upon social security and medicare, making those payments primarily over automobile insurance coverage, will pass the burden of victim compensation from both the individual involved and the class of automobile drivers to the general public which must support social security and medicare through payroll taxes. Here, again, is a thorny problem of cost allocation which we believe is best left to state experimentation to determine the wiser course to follow.

Throughout this report, we have studiously avoided reference to constitutional and policy questions of federal involvement in traditionally state activities. We have hoped to illustrate the practical cost-related aspects of the various existing state insurance plans. I think it can be clearly stated that the prospect of federal legislation in this area has prompted many of the states to undertake a plan of no-fault insurance. We think it foolish, now that the federal government has stimulated these varied state plans, not to take advantage of the empirical data being collected through actual operation of these different plans. If no-fault insurance is perceived by this committee and by the Congress as being necessary for the national good at this time, we would suggest a different approach than those yet proposed. Notwithstanding the objections of the various states to any plan of no-fault insurance, we would suggest that Congress merely require all states to enact some form of no-fault insurance. This would more than double the experimental laboratory for this vital area of day-to-day life. If, in the future, a sense of national urgency and need for a uniform plan of automobile insurance is seen, then the Congress can make an informed decision over which plan is best for the entire country, based on the experience gained by the states in the actual operation of their own plans. The imposition of federal guidelines and minimal requirements at this time will cut off forever the process of experimentation and reform of automobile insurance coverage. The Florida Bar opposes any federal intervention in this area for policy reasons. But, we have hopefully shown in this report, beyond those policy reasons, there exists a factual basis for refusing to impose any federal regulation of our existing no-fault insurance plan, as well as the existing no-fault plans in other states.

Very truly yours,

F. LAWRENCE MATTHEWS.

[From the Florida Bar Journal, November 1974]

A TECHNICAL LOOK AT FEDERAL NO-FAULT INSURANCE

(By F. Lawrence Matthews)

Hearings on Senate Bill 354, the most likely form of federal no-fault insurance have been completed by the House Committee on Interstate and Foreign Commerce. Since there has been no widespread hue and cry against this federal no-fault insurance, and the printed and electronic media are strongly in favor of it as a piece of "consumer" legislation, I expect that we will have federal no-fault insurance within a short period of time. The Florida Bar Committee on No-Fault Insurance has already recommended that all lawyers express opinions on Senate Bill 354 to the public and to the Congress while it is still pending.

Florida already has a No-Fault Insurance Act. Most people, whether they are lawyers or not, assume that the proposed federal legislation is similar to Florida's act. It is not. Most of the publicized controversy over the proposed Federal no-fault insurance plan concerns whether the Federal Government should invade an area traditionally regulated by the states. Most of the publicity put out concerning the proposed act, whether by its proponents or opponents, has been in broad sweeping terms directed to the policy arguments about no-fault insurance and federal regulation of the insurance industry. The time has come for a technical analysis of some of the important features of the proposed federal legislation.

Senate Bill 354 has three sections. The first section, general provisions, defines the terms to be used and controls how the system will work procedurally. Title two of the proposed federal plan gives the substantive rules to be embodied in a state no-fault insurance plan. The third section provides an alternative plan which would become binding upon each state which does not enact a plan meeting the minimum national standards contained in the second part. The first alternative state plan, the one which has gotten all the publicity, is roughly similar to Florida's No-Fault Insurance Plan. There are first person and work-loss benefits, and the right to sue is limited to certain specific types of cases, such as deaths. There is no threshold of medical expenses which would allow an individual to sue who did not otherwise meet one of the required exceptions to tort immunity. The alternative state plan, which would become mandatory if a state has not enacted a plan satisfactory to the Secretary of Transportation, abolishes all automobile negligence actions. This alternative, and its mandatory imposition upon states which fail to enact model plans, has received no publicity at all.

The basic benefit offered by the federal no-fault insurance plan, like Florida's, is the payment of "special damages" to an insured without regard to fault in the accident. Florida's minimum required protection will cover all reasonable medical expenses and work-loss up to a single limit of $5,000. Senate Bill 354 puts no limitations on the amounts payable for reasonable medical services and has a separate work-loss limit which may reach an aggregate total of not less than $15,000. On its face then, the federal plan appears to offer substantially higher benefits than Florida's P.I.P. with the only additional restriction on tort liability being the elimination of the $1,000 "threshold."

The federal plan proposes to "pay more people more money" and at the same time reduce premiums. This task appears impossible. The hoped for result of Senate Bill 354 is achieved through deception. The type of insurance plan which is envisioned by Senate Bill 354 is a "last pay" type of plan. The benefits available will become available only when all other sources of payment have been exhausted. Should the claimant have workmen's compensation coverage, or his own private health plan which does not have an excess escape clause, those plans, along with any expected governmental benefits, such as Social Security or Medicare, would have to be completely paid before the claimant can draw upon the benefits in his no-fault insurance policy. This may have the effect of reducing automobile premiums, but only by shifting the burden of payment to other sources, each of which would have to be funded by either tax dollars or individuals contributions. The effect would be to penalize any individual who is prudent and arranges for hospitalization or medical insurance without the compulsion of law. Those individuals will now have to pay two premiums to get the coverage for automobile accidents that someone less prudent would get with paying only one premium. They cannot cancel their hospitalization policy because they still need the protection for illness and injury not related to automobile operation. Another example would be the individual who is entitled to receive some governmental medical assistance, whether that is termed Medicare, Medicaid, Social Security. Mention need only be made briefly concerning the number of people in the State of Florida who are retired and entitled to the benefits of Medicare or Social Security. While they would continue to pay their full automobile insurance premium, the burden of payment would be shifted under Senate Bill 354 to the various governmental programs. The net result would, of course, ultimately be an increase in taxes to assume the costs of payments for medical and work-loss expenses related to automobile accidents.

Another way that Senate Bill 354 attempts to reduce premium costs is by appearing to give benefits which do not, in fact, exist. One way this is accomplished is through the mandatory offering of deductibles to the insured. These optional deductibles, if taken, statistically exclude about 10 percent of all injured victims from any first party recovery. Senator Howard Baker, dissenting from the majority report of the Senate Commerce Committee, felt that premium pressure would make it likely that a significant proportion of the driving public would find it necessary to take such deductibles, thereby reducing or eliminating any benefit at all which they might receive from "no-fault" insurance. Expected benefits are also elusive in the area of work-loss. The $15,000 minimum work-loss benefit has received publicity. How that work-loss benefit will be computed is complicated and usually never explained. The work-loss benefit will be the lesser of either the insured's actual income or $1,000 per month multiplied by a fraction whose numerator is the average per capita income per state and whose denominator is the average per capita income in the United States. Since the average income of a family of four in urban areas of the United States is almost $12,000 at the current time, it means that every person who is supporting a family of four, and whose income is above the average, will only be entitled to recover some part of his regular income. Every person who is employed and making less than the average income necessary to support a family of four will be entitled to just his actual work-loss.

DISCRIMINATES AGAINST MIDDLE CLASS

It is my opinion that this provision is highly discriminatory against middle-class citizens in states such as Florida. If you have a person who is making more than $12,000 a year in the State of Florida, where the per capita income is less than the national average, and a person in an industrialized state, such as New York, doing the identical work for the identical pay, then the injured worker in New York is entitled to recover more work-loss benefits than the injured worker in Florida. The conclusion that federal no-fault will insure work loss up to at least $15,000 is highly misleading. There may be some severely and permanently disabled persons who will be able to collect the maximum work-loss benefits. The large majority of injured claimants, however, even if permanently injured, will not be out of work long enough to recover the maximum work-loss benefit.

The theory behind tort law is to shift the burden of payment from the innocent party to the wrongdoer. The movement for no-fault insurance arose basically from a conclusion that there was no assurance that the wrongdoer would be solvent and be able to accept the burden of payment shifted to him under tort law. In addition, it was finally recognized that there may be many accidents in which no one is legally at fault but in which there still are uncompensated victims of the accident. No-fault insurance seeks to shift the burden of payment back to the victim of the accident and require him to purchase insurance for his own benefit. Senate Bill 354, under public pressure to reduce automobile insurance premiums, shifts the burden partially to the insured and his own resources, and partially to other forms of either public or private insurance, other than automobile insurance. The old maxim "you get what you pay for" remains true and Senate Bill 354 does not pay more benefits for less premiums.

This bill, and the concept of federal no-fault insurance, has been sold to the media and to the public as a solution for high automobile insurance premiums. This appears to be the prime criterion for the passage of the bill. Consider the articles and arguments you have heard in favor of federal no-fault insurance. They, and the ones you are likely to hear in the coming weeks and months, answer all arguments with the statement that it will reduce insurance premiums. Disruption of traditional federal-state relations, abrogation of trial by jury, restrictions of benefits recoverable, and any other objections to this bill are justified with the allegation that it will reduce premiums.

Whether it actually will is by no means certain. The costs of the federal no-fault insurance plan have been estimated, and as estimated show a savings in the overall cost to society by society as a whole. The figure suggested indicates substantial savings. Past experience, however, indicates the governmental provisions of cost of legislation usually wind up being seriously deficient. Two of the caveats by the actuaries who prepared the cost estimate bear close examination and are particularly important when taken in the context of traditional governmental understatement of legislative cost. Those caveats are:

(2) S. 354 is a powerful piece of consumer legislation that would, if effective, force insurance carriers to deal more liberally with their policyholders and claimants. Provisions for accomplishing this are particularly difficult to price, however, and their cost implications are generally beyond the capabilities of our model and thus are not reflected in our premium change conclusions. *The important thing to recognize is that increased or accelerated payments by the carriers sooner or later must result in corresponding premium increases.*

(3) S. 354 would provide federal standards for state enactment of no-fault automobile insurance legislation. Our conclusions in general show that premium decreases could be expected from enactment of these standards. It should be noted that these conclusions result largely from a substantial abolition of tort liability coupled with significant no-fault benefit limitations, however, and not in the slightest from anything inherent in federal no-fault legislation that saves more money than corresponding or other cost-conscious state legislation. (Emphasis added.)

The most important statement is that the actuaries believe that there is nothing in the federal act which would save money under state legislation. In fact, the opposite may prove to be true. Florida with its $5,000 combined medical expense and work-loss benefit has had no-fault insurance without the premium being noticeably reduced. Insurance companies are still asking for substantial rate increases, even though there have been limitations put on tort liability. If the available benefits are increased to unlimited medical expense and a separate $15,000 work-loss benefit, Florida insurance premiums must increase. A significant expense has been omitted from their computations. Each state already has an administrative framework set up to regulate the insurance industry. Nothing in the federal act would reduce the size of that bureaucracy. On the other hand, a new bureaucracy would be created in the Department of Transportation to oversee and to administer each of the state acts. This new bureaucracy, regulating the regulators, would have to be paid for out of tax dollars, not only is there a question of whether such an additional administrative expense is justified, but also there is a question of whether it is fair and equitable for taxpayers who are not drivers or owners of vehicles to shoulder part of the cost of administering automobile insurance programs.

A question is also raised whether the individual insureds would really save money under the proposed federal no-fault scheme. The cost estimates showing great savings are predicated on the cost of first-party benefits alone. All prudent persons should also carry liability insurance. In addition, since the no-fault benefits are less than the average living expense of the typical family of four, those persons who have hospitalization coverage will undoubtedly wish to continue that coverage and thus be unable to save money from the mandatory first-party benefits. The actuaries admit that their analysis is weakest in the large-loss area and it is precisely in this area that people need the most protection.

The actuaries also reach a conclusion which is stated in average terms. The average no-fault premium compared with the average current liability premium, is supposed to be reduced. But this average includes all types of vehicles and does not take into account, in its final conclusion, the differences in rating territories and rating experiences. Owners of commercial vehicles, who presently pay large liability premiums, would find their no-fault premiums greatly reduced, since most occupants of commercial vehicles will be covered by workmen's compensation. Therefore, the underwriters of these automobile risks will not have much exposure. Areas and driver classifications which presently have high ratings will continue to have high ratings, and perhaps there even will be an underwriting switch causing the premiums in favorable classes to increase while other nonfavorable classes are decreased.

Under current rating systems, the young married man between the ages of 25 and 40, living in the suburbs, with a couple of children, is the best risk from a liability standpoint, and his premiums are markedly lower than the teenager or the person who is over 65. Since these drivers have over the years presented the insurance carrier with the least exposure, they get the smallest premium. Let the insurance company exposure be based not on the criteria for judging liability insurance, but on potential medical expense and work-loss benefits, and the situation is reversed. The most significant wage-loss exposure is in the same age group which now gets the preferred liability rating. The teenagers and the elderly do not have nearly the same work-loss potential. In addition, the several member families, insured under the same policy in a suburban setting present a much greater potential medical expense exposure than the single person or the elderly couple whose children have grown up and left home.

ACTUARIAL STUDY

The actuarial study commissioned by the Senate Commerce Committee showing savings in the liability portion of the insurance premium payment has been coming under increasing attack. In addition to the hidden limitations on coverage mentioned above and the unstated bureaucratic expense, there are two misleading factors which the accountants have figured in their report which lead to a false conclusion that costs would be saved. Presently in the insurance industry, about 40 percent of the premium dollar is paid out in the form of liability claims. The other 60 percent is consumed by the insurer in sales and commission and expense, underwriting overhead, claims expense, and company profits. Should the loss ratio, the ratio between payments made to claimants and premium received, inch above 40 percent, there is a resulting decrease in the insurance company's profits. The accountants who prepared the study for the Senate Commerce Committee were told to assume that 60 percent of the premium dollar would be returned to claimants.

While elimination of most third party claims may result in insurance companies being able to operate more efficiently, and thus return more premium to the insureds in the form of claim payments, that has yet to be seen. One of the studies presented to the Senate Committee on the Judiciary showed there has been little if no difference in the loss ratios between casualty third party insurers and traditional first party accident and health insurers. To insist arbitrarily that the accountants assume without proof that the amount of benefits returned to claimants would increase by 20 percent introduces an automatic 20 percent "fudge factor" into the equation and artificially reduces the amount of premium necessary to generate an equal amount of claim payments. One of the beneficial aspects of no-fault insurance is that it can only be used within a scheme of compulsory or mandatory insurance. It is a known actuarial fact that as you increase the pool of insured risks, the individual cost of the insurance will drop. Under compulsory insurance, the number of insured drivers, will, of course, increase and this, by itself, will naturally bring about some reduction in rates which has no relationship to the beneficial or detrimental effects of federal no-fault insurance.

FEDERAL NO-FAULT

Combining the hidden cost limitations and the independent "fudge factors," it is no wonder that the actuarial study done for the Senate Commerce Committee shows some decrease in costs. What is needed is not a theoretical study done by accountants employed to justify the cost expenses of the plan but empirical research to see what has happened in the states which have enacted no-fault insurance. Then there will be concrete information concerning the effect of no-fault insurance on automobile rates.

FLORIDA LAW WOULD CHANGE

Beyond questions of whether or not this specific plan will actually reduce insurance premiums, there are several features of this proposed legislation which would change Florida law and be more favorable to insurance companies than the existing law. A review of the entire act and the committee reports shows several underwriting considerations have been considered for the insurer. In each case the policy decision on whether the underwriter providing the no-fault coverage should be protected in a controversy with other types of carriers, entities, or claimants was resolved in favor of the insurer providing the no-fault benefits. Some brief examples will illustrate this point. The insurer may cancel its policy of automobile insurance at any time for any reason within 75 days after the policy becomes effective. This is an extraordinarily long period of time and grants the companies much more latitude than they have nationwide now.

Florida law allows an insurer to avoid a contract if the insured misrepresents or gives inaccurate information to the insurer, no matter how innocent the misrepresentation or incorrect information is. Under Senate Bill 354, the insurer, his agents and employees, and any person having dealings with them who provide the company with information upon which the company relies are immunized from any liability. This goes expressly against the growing trend in federal, state, and local legislation to restrict the activities of commercial credit investigators and protect individuals' rights to privacy. The effective tool of a damage action against the investigator and the insurance company which relies on that investigation would be forever lost to the consumer. There will be no actions for extra contract damages against insurers absent proof of fraud, which is, in most cases, not susceptible of legal proof.

Witness after witness appeared before the United States Senate Committee on the Judiciary, pointing out the problems in the cost estimates prepared for the Senate Commerce Committee. These witnesses all came to the same conclusion. Since the actuarial study was suspect and there were 19 states at that time, now 21, which had different no-fault insurance plans, it would be much wiser to let the experience of different approaches to no-fault insurance operate for a few years to demonstrate which, if any, no-fault insurance plan actually resulted in substantial premium reductions. Then, if a federal plan was thought desirable or necessary, the best and most effective features of the various state plans could be combined in a federal plan which would have the benefit of the states' experience and be proven effective. There has been such a push on for immediate passage of a federal no-fault insurance plan that these arguments were unsuccessful, and the Senate Judiciary Committee, and finally the Senate itself, approved Senate Bill 354 and sent it to the House of Representatives.

As with the Florida act, the amount of medical expense to be paid is "reasonable." But to whom? Treating doctor, the insurer and the claimant will all have conflicting ideas on what is reasonable treatment for any specific injury or condition. No mechanism is in this act, or any of the no-fault insurance acts for that matter, which allows resolution on disputes over the reasonableness of the medical charge. "In practice, the insurer will determine what is reasonable and the doctor if he is not satisfied with that, will then bill the injured person for the excess over the amount paid by the insurer. If this is to be a piece of "consumer" legislation, as it's being touted, it would be a simple matter to have any disputes over the reasonableness of the fees be solved between the insurer and the medical facility and have the injured person not billed by the medical facility. An example of this is the Champus Program, where the doctor must agree that he will not bill the patient for any difference in a disputed bill while treating a serviceman in a civilian facility.

While Senate Bill 354 allows insurers to arrange for medical payment plans in excess of the no-fault benefits, this is allowed only where those plans are specifically made excess over any other valid and collectible insurance. On one hand, this opens up a lucrative new market for the insurer since it will allow them to write hospitalization or disability income insurance with a minimum exposure. Many companies are having experience with this in offering insurance above medical benefits. On the other hand, every individual who has been prudent enough to obtain a policy of disability insurance or hospitalization insurance at the present time may find that he is paying two premiums for the same exposure. This windfall for the no-fault carrier could be easily avoided through the use of a "grandfather" clause or similar device, but is not.

Earlier in this article I mentioned how collateral sources of automobile benefits would have to be used before the automobile policy came into effect. To further help each individual carrier to reduce his exposure for payment, Senate Bill 354 allows the same benefits to be divided prorata between two or more insurers if they both are exposed to liability.

UNIONS FAVOR BILL

At the present time, strongest legislative push in favor of the passage of Senate Bill 354 is from the AFL-CIO. It is easy to see why. The organized unions who comprise the AFL–CIO draw their strength, both politically and economically, from middle income workers in the industrialized states where the per capita income is higher than the national average. The union members in the state would then fall within the only group which would be benefitted by the passage of Senate Bill 354. Benefitting from employer paid workmen's compensation insurance and partially employer-paid group medical plans, these union members would be able to take advantage of the more liberal work-loss provisions for people in those states without suffering the complete effect of having to pay both an automobile and a health premium. In addition, automobile plans would then be susceptible of being written on a group basis, which could become another benefit wholly or partially funded by the employer and resulting in additional savings to a union member.

The same criteria do not apply to the population as a whole and particularly those people who live and work in states like Florida. To call this legislation "consumer oriented" is a misnomer. It is a guarantee for the insurer that they will have customers, through conpulsory insurance, and they will not have any risks through unpredicable casualty claims. Benefits will not necessarily be increased and premiums most certainly will not be reduced.

The acknowledgement that thousands, if not millions, of Americans are injured each year in automobile accidents who under existing systems cannot be compensated for one reason or another and the legislative goal to try to compensate these victims of automobile accidents are both noble expressions of our social conscience. Economic and political pressures to reduce automobile premiums are also a reality which must be faced.

General unawareness of what their insurance policies cover and the limits of that coverage, plus the established belief that the accident always happens to the other guy lead most people to look no further than their latest premium statement before concluding that something, anything, must be done. No-fault insurance on a national scale is coming, whether it be by individual state enactment or federal legislation. The legal profession, because of its knowledge, training, and experience, owes an obligation to the public that this coming nation-wide no-fault insurance be the best, fairest, and most equitable compromise between the rate paying public, the insurance company, and that part of the public we are in most common contact with, the injured claimant. While no-fault insurance may be a great benefit to the population as a whole, and while there are good features in Senate Bill 354, there are bad features which could and should be eliminated before this bill ever becomes law.

SOURCES

Instead of line by line footnotes, the reader is referred to two governmental publications:

The first is the Committee Report of the Senate Commerce Committee on Senate bill 354.

The second source is titled "Hearings Before the Committee on the Judiciary on No-Fault Insurance—Senate Bill 354."

Both are available from the Government Printing Office in Washington, D.C., and were the sources of the facts and opinions contained in this article. Should the reader desire more background on federal no-fault insurance, the Government Printing Office can also provide the Committee Report from the Senate Committee on the Judiciary on Senate Bill 354, which has just become available, and the Hearings Before the Committee on Interstate and Foreign Commerce, United States House of Representatives, on No-Fault Insurance.

RESOLUTION

Whereas, a new Congress has been elected and assumed office in Washington; and

Whereas, The Florida Bar has previously gone on record opposing Federal No-Fault Insurance and specifically, a proposed piece of legislation known as Senate Bill 354, purporting to set up a national no-fault plan; and

Whereas, The Florida Bar again wishes to reaffirm its opposition to Federal No-Fault Insurance and Senate Bill 354; it is therefore

Resolved, That the Florida Bar opposes enactment of Senate Bill 354 for eacn of the following grounds:

1. Senate Bill 354 represents an unwarranted intrusion by the federal government into the regulation of the insurance industry. Regulation of the insurance industry has traditionally been a matter of state rather than federal control and not only would Senate Bill 354 represent a serious alteration in this traditional division of governmental spheres of authority, but also may be directly in conflict with the McCarran Act.

2. While Congress may have the power to regulate the Insurance industry under the Commerce Clause of the United States Constitution, Congress lacks the power to regulate rules of substantive tort liability since these actions have been considered local and transitory throughout the entire history of our Anglo-American jurisprudence and therefore not within the scope of the powers delegated to the federal government by the states.

3. Federal legislation abolishing or restricting the right of individuals to sue for damages in common law negligence actions where the amount in controversy is in excess of $20.00 violates the Seventh Amendment of the United States Constitution. If such rights are to be limited or abolished, this is solely a question of state constitutional law to be determined by the several states of the Union based on their individual state constitutions.

4. The alleged justification for Senate Bill 354, a reduction in the rates charged for automobile insurance, has not been proven. The actuarial study relied upon by the Senate Commerce Committee in approving Senate Bill 354 has come under increasing attack. Its hypothetical conclusions that the proposed federal no-fault insurance plan will reduce insurance premiums are based on the theoretical estimates. In addition, the actuaries themselves concede that there is nothing inherent in the federal no-fault insurance plan which would save money over state no-fault insurance plans. The Florida Bar believes that passage of this insurance plan not only has severe constitutional questions, but also does not demonstrate it will accomplish the stated aim of the legislation, reduction of automobile insurance premiums. With 21 states having enacted no-fault insurance plans of varying types, The Florida Bar believes that the wiser course of action is to refrain from considering any federal plan until there has been sufficient experience developed under the various state plans to demonstrate which, if any, of the various state plans does actually reduce automobile insurance premiums while achieving the beneficial effect of compensating automobile accident victims.

5. The formula contained in Senate Bill 354 for computing work loss payable to injured persons unfairly and unconstitutionally discriminates against wage earners in a state, like Florida, where the per capita income is less than the national average while unfairly and unconstitutionally favoring employees in states where the per capita income is higher than the national average.

6. The work loss formula contained in Senate Bill 354 unfairly and unconstitutionally discriminates against women, children, the elderly, the poor, the unemployed, and the under-employed by granting greater compensation to the employed while restricting the rights of all to recover the total amount of their damages.

7. By this resolution, The Florida Bar does not mean to imply that it opposes the concept of no-fault insurance with mandatory first and third party insurance coverages as a valid exercise of state concern for the compensation of all injured victims of automobile accidents and reduction of insurance premiums.

Mr. VAN DEERLIN. It is about 12:40 p.m., and we have two additional witnesses to hear, so the question is do we break for lunch and come back or do we ask the witnesses to bear with us and complete the hearing uninterrupted?

Mr. STUCKEY. Can we continue in the best traditions of our Government and be hardworking, dedicated public servants and just continue with the hearings?

[Discussion off the record.]

Mr. VAN DEERLIN. The next witness will be our first out-of-State witness, Mr. Jack Hutto from Brunswick, Ga.

STATEMENT OF JACK HUTTO, PRESIDENT, GEORGIA TRIAL LAWYERS ASSOCIATION; ACCOMPANIED BY CHARLES H. HYATT, CHAIRMAN, NO-FAULT AUTOMOBILE REPARATION COMMITTEE, STATE BAR OF GEORGIA

Mr. HUTTO. I have Mr. Charles Hyatt, who is also coming in from the back with me. Charley is with the State Bar. We have submitted a paper that we put together last night about 12 o'clock. So probably the content of it probably shows that, but as usual we were working at the last moment to try to prepare it so you would have something to follow with us.

I do not like to read a prepared statement, but I propose in the interest of time I will do that and then open up to questions because I am sure from listening to the last few, you are going to have quite a few questions.

So, with your indulgence, I will read this and I will stop at any time.

As president of the Georgia Trial Lawyers Association and Charles Hyatt, on my left, is chairman of the Automobile Reparations Committee of the State Bar of Georgia, it is the position of the Georgia Trial Lawyers and the State Bar of Georgia to oppose any national no-fault legislation.

Our opposition is not predicated solely on the basis that we oppose no-fault theories but primarily on the fact that we now have no-fault legislation enacted in Georgia which became effective on January 1, 1975, and implemented on March 1, 1975, commonly called Georgia Motor Vehicle Accident Reparations Act.

Mr. SCHEUER. Could I ask the witness what he means when he said we oppose no-fault theories?

Mr. HUTTO. Well, no-fault theories. I am opposed to any no-fault theories that the—the tort system is based on fault and recovery is based on fault and if you are at fault you do not recover, but if you want to recover when you are at fault, in my opinion what you do is insulate yourself with accident and health policies and that in essence is what no-fault insurance is, a great accident and health policy.

Mr. SCHEUER. Did your Bar Association oppose the Georgia no-fault legislation?

Mr. HUTTO. Yes, sir.

Mr. SCHEUER. So you are opposed to no-fault legislation even on the State level?

Mr. HUTTO. Yes, sir.

Mr. SCHEUER. Thank you very much.

Mr. MCCOLLISTER. How do you account for the fact the other gentleman from Georgia is one of the most outspoken proponents of no-fault?

Mr. STUCKEY. I didn't know that. I don't appreciate the gentleman putting words in my mouth. If you recall, I came to your rescue last year.

Mr. VAN DEERLIN. Will the witness proceed, if he can.

Mr. HUTTO. Mr. Stuckey and I have talked about that quite often.

Mr. STUCKEY. The gentleman from Nebraska will recall last year I came to his rescue on many occasions.

Mr. HUTTO. At any rate, the Georgia no-fault legislation is in its infant stages and the legal profession is trying to understand what type of bill has been created and its effect upon the insured public. We believe that the passage of a national no-fault bill would confuse the issue even more without giving our State bills time to be tested as a practical matter. Further, some of the reasons we are opposed to national no-fault legislation are as follows:

1. That the Federal Government will set up another bureaucracy in an attempt to enforce and administer a national no-fault bill which will be extremely burdensome to the taxpayers of the country. The Secretary of Transportation, William T. Coleman, Jr., has predicted costs of $2.2 million for the first year; $2.1 million for the second year; and $1.5 million each year thereafter merely for implementing Federal no-fault insurance.

2. Allstate Insurance Co. has made certain projections and based upon these projections, the National Association of Independent Insurers, NAII, has calculated the total cost of S. 354 to increase the premiums to the American private passenger car-owning public to approximately $1.25 billion annually.

3. Many of the insurers have experienced startup cost impact for implementing State automobile no-fault programs and should S. 354 pass would reoccur and these additional startup costs would have to be passed on to the consumer public.

4. Different problems exist in different States, and the citizens of one State should not be required to assume or pay for those problems existing in other States, that is, the problems existing in New York City, Miami, and other large metropolitan areas as opposed to Georgia which is still predominately a rural State with few large metropolitan areas.

5. No-fault legislation, State and Federal, leaves a hiatus for the protection of the average citizen, that is, who is to fill out the forms for those who recover under no-fault?

There is no provision for that and under the no-fault plan in Georgia the average person walks in with all of the forms to fill out and he comes to my office for me to fill them out and who is to pay for filling out of the forms? There is no provision in the law for that.

The client needs and expects help in preparing his claim under no-fault. So it is not just a simple matter of informing the insurance carrier you had an accident and they take the initiative. The injured client has to take the initiative to fill out these forms to make his recovery under no-fault.

Believe it or not, the preparation of these papers and the proofs of loss and so on, that is a complicated procedure, as is the trial of a lawsuit and you just don't do it and the average citizen just cannot do these things adequately without the kickback of the insurance company of the papers and saying redo it again and let's get the thing right.

6. In Georgia, we are not so far behind in our court cases that the clients are suffering. We get the cases to trial we think in a reasonable time. As I heard the Florida Bar speak here, they were ahead before the no-fault and now they are getting behind on their docket because of the additional caseload.

An April 1970 DOT study, Automobile Accident Litigation, shows that the present automobile accident litigation system is actually a very efficient system, largely because litigated claims constitute a minuscule proportion of total claims. In 1968, for example, approximately 4.4 million persons were injured in motor vehicle accidents in the United States. Of these, only 220,000 lawsuits were filed. Other studies indicate that only 7 percent of all lawsuits filed are ever carried to verdict. Therefore only about 15,400 or 0.35 percent of all potential claims resulted in trials reaching verdicts. This means, roughly, that only 1 injured person in 290 ever needs to use the full court system for a jury verdict.

Not only is the present problem of court congestion not as great as is claimed by proponents of S. 354, there are some indications that the bill would create more litigation than it eliminates. S. 354 provides for unlimited benefit payments for allowable expenses under section 204. There is every reason to believe that this will encourage inflated claims for medical bills, and even overtreatment. It is very possible that this opportunity for human nature to assert itself will result in increased litigation.

Also section 206(a)(5) which allows noneconomic detriment damages only if the accident results in "death, serious and permanent disfigurement, or other serious and permanent injury would likely create great amounts of litigation in each State as the courts try to determine the precise injuries which will be considered sufficient to allow the award of noneconomic detriment damages.

7. Collateral sources.—Except for certain circumstances under the assigned claims plan, S. 354 provides that benefits received, or entitled to be received, from social security, except for medicaid benefits, workmen's compensation, any State-required temporary, nonoccupational disability insurance, and all other benefits, except for life insurance benefits, received, or entitled to be received from any government are primary to benefits under S. 354, unless the law authorizing such benefits makes them secondary.

Accident and health insurers point out that 182 million Americans are covered by private health plans at present, and that three-quarters of them have group coverage. They argue that individuals should not be compelled to purchase automobile insurance to protect themselves from the same risk against which they are already protected under their medical coverage. Automobile insurers argue that making their coverage secondary, or excess, would cause delay, confusion, and duplication of efforts. Also, as only approximately one-half of all Americans drive, many nondrivers would be forced to subsidize, with higher rates, the drivers who also have group coverage.

It is impossible to resolve this dispute in this brief section, but it is important to note that S. 354 makes accident and health insurance primary, subject to the State's decision to make it secondary. This constitutes a reversal of the traditional pattern of insurance in America. This step should not be taken without the most compelling reasons being present. As far as we can see, the case for this reversal is unpersuasive, and the present system should be maintained.

8. Property damage in the national no-fault bill.—The basic restorations benefits do not include benefits for damage to property. Why? Once again this is a coverage question which can be handled under the collision aspect of a policy, however, who is to represent the insured in a dispute over $200 or $300 or $1,500 to $2,500 claim? Economically this is not feasible for the insured who have this type of controversy with the insurance company to hire counsel to contest same and this too leaves a hiatus in the no-fault legislation.

9. Costs.—Allstate Insurance Co. has made a study of what national no-fault would do to costs. This study shows that the insurance cost increase to motorists in 45 States would range from 4 percent to 97 percent. This actuarial study was based on a computer model which has been proven in the real world experience of no-fault and which would reliably predict automobile insurance costs. For example, the average Utah Allstate policyholder would pay $41 more for his automobile insurance if the national no-fault bill is passed. In Georgia, we have one of the lowest rates now in the Nation. Why should we be saddled with the problems of automobile insurance in the other parts of the Nation? We believe that State's rights are an important part of our government and that we should be able to control our own destinies in this matter and especially not be saddled with the economic burden imposed by other States which may be caused as a result of their local laws or social problems. Allstate shows that Georgia rates will increase to 69.3 percent. How can one ever say that this would be fair for the Georgia or Utah policyholders?

Mr. VAN DEERLIN. You mean they will increase by 69 percent?

Mr. HUTTO. Yes, sir. Charley and I decided since you gentlemen hail from these States, we will put your States down to show what kind of experience you may expect in your States.

10. Based upon the projections made by Allstate Insurance Co. as to future costs of S. 354 no-fault when enacted on the States represented in this subcommittee, we exhibit the following figures as to what can be expected as to costs for the said program.

Mr. Chairman, your State of California would increase 37.3 percent.

Mr. VAN DEERLIN. Well, in that case I will close the hearings right now.

Mr. HUTTO. Georgia is 69 percent, Mr. Stuckey, and Illinois is 23 percent and Michigan, they would go down, minus 4.4 percent.

Mr. VAN DEERLIN. Good, he is not here.

Mr. HUTTO. Nebraska is 84.7 percent.

New Jersey increased 16.4 percent and New York would go down 0.5 percent.

Mr. VAN DEERLIN. Mr. Scheuer is here.

Mr. HUTTO. And Texas would increase 24.4 percent.

In other words, gentlemen, you're going to go back home and explain to your constituents with the exception of Michigan and New York that the cost is going to appreciably rise if the Congress enacts S. 354, and the benefits will decrease.

SUMMATION

No-fault is being sold to the American public as a way to reduce premium costs at the expense of the insurance companies and the trial bar. It has been heralded as reform legislation to cure alleged ills now existing. The national news media has taken up the fight and espoused this reform legislation; however, they have chosen to overlook the projections by one of the Nation's largest insurers, Allstate Insurance Co., showing a sweeping premium increase under S. 354. If the American public is informed as to the true facts and is shown that accident victims under S. 354 are obligated to insure themselves and give up their right to go to court for a redress of wrongs committed and are subject to limits on loss of wages, medical benefits, funeral benefits, and the like, and that this no-fault legislation is not applicable to the physical loss or collision damages done to automobiles that the public will en masse reject this theoretical creature which is going to substantially increase the cost of their insurance premiums and reduce their rights as they now exist.

Regardless of what the reformers say, our courts are working and they are constantly improving the system. We do not need any more Federal bureaucracies to burden the harassed taxpayer. Statistics show that 1 out of every 6 employees now are employees of the Government. Do we need more Government employees? Statistics show that 1 out of every 3 people in this country receive some sort of Government benefit. How much more can the Government give at the expense of the taxpayer?

Reform legislation should be investigated as this theoretical panacea is now being investigated, but when the facts show that Federal no-fault simply is not the correct method, then let the States implement and control the insurance industry as they have done in the past so that we will have adequate time to see the real effects.

That is our statement and, of course, if you have some questions about what is done in our State or anything else, we would like to answer them.

Mr. VAN DEERLIN. Mr. McCollister.

Mr. MCCOLLISTER. I don't have any questions, Mr. Chairman. I thank you gentlemen for your statement. I will say only in passing that an increase of 84.7 percent of Nebraska's premiums is the best platform on which one would hope to achieve some kind of statewide approval in another office.

Mr. VAN DEERLIN. Mr. Stuckey.

Mr. STUCKEY. Thank you, Mr. Chairman. The only question I would ask is how would you say that the Georgia no-fault system has worked? What have been the results? Are people happy or unhappy with it?

Mr. HUTTO. Charley, do you want to answer that?

Mr. HYATT. We just have had it in operation for 4 months, so we really would be making just a guess. I really can't voice an opinion. We have a 2-year statute for personal injuries and a 4-year statute for property damage in Georgia and that 2 years, a lot of lawyers I assume are playing a waiting game trying to figure it out. It is amazing in the seminars we conduct over the State explaining no-fault to lawyers and to people, the loss of concept and the concept of trying to mix tort and first party benefits is so far in to the system that we were all raised on that, it is hard to get it.

The best explanation I give to our Georgia no-fault laws is we have the same old liability features with an attachment or leech, as we will call it, slapped on it of a health and accident policy which you have to buy and by having to take it you release certain rights in tort. We really don't have any experience and we are not in a position to give you the hard facts that the Florida Bar has.

Congressman Stuckey had asked Jack and myself to come here and give our feelings because we are a neighbor State and we are in this area.

But here is another fact that we didn't set out here. Massachusetts had a very peculiar reason for having to have no-fault. They had compulsory bodily injury claims and had insurance for years. They had lawyer involvement in claims in a percentage of something like 76 percent of all accidents. They had an astronomical figure. In other words, a fellow knew in Massachusetts when he had a fender bender, as we call it, and he wanted to get his fender fixed, what he did, he jumped out and got a hold of my back, and that is a bad example for me because I fell the other day and hurt my back.

Mr. VAN DEERLIN. Do you want a good lawyer?

Mr. HYATT. No. I am afraid I am the culprit of my own wrong, but we accept those things, we accept our own wrongs. But, be that as it may, in Georgia in contrast with Massachusetts, do you know what our lawyer involvement was, 18 percent as opposed to 76 percent in Massachusetts? The difference, if we are going to say why there is a difference, is in people, you see.

Mr. STUCKEY. We have a better class of people in Georgia than we have in Massachusetts.

Mr. HYATT. I ought to agree. No, I didn't mean that. You take these three Florida lawyers that sat here, they are astute advocates and we are drivers. They could not try a case in Georgia in certain areas and get away with it. The juries would not let them interrupt.

I am not taking it away from them. That is the way it is. The same way in Massachusetts, some people would rather fight than switch. It is not a lack of character, but is a lack of whatever you want to call it. Be that what it may be, in deference to my aging back, that is the reason that you need a study and let this thing try to work in the States. Let us try to work it. We had some innovations in Georgia. We almost, or we have a hybrid of the Delaware plan in Georgia and it may work, that the premise in Delaware is if you take the icing off the cake, the fellow with the small claim is going to go away and he is not going to sue, you see. We kind of got a hybrid of that in our claim.

Mr. STUCKEY. I would suggest this is what several of us have advocated and still are advocating. It is that we give the States the opportunity to come up with any innovative ideas they can and see what has worked in other areas. You are talking about a major step when you say we are going to come up with one uniform no-fault bill without really knowing what we are getting into. I think this is what has been said earlier today, let's do give no-fault an opportunity to see if it will work. If it does work, let's pick up the better features, and those that don't work of course let's disregard them.

I also happen to have been, I guess, one of the few people that believe if you would leave the various States alone, all 50 States would adopt some form of no-fault.

Mr. MCCOLLISTER. Will you yield?

Mr. STUCKEY. Delighted.

Mr. MCCOLLISTER. I want to make amends for putting the gentleman in an awkward position earlier. We have three votes on that proposition now and why don't we call for the question and end it right now.

Mr. STUCKEY. That is a turnaround.

Mr. VAN DEERLIN. Mr. Rinaldo.

Mr. RINALDO. No questions.

Mr. VAN DEERLIN. Mr. Scheuer.

Mr. HYATT. Well, let me say something in that I represent the State bar of Georgia, or the no-fault committee of the State bar, and our position, as voted by the board of governors of Georgia, which I happen to be a member of, is that we, in our official position, that we are not opposed to an equitable no-fault. Now whatever that may be, the Lord only knows.

Mr. SCHEUER. Would you oppose the legislation that is currently operative in Georgia?

Mr. HYATT. We opposed it in certain ways. We were in favor of the Delaware plan because we concede as lawyers, however if you take the icing off, the people lose interest. The fellow who gets mad is the fellow who loses his wages or some adjuster who steps on his foot or does something and then that drives him to the lawyer's office.

Lawyers, they don't, to my knowledge, stand right on the corner and yell, "Give me your claim." People have to get there for some reason, you see.

Mr. SCHEUER. In your testimony on page 1, you say that you oppose no-fault theories. That seems to be a philosophical opposition to the basic principles of no-fault insurance. Now is that true?

Mr. HYATT. What we are talking about is first party benefits when we say it and we are not opposed to the equitable no-fault, which is a first party benefit that a person can obtain. What we are opposed to is the taking of the right of a person for redress at the courthouse.

Mr. SCHEUER. You would oppose any threshold then?

Mr. HYATT. Yes, I would.

Mr. SCHEUER. Did both of your organizations, both the Georgia Trial Lawyers and the State Bar of Georgia oppose passage of the present no-fault legislation in Georgia?

Mr. HYATT. We opposed part of it and I think the present bill we opposed it because certain parts we did not like. You know, or as you know, a bill that goes in does not always come out the same way.

Mr. VAN DEERLIN. On final passage, you would have voted no, is that correct?

Mr. HYATT. We would have because we thought and were convinced that the Delaware plan, as we call it, the Delaware plan would be a remedy and I am not the best politician as you can see, so I don't know the workings of the legislature but I would say that we did oppose it in its final form.

Mr. SCHEUER. Would you oppose some kind of loose framework we discussed this morning, whereby we would leave maximum discretion to the States and would leave jurisdiction in the State insurance commissioners and give them adequate time to comply with just a few general standards that we would set out, a few minimum standards, and really rely on a process of safe experimentation, perhaps for 3- or 4- or 5-year period and then having an evaluation of all of that State experience, before the Congress made a lot of fine-tuned decisions, would you oppose that very loose plan?

Mr. HUTTO. I would oppose any legislation on a national level. I don't oppose the studying of it on a national level but I don't know why you have to enact legislation to see what is going on in the States because you all come from different States and you can study the problem without enacting legislation.

Mr. SCHEUER. Maybe one reason is because more than half of the States have done nothing and we would like to see this process of experimentation take place on a systematic basis right across the country in all of the States and then collate all of that information and distill it and have people like you, experts like you come and testify about the experience in your State and nearby States and have enough experience uniformly across the country that after a period of experimentation we could fine-tune then a piece of national legislation.

In other words, we would avoid the buckshot approach whereby less than half of the States have done anything.

Mr. HYATT. Let me say, one of the reasons which I gather from the questions was the fear of the thought that other States are not going to do anything, the other 26 States are not going to pass no-fault legislation and therefore there will be nothing to study in the balance of the States.

Here is the reason that they probably will pass it. That is because the news media, it is a favorite topic with the news media and it has a sound ring of no-fault. We have a thing in Georgia called no-fault divorce and that is what the man on the street calls it and what it is is irreconcilable differences, which is, well, other States call it some other term but the common man calls it no-fault because some newspaperman picked it up and put it in the paper as no-fault and everybody that comes into your office about a divorce they say I want to get a no-fault divorce.

Well, it has a nice sound to it even in the trial of cases lawyers pick it up and say fault where we used to say liability and they say fault.

Mr. SCHEUER. Are you suggesting we are going to have no-fault insurance programs in those States with the highest percentage of unhappy marriages?

Mr. HUTTO. Let me say this. How are you ever going to study a problem if you don't have pro and con? If everybody goes no-fault and you don't have anything to compare it to, what happens? But if you have some that are no-fault States and some without no-fault, then you can compare it. But if everybody has the same thing what will you compare it with?

Mr. SCHEUER. I don't think anybody on the committee is trying to mandate a uniform State approach at this time.

Mr. HUTTO. I mean, if I read H.R. 1900 and S. 354, when it goes on the national level, that is uniform, isn't it?

Mr. SCHEUER. I don't think anybody on the committee is wedded to that particular bill.

Mr. HUTTO. I mean if we are going to do something about making sure that everybody's medical bills are paid and the doctors can charge whatever they want to as long as they have coverage, because you know, that is a very viable thing and when you go into a hospital they want you to sign insurance benefits immediately. So why don't you just pass a law in Washington that everybody that gets born must have accident and health insurance and do away with no-fault?

Mr. SCHEUER. I think we are coming to that very swiftly.

Mr. STUCKEY. Don't suggest it.

Mr. SCHEUER. I think you will have a national health program in the next year or two that will do just that.

Mr. HUTTO. Then what we are leading to then, what you are saying is we are going to have this.

Mr. SCHEUER. And probably the civilized country, we are probably the only civilized country on Earth that does not have that kind of system.

Mr. HUTTO. There are qualities and quantities of that. When you say we are going to have that kind of health insurance and I understand what you are saying, then why not let the Government, if that is true, why not put the insurance companies out of business and let the Government administer both?

Mr. STUCKEY. Don't suggest that either.

Mr. SCHEUER. I think you have raised a serious question that will be discussed in great detail.

Mr. HUTTO. I have been reading a lot about it.

Mr. SCHEUER. I think the role of insurance companies in national health programs is a very problematic one and we will put many hundreds of hours into thinking about that question you raised and I am glad you raised that for us today.

Mr. HUTTO. I hope it is more efficient than the Post Office Department.

Mr. SCHEUER. Wait a minute. The Post Office Department used to be a public function and now it is not a public function but a private function and I am not sure we are very pleased with the results of turning that back from the public sector into some form of private sector operation. There is very little evidence there has been a substantial improvement. I was one of the ones who voted for that change and I am not sure that the evidence justifies it.

Mr. HUTTO. May I say one other thing that concerns me and the organization that I belong to, is primarily that of representing the average person on the street, the little man, so to speak, we do not represent corporate America or the insurance companies. I am concerned that the people, the average citizen have access to the courts, because the progress that has been made in this country by the average citizen has been through the courts and you eliminate the ability for the lower man to get to court and have his case heard then you are going to eliminate his right in many respects.

If you start arbitrating and start it being administered from Washington you will seriously impair this man's ability to have redress at home and I think he ought to be able to go to his court at his home and get redress.

Mr. SCHEUER. I take it this represents your philosophical objection to any kind of no-fault program at the State level as well as the Federal level?

Mr. HUTTO. Well, we have it State level and I accepted it.

Mr. SCHEUER. You had opposed it?

Mr. HUTTO. I opposed but I am now going to try to see what I can do to see that people get protected under it.

Mr. VAN DEERLIN. Mr. Metcalfe.

Mr. METCALFE. I have no questions to ask other than to express my thanks to my distinguished colleague, Congressman Stuckey, for inviting you here to give us an entirely new insight into the total no-fault picture and you are to be complimented for giving us that information and to broaden our perspective and helping us to come to some decision.

Mr. SCHEUER. I appreciate the witnesses' raising for us the thoughtful and challenging role of the insurance company in health insurance as well as accident insurance.

Mr. VAN DEERLIN. Have either of counsel any questions to complete the record?

Mr. KINZLER. Just one, Mr. Chairman. Mr. Hutto, you supplied for the record the Allstate cost figures for the States that these various Congressmen represent. If I understand correctly, those figures were for last year's Senate bill and not this year's, that is, they do not include the subrogation provision for commercial vehicles, so I wonder if you would be kind enough to supply for the record at your convenience the figures for those States with the subrogation provision in S. 354, as it was reported from the Senate Commerce Committee this year?

Mr. Hutto. I will be glad to.

Mr. VAN DEERLIN. We will be glad to receive it.

[At the time the hearings were printed the material requested had not been received.]

Mr. VAN DEERLIN. We thank both of you for coming all the way down here from our neighboring State.

Our next witness will be the representative of the American Association of Retired Persons from Cape Coral, Fla., Col. Henry LaRaia.

Mr. MCCOLLISTER. Mr. Chairman, I ask unanimous consent that the colonel be permitted to summarize his testimony, if he so chooses.

STATEMENT OF HENRY LaRAIA, NATIONAL RETIRED TEACHERS ASSOCIATION AND THE AMERICAN ASSOCIATION OF RETIRED PERSONS; ACCOMPANIED BY DAVID F. DUNNING, WASHINGTON OFFICE LEGISLATIVE REPRESENTATIVE

Mr. LARAIA. Yes, I can, Mr. McCollister. Since hearing all the preceding witnesses this morning, I will eliminate any duplication. However, I disagree in part with those witnesses that spoke, representing insurance companies and those lawyers representing the legal profession in not endorsing Federal no-fault insurance. One of the lawyers representing the Florida bar finally agreed after your committee questioned him, that some form of national no-fault should be enacted. I agree with him, we should have no-fault insurance laws on a Federal level.

We look to you our lawmakers to help the rest of the States that have not passed no-fault insurance, to give them guidance in some way so that we can get Federal no-fault immediately.

To benefit the people of the United States, particularly in our association, the American Association for Retired Persons, where we have 650,000 people in Florida and 8.4 million people in the United States that travel from one State to another, we must have some kind of protection and if it is not you that gives us the protection then we have to wait until all of the States get around to passing their ideas of some form of no-fault insurance even though a lot of it passed by legislation might be unconstitutional, as happened in the State of Illinois when in 1971 or 1972 the Illinois Supreme Court knocked out no-fault entirely.

Isn't that true, Mr. Metcalfe?

Mr. METCALFE. Not in Illinois.

Mr. LARAIA. Illinois in the case of *Grace* v. *Howlett,* in April 1972.

Mr. METCALFE. That is correct.

Mr. LARAIA. Because it was declared unconstitutional, the Illinois Legislature didn't do their best homework the first time, but finally enacted a better no-fault insurance for the State of Illinois.

Possibly what should be done with no-fault on the Federal level, is to let the Federal Government enact the law and with guidance let the States enact their no-fault and if necessary let the courts rule on any part that may be unconstitutional.

When those insurance people speaking this morning stated to you that they don't want the no-fault because it might hurt them financially, then let me say that it might be their faulty administration within their own organizations. I don't know the answer. But it is possible they might have too many people in their executive branch or departments that are getting very high salaries.

I get a little hot about this sometimes but let me answer one question here that Mr. Metcalfe, the Representative from Illinois, asked the representative of the Florida commissioner's office in Florida. Mr. Metcalf asked if every automobile owner in the State of Florida knows that they have compulsory insurance in the State of Florida. The insurance representative said he was not sure, but a safety inspection by the car dealer is authorized by law when the car is sold to a customer but the succeeding year he had to go to an inspection station controlled by the State to get that vehicle inspected.

A Florida law was passed stating that when a person has his automobile inspected he must bring his insurance policy or a financial card from the insurance company showing that he has insurance for his vehicle. A Florida licensed car must be inspected yearly and cannot be driven until after insurance is secured.

But I certainly disagree with all of these people when they say, "We won't need a no-fault." I look forward to the Federal Government saying, "Yes, we need it", and then let the Federal Government give the States guidelines for no-fault insurance.

Mr. MCCOLLISTER. Colonel, may I interrupt to ask you what do you believe are the primary benefits of no-fault?

Mr. LARAIA. I think everything is a benefit now.

Mr. MCCOLLISTER. Let me take a couple. Cost—do you think it is lower cost?

Mr. LARAIA. Lower cost?

Mr. MCCOLLISTER. Yes.

Mr. LARAIA. Well, whatever the individual person feels that he needs, because we have a poor person and a rich person, and if a rich person's salary is $40,000, or $50,000, or $60,000 a year, let him pay a premium that he can afford.

Mr. MCCOLLISTER. Do you believe no-fault insurance will give the premium payer the opportunity to pay less?

Mr. LARAIA. From the results I have seen in the State of Florida I would say no, because we have not received a decrease in insurance, which is one of the basic points of no-fault.

"Should we have no-fault because it will help decrease the premium?" Not in the State of Florida.

Mr. McCollister. It might be helpful to you to know that almost all of the witnesses before our committee in Washington have said that no-fault will not result in any premium savings.

Mr. La Raia. OK. Then it is the opposite opinion of what happened in Florida when we tried to push no-fault as a matter of law.

Mr. McCollister. Because everybody believed it would save money?

Mr. La Raia. Yes, sir.

Mr. McCollister. Second, do you believe, or you are surely interested also because you believe no-fault will pay quicker?

Mr. La Raia. Absolutely. We have experienced that, and from my survey among our people here, the 650,000 people in Florida in the American Association of Retired Persons and the National Retired Teachers Association, said yes, their claims are paid between 10 to 15 days after a claim is filed.

Mr. McCollister. Yes, sir.

What other reasons, other than the original belief that it would save premium dollars and that you would get paid quicker, what other reasons do you have for support of no-fault?

Mr. La Raia. Well, sir, because when a person is laid up in some type of accident or even if his automobile is smashed and he has no other means of transportation, we look forward to the insurance company under no-fault to pay those damages immediately whether it is for liability or whether it is for injury.

When one of these lawyers here from the bar association states, "We don't need Federal laws the State can take care of its own because we are going step-by-step into finding out the best solution," also, I believe the two previous men from Georgia said, "We need possibly a look at the insurance companies to determine whether or not insurance laws should be changed so that everybody will benefit by it." From that they do not seem satisfied with State laws and insurance policies.

No-fault automobile insurance is not the right to sue. It is a right to protect those people to seek compensation for the injuries they receive, or to repair their automobiles so that they will have transportation again.

I feel if it comes down to this, that we should have an insurance for automobiles as we have for health and other types of insurance, then let's go to that, because these people must look to something to pay for their illness or injuries, damages, repairs. Perhaps the present type of automobile insurance is not right.

Mr. McCollister. Let me ask another question. Do you believe that people should have the right to sue for pain and suffering?

Mr. La Raia. Well, when it comes to a millionaire who can pay a higher premium, and he does not get all he wants, yes.

Mr. McCollister. I am not talking about economic loss, but talking about pain and suffering. Does a person have a right to sue for that? Should a person have the right?

Mr. La Raia. Since I am an advocate of no-fault insurance, I feel they should not have the right to sue providing there is a sufficient amount of money coming in from the insurance company to pay full compensation to the individual that seeks the benefit.

Mr. McCollister. Are you saying then that at no point should they have the right to sue for pain and suffering?

Mr. LaRaia. Well, after listening to these previous gentlemen that spoke before me, they all seemed to agree there should be some method of suing, or to get some compensation, but if these insurance companies act correctly, there should be no area where one should sue if they are satisfied in their claims. Even the doctor that spoke this morning said he received $7,000. Was that claim adequate for his profession in lost wages? He seems to indicate, yes, but then again he says no. You see, he is on the defensive. He does not know one way or the other. I hope he is satisfied eventually, but in Florida we found out where some people received injuries, remained in the hospital for a long length of time and some of the insurance companies took care of those individuals in the hospital and paid their claims as the claims were filed. So the right to sue is a matter of opinion I suppose, but in my opinion I say no.

Mr. McCollister. OK.

Thank you.

Mr. LaRaia. On my left is Mr. David Dunning, our Washington office legislative representative on a national basis, and I am a member of the Florida Joint State Legislative Committee.

Now I will delete a lot of data from my paper after hearing a few of these people that appeared before me because some might be duplication, and I will be as brief as possible.

Mr. McCollister. The gentleman on your left is a remarkably well-preserved senior citizen.

Mr. LaRaia. Yes. Dave came down from Washington last night, and I came down from Jersey, and unfortunately I didn't have too much time to be prepared here. I wrote this up a week ago. My brother died, and I got in here last night myself. So there might be times—well anyway, I want to read some of these notes.

The pros and cons of no-fault legislation has been debated at great length during recent years. The opponents have consistently said, "Give the States time to pass sound legislation and they will handle the matter." The Ford administration most recently has expressed the same view, but we take exception to the position that "the progress that has already been achieved by the States should be viewed as truly remarkable."

On the contrary, it seems to us that progress by the States has been far less than desirable in the light of the urgency of the problem. It has taken 4 years for every State legislature to consider this legislation. The Department of Transportation has given passing marks to eight of those States who have at least signed into law a degree of no-fault reform. Among these eight States, the Florida law is used as a constructive move away from the problems of tort liability.

The committee I'm confident will hear from other witnesses today outlining what they view as serious problems with the Florida law regarding such things as abuse of the $1,000 medical threshold, the possibility of duplicating benefits for the same injury because of the equitable distribution law and also the possibility of the exhausting first party benefits. In general, our associations are pleased with the Florida law.

As I am sure the committee is aware, the Florida law is the second law in the United States to restrict tort liability, which we consider absolutely necessary. While cost savings as a result of restricting tort liability is important, a most important objective of no-fault reform is prompt payment when an accident occurs and adequate payment in relation to the damages suffered.

The no-fault insurance law seems to be very effective in the minds and contentment of our people in that, knowingly in the event of an accident, their insurance coverage immediately pays off the benefits by its insurer regardless of fault, thereby preventing long delays to determine fault through court action, adding additional expense to the insurer. It is a peace-of-mind factor to our older people.

I personally have interviewed many of our members who have been involved in minor motor vehicle accidents and their experiences have been that benefits have been paid within the period of 14 to 21 days after the claims have been filed.

One of the few examples I discovered in my research regarding injuries sustained in an automobile accident was the following: Mr. and Mrs. Cee from Cape Coral, Fla., were sideswiped by a hit-and-run car, pushing their car partially into a canal. Mr. and Mrs. Cee received minor hand and head cuts. Both were treated at the hospital and released. The insurer paid their benefits within 15 days. Notwithstanding these advantages, the Florida plan has serious defects which adversely affect not only our members but all Florida motorists.

Today, there are several broad groups of people who fall at the lower end of the economic spectrum and yet they either pay higher than average premiums for automobile insurance or at least have serious market problems. By and large, most of those segments which are now at the upper end of the risk spectrum tend to improve as risk under no-fault. For example, young people are responsible for a disproportionately large percentage of all automobile accidents and losses under the tort system and, consequently, pay substantially higher than average premiums. Under no-fault, we will be more concerned with the driver's economic loss than the damage he does to others and the young person tends to become a better risk. His wages are usually below average and his medical bills probably will be substantially below average simply because, being young, he is less prone to severe injury and physically capable of faster recovery.

Another broad category of people who could be significantly affected by the introduction of no-fault is the elderly. Here, too, we have a group of people in which wage loss is obviously much lower than average. In this case, the bulk of economic loss is medical expense. As you are all well aware, we already have a system of national health insurance applicable almost universally to elderly people. This system, medicare, has been in existence since 1966. It was created in recognition of the very expensive medical needs of the elderly at the very time when their income level has been sharply curtailed by retirement or semiretirement.

Medicare differs from any other form of health insurance currently in existence in this country primarily because of its near universality and its uniformity of coverage. Medicare is available to every U.S. citizen over 65 with relatively few exceptions. Further, coverage under medicare is uniform for all those who are eligible. After a $90 deductible, part A covers semiprivate hospital care without charge for 60 days and with a $23 per day charge for an additional 30 days. It also covers care in a "skilled nursing facility" without charge for 20 days and at a charge of $11.50 a day for an additional 80 days. Part A also covers posthospital care at home for as many as 100 visits in a 1-year period.

One of the sad facts of life in automobile accidents is that older people, when involved in an accident, do sustain greater economic loss than do younger people. The Department of Transportation automobile insurance and compensation study shows that the average economic loss for bodily injury claimants under 65 was slightly below $500. People age 65 and over had economic loss in excess of $700. Since the vast majority of people 65 and over are retired, their wage loss is minimum and often nonexistent. There economic loss is almost entirely composed of medical expenses. If we were to compare the medical expenses of older people to the medical expenses of younger people, we would find the ratio to be more than two to one. The higher medical loss sustained by people 65 and over is simply the result of the aging process. People 65 and over are more brittle than younger people and are therefore more inclined toward broken bones. Further, the rate of recovery from a given accident is very slow.

A serious defect of the Florida law is, in our view, that this does not consider medicare to be a primary source of benefits. No-fault, written in excess of medicare, would make automobile insurance considerably less expensive to older people than is now the case. Representatives of the insurance industry said that they believe drivers and users of automobiles should bear the cost of automobile ownership and, therefore, the cost of automobile insurance should be internalized. Internalization means that the automobile owners' share of economic loss should ultimately be paid by that owner in the form of automobile insurance premiums. As general philosophy, there is merit in this approach, but older people are a unique problem. Under no-fault, they would contribute a disproportionate part of the total economic losses because they are old and not because they cause an excessive portion of accidents. Not long ago, the National Safety Council showed that about 9 percent of all licensed drivers in the United States are 65 and over, yet they are involved in only 6 percent percent of all accidents.

In short, the benefits of medicare should be utilized by those receiving social security and companies should be required to sell no-fault insurance as excess benefits over those provided by medicare, at substantially lower premium rates.

A related issue is the limited wage loss exposure a person 65 or over experiences. There are areas in which the elderly driver will not incur the greater wage loss of his more affluent neighbor, particularly where the elderly retired driver experiences no wage loss. First party benefits are, theoretically, based upon the loss exposure of the insured party. If the elderly retired driver does not stand to lose as much as the wage earner then the lower benefits to be paid out by the insurance company should be reflected in lower premiums.

Very recently, a bill was introduced in the Michigan Legislature under the title of H.B. 5222, which adds a new chapter to the casualty and rating statute in that State. Essentially, it "amends the no-fault law by providing that rates on no-fault insurance must reflect diminished exposure to loss occasioned by coverage of retirees, persons not employed, persons without dependents, and persons with income below maximum work loss benefits levels." A dramatic example of how the insurance industry treated this provision before amendments were added was demonstrated in an article in the February 25, 1975, edition of the Wall Street Journal, which I would like to submit for the record. The article very briefly mentioned that laid-off workers in Michigan were finding a considerable bonus relative to auto insurance premiums due to their own employment. With benefits tied to earning power, the States' no-fault insurance law requires lower premiums for persons with lower income. Some persons were finding as much as a 35 percent premium decrease off their auto insurance checks. After checking with the insurance commissioner in Michigan, this is not necessarily reflective of what would happen to the same auto insurance premium for those 65 and over. However, we have been assured that the results would be nonetheless a considerable savings which this age group has never before experienced.

Further, our State Legislative Department in Washington has recently been requested by other States such as Illinois, Wisconsin, and Indiana, to suggest appropriate wording for amendments outlining equitable rate determinations which would be made by the insurance commissioner as a result of limited wage loss exposure for the elderly retired driver.

Most recently, the Senate Commerce Committee in Washington voted out a bill, S. 354, which will be considered by the full Senate in the near future. We were pleased that the Senate Commerce Committee has included in this legislation provisions which would allow equitable rate determinations with respect to wage loss exposure.

In ending, we hope that we have responded to your invitation to comment upon the impact of the Florida no-fault law on the retired driver. It appears to me that residents of this State enjoy a considerably better method of auto insurance as opposed to the other States now under no-fault. I've been advised that every other State legislature has considered the no-fault approach to auto insurance. I'm discouraged at the progress which has been shown. In my view, it is unrealistic to rely on a majority of the State legislatures to pass meaningful no-fault legislation. I, therefore, believe that a sound no-fault reform bill must be reported this session of Congress.

Thank you very much for the invitation to be here today and I, of course, will be glad to answer any questions you may have.

[The newspaper article referred to follows:]

[From Wall Street Journal, Feb. 25, 1975]

SILVER LINING

Laid-off workers in Michigan find one bonus amid their plight: Their auto insurance premiums are falling. With benefits tied to earning power, the state's no-fault insurance law requires lower premiums for persons with little income. The cut could trim up to 35% off the auto insurance checks. one official says.

Mr. VAN DEERLIN. Thank you, Colonel.
Mr. McCollister.
Mr. McCOLLISTER. I don't have any questions. The colonel's statement is quite well prepared and direct, and I thank you.

Mr. LaRaia. Thank you. Let me add one more point to this. My son had studied at the law school at the Oklahoma University Law School after he retired as a major in the Army. He was a bright student, but I wanted to point this out, that the law schools now are putting this no-fault insurance in their curriculum. In other words, they are teaching students about no-fault insurance.

There is another advantage to Federal no-fault insurance, because those law students as lawyers are going to be in the future our legislators in the various States and will understand no-fault insurance.

Mr. McCollister. We hope not all of them.

Mr. LaRaia. My son was finally grabbed upon graduation from law school by Exxon, took the bar examination in both Oklahoma and Texas and now in California, working for Exxon on the Alaskan pipeline. He wrote a paper in his third year of law school published in the Law Review.

I have just one little paragraph from his notes which is the basis of this whole thing. He says:

> The idea of providing no-fault protection to persons involved in automobile accidents is not a new one, but in recent years the outcry for improvement in automobile accident compensation systems has brought about proposed plans which have come to be classified under the heading of no-fault. Generally, the plans came to improve the present compensation system by assuring prompt payment to victims of medical and economic losses, to reduce automobile insurance premiums, and that is important, by increasing efficiency, and this is wherre the insurance companies are lacking, efficiency, in my opinion, and possibly in the insurance industry, and to eliminate the court congestion which is due in large part to automobile personal injury litigation.

When we had a couple of lawyers up here that said we increased the judicial system in Florida in order to handle these cases I can assure you a lot of the cases never reached the court because of no-fault. Prompt payment by the insurance companies prevented the cases from going to court. We are paying more judges than we need in Florida and I hope we can use them elsewhere because we have a lot of crimes in Florida which they can try.

Mr. Van Deerlin. Mr. Stuckey.

Mr. Stuckey. No questions.

Mr. Van Deerlin. Mr. Metcalfe.

Mr. Metcalfe. I am very much impressed by the colonel's statement.

Mr. LaRaia. I wonder if you can speak louder, I am a little deaf.

Mr. Metcalfe. I would like to say this, Colonel. In your military background, you know how to address questions and speak very frankly, therefore, I would pose this question to you, which I have previously asked and maybe I will get a new perspective.

I am not thoroughly convinced there is need for additional time before we seriously consider writing up a bill because no-fault insurance is nothing new, it is 25 years old.

Mr. LaRaia. That is right.

Mr. Metcalfe. As a matter of fact, both Professor Keeton and Professor O'Connell made an examination of the automobile reparations system back in the 1950's and all the way up to 1965, and since then, of course, Florida has had a no-fault insurance bill since 1971, when they started, and passed it in 1972 and Massachusetts since 1971, so it appears to me that, and I would like your judgment, please, but it appears to me that we have studied it enough and have had enough expertise from the States that have already passed it, the 24 States, to give us a barometer as to what we need.

That is the reason I had raised the question with one of the previous witnesses as to how much more time do we need to study this and examine all of the ramifications and I would like your reaction as to whether or not we are prepared now to go ahead and write a no-fault insurance bill nationally?

Mr. LaRaia. I agree 100 percent, Mr. Metcalfe, and I say that in my text here, we have spent too much time in these hearings and we should go right back to Washington and get this out before the whole Congress, a compromise between the Senate and House, and put it on the floor, so we can pass no-fault insurance on a national level and it should be done in this session of Congress. That is right, absolutely.

Mr. Metcalfe. Thank you very much, and thank you, Mr. Chairman.

Mr. Van Deerlin. If not in this session at least in this Congress.

Mr. LaRaia. In this Congress.

Mr. Van Deerlin. Mr. Scheuer.

Mr. Scheuer. I appreciate the gentleman's testimony very much. It was very helpful. Thank you.

Mr. Van Deerlin. Mr. Rinaldo.

Mr. Rinaldo. You mentioned you were very much in favor of no-fault and familiar with the Florida law. What don't you like about the Florida law that you would like changed at the national level?

Mr. LaRaia. Well, Mr. Dunning will answer that one possibly.

Mr. Dunning. We have found, Congressman, there are of the 24 States that have passed it, the group here is able to take advantage of the medicare program. Twenty-four of the States have passed and only five of those have made medicare primary. In other words, included in that are first party benefits and then the insurance package for any additional medical losses would cover for that.

In some cases we found that worth as much as 50 medical. That is not considered primary in this State. It is in most of the Federal bills.

Another one which has been introduced in a few other States is the work loss exposure, which is prevalent to the elderly retired person and that is one thing that has, very recently, in the last year and a half, has come up. But our position is that I think too much emphasis probably was put on the cost savings. There are so many at Allstate, the Milliman & Robertson study overemphasized it and I am sure it is important but the need for abolishing tort and getting prompt payments and adequate payments to the accident victims is our need and in our view is much more important than the costs and we will struggle with the system, but in the absence of the other States acting, we think the Federal or Senate bill should go ahead.

Mr. Rinaldo. Thank you. No further questions.

Mr. Van Deerlin. No questions by Mr. Kinzler and Ms. Nord.

We appreciated your attendance here today, Colonel, and especially your patience in waiting so long to testify.

Mr. Van Deerlin. We have one further public witness, Mr. John Paul Skandamis, Daytona Beach, who has had more than one experience in auto accidents and is going to describe his experience to us.

STATEMENT OF JOHN PAUL SKANDAMIS, DAYTONA BEACH, FLA.

Mr. SKANDAMIS. Mr. Chairman, I am thankful for my Lord Jesus Christ and for the strength He gives me to come here, and for this committee for listening.

The experience I wanted to relate, as a public citizen of the State of Florida, spans some 12 years. I have had three automobile accidents in that period of time, two without no-fault insurance and one after no-fault insurance here in Florida.

I read of the hearing here in the local newspaper. It said that they wanted testimonies, and that is what I have. I prayed about it, and and it seemed that I was led to come here, and I thank you, because I live just about a half-block away. I appreciate all of you coming here.

I am a public school teacher, and I teach now in Jacksonville, Fla. My parents moved here from south Georgia in June 1963. My father was a semi-invalid without social security, without any retirement income, and only lived on limited savings. We settled nearby here and while I was driving him down the street, this street here, we had an automobile accident. A car ran into the back of us. We were covered by an auto insurance company located in Alabama and medical pay from my car insurance with State Farm.

We received some whiplash injuries, my mother and father, and I. The accident took place about a week after we got here. I was not accustomed to the driving situation. We went to a lawyer. We sued for medical payments and damages. The injuries were not severe.

I had an opportunity to go to the State of Michigan to teach school, and I had to turn it down. I was fortunate that I found a local teaching position, for a year, here in mathematics, in a junior high school. My father could not get auto insurance for his car after that accident. They cancelled him. I was not responsible, or charged for the accident. And for about a period of a year we received medical treatments.

Mr. MCCOLLISTER. Did you say you were not charged with responsibility for the accident?

Mr. SKANDAMIS. Yes. A person from Connecticut, a young student visiting Daytona collided with us because he was following too close. Near here, near this motel.

Well, settlement took a year. We had a lawyer and the case was favorable, but it took a year for the people to pay these bills. I lost the opportunity to go to a better paying job in Michigan. I had been teaching school in Georgia before the year I taught here in Daytona Beach, 1963-64.

We finally settled the case within a year and paid the bills.

The next year, 1964-65, I was unemployed due to a lack of proper certification and other difficulties. My father could not purchase car insurance. Also my car could not be maintained properly and it was covered by State Farm Insurance Co. One day it would not start, April 1965——

Mr. MCCOLLISTER. Wait a minute. You said your father could not get car insurance?

Mr. SKANDAMIS. Yes. He could not, because of his age.

Mr. MCCOLLISTER. Right, but how were you then covered by State Farm?

Mr. SKANDAMIS. I had my own automobile.

Mr. MCCOLLISTER. Okay.

Mr. SKANDAMIS. And he was near 70 at the time. We have had a lot of retired people in this area. During the second year 1964–65, here in town, I went to hear Rev. Oral Roberts at the speedway grounds. They had a local crusade. While returning, I was using his car, my father's car without insurance. And, now in his car, I was covered under my State Farm policy, under the nonowned vehicle clause, while using his car, temporarily. My car, the day before the accident or on the day of the accident would not start. My battery was dead.

I was not able to maintain my car as I had been accustomed to doing, being unemployed and having lost nearly $5,200 in salary that second year here in Daytona Beach.

Returning from the crusade in my father's car, not insured, my brakes failed on his car and I hit a car in front of me and it ran into the back of two cars. I was responsible for the accident. It was my fault. The brakes should have been repaired. I didn't realize they were that defective until I started driving it back home.

From the accident I was taken to the hospital, examined, and released. I went back to hear Rev. Oral Roberts that night, April 9, 1965. On Monday the insurance adjuster came, Bob Boyers, State Farm adjuster, and claimed they would not cover me. They made an investigation. Then, Mr. Lane, the claims superintendent wrote the accident was not covered because I didn't have a current automobile tag on my car.

Having moved from Georgia to Florida, the time for vehicle registration had been a little different, and we had not adjusted to that, and so they, State Farm, refused to cover the automobile accident. And I told them the reason I didn't drive my car was because my car would not start. Yet, they paid an emergency road service charge of $1 to get my car started after the accident.

So, I had to find my own attorney, and it took 4 years to win the victory against my own company for coverage. State Farm, I think, paid something like $3,000. I didn't derive any benefit except this: I had heard a man named E. Stanley Jones, a missionary evangelist, who said, "If life kicks you, let it kick you forward." So around April 1965, being unemployed, I had thought about this young fellow that hit us in 1963 and had injured us, and the need for traffic safety. I wrote to the State Department of Education, and got a scholarship of $100 from Allstate Insurance to go to the University of Florida, which I did in the summer of 1965 and studied driver education.

After I had finished I came back here and my father said, "Well, son, after all of these years"—I was about 30-years old then—"After all of these years of driving you finally learned how."

He was right. I had been driving for years and countless thousands of miles without really learning the proper way. There had been so many changes made, you know, in automobiles, shifting of gears and interstate highways and all of those things that came into existence since I was 16. So I had really learned how to drive safely.

I found a job through the University of Florida. I went to Duval County. They had a driver education program. They had a need for teachers to teach this subject, and I taught it there 6 years. I got the job and I taught 6,000 of their students to drive safely. No one was injured, not even a dented fender. I have had students say, "Mr. Skandamis, my parents are afraid to drive with me at home, you are not afraid," and she had just run right through a red light. I went to a church one night soon after I got up there and got the job. I took a course on the subject of prayer. At the beginning of the course we had to tell why we were interested in prayer. When my turn came I said, "I am a driver education teacher." They laughed. I did get a lot of spiritual help from prayer and the Holy Spirit did help me in teaching my students to drive safely.

We taught in teams of four, 1,000 students a year, in a multiphased program from classroom for 30 hours and 6, range, simulation, and on the street. Actually putting them behind the wheel of a live automobile with 200 horses under the hood and putting them on interstate within 2 months' classroom time.

During this time of teaching I became quite aware of the need for insurance. Meanwhile, all of this time, the *State Farm* case was pending. It was not until after I got the job that I realized that I may lose my driver's license if State Farm won the case. So, I kept praying about it, and my lawyer here locally, did win the case and settled it.

Now, I am here, encouraged that you people are interested in no-fault insurance. I think it is needed, greatly needed and there are 2 million people a year, according to statistics of a few years ago, injured every year in the United States. In the last 12 years that would add up to 24 million people; 50,000 are killed every year or thereabouts. Well, more or less, in that time, that is almost 600,000 people killed in car accidents.

We need more prevention than we need cure. We need more education for the driving public. We have 100 million cars. Teenagers are responsible for more accidents than the older public, but even the older public needs safety education. They also need a good insurance policy and a seat belt and the grace of God to drive safely.

Now, I was in the program 6 years. My seventh year I taught psychology at Lee High School in Duval County. One of the famous schools here in Florida. I taught there a year. Because of a change of population, and integration, and the opening of two new high schools, I was moved some 30 miles away to teach English, where I have been for the last 3 years.

Now, 2 weeks after I was moved to teach English I had my third automobile accident. It was on October 12, 1972.

Mr. STUCKEY. Was it after no-fault?

Mr. SKANDAMIS. Right after no-fault, about a year after no-fault. I had my cars covered all of this period of time.

Mr. STUCKEY. With State Farm?

Mr. SKANDAMIS. No. Allstate. I am partial to Allstate because they want to help people. They gave me the scholarship. Also, Aetna and some of the others have safety equipment. They have designed simulators. They have safety programs and equipment to teach this particular high school population.

Now, in the third accident was a woman teacher rushing to school, who ran a stoplight—she was charged by the police—and collided with my car. As a result of the accident I was in the hospital for 5 days. I had a whiplash injury. At the time of the accident I had my seat belt on. I am thankful for that.

I didn't go immediately to the hospital but I did go to my doctor, after I said my prayers, and asked others to do so too. I put on a neck collar, as my wife was interested in going to South Carolina to a wedding of a niece. So we went to the wedding. When I returned I went to the hospital, admitted by the doctor for cervical strain. But, within 4 hours after the accident I had a cash settlement under no-fault insurance, where, before no-fault insurance in Florida, it took me 4 years to get a settlement with State Farm Insurance Co. on October 12, 1972, they—Travelers Insurance Co.—gave me a check for $700 for my car, and after about a week in the hospital I got another $700 for the hospital bill. Within 2 weeks I had repaired the car. I had no trouble with the no-fault insurance.

Now, Mr. Chairman, in a study made by Northwestern University, I remember reading, while at the University of Florida, that there are 4.3 errors made in driving accidents. The Northwestern University in Evanston had made a traffic study of some 40 accidents, scientifically—hours of interviews with the people involved in the accidents, and the doctors and this, that, and the other, and one of the conclusions they came out with that in every accident there was at least 4.3 errors made by drivers in every accident studied.

So, I don't know that the term "no-fault" is really true. I think it is a misnomer. I think everybody is at fault in an accident, somehow or other, you know. Between now and tomorrow, there will be 5,200 people injured in automobiles and yet you won't see it in the national headlines.

An airplane will crash in New York, as it did a few weeks ago, 100-and-something killed. Well, Congressmen, between now and tomorrow 150 people will be killed in automobile accidents, and will have a funeral that they were not planning to go to, and 1,000 will be killed this week, and over 35,000 injured in a week from an automobile. And yet we play up in big headlines in the newspaper "100 Killed In An Airplane Accident," and yet every day in America 1,000 people are killed on the average.

Mr. VAN DEERLIN. Every day?

Mr. SKANDAMIS. Every week, excuse me. 50,000 a year killed, 2 million injured in a year's time. Divide 365 into 2 million, you will get about 5,200 a day, and they are not intended to happen. These people need protection, and that is what I understand you are speaking about here, to protect the public, to protect the consumer.

You see, I had paid for my coverage with State Farm in my second accident, yet they denied me coverage and a hearing on the basis of a tag, a minor thing. I had the coverage and they eventually paid it off. The lawyer I retained was a good one, but he couldn't get into court. It took 4 years to close.

Mr. VAN DEERLIN. And that was partially an interstate problem because you had a Georgia tag and moved to Florida?

Mr. SKANDAMIS. That is correct. My father couldn't get insurance. Had he had his insurance, we would not have had this problem. So I let that turn me around, and used it to make me better, I am a better and safer driver, and I still have many more years to drive, and I guess we drive 50 or 60 years in our life. We spend more time licensing a person to get a barber's license in Florida, some 9 months, I think. Far more time than they need to pass an examination to get a Florida driver's license. The laws have changed from the time that I first learned to drive at 16, you know. Where there was a very limited education available. My father was as good a teacher as he could be. He was concerned. But cars changed from manual shifts to automatics, from cars without air-conditioners and cars with running boards to no running boards and air-conditioned cars. From two lanes to four lanes in interstate highways and changes in traffic signals and great population growth in driving.

Mr. VAN DEERLIN. Any questions for the witness?

Mr. SCHEUER. No questions, Mr. Chairman.

Mr. RINALDO. No questions, Mr. Chairman.

Mr. VAN DEERLIN. You certainly are a most absorbing witness.

Do either counsel have questions?

Ms. NORD. No questions.

Mr. KINZLER. No questions.

Mr. SCHEUER. Mr. Chairman, I would like to observe to the witness that this is not only a bipartisan committee, but an interfaith committee, and I assume that your prayers were meant to be interdenominational prayers for all members of the subcommittee?

Mr. SKANDAMIS. Yes.

Mr. SCHEUER. Thank you, Mr. Chairman.

Mr. VAN DEERLIN. Thank you so much for coming to volunteer this testimony.

Are there further public witnesses to be heard before the committee recesses?

Thank you very much.

That concludes the hearing for today. The hearings will resume at the call of the Chair.

[Whereupon, at 2:30 p.m., the subcommittee adjourned, subject to the call of the Chair.]

NO-FAULT MOTOR VEHICLE INSURANCE

THURSDAY, JULY 17, 1975

House of Representatives,
Subcommittee on Consumer Protection and Finance,
Committee on Interstate and Foreign Commerce,
Washington, D.C.

The subcommittee met at 1:30 p.m., pursuant to notice, in room 2322, Rayburn House Office Building, Hon. Lionel Van Deerlin, chairman, presiding.

Mr. VAN DEERLIN. The subcommittee will renew its hearings on several bills dealing with no-fault auto insurance.

We are privileged to hear first this afternoon from the distinguished former Solicitor General of the United States and constitutional authority, Mr. Erwin N. Griswold.

Welcome to the subcommittee, Mr. Griswold. We stand to be interrupted at any time because of the bill establishing a new committee to look into CIA activities. It is a rather volatile subject and we may have numerous votes, but we are here to learn from you and we invite you to proceed.

STATEMENT OF ERWIN N. GRISWOLD, ESQ., ON BEHALF OF STATE FARM MUTUAL AUTOMOBILE INSURANCE CO., BLOOMINGTON, ILL., AND THE AMERICAN INSURANCE ASSOCIATION

Mr. GRISWOLD. May I say I am interested in the CIA subject, too, but I shall not undertake to deal with that at this appearance.

Mr. Chairman, and members of the committee: As the chairman has said, my name is Erwin N. Griswold. For the past 2 years, I have been engaged in the private practice of law as a member of the firm of Jones, Day, Reavis & Pogue here in Washington and I appear here today on behalf of the State Farm Mutual Automobile Insurance Co. of Bloomington, Ill., and the American Insurance Association.

It is just a year ago, indeed a year ago tomorrow, July 18, 1974, that I appeared before this subcommittee to express my opinion on the constitutionality of S. 354, which would provide Federal standards for no-fault insurance, and other similar legislation. S. 354, as it passed the Senate last year, is substantially identical to H.R. 1900, which is before the subcommittee now. The views I expressed then were presented in full before the committee, and are available in the printed hearings.

A year's further thought on the questions, and the developments which have occurred during that time, have not led me to change the views I expressed at that time; namely, that the provisions of H.R. 1900, if enacted by Congress, would be a valid exercise of congressional

(551)

power under the Commerce clause and the Post Road clause, and would not violate any prescription of the Constitution, express or implied.

In particular, I concluded that Congress may, as provided by H.R. 1900, set minimum Federal standards for no-fault reparation of auto accident victims, yet leave administration of these standards to State courts and State insurance departments.

Administration of the no-fault standards in H.R. 1900 would require of State insurance departments no tasks which they are not well equipped to perform, and would involve responsibilities which these departments generally already handle pursuant to State law. As I noted, this type of scheme appears to promote the values of federalism, since it establishes nationwide standards for reform, without totally displacing local administrative authority.

Just before I testified here a year ago, the U.S. Court of Appeals for the Third Circuit in Philadelphia decided a case which appears to give strong support for the view that H.R. 1900, if enacted, would be constitutional. This is *Commonwealth of Pennsylvania* v. *Environmental Protection Agency*, 500 F. 2d 246, decided on June 28, 1974, in an opinion written for a unanimous panel by Judge Van Dusen.

In this decision, the court upheld the constitutional validity of the clean air amendments, enacted by Congress in 1970. These amendments require that the States, in certain circumstances, carry out the steps which are necessary to meet Federal standards with respect to air quality—just as H.R. 1900 provides with respect to compensation of auto accident victims. The third circuit viewed the relevant constitutional authorities in quite the same light as I did in my opinion.

In his opinion, Judge Van Dusen dealt directly with the question of federalism. In holding that—

> The Administrator (of EPA) acted within the Federal commerce power in requiring the Commonwealth (of Pennsylvania) to enforce its (EPA's) transportation plan.

Judge Van Dusen said:

> We believe that this approach represents a valid adaption of federalist principles to the need for increased Federal involvement. The only alternative implementation would be for the Federal Government to assume some of the functions of traffic control and vehicle registration and directly enforce the programs contained in the various transportation control plans. The Administrator has determined that this would not be a practicable way of attaining national air quality standards * * * and we fail to see how this would represent less of an intrusion upon State sovereignty.

As recognized by the court in the *Pennsylvania* case—500 F. 2d at 262—this is simply a reflection of the view expressed by the Supreme Court in *Parden* v. *Terminal Ry. of the Alabama State Docks Department*, 377 U.S. 184, 192 (1964), where the court said:

> By empowering Congress to regulate commerce, then, the States necessarily surrendered any portion of their sovereignty that would stand in the way of such regulation.

Another development in the past year is the decision of the Pennsylvania Supreme Court in the case of *Singer* v. *Sheppard*, decided on June 25, 1975. This case upheld the validity of the Pennsylvania no-fault statute under the State's constitution. It is relevant here because of the answer which it gives to the argument made by opponents of bills setting up Federal standards that States might be barred from enacting plans under title II by their own constitutions. As I noted in my opinion, the "barriers" to no-fault which opponents found in State constitutions may be interpreted in a manner harmonious with the no-fault concept.

Finally, I would refer to the decision of the Supreme Court in the case of *Fry* v. *United States*, decided on May 27, 1975. This case upheld and applied the Court's earlier decision in *Maryland* v. *Wirtz*, 392 U.S. 183 (1968), in holding that the 1970 Economic Stabilization Act's ban on salary increases was constitutionally applicable to salaries paid to State employees, specifically employees of the State of Ohio. The argument was made—

That applying the Economic Stabilization Act to State employees interferes with sovereign State functions and for that reason the commerce clause should not be read to permit regulation of all State and local government employees.

This argument was specifically based on the 10th amendment as well as upon the construction of the commerce clause. As I have said, the Court upheld the validity of the wage regulations as applied to State salaries, reaching this result on the "principle that States are not immune from all Federal regulation under the commerce clause merely because of their sovereign status."

Although these developments support the conclusion I expressed last year that H.R. 1900, if enacted by Congress, would be constitutional, I understand that it may no longer be necessary to face this problem directly, at least as far as the Senate bill is concerned. The Senate Commerce Committee has now modified S. 354 to eliminate this basis for constitutional debate.

Under these amendments, the States will be given the opportunity to enact title II; and if any State does not choose to do that, it will be given the opportunity to administer title III. If, however, any State chooses to do neither of these things, then title III will be administered in the State by Federal authority. Under this arrangement, no State is forced to do anything. There can be no doubt since the *South-Eastern Underwriters* decision—*United States* v. *South-Eastern Underwriters Ass'n*, 322 U.S. 533 (1944)—that Congress has power under the commerce clause to regulate and administer insurance within the States. If a State decides to do this itself, it is free to do so, under the provisions of the McCarran Act. But, if a State does not wish to administer a statute which meets Federal standards under title II or title III, then it is under no compulsion to do so. This should serve to eliminate any question based upon concepts of federalism.

As I have already indicated, it is my judgment that these amendments are not constitutionally required. However, they make eminent good sense politically, in both senses of that term. Under H.R. 1900, with this amendment, the States can have it either way. They can pass and administer a title II program. Or they can accept a title III program on either a State or federally administered basis. No State is required to take any action at all, and, specifically, no State is required to administer a Federal or any other act.

Of course, the likelihood of a State's accepting title III on either basis, particularly a federally administered basis, appears extremely remote. Nevertheless, the objectives of the amendment to S. 354 could be significant as a symbol of the willingness of Congress to accommodate all State concerns consistent with the implementation of Federal policy in establishing minimum standards for no-fault insurance.

Since there can be no doubt as to the power of Congress to regulate insurance of motor vehicles on the Nation's highways, there can, I believe, be no doubt of the power of Congress to establish minimum standards for such insurance. The only substantial issue which has been previously raised is the contention that Congress could not compel the States to administer a Federal law consistently with proper standards of federalism. Since the amendments to S. 354 and possible amendments to H.R. 1900 remove this compulsion, this constitutional contention is fully answered.

Although I adhere to my previously expressed opinion that S. 354 and H.R. 1900 would be constitutional without these amendments, I can see merit in eliminating the question of compulsion. The amendments to the Senate bill constitute a practical and legal modification of the bill.

On this basis, the only question pending before the Congress is the wisdom of establishing Federal standards in this area. One of the important elements of federalism is our unity in diversity. One of the great things about the United States is that we have a single economy, a common market. Transportation is now quick and easy, and many trips on the highways, both by automobile and truck, involve interstate travel. Our forefathers, with great prescience, gave Congress the power to regulate interstate and foreign commerce, and one of the reasons for this was the desirability of providing for a considerable amount of conformity. Quite apart from the pervasive degree of Federal involvement in the creation of the motor transportation system, the Federal concern with the proper conduct of that system is clear to anyone who uses our great interstate highways.

In this view, the objectives of H.R. 1900 are no different from those of, say, the Federal Employers Liability Act, applying a uniform standard to injuries on the Nation's railroads, or of the National Traffic and Motor Vehicle Safety Act of 1966, which, like H.R. 1900, is a me at the amelioration of the Nation's auto accident injury toll.i d

It is true that H.R. 1900 involves insurance, but since the *South-Eastern Underwriters* decision, it has been clear that the business of insurance is interstate commerce, and subject to regulation by Congress. It is only through congressional grace, evidenced in the McCarran-Ferguson Act, that insurance is a field primarily regulated by the States. H.R. 1900, especially with the suggested amendments, accommodates fully the tradition reflected in the McCarran-Ferguson Act.

There may be those who say that Congress should stay its hand in the field of no-fault reform, unless State reparations systems are engulfed by a massive and dramatic "crisis." But federalism does not contemplate that Congress should feel so constrained. Congress does not have to wait until accident victims organize or institute mass demonstrations or attempt civil disobedience to protest the deficiencies of the status quo.

While I do not purport here to discuss this legislation on the merits, it would seem that Congress would have every right and reason to consider the auto accident problem a matter of crisis proportions, albeit perhaps a relatively silent crisis. Surely, with tens of thousands of deaths and millions of injuries annually, this must be one of the

Nation's most serious public health challenges. One can hardly think of a more appropriate use of the commerce power than the adoption of reforms designed to assure comprehensive compensation for victims, in a manner which is both efficient and conducive to further initiatives to improve the reparations system.

Finally, I would suppose that Congress is especially well qualified to determine the requirements of national policy in light of the claims of State authority. Both the States and the localities of the country are represented in the Congress, and both the Members of the Senate and of the House of Representatives are fully conversant with the needs and interests of their constituencies. Thus, the Congress has built into it a substantial degree of local orientation, and can readily harmonize differences in points of view between the Nation and the States. I believe that this is very satisfactorily accomplished in H.R. 1900, with or without the amendment adopted by the Senate Commerce Committee.

My particular concern is with the constitutional validity of the proposed statute. As I have indicated, it is my conclusion that H.R. 1900 complies with the provisions of the Constitution.

Thank you, Mr. Chairman.

Mr. VAN DEERLIN. Thank you, Mr. Griswold.

Your statement was both informative and poetic. The use of the term "silent crisis" is a very good one, I think, and we gathered at earlier hearings, judging from the protests against some of the practices imposed on motorists by insurance companies, that the crisis may become less and less silent all the time.

I would say, combined with the Attorney General's testimony before the Senate committee, your testimony today gives us now two preeminent constitutional scholars who say that under certain conditions Federal no-fault law would undoubtedly be constitutional.

I think the Attorney General's caveat was that the bill must contain an amendment to allow the States to choose whether or not to support the mechanisms in title III. With that amendment, he found no constitutional objections.

We are still left, as you note, with the question of whether Federal Government involvement is an advisable step to take. The States have been in it for about 5 years now and there have been suggestions we should wait a while longer to give additional States an opportunity to come aboard.

I would be interested—since you have suggested the comparison with the Federal Employer's Liability Act under which we are applying uniform Federal standards to injuries on a transportation system that the Federal Government has helped to build—in whether you can expand a little and tell us what would be the proper objective of Federal standards in no-fault insurance. Would it be to compensate the inevitable victims of an inherently dangerous system, that is, today's automobiles on today's highways—highways which the Government has created?

Mr. GRISWOLD. Yes, I think that is such a case.

Mr. MCCOLLISTER. If you will yield for a moment.

Mr. VAN DEERLIN. Of course.

Mr. MCCOLLISTER. Before Dean Griswold responds, since we already heard from his client in this regard, I would like to know whether we are hearing State Farm's view or your own, personal, view without regard to your relationship with State Farm?

Mr. GRISWOLD. Well, that is a little hard to answer, Mr. McCollister. I made it plain that I am appearing here on behalf of these two agencies. However, to the extent of my ability, I am stating my view. I have not undertaken to twist or distort my view on their behalf, but I cannot, or I want to make it plain that I am not appearing here as I might have if I had been an academic, as I long was, simply stating independently my view; but I am, to the best of my ability, stating my honest view as to the conclusion, as to my conclusions as to constitutionality of these provisions.

Mr. MCCOLLISTER. I was not referring to that, but I think the question that our chairman put to you, perhaps I misunderstood the question.

Mr. VAN DEERLIN. Well, I thought it was with great propriety that Dean Griswold mentioned at the outset that State Farm is his client. I feel sure that the witness' legal conclusions would not be for sale to any bidder.

Mr. GRISWOLD. Well, on the general subject, of course, I became interested in this problem more than 10 years ago when I was at the Harvard Law School and was instrumental in obtaining the money to finance the research which was done first by Prof. Robert E. Keeton of the Harvard Law School faculty and he brought Jeffrey O'Connell of the University of Illinois faculty in to work with him, and the Keeton and O'Connell books and articles have been prominent in this area; and I generally support the line of argument which they have made, which is that no-fault insurance, by eliminating what at least for the smaller accidents is really an irrelevant question; namely, the issue of fault is sound because, like workmen's compensation, we know that with 100 million vehicles on the highways there will be a certain amount of accidents and there ought to be an effective way for providing for losses which result from those injuries.

It occurred fairly early, in fact to Mr. Ballantine in the Columbia study, back in the 1930's, that there was an enormous amount of wastage in the legal system in litigating the issue of fault which made it very difficult to get any certainty and which led to inevitable substantial delays.

So, the basic concept of no-fault is simply what its name indicates, that you are not interested in whose fault it was, but you are interested in the amount of the injuries and in prompt payment, and the no-fault system does provide an effective and efficient way for providing that.

You can have no-fault all the way down the line. There are people who think that there is merit in the traditional tort system, so it is usual to put in a limit or a threshold, as it is sometimes called, beyond which the tort system will continue to operate.

One reason, as I see it, why it is not very sound to let this continue to develop in the States is that those thresholds vary widely in every State bill from, in effect, zero in some cases to fairly substantial amounts in others, which makes it really impossible to compare the results which are obtained in the States. That is one reason why I think there not only ought to be a Federal no-fault statute, but that that statute ought to set minimum standards so the States could have stricter standards if they wanted to; but they ought to go at least that far.

Mr. McCollister. Dean Griswold, does the evidence of the States suggest that that minimum threshold should be something fairly clear in your view? Can you tell me what you believe that threshold should be?

Mr. Griswold. Well, since you are trying to minimize litigable issues, I think it is fairly important to have a way of defining what is within the threshold and what is without it that involves as little opportunity for controversy as possible. I think that S. 354 and H.R. 1900 do that in a very acceptable way and I don't know of a better way than is embodied in those two bills.

I don't mean to say that is the only conceivable way. Any line-drawing problem involves a certain amount of arbitrariness, but I think that is a good place to draw the line.

Mr. McCollister. That is the very reason I have felt that we ought not have that arbitrariness at this point until there has been a greater experimentation period for the States to test those various thresholds in light of experiences of the States in order that we might not draw that line arbitrarily.

Mr. Griswold. One problem I have with that is, that under the present system with no Federal standards, we have at most 18 or 20 States which have done this, which means that 30 States have not even started after 10 years. Of those 18 or 20 States, only 3 or 4 or 5 have what can really be called a no-fault statute. The others have thresholds so low that they don't really achieve the objective.

My thought would be that we had spent enough time discussing this so that, if we really are to make progress, we ought to have a federally enacted minimum standard.

Mr. Van Deerlin. We found on Monday, Mr. Griswold, that the $1,000 threshold in the Florida law has proved an insurmountable temptation to certain doctors and lawyers in Dade County, the seat of Miami. They find that if the victim is up around $500 or $600, the lawyer can find the right doctor to build the medical bills up to take him past the $1,000 threshold. Did you suggest a moment ago there might be something other than a flat financial threshold that might help remove the controversy?

Mr. Griswold. There are provisions, I believe, in some of the statutes for broken arms and legs and the loss of an eye or of a limb or certain objective things like that, which would do it. But I think it is hard to get away at some point from a dollar amount. Perhaps a way to handle it would be to put the dollar amount higher and then to try to have some effective disciplinary proceedings in both the legal and medical professions in Dade County and elsewhere.

Mr. Van Deerlin. Do you think, Mr. Griswold, that to continue with a system in which some States have no-fault laws and as many or more do not, do you think this gives us a hopeless state of confusion for the interstate traveler, where, in some States no-fault laws apply and in others, the tort system applies.

In a great mobile society, I assume you do think this is an unsatisfactory way to leave the law?

Mr. Griswold. I think this leads to great uncertainty and great confusion. Two weeks ago, I was in the province of Quebec in Canada, just across the New Hampshire line, and, in the interval, I have driven back and in that period I was in 10 different jurisdictions starting with Quebec, New Hampshire, Vermont, Massachusetts, Connecticut, and New York and Pennsylvania and Delaware and Maryland and, finally, the District of Columbia. Fortunately, I didn't have any automobile accident along the way.

I would find it more comforting to have more assurance than I have as to what kind of coverage I actually had with respect to the situation if an accident had happened in any one of those places and it seems to me this country, as it has developed, the exact spot of an accident is more or less irrelevant in terms of what should be the provision for compensation for losses resulting from injuries on the highways, particularly on the great interstate highways which have been financed by Congress and over which much of my route lay.

Mr. Van Deerlin. Mr. McCollister.

Mr. McCollister. Dean Griswold, were you similarly discomforted by the fact that in the eight jurisdictions you traveled in had differenty traffic laws and cannot a similar argument be made, since the traffic laws applied to every driver and, fortunately, the accident happens to only a few drivers?

Mr. Griswold. Mr. Congressman, I think that is an excellent opportunity for me to answer. The traffic law with which I was most concerned was the speed limit, and that was 55 miles an hour and that is the result of a Federal enactment.

Congress has passed a national standard which meant that 55 miles an hour was the maximum limit and I tried very, very hard all the way to keep my car going about 54 miles an hour while many cars passed me.

Mr. McCollister. As it happens, I will have lunch today with a couple from my district who have made claims about that same path you have traveled and they have talked about the wide ignorance, or rather, not applying to the law in that same route traveled and they spoke of the same number of vehicles that passed them that you just spoke of. Doesn't that say something about the application of such a law as relates to different States?

Mr. Griswold. No, I don't think so. As a matter of fact, despite what I said about people passing me, which is true, it is perfectly obvious to me as I drive the highways, the average speed has been reduced by probably 10 miles an hour.

Mr. McCollister. Are you suggesting, sir, we ought to have Federal jurisdiction over all traffic laws, that we ought to have one national law?

Mr. Griswold. I think it would be worth considering at an appropriate time, whether there should not be a Federal statute setting up minimum standards to be administered by the States.

Mr. McCollister. According to title III, if a State chooses not to administer those laws, then would we have the FBI administering all of the traffic laws?

Mr. Griswold. I would hope it would not be them because I think they have other things to do, but we would have to set up a national highway control or something or other, particularly on interstate highways. That would give me concern.

As a matter of fact, you have it here on the George Washington Parkway that is administered by the Federal Government. If you violate a regulation there, you get taken before a U.S. magistrate, not before a judge of the court of Virginia.

Mr. McCOLLISTER. Dean Griswold, changing the subject back to the legal wastages you referred to earlier, do you believe that subrogation ought to be prohibited?

Mr. GRISWOLD. Well, let me be a little more clear as to what your meaning is in this case.

Mr. McCOLLISTER. While we were in Florida on Monday, one of the witnesses, or I guess several of the witnesses suggested that the contest between insurance companies, every insurance policy containing some subrogation rights for one company to recover from another company, suggested that in balance what a company gained from its claims awarded from another company is lost in claims it had to pay to all other companies and that the net result of this was pretty much a push and in the meantime all of this legal expense was wasted in one company challenging another company's liability under various laws.

So, they have suggested or some have suggested that as part of a national no-fault bill that subrogation should be forbidden.

Mr. GRISWOLD. I don't think I am prepared or qualified to answer that, Mr. McCollister. That is a question of the administration of the insurance laws. I had understood that that question was largely worked out administratively by the insurance companies and without very great difficulty, but I may be wrong on that. In any event, I am not an insurance administrator.

Mr. McCOLLISTER. At least there are those who contend that much of the legal expense of insurance companies in defending themselves or in pursuing claims against others, come as a consequence of their subrogation procedures and not all of it coming as a consequence of the full question of fault that we are talking about.

Mr. GRISWOLD. That surprises me. I would not think it would be the case, but I am not qualified to make an answer.

Mr. McCOLLISTER. I don't think that any, if I remember the charts we have of the 24 States, I don't believe there is any State, unless perhaps Michigan, which eliminates subrogation and there is none in H.R. 1900.

Mr. VAN DEERLIN. Majority counsel.

Mr. KINZLER. Dean Griswold, you talked about the difficulties in going from State to State in terms of knowing what the insurance coverage is.

How difficult would you anticipate the conflict of law problems would be without a Federal standard plan?

Mr. GRISWOLD. I used to teach "conflict of laws" in my academic days and this whole area, as any student in the field knows, has become bizarre.

Roughly speaking, I used to tell my students that the only answer that clearly appeared from the cases was that the plaintiff wins. But to try to rationalize that and to try to find a consistent basis on which the courts were proceeding, was, let's say, as of 10 years ago, very hard to find.

Mr. VAN DEERLIN. And they get killed in New Mexico.

Mr. GRISWOLD. And while they were in Connecticut they ran into a car and that bounced them across the State line into Massachusetts where they hit a tree.

I mean, you can make beautiful examination questions out of it, but it does not seem to me to be a very sound way to administer a compensation system for losses resulting from inevitable accidents.

Mr. KINZLER. You also indicate in your statement that a Federal standards approach would help to promote values of federalism by making implementation of no-fault a joint venture.

Is this analogous to what the Congress did in the Clean Air Act, in that they took Federal standards and left a State system which had been in existence for some length of time to administer large portions of it?

Mr. GRISWOLD. Yes, I think that the system of setting up minimum Federal standards and then having the States administer it, is really a clear way of promoting federalism. There is much to be said for local administration, where the States will have more offices around in the cities than the Federal Government can have for this, and the local people will know the situation and so on, and it will, in many situations, be more comfortable for the local person to deal with the local officials than it would be for him to think in terms of Washington, which, if you are in Peoria or Pocatello, is very far away.

Even though there is a Federal office somewhere, it will be in Springfield or Boise, which is likewise far away.

So I think you get a good deal of the benefits of cooperative federalism by having State administration while getting the benefit of a uniform administration of our common market through having Federal standards.

Mr. KINZLER. Thank you very much.

Mr. MCCOLLISTER. If you will yield, I think there is still another advantage. Think of the money we could save by doing away with the State legislators that wouldn't have anything more to do.

Mr. GRISWOLD. There will still be plenty of things for them to do, at the very least, trying to find ways to raise the revenue to meet all of the costs which they have to deal with.

Mr. VAN DEERLIN. Ms. Nord?

Ms. NORD. Thank you.

Following through on Mr. Kinzler's question with regard to conflict of law problems, Dean Griswold, in your statement you spoke of the need for uniformity in this area. Is this not a problem that can be taken care of contractually merely by putting a rider on the insurance policy?

Mr. GRISWOLD. I don't see how a rider on the insurance policy can possibly affect what the laws of the various States are, nor do I see how it can control the conflict of laws decision unless the other party who is unknown at the time you take out the policy also joined in the policy.

Ms. NORD. Can you not purchase a rider to your policy that would cover you if you are residing in a no-fault State and you have an accident that is in a tort State, that sort of situation?

Mr. GRISWOLD. Often the question in these conflict of laws cases is essentially between the two insurance companies, namely, whether the driver's insurance shall apply or whether the other car's insurance shall apply.

The people are covered, although a good many of these cases involve guest statutes and things of that sort, where, unless you have the guest when he came into your car sign the rider, the rider would not be binding on him.

I think it would be very hard to do. I think you could help it by imaginative, farsighted, forward-looking provisions in the insurance policy, but I don't think you could begin to cover all of the situations that would come up, particularly because you could not bind the other party to the accident.

Ms. NORD. Thank you.

Mr. VAN DEERLIN. Any further questions for the witness?

Mr. Kinzler?

Mr. KINZLER. Following up on Ms. Nord's question, while a binder from an insurance company might well give you your first party benefits in a tort State, don't the people in the no-fault State have to pay higher premiums because they have to insure themselves against the possibility of one of their people being at fault in a tort State and thus being subject to a tort judgment?

Mr. GRISWOLD. This would undoubtedly be taken into account in determining the loss experience and the loss projections and I would think it would likely affect the premium paid by the people in the no-fault State.

Mr. KINZLER. So this system might well vitiate some of the cost effectiveness of no-fault?

Mr. GRISWOLD. I am sure it would.

Mr. VAN DEERLIN. Thank you, Mr. Griswold, for your helpful testimony this afternoon.

Mr. GRISWOLD. Thank you, Mr. Chairman.

Mr. VAN DEERLIN. We are grateful to you for rearranging your time from morning to afternoon.

Our next witness is Mr. Guido Calabresi, professor of law, Yale University.

STATEMENT OF GUIDO CALABRESI, PROFESSOR OF LAW, YALE UNIVERSITY SCHOOL OF LAW

Mr. CALABRESI. Thank you, Mr. Chairman and committee members.

My name is Guido Calabresi and I am a professor at Yale University in the law school. I want to thank you for the opportunity to present to you some of my views on various approaches to no-fault. These are academic views of an academic and are not views of an association or any other particular group.

I think Dean Griswold has spoken more than adequately on the constitutional issue and I don't propose to talk about it.

Apart from the question which was raised by the Attorney General, which did not in itself make H.R. 1900 or its Senate equivalent unconstitutional, and which could be cured through the language the Attorney General proposed, I don't believe there are any serious constitutional questions in well drawn carefully written no-fault law of the sort that S. 354 or H.R. 1900 are.

Most of the so-called constitutional issues are really questions of legislative policy, that is, questions for you and not for the court. They are questions of the appropriate role of State and Federal Governments and it is to those I would like to turn.

I think that relatively few people believe that the existing system of accident law compensation is anything short of a scandal.

Mr. McCollister. Which system is that, the system which applies in the 24 States which have enacted legislation or the 26 which have not?

Mr. Calabresi. The system which applies in the 26 which have not; and in large part I must say the same applies to the systems in force in the 20 or so States that have patched, rather than reformed traditional tort law.

I think the Department of Transportation study and Secretary Coleman's testimony are eloquent on the problems of the existing system.

Most of the people who prefer the so-called fault system—it's crucial part is not that it is a fault system, but that it is a third party liability system—and I will come back to that issue later, but most of the people who support the so-called fault system have a particular interest in it.

That does not mean that their judgment is wrong, but I think it is an interesting fact that most of the people who do not have a particular interest in the existing system suggest changes.

Because most people are in agreement that something should be done, the main thrust of the policy discussion understandably has turned to the question of "State or Federal" reform.

I must say that one's view of whether changes should be mainly enacted by the States or mainly by the Federal Government depends at least in part on what one thinks is wrong with the preexisting system, because there are some aspects which are better done by the States—or might in theory be better done by the States—while others are preeminently Federal issues. It is to these aspects I would like to turn.

I suggest there are two fundamental functions of accident law. One is to compensate victims for unnecessary suffering and so avoid unnecessary socioeconomic dislocations.

The second is to induce safety and to deter those injuries which are avoidable, that is, which are worth avoiding, because not every injury, as much as we would like to think so, is worth avoiding.

The object of legislation has to be to accomplish both of these in an effective and inexpensive way, consistent with our free enterprise system.

As a conceptual matter, the first of these, compensation of victims, could be left up to the States. It is in the nature of insurance, and once a decision was made by the McCarran Act to leave insurance to the States, as a conceptual matter one could say:

Leave compensation to the States, let them set up whatever system of social or other insurance which covers however much they want covered.

As a practical matter, I don't think that will work. I think the opposition of certain groups has made the establishment of a truly effective system of compensation almost impossible for the States to achieve, unless there are Federal minimum standards that require it.

More important, even if it were possible for the State to pass compensation laws which are adequate, the interstate nature of auto traffic is such that laws of that kind would create impossible burdens, in part on interstate commerce, but even more crucially on consumer citizens.

I refer here to the conflict of laws problems which majority counsel raised.

I would note that the one time I really got involved with a statute of this sort was for the legislative auditor of the State of Hawaii, because Hawaii is one of the few States in which one can genuinely enact automobile insurance reform without significantly worrying about interstate commerce.

I would also note that almost to ridicule the suggestion that this could be done adequately by the States, a member of the other Chamber, a few years ago, introduced a bill providing first party insurance coverage in the District of Columbia. I think that emphasized dramatically the problems which would be involved.

The National Legislature would have been acting like a state in passing such a law for the District of Columbia, for that is its jurisdiction. But how would such a law deal with all of the people going back and forth from Maryland, Virginia, and so on?

One could say, "Why hasn't the same problem been evident with existing tort law? After all, these are the same jurisdictions and they have been dealing with this area without undue conflict problems?"

I think the answer is that the common law had a basic unity. It was a unity which arose in England so that essentially there was one law in most States. It was a third party system based on fault. There were a few minor areas, generally where States had passed legislation to change things, where there was not that unity, wrongful death statutes, guest statutes, things of that sort.

It is to those areas that Dean Griswold automatically went when he spoke about conflict of laws problems, because there one didn't any longer have the unity of the common law. One had different laws and of course there were constant conflict problems when people from different States with different guest statutes, different wrongful death statutes got involved.

Those would multiply, those which were minor problems would be multiplied many many times, if no Federal standard were set up now, because now we are faced with a situation where we would have laws which, in their fundamental basis, would differ from State to State.

The thrust of this is that the consumer, the purchaser of insurance, to protect himself would have to buy insurance riders (and of course he could buy riders, Ms. Nord, to protect himself in the first instance) but the effect of that approach would be that he would have to buy insurance policies which would pile one type of coverage on top of another and that always ends up being much more expensive.

In a perfect world, it might be that one would get a diminution of some premiums if one were trying for some others, but I think all of us who have had to buy workmen's compensation insurance for household help, have noticed it has not diminished our homeowners' insurance. Theoretically, it should, but when you have to buy two types of insurance to cover two types of things it always ends up you pay more for both.

That would be the inevitable effect, I think, of trying to avoid this problem through insurance riders which would cover the insured apart from jurisdiction.

I think it is no accident that when railroads were the fundamental basis of interstate transport in this country (under the "old" Supreme Court, I mean the court of Mr. Justice Hughes, not Mr. Chief Justice Hughes) Mr. Justice McReynolds went so far, incorrectly I think, as to say, "One could not permit State workmen's compensation laws dealing with railroad accidents," because one was dealing too much with something which went across State lines.

The notion then that when one is dealing with something that goes across State lines in this way, the basic insurance system ought to be a Federal system, is I think something which goes back, not to the time of an expansive view of interstate commerce, but to one of the most traditional views of interstate commerce.

I would not have agreed with Mr. Justice McReynolds on this as a matter of consitutional imperative, but, as a matter of policy, that there should be Federal standards for compensation when interstate transport is involved, I would agree.

Let me turn to the second issue, that of safety. That is less generally discussed and much harder to deal with in short order, but since it has very important consequences insofar as the question of Federal and State treatment of this area is concerned, and since it is rarely discussed, I would like your indulgence to talk about it even though it is a little dense.

I think there are two parts to the question of safety. The first goes to individual behavior, getting somebody to drive carefully. That part I would suggest is essentially a State issue. It is a part of the issue which deals with State traffic regulations. It is much more akin to criminal law. It is the kind of thing about which individual States can make individual judgments.

I am happy that H.R. 1900 specifically permits States to enact uninsurable tort fines, if they wish, in order to induce that kind of safety by individual drivers.

That has classically in our system been a State issue and I would like to keep it that way. I don't want a Federal law which tells people whether one road is suited for 55 miles per hour or another for 45. I think we can do that kind of thing better through the States, through State criminal laws and through a new device, mentioned in the statutes, uninsurable fines, civil fines, to induce safety by individuals.

There is, however, another equally important—indeed to me more important—trade-off between safety and convenience and expense in the automobile accident field and that goes to how cars are made and what categories of drivers drive; that is, an accident law system must provide inducements to make automobiles which are safe.

Mr. McCOLLISTER. I hope you are not proposing some sort of ignition interlock system?

Mr. CALABRESI. I am certainly not. It is entirely because of the defects of such mandatory requirements that I believe we have to move to a first party system. It is entirely because of that. Let me go on with this.

You see, basically, a third party system of accident law causes the rates to depend—the insurance rates you and I pay—to depend on the likelihood of my hitting the guy out there.

My rates do not depend on the likelihood that I may injure myself, my passengers, or other people in my car. The result is that there is no incentive in our system—in a financial sense—to cause cars to be made which provide for in-passenger safety.

Mr. McCOLLISTER. That is not true of the whole insurance premium but only of bodily injury.

Mr. CALABRESI. That is true of bodily injury, it is not fully true as to property damage, but even then the first party safety incentive is lessened by the fact that one can sue for a third party's fault; that makes the incentive much less.

Now, if one has this kind of third party system, it is natural that the automobile companies will not worry, because they have no financial incentive to worry, about making a car which is safer for the driver. That is, if they have to put in an air bag or a type of seatbelt or some complicated interlock system, what they do is tell the consumer,"One, you have to pay more; two, it is a bother to you, and three, your insurance premiums do not go down."

The consumer does not like that and it is understandable that he does not like it. Why have we gotten legislation which has required these things? We have gotten legislation which has required these things on a national basis because we have not had free enterprise incentives to have better first party devices created.

Turn the matter around and go to a first party system of insurance; now an automobile manufacturer can say, "I have devised"—Lord knows I trust the automobile manufacturers more to devise safety systems than I do some Bureau down here—"I have devised a system"—and I trust the automakers to do it, though only if they have an incentive—"I have devised a system of making a car with seatbelts or air bags or something, which I believe will sufficiently lessen serious accidents so that your insurance premiums will go down enough to cover the cost of that system."

Mr. McCOLLISTER. If I might interrupt at this point, a cost-benefit study to the cost of air bags versus the cost of reduction of insurance premiums?

Mr. CALABRESI. Sir, that was a question which was asked me by Senator Buckley in the other Chamber and I told him I did not make such study.

The answer I gave to his question was that the object of auto-safety laws must be to put the incentive in the appropriate place, to create an incentive to invent worthwhile safety devices. If then even with an incentive to install it a particular safety device is not worthwhile; if accidents do not justify air bags, well, air bags will not be put in.

at all.

The reason I prefer a first party system is because, if there is such a system, then there is the kind of incentive on auto manufacturers to devise precisely those systems which are worthwhile.

You know, when the President of the United States says, "The trouble with those requirements which we enacted is that we have no idea if they make sense in terms of any cost-benefit ratio" my answer is, the tradition in this country is to create a way so that the market itself introduces this kind of cost-benefit analysis.

Mr. McCollister. We have been around the track before, and are you familiar with our Automobile Damageability and Cost Reduction Act of 1972, perhaps, where we had the subject of automobile bumpers before us and we mandated 5 miles an hour bumpers in the front and 2½ miles an hour bumpers on the rear at a cost of something more than $200 extra per bumper and that we were to get all sorts of benefits from this because of the reduction in damage and because of the resulting reduction in insurance premiums, and it has been my observation there has been virtually no reduction in insurance premiums because of this and that all we had to do is pay more for our automobile bumpers.

Mr. Calabresi. Mr. McCollister, I would suggest that that exactly proves my point. What you were asked to do was to decide for yourself what kinds of bumpers would be worthwhile and with all respect for you and your staff, that is not something which you or I am in a position to do. That is why I refuse to get into that kind of cost-benefit analysis. But what you can do is create the kind of incentive in the system which will cause an automobile manufacturer to do it.

Consider again what the current third party system is. Under the current third party system basically, what you pay in your insurance premiums does not depend on how well your car is designed to protect you.

That is why a small frail car gets lower insurance premiums than a car which is safely built. Under a first party system there is an incentive on the manufacturers to put in precisely those safety devices which are worth their cost, because, when one includes insurance costs, they can then sell that car for less.

It is to avoid putting you in the situation of deciding for or against a particular Nader-type reform that I think we must move to a first party system on the issue of safety.

Mr. McCollister. I have listened even more attentively than I ever have.

Mr. Calabresi. I have been talking about the issue of safety now, and the issue of compensation is quite a different matter. It is, however, a lucky coincidence that one can accomplish compensation more economically through a first party system of the sort proposed and at the same time accomplish the kind of free enterprise incentives which we need rather than the kind of regulation you enact.

Mr. McCollister. Just a footnote to the bumper question, that was a substitute that we felt we could compromise on, a substitute that prevented us from trying to select the design of the fender, door panels, headlights, grills, and I don't know what else that would have put us even more in that business of trying to design those things.

Mr. Calabresi. But, again, sir, you see, if you had created incentives, and this kind of law would do so, you then would need to do less by regulation and more through allowing people to respond to the fact that as they come up with a better car they will make an honest buck out of it.

Mr. McCollister. You have hit my Achilles' heel.

Mr. Calabresi. I hope so, sir, though I did not know it was your Achilles' heel.

Well, now, how does this relate to the question of State versus Federal laws? The answer is unfortunately that, in order to get incentives which work, one has to have a degree of uniformity; only then can the manufacturers respond.

That is, if they cannot say, "Look, if we put this safety device in your car your insurance rates will go down," no incentive to safety will have been created. Incidentally, if insurance companies do not give lower rates, the auto makers could themselves enter the insurance business as a first party insurer. There would be nothing peculiar about an automobile company, if it thought it had a safer car and insurance companies were not responding, setting up its own insurance company, and qualifying in the various States to do this.

But it would be difficult for them to do any of this, very difficult, to offer, in effect, lower priced cars, lower premiums—and let's all remember the cost of the car to the usual driver is more the accident costs as reflected in insurance costs than any other car costs, so that if one can reduce that part of the cost one can reduce substantially the cost of the car to the buyer—it would be very difficult for the manufacturer to put that kind of worth while safety device in if it were dealing with laws which were different from State to State, because some States were experimenting one way and some were experimenting another and some were doing something else again. And this difficulty goes to the essence of interstate commerce, of an economic system having the kind of incentives which it needs. So much is this so that in the absence of the uniform type of incentives I have described, we find demands for precisely the type of legislation which I gather you oppose.

the house we own.

A first party system enables a person to insure his salary and therefore inevitably it is going to be more to the advantage of the lower income groups.

Mr. McCollister. I agree with you and I think the States ought to enact those kinds of laws.

Mr. Calabresi. That is why I say, sir, as a matter of compensation, as a matter of theory, if it were just the compensation or fairness side, I would say have the States do it, although, as a practical matter, I find myself troubled by several facts; one, that they have not done it adequately, because they have all retained the third party side to an extent which negates these effects—virtually all of the States which have enacted laws of that sort have retained the third party side to a large extent—two, that State action would create conflict problems of a sort which would be inordinately expensive; and, finally, three, your Achilles' heel, sir, that the free enterprise incentives toward safety which are needed will only work if we have minimum standards of a first party sort, sufficient to create real incentives, sufficient to have the automobile manufacturers—to take only one group, because there are others who could do the same sort of thing—develop ways of protecting drivers and passengers from injuries.

I am as keen on federalism as anyone, I think. I think the type of argument I made with respect to free enterprise suggests sensitivity to diversity, because after all free enterprise is diversity and is competition, so I am aware of the advantages of having the States do things.

On the other hand, I don't think one serves federalism by asking States to do that which either they cannot as a practical matter do or which, even if they do, will fail to accomplish the aims for which they did it.

All that does is convince another gneration of legislators that States cannot act, or cannot act successfully. I think one only serves federalism by giving States those things to do which they can do. I am very much afraid if we do not pass this kind of law allowing to the States the administration of insurance coverage and allowing to the States that part of safety which deals with individual behavior, but setting minimum standards on that part of safety which goes to structural changes in how automobiles are made and which categories of people drive how much, that is, on those issues which are basically issues of interstate commerce; unless we do that, I think we will end up in the way in which we were heading before these first party laws were proposed, with a system which covers all of the ills one has in automobile injuries through general social insurance and then attempts to legislate safety and inevitably will legislate nationally thus stultifying both the enterprise system and "federalism."

My comments have been somewhat to the side of the principal arguments for no-fault, administrative cost savings, pressures on courts, and removal of scandal in the sense of, oh, expensive litigation which unfortunately in this and other areas like malpractice has been doing neither citizens nor States, in their hurried attempts to patch together a response, much good.

I associate myself with what I know has been said before on this, for example, the Department of Transportation study which outlines the needs for a fundamental change in this area.

What I tried to talk about has been somewhat to one side of that because I think they are the less-discussed issues.

Mr. McCollister. Do you associate yourself, sir, with the remarks of many witnesses before us who have pretty much agreed that premium costs are going to go up?

Mr. Calabresi. Premium costs are going to go up, you know, by itself is a funny kind of a statement if one says, premium costs are going to go up because you have inflation, that may be the case.

I would say that most of the witnesses whom I have heard testify that premium costs would go up, and I have read the hearings, are the same witnesses or represented the same groups who suggested that premium costs would go up when the first minimal types of no-fault laws were passed in the States.

Mr. McCollister. Now, even State Farm said you couldn't base the argument for lower costs of no-fault on lower premium costs. They talk about the whole system, better distribution of the system.

Mr. Calabresi. The other side about "premium costs will go up" is that costs are entirely a matter of how much one is giving.

To give the same amonut to the consumer as he gets out of the current third party system, through a first party system, would cost less.

If you choose, and you may well choose, to give the consumer more in the way of insurance, also because doing so creates incentives toward safety, then what you chose may well end up costing more.

What comes out at the end for what you put in is more under a first party system. How much one wants to get out at the end is a different issue and it is one which depends on how much insurance coverage one wants.

My own feeling—and this is really somewhat to one side, and if you want "heretical"—is that insurance premiums might very well properly go up. If the result of that use was the kind of coverage people want and the kind of incentives to make a car which is safe—that is, to have the insurance premiums genuinely cover accidents so that auto manufacturers could truly engage in a cost-benefit analysis between safety measures and their costs—then such a use would be desirable.

If that is what happened, I wouldn't mind a bit. Because you know to have premiums go down can also be undesirable. If the result of premiums being lowered is that there are people who are injured and who bear the costs of those injuries is simply to choose a different person to bear the premium cost and not to lower accident costs a bit. It is not more costs being put on the system but shifting them one from another

Mr. VAN DEERLIN. Mr McCollister was quite accurate in citing the testimony which warned against seeking to sell a national no-fault system on the basis of reducing premium rates. But I believe there is nothing in the record in the way of testimony or any studies that have indicated the inevitability of rates going up—is that right, Mr. Counsel?

Mr. KINZLER. We have in the subcommittee record in this Congress only one study. That is a study by State Farm which indicates an average premium reduction of 10 percent nationally on existing rates.

Mr. VAN DEERLIN. Projected?

Mr. KINZLER. Projected 10 percent decline nationally. Another study, and it is not within the hearing record, was done by Allstate, which is on the other side of the issue. Their initial projection for H.R. 1900 and S. 354 was a national increase of 17 percent in rates. Since that time Allstate has done a costing of S. 354 as it came out of the Senate Commerce Committee, which had a major change dealing with the subrogation of commercial vehicles accident losses. Those figures reduced the nationwide increase to 4.4 percent and Nebraska dropped down to 36.8 percent.

At the point Allstate indicated to the committee the difference between their plus 4.4 percent and State Farm's minus 10 percent, relates to two things. Two-thirds of it relates to the question of what you estimate for survivors benefits and H.R. 1900 only requires survivors benefit to be reasonable. Allstate assumed a reasonable level of $15,000 and State Farm $5,000 and if you reduce the 15 to 5, which the States are free to do under H.R. 1900, Allstate's figures would be in the minus category.

The other third of the difference comes from Allstate's estimated increased utilization factor, a higher factor than State Farm has, and those are the only figures we have here.

Mr. CALABRESI. Congressman McCollister, when I was involved with a proposed law in Hawaii which suggested broader benefits than H.R. 1900, various studies were made by insurance companies, both pro and con, for the legislative auditor of the State of Hawaii and in that jurisdiction the indication was one could go quite a long way, that is, beyond H.R. 1900, and still come out with actual savings.

My point is not to say that I am not for savings because I obviously am for savings in consumer premiums. But the position I take with respect to these laws, is that the important thing is that they do two things; (a) create appropriate incentives toward safety, toward a tradeoff between safety and not making cars too expensive, and (b) establish a system of compensation which works so that we do not have pressures for a type of total social insurance which would remove all incentives for safety.

I am bound to say I would be willing to pay, because I think it fundamental to our system to have a system of accident law of that sort, I would be willing to pay higher premiums for that. When instead, the figures come out, at worst, ambiguous, and, at best, suggesting that this can be done at lower premiums because of the undoubted administrative cost and wastage of the current system, then I find myself saying "This may be one of those remarkable situations in which "one can have one's cake and eat it, too."

I want to thank you, Mr. Chairman.

Mr. McCollister. I interrupted this man's testimony on previous occasions and found him to be absolutely delightful and even a little persuasive and I have no further questions.

Mr. Van Deerlin. I wonder if we shouldn't schedule him several more times before the hearing is completed.

Mr. Kinzler. I would like to clarify one thing in the record alluded to before which is your testimony before the Senate with respect to the question of air bags. You indicated that one company, even without the first party system, has offered a 30-percent reduction in air bags and you and Senator Buckley engaged in a colloquy as to the cost-benefit analysis of that.

Senator Buckley basically said if you received a 30-percent reduction on the $50 premium you would save $15 a year and he didn't see how it was much incentive to buy a $250 air bag.

After your testimony, Les Cheek of the American Insurance Association, a more knowledgeable expert in insurance, took the stand and suggested the following:

America spends approximately $8 billion a year for bodily injury liability. If there were an industrywide 30-percent discount, that would amount to about $2.4 billion a year worth of savings.

If one assumes that about 8 million cars are sold a year, with an air bag cost of $200, which is probably closer to the actual cost, you are talking about a one-time expense of $1.6 billion.

If you then assume that most people use their cars for about 10 years, which I think they will as car costs increase.

Mr. Calabresi. Assume only 5 years and you come out with a dramatic figure.

Mr. Kinzler. Right, you can use 5 years multiplied by $2.4 billion and you come out to $12 billion of savings as compared to $1.6 billion cost. Those are all estimates, but that is the kind of thing you are talking about.

Mr. Calabresi. That is the colloquy that I was referring to, but, again, my point is not based on those figures. It is clearly the case that a significant reduction in premiums of the order of 20 or 30 percent, which might be available if a particular safety device were put in, would go a very long way toward inducing the installation of a lot of safety devices. But quite apart from that, my point is that under existing law there is no incentive to put in safety devices regardless of whether they would turn out to be worthwhile. Under a first party system, there would be an incentive to do just that; it would be an incentive to put in just those devices which are worthwhile.

We can have a discussion with different people playing with the figures, but the one thing I can be pretty sure of is that if an auto manufacturer can end up selling a car for a lower price—including insurance premiums—because he puts in a safety device, that auto manufacturer will do it.

The other thing I am sure of is that today there is no incentive which will cause an auto manufacturer to do that.

Mr. McCollister. Referring back I asked majority counsel as to Cheek's figures and they went by pretty quickly, but it seems to me that 30-percent savings applies to the total premiums paid of some $12 billion, it seems to me, and that 30-percent savings does not reduce all of the cost and would apply, I mean it does not reduce acquisition costs and does not reduce all of the administrative costs, but mostly apply to that portion of the premium that is paid out in claims and even saying 60 percent of the premium that is paid out in claims you would have to have a 50-precent reduction in the claims to get a 30-percent savings in the benefits and it seems to me could be, or I guess what I need to do is to have those figures made available to me.

Mr. Calabresi. The 30 percent, Congressman, was derived from the fact that, essentially as a show measure because they get no real benefit from it since they are paying third-party payments, one insurance company was offering that to its consumers.

Now, the idea, the reason, that those figures were being played with was based on the fact that if this was an accurate figure, this 30 percent—and we can assume it must be a minimum, is what proponents of those figures were saying, though I agree with you that assumption is uncertain—then this is the kind of savings which could be gotten.

Again, the point is not to argue in favor of a particular device as being worth its cost as against another device, but to show how a system can be established which will enable enterprise to work.

Mr. McCollister. No further questions.

Mr. Kinzler. Mr. Calabresi, we heard over the course of these hearings that no-fault auto insurance is a rather new concept that goes back to the Department of Transportation study in 1970 or 1971, and some have indicated it goes back as far as the Keeton-O'Connell study back in 1965. Is no-fault auto insurance or some type of no-fault auto insurance that recent or, if not, how much further back would it go?

Mr. Calabresi. Well, it goes back a very long way. A plan of this sort was proposed, called the Columbia plan, in the twenties. Its principal problem was that it was a third party no-fault plan and so it had substantial technical disadvantages. The cost of it would have been much higher than the new one.

My own writings on this go back to the late fifties and early sixties, and suggested that, for theoretical reasons, based on economic theory and other such things, such a no-fault approach would in fact increase safety rather than diminish it.

Moreover, in terms of tort law, the tradition of no-fault is a far older one than the tradition of fault.

"Fault," as a system of law, developed in the United States in the mid-19th century. It came into its own in the mid-19th century and until then, for about 200 years in the Colonies and the early States, if somebody injured somebody else, they were liable on a no-fault basis so long as the injury was direct.

"Fault" is a Johnny-come-lately in terms of legal developments. That this is so has always been known in academic circles. As early as 1914, Professor Smith wrote an article in which he discussed the relationship btween workmen's compensation, which obviously was a no-fault system of sorts, and a fault system in the rest of law, and suggested that it might well happen, that through expansion of certain concepts, courts would go back to the common law as it was before 1850, that is, back to no-fault liability.

And there are many who feel that what has happened in tort law has been something of that sort, that is, that we have had an increasing scope of liability—the sort of thing Dean Griswold meant when he said that the basic rule is that the plaintiff always wins—to the point that liability exists almost on a no-fault basis. And yet it is a no-fault basis which, being a third party, no-fault basis, turns out to be a very expensive one and one which does not give very many of the kinds of incentives I suggested.

Mr. KINZLER. Just going back in the 19th century for a moment, you said that the fault system was preceded by a no-fault system for 200 years in the Colonies.

The trial lawyers have suggested it was not in fact a no-fault system, but was an absolute liability system and that is a different animal than no-fault. Would you so characterize it?

Mr. CALABRESI. Well, if absolute liability means you are liable regardless of fault I don't know what one wants to call it except no-fault. If they say it is different from this system because this system is a first-party system, while that was not, I think that is substantially accurate, but I don't know that that has anything to do with the basic question which was "Are you holding somebody liable?" or "Are you making somebody pay, regardless of whether that particular person is at fault?"

The absoluteness was not actually absolute. It was a strict liability system, not an absolute liability system. The difference is that most writers call an absolute liability system one that might apply regardless of a casual link while a strict liability system in the jargon, and it is only jargon, is one in which certain kinds of casual relationships are required. And that kind of casual relationship is precisely involved in these bills, so technically these bills, like the old common law, involve strict liability systems.

Mr. KINZLER. Thank you very much.

Mr. VAN DEERLIN. Ms. Nord?

Ms. NORD. One brief question, Professor Calabresi.

It is my understanding that at some point before Congress made mandatory the 5-mile-an-hour bumper, several insurance companies did offer a reduction in collision premiums for cars with this bumper; however, the auto companies found that consumers were not terribly interested in purchasing more expensive automobiles. I am wondering if this is at least a small test of your theory?

Mr. CALABRESI. No. It really isn't. In the first place, at most, it suggests that when one took only one type of damage, the collision part, rather than considering also the effect that better bumpers might have on personal injuries, then the kinds of bumpers which were being suggested at that time were not worth their cost.

But more important, to say that putting a first-party incentive does not result in a particular safety device being put in, is not to say that the approach is wrong, it is to say that that device might not be worth it.

That is precisely what we are about, to have the kind of law which gives us a test so that we can say "Is the device worth it?"

Now, there are technical reasons of a sort which go to "What was it that collision insurance covered," "What is it that is generally uninsured in collision insurance because of deductibles," and "What kinds of injuries would these bumpers have stopped?," which leads me to think that probably that particular situation didn't say much of anything one way or another even to the relative merits of those bumpers as against pure collision damage. But even if it had, even if we were to assume that the result of all of that showed that this type of bumper change was not worth it, as far as I am concerned that would have been a very useful thing to have as part of the system so that we would know what changes are worth making.

It would be a direct response to the kinds of questions which the President of the United States, perfectly properly, suggests should be asked of safety devices.

Ms. NORD. Thank you.

Mr. VAN DEERLIN. Thank you, Professor.

I guess we got you off in plenty of time for your plane back home, which is mainly because we were not interrupted at all by the votes on the floor.

I am very grateful to you for being with us and for your suggestion that we might have increased safety as a happy fallout of the national no-fault law.

Mr. CALABRESI. Thank you very much for the opportunity, sir.

Mr. VAN DEERLIN. You are very welcome.

The hearings will resume Tuesday, the 22d.

[Whereupon, at 3:45 p.m., the hearing was adjourned, to reconvene on Tuesday, July 22, 1975.]

NO-FAULT MOTOR VEHICLE INSURANCE

TUESDAY, JULY 22, 1975

House of Representatives,
Subcommittee on Consumer Protection and Finance,
Committee on Interstate and Foreign Commerce,
Washington, D.C.

The subcommittee met at 1:30 p.m., pursuant to notice, in room 2322, Rayburn House Office Building, Hon. W. S. Stuckey, Jr., presiding, [Hon. Lionel Van Deerlin, chairman].

Mr. STUCKEY. The subcommittee will come to order.

The first witness this afternoon will be Mr. John G. Cook, president of the National Association of Mutual Insurance Agents.

Mr. Cook, come up, please. We would be delighted to have you summarize your statement, and submit the entire statement for the record. Or if you prefer, you can read it.

STATEMENT OF JOHN G. COOK, PRESIDENT, NATIONAL ASSOCIATION OF MUTUAL INSURANCE AGENTS; ACCOMPANIED BY HAROLD W. TRAUB, PRESIDENT-ELECT, NAMIA

Mr. COOK. Thank you, Mr. Chairman and other members of the committee. I will read our statement, as it is very brief.

My name is John G. Cook, of Orlando, Fla. I am the president of the National Association of Mutual Insurance Agents, and I am also the president of the John G. Cook Agency, Inc., of Orlando, Fla. NAMIA is a national organization of more than 23,000 independent property and casualty insurance agents with members in all 50 States and headquarters in Washington, D.C.

With me today is the president-elect of NAMIA, Harold W. Traub, who is the president of the Paul Zurlin Agency in Lakewood, N.J.

Since April 1971, NAMIA has appeared before this subcommittee three times. Our support of national minimum guidelines has been stenghthened because of the apathetic response in the State legislatures and lack of creative thinking by a large segment of the insurance business. The States have not resolved the basic problem with the fault system, that is, returning a major part of the insurance dollar to the victims of an automobile accident. The following quotes from the Department of Transportation's automobile insurance and compensation study are still valid today:

* * * 44 cents out of every premium dollar collected is used to compensate accident victims for their losses. Of this amount 8 cents is duplication of payments from other sources and 21½ cents is used to pay for general damages (i.e., "pain and suffering" or intangible losses), leaving 14½ cents to compensate for otherwise uncompensated economic losses.

This analysis indicates further that the remaining 56 cents is needed to operate the auto liability insurance system. General overhead—including acquisition expenses, taxes and profits—requires 33 cents from every premium dollar. Claims administration costs—including salaries and fees for claim investigators, defense attorneys and plaintiff attorneys—consume the remaining 23 cents.

The above information was available in March 1971. The insurance industry as a whole has been discussing adaptation of the no-fault principle to the problem of automobile accident compensation since 1919. Yet, on this date, July 22, 1975, only 16 States have passed no-fault laws that restrict tort to any extent. Of the 16 no-fault States, only 4 have enacted medical thresholds of at least $1,000— Florida, Hawaii, Minnesota, and North Dakota.

As insurance agents, we are engaged each day at the point of sale, and we obtain the true reflection of dissatisfaction from members of the motoring public who are not pleased with the current automobile reparations system. We find the insurance buyer is a much more articulate consumer today. He will not tolerate arbitrary cancellations and insurance he cannot afford to buy. He views his insurance premium as a part of the cost of getting a new license plate. He does not want to feel that in buying car insurance, he has merely purchased the capability to handle a law suit should one come his way. He is willing to accept the responsibility of protecting the other driver, but he feels his insurance should give him the same first-party coverage as does his fire and health insurance.

It is our belief that pressure will increase on Federal and State legislators to make the automobile insurance mechanism more responsive to these consumer demands.

We are strongly committed to the State regulation of insurance and to States' rights in general. However, we are seeing that in the absence of more widespread and meaningful State action, the insurance buyer is turning to Washington for satisfaction. To avoid a complete takeover of the automobile reparations system by the Federal Government, it is essential that a minimum standards bill be enacted by the U.S. Congress as soon as possible. We believe that this will do more than anything else to keep the regulation of the automobile insurance business at the State level.

The National Association of Mutual Insurance Agents has found that H.R. 8441, a national minimum guidelines bill introduced on July 8, 1975, by Congressman Matthew J. Rinaldo of New Jersey, meets the policy and recommendations of our National Association of Mutual Insurance Agents. We find that H.R. 8441 offers a constructive alternative to both H.R. 1900 and H.R. 1272 as it takes a course between a national maximum standards bill and very limited guidelines bill. It would allow the insurance-buying public to receive the benefits of no-fault while giving the industry and government a period of time to develop hard data on the cost of changing from a fault to a no-fault compensation system. Improvement could then be made upward. As we know too well, very few programs are reduced once they are in operation.

H.R. 8441 provides:

1. That automobile insurance remain the primary source of recovery in automobile accidents.

We are extremely concerned about the primacy language in H.R. 1900 and H.R. 1272, which holds that the entire no-fault benefits as required in the bill would be excess of all statutory benefits. The medical and rehabilitation benefits would also be excess of all other sources in H.R. 1900 unless the State determines that primacy of other sources would "affect adversely or discriminate against" the insured's interest.

We wholeheartedly support the concept that basic compensation for automobile accident injuries should be paid by automobile insurance—not by health care payment systems. This matter is of such importance to the insurance-buying public and the independent insurance agent, that we developed a White Paper on the entire question of automobile insurance remaining the primary source of recovery in automobile accidents. Our White Paper on Primacy is attached to this statement as exhibit I. We would appreciate its inclusion in the official record.

Mr. STUCKEY. If there are no objections, it is so ordered.

Mr. COOK. Thank you, Mr. Chairman.

2. A benefits ceiling which would pay the medical expenses and lost wages of a very high percentage of automobile accident victims, to avoid the higher premium cost we believe will accompany unlimited benefits.

Most of the major bills now before the Congress provide benefits in excess of what individual States have found to be prudent and desirable, particularly as an initial reform step. This does not mean, however, that higher benefit provisions would not be ultimately desirable. We believe a prudent approach would be to establish a benefit level that will pay the medical expenses and lost wages of a very high percentage of automobile accident victims. An approach that offers high benefits will undoubtedly be accompanied by high premium costs. This could be avoided by limiting the medical, rehabilitation, work loss, and replacement services to an aggregate $50,000 per individual injured in the accident. Statistics show that this ceiling on benefits will compensate more than 99 percent of all persons injured in automobile accidents.

We would also like to suggest that if medical and hospital expenses are less than $50,000, an allowance should be made for additional disability income coverage representing 85 percent of gross income after missing 5 consecutive working days, for 12 months or a maximum of $1,000 per month. We would suggest maximum combined medical, hospital, and disability income benefits not to exceed $50,000 with higher limits optionally available at additional costs.

Mr. Chairman, unlimited medical payments are threatening no-fault rate increases. Employers Reinsurance Corp. has released hard data from Michigan showing total reserves of $6,650,000 for 33 cases, an average of over $200,000; 14 of these 33 cases were single car accidents. The reserves established on the 14 one-car accidents are $2.7 million— an average of more than $190,000. Previous to no-fault, only the damage to the car and $500 to $1,000 medical payments were covered. A $50,000 lid on mandatory first-party benefits would not impact adversely on the automobile reparations mechanism.

3. A numerical threshold for pain, suffering, and inconvenience.

All the bills now before Congress would eliminate tort liability almost completely and drastically restrict an automobile victim's right to recovery for general damages. States which have enacted no-fault bills have followed a more moderate approach. For example,

Massachusetts has a $2,000 tort exemption and a $500 medical-general damages threshold. Florida has a $5,000 tort exemption and a $1,000 medical threshold.

We believe that the threshold approach should be tested in the marketplace before common law tort rights are completely eliminated. We, therefore, suggest a numerical threshold of $2,000 for pain, suffering, and inconvenience. In other words, the right to recovery for general damages would be protected when the victim's medical expenses exceeded $2,000. The threshold test would not apply in cases in which the victim has suffered permanent disfigurement, dismemberment, or permanent loss of bodily function.

4. A provision allowing for inter-company subrogation.

An appropriate form of subrogation should be included in any minimum standards proposal. In the absence of subrogation, expense shifting will occur to the detriment of the good driver. I believe it is unnecessary to point out to this subcommittee the potential political repercussions of a reparations system which charges higher rates for good drivers and lower rates for bad drivers. Under the present system, the cost of a loss is imposed on the person whose carelessness has caused the accident. Losses are allocated equitably between classes of policyholders.

Our association urges that provision be made for allocation of loss on the basis of fault by intercompany subrogation and by use of an intercompany arbitration system which would prevent disputes between insurers from burdening the courts. Such a subrogation-arbitration system has been tested and found practicable and inexpensive in loss-transfer between automobile collision and automobile property damage insurers. Such a system has also been used in several no-fault States with respect to losses arising from bodily injury. Actuaries indicate that the cost of this subrogation-arbitration system is so small that they would not include it in their estimates of the expense of loss adjustments under a no-fault system.

We believe that insurers whould be granted temporary subrogation rights for 3 years, and require them during this period to compile detailed statistics on their gains and losses from subrogation. These would be filed annually or semiannually with State insurance departments with the experience data obtained.

The prime purpose of no-fault restoration benefits is to provide prompt payment to injured victims and to reduce court congestion.

A plan of subrogation whereby restoration obligors may seek reimbursement from other restoration obligors in arbitration proceedings based upon a determination of fault is not inconsistent with the essence of no-fault benefits. To eliminate frivolous arbitration claims, only benefits which exceed $2,000 would form the basis for such an arbitration claim. To maximize flexibility, the arbitration hearings would be conducted in accordance with procedures established by the commissioner on a State-by-State basis.

The National Association of Mutual Insurance Agents once again offers its assistance to this committee. We want a bill now. It is the firm belief and opinion of our association that no-fault automobile insurance will:

(1) Restore consumer confidence in the private insurance mechanism; (2) relieve the burden on our courts; (3) reduce costs by more

efficient operations; and (4) heal the injured on a more equitable basis so they will not be a burden on society.

Our national association believes that a national minimum guidelines bill, such as H.R. 8441, is good legislation. Its passage will at long last guarantee no-fault benefits to all citizens. It also will provide the guidance needed to solve the maze of laws which now exist in our States.

Mr. Chairman, I thank you very much.

[The exhibit to Mr. Cook's statement follows:]

PRIMACY

The National Association of Mutual Insurance Agents has long been an advocate of automobile insurance reform in the United States. We believe that no-fault automobile insurance is an idea whose time has come, as no-fault legislation will be implemented in additional states in the upcoming year. There is one area of debate that remains to be explored; that is the question of primacy.

Primacy refers to the controversy over which carrier, health insurance or automobile insurance, will pay benefits to the injured victim of an automobile accident. This Association believes that medical benefits, lost wages and other economic losses should be paid by the automobile insurance industry.

It is the contention of the National Association of Mutual Insurance Agents that those who drive should assume the cost of insurance. Currently, health insurance is part of the fringe benefit package made available by many employers. If, as a result of no-fault, automobile injuries were added to a program's loss experience, an employer could suffer an increase in cost corresponding to the adverse loss ratio. In order to keep his cost within reason, the employer might be forced to reduce the coverage available to his employees. In effect, those who do not drive would suffer for those who do.

If health insurance were primary, there is no question that this cost would be passed on to the non-driving public. It is important now as never before in our nation's economic history that those who engage in a particular activity should pay for that activity. The non-driving public includes millions of Americans on fixed incomes, such as those living on social security and annuities. Now is not the time to penalize those who are straining under the burden of double-digit inflation.

In any fragmented approach there would be a corresponding duplication of cost if health insurance were to be the primary provider of benefits. A recent survey estimated additional cost to be $75 million in New York State alone. In response to that survey, Benjamin R. Schneck, Superindendent of Insurance of the New York State Department of Insurance, recently issued Regulation 62 requiring Blue Cross and Blue Shield to exclude no-fault automobile insurance from health insurance contracts.

At the present time health carriers are not equipped to investigate claims in the same manner that automobile carriers do, because they are not compensating the victim for all of his losses. They would have to hire and train additional staff which would further increase the cost of health insurance.

Under the present system, when an individual is involved in an accident, his insurance company undertakes an investigation, and the adjuster is then free to pay all facets of compensation, including medical bills, loss of earnings, repair of property damage and any liability. If health insurance was primary, two investigations of every accident would be required. This means, of course, that the victim would have to negotiate with two different companies to secure his compensation. This duplication is wasteful and serves no purpose to the public whatsoever. The average driver is not concerned with what primacy means in regard to the coordination of benefits clause in his contract. He responds only to the delay and frustration which results in his time of greatest need.

Some states have passed laws which provide for options to the consumer as to whether health insurance or automobile insurance should be the primary provider of benefits. This creates problems in administration. For example, under the no-fault law recently passed in Pennsylvania, if an employee's health insurance is primary and his job is terminated, he could be left without coverage. Since his automobile insurance coverage excludes those benefits formerly provided by the health carrier, in the event of an accident he would be left without medical benefits. It would be incumbent upon him to notify his automobile insurance carrier to add this coverage which would raise the cost of his premium at a time when he can least afford it.

Another area that should be considered is that of revenue to the state. Currently, automobile insurance carriers pay a substantial tax on premium earnings. Some health carriers, like Blue Cross and Blue Shield, are not profit making organizations and so do not pay taxes. States would suffer a great loss of revenue if automobile insurance were to be excluded from first party benefits. This would substantially effect a state's ability to fund existing programs. For example, the police pension fund in Pennsylvania is provided for by the premium taxes from insurance companies. Without these revenues the program would either be discontinued or the state would suffer some increase funding requirements.

The solution to this problem is obvious. Automobile insurance should be the primary provider of benefits resulting from an accident. The ruling of the New York State Insurance Department is sensible, and it is the hope of this Association that other states will follow New York's lead.

We are convinced that if health insurance were to be primary, the public would suffer confusion, administrative chaos, and premium increases from the duplication of effort. Equally important, the loss of public confidence in the insurance industry would be decreased. This frustration may lead to the destruction of the private insurance mechanism in this country.

Fair and simple claim handling at the lowest possible cost should be the goal of insurance reform. It is the belief of the National Association of Mutual Insurance Agents that this can be done by retaining automobile insurance as the provider of benefits as a result of automobile accidents.

Mr. STUCKEY. Thank you, Mr. Cook.

Mr. Rinaldo, any questions?

Mr. RINALDO. Yes, I have a couple of questions.

First of all, I want to thank Mr. Cook for his testimony. I would like to ask, if the people who actually pay out the money are in favor of unlimited medical benefits on the basis that they will cost only—I believe the figure given was—one-tenth of 1 percent more than the $50,000 benefit, why are the insurance agencies so opposed to it; do you have figures to show that unlimited medical would cost more; and do you think the percentage that is being used is unreasonable?

Mr. COOK. That is a pretty long question, Mr. Rinaldo.

Mr. RINALDO. I recognize that fact.

Mr. COOK. Before I answer your question, Mr. Rinaldo, I would like to introduce Mr. Harold Traub of Lakewood, N.J., president-elect of our national association.

Mr. RINALDO. Very good. We are pleased to have you here.

Mr. COOK. We believe that most agents are not opposed to good legislation that provides better services and better coverage for their customers, but we do believe that excessive costs are not in his interest and therefore, we feel we must establish at some point a maximum amount, with the right of the consumer to buy more coverage if he so desires.

Now, I don't know if I answered your question fully.

Mr. RINALDO. I guess it was a rather difficult question and perhaps you were not prepared for it.

I agree that you did not answer fully, but I also recognize the difficulty in answering a question like that off the cuff without any prior awareness.

So, under the circumstances it would be appreciated if you would submit for the record a complete answer to the question.

Mr. COOK. Mr. Rinaldo, I was about to suggest, if you would let us have the specifics, we would be happy to provide the answer for you.

Mr. RINALDO. Thank you very much.

That is all I have.

[The following material was received for the record:]

RESPONSE TO QUESTION ON UNLIMITED MEDICAL EXPENSES

Those who advocate federal legislation with unlimited coverage for medical expenses and high benefits for wage loss, appear to do so because of their appraisal of the problem of the seriously injured. These appraisals often refer to the Department of Transportations' study which blew up a sample of 1,376 accident victims to a theoretical estimate of 500,000 fatalities and seriously injured persons in one year. Yet the professionals who conducted the study warned against the "speculative" nature of the projections of future losses, the "substantial errors in classifying the various individuals, the arbitrary criteria used for defining serious injury", and the fact that the "study does not provide reliable estimates of aggregates." We would refer here only to the extrapolated statement in the report that the seriously injured had $5.1 billion of compensable loss in a single year. Three billion dollars of this loss is for future wages beginning thirty months after the accident. This future wage loss was what the victims or their survivors recalled more than two years after the accident. In a parallel study, the U.S. Public Health survey rejected data based on events more than ninety days old having found that recollection beyond that point is not reliable.

In contrast, in the sixteen-company survey of 23,635 cases (in which the economic loss was determined with great accuracy) the number of injured persons with economic loss in excess of $5,000 was 1.6%. The number of injured persons with economic loss in excess of $25,000 was one-tenth of 1%.

Fifty thousand dollars in first-party benefits would guarantee payments covering 100% of the economic loss of 99.9% of all automobile accident victims. This clearly meets the most important reform criteria by providing guaranteed benefits to the vast majority of automobile accident injury victims. Payment for the excess expenses of the 1% of accident victims with losses over $50,000 would be covered by optional first-party coverages which may have been selected by the insured, and by tort recoveries from others who have negligently caused injuries.

Mr. STUCKEY. Mr. Kinzler.

Mr. KINZLER. Mr. Cook, following on Mr. Rinaldo's question, you say you don't think the consumers should be forced to pay an unreasonable premium.

Do you consider today's premiums in most of the States unreasonable from a consumer's viewpoint?

Mr. COOK. I think many times the consumer feels his rate is too high.

Mr. KINZLER. Well, assuming the consumers will always feel that way, do you feel they are too high?

Mr. COOK. I feel they are not high enough in many cases in order for the insurance industry to survive. I could cite to you some examples of companies that have been forced to withdraw from certain territories because they could not get an adequate rate.

Mr. KINZLER. The reason I asked this is because you say, in supporting Mr. Rinaldo's bill, that you don't think the consumers should be forced to pay higher premiums, and you didn't say higher premiums but you said unreasonably higher premiums.

But I refer you to the figures submitted to the subcommittee by State Farm Insurance Co., which indicates rather than higher premiums with H.R. 1900, which includes unlimited medical benefits, in fact there would be a national decrease or decline of 10 percent in those rates.

Mr. TRAUB. I understood that was State Farm only, that Allstate indicated an increase of 17 percent.

Mr. KINZLER. Right. Allstate has since that time indicated that the Senate-passed bill, which includes a commercial vehicle subrogation provision, would result in a 4-percent increase nationally if one assumes $15,000 worth of survivor's benefits, and if you assume

$5,000 worth, you come out with about the same figures as State Farm.

Since H.R. 1900 simply says a "reasonable" amount of survivors' benefits the States would be permitted to adjust the level, in fact, they could go lower, down to $1,000, if they wish. If we are talking about legislation which gives significantly higher benefits to the consumer for lower premium, what objection would you have?

Mr. Cook. No objection whatsoever to a better product for a lower price to the consumer, but we must maintain enough premium for the business to remain solvent.

Mr. Kinzler. Right. Both State Farm and Allstate, being sensitive to their own needs, have added a figure that would return them a reasonable profit.

Mr. Cook. Yes.

Mr. Kinzler. In your statement, you talked about reinsurance problems in Michigan.

There are before this subcommittee two letters from the insurance commissioner of Michigan in which he indicates not only that small companies have not had reinsurance problems the State of Michigan is aware of, but that he had invited representatives of the insurance industry at public meetings to come to the department with any reinsurance problems, they encountered and there has been no response.

Could you expand on the problems you are aware of that maybe the commissioner is not?

Mr. Traub. While I am not familiar with Michigan, but I am aware of the situation in New Jersey.

Mr. Kinzler. That is helpful, because we have a letter from the commissioner in New Jersey, which also indicates there are no serious problems.

Mr. Traub. There are no problems?

Mr. Kinzler. Right.

Mr. Traub. Mr. David Green, president of the Motor Club of America, a domestic company in the State of New Jersey, has indicated severe difficulties in obtaining reinsurance under the unlimited no-fault program in the State of New Jersey.

Mr. Kinzler. Right.

Mr. Traub. This is the converse of what you are saying.

Mr. Kinzler. Yes. Following on that, is the problem for a small company that the pool is not large enough or that you can't actuarialy cost such unlimited benefits?

Mr. Traub. I would have to answer you by saying simply there is not sufficient data to determine the cost import on domestic companies.

I don't believe anybody at this point is qualified to make a solid judgment. Everybody is making judgments based on assumptions at this point.

Mr. Kinzler. Well, we do have some statistics with respect to the number of deaths, serious injuries, different economic levels, all from the Department of Transportation study, which I believe is the foundation of both Allstate's and State Farm's costing of an unlimited program.

My point is, and let me follow this a little more and maybe we can find an answer, that if the problem is that the small companies do not have a large enough pool to enable them to spread the risk in any particular aberrational year, I believe H.R. 1900 and S. 354 would leave the State Commissioner free, if he chooses to develop a kind of assigned claims plan for the whole State where you could pool everybody's losses and, perhaps allocate the costs over a 10-year basis, so no individual company is subject to these kinds of aberrational losses you are talking about.

Mr. COOK. I think that is a reasonable approach, and could be done. We are interested in market available, so that insurance is available.

Mr. KINZLER. Yes.

Mr. COOK. One of our main goals is to preserve a market. We don't want to see any insurance company damaged by legislation. This is not our goal.

We are independent agents, but we do need to have a viable market.

Mr. KINZLER. Right, but such a provision or the availability of such a provision would alleviate some concerns you expressed with respect to the unlimited medical, would it not?

Mr. COOK. I am not sure it would, because we still don't know what the future costs of serious and permanent disabling injuries would be.

Mr. KINZLER. That is a problem with respect to any legislation regarding medical cost.

Mr. COOK. True.

Mr. KINZLER. One more question, if I may.

You suggest a numerical threshold of $2,000 in medical benefits before permitting suits for obtaining pain and suffering.

This subcommittee was in Florida last week, and they have a $1,000 threshold and what the subcommittee found was that it was a disaster, that the lawyers and the doctors were simply colluding to get over that threshold. Won't you have the same problems with a $2,000 threshold?

Mr. COOK. We think the problem would be reduced considerably going to $2,000 because it would be more difficult to inflate a minor injury up to the $2,000 than for $1,000 for example.

Mr. KINZLER. Are we not perhaps better off trying to deal with something other than a dollar threshold? Don't we have potential problems where you have medical costs that very in different States, that is somebody can have a right to sue sooner in one State than another. Don't you always have these kinds of problems with a dollar threshold?

Mr. COOK. I think you make a good point. We believe in some way there must be some kind of a threshold; however, if there is a better method, then we should find it.

Mr. KINZLER. All right, but as opposed to some other approaches suggested here, such as death and disability with a 3-month period and permanent and serious injury or disfigurement, there are things that are not subject to the collusive kind of behavior that the $1,000 threshold might be and would be more equitable from State to State perhaps?

Mr. COOK. Are you speaking of a time limitation?

Mr. KINZLER. Yes, whether that might be a more equitable kind of approach than a dollar threshold?

Mr. COOK. I suppose that in some cases it might be.

Mr. KINZLER. Yes, sir.

Mr. COOK. We do see cases of individuals under no-fault in Florida, however, stretching out the time of their disability.

Mr. KINZLER. Right.

Mr. COOK. So we have those who abused the system in any way that they find practical to abuse it. We will always have these people with us; it is difficult to find that perfect solution.

We are hopeful that no-fault automobile insurance will be a better way to compensate auto accident victims than the present system.

Mr. KINZLER. OK. Let me suggest, that if you, in the next month or so, are still so inclined, if you could perhaps reconsider the question of threshold and can devise some language that you think might be more successful in trying to get at the point you are concerned about, submit it to the subcommittee. It would be appreciated.

Mr. COOK. Mr. Kinzler, we have a staff here in Washington, working with this type of question constantly, and I am sure they will be keeping right up to date with it, and we will be delighted to provide you with any new thinking we might have. We are pleased to have this opportunity to appear before the subcommittee today.

Mr. STUCKEY. Mr. Cook, I think we have one more question by Mr. Rinaldo.

Mr. RINALDO. Thank you, Mr. Chairman.

We have had witnesses before the committee that stated in the absence of subrogation, expense shifting will not occur to the detriment of the good driver. They have gone on to say that insurance companies will always take into account various factors such as accident records, age of the insured, and so forth, in order to determine the premium question.

I would like your comments in regard to that particular statement.

Mr. COOK. Maybe I should say in the beginning, I believe there are certain drivers within the population of drivers who are uninsurabel at any price. In the area of intercompany subrogation, we can offset whatever the costs are, one company against another. But there does need to be a measure of "Where does the loss originate and in what groups does it originate?"

We need to be able to make these determinations. I don't think we will ever be able to get away from that.

I would expect that the company would continue to evaluate the people who want to insure with them and whom they wish to insure from that standpoint.

Mr. RINALDO. So, in effect, you are agreeing with the statement?

Mr. COOK. Yes, sir.

Mr. RINALDO. All right, thank you. That is all, Mr. Chairman.

Mr. STUCKEY. Thank you, Mr. Cook.

Mr. COOK. Thank you very much, gentlemen.

Mr. STUCKEY. Our next witness is Mr. Lawrence Jones, president of the AIA. Mr. Jones, it is good to have you with us again.

STATEMENT OF T. LAWRENCE JONES, PRESIDENT, AMERICAN INSURANCE ASSOCIATION

Mr. JONES. Thank you.

Mr. STUCKEY. It seems like some of us have gone through these same hearings three or four times; this is a repeat.

Mr. JONES. Yes; several of us have. I guess this is the fourth time in 3 years for us. But you picked up a few new colleagues this time on your subcommittee.

Mr. STUCKEY. The committee does seem to be growing.

Mr. JONES. Yes; I would like to submit my prepared remarks for the record, rather than reading them, if I could.

Mr. STUCKEY. We will be delighted for you to summarize, and we will insert your printed statement in the record.

Mr. JONES. Yes, Mr. Chairman. As you stated for the record, my name is T. Lawrence Jones, president of the American Insurance Association, an organization of 138 member companies, marketing nationally all forms of property and casualty insurance, and representing about 30 percent of the automobile insurance market.

Nearly 7 years ago, our association concluded that our industry was capable of designing and producing a product that we had never had in this country; that is, a true auto accident reparations system that would bring insurance benefits to everyone who suffers loss through auto injury and service them fairly, quickly, and efficiently without the need of establishing fault or liability.

Such a system was first recommended by a column by a university study team more than 40 years ago, so it is not a new idea. It is now endorsed by the executive, or the concept of no-fault automobile insurance is endorsed by the executive branch of our Government, by leading consumer organizations, labor organizations, the Nation's press, by the insurance industry as a whole, and by the most prestigious of the bar associations. Yet the pace of reform is at the speed of the tortoise. Progress has been very slow and agonizing. All of the States have considered no-fault at least once. Many have done it four or five times. California, which is normally a pace setter, is giving in the ninth consideration this year.

For every month or year that passes, the delay in converting from a fault to a no-fault system means that about 1 million automobile accident victims each year reveive nothing under the automobile liability system. As Cook pointed out to you, after 7 years we have 16 no-fault law States, and even there the laws vary considerably as to their benefits and tort restrictions.

It is our considered opinion we are not going to get adequate, prompt auto accident reparations reform unless it comes from Congress. We would prefer reform to come in the form of national standards for State action rather than any preemption of the field.

All of the bills before you have merit, Mr. Chairman; all are directed toward reform of a system that has outlived its usefulness, but in our opinion only S. 345, as recently reported by the Senate Commerce Committee, fully realizes the potential of using the federalist system to its maximum advantage, with the Federal Government and the States each carrying their own responsibilities.

We have developed a form of score sheet on which we have set out five criteria we think are important for a good no-fault bill, then rated the bills before you in terms of these criteria.

Mr. STUCKEY. We will make that a part of the record. Thank you.

Mr. JONES. I would like to touch briefly on some of the key issues as we see them in the bills before you. Of course, we have done this in much greater detail in our prepared statement.

First, we believe an effective auto accident reparations system should provide unlimited medical, hospital, and rehabilitation benefits to all auto crash victims.

Every major study of the fault system has identified the undercompensation of the seriously injured victim as the cruelest defect of the old system.

We are in a unique position in dealing with automobile accidents to provide medical and hospital expense coverage from what we in the industry call the first dollar; that is, there is no need for deductibles or coinsurance features. If the insured loss arises out of a traumatic event, then there is no need to create safeguards against overutilization of medical and hospital facilities.

We think it would be a serious disservice if this basic objective were lost and the no-fault system did not provide unlimited coverage for medical expense.

We seriously question the allegation that some smaller insurance companies will be unable to afford reinsurance for unlimited medical benefits. We have not observed this occurring and we have no reason to believe it to be the case.

We are aware that this allegation has been made a number of times. We can only understand the allegation in the context of companies that are not familiar with buying reinsurance for this type of peril or risk. But those that have been writing workmen's compensation insurance, where we have unlimited medical and rehabilitation in 47 of the States—47 or 48, depending on which way you count them—those that are experienced, they know that it can be obtained and know how to do it.

Second, we are opposed very much to a transfer of loss costs among no-fault insurers on the basis of policyholder fault, except in the case where we have the private passenger vehicle involved in an accident with he commercial vehicle. Loss cost transfer has been characterized as a "behind-the-scenes tort liability system," and it has been defended on grounds that only the insurance companies would be involved, not the public, but our companies feel that loss cost transfer would deprive them of the ability to price their product more accurately for the risks that they would be covering under a first-party system.

Also, loss cost transfer is quite expensive. Some of our companies early in their experience in Massachusetts keep track of their loss cost shifting, and one in particular did it or 6 months and found he came out $50 ahead, after transferring a great number of dollars to other people and receiving a great number of dollars back. He did not accomplish anything worthwhile, and it cost him a great deal of money to do it.

Our figures are that it costs approximately 5 percent of the premium dollar to go through this kind of transfer.

Third, we think the subcommittee should consider including property damage under the no-fault system. In our original study in 1968, we recommended that this be done. Now we have supported State laws in which property damage was not included in the system, the defects in the old system that needed attention were mostly on the bodily injury or personal injury side and not on the property damage side.

But we have had a first-party no-fault property damage coverage, which we call "collision coverage," since 1904. It is complementary and in many situations duplicative, but it is there for those people that want that kind of coverage so a no-fault for property damage has not been an important factor in State legislation, at least not as important a factor as the other.

I would point out, however that if a no-fault property damage system were established nationally the insurer would have incentives to be concerned about the crashworthiness of the car and thus to develop a classification system which would not be possible under the tort law, to give better rates to those cars that are more crashworthy.

Fourth, the subcommittee should consider whether the seriously njured might be better served if tort liability were eliminated or abolished with respect to wage loss as well as with respect to hospital expense.

Under these circumstances, the individual, the insured, could elect what first-party coverage he wanted for his wage loss. We would get away from the problem we have under the tort liability system, where, in essence, the less affluent subsidize the more affluent.

Under the fault system, it is just as likely that you will have an accident with someone with a greater wage loss than the average than with someone with a less wage loss than the average, so you pay premiums based on the average. Thus, the less affluent contribute proportionately more to the fund than do the more affluent.

Fifth, you may want to consider a schedule of benefits to provide first-party compensation for noneconomic losses in some cases, as opposed to allowing lawsuits for such losses in cases of death or serious injury.

This approach would be somewhat like that in H.R. 1272, but we would strongly recommend that you not do this in all cases, as H.R. 1272 would, and that it be limited to the seriously injured and that it be done on the basis of an optional schedule of benefits.

In our original report in 1968, we recommended that there be, on a basis where it could be measured objectively, additional compensation for the seriously injured that covered noneconomic loss.

We have also endeavored to have State legislation drafted in such a way that a company could optionally offer additional coverage on a schedule of benefit basis, if it chooses to do so.

We don't think it ought to be made a part of the compulsory system for this reason: Auto insurance for many people is just part of the cost of getting to and from work and, thus, in the mandatory system you shouldn't include anything more than the minimum coverage needed.

If it adds to an individual's cost to have noneconomic loss coverage on a first-party basis, he should be given the option as to whether he wants it or not. It is not coverage to repay an economic loss that he had, it is coverage on a noneconomic loss.

He also should have an option as to what schedule of benefits he wants. Someone may want a schedule of benefits that begins at $10,000. Another man may want to have a schedule of benefits that begins at $100,000. Under those circumstances, they can make their own election and choose the one they think most appropriate to them and can get that sort of coverage, and we have tried to see that legislation permitted that.

The companies have not felt that there was a great market or demand for it at this time, and they have not developed the coverage or tried to sell it.

But if this subcommittee considers that idea further, we would urge that they consider it on a schedule of benefits, or some other controlled basis, and on an optional basis.

We would say in summary that S. 354, as reported by the Senate Commerce Committee represents a lot of study, and is a well thought out and constructive bill. We urge you to consider it above all the other bills before you.

We recognize that the auto insurance system, as an institution, needs to be revitalized and renewed. Crash victims need to be restored. The prospects of accomplishing this by the end of the century are bleak, unless the U.S. Congress takes some action.

[Mr. Jones' prepared statement, with attachments, follow:]

STATEMENT OF T. LAWRENCE JONES, PRESIDENT, AMERICAN INSURANCE ASSOCIATION

Mr. Chairman and members of the subcommittee, My name is T. Lawrence Jones. I am president of the American Insurance Association, an organization of 138 insurers whose members market all kinds of property and casualty coverages—including approximately 30% of the nation's automobile insurance—throughout the United States. We appreciate this, the third opportunity we have had during the past four years to testify before you on the subject of federal no-fault auto insurance legislation.

As several of you know from our past appearances here, we have advocated a complete no-fault auto insurance system since 1968, but nevertheless have rather consistently supported the enactment of more modest reform legislation at the state level. In June of 1973, after five frustrating years of effort in the state legislatures, we announced our support for S. 354, the 93rd Congress version of one of the bills currently before you. It was our view in 1973, and it is more firmly our belief now, that the enactment of federal legislation establishing minimum standards for state no-fault laws is the only way to achieve reasonably soon, meaningful reform of the way in which the victims of auto accidents are compensated. We also believe that further delay in the enactment of such legislation deprives the public of needed compensation and threatens both the automobile insurance industry itself and the state-by-state regulation of the business of insurance.

Other witnesses at these proceedings have told you of the virtues of the no-fault system from the perspective of the insurance-buying public and from the point of view of the accident victim, particularly the seriously injured accident victim. We would like to share with you briefly why our members, as profit-oriented enterprises, advocate no-fault reform.

For most of our members, auto insurance is a major product, constituting up to 40 percent of their volume. It is also a major headache, in that the fault system on which liability coverage is predicted makes it necessary for our members to deal with most claimants not as valued customers, but as adversaries in the expensive and time-consuming process of determining who was "at fault."

Moreover, the fault system of auto insurance is at odds with the fundamental purpose and practice of insurance, which is to compensate the losses of the few from the pool of contributions by the many who are exposed to a risk or peril. As the Department of Transportation's 1971 report, "Motor Vehicle Crash Losses and Their Compensation in the United States," observed:

. . . Today, our society need not settle for a reparations system that deliberately excludes large numbers of victims from its protection or that gives clearly inadequate levels of protection to those who need it most. With only 45 per cent of those killed or seriously injured in auto accidents benefiting in any way from the tort liability insurance system and one out of every ten of such victims receiving *nothing* from *any* system of reparations, the coverage of the present compensation mechanism is seriously deficient. (Italic in original.)

Over the years, courts and legislatures, recognizing the unresponsiveness of a fault-based insurance system to the needs of an automobile-oriented society, have sought through a variety of devices to convert this system into one that would compensate a larger number of accident victims. The substitution of "comparative" negligence for "contributory" negligence in many states is an example of these attempts to convert a legal liability system into a compensation system without changing the basic necessity of assigning blame. No-fault, in our members' view, is the logical culmination of these efforts, and the only appropriate response to our society's demand for a more humane, rational and efficient system of compensating the victims of automobile accidents.

Our members believe that no-fault will convert a product that is both a public relations albatross and a remarkably inefficient means of compensating accident victims into a product with which the motoring public will be pleased and of which the insurance industry can be proud.

Our members also see in no-fault an answer to those who argue that the ills of the auto insurance industry can be cured only by killing the patient and assigning its functions to a system of national accident and health insurance. We recognize that if we do not solve our own problems, someone else will solve them for us at our expense.

In another era, the pace of change that is taking place now at the state level in the system of compensating auto accident victims—16 no-fault laws in 7 years—would have been acceptable. It took 40 years, for example, for all the states to change their systems for compensating the victims of work-related accidents and illnesses. But the 2.5 million Americans injured, the survivors of the 50,000 Americans killed in the 14 million accidents on our highways each year, and the millions of Americans who buy auto insurance cannot, will not, and should not have to wait so long for a reform as long overdue as is no-fault.

We believe, on the basis of seven years of effort to enact no-fault laws at the state level, that many state legislatures either cannot or will not enact meaningful reform measures within the foreseeable future. It is our considered opinion that adequate, sound and prompt auto accident reparations reform must come from the Congress.

The property and casualty insurance business is by and large a state-regulated industry. Our members support state regulation of their business. In supporting the enactment of federal standards no-fault legislation, we are seeking to reform the legal rules governing the compensation of auto accident victims without altering the pattern of insurance regulation. We hope and expect that the states will continue to regulate the auto insurance business under the no-fault system as they now do under the fault system of auto insurance.

With this background, let me first briefly list the features we consider essential in a federal no-fault bill and then address each of the bills before the Subcommittee in terms of these criteria.

The features we consider essential in a no-fault bill are as follows:

(1) High "first-party" benefits for economic loss, including unlimited medical, hospital and rehabilitation benefits; wage replacement sufficient for most accidents and reasonable household services coverage;

(2) Abolition of lawsuits for economic loss covered by these "first-party" benefits, and restriction of lawsuits for non-economic loss to cases involving death, serious injury or disfigurement, or more than 90 days of total disability (we preferred 6 months of total disability, but have indicated our support of 90 days as passed the Senate last year and as reported by the Senate last year and as reported by the Senate Commerce Committee this year);

(3) Prohibition of any transfer of loss costs among no-fault insurers based on policyholder fault, except in cases involving both private passenger and commercial vehicles;

(4) Primacy of the compulsory no-fault auto insurance coverage over other benefit sources. We recognize the existence of the workers compensation system and certain existing state and federal programs, but we believe all future programs should exclude losses from auto accidents covered by the compulsory no-fault auto insurance coverage. We also recognize the desirability of coordinating to the extent feasible coverage under no-fault auto insurance with other benefit sources, both as a sound insurance principle and as a means of achieving overall cost savings; and

(5) Establishment of federal minimum standards for state no-fault laws, rather than federal preemption of auto accident reparations insurance system.

(1) Three of the bills before you—H.R. 1272, H.R. 1900 and S. 354—meet the criterion of high first-party benefits. H.R. 8441 fails to meet this criterion, providing instead for a combined medical, wage and other benefit limit of $10,000.

first dollar of loss.

This being the case, it is tragic that all but three of the 16 state no-fault laws deny adequate protection to the accident victims who fare worst under the fault system—the seriously injured.

In our view, the provision of anything less than unlimited medical, hospital and rehabilitation benefits would be a disservice to the basic objective of a no-fault reparations system, which is the *restoration* of persons injured in automobile accidents.

It has been alleged that the requirement of unlimited medical, hospital and rehabilitation benefits will so increase reinsurance costs for smaller insurance companies as to perhaps put some of them out of business. We have not observed any such experience occurring. We have not ever seen any substantiation of these allegations and they have been repeatedly denied by the Insurance Departments of the two states—New Jersey and Michigan—with experience under no-fault laws providing unlimited medical, hospital and rehabilitation benefits. In any event it is an unusual argument. The public welfare should be served regardless of the resources of certain insurers. Society would not tolerate the deferment of a cancer cure because some medical institutions could not afford the new equipment.

First, the no-fault auto insurance system is similar to the workers' compensation laws of the 50 states and the District of Columbia in that it provides benefits to workers without questions regarding liability based on fault. Fully 47 of these laws place no limit on the amount of medical, hospital and rehabilitation benefits available to the victims of work-related accidents and illnesses. Thus, unlimited medical benefits are not a novelty for the insurance industry; indeed, the industry's efforts in the full rehabilitation of work accident victims are one of its proudest achievements.

Second, more than 400 insurance companies are either members or subscribers of the National Council on Compensation Insurance, the principal statistical agency for workers' compensation carriers. These 400-plus companies obviously include a large number of smaller companies, none of which, to our knowledge, has ever, experienced any difficulties in obtaining reinsurance for, or maintaining solvency in the face of, their unlimited exposure for medical, hospital and rehabilitation benefits.

Third, most work-related accidents, like auto accidents, result in traumatic injuries, so that the experience of insurers under workers' compensation laws is analogous to what can be expected under a national no-fault system for the treatment of auto accident victims, and can be utilized by primary insurers and reinsurers alike to establish adequate rates for no-fault insurance and reinsurance.

Fourth, as was pointed out in the Senate Judiciary Committee's favorable Report on S. 354 last year (S. Rept. No. 93-757), every company's reinsurance needs are unique:

In negotiating reinsurance protection for medical, hospital and rehabilitation coverages, the "unlimited" nature of the company's liability is generally less important that *the point at which the reinsurance attaches* in a given situation. In such contracts, the term "unlimited" is actually a misnomer, in that it is possible to calculate with reasonable precision the maximum possible loss under the most extreme circumstances. Once the maximum potential loss has been calculated, reinsurance can be negotiated in multiples of hundreds of thousands or millions of dollars. Reinsurance protection of up to $5 million per occurrence is readily available at reasonable prices. (Italic added.)

The price that a primary insurer pays for its reinsurance is a function of the dollar amount of each loss that it wishes to retain. The amount of the "retention" is always within the control of the primary insurer; accordingly, so is the price it pays for its reinsurance. The higher the retention, the lower the cost of reinsurance.

The Judiciary Committee Report also points out that because the frequency of large medical, hospital and rehabilitation expenses in auto accident cases is so low, "unlimited medical benefits can be provided for 0.1 percent more than the premium for $50,000 of such coverage."

There is no question in our minds that small companies will be able to obtain the reinsurance they need to complete effectively under the no-fault system, so long as regulators recognize the need of both primary carriers and reinsurers for rates that adequately reflect loss exposure.

H.R. 1272 is unique among the bills before you in that it provides not only generous first-party economic loss benefits, but also unlimited non-economic loss benefits, payable on a first-party basis and calculated according to the damages rules of the victim's state. The virtue of this first-party approach to non-economic loss is that it would provide all the victims of all accidents with benefits in excess of their out-of-pocket losses. The burdens and costs of the approach, however, outweigh its virtue, in our view.

First, by its very nature, non-economic loss defies quantification. The imprecision of non-objective damages is the fundamental cause of the overcompensation of small claims under the fault insurance system. Insurers now overpay even questionable liability claims because it is cheaper to do so than to contest liability. Indeed, many disputes under the fault system involve questions, not of liability, but of damages for non-economic loss. The payment of non-economic loss benefits on a first-party basis would eliminate all countervailing questions about responsibility and contributory conduct, but would eliminate few of the disputes over the amount of damages payable. As the tort system now does, the system proposed under H.R. 1272 would invite dramatization and exaggeration of automobile accident injuries, and we believe in time would increase rather than decrease the amount of litigation arising out of automobile accidents, even where the system is designed to delay litigation to a substantial extent.

Second, it is simply not possible to pay *all* accident victims not only all or most of their economic losses but also their noneconomic losses, without substantially increasing the cost of automobile insurance. Indeed, no-fault can provide sufficient resources for the payment of economic losses only be eliminating payment for non-economic losses in less serious cases—if auto insurance costs are to be stabilized or reduced.

Third, it has been our view since 1968 that as long as "pain and suffering" and other forms of non-economic loss are not susceptible of objective measurement they have no place in a compulsory or mandatory reparations system. The workers' compensation system does not recognize non-economic loss as such, but does afford scheduled benefits, over and above for economic loss, for permanent partial and total disabilities. In our original no-fault auto insurance proposal, which, like H.R. 1272, would have entirely eliminated tort liability arising out of automobile accidents, we recommended that: " . . . the insurance system provide extra payment to persons who sustain permanent impairment of disfigurement in automobile accidents to compensate them for such injuries which cannot be measured by economic loss. . . . (Benefits) should vary according to the degree of impairment or disfigurement."

We agree with H.R. 1272's abolition of tort liability and with its goal of providing some benefits over and above economic loss. But we do not think that supplemental payments should be made in all cases, and we do not believe that they should be made even in serious cases without establishing a schedule of benefits in order to improve service, reduce litigation and control the system's costs.

We do not believe that it would be possible without some increase in auto insurance costs to establish a no-fault system that would provide unlimited medical, hospital, rehabilitation benefits; monthly wage loss benefits without time limitation; and scheduled benefits for permanent partial and total disabilities— even with the total abolition of tort liability for auto accident injuries. Of course, it would depend on the schedule of benefits for non-economic loss. Even then, we do not think the scheduled benefits should be part of the compulsory system, but should be offered optionally and on the basis of several different schedules.

(2) H.R. 1272, H.R. 1900 and S. 354 also meet our criteria for restrictions on the tort remedy for auto accident injuries. H.R. 1272, as noted above, entirely eliminates tort liability for bodily injury, while H.R. 1900 and S. 354 contain identical 90-day disability thresholds for non-economic loss claims. H.R. 8441 however, proposes no thresholds at all, but contains an evidentiary restriction in suits for non-economic loss that we regard as inadequate to safeguard abuse of the first-party benefit system.

We note that H.R. 1272 also abolishes tort liability for property damage. Our own proposal in 1968 called for the elimination or property damage liability. We have not opposed no-fault legislation that did not include elimination of property damage liability, because the abuses that most demand reform of the bodily injury liability system are not so prevalent in the settlement of property damage claims and a complementary and duplicative first-party no-fault collision coverage has been available since 1904. We would like to point out, however, that just as no-fault bodily injury coverage will provide economic incentives to insurers to reduce the frequency and severity of bodily injury and death of their policyholders, so, too, would no-fault property damage coverage increase insurers' concern with the relative crashworthiness and damageability of automobiles that they insure.

As we said earlier, we would prefer to see a complete substitution of first-party benefits for the tort liability insurance system. In our view, this approach would best meet the needs of the seriously injured accident victim. If tort liability is not entirely abolished, there should at least be unlimited medical, hospital and rehabilitation protection, so that the physical restoration of the seriously injured accident victim need never be dependent on the circumstances of the crash.

The retention of residual tort liability in most of the bills before you poses problems for seriously injured accident victims who have elected minimum wage replacement benefits ($15,000 in H.R. 1900 and S. 354; something less than $10,000 in H.R. 8441). Though these bills prohibit a claimant who has elected the minimum package from recovering in tort any excess wage loss sustained during the period in which his benefits were being paid at the maximum $1,000 per month permitted under the minimum coverage, they nevertheless contemplate permitting suits for all wage loss sustained beyond that period, unless the claimant has purchased supplemental disability coverage.

It seems to us that the seriously injured might be better served by a system in which tort liability were entirely abolished, but in which wage loss benefits elected by insureds would continue for the duration of their disability. Such a system would serve to increase individual reliance on first party coverage and prevent the subsidy of the affluent by the less affluent that is inherent in the third-party liability system of auto insurance, as was pointed out and developed in the Department of Transportation study.

Whether the abolition tort liability is partial or total, it is plainly essential to reform of the automobile accident reparations system and to the stabilization of auto insurance costs. The 31.8 cents of every automobile bodily injury insurance premium dollar now devoted to the process of fault-finding cannot be turned into first-party benefits unless it becomes unnecessary to determine fault in the great majority of cases.

(3) H.R. 1272 and S. 354 meet our criteria with respect to prohibitions on lost cost transfer among insurers based on policyholder fault. Both bills prohibis such transfers among insurers of private passenger vehicles, and S. 354 permits them only in cases involving private passenger and commercial vehicles where loss exceeds $100. H.R. 1900 and H.R. 8441 do not meet these criteria: both permit loss cost transfer between private passenger and commercial vehicle insurers only in cases where loss exceeds $5,000; and H.R. 8441 permits such transfer in any case where loss exceeds $2,000.

We are opposed to allowing private passenger vehicle insurers to shift no-fault loss costs among each other on the basis of policyholder fault because such loss shifting would turn the no-fault system back into a "behind-the-scene" fault system and would frustrate no-fault's potential for changing the way in which auto insurance premium costs are assessed.

It has been argued that no-fault loss cost transfer based on policyholder fault (loosely called subrogation) is necessary to assure that drivers who "cause" accidents will continue to pay more for their auto insurance than those who do not. This argument suggests that insurers are the enforcers of our traffic laws, and that high insurance premiums or denial of insurance coverage will force "bad" drivers off our highways. We have enough experience to know that we cannot price "bad" drivers off the road, and we believe that the role of insurance is to compensate, not punish. The removal of "bad" drivers from the highways is the function of our law enforcement and judicial officers, not insurers.

The argument in favor of loss cost transfer based on fault also suggests that without it, no-fault insurers will not care who "causes" accidents, and therefore will not adjust rates on the basis of accident-causing propensity. This is not so. Rates will reflect this propensity, which can be determined far more objectively from Motor Vehicle Department records of conviction for, or forfeiture of collateral with respect to, moving traffic violations than by loss cost transfer based on an "undercover" determination of policyholder fault.

Loss cost transfer on the basis of policyholder fault has the effect of converting the no-fault system into a fault system. If insurers are permitted to shift, on a fault basis, dollars paid to policyholders on a no-fault basis, it follows that they will have to continue investigating every accident, no matter how minor, in order to establish the fault basis for the loss cost transfer.

First of all, this would be an expensive process, adding at least five cents to every dollar of no-fault premiums. And this expense would be wasted, since four years of experience with such a loss cost transfer system in Massachusetts have shown us that no-fault insurers lose as many cases as they win, and pay out as many dollars as they take in.

Second, if premium costs are to be based on fault, which would be the objective if loss cost transfer is permitted, the potential of no-fault to inject greater equity into rating classification systems would be entirely lost. Under the fault system, a a third party is a principal beneficiary of the insurance contract, and that party's loss can never be calculated in advance. As a result, rates must be based on the average loss in particular rating classifications and territories. Thus, a $50,000 a year executive and a $10,000 a year laborer in the same rating classification and territory pay identical rates for similar amounts of bodily injury liability protection, even though the executive stands to take proportionately more out of the system as a claimant than he contributes as a policyholder, and the laborer stands to gain proportionately less than he contributes. If loss cost transfer is permitted under the no-fault system, this inequity will be perpetuated.

If loss cost transfer is prohibited among private passenger vehicle insurers under the no-fault system, policyholders' rates will reflect to a greater extent their own loss-incurring potential, rather than the average loss. Under such a system, the youthful driver with no dependents and a low income and the elderly driver with no wage loss exposure can expect their rates to reflect their own losses rather than those of the average party claimant, assuming that their driving records are good. Absent loss cost transfer, the no-fault auto insurance rating system will be much like those for other first-party insurance systems, where the rate is based largely on what the policyholder stands to lose if the event insured against takes place, and on the frequency with which that event is likely to occur.

We recommend, however, that loss cost transfer be permitted among private passenger and commercial vehicle no-fault insurers in accidents involving both types of vehicles, since the greater weight of commercial vehicles such as trucks virtually guarantees that they will inflict far more damage than they will sustain. Unless loss cost transfer is permitted in private passenger—commercial vehicle accidents, private passenger no-fault policyholders will have to shoulder a disproportionate share of the loss costs in such accidents. We estimate that the absence of such a transfer system, or a system with a deductible greater than $100, would reduce no-fault's potential savings for private passenger vehicle owners by as much as five percentage points. (4) S. 354 and H.R. 8441 meet our criteria with respect to the primacy of compulsory automobile insurance benefits over benefits from voluntary coverages. H.R. 1272 is deficient in that it makes no-fault benefits excess of virtually all other benefits and H.R. 1900 contains, in Section 208(c), language that would make group health insurance plans meeting detailed requirements primary to no-fault auto insurance medical benefits.

We believe that the ability of an accident victim or his survivors to look to a single source for all economic loss benefits under the no-fault system is one of no-fault's great advantages. A single benefit source, compulsory for all vehicle owners, makes it possible to minimize duplication of coverage and to achieve the greatest cost savings for the motoring public. Other benefit sources can exclude coverage for auto accident injuries in the certain knowledge that these will be provided under the no-fault policy, and duplication is thereby avoided. Similarly, the handling of auto accident costs through single claims mechanism maximizes cost savings through avoidance of a multiplicity of claims handling systems.

S. 354 recognizes in Section 208(a) the primacy of no-fault benefits to other than certain specified systems (such as workers' compensation and Social Security) and encourages the states in Section 209(a) to minimize duplication of benefits and achieve cost savings through programs of benefit coordination. We think the flexibility of S. 354 on this point is appropriate in a minimum national standards measure, and we recommend it to you.

(5) H.R. 1900, H.R. 8441 and S. 354 all conform to our belief that reform of the auto accident reparations system can be achieved through federal minimum standards that leave in place the traditional insurance regulatory functions of

the states. H.R. 1272, however, would totally preempt state reparations reform and insurance regulatory activity, a step we think unnecessary to the achievement of reform and inappropriate to a federal system.

Congress has long been concerned with the compensation of persons using federally assisted or federally regulated transportation systems, or transportation systems whose role in interstate commerce makes uniformity of compensation essential. In enacting the Employers' Liability Acts (45 U.S.C. §§ 51-60) beginning in 1906 and the Longshoremen's and Harbor Workers' Compensation Act of 1927 (33 U.S.C. §§ 901-945, 947-950), for example, Congress recognized the importance of American railroads and port facilities to the free flow of commerce by establishing uniform rules for the compensation of railroad workers and stevedores, despite the availability of tort or other remedies under state law.

Federal assistance to the railroads in the form of land grants, and to the maritime industry in the form of shipbuilding and operating subsidies and rivers and harbors construction efforts, is dwarfed by the scale of federal assistance in the construction of our highway system. That system has become our primary transportation system, and the personal injury, loss of life and property damage on our highways vastly exceeds the extent of injury and death among railroad or harbor workers. Just as railroad workers and stevedores required Congressional action to assure them of uniformity and adequacy of compensation, so, too, do the victims of accidents on our highways.

In treating the needs of railroad and harbor workers, Congress preempted fields in which the states were either unable or unwilling to act. In the case of railroad workers, relief was required because employers had persuaded state legislatures to place limits on common law remedies and because no state had a workers' compensation law. In the case of harbor workers, the states' jurisdiction over navigable waters was at best questionable and, in 1927, substantial numbers of states did not have workers' compensation acts.

In our view, Congress clearly has the power, under the Commerce Clause, to preempt the states both as to the law governing the compensation of highway accident victims and as to the regulation of insurance. And a preemptive act would be consistent with previous Congressional enactments governing the compensation of the victims of transportation system accidents.

But we would suggest that despite Congress' clear power to preempt the states both as to the legal program of auto accident victim compensation and as to the regulation of insurance carriers providing the required benefits, the needed quality and uniformity of reparations reform can be achieved while (1) giving the states a choice between their own reparations system and a federally administered system and (2) recognizing and preserving existing state mechanisms for the regulation of insurance carriers. While the inability or unwillingness of most of the states to enact reform legislation clearly requires Congressional action, they do not compel complete preemption of the field. If the states are given a limited number of criteria deemed essential to a uniform compensation system, they can frame their own programs meeting or exceeding those criteria or choose an alternative federal program administered either by themselves or by the federal government. Much the same choice has been given the states under the Clean Air Act and the Occupational Safety and Health Act.

A number of states have accepted federal administration of their occupational safety and health programs because they were not equipped to do the job themselves. This is not the case with respect to state insurance regulation. At least since 1948, all the states have had professionally-staffed departments of insurance. Thus, the states are equipped to regulate insurers under federal no-fault legislation, and it makes sense, we believe, to frame the bill so as to allow the states to continue to do under the no-fault system what they have long been doing under the fault system. Of the bills before you, S. 354 gives the most recognition to the role of the states under our federal system, while at the same time establishing the basic criteria for a nationwide system of reasonably uniform no-fault compensation laws for the victims of auto accidents.

In conclusion, Mr. Chairman, all the bills before you have merit; they are all directed at reform of a system that has outlived its usefulness. But only S. 354, in our view, achieves the needed reform in a manner that fully recognizes the partnership between the states and the federal government, a partnership—which we, on occasion, call federalism—that is one of the keys to the genius of this nation's governmental system.

Thank you for your attention. We would be happy to answer your questions.

DISTRIBUTION OF THE PREMIUM DOLLAR—STOCKS, MUTUALS, AND RECIPROCALS; PRIVATE PASSENGER AND COMMERCIAL AUTOMOBILE LIABILITY

[In percent]

	Tort system	No-fault
Operating expense (commissions, other acquisition, general administrative, and taxes)	26	26.0
Loss adjustment	[1] 12	[2] 9.5
Losses incurred	60	60.0
Underwriting profit	2	4.5
Total	100	100.0

[1] Actual.
[2] Estimated.

Period 1963 through 1973, stock insurance company loss ratios—all-company ratio of losses incurred to total premium

```
                                                        Loss incurred
                                                        ratio (percent)
Type of insurance:
    Automobile liability_____  64.1
    Automobile physical damage_____  59.2
    Ocean marine_____  67.9
    Inland marine_____  55.5
    Homeowner's multiple peril_____  59.6
    Commercial multiple peril_____  50.3
    Fire_____  54.8
    Allied lines_____  53.8
    Miscellaneous liability_____  51.0
    Glass_____  50.4
    Nongroup accident and health_____  49.5
    Fidelity_____  48.7
    Burglary and theft_____  47.8
    Credit_____  46.4
    Boiler and machinery_____  36.2
    Surety_____  29.2
Group Insurance:
    Group accident and health_____  84.0
    Workmen's compensation_____  65.2
```

HOW NO-FAULT BILLS SATISFY AIA CRITERIA FOR DESIRABLE REFORM

Criteria	S. 354	H.R. 8441	H.R. 1272	H.R. 1900
1. Unlimited medical, hospital and rehabilitation benefits; sufficient wage replacement and reasonable household services coverage.	Yes	No	Yes	Yes
2. Abolition of lawsuits for compensable economic loss; restriction of suit for noneconomic loss to cases of death, serious injury or disfigurement, or more than 90 days of total disability.	Yes	No	Yes	Yes
3. Transfer of loss costs based on fault restricted to cases involving both private passenger and commercial vehicles.	Yes	No	Yes	No
4. Primacy of compulsory no-fault auto insurance coverage over other benefit sources.	Yes	Yes	No	No
5. Establishment of Federal minimum standards for State laws, rather than preemptive federal system.	Yes	Yes	No	Yes

Mr. STUCKEY. Thank you, Mr. Jones. We certainly appreciate your statement. It is always good to have you appear before the committee. Maybe this will be the last time for all of us. I think it is both yours and my fourth time around.

Mr. Rinaldo.

Mr. RINALDO. Thank you, Mr. Chairman.

Mr. Jones, in your statement the concept of a reckless driver not being liable to a third party disturbs me. Don't you think this complete nonliability will, among other things, have an extremely adverse effect on people's driving habits?

Mr. JONES. No, Mr. Rinaldo. I would urge you to read one of the studies that was done on a contract basis for the Department of Transportation in that comprehensive study they did. Their study sought to determine if the insured tort liability system had operated in such a way as to make people more careful. It found that because we let a man transfer any obligation he has to the insurance company by buying his insurance, he has escaped the impact of that liability and hence its potential deterrent effect.

One professor in California says the combination of liability and insurance is born in sin, in that the law has said there is legal liability for the person, but then we let him buy liability insurance at the same rate as other people in his classification and in his territory, and he transfers that liability away from him; so there is no impact on him as an individual to make him drive more carefully.

Mr. RINALDO. Are you saying that personal injury actions, and any additional liability does not serve to deter a reckless driving attitude?

Mr. JONES. We don't think there is any evidence that it does, and the DOT study showed there is no evidence that it did.

We have always been an industry that strongly supported enforcement of the traffic laws and police enforcement of traffic laws, and we think that is where the reckless driver should be dealt with.

Mr. RINALDO. We are also speaking of a deterrent that creeps into that system as a result of a person assuming liability. For example, there is an analogy between the facts in the study and the broad spectrum of people in this country that argue against the death penalty. On the other hand, there is another group who feel that the death penalty in the case of murder presents a certain deterrent.

In the case at hand when you say that you prefer that the reckless driver assume no additional liability, then you are removing, as far as I am concerned, a deterrent to a person's or I should say even an incentive to go out and become a better driver.

Furthermore, if the philosophy on which you predicate your statement is correct, then, of course, we might as well do away with point systems in existence in many of our States.

Mr. JONES. Not at all. Under this first-party system, the point system would be more significant and work better. There is nothing under the liability system in terms of classification and penalizing a bad driver that cannot be accomplished under the first-party system. You are doing it directly.

You are concerned about that driver and what his past experience is and if his past experience under whatever system a State has justifies a higher classification, you will be giving him a higher classification.

Mr. RINALDO. Then you feel that all types of noneconomic detriment could possibly be devised into some sort of schedule?

Mr. JONES. We think that is possible.

In effect, you do that in the workmen's compensation system.

Mr. RINALDO. In effect, you do, but in workmen's compensation, you have scheduled injuries for example, for an arm; they award you x amount of dollars for the arm. But in most cases where there is arm loss they also throw in a neurological claim because they feel the schedule system does not compensate the injured person adequately.

Mr. JONES. One of the things that has been of interest to us is what the Swedish companies have done; and, of course, they operate under a completely different legal system. The Swedish companies pay for pain and suffering on a third-party basis. They have gotten together and have agreed among themselves as to what they will pay for different injuries, because they want to be sure not to pay the rich man more than the poor man for the same injury. So they have an informally developed schedule of payments that they make for pain and suffering. I am sure it is not always equal, but they try to make it equal for equivalent injuries. A schedule of benefits enables an insurer to control costs while compensating for pain and suffering.

Mr. RINALDO. You cause me pain and suffering because I disagree with this part of your testimony.

Thank you, Mr. Chairman.

Mr. BRODHEAD [presiding]. Thank you, Mr. Rinaldo.

My name is Bill Brodhead, and I am a member of the committee and I am acting as chairman for a while.

I want to say that, for the benefit of our witnesses, that the reason that there are so few of us here is that the full committee, Interstate and Foreign Commerce Committee, has two bills up on the floor, being debated right now, the disapproval of the President's decontrol, and also H.R. 7014, the Energy Conservation and Oil Policy Act, which is also on the floor. That is the reason why so many of the Members are finding it difficult to be here.

At this point, our counsel, Mr. Kinzler, has some questions.

Mr. KINZLER. Thank you, Mr. Chairman.

Mr. Jones, if I understand you correctly, you do not suggest that a workmen's compensation type pain and suffering schedule should be in place of the threshold permitting recovery in suits of death, dismemberment, permanent serious injury, so forth, the provisions in H.R. 1900 and S. 354?

Mr. JONES. The schedule could be an alternative to lawsuits, or they could be there together. But it would seem to us that if you took the approach of having noneconomic loss compensated for on a schedule of benefit basis, you might consider substituting it in place of any sort of threshold or any sort of tort action.

Mr. KINZLER. But it would be, in the first instance, a mandatory offering and only if you choose it would you then lose your right to recover; is that correct?

Mr. JONES. That could be done, yes. That would be an appropriate way to do it.

Mr. KINZLER. In your statement you indicated the basic objective of a no-fault reparations system is restoration of a person injured in auto accidents.

Does this mean you view unlimited medical and rehabilitation coverage as the most important element of a no-fault plan?

Mr. JONES. Yes. That is the great virtue of a no-fault plan. We are in a position to provide complete protection for medical and rehabilitation costs. We think it is entirely reasonable within the total insurance system to do it. That would be the greatest beneficial change over the existing tort liability system.

If you will recall from the DOT study it is the seriously injured person that fares the poorest under the existing system. No-fault would give him the assurance that he was going to get all of the medical care he needed when he was seriously injured, and that his family would be able to pay the bills if he were unable to work.

Mr. KINZLER. About how much would it cost on the average premium for unlimited medical coverage, as compared to a $50,000 or $100,000 "cap" on medical?

Mr. JONES. We had various companies tell us they didn't think it was going to cost over 1 percent more in fact less than 1 percent more, to cover medical above $50,000 in expenses. They also said it would be less than what they have to pay for workmen's compensation medical, because the type of injury that they get out of the workplace is much more the kind that makes for long-term disability than they have out of automobile accident cases.

Mr. KINZLER. I would like to come back for a second to the reinsurance question. I note from your testimony you don't place very much credence in the difficulties there, but assuming that the committee were to determine that there was a legitimate reinsurance difficulty, let me pose the same question I posed to Mr. Cook. Would it be possible to solve that problem by simply having a greater pooling of people so as to handle it on a statewide basis?

Mr. JONES. Yes. You definitely could.

You could set up some all-industry mechanism, or you could enact legislation like the Federal Riot Reinsurance System, which gives you the ultimate protection of spreading the cost over the broadest base.

Mr. KINZLER. And under both H.R. 1900 and H.R. 8441, the States would be free to do such a thing if they saw this as a problem, would they not?

Mr. JONES. As I understand the bills, yes.

Mr. KINZLER. In your statement you say that any no-fault bill should contain wage replacement sufficient for most accidents.

Now wage replacement, of course, is something which varies from State to State, likely medical problems, which are similar in any given State. How high would you suggest that this amount be? There is $15,000 in the Senate bill and H.R. 1900. Is there some kind of magic figure here or could we go higher or lower than that?

Mr. JONES. You could easily go higher or lower. A lower limit would cover a substantial amount of the loss involved, but would also lead to more lawsuits. Our original proposal was to cover wage loss, without time limitations, but with what we call an internal limit of $750 a month. Really, that amount would have then covered most of the accidents and we felt that any grading under that amount could be taken care of by classification. We recommended that people be permitted to buy coverage for amounts beyond the $750 basic monthly limit.

We have supported laws on the State level that placed a time limit on wage loss protection, or even combined it with the medical expenses, because it is possible to cover the entire wage loss in a large percentage of accidents with a low figure.

So the subcommittee could use a lower figure than $15,000 as long as the bill permitted us to sell amounts greater than that to people that need it. But our preference would be for the higher figure, to keep most cases in the first-party system.

Mr. KINZLER. So your suggestion, basically is that H.R. 1900 and S. 354 are minimum standards bills; that unlimited medical is really a minimum standards, but that the wage loss is something that the subcommittee could raise or lower.

Mr. JONES. That is right.

Mr. KINZLER. One final question:

You have been kind enough to raise for the first time, I think except for Mr. Eckhardt's bill, of course, the question of no-fault property damage in these hearings.

As you know, the Florida Supreme Court ruled their so-called triple option unconstitutional. Of course, we have lost two members of that Supreme Court since then. But would you suggest, or would you be suggesting a double option whereby people are given a choice between no-fault or the existing system so that in no case would they be worse off than they presently are? Is that what you had in mind?

Mr. JONES. Well, we support the triple option. We support it as the best alternative to make available.

The double option that our companies would prefer, and that, I think would work over time—although there are a lot of people in the industry that disagree with us—would be that you either purchase collision coverage or you choose to be uninsured or self-insured. But tort liability would be eliminated. If you give the man an election to retain his tort rights or to go to the first-party system, I think you don't give him enough options. If you do what you propose, you are either going to have a pretty complicated assigned case plan or you are going to make me, if I elect to buy collision coverage, do what I do today and also buy property damage liability coverage.

What we were trying to do in our proposal was to let you substitute your first-party collision coverage for your property damage liability coverage.

If you give the other man the right to elect to stay under the tort system, then you either have to continue to carry property damage liability or the State has to see that an assigned case plan is set up to which the person electing tort, involved in an accident with someone that has not elected tort can go to have his claim handled. That would be what the assigned case plan would do.

Mr. KINZLER. Perhaps, then, you could remedy some of that by permitting a fairly high deductible?

Mr. JONES. They tried to use a deductible in Florida.

Mr. KINZLER. A deductible with an obligatory mandatory purchasing as opposed to a separate one?

Mr. JONES. Yes.

Mr. BRODHEAD. Thank you, sir.

Mr. JONES. Thank you, sir.

Mr. BRODHEAD. I will point out to the other people here that a transcript is being made of this testimony today and it will be available within 48 hours to all members of the committee.

Mr. Blume, are you ready, sir?

Will you state your name and address for the record, please?

STATEMENT OF PAUL BLUME, VICE PRESIDENT AND GENERAL COUNSEL, NATIONAL ASSOCIATION OF INDEPENDENT INSURERS

Mr. BLUME. My name is Paul Blume, vice president and general counsel of the National Association of Independent Insurers.

In the interest of time, Mr. Chairman, I will just highlight two features of my statement and file the statement for the record.

The two features I would like to highlight are the State versus Federal issue and the small company issue, if it would please the committee.

Mr. BRODHEAD. That is fine. If you like, your full text will be entered into the record.

Mr. BLUME. Yes, Mr. Chairman. Those two features of my statement appear on pages 6 and 18 of the full statement.

Mr. BRODHEAD. Fine. Without objection, your full statement will be entered into the record.

Mr. BLUME. Thank you, Mr. Chairman.

Mr. Chairman and members of the subcommittee, we appreciate this opportunity to comment on H.R. 1272, H.R. 1900, and other motor vehicle no-fault insurance acts that are before this committee.

The basic position of our association and its member companies on this issue can be summarized as follows: (1) We favor constructive reform of the existing automobile accident reparation system. (2) We believe such reform can and should be accomplished by the States, with ample opportunity for reasonable experimentation. (3) We are opposed to congressional imposition upon the States of a federally conceived no-fault system either directly or by promulgation of mandatory standards for State action.

The main reasons for our opposition to the concept embodied in both H.R. 1272 and H.R. 1900 are:

The States have already moved to solve the reparations problem, with 24 States representing over half the population in the United States passing legislation to improve their tort systems.

These bills would create an additional costly and duplicative Federal bureaucracy at a time when the existing bureaucracy is already being closely scrutinized and criticized by both the White House and Congress as being too costly and remote from the people.

States are far better equipped to determine the local needs and desires of their people and should be permitted to develop plans fitted to such needs.

Insurance costs will increase substantially and would cost the American public $1.25 billion in increased insurance premiums.

A Federal no-fault system would be particularly harmful to the small and medium-sized companies and would deprive the public of the market capacity and competition that has historically been provided by this segment of the industry.

Provisions in the Federal bills making auto insurance secondary for medical expenses would create costly and duplicative procedures that would be better left to the source that pays most of the loss— the auto insurer.

The issue of whether the State or the Federal Government should handle the development of auto accident reparation systems in the several States and the attendant responsibility for regulation of the insurance covering autos is, to our way of thinking, the basic one facing this Congress.

The no-fault bills before you, both H.R. 1272 and H.R. 1900 and its companion in the Senate, S. 354, would take this authority away from the States. No longer would the traditional right of States to design their own tort systems be harbored there. Instead, they would either have to develop laws in conformity with set standards as prescribed in H.R. 1900, or this right would be completely preempted as in H.R. 1272. We deem this drastic change both unnecessary and completely undesirable.

First of all, under the traditional concepts of federalism, Congress normally does not act in an area that is covered by State law unless the States have neglected or refused to act. This is just not the case here.

Twenty-four States representing over half the population of the United States have enacted changes in their reparation systems to deal with the problem, and the remaining 26 States are giving the subject careful study and consideration.

Some critics say that the States are not moving fast enough. In answer, we would submit that serious consideration by the States of well over 600 no-fault measures and action in 24 States to date is a commendable record. This is especially so when one considers that it was only a few years ago that the DOT report was presented, and that the task confronting the States is so difficult—involving as it does the reordering of a cluster of vital, deeply rooted rights, responsibilities, and relationships.

There have been countless instances we could point to where the Congress itself has wrestled for many, many years with problems of no greater complexity than this one before taking definitive action. And we repeatedly witness instances of sharp disagreement within the Congress as to which of many proposed solutions to a problem best serves the public interest—including the no-fault problem itself. The State legislatures should therefore not be criticized for taking the time and care they find necessary to shape the solutions to this intricate and controversial issue that they believe best serve the interests of their citizens.

There are many aspects of no-fault that the experts in government, the industry, the bar, or even consumer groups know nothing about. How well does a partial limitation on a person's right operate, and to what extent should these rights be limited? What is the actual cost of first-party benefits, and should there be limits on such benefits? How well do the compulsory features work, and what is the cost of policing? Does the assigned claims plan adequately fill the gap? These and many more questions can only be answered in the real world of actual operation of no-fault plans. The States provide an excellent laboratory for experimenting with the many features that have been developed for the first time under no-fault experimentation without the costs contemplated in a 50-State program on an all-or-nothing basis. As Secretary Coleman stated in his testimony:

The State governments and legislatures can provide invaluable experimentation, innovation, and wisdom in the development of social policy. But we will stifle this resource with excessive intervention.

Already, State experimentation is developing invaluable experience data in such areas as unlimited benefits, overutilization, fraud, malingering, and other abuses, cost, and policing. These data will prove to be exceptional resources and tools in the further development of meaningful reform. On this basis alone, the experiment should be permitted to continue.

One aspect of this whole issue of State versus Federal management of auto operation is of vital importance to us; namely, regulation of insurance.

In H.R. 1272 it is fairly clear that responsibility for such regulation rests with the Federal Government.

In H.R. 1900 it is equally, if not more certain that the Federal Government will usurp the power of States in several important categories and create a dual system of regulation with all of the corresponding costs and burdens on the industry and the public.

We feel this is entirely contrary to the mandate of the McCarran-Ferguson Act which provides:

. . . the Congress hereby declares the continued regulation and taxation by the several States of the business of insurance is in the public interest.

It is certain from this language the policy of Congress is that the States should regulate the insurance business and not the Federal Government. This policy has been reviewed several times over the years, particularly by the Senate committee and there has not been up to this time any suggestion for change in the policy. Yet, under this legislation, the authors have attempted to erode away such authority under the guise of reformation and reform.

As was so succinctly put last year by the President of NAIC, the National Association of Insurance Commissioners, Mr. Johnnie Caldwell, of Georgia, I quote:

In short, the power to determine complaince with title II, coupled with pervasive investigatory and reporting authority, in fact transfers to the Federal Government far-reaching regulatory authority over automobile insurance. Such authority could be used to cover virtually every aspect of an automobile insurer's activities and the operation of State insurance departments. Furthermore, S. 354 mandates the States to establish certain regulatory mechanisms which would be continually subject to federal review. As currently structured, S. 354 is designed to circumvent the long-standing policy espoused in the McCarran Act.

Congress has spoken through the McCarran-Ferguson Act that the regulation of insurance by the several States is in the public interest.

We see no reason to change this policy either directly or indirectly. The States have evidenced expertise and ingenuity in regulating insurance and the no-fault injury law should not do indirectly what Congress has not seen fit to do directly—erode away another cornerstone State authority that has served the public responsibly over the years.

Not only is this contrary to congressional policy and an erosion of State authority, but from a practical standpoint, we can foresee the creation of a costly duplicative Federal bureaucracy that will do nothing more than generate redtape and additional expenses to the detriment of the public and the insurance business alike.

There have been several articles recently on the services performed by government as compared to the promises made by those who supported those programs. Governor Brown of California, in an interview for Newsweek magazine, said:

> Action has been the catchword but people feel that things are being done to them, not for them. Sometimes non-action is better. Sometimes we need fewer programs, less planning, more space to live our lives.

Here, there is enough action. States have been moving to solve the reparations problem. Action by the Federal Government here will end up by extending that feeling of things being done to the public rather than for the public with the unnecessary and needless additional costs created by this legislation.

President Ford said recently, and I quote:

> Government regulation has become counterproductive and remote from the needs and interests of businesses and consumers alike.

The creation of an additional level of regulation of the insurance business in Washington would seem to us to fit this description very well. The States are not as remote from their people and have proven capability for regulating the insurance business. Such regulation should remain there.

Now, with respect to the small company problem, consider the state of the property-casualty industry at this moment:

In 1974, the industry suffered its largest underwriting loss in history—over $2.5 billion. The combined loss and expense ratio of the industry was the worst it has been since the Depression year of 1932.

Companies lost in the neighborhood of $6 billion due to the depreciation of their investments, and policyholders' surplus—the financial backup that determines how much business we can write—was reduced by 24 percent as of year's end 1974. The first two quarters of 1975 are proving to be even worse as far as underwriting results are concerned.

In these circumstances, more than ever, our industry can ill afford to risk the open-ended new exposures to loss which H.R. 1272 and H.R. 1900 (S. 354) will thrust upon them. And whereas in previous testimony we mentioned this concern principally in the context of the small companies, today we extend that concern to many medium-sized and larger companies.

Small companies will still be the hardest hit by this legislation. They will be placed at a serious if not fatal competitive disadvantage by the generous procedural and tooling-up burdens imposed under the bill, and by the nationally dictated regulatory controls and regimentation that will follow its enactment as surely as night follows day. And they will be the least able to withstand the traumatic impact of a succession of catastrophic medical/disability losses, or the tremendous increase in reinsurance premiums needed to provide at least a partial layer of protection against such losses. This has been documented not only by company executives themselves in testimony before this committee and the Senate Commerce Committee, but also by a statement filed with the chairman of the Senate Commerce Committee by Charles W. Havens III, president of the Reinsurance Association of America. He said, simply stated:

> The seriousness and frequency of injuries requiring extensive medical expenses in excess of $50,000 have been greater than anticipated. This has resulted in some primary companies experiencing significant increases in their reinsurance costs . . .

But a number of recent developments indicate that these adverse consequences won't be limited to small companies. The highly inflationary impact of this legislation as projected by Allstate, coupled with the general inflationary forces already at work pushing up the prices of the basic ingredient of auto insurance, such as medical/hospital care costs, will make it difficult if not impossible for companies of all sizes to keep rates in tune with loss trends. We have just seen the surpluses of some of the very large companies—particularly those which have been in the habit of relying on investment gains to offset bad underwriting results—drop to dangerously low levels in relation to their current premium volumes. A continued worsening of operating losses—which this legislation would bring—could force those companies either to sharply cut their book of auto insurance business or face serious financial trouble. Either of those contingencies—one a market capacity crisis and the other an insolvency threat—is a peril with grave consequence to our business, and more important, to the public.

For the reasons we have set forth, we respectfully urge Congress not to adopt this legislation which would establish a Federal automobile accident no-fault system or impose mandatory no-fault standards upon the States. We, on our part, will continue to work diligently for constructive reform and improvement of the State automobile accident reparations systems in the light of the growing body of real-world experience being developed under the various State no-fault programs.

That concludes my oral statement, Mr. Chairman, and I will be happy to answer any questions.

[Mr. Blume's prepared statement follows:]

STATEMENT OF THE NATIONAL ASSOCIATION OF INDEPENDENT INSURERS

We appreciate this opportunity to comment on HR-1272 and HR-1900, the proposed No-Fault Motor Vehicle Insurance Acts. The basic position of our Association and its member companies on this issue can be summarized as follows: (1) We favor constructive reform of the existing automobile accident reparation system. (2) We believe such reform can and should be accomplished by the states, with ample opportunity for reasonable experimentation. (3) We are opposed to Congressional imposition upon the states of a federally-conceived no-fault system either directly or by promulgation of mandatory standards for state action.

The main reasons for our opposition to the concepts embodied in both HR-1272 and HR-1900 are:

The states have already moved to solve the reparations problem with 24 states representing over half the population in the United States passing legislation to improve their tort systems.

These bills would create an additional costly and duplicative federal bureaucracy at a time when the existing bureaucracy is already being closely scrutinized and criticized by both the White House and Congress as being too costly and remote from the people.

States are far better equipped to determine the local needs and desires of their people and should be permitted to develop plans fitted to such needs.

Insurance costs will increase substantially and would cost the American Public $1.25 billion in increased insurance premiums.

A federal no-fault system would be particularly harmful to the small and medium-sized companies and would deprive the public of the market capacity and competition that has historically been provided by this segment of the industry.

Provisions in the federal bills making auto insurance secondary for medical expenses would create costly and duplicative procedures that would be better left to the source that pays most of the loss—the auto insurer.

NAII is a voluntary national trade association of almost 600 insurers.[1] Our organization is truly a "melting pot" of the casualty and fire insurance business

---

[1] 411 members and 184 statistical subscribers.

in America. Our members range in size from the smallest one-state companies to the very largest national writers; they comprise both stock and non-stock corporations; they reflect all forms of merchandising—independent agency, exclusive agency, and direct writers; and they include insurers which serve a general market and those which specialize in serving particular consumer groups such as farmers, teachers, government employees, military personnel and truckers.

The total automobile accident problem, of which today's subject is one part, has long been a matter of study and action by NAII and its companies. Our Association's comprehensive testimony and accompanying data presented in the 1969 investigation by the Congress into the subject of auto damages and repair costs helped launch the battle for better bumpers and saner auto design. We have continued our safety and loss prevention efforts through the years, the most recent example being the leadership provided by NAII early this year in testifying for the entire casualty insurance industry in opposition to the proposed rollback by the National Highway Traffic Safety Administration of their existing bumper standards. That testimony was instrumental in causing NHTSA to drop its rollback proposal and retain the 5 m.p.h. barrier test requirements.

This point is mentioned to demonstrate that while we have been giving a great deal of attention to the question of how to improve the systems for financially compensating the victims of auto accidents, we have by no means been neglecting the root problems of how to prevent accidents in the first place, and how to reduce injuries and vehicle damages in those accidents that do occur. Those problems, we believe, continue to merit top priority consideration.

MAJOR ISSUES TO BE DETERMINED IN THE NO-FAULT CONTROVERSY

The no-fault issue has been the subject now of continuous debate for almost 10 years and yet there is really no debate as between proponents and opponents on whether or not reparations reform is needed. Most, if not all of the participants have agreed that it is. The only real questions now are: First, what and how much to give in benefits and to take away in existing rights, and exactly which categories of consumer and accident victims are to do the receiving and which are to suffer the taking away. Secondly, which level of government is to develop and manage whatever system is finally decided upon. Third is cost. Fourth is the effect on competition; and fifth, who should be the primary benefit provider?

TYPE OF REFORM NEEDED

The first issue is one that constitutes a major source of uncertainty and disagreement surrounding the whole no-fault subject.

At one end of the spectrum are persons and groups who believe that the existing fault-based system has really very little wrong with it, and requires only minor improvements—procedural reforms to speed up the negotiation and adjudication process, and perhaps the required offering of a minimum amount of add-on no-fault benefits—but with no significant restrictions upon existing rights of recovery in tort.

At the other end of the spectrum are those who propose total or near-total abolition of the concept of personal accountability in tort and the right of recovery of general damages, and substitution of unlimited or very high limit no-fault benefits.

It is obvious that markedly different value judgments are used in arriving at these two diametrically opposite positions. Those who propose only minor adjustments in the present reparation system assert that the principles of accountability for negligence and right of recovery by innocent parties of all elements of damage are of such value as to justify the cost and time factors attached to them. If no-fault benefits are desired, they should be offered on an additive basis, according to this point of view.

Those at the other end of the spectrum view determinations of who is at fault in auto accidents to be not worth the time and cost involved. And they believe that the desirability of providing guaranteed economic loss payments for everyone, the negligent included, outweighs the desirability of preserving for each innocent accident victim the right of recovery for all elements of his damage against a negligent party.

There are those also who have taken a middle ground between the two extremes. NAII has taken this tack and we believe rightfully so.

Over the past several years we have been advocating improvements in auto reparation systems. We have, through a process of evolution been refining many of our ideas to aid lawmakers and officials at the state level in the experimentation process in every way possible toward achieving meaningful, middle-of-the-road no-fault reform. In this regard, we have developed programs in various states embodying the following principles:

A provision for payment of basic economic benefits directly to the injured insured on a timely basis.

A requirement that all insurers offer optional excess limits no fault coverage.

Cost-balancing provisions including restricting tort recovery for non-economic loss to the more serious injury cases—i.e., those exceeding a reasonable medical or time threshold or involving death, dismemberment, permanent disfigurement of serious permanent disability.

Recognition of the important concepts of auto insurance primacy, of coverage following the vehicle (with the insurer of the person secondarily liable) and of loss cost transfer by subrogation and mandatory inter-company arbitration.

Preservation of the existing right of recovery for negligently inflicted vehicle property damage.

Establishment of assigned claims plans to extend no-fault benefits to non-car owning families and to other categories of deserving but unprotected claimants.

Many of these principles have been adopted by the states in their efforts at reforming their individual systems and more are now considering them.

We believe there are many advantages to this approach: It greatly expedites the claim payment processes and increases the overall cost efficiency of the present system by compensating basic economic losses on a no-fault basis. It preserves tort recovery of excess economic losses, plus general damage in the more serious cases. It assures that motoring will pay its way by keeping auto insurance as the primary compensation source. And, by retaining the fault concept, it preserves personal accountability and assures that the greatest proportionate share of the auto accident premium burden will remain on the shoulders of those who cause most of the accidents and losses.

STATE VERSUS FEDERAL MANAGEMENT OF THE AUTO ACCIDENT REPARATIONS PROBLEM

The issue of whether the state or the federal government should handle the development of auto accident reparation systems in the several states and the attendant responsibility for regulation of the insurance covering autos is, to our way of thinking, the basic one facing this Congress.

Both HR-1272 and HR-1900 and its companion in the Senate, S-354, would take this authority away from the states. No longer would the traditional right of states to design their own tort systems be harbored there. Instead, they would either have to develop laws in conformity with set standards as prescribed in HR-1900 or this right would be completely preempted as in HR-1272. We deem this drastic change both unnecessary and completely undesirable.

State action

First of all, under the traditional concepts of Federalism, Congress normally does not act in an area that is covered by state law unless the states have neglected or refused to act. This is just not the case here. Twenty-four states representing over half the population of the United States have enacted changes in their reparation systems to deal with the problem and the remaining 26 states are giving the subject careful study and consideration.

Some critics say that the states are not moving fast enough. In answer we would submit that serious consideration by the states of well over 600 no-fault measures and action in 24 states to date is a commendable record. This is especially so when one considers that it was only a few years ago that the DOT Report was presented and that the task confronting the states is so difficult—involving as it does the re-ordering of a cluster of vital, deeply-rooted rights, responsibilities and relationships.

There have been countless instances we could point to where the Congress itself has wrestled for many, many years with problems of no greater complexity than this one before taking definitive action. And we repeatedly witness instances of sharp disagreement within the Congress as to which of many proposed solutions to a problem best serves the public interest—including the no-fault problem itself. The state legislatures should therefore not be criticized for taking the time and care they find necessary to shape the solutions to this intricate and controversial issue that they believe best serve the interests of their citizens.

There are many aspects of no-fault that the experts in government, the industry, the Bar or even consumer groups know nothing about. How well does a partial limitation on a person's right operate and to what extent should these rights be limited? What is the actual cost of first party benefits and should there be limits on such benefits? How well do the compulsory features work and what is the cost of policing? Does the assigned claims plan adequately fill the gap? These and many more questions can only be answered in the real world of actual operation of no-fault plans. The states provide an excellent laboratory for experimenting with the many features that have been developed for the first time under no-fault—experimentation without the costs contemplated in a 50-state program on an all or nothing basis. As Secretary Coleman stated in his testimony:

"The state governments and legislatures can provide invaluable experimentation, innovation and wisdom in the development of social policy. But we will stifle this resource with excessive intervention."

Already, state experimentation is developing invaluable experience data in such areas as unlimited benefits, over-utilization, fraud, malingering and other abuses, cost and policing. These data will prove to be exceptional resources and tools in the further development of meaningful reform. On this basis alone the experiment should be permitted to continue.

Uniformity

One contention encountered repeatedly is that federal no-fault or federally-dictated state no-fault standards are needed because basic countrywide uniformity in the reparation of auto accident losses is essential. Uniformity is said to be desirable in order to avoid confusion and uncertainty that would allegedly be engendered by a multiplicity of non-complementary state systems.

This same argument is advanced each time a proposal is introduced calling for the handling of another state-exercised function to the federal government. If it were given full sway, we would soon no longer have a carefully balanced multi-level system of national and local government functions, as contemplated under our Constitution, but a system where every aspect of the daily lives of our citizens is controlled and directed out of Washington.

A certain amount of state-by-state individuality is and always has been a familiar characteristic of our way of government, and has been one of the sources of strength of our Federalist system. Rseaonable variety and experimentation in approach are necessary and desirable: They are especially appropriate where, as here, there are new and untried concepts to be tested, and where, as here, controversial issues are presented on which there is no easy, universally accepted answer.

It has been suggested that basic countrywide uniformity in reparation systems is needed to avoid confusion, uncertainty and chaos, as well as to eliminate possible burdens on interstate commerce. As best as we can tell, these contentions center mainly around a concern for the motorist engaged in interstate travel into a jurisdiction whose laws differ or may differ from those of his home state.

The problem is not a new one, of course. There have always been some differences among the various states on such matters as:

The basic laws and rules governing liability and rights of recovery (contributory versus comparative negligence systems, presence or absence of guest laws, varying wrongful death limits, etc.)

Whether or not auto insurance is compulsory, the minimum statutory limits of liability insurance coverage under such compulsory laws or under the financial responsibility laws, and variations in the procedures governing accidents under those laws.

Whether or not special funds or statutory coverages exist to protect against the uninsured motorist hazard.

These differences have not, to our knowledge, produced chaos, irresolvable uncertainties, or significant burdens on interstate commerce. This is largely because the automobile insurance industry has responded by providing in their policies for coverage in accordance with the tort laws and financial responsibility or compulsory laws of all states where the insured may travel.

Similarly, with the advent of state no-fault laws, the insurance companies have been rapidly expanding their coverage voluntarily to satisfy the requirements of the laws in all states into which their policyholders travel. Our industry, the state insurance departments and the state legislative committees are watchful of any possible coverage gaps or areas of vulnerability to interstate travelers which might arise under the new no-fault laws, and through the sum total of our and their efforts the problem has been rendered a de minimis one.

Accordingly we do not believe that immediate, countrywide uniformity in auto accident reparation laws is necessary to prevent chaos and undue burdens on interstate commerce. What is important is the fact that the state reparation systems and attendant insurance coverages now possess and will continue to possess *compatibility* for purposes of interstate travel. Out of state-by-state experimentation will, in due course, come increased uniformity—a sound degree of uniformity based on experience. This is exactly what was contemplated by the Department of Transportation in its March 1971 Report, which made the following recommendation:

"To explain further the kind of a system that we believe the States should now strive toward, it may be useful to describe what its *ultimate* configuration might look like following a suitable period of expirmentation and testing. *It should be emphasized that this is a goal to be achieved over time, not an action blueprint for tomorrow. Moving in stages toward such a goal would allow us to test its virtues and discover its faults, thereby giving us new knowledge that could serve to modify the goal itself. A little observation is worth a great deal of speculation, and State experience with diverse plans will provide us with that opportunity for pilot project testing which must precede massive reform.*

"This system, as we see it now, should be based on universal, compulsory first-party insurance for all motor vehicle owners covering all economic losses above voluntarily accepted deductibles up to reasonably high limits. Insurers should be free to offer additional insurance coverage above these limits. Victims should retain their present right to sue in tort for specified intangible losses, but the right should be restricted to the truly serious cases. Victims should not be able to sue in tort for economic losses compensated by their own insurers or voluntarily accepted as a deductible. *The system should be implemented in stages at the State level. The private insurance industry should service the system, which should continue to be regulated by the several States.*" (Italics supplied)

Constitutional questions

Attorney General Edward Levi in testimony before the Senate Commerce Committee outlined serious constitutional flaws in the federal minimum standards bill (HR-1900 and S-354). We had previously alluded briefly to these problems in testimony before the Senate Judiciary Committee, the Senate Commerce Committee and this Subcommittee and had retained Professor Philip Kurland of the University of Chicago for his expert testimony on this aspect of the bill. (Professor Kurland filed a statement with this Subcommittee's predecessor, the House Subcommittee on Commerce and Finance, copy of which is attached to this statement.)

It is readily apparent from the drastic changes made in the Senate Commerce Committee draft of S-354 that these problems were *not* imaginary.

We do not hold ourselves out as constitutional experts but the letter from Attorney General Levi to Senator Magnuson indicates that all constitutional questions have not been answered by the amendment. He says, "I know you realize that other constitutional challenges are made—as for example, the discrimination imposed by the differences between Title II and Title III. There remains also the legislative question as to the wisdom of the measure from the standpoint of Federalism."

Suffice it to say that serious consideration should be given to these questions before any action is taken on legislation such as HR-1900.

Federal regulation of auto insurance

One aspect of this whole issue of state vs. federal management of auto reparations is of vital importance to us—regulation of insurance. In HR-1272 it is fairly clear that responsibility for such regulation rests with the federal government. In HR-1900/S-354, it is equally if not more certain that the federal government will usurp the power of the states in several important categories and create a dual system of regulation with all of its corresponding costs and burdens on the industry and the public.

This is clearly contrary to the mandate of the McCarran-Ferguson Act (Public Law 15, 78th Congress) which provided:

". . . the Congress hereby declares that the continued regulation and taxation by the several states of the business of insurance is in the public interest."

It is certain from this language that the policy of Congress is that the states should regulate the insurance business and not the federal government. This policy has been reviewed several times over the years, particularly by the Senate Antitrust and Monopoly Subcommittee and there has not up to this time been any suggestion to change that policy. Yet under HR-1272, HR-1900 (S-354), the authors have attempted to erode away such authority under the guise of reparations reform. As was so succinctly put last year by the then President of the NAIC, Mr. Johnnie Caldwell of Georgia:

"In short, the power to determine compliance with Title II, coupled with pervasive investigatory and reporting authority, in fact, transfers to the federal government far-reaching regulatory authority over automobile insurance. Such authority could be used to cover virtually every aspect of an automobile insurer's activities and the operation of state insurance departments. Furthermore, S-354 mandates the states to establish certain regulatory mechanisms which would be continually subject to federal review. As currently structured, S-354 is designed to circumvent the long-standing policy espoused in the McCarran Act."

Congress has spoken through the McCarran-Ferguson Act that the regulation of insurance by the several states is in the public interest. We see no reason to change this policy directly or indirectly. The states have evidenced expertise and ingenuity in regulating insurance and the no-fault issue should not indirectly do what Congress has not seen fit to do directly—erode away another cornerstone of state authority that has served the public responsibly over the years.

Not only is this contrary to Congressional policy and an erosion of state authority, but from a practical standpoint, we can foresee the creation of a costly duplicative federal bureaucracy that will do nothing more than generate red-tape and additional expenses to the detriment of the public and the insurance business alike.

There have been several articles recently on the services performed by government as compared to the promises that were made by those who supported those programs. Governor Brown of California, in an interview for Newsweek Magazine said, "Action has been the catchword but people feel that things are being done to them, not for them. Sometimes non-action is better. Sometimes we need fewer programs, less planning, more space to live our lives."

Here, there is enough "action". States have been moving to solve the reparations problem. Action by the federal government here will end up by extending that feeling of things being done to the public rather than for the public with the unnecessary and needless additional costs created by this legislation.

President Ford said recently:

"Government regulation has become counter-productive and remote from the needs and interests of businesses and consumers alike."

The creation of an additional level of regulation of the insurance business in Washington would seem to us to fit this description very well. The states are not as remote from their people and have proven capability for regulating the insurance business. State regulation should remain there.

Cost of Auto Insurance Under Federal No-Fault Proposals

The proponents of federal no-fault by their repeated promises of substantial cost savings have conditioned American consumers to expect large cuts in their premiums. This, we believe, is a serious distortion of the basic facts.

Originally, the predecessor bill to HR-1900 was costed by the firm of Milliman and Robertson back in 1973. Their analysis was relied on by proponents of the legislation up to early 1975 even though several key features of the legislation had been changed and additional analysis and new cost data had been provided both by ourselves and the Allstate Insurance Company, one of our members, in testimony before this Subcommittee.

(For details of this analysis, see testimony of Arthur C. Mertz, Executive Vice President of the NAII, before the House Subcommittee on Commerce and Finance on July 14, 1974.)

Essentially, we had determined that the Milliman and Robertson costing was seriously deficient in several respects including the failure to begin with actual existing rates in every state; the failure to cost out commercial and private passenger automobile separately; and faulty assumptions on the ratio of general to special damages, increased utilization of medical benefits and the losses of irresponsible motorists forced to purchase coverage under the compulsory provisions.

This was buttressed further by Allstate's costing of the bill for 10 states initially and finally for all 50 states completed for submission to the Senate Commerce Committee on April 30, 1975. Their figures indicated massive auto personal injury rate hikes—ranging all the way up to 97%—in 45 states, and only trivial reductions in the other six states. We estimated an overall increase of some $1.25 billion annually. While these cost projections would still apply to the House version of the bill, HR-1900, the Senate version has been amended to reduce the threshold amount for subrogation from $5,000 to $100. This amendment, if it does what we think is intended, alters, to some degree, the Allstate cost estimates necessitating an updating of cost projections. This was done in a letter to Mr. Sutcliffe, Counsel to the Senate Commerce Committee, dated July 3, 1975.

Still, even with this adjustment, the cost of auto liability insurance will be raised substantially—all the way to 76%. Again applying these projections on an overall basis, the cost to the American public would be approximately $250 million. (A copy of the cost projections by Allstate is appended to this statement.)

There is a substantial difference of opinion on this matter of cost. The proponents of the bill now have finally completed their own costing with, of course, diametrically opposite views. Basically, the difference lies in assumptions on survivor's benefits and increased utilization of medical benefits. Allstate uses a $15,000 assumption for survivor's benefits and a 20% higher assumption for increases in utilization in the medical portion of personal injury protection, while the proponents use $5,000 and no assumption for over-utilization.

These Allstate assumptions are, in our opinion, far more realistic because they more accurately reflect the experience generated in the real world of present no-fault states and the intent of the legislation. Certainly in a proposal that would provide unlimited medical benefits and $15,000 in wage loss benefits, the authors would not suggest that survivors receive only $5,000. As was brought in the Allstate letter, the National Conference of Commissioners on Uniform State Laws in drafting UMVARA (the model from which HR-1900 and S-354 were adapted) recommended that survivor's benefits equal wage loss benefits. It should also be noted that in the two states that presently have unlimited medical benefits and are the closest to the federal minimum standards bill, the survivor loss benefits are equal to the income loss benefits.

With respect to increased utilization, we feel that the Allstate factor is absolutely necessary in any costing of no-fault, particularly where there are unlimited medical benefits.

The evidence of increased utilization in other similar plans such as medicare and medicaid, the present indications that the medical profession, the hospitals and other health care providers are increasing utilization because of the threat of malpractice claims, and the evidence of fraud or malingering in some areas where no-fault is in effect, all lead to only one conclusion—that there will be an increase in utilization where the benefits are available, and that it should definitely be considered in any costing of the system.

We are firmly convinced that the benefits provided under HR-1272 and HR-1900 will lead to massive increases in private passenger personal injury premiums. Some people differ with this conclusion. We cannot believe, however, that this Committee or the Congress would embark on a sweeping, untested no-fault program on the basis of the cost evaluation record now before you. The uncertainty alone, particularly in these tough economic times, should be enough to make any legislator pause before plunging.

Impact of Federal No-Fault on Competition

In the light of these cost considerations, we submit that state-by-state experimentation and modification are the best and safest paths of reform. Safety and caution are more than ever imperative in the hazardous economic landscape that confronts us. Even a minor miscalculation here could be disastrous.

Consider the state of the property-casualty industry at this moment: In 1974, the industry suffered its largest underwriting loss in history—over $2.5 billion. The combined loss and expense ratio of the industry was the worst it has been since the Depression year of 1932.

Companies lost in the neighborhood of $6 billion due to the depreciation of their investments, and policyholders' surplus—the financial backup that determines how much business we can write—was reduced by 24 percent as of year's end 1974. The first two quarters of 1975 are proving to be even worse as far as underwriting results are concerned.

In these circumstances more than ever, our industry can ill afford to risk the open-ended new exposures to loss which HR-1272 and HR-1900 (S-354) will thrust on them. And whereas in previous testimony we mentioned this concern principally in the context of the small companies, today we extend that concern to many medium-sized and larger companies.

Small companies will still be the hardest hit by this legislation. They will be placed at a serious if not fatal competitive disadvantage by the onerous procedural and tooling-up burdens imposed under the bill, and by the nationally-dictated regulatory controls and regimentation that will follow its enactment as surely as night follows day. And they will be the least able to withstand the traumatic impact of a succession of catastrophic medical/disability losses, or the tremendous increase in reinsurance preminums needed to provide at least a partial layer of protection against such losses. This has been documented not only by company executives themselves in testimony before this Committee and the Senate Commerce Committee, but also by a statement filed with the Chairman of the Senate Commerce Committee by Charles W. Havens, III, President of the Reinsurance Association of. America. He said, "Simply stated, the seriousness and frequency of injuries requiring extensive medical expenses in excess of $50,000 have been greater than anticipated. This has resulted in some primary companies experiencing significant increases in their reinsurance costs. . . ."

But a number of recent developments indicate that these adverse consequences won't be limited to small companies. The highly inflationary impact of this legislation as projected by Allstate, coupled with the general inflationary forces already at work pushing up the prices of the basic ingredient of auto insurance, such as medical/hospital care costs, will make it difficult if not impossible for companies of all sizes to keep rates in tune with loss trends. We have just seen the surpluses of some of the very large companies—particularly those which have been in the habit of relying on investment gains to offset bad underwriting results—drop to dangerously low levels in relation to their current premium volumes. A continued worsening of operating losses—which this legislation would bring—could force those companies either to sharply cut their book of auto insurance business or face serious financial trouble. Either of those contingencies—one a market capacity crisis and the other an insolvency threat—is a peril with grave consequence to our business, and more important, to the public.

These considerations fortify the position earlier asserted that the only safe and sensible avenue to sound auto accident reparations reform is by additional experimentation and experience-gathering under the emerging forms of state no-fault programs. To make a countrywide plunge with a program of the magnitude contemplated in these bills would in our opinion be a most dangerous move.

Primary Benefit-Provider—Auto Insurance

HR-1272 and HR-1900 as presently constituted place in serious jeopardy the continued position of automobile insurance as the primary benefit source for automobile accidents. (The recent Senate Commerce Committee amendment to S-354 calling for states to institute programs for "coordination of benefits" among providers of no-fault insurance and other sources of coverage, does not in our view, alter this opinion.) These developments provide further grounds on which we strongly oppose this measure.

Our Association and other segments of the casualty-property insurance business have long urged that whenever the occasion arises for avoidance of duplication between benefit systems, automobile insurance coverage should remain the primary source of reparations for economic losses arising out of automobile accidents. This position is well grounded in terms of fundamental public policy as well as upon considerations of practical operational efficiency and simplicity.

Motoring serves important functions in our economy. At the same time, it subjects our society to serious hazards in the form of deaths and injuries, and to problems and burdens including traffic congestion, air and noise pollution, and consumption of natural resources.

Sound public policy dictates that to the greatest extent possible those who engage in a fundamentally dangerous or socially burdensome activity should shoulder the full costs of that activity.

It is because of this principle that our society requires the costs of compensation of workers injured in industrial accidents, the costs of abating factory-produced air pollution, and the costs of paying for injuries to consumers from defective products to be borne not by the victims or by the public at large but by the self-same enterprises whose activities create the hazards. Similarly, the principle has long been observed in this country that "motoring should pay its own way".

The auto owner or truck owner, of course, pays the full, non-subsidized cost of his vehicle upon purchase. Through gasoline taxes he supports the cost of maintenance of the highways he uses. And through the obligations imposed on him by state financial responsibility, no-fault and negligence laws, he is made to shoulder still another significant cost element attached to motoring—the cost of compensating the losses inflicted in the course of that pursuit.

In this connection, reference should be made to the tremendous, continuing contribution to the cause of vehicle and traffic safety being made by the automobile insurance industry, both through the work of the Insurance Institute for Highway Safety to which we contribute major support, and through the direct activities of our Association, its individual members, and others in our business. Those efforts have played a major role in bringing about significant improvements in which vehicle design and crashworthiness and in highway safety. They can be expected to reap even greater benefits for the public in the immediate future, provided our industry's very basis and motivation for injury and loss reduction is not destroyed by having much of its area of operations swallowed up by making other benefit sources primary.

As one additional particular in this regard, it should be noted that Section 205 of the Motor Vehicle Information and Cost Savings Act adopted by this Congress in 1972 gave explicit recognition to the unique and crucial role which automobile insurers can play in gathering vital accident data relating to the crashworthiness (and damageability) of different makes and models of automobiles. As the results of many months of meetings between our industry and the National Highway Traffic Safety Administration, certain of the types of data referred to in that Section are now being supplied to NHTSA, and it is contemplated that additional types of data will be furnished in the future.

As a practical matter, the kinds of vehicle accident information NHTSA needs and is requesting from auto insurers pursuant to this important statute could never be retrieved, developed or supplied by general health-care benefit providers. Were no-fault legislation to be adopted without preserving the primacy of automobile insurance in motor vehicle accident cases, we cannot visualize how the important obligations being shouldered by our industry under the Motor Vehicle Information and Cost Savings Act could continue to be properly and credibly fulfilled.

In conclusion, the principal reasons why we strongly urge recognition of the primacy of automobile insurance in any no-fault legislation are:

It will avoid needless duplication of benefits.

It will support the vital safety objectives underlying the Motor Vehicle Information and Cost Savings Act of 1972, and the National Traffic and Motor Vehicle Safety Act of 1966, as well as the many valuable safety programs and efforts engaged in by the automobile insurance business.

It will be consistent with such existing laws as the Federal Employees Liability Act and Title XIX of the Social Security Act (Medicaid) which provide for set-off or recoupment of benefits where a third party is legally liable.

It will be consistent with the primacy recommendations made by the Department of Transportation on the completion of its study of the auto accident reparations system.

It will keep all types and elements of losses arising out of the same automobile accident within one reparation system, thereby promoting efficiency, eliminating confusion, and expediting the entire claim-payment function.

In connection with the last point, we cannot emphasize too strongly the inefficiencies that would result from fragmentation of the various portions of the total losses arising in auto accidents. Shifting that portion of the losses to medical health or disability insurers would not in any way relieve auto insurers of any of their obligations to investigate, verify and pay claims covering all the other elements of loss covered by automobile insurance policies. Those other elements include, of course, a host of possible items such as residual health—care expenses, residual bodily injury liability, property damage liability and collision and comprehensive losses.

CONCLUSION

For the reasons we have set forth, we respectfully urge the Congress not to adopt HR-1272, HR-1900, or any other legislation which would establish a federal automobile accident no-fault system or impose mandatory no-fault standards upon the states. We on our part will continue to work diligently for constructive reform and improvement of the state automobile accident reparation systems in the light of the growing body of real-world experience being developed under the various state no-fault programs.

State:	Cost of S. 354 as favorably reported by Commerce Committee [1]	State—Continued	Cost of S. 354 as favorably reported by Commerce Committee [1]
Alabama	+18.1	Nebraska	+36.8
Alaska	+17.1	Nevada	+14.1
Arizona	+17.5	New Hampshire	−9.0
Arkansas	+9.5	New Jersey	+4.9
California	+2.9	New Mexico	+20.8
Colorado	+37.5	New York	−10.3
Connecticut	+2.0	North Carolina	+7.9
Deleware	+2.1	North Dakota	+39.8
Distict of Columbia	−10.4	Ohio	+7.4
Florida	+9.3	Oklahoma	+0.0
Georgia	+52.0	Oregon	+22.0
Hawaii	+3.2	Pennsylvania [3]	+24.8
Idaho	+34.3	Rhode Island	−11.4
Illinois	−7.3	South Carolina	+17.8
Indiana	+25.0	South Dakota	+36.3
Iowa	+24.1	Tennessee	−6.1
Kansas	+76.1	Texas	+10.5
Kentucky [2]	−7.9	Utah	+39.2
Louisiana	−1.0	Vermont	+28.7
Maine	+2.7	Virginia	+30.8
Maryland	−11.3	Washington	+18.2
Massachusetts	−11.6	West Virginia	+1.2
Michigan	−14.6	Wisconsin	+4.4
Minnesota	+45.5	Wyoming	+31.0
Mississippi	−2.1		
Missouri	−1.1	Countrywide	+4.4
Montana	+32.5		

[1] This pricing is based on those insureds who carry bodily injury liability, uninsured motorist coverage, medical payments, or personal injury protection coverage (PIP) in no-fault states, and any excess medical payments or excess PIP coverages. While these coverages are respresentative of approximately 85% of Allstate insureds, they substantially exceed those coverages required by law in most states. Thus, that group of insureds which carry only the minimum required by law, which presumably would include most low-income persons, will experience even greater price increases or lesser price decreases, depending on the state in question.

[2] Kentucky cost projections are based on Kentucky premium levels under that state's tort system. Optional no-fault program becomes effective in Kentucky July 1, 1975.

[3] Pennsylvania present premiums are based on projected no-fault costs as of July 19, 1974.

Mr. BRODHEAD. Thank you very much, Mr. Blume, for your most useful testimony.

Mr. Rinaldo.

Mr. RINALDO. No questions.

Mr. BRODHEAD. Mr. Kinzler.

Mr. KINZLER. Thank you, Mr. Chairman.

Mr. Blume, in your testimony, you indicate fully 24 States have moved to solve the reparations problem, but you don't indicate they moved to no-fault legislation. Would you contend that all 24 of those bills are no-fault laws?

Mr. BLUME. That depends on what you mean by "no-fault."

Mr. KINZLER. I ask, what is your definition?

Mr. BLUME. There are differences of opinion as to what no-fault is, and that depends on the State. We, of course, oppose some of this legislation, but we feel that the States should be left to their own devices as far as what they feel is necessary in the no-fault area.

Many people define no-fault as being first party benefits. Others define it as including some limitation on a person's tort rights. We feel that the States should be permitted to experiment with both devices.

As I said, we opposed some of the no-fault legislation that has occurred in the States, but quite frankly, we feel the experimentation will be useful.

Mr. KINZLER. Mr. Blume, do you consider the eight States which are called add-on States to be no-fault laws, and do you support them?

Mr. BLUME. As I indicated, we have not supported some of that legislation, and that includes add-on. As I said, we would prefer to leave the States to their own devices insofar as what plan they feel is necessary for their State.

Mr. KINZLER. That would include, if the State chooses to adopt no plan whatever, that would be perfectly fine?

Mr. BLUME. That is correct.

Mr. KINZLER. How long have the States been dealing with reforms of the reparations system as you define it?

Mr. BLUME. You can take two dates. I think Mr. Jones indicated that no-fault is not a new principle. It started way back in 1930's when the Columbia University study came out. I don't think any States at that time seriously considered no-fault legislation. I think the earliest date that I know of that a State considered no-fault was in 1969 in Massachusetts, but I think most of the States began to study no-fault seriously after the DOT study came out in 1971, which is approximately 4 years ago.

Mr. KINZLER. Right. There is an interesting summary in the recent report of the Senate Commerce Committee; a chart indicating that in 1967, the following States considered no-fault legislation: California, Illinois, Massachusetts, Michigan, Minnesota, New Jersey, and New York. Now, that is 8 years ago.

Mr. BLUME. You say "considered,' but I say they didn't seriously consider it until after the DOT study was submitted. I myself lobbied in Illinois in 1967, and sure, there was a bill introduced in Illinois, but I don't think it was even considered by a committee. We can all say that legislation has been introduced, but whether it was seriously considered is another question.

Mr. BRODHEAD. Excuse me. Would you characterize this as serious?

Mr. BLUME. Yes; I would.

Mr. BRODHEAD. All right, Mr. Kinzler, proceed.

Mr. KINZLER. I compliment the chairman for getting some agreement for the first time.

Mr. Blume, would you put any time limit whatsoever on State experimentation with respect to reforms to the auto insurance reparations system?

Mr. BLUME. That is an interesting question.

Mr. KINZLER. I thought it was.

Mr. BLUME. I have heard with interest some of the questions on that in previous hearings.

Quite frankly, I think it is very difficult to put a time limit on reform at the State level. Now, that is for this reason: You have varying dates on which no-fault automobile acts were enacted at the State level.

For example, in Michigan, I think the effective day of the Michigan law was October 1, 1973, about what—a year ago, or a year and a half ago, or 2 years ago—almost 2 years ago, and yet that is an unlimited medical benefit law, with a verbal threshold. I don't think you can characterize it as a medical threshold or time threshold. It is a verbal threshold, whatever that means.

I frankly think that law needs careful study for a period of time because many of those serious injury cases will not mature for quite some time.

I would hope the Congress would be more flexible in reviewing State action to no-fault similar to what they have done as far as insurance regulation itself is concerned.

For example, they have periodically reviewed whether the States are adequately regulating the insurance business. There is a lot of flexibility in the way they do it.

I would hope that Congress would consider that same policy in this area.

Mr. KINZLER. Mr. Blume, are you suggesting we really should not consider no-fault legislation not only now but not 10 years from now and not 20 years from now?

Mr. BLUME. Not necessarily.

Mr. KINZLER. OK. You say in your statement that the States are far better equipped to determine the local needs and desires of the people and should be permitted to develop plans fitted to such needs.

Can you tell me how the medical needs of the seriously injured victims vary between the States in such fashion so that the local States could fashion a more appropriate remedy than the Federal standard of unlimited medical benefits?

Mr. BLUME. I think you have to consider that question carefully with the costs at the State level. We happen to feel that the cost of unlimited medical benefits will be too high. In other words, we feel that people have champagne tastes with a beer pocketbook when you have unlimited medical benefits.

Mr. KINZLER. Would you subscribe to Allstate's costing of unlimited medical benefits or not?

Mr. BLUME. To a certain degree, yes, we would.

Well, I will say this first: There are some real world data now being presented that indicate thay they may be conservative.

For example, I think there was testimony earlier where it was said that reinsurance under the Michigan law where there is unlimited medical benefits would be very, very costly. Mr. William Fee of Employers Reinsurance Co. expressed that opinion in a recent speech.

I can even quote to you from that speech. He said the only way no-fault can succeed, in the public's opinion, is to achieve some premium reduction and with the facts coming to light now on the unexpected frequency and unexpected high cost of unlimited medical benefits, any premium reduction is highly unlikely.

It seems to me that, as I said, Allstate's figures may be in this situation conservative.

Mr. KINZLER. There have been three significant cost studies made, Milliman & Robertson, Allstate's and State Farm's, and are you stating you are not agreeing with any on unlimited benefits?

Mr. BLUME. We would agree with Allstate's up to now, but, as I said, there is other evidence.

Mr. KINZLER. How about considering it up to now for purposes of this question. According to Allstate's figures with unlimited benefits, with a higher factor than State Farm's for increased utilization of medical benefits, if one drops their assumption for survivors' benefits from $15,000 to $5,000 which is permissible under S. 354 and H.R. 1900, almost every single State would be in a minus category and if they drop it to $1,000 which is also permissible under the bills, the average would probably be closer to minus 19 percent nationally.

Mr. BLUME. First of all, I think you have to make a distinction between S. 354 passed out of the Senate committee.

Mr. KINZLER. I'm talking about this year's bill.

Mr. BLUME. This year's bill, H.R. 1900?

Mr. KINZLER. Let's talk about S. 354.

Mr. BLUME. That has the subrogation and I understand from Allstate, it will cost less. H.R. 1900 does not have the subrogation feature as S. 354 has. But, if you want to stay with S. 354?

Mr. KINZLER. Yes, I would, please.

Mr. BLUME. I would agree with Allstate that the $15,000 survivors benefit assumption is probably much more accurate than State Farm's and probably more realistic.

Mr. KINZLER. This is not a question of accuracy, but a matter of States with freedom to raise or lower the number.

The "reasonable" provision of the Senate bill indicates they can go as low as $1,000.

Mr. BLUME. That is right, but there is an indication in Allstate's letter that nine States had a survivors benefit equal to wage loss benefit, which is a minimum of $15,000 under S. 354.

Mr. KINZLER. Of those existing laws, also, only one of them I believe reaches the $15,000 level; so we are talking about apples and oranges, I suggest, Mr. Blume.

Mr. Blume, you talk about a minimum standards bill and here we have a provision which permits the States to adopt survivors' benefits at any level they chose down to about as low as $1,000, and you insist they go to $15,000 even though it would take a State like Nebraska from maybe minus 15 percent to plus 30 percent. That does not sound reasonable to me and I don't see how we can deal with that kind of assumption.

Mr. BLUME. I think it is fairly reasonable, a State there likeNebraska would go to a minimum, a person who is living as far as wage losses is concerned should get that amount. I think a $15,000 assumption is probably more reasonable.

Mr. KINZLER. You would support then not only unlimited medical benefits, but $15,000 for survivors and $15,000 for wage loss?

Mr. BLUME. No, sir.

Mr. KINZLER. I just wanted to understand you.

All right, Mr. Blume, your testimony spends a fair amount of time talking about support for the National Highway Traffic Safety Administration.

How would you respond to Mr. Calabresi's testimony that we will lose free market incentives for safety unless all States have no-fault laws?

Mr. BLUME. Well, I respect Mr. Calabresi as an eminent legal scholar, but I think, as I recall, I refer to the National Highway Transportation Safety Act and the statistics that were to be gathered there in the context of our efforts to be primary under any type of no-fault legislation and the fact that we have already developed statistical plans with the Federal Government to collect statistics, and we feel that that is the best and easiest way to collect them, by having the right to be primary and to be able to develop statistics on that basis. I don't think I referred to any other, did I?

Mr. KINZLER. You did, but for the sake of brevity, let me close with a couple of questions to keep it as short as possible.

In my never-ending search for an area in which we agree, Mr. Blume, let me say on page 12, you quote the Attorney General's letter to Senator Magnuson to the effect that all constitutional questions have not been answered by his suggested amendment.

Unfortunately, you did not quote the Attorney General's entire last sentence, and the missing first part reads, as follows: "While I believe this suggested amendment would answer the major constitutional questions in the bill," then you go on to quote the rest of it.

Is not the real meaning of the Attorney General's letter in the total context that he feels the amendment would answer the major constitutional questions, but other people raise other constitutional questions to which he does not personally subscribe?

Mr. BLUME. Well, you are making that statement. I read it differently. I felt there were other problems with the legislation, but it is matter of opinion.

Mr. KINZLER. Let me indicate the Attorney General was invited, and Mr. Kurland, who testified on behalf of NAII, was invited to appear, and Mr. Dorsen also was invited to appear before the subcommittee. All of these people raised constitutional objections in the past, and none of them have chosen to come before the committee.

My final question, and this is a very important question which we have dealt with all day long, and you deal with it in your statement, too, is the question of reinsurance.

In your testimony, you quote Mr. Havens, president of the Reinsurance Association of America, to the effect: "Some small companies are having reinsurance problems because of the high number of serious accidents."

I might point out Mr. Haven's letter did not suggest a $50,000 cap on benefits, and you did not either.

In fact, he told me yesterday the association reached no consensus on a figure, but they couldn't advance an argument for less than a $100,000 cap, because they would want even the most seriously injured persons to have a guarantee of prompt accident care to start back on the road to recovery.

If the subcommittee chooses to go ahead with a Federal minimum standards bill, how would you suggest we remedy any possible reinsurance problems?

Mr. BLUME. I feel that you could remedy it best by not having any legislation at all, but by having the States do their own thing.

It is a very difficult problem. I am not sure of what you are suggesting. Are you suggesting you are going to place a limit on the benefit levels in S. 354 or H.R. 1900?

Mr. KINZLER. What I suggest is if the cost between, say, $100,000 of medical benefits and unlimited medical is a reasonably small amount, say, 5 percent—and we have heard of lower figures—but the problem is that the small insurance company cannot absorb an aberrational year of bad losses. Is there not a way where we can, in effect, increase the pool so as to spread the risk over a larger number of people rather than deprive the consumer of benefits in case he happens to be in a $1 million accident?

Mr. BLUME. I don't see how you can do it on the Federal level, but on an individual State basis, as a matter of fact, it was suggested in New Jersey, and I am not necessarily subscribing to this, but I believe the Deputy Commissioner of Insurance in New Jersey suggested they use the unsatisfied claims and judgments fund as a pooling device for smaller companies. But I think it varies State by State, and that is why we feel there should be experimentation at the State level.

That is why we don't feel there should be any Federal standards or Federal legislation in the area.

Mr. KINZLER. If there indeed were Federal legislation, would you accept the H.R. 1900 and S. 354 approach, which would leave the particular matter entirely to the State?

Mr. BLUME. No, sir, we would oppose this.

Mr. KINZLER. That is not the question I asked. If there is Federal legislation?

Mr. BLUME. You mean if it were passed?

Mr. KINZLER. If it were passed.

Mr. BLUME. And signed by President Ford?

Mr. KINZLER. Yes; and signed by President Ford, and there had to be a provision dealing with reinsurance, would you prefer it be left as is; that is, the States would have the right to develop such a plan, or would you prefer something else?

Mr. BLUME. Yes.

Mr. KINZLER. OK. I think at long last, we found something to agree upon, and given that, I will gladly give up.

Thank you very much, Mr. Blume. Your testimony has been very useful.

Mr. BRODHEAD. Thank you, Mr. Blume, and we are ready for our next witness.

Mr. Huff, would you state your name and address for the record, please.

STATEMENT BY WILLIAM H. HUFF III, INSURANCE COMMISSIONER, STATE OF IOWA, AND PRESIDENT, NATIONAL ASSOCIATION OF INSURANCE COMMISSIONERS, ACCOMPANIED BY RICHARD HEMMINGS, COUNSEL; AND ROBERT BAILEY, STAFF ACTUARY

Mr. HUFF. Mr. Chairman, I am Bill Huff, president of the National Association of Insurance Commissioners and insurance commissioner for the State of Iowa. With me today, on my right, is Dick Hemmings, legal counsel for NAIC, and Mr. Bob Bailey is staff actuary and head of the data bank system for the NAIC.

We have a very detailed statement, Mr. Chairman, if I can make it a part of the record and summarize it and stay within the 10 minutes?

Mr. BRODHEAD. Fine. Without objection, your full statement is entered. We are pleased to have you with us and are grateful that you took the opportunity to come a long distance to be of assistance to the committee.

Please proceed.

Mr. HUFF. Thank you.

I would like to thank the subcommittee for the opportunity to appear and present some of the concerns of the NAIC over the proposed no-fault automobile reform proposals which you are considering.

We have submitted to you, for the record, a complete written statement of the NAIC's position on the bills pending before you.

It has consistently been our position throughout the Congressional proceedings on no-fault auto insurance that Federal legislation at this point would be inappropriate and undesirable.

There have been no new developments of any kind that have altered our judgment and we continue to oppose the basic legislative changes in auto insurance at the Federal level.

Our position is not primarily based on a choice between States rights and Federal regulatory expansion, Indeed, we recognize the power of Congress to totally preempt the field in all aspects of insurance regulation.

Rather, it is our firm conviction, based upon years of experience with insurance regulation, that a national uniform approach to no-fault automobile insurance is not in the public interest at this time.

Furthermore, it is our opinion that each of the no-fault bills before you presents a regulatory scheme that will prove to be unnecessary and undesirable if enacted on a national scale.

The attempt to homogenize the circumstances and variables of the several States through the imposition of a standard uniform surrender of tort rights, in exchange for a uniform package of first-party benefits, will, either in the Congress before enactment or by the public, after enactment, be recognized as a basic and costly error.

At the outset, I would underscore the fact that NAIC has no vested interest in maintaining, modifying, or eliminating any third-party legal liability system. The States are regulating both fault and no-fault types of coverage.

We are fully aware of the inequities engendered by the fault system and have officially taken the position that the States should proceed with at least a modified no-fault program.

The NAIC has not adopted any model no-fault legislation because we believe it would be premature to recommend any uniform approach at this time.

The primary reasons for encouraging State by State experimentation are as follows:

One, to determine what compromises the public wants and is willing to accept.

Two, to reflect local circumstances significantly varying throughout the Nation for example average liability claims and judgments, medical costs, and so on, and

Third, to allow time to work out incorrect legislative assumptions and problems in a reform package designed to overhaul the complex automobile insurance system based on fault.

The reasons which have at present foreclosed the present NAIC action on no-fault reform equally apply in our opinion, to the possibility of Federal legislation.

The experimental efforts at the State level are uniquely suited to sifting through the multitude of factors, concepts, attitudes, and values which vary from area to area.

The citizens from different States may not be equally benefited or hurt by or receptive to a mandated nationwide program.

We need only note the diversity of the Federal proposals before you to understand the lack of consensus on no-fault reform. At a bare minimum, Congress should reflect on whether it should adopt legislation which would preempt the legislative determinations of the 24 States which already have no-fault plans, and ones they believe are best suited to their local circumstances.

Also, I would direct your attention to the conclusion of Professor Keeton in testimony before this committee a year ago that with the S. 354 national standard approach, Congress cannot assume any State will comply with the so-called standard absent amending legislation.

We believe that any universally applicable no-fault reform proposal, if enacted, would today be premature. A Federal no-fault scheme would freeze in the mistakes and will prevent self-determination in the States.

In addition, some of the claims and assumptions underlying the Federal proposals are likely to be inaccurate or clearly erroneous.

For example, premium cost savings have been highly acclaimed by the proponents of S. 354 as a compelling reason for consumers to support and for Congress to enact a Federal bill. But the facts disclose, in perspective, that premium cost savings, if any, will likely be insignificant, and when you deal with averages it presents a dangerous situation, which I can refer to later. I assume Mr. Kinzler will ask some questions about that.

As a matter of fact, the evidence cited in the Milliman & Robertson study used to support cost savings claims is now 2 years old and the underlying data is 6 years old. We regard that study as obsolete and not reliable for any claims of certain cost savings.

An example of the potentially erroneous assumption made by the drafters of S. 354 and H.R. 1900 is that the adverse cost impact of greater benefits of title III relative to title II will be offset by the virtual elimination of tort suits.

Title III allows no overall maximum limitation on survivors loss benefits, but rather a weekly limit of $200 per week.

Over a period of 50 years an eligible survivor could collect $500,000. However, even the out-of-date M. & R. statistics show that death claims are the single greatest cost component of first-party benefits when set at the high level.

We are not aware of any documentation underlying the scheme of title III. Notably, the cost estimates on S. 354 have focused on title II.

Another example of the premature nature of both H.R. 1900 and the Senate Commerce Committee's reported version of S. 354 are the provisions requiring consultation on detailed information on the impact of title II no-fault plans in several specific areas, such as cost, competition, and senior citizens. It can be argued that it is irresponsible to collect such information after adoption to fill the void that currently exists in essential information.

In short, the NAIC encourages State-by-State experimentation, unencumbered by uniform requirements or standards when it is not yet known whether a national solution is even feasible.

To date, some 24 States have enacted some form of no-fault automobile insurance reform legislation and it is evident that the momentum exists for meaningful no-fault reform in the States.

The advantages of State regulation should receive your deliberate attention before you conclude that the national interest requires Congress to enact a proposal that would wrest or tend to wrest the insurance regulation away from the States.

State insurance regulation has been in place for over 100 years, and the regulatory offices have in excess of 5,100 employees and a combined budget of over $70 million.

There are more points for applying citizen pressure in the States than would exist at the Federal level. The mere fact that State legislation exists is a powerful argument for its continuance, because it is generally less costly to improve the existing institutions than to start new ones. The pluralism and diversity of State regulation provides numerous opportunities for creative legislation.

Finally, local decisionmaking is more likely to be tailored to local problems, desires, and values.

Federal proposals that impinge upon the effectiveness of State insurance regulation would be contrary to a viable concept of federalism and should be abandoned by your committee.

Turning now to the specific proposals before you, I believe that the reasons upon which we would base our opposition to H.R. 1272 are obvious. That bill would totally preempt State regulation of automobile insurance.

While the bill's social objectives may be desirable, we believe that the complete provision of first-party benefits for economic and noneconomic loss would simply be too expensive to be practical.

H.R. 1900 would be unconstitutional if enacted, as indicated by the United States Attorney General's testimony before the Senate, and by the Senate's subsequent revisions to S. 354.

Contrary to the suggestions of the proponents, the standards bill would create a massive Federal regulatory role colliding with the public policy expressed in the McCarran Act—that insurance regulation which should be vested in the States.

Although the Senate Commerce Committee sought to deal with the constitutional problems of S. 354, the reported version of the bill remains, in our view, impractical and unacceptable.

The Senate 1975 revisions will virtually assure a direct Federal regulatory role under title III. According to the bill, title III is to be "implemented and administered and operated and maintained exclusively by the Secretary of Transportation."

This result is contrary to the explicit findings of Congress stated in section 102(a)(7), that direct regulatory action is neither necessary nor desirable.

In addition, S. 354 would create anything but uniform national standards because of the peculiar inclusion of two quite different no-fault plans in titles II and III, a result which also contradicts the purported findings of Congress in section 102(a)(7) that uniformity is necessary. Unlimited first-party benefits are likely to adversely affect small insurers because of increasing reinsurance premiums.

Although H.R. 1900 and S. 354 call for review of the impact of the legislation on competition between small companies within the motor vehicle insurance industry, reports on such reviews may be too late to lead to a remedy of the elimination of such companies from the market.

In general, we believe that the title II guidelines of S. 354 and H.R. 1900 severely limit the range of State regulatory prerogatives.

For example, the descriptive threshold for resort to tort liability is inherently vague and will probably require a course of judicial interpretation in every State.

On the other hand, a straight dollar threshold could be subject to abusive attempts to artificially inflate the degree of economic loss. The obvious lesson of this observation is that flexibility should be preserved for State experimentation and the accommodation of local circumstances.

For these reasons we urge the committee to abandon Federal no-fault proposals before you. If Congress inevitably determines that a national no-fault reform is necessary, additional approaches should be considered.

Several alternatives in H.R. 7985, or the later version which I guess is H.R. 8441, may slightly improve the approach of the standards bills. For example, the variations between titles II and III could be eliminated.

However, we remain opposed to any Federal legislation that would restructure the automobile accident reparations system.

The public interest requires State-by-State experimentation to test various approaches, benefit levels, benefit restrictions, and costs.

Mr. CHAIRMAN. That concludes my oral testimony, and I will be glad to attempt to answer any questions you might have.

[Mr. Huff's prepared statement follows:]

STATEMENT ON BEHALF OF THE NATIONAL ASSOCIATION OF INSURANCE COMMISSIONERS ON NATIONAL NO-FAULT LEGISLATION

Mr. Chairman and members of the committee, my name is William H. Huff III, Commissioner of Insurance in the State of Iowa, and President of the National Association of Insurance Commissioners (commonly referred to as the NAIC). Having its inception in 1871, the NAIC is the oldest voluntary association of state officials. The NAIC membership consists of the principal insurance regulatory officials of the 50 states, the District of Columbia, Guam, Puerto Rico and the Virgin Islands.

We appreciate this opportunity to again appear before this Subcommittee to express our views on the no-fault automobile insurance bills which are before you. We have serious reservations about the approaches and certain provisions of the bills and believe the overall impact will, in the long run, be inimical to the interests of the insurance buying public. The seriousness of our concern over federal activities is manifest by the previous NAIC deliberations on the subject, numerous congressional appearances with testimony before the Senate Commerce Committee,[1] testimony before the Senate Judiciary Committee,[2] and prior testimony before the House Subcommittee on Commerce and Finance.[3]

We wish to highlight at the outset the fact that the NAIC has no vested interest in either eliminating, modifying, or continuing the third party legal liability system which has in the past been prevalent in the automobile insurance system. State insurance regulators have diverse experience in regulating both fault and no-fault types of coverage. Our one overriding interest is the evolution and progressive development of the automobile insurance system in a manner best designed to serve the public interest.

[1] Hearings before the Committee on Commerce on S. 945, Pt. 4 (1971) p. 1666 et seq. and Pt. 5 (1971), p. 2354, et seq. and/or S. 354, April 30, 1975.
[2] Hearings, before the Committee on the Judiciary on S. 354 (1974), p. 1192.
[3] Hearings before the Subcommittee on Commerce and Finance, Pt. 2 (1971), p. 581.; Pt. 1 (1974), p. 925.

I. THE DESIRABIITY OF FEDERAL NO-FAULT LEGISLATION

A. *The need for state by state determination of the type of no-fault plan that best meets the needs of state citizens.*

No-fault automobile insurance is essentially a system of first party insurance which provides some combination of medical, disability, or property coverage with an accompanying elimination of tort liability in some degree. This kind of insurance is neither new nor revolutionary.

At the same time, however, applying the no-fault concept in the area of automobile insurance involves fundamental conceptual changes in a complex, ongoing system in terms of both social and legal policy. While the dichotomy in operation of a fault versus no-fault system is easy to understand, there underlies any legislative choice a veritable forest of subsidiary issues and questions of should be taken into account.

Proponents cf no-fault are urging that virtually all injuries be compensated regardless of fault. The conflicting objectives are apparent, i.e., lower cost versus increased benefits. Alternative approaches have been suggested that include: (a) retaining the status quo; (b) improving the tort liability system with judicial reform, shifting to comparative negligence, regulating contingency fees, etc.; (c) relying on evolutionary reform combining fault and no-fault coverages; (d) establishing a total no-fault system, or (e) utilizing government insurance. In both the federal and state efforts to seek some resolution of the various issues, numerous groups have advocated certain kinds of changes and announced their vital concern with the ultimate result. The groups include policyholders, claimants, attorneys, providers of medical services, insurers, agents and unions. Local considerations in each state affect the basic questions such as what benefits the public wants, what privileges the public is willing to forego, and what cost level is acceptable.

At present, 24 states with over 53% of the national population have enacted some form of no-fault legislation.[4] The approaches vary, and it is only by a process of trial and error that the public will ascertain the true costs and benefits of the various no-fault plans. The experimental efforts at the state level are uniquely suited to sifting through the multitude of factors, concepts, attitudes and values which vary from area to area. Not all states are alike and public policy changes can best be made on a state-by-state basis. At a bare minimum, Congress should begin to reflect on whether it has sufficient widsom to preempt the legislative determinations of the 24 states which have enacted mandatory or voluntary no-fault plans which the states believe are best suited to local circumstances.

The NAIC has consistently opposed adoption of basic legislative or regulatory changes in automobile insurance at the federal level. Citizens of different states may not be equally benefitted (or hurt) by or receptive to a mandated nationwide program. Medical costs in Nevada are not the same as those in New York. Liability claims in California are generally not the same as those in Iowa. The level of first party benefits and the degree of exemption from tort liability would most effectively be determined in a manner designed to accommodate local experience.

Ultimately, the best solution for one state may be inappropriate in another. We perceive no reason justifying a mandated nationwide program that would encumber, inhibit, or eliminate the state-by-state development of better forms of automobile insurance.

The objectives and convictions of proponents of federal no-fault programs are doubtlessly of long-considered and worthy origins. However, past experience with massive federal programs engenders a degree of skepticism. Putting aside the relative capability of the states to better deal with their local affairs, no theoretical or circumstantial basis exists to readily assume that the federal government is uniquely capable of ameliorating all deficiencies in the course of human affairs. Mandating a massive uniform federal program involves a sizable risk and may prove to be unworkable and/or very costly. The potential damage and disruption could be of great magnitude.

Congress cannot ensure that a nationwide no-fault program will not be successfully challenged in the courts or that Congress will not determine that midstream corrections are necessary to remedy unrecognized defects (An example of which is noted on page 13 of this statement). No-fault laws have been challenged in several states, indicating the existence of potential problems with any no-fault plan that must be ironed out. Insurance companies necessarily make large

---

[4] Ark., Cal., Conn., Del., Fla., Ga., Hawaii, Kans., Ky., Md., Mass., Mich., Minn., Nev., N.J., N.Y., N. Dak., Oreg., Pa., S.C., S. Dak., Tex., Utah, Va., and Puerto Rico.

expenditures in preparation for marketing under a particular regulatory scheme. If a national no-fault plan is overturned or substantially altered, consumers will be faced with paying for the costs of the unsuccessful nationwide experiment. State experimentation at least limits the potential marketing costs in working out feasible no-fault systems. It would be imprudent to mandate a nationwide no-fault scheme for over 200 million people in 50 states and then step back to see if it works while there exists a viable state by state alternative.

The states are not asking for national intervention, but rather that Congress recognize the rights of states to solve their own state problems with the concomitant right to attempt various solutions. One need only note the diversity of federal proposals before your committee to understand the lack of consensus on no-fault reform.

B. Enactment of a national no-fault scheme would be premature

Inherent in any change affecting millions of persons on a nationwide basis are numerous unforseen ramifications. The enactment of any of the proposed national no-fault plans would impede meaningful experimentation on a state-by-state basis that can efficiently ascertain virtues and defects of the various state approaches, thereby (a) destroying flexibility, (b) freezing in mistakes, and (c) preventing self determination. This does not suggest that a particular national plan is appropriate or inappropriate in a given state but rather it would be inappropriate and premature as a nationwide standard.

All of this is not to argue for the status quo. The NAIC and the states have proceeded with their efforts to bring about constructive change in the automobile accident reparations system. The NAIC has recommended that states enact, at a minimum, some type of "modified no-fault" legislation providing for losses suffered in automobile accidents.[5] As previously noted, 24 states have done so to date.

(1) *Costs.* The proponents of national no-fault plans have seized upon the issue of premium cost savings as a matter of great consumer interest. While alleged cost savings have drawn the attention of consumers, the cost issue is probably only understood by the consumer (and perhaps Congress) to mean a very significant increase or decrease.

Most of the pending no-fault proposals before Congress address the reformation of the automobile accident fault system solely in terms of bodily injury coverage. Nationwide, the premiums for coverage of personal injury comprise about one-third of the total automobile insurance premium.[6] The proposed no-fault reform proposals therefore would affect only one-third of the premium dollar. The overall cost of operating an automobile averages about 16¢ per mile. Insurance represents only 1.6¢ of that figure,[7] and most no-fault reform proposals would impact on only one-third of the insurance costs.

On reflection, it should be clear that the significant and true consumer appeal of no-fault reform is payment of BI claims without regard to fault. Those who highlight cost savings are, in our opinion, misleading the consumer.

Notwithstanding this observation, costs should be taken into account as *one* factor in evaluating a potential legislative reform of the automobile insurance system. The generation of credible cost data is an expensive and time consuming process.

One of the more frequently cited cost studies of no-fault reform is that of Milliman & Robertson. That study was jointly sponsored by the NAIC and the U.S. Department of Transportation. The study itself is now two years old, the data underlying the study is six years old, and we regard it as obsolete.

In addition, more recent and conflicting actuarial cost studies have been prepared by others, such as the Allstate and State Farm Insurance Companies. The conflicting industry estimates underscore the need for a new independent study. Firm facts that would be useful in comparing fault and no-fault insurance are now available in raw form in the several states. Because the availability of such cost data is one relevent factor in evaluating no-fault reform—particularly when proposed on the national level—it appears to us to be imperative to develop new credible and reliable cost data based on the available experience in the states

In the Senate, the proponents of S. 354 have been using the outdated Milliman & Robertson study to argue that the bill would result in premium cost savings. But even at the time of the preparation of the study, Milliman & Robertson

---
[5] 2 *Proceedings of NAIC* 617 (1971).
[6] *Statistical Abstract of the U.S.*, 1974, U.S. Department of Commerce, p. 562.
[7] Id. p. 560.

were very conscious of the uncertainties involved in their estimates and attached strong caveats to their reports warning against excessive reliance on the "numbers generated by this system." The M & R report stated:

Although the conclusions presented in this report are probably the best estimates available, it should nonetheless be recognized that they are subject to a high degree of uncertainty as well as being very susceptible to misrepresentation. It thus becomes essential to specify that those conclusions neither be used nor released except in conjunction with a thorough understanding of the following (six) caveats.[8]

In those states which have enacted no-fault laws, it is probable that the enactment of another national plan would result in significant cost increases in contrast to the out-of-date figures in the M & R reports, which assumed that each state still had a fault system. It is one thing for the states to use tentative cost estimates to enact new and experimental legislation. However, it is quite another thing for the Federal government to enact an all-embracing, permanent national scheme based on mere estimates when the firm facts, produced by state experience, are available.

2. *Legislative Design.* When insurance reform is necessary, it is not necessary to affect the whole nation, as would be essential with a single national plan. The experience in the states has proven that a legislature enacting no-fault legislation at this time can only hope to anticipate what the public will accept in terms of (1) benefit levels, (2) restrictions on tort rights, and (3) costs. The best way for the public to make effective judgments in these areas is to "live with" actual no-fault laws over an adequate period of time. From such experience under different pilot legislation, legislatures can then make informed revisions of the early legislation, giving the public what it wants and what it will pay for.

When a uniform approach to legislative and regulatory insurance problems is indicated, the NAIC and other state associations serve as an effective source for developing and recommending model state plans. On the very complex no-fault reform issue, it has been the position of the NAIC to encourage state experimentation. At this date, we believe it would be premature to recommend any uniform approach. The primary reasons for encouraging state by state no-fault experimentation are: (1) to determine what compromise the public wants and is willing to accept; (2) to reflect local circumstances which vary considerably throughout the nation (e.g., average medical costs, liability claims and judgments, wages, etc.); and (3) to allow time to work out incorrect assumptions and problems in a legislative package designed to overhaul the complicated automobile insurance system based upon fault.

A number of assumptions have been made in designing the federal proposals that may prove to be incorrect. For example, in S. 354 and H.R. 1900, the alternative federal plan under Title III mandates greater dollar benefits overall than does Title II. The Senate Commerce Committee assumed that the greater benefit package and its adverse cost impact would be offset by the more severe restrictions on tort under Title III than those under Title II.[9] One the more costly Title III benefit provisions is for survivors loss (Section 302(c)). There is a weekly maximum limit of $200, but no overall maximum limitation. Over a period of 50 years,

---

[8] "(1) Average premium change indications will not apply uniformly, but rather will vary considerably by type of vehicle insured. Inclusion of motorcyclists under the no-fault law, for example, may be expected to increase premiums greatly for this group of motorists.

(2) The study did not deal with changes in rating classification and territorial relativities, which may be substantial. Generally speaking, urban areas of a state may be expected to experience results that are more favorable than shown, and rural areas results that are less favorable.

(3) The cost implications of the input assumptions and supporting data base to the model should not be overlooked nor underestimated. This is particularly true where there is a combination of uncertainty and cost impact, such as of psychological factors affecting tort action rates and of large first-party loss projections based on sparse data of limited applicability to no-fault auto insurance.

(4) The study deals exclusively with the relativity between the proposed system and the tort liability system currently or most recently effective in the 1974 levels. No attention has been given to possible inadequacy or redundance of existing premium rate levels.

(5) The study addresses the automobile insurance system only, and not the effects of changes in that system or other lines of insurance or public institutions or other personal risk assumption.

(6) The findings presented in this report reflect no more than an attempt to predict the relative cost implications of passage of a particular bill, and not the effects of various other influences on automobile insurance premiums. Such influences are many, and include changes in automobile safety features, enforcement of driver standards, marketing and administrative practices, public attitudes toward seat belts and drunk drivers, and general economic conditions, among others."

Exhibit B, Caveats Pertaining to Numerical Results, pp 12–13, *Cost Estimate of No-Fault Automobile Insurance,* Millimarr & Robertson, Inc., November 7, 1973.

[9] Report of Senate Commerce Committee, p. 72, August 15, 1973.

the $200 per week benefit would result in over $500,000 of first party benefit payments for every death for survivors who are entitled to the relatively modest $200 per week figure. Virtually all of the costing estimates have focused on a Title II no-fault scheme. Assuming an overall limit of $50,000 on death claims the M & R study discloses (for a Title II plan) that death costs would be the greatest single cost component of first party benefits. We consequently cannot understand the basis for the Senate Commerce Committee's assumption that the adverse cost impact of the greater Title III benefits will necessarily be offset by the elimination of tort suits. In any event, cost estimates for both Title II *and* Title III should be developed in order to accurately characterize the consumer cost impact of S. 354.

Both H.R. 1900 (Sec. 201(b)) and the reported Commerce Committee version of S. 354 (Sec 202(d)) include provisions requiring the compilation of detailed information on the impact of state no-fault plans in several specific areas. It can be argued that it is irresponsible to collect such information after adopting a virtually irreversible program in order to fill the great void that currently exists in essential information, especially when there exists the laboratory of various state laws. Unfortunately, Congress does not appear willing to follow the logic of this observation. The argument is being made that we need a uniform system—now. But, in fact, experience has taught us that what we need more at this point in time is flexibility. A federal no-fault bill would "freeze" no-fault into a single approach at the very time when experimentation is most needed. In contrast the states are actively testing various approaches in accordance with local values and preferences. Furthermore, early mistakes can be more easily rectified in a state whereas in a federal program defects are more likely to assume unmanageable and national proportions.

In short, the NAIC encourages experimentation—and experimentation on a large scale is actually under way. In addition to the 24 states which have enacted no-fault legislation, the other states are closely watching the results of the experiments to ascertain the best and most acceptable combination of benefits, restrictions on benefits and costs for enactment in their own states. State experience should be considered before reaching any final conclusions on the best approach or approaches, something which the Congress has not yet taken time to do. Federal action now would be premature.

Furthermore, it might be pointed out that in automobile insurance, the policyholder is billed at least once a year, and in many cases more often. Thus, the policyholders are reminded periodically what the legislature has done *to* them as well as *for* them. The effect of federal no-fault legislation will be to put every member of Congress into the middle of subsequent premium rate and benefit level controversies.

II. ADVANTAGES OF STATE INSURANCE REGULATION

Most of the no-fault proposals that are before your committee would involve a substantial preemption of state insurance regulation. In the case of H.R. 1272 the preemption would be virtually complete. The Senate Commerce Committee's reported version of S. 354 ensures a federal regulatory role in some states. We believe on the basis of our regulatory experience that the Congress is ill-advised and the federal government ill-prepared to assume a direct role in the regulation of automobile insurance.

In light of the Supreme Court's interpretation of the scope of the commerce clause,[10] few would argue on the basis of judicial precedent that Congress does not have the constitutional authority to regulate insurance as an incident of interstate commerce.[11] But, as we broaden the commerce clause constitutionally and concomitantly broaden the powers of Congress, we will ultimately reach a point where there is no subject of legislative concern in which Congress cannot meddle as a matter of right. However, we doubt that most Americans, faced squarely with the proposition of one centralized government, would favor the transference of any and all regulatory authority to Washington. We submit that Congress should pause whenever it has occasion to consider the preemption of function historically performed by the states.

We are not aware of the circumstances or public policy that would justify an act of Congress designed to wrest automobile insurance regulation from the states. On the contrary, most of the proponents of federal no-fault have maintained that

---

[10] U.S. Const. Art. I Sec. 8.
[11] U.S. v. South-Eastern Underwriters Ass'n, 322 U.S.

state insurance regulation should be left in place. A review of the development and advantages of state insurance regulation should proceed any intrusion into this historically state performed activity.

A. Development of State Regulation

In part due to Paul v. Virginia (1868)[12] which held that insurance was not interstate commerce, the regulation of insurance developed at the state level. As a consequence, insurance was not subject to congressional jurisdiction under the commerce clause. However, in the *SEUA* case (1944),[13] the Supreme Court reversed this position. To assure that state insurance regulation was not upended under the commerce clause, Congress determined that state regulation of the business of insurance is in the public interest. Specifically, the McCarran Act (1945) provides:

Congress declares that the continued regulation and taxation by the severa States of the business of insurance is in the public interest, . . .[14]

Thus, the regulation of insurance continued to develop at the state level and has done so at an accelerated pace in recent years.

State insurance regulation is dedicated to protecting the public interest by focusing on at least four fundamental regulatory objectives; (a) assuring the financial integrity underlying the security promised (preventions of insolvency, guaranty funds); (b) quality of the product; (c) availability of the product; and (d) fairness to the insurance consuming public. To achieve these goals, a broad and detailed state regulatory mechanism has evolved. For example,

(1) Insurers must obtain and continue their licenses in order to do business. This, in turn, requires complying with statutes and regulations pertaining to formation; financial standards concerning assets, capital and surplus, permissible investments, adequacy of reserves; and qualifications as to character of management, experience and knowledge of the business. Licenses may be suspended or revoked for failure to comply with the law or when the public interest so requires.

(2) Insurers must file comprehensive annual and other periodic reports under oath in each state in which they do business. The NAIC annual statement requires detailed information concerning financial condition, underwriting, investments, reserves, etc.

(3) Insurers are subject to comprehensive periodic examinations among other things, to ascertain the financial condition of the company, the results of operation, corporate investment and underwriting practices, whether the company is meeting its obligations to its policyholders, etc.

(4) By virtue of statutory standards on policy content and the commissioners' policy form approval or disapproval power, much of the source of misrepresentations or other unfair practices is deterred in advance.

(5) Control is exercised over the pricing practices of property and liability insurers by implementing, either through prior approval or subsequent review, the standards that rates shall not be excessive, inadequate nor unfairly discriminatory.

(6) Market practices are controlled by, among other things, laws governing the qualifications and licensing of agents and brokers, prohibitions against certain practices such as false and misleading advertising and representations, defining standards of fair competition, control over policy forms, rate controls in several areas and department investigations of complaints.

(7) The insurance commissioner may, for a variety of causes, (e.g., insolvency, refusal to comply with orders, failure to remove officers, etc.), apply for a court order of liquidation, rehabilitation or conservation.

(8) Among the sanctions available for enforcement of the insurance laws are criminal and civil penalties; cease and desist orders; injunctions; removal of officers and directors; fines; and revocation (or refusal to renew) licenses of agents, adjusters, brokers, and insurers. These express powers and sanctions, plus the informal powers, sanctions and alternative modes of relief stemming therefrom, extend far beyond what is being talked about in connection with any of the proposed federal bills.

Supplementing the efforts of the individual states has been the NAIC which is a 100 year old organization consisting of the insurance commissioners of the several states. The NAIC has sought to promote uniformity where appropriate, develop model laws and regulations for use in various states and has conducted

---
[12] 75 U.S. (8 Wall.) 168 (1868).
[13] U.S. v. South-Eastern Underwriters Ass'n., 322 U.S. 533 (1944).
[14] 15 U.S.C.A. Sec. 1011.

various types of studies and research projects. The NAIC, as a whole, meets twice a year. Various committees meet during the interim. In addition, a central research office has been established. Thus, the NAIC provides a flexible and timely facility to develop and implement change. In short, the NAIC has served as a mechanism to improve regulation and has provided impetus for change.

This discussion is not intended to be comprehensive but rather simply highlights the comprehensive nature of insurance regulation as it continually evolves to meet changing needs.

B. Federalism and State Regulatory Advantages.

The dispersion of power between the state and federal governments is advantageous and in the public interest. This constitutional tenet is rooted in sound public policy. Undisciplined power tends to become unresponsive at best and corrupt at worst. Effective implementation of the concept of federalism is fundamental to the exercise of such discipline. This concept requires a dispersion in ultimate decision making power and responsibility, and not merely superimposing a federal regulatory agency on top of that of the states. Enactment of any of the federal no-fault proposals would severely challenge the concept of federalism by ignoring the inherent advantages of state regulation. We recognize that the Senate Commerce Committee has sought to remedy the constitutionally obnoxious character of S. 354 with changes in the bill reported from the Committee, but the issue of states rights is as much a matter of practicality and sound public policy as it is constitutional. In order to avoid the serious constitutional impediments in S. 354, the sponsors have decided to create a direct federal regulatory role for the Secretary of Transportation. This is in contravention of Section 102(a)(7) which states the policy of Congress to avoid direct regulation. H.R. 1272, of course, makes no pretense of maintaining state regulation. We urge you to recognize the myriad reasons for maintaining state regulation prior to any preemption.

(1) *Advantages of State Insurance Regulation.*

Among the advantages of state insurance regulation are (a) its existence, (b) pluralism, (c) threat of a federal alternative, and (d) regulation closer to the people. Let us deal briefly with each of these areas which should receive your deliberate attention before concluding that the national interest requires Congress to wrest insurance regulation from the states.

(a) *Existence.* The state insurance regulatory system already exists. It utilizes over 50 offices (at least one in each state and multiple offices in several states), employs over 5,100 persons with combined budgets of approximately $70 million.

As a general proposition, it is more effective and less expensive to improve upon and add to existing institutions than to start new ones.[15] This is particularly true with respect to institutions, such as the state insurance regulatory mechanism, which have demonstrated a willingness to change where appropriate, which have a facility for change, and whose goals in affording protection to the public are similar to the objectives of the national no-fault program. Assumption of regulatory power by the federal government could sweep away much of the experience and expertise existing in state insurance departments. Such a shift would throw into doubt for years many of the rules under which the business has been accustomed to function. From the customers' viewpoint, the known local points for applying citizen pressure would be removed, dispersed, or obscured. Furthermore, there is no assurance that the resulting quality of federal regulation will justify the dislocations incident to the change in locus of regulatory authority.

The history of several federal agencies does not give rise to overconfidence. Nothing is so unsure as predicting the full range of consequences of a major change in a complex system. Thus, the fact that the state insurance regulatory mechanism already exists is in itself a powerful argument for its continuance.

(b) *Pluralsim, Experimentation and Vitality.* A second sdvantage to state regulation is the pluralism and diversity with the system. It involves regulatory agencies of limited size. It seems clear that the economies of scale taper off as size increases beyond some point while problems of bureaucracy become proportionately worse.

The field of government regulation is imperfectly inderstood. This lends support to utilizing a number of agencies rather than just one. Such a system is conducive to experimentation and will confine the impact of an experiment until

---

[15] Although vesting regulatory authority in DOT would utilize an existing agency, to do so is new in that DOT has not functioned in the insurance regulatory area.

it has been tested. The dispersion of decisional responsibility and power tends to restrict the gravity of the impact of mistakes or miscalculation to a limited area and segment of the population. On the other hand, a dramatic and effective innovation by a particular state is apt to be adopted elsewhere after a period of time and testing.

Pluralism also affords a more fertile environment for greater vitality than does a single national agency. The scope for top creative leadership is greater in a small organization and the likelihood of creative leadership is greater in a system having several tops. The work of one or more vigorous agencies is contagious. It tends to be imitated, competed with and used as a standard in other states. The problem of keeping regulatory agencies, whether state or federal, inbued with the sense of vitality, capable of self-renewal and change is now and, certainly in the future, a graver public concern than an occasional awkwardness of a multi-state regulatory system.

(c) *The Threat of a Federal Alternative.* An extremely important and unique advantage to state regulation is that the threat of a national alternative always hangs over it. State insurance regulatory agencies are subject to review, investigation and embarrassment by Congress which admittedly has the power to abolish the system if it so chooses. As one former insurance commissioner said, "This concentrates the mind wonderfully." Such congressional oversight no doubt stimulates state regulators to do a better job.

In contrast, if a national regulatory agency becomes involved, it would not be as skeptically watched or credibly menaced. Congressional oversight of federal regulatory agencies has not been demonstratively better than state legislative oversight of state agencies. In other words, congressional oversight of federal agencies has yielded fewer benefits and more adverse side effects than congressional oversight of state insurance regulation.

(d) *Regulation Closer to the People.* It is an old cliche that the states are closer to the people than is the Federal Government. The individual member of the public possesses more readily available means to seek redress, to answer inquiries and to apply pressure at the state level. For example, an insurance commissioner and top members of his staff are more accessible than comparable members of the President's cabinet. Furthermore, there are over fifty commissioners, contrasted to one cabinet secretary, to whom resort can be had. State legislators, who can and do make forcefully known to the commissioner of insurance problems of their constituents, are also more accessible and tend to be more responsive to an individual's problems. When ultimate responsibility is vested in Washington, the response tends to be more sluggish and less attuned to the individual's needs and demands.

To the extent that the federal proposals would adversely affect the state insurance regulatory mechanism, we believe they are contrary to the public interest, contrary to a viable implementation of the concept of federalism which is a keystone of our system of government, and should not be enacted.

The more local the decision making, the more accountable to constituents are the decision makers. It is also more likely that the decisions will be tailored to local problems, desires, and values. Unfortunately, these basic considerations are often overlooked in the urge to see one particular viewpoint adopted. We suggest the importance of considering federal no-fault legislation in this context.

(2) *Local Legislative Policy*

The enactment of a federal no-fault bill would mandate a national no-fault system of certain specifications. No-fault insurance reform, whether good or bad for a particular state, would be required. This would be true regardless of what the states have done. Every state has considered whether to adopt some type of no-fault insurance legislation. This has been done by duly elected representatives of the people of each state who are accountable to the electorate therein. It is difficult to imagine a federal action more directly conflicting with the fundamental concept of a federal system of government than that embodied in the proposed federal no-fault legislation, especially when no state has ignored the issue but rather every state has actively considered it.

The counter argument raised is the alleged need for uniformity among the states in order to enable a no-fault system to work. This argument lacks substance since an insurance policy can be drafted to accommodate state variations as a motorist travels within different states. The insurance business is long accustomed to techniques which accommodate the different public policy determinations of the various states. Furthermore, even if the uniformity argument had some validity, its importance would pale in the face of the countervailing fundamental considerations concerning the nature of federal-state relations and the importance of effective accountability to the electorate in a democratic system.

III. REGULATORY DESIGN AND ANTICIPATED PROBLEMS IN THE FEDERAL NO-FAULT PROPOSALS

We have already discussed the basic problems involved in a single monolithic, national approach to no-fault automobile insurance reform. The reordering of the underlying basic legal rights founded on historic common law doctrines should not lightly be tampered with or abandoned. Alleged cost savings should certainly not be the talisman for congressional initiative. Uniformity has not been demonstrated to be either necessary or desirable. On the contrary, a single national plan is likely to impose a high common denominator of universal application in the states that will ignore local variations and circumstances. The very compromises that comprise the entire theory of no-fault reform obviously vary in the existing state no-fault plans as well as the several proposed national reform measures. The developmental history of S. 354 is replete with shifts in benefits assured and rights to be surrendered. No one can yet promise the perfect answer. The basic flaw in all federal no-fault reform proposals is that they necessarily presume that the great complexities of no-fault reform in every state are reducible to a single national answer.

We are not prepared to say that any part'ᵣu'ɑʳ national no-fault proposal is entirely inappropriate for any particular state. 1 ther, our point is that you don't know whether or not it is appropriate nor do w . Furthermore, stamping out state prerogatives and flexibility for the sake of demonstrating congressional power is unacceptable per se. The very diversity of congressional proposals demonstrates the lack of consensus and diversity of value judgments involved. A brief review of the several bills before your committee discloses many points of concern to us.

A. S. 354

The Senate national standards no-fault bill as reported from the Senate Commerce Committee on June 27, 1975 has been revised to eliminate several areas of potential concern. However, the bill remains impractical and unacceptable. It is interesting to note the course of development of the present bill. Relatively late in the development of S. 945, the precursor of S. 354, it was decided to use a "federal standards" approach in order to enable states to continue their historical role in insurance regulation. The predecessors of S. 354 started at a point involving direct federal regulation and we have now come full circle to that same point. The bill in present form remains totally inconsistent with the basic principles of the McCarran-Ferguson Act.

Actually, the Senate bills 945 and 354 were designed to incorporate two very different no-fault plans: (1) the so-called national standards under Title II, and (2) the federal (or alternative state) plan under Title III. Despite benefit changes under both titles, the essential distinction between Titles II and III remains. Title III would involve a more radical shift from a fault system by virtually eliminating tort liability and mandating a broader benefit package than that meeting Title II requirements. The apparent purpose of the diverse approaches in the same bill is to coerce states to enact a Title II plan and to eliminate trial lawyers opposition to a state plan meeting the requirements of Title II.

This tandem arrangement in a serious federal proposal has always been somewhat puzzling in light of the fact that one of the stated arguments for federal legislation is the desirability of a uniform approach. In fact, the need for uniformity of the essential elements of a federal no-fault system is stated in S. 354.[16] The current version of S. 354 states, as a finding of Congress, that a fair no-fault reform law would eliminate "the need to determine fault, except in cases involving serious injuries." [17] Notwithstanding this congressional finding, Title III goes on to abolish any right to sue in tort for serious injuries caused by an insured but negligent driver.[18]

In general, the federal guidelines seriously limit state initiatives over a wide range of regulatory prerogatives. Section 202(e) severely limits the time within which a state may adopt a plan consistent with Title II or conform existing law to the standards involving availability of insurance, payment of benefits, amounts

---

[16] S. 354, Section 102(a)(7).
[17] S. 354, Section 102(a)(5)(B) (emphasis added).
[18] Id. Section 303.

and manner of charging attorney's fees, assigned claims, rating and public dissemination of rating information and so on. The time constraints take on added significance in light of the observations of Professor Keeton before your committee last year that presently not one state no-fault law can be said to conform to the national standards.[19] Section 204 provides for unlimited first party medical and rehabilitation benefits, and work loss benefits of at least $15,000. There are at least two adverse effects that may stem from these provisions: (1) they will tend to be anticompetitive and (2) they will limit the composite flexibility of states in determining the program of benefits best suited to local needs.

Any provision requiring unlimited benefits is likely to escalate the reinsurance premium for small companies relative to larger insurers, forcing them to increase rates and become less competitive. We do not believe that the elimination of small independent insurers from the automobile insurance market is in the public interest. Exploration of the anticompetitive effects of federal no-fault legislation should occur before enactment rather than after as contemplated by in Section 202(d)(1)(D) of S. 354.

In Section 206, the bill would partially abolish tort liability. Resort to tort liability is possible only if disfigurement or injuries are serious or permanent, or if there is disability beyond 90 days. Precisely what this descriptive threshold means is unclear. Because of the vague nature of the threshold, it is likely that each state will have a course of judicial interpretation. On the other hand, a more precise dollar threshold may be subject to abusive attempts to artificially inflate the degree of economic loss. The lesson to be learned from this observation is that flexibility should be preserved for state experimentation.

Uniform standards in this type of legislation may jeopardize the values of federalism. The virtues of experimentation endemic to our federal system are compelling in areas such as this, where the fundamental regulatory changes sought are complex and loaded with ancillary societal issues.

Finally, it should be explicitly recognized that the Senate Commerce Committee revisions to S. 354 this year will ensure a direct federal regulatory role under Title III in some states. The NAIC did recommend to the Senate Commerce Committee several changes in the structural design of S. 354 to eliminate what we believed to be grave unconstitutional requirements placed on the states. The legislative precedent that would be created absent the revisions would pose a serious challenge to our system of government. To eliminate the constitutional problems, however, the Senate Commerce Committee has now provided (Section 202(g)) that the Secretary of Transportation will regulate a no-fault insurance program in states which do not enact a Title II plan and cannot perform all of the functions implicit in a Title III plan.

The review board established in Section 201 would be required to throw a state not complying with all of the requirements of Title II into a federal Title III plan. For example, a state insurance department unable to provide consumers with rate information "adequate to permit them to compare prices, about rates being charged by insurers for no-fault benefits"[20] would result in a federal takeover of regulatory authority in that state. Other provisions in a state plan that are not being regulated to the satisfaction of a small group of consumers could presumably be pressed by the new consumer advocacy agency if that legislation [21] is enacted. On the consumer rate information requirement—for illustrative purposes—although desirable, there is some doubt as to the feasibility of compiling, preparing, and distributing meaningful and accurate information to each consumer on a timely basis by either the state or federal governments. We submit that it is grossly unreasonable that a federal regulatory takeover (which the bill itself indicates to be contrary to the Congressional intent [22]) be so weakly held in abeyance. Consequently, it is our view that even if Congress should decide that federal legislation is necessary in this area, the operational mechanics of S. 354 remain unacceptable.

The federal bureaucracy that will be created under Title III could eventually lead to the complete federalization of automobile insurance regulation. The practical effects of this federal regulatory responsibility are virtually ignored in the substantive provisions of S. 354. The bill as currently drafted merely directs the Secretary of Transportation to carry out the enumerated regulatory activities.

---

[19] Hearings before the Subcommittee on Commerce and Finance, Pt. 1 (1974), p. 404.
[20] Ses. 109(b).
[21] S. 200, as passed by the Senate.
[22] S. 354, Sec. 102(a)(7).

B. H.R. 1900

Representative Matsunaga's bill, of course, has not been revised to reflect the recent changes made in its Senate companion S. 354. Consequently, our criticisms of S. 354 as introduced in the 94th Congress still apply in full force to H.R. 1900.

We believe that the impact of H.R. 1900 on state insurance regulation would be substantial and fundamental rather than limited as suggested by the proponents and the bill itself.[23] A brief review of some of the provisions in H.R. 1900 which create a massive federal regulatory role illustrates the collision of the bill with the policy expressed in the McCarran Act—that insurance regulation should be vested in the states.

1. Title I

(a) Section 105(a)(5) requires the Commissioner to afford coverage to the "economically disadvantaged" at rates which are not so great as to deny access to coverage. If rates without this provision would be too high, then it must contemplate some sort of a subsidy which is contrary to state insurance laws which prohibit excessive, inadequate or discriminatory rates. Moreover it is impossible for anyone to determine at what point rates are not so great as to deny coverage or that those conducting federal review will be satisfied.

(b) Section 105(b) superimposes a detailed regulatory structure to govern cancellations and renewals. Virtually every state regulates insurers' power to cancel, refuse to renew, or cause other termination of insurance. However, S. 354 would ignore the regulatory role of the states by setting its own requirements instead of incorporating state law to ensure consistency of the federal standards with laws already existing in the states.

(c) Under Section 108, assigned claims plans are established, which among other things, provide for assignment of claims unpaid because of insolvency of financial inability of the insurer. The provision ignores the existence of guaranty fund laws which have been enacted in 47 states.

(d) The State Commissioners would be required to put mechanisms into effect under Section 109(b) to provide consumer information on rates and comparison of prices. Certainly this is desirable. This mandate overlooks, however, the feasibility of compiling and distributing meaningful information on a timely basis.

(e) Section 109(c) would make state medical and rehabilitation services accountable to the Insurance Commissioner. The Commissioner is to review their necessity and consistency with the goals of S. 354, and make sure that rates are fair and reasonable. Besides the fact that this responsibility is somewhat far afield from insurance regulation, it illustrates the intrusion of S. 354 into the internal affairs of sovereign states.

(f) A further example of the intrusion is apparent in Section 109(d) which authorizes the Commissioner to coordinate with other agencies in the creation and maintenance of emergency medical service systems. This detailed ordering of state functions within state government is somewhat presumptuous and probably unconstitutional.

2. Titles II and III

In Section 201, the Secretary of DOT is given the power to determine compliance of state plans enacted under the requirements of Title II. In Subsections 201(d) and (h)—The Percy Amendment—the Secretary is also given far-reaching power by the requirement that the Commssioner provide all relevant, requested information, without regard to cost or the value of such information to the Commissioner in carrying out state responsibilities. The Secretary could compel the states to provide virtually unlimited information, and he would have wise discretion in applying not only the national standards, but also the broad purpose Section (Section 102(b) which refers to "low cost," "comprrhensive," and a "fair system" of automobile insurance.).

The pervasive and ultimate power of the Secretary would arise from his ability to demand changes following his authority to conduct sweeping investigations. As leverage for compliance, he could determine that a state no longer complies with the national standards under Title II or the purpose section and thereby put into effect the "alternative state no-fault plan" (Title III in accordance with the specific direction of Section 201(e)(3)). Under Title II or Title III, the Commissioner would be subject to the same specific responsibilities and the Secretary would continue his periodic review. The McCarran Act would be seriously undermined, not on the merits of desirable change, but through circumvention.

---

[23] H.R. 1900, Sec. 102(a)(7).

The bill, in effect, makes state insurance departments subordinate agencies of the federal government. This, we submit, is neither consistent with the stated purposes of H.R. 1900, its sponsors, the interests of the insurance consuming public, or the Constitution of the United States.

3. Constitutionality of Interference

If H.R. 1900 were enacted, state officials would be charged with carrying out complex requirements of federal law under direction and oversight of active federal regulatory authority. What is constitutionally obnoxious about the bill is the manner in which it would impose duties and burdens on state officials without affirmative action of state legislatures.

The constitutional law cases and other federal legislation cited as authority for H.R. 1900 are not relevant to the specific unconstitutional character of the bill. The degree of federal intrusion into the affairs of sovereign states would be unprecedented.

On June 5, 1975 the Attorney General testified before the Senate that it was his view that S. 354 was unconstitutional. The Senate Commerce Committee has now recognized these constitutional impediments by its revisions to S. 354. The current version of S. 354 clearly establishes a federal regulatory role. The choice now before you on H.R. 1900 is apparently one of reporting an unconstitutional bill or revising it to preempt state insurance regulation. Since neither choice is in the best interests of the state or federal governments, nor, most importantly, the insurance consuming public, we urge you to abandon this legislative proposal.

C. H.R. 7985

The bill introduced by Representative Rinaldo is a version of H.R. 1900. To the extent that it incorporates provisions challenged in our remarks on H.R. 1900, we would voice the same criticisms.

However, the basic approach of H.R. 7985 does seem to offer a few significant alternatives to the approaches of S. 354 and H.R. 1900. Throughout the Congressional proceedings on no-fault reform we have consistently opposed federal intervention. Our position on this remains unchanged. Nonetheless, if Congress is determined to enact some form of federal no-fault legislation, regulation should be left exclusively in the states. This result appears to be contemplated by H.R. 7985.

Some of the provisions of H.R. 7985 would substantially improve the operational design of H.R. 1900. Sections 104(a)(2) and 204(a) would allow states greater flexibility of setting total first party benefits at a level of $10,000 or higher. These provisions would be more acceptable than the corresponting provisions in H.R. 1900. Aothough states would continue to be overly limited in designing required benefit packages, the alternatives of the other proposals are far moree objectionable.

The concomitant provisions in Section 206(a)(4) and (5), allowing more flexible restrictions on tort liability, would of course be necessary with the greater flexibility reserved to states in setting first party benefits.

Finally, H.R. 7985 appears to be the only version of a national standards bill that in fact establishes *one* set of standards for state no-fault reform. The elimination of a separate and distinct set of no-fault requirements under Title III is in keeping with the purported intent of all of the national standards proposals. We do not understand the reason why two substantially different no-fault reform measures are incorporated in H.R. 1900 and S. 354 under their respective Titles II and III, in light of the fact that each of the bills specifically recites the Congressional finding that uniform standards are necessary.

Again, we believe that federal no-fault legislation is completely unnecessary and undesirable. However, if a uniform national standards plan is deemed essential by Congress, it would appear to be logical to establish only one set of standards, as does Section 301 of H.R. 7985.

D. H.R. 1272

Our comments on Representative Eckhardt's H.R. 1272 are brief because we view that bill as a total federal preemption of state regulation of automobile insurance. Our preceding comments fully develop the reasons why the policy of the McCarran Act should be preserved in this area, and automobile insurance regulation left to the states.

The regulatory pattern that would result from the enactment of H.R. 1272 would produce a dual system of insurance regulation on a broad scale. Presumably,

Mr. BRODHEAD. Thank you very much. Do either of you gentlemen have anything to add?

Mr. BAILEY. No, sir.

Mr. BRODHEAD. Mr. Kinzler.

Mr. KINZLER. I have a couple of questions, if I might.

You indicate that the NAIC has not seen fit to develop a uniform law; is that correct?

Mr. HUFF. Yes. We have a resolution encouraging experimentation and some limitation on text.

Mr. KINZLER. What is the status of the National Conference of of Commissioners on Uniform State Laws? Who are they appointed by and how does that body exist; do you know?

Mr. HUFF. I don't know. They are not connected with us.

Mr. KINZLER. They are connected with the States and the Governors, if I am not mistaken.

Mr. HUFF. That is correct.

Mr. KINZLER. They have indeed devised a uniform law, is that right?

Mr. HUFF. UMVARA?

Mr. KINZLER. Right; devised in 1972. Do you know offhand how many States with laws would generally be considered in with that?

Mr. HUFF. My offhand guess is none.

Mr. KINZLER. Right. The only one that would be close would be Michigan.

So we have some idea, speaking on behalf of the States, as to what the uniform law would be?

Mr. HUFF. The problem with the uniform laws, if you have ever read UCCC, they tend to be so complicated and to some extent impractical that many States have difficulty accepting it.

Mr. KINZLER. They have been adopted by some States?

Mr. HUFF. Yes; no question, but it is one of the most difficult documents to comprehend around.

Mr. KINZLER. Mr. Huff, if I were a legislator in your State, and I were to come forward with a bill that offered to increase the number of injuries compensated by 40 percent, and increase the dollars available to compensate injuries by 43 percent and told you it would reduce the average premium by 5.3 percent less for each private passenger vehicle, what would you say?

Mr. HUFF. I would say you are full of baloney. That is like saying the guy has his head in the oven and feet in the refrigerator, and the average is just right.

Let me give you an example of the premium. I read the State Farm and Allstate testimony, and the State Farm, as you recall, anticipated a reduction and Allstate anticipated, as I recall, a 4 percent increase on the average premium using the $100 subrogation.

The total premium in territory 8 in Iowa for a safe driver, accident-free driver, this is State Farm—this includes $50,000, $100,000 B.I. liability and $10,000 property damage, $2,000 medical pay, and uninsured motorist, and I used $50/$100 because Allstate indicated that was somewhere close to their average. They used then a 73 percent reduction in bodily injury premium and S. 354, of course, wipes out medical pay.

Anyway, the total premium including $10,000 P.D. liability, in territory 8, which is our rural territory, and which is most of our State, is $52.60.

Now, Allstate's cost, for the first-party benefit package under S. 354 is $50.38 under the $100 subrogation.

So, if you subtract out the property damage and the medical payments from the figure they have I have to guess a little because State Farm in Iowa combines B.I. and P.D. liability, but take Allstate or, as I figure, it is $9 differential, $9 more for B.I. than for property damage both in territory No. 1, which is Des Moines, and territory 8. They are now paying for the people damage portion $39 and they would have been paying under S. 354 around $69, $50.38 for first party benefits plus about $10 for residual B.I. liability.

The problem you get into in a rural State, talking about Iowa now, you know when you say people are injured, you quote figures that talk about percentages uncompensated, and you say, "There are more people going to be compensated." I say then, "Under what system?"

Because to say they are uncompensated is not correct. They are compensated either under the health or disability income program or something.

Anyway, in the rural areas they are compensated like this. If you have a disability situation in most of the rural areas, what happens is the neighbors come over and have a picnic, plow the field or plant the corn or run the combine, or feed the cows—whatever it is

The wage loss is, or what I am getting at, rather, is the wage loss is not that much of a problem, but that is where your single car accidents are. They are hitting cows and trees, not other cars.

The high premium cost in a rural area in Iowa is collision and comprehensive because you have gravel roads and you have trees to hit and cows running on the roads, and everything like that.

So, while, you know, I don't necessarily disagree with State Farm, because I think State Farm and Allstate are fairly close, but just two assumptions are different:

One, as you indicate, is the 15 versus 5, and I, too, with Mr. Blume, tend to agree with him that, even a State like Iowa where it would cost more to attempt to match wage loss with survivors benefit.

The other is on the question of utilization. I think that from Allstate's indications, there has been overutilization in many States that passed no-fault.

You know, if you read Allstate's testimony to the Senate, their indication was that the Oregon bill worked better and was closer to projections of what would happen than in the other States.

I guess what we are saying is, they might be right and maybe on an average there might be a reduction of 5 percent in Iowa but there is no way to average this out.

What you are going to see with a proposal like S. 354 is a tendency, and Congressman Rinaldo had gotten to it, a tendency with the good and bad drivers, and you are not going to have a complete shifting of them, but a tendency to bring them together because you are going to see shifting from the ability to cause loss from the ability to sustain loss. I guess that is a long answer.

Mr. KINZLER. I forgot my question.

If you are driving along a rural road in Iowa, and you swerve to avoid that proverbial cow and you hit a tree and are seriously injured, what kind of recovery would you have? You certainly have nothing under the tort system; correct?

Mr. HUFF. Correct. You would have medical paid loss, and if you have the Farm Bureau Blue Cross/Blue Shield coverage, you have full comprehensive coverage plus $250,000 major medical.

If you bought a disability income policy, you have that, but as I say, most of them don't buy it out there because their neighbors help them out.

Mr. KINZLER. Right, but say you were seriously injured, to make it fairly obvious, let's say that you became a quadraplegic so your neighbors could only do so much and certainly couldn't help your medical costs—you would have whatever the limitations were of your own insurance on medical.

Mr. HUFF. Plus your health insurance.

Mr. KINZLER. Right. What I am trying to get at is this, one of the professed advantages of no-fault is in the rural States where we are talking about exactly what you talked about; for example, that there are a lot of single car accidents at high speeds where recovery is far less because these people do not have access to the tort system They have access to other systems, and there are medical and other systems as you point out, but they don't provide nearly as much as the potential tort remedy.

What I suggest by the figures, and they are anything but "written in stone," is that you can't simply compare premiums.

There is the matter of increased benefits, of increased payout. We are talking about a system which demonstrably increases the payout from the insurance company. I mean, the amount of money that the consumer holds onto at the end without attorney fees, from 40-some-odd percent to over 60 percent.

Mr. HUFF. Let me make, if I might, two points on that: One, I fail to see the difference between the individual driving down the country road and hitting a tree and the individual who falls down the steps and becomes a quadraplegic or the individual who is in a boat and gets injured.

The other point I would like to make, when you are talking about this dollar thing, and it is one of the problems you have, recognizing that most of your carriers in the State offer an add-on type coverage as an optional benefit.

The problem is that the only way that they are able to sell that is to roll it on at no increase in premium and then the policyholders tend to buy it the next year.

I think one of the reasons that there is nobody around buying these things, and I don't think an insurance company would want to write them if purchasers had a different attitude about things, is that nobody thinks they are going to get in an accident, and most of them don't. To tell the farmer in Iowa that he is going to get all of these great benefits and it will only cost him $2 more when he doesn't think he will have an accident next year is why the agents have some problems and we will have problems trying to explain to them why their premium went up so much.

Mr. KINZLER. Sir, it is a little difficult in legislating to deal with anything but averages.

Mr. HUFF. I understand that.

Mr. KINZLER. We can't pull out that individual farmer because it just does not work and we can only look at the averages.

Mr. HUFF. That is half of our State.

Mr. KINZLER. But Allstate is including farmers and we are still talking about minus 5.3 percent.

Mr. HUFF. These are State Farm figures.

Mr. KINZLER. No. I am using—yes; State Farm figures or Allstate's, assuming a reduction from $15,000 to $5,000 of survivors benefits, and a minor calculation for increased utilization.

Mr. HUFF. Well, you know I just can't see that, and I assume, if they use $5,000, the figures come out very close, State Farm's and Allstate's. And they must be using about the same dollar figure that Allstate is for the cost $50.38.

And if you are talking about territory 8, territory 8 in Iowa, obviously we are a rural State, not about half of the population, so you are talking about maybe we will say a fourth of the population now paying $52, including property damage liability, which is not affected.

And, you know, it is difficult. The people saving the money on this, in my opinion, in Iowa, are the younger drivers that have relatively little wage loss and probably even the older people, the retired, with medicare and who have a wage loss, and those that have a higher income that are going to tend to be those that, with maybe a lot of children, that are good drivers now are probably going to pay more even though you talk about averages.

I recognize your problem, and I tried to get information from the companies to break it out by territory. It is like pulling teeth without

Novocain. You can't get it, and it is because of too many assumptions, and they make enough assumptions in pricing S. 354, but they would have to make substantially more.

I think that is one of the problems you see in attempting to price title III.

In my opinion, title III should not have different benefits or standards than title II, and I don't think Congress should assume that there are not going to be some States that say to Congress: "To heck with you, you take the heat on this thing. We are not going to pass title II. You implement title III, and you take the heat for whatever increase results."

That is why I think you should consider having title III be the same as title II, and just it is a question if the State does not act, then they get title III under the DOT, but it is the same as title II.

Mr. KINZLER. Thank you, Mr. Chairman.

Mr. BRODHEAD. Thank you, Mr. Huff.

All of this talk about averages reminds me of the story that an old lawyer once told me. He said: The average person that has dealt with me has been treated fairly. He said: When I was a young lawyer, I lost a lot of cases that I should have won; and now that I am a crafty lawyer, I win a lot of cases that I should lose.

Thank you very much.

Mr. Edward J. Kremer, would you state your name and address for the record, please.

STATEMENT OF EDWARD J. KREMER, CHAIRMAN, FEDERAL AFFAIRS COMMITTEE, NATIONAL ASSOCIATION OF INSURANCE AGENTS, ACCOMPANIED BY DONALD W. PERIN, JR., DIRECTOR OF RESEARCH

Mr. KREMER. Mr. Chairman, my name is Edward Kremer, and I am an independent insurance agent from Salisbury, Md., and with me is Mr. Donald W. Perin, director of research from the New York office of the National Association of Insurance Agents.

We represent one of the 10 largest trade associations in the United States, with a membership consisting of 50 State associations, plus the District of Columbia, over 1,200 local boards situated in various major cities and counties, over 33,000 independent insurance agency firms, and over 125,000 licensed insurance agents scattered strategically throughout the country to serve the insurance buying public.

Mr. Chairman, I might say here and now in anticipation of a request for brevity, our statement, which I will read in total, will take less than 10 minutes.

Mr. BRODHEAD. All right, we are going to have a little problem because there is a vote on the floor, and I think it is one I have to get to.

We are going to have to recess for a few minutes while I run over and cast my vote, and we will come back in 11 minutes at 4 o'clock, if it is all right with you.

Mr. KREMER. Yes.

[Brief recess.]

Mr. BRODHEAD. Please continue, sir.

Mr. KREMER. Thank you, Mr. Chairman.

In my introduction before, I believe I omitted the fact I am appearing this afternoon as chairman of the Federal Affairs Committee for the NAIA, and appreciate the opportunity to comment on H.R. 1272 and H.R. 1900 and other bills pending which would require no-fault motor vehicle insurance as a condition precedent to using a motor vehicle on public roadways.

As pointed out to the Senate Commerce Committee when we testified on S. 354 just 3 months ago today, no-fault auto insurance is not a new subject for our association. Many man-hours have been devoted to in-depth study by our people over the past 5 years. The problems inherent in developing an effective and efficient automobile accident reparations system are well understood and appreciated by our organization. We first testified before the Senate Commerce Committee some 4 years ago—May 1971—when the original Hart-Magnuson bill, S. 945, was under consideration and which, if it had passed, would have put the Federal Government directly into the no-fault automobile insurance business. We opposed that legislation, and in the ensuing years have consistently opposed similar Federal legislation which would remove insurance from the jurisdiction of the individual States and place it under Federal control and regulation.

Of the bills presently before you, Mr. Eckhardt's bill, H.R. 1272, is also designed to impose a national no-fault automobile insurance system upon the citizens of the United States under the jurisdiction of the Federal Government. A second bill, Mr. Matsunaga's H.R. 1900, is virtually a carbon copy of the 1975 version of S. 354, prior to the recent revisions made by the Senate Commerce Committee, which would establish Federal guidelines for a national no-fault auto insurance system.

We have also reviewed Mr. Rinaldo's bill, and while we are not supporting any Federal legislation at this time since we do not believe adequate time has been afforded the States for experimentation, we are favorably impressed with the treatment of the primary issue.

Just as we opposed the original 1975 version of S. 354, we also oppose H.R. 1900, or any other legislation which may be introduced to provide a mandated Federal no-fault automobile insurance scheme to be imposed upon the several States, whether it be veiled as "national standards," "Federal guidelines," or some other euphemism. We are firmly convinced that such legislation would ultimately lead not only to complete Federal control of the automobile accident reparations system, but also to the total abolition of the principle of tort liability.

When we testified before the Senate Commerce Committee 3 months ago, we called the attention of the committee to a comprehensive resolution adopted by the National Association of Insurance Commissioners in 1974, following the passage of S. 354 by the Senate, which was sent to all Members of the U.S. Senate and House of Representatives. The resolution was too lengthy to quote in its entirety; however, we quoted in relevant part:

Whereas, S. 354 does not simply provide minimum standards but, rather would impose a rigid and unyielding automobile insurance system with significant Federal regulatory demands on all citizens while at the same time, placing severe limitations on the ability of the individual states to accommodate localized needs as well as their ability to regulate the business of automobile insurance in the best interests of the citizens within their borders;

Whereas, the continuation and expansion of the State-by-State experimentation process is the only viable means by which different no-fault concepts, structures, cost-benefit relationships and public acceptance can be adequately tested;

Now, therefore, be it resolved that:

1. The NAIC reaffirms its conviction that the respective States should continue and increase their efforts to enact and experiment with no-fault programs compatible with the needs and desires of their respective citizens;

2. The NAIC reaffirms its opposition to the enactment of S. 354 or other similar Federal no-fault automobile insurance plans.

We don't mean to be redundant. You heard from NAIC again today, but, gentlemen, we agree with them thoroughly.

Gentlemen, these are the publicly expressed convictions of the State officials who would be forced to administer the no-fault programs prescribed by H.R. 1900 if it should become law.

Just a week after our testimony, President William H. Huff III, Insurance Commissioner of the State of Iowa and president of the NAIC, appeared with Dick L. Rottman, Insurance Commissioner of the State of Nevada and vice president and chairman of the NAIC Executive Committee, before the Senate Commerce Committee to express their views on the 1975 version of S. 354. Their statement focused on three major areas: (1) The undesirability of Federal no-fault legislation, (2) predictable interference of the proposed Federal legislation with State insurance regulation and, (3) federalism and the unconstitutional nature of the design of the Federal legislative proposal. We strongly support these comments made on behalf of the National Association of Insurance Commissioners as they are so germane to the problems we visualize as being involved in the legislation the subcommittee is considering.

Earlier we expressed our firm conviction that legislation such as H.R. 1900 would ultimately lead not only to complete Federal control of the automobile accident reparations system but also to the total abolition of the principle of tort liability. It does not take much imagination to trace the probable course of events: Automobile accident victims would no longer be compensated through an automobile insurance system, paid for by the motoring public, under the jurisdiction of the State regulatory authorities and operated under the private sector. In successive steps, accident and health insurance, or benefits of other health care providers would be made primary, complete control of the system would pass to a Federal bureaucracy, and this would be followed by the absorption of the total mechanism under a national health program of the social security system. We are not only convinced that it could happen, but that it will happen if the legislation before you becomes law.

A review of the provisions of H.R. 1900 raises some questions:

Reference under title I, sec. 102(a)(5) to "the present basic system" seems to refer, by the definition which follows, to the tort liability system. Have the drafters of the bill perhaps overlooked the 24 States which have already passed no-fault automobile legislation? Is it clearly understood that if H.R. 1900 should become law, it would mullify the no-fault automobile insurance statutes of all those States with the possible exception of one—Michigan?

Under title I, sec. 102(b)(2) it is the stated intent of Congress to pass Federal legislation "which enables each State to participate legislatively, to administer without interference, and to continue regulating the business of insurance." Yet, under title II, sec. 201(h) the Secretary of Transportation is required to make a detailed annual "review of the operation of State no-fault plans" and "report to the President and Congress—on the results of such review and determination together with his recommendations thereon." These provisions seem to contradict each other. How can a State continue "to administer without interference," and continue "regulating the business of insurance" if the insurance commissioner is second-guessed by the Federal Government on an annual basis?

Under title II, sec. 204(f), the drafters of H.R. 1900, in their wisdom, provided for the primacy of automobile insurance by permitting any other benefit provider, such as a health insurer, to "coordinate"—that is, eliminate—benefits if benefits were payable under a no-fault automobile insurance policy, and also provided for "an equitable reduction or savings in the direct or indirect cost to the purchasers of benefits other than no-fault benefits." This provision would be commendable under any no-fault law to avoid payment of duplicate benefits and to have the cost of motor vehicle accidents paid by motorists and not be subsidized by the general public through their health insurance policies.

But, the new provision under title II, sec. 208(c) virtually reverses this thinking and forces the States to recognize qualified group accident and health insurance policies as primary if the group health insurer wants them to be primary and meets the stipulated requirements. With the problems our economy is suffering today, and the thousands of employees who have lost their group health insurance coverage by becoming unemployed, has anyone considered what havoc this provision would raise? How many workers who become unemployed would be astute enough to notify their no-fault auto insurers and affluent enough to pay the additional premium which would be required to again make the auto insurance primary?

Gentlemen, to avoid any misunderstanding, the National Association of Insurance Agents favors no-fault automobile insurance. Anyone who is familiar with the well-documented studies of the Department of Transportation would find it hard to contend that automobile accident reparations have been handled efficiently or equitably under the pure tort liability system which still exists in many of the States today.

We readily acknowledge that the fault system has been cumbersome, that it has many deficiencies and that some system of immediate first-party payments, without regard to fault, is desirable.

Where we come to the parting of the ways with the proponents of H.R. 1900 lies in the method of reaching the desirable end. We do not feel that the State-by-State approach is too slow or that Federal legislation is the only way to attain meaningful reform of the automobile accident reparations system. The tort or fault system establishing rights and responsibilities of individuals to society was hundreds of years in its formation through statute and through court interpretations. In a span of less than 5 years some 24 States, representing over one-half of our population have passed some form of no-fault automobile insurance legislation which, to varying degrees, modified laws which have been centuries in the making.

We agree thoroughly with the National Association of Insurance Commissioners that there is great virtue in State-by-State experimentation with a variety of no-fault laws designed to meet the unique situations of each individual State. We believe that this readymade proving-ground should be utilized to the utmost before consideration is given to any federally mandated no-fault program.

Despite the consideration of the constitutionality of S. 354 by the Senate Judiciary Committee last year, this issue does not appear to have been settled to the satisfaction of all concerned. The experiences suffered by some of the individual States which have enacted no-fault laws and have had them declared unconstitutional in whole—Illinois, or in part—Florida, should be carefully observed. What a tragedy for the Nation it would be for H.R. 1900 to be adopted and subsequently be declared unconstitutional.

We commend your subcommittee for its interest in this problem, and particularly for your decision to hold hearings on H.R. 1900. Changes in our economy the past year—inflation, unemployment, the energy crisis, to mention a few—all should be carefully considered for their impact, and the substantial effect of the changes in S. 354 as a result of amendments from the floor of the Senate last year should be examined in detail before a program is adopted which we feel would be disastrous.

Thank you for the opportunity to present the views of the National Association of Insurance Agents and to add our voice to those others in the industry who oppose the Federal legislation. We pledge our Association's continuing efforts to encourage the enactment of effective no-fault automobile insurance.

Mr. BRODHEAD. Thank you very much, Mr. Kremer.

We are most grateful for your cooperation. We don't have any questions for you at this time. Thank you.

Mr. KREMER. Thank you.

Mr. BRODHEAD. Mr. Robert Spolyar.

Would you identify yourself for the record, please?

Mr. SPOLYAR. Yes, Mr. Chairman.

STATEMENT OF ROBERT J. SPOLYAR, VICE PRESIDENT, LEGISLATIVE SERVICES, AND COUNSEL, NATIONAL ASSOCIATION OF MUTUAL INSURANCE COMPANIES; ACCOMPANIED BY ALDEN A. IVES, CHAIRMAN, NAMIC

Mr. SPOLYAR. My name is Robert J. Spolyar. I am vice president of legislative services and counsel for the National Association of Mutual Insurance Companies, commonly referred to as NAMIC, Indianapolis, Ind. My offices are also in Indianapolis.

We represent over 1,000 liability mutual insurers, mostly small, farm mutuals not involved in automobile writing, so one-third of our membership roughly is so involved.

With me is Mr. Alden A. Ives, chairman of the National Association of Mutual Insurance Companies and he is chief executive officer of a company in Connecticut, a mutual company that writes automobile insurance. He is also, incidentally, former treasurer of the State of Connecticut.

We have a statement I would like, Mr. Chairman, to be entered into the record, and I see no reason to read it in the interest of brevity, and I would like to have you accept it into the record, if you will.

Mr. BRODHEAD. Without objection, your statement will be entered into the record at this point.

Mr. SPOLYAR. Thank you, Mr. Chairman.

Basically, our position is to support State-by-State activity in the area of no-fault automobile writing of legislation, but we realize that this argument has been reiterated over and over and has not convinced a great number of people that the necessity for Federal legislation does not exist.

So, within the context of the fact we still feel that experimentation at the State level is the best way to proceed, we would like to offer some comments, briefly, as to how the two bills primarily here for consideration, H.R. 1900 and H.R. 1272, could be improved.

With respect to the H.R. 1272, our remarks are in the report. We think it preempts the State insurance commissioner as a regulator of insurance and for this reason, coupled with a deep belief in the principles behind the McCarran Act involved, and the effectiveness, proven effectiveness of State regulation of insurance, we cannot in any way support this proposal.

H.R. 1900 has some attributes we see as alleviating to some degree difficulties in the reparations systems for certain States, however we feel that if a minimum standards bill is passed in the form of H.R. 1900 or in any other form, the standard should be truly minimum.

We have one or two areas we would like to point out. As of now, we feel that it must be realized that there are great differences among the several States with regard to problems in automobile insurance writing. These differences are geographical. Commissioner Huff pointed out succinctly the fact that the accident types in Iowa are quite different than those in New York, Illinois, and Michigan in many cases.

The congestion in the courts vary across the country. The sociality of the people, the entire situation can be very different as between Arkansas and New York; and recognizing this and no-fault automobile insurance or some form thereof is best answered in many areas, we would like to submit that perhaps no-fault is not the best answer in all States.

But we feel, as to this business of reinsurance poblems for small companies, it hits us particularly hard because we have companies growing which perhaps would like to enter the automobile writing field and I think we can all agree this would be to the benefit of the consuming public and we feel there is a real chance this would occur.

If reinsurance companies are reluctant to deal with brand-new writers, small, medium-sized writers, because of the fact there is no limit to potential losses, we think that ultimately the consumer will be done a disservice and he would be better served by placing a cap on the amount of benefits he could claim under any given insurance department.

Now, we also would like to reiterate our position in favor of continuing automobile primacy. The reasons have been reiterated here previously succinctly, I think, and they have great potential for coverage of groups, great requirement for coordination as people change jobs, and go from a group hospital plan to no group hospital plan, or a reduced plan.

The current system is a good one. We feel that people think when they have an accident, they should deal with one insurance company and not two, and we see no reason for elderly people who do not drive who need health insurance to be subsidizing in any fashion the drivers of the Nation.

With these points I have made, I would like to answer any questions from you, Mr. Brodhead or Mr. Kinzler, which you may feel appropriate.

[Mr. Spolyar's prepared statement follows:]

STATEMENT OF ROBERT J. SPOLYAR, VICE PRESIDENT, LEGISLATIVE SERVICES, AND COUNSEL, NATIONAL ASSOCIATION OF MUTUAL INSURANCE COMPANIES

My name is Robert J. Spolyar. I am Vice President of Legislative Services and Counsel for the National Association of Mutual Insurance Companies (commonly referred to as NAMIC), Indianapolis, Indiana. My offices are also in Indianapolis. I am a member of the Indiana Bar and admitted to practice in Federal Court (Southern District of Indiana).

With me today is Mr. Alden A. Ives, Chairman of NAMIC. Mr. Ives recently left his post as Treasurer of the State of Connecticut. He is the Executive Vice President of Patrons Mutual Insurance Company of Glastonbury, Connecticut, an interstate fire and homeowners, property and liability underwriter of nominal size.

Washington Counsel for our Association is Mr. Jerome P. McGranaghan, 1120 Connecticut Avenue, N.W., Suite 310, Washington, D.C.

NAMIC is made up of 1,024 member companies, approximately ⅔ of which are quite small. These companies restrict their writings (by choice and by law) to farm risks. The age of many of them exceeds 100 years. They are spread throughout 43 states and, mutual in nature, they comprise the original consumer movement.

Among the remaining ⅓, many of the companies do write automobile coverages. They range down in size from the very largest to moderate sized companies. In appearing today, we speak only for the Association as a whole and not for any individual member companies.

Heretofore, NAMIC has been against the passage of Federal bills proposed which would affect the automobile reparations system. This is not to say that our Association is opposed to the no-fault concept. Quite the contrary, we have urged that all state legislatures take a close look at the potential advantages that reform of the traditional tort mechanism may bring.

Our opposition, rather, has been based upon the realization that tremendous differences exist in the type of auto insurance compensation problems faced by the several states, and that a Federal bill, if appropriate at all, would need to recognize these differences. This realization, coupled with a deep belief in the advantages of state regulation of insurance, account for our reluctance to support any of the proposals seen to date, including the ones before this Committee.

We are not here, however, to take up your time with a rehash of the reasons why federal legislation is not the answer. Though some of these reasons are valid in our opinion, their previous recitation has not convinced this Committee that the American consumer is either presently well-served by traditional reparations systems or that he or she will be well served by reforms that have taken place in many state capitals in the past few months.

We are here instead, to focus your attention on the need to make any bill that you may determine to report out, one that lives up to the "minimum standards" label and to ask you to refrain from doing harm to the proven effectiveness of state regulation and auto insurance primacy for medical payments.

One bill before you, H.R. 1900, contains the potential to unintentionally maximize the standards and ill-serves the consumer by de-emphasizing the role of his state insurance commissioner (to whom he has ready access) and mixing his insurance policies to a degree that this out of pocket expense goes up at the same time that the potential for gaps in his coverage does. We want to confine our brief remarks to these areas.

The other bill under study, H.R. 1272, effectively preempts the state insurance commissioner's position as regulator, and we wholly oppose this measure for this reason and without further comment.

As to minimum standards: It is the stated desire of the creators of H.R. 1900 type legislation to provide the states with minimum standards, above which each can tailor a statute best serving its unique character. Copsistent with this, a beginning limit on wage loss is contained in the measure before you.

Strangely, however, no such limit exists regarding medical payments for which a company may become liable.

This omission has the effect of maximizing the desired minimum standard, creating reinsurance problems for the small auto writing company (and discouraging the small company trying to enter the auto field, to the detriment of the consumer) and to some degree, creating underwriting difficulties for all companies.

We submit that a better approach would be to delete the limit on wage loss and to create a total limit on all first party payments, medical and wage loss (regardless of fault), for which a company would be liable. Above this amount, the injured party should be able to exercise a claim in tort.

The net effect would be to accomplish the goal supporters desire without discouraging competition and state innovation. Further, the confidence with which underwriters could proceed should accrue to the consumer's benefit at premium payment time. If a state decided that its citizens would be best served by removing this proposed limit, it would be free to do so.

As to primacy in medical payments by automobile insurers: the intent of the authors was surely to eliminate duplication thereby reducing the cost to consumers. We feel that the opposite will be true if the Mondale-Stevens amendment, added just before the Senate version passage last year, is allowed to remain in H.R. 1900, with the tragic "bonus" of potential coverage "gaps" and a resultant weakening of the insurer-insured relationship.

We are aware that the amendment in question leaves, to a great degree, the final determination of primacy to the legislature and insurance commissioner in each state. This is good. In our opinion, however, the "burden of proof" that auto insurers should remain primarily liable, is on the auto writing companies. We think it is misplaced and that this Committee should consider eliminating any provision in H.R. 1900 that places primary liability for medical payments at the doorstep of hospitalization insurance writers. Here's why.

Under the bill before you now, auto insurance protection is compulsory. Hospitalization coverage is not. The most casual observer can sympathize with the plight of the auto underwriter trying to arrive at a fair premium (necessary to prevent inequitable assessment of other policyholders).

Does the insured have hospitalization coverage at all? What are the limits? How long does the contract run? If he (or she) loses the job upon which such coverages are based, will the auto writing company be notified? In short, the amount of coordination between insured, agent and company required to make such a system work would be staggering.

And for what gain? None that we can see. No charge has been made that auto writers have been derelict or inept in this area.

The public expects their auto insurance company to handle all expenses attendant to an auto accident. They will be neither well served nor happy about having to deal with a second insurer for no apparent reason.

With the job mobility present today in our society, the motorists will be even less enchanted with any requirement that changes in hospitalization limits be forwarded (by themselves) to their auto insurer each time such occurs.

The consumer needs less complexity in his life—not more.

Should he be held responsible for not reporting a temporary loss of hospitalization coverage which unhappily precedes an auto accident? Or should the auto writing company pay the full claim and penalize other policyholders possessed of better memories? That is the choice faced by the company claims department when this scenario occurs, as it surely will.

If this presumptive hospitalization primacy is enacted as written and not successfully rebutted in a given state by the auto insurance carriers, we feel the following will be the price tag:

1. Increased administrative and sales expense.
2. An unnecessary load upon the consumer to keep all companies involved informed of his hospitalization coverage changes.
3. Increased friction between the consumer and both insurance companies involved.
4. An increase in the incidence of coverage gaps.

5. Potential inequitable assessment of those policyholders who discharge their responsibility to report changes in hospitalization coverages to their auto carriers.

6. An unintentional geriatric subsidy (by senior citizens who do not drive but must have health insurance) of driver health insurance premiums.

Coordination or "dovetailing" of benefits is a way that maximizes the efficiency of the system. We urge its inclusion in the measure before you and the removal of the presumption that the automobile insurer should be secondary in medical payments.

As to weakening of the concept of state regulation of insurance; we ask you to eliminate or soften the very stringent annual reporting requirements contained in H.R. 1900 as it sits before this Committee.

We ask this of the Committee for two reasons: one philosophical and one very practical.

This Association feels very strongly that all the reasons for encouraging state regulation of the business of insurance underlying enactment of the McCarren Act are still valid today. End of philosophical argument.

On the practical side; many, if not most, state insurance commissioners are charged with a wide range of responsibilities without commensurate budgeting and manpower allocations. For example:

One of the many critical responsibilities the Commissioner has is the monitoring of the continued solvency of companies doing business in his state.

Particularly in economically troubled times, this becomes extremely burdensome. Any diversion from this task becomes dangerous, not only to other insurance companies, but to the insuring public as well. Recent examples of company failure illustrate how dangerous.

Therefore, it is important that any resource distraction, from this and other essential responsibilities, be accepted only for the most critical reasons.

We in NAMIC do not feel that studies involving no-fault cost-savings methods of refunding these cost-savings, the impact of no-fault on farmers, speedlimit effect, etc., meet this test of criticalness.

We realize that the legislation before you provides for ". . . grants on a fair and equitable basis . . ." to help offset this added cost, but the potential depth of the requisite studies mandated, compared with what we see as a speculative and indefinite reimbursal from the Federal Treasury bodes ill for state insurance departments and the insuring public.

In short, we see more potential harm to the consumer than help at the cost of at least some erosion of the state regulation concept and we ask you to carve out and discard the appropriate sections.

In summary gentlemen, we have attempted to lay before you, concisely and specifically, the aspects of Federal legislation in the area of auto insurance that are most disturbing to our membership. Since the small farm mutuals which account for ⅔ of our Association's members have no other organized voice, we were dutybound to do so.

We would be happy to elaborate upon our testimony today, if desired by the Committee or Staff.

We find much in common with proponents of a Federal solution. Essentially we are aiming at the same goal—improvement in the existing system of automobile injury reparations, from the consumers' point of view. As representatives of companies that were largely formed because individual farmer-consumers could not get satisfaction in the marketplace, it follows that we think of consumerism as not only a good moral policy, but as good business.

It is with this background then that we endorse experimentation with reforms at the level to which the consumer has the easiest practical access—the state. A Federal minimum standards bill would not necessarily prevent this experimentation and consumer input, but H.R. 1900, as written, has precisely this suppressive effect.

Thank you for the opportunity to appear before you today and for your kind attention.

Mr. BRODHEAD. Mr. Kinzler.

Mr. KINZLER. You indicated that under no-fault an elderly person who no longer drives would be subsidizing other people. How would that be if he does not have an insurance policy?

Mr. SPOLYAR. Well, if the health insurance was primary, I would assume he would need health insurance.

Mr. KINZLER. You mean if it were national health insurance or private health insurance?

Mr. SPOLYAR. Let's say private health insurance. In that situation he or she would be paying premiums which at least in part would go to subsidize drivers in the event that health insurance payments were proper.

Mr. KINZLER. OK. Thank you.

Mr. BRODHEAD. I have no questions. Is there anything you would care to add?

Mr. IVES. No, sir.

Mr. BRODHEAD. Thank you for being with us.

Our final witness is Mr. H. Paul Carpenter. Would you state your name and address for the record?

STATEMENT OF H. PAUL CARPENTER, VICE PRESIDENT AND GENERAL COUNSEL, MERIDIAN MUTUAL INSURANCE CO.

Mr. CARPENTER. I am Paul Carpenter, vice president and general counsel of Meridian Mutual Insurance Co. of Indianapolis, Ind., and in view of the hour, let me merely try to summarize the statement which I would appreciate being entered in the record in due course.

Mr. BRODHEAD. Without objection, your statement will be entered into the record in its entirety. Proceed, sir.

Mr. CARPENTER. My company is a regional insurance company that does business in four States: Michigan, Indiana, Ohio, and Kentucky, and within those four States, we work with three varieties of automobile reparations plans.

Michigan has made a very sweeping revision of the system. Kentucky has revised its system to a no-fault system that retains a typical Kentucky peculiarity of individual choice. Indiana and Ohio to date retain pretty much the classic fault system.

In our area of doing business, an insurance company has to provide the things that people need and the things that people want. If you don't do this, they go to another insurance company. And from that background, we find ourselves very successfully insuring literally thousands of people every day who cross State lines into and out of different types of automobile accident systems.

The argument has been made many times that a greater uniformity or complete uniformity or minimum standard uniformity is just an absolutely necessary thing to prevent confusion and chaos, a long list of adjectives, uncertainty.

In our experience—and remember, we do daily deal with people in and out of three different varieties of accident systems—this just has not proved to be the case.

The reason it has not proved to be the case is that we have adjusted to provide an insured with the kind of coverage that he is required to have no matter where he drives his car. So that an insured in Michigan who drives into Indiana takes with him his Michigan first-party benefit coverages and an insured from Indiana who drives into Michigan takes with him his Indiana coverages, and he also has whatever coverages are required of him under the Michigan no-fault law.

In the case of an Indiana driver who drives into Michigan, we provide him with a coverage that he did not even purchase back in

Indiana, that incidentally is not required of us to provide him under the Michigan no-fault law. It is set out as a precise example in the written material and this does not create any confusion or uncertainty or complexity as far as the policyholder is concerned.

In effect, he is always in the position of having the ability to elect the most advantageous automobile insurance accident system that is is available. The result of this, as we see it, is that our insured are protected by a national system of protection.

Now, it is not a uniform system, but it is a national system. It follows them wherever they go. It provides them with whatever coverage the legislature of a given State, such as Michigan or Kentucky, has determined that every car operating on the highways of that State should have, and at the same time the policy is uniform only in its automatic assumptions of any coverage that is needed to comply with a State's law.

Literally, thousands of our insured every day go back and forth across the border from Indiana to Kentucky or Michigan to Indiana and the system basically works out very, very well.

From this, we conclude that 50 State uniformity just is not necessary to protect the interestate motorists, so who does it protect? Why do we need uniformity between the States?

From the view of a smaller regional insurance company, and we admit we are prejudiced, we see the principal beneficiary as being the giant insurers who can then provide a uniform product to everyone, one that is well-fitted to the great big computer on the 37th floor, but a product that is not necessarily fitted to the needs of an insured in Michigan or Kentucky or Indiana.

Now, I personally, my company, actively and sincerely supports this philosophy of reform of the automobile accident system. We have supported no-fault legislation and we are not anti-no-fault. We are firmly anti-federally imposed uniformity.

The classic pattern of Federal regulation has been that, as rules and regulations are developed, they are developed after consultation with the giant nationwide companies that can afford to have someone here in Washington all of the time, and I was impressed by the references to, you know, old adversaries and old friends here today.

My company cannot afford to have a full-time friend or adversary. This is the second time in my life I have ever been on Capitol Hill. But the weakened position for smaller insurers, the weakened competitive position that will, in our view, inevitably result from Federal minimum standards bills is not a necessary tradeoff. It is not something that has to happen in order to prevent chaos for interstate motorists. There is sincerely not that chaos today.

Again, we feel that this federally imposed system is going to serve primarily the anticompetitive interests of giant national insurers, and further concentration of economic power in a decreasing handful of giant insurers is not necessarily or in our view at all in the interest of the motorist consumers of automobile insurance.

These are the reasons, Mr. Chairman, that we are just fundamentally opposed to H.R. 1900, H.R. 1272, and the other bills that impose Federal standards which ultimately become Federal uniformity.

Thank you.

[Mr. Carpenter's prepared statement follows:]

STATEMENT OF H. PAUL CARPENTER, VICE PRESIDENT AND GENERAL COUNSEL, MERIDIAN MUTUAL INSURANCE CO.

I am Paul Carpenter, Vice President and General Counsel of Meridian Mutual Insurance Company, a mutual insurer serving approximately 150,000 policyholders in the states of Indiana, Michigan, Kentucky and Ohio.

Our four-state area provides a rich diversity of automobile accident reparation and insurance plans. Michigan is noted for its most sweeping revision of the fault system; Kentucky has adopted a modified-fault system, retaining a strong element of individual choice; while Indiana and Ohio have, to date, retained the fault system.

The vigorous competitive climate of our area makes it necessary for a successful regional insurer to be innovative, to provide protection that is broad, needed and dependable, and to consider always the needs and desires of the people we serve.

Meridian successfully insures literally thousands of motorists who daily commute across state boundaries, into and out of jurisdictions which have determined to apply varied rules and systems to the auto accident.

The bare-boned statement has been made in the findings and purposes section of federal standards no-fault bills, and in testimony before this Sub-committee and other committees of Congress, that uniformity in the essential elements of motor vehicle accident and insurance law is necessary to avoid confusion, complexity, uncertainty and chaos.

In Meridian's experience, protecting insureds residing in four states with three different accident systems, this simply has not proved to be true.

Our Indiana and Ohio insured is automatically provided (at no extra cost) with any additional protection which is required of him by *any* state into which he drives. In addition, he may, and is encouraged to, purchase excess first-party no-fault benefits which apply to accidents in *any* state or province in which he drives. Similarly, the first-party no-fault benefits provided to Michigan and Kentucky residents follow them into other states, and they are also protected by all required coverages of the state into which they drive.

The practical effect on the motorist-consumer of auto insurance is that he can elect to apply the auto insurance coverages most beneficial to him whether it be the coverage he has purchased in his state of residence or the coverage that is required in the state into which he drives.

This result is not particularly complex. It is not nearly as confusing as trying to remember whether or not a right turn against a red light is O.K. in particular states, and it has certainly not created chaos.

Much of the confusion has been in our failure to explain adequately to you the difference between a *national* system of auto insurance and a *uniform* system. The interstate motorist, whether a tourist driving across the country or the daily commuter driving across the river from Jeffersonville, Indiana, to Louisville, Kentucky, presently is protected by a nationwide auto accident insurance system. It is national in that it provides the benefits determined to be necessary by each state and province of Canada in which the car is operated. That national system is not uniform. Rather, the states can and do properly recognize individual and geographic differences in insurance needs.

As a four-state regional insurer, we are demonstrating that a uniform national auto accident insurance system is not essential to prevent a chaotic situation for interstate motorists.

Just one example: Michigan has abolished tort liability for damage by one automobile to another. Thus, recovery for damage to your own car is recoverable only under some form of collision insurance. A Michigan motorist without collision coverage cannot recover for damage to his car even though he has been "rear-ended" without the slightest fault on his part. Many insureds outside Michigan do not carry collision coverage, consciously electing themselves to carry the risk of damage to their car, but expecting to recover from other drivers who are solely at fault. Meridian provides Michigan non-residents with a limited collision coverage when they drive in Michigan so they can in effect elect to recover from their own insurer the amount they would have recovered from the at-fault driver if the accident had happened at home.

While this example may seem complex, there is nothing complicated at all about it from the viewpoint of our policyholder.

Fifty-state uniformity in the auto accident insurance system is not necessary to protect the interstate motorist.

Please consider whether the primary beneficiary of uniformity would be the consumer, or would it be the giant insurers who could then provide a uniform product to all their insureds, with maximum consideration of administrative convenience and minimum regard for individual or geographic differences in the needs and desires of individual consumers?

We support the philosophy of deliberative reform of the auto accident insurance system. We do, however, oppose the philosophy that uniform federal standards for auto insurance should be imposed upon people who have different auto insurance needs and desires.

The classic pattern of federally guided or imposed regulation has been to consult only nationwide giant companies with a resulting inbuilt favoritism for the giants. The weakened competitive position for smaller or regional insurers, which would result from uniformity, is not a necessary trade-off to prevent chaos for the interstate motorist. A federally imposed uniform nationwide determination of what the motorist needs serves primarily the anti-competitive interests of giant nationwide insurers. The concentration of economic power in a handfull of giant insurers as a result of S-354, HB 1900 and HB 1272 is not, in our view, in the best interests of the motorist who must ultimately pay the cost of auto accidents.

Mr. BRODHEAD. Thank you.

Mr. Carpenter, could you perhaps give me a little detail on how it is that you feel that should this proposed legislation be enacted into law, that your ability to compete would be diminished over, or as compared to your ability to compete under the present system?

Mr. CARPENTER. We feel that our ability to compete under the type of bill that is now under consideration would be diminished, principally because under the review system, type of coverage would become straitjacketed to where we could no longer provide the extras, the things that we currently provide that people in the southern tier of counties in Michigan happen to like, and they must like it; they buy it in preference to others, and they would straitjacket us from providing, as we do, now some differences in coverage between Kentucky policyholders, Indiana policyholders, and Michigan policyholders.

This is our concern and that, as it comes to a uniform product, then there is not the reason—or the reason that our company sees for its existence in a small area, which is to provide for the unique needs of people that live in that area, needs that inevitably are not recognized by a giant insurer from a thousand miles away.

Mr. BRODHEAD. I see. Thank you.

Any questions, Mr. Kinzler?

Mr. KINZLER. Just a few.

Mr. Carpenter, you insure in Michigan?

Mr. CARPENTER. Yes.

Mr. KINZLER. I gather you are insuring rather successfully in Michigan. In Michigan, the law, as it exists now for a State which, of course, is both industrial and moral, is pretty similar to the provisions contained in S. 354 and H.R. 1900.

Are you having trouble with the uniformity that exists in Michigan now?

Mr. CARPENTER. The uniformity within the State of Michigan as determined by the Legislature of Michigan, you know, this is what the people of Michigan want and need. Therefore, we provide it and in fact, we go beyond it in a few areas.

Mr. KINZLER. If all States were to decide that the Michigan law was the ideal law for them, in fact, were to adopt the UMVARA uniform State approach, would that put you out of business? Would it really hurt your competitive position?

Mr. CARPENTER. I think if the Michigan law is the best possible law, other States will inevitably adopt it.

Mr. KINZLER. All right, but you would be able to survive in such a climate, I gather?

Mr. CARPENTER. We would survive in such a climate because the other States that adopt it would still allow, I would hope, for the peculiarities of their own States.

Mr. KINZLER. The reason I pose it is because I don't see what the difference would be between the States adopting UMVARA and the States being required to meet the Federal minimum standards of S. 354, which are similar to UMVARA.

Mr. CARPENTER. That presumes that the UMVARA standards are S. 354's standards, and are the best solution for all States. I personally am not wise enough to answer that question. I think only time and experience will answer it.

Mr. KINZLER. All right, I still have a couple of more questions.

You indicated you are concerned about potential increases in concentration in the insurance industry. Do you have at your command or could you supply the subcommittee with some statistics on the level of concentration in the insurance industry? It is my understanding it is not peculiarly high, but I am not an expert.

Mr. CARPENTER. At the present time, the concentration in insurance, and I am speaking from memory of some academic articles I have read, is relatively low, particularly in the property and casualty field. The thing that scares us to death is that this is going to increase that concentration.

Mr. KINZLER. Of course, H.R. 1900 and S. 354 would not affect the property damage law as it exists now.

One final question, if I might. You indicate that there are no problems with the person traveling from, say, the no-fault State of Michigan to the fault State of Indiana, because the coverage of Michigan applies in Indiana?

Mr. CARPENTER. Right.

Mr. KINZLER. Does not the consumer pay a certain price, additional price, for that coverage in his total premium, not because he goes from one State to another, but because there is a possibility when he is in Indiana that he will be at fault in an accident and would therefore be responsible for the damages? Does not this possibility mean that you have to increase the premiums of everyone in Michigan to protect against that possibility?

Mr. CARPENTER. I would answer that by describing the rating process. First of all, every Michigan policyholder presently carries bodily injury-liability insurance.

The Michigan act did not do away with it. A Michigan driver can have a major liability claim because of the exceptions in the statute, the permanent and serious disfigurement case, the death case, these are areas in which tort law in the wisdom of Michigan, right or wrong, still applies. So the Michigan driver must carry still his—he is required by statute to carry bodily injury liability.

That same bodily injury liability protects him wherever he drives, whether it is in Michigan, Wisconsin, Indiana, or a Canadian province. And the losses under that, the losses, or the bodily injury losses to a Michigan automobile will ultimately wind up in the rating process as claims paid under that coverage on Michigan cars and ultimately wind up in the rate of a Michigan motorist.

Mr. KINZLER. In effect, without a uniform system, the Michigan motorist would pay a little more than he would have to if all of the surrounding States had the same minimum anyway?

Mr. CARPENTER. I think that is a presumption I am not wise enough to agree or disagree with.

Mr. KINZLER. OK. Thank you very much.

Mr. BRODHEAD. Thank you, Mr. Carpenter. Your testimony has been most helpful.

Mr. CARPENTER. Thank you.

Mr. BRODHEAD. Unless anybody has anything further to add, that concludes today's hearings, and I thank you all for your patience and and attendance here, and the subcommittee is very grateful to you.

The hearing is adjourned, and we will meet tomorrow at the same time in this same room.

[Whereupon, at 4:45 p.m., the subcommittee adjourned, to reconvene on Wednesday, July 23, 1975, at 1:30 p.m.]

NO-FAULT MOTOR VEHICLE INSURANCE

WEDNESDAY, JULY 23, 1975

House of Representatives,
Subcommittee on Consumer Protection and Finance,
Committee on Interstate and Foreign Commerce,
Washington, D.C.

The subcommittee met at 1:30 p.m., pursuant to notice, in room 2322, Rayburn House Office Building, Hon. Lionel Van Deerlin, chairman, presiding.

Mr. Van Deerlin. The hearings on the no-fault auto insurance bills will come to order.

We are going to rearrange the order of witnesses briefly so that our first witness will be Hon. Paul Sicula, member of the State House of Representatives of Wisconsin, from Madison.

STATEMENT OF HON. PAUL E. SICULA, MEMBER OF THE HOUSE OF REPRESENTATIVES OF THE STATE OF WISCONSIN, ON BEHALF OF THE CONFERENCE ON INSURANCE LEGISLATORS AND THE NATIONAL CONFERENCE OF STATE LEGISLATORS

Mr. Sicula. How do you do.

Mr. Van Deerlin. Welcome to the subcommittee.

Mr. Sicula. My pleasure to be here.

Mr. Van Deerlin. We will just ask you to proceed in any manner you choose.

Mr. Sicula. Fine.

Thank you for the privilege, on behalf of the Conference on Insurance Legislators, of which I am a member, and I am also on the executive board of the conference.

Since I have been chairman of the assembly's insurance management committee in the State of Wisconsin for the last 4 years and member for the last 8 years and also on behalf of the National Conference of State Legislators, of which I am a member, and I am also pleased to speak in their behalf on this issue.

The adoption of a national no-fault or mandated Federal standards is not an acceptable option to individual State action, in my opinion, and, in our opinion, on behalf of the organizations I represent.

State response is particularly appropriate since insurance needs and conditions vary so dramatically from State to State. National no-fault law cannot take into account the State differences in medical costs, urban-rural composition and accident statistics. No single bill could conceivably facilitate the myriad requirements of all the different States with their different populations, economies, existing laws, and political and philosophical backgrounds.

Further, the enactment of a Federal standards bill or a national no-fault bill would impede meaningful wide-range experimentation on a State-by-State basis to ascertain the virtues and defects of different approaches and thereby (1) destroy flexibility, (2) freeze in mistakes, and (3) prevent self-determination.

As in many other cases, State laws on the automobile compensation system and, indeed, tort compensation in general differ greatly. The national standards that you suggest to impose H.R. 1272 and H.R. 1900 may be right for the State of Massachusetts, but wrong for the State of Wisconsin; may be right for the State of California, but wrong for the State of Minnesota; may be right for the State of Florida, but wrong for the State of Oregon.

Twenty-three States have enacted some sort of no-fault legislation to date. Many other States, including Wisconsin, have attempted to enact no-fault legislation. None of those States, and in fact the entire United States, deserves the unmerciful, costly, naive, and ill-advised proposals outlined in H.R. 1272 and H.R. 1900.

While I understand that H.R. 1900 proposes to instruct the States that they have a certain time limit to enact their own form of no-fault legislation, and while I understand that the purpose behind this type of legislation is to give the impression that the Congress is inviting the States to act for themselves, in reality the bill does not accomplish that purpose.

As I am sure you are well aware, the bill sets up certain minimum standards that must be met by any no-fault State plan or the Federal bill will take effect. That will virtually replace every State no-fault law on the books and goes far beyond what would be contemplated in even the most serious crises. Those minimum standards in reality, then, are being uniformly thrust upon each and every State of these United States, including those States that already have no-fault laws.

As far as I know, in fact, the Federal no-fault law as proposed by H.R. 1900 and S. 354 is more drastic than any State law that is presently on the books with the possible exception of the State of Michigan.

It is unfortunate that this political body would consider a piece of legislation as H.R. 1900 that does not address itself to the complaints of thousands and thousands of people when they think of automobile insurance. These people are concerned about cancellation, nonrenewal, and changes in premium or coverage. Stronger regulation is needed which would require that:

(1) No insurer may cancel or refuse to renew an automobile liability insurance policy solely because of the age, residence, race, color, creed, national origin, ancestry, or occupation of anyone who is an insured.

(2) No insurer may cancel or refuse to renew a policy of motor vehicle liability insurance, as to any resident of the household of the named insured, except for: (a) Failure to pay the premiums on the policy when due; (b) fraud in any material representation made by the insured in the application of the policy; (c) conviction of the insured of homicide resulting from the operation of a motor vehicle; (d) conviction of the insured of operating a motor vehicle while under the influence of intoxicating liquor or a controlled substance; or (e) accumulation of nine or more demerit points in 1 year on his

record in the motor vehicle division of the Department of Transportation.

(3) No insurer may increase a premium on any policy of motor vehicle liability insurance, as to any resident of the household of the named insured, unless the increase is part of a general increase in premiums approved by the Commissioner and does not result from a reclassification of the insured, or reduce the coverage under any such policy unless the reduction is part of a general reduction in coverage approved by the Commissioner of Insurance in that State or to satisfy the first-party no-fault benefits.

As a politician who has been in the center of this controversy for 6 years and has conducted exhaustive public hearings, debates, and appearances, I fail to see how politicians can fail to address themselves to those problems, and they are talking about auto reparations reform.

There has been no great clamor by the people for enactment of State or Federal no-fault that curiously reduce the rights of those persons to seek redress from the courts. Rather, it is politicians responding to fancy slogans and not the desires of the people that has perpetuated the no-fault movement.

In a referendum in November 1972, for example, the Colorado voters rejected the no-fault concept and a detailed proposal of the $2,000 threshold play by a 3-to-1 margin—598,815 votes to 209,849. Despite this large margin, the 1973 Colorado Legislature proceeded to enact a threshold no-fault bill which became effective April 1, 1974. Politics was also instrumental in overlooking the needs and desires of the American citizen when the Minnesota Legislature enacted a $2,000 threshold no-fault bill after receiving recommendations to the contrary from a 14-month study conducted by the Minnesota Automobile Liability Study Commission.

H.R. 1900 was introduced as the remedy for the human consequences and needs of automobile accident victims. Yet this bill is a drastic revision of our present automobile system both as it affects person's remedies under the law for injuries done to them and underwriting practices of all people affected by the automobile.

Tort remedy for injured persons is all but abolished except in the most extreme and catastrophic cases, probably comprising somewhat under 5 percent of automobile accident victims—"Auto Personal Injury Claims," Department of Transportation study, 1970, pp. 19 and 24. Also, 80 percent of those 95 percent will lose 78 percent of benefits they currently receive—"Economic Consequences of Auto Accidents," Department of Transportation study, 1970, pp. 47 and 50.

On a nonfault basis, H.R. 1900 and H.R. 1272 are ordering first-party accident, health, and disability protection to each and every owner and driver of an automobile is an almost unlimited amount that he must have, whether he needs it or not whether he can afford it or not, whether he is a good driver or not, in order to drive an automobile.

I suggest to you that in an attempt to legislate for the most catastrophic economic losses in auto accident cases, comprising a small percent of all accident victims, we are going to abolish auto accident claims and at the same time raise automobile insurance premiums by more than 25 percent.

No-fault "sold" to the people in Massachusetts and Florida on the basis that automobile insurance premiums would go down. After 3 to 4 years of experience, they have found that in actuality, premium rates have gone up, and the people are not happy with the no-fault system if they have the misfortune of having to experience it by virtue of being in an accident, especially if you happen to be a workingman in the State of Massachusetts who finds out he must exhaust his collateral wage loss protection and medical protection with his employer before he can sue the negligent person that collided with his automobile.

EXAMPLE: DIFFERENCE BETWEEN STATES

With deep respect to those Senators and Congressmen from the State of Massachusetts, I think it's fair to say that Massachusetts had the worst automobile insurance system and laws in the country both before and after no-fault insurance. By the same token, it is recognized throughout the country that Wisconsin has been a model State in the area of automobile reparations, laws, and insurance rates. Former Wisconsin Insurance Commissioner S. C. DuRose admitted in an article for an insurance magazine the following:

Right now, in Wisconsin the automobile insurance system pays more dollars to more claimants and pays them quicker and with fewer lawsuits than that of any other State in the Country.

That is quite a contrast to the State of Massachusetts.

Wisconsin long ago abolished archaic and antiquated defenses and obstacles in the law that denied many people to recover even one cent as a result of damages suffered in an auto accident or any accident. Wisconsin does not have a contributory negligence system in which 1 percent negligence on the part of a driver bars any recovery for him in a tort claim, as was the case in Massachusetts. In Wisconsin, a person can be up to 50-percent negligent, and still recover 50 percent of his entire claim, whether it is for medical bills, lost wages, or general damages.

Insurance rates in Massachusetts before and after no-fault are four times higher than the State of Wisconsin. The Department of Transportation study showed that prior to no-fault, 75 percent of the people of Wisconsin paid less then $75 for automobile liability insurance; 88 percent of the people paid less than $100 and 96 percent of the people paid less than $150 for liability insurance. In contrast, 88 percent of the people in New York paid more than $75 for liability insurance prior to no-fault. The rate is even higher in Massachusetts.

Wisconsin long ago abolished charitable municipal and parental immunities which denied legitimate claimants the right to sue those exempted groups. Many States still have those immunities.

Wisconsin does not have a host-guest law which bars the passenger in an automobile from having the right to sue the driver of an automobile in an automobile accident case as in the law in many other States.

Wisconsin has done away with "assumption of risk" and "last clear chance" doctrines, which again barred many people from legitimate claims in auto accident cases and from suing in court.

Wisconsin now requires mandatory offering of no-fault medical payment protection and increased its limits of liability to 15–30 about 4 to 6 years ago.

A Department of Transportation study showed that in Wisconsin you have the least claims-conscious society. By that, I mean that 24.5 percent of those people receiving a bodily injury in an auto accident in Wisconsin actually hired an attorney and proceeded further than the insurance company's office, as contrasted to the national average of 46 percent and to the Massachusetts average of 79.8 percent prior to no-fault.

In Wisconsin, 95 percent of all claims are settled within 1 year from the date of the accident. Twenty-seven percent are settled within 1 month from the date of the accident.

In Wisconsin, only 4 percent of all claims actually proceed to a court and of that, eight-tenths of 1 percent wind up in a trial.

In our most populous county, Milwaukee, in 1974, out of 23,000 civil cases filed, 1,700 of those cases were for an automobile accident situation. In other words, only 6.6 percent of all civil cases, not criminal, not juvenile delinquency cases, but civil cases were actually as a result of an automobile accident case.

Certainly, you cannot say in Wisconsin you have a serious court congestion problem which would justify serious revision of who can go to court in an automobile accident case.

I apologize for bragging about the Wisconsin situation and belaboring before this national committee about the advantages of one particular State. However, this has to be done in order to emphasize that a national, uniform dosage of medicine which drastically changes a system which is excellent in our State may not be the answer. That is why this subject is best left to the respective States to handle. The people in the State of Wisconsin already have first-party protection for medical payments and lost wages through one plan or another including the automobile liability system or the automobile policy system in probably well over 80 percent of the cases.

H.R. 1900 and H.R. 1272 in many respects abolish their rights and do not give them very much in return. What's even sadder, is that there is no guaranteed reduction of insurance rates accompanying the abolition of very substantial rights that the people have enjoyed in our State for some time by law and by our State constitution. In fact, rates will go up in most cases in the State of Wisconsin and if you happen to be a victim those rates really go up as to you.

Many no-fault bills, under the guise of financing no-fault payments, or under the guise of "redistribution of benefits," or under the guise of eliminating the small, worthless claim from the system, or under the guise of eliminating the attorney in this area suggest the necessity of some sort of threshold formula system which eliminates the right to sue the negligent party for general damages.

There is no uniformity among States or even proposals as to what is an appropriate threshold. H.R. 1900 perhaps has the highest threshold, except for a total abolition, that all but eliminates tort action for the vast majority of claimants. These thresholds range downward from $2,000 in Minnesota to $200 in New Jersey. The idea being that unless the claimant has expended that necessary monetary amount for medical bills, has incurred that ambiguous but limited description of physical injury, tort remedy is gone.

In reality, that is the sole, underlying issue that creates the controversy in my State and around the country on the subject of no-fault insurance when subject thresholds are included in proposals. Such a medical threshold is discriminatory, as medical costs vary considerably within and between the States. Average hospital costs range from $77.44 per day in Louisiana to $159.85 per day in Alaska.

Insurance companies and others use every argument that they can think of, without factual justification and basis, to support a threshold-type bill. On the other side, lawyers, like myself, argue vehemently that a threshold system or a complete abolition of the tort remedy as in H.R. 1272 is unfair, unjustified, unwarranted, and unsubstantiated in fact.

Unfortunately, lawyers are castigated because of our own alleged self-interest. Let me say that the fact that lawyers like myself have an interest in this matter does not ipso facto mean that we are wrong. To the contrary, we are right. Not only are we right, but every poll, survey, and indeed referendum as took place in the State of Colorado bears out that the average person, voter, claimant, and consumer support the lawyer's position on this matter when it is adequately explained to them:

Read into my record will be some data that will support their arguments, but let me say in my own area where a letter was sent out to my constituents which asked whether you favor a no-fault system, 61 percent said "yes," 22 percent "no," and the rest were undecided.

The next question was, "If a no-fault law is adopted do you believe an injured person's right to sue for pain and suffering and loss of future earnings should be abolished?"

Of those that answered, 12 percent said "yes"; 71 percent said "no."

No legislative proposal that attempts to eliminate attorneys from any field is desirable if in fact that proposal does three, to four, to five times more damage to the people it's intended to serve.

Do not underestimate the impact of the threshold formula system. The Department of Transportation studies show that 85 percent of all persons injured in automobile accidents incur less than $500 in medical bills and that 90 percent of all people injured in automobile accidents incur less than $1,000 in medical bills. Yet, the Department of Transportation studies further show that the great majority of your automobile insurance premiums do not go to medical bills, attorney fees, court costs, administration expenses, or pain and suffering payments. Somewhere between 63 and 65 percent of your automobile insurance premium goes for nuts and bolts, fenders and bumpers, and other property.

In other words, regardless of what you do in a no-fault bill you are really dealing with a very small percentage of what you pay for automobile insurance.

The fact is that the largest percentage of the personal injury award goes to that thing called general damages whether that's for pain and suffering, loss of human enjoyment, embarrassment, humiliation, loss of earning capacity or potential, or what have you.

The facts are that since actual economic and medical loss in an accident totals very few dollars, the claimant seeks and is entitled to some sort of monetary compensation for these intangible things. If that were not so, it would be safe to say that virtually every claim would be settled between the injured and the insurance company. In fact, the overwhelming reason a great and vast majority of people choose to pursue a claim further, that is, contact with the adjuster of an insurance company is because they feel that they are entitled to more than just repayment for their mere economic loss.

An individual may or may not hire an attorney to assist him in this particular claim. One thing is certain, the mere right to an attorney, the mere right to pursue his claim further in the insurance company's office, gives to that injured party power and strength that cannot be replaced if you eliminate those rights. And I might add that most of the complaints against insurance companies do not come from complaints against the defendant insurance companies but those complaints come from complaints against your own insurance company.

In our State over 40 percent of the complaints to the insurance commissioners received were those persons complaining against their own health and accident carrier. In other words, their own no-fault insurance company. They complained more against him than they did against the defendant's insurance company.

Those who decry the "stake" of the claimant's lawyers in the final distribution of the premium dollar should, in all fairness, point out that the insurance industry tucks away annually nearly as much money in the investment profits it makes with policyholders' premiums as all the claimants' lawyers make in automobile cases.

Insurance agents take more in sales commissions than lawyers do in fees. Doctors take more of the insurance dollar than lawyers. Automobile repairmen take far more of the insurance dollar than lawyers do. This is not to suggest that any one of these professions or trades do not earn their compensation. They undoubtedly do. But lawyers earn their keep as well, and their presence benefits not only the one out of three claimants who hires a lawyer, but in a very real sense their presence gives protection and benefit to the two out of three claimants who settle without a lawyer.

Department of Transportation studies show this, commonsense convinces us of this, and equity and fairness rationalizes this approach. The "Economic Consequences" study of the Department of Transportation, table 40FS, page 322, reports that in cases of economic loss exceeding $25,000, with counsel averaged a tort recovery of $25,494 and claimants without counsel averaged only $3,821. Perhaps this system did not work as well in Massachusetts as it does in Wisconsin among other States; that doesn't mean that a drastic bill such as H.R. 1272 or H.R. 1900 is the solution uniformly across this land to whatever problem does exist.

In Wisconsin we have a State provision in our constitution which says that every person shall have a remedy for a wrong done to him. The attack on the Illinois threshold of $500 was based on the 14th amendment language of equal protection and due process type of arguments.

Any threshold bill which arbitrarily and capriciously says that certain people are injured and certain people are not, depending on whether they've suffered 6 months' disability as contrasted to 5 months/3 weeks, incurred $480 in medical expenses as contrasted to $501, or some other ambiguous, limited physical description of an ailment, comes under attack of trying to apply it fairly across this land. This is so because human beings differ in the way they react to injuries they receive.

That is why some people can play professional football with an injury that would otherwise disable another human being for 6 weeks. Thatyis why a country doctor may charge a medicalgbill of $150, whereas the corresponding treatment in the city may cost $500, $600, or $700.

That is why awards in this area vary from location to location; State to State; economical strata to economical strata. There is no sure and definite way to satisfy and uniformly apply monetary awards in compensating people for their injuries.

In the only attempt to do this, the workmen's compensation field, there has been gross dissatisfaction throughout this country in the inadequacies of that system which came about totally for different reasons than the so-called no-fault automobile discussion.

If two people—a claimant and an insurance company—cannot agree on what is a fair award to them, they do have a system that works fairly well in this country. It's called "a cause of action" where a jury of their peers evaluating and in most times compensates people fairly for their injuries. It does not even have to be a jury system, in cases of uninsured motorist claims or in cases of arbitration systems as is the case in Philadelphia, a disinterested party usually can judge how much each individual is entitled for his compensation.

I am not saying that the automobile system in this country is perfect. I am not insisting that this body pass a law identical to the Wisconsin situation and bring all States up to this area.

However, I am suggesting that the problem is much too complicated and diverse to look for one simple, uniform solution. However, I would suggest that in Wisconsin we are going to take meaningful steps for reform in the area of insurance laws.

We are going to redress the problems that people pose with regard to the automobile insurance system. Claims such as unfair cancellations of policies; arbitrary rate structuring; unfair rate renewal increases; mysterious rating practices of the almost exempt insurance industry throughout this country; more powers for insurance commissioners to regulate the insurance industry in all facets of life.

It is my hope that in the next session of the legislature, Wisconsin will pass a no-fault bill without a threshold restriction. I feel that every person should be entitled to first party medical payments and economic loss payments without regard to fault in the vast majority of the cases.

At the same time he should not get double payment for his medical bills or lost wages. Yet, with reform in this area we must be careful so that the good driver still rates better than the bad driver; so that the man who drives a high-speed, high-risk car still pays more for his insurance than the man with the economical automobile or station wagon; and so that the injured party recovers more money instead of less, so that the elderly citizen does not have to buy lost wage protection as your bill suggests in order to drive a car and have an opportunity to collect under that lost-wage package because he is not employed.

A number of bills have been proposed to the Wisconsin Legislature. I would suggest that if Congress must act, that minimum standards such as follows are more appropriate:
  1. Mandatory automobile insurance;
  2. First-party medical benefits of up to $3,000 required;

3. Income loss protection of up to $750 per month required;
4. A $5,000 death benefit required;
5. A $1,500 funeral expense required;
6. A $15 per day compensation for essential service loss of a non-income wage earner;
7. All of these first party benefits above described be satisfied by responsible private health carriers or through wage continuation plans at work, so that the automobile owner is not forced to pay for things that he already has;
8. Rate regulation and rate-structuring power vested with the Insurance Commissioner's office so that he can take into account such things as unearned income from premiums and from reserves—the ability to take into consideration income from investments of insurance companies in setting rates;
9. The Insurance Commissioner should have the power to deal with arbitrary and unfair cancellation of insurance policies, nonrenewal and rate increases which are unjustified;
10. Certain prohibited practices with regard to cancellation, nonrenewal of policies, raising of premiums should be defined and set down;
11. The automobile insurance buyer should have the right to appeal to the Insurance Commissioner and arbitrary treatment of him with relation to a cancellation, rate increase or nonrenewal situation;
12. Abolition of archaic and antiquated laws on the books of many States, such as the host-guest law; assumption of risk; contributory negligence; parental immunity; municipal immunity so that more people will have the right to collect more money under a fairer system as we already have in the State of Wisconsin.

I hope that you will consider my testimony under a rational, logical, and factual basis and demand of those who would seek to drastically change a system that works well, at least as well as other systems, demand from them strong burden of proof before you act in an unwise manner regardless of the political sexiness of the situation.

I thank you for the opportunity to speak and I will be more than happy to answer questions, if you have any.

Mr. VAN DEERLIN. Thank you, Mr. Sicula. I don't know how sexy I would judge this subject to be. I think if it were as sexy as you suggest, we might have more members on hand to hear the testimony this afternoon.

Mr. SICULA. I am used to that in my own legislative experience. It is tough listening to us politicians sometimes.

Mr. VAN DEERLIN. However, our faithful staff is always here. Mr. Kinzler.

Mr. KINZLER. This is what happens when you have compulsory staff attendance.

Mr. Sicula, you talked in your testimony about your difficulties in Massachusetts with no-fault. I was wondering if you had some figures on the experience in Massachusetts at hand. If not, I assure you I do. Why don't we deal with mine, then; all right?

Mr. SICULA. Well, if we deal with yours, maybe I will recall some I have in my memory.

Mr. KINZLER. OK; fair enough. I have here a chart for private passenger car average compulsory bodily injury rate for the State of Massachusetts for the period of 1967 to 1970. The figure—and it is, of course, pre-no-fault—is $66.75. The figure today is $36.10. Now let's look at Boston cars, which, of course, as you know, have a somewhat different rate. A person under 25, for example, between 1967 to 1970 paid an average of $374 for his bodily injury insurance and in 1975 he pays $146. There are comparable rates here also for other people. These obviously offer a significant reduction, so what concern do you have with the Massachusetts rates?

Mr. SICULA. I suppose it would be safe to say that the Massachusetts driver has benefited under the no-fault system because of the figures you cite. However, in reality, the driver is paying more, for instance, in Massachusetts.

How is he paying more? Sure, they reduced the liability portion of their premium somewhat. They reduced the amount of claims substantially; so, as a result of the liability portion of the premium, the insurance commissioner had to sue the industry of insurance writing in Massachusetts for excess profits.

So it is safe to say that you can reduce the price of part of the package if you reduce the remedy almost to nothing. So if they reduced the bodily injury by 50 percent, reduce your rights by 90 percent, you have made some inroads.

However, that does not tell the whole picture, Mr. Kinzler, of what they did in Massachusetts, because they abolished 90 percent of all tort right, so they lowered the liability portion, so that went down.

On the other hand, they mandated first party medical and wage loss protection, so that went up.

Now, in addition to that, under the Massachusetts law, you cannot collect under your medical protection or lost wage package of your automobile policy unless you exhaust your own collateral sources; so, for the labor man and the working man who had a comprehensive health care package, he had to exhaust that first before he could go to his policy to get a medical bill paid even though he was "rear ended" by a drunk driver driving down the street, hitting the rear end of his car. So they raise that portion.

In addition, they raised the collision coverage, which is inflexible, dealing with 63 percent of your premium, but raised it in an unconscionable manner, said you had to buy a deductible portion for collision. Now, if somebody caused the accident and caused $200 damage to your car, you couldn't collect from that negligent driver unless you bought back the right from your own company to collect your deductible against the other fellow's insurance company.

So when you total up the entire package for Massachusetts, sure, the liability portion went down a few dollars, although when it trickled down to the consumer, especially in Boston, it didn't amount to much, but it went up on the midpaying lost wages part and on collision and on collateral source, so there is nobody that can really say he is paying less for insurance in the State of Massachusetts. If you are a victim of a bodily injury and lost your right to sue in 90 percent of the cases, the tax to you is even greater.

Mr. KINZLER. I would be interested in seeing where your 90-percent figure comes from. You talk about collision coverage and compulsory property damage. Let us look at the compulsory property damage portion for a minute. The 1970–71 premium was $17.29.

Mr. SICULA. Is that for a bicycle?

I am sorry; $17 for collision in Massachusetts?

Mr. KINZLER. No; this is compulsory property damage liability.

Mr. SICULA. Other people's property. We are talking about collision, your own car; that is where it is costly in Massachusetts and created probably the problem for the last 15 or 20 years in Massachusetts—high cost of your own collision coverage.

Mr. KINZLER. We don't have adequate collision figures here but I have seen figures for the total premium cost to different Massachusetts people and that figure is, if I recall correctly—and my memory also is short on this subject perhaps—approximately the same today as it was 5 years ago. If that is indeed accurate, that is a pretty good experience for any State; is it not?

Mr. SICULA. I challenge the accuracy of that statement. I think when you find the collision figures, the only way they brought them into line is that they put in this deductible portion, so that many Massachusetts drivers are driving with high deductibles. As a matter of fact, that is what made Massachusetts so claims conscious in the last 20 years, because many people, to offset high deductibles in their car, became injured.

Mr. KINZLER. Mr. Sicula, do you have a profile of the economic loss and the average recovery for the average person in the State of Wisconsin? In other words, under the Department of Transportation study which you cited, people with less than $10,000 economic loss—those who had a tort action—recovered between 110 and 450 percent of economic loss, while the people with the most serious economic loss, over $25,000 worth—those who had a tort action and those who did not—recovered on the average only 30 percent of economic loss. Are those figures different in Wisconsin?

Mr. SICULA. We don't have any such figures like that for Wisconsin—at least I don't—and they are rather meaningless, Mr. Kinzler; I will tell you why.

Mr. KINZLER. Please do.

Mr. SICULA. The fact is, in the Department of Transportation study, which relied somewhat on this argument that in the catastrophic cases, the claimant was receiving so little, what we have to do is take care of that 1 percent. They missed the point. The reason he received so little is because the States that regulate insurance could not raise their bodily injury liability. Many States have 5-10 and we had a minimum of 15-30, although a great portion covers $100,000 to $300,000.

Mr. KINZLER. Does it cost more than 5-10 to buy $100,000/$300,000 than it does to buy $5,000/$10,000 coverage?

Mr. SICULA. As a matter of fact, $100,000 to $300,000 in terms of dollars is very little difference in the cost to the driver. The reason why is, fortunately, as bad as our highway problem is, 90 percent of the people in an automobile accident suffer a wage loss of under 2 weeks and a medical bill of under $1,000.

So, in an attempt for the Department of Transportation and UMVARA and S. 354 and H.R. 1900 to legislate for the catastrophic losses of the 1 percent, you could abolish the program for the rest of the 99 percent and never really take care of that catastrophic situation and it really misses the point. The fact is that the insurance commissioner in Wisconsin said that more people received more money with fewer lawsuits.

Mr. KINZLER. It would be useful to have some of the payout figures if you could supply it, because much of the contention on behalf of supporters of no-fault is that rather than receiving approximately 40 or 44 cents on the premium dollar in terms of benefits on the part of consumers, you receive a good 20 cents more.

Mr. SICULA. I never could understand that.

Mr. KINZLER. If Wisconsin is doing better than other tort States, it may be 47 cents, and that is not much of a beginning.

Mr. SICULA. I could never understand that argument. In fact, it is the entire portfolio really of the so-called pressure no-fault arguments. The injured person is going to receive more of his premium dollar.

The fact is, if you are not injured, you receive zero of your premium dollar. The fact is, in other studies it is shown that the only way to return more of the dollar premium-wise is to let the Government run the business. Social Security returns more of the premium dollar because they don't pay agents' commissions. It is an argument that really does not wash.

Mr. KINZLER. We have a bill before us which would eliminate the State governments entirely from this, and it might lead to that lowering of the premium.

Mr. SICULA. This is the way. Put the State in the business of writing insurance; then you have a more realistic viewpoint.

I will say this: I will predict, no matter what bill you pass, the way it is drafted you will have the same portion of the premium dollar allegedly being eaten up for expenses, agents' commissions, as you have now, because in all of the bills there is still somewhere behind the scene a determination of fault, and there is still somewhere behind the scene an agent's commission and executive's salary, and the fact is that it is a "red herring" across the arguments.

Mr. KINZLER. Where is the determination of fault in S. 354 with respect to bodily injury—you say, somewhere behind the scenes there is determination of fault. Where is it?

Mr. SICULA. In a portion, if it is catastrophic, you still have a right to go to court.

Mr. KINZLER. In the situation you described previously, which is 1 percent of the cases, a little less than 1 percent——

Mr. SICULA. How do you know, as an insurance industry spokesman, at the outset you may not have to determine fault? By the same token, collision coverage—there is still a fault situation in that.

Mr. KINZLER. We are talking strictly about bodily injuries because those are the only places the claimed savings are supposed to exist, not property damage, with respect to S. 354.

Mr. SICULA. In fact, the claim savings system to investigate fault takes the same amount of time; whether it is property or bodily injury, you still have to determine who is at fault. By the same token, in S. 354 you have some provisions probably for subrogation against the various insurance companies who may be making a contribution, both first party and other defense.

Mr. KINZLER. Only with respect to commercial vehicles, which, as you know, is a very small percentage.

Mr. SICULA. All right. So then, in other words, you are stating that there will be mandated collision nonfault coverage that I will buy for my car under S. 354, and my company will pay that damage regardless of the fact if it happened to be parked down the street and the guy barreled into it.

Mr. KINZLER. In H.R. 1900 and S. 354, we are not talking about property damage.

Mr. SICULA. But the investigative staff is the same. As a matter of fact, there are far more property claims in the country than bodily injury. You won't save a dime on investigation from that standpoint as long as you still have a fault system in it; and if you don't have a fault system in it, then you penalize the good driver.

Mr. KINZLER. Thank you, Mr. Sicula.

Mr. VAN DEERLIN. Ms. Nord.

Ms. NORD. Thank you. We have heard from a number of witnesses that people are tired of inequities that flow from the court system, and Mr. Sicula, you are a State legislator. I am wondering if you can tell me what kind of pressures you have been getting from the people you represent in Wisconsin.

Mr. SICULA. Two—slim and none. And I have been in the center of this controversy for 6 years as a lawyer and chairman of the Insurance and Banking Committee who have had the bills in my committee. I made it clear to anybody who wants to listen to me that I oppose any no-fault bill that restricts your right to sue.

I suppose it can be said, then, that if anybody were to be on the block politically on this issue, it would be me. I have said at the outset that I would not report any bill out of my committee that did those things. I have received no letters from constituents of mine. I ran last election unopposed. I ran endorsed by labor, and it blasted on my position on no-fault.

At least in the last 4 or 5 or 6 months, at the advent of the malpractice crisis, there has been no clamor for any action on the subject of no-fault whatsoever.

When the bill was debated in our legislature at the last session, when it had the Governor's office favoring it, labor favoring it, this was a threshold bill, many of the newspapers favoring it, we had nobody appear at the public hearings other than private interest groups.

The legislature defeated the bill. No one who voted against the bill was defeated in the following election for that reason. What else can I say?

Mr. KINZLER. Will you answer one other question?

We have heard, for example, the Consumer Federation of America testify they had worked very hard on a State level to try to enact State no-fault bills.

State Farm has indicated they worked very hard at the State level, and because we have seen insignificant increases made in the numbers of bills enacted on the State level, we need a national plan, and I wonder if you can refute that.

Mr. SICULA. There has been sizable action among the States to enact some sort of no-fault law.

We in Wisconsin are out to increase the present no-fault benefits we presently have. The fact that various groups work State by State to enact State laws is one thing, and I understand there is 23 or 24 that have no-fault legislation and it may be more.

As far as a certain number of States having to enact no-fault law in order to persuade you Federal people not to, I don't know what magic number that is.

New York has a no-fault law, California enacted a no-fault law, and I would think there would be a lot of motivation not to have one.

I don't care if there is one State that has a no-fault law or 49 States, it is not the type of problem suitable for one national Federal suggestion and I hope you understand that was the main purpose of the speech. It is unfair to compare Massachusetts with Wisconsin or any other State.

Mr. Kinzler is right. It was a mess in Massachusetts for a lot of reasons. There were a lot of things that should not have happened in the system. But for you to enact a Federal bill you would have to really deal with the Massachusetts problem.

Is that fair especially in Boston where it is just astronomical, to take that situation and then legislate for Salt Lake City or Takoma, Wash., Milwaukee, Wis., or Superior, I think it would be a drastic situation that will increase the cost of insurance greatly to the greatest amount of drivers.

Mr. VAN DEERLIN. Thank you, Mr. Sicula. Next, a panel we have been awaiting with great suspense made up of Mr. Robert E. Keeton, Langdell professor of law from Harvard and Mr. Craig Spangenberg from Cleveland, making his second appearance in this set of hearings before the subcommittee.

I hope Mr. Spangenberg is going to talk to this?

STATEMENTS OF A PANEL CONSISTING OF ROBERT E. KEETON, LANGDELL PROFESSOR OF LAW, HARVARD LAW SCHOOL, AND CRAIG SPANGENBERG, ESQ., CLEVELAND, OHIO

Mr. SPANGENBERG. I heard some numbers and I know they are incorrect and I hoped you would like to hear the correct ones.

Mr. VAN DEERLIN. Mr. Keeton.

Mr. KEETON. Thank you very much for the opportunity of appearing here, Mr. Chairman.

I have a prepared statement which, if I may, I will file with the committee and speak briefly to several of the basic policy issues and then stand ready to respond to questions you may have.

I speak first of the problem of standards of reform. I start with the proposition that the fault and liability insurance system for automobile accident compensation is a demonstrated failure. In the first place, it is inequitable, greatly unfair, both in its distribution of benefits and its distribution of the costs among the policyholders who pay for the system. Second, it is wastefully expensive and in addition to being wasteful, has produced extraordinarily high costs.

It seems clear that the standards by which we should judge whether a piece of legislation will effectively change this greatly unfair and wastefully expensive system are two.

First, good reform legislation must provide first party benefits that are quite substantial. None of the fault and liability insurance systems operating in the States have substantial first-party benefits for bodily injury.

All of them have substantial first-party benefits on an optional basis for property damage which we refer to as collision coverage. But they do not have adequate provisions for first-party benefits for bodily injury. That means that the persons who are injured, even though they have paid very substantial sums into an insurance system, are not able to receive any benefits unless they happen to be able to make their case on fault and also happen to be lucky enough that the person against whom they make it is financially responsible to the extent of their losses and rarely is that true, since, in none of the States, is the amount of the compulsory liability insurance premium adequate to assure that.

Moreover, in addition to this lack of adequate provisions for first party benefits, there is the great problem of waste and inequity growing out of the fact that the greater part of these enormous sums we are committing to buying automobile insurance are committed to an automobile liability insurance system under which the costs are high in relation to the benefits received.

The 44 cents on the premium dollar—which has been calculated, not simply by me, but by many others and confirmed by the New York Insurance Department Actuary shortly after we first calculated it—is a calculation of how much of that premium dollar comes out in benefits to someone who is injured.

There is no conflict here with respect to the basic data we are talking about. But those opponents of no-fault insurance who point to a figure in the neighborhood of 67 percent or sometimes even higher, sometimes up into the 70's, are pointing to precisely the same data but describing them from a different point of view. They include in what they refer to as policyholder benefits not only the amount that goes to someone in compensation for losses but also the total amounts expended in fighting over fault on both sides, that is, attorney's fees and claims investigation costs on both sides.

An additional reason the figure sometimes goes into the mid-70's instead of the high 60's arises when the premium is too low for the company to receive underwriting profits under that strange accounting system that the industry still insists on maintaining in which they totally disregard investment income. When costs run so high that they do not have underwriting profits, then instead of working on a base of 100, they are working on a base of something like 107 to 110. A figure of 75, which is the figure you sometimes see stated, is in relation to a base of about 110, so it comes back to approximately 65 to 67 percent.

The difference between the 44 and the 67 is the claims administration cost in the system.

So there is no real difference about what the data show, and I submit that in evaluating the system as an insurance system for compensating for the accidental losses sustained in automobile accidents, we should not count as benefits the administration costs that the system incurs because of its peculiar requirements of fault. Rather, we should ask ourselves, "How well is the system performing in using the money we are committing to it in taking care of the injured people?" When we look at it that way, we come out with 44 cents, or as some have calculated it, an even lower figure. The 44-cent figure is one that can easily be demonstrated.

The second requirement for a good reform law therefore is one that will correct this wastefulness and this inequity of using a high percentage of even that 44 cents in compensating the least seriously injured persons.

All of the economic studies that have been made, beginning with the Columbia study in the early thirties and extending to the most recent study, have confirmed the proposition that persons with relatively minor injuries are being paid many times their losses whereas the persons with the most grievous injuries are underpaid, not even paid enough to equal their losses.

So it is not simply wasteful but it is also terribly unfair to require people to pay into a system that produces this inequity in benefits.

The only way to correct that inequity is a substantial tort exemption.

S. 354 and H.R. 1900 both have excellent tort exemptions. H.R. 1272 has an even stronger one, which goes beyond the kind of tort exemption I myself would recommend.

The other two are at levels that I do recommend to the committee as being wise tort exemptions.

Let me emphasize another point: Opponents of no-fault are constantly saying that it takes rights away. Let me emphasize that the most deserving victims—those persons most severely injured and injured by someone else who was at fault—would receive more, not less, under each of these bills. More, not less.

It is those persons who have fault claims that are meritorious but have minor injuries that may receive somewhat less under these bills. It is not the persons who are the most deserving, those who are the most severely injured.

Since one of the inequities is that the persons with the lesser injuries are being overpaid in comparison with those with the more severe injuries, the good no-fault bills are substantially improving the equity. They are taking nothing away from the most deserving victims, the most severely injured, but adding to their benefits.

Let me turn now to a second major problem. What should our priorities be in concerns about automobile insurance reform, in concerns about what the law requires of people in relation to automobile insurance?

The answer is closely related to the point I just made. I submit that our first priority should be adequate compensation for the most deserving victims—those who are most seriously injured and who also have meritorious fault claims.

That is where a good no-fault law puts its priorities.

I submit that it is not an appropriate priority to require that citizens buy into a liability insurance system that will pay pain and suffering benefits at low levels of injury and cut off the amount of potential benefits by having a low limit of liability. That is precisely what the liability insurance system does.

Let me put it another way. There has been some discussion from time to time about paternalism in this system. Of course, in a sense there is paternalism in the automobile insurance law of every State of this Nation. Whenever there is any kind of compulsion to require insurance, taking away rights to drive, for example, if you don't have it, there is that element of paternalism in which somebody enacting the law, the State legislature, whoever it may be, is saying "We will require you on pain of certain sanctions being imposed if you don't meet it, to buy this kind of coverage specified in this law."

I am not objecting to these laws on the ground of paternalism. We have long since accepted the need for an element of paternalism not using it in a pejorative sense.

I do say though that when any legislative body undertakes to make a decision for the citizens, undertakes to make this paternalistic decision, it is terribly important that priorities be kept in order.

The liability system puts a high priority on the purchase of automobile liability insurance in order to be able to drive in these United States—on purchasing that kind of coverage which will provide to everybody in the sytsem through the mutual fault coverages, compensation for pain and suffering. As we know from the data, it has worked out in practice that payments are seven times the amount of the economic loss when the economic loss is less than $100. But State laws cut off the required coverage at a very low limit—in most States at $10,000, with few States going somewhat higher than $10,000.

That, I submit, is an erroneous order of priorities, to require people to spend their insurance money for that purpose rather than to spend it for the higher benefits for the economic losses and then making available on an optional basis the pain and suffering coverage for those who wish it. This more sensible ordering of priorities is what these no-fault laws would do.

I will speak more of costs in a moment, but at this point let me just make this brief comparison. The good no-fault laws, including H.R. 1900 before this committee now, would not increase the total amount of premiums that the public are putting into automobile insurance. Indeed, it is my own estimate that it would decrease it somewhat. But I accept, for the basis of judgment, the data we are getting from the industry studies that show that the total cost would remain at about the same level. But what would we get for our money? What would be the comparison?

Instead of this compelled purchase of coverage that pays us several times the loss in minor injury claims and does not give guaranteed protection above $10,000 or some such figure as that, with good no-fault law we would get life-time protection for medical expense, at least $15,000 of wage protection, something of that same order for protection in death benefits, all of that plus liability protection. We would get all that for about the same price that we are now paying for this other package.

I submit then that if we get our priorities straight, the protection of the economic losses that are resulting from automobile accidents should come first. I say all of that recognizing that these are accidental injuries, and supporting, as I do, through the rating system, causing the worst drivers to pay their fair share of the burden, I favor a rating system that does that in a feasible way.

I do not favor a compensation system that undertakes to make the right to benefits payable only on the basis of fault and then gives the right to recover several times economic loss, as a piactical matter, on the small claims.

Let me turn now very briefly to another one of the major questions: Should this kind of law be extended to property damage? I would make these points in that connection.

No. 1, there are possible savings there, but they are very minor compared with the savings that are possible through a bodily injury system. So we should not expect the extension of the no-fault principle to property damage to make a great deal of difference.

One of the reasons for this is that we already have, and always have had since the very invention of automobile insurance, an optional kind of first party property insurance in our collision coverage.

The second point I would make is that we should not expect a property damage system that retains subrogation claims among insurance companies to help at all, because that really is retaining the property damage fault system.

Our legislature in Massachusetts deserves great praise for what they did, in my judgment, in 1970 and in 1971.

In 1970, that is in passing bodily injury no-fault law and in 1971, passing the property damage no-fault law that became effective in 1972.

I regret to say I cannot state the same judgment about what they have done effective January 1st of this year. They restored the subrogation rights in the property damage system and that has produced a rate increase for property damage liability coverage, effective January 1st. On average it is an increase of 165.3 percent, which gives you some notion of what it means to go back to the system in which you are dealing with fault again, even though it is only between companies.

Now, I hasten to add, that figure standing by itself is very misleading, because that is 165.3 percentage increase on a base that is a much lower base of dollars than the amount of the collision premium, and the collision premiums go down slightly to match this heavy increase in property damage liability.

But the percentages look very different. The decrease in collision coverage premium for $50 deductible in 1975 was 11 percent when some of this money was passed back over to the property damage liability system. Compare this 11 percent decrease with the 165.3 percent increase on the property damage liability.

But the dollars involved were a base of $17.75 on the property damage side and $155.17 on the collision side.

So that comparison by itself, if you put in percentages, it is not revealing as it is when you put it in dollars.

I want to make one other point about that comparison, though. Because another thing that happens when you shift the money from collision coverage over to the property damage coverage, which is what the change in 1975 did, is that you restore a great inequity that exists inherently in the fault system and the rating that goes along with it.

Let me try to illustrate it with a particular example. When Massachusetts adopted the no-fault property damage law in 1972, they not only gave us some savings—small savings but some savings—in the total property damage premium for the combination of property damage liability coverage and collision coverage. They also redistributed costs very substantially.

That came about for this reason. On the property damage liability coverage, the companies do not take into account the value of your car when they set your premium.

So the new Cadillac owner with a car worth $10,000 or more pays the same property damage liability premium as another person in the same rating category, age, and so forth, who owns a well-used compact that is worth $500. They pay precisely the same premium.

Imagine the outcry if two homeowners paid fire insurance premiums on a $5,000 house and $100,000 house and paid the same number of dollars. That is exactly what is happening on property damage liability premiums.

It is so grossly unfair when you see it in fire insurance contracts, nobody would think of rating that way.

That is exactly what we have been doing in property damage liability coverage all along. We stopped doing it in Massachusetts for 3 years. We went back to doing it this year. Why? It is puzzling to me in a way, but I think I understand what happened.

When the shift in costs occurred in 1972, the owners of cars on the roads in Massachusetts that were worth less than average value of all cars got very substantial savings on their total property insurance package.

In contrast, higher costs were paid by owners of the new Cadillacs and other high-value cars, and, incidentally, that includes the new Ford, worth well above the average of the value of all cars on the road. A new Ford is probably worth twice the average value of all cars on the road. The owner of a new car paid a higher percentage of the total insurance premiums during that period 1972 to 1974. Those people with the higher priced cars are also, you can see, among the best customers of the insurance agents. They screamed and they were heard. The legislature heard them and responded.

So Massachusetts, although it is still being said it has a property damage no-fault system, does not have a true property damage no-fault system any more as of January 1, 1975, because we restored subrogation right. This means the companies still fight over fault between themselves to decide who finally pays for the property damage premiums and the result is we go back to the old proposition that the Cadillac owners are subsidized by the compact owners.

Now, that is a good example of what should not be done if this committee recommends that property damage be included. I would recommend that property damage be included, but I do so also, with a realistic appraisal, that it is not going to make a great deal of difference in the average premiums. It will greatly improve the equity among car owners by causing the high value car owners to pay their fair share instead of passing part of their costs over to the owners of low value cars.

The previous speaker spoke of the lack of equity between the owners of different cars on the road.

It seems to me that this is the plainest lack of equity that one could imagine, and it is one that should receive attention.

Now, having spoken of costs in this connection, I turn to some comments, if you will permit me, Mr. Chairman, on savings and what should be done with them.

First, I have submitted a supplemental statement, which I prepared earlier this week, but before I say today's newspapers, and if I then had today's newspapers before me I would have added another line on this chart that appears on the front page of the supplemental statement.

This chart shows pictorially what has happened to the compulsory bodily insurance premiums in Massachusetts.

In that connection, incidentally, let me correct an error made by the previous speaker.

This compulsory premium includes not only the liability insurance coverage of $5,000, which it included both before and after 1967. It also includes all of the no-fault coverage. So his statement that these savings were counteracted by an increase in these no-fault coverage costs is just flat erroneous.

This is the no-fault coverage package that includes both the no-fault benefits and the compulsory liability insurance premium. This chart shows pictorially how the cost of this combined package has been going down. The cost of the compulsory system was level for 4 years, when the rates were frozen in 1967 to 1970. When the new no-fault law went into effect there was an immediate 15-percent reduction followed by a 25-percent rebate and followed by smaller savings year by year since then.

Actually, it is clear to me that those smaller savings represent not a real downward trend in costs, but squeezing out the excess profits that were still there in the first few years. That squeezing out has not been concluded yet because, as indicated on the third page of my supplemental statement, a report released in the middle of June showed over 10 percent profits of the companies on this compulsory coverage in Massachusetts in 1974. This is at a time when they still have those reserves that I would expect to be too high. So when we come, let us say, to 1978 or 1979, and actual costs have been substituted for those reserves, I think that profit is going to turn out to be a bigger figure. So I think some more squeezing out will occur. After the squeezing out is finally finished this bottom line should probably turn up.

The reason it should turn up is that it is, after all, tied to the price index, to the cost of medical services, to wage levels, and so forth.

That leads me to say that the other line I would have added to the chart, had I had today's news before me, is one that concerns what has happened to the price index.

Today's newspapers report that the price index, with 1967 being rated as 100, reached 160.4 in June 1975.

If you apply that to this chart, you will find that it produces a line that comes out just slightly higher than the top line. In other words, this underscores the conservatism of my projection of what would have happened to automobile insurance premiums in Massachusetts if the law had not changed.

Of course, the real comparison we want is "What would our costs have been if the law had not been changed" and "What are they today."

Now, the response I keep hearing over and over again from opponents is, "Oh, but the property damage costs have gone up."

Well, of course! Inflation has continued to affect the cost of repair of automobiles during that period of time. We have also, incidentally, had a couple of other factors on comprehensive coverage, which is not remotely affected by the no-fault law, and it has gone up faster because in addition to having the repair costs go up we had the crime rate go up. The theft rate is up.

So the comparison of what has happened to property damage rates in Massachusetts with what has happened to bodily injury rates, instead of indicating that the no-fault system has failed, simply underlines what the savings have been. It shows what does happen to a coverage that is not affected by the system, such as the comprehensive coverage.

This same projection here of what would have happened to the bodily injury cost is also a projection of what you would expect to happen to the property damage cost. And it has happened!

Let me add also that the figures I have submitted here in the tables, and in that chart as well with the exception of those two projected lines, are the solid data. You can't argue with them. They are the facts. They are produced by the Automobile Rating Bureau in Massachusetts, which gathers the data on the basis of which the Commissioner sets the rates.

These are data from that rating bureau about what the rates have been. I used the averages here. If your committee would like a breakdown on that, the Automobile Rating Bureau in Massachusetts has been very gracious in making information available and I am sure it would make available a lot more supporting data than I tried to pull together here.

Mr. VAN DEERLIN. I have to take another 10-minute break, Mr. Keeton, to answer those bells.

[Brief recess.]

Mr. VAN DEERLIN. Mr. Keeton, will you proceed.

Mr. KEETON. Yes, thank you, Mr. Chairman.

I have spoken at some length about the rate impact in Massachusetts, because there has been so much misinformation about Massachusetts. I think I should say a word or two about another argument that is constantly made—that Massachusetts is all alone and unlike any other part of the country. I think that is clearly a mistake, too.

Mr. VAN DEERLIN. George McGovern would agree with you.

Mr. KEETON. It has even in that instance, I would submit, only been different in degree from other parts of the Nation, and I think the same thing is true here. That is, I think it is clear that Massachusetts had this diseased system in a more advanced state than any other State in the Union, but the disease is basically the same. And as we look around all of the other States, we see the comparison. The Status having the congested population centers also have higher insurance rates and mainifest more severely these symptoms I have been pointing to.

As a matter of fact, if you break down the Massachusetts data according to counties, you find that out in the Berkshires the situation is not nearly as bad as it has been in Boston, and that shows up in some of these data that are in this supplementary statement.

The savings from the system have not been as great out there as in Boston, but the savings have been there. So, the point I am making is that, while Massachusetts is distinctive in the degree to which it had this problem, it is not basically different from the other States.

The basic problem is with the system, not with the States where it is applying. So, savings can be achieved, and the data that your committee is receiving from industry sources and from the actuarial study confirm this. The question of choice that faces one at this point is, "What should be done with the savings?"

"What level should one seek to achieve—what should be the strength of the tort exemption? And then what should be done with the savings?"

In that respect, the legislation that has been passed in 17 States that have true no-fault laws with a partial tort exemption has been good, as a movement in the right direction. I submit that it has not gone far enough. Only the Michigan statute really comes close to meeting the criteria in H.R. 1900 and in the new Uniform Motor Vehicle Reparation Act, UMVARA.

The choice that is available to us can be described in these terms: certainly, at no increase in cost—and I believe at some decrease in cost—we could have a good no-fault system in lieu of the fault system.

The system we now have, in the States that do not have a no-fault law, is a system in which, if you are not able to make out a claim on fault, you have nothing, and, if you are, you don't have any assurance of getting more than the limit, $10,000 in most States, somewhat more than that in others. That package does have the advantage that you get this opportunity to recover a lot more than your loss for pain and suffering, if you get over all of these hurdles.

In comparison with that, you could have the no-fault package, in which you are assured of your economic recovery up to $15,000 for wage loss and lifetime medical expense, rehabiliation expense, which is terribly important. You could be assured of that.

I think, if most citizens were given the choice and understood that in order to get this chance at pain and suffering recovery, you have to give up this assurance of economic loss, but you can instead give up that chance at pain and suffering and get the assurance of economic loss, they would take the latter.

That is what H.R. 1900 and S. 354 propose to do. I would recommend one modification; that is, I think it is appropriate to offer people the choice to have that pain and suffering award if they want it.

That is feasible. Bills have been drafted. We drafted several in Massachusetts. They were not passed because the final compromise measure did not include this added protection coverage in it. But it is feasible to mandate that the companies offer to a person this option so that if one wants to buy a coverage that would provide all of the benefits one could get now, plus the assurance that we have been talking about of a lifetime coverage, it would be there to be purchased.

I personally think relatively few people would buy the pain and suffering coverage, but I think they ought to be given that choice. That certainly is a better solution.

Mr. VAN DEERLIN. Would the premium be prohibitive?

Mr. KEETON. I think it would not be.

I am talking about coverage that pays pain and suffering benefits only when another person was at fault—just as is the case in the fault system. One can get some sense of what that premium might be by looking at the amount we are saving by eliminating the pain and suffering claims through these tort exemptions. On that basis, at the outside probably would not be more than 30 to 50 percent above the premium we are talking about now. That is an outside figure of what that cost would be. It probably would not be that high.

But what we are talking about is, how you use that money that is saved by the tort exemption. The present system forces you to buy this protection that gives you a chance at the higher recovery, but does not give you lifetime protection for economic loss.

I would say, if we are going to force people to do something, that is not the right thing to force them to do. Let them have that kind of coverage if they wish but the coverage that is forced upon them ought to be the coverage that takes care of economic loss.

Just a word, briefly, about the Federal-State relations problem. I preferred that this matter be handled in the States. Professor O'Connell and I so recommended in our original proposal in the midsixties.

I now support a Federal minimum standards bill, not a Federal prexemption bill. I do so for the reason that the track record of the last few years has shown that the pressure groups that have their influence upon the State legislatures will prevent the enactment of a good no-fault law that is in the public interest in this area for a long time to come. It is time for Congress to step in with a minimum standards bill that would still leave it to the States to operate the systems and regulate insurance, but would assure that each State has a bill that at least meets these minimum standards. A person who is traveling interstate then has some similarity of systems to work with and that eases the problems. It reduces both the problems of unexpected results that might otherwise occur for the victim and the problems of cost of administration that result from systems that are too different in different States.

Thank you, Mr. Chairman.

[Mr. Keeton's prepared and supplemental statements follow:]

STATEMENT OF ROBERT E. KEETON, LANGDELL PROFESSOR OF LAW, HARVARD· LAW SCHOOL

Mr. Chairman and members of the subcommittee, I am grateful for the opportunity of appearing before you today. My submission focuses primarily on the major issues of public policy underlying what has come to be called "no-fault automobile insurance."

STANDARDS FOR EFFECTIVE REFORM

In its practical performance, the fault-and-liability-insurance system for dealing with injuries to persons in car accidents is a demonstrated failure. It is unfair both in the distribution of its benefits and the assignment of shares of the cost, and it is inefficient and wastefully expensive.

The key to effective reform is twofold. First, the law must establish a system of automobile insurance under which you buy self-protection on a no-fault basis instead of just buying "liability" insurance to pay somebody else you injure. Second, the law must abolish "liability" claims altogether unless injuries are serious or severe.

Under a system with this key, two-fold feature, you would be paid for your medical expenses and wage losses under the no-fault self-protection insurance. And you could buy as much self-protection as you wish, instead of being at the mercy of another person's option to choose a high or low policy limit, as you are under "liability" insurance.

Although "no-fault" is not a term I would have chosen to describe a law that meets these two standards, it is the term that has caught hold, and I accept it. It is imperative, however, that we distinguish between the laws that meet these two standards (which I will refer to as "real no-fault" laws) and those that do not.

The so-called no-fault laws of a few states, Arkansas, Delaware, Maryland, Oregon, South Carolina, South Dakota, Texas, Virginia, and Wisconsin do not have the second of these two key provisions. They are bad models to follow. They would not correct the waste, inefficiency, and unjust distribution of benefits and burdens of the fault-based system. They are merely "add-on" laws.

The add-on laws are being called no-fault laws by people who are basically opposed to a real no-fault system and hope to head it off by compromise. Those laws are corruptions of the no-fault principle. They will just add more insurance costs to the burden the public is already bearing. And they will not correct the injustice of overcompensating for minor injuries while undercompensating for serious and severe injuries.

In contrast with the "add-on" laws, a real no-fault system gives better protection at lower cost. Your medical expenses and wage losses are paid promptly under your own self-protection coverage. And your insurance costs you less because a real no-fault system reduces the overhead and cuts out wasteful, heavy overpayment of claims against you for minor injuries.

Under the fault-and-liability-insurance system, your insurance company usually settles small claims made against you just to get rid of them. And as a result you pay higher "liability" insurance premiums. Your company does this because under the "liability" system a claim of pain and suffering has a substantial amount of nuisance value, on top of any value it may have on the merits. The reason is that it would cost the insurance company more than $1,000 to fight the case through an appeal. In practice, the insurance companies find it less expensive to pay than to fight. And when the claimant's out-of-pocket loss is less than $100 and he has an attorney, on average the companies pay more than seven times the out-of-pocket losses to settle. In contrast, the insurance companies find it worthwhile to fight in cases of serious injuries, and a claimant who has out-of-pocket losses of $2,500 or more has to be lucky just to get his out-of-pocket loss paid. ▶Let it be emphasized that a good no-fault law (one with a realistic partial tort exemption) does *more* for the victims who are most deserving—those who have been severely injured by someone else's fault. Rather than taking away some of their rights, as opponents charge, it preserves their tort claims and provides no-fault benefits too. This is the kind of law that will best serve the public interest all across the nation.

ENACTED LAWS

Among the real no-fault laws (as well as the "add-on" laws that do not provide a partial tort exemption), no two statutes thus far enacted are identical. The variations are substantial enough to cause confusion and concern among motorists who are quite properly worried about the possible consequences of accidents during travel outside their home state.

In one respect, the real no-fault laws are all alike. Each contains some kind of partial tort exemption. That is, in addition to providing benefits without regard to fault to cover losses from bodily injuries caused by car accidents, the statute eliminates tort claims (that is, claims based on fault) for some injuries. The claims for injuries of a less serious nature are eliminated. Persons who suffer more serious injuries still have their tort claims, in addition to the new no-fault benefits. A good statute also dovetails these two kinds of benefits to avoid double recovery for a single item of loss—and to avoid double cost for the system.

▶ Two of the partial-tort-exemption statutes—those in New Jersey and Connecticut—eliminate tort recoveries for *minor* injuries only.

Thirteen eliminate tort recoveries for what I would call *minor* and *substantial* injuries but preserve tort recoveries for what I would call moderate, serious and severe injuries. These are the statutes in Colorado, Florida, Georgia, Kansas, Kentucky, Massachusetts, Minnesota, Nevada, New York, North Dakota, Pennsylvania, and Utah.

▶ Two statutes eliminate tort recoveries for *minor, substantial,* and *moderate* injuries but preserve tort recoveries for serious and severe injuries. These are the statutes in Hawaii and Michigan.

By way of comparison, UMVARA—the Uniform Motor Vehicle Accident Reparations Act proposed by the National Conference of Commissioners on Uniform State Laws—would eliminate tort recoveries for *all except severe* injuries.

EXTENSION OF NO-FAULT TO PROPERTY DAMAGE

Much of the current controversy centers on extension of the no-fault principle to damage to cars as distinguished from injuries to people. I submit three propositions about application of the no-fault principle to damage to cars.

First. The possibilities for improvement of the system in this area are very modest in comparison with the dramatic improvements effected by a real no-fault system for injuries to people.

Second. In relation to car damage, as in relation to injuries to people, an "add-on" law is no improvement at all. We have had an "add-on" car damage coverage ever since car insurance was invented. We call it collision coverage. The current Massachusetts car damage coverage is such an add-on coverage. It does not eliminate tort claims for car damage. Instead, it just converts them from claims against drivers to "subrogation" claims against their insurers. The key disadvantages of "fault" claims are still there in the system. The current Massachusetts car damage system will not help and should not be copied anywhere else. Temporarily (1972-74) Massachusetts had a slightly improved car damage system, about which I will comment further in the supplement to this statement. Some features of that system deserve to be copied elsewhere; others do not.

Third. The "no-fault" principle for car damage is not capable of doing anything about rising repair costs and rising theft rates, both of which are causing increases in car insurance costs.

Some opponents of "no-fault" persist in advancing the argument that rising rates for *insurance against car damage* prove that "no-fault" does not work. This is a fundamental fallacy, based on failure to recognize the vast difference between insurance against damage to cars and insurance against injuries to people. It is not a failure of fire insurance when rates go up with inflation and rising construction and repair costs. Nor is it a failure of no-fault car insurance when rates go up with inflation and rising repair costs. Indeed, as an analysis of costs will show, the inevitable fact that rates for insurance against damage to property (whether houses or cars) are tied to inflation and rising repair costs merely underscores the success of no-fault insurance against injuries to people in maintaining a downward trend in costs during a period of general inflation.

EQUITY IN DISTRIBUTION OF COSTS (A NEED FOR AMENDMENT OF H.R. 1900)

With respect to the tort exemption, the provisions of H.R 1900 are, I submit, excellent. However, in one respect this bill would force upon the states an inequity that is indefensible.

Because of Section 111 (a), the major impact with respect to cost savings would be to give the savings primarily, and perhaps exclusively, to the owners of heavy cars and trucks. This runs directly contrary to equity and fairness, since the weight of the heavier vehicles sharply increases the number and severity of injuries to passengers in lighter vehicles with which they are in collision.

Honorable Eugene Burdick of North Dakota, past president of the National Conference of Commissioners on Uniform State Laws, and Professor Roger Henderson of Nebraska, Co-Reporter for the Conference's Special Committee on Uniform Motor Vehicle Accident Reparations Act, have suggested an appropriate way of curing this same defect in S. 354. Their suggestion applies as well to H.R. 1900. They recommend that Section 111 (a), paragraph (1), subparagraph (B), be amended by addition of the underlined words to read as follows:
 . . . a restoration obligor- . . .
(B) may not directly or indirectly contract for, or be granted by a State, any right of reimbursement *based upon a determination of fault* from any other restoration obligor not acting as a reinsurer for no-fault benefits which it has paid or is obligated to pay as a result of injury to a victim.

In addition to supporting their recommendation, I submit that paragraph (3) of Section 111 (a) is both unwise and unfair. It is an apparent compromise aimed at doing a little, but very little, about the inequity of subparagraph (B). If subparagraph (B) is amended in the way stated above, there is no longer any need for paragraph (3). If paragraph (3) is retained, however, it should be amended by striking the concluding phrase, "Provided, that in such event such right of reimbursement may be granted only with respect to benefits paid for loss in excess of $5,000." This phrase causes car owners, through payment of their insurance premiums, to subsidize owners of commercial vehicles in an annual sum equal to $5,000 times the total number of occupants of passenger cars seriously injured in the car-truck accidents to which the provision applies. Moreover, all the cases to which this provision applies are cases in which the injuries were caused *by the fault of the owners or operators of the commercial vehicles.* I submit; that merely to identify this effect of the $5,000 clause is to demonstrate how unfair it is.

THE CURRENT CHOICE

Costs of insurance under a genuine no-fault system—one coupling no-fault insurance with partial elimination of tort actions—have proved to be far lower than Professor O'Connell and I imagined when we offered the Basic Protection Plan in 1965. Of course there continue to be wide variations in cost estimates, even after the surprisingly favorable experience in Massachusetts has developed. But the difference in estimates has been narrowing with increasing data and more studies. For example, the estimates submitted to the Special Committee on UMVARA from the three major segments of the industry, who disagree sharply about the desirability of no-fault insurance, ranged only from modest savings to modest increases in comparison with costs of the existing system, on average, for policyholders carrying liability insurance coverage of $25,000 per person and $50,000 per accident. An appropriate way, then, of putting one question of choice now before us is this: You can have either of two forms of insurance for approximately the same price. The *first* gives you a right to recover for both economic losses and pain and suffering if you have a valid claim based on fault, but no right to recover either kind of damages in other cases and no assurance of the financial responsibility of the negligent party above $25,000. The *second* gives you a guaranteed life-time coverage for economic losses regardless of fault but no chance of recovering damages for pain and suffering unless you sustain a very severe injury. Which would you take?

I submit that among those who fully understand the range of coice and have no special axe to grind, the answer is clear. Year by year since the mid-1960's, as public understanding has increased, public support for true no-fualt laws has increased. Lifetime no-fault coverage for economic loss is plainly the best choice. Under a good no-fault law, most people could continue to pay about the same insurance costs as they will pay if the law is unchanged, and would receive this greatly improved protection. That, I submit, is a better answer than enacting a "scaled-down no-fault" law that would greatly reduce insurance costs. Perhaps the more cautious aproach of scaling down the law was defensible when Massachusetts was pioneering in 1970. A better choice is available now.

FEDERAL LEGISLATION

My initial hope was that the states could and would deal with this problem effectively, without federal legislation. I continue to prefer that the problem be dealth with, as far as it is feasible to do so, at the state level. With regret, I have come to the view that in the absence of federal legislation, action will be both too slow and too different, state by state, to serve the public interest. I respectfully recommend, however, that federal legislation set minimum standards for satisfactory no-fault laws rather than totally preempting state laws in this area. I would urge that those standards require that the partial tort exemption eliminate tort actions except in cases of serious or severe injury and that the no-fault benefits be at least as great as they are in the Michigan law.

Thank you for the opportunity of appearing before you.

The Impact of No-Fault on Insurance Costs

The most important reasons for adopting a good no-fault system are that it will be fairer and more efficient in the way it treats people involved in accidents—both victims and drivers. Although I would give lower priority to a third objective—reducing premium costs—that objective inevitably receives much attention.

Exhibit 1 shows what has happened to *compulsory bodily injury* insurance rates in Massachusetts from 1951 through 1975.

Exhibit I

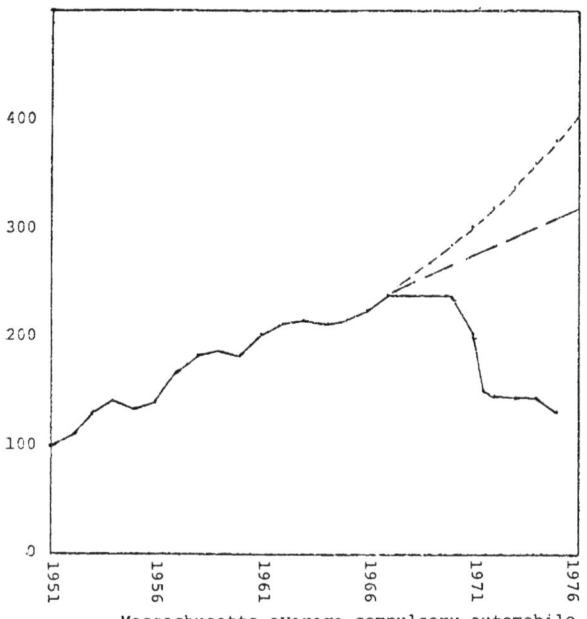

———— Massachusetts average compulsory automobile bodily injury insurance premium-private passenger cars
— — — Straight-line projection of average premium beyond 1967.
- - - - - Curve projection, 6% increase per year, of average premium beyond 1967.

For the years 1968–70, rates were frozen at 1967 levels, first by administrative order and later by statute, while legislative consideration of "no-fault" and other reform proposals proceeded. The bodily injury "no-fault" law was enacted in 1970 and became effective January 1, 1971.

Exhibit 1 uses the 1951 rates as a base of 100 and compares later rates with this base. The figures in Exhibit 2 enable one to make a rough translation of the meaning of these comparisons in dollars of premiums for different classes of policyholders. The translation is not exact, however, since the differential between premiums for different classes has been modified from time to time, and the annual figures used in preparing the chart were *average* annual premiums for all private passenger cars in the state.

EXHIBIT 2

PRIVATE PASSENGER CAR AVERAGE COMPULSORY BODILY INJURY RATES

	All cars in State	Boston cars Under 25 [1]	Class 10 [2]
1951	$27.78		
1952	30.42		
1953	36.03		
1967 to 1970	66.75	$374	$117
1971	53.57	318	99
1972	40.24	237	74
1973	39.54	196	61
1974	39.54	196	61
1975	36.10	146	45

[1] Under-25 male owner, no driver training.
[2] No regular driver under 25 yrs of age.

Exhibit 3 presents the same information as Exhibit 1 (except for omitting the straight-line projection beyond 1967) but does it in tabular form.

EXHIBIT 3.—*Massachusetts Compulsory Bodily Injury Insurance Rates, 1951–1975*

(Rates for later years are stated in comparison with those for 1951; the 1951 rates are stated as 100 for ease of comparison)

Actual rates:
  1951=100
  Up 9.5%—1952=109.5
  Up 18.5%—1953=129.8
  Up 9.3%—1954=141.9
  Down 6.3%—1955=133
  Up 5.2%—1956=139.9
  Up 19.6%—1957=167.3
  Up 9.1%—1958=182.5
  Up 3.2%—1959=188.3
  Up 9.1%—1958=182.5
  Down 2.9%—1960=182.8
  Up 10.9%—1961=202.7
  Up 5%—1962=212.8
  Up 1.2%—1963=215.4
  Down 1.7%—1964=211.7
  Up 1.6%—1965=215.1
  Up 5%—1966=225.9
  Up 6%—1967=239.5
  Frozen—1968=239.5
  Frozen—1969=239.5
  Frozen—1970=239.5

NO-FAULT LAW EFFECTIVE

Rates:
  Down 15%—1971=203.6
  Rebate 25.9%—150.9
  Down 27.6%—1972=147.4
  Down 1.7%—1973=144.9
  No change—1974=144.9
  Down 9.6%—1975=131.0

PROJECTION UNDER FAULT LAW WITHOUT FREEZE (AT 6% ANNUAL RATE)

  Up 6%—1968=253.9
  Up 6%—1969=269.1
  Up 6%—1970=285.2
  Up 6%—1971=302.3
  Up 6%—1972=320.4
  Up 6%—1973=339.6
  Up 6%—1974=360.0
  Up 6%—1975=381.6
  Up 6%—1976=404.5

In June, 1975, companies writing automobile insurance in Massachusetts reported to the Commissioner that they had sustained a $9,695,000 "underwriting profit" on the compulsory bodily injury liability coverage for 1974. At the same time they reported a $76,100,000 "underwriting loss" on other automobile insurance coverages, for a new "underwriting loss" of $67,481,000 on all automobile insurance coverages combined. The Standard (Northeast's Insurance Weekly), vol. 196, No. 25, June 20, 1975, pp. 1, 8. The dollar amount of the decrease in compulsory automobile insurance rates for 1975 was $8.7 million. The Standard, vol. 196, No. 2, January 10. 1975, pp. 1, 17, 19. According to information from the Massachusetts Automobile Rating Bureau, this was a decrease of 9.6%. Thus the latest report of company profits of $9.7 million on bodily injury compulsory coverage in 1974 indicates a profit in excess of 10%, despite all the rate reductions that had occurred.

All of the foregoing figures concern *compulsory bodily injury* rates only. Part of the misinformation spread abroad is the assertion that the no-fault law caused the motorist's total automobile insurance bill to go up rather than down *because* all the *property* insurance coverages went up. What opponents of no-fault fail to disclose in making this asserting is that the *property* rates would have gone up anyway. Indeed, the no-fault law passed in 1970, and effective through 1971, applied to bodily injury only. Only later was the law amended to apply to damage to vehicles as well as people, effective in 1972. Thus, all of the increases in *property* rates for 1971 were based on projections from past experience under the same *property* coverages, and the no-fault law had no effect on them at all. These *property* rate increases were dramatic, since property rates, as well as bodily injury rates, had been frozen. They ranged from a little over 25 percent for collision and comprehensive coverage to 38 percent for property damage liability coverage.

For 1971, then, *property* rate increases, for coverages not affected by the no-fault law, offset no-fault savings. But it was not the no-fault law that caused this increase in *property* rates. Rather, the increase was simply another manifestation of the long-standing pattern of escalating rates, aggravated by the fact that the 1971 increase was the accumulated increase for the years of the rate-freeze.

The *property* damage no-fault law effective in Massachusetts from January 1, 1972, through December, 1974, produced modest savings *on average in comparison with what those rates would have been* in 1972–74 if the law had remained unchanged. It also redistributed premium costs by causing high-value car owners to pay a larger share of the costs and low-value car owners a smaller share of the costs. This led to some complaints by high-value car owners as well as opponents of no-fault insurance, but I submit that this redistribution of costs corrected another inequity of the old system—the inequity that under traditional property damage liability insurance two car owners in the same rating class pay exactly the same premium even though one owns a new Cadillac and the other owns a well used compact. Imagine the outcry if two homeowners with homes that differ in value were charged the same amount for full-coverage homeowners policies!

Unfortunately, the complaints of the owners of high-value cars, who paid a *higher percentage* of the total car-damage insurance costs in 1972–74, were louder than anything heard from the owners of low-value cars or anybody else. And their insurers backed up their complaints. As a result, the legislature fully restored insurance company subrogation claims for car damage effective January 1, 1975. This means both higher costs for car damage and restoration of the old inequity under which the value of a high-value car is totally disregarded in setting the insurance rate of the owner for property damage liability insurance coverage. Of course this aspect of the Massachusetts law is a prime example of what not to do, though the Massachusetts lawmakers deserve high praise for leading the nation in introducing a no-fault bodily injury system.

Rate changes on coverages for damage to cars appear in Exhibit 4 (two pages, attached).

Comparisons for total automobile insurance costs for average policyholders—including both bodily injury and car damage coverages—appear in Exhibit 5.

EXHIBIT 4

AVERAGE RATES FOR MASSACHUSETTS PRIVATE PASSENGER CARS COVERAGES FOR DAMAGE TO CARS

	(1) Compulsory property damage liability		(2) Collision coverages				(3) Col. 1+2				(4) Option 2 coverages (must show fault)				(5) Col. 1+4				(6) Comprehensive coverage	
			$50 deductible		$100 deductible		$50 deductible		$100 deductible		$50 deductible		$100 deductible		$50 deductible		$100 deductible			
Year	Amount	Percent	Amount	Percent	Amount	Percent	Amount	Percent	Amount	Percent	Amount	Percent	Amount	Percent	Amount	Percent	Amount	Percent	Amount	Percent
1970	(¹)	(¹)																		
1971	$17.29	+38.4																		
1972²	19.29	+11.4		+7.8		+14.8														
1973	17.75	−11.0		+2.9		+2.5														
1974	17.75	Same	$155.17	Same	$141.74	Same	$172.92		$159.49		$34.34	Same	$29.12	Same	$52.09		$46.87		$36.55	+6.4
1975³	46.51	+165.3	138.14	−11.0	129.40	−8.7	184.65		175.91		10.17	−70.4	3.00	−89.7	56.68		49.51		50.66	+4.8 Same +38.6

¹ No change.
² The "no-fault" property damage law became effective on Jan. 1, 1972. It included a tort exemption that generally precluded claims between Massachusetts private passenger car owners and their insurers for damage to cars.
³ Effective Jan. 1, 1975, subrogation rights were restored to insurers. Thus, a collision insurer may now claim against the other driver's property damage liability insurer, though the nominal tort exemption in favor of the other driver is still in the law. The dramatic changes in 1975 rates for property damage liability and collision coverages are mostly due to this change in the law.

Source: Data supplied by courtesy of the Massachusetts Automobile Rating and Accident Prevention Bureau.

EXHIBIT 5

COMPOSITE COSTS IN MASSACHUSETTS—AVERAGE PRIVATE PASSENGER CAR RATES WITH $50 DEDUCTIBLE COLLISION AND FULL COMPREHENSIVE COVERAGE

	Col. 3 from exhibit 4—$50 deductible collision	Col. 6 from exhibit 4—Full comprehensive	(7) Compulsory bodily injury	(8) UM, extra-territorial, and increased limits to $20,000/ $50,000	(9) Total package
1974	$172.92	$36.55	$39.54	$28.27	$267.28
1975	184.65	50.66	36.10	42.08	303.49

Mr. VAN DEERLIN. Thank you, Mr. Keeton. Mr. Spangenberg.

STATEMENT OF CRAIG SPANGENBERG

Mr. SPANGENBERG. I will speak briefly on the 44 cents' point, on the Massachusetts' point, and then get to the real reason I came here.

You are in trouble. You have cost projections from Allstate, three different sets, cost projections from State Farm, cost projections from AMIA, plus the original Milliman & Robertson cost projections, which comprise six different sets, and I doubt anyone on your committee now knows how to read any of those cost predictions with some knowledge of what the actuaries were saying.

For a quick example, all over Washington this week, I have heard that Allstate said the average rate increase would be 4 percent, and that is a happy number, because it is within the same ball park as State Farm, which said the average decease would be 10 percent.

But all you have to do is take your little pocket calculator, add up the 50 State rates and divide by 50, and you find State Farm's minus 10 is minus 8, and Allstate's plus 4 is really plus 14, and it will take you 2 or 3 days if you backtrack, as I did, to find out how an actuary can make that kind of statement and suddenly learn they were not talking about countrywide figures at all, but what happened to their policy owners. They write more policies in the States which would have small increases.

One way to handle it is to take the per State increase and see how many automobiles there are in that State, because someone will sell a policy if your compulsory law goes through.

I have done it, and it took a lot of hours of calculating to find the total automobile population in the United States per State and then do an indexing factor, so I could apply it. I will be happy to leave the indexing factor with you, Mr. Kinzler and Ms. Nord, so you don't have to do it again.

When you get through that, you will find that Allstate is really predicting an 18-percent increase for the average automobile owner in the United States, if other companies have to follow the same kind of rate increase they are predicting.

Now, that is important to you. Massachusetts is really not. The average breakdown of the personal injury premium is 40 cents for expenses and 60 cents for payout, and not 44 cents for payout. I document that with 13 years from the Best's aggregates and averages.

It is obvious you can save 60 percent of the premium, if you didn't pay anybody. That would leave the insurance company happy. They could sell the policy. They could investigate it. They could earn that 40 cents and then pay nothing.

Now, the reason Massachusetts had such fantastic savings is they predicted no-fault would increase, would result in paying 30 percent more claimants with a combination of tort and personal injury protection. An extraordinary result is that, after their 5 years' experience, they found they paid not 30 percent more but 40 percent fewer, including all of those who were getting personal injury protection.

Now, how do you arrive at this 70-percent decrease in the people you pay as against those you predict?

They also found they were not paying 60 cents in benefit, but 24 cents in benefits, so the public was getting completely raped even with a 15-percent reduction. So, they ordered a mandatory 25 percent reduction to get the payout up to 48 cents instead of the 60 cents that was being enjoyed in the other States, and they have been fighting the battle ever since.

And the reason for it is well-known in the insurance industry, and I have heard half a dozen executives explain that, for 30 years Massachusetts had compulsory BI, but no compulsory property damage insurance, so when you heard your fender crunch, you didn't know if the fellow had property liability insurance, but you knew he had bodily injury, so you got out of the car holding your neck and saying, "You knocked the daylights out of my neck." And he would say, Don't worry, my company will pay for it, and they did, paying for fenders with the pretense it was for personal injury.

The result in the statistics would be that Massachusetts, in the Federal Highway Department statistics, showed three times the national average injury rate, but only 60 percent of the national average death rate, which makes you think they were the world's most fragile and most easily injured people, but had such a tough hold on life they didn't die from injuries.

All that happened was, they were paying for fenders with bodily injury money, so when they went to no-fault, that money went out, but went to property damage liability and the rates went up 38 percent.

Mr. Van Deerlin. This is all connivance with doctors?

Mr. Spangenberg. No. I just said it involved connivance with insurance agents and adjusters everywhere, who knew what was going on. It was a game they played, and when they had to change the game, property damage liability insurance rates went up 38 percent the first year and people screamed. And they said, "We will take care of that, abolish property damage liability and you can't scream about that."

That threw it on the collision rates, and now you come into a study, which happened to give the bodily injury rates and what has happened to the collision rates, and you find that Massachusetts' rates have gone up. And I have done it, and they are twice as high as the Ohio rates, which have gone down on the same combination. So, don't tell me this "disease" is all over the country.

We don't have it in Ohio, and we don't want it. And since we don't have the disease, we don't want your sulfanilamide.

Getting to the next one—44 cents that insurance companies pay out—I brought here today Best's books for the last 2 years, and you can read them yourself, if you don't believe me. I will put it on the blackboard.

What really happens, this is all of the mutual insurance companies in the whole United States of America. You have been told by Professor Keeton that the only way you can get 60 cents is by adding loss adjustment expense. That is the insurance company approach. They say, "When we defend you, we do you good, therefore, it is a benefit, and therefore the benefit we pay is really 73 cents."

I have never used the figures of Mr. Keeton. Premiums were over $3 billion. Loss, tabulated as Incurred Losses, are 60.8 percent of the premium. Adjusting expense for mutuals is 13.4 percent. That is higher than the stock by about 2 percent. All other expense is 22.3 percent of the premium. So, I can only get to 60, if they lose money.

Profit is 3.5 percent. Now, it is not always a profit. But for the last 11 years that I have been cracking Best's aggregates and averages, I will tell you the payout is about 62 cents of the premium dollar. The adjustment expense for private passenger stocks and mutuals and reciprocals and commercial auto liability, stock mutuals, reciprocals, has been about 12 percent of premiums. "Losses Incurred" have hung right in there 60, 62, 62, 63, 64 cents, depending on how things go. Adjusting expense, longtime average 12 percent, which I have not counted as payout. Profit is 1 or 2 percent. But that is underwriting profit. I know the Chinese algebra of insurance company accounting. I will tell you, $1 of premium equals $1 of reserve.

Now, any banker, if you went to him, with $8 billion, would give you 7 percent today on a year's CD. Well, the insurance company gets it for nothing just for running the business, investment profit on the $8 billion that goes into the total personal injury liability premiums today produces investment income which is not counted as income for underwriting purposes.

None of it is in that figure. Instead of paying interest to get it, they just run the insurance company. So the whole insurance industry would be absolutely delighted if they could break even, provided they knew they could break even, but when their losses get more than the investment income is producing, of course they complain about it.

Now, I know how Professor Keeton got the 44 cents. You do that by calculating how much the claimant had to pay to his lawyer, and you guess at the figure.

All right, but the statement given was the company pays 44 cents so it is a wasteful system. That statement is absolutely incorrect. The company pays 62 cents and the company does not pay the plaintiff's lawyer. The plaintiff may or may not.

Now, another difference between Massachusetts is, according to the latest blast I read from Allstate, 80 percent of claimants in Massachusetts hire lawyers. The last number I had was 68 percent do. But only one out of five do in Georgia and about one out of four in Ohio, so that is different and very different.

Now, it may be that the rest of us are going to get the disease, but I doubt it. I think there are significant differences that explain the whole Massachusetts experience.

Now, with that tirade over, let's turn to your problems in understanding costing figures.

Now, I will give you some quick rundowns of what the difference is between prediction and actual fact. To an insurance company actuary, when he has to predict what something will cost, he says "How many policies will we write" and "What will be the frequency?"

I will take a minute to define words so we can talk "frequency," "severity," and "index."

"Frequency" to an actuary means "How many claims will we get in, per 100 policies sold," and under the tort system it runs usually somewhere in the range of 3 percent, maybe 2.3 or 3.1 depending on whether it is bad risk drivers or preferred risk drivers.

Just, for example, 3 percent is a fairly common frequency figure. If you sell 100 policies, you will get three claims from somebody.

Severity—how much does it cost us to close the average claim, not adjusting expense, but how much do we have to pay per average c aim?

And over the years that figure varies, but for example, let us assume the average claim would cost $1,000. Fifty percent of them will be $100 claims, you know, the rest will go on up to the limits of your policy, but that is also called ACC, average claim cost.

Frequency times severity gives me "index." What will it cost us per policy?

If 3 percent of the policies produced claims, and average claims cost is $1,000, the index is $30, called pure insurance cost to which the actuary then adds loss adjustment expenses, a percentage, and all of his operating experience as a percentage.

You can find that for every company, even to what they spend for postage in Best's aggregates and averages every year.

Year after year, I think you will find that retention of profit plus administrative expense plus loss adjustment expense will equal 40 cents.

Now, what is the prediction of all of the vast savings under no-fault? The prediction is it will still cost 40 cents. That is the M. & R. prediction, State Farm prediction and Allstate prediction when you track through all of their figures.

State Farm does not tell you what it will be. It simply says: We think the expense will be about what it now is for our first party coverages like collision and comprehensive.

Fortunately, I can turn to the book and what does State Farm pay in adjustment expense for collision and comprehensive? When you take their numbers, what they say they pay for collision and comprehensive adjustment expense, just about what the average company pays for bodily injury liability expense, so they are not predicting any expense savings for the general run of insurance companies.

Milliman & Robertson says administrative expense will remain the same, but may go higher and they have elaborate formulas for the adjustment expense and at best they predict you might save $2\frac{1}{2}$ percent of the premium. You might. That is a prediction.

Now, we get to the problem. You have a no-fault bill and how do you cost it?

All of the companies I have named, and I can add to it American Mutual Insurance Alliance and American Insurance Association, have said they don't know how to cost no-fault because they don't know what kind of claims will come out of no-fault.

No one has a record. No one knows how many first party actions there are, single car, and no one really knows how many passengers are in the car of the driver who is on the wrong side and hits you head-on or how many of those drivers there are, because all you know is what is in the tort system and they are not known unless they have sued their own driver.

In 1969, a massive study was done on the tort system called "Personal injury claims" and also referred to as the "closed claim study" and 19 insurance companies in 16 States, or vice versa, took all of the claims settled in 10 days and then made up elaborate questionnaires, what was the wage loss, what was the medical expense, and whether they are single car or multicar, two cars or more than two cars, involved, distinctions between right side-wrong side, how many rear end collisions, just the most tremendous detailed exposition of what had happened in the tort claims.

All of that data was put on computer tapes after they edited out the known errors, as a result of which we got two volumes of statistics that none of you will read or should try to of what happened in tort.

Mr. VAN DEERLIN. We will stop now briefly, please, for another vote.

[Brief recess.]

Mr. VAN DEERLIN. My apologies, Mr. Spangenberg.

Mr. SPANGENBERG. I almost forgot where we were. But maybe I can pick it up. I think I was discussing personal injury claims and in fact that is the biggest body of data there is, but it is all data on tort.

The actuary predicting no-fault then has to take that data and try to guess at how many more claims will come in and what is the severity or what it will be? They all confess they do guess, for one thing.

State Farm and M. & R. said it is the best body of data there is. State Farm said, "We followed it closely." That is an extraordinary statement, in view of the fact that the entire personal injury claim study is based on closed claims, and the statement of economic loss that is used from it is economic loss to date of settlement.

The study itself had shown this and, Brother Kinzler, if you read it as you told me you have, you know it said the study completely ignored 83 percent of the actual loss in death cases and 90 percent of the actual loss in serious disability cases because they went on after date of settlement and the study had no way of calculating them and did not.

Other studies have shown about a total of a 63-percent error factor in the personal injury claim study of what economic losses were.

That study is entitled "Economic Consequences of Automobile Accident Injuries," in which they tried to predict the long-range losses.

The result of that study is absolutely startling, that 1 percent of all victims have claims over $25,000 in economic loss, wages, medical. The claims average, for that 1-percent group, over $76,000 apiece and the aggregate is, or was at that time, $3.6 billion out of a total loss of less than $6 billion in the total losses of all victims.

The fact is, if you believe "Economic Consequences," 2 percent of the population has losses over $10,000, but their loss is 84 percent of the total loss.

With those figures well documented, it is extraordinary to me that I can see such a fraudulent statement as I read in the final report of the Senate Commerce Committee, that says: "The work loss benefit level of $15,000 will assure that approximately 98 or 99 percent of all wage losses will be compensated."

Now that is not true. It cannot be true. No insurance man would ever say that. What they are saying is "Under personal injury closed claims, 98 percent of all wage loss up to date of settlement would be compensated by a $15,000 figure."

But they know very well that you are talking about 83 percent more than that, which is not compensated by the $15,000 figure. I think that the figures should be used carefully and there should be explanations of what they mean, whether you are dealing with closed claims or true economic consequences.

The result of the economic consequences study is, that if you adopt Professor Keeton's theory, "No-fault should really pay all losses forever—medical, wage, and death"—then this has to more than double the premium. Every insurance company actuary knows it, too, and they know they can't sell it to the American public because we had 8 years of propaganda about how no-fault is going to reduce premiums and if you add general damages to it, on Congressman Eckhardt's model, I am afraid you are talking about more than triple the premium.

It just cannot be done if you talk total full lifetime economic losses and to say today, Professor Keeton, you would not have to increase the premiums very much to do that means you are talking "closed claims" data and not the economic consequences survey.

What have the actuaries done that recognize the deficiency of the closed claim survey? They take an estimate of how many more claimants there will be the State Farm says 60 to 110 percent more than, depending on the State, and they estimate there will be more receiving. This is known, the single car accident produces far more severe injuries on highways. They are the fellows that leave the highways and impact against a tree and so forth.

State Farm estimated a 10-percent increase in severity new claimants who are brought in. Allstate has different estimate figures. To some extent I have written it up, but it is a little tiresome to go through it step by step because they are all guesses.

Now, it is a result of this guessing game of what the losses will really be, how many more claimants will really come in and what the severity will be, you get a whole system of different charts.

State Farm and Milliman & Robertson are very close together. Allstate is higher. "AMIA" is in the middle. "AIA" would be lower if actuaries used them but they don't use them, because AIA forgot death costs and limited all permanent disability claims to 99 weeks because their computer model has two digits on it. It is an erroneous study and it is no longer quoted.

The real test of how good the estimate will be, I think, is what has really happened.

Now, Bob and I both know what the estimates were. We had the actuaries out in the conference of the commissioners special study committee on UMVARA to cost that at the various levels with the same wild disagreement and pretty good cross-examination of the experts. Charles Hewitt, who is, I think, the best actuary in the world, came in for Allstate and said, "This is my formula." And that was before New York Life hired him away to set up their casualty department.

I think Hewitt's formula is still the Allstate formula, although other people are now guessing in figures.

The real test of all of these cost estimates is to see what has really happened in the States which enacted no-fault laws. You can't get data from many of them because they have not been going long enough.

You have to have the plan going a year to get the data. It takes another year to analyze data, so you are always 2 years behind. But we have data available from a series of States, and let me hand you a set of these so you can follow them because it is hard to follow orally stated numbers.

The top page is just an index of what different States have done with no-fault bills. The data I want to get with is the, let's see, one, two, well, the costing model reconciliation has a sheet. What has really happened in Florida, Kentucky, New Jersey, Maryland, and Oregon as between the model and what really happened in fact?

You will find that Florida starts off with a model indication of $80 and first year experience of $92.

Now, what does that mean? The average premium for the Allstate book in Florida when no-fault came in was $80.

Milliman & Robertson's formula would produce a 15-percent savings if Florida adopted its no-fault law. The legislature said, "Let's put your money where your mouth is. We will mandate a 15-percent premium reduction."

So premiums were artificially reduced to $68.20 just because some actuary said that is the good thing that will happen with no-fault.

Charley Hewitt's formula said, "Wait and see, it is going to cost $85, and at $68.20 we have to lose money."

Mr. Hewitt was right; they have lost $14.6 million in Florida in the first year because his model was too low.

The actual experience in Florida indicated the premium should have been $92.

The same is true in Connecticut; it cost more than Allstate's model said it would. It cost more in New Jersey than the model said it would. It cost less in Maryland than the model said it would and less in Oregon. Those two States have no threshold.

You have another sheet of what has really happened with threshold. At least I hope you do. I had one. I know I had one. Would you give me a minute, Mr. Chairman?

Mr. KINZLER. We will give you the schedule, if you like.

Mr. SPANGENBERG. Here it is. You don't have one either.

Now, let's back up for a moment. We can demonstrate, and can demonstrate over and over again if you study the literature, that all expenses runs under both systems about 40 percent of the premium dollar.

The studies on what happens to the benefit dollar are difficult because they come from the closed claim study, too. What happened there is that if you had a $10,000 policy, absolute liability, bad injury, you settle early for a discount as insurance companies do, you know,

$9,500. "Why don't you take that and sign off now, you won't have to hire a lawyer." That is commonplace.

By that time, the fellow only had $3,000 or $4,000 in wage loss and medical expense. Closed claim says: Economic loss was $3,000 or $4,000, and the rest was general damages.

Well, it was not. The rest was the money he was going to lose next year and the year after and year after because of a disability.

So, when the serious cases losses would go on after settlement, there is a lot of money really paid for in the settlement that was economic loss and gets called damages, so the actuaries have to do a guess figure adjustment of that.

And M. & R. and State Farm generally say economic loss in the tort payment dollar takes 50 percent of the dollars or of the benefit dollar, rather, or 30 percent of the premium and general damages runs the other 50 percent of the benefit dollar or 30 percent of the premium.

Now, if you adopt a plan that says, "We are going to double the benefits but leave tort for some seriously injured people," and I have heard that said around Washington, what you are saying is, "We will increase economic loss by two, so it will take 60 percent of the premium dollar, and we will cut, with a big threshold, general damages in half," which is the maximum prediction of Milliman & Robertson, or 15 percent of the premium dollar, and then you will keep 40 cent and pay out 75 cents.

Now, there is no way you are going to do that without losing 15 cents on every premium dollar, and it cannot happen and will not happen.

So any scheme that pays more total benefits than is now paid will cost a premium increase, and it has to. That is, unless you do some other magic.

There is one gimmick I hope we have time to do that is in itself worthy of your attention, because, like the others, "It ain't really so."

But starting with this basis, you are going to increase economic loss by something. Start with the 30, if you have "PIP" benefits, "Personal Injury Protection," restoration benefits plus, what shall we say, 50 percent more, and it will cost 45 cents of the premium to pay it.

Then you can break even. You pay 50 percent more economic loss benefits and cut general damages in half and you break even.

Now, that has been the theory in many States. Indeed, Massachusetts thought they would cut general damages so much that they would have a savings. Florida thought the same thing.

In Florida, $1,000 threshold, the frequency dropped to 35 percent. That is about one-third as many people brought residual liability tort actions after meeting the threshold and as has brought tort actions before under the past system.

The severity, however, increased to 3.3; that is, the average claim cost in Florida has increased 330 percent, which is far more than Milliman & Robertson predicted. Milliman & Robertson's predictions was that the frequency would be 25 percent, the severity would go up to about 220 as I remember the figure, and the resultant cost to the system would be that residual tort would cost about 56 percent as much as prior tort had cost; that is, pretty much they thought could cut it in half.

The index in Florida, however, is now 1.15. That means the cost of paying residual tort claims in Florida costs 15 percent more than the entire tort system had cost before, and in addition to that you are paying the personal injury premiums for the personal injury protection benefits.

So that Florida costs have had to increase, and they have increased by 15 percent.

New York, with $500 threshold, reduced its tort claims to an index of 0.60, or 40 percent fewer tort claims were filed, and three out of five people, or three out of the five people who would have had a tort claim, still have it at a $500 threshold.

The severity index has risen there to 1.5. This is higher than Milliman & Robertson predicted.

Index equals 0.9. M. & R. had predicted the index should be something under 0.6.

New Jersey, with a $200 threshold, gets a 0.6 index on frequency; that is, 40 percent of the tort claims are knocked out.

The average claim goes up 1½ times, and the index is 90, and they saved 10 percent of the old tort costs on the residual tort claims.

Connecticut has a $400 threshold and their frequency, with a $400 threshold, the frequency has gone down to 0.3. No one thought it would happen. That is only 3 out of 10 of the old tort claimants now make a tort claim with a very low threshold, but the average severity has gone up to 3.5 and the combined cost is now at an index of 1.05. This 30 percent who may still file for a claim get 5 percent more than everyone got in tort before.

That is with a threshold half way between New York and New Jersey.

Now, it is no wonder that Allstate has testified over in the Senate: "We don't know what will happen in no-fault. We need time to experiment because nothing works out the way it should and all we can say is we are still in favor of no-fault on a State-by-State basis. We know some States will experiment and will have to change the experiment because it will not work, but none of our actuaries, who we think are the best in the business, can tell you in advance what any plan will do." When they submit to you your cost figures that you think are somewhere in the ball park with State Farm, they know that their cost models have been producing lower results than really happened and they don't know what will happen in the Federal bill either, except if the average increases in the other States happen under the Federal bill, we are all in for a very large premium increase indeed.

Let me argue another point: What happens if you take a plan that has no tort restriction, none at all, and say, "We will pay your benefits as you lose them, you can have a tort suit, but if you go to tort and sue, whatever we have paid you must be paid back."

Now, the name of that is "add-on take-off".

They buy first party benefits, true no-fault benefits, they keep the tort claim, if they want to pursue it, but, if they do and recover, they have to pay back the first party benefits to the insurer. That is add-on take-off.

Now, we have two States that tried that and one is Maryland and one is Oregon and they came to quite different results, because Maryland made what I think is a serious mistake.

In Maryland, they had a benefit bill in which you got first party benefits and had a free right to sue in tort. That produced a frequency figure of 0.8, but it produced a severity figure of 1.5, that is 50-percent increase in tort claims out of that 80 percent, which I think you might have expected if you know the breakdown between little claims, but a combined index of 1.2.

Where did they go wrong? They forgot to take off. They get the first party, keep it and keep the tort, too.

Now, it is worth while in Maryland to get double recovery and every time you could spend on a doctor you should because the jury will give it back and your own insurance company will give it to you. I say, "Don't go that route."

Oregon said "Add-on, take-off, the true plan." Frequency 0.75, residual tort claims have been reduced by 25 percent. Even though no one has to give up the tort claim, all he has to do is give back the first party benefits.

The severity factor in Oregon, because of the take-off, has gone up to only 1.2, instead of Maryland's 1.5, and resulting index is 0.9.

Now, check your sheet. What State has done the best? The best? Oregon has done the best, with no threshold. They have done as well as New York with a $500 threshold, as well as New Jersey with a $200, and better than Connecticut with a $400 threshold and 25 percent better than Florida with $1,000 threshold.

Fair warning, Milliman & Robertson, your favorite actuaries, say: You can relate name calling thresholds to money. And 2 month's disability equals $600 medical. If you follow through their charts, 3 months disability is about $1,000 medical. What Milliman & Robertson are saying is, if you have to spend $1,000 for treatment, you probably will be disabled on an average about 3 months. Medical expenses of $600 are equivalent to the 2 month's disability threshold.

Medical expenses amounting to $2,000 is equivalent to a 6-month threshold.

Well, that is a guess, too, but, if you believe it, you should remember that the index in Florida went up to 1.15 with the biggest threshold. Why is that so? What happened in Oregon is called by the insurance folks, and it is a good word they adopted, the happiness factor.

Most people with smaller claims just want their losses paid. They can't get them paid. The adjustor gives them a hard time.

Now, under Oregon no-fault the adjustor has to be sweet. He has to pay them; he goes in and pays them right away. He says: "Here are all of your losses. You don't want to have a tort suit, do you? Any losses you have we will pay—your wage and your medical."

It works. The claimants go to a lawyer, particularly when they say you get a couple of hundred more, but you have to then pay the lawyer and pay these people back, so what is the point? So, they don't bring the lawsuit. That factor works.

Now, suppose you say to the victim:

You aren't going to have a tort suit. Although you were on the right side of the road and he was on the wrong side and he creamed you and he was drunk and you are mad at him and your wife is bleeding and battered and your kids are hurt and you are hurt and you know you are going to hurt and you want a tort suit. What happens?

You can't have it until you pass our threshold.

What is that?

You have to spend $1,000 of medical.
Where am I going to get $1,000?
We will give it to you.

Do you think he is not going to spend $1,000 for medical if he finds a doctor who is willing to treat him and why shouldn't the doctor be willing to treat him? He hurts and his doctor says: "Come on an, we will give you physical therapy, massage, and stretch your neck."

This is probably good for him, but it is not going to cure him any faster. I think you can get as much good out of standing under a hot shower.

Well, you get a crick in your neck; wrap a towel around your neck and put that on your neck and get a real hot soaking. That is deep heat. You can get it done by a pretty girl, and a massage, too, if you want to spend $15 a session for physical therapy. If I could get that benefit and move myself toward a threshold I guess I would.

You know, the average fellow says: "Try to cheat me and I will fight back and if you treat me fair I will be fair with you." That is human psychology. All you see in these results is what happens to people.

When Congress gets over the idea that everyone is a plastic chip that you can move around and handfeed through a computer and say, "Your hurt does not count, show us your wage stub."

He says, "Forget that, I hurt. I enjoyed life and I have only one to live and you are taking away 3 or 4 months of it. When I don't enjoy it I want to be paid for it."

Now, every public opinion poll has said that is the way the American people feel about it. Even the public attitude study of DOT leans on that one.

Keeton and O'Connell say that in their book. They know that is how people feel. That is why you save tort, but you save it in part, allowing only the people badly hurt to sue. When you let people who are hurt really badly do the suing, you are dealing with the people who are going to get the large recovery and you are saving the big cases and you are going to get a severity factor out of S. 354 or H.R. 1900 of about 300 percent.

There is no way you can leave any tort and save enough to pay the benefit levels you are talking about.

Allstate knows it. That is why they have an 18-percent average increase, they know it from the model; and that is going to translate in real life on real experience to around 22 percent, I would think.

If history repeats itself, that is, if these States are models.

My final plea to you as responsible members of our National Government: I have been studying it for 8 years and I have gone through 24 volumes of these red books and I have been through every cost study and I have testified all over the country and debated with Brother Keeton and we have both been on advisory committees and the more we know about it the more we realize what really happens depends on people's reactions to what you are doing to them and whether they think it is fair.

The more I worked in the field, the more I realized that any statement that you make, about how little the innocent victim is recovering, is necessarily fraudulent because you completely ignore what he kid.

If you say, "Well, no, I think I am going to get covered by Salida Mutual Insurance," they say "Please wait."

Now the health deliverers like the Blue Cross system. Why not make it primary? What is so magic about saying there should be one source where you get all of your benefits?

I want to know what does the fellow who is giving me the benefits want?

He wants Blue Cross-Blue Shield, then I have no problem. I think all health insurance ought to be primary. Everything else should be primary. Auto excess means when you run out of that, if you run out of the union fringe, add the auto. Right?

You would save about 30 percent on a premium as nearly as I can figure it if you do that because you are really whacking the economic losses down to something you can handle.

On that basis, you could pay I think $5,000 in benefits, that is about the State median, you know, in the experimental States. That would certainly pay 97 percent of the people right now. If you paid an excess amount about 98.5 percent of the people.

Now, 49 out of 50 is not bad, and it would save them some money on premiums.

I would like to see someone try it, but I think the insurance company would scream bloody murder and you would have more lobbyists than you would know what to do with as soon as you talk "excess."

Because it cuts premiums and that is not the name of the no-fault game. No-fault started in 1968 when you passed the safety standards for automobiles. It didn't take any genius, when you padded the dash, padded the arm rests and padded the visor and put in a better windshield, to know that a head couldn't go through the glass and hang up half way through and slice up and down as the car came to a stop.

That is what we used to have. I have seen them with over 400 stitches just in the face. That windshield was changed in 1966. I should never see one again. Those cars are now off the road. I think I have seen my last exploded heart a year and a half ago, when it came in, her husband driving a 1966 Chevrolet head-on collision in a city street. It could not happen since 1968 because that is when you mandated the collapsible steering column and that injury is gone.

We have not seen a whiplash in our office for 5 years, a real injury, at 15 miles an hour the back of your head going over the back of your seat so far the back of your head actually hits the back of the front seat and it is instant dislocation of the neck and your ligaments are not strong enough to hold it back. That is whiplash.

They put a little head rest so your head can't go back and there is no whiplash. It didn't take reforming the insurance system to end that injury, but a change in the car.

Now, we will add to that a 55-mile-an-hour speed limit and I have just seen New York Lifes' figures on that, a 20-percent reduction in automobile deaths. They think it is due to the speed limit, it is high speed crashes that cause the deaths and there is less high speed, although there are still some.

If you start mandating real automobile safety you know very well that you are going to reduce injuries and if you reduce injuries, you reduce claims and if you reduce payouts you reduce premiums and if you reduce premiums you are reducing investment losses.

I am a little cynical after working on this since 1968, because I think all of this propaganda we hear about "We want to save premiums," that comes from the industry, is not true, has not been true; that all no-fault is designed to do is to pay enough more so they can keep premiums up or increase them a little.

Because I have not seen a plan yet that saved anybody anything even in Massachusetts where all you did was switch it to another line of insurance.

I am not interested in switching rates. I would like to see you mandate an excess plan that would really save me money, as it would.

The insurance company would have to take less and the consumer would get more and you can do it with no threshold at all. That can be done and that would reform the system.

While you are reforming, why don't you reform the tort system too? Do you still want the seriously injured man to be paid? Everyone knows comparative negligence is better and why shouldn't it be in the standards? Why shouldn't decent limits be in the standards? Not a province in poor old Canada has limits less than 50; unlimited in Great Britain; and $200 000 in West Germany and we piddle along with 10–20 here in the United States.

You want to help the guy who is right. I think you could say something about limits, too. But maybe you really don't want to reform the tort system, I don't know.

Mr. VAN DEERLIN. Well, maybe we could toss the ball back to Mr. Keeton in a while.

Mr. SPANGENBERG. Yes. In no-fault, and I am closing, I think we need more experiment. The point of the last sheet you have shows what the States have done and there is not a single State whose no-fault plan can continue to exist if you pass S. 354.

Not even Michigan meets it. Michigan says: The threshold is any serious impairment of bodily function whether temporary or permanent. It is one of the lowest thresholds there is, so that has to go. The rest of the benefits don't meet the standard, so you will kill 24 experiments.

We don't know what is going to happen in Michigan. It has not gone long enough. I would like to have Michigan and Arkansas and Texas data because every plan is different. When I get enough different data in, and I talk like I am going to move the insurance industry, I won't, but I know what will happen and I know what actuaries will do when they get data.

When they have their hard data then they can do some real predicting and we will be getting it from 24 States, but we won't get if it Congress says, "We know best." The sad fact is none of you know enough to pass a plan with any prediction of what will happen and you can't know it until more experiments are completed.

I beg you let us experiment in the States.

Thank you.

Mr. VAN DEERLIN. Will you proceed, Mr. Keeton.

Mr. KEETON. Mr. Chairman, I will be very brief. I first want to express my admiration for Mr. Spangenberg's great advocacy. We have another enterprise in which we work together in trying to train young trial advocates, and I hold him out as one of the models of the supreme advocate. Even after having traveled the circuit with him on this subject and having heard him before, I can almost believe until I pinch myself and wake up to the proposition that he has just been trying to sell us.

I refer, for example, just one example, to the proposition that is now represented on the board over there. Do you realize that what he has told us is that if, instead of having any kind of tort exemption at all, you just add on more coverage, that it will cost less?

Mr. SPANGENBERG. You take over.

Mr. KEETON. That is the proposition. You add on coverage that was not there before, and you provide for no duplication between the two. But nevertheless he says that by adding the extra it will come out that it costs you less.

On the other hand, if you produce a tort exemption which says the insurance company pays out less, it will cost you more. That is the proposition. That is what it adds up to. I submit that that is a little difficult to believe.

Now what is his theory? He finally got around to trying to tell us why it would be true in theory because on its face it is an absurd proposition. Why did he tell us it would happen? He says that because of what he refers to as the happiness factor—people will be so happy they got something more than they had before—they won't sue for what they could have sued for under the previous system.

Now, there is, of course, another proposition that has been asserted by the industry. Every time anybody proposes such a system to them and proposes that they rate it at something lower than what they would have charged, the industry talks about financing claims.

I emphasize, as I did before, that the relevant comparison is: What are the rates under this system compared with what they would have been under the old system?

We are not making a proper comparison if we look at rates for 1 year under one system against rates for another year under a different system. The relevant comparison is rates for the same year.

Now, if it is asserted that an add-on system will reduce rates and you ask yourself "How could that possibly be?" I think you have to take into account another factor—it is a well-known phenomenon in the industry. First party benefits run the risk of doing what the claims men call "financing more claims." They take away the bargaining weapon that the insurance company has because of the injured person's need for cash.

Now, I personally think that taking away this bargaining weapon will result in somewhat higher payments to the most severely injured persons, and I think that is right. That is the way it should be, because they have sometimes been settling their claims for less than they were truly worth because of the necessity of getting some cash promptly.

So, working on the opposite side from this so-called happiness factor is this proposition that you give an improved bargaining position to the claimant and do what claims men refer to, in somewhat of pejorative sense, as financing claims.

Then I submit that not only is this proposition absurd on its face—this proposition that by increasing the coverage and changing nothing else, you can reduce the costs—but also when you start talking about "What would be the incentive factors to people operating under the system?" you will have a lot more people using these no-fault benefits to finance tort claims than you will saying "I am so happy that the insurance company is giving me this that I won't pursue the rights I have."

Let me just point to another consequence of this: If Mr. Spangenberg were right, then all of the trial bar would be financially advantaged by the enactment of tort exemption bills. That would be one of the implications of this proposition he just tried to sell us.

I think that once you pinch yourself and wake up after hearing this excellent advocacy, you realize that there was something wrong with the proposition somewhere along the line.

Now, I have made the point that the true comparison that we are interested in is: What would the cost be for a given time and place under each of the two systems?

The Oregon bill went into operation, as I think Mr. Spangenberg will agree, at about the same time that the industry had a favorable turn in general loss experience. We can speculate about what the reason for it was. I personally believe that it was partly another factor. Improvements in automobile safety reduced the severity of accidents. But whatever the reasons may be, whether safety factors, or general economic factors, they affected the whole country. There were others speculating it had something to do with the whole economy. That one never quite satisfied me.

I think a more likely explanation is reduced severity of accidents and reduced severity of injuries from equally severe impacts, because of the safety factors introduced by car manufacturers. They have produced a modest reduction in actual losses and, of course, that should be reflected in a modest reduction in premiums.

At any rate, if you look at Best's, to which Mr. Spangenberg referred several times, there was a dramatic turnaround throughout the Nation in the experience with liability insurance when this shift occurred, and it occurred simultaneously with Oregon's law going into effect.

If we discount for that dramatic turnaround nationwide, we don't have Oregon's rates going down under that law but we have them going up slightly, which is exactly what you would expect from the enactment of such a law.

Just one other point I would like to make. Again the Massachusetts data—you cannot explain what has happened in Massachusetts on the ground of switching claims from bodily injury to property coverages. Let me be specific again about that 38.4 percent increase in the property damage liability rate in 1971. That was an increase that occurred when no change had been made in the property damage law; the only change had been made in the bodily injury law.

Mr. Spangenberg says that only means that people who were collecting under the fraudulent claims of the sore back have now started collecting against the property damage. That will not explain a 38.4-percent increase. That rate was set by the State. It was set by the State actuary.

He explained in a public hearing the reason he put that 38.4 in there. There was nothing said about switching of this kind; that 38.4 was a projection of experience on the property damage coverage only, on the assumption that the bodily injury law would not affect it at all.

The reason it was that high was that, while this controversy was going on in Massachusetts, that rate had been frozen for 4 years, so the 38.4 percent represents an accumulated 4-year increase; the same thing would have happened in the bodily injury rates if we had not had a change in the laws, maybe not exactly the same figure but something approximating that.

Now, to underline the point that I have just made, look at what happened—and this appears on exhibit 4 attached to my statement—look at what happened in 1972, 1973, and 1974 to that same property damage rate: Up 11.4 percent in 1972, down 11 in 1973, still at the same in 1974.

Now you put all of that together and that means that the 1974 property damage liability rate in Massachusetts, which is the one that ought to reflect all of this increase in costs, if truly that shifting had occurred, that rate in 1974 was just above 38 percent higher than it had been back in 1967, when the rate was first frozen.

Look at it from another point of view. The average motorist in Massachusetts in 1974 was paying $17.75 for property damage liability coverage. Back in 1967 that figure would have been a little over $13. That is the difference. That is $4. Look at the savings on the other hand in the bodily injury coverage. They are on the order, for the average motorist, of a difference between $66 in 1967 and $36 in 1974, a $30 savings.

Even if the whole $4 was attributable to that shift, that is $4 out of the $30 saved. It is impossible to explain what happened in Massachusetts on the theory of shifting.

Now, Mr. Spangenberg and others keep talking about the total of the policy costs. That, of course, includes a lot of coverage that could not possibly be affected even if the phenomenon he alleges occurred. The comprehensive you can't possibly explain on that basis. I repeat, then, it is simply clear that the Massachusetts experience cannot be explained on that basis.

Mr. Van Deerlin. You don't have to catch planes, I trust.

Mr. Spangenberg. I stand on my statement; the real reason is that he is paying for 40 percent fewer people.

Mr. VAN DEERLIN. I am talking about taking a break to go to vote.
Mr. SPANGENBERG. Excuse me.
[Brief recess.]
Mr. VAN DEERLIN. Mr. Keeton, will you proceed.
Mr. KEETON. Thank you, Mr. Chairman. I know you and the staff have questions and I think I will forgo any further statement and respond to any questions you might wish to ask.
Mr. SPANGENBERG. I will be brief, Mr. Chairman. In Massachusetts, I thought I said, the major reason was that they didn't pay people, a 40 percent reduction in claimants paid, and that is documented in three articles in the Journal of Risks in Insurance, and about half of the articles here were on the phenomenon of Massachusetts, and I stand on my statement that the reason the rates went down is that far fewer people were paid and paid less and, as soon as you start paying less benefits, rates have to go down.

The disturbing thing is that expenses of Massachusetts went up, and total insurance cost of the policy, the total premium, has gone up in his State. On the other thing, you couldn't expect what has happened in Oregon to happen because it does not make sense, Professor Keeton says.

"Somehow you have got to pinch yourself because I am an advocate." I never advocated a fact unless the fact was the fact, and the fact is the advocacy and I have been quoting facts. I have not given you oratory but tables and statistics and data.

Mr. VAN DEERLIN. You don't resent being called an able advocate?

Mr. SPANGENBERG. I don't resent that. An able advocacy consists of doing research and preparation to get the facts and then let them march around; that is how you are being an advocate, and that I do.

Let us match one simple statistic. Milliman & Robertson made an early cost study: What will hapen in a State if they paid no-fault benefits and have no threshold and simply allow people to sue if they want to, if it is an offset State? They did one for Oregon. This is not Spangenberg, the advocate; this is Milliman & Robertson, the favorite actuaries of the Senate Commerce Committee.

Prediction for Oregon: With no threshold, block 4 of appendix 2 of their three appendixes, Oregon, no threshold, they said: Frequency will decrease to 85 percent, or 0.85, frequency. Severity will increase to 1.05 percent. The resulting index will be 0.894. That is what they said.

Fact: They were right for the wrong reason. Fact: Frequency was not 0.85 but 0.75. Dropping more cases out, increase of severity somewhat and severity was 1.2 and index 0.9. Total agreement.

What happened is what was predicted would happen by Milliman & Robertson.

If you are interested in the rest of their predictions, the Senate Commerce Committee report, page 49, lists—and I think it was supposed to terrify us—what will happen in the United States if you pass all of the benefits of S. 354 with no threshold at all. And what they really said was: Rates would go up an average of 9 percent. Now, maybe you think that that is unimaginable but that is the actuarial prediction that has been quoted in the final report of the Senate Commerce Committee on page 49.

Now, one reason the total cost does go down—and you should know this; I want to leave you with complete accuracy—all but one of the three Allstate cost figures, all of the State Farm figures, and all of the Milliman & Robertson figures assume that the motorist in the State buys a medical payments policy. They do it by assuming the average of medical payments, so every motorist buys whatever the State average of medical payments coverage is in the State. In fact, only 80 or 85 percent buy them but the assumption is that everyone has the 85 percent of the total amount, or of the total average amount.

Curiously enough—and I don't know the logic of it—when they count the cost of the tort system, they always count the costs of the medical payment. When they count the number of victims who get paid, they do not count the number of medical payment victims who recover.

So, when you see "50 percent more victims will be paid at such-and-such a cost," remember they are not counting all of the victims who now get medical pay, and the true number should be about 30.

That is one reason Brainard's predictions are different from Milliman & Robertson. because he counts the number of people who got medical pay, which I think you should, so there is that curiosity.

The figure you have is assuming that people do buy medical pay and with no-fault don't have to buy it, what is the difference? The present premium plus 9 percent. It is the same basis on which State Farm and Allstate in their later tabulations did it. So I have done it, too, and I am sorry that I kind of assumed that you would know that little mathematical gimmick is in the figures, but it is.

So when I say the premium in Oregon has not increased, it has not increased at all for the people who already would be buying medical pay. They pay no more.

The pure tort premium turnaround was not 72; it was 71. It was a year ahead of the Oregon switch. So any comparison of what really had happened in Oregon in the last 3 years is valid.

If you have any doubts as to whether I have misled you by bringing "advocacy" here, why don't you get on the phone and call Lester Rawls. He has been commissioner of Oregon ever since the bill went into effect and is very knowledgeable and learned and he will tell you what happened in Oregon and can give you rates.

They are about a third of the rates of Massachusetts and he would be happy to brag about it. He knows Oregon has had a good experience and wants to keep the experiment going. They recently increased the benefits in Oregon because it works so well. So they are up to pretty good levels.

The final point has to do with a statement made earlier, and you have to understand that if you want to understand the actuarial tables. When State Farm, or when Milliman & Robertson does a cost study, if you track through the actual tables, which I have done for this vast volume of stuff, you find that no-fault costs more, as you know it has to. That is because it pays more and they assume expenses will be about the same.

But then it turns out that there will be a premium reduction. Now, how can you do that? The way they do that is something that you must be aware of. They say: Under the tort system, only about 80 percent nationally of all drivers buy insurance, 80 percent of car owners buy insurance. So the total tort system should be divided by 80 to get a cost per insured; and we assume that, under no-fault, half of the uninsured people will buy insurance, so 90 percent will be insured.

So, to get a cost per insured, you should divide total no-fault costs by 90. Well, that is 12 percent higher, so you can have no-fault benefits that cost 12 percent more and then divide by 12 percent more and you are back to even, you see. It is a very dangerous assumption to think that in the real world you can do that.

As Professor Webb and Professor Brainard analyzed, more brilliantly than I can, in their testimony last year, this is not an argument in favor of no-fault at all. This is an argument in favor of compulsory insurance; because, if you made tort system compulsory, you should get the same result, and then you would divide tort by 90 as well, and then you would find that no-fault costs more. And it still might not be true, but on paper it would come out the same.

The only State which Milliman & Robertson ever had to cost that had compulsory tort and compulsory no-fault was Kentucky, which has the constitution provision saying you cannot take away a traditional common law tort claim, so they passed a compulsory no-fault law; but, to satisfy their constitution—and in their attorney general's opinion, by itself it would be unconstitutional—they added a clause "You may elect not to take no-fault but, if you do, you must stay under tort and you must buy tort liability insurance." Then if you elect tort, you don't get first-party benefits but, if the no-fault driver hits you, you have your tort claim against him. The no-fault driver, if you are wrong, does not have a tort claim against you unless he passes their $1,000 threshold.

So you have on the same highway same people, same everything,. two classes of drivers, compulsory tort and compulsory no-fault; Milliman & Robertson costed that and it will cost 12 percent more for no-fault—yes, 12 percent more for no-fault. They couldn't do the fancy division when both systems are compulsory.

The great danger to your committee is what has happened in States which went compulsory. It is easy to say divide by 80 for tort and divide by 90 for no-fault. That really assumes something else. That assumes the new class of motorists you bring in will have the same accident rate, same frequency rate and severity rate, that they will be like the ones you already insured. If that is so, then you get more premiums; you know, you can spread the cost.

What has really happened? Ask the insurance industry and you will get the same answer from all of them: The uninsured driver who was compelled to buy insurance and bought into the system is the worst risk we have ever seen. He is worse than the present assigned risk claim, his accident frequency rate is atrocious and his severity is higher.

I can give you Allstate's figures for the State of New Jersey, which explains why New Jersey is now predicting a rate increase. For the previously uninsured drivers brought into New Jersey by compulsory New Jersey's no-fault, frequency went up 219 for them, 219 percent, more than twice as many accidents per 100 policies as the previously insured drivers had, and severity went up 58 percent—not only more accidents but worse accidents. And now you have compelled the companies to insure them.

Mr. Van Deerlin. Obviously they are a less responsible element of society.

Mr. Spangenberg. Net loss—net loss. It costs more to bring them in than you save by bringing them in. I insist you can't use the Milliman and Robertson flat gimmick—"we will divide by 80 and divide by 90"—when the 10 percent is going to produce a net loss rather than a net savings.

I think the solution to that is in the recent solution by the insurance industry—in fact, if they had done it 20 or 30 years ago, I don't think we would have ever heard of no-fault. That is uninsured motorists' coverage. A responsible driver can protect himself against the uninsured driver by buying uninsured motorists' coverage, and that one I buy. It is the best buy I get—about $3 in Ohio, $2 in New Hampshire and about $2 in Oregon—very low rate.

I insure the fellow who hits me. The only problem is that I can't buy enough of it. I can buy it only up to the minimum limits in Ohio, which is $12,500. That is all I can get because they won't sell me more.

I have sponsored, for some years—and I argued in some States' legislatures which have passed laws and I have had a lot of help on it because a lot of people believe it is good—why not have underinsured motorists' coverage? If I buy 100, 300, to protect the guy that I might hit or 300, 500—and I don't want to brag about my own limits; they are pretty high; I think I have a good goal to protect and that is what liability insurance is all about—I would sure like it if I was protected against him, and he may have the $12,500.

I would be happy to pay a premium that says: Whatever limits I buy for liability I can buy for the underinsured motorist. Only three or four States have mandated that; but in your markup, if you go to a mandatory standard that is a good one, that is compulsory underinsured as well as uninsured motorists' coverage, and it is a lot cheaper than making the presently underinsured motorists buy insurance—for statistical reasons that is so—and it is the cheaper way to do it.

It does leave him unprotected, but he has lots of other protection from all kinds of programs and mostly welfare; and I know the argument—"You shouldn't make the automobile public pay for it." The automobile public is the public. Who is there in the United States who does not use the automobile, bus, truck, taxi—not many taxis but buses, sure—ride with friends, hitchhike, thumb? Everyone is the automobile public. They are the same people who are the public public and I don't see why we make a fuss about "We have to make the automobile public do this or that."

Mr. Van Deerlin. Mr. Kinzler.

Mr. Kinzler. Mr. Spangenberg, both in this hearing and in our previous hearing, you indicated that it is not really fair to look at the tort system by itself as a reparations system for automobile accidents because a large percentage of the recovery that people actually receive comes from other systems.

Mr. Spangenberg. Yes.

Mr. Kinzler. Do you recall approximately what the total recovery is for all injured victims, of just their economic loss, with all systems of recovery included, according to the Department of Transportation report?

Mr. Spangenberg. It will take a minute to go to the book and get it.

Mr. KINZLER. Well, it is in the neighborhood, depending on how you cut in, serious or all injuries, somewhere between 50 and 60 percent.

Mr. SPANGENBERG. Depends on the study.

Mr. KINZLER. Economic Consequences, using the Department of Transportation report.

Mr. SPANGENBERG. Which one?

Mr. KINZLER. Final volume.

Mr. SPANGENBERG. All right.

Mr. KINZLER. You indicated also that the 30-percent figure for recoveries for people with economic loss of $25,000 or over was a somewhat phony figure because it did not count the other systems.

Now, the chart in this particular volume, table 9, talks about the ratio of net recovery to losses with tort, tort as well as all other sources, and without tort, and both of those are 30 percent.

Mr. SPANGENBERG. And you walked into one, haven't you, because that has to be an error. How can you say that the recovery with tort is the same as recovery without tort? What you are saying is that there is no tort recovery if your loss is over $25,000. That makes no sense and we both know it. I don't think you thought it through. It has to be a misprint, and I don't know what the right number is because it is buried back in the index in the second volume somewhere.

Mr. KINZLER. Mr. Keeton, is that a misprint?

Mr. KEETON. If I understood the figure you quoted with the same percentage recovery—one without tort and the other with tort?

Mr. KINZLER. Right.

Mr. KEETON. Well, if that is the way it appeared there, unless there is some other explanation, it seems to me that it does imply no tort recovery, which must not be correct.

Mr. SPANGENBERG. It is not true for any other number and is an anomaly in the record, and I asked about it before and it bothered me when I saw it and I never heard it explained as to how it could be, but is is obviously impossible. Mr. Sutcliffe asked me about it in the Senate hearings and got the same kind of answer.

Mr. KINZLER. We will see if we can clear it up.

You also talked about the possibility of reforming the existing tort system.

Mr. SPANGENBERG. Yes.

Mr. KINZLER. At various times we have heard about changing contributory negligence to comparative negligence. Certainly any reform would include the abolition of guest statutes and perhaps also the elimination of statutory limits on recovery on wrongful death actions, and universal compulsory insurance?

Mr. SPANGENBERG. I never said that and never will. I just explained why you can't get me to support compulsory insurance.

Mr. KINZLER. Another change is the increase in bodily injury coverage from $10,000/$20,000 in most States, say, $50,000/$100,000?

Mr. SPANGENBERG. Fifty—single limit or——

Mr. KINZLER. Yes; the death is in the right ball park as far as that. You indicated also if you went to universal compulsory insurance, that would give you a larger base so your costs would go down?

Mr. SPANGENBERG. I did not. I just spent 5 minutes on the reverse.

Mr. KINZLER. You said you would bring higher cost people into the system?

Mr. SPANGENBERG. Yes, I said that.

Mr. KINZLER. But would the costs for everyone go down or up?

Mr. SPANGENBERG. Go up. You would now subsidize the bad drivers.

Mr. KINZLER. Right, but are we talking about a 5- or 10-percent increase or 2- or 3-percent increase?

Mr. SPANGENBERG. I say it is cheaper with underinsured motorists coverage and that is the reason I said this.

Mr. KINZLER. In light of your discussion of these proposals and similar discussions by other people, it seems worthwhile to look at a uniform system. I have some figures here which I am sure you are interested in looking at and examining—and I will give you the details afterward——

Mr. SPANGENBERG. Thank you.

Mr. KINZLER (continuing). Which is the costing of a plan with the five specific topics I mentioned. The estimated costs of a plan consisting of the five forms I mentioned show an increase of 53 percent—for the average person, an increase of 53 percent in metropolitan areas and an increase of 65 percent for rural areas.

The reason I raise these figures is if the existing system is not doing the job, then we have to look to some kind of reform; and, if those are the kinds of costs we are talking about in this type of reform, then I question whether this is the way to go about it.

Mr. SPANGENBERG. I will be glad to look at the figures. I can tell you, as you named them they don't sound right. They can't be right. And I don't know the basis. You are talking as opposed to what?

Mr. KINZLER. As opposed to the existing tort system.

Mr. SPANGENBERG. With minimum coverage or average?

Mr. KINZLER. With the 10–20.

Mr. SPANGENBERG. Well, none of these other figures you kicked around up there are with a minimum. They are with the avaerge amount of coverage in the State. There are extensive statements by M & R as to what it is. The average coverage is up around 25; so, to change it to 25 would not change anything, you see.

Mr. KINZLER. But we are changing the mandatory to $50,000/ $100,000. It is from 10–20 minimum not from what the people are actually carrying.

I say I will give you the figures but let me go through one thing besides that. We heard from you again today that Best's Aggregates and Averages talk about 60-plus-percent insurance company payout, and that is an accurate figure?

Mr. SPANGENBERG. Yes.

Mr. KINZLER. Now, as you indicated before, that pay-out is not necessarily what the beneficiary——

Mr. SPANGENBERG. I have used it with absolute precision. That is what they do pay. They do not pay 44 cents.

Mr. KINZLER. Right. Nobody is arguing it and I don't think Mr. Keeton argued it.

Mr. SPANGENBERG. He didn't mention plaintiffs' fees but investigative expenses and loss.

Mr. KEETON. I did. I said: Attorneys' expenses on both sides. And I meant one side to be the plaintiff's side.

Mr. SPANGENBERG. I am well aware if you start deducting attorneys" fees, you will, of course, reduce what the average consumer receives.

You will not reduce what all of the consumers who do not hire attorneys receive.

Mr. KINZLER. Will you reduce that average figure from over 60 down to 44 cents?

Mr. SPANGENBERG. Who would?

Mr. KINZLER. Will you reduce it?

Mr. SPANGENBERG. I certainly will not, because you don't have any data, any data that allows you to do it.

Mr. KINZLER. All right. If we go back to the Department of Transportation report, look at the automobile accident litigation and the automobile personal injury claims, according to these two volumes, attorneys represented only 46.2 percent of all paid claimants but these claimants incurred 73.2 percent of all economic loss to date of settlement and received 77 percent of all payments, on the assumption also made that the average claimant's attorney's fee was 35.5 percent.

Mr. SPANGENBERG. Yes, on the assumption.

Mr. KINZLER. That is the assumption made in here; of gross payments, attorneys' fees amounted to 27.3 percent of total payments to all claimants and an additional assumption of claimants' other litigation expenses averaged $250 per suit filed and these expenses amounted to an additional 3.2 percent of total payments to all claimants.

If you take those figures and apply them to a dollar, we end up not with Mr. Keeton's figures on the 44-cent figure but with the Department of Transportation's figures, and their net benefits to claimants is 40 cents.

Mr. SPANGENBERG. Yes, if we do. But don't say——

Mr. KINZLER. Do you disagree with the figures?

Mr. SPANGENBERG. Of course. I have read all of the reports with care. Now, you say: "if it is assumed that the average attorney's fees is 35 percent." Well, anyone would be a nut to assume that. The maximum is 33⅓ percent in most of the places I know about. It is different in Massachusetts; they may charge 40 percent there.

Mr. KEETON. You are talking about higher claims. Thirty-three is not a maximum in any State with respect to the smaller claims.

Mr. VAN DEERLIN. What is the normal contingency fee?

Mr. SPANGENBERG. Twenty-seven percent on settlement and 33 percent on suits, and you will find those fees all over the United States in which I consider to be decent States with decent population and decent attorneys.

Mr. VAN DEERLIN. Excluding Massachusetts, of course?

Mr. SPANGENBERG. Massachusetts and New York are special and so is Chicago, Ill., and so is Los Angeles, Calif.

Mr. VAN DEERLIN. We heard last week Miami may be.

Mr. SPANGENBERG. Miami may be special.

Mr. KEETON. The figures you have given apply to larger claims, but where contingent fees are even regulated by courts, as they are in relatively few jurisdictions, they always have a higher percentage for the claims under $500, under $1,000, sometimes a break to $2,000 and $2,500.

Mr. SPANGENBERG. Of course.

Mr. KEETON. Isn't that also a common practice?

Mr. SPANGENBERG. Bob, there are places so bad the courts have had to step in and regulate the fees and, believe me, that is a rarity in the United States and I am sure you know it. And then they say 50 percent of the first thousand and then 40 percent of the next $2,000 and one-third of the next $5,000 and then 25 percent and then 20 and then 10 percent over 100.

But when—well, yes, "or"—and every one of them is "or"—"or one-third maximum." Well, that is where they had to regulate, but that does not mean that every attorney in that jurisdiction charged that level of fees that the court thought was the maximum that could be tolerated.

Now, you said, "if we assume," and I will tell you where assumption came from; it came from part of the questionnaire in the economic consequences study in which they asked people if they had attorneys and if they paid them.

The economic consequences study itself says, "Unfortunately the people who answered were people who had been through litigation, so we have a skewed figure." which is the polite way to say, "It is not so." Of course you are going to pay more if you litigate than if you settle without litigation.

I think there were only 346 people who answered the questionnaire. Now you are saying: Don't I believe figures where 346 people, most of whom had been through litigation, said that is what they paid their attorneys?

That is in the survey done. It is that kind of figure which was said must be the average attorney's fee in the United States for all claims in which people go to a lawyer.

Now, the figure is not correct. You have asked me before if I know the right one. I don't. I don't know of anyone who does. Allstate, in its last submission, said: Generally State Farm thinks that the attorneys' fees might be as much as 25 percent, but we don't think that can be so, knowing the number of people that do not hire attorneys.

They cite that only one of their claimants in Georgia out of five ever go to attorneys, so I think it is something less than 25 but we don't know what.

Mr. KINZLER. What they are dealing with here are on people who do retain attorneys—that is basis of the 35.5 percent figure.

Mr. SPANGENBERG. Let's take your bill, Mr. Kinzler, and you go through the frequency and severity figures and you had better be sure that every one of those people who got the big claim had to have a lawyer to get through the no-fault maze in that State.

You found that in Dade County, I am sure, and you will find it in any of the no-fault States, that the people who have to beat a threshold and wrestle around their cases are the people who hire lawyers; and, when you see 115-percent severity, would you please apply your own attorney fee percentage to that number and not pretend no-fault will pay everybody without attorneys and somehow you have saved that cost.

Mr. KINZLER. That brings up another point we went through last time and—if I can find the relevant chart—you indicated that, if you have residual tort for serious injuries, it would not save much because thsoe are the cases that generate most attorney's fees. Is that correct?

Mr. SPANGENBERG. That is right.

Mr. KINZLER. If we look at table 44 of Economic Consequences, volume I, appearing on page 76, percentage distribution, attorney's fees——

Mr. SPANGENBERG. You said "Economic Consequences." That is table 5.

Mr. KINZLER. I am sorry, that is not the correct volume. It is in the automobile personal injury claim file.

That is on page 76. The table is for percentage distribution of attorneys, clients, law suits, and fee income by size of total payment.

The cases of $10,000 to $25,000 of economic loss, constitute only 16 percent of plaintiff's attorneys' fees and those over $25,000 constitute 12 percent.

I would assume that if you are talking about death, disability, permanent or serious injuries, you are talking about something from $10,000 and up as a general rule?

Mr. SPANGENBERG. Yes. You are too fast for me. Let me follow you on this.

Mr. KINZLER. Okay. All right, the suggestion is that the most serious cases do not necessarily yield the largest percentage of plaintiff's attorney's fees, because attorneys make an awful lot of money at the end of the system where there are a lot more cases, as you told us and quite accurately so.

I feel ill equipped to discuss this with you with your computer.

Mr. VAN DEERLIN. Mortal man works at the machine.

Mr. SPANGENBERG. Go ahead. I am anticipating where you will come out, and I thought I might be prepared.

Mr. KINZLER. I thought I had come out already. If I am not mistaken, Mr. Keeton's approach and the Department of Transportation's approach in calculating what the reduction in plaintiff's attorneys' fees would be under a no-fault system, reduced the figure for plaintiff's attorneys' fees from about 15.9 to 8 percent of the premium dollar, about a 50-percent reduction. Would that be consistent with your figures?

Mr. SPANGENBERG. Too high.

Mr. KINZLER. That figure, the 8 percent, would be too high?

Mr. SPANGENBERG. They are postulating a much larger reduction than can occur if you believe the Milliman & Robertson cost estimates, the Milliman & Robertson study of what the average recovery would be under the $600 threshold, which is as close a table as we have to the 3-month disability threshold. And they are postulating that the average recovery in that case is only going to be about $2,500 average, which means there will be a lot of them at 2 or 22, and then they will go up to 50 and 100, but they are postulating rather low average recoveries.

In order to make recoveries, the people have to hire an attorney, so the best I can do on what I hope is an impartial and informal judgment is that if the table is so, if the M. & R. estimates are so, then you are talking about attorneys' fees that would be in the range of 75 percent of what they now are.

But if the actual experience in the no-fault States with thresholds would show much greater recoveries than the M &. R. estimates is so, then you are up to 80 or 85 percent as much in attorneys' fees; that is, I do not think that the quality of attorneys in this country who do handle serious litigation will suffer any economic loss, as you used the term from the no-fault bill.

I think I am not infected in any way with any personal interest. There are some attorneys in every metropolitan area who make a specialty of catching minnows and gather in a great many small claims.

When you take the minnows and grind them into fishmeal, it is nourishing, but those people will no longer function in the system.

It may be a great loss to them. I am not sure it is a great loss to me. I am not concerned about the small claim.

Mr. KINZLER. Mr. Keeton, you cut the figure by half. Where do you differ from Mr. Spangenberg?

Mr. KEETON. I agree with Mr. Spangenberg that the expert trial lawyers, like himself will not be financially disadvantaged by enactment of a no-fault system, because the tort claims of the kind that they are handling and actually trying in the automobile system and other parts of the tort system, are the ones that would still be saved under the tort threshold.

I disagree with him about the percentage of attorneys' fees that that group represents in the total of attorneys' fees that go into the statistics for the total system, and I think my difference is borne out by the study made by the Council on Law-Related Studies on what has happened to the Massachusetts bar as a result of the operation of the no-fault system up there. That study included a questionnaire submitted to, if I remember correctly, something like 3,500 of the 18,000 lawyers throughout the State of Massachusetts, whose names they could find on the rolls of those authorized to practice in Massachusetts.

They got what the pollsters regard as a high response rate from the questionnaires. On the basis of that, they came to the conclusion that 10 percent of the total bar in Massachusetts, lawyers in all kinds of law practices, were so substantially affected by the operation of the no-fault law that they made major changes in their career patterns following enactment of that law.

Eighty percent were not substantially affected, and in another 10 percent there was uncertainty when this study was made about 18 months after the system first went into operation. They had under discussion—and I don't know whether they decided whether or not to do it—an effort to update that study by following it through to see what happened to the other 10 percent. But it seems clear to me that if that large a percentage of all persons authorized to practice—which would, of course, include a number of people really engaged in corporate enterprise rather than in the practice of law—if that large a percentage of the total were substantially affected, it does not seem a fair inference that the system is only reducing attorneys' fees by 25 percent or even less according to Mr. Spangenberg's point. I think our estimate was probably conservative.

Mr. SPANGENBERG. Well, the 25 percent was Allstate's estimate criticizing—no, 25 percent was State Farm's estimate which Allstate in its submission recently, 2 weeks ago, criticized, saying it is too high, but they don't know the lawyer number, so it is not my figures.

That is two distinguished insurance company groups, you know.

Let me quote Massachusetts again. I think I know pretty well what happens in what I think is a great State, Ohio, and I only have to look at this volume to see that under the tort system, 78.8 percent of all Massachusetts claimants hired attorneys.

I know that your accident rate was 684 or 687 per 100 million miles driven, against a national average of 256 injuries per 100 million miles driven. I hope it impresses you.

Illinois, it is not a big problem. There are not many injuries per 100 million miles. Ohio is 159 injuries per 100 million miles driven, and our rate of hiring attorneys is much less. It is startling to me after Massachusetts adopted no-fault, the official report of the highway department for the next 2 years showed the injury rate in Massachusetts dropped from 674 to something into 300; that is, came close to the national average.

I don't know anything in no-fault that reduces accidents and injuries. It didn't change in other States. So Massachusetts is a queer place.

Mr. KINZLER. Mr. Keeton, we have two strange things now about Massachusetts to discuss; according to Mr. Spangenberg, both the dramatic reduction in the accident rate and also his explanation of your figures on bodily injury premiums, that was done by simply paying fewer people fewer dollars. Would you please respond to those statements?

Mr. KEETON. Yes. It is true that the number of reported injuries—which of course, is the only thing we have data on in the absence of a field study independently, which nobody has done—it is true that the number of reported injuries went down dramatically in Massachusetts after the no-fault bill was in operation. I don't think there is anything mysterious about that at all.

Now it is a very common experience in a fender bending accident that people in the car are thrown around a bit. They get some bruises. If we have a tort system, those bruises are worth a substantial amount of money. Indeed in the marketplace they are worth a whole lot more in relation to what they are than rather serious injuries. It seems clear to me that what was happening in Massachusetts before no-fault went into effect, and what does happen in other jurisdictions, though I agree it happens to a greater extreme in Massachusetts, is that the people who had minor bruises from being tossed around in fender bending accidents made claims. And when they made claims, of course they also made a report of the accident. So not only were there more reported injuries, but also more reported accidents under that system.

Now, after no-fault went into effect, there was no longer any profit to be made by that kind of report and it was trouble to do it, and so it was not done. I think virtually everybody who was observing the situation was surprised that the amount of that reduction of reported accidents was as great as it was, but that to me was only a demonstration of the efficacy of the no-fault system. It demonstrated it was more needed and more efficacious than even the strongest proponent predicted.

Mr. SPANGENBERG. I quote to you, Mr. Kinzler, if I may, from the Journal of Risks and Assurance, technical journal of actuaries, from an article published in 1973, March edition.

"Massachusetts loss experience under no-fault analysis and implications" written by a Professor of Actuarial Science at the University of Rhode Island, "The overall reduction of 40 percent in total claims" and that is both no-fault and personal injury protection, "is due to the fact that no-fault compensated for an increase of 42,540 in PIP," no, no, liability claims, that is, the no-fault benefit claims, "by bringing about a decrease of 89,453 in liability claims."

"As Exhibit 5 shows, the principal impact of no-fault on the 1971 loss experience was a 76-percent reduction it produced in tort claims."

Then, this goes on to say that "The overall reduction of 40 percent was totally unexpected, the dramatic cost result in savings could not have been achieved without this totally unforeseen reduction in the number of total claimants" and that the anomaly had not yet been explained and no satisfactory explanation can be reached.

By way of contrast, may I say that every State that I know of, that has now reported a no-fault experience other than Massachusetts has shown a predictable increase in total claims paid. Florida actually paid more people. New York paid more people and New Jersey and Colorado, everybody pays more people.

Massachusetts is the only State that pays 40 percent fewer people in combined tort and the no-fault claims.

Mr. KINZLER. That was the other half of my question.

Thank you. Mr. Keeton.

Mr. KEETON. What is the question? Why is the total number of persons paid in Massachusetts lower?

Mr. KINZLER. And is that the basis for the lower costs?

Mr. KEETON. Yes; it is part of the basis, yes. That difference, that other 40 percent who were making claims under the old system were all making liability claims and they were in that body of claims in which the actual out-of-pocket losses were relatively low and the State average for a loss that was under $100 was that it was settled for 10 times the economic loss. If it was, say $75, it would be settled for $750. That was a statewide average for all claims regardless of how meritorious they were. Of course it included some meritorious on fault and some pretty weak, but the general proposition was that companies were settling rather than incurring the costs of fighting those.

That same figure, incidentally, for Boston was not 10 to 1, but 18 to 1. The big body of claims drawn out—the 40 percent drawn out— are mostly those very small economic loss claims. And there is another thing that happened in Massachusetts that I think helps explain the result, although none of us had the wisdom to see it ahead of time and forecast it. It is easy in hindsight to see why it happened.

That is, that the whole fight over the introduction of the no-fault and the threat of the insurance companies to withdraw from the State immediately after it was passed, before some court action was taken to declare invalid the 15 percent mandated reduction on coverages that were not effective, has led people to fear they would not be be able to get coverage if they had a claims record. Indeed for a period of a few months companies were not taking any new business. As a result of that, I think the system in Massachusetts has actually functioned with an operative deductible even though there is theoretically no deductible on the books. Take a person who has a $50 medical bill to find out that he had nothing but bruises you know mostly X-rays, for example. Now that person does not bother to make a claim because he does not want it on the record. I think that helps to explain that 40 percent figure.

Now, of course, it is true that without a field study and maybe even with it it would be impossible to determine exactly what caused that reduction, but there are two among the many speculations that make sense and I think explain it.

One is this fear of not being able to get insurance or having to pay higher rates as a result of the claim record which has caused the people not to make the small claims that they were making to collect several hundred dollars more than loss.

The second is that it is no longer possible to make the really fraudulent claim, the numbers of which I don't think were really as high as the cases of the type I just explained.

Those were the two suggestive explanations that make sense to me, and as a matter of hindsight I think they account for the reduction in the numbers of claims and also of course for reductions in numbers of reported accidents. People just don't report fender-bender accidents any longer when they don't want to make a claim.

Mr. SPANGENBERG. Gee, I am glad you have said that. I have heard it too, and I know there was a public opinion poll that said people were not making claims under $50 for fear of getting cancelled or not renewed, but I thought that wasn't a very good argument for a no-fault system.

We have got to pay money for this protection and then we don't make a claim, I don't think that's good.

Mr. KEETON. I think it's an excellent argument and one which you have in fact supported when I recall to you another proposition. You have argued that automobile ought not to be primary, and what's happened here, this $50 bill that is paid by Blue Cross is not being claimed again in tort, whereas it was under the old system. Don't you favor squeezing that out of the system?

Mr. SPANGENBERG. No, no, because on that system I pay for the predictive risk that the loss will occur, which is why you have that big 10 percent figure that haunts you in Massachusetts.

Where if—let me give you just a simple mathematical argument—if your personal injury protection benefit for all the policyholders in the country had to pay for say $1 million of benefits, and then you made it all excess and you only had to pay out, the company only had to pay out $200,000 in benefits, they would have to reduce the premium.

If the total payout is reduced, the premium has to reduce. So the fact that some people claimed and some didn't would be reflected in the premium. And my premium would be much lower, I wouldn't make the claim because I have the Blue Cross and the other coverages, but I don't want to pay premiums to get double recovery.

I know that's a bad investment. I would like to pay a premium that allows single recovery for everyone, which the excess system does. Then the premium does go down. You would agree with that, wouldn't you, Bob?

Mr. KEETON. Certainly, and you have answered your own argument by making the point that you pay the premium for whatever the coverage effectively is. If we have this duplication you will have to pay higher premiums; if we can squeeze it out you don't. And I think the voluntary deductible makes great sense.

Mr. SPANGENBERG. Well, maybe so, but I still don't like the system in which some people make the claim they are entitled to and some people are afraid to make it for fear of being cancelled. That to me isn't right. That's different from excess and you're in favor of excess, aren't you, really?

Mr. KEETON. You would prefer a system in which some people make fraudulent claims——

Mr. SPANGENBERG. No.

Mr. KEETON. And get away with it?

Mr. SPANGENBERG. No, I will leave that to you.

Mr. KEETON. You have yours.

Mr. SPANGENBERG. I will leave that to you, wherever you may be.

Mr. KEETON. You have yourself argued that's the way the system is functioning. And believe me, Massachusetts is not going to be unique in that effect. I believe that citizens everywhere have about the same inclination in the United States to respond to the incentive structure of the system.

Mr. SPANGENBERG. Oh, don't say that.

Mr. KEETON. And if you set up the incentive system to make profit by making fraudulent claims, the incidence of fraudulent claims will increase.

Mr. SPANGENBERG. There are differences in cultures, Mr. Keeton, and you know the numbers show them. There are differences in cultures. I guess I will close by saying I am glad you fixed that problem in Massachusetts with your bill, and we certainly don't need a Federal bill now all over. You have got it all cured and so let us go and fix it for the rest of the country in the right way.

Mr. VAN DEERLIN. Well, thank you both very much for being here. Speaking of separate cultures, I must now return to my subject culture on the House floor, in hopes that it is the last vote of the day over there.

We very much appreciate your both being with us and giving us this very interesting format of discussion.

Mr. SPANGENBERG. Thank you very much for your patience, Mr. Van Deerlin. It has been with great pleasure.

Mr. KEETON. Thank you.

Mr. VAN DEERLIN. The subcommittee will adjourn until tomorrow.

[Whereupon, at 6:12 p.m., the hearings were adjourned, to reconvene at 10 a.m., Thursday, July 24, 1975.]

NO-FAULT MOTOR VEHICLE INSURANCE

THURSDAY, JULY 24, 1975

House of Representatives,
Subcommittee on Consumer Protection and Finance,
Committee on Interstate and Foreign Commerce,
Washington, D.C.

The subcommittee met at 1:30 p.m., pursuant to notice, in room 2322, Rayburn House Office Building, Hon. Lionel Van Deerlin (chairman) presiding.

Mr. Van Deerlin. The subcommittee will come to order for a continuation of hearings on bills looking into no-fault auto insurance.

Our first witness this afternoon will be Dr. Carl Granger, representing the American Academy of Physical Medicine & Rehabilitation and the American Congress of Rehabilitation Medicine.

Dr. Granger, welcome to the hearing.

STATEMENT OF DR. CARL V. GRANGER, PRESIDENT-ELECT, AMERICAN ACADEMY OF PHYSICAL MEDICINE & REHABILITATION, MEMBER, AMERICAN CONGRESS OF REHABILITATION MEDICINE; ACCOMPANIED BY RICHARD E. VERVILLE, COUNSEL

Dr. Granger. I would like to be joined by counsel of the organizations, Mr. Richard Verville.

Mr. Van Deerlin. I have my counsel, and you are entitled to yours.

Dr. Granger. I represent the American Congress of Rehabilitation Medicine and the American Academy of Physical Medicine & Rehabilitation. The Congress is a national organization of physicians, nurses, therapists, psychologists, and social workers in the medical rehabilitation field. The American Academy of Physical Medicine & Rehabilitation is a scientific organization of physicians specializing in rehabilitation medicine.

Both organizations support Federal legislation establishing a national no-fault auto insurance program including appropriate medical care and comprehensive rehabilitation care.

We believe that such a system is important for the restoration of those injured in auto accidents. The current tort system is counterproductive in terms of assisting in the restoration of the injured, and we do not believe that the States have adequately dealt with the matter to date.

The interest of the two organizations I am representing today in no-fault auto insurance stems from the experience of the professionals in these organizations with caring for those injured in motor vehicle accidents.

A substantial part of the caseload of a rehabilitation facility or a private practitioner involves patients disabled from auto accidents. Our caseload generally involves those who are most seriously disabled, such as those with spinal cord injuries, since it is they who need medical rehabilitation. It is also they who fare the worst under the present tort system, as my testimony will explain.

I thought my testimony should open with a general description of the rehabilitation process for the physically disabled, since many of you may not be fully aware of its scope.

THE REHABILITATION PROCESS

The process of rehabilitation for those injured in auto accidents is no different than it is for any other disabled person because it is tailored to the specific needs of each individual.

The process involves a continuum of medical, social, and vocational rehabilitation. We in the field of physical medicine and rehabilitation emphasize medical rehabilitation, but are also involved in the social and vocational aspects of rehabilitation which often include education, training, and counseling with regard to vocational goals.

Our goal is restoration of the patient to his optimum functional capacity, which includes return to gainful employment where possible, or at least improving the capacity of the patient to independently perform his usual activities of daily living other than work.

The main point with regard to rehabilitation services is that there be a comprehensive plan for the disabled person setting forth goals in terms of physical, mental, social, and vocational functioning. In the medical sense, this plan is supervised by a physician. The physician also assists in the planning of the vocational services.

The key to both the medical and vocational phase is that the providers of service focus on measurable progress in terms of functional capacity. Periodic review for achieving skill in independent functioning is a substantial method for quality and cost control on the program.

The services that are provided in the medical phase of rehabilitation include a physician's diagnostic and therapeutic services and his supervision of the case; the services of nurses competent in rehabilitation nursing; physical, occupational, and speech therapy services; other therapy services such as audiology and blind training for those with hearing and visual impairments respectively, and inhalation therapy for those with respiratory problems; psychological and social services; and rehabilitation counseling services. Also involved are the prescription, provision, and fitting of prosthetic and orthotic devices where they are needed.

In the vocational phase, the services include vocational testing and counseling, job training and placement services, the provision of occupational tools and licenses, et cetera, as well as psychological and other counseling services.

All of the professionals involved deal with rehabilitation in a team approach. It is one area of medical care where there is a close working relationship between medical and allied health service providers.

It should be noted that there are two objectives related to the provision of rehabilitation services in the medical rehabilitation field, and the law must recognize both.

One objective is the progressive improvement in physical and mental function, and the other objective is the maintenance of an improved condition, including prevention of deterioration in that condition.

Many Government programs, including workmen's compensation, medicare, and medicaid, often terminate reimbursement for services related to maintaining an improved condition or preventing its deterioration. The result is that the disabled person may regress, and then the insurer will pay more when it starts reimbursing for the rehabilitation of that individual.

Generally, the major categories of physical disablement resulting from motor vehicle injuries that are appropriate for comprehensive rehabilitation services, are amputations, multiple trauma or complicated fractures, and injuries to the nervous system (nerves, spinal cord, brain).

The combination of acute medical care and rehabilitation for these catastrophic cases can be as high as $50,000.

For those patients too severely injured to regain independence, rehabilitation can assist in recovering partial function. The result is that less expensive resources and less human assistance will be needed for long-term maintenance.

Despite permanent injury, some patients are able to achieve long-term personal adjustment and function as handicapped homemakers, students, workers, or professionals. The savings involved in having these people become productive workers or regain enough function to free those who would otherwise care for them to work, are enormous.

A young college student with a severe spinal cord injury resulting from an auto accident was rehabilitated in 120 days at a cost of about $13,000. This happens to be an a typical figure in that it is quite low. He was completely paralyzed at admission, and upon discharge had almost totally regained his function.

If he had not improved, the cost of maintaining that boy for 50 years would certainly have exceeded the costs of rehabilitation by a multiple of 10. Beyond that, the boy will be able to work and probably contribute 10 times the cost of his rehabilitation in taxes.

For maximum effectiveness, rehabilitation principles and practices must be applied early after onset of the disabling condition rather than after the opportunity for maximum benefit has passed. The boy just mentioned entered the Texas Rehabilitation Institute soon after his accident.

The program should be one of anticipatory management, that is, anticipating probable problems and most feasible care rather than reacting after unnecessary complications have occurred. It is essential, therefore, that service delivery systems for the disabled assure the prompt referral where appropriate to a rehabilitation program.

THE PRESENT TORT-INSURANCE SYSTEM

The present tort-liability system is counterproductive both economically and in terms of enabling the restoration of the individual to his optimum functional capacity. The present system emphasizes the bargaining-litigation-settlement contest in an adversary atmosphere. There is little incentive for provision of assistance to restore the injured victim to optimum productivity.

The disabled person is the focus of conflicting efforts toward financial settlement of the case rather than servicing his needs. Essentially the system focuses on retribution, not restoration.

As a result of these contradictions, the experience has been that small losses are routinely overcompensated with or without attorney representation and large losses are tragically undercompensated. The seriously injured are also not referred for rehabilitation pending litigation. This failure of timely referral is one of the most tragic failures in the system.

This is all quite senseless since insurance carriers will pay out less money in benefits where the victim is rehabilitated and returns to work rather than being permanently disabled.

Information from research done by the Liberty Mutual Insurance Co. regarding those with spinal cord injuries who were promptly referred for rehabilitation as compared to those who were not has indicated a substantial savings to the carriers in providing rehabilitation.

From experience cited from Department of Transportation studies, it is overwhelmingly evident that the present system fosters a regressive mentality that fails to provide for human needs. One survey finds that no rehabilitation program was even suggested to 88.6 percent of seriously injured accident victims; this is an alarming indication that a vitally important resource is virtually unused by the private automobile insurance industry.

It is apparent that claims adjusters who control the system are either unaware or are unsympathetic to the plight of severely disabled accident victims.

Secretary Volpe, in March 1971, summarized that:

> The existing system ill serves the accident victim, the insuring public and society. It is inefficient, overly costly, imcomplete and slow. It allocates benefits poorly, discourages rehabilitation and overburdens the courts and legal system. Both on the record of its performance and on the logic of its operation, it does little if anything to minimize crash losses.

NO-FAULT INSURANCE

No-fault insurance, on the other hand, as represented by the bills before this subcommittee, offers the accident victim an opportunity to protect and restore his health and his normal functions rather than simply to protect himself from a liability suit from a stranger.

It provides five highly important components to accomplish the goal of meeting needs of the severely disabled accident victim:

First, it focuses on meeting the needs of the injured, not on determining culpability;

Second, it provides the individual the financial wherewithal to secure necessary services through coverage of medical and comprehensive rehabilitation services;

Third, it provides the incentives in the direction of human restitution rather than retribution;

Fourth, it does not siphon off resources paid in by way of insurance premiums for a wasteful and dehumanizing bargaining-litigation-settlement contest; and

Fifth, it avoids catastrophic drainage of financial resources of the victim and his family that leads to their being forced to become welfare and medicaid recipients.

By removing the element of fault from the insurance scheme and focusing on covering the maintenance, treatment and rehabilitation of the injured, the incentives will all be to provide care for the seriously injured person. No longer would appropriate care be delayed and perhaps never covered at all.

We also believe that to be successful in reaching the goal of restoration, Federal no-fault provisions must include a number of specific programmatic provisions:

One: Substantial coverage of comprehensive rehabilitation services, both medical vocational, necessitating a clear definition of rehabilitation services in the law;

Two: An approach to rehabilitation that stresses patient outcomes and reimburses for services that will improve function or prevent deterioration—this, too, relates to the definition of rehabilitation;

Three: A program of reporting and review that stresses measurable outcomes and makes the providers of rehabilitation care accountable for quality and cost;

Four: Accreditation standards for institutions to be reimbursed;

Five: A mandatory referral system to assure that the disabled receive rehabilitation where necessary; and

Six: Positive economic incentives to encourage full rehabilitation and return to work.

THE BILLS BEFORE THE SUBCOMMITTEE—S. 354 AS REPORTED, H.R. 1900 AND H.R. 7985

We have worked closely in the development of S. 354 and believe that it substantially meets the above criteria, although we think there needs to be more legislative history regarding the scope of the cost and quality control program in section 109.

H.R. 1900 and H.R. 7985 are similar to S. 354 as introduced and lack some of the clarifying amendments in the scope of rehabilitation coverage provision of S. 354 as reported, but have more clarity regarding the cost and quality control program in section 109.

S. 354 as reported and H.R. 1900 and H.R. 7985 all contain broad and substantial coverage for rehabilitation and a clear definition of rehabilitation which focuses on the progress of the patient in terms of function.

S. 354 as reported includes a clarifying amendment which refers to rehabilitation as a program to improve function or prevent deterioration in condition and the House bills do not. We would urge the inclusion of prevention in the definition of rehabilitation as in the Senate bill.

The Senate bill as reported and the House bills contain requirements regarding a State regulatory program to assure accountability to the public for the quality of care and the reasonableness of costs; but unlike the House bills, the language of the Senate bill as reported is not specific as to how such a program would measure quality or control costs.

The House bills and the Senate bill as introduced tie the review program to the definition of rehabilitation and the assessment of the functional capacity of the patient. In this respect, we favor the House bills and the Senate bill as introduced; but otherwise, the general flexibility of the Senate bill as reported regarding the State regulatory program represents an improvement over the Senate bill as introduced and the House bills.

In all bills, however, there should be emphasis on standards relative to quality control programs utilizing professionals in the relevant fields analogous to the PSRO program under medicare and medicaid.

All three of these bills have the provisions we believe are necessary regarding accreditation, referral, and economic incentives. With regard to the latter, we only raise the question, for which we have no answer, regarding the need to allow the disabled to keep more of their earnings as a positive incentive to return to work.

Under the three bills, 10 percent of earnings could be kept. We had previously recommended a sliding scale system in which earnings and compensation were linked. This is a terribly difficult area, however, and we would recommend that expert testimony from specialists in income maintenance economics be consulted if the issue is dealt with.

H.R. 1272

H.R. 1272 includes broad and substantial coverage for medical care and rehabilitation. However, we believe the definition of rehabilitation used in the other bills should be used in H.R. 1272. It would leave less room for dispute in implementation and would tighten control by focusing on measurable patient goals instead of a list of services.

The specific language of H.R. 1272, because it lists specific services, runs the risk of failure to cover some which are not listed; for example, equipment and appliances, care in a skilled nursing facility, speech therapy, inhalation therapy, psychological services, medical social services, vocational training and placement services.

H.R. 1272 also should include rehabilitative care necessary to restore function or prevent deterioration in condition.

We would also urge the inclusion in H.R. 1272 of: (1) a quality and cost control program for all care provided; (2) a facility accreditation program for all providers who may be reimbursed under the qualifying insurance programs; and (3) provisions to encourage insurors to refer individuals promptly for rehabilitation.

H.R. 1272 does not in any way prohibit such programs from being established by the Secretary of Transportation, but we believe the bill should actually include such programs with broad guidelines leaving the Secretary discretion in implementation.

With regard to a program of quality and cost control, we suggest the program of S. 354 as reported together with the suggestions made in our testimony regarding standards for quality based on functional improvement. The accreditation and referral provisions of S. 354 as passed and the two other House bills are appropriate as references for any change in H.R. 1272.

CONCLUSION

In conclusion, we urge the enactment of a national no-fault program including the objectives and provisions we have referred to in this testimony. We think all of the bills before the subcommittee would establish such a program, although we do urge some definitional and other changes of a relatively minor nature, as we have mentioned.

We appreciate the opportunity to present our views to the subcommittee. I hope you will call upon us if we can be of any further assistance to your deliberations on this important issue.

Thank you very much.

Mr. VAN DEERLIN. Thank you Dr. Granger.

You have said "seriously injured" under the present tort system are not referred for rehabilitation pending litigation. This is one of the outstanding gaps in the present system. I can think of only one reason that there might be this delay. I was wondering what you had in mind? What causes the delay? Why does this occur?

Dr. GRANGER. Well the financial incentive is to be disabled rather than to be rehabilitated if anyone has a significant impairment.

Mr. VAN DEERLIN. You mean for court room purposes?

Dr. GRANGER. Courtroom purposes?

Mr. VAN DEERLIN. Impressing juries?

Dr. GRANGER. Juries for one, and just in life style, one would expect to be supported as long as one were in the category of remaining disabled rather than being rehabilitated. There is not any financial incentive toward the rehabilitation process.

Mr. VERVILLE. I would like to expand on it a bit so that lawyers don't sound quite as malicious or evil as they may sound in that characterization, not only because I am a lawyer but also because I think it is somewhat accurate.

I think what happens also is that the lawyer who is handling a plaintiff's case gets to the point where he may be near trial, and the patient has probably had emergency medical service and his or her acute care.

Then the question is: What does the patient look like? What is the nature of the disability? And that relates to how much your damages may be when you go to trial and at the same time the lawyer may not know that there is such a thing as rehabilitation. If he does know, he may not be aware of the fact that it makes a difference that the person gets to it quickly.

So the lawyer may just conclude: Look, this person has a bad disability. He needs to be compensated. If there is something called rehabilitation he may not need it now and he may conclude that his client ought to just wait for the rehabilitation, until after the case.

Mr. VAN DEERLIN. You mean possibly dumb rather than malicious?

Mr. VERVILLE. Yes, and I think it is very possible to be dumb. I think we feel it happens a lot. I know the transportation department study indicated that. I think the personal experiences of physicians that are in our organization support that proposition.

Dr. GRANGER. One of the elements in the process of rehabilitation is to break the "sick role" and the "sick role" is one in which the patient expects to be waited on, expects to be dependent, and one in which those providing services, physicians, nurses and so forth, expect to wait on a "sick" person. Because of this the patient develops a sort of psychological "set" of being dependent. Unless we work with the patient toward his own restitution and restoration early, it is hard to reverse that psychological "set" that the patient may get into. It may not be established in any malicious way, but rather becomes sort of a habit, or a learned response to chronic handicap.

So that is the reason it is important that the rehabilitation process starts early on patients who have impairment severe enough to require the process in the first place.

Mr. VAN DEERLIN. Of course, rehabilitation delayed is much more difficult, I suppose?

Dr. GRANGER. It is, it is difficult because the patient is less amenable to change. He becomes adapted to a lifestyle of being dependent on others around him including family members that become adapted that way.

Mr. VAN DEERLIN. What the Army calls goldbrick?

Dr. GRANGER. No, that is a kind of malingering perhaps, but this is an unconscious psychological adaptation to being handicapped. Although many people who are handicapped do not need to adopt that kind of role.

Sometimes under the tort system, it would take a rather unusual personality to overcome those obstacles that are psychological, whereas with a no-fault system we would hope those obstacles would not be present and Joe Blow, ordinary citizen, might have motivation to become rehabilitated to his maximum potential.

Mr. VAN DEERLIN. Mr. Kinzler.

Mr. KINZLER. Thank you, Mr. Chairman.

Is there any information to indicate that the later rehabilitation that is occasioned by the tort system might lead to more permanent injury, that is, something that might be remedial at one point is no longer remedial 2 or 3 years later?

Dr. GRANGER. It is hard to produce firm data to prove that. I think everyone that practices in the field will testify that is their impression and so forth, but there is not hard data to substantiate that. Although in certain cases such as neuromuscular paralysis, we know joints that do not move become tight and painful, and the major parts of the program might be devoted to loosen that particular joint before one moves on to other stages of achieving independence.

Patients with paralytic condition of the spinal cord can get sores because they have not gotten into a rehabilitation program early enough. Early prophylactic measures include frequent turning of the body to relieve pressure points, for example.

So, in a fragmentary way, there is plenty of evidence, but it is hard to pull together in any standardized study.

Mr. VERVILLE. There was a study done at New York University Medical Center we can make available to you, which dealt with spinal cord injured patients who were referred for rehabilitation within 21 days after the onset of the problem.

That study dealt with the cost savings involved when you looked at the people who were not referred within that 21-day period and the costs that were involved in keeping him in a hospital or nursing home over a time. The information that I received from the New York University Medical Center in the study was to the effect that you could save in these badly injured spinal cord cases up to 100 days in inpatient care, but I will have to get ahold of that for the record.

Mr. VAN DEERLIN. We were just wondering if you might provide it.

[The following material was received for the record:]

Model Regional Systems of Spinal Cord Injury Care

During the period 6/15/72 to 4/30/74 a full time physiatrist, a rehabilitation nurse coordinator, and consultant technical and medical computer biostaticians are on staff and have developed a data collecting system which will be completed in a few months for this Model Systems Program. A full-time medical social worker was added on March 1, 1973 and her work is that of a community outreach person. Coordination has been developed with counterpart staff personnel of the Acute Care Program which was activated January 1, 1974 by the Department of Neurosurgery under Dr. Joseph Ransohoff with funding by NIH NINDS (N.S.) #71255346.

Staffing patterns in education have been developed so that spinal cord patients may now be admitted to the Institute of Rehabilitation Medicine as soon as their acute status has become stabilized. This also allows for a faster flow of the subacute spinal cord patient into the rehabilitation system.

Renovations have been made at the Institute of Rehabilitation Medicine to provide a core of offices that are used by Model Systems (SRS) Program.

The building of a data base for computer storage, retrieval, and analysis has progressed productively in consultation with other Regional Centers. Necessary hardware and personnel to meet these needs have been approved by SRS and have been acquired.

Funding problems in hospital reimbursement for rehabilitation services which would delay flow of the patient into and out of the system have been identified and steps to rectify these at city, state, and regional levels have been in progress.

A Regional Spinal Injury Center for the Rehabilitation Management and long-term comprehensive follow-up of spinal cord injured patients has been established at the New York University Medical Center. The Center functionally interdigitates with the Acute Spinal Cord Injury Clinical Research Center at the New York University Medical Center. The latter is conducted by the Department of Neurosurgery under the direction of Dr. Joseph Ransohoff, Professor and Chairman, and was activated on January 1, 1974.

The present request is for a one-year continuation period. The present year has been devoted to the completion of sophisticated data computer input and retrieval system for storage of spinal cord rehabilitation and follow-up information and statistical analysis.

The Regional Center has been operational since June, 1973 and delivers a comprehensive rehabilitation program, multidisciplinary in nature and in keeping with the spinal cord injured patients' special restorative needs. Staff includes physiatrists, a complete consultant staff, and a multidisciplinary team of allied health professionals needed for delivery of comprehensive rehabilitation services.

Follow-up of patients subsequent to discharge will continue on a regular basis for their lifetimes.

New York University Medical Center,
Edward W. Lowman, *Project Director.*

35. NARRATIVE DESCRIPTION OF PROPOSAL

A. *Introduction*

1. *Objectives.*—Trauma to the spinal cord is a leading cause of catastrophic and permanent injury. 10,000 new cases occur each year in the United States. Because the mechanism of the accident so often involves moving vehicles, water sports, the younger segment of the population is predominantly affected. The care of the spinal cord injured is so multidisciplinary that the organization and efficient operation of a team of health personnel dedicated to delivering intensive and long-term services is essential. This level of health service delivery is not within the fiscal and functional scope of the local community or general hospital. Indeed, too often the focus of care at this level does not include measures adequate for the prevention of serious complications which can exert long-lasting deleterious effects on the prognosis for rehabilitation.

The experiences of spinal cord centers both here and abroad indicate that considerably more than 50% of the spinal cord injured can be returned to productive lives. The attainment of the desired level of therapeutics, professional education and research is best achieved within the atmosphere of a large center where all needed services can be closely coordinated and integrated.

The major objective of this project is to provide and demonstrate the end result effectiveness of a systematized care system for the treatment of the spinal cord injured man. Specific objectives of this system of care are (1) minimization of neurological deficit consequent to acute spinal cord trauma, (2) early entry into an acute rehabilitation system for rapid institution of restorative services as well as prevention of complications, (3) maximization of the restorative end results as well as lifetime follow-up to assure that these results are maintained (4) the evaluation of the cost effectiveness of such a spinal cord injured care system through systematized data collection, storage flexibility and accessibility for retrieval and analysis.

2. *Background.*—The Institute of Rehabilitation Medicine of New York University Medical Center has long been recognized as a center of excellence for the rehabilitation of spinal cord injured patients. More than 2000 such patients have been treated here within the past decade. The continuum of care delivery which is now available with the new Model System was not always possible in the past. The average delay in transfer of the patient from the acute orthopedic or neurosurgical department to the rehabilitation system has frequently been from four to six weeks or longer and the incidence of accompanying complications has been high. Post discharge follow-up has often been focal, irregular and fragmented in nature but has included urological follow-up, medical examinations, vocational follow-up surveys, emergency incidences, etc. Interaction with the community has frequently been insufficient as reflected by the paucity of adequate housing, facilities, the lack of available public transportation, the improving but still difficult problem of finding accessible, adequate and high quality educational institutions for spinal cord patients once they are rehabilitated and returned to the community.

A systematized data storage base has been lacking in the past. Although data has always been collected on spinal cord injured patients, the lack of a uniform data system has prevented statistically tapping this source in an optimal way. Due to the specific personalities and vocabularies of the people gathering data, many cause-effect, trends and correlations dealing with these patients have been left unanswered in the past. The new Model System is coping with this problem by monitoring that all people who do collect data consider specific given problems and report these problems in a uniform fashion.

3. *Rationale.*—As a result of this system of delivery of care from the site of injury into lifetime follow-up there is every reason, based upon extensive clinical experience, to believe that the objectives (A-1) will be achieved and that the former looser and fragmented system of care will be improved.

B. *Specific aims*

To produce a higher effective restorative outcome with an improved and shorter term care delivery system for the spinal cord injured man and to equate these outcomes in terms of cost effectiveness.

C. *Methods and procedures*

The spinal cord program at New York University Medical Center is unique in many ways. Under the NINDS grant #71255346, the Department of Neurosurgery under the direction of its professor, Dr. Joseph Ransohoff, has developed a system of acute care delivery for the acute spinal cord injured. Activated on January 1, 1974, this acute care phase has been developed with the rehabilitation of the patient in mind. (See Addendum #1). Addendum #1 shows how the whole rehabilitation team is brought into action while the spinal cord patient is still under the primary care of the neurosurgeon.

Due to the unique population spread in New York City, with high-rise and high density population areas spilling out into average density suburbia, Dr. Ransohoff has made his spinal cord center available to 230 neurosurgeons in Departments of Neurosurgery within a 50 mile radius of New York City. This allows other medical service facilities to participate in his grant effort and since his system is interdigitating into ours, many of these patients are fed into our early pick-up rehabilitation oriented system. This concept adds broad dimension to the program for, as a large catch basin for care delivery, it will funnel patients earlier and in larger volume into the rehabilitation system within the New York University Center complex (Institute of Rehabilitation Medicine, Bellevue Hospital and Goldwater Memorial Hospital.) Upon entry into the system, the patient is followed throughout by the Neurosurgical Service, New York University Medical Center and when he is transferred to our Rehabilitation unit, close continuing supervision is maintained. Since the Rehabilitation unit is physically united to the Neurosurgical Department through interconnecting corridors located on each patient floor, patients can easily be transferred back to the Neurosurgical unit if their neurosurgical status warrants, and any patients located in the Neurosurgical unit can as easily be transferred to Rehabilitation as needs occur. While in the Neurosurgical unit, the patients are followed by a physiatrist and rehabilitation nurse from our Rehabilitation Center as well as by all needed paramedical personnel such as occupational therapists, physical therapists, etc. This makes it possible to start early bedside therapy, to initiate early bowel and bladder training programs and to provide expert rehabilitation nursing care from the very start of hospitalization. Since both the Neurosurgical Service as well as the Rehabilitation service work so closely together, the result is a unitized system with constant follow-up. The resultant effect of the system is that teaching occurs in both directions: that is to say, rehabilitation concepts are brought into play early or almost immediately as the patient enters the acute phase of his illness and close neurosurgical follow-up is maintained throughout the entire stay of the patient in the rehabilitation facility.

A data collection system has been developed using common format for both acute and rehabilitation phases of care. A common pool of consulting medical and surgical staff is identical for both acute and rehabilitation phases.

To assure and facilitate the interdigitation of the National Institutes of Health and the Rehabilitation Services Administration phases of the program, coordinators facilitate information sharing on a medical, nursing, therapeutic and social service level so that the total care of the patient from the moment of his entry into the system at the acute stage and up to and including lifetime follow-up after rehabilitation will become a longitudinal continuum of care rendered by a group of medical and surgical specialists who have known the patient from the very onset of his injury. At one point in time, the patient can be seen or moved to any department in our medical complex. Primary care for the patient can be shifted back and forth (with the same team still participating) as the patient's needs arise. This flexibility maintains a unified systematic approach while still meeting in an optimum fashion any individual patient's particular needs. This means that a patient gets the appropriate care at the proper time.

The patient's total management consists of three stages: i.e. (1) which extends from the moment of injury up to his discharge from the Neurosurgical Intensive Care Unit when his vital signs are stable. Stage (2) starts at discharge from the Neurosurgical Intensive Care Unit. At this stage the patient is admitted into the Rehabilitation facility, becomes part of the RSA component of our total care system. He is bed-bound, and still requires close medical and nursing supervision. A patient at stage (3) no longer requires intensive medical and nursing supervision. He can be taken out of bed and can be placed on a regular intensive rehabilitation program.

Staff for stage (1) (acute care), that is, for the acute NIH component, in addition to neurosurgeons, medical and surgical consultants, comprises a physiatrist, a rehabilitation nurse clinician, social workers, a computer systems data designer, and data collectors. This staff is working in close liaison with the FSA sponsored spinal cord component which now consists of a director, a full time physiatrist, a rehabilitation nurse coordinator, a research clinical scientist, a coordinator clinical psychologist, a job placement counselor, a computer systems designer, programmer, data analyst, community liaison social worker, a project secretary and two data input teletypists.

With the transfer of the patient from the Neurosurgical Unit Stage #1 following medical stabilization, he is admitted, depending upon his condition, to rehabilitation as a sub-acute patient (Stage #2), or as a regular rehabilitation patient (Stage #3). Those patients who come in as sub-acute patients are generally bed-bound, require intensive nursing care and are placed on a rehabilitation program designed to their particular needs. All therapies are brought to and carried out at bedside. In some cases, this sub-acute phase, Stage #2, can go on for several weeks before the patient is progressed into Stage #3 which is the intensive rehabilitation program where he continues to be followed by the same therapists. In certain cases where individual special care is not required, the patient may be immediately progressed from Stage #1 to Stage #3. During Stage #3 the patient no longer receives therapy at bedside but receives all therapies in the areas of the Institute especially designed for each type of therapy. This method of treatment programming has been tested and is not only feasible but highly desirable as a means of preventing physical complication in shortening the entire process of rehabilitation. During Stages #2 and #3 the physiatrist has now become the primary physician responsible for the patient's care, and is in constant communication with the orthopedic and neurosurgical teams who now function on a consultant basis.

A full-time Rehabilitation Nurse Coordinator is associated with the Spinal Cord Center. Her duties are varied. They include training intensive care unit nurses in rehabilitation nursing procedures. This includes bedside teaching and demonstrations, attending and directing team conferences and participating in the ongoing In-Service Nursing Education Program. Her activities in the Neurosurgical Intensive Care units both at University Hospital and at Bellevue Hospital are essential. Further, she is also available in the same capacity on a consultant basis to any of the Neurcsurgical Departments in the Greater New York City area that care for Spinal Cord Injured patients. The major thrust of this effort is to bring rehabilitation techniques to acute hospital settings and to create a unified system of nursing care in all hospitals involved with SCI patients.

She helps coordinate the transfer of the patient to the Rehabilitation Unit and personally sees that the nursing care which has been instituted in the intensive care unit is continued without interruption. Team conferences and participation in the In-Service Nursing Education Program is also continued at this level.

This Nursing Coordinator also is available for lecturing and teaching the various community oriented nursing services such as the Visiting Nurses Association and other community nursing groups as well as groups associated with patient sponsorship such as Blue Cross, Blue Shield, and Office of Vocational Rehabilitation. The purpose here, again, is to maintain a unified continuous system of care. The educational aspects of her duties also require her to address other types of groups in the community especially those concerned with the more technical aspects of our program. She also plays an important role in the out-patient follow-up of spinal cord patients and arranges for nursing care advice whenever needed. She is concerned with all of the patient's problems including sexual problems where she serves as an important adjunct in discussing these problems with both patients and spouses. She is also part of the Sexual Attitude Reassessment Team. She maintains close communication with the nursing staffs of other rehabilitation centers who are planning to fcrm an association for rehabilitation nursing in the United States. A meeting is being held in July in Texa's in order to discuss plans for setting up such an organization. A nursing manual for out patients and their families is in production and will be useful for the everyday care problems that the patient encounters at home.

The social worker concerned with community outreach deals with the problem of interpreting community needs to this department as well as developing new and better relationships with the various community resources that the patient will be dependent upon once he is reintegrated into the community. Enclosed is addendum #2 detailing the scope of these activities. It should be emphasized that this professional is not engaged in case work but exclusively community problems and community relations.

The overall activities of the data collecting part of the project is represented in addendum #3. Briefly, a data collecting team has been organized. Documents concerned with the evaluation stage of the patient's rehabilitation have been formulated, finalized and are being used and this data is now being transferred by two teletypists intc computers. Documents reflecting the progress of the patient in all areas during his rehabilitation phase have been formulized in most of the areas and those not yet finalized should be finished by the time this grant request is submitted. This mass of data will be entered into the computer as we go into the next stage of this program within the next few months. Our program designers are at present working on this material so that periodic progress reports covering all aspects of therapy as well as medical status can be available to us as a computer print-out. The total bulk of data will also be capable of being arranged so that a document will be generated giving the information generally contained in a discharge summary. Data concerning the outpatient status of the patient will also be entered into the computer to allow closer control of patient follow-up. We will then be ready to proceed to the analysis of all this data.

Since the major effort in the rehabilitation of the spinal cord patient is geared to his return to society in a productive capacity, the rehabilitation counselor's role is all important. The work of this counselor involves working out goals with the patient once he is "ready". However, the patient is seen initially by the Vocational Counselor as soon as he enters the rehabilitation component of the system. The goals usually deal with two major areas—education or employment. The first may involve going back to school for completion of an already started course of study, or the redirecting of scholastic goals in a direction consistent with the patient's disability. Once realistic goals have been established, the counselor then proceeds to help find a school where this patient may be enrolled. The establishment of special education programs in a few colleges and universities is a hopeful trend. However, there is a large need for expansion of such programs (answering a patient's special needs, architecturally accessible campuses, funding for education). The second large area that the Vocational Counselor deals with concerns employment goals. This consists first of all of exploring each patient's employment potential. In certain cases this may mean retraining. Once exploration and possible goals are reached, the problem becomes one of finding an employer who is willing to hire a handicapped person. In many cases, the vocational counselor works closely with cooperative employers to help redefine and redesign a patient's former job so that he may return to work with the same employer in a redesigned job adapted to his functional potential. (See addendum #4)

The psychological and social problems which accompany spinal cord injuries both from the patient's point of view and the family unit are such that close psychological supervision, counselling and follow-up are essential to the reconstructive goals of rehabilitation. Because of this, the patients as well as family members are seen by our psychological staff. This program is being supervised by the clinical psychology supervisor attached to the spinal cord center. The immediate needs of the patient are dealt with on a one-to-one basis with follow-up during the entire stay at IRM as well as on an out-patient basis after discharge as needs occur. In addition to his, seminars in personal functioning, again under psychological supervision, treat with all aspects of the patient's disability. This program utilizes a group therapy approach. The patient's loss of motor power, loss of sensation, bowel and bladder dysfunction, sexual dysfunction, which have already been discussed on a one-to-one basis are there discussed in a group setting. Patients are encouraged to interrelate, verbalize feelings, exchange ideas and discuss solutions that they have found useful. In addition to this, Sex Attitude Reassessment (SAR) seminars have been set up for patients where they can reassess their attitudes and feelings about their own sexuality and sexual performance and consider alternatives when this is necessary. Since the whole attitude of sexuality can be influenced by the attitudes projected by our own staff members, plans are now being made to have special workshops for these staff members. For this reason we have held two workshops geared solely to the initial training of counselors. These workshops are to be followed up by a training program in group dynamics. There are now 19 staff members who are being trained to be counselors. We hope to augment this number during the next year and also to include disabled people in our training program so that they, too, may take on the role of counselors in the future workshop programs.

Since a spinal cord injury involves not only a patient but his family, in addition to the person-to-person psychological aid that is available, we have also initiated family group counselling sessions. The reaction from both the participants as well as from the patients is such that family group sessions will continue to be an integral part of our therapy armanentorium. (See addenda #5 and 6.)

The importance of the urological problem in spinal cord injured patients is recognized by all. For this reason and to concentrate the responsibility of care, we have two GU nurses directly responsible to the chief of the urological service working in close conjunction with the psychiatrist. These GU nurses follow all aspects of urological management of our patients. During the past year, we have added a third GU nurse on a trial basis. This added coverage has proven successful and led to better management of our patients so much so that when the trial period is over, this nurse will be retained on staff and salaries will be taken over by e Rehabilitation Institute budget rather than by the Spinal Care Project fundh

As part of our community outreach program most team members are called upon to tell our story to varied organizations. A motion picture film dealing with spinal cord injured patients, their adjustment to their disability, the way in which they meet barriers set up in the community, has been made. The unique quality about this film is that we were able to indoctrinate and educate the film makers into the problems of spinal cord injuries. This training is reflected on film by the empathy and warmth in which the subject is treated. In addition to using this film as instructional with various community groups, we also hope to give this film wider exposure by having it scheduled on network television. As part of a Public Broadcasting Corporation one-hour television production (a tribute to Dr. Howard Rusk and his contribution to rehabilitation medicine) a section of this program was reserved to discussing spinal cord injuries, its problems and the rehabilitation of these patients.

The many problems involved in the altered physiology of the body following a spinal cord injury has led to research in various fields. In the past, as now, we have studied catacholamine changes that occur in our patients and the effect that these changes produce on various body functions and this project is being continued. We are studying calcium metabolism, since the metabolic changes that occur can cause complications such as osteoporosis, urinary tract stones, and ectopic calcium deposits. In the near future we plan to expand our studies to include the area of endocrine gland dysfunction in the spinal cord injured man. This may help to explain problems such as gynecomastia and hypospermia as well as testicular atrophy. Blood and urine samples have already been collected and stored so that they can be analyzed once we are ready to start these studies. (See addendum #7). These clinical studies are supported by private research funds.

D. Data of results to date

The following data concerns Spinal Cord Injured patients who were discharged during 1973–April 30, 1974 as well as those who are still receiving inpatient care at the Institute of Rehabilitation Medicine (I.R.M.) Data is reported separately for these two groups of patients.

Table I shows the lowest cord level preserved whether complete or incomplete, unilateral or bilateral at the time of injury. As shown, 41 patients developed quadriplegia, 26 paraplegia following the initial insult to their spinal cords.

TABLE I.—CORD LEVEL AT TIME OF INJURY

Level [1]	Number of patients	
	Discharged	Inpatients at present [2]
Cervical:		
2	0	1
3	3	2
4	1	7
5	7	10
6	6	2
7	0	0
8	0	0
Thoracic:		
1	1	1
2	0	0
3	0	1
4	2	3
5	1	1
6	0	0
7	2	0
8	2	1
9	2	3
10	1	1
11	2	0
12	2	2
Lumbar: 1–5	0	0
Cauda equina	0	0
Total	32	35

[1] Lowest cord level preserved at time of injury; whether complete/incomplete, unilateral/bilateral or of unequal levels.
[2] Inpatients as of Apr. 30, 1964.

Table II shows the type of accident which caused the Spinal Cord Injury. Transportation, Sports and Gunshot Wounds stand out as the major causes of Spinal Cord Injury. Vehicular accidents alone are equal to the next two major causes (sports, gunshot wounds) combined.

TABLE II—TYPE OF ACCIDENT

	Inpatients at present	Discharged	Total
Transportation:			
Automobile	11	15	26
Motorcycle	1	1	2
Bus	1	1	2
Hit by automobile	1	0	1
Total	14	17	31
Sports:			
Water	6	4	10
Field	1	2	3
Gym accidents	0	2	2
Total	7	8	15
Personal assaults:			
Gunshot wounds	6	3	9
Stabbing	0	0	0
Blunt trauma	0	0	0
Total	6	3	9
Other:			
Falls	6	3	9
Falling or flying objects	1	1	2
Hit by horse	1	0	1
Total	8	4	12

Table III shows the distribution by sex, males leading females 4 to 1.

TABLE III

	Inpatients at present	Discharged	Total
Male	27	27	54
Female	8	5	13

TABLE IV.—AVERAGE AGE OF PATIENTS AT TIME OF INJURY

Inpatients at present (35)	Discharged (32)
24.3	26.3

More single people than married are represented at a ratio of 2:1. Table V.

TABLE V.—MARITAL STATUS

	Inpatients at present	Discharged	Total
Quads married	6	4	10
Quads single	16	13	29
Quads separated	0	1	1
Paras married	5	7	12
Paras single	8	7	15

TABLE VI.—NUMBER OF CHILDREN

	1	2	3	4	5	Total
Inpatients at present	1	4	3	0	1	9
Discharged	5	0	2	0	2	9
Total						18

Most of our patients were legal residents of New York State (38) as could be expected. Patients from nearby adjoining states (Connecticut and New Jersey), 11 represent a smaller amount than would be predicted but this is expected since out-of-state sponsorship has always been and still is a problem. Table VII.

TABLE VII.—LEGAL RESIDENCE AT TIME OF INJURY

	Inpatients at present	Discharged	Total
Colorado	0	1	1
Connecticut	2	2	4
Florida	1	2	3
Indiana	1	0	1
Maryland	1	1	2
Massachusetts	1	1	2
Mississippi	0	2	2
New Jersey	6	1	7
New York	20	18	38
Pennsylvania	1	0	1
Tennessee	0	1	1
Washington, D.C.	1	0	1
Panama	0	1	1
Puerto Rico	1	0	1
Switzerland	0	1	1
Virgin Islands	0	1	1
Total	35	32	67

Time elapsed between time of injury and admission to the system is shown in Table VIII. Patients selected for inclusion in the sample of "System" and "Non-System" patients were screened according to the following criteria. An Immediate System patient must have been an inpatient at both University Hospital and the Institute of Rehabilitation Medicine and been brought into the system within 48 hours. Intermediate System patients must have been admitted to Institute of Rehabilitation Medicine within 2 weeks of their injury without having been University Hospital patients. Delayed System patients are patients brought to Institute of Rehabilitation Medicine within 8 weeks of their injury. Non-System patients are patients who have not received their acute treatment at University Hospital and that were admitted to Institute of Rehabilitation Medicine more than 8 weeks after injury.

TABLE VIII.—Number of system and nonsystem patients

System:
- Immediate _____ 8
- Intermediate _____ 0
- Delayed _____ 17
Nonsystem _____ 42

Total _____ 67

Table IX shows the Average Stay at the Institute of Rehabilitation Medicine of Discharged System (3 categories) and of Non-System patients. It can be seen that the stay of Discharged System patients at I.R.M. was longer than for Non-System Patients.

TABLE IX.—AVERAGE STAY AT INSTITUTE REHABILITATION MEDICINE

	Number of patients (1st admission)	Average days
System:		
Paras	9	131.88
Quads	7	208.75
Nonsystem:		
Paras	5	94.2
Quads	14	198.14

Table X shows *total hospitalization* days of Discharged System (3 categories) and Non-System patients.

TABLE X.—AVERAGE STAY FROM DATE OF INJURY TO DISCHARGE FROM I.R.M. FOR INITIAL REHABILITATION [1]

	Number of patients	Average days
System:		
Paras	8	179.37
Quads	4	255.0
Nonsystem:		
Paras	2	244.0
Quads	8	355.63

[1] Excluded from this group is 1 patient who expired after 17 days at I.R.M. Also excluded are 2 children who were discharged "early" because they were homesick.

The total hospitalization (*acute care and rehabilitation*) for System paraplegic patients was 64 days less than for Non-System patients. For quadriplegic patients, System patients were hospitalized 100 days less than Non-System patients. Table X.

Table XI shows educational level of both inpatients at present at Institute of Rehabilitation Medicine and discharged patients. About half (34) of this patient population had completed the 12th grade and 23 had gone on to additional education.

24 patients had not completed high school. One patient brought up in China stated that he had never received schooling. Another patient was in a pre-school at the time of his accident.

TABLE XI.—EDUCATIONAL LEVELS AT TIME OF INJURY

	Inpatients at present	Discharged	Total
Preschool child	0	1	1
No schooling	0	1	1
Elementary school	7	5	12
High school students	11	8	19
High school graduates	10	1	11
Junior college	0	1	1
College students	4	7	11
College graduates	1	3	4
Graduate school graduates	1	3	4
Vocational school	1	0	1
Graduate school students	0	2	2
Total	35	32	67

Table XII. Vocational status at time of injury.

TABLE XII.—EMPLOYMENT STATUS AT TIME OF INJURY

	Inpatients at present	Discharged	Total
Blue collar, unskilled	0	4	4
Blue collar, skilled	7	1	8
White collar	9	10	19
Employed	16	15	31
Homemaker	1	1	2
Preschool	0	1	1
Students	13	18	31
Nonemployed	2	3	5

Table XIII. Vocational status after discharge.

TABLE XIII.—VOCATIONAL OUTCOME FOLLOWING DISCHARGE

	Paraplegics	Quadriplegics	Total
School	4	8	12
Employed	4	0	4
Homemaker	1	0	1
Seeking Employment	0	2	2
Retired	2	0	2
Plans unknown at this time	1	3	4
Out Patient Program	1	0	1
Discharged to chronic hospital	1	4	5
Deceased	1	0	1
Total	15	17	32

E. Significance

The unique aspects of the New York City program are:

1. The interdigitation of the acute care phase which is funded by NIH with the subsequent continuum of care thereafter sponsored by SRS.

2. The initiation of early admission to the rehabilitation center for the subacute neurosurgical patient.

3. The follow-up of a control group of spinal cord patients will serve as a control group for data comparison with the Model System group.

F. Facilities available

The Institute of Rehabilitation Medicine of the New York University Medical Center is a 152 bed Rehabilitation Hospital with complete facilities and staff personnel in physiatry; hospital administration, occupational therapy, physical therapy, speech pathology, psychological service, functional training (activities of daily living), social service, rehabilitation nursing, urological nursing, therapeutic planned recreation, X-ray (including cystoscopy), orthotic-prosthetics, clinical laboratory, and vocational testing and counseling. Its consulting staff consists of a wide spectrum of specialists in medicine, surgery, orthopedics, neurology, neurosurgery, plastic surgery, dermatology, urology, etc., all from the New York University Medical Center of which the Institute is an integral unit. It provides in and outpatient care for both adults and children. In addition, it delivers all rehabilitation therapies needed by patients acutely hospitalized in the University Hospital.

Staff personnel total 766 of which 422 are in clinical services and 344 in research. Among these are 41 physicians, 62 physical therapists, 19 occupational therapists, 17 psychologists, 9 social service, 11 speech pathologists, 4 vocational counselors, 53 registered nurses, 3 therapeutic recreation workers, 2 X-ray technicians, 3 orthotists, and 5 clinical laboratory technicians. In addition, on the nonprofessional level are 93 nursing aides, 42 physical therapy aides.

G. Characteristics of applicant and affiliates

The project director is the Clinical Director of the Institute of Rehabilitation Medicine who with additional medical staff has day to day contact and responsibility for prescribing and supervising both medical and physiatric care of patients. A full time physiatrist functions under the project director and his sole responsibility is to the Spinal Cord System. He coordinates care delivery with the physiatrist who follows the patient during his neurosurgical acute phase. He coordinates the continuum of care, supervises data collection and processing and follow-up. Working with him is a Spinal Cord Systems Team consisting of a rehabilitation nurse coordinator, a medical social worker who functions in a community liaison capacity, a psychologist, vocational counselor, computer terminal clerks and an administrative secretary. The purpose of this team is not to take over the day-to-day delivery of the services now performed by the present multidisciplinary staff. Instead the Spinal Cord Systems Team is added on to direct, supervise, and assure coordinated service delivery. The team members provide education both within the Institute and in the field and is available for consult. It is also responsible for maintaining efficient high level of quality data collection. It outreaches into the community to facilitate the patient's entry into the system as well as a smooth reintegration back to his community. It is responsible for maintaining the continuing follow-up relationship that must exist with the patient following his discharge.

Many major problems are still being resolved including financial resources for payment of rehabilitation services within the hospital and post-discharge needs of the patient. A meeting with the State Director of Vocational Rehabilitation Program was held jointly with Medicare and Medicaid representatives in an attempt to define the role of each agency in regards to patient sponsorship to make sure that resources available from these different agencies can be brought into play as soon as possible and at the time at which the patient needs them.

Another area which is being resolved is that of informing insurance companies that deal with long-term disability of the need for early identification of spinal cord patients, of the necessity to rehabilitate these patients rapidly and thoroughly so that they can resume a productive life. With this idea in mind, we have held all day workshops for insurance company personnel. The result has been an increased awareness of rehabilitation potentials for their clients who can benefit from a program such as ours. In addition to these workshops, members of the team also meet with insurance people on a one-to-one level to discuss particular cases in an attempt to institute rehabilitation as rapidly as possible. These one-to-one contacts will be continued and more workshops are planned for the coming year.

H. Support Data and Other Information

The Institute of Rehabilitation Medicine has long had close relationships with the Rehabilitation Services Administration; Regional Office, Social and Rehabilitation Service; Division of Vocational Rehabilitation, New York State Department of Education; New York City Department of Health, New York City Department of Hospitals; Mayor's Council on Rehabilitation; and other governmental and voluntary agencies concerned with rehabilitation.

Eugene J. Taylor of the Institute's staff served for many years as Vice-Chairman and then Chairman of the Governor's Council on Rehabilitation. He also served as the Chairman of the New York State Vocational Rehabilitation Planning Council, and served two terms on the National Advisory Council on Vocational Rehabilitation.

The Director, Howard A. Rusk, M.D., has served as consultant for many years to the Rehabilitation Services Administration, and many members of our faculty have served as members of study sections for the National Advisory Council on Vocational Rehabilitation, and panels on the training activities of the Rehabilitation Services Administration.

Currently, under its designation as a regional Research and Training Center, the Institute has a formal Advisory Council consisting of representatives of the Regional Office of the Social and Rehabilitation Service, state agencies within the region which work with the Regional Office of the Social and Rehabilitation Service, and interested civic leaders.

Dissemination of project results

The academic staff of the Department of Rehabilitation Medicine of the New York University Medical Center contributes prolifically to the medical literature. Subjects range from highly scientific technical and basic research reports to reports at very practical levels of direct patient applicability. All disciplines within the wide spectrum of professionals on the rehabilitation team contribute to the medical literature appropriate to their spheres of interest, and this in turn reaches their specific professional colleagues. The results of the spinal cord center's activities will be similarly widely reported in this same wide-spectrum pattern of scientific information dissemination.

The second major media whereby the results of the study are disseminated is via teaching programs which is one of the major activities and responsibilities of the Institute of Rehabilitation Medicine under its designation as Research and Training Center #1 by the Social and Rehabilitation Service of the U.S. Department of Health, Education and Welfare. Teaching activities include: postgraduate training courses for physicians (5 courses in 1973); residency training of physicians (47 currently in training); advanced course training in rehabilitation methods for physical and occupational therapists and for registered nurses (a 4 weeks' course, 3 times a year, for 100); clinical affiliation training of physical and occupational therapists (200 a year); summer fellowship programs for medical students (13 per summer); supervised field work training of rehabilitation counseling students (6 per year); training in placement techniques for the severely disabled for rehabilitation counseling students, counselors and personnel specialists; etc. In the past 11 years, 17,805 rehabilitation personnel have trained in a short term (16,050), or long term (1,755) program at this center.

Addendum No. 1

SPINAL CORD TRAUMA STUDY

PROTOCOL

The following is the list of primary physicians and consultants to be notified of the admission of any patient sustaining a spinal cord injury. If the first person in any category listed cannot be reached, then attempt to call the second person, etc.

To be notified immediately upon admission

Neurosurgery: *Extension*
  1. Dr. V. Benjamin ----- 2615/2885/2855.
  2. Dr. J. Ransohoff ----- 2885/2858.
  3. Dr. E. Flamm ----- 679–0100.

Please notify Alan Dahart, R.N. ext. 2911 or page him regarding *ALL* spinal cord trauma patient admissions.

Neurology:
  1. Dr. B. Fischer ----- 4181.
  2. Dr. C. Randt ----- 2756.
  3. Dr. J. Feigenson ----- 2756.

Neurophysiology:
  1. Dr. N. Spielholtz ----- 3760.
  2. Dr. J. Goodgold ----- 3870/2191.

Neuroradiology: 1. Dr. I. Kricheff ----- 4065/2819.

To be notified immediately or as soon as possible within first 24 hours of admission

Pulmonary unit: Dr. J. Sokolow ----- 3846.
Orthopedic surgery: Dr. R. Lusskin ----- 3254.
Urology: Dr. P. Morales ----- 3252.
Anesthesia: Dr. R. Hsu ----- 3134.
Spinal lab studies: Dr. E. Naftchi ----- 3842/3766.

To be notified during or as soon as possible after first 24 hours

General surgery: Dr. M. Worth ----- 2611/3924.
  (if necessary)—except Bellevue patients
Infectious disease: Dr. R. Chase ----- 3331/3030.
Rehabilitation:
  Dr. M. Berard (IRM) ----- 2295/2296.
  Dr. G. Fleischer ----- 2055.
Social service: Ms. Pat Malone ----- 3361.
Randomization process: Dr. D. Quatermain ----- 679–0100.

Addendum No. 2

REPORT OF SPINAL CORD PROJECT COMMUNITY SOCIAL WORKER

Goals for the past year have been:

1. To establish a consumer group which can take action on issues of concern to the disabled. In December 1973 we founded the New York Metropolitan Chapter of the National Paraplegia Foundation. The National Paraplegia Foundation is the only civilian organization devoted to the interests of the spinal cord injured. One of the first issues we dealt with was organizing a letter writing campaign to insure special provisions for the handicapped in the event of gas rationing since our members cannot use mass transit. We are interested in promoting opportunities for socialization for our members and hope that as spinal cord injured patients are discharged from IRM, they will join with us. I was elected Corresponding Secretary of the Chapter and appointed Executive Secretary by the President.

In the last few years, the thrust among all disadvantaged groups is toward self-help organizations. This is also true of the disabled who are working towards a coalition so that they can become an effective force in the community. As a first step in this direction, we are planning a voter registration drive this year.

2. To contact other groups in the community working on similar issues:

(a) I have worked on the National Association of Social Workers and National Rehabilitation Association Program and Publicity Committees of the "Conference on Housing Alternatives for Handicapped Adults." This city-wide conference, the first of its kind to focus on the needs of the handicapped, has been planned to provide information on housing and what the possibilities are.

(b) I am a member of the United Neighborhood Housing Forum which is a loose organization of many groups in the community concerned with providing more low cost housing and preserving our existing stock.

(c) As the only member of the Community Council of Greater New York's Committee on Recreation and Group Work who is representing the disabled, I have felt it important that the needs of this underserved group be constantly brought to the fore. Our spinal cord patients are a very young group who want to remain active and are too often "shut out" of activities by thoughtlessness and architectural barriers. As one means of focusing on the recreational needs of the handicapped, I have been planning a conference to be jointly co-sponsored by IRM and a recreational agency. The conference would deal with what disability means, how to overcome architectural barriers, integration of the handicapped into ongoing programs, and specialized groups for handicapped.

(d) The East Midtown Community Council is a coordinating group of agencies, churches and elected governmental officials with health, welfare and social issues in the midtown area where the Institute is located. We have played host to a meeting of this Council including a tour of our facilities. I am on sub-committees on housing and hotel occupancy. Much hostility has been generated in the past between the local community and the large medical institution within that community. By keeping communication open, I hope to work to better community relations.

(e) I am a member of the SSI (Supplemental Security Income) Monitoring Committee of the Community Council. The Federal takeover of the assistance programs to aged, blind and disabled, has benefitted many but has also resulted in hardships and inequities for many others. This Committee is monitoring the effects of SSI, suggesting changes and coordinating community action. My particular area of concern is the need for supplementation of housing allowances in addition to the flat grant. It will become increasingly difficult to discharge disabled patients from hospitals since they will not be able to find appropriate housing within their means.

3. To support and work with the Mayor's Office for the Handicapped. I serve on several of the Advocacy Committees (Housing, Architectural Barriers, Transportation). In addition, I work closely with individual staff members to coordinate efforts in support of legislation and other projects of benefit to the disabled community.

4. To build awareness of the needs and problems of the physically handicapped.

(a) I have contacted legislators on all levels of government and am in frequent touch with their staff members.

(b) I have met with various state and city officials. One result of this was a change to greater accessibility in the design plans for new facilities at Harlem River State Park, the first New York State Park within the city. Within New York City, the Chairman of the City Planning Commission has promised to develop a program that will aid the handicapped. (See attached letter)

Most of the above objectives cannot be met in one year but are ongoing projects. Next year I hope to start an adult education program within IRM, particularly geared for quadriplegics. These will be courses designed to widen the horizons of our patients so that they might discover other interests and ideas to pursue when they leave the hospital.

There is much more work in this field than one person can handle. It also provides an excellent learning opportunity for a community organization student. Consequently, since we are part of New York University which has a School of Social Work, we are offering a field work placement for a community organization student for next year.

CITY PLANNING COMMISSION,
New York, N.Y., April 9, 1974.

Ms. ROXANE BRODY,
Community Liaison, Spinal Cord Center, New York University Medical Center, New York, New York

DEAR Ms. BRODY: I have spent the past several weeks meeting with staff preparing the work program for the next six to twelve months for the agency.

One of the items that we will be devoting time and staff to is development of a program to aid the handicapped through rational planning that considers their needs.

It occurs to me that it might be useful in advancing these efforts to create a joint task force with City, community and institutional representatives to pursue this matter.

I will be making staff assignments shortly and suggest that we schedule a follow-up meeting at that time to launch the project.

I look forward to the opportunity of working with you on these and related issues.

Sincerely,

JOHN E. ZUCCOTTI,
Chairman.

Addendum No. 4

VOCATIONAL SERVICES DEPARTMENT

Rehabilitation counseling and vocational services are available on admission and are provided as soon as a patient is "ready" to use them. The vocational rehabilitation process is viewed as a joint endeavor wherein the counselor and patient together seek to develop experiences and services leading to successful vocational adjustment. Individualized services, flexibility, innovation, imagination, continued reassessment and patient advocacy efforts are vital ingredients of this process. Furthermore, our program seeks to move the spinal cord injured into the mainstream of the world of education, vocational training and work; to eliminate as much as possible experiences in "ghetto" agencies servicing only the disabled. Vocational evaluation through formal testing and work samples— the procedure generally carried out in vocational rehabilitation centers—is we believe, an unreliable vocational index and too often results in the constriction of the training and employment opportunities available to the disabled. Our vocational program is engaged in developing services and relationships with business, industry and government that will make it possible for increasing numbers of severely disabled to be evaluated, trained and employed through the same methods applicable to the non-disabled.

JOB PLACEMENT: EXPANDING EMPLOYMENT HORIZONS

We are convinced that there is an untapped reservoir of cooperation in the business community that is ready to participate in defining and solving the employment problems of the spinal cord injured. We have been demonstrating this through our Committee for the Specialized Placement of the Handicapped and through our increasing involvement with employers—private and governmental. The Committee for the Specialized Placement of the Handicapped, consisting of executives of business and representatives of government, meet monthly at this Center. The Committee members meet job applicants, provide advice in job seeking and develop job contacts. They are also active in employer education and in issues related to rehabilitation, for example, transportation.

There have been increasing requests for advice and assistance and also increased outreach activity on our part. Some of our activities include:

1. Seminars and consultation for employers.
2. Employers and placement specialists have observed meetings of the Committee for the Specialized Placement of the Handicapped. A video-tape was made of a Committee meeting to be utilized for teaching and demonstration purposes with professionals and employers.
3. The Director of Placement Services has on request provided consultative services to OVR, college counselors, rehabilitation centers and hospitals.
4. Moss Rehabilitation Center, Philadelphia; United Cerebral Palsy of New York and the New York City Board of Education Placement and Referral Center for Handicapped Students have consulted with the Placement Director on the formation of a Placement Committee. Further meetings will be held at their locations to assist in implementing plans for a Committee.
5. We are developing contacts with new job sites where patients can be exposed to an expanded diversity of occupational opportunities for evaluation, training and placement.
6. The Placement Director was keynote speaker on Employment of the Handicapped at the Annual Conference of the City University of New York's Career and Placement Association.
7. We have provided supervised field experience in placement for students in graduate rehabilitation counseling programs and given lectures on placement to rehabilitation counseling classes.
8. A presentation on placement of the severely disabled and motivation for employment was made jointly by the Placement Director and Chief of Psychological Services at an all-day seminar for the Connecticut General Life Insurance Company.

Because, we are serving patients from an early stage in their rehabilitation process, we find that instituting placement plans is not indicated until considerably later on. Frequently, it is necessary to have the patient return home for a period of time before more definite employment plans can be introduced or are even welcome. However, ongoing contact and sustaining interest are necessary until that point is reached.

IMPROVING SERVICES FOR STUDENTS

Of special concern to us are high school and college students with spinal cord injury and other severe disabilities—a group that has suffered from profound neglect. Because of inadequate educational programs, the paucity of effective counseling services and exclusion from job opportunities during their school years, this group generally reaches the age for vocational decision-making lacking the experiences, the self-esteem and self-concept essential for realistic occupational choice and planning. Educational and vocational counseling programs are sorely deficient if they do not provide the student with opportunities for meaningful paid work experience. Experience in real jobs exposes the disabled student to the demands and rewards of the world of work and enables the young person to develop the vocational awareness, work and social skills essential to vocational growth and successful job performance.

An important activity initiated and developed by our Vocational Services Department was an all-day "Institute" for the New Tork City Board of Education on the theme of "Recognizing the Potential of the Severely Physically Disabled Student." More than 100 people attended—teachers, school counselors, supervisors, administrators, etc., plus the OVR counselors serving the schools. The "Institute" which was received enthusiastically, sensitized the participants to the untapped potential of the severely disabled and to the rehabilitation technology and services that will make it possible for the most severely disabled to achieve functional independence and employment.

The Director of the Vocational Services Department and the Director of Placement have served as consultants in planning and will participate in a 3-day program for representatives of all the New York State Community colleges. The purposes of the program is to improve and expand educational services for the disabled students in these campuses.

MAYOR'S OFFICE OF THE HANDICAPPED

The Mayor's Office of the Handicapped, now more than a year old, has the responsibility for assessing the unmet needs of the handicapped and seeking to improve the services and opportunities available to this group. Our staff has played a very active role as consultants and committee members dealing with such problems as employment, hiring practices and discrimination, transportation, education and training.

INCREASED DEMAND FOR SERVICES

With the establishment of this center as a model Regional Spinal Cord Injury Center there has been an increase in the unmet needs of patients admitted early post injury. Serving patients during the earlier stages of adjustment to disability requires more time and more intensive counseling.

Another consequence of early admission is that patients are discharged medically while still requiring intensive vocational services. Therefore, it is necessary to plan for an expansion of our capability for providing counseling and vocational services to patients following discharge.

The earlier admission of quadriplegics and the increase in the number of admissions with high lesions necessitates additional services in our school programs to provide bedside instruction, and assistance by amanuenses.

OVR services and funds are essential for a successful vocational rehabilitation program. There is a need to re-examine OVR procedures that are obstacles to an effective program.

In terms of spinal cord injured, where they enter college programs, it is essential for OVR to sponsor their graduate programs in order to effect a worthwhile career. For example, a B.A. in Psychology is meaningless for someone who wants to eventually practice as a Psychologist.

Addendum No. 5

PSYCHOLOGICAL SERVICES

GOALS

1. Development of a comprehensive system of collection of psycho-social data, which can be fed into a computer, that will supply useful bases for management of patients, as well as supply data for the testing of hypotheses for research purposes. Such a document has been constructed for the adult services. Because of staff changes, a similar document for the Children's Service is not quite complete.

Plan: After we have collected data on a sufficient number of cases, we hope in the coming year to investigate whether specific items of the document can be used to predict when a patient is ready to participate in particular psycho-social-medical programs.

2. Greater increase in communication across disciplines.

a. Seminars in Personal Functioning, jointly run by a physiatrist and a psychologist are not part of the regular program for spinal cord patients on one adult service.

b. We are in the process of setting up a program for staff from various disciplines to train them in management of problems relating to patient's sexuality. To do so, we need to train group facilitators. The psychology department has been given the responsibility for training, evaluation and supervision of these facilitators.

c. Small training groups in how to communicate with patients, conducted by psychologists, are now a regular part of the program for:

(1) Residents: They have accepted the program so well that they now have expanded the meetings to include coping with their own problems as residents. It is hoped that these meetings will contribute materially not only to the effectiveness of the residency training program, but, through it, also to the effectiveness of patient-care.

(2) Physical Therapists: One effect of the meetings has been permitting family-members to attend P.T. classes with patients so that families can become more familiar with the extent of the patient's disability and to know of his abilities as well. The psychology department helps with the decision of when the family member should be invited to attend. For example, for a patient in the midst of a struggle for independence from his family, the family member would not be invited to participate until the patient is well on his way to resolution of that problem.

Addendum No. 6

NEW PROGRAM: SOCIAL SERVICE DEPARTMENT

The Institute of Rehabilitation Medicine's Social Service Department has initiated and developed a group program for family members of the spinal cord injured patients. The purpose of the weekly 1½ hour meetings is to:

(1) Improve the delivery of services so patients by helping family members to deal with adjustment problems by means of the group process.

(2) Bring family and staff closer so that there is an increased mutuality of understanding of their respective roles as members of the rehabilitation team.

(3) Help educate family members about the rehabilitation process. Every rehabilitation discipline will be represented on a week-to-week basis.

(4) Provide an opportunity for family members to get closer to each other and help them share their common concerns and needs.

(5) Help family members to mobilize community resources in behalf of the patient.

EVALUATION OF GROUP MEETINGS

The first group has met for eight sessions and the attendance has been excellent (98%). Family members have begun to get closer to each other and share intimate and painful experiences in an attempt to get closer to their feelings and get help from each other. The family members have also received an education in regard to what the members of each department contribute toward the patient's rehabilitation. The program has been very successful and will be expended in the near future.

Addendum No. 7

CLINICAL BASIC RESEARCH

GOALS FOR LAST YEAR

To determine the cause of and prevent excessive bone demineralization in patients wih paralysis due to spinal cord lesions. To arrest and treat complications of osteoporosis by controlling calcium and phosphate metabolism with thyrocalcitonin therapy.

HOW THE GOALS HAVE BEEN MET

In order to study mineral metabloism after trauma to the spinal cord, animal models (rats) were used. Immediately after transection of the spinal cord (T5 level) rats were placed in metabolism cages and urine and feces were collected daily. Calcium, magnesium and phosphorus levels were determined and metabolic balances were calculated. The survival rate after spinal transection was about 25%; animals developed hydronephrosis. Beginning at day-five and continuing until day-ten post transection calcium, magnesium, and phosphorus excretion was markedly elevated in all animals. In another group of rats thyrocalcitonin therapy was initiated one day after spinal cord transaction. Thyrocalcitonin improved survival rate (85%) and calcium, magnesium, and phosphorus balances in all the animals. Further, hydronephrosis was reduced considerably.

In spinal cord injured patients hypercalcemia and calciuria can lead to bone demineralization, ectopic bone and bladder stone formation. In order to elucidate the onset of hypercalcemia and calciuria in these patients blood and 24-hour urine specimens were collected immediately post trauma and then weekly thereafter. Total and ionic calcium are currently being determined in the serum; calcium, magnesium and phosphorus levels are concommitantly determined in the urine. The use of thyrocalcitonin therapy to reverse bone resorption has been initiated. In addition, osteodensitometry, ^{18}F uptake, acid and alkaline phosphatases are being determined before and after thyrocalcitonin therapy.

GOALS FOR NEXT YEAR

To critically examine endocrine function in spinal cord injured subjects by using radioimmunoassay and gas-liquid chromotography to determine major hormones in the blood and urine.

Plasma c-AMP levels will be determined in spinal cord traumatized cats before and after the injury. Subsequently plasma c-AMP levels will be determined in spinal cord injured patients.

Mr. KINZLER. Finally, you suggest a number of revisions to both the Senate and House bills. It would be useful to the committee if you could supply us with some specific legislative language so when the subcommittee gets to deliberating, it will be available.

Mr. VERVILLE. I would like to ask one question, and this occurred to us when having lunch and looking through the bills. We were going through H.R. 1272, and it occurred to Dr. Grange and me, after looking at the question, to feel the way we did.

There was a possible problem in the way medical and rehabilitation care was treated as a definitional item. It is treated as an economic loss. I wonder whether it is intended that the person therefore would have to pay out of his own pocket his medical and rehabilitation care expenses before he can then get reimbursed from the insurance company, because the notion of economic loss implies that he must have lost something personally.

The language refers to "expense necessarily incurred." I wonder if it was meant that the patient had to pay out of his pocket. It is clear he cannot pick it up through a private insurance or public insurance program because in the definition of "net economic benefit," that is what is excluded. So that person in the hospital could not use some other insurance to carry him through the period until he could go to the auto insurer to get that money because it would be then used to reduce his benefit.

It sounds like he might have to pay out of his pocket, and it would be terribly difficult for people with catastrophic injury. They couldn't do it and would end up as medicaid patients possibly.

Mr. VAN DEERLIN. Ms. Nord?

Ms. NORD. Thank you, Mr. Chairman.

I have just one question. We have heard much testimony during these hearings indicating that the reason we need a national no-fault bill is because the States are not moving quick enough in this area.

I am wondering to what extent the organization you represent has made an effort to work with the States to enact State no-fault bills?

Mr. VERVILLE. I know that there was work done in New York and Minnesota by people in the association.

Dr. GRANGER. Michigan and Puerto Rico, I think, also.

Mr. VERVILLE. People tried in the State of Washington, but I gather from one of the charts I have looked at, they have not succeeded yet. The lack of uniformity, even if you get success, it is still a problem, however.

Dr. GRANGER. One of the main problems from State to State is the threshold level which triggers the tort proceeding.

In Massachusetts, the threshold of $2,000 served to take away the nuisance cases, but it does not work in terms of serving the severely disabled, and also one has to protect himself both ways.

In other words, you have a mandatory no-fault policy, plus you have to protect yourself against litigation from someone else should you be found at fault in causing the accident.

Mr. VERVILLE. We have looked at that. As of November, there were supposedly 25 or 26 State plans, and our conclusion is, using the tests that those plans should provide $50,000 in medical and rehabilitation care and certainly can't provide less than $25,000, that only 6 or the 25 plans are adequate.

Ms. NORD. What do you think of a plan such as Oregon's add-on plan where you get your first-party protection, but you still retain the right to sue?

Dr. GRANGER. We wonder what that does to incentive for rehabilitation.

Again, the point of demonstrating, say in court, the appearance of being handicapped perhaps more than one need be or for a longer period than one need be. I cannot answer that except it is an issue.

Mr. VERVILLE. It looks to me like the Oregon program would not be very good from our perspective.

First of all, it does not have the coverage in there for—well, it has up to $5,000 for medical incurred in the first year. It has no rehabilitation. You might squeeze some medical rehabilitation under "medical," but $5,000 is not very much. So the person is not going to get much rehabilitation covered anyway. That is one problem.

The other problem would be what Dr. Granger says. With that kind of limit on the reimbursement. I have not had quite a chance to think through what the wage loss limits are like, but if they are fairly low, there certainly seems an incentive there to not get that person into a rehabilitation program.

Ms. NORD. Thank you.

Dr. GRANGER. One of the things we are concerned with from our organizational point of view is the care of the severely catastrophic cases, these severely injured, and we find that as we move across time, many of these policies lapse and you have to leap from one mountain to another to get a person to get the full service benefits that he would require over a time to get him fully rehabilitated.

Yet, while each of these cases has a tremendous bill—for example, $50,000 or $25,000 or maybe $10,000—they absorb in financial terms an inordinate amount of money. On the other hand, they compose relatively, a rather low percentage in terms of number of people requiring medical service—it would be under 5 or maybe 2 or 1 percent—so in total dollar amounts, it is not that much when you think of insuring the total population.

At the same time, comprehensive, no-fault catastrophic coverage would tend to direct these people from the necessity of going onto public medical benefit programs, medicaid and so forth. So we are really looking at the program which serves the severely handicapped as well as the moderately or the less severely injured persons.

Mr. VERVILLE. One of our pieces of information with regard to the Blue Cross UAW plan which we worked on, and I think I have the right reference, it is a catastrophic plan and it does improve medical rehabilitation benefits but it is just a medical plan, they went from a plan with just 90 days in the hospital care, limited to that, and some physician services on an outpatient basis to a $250,000 coverage policy and the information we had from them was that costs only 25 cents a month in premium.

That is how small the population is that needs to go from regular 90-day inpatient acute care coverage to a $250,000 catastrophic program and I think it is relative to this bill as it is naturally to national health insurance, to try to figure out what the benefits are and the costs.

Dr. GRANGER. We are very much in favor of a cost containment kind of program and quality control type of program.

We would like to see it and I think the Senate version as it has come out was looser than we recommended, but it is a problem of how specific to make it in a national bill.

Mr. Van Deerlin. We thank both of you for your appearance here this afternoon.

The chairman of the National Committee for Effective No-Fault, Mr. Gary Frink.

STATEMENT OF GARY FRINK, EXECUTIVE DIRECTOR, NATIONAL COMMITTEE FOR EFFECTIVE NO-FAULT

Mr. Frink. Mr. Chairman. How are you?

Mr. Van Deerlin. Fine. It is high time you appeared before this subcommittee.

Mr. Frink. We are glad to be here.

I wish to commend you, Mr. Chairman, for the patience and diligence you have demonstrated in sitting through these many hours of what must seem like endless testimony to you.

Mr. Van Deerlin. Well, it did seem pretty endless yesterday, which was another day.

Mr. Frink. I have a statement which we have rewritten to cut it down to five and a half pages.

Mr. Van Deerlin. I bet you know it by heart.

Mr. Frink. Yes, I bet I do.

My name is Gary R. Frink. I am executive director of the National Committee for Effective No-Fault (NACENT), a coalition of labor, consumer, insurance, and other supporters of Federal legislation setting minimum standards for State no-fault automobile insurance systems.

Among those affiliated with the National Committee for Effective No-Fault are:

The 14-million-member AFL-CIO; the 1.5-million-member United Auto Workers; the 2-million-member International Brotherhood of Teamsters; the 120,000-member United Mine Workers of America; the Consumer Federation of America, serving more than 30 million consumers; the 8.4-million-member American Association of Retired Persons-National Retired Teachers Association—and you will be hearing from Mr. Martin later—the American Insurance Association, whose 138 member companies write auto insurance for 30 million Americans; and the Car and Truck Rental and Leasing Association, with a membership in excess of 3,000 firms.

We welcome this opportunity to testify before you today, and we come to you aware of the great amount of testimony you have heard on this issue over the past several weeks. Our purpose today is to draw your attention to the person who seems to have been forgotten in much of the testimony that you have heard thus far—the injured accident victim. It is this person whose needs underlie our support for legislation setting Federal minimum standards for State no-fault laws.

The high benefit levels and tort thresholds incorporated in H.R. 1900 and S. 354 seem to us to be the minimum, if we are to provide adequate compensation to the injured at reasonable cost.

As Congressman McCollister has already indicated during these hearings, the question is no longer no-fault versus tort; it is this: Do we continue to watch the States struggle laboriously to enact widely varying no-fault laws of questionable value to the seriously injured automobile accident victim; or do we enact promptly a Federal minimum standards no-fault law which allows the States to continue regulating the business of insurance, while guaranteeing that most of the economic losses of all injured accident victims will be compensated?

Let us look at some of the State no-fault laws from the perspective of the seriously injured accident victim.

The subcommittee has heard testimony from those who have lived under the Florida no-fault law. In Florida, the law has worked well for the not so seriously injured person, in that he receives first-party benefits he may not have had access to prior to the no-fault law.

However, the Florida law has failed to improve the lot of the seriously injured accident victim. The low level of first-party benefits has contributed to abuse of the law's $1,000 medical threshold. The collusion on the part of some orthopedic surgeons and plaintiffs' attorneys to pierce the threshold in order that more victims may continue to sue in tort, would be less prevalent if first-party benefits were higher.

Florida's no-fault law, and the other 15 no-fault laws, have certainly helped the vast majority of injured persons recover their out-of-pocket expenses; but most of these laws leave out the very seriously injured, who, studies have shown, have traditionally fared worst under the tort system. Because the seriously injured are not being served in most States today, NACENT is convinced that the only means of achieving adequate reform for those most in need is to require State action through the establishment of Federal minimum no-fault standards.

The name of the no-fault battle in which we are all participating is reform. We are attemping to reform a system which does not effectively meet the needs of millions of American citizens; we are attempting to reform a system which overcompensates spurious or slight automobile accident injuries, and tragically provides no compensation for or undercompensates those who are seriously injured or those who survive the thousands of people who die annually in American automobile accidents.

The trial bar talks to you about the right to sue; what we are attempting to bring about is the right to recover, as much as this is humanly possible for those maimed, or for the survivors of those killed, in automobile accidents.

I suspect that there are few in this room who have not been personally touched, or had friends or relatives touched, by the tragedy of serious injury or death on the highway. My father was killed in an automobile accident on December 22, 1961; he was on his way home from work in his automobile when he came over a rise in the road and encountered a pickup truck turning left from the right shoulder of the road. It was deep dusk, and the driver of the truck knew that his vehicle was without lights; he was attempting to return home before total darkness. He did not make it, nor did my father.

It is axiomatic that nothing could restore my father to life, but if no-fault had been in force in Michigan at that time, it would have provided my mother and teenage sister great relief from the financial anxiety which inevitably followed my father's death. Suffice it to say my mother was left a widow of modest means. At the time, I was a law student at the University of Michigan and not in a position to help them financially. We filed a lawsuit in April of 1962. The defendants' insurer never questioned liability; the only issue was damages.

In September 1963, that lawsuit was settled. As I remember, my mother settled for near the defendant's policy limits of $10,000; beyond that, the defendant was judgment proof.

For almost 2 years my mother and sister did not know if they would be compensated in any way as a result of my father's automobile death. After a wait of almost 2 years, my mother received less than $7,500, after attorney's fees.

If S. 354 had been effective in Michigan at the time of my father's accident, and assuming that he carried only basic coverage, my mother and sister would have received $15,000 in survivor's benefits; in addition, $1,000 would have been available to pay the funeral director, and a lump sum death benefit would have been paid her. But most important of all: These payments would have begun almost immediately after my father's death; there would have been no 2-year suspense to determine if my mother and sister would be compensated at all. In addition, I think it is important to realize that after these benefits would have been exhausted, my father's estate would still have had the right to file a lawsuit.

The trial lawyers would have us believe that Federal no-fault automobile insurance standards would take away our cherished right to sue in automobile cases, but in the serious injury and death cases, this clearly isn't true.

In the cases of serious injury or death, after one's own insurance carrier pays for unlimited medical and lost wages and survivor's benefits, one will still have the right to sue.

The lawsuits that S. 354 will restrict are the spurious and the minor claims—and these are the lawsuits that are clogging the courts and draining away the bodily injury premiums which should go to the seriously injured or survivors.

The name of the game is reform—and reform that inevitably must come. The automobile accident serious injuries and deaths are too tragic and too common to leave to the random gamesmanship of litigation. A rational, compassionate compensation system must replace the liability still prevailing in most States.

Much has been made in these hearings about the costs of S. 354 or other no-fault bills. Allstate says up, State Farm says down; but if you use the same benefit data, the difference in the two cost estimates is small indeed. What must be remembered is the chief issue in all of this: Timely, adequate compensation for the doctors and hospital bills, and lost wages for the people who are the statistics in the carnage on the highways in every State of the Union. The States are not going to do it, only 16 have passed laws since 1967; only 1 of these meets the standards of S. 354. If the job is to be done, you must do it.

Thank you very much. I will take questions.

Mr. VAN DEERLIN. Very direct, Mr. Frink, and I will say, without exception, your statement was the most personally dramatic we have had in the hearings.

Mr. FRINK. Thank you, Mr. Chairman.

Mr. VAN DEERLIN. Your father's death is what prompted your taking up this cause?

Mr. FRINK. I wouldn't say it prompted my taking up the cause, but it does give one a little bit more of a commitment than one might have had.

Mr. VAN DEERLIN. You say that there would have been an immediate $15,000 payoff in that case rather than having to wait 2 years for that amount. Can you tell us a little bit more about what is behind that statement? Was it the face value of your father's policy?

Mr. FRINK. No. In my father's case, we sued the tortfeasor, and he had policy limits of $10,000, so that was all there was; my mother settled for something less than that.

Now, if no-fault had been in effect, the $15,000 would be the lost wages, the minimum lost wage, and my father was 58 at the time and had an expectancy of 7 more working years.

Mr. VAN DEERLIN. I hope it is more than that at the age of 58. I am having a birthday tomorrow.

Mr. FRINK. I saw that in the paper. Your birthday was prominently displayed in the Washington Post.

Mr. VAN DEERLIN. I think the less you want it, the more attention you seem to get.

Apparently your father, under the present system had the best of everything going for him because, from your description of the accident, there was apparently no question as to fault.

Mr. FRINK. None. It was never questioned.

Mr. VAN DEERLIN. The defendant had no lights.

Mr. FRINK. The driver of the pickup truck admitted he was trying to sneak home because he didn't have lights; that is why he was on the right-hand shoulder. He was waiting to make a left turn, but he couldn't see beyond the rise behind him, and you know, it just happened.

Mr. VAN DEERLIN. We have had testimony that even in a case like your father's, had there been any extenuating circumstances such as a lapsed driver's license or something like that, that your father could very well have not been in the clear?

Mr. FRINK. Yes; in Michigan at that time, any contributory negligence would have left my mother without any avenue of recovery.

Mr. VAN DEERLIN. It is a very poignant situation.

Mr. FRINK. It was very real, yes.

Mr. VAN DEERLIN. But as I pointed out, here he had the best of everything going for him, didn't he?

Mr. FRINK. Correct.

Mr. VAN DEERLIN. Under this system?

Mr. FRINK. Correct.

Mr. VAN DEERLIN. And this was still the only reward?

Mr. FRINK. You see, my mother was dependent for recovery on the coverage that this unknown person carried, not on the coverage that my father carried; in my statement, I say, "Under no-fault if he had just the basic coverage," but my father was the kind of man who in the normal course of his business would have taken additional coverage, so the compensation really would have been greater under no-fault.

But under the present tort system, you don't insure to protect yourself; you insure to protect others against the harm you can do them, and it is a very difficult thing to deal with, as the insurance people will tell you.

Mr. VAN DEERLIN. Mr. Kinzler.

Mr. KINZLER. I have no questions, thank you.

Mr. VAN DEERLIN. Ms. Nord.

Ms. NORD. Mr. Frink, you are reading the term "work loss" to be the same thing as survivors benefits?

Mr. FRINK. No; but as it was explained to me, there would be a separate survivor's benefit fund of x amount of dollars.

Ms. NORD. A reasonable amount?

Mr. FRINK. Yes.

Ms. NORD. So your family would have recovered the work loss and the survivors benefit in addition to that?

Mr. FRINK. Yes.

Ms. NORD. Your father had no life insurance, I take it?

Mr. FRINK. He had some modest life insurance, from his employment.

Ms. NORD. Thank you.

Mr. VAN DEERLIN. Thank you, Mr. Frink.

I know you will be watching closely the efforts of the subcommittee, and I daresay that you will be helping to rouse support for action on this legislation.

Mr. FRINK. Yes, sir. Those of us who are in favor of S. 354 are very pleased, and it wouldn't be an overstatement to say that we are amazed at the pace at which you are going; we appreciate it and are very, very pleased. Thank you again.

Mr. VAN DEERLIN. Thank you for being here, Mr. Frink.

The next witness is Mr. John B. Martin, legislative consultant for the American Association of Retired Persons. How do you do.

STATEMENT OF JOHN B. MARTIN, LEGISLATIVE CONSULTANT, NATIONAL RETIRED TEACHERS ASSOCIATION AND AMERICAN ASSOCIATION OF RETIRED PERSONS, ACCOMPANIED BY DAVID F. DUNNING, LEGISLATIVE REPRESENTATIVE, FEDERAL LEGISLATION

Mr. MARTIN. I am happy to be here today.

I am John B. Martin, legislative consultant for the National Retired Teachers Association and the American Association of Retired Persons whose combined membership represents approximately 8.4 million elderly Americans.

Part of my background is a long affiliation or association with problems of the elderly including service as U.S. Commissioner on Aging, so that in representing AARP, I am following through on problems that the elderly have had for a long time in this country. These hearings are very important to the solution of one of those problems.

With me today is David F. Dunning, our legislative representative for Federal legislation.

Our interest in no-fault insurance is based upon the substantial number of our members who are carowners and who depend heavily on the automobile as the sole means of transportation. Being retired means a heavy dependence on pensions, annuities, and social security benefits for a primary source of economic survival. Naturally, when a retired person is injured and must await settlement of claims for injuries sustained in an accident, any long delay is a great burden for the elderly person.

Unfortunately, when one of our members sustains injuries in an automobile accident, it is often serious, often more serious than with younger persons, and healing sometimes takes longer. Even with the many available Federal and State programs, medical expenses may often exceed these benefit levels. For too long the elderly accident victim has been put under severe economic pressure from medical payments and other expenses while awaiting the outcome of long-delayed tort liability litigation.

We favor a system which would eliminate fault in those accident cases covered under a comprehensive no-fault system. We believe this would significantly reduce the amount of time and money expended by insurance companies and plaintiff attorneys to make fault determinations and would thereby result in prompt and adequate reimbursement—and I stress those words "prompt and adequate" reimbursement—for actual losses and cost savings to the insurance company which would result in lower premiums to the consumer.

Let me state briefly those provisions which we feel are essential in any no-fault plan.

One, overall we favor a minimum Federal standard approach in order to establish basic uniform no-fault insurance laws in the 50 States. The progress toward sound no-fault demonstrated thus far, even by those States with some form of no-fault law, has left open serious coverage gaps leaving those who need it most with inadequate levels of protection.

While we at one time strongly favored experimentation by State legislatures, it should be clear that the results of 7 years' work by many of the State legislatures is inadequate and insensitive to the needs of the driving public of most of the States.

Two, a satisfactory bill should contain high first-party benefits for economic loss, including unlimited medical, hospital, and rehabilitative services, substantial wage loss benefits, and reasonable replacement services benefits.

I was much impressed with Dr. Granger's testimony here just a short time ago on the need for rehabilitative services. This is an important element in the whole picture, and I think it has had too little attention.

Three, we believe that restrictions on the right to sue are essential in achieving the principle objective of no-fault. The right to sue should be limited to economic loss in excess of benefits, and for non-economic loss the right to sue should be limited to cases involving death, serious injury or disfigurement, or more than 90 days of disability.

Four, the elimination of the right of subrogation between insurers whereby a transfer of loss costs occurs between two insurance companies is essential. An exception may be made for cases involving passenger and commercial vehicles.

Five, the benefits of medicare are available to those persons eligible for social security, and Social Security and companies should be required to sell no-fault insurance as excess benefits over those provided by medicare at substantially lower premium rates.

I should like now to comment on some of these provisions in more detail.

Loss cost transfer between insurance companies or subrogation, as it is called, on the basis of their determination as to which policyholder is to blame for an accident in effect converts a no-fault system into a fault system. Under a true no-fault system, insurers would have to look at their own policyholders' loss-incurring potential, whereas under the fault system they look at their policyholders' loss-causing potential.

Our associations feel that by allowing subrogation under no-fault insurance, companies are led unfairly to base their rating system on loss-causing potential. We feel that this discriminates against the lower income policyholders who are expected to subsidize their more affluent neighbors. Without subrogation, a person insures himself against his own loss potential on what he stands to lose.

Under a true no-fault system, each insured person should pay into the pool primarily according to his loss-incurring potential, not according to his loss-causing potential. This concept would be seriously eroded, we believe, if insurance companies use the fixing of fault to determine reimbursement between companies. We recommend that whatever bill is reported by this subcommittee prohibit subrogation except as between insurers of passenger and commercial vehicles.

If subrogation is eliminated among private passenger vehicle insurers under the no-fault system, policyholders' rates will reflect to a greater extent their own loss-incurring potential, rather than the average loss. Under such a system, the retired driver with no work loss exposure could expect his rate to reflect his own losses rather than that of the average third-party claimant. We believe strongly that if one purpose of insurance is to insure against wage loss and there are no wages, because of the policyholder is retired, a premium should properly reflect this fact.

In short, an insurance rate for auto premiums should be based largely on what the policyholder stands to lose. We, thereforere, commend for whatever bill is approved by this committee, that it provide that rates on no-fault insurance reflect diminished loss exposure, as in the case of the retired elderly driver with no wage loss potential.

Another provision which is of extreme importance not only to the elderly but to all motorists, is unlimited medical, hospital, and rehabilitation benefits. Undercompensation for those seriously injured and overcompensation for minor injuries may well be the most serious defect in the present fault system. The most important thing to our members in auto insurance is to have their medical and hospital bills paid promptly and to be rehabilitated as soon as possible.

Being involved in a serious auto accident for an elderly person is catastrophic, but adding to their considerable concern is not knowing whether medical bills have exceeded coverage. Proponents have said unlimited medical, hospital, and rehabilitaion benefits are expensive. From the reports we have seen from the State insurance offices of Michigan and New Jersey, this is simply not true. In the State of Michigan, our associations represent approximately 570,000 elderly people. We have followed closely the very comprehensive Michigan law which provides unlimited medical, hospital, and rehabilitative benefits.

Operation of the law has been characterized by adequate and prompt payment. We find that not only have premiums dropped on the average of 14 percent, but those seriously injured have benefited substantially from the unlimited medical benefits provided under the Michigan law.

Further, I should like to quote one of our members, Col. Henry LaRaia, who testified before this committee in Daytona Beach, Fla. Colonel LaRaia's remarks were concerned with the adequacy of benefit levels in the State of Florida:

We find that adequate benefit levels provide a source of contentment for our people knowing that adequate protection is offered for seriously injured victims of automobile accidents, but it also gives others who are not injured the security of knowing that there is a sound system available to them.

The pros and cons of Federal no-fault legislation have been debated at great length during recent years. The opponents have consistently said, "Give the States time to pass sound legislation and they will handle the matter." The Administration most recently has expressed the same view, but we take exception to the position that "the progress that has already been achieved by the States should be viewed as truly remarkable.'

On the contrary, it seems to us that progress by the States has been far less than desirable in the light of the urgency of the problems and the quality of the solution that is available. It has taken 4 years for every State legislature to consider this legislation. The Department of Transportation has given passing marks to eight of those States who have at least signed into law a degree of no-fault reform.

Actually, only one of those States—Michigan—measures up to the kind of standards which are embodied in S. 354. This kind of so-called "progress" is not swift enough. Results of State action in 1975 provide clear evidence that the momentum is dropping rapidly. With a majority of the legislatures adjourned at the present time, only one State—North Dakota—has enacted some form of effective no-fault law in 1975.

So we would say, Mr. Chairman, that we strongly approve the provisions of S. 354. We believe it is a good bill and we think it has been tailored and worked upon to the extent that it provides adequate protection for the policyholder and that it does not abuse the rights of citizens to sue when that seems to be appropriate.

We think that the most important thing, as I have emphasized in my statement, is that policyholders be paid promptly and that they be paid adequately and neither of these things is true under the present system.

It is simply that the fault liability system, tort liability system simply does not work that way, guaranteed in many cases, as Dr. Granger indicated, with regard to rehabilitation. It is guaranteed to delay settlement and guaranteed to hold off the things that ought to be done for people injured in automobile accidents.

We have a small chart here on how no-fault bills satisfy our criteria for desirable reform. We would be glad to introduce this into the record, if you would like to have it, Mr. Chairman.

HOW NO-FAULT BILLS SATISFY NRTA/AARP CRITERIA FOR DESIRABLE REFORM

	S. 354	H.R. 8441	H.R. 1272	H.R. 1900
1. Unlimited medical, hospital and rehabilitation benefits; sufficient wage replacement and reasonable household services coverage.	Yes	No	Yes	Yes.
2. Abolition of lawsuits for compensable economic loss; restriction of suit for noneconomic loss to cases of death, serious injury or disfigurement or more than 90 days of total disability.	do	do	do	Do.
3. Transfer of loss costs based on fault restricted to cases involving both private, passenger or commercial vehicles.	do	do	do	No.
4. Primary of medicare benefits over no-fault auto insurance.	do	Yes	do	Yes.
5. Establishment of Federal minimum standards for State laws, rather than preemptive Federal system.	do	do	No	Do.
6. Equitable rate determinations based upon limited or no wage loss exposure.	do	No	do	No.

Mr. VAN DEERLIN. In addition to the longer recuperation that most elderly require after an accident, isn't it true also that the elderly are likely to be the most frequent victims of pedestrian accidents?

Mr. MARTIN. Yes, that is certainly true, because, just because of the fact that they are apt to move more slowly. Their eyesight is apt to be not quite as good. They're apt to get caught on crossings where the lights are too rapid and when they do get hurt there are longer periods in the hospital and the injury is apt to be more serious, so that this, for our people, and when I say "our people" I mean those who are not just over 65 but are over 50 or 55, is a very serious thing and we think it is important even to the people who have not reached retirement age.

Mr. VAN DEERLIN. You touched my responsive chord.

Well, the point of my question was then to ask if any of the proposals before us give adequate attention to the needs of persons injured who are not in automobiles.

Mr. MARTIN. Yes. My understanding is that this covers the injury to, or S. 354 covers injury to the pedestrian and he would be compensated for by the insurance company, whose policyholder struck the pedestrian. This is important in both, well, particularly in cities where traffic has become more and more congested and where the problem of getting across the street is a problem even for people who are able and fleet of foot, but much more so for those who are not.

Mr. VAN DEERLIN. Mr. Kinzler.

Mr. KINZLER. Mr. Frink described a situation which was an open and shut tort case and it took his family 2 years to receive any money.

I would assume it would be that much harder, taking the chairman's example on the pedestrian being hit by a negligent driver, it would be that much harder for an elderly person who had to wait 2 years to recover?

Mr. MARTIN. Well, that is true, because most of these elderly people are living on much smaller incomes. Forty percent of our older people are in the poverty or near poor categories. People don't realize that, but it is a dramatic figure and it means they don't have any money left over to support themselves or carry along for a year or 2 years if they are disabled and have to pay out medical expenses to meet the normal expenses of living. So that it is much more of a hardship for people like that than it would be for people who have steady and perhaps rising incomes coming in.

Mr. KINZLER. At one of our early hearings, the subcommittee was told that the elderly would be people who would lose out under a no-fault system because they already have medicare and medicaid and other coverage and no-fault would force them to buy more insurance. Obviously you don't believe that.

Mr. MARTIN. We don't believe that because we understand medicare is primary under this system and we believe that this is important also from the standpoint of cutting or rather lowering premiums.

Obviously if that portion of the expense of the accident is going to be taken care of by medicare, the policy ought to sell for less and allow people to benefit by the reduced premiums.

Mr. KINZLER. Finally, you indicate that you urge Federal action in light of the urgency of the problem. We have been told by a number of witnesses that we should leave it to the States and let them have a chance to act.

How would you suggest that this problem is more urgent than some of the other things we left to the States such as uniform commercial code and other uniform State laws?

Mr. MARTIN. Well, I think it is more urgent just because I think the forces resistant to State legislation are, if anything, stronger.

As we have watched what has happened in these various States, and we have our legislative committees working in every State, we are impressed by the fact that the trial bar in particular has been able to put off legislation or to defeat legislation, or almost worse, to go along with legislation that looks like no-fault legislation but it is really only add-on legislation. And we think that the situation is very resistant to change in the States. It took 40 years to get the States to set up adequate workmen's compensation programs.

We certainly don't think that people in the United States are going to sit around and wait 40 years for the States to enact decent no-fault laws.

Mr. KINZLER. You see the problem that no-fault seeks to address is more important and thus requires faster action than something such as the regulation of commercial paper and so forth?

Mr. MARTIN. I certainly do. I think it is, because it involves personal injury and this is certainly one of the most urgent—I mean the correction or dealing with that situation is one of the most urgent problems that I can imagine.

Mr. KINZLER. Thank you, Mr. Martin.

Mr. VAN DEERLIN. Any questions?

Ms. NORD. No questions.

Mr. VAN DEERLIN. Mr. Martin, we very much appreciate your appearance before the subcommittee. It very nicely complements the testimony we got from Colonel LaRaia at Daytona Beach.

Mr. MARTIN. Thank you very much. It was a pleasure to be here today.

Mr. VAN DEERLIN. Our final witness for today is Mr. Jim Scott, program supervisor for workmen's compensation and no-fault insurance programs for the Division of Vocational Rehabilitation of the National Rehabilitation Association with headquarters in Lansing, Mich.

STATEMENT OF JAMES W. SCOTT, PROGRAM SUPERVISOR, WORKMEN'S COMPENSATION AND NO-FAULT INSURANCE PROGRAMS, DIVISION OF VOCATIONAL REHABILITATION, NATIONAL REHABILITATION ASSOCIATION, ACCOMPANIED BY FRED R. TAMMEN, LEGISLATIVE ANALYST, NATIONAL REHABILITATION ASSOCIATION

Mr. TAMMEN. Mr. Chairman, I am Fred Tammen, legislative analyst for the National Rehabilitation Association and we are pleased to have Mr. Jim Scott represent the association in these hearings.

Mr. Scott has had considerable experience working as a supervisor in the Michigan State Vocational Rehabilitation Agency and working in particular with the State no-fault insurance programs and the workmen's compensation programs, so we feel that he brings a considerable wealth of experience to these hearings.

Mr. Scott?

Mr. SCOTT. Thank you.

Rather than read my statement, I would prefer, with your blessing, to kind of highlight some things and attempt to convey the kind of experience we are having in Michigan.

I am pleased to know that Michigan meets the standard in terms of Federal criteria. However, I would like to highlight some of the problems we are experiencing that might point to some things that should be included in Federal legislation.

Before I begin, however, I would like to clearly state that the National Rehabilitation Association wants to go on record as being in support of the concept of national no-fault auto legislation.

The fact of the matter is that under the fault system, the severely disabled auto accident victim receives a quick trip to poverty rather than a trip to a rehabilitation center for rehabilitation services.

Our statement makes reference to the fact that we do not posture ourselves as experts in terms of insurance. However, NRA members are professional consumers of the insurance dollar, in terms of the recommendations we make to insurance companies. My base of experience is primarily in the workmen's compensation area. The Michigan Vocational Rehabilitation Service is just beginning to interact with no-fault auto insurance carriers.

I am a personal consumer of Michigan's no-fault law in a sense that I carry a plastic plate in my skull, courtesy of Aetna Life and Casualty Insurance, which is a result of a skull fracture I had in an auto accident. I can attest to the fact I did not have to engage in a court case to get those benefits, and benefits were paid promptly.

I had some problems with Aetna in terms of the speed of their processing, but basically no hassle, and from the experience I have had, I can appreciate what we are hearing from States that are still under the fault system, that is, the problems of delay, and the very articulate statement made by Dr. Granger relative to the rehabilitation services that are not being provided.

I want to highlight the fact that the important thing in terms of the legislation is to get disabled auto accident victims to the kinds of facilities that Dr. Granger referenced.

As far as the vocational rehabilitation agency is concerned, we would like to direct the committee's attention to the need for a mandatory referral system to the State vocational rehabilitation agency when the medical restoration process is completed. At this point, the individual faces a problem in terms of the future economic consequences of disability.

Questions like can he return to his old job, does he need to be trained in a new occupation, must be answered.

The VR agencies that interrelate with the kind of facilities Dr. Granger and the NRA statement describe will be on the scene but the reality of the situation is those facilities do not exist in sufficient numbers.

We make reference on page 8 to the idea of an industry assessment model to provide a funding mechanism to assist in development of such facilities.

The current reality is that the individual probably will receive immediate service at a local hospital and the physical restoration facility that can do the job is some distance away. The problem still remains of how to trigger that insurance company's behavior to get that person to the right facility at the right time.

I make some specific recommendations in terms of principles on page 4 where we talk about the cost of the rehabilitation benefits. It is our feeling that the total cost of all medical and vocational rehabilitation services required for the restoration of an individual for independent living and vocational competence should be an obligation of the insurer.

Speaking from the standpoint of an individual who works in a State office of a vocational rehabilitation agency, I see the similarities between this kind of recommendation and a recommendation made by the National Commission on Workmen's Compensation in terms of all costs being paid.

An important part of our service delivery system is our staff. The first point on page 4 should be understood to mean that the auto insurance carrier should be responsible for the vocational rehabilitation agencies' staff costs.

I received considerable education from the last speaker relative to the implications of the subrogation issues.

One of the problems that the committee should be aware of that exists in Michigan's law is section 3109.

It allows the insurance company to offset their benefits based on the provision of government benefits.

As Mr. Martin told us there is some good in an offset which results in reduced premium for retired individuals. However, if the insurance company can tell us, as one major insurance company did in Michigan, that since vocational rehabilitation is a government agency, vocational rehabilitation has the responsibility for vocational rehabilitation and not the insurance company.

There is really an injustice in that situation. I know that the insurance industry is quite skilled in dealing with the proper subrogation and offset devices for their own interests. I suggest that you look at it from the standpoint of the implications for the public agencies and whether or not they should have to shoulder the burden via offset provisions.

The issue of referral is specifically dealt with in our recommendations. Because the committee has made a specific request for language, please reference our recommendations on page 10 for a referral provision.

When you deal with the developments of a referral system and the provision of rehabilitation benefits, I think you should also keep in mind a very basic problem and perhaps learn some lessons from workmen's compensation legislation.

Simply putting the provision in the law is not going to motivate all insurance companies to buy the rehabilitation concept and engage in it.

A small survey I did last week to see what was happening with our no-fault auto cases tells us about in one-third of those cases the insurance companies are refusing to participate in vocational rehabilitation.

They may have provided adequate medical services, they may be providing income replacement, but if they can refuse the provision of vocational services, then the provision might as well not exist.

When we approach our Insurance Bureau in terms of the compliance issue, we are told that they are not like the Workmen's Compensation Bureau, that is, they cannot order an insurance company to perform.

I would recommend that this committee provide some "teeth" in the law so that the State vocational rehabilitation agencies and the rehabilitation agencies described by Dr. Granger do not end up paying bills that should have been borne by the auto insurance industry.

I might also point out both in the Senate bill and House bill, section 109(c)—the accountability model—is a literal expression of what we do in Michigan in terms of our counselors providing recommendations to insurance companies for payment directly to the vendor.

That completes my statement, and I would be open to your questions.

[Mr. Scott's prepared statement follows:]

STATEMENT OF THE NATIONAL REHABILITATION ASSOCIATION

Mr. Chairman, I am Jim Scott, representing the National Rehabilitation Association. The NRA, a 50 year old organization representing both handicapped people and the programs that serve them, welcomes this opportunity to appear here before the Subcommittee on Consumer Protection and Finance in support of the rehabilitation provisions as contained in the National No-Fault Motor Vehicle Insurance Acts of 1975 (HR 1900 and HR 1272).

The National Rehabilitation Association does not pose as an expert on automobile insurance nor any other kind of insurance. Its members do have expertise in the assessment of disability and the providing of rehabilitation services to all individuals with various types of disabilities. Accordingly, our comments shall refer principally to how National No-Fault Motor ¡Vehicle Insurance can contribute in the most effective way to the rehabilitation of accident victims.

First of all Mr. Chairman, the National Rehabilitation Association supports in principal, the idea of National No-Fault Motor Vehicle Insurance standards. It does so because it is concerned with any development which promises to decrease the number of accidents, make adequate reimbursement for loss in accidents, and assure maximum recovery of every individual from his injury. We do not, of course, consider that National No-Fault Motor Vehicle Insurance standards is a panacea for the many ills that now exist, but we strongly believe that it will make a valuable contribution to the solution of many of our problems. For several years now both Houses of Congress have considered the development of federal standards governing state's no-fault automobile insurance laws. The NRA sincerely hopes that these hearings will be followed by prompt action on the part of the Subcommittee and full committee and finally by the House so that these minimum standards can be implemented at the earliest possible date.

First, let me explain what we mean by rehabilitation services. It is sometimes difficult, for instance, to distinguish between medical service and rehabilitation service. Rehabilitation services are the services that are required to restore the individual to maximum physical and mental functioning and vocational competence and which may not be included in routine medical care.

While the principal of rehabilitation may be practiced in many ways, the central focus for provision of rehabilitation services is the rehabilitation facility. In such facilities, physicians, nurses, physical therapists, occupational therapists, speech and hearing therapists, vocational evaluators, psychologists, counselors, and others operate as a team in identifying the nature of an individual's problems, assessing his limitations and abilities, and helping him to make a maximum recovery, including the ability to work and earn a living. This coordinated approach is found to be far superior to any other method in helping the individual obtain maximum ability to function. In this setting, an individual may be receiving physical restoration, learning to walk with crutches or canes, to use a wheelchair, to control bowel and bladder functions, and to perform the many tasks of daily living which most of us take for granted. But at the same time, if the individual is to require vocational adjustment, an assessment can be made of his vocational skills and attitudes, and vocational training can be done while the individual is still undergoing physical restoration. When the maximum benefits have been achieved in a rehabilitation facility, the individual returns home where rehabilitation is continued if necessary.

Mr. Chairman, this is what we mean by rehabilitation. It is generally agreed that this kind of rehabilitation cannot be practiced in the average hospital in the United States. It certainly cannot be practiced in the average physician's office. Unfortunately, we do not have enough rehabilitation facilities in the United States to assure that every individual who needs such services has them available. In fact we are told that a very small percentage of the spinal cord injured individuals actually get the rehabilitation services that rehabilitation professionals know how to deliver. An important part of any national rehabilitation effort should be to expand and improve rehabilitation facilities.

As already stated, the National Rehabilitation Association is not an expert in the technical aspects of automobile insurance, nor any other kind of insurance. Its concern is that any no-fault insurance act which is passed by Congress and signed by the President will contain provisions that will assure, so far as this is possible, that every injured individual will have the best possible opportunity to benefit from total rehabilitation services. In doing so we think several principals are important. These include;

(1) The total cost of all medical and vocational rehabilitation services required for the restoration of the individual to independent living and vocational competence should be an obligation of the insurer.

(2) Medical and vocational rehabilitation services should be defined comprehensively enough to assure that all services which can make a significant contribution to the rehabilitation of individuals will be available.

(3) The legislation should recognize the rehabilitation facility as an institution which provides a comprehensive, coordinated approach to helping handicapped individuals achieve their rehabilitation goals. It should assume that many injured individuals will receive their rehabilitation services in such institutions.

(4) The referral of injured individuals to state vocational rehabilitation agencies should be mandated and the state vocational rehabilitation agency should be the focal point for the delivery of rehabilitation services to injured individuals. I shall briefly speak on each of these points.

So far as we know, the authors of all no-fault automobile accident legislation had the same thing in mind, so far as the rehabilitation of injured individuals is concerned. They desire to see that they are as completely restored medically and vocationally as possible. All such legislative proposals recognize in one way or the other that the provision of medical care alone does not mean complete rehabilitation. Although it is a necessary first step, it may fall short of helping an individual achieve his maximum rehabilitation potential. It is important, therefore, that benefits are defined clearly and comprehensively, so as to make certain they will meet all of the needs of the injured person.

If the insurance premiums do not bear the full cost of rehabilitation, this will mean that funds to rehabilitate victims of automobile accidents will have to come from appropriations from the general funds of the state and federal governments.

Experience has shown that Federal administration will not recommend, and Congress will not appropriate, from general funds sufficient sums to pay the total cost of rehabilitation services for all that need them. What is true of the Federal government is true of the states. The only way to assure that the automobile accident victims will receive all of the rehabilitation services they need is to see that they are paid for from the insurance premium collections.

The definition of medical and vocational rehabilitation services as contained in definition (16) of HR-1900 appears sufficiently comprehensive to assure that all services that can provide a significant contribution to the rehabilitation of an individual will be available. We suggest that a similar definition be contained in any legislation promoted by this Subcommittee.

In the first part of the statement we referred to the rehabilitation facility as an important institution for the provision of rehabilitation services. The rehabilitation facility has been developed as a result of the fact that all of the needs of certain classes of handicapped individuals cannot be met in one or more traditional institutions which provide medical, educational, and other services. The rehabilitation facility is a child of the twentieth century, and the last twenty-five years have seen it assume an important and generally recognized place among the institutions providing vital services to persons with significant impairments. The nature of the institution is such that it does not very well come under the definition of a hospital, a school, convalescence center, etc. This being true, the legislation should recognize the rehabilitation facility as being a facility in which it is expected many injured individuals will receive their rehabilitatiou services. The legislation should either have a definition of a rehabilitation facility, or the report accompanying such legislation should clearly recognize the importance of the rehabilitation facility and the provision of rehabilitation services.

It is generally recognized that *prompt referral* of an injured individual to a rehabilitation agency is the most important single factor in determining whether or not such individual will accept and benefit from rehabilitation services. All too often, many months pass before an individual is so referred. Particularly, this has been a problem in workmen's compensation programs which, I might add, need overhauling as badly as do automobile insurance programs. The no-fault insurance law should mandate the referral of injured individuals to the vocational rehabilitation agencies. In our judgement, every individual expected to be permanently injured should be referred to the rehabilitation agencies during the course of acute medical treatment. Any other individual who is expected to be disabled as much as six months should also be referred. (On an accompanying sheet I shall propose precise language dealing with the referral process.) What we are trying to do is simple, i.e. to assure that all individuals likely to require rehabilitation services are referred promptly while, at the same time, preventing a flood of referrals to the state vocational rehabilitation agencies which would waste valuable staff time and identify very few individuals who would need the services of agencies. It should be emphasized that the state vocational rehabilitation agency should be the focal point for the delivery of rehabilitation services to injured individuals. There are large and well established agencies. They have contracts with rehabilitation facilities, vocational schools, hospitals, etc. which puts them in an admirable position to assess the need and potential of handicapped individuals and to secure the appropriate services as promptly as possible. Related thereto, these agencies may be said to be in the best position to protect the interests of the injured individual. The standards they use for the approval of institutions to provide rehabilitation services will assure that only properly accredited institutions are used. The traditional economical way in which they administer their programs will assure good services at reasonable costs.

The accountability program requiring periodic reports by the state vocational rehabilitation agency as required in section 109(C) is new to this year's bill. It was not contained in previous legislation, however, reporting systems and reporting requirements are certainly not new to the vocational rehabilitation agencies. Their current reporting system is a comprehensive one providing for a detailed rehabilitation plan and sufficient progress notes. The accountability required by HR-1900 would certainly be compatable with that which is already being done by the vocational rehabilitation agencies and such provisions would not be opposed by this association.

Provisions contained in paragraph (D) of section 109 which assures the availability of services should be strengthened by allowing the Secretary to assess each insurer an additional amount not to exceed ½ of 1 percent of the total amount of premiums collected each year from the sale of no-fault policies. We recommend that ¾ of this amount collected be distributed in proportion to the amounts collected in each state to the state vocational rehabilitation agency or agencies having an approved state vocational rehabilitation plan to be used to finance research, training and development projects designed to increase knowledge and improve delivery of rehabilitation services to individuals injured in motor vehicle accidents. A portion of the amount accessed by the Secretary should also be made available for the renovation, expansion or construction of a rehabilitation facility to help assure that comprehensive rehabilitation services will be available to the accident victim. We further suggest that the ¼ percent of the remaining assessment be made available to the Secretary of HEW to be expended for projects of a similar nature which can be operated most effectively on an interstate basis.

This type of funding proposal would be a positive force in assuring the availability of resources through trained counselors, research and adequate facilities.

Mr. Chairman, the NRA wishes to reiterate its appreciation for the opportunity to present its views on no-fault motor vehicle insurance bills being considered by this Subcommittee. We hope that your Subcommittee will, at a very early date, report a bill that will assure comprehensive rehabilitation services to those individuals who are injured in automobile accidents. If our Association can be of further assistance in this Subcommittee's deliberation, we will be happy to do so.

AMENDMENTS TO HR-1900 AND HR-1272

Substitution of paragraph (D), section 111 of HR-1900

"A basic restoration obligor shall promptly refer to the appropriate state agency administering or supervising the administration of a state plan for vocational rehabilitation services approved under the Vocational Rehabilitation Act (29 USC 35) each person incurring injury which is expected to be permanent and is of such severity so as to interfere with a person's ability to perform work and earn a living, provided however that each person whose benefits are paid for or expected to be paid for six months or more shall so be referred."

NOTE.—HR-1272 contains no provisions for referral of accident victims to vocational rehabilitation, therefore, the above statement should be added as a new section.

Mr. VAN DEERLIN. Thank you, Mr. Scott.
Mr. Kinzler?
Mr. KINZLER. I have no questions, thank you.
Mr. VAN DEERLIN. I would like to develop just a little bit, and probably with Mr. Kinzler's help more than my own input, the difference between the term "offset" and "subrogation" as it has come to be applied to no-fault insurance.
Mr. SCOTT. Well, as I am using the term "offset," I am simply indicating there is a provision in Michigan's law that allows the insurance company to take the deduction off of their benefit because there is a Government benefit being provided.
"Subrogation" is, as I define it, in the area of providing a mechanism for the insurance company to gain reimbursement.
Mr. VAN DEERLIN. To go after one another?
Mr. SCOTT. To go after one another in effect. As I say, Government agencies have no subrogation rights in a given case. The facilities we have already described, and our State rehabilitation agencies, upon the refusal of the insurance company to participate, have to incur the costs. We should have a mechanism to get carrier dollars back into the public till.
Now, the model the Michigan vocational rehabilitation service has followed in workmen's compensation in which we tried to train specialists to work with insurance company dollars has a diminishing return. It is ineffective when you talk about the number of insurance companies that have to be sold on the concept.

So, if you wish to preserve legislative intent, in terms of making sure the rehabilitation benefit is there, and that insurance companies pay for it, I think you should direct your attention to the language in this statement for the provision for the fund or assessment model that would assist development of these facilities—steps in that direction would probably pay more benefits in defining the linkage between the auto insurance industry and the State vocational rehabilitation agencies.

In the context of how "VR" operates in the country, the Social Security Administration does set aside a set amount of dollars for rehabilitation of social security recipients. That model operational is in 50 States.

A similar type of model can be developed to define the linkage between the rehabilitation community and the insurance industry and preserve legislative intent.

Mr. KINZLER. I assume then you are talking about coordinating different insurance systems rather than a system whereby the insurance companies would determine who is at fault in the accident and pay the money back and forth?

Mr. SCOTT. Right.

Mr. KINZLER. That is very useful for our purposes.

Thank you, Mr. Chairman.

Mr. VAN DEERLIN. Thank you very much, Mr. Scott, for giving your views to the subcommittee.

This concludes the hearings for this afternoon. We will resume at 10 o'clock tomorrow morning.

[Whereupon, at 3 p.m., the subcommittee adjourned, to reconvene at 10 a.m., Wednesday, July 25, 1975.]

NO-FAULT MOTOR VEHICLE INSURANCE

FRIDAY, JULY 25, 1975

House of Representatives,
Subcommittee on Consumer Protection and Finance,
Committee on Interstate and Foreign Commerce,
Washington, D.C.

The subcommittee met at 10 a.m., pursuant to notice, in room 2322, Rayburn House Office Building, Hon. Lionel Van Deerlin, chairman, presiding.

Mr. Van Deerlin. The subcommittee will resume hearings, looking into several no-fault insurance bills.

Our first witness is Mr. Lyle W. Allen, representing a Special Committee on Automobile Insurance Legislation for the American Bar Association.

Mr. Allen.

STATEMENT OF LYLE W. ALLEN, SPECIAL COMMITTEE ON AUTOMOBILE INSURANCE LEGISLATION, AMERICAN BAR ASSOCIATION; ACCOMPANIED BY SHANLER D. CRONK, STAFF ATTORNEY

Mr. Allen. Good morning, Mr. Chairman.

As the chairman stated, I am Lyle W. Allen, and I practice law in Peoria, Ill. I am a member of the Special Committee on Automobile Insurance Legislation of the American Bar Association, and in the absence, unavoidably, of Mr. Ghiardi of Marquette University Law School, who is our chairman, I have been designated by the president of the ABA to appear.

Certainly since the midsixties the American Bar Association has been active in the field of tort reform, particularly with respect to automobile claims. In February 1968, a Special Committee on Automobile Accident Reparations was formed and submitted some 52 recommendations for reform in the tort areas, more particularly in automobile claims. A number of those recommendations have been adopted.

In 1971, the association created the committee of which I am now a member and which I represent before your committee today. The purpose was to monitor and to evaluate new developments in the reform movement, such as the Department of Transportation study of motor vehicle crash losses.

In August 1972 our special committee filed its first recommendation and report with the association's house of delegates, and it was approved there. That report provided that we recommend to the States that certain minimal requirements for automobile accident coverage be enacted, and more specifically: $15,000 limits for bodily injury to one person and $30,000 for all injured in one accident, and $5,000 property damage; that uninsured motorist coverage be extended with limits of 15 and 30, and that, more importantly from the standpoint of this committee's inquiries, the association went on record as endorsing the basic no-fault concept in recommending that all States should adopt laws which require minimum first-party coverage of at least $2,000.

There is no magic in the figure of $2,000 but the studies of the association's committees brought to light the fact that $1,500 will cover some 93 percent of the victims of automobile accidents and that another 3 percent can be covered for another $500, and that $2,000 would thus cover the economic losses of about 96 percent of the accident victims.

The final recommendation adopted in 1972 declared the association's opposition to Federal no-fault and expressed support for continued State action in this area for appropriate changes in the automobile accident reparations system.

Our commitment to State action has been reinforced from time to time, has remained steadfast, and it was most recently reinforced by action of our house of delegates in 1975 in a February meeting in Chicago.

Copies of the resolutions adopted by the house of delegates and ABA have been appended to the prepared statement which I am privileged to give to this committee this morning. This statement is of course in printed form. I intend in the few minutes allotted to me to hit some of the highlights of it.

One of the problems to which we address ourselves and which we believe the Congress should address is the fact that the automobile accident reparations systems vary widely from State to State and can be dealt with most effectively and fairly by action of the States.

The whole tradition of our history of the regulation of insurance fits squarely with the policy declaration of the McCarran-Ferguson Act to the effect that this is a State problem.

I am sure you have been advised by others who have appeared and who will appear that some 24 States have now adopted some type of no-fault automobile accident reparations system. They vary from State to State, with differing types of provisions, and differing types of changes have been made in the several States.

In addition to those 24 States which have acted, the other 26 all have before them a combination of plans, literally hundreds of them, which have varying effects upon the automobile accident system.

For example, Illinois presently has two bills alive for the fall session of our legislature, and it is expected California will debate the problem in the fall. The other major State, in population at least, which has not acted is Ohio, and it is my understanding their attention has been diverted by the medical malpractice insurance problem.

We should also note that four States have had legislation vetoed by the Governor and that one enacted plan was declared unconstitutional by the State supreme court.

In addition to those States which have enacted and are enacting, Iowa, Mississippi, and Washington have all implemented study commissions which have undertaken to report to the State legislature the need for reform and the type of reform which should be enacted.

Since 1971, when the DOT study appeared, it is apparent that some 53 percent of the citizens of this country are now covered by a type of no-fault automobile accident system. We believe that the types of systems which are currently in effect do not cause people to suffer by their differences but rather that the differences are important to a collection of information which will be beneficial in the long run in finding out which, if any, of the systems is best insofar as the automobile-driving citizen is concerned.

We think that ratemaking, for example, within the individual States, reflects the geography of the State, the road conditions, population density, and propensity of citizens of a State to sue, factors which can be more accurately evaluated on an individual State basis.

During earlier hearings, representatives of the National Association of Insurance Commissioners have supported the concept of State-by-State analysis, and I thought it was important that their representatives testified that the basic questions to be addressed concern the benefits the public desires, the privileges and rights which the public is willing to forgo for those benefits, and the acceptable cost level.

The cost level particularly is the subject of great concern. It has been the subject of analysis both before the fact and after the fact. You have been made aware, I am sure, of the Milliman & Robertson, the Allstate, and State Farm studies, all of which attempt to project figures with respect to possible future conclusions.

Some of the relevant studies which have been made after the fact, for example, in New York, New Jersey, and in Oregon, are interesting.

A New York Times article in February 1975, that is, February 21, reporting on a New York insurance department study, indicates that it tends to show that the high-risk driver rather than the low-risk driver was receiving the largest reduction in the amount of insurance coverage, or rather the amount of insurance for which he was expected to pay. That is his premium, in other words.

This is a factor which ought to be considered in connection with establishment of a no-fault system.

The study in Oregon tends to indicate premiums have stabilized there where they have a so-called add-on system adding no-fault benefits onto existing coverage, tending to give the person who is injured in an accident a right to sue as well as to have the benefits of these economic payments which are recommended by the ABA and others.

The premium in Oregon seems to have been stabilized by their system, whereas in New Jersey, where a more comprehensive type of no-fault has been enacted, the insurance companies, the major part of them, just this month have gone in asking for some 34-percent increase in premium.

This is a highly touted feature of Federal no-fault, the impact that its proponents assert it will have on automobile insurance premium costs. Certainly this committee ought to be looking into the fact that the costs of third-party accident benefits, the costs—and I will provide a synopsis by saying that all of the insurance affected by no-fault type of legislation is the very least cost of operating an automobile and it is the smallest cost of the insurance premium which the public pays to obtain insurance coverage.

I have alluded to the Milliman & Robertson study and to the Allstate figures. The results of the Allstate study indicated that Senate bill 354 would increase costs for the vast majority of American automobile insurance buyers, and in some cases the increases would be fantastically large.

Now whether they are correct or whether Milliman & Robertson is correct is not for us to decide, but we do believe that some experimentation at the State level will provide the type of necessary information for an analysis of what kind of changes we need to have in the automobile reparations system.

Again with respect to the studies concerning themselves with costs, it is difficult to draw any conclusions which are meaningful without data which tells us what people actually pay after no-fault has been enacted.

One of the bills, and I believe it is H.R. 1900, gives recognition to this fact by calling upon the commissioners of insurance of the several States to keep statistics to inform the Department of Transportation concerning the continuing assessment of the effects of the legislation upon the insurance premium.

At this particular stage we believe that we do not need Federal legislation which would establish a system plagued by the typical problems of Federal regulation, problems which are inherent in the bills which are before this committee.

The American Bar Association, in keeping with its resolutions which are appended to our report, asks that the committee reject the concept of Federal regulation of insurance through a Federal no-fault system.

Thank you.

[Mr. Allen's prepared statement and appendixes follow:]

STATEMENT OF LYLE W. ALLEN ON BEHALF OF THE AMERICAN BAR ASSOCIATION

Mr. Chairman and members of the subcommittee: My name is Lyle W. Allen and I am a practicing lawyer in Peoria, Illinois. For the past two years I have served on the American Bar Association's Special Committee on Automobile Insurance Legislation, and appear before you as the designee of the Association's President, James D. Fellers. The current chairman of the Special Committee, Professor James D. Ghiardi, had hoped to represent the Association today, but was unable to rearrange a prior commitment and asked that I express his regrets to you.

Reform of the automobile accident reparations system has been a subject of concern to the Association since the mid-1960's when criticism of the existing tort system began to surface. In February, 1968, the Special Committee on Automobile Accident Reparations, the predecessor of the Special Committee, was created to investigate the system and its asserted deficiencies. That study resulted in 52 recommendations for reform in such areas as court delay, the substantive law and the law of damages, insurance and legal costs, automobile insurance coverages and availability, and highway safety. A number of the recommendations have been included in plans adopted by the various states and improved the automobile accident reparations system during the past few years.

In 1971, the Special Committee was created so that the Association could monitor and evaluate new developments in the reform movement such as the Department of Transportation Study of Motor Vehicle Crash Losses and Their Compensation in the United States, federal no-fault legislation and no-fault plans enacted or under consideration by various states.

In August of 1972, the Special Committee filed its first recommendation and report with the Association's House of Delegates, a copy of which is appended to this statement. In addition to reaffirming the conclusions of the earlier study of its predecessor it recommended that each state adopt laws providing automobile liability coverage of at least $15,000 for bodily injury to one person, $30,000 for all bodily injury associated with one accident and $5,000 for all property damage from one accident. Further, it recommended that each state also adopt laws providing uninsured motorist coverage with limits of at least $15,000 for bodily injury to one person and $30,000 for all bodily injury associated with one accident. Most importantly, the Association went on record as endorsing the basic "no-fault" concept in recommending that all states should adopt laws which require minimum first party coverage of at least $2,000.

The final recommendation adopted in 1972 declared the Association's opposition to any federal no-fault automobile insurance legislation and expressed support for state action as the vehicle for appropriate changes in the automobile accident reparations Of course, we support state action which includes the substantive recommendations in the 1972 report.

Our commitment to state action in this area has remained steadfast since that time and has recently been reinforced by the adoption by the House of Delegates of the Special Committee's most recent recommendation in February, 1975. That recommendation exhorted those states not yet having done so to enact, as expeditiously as possible, appropriate automobile accident reparations reform legislation encompassing, but not limited to, the aforementioned substantive provisions of the Association's posture. A copy of this most recent resolution as adopted by the House of Delegates is also appended to this statement.

The ABA has always predicated its involvement in the no-fault controversy on the belief that the problems with the automobile accident reparations system vary widely from state to state and can be dealt with most effectively and fairly by action of the states. The states have traditionally assumed the responsibility for the regulation of insurance, a responsibility squarely placed with them by the policy declaration of the McCarran-Ferguson Act.

While the ABA will not be satisfied until all states have taken appropriate action, progress which has been made, and that which is anticipated, is encouraging. There is credible evidence that meaningful reform can be implemented at that state level if the states are given time to let their legislative processes run their course. You have been advised that 24 states have now enacted some type of no-fault legislation, and while this fact is a yardstick of substantial progress in its own right, it by no means fully or fairly discloses the full scope and depth of state action.

From our ongoing efforts to keep abreast of the legislative, executive and judicial developments in each state, we have been able to monitor the full breadth of state activity on this issue. Literally, hundreds of legislative proposals have been and are being considered by the state legislatures in the 26 states which have not yet enacted no-fault reform measures. Some, such as California, will continue to deliberate on this issue well into the fall. Additionally, amendments to existing enacted no-fault plans reflecting the lessons of actual experience are constantly being considered, and enacted.

It should also be noted that four states have had legislation vetoed and that one enacted plan was declared unconstitutional by the state supreme court. A number of no-fault plans have been and are being further refined and clarified by attorney general and supreme court advisory opinions.

Particularly significant are the studies which a number of states have commissioned in order to develop a sound basis for the enactment of no-fault legislation. Studies such as those in Iowa, Mississippi, and Washington clearly indicate the desire of the state legislatures to enact reform legislation on the basis of developing experience. Obtaining a sound basis for no-fault legislation is now possible because a multi-specimen laboratory for experimentation has resulted from the variety of state plans enacted. Common questions about no-fault are developing and as their answers begin to surface there is every reason to believe that the pace of state enactments will increase.

The primary catalyst of the movement to reform the automobile accident reparations system, the previously mentioned DOT study, did not appear until 1971. Since that time, nearly one-half of the states have enacted reform legislation extending coverage to over 53% of our citizenry. When compared to the length of time it took to obtain nationwide implementation of workmens' compensation, it might be concluded that we are dealing with a relatively young issue. We agree with Secretary Coleman's June 17 statement to the Subcommittee that while we may not know precisely how long a "reasonable time" is for state action, we do know that it has not yet run.

Regulation of automobile insurance has developed as a state responsibility not by chance, but because the variables which comprise the automobile accident reparations system have always differed from state to state. Rate-making, for example, reflects geography, road conditions, population density, and propensity to sue, factors which can more accurately be evaluated by the individual states. Supplanting the existing system with one of uniformity established by federal legislation is inappropriate for two reasons: there is little likelihood that any such uniform system could better deal with these variables or that such a system would improve the state regulatory mechanism currently in place. Improvements in a system can be more effectively and less expensively accomplished by working with existing institutions rather than starting new ones.

Basic social policy questions posed by the no-fault concept also would seem better addressed at the state level. During earlier hearings representatives of the National Association of Insurance Commissioners testified that basic questions to be addressed concern the benefits the public desires, the privileges the public is willing to forego for such benefits, and the cost level that is acceptable.

State governments, being closer to the people, are in the best position to determine the answers and respond with tailor-made legislation. State insurance commissioners are more accessible to individual citizens, and state legislators can more forcefully make known to their state commissioners the insurance problems of their constituents than they could to the appropriate authority in Washington.

As the Subcommittee has heard from a number of witnesses, examination of various types of no-fault plans has raised significant questions about the theory of no-fault, questions which merit further examination and experimentation. States have experienced unanticipated increases in the severity of bodily injury claims negating the cost savings resulting from decreases in the frequency of such claims. In some states where plans do not restrict the right to maintain tort lawsuits, the frequency of bodily injury claims has been reduced to the same extent as in states where plans incorporate tort restrictions. Some states have experienced an unanticipated over-utilization of no-fault benefits, the result of which is to drive up the system's cost.

Against this background, a host of new questions warrant investigation. Have jury attitudes changed so that a victim who qualifies to maintain a tort lawsuit is thought to be deserving of a high award? Is there a trend developing whereby third party actions are financed by the speedy first party coverage payments? To impose an extensive, federally mandated system, whether by minimum standards or actual federal preemption, on this country when cautious experimentation with state plans can provide the answers to these and other questions would be reckless and imprudent.

While the experience of existing plans has isolated problem areas in certain states, primarily with regard to costs, it has also been demonstrated that state no-fault plans, specifically tailored to the varying needs of each state's citizenry, can be successful in quickly and adequately compensating accident victims for for their significant economic losses. These results often have been accompanied by a decrease or a stabilization in insurance premium costs. In short, state plans can work and are working.

Even the DOT Study on Motor Vehicle Crash Losses and Their Compensation recommended that automobile accident reparations reform be accomplished by experimentation at the state level, a position still reflected by the Administration. The same conclusion has been drawn by the National Association of Independent Insurers and the American Mutual Insurance Alliance. Also endorsing this approach are the National Association of Insurance Commissioners, the Council of State Governments, and the National Governors' Conference which recently stated:

"We believe that individual state action and interstate cooperation can provide a no-fault system which is uniform enough to meet the needs of interstate vehicle accidents and flexible enough to suit the conditions in each state without increasing rates."

The American Bar Association, during its several appearances before various Committees of both Houses of Congress, has repeatedly asserted that the federal legislation is not needed to reform the automobile accident reparations system. Though H.R. 1272 and H.R. 1900 differ in some respects from earlier federal proposals, our examination of them has given us no reason to depart from this conclusion.

In seeking to hold federal legislation out as the panacea for a troubled reparations system, one virtue often cited is the basic uniformity it would achieve. We submit that such uniformity is not needed for reform of the system, and in fact, would retard efforts presently underway.

H.R. 1272 would establish a uniform, federally regulated automobile accident reparations system. The authors of H.R. 1900 apparently intended to establish uniformity only in the sense of certain "minimum standards" and allow the states to further shape and regulate their own reparations system. Comparing the standards, taken together, to existing state no-fault legislation indicates a high degree of uniformity would result if applied in every state.

Advocates of federal no-fault often suggest that basic nationwide uniformity of automobile accident reparations sytems is needed to avoid the chaos and confusion in interstate driving which would result from a "hodge-podge" of different systems in different states. We find these fears to be ill-founded. There have always been differences from state-to-state in the laws governing liability, rights of recovery, compulsory insurance, minimum liability insurance coverage limits etc. The insurance industry has avoided uncertaintly and burdens on interstate driving through the use of such devices as policy endorsements. Industry representatives have repeatedly indicated that different state no-fault plans can be made compatible in a similar manner. We consider the absence of such chaos and uncertainty in the eastern seaboard no-fault states to be a reliable indication that such concerns are without foundation.

That aspect of the inherent uniformity of federal legislation which is most distressing to us is its lack of flexibility to allow the states to experiment with different elements of a total no-fault system so that they might determine the best possible mix. The need for such experimentation was set forth above, but both H.R. 1272 and H.R. 1900 have effectively precluded experimentation with variables such as benefit levels and limitations on tort lawsuits. Section 201(d) of H.R. 1900, requiring the Secretary of Transportation to periodically review and evaluate the results of the legislation in each state in certain specified area, is an admission that there is much uncertainty about the effect it will have. Inasmuch as this is a clear recognition of an informational void, it would appear to be irresponsible to attempt to collect that information subsequent to the adoption of an irreversible uniform system. This inconsistency is more difficult to understand since states are already actively experimenting with different approaches designed to suit local needs.

Objecting as we do to the rigid approaches of H.R. 1900 and H.R. 1272, we are also troubled by provisions which could affect other traditional legal concepts not exclusively within the scope of the automobile accident reparations system. For example, H.R. 1900 now dictates that the right to sue in tort must be determined by the law of the victim's principal place of residence, if he has one. Uniform imposition of this provision in the states would summarily nullify the great strides recently made in conflict of laws rules which are intended to provide equitable results in particular cases.

The second highly-touted feature of federal no-fault is the impact that its proponents assert it will have on automobile insurance premium costs to the consumer. At a time when the troubles of our economy have affected every consumer pocketbook, the cost of automobile insurance in a no-fault system is certainly a matter for legislative concern. Nevertheless, before becoming preoccupied with making projections about the cost savings that will be in any no-fault system, we must understand what no-fault reform was intended to achieve in the way of premium costs.

As we cautioned the Senate Commerce Committee earlier this year and this Subcommittee last year, we cannot afford to forget that no-fault was conceived to provide compensation to as many automobile accident victims as possible for their significant economic losses, to insure that such compensation was adequate for both minor and severe injuries, to make insurance coverage available to as many persons as possible, to increase the efficiency of the reparations system in terms of the speed of the reparation and the percentage of the premium dollar returned to victims, and to reduce the overall cost of the insurance system which could result in reductions in the average premium paid. In the long run, no-fault will surely be judged by its performance against all its objectives.

Secretary Coleman placed this issue in its proper perspective in his statement when he observed:

"First, from the perspective of the public policymaker, cost savings, while admittedly important, should not, and in my view do not, constitute the primary purpose of no-fault reform. Much more important, for example, are the adequacy of victim's benefits, the certainty and universality of their insurance coverage, and the elimination of the adversary process from the benefit decision."

Consider also the impact of bodily injury automobile insurance on today's consumer in today's economic setting. A DOT study of the cost of operating an automobile published in April of 1974 demonstrated that the cost of those automobile insurance coverages with which no-fault is concerned is the smallest portion of an individual's total cost of operating an automobile. These coverages cost the consumer less than taxes, garage parking, and tolls, gas and oil before taxes, maintenance, accessories, parts and tires, and original vehicle cost depreciation. Since the publication of that study, we have seen a tremendous increase in the cost of gasoline, parts and garage services which would likely reduce the proportionate bodily injury insurance premium cost still further.

Unfortunately, federal no-fault proposals, and in fact most state proposals have been sold to the public as cost savings devices. While it is likely that cost savings often can occur, the fact is that a properly balanced no-fault system with adequate benefit levels may distribute better insurance benefits without reducing the overall premium costs. We must not mislead the American consumer to the extent that he equates no-fault reform with guaranteed premium reductions and is blinded to the important reform that is achieved.

Keeping in mind the purpose of no-fault reform, we have attempted to determine what the cost results of the proposed federal legislation will be. The basis for the first cost projections was the much discussed Milliman & Robertson, Inc., Cost Estimate Study which attempted to project the cost impact of S. 354 in each of the states. Generally speaking, the conclusion drawn from the study was that substantial reductions in the average premium paid would result in every state that enacted a no-fault system which included the provisions set out in S. 354. After examining this study, we concluded, as did many others, that its projections were highly speculative and subject to only limited application.

The study itself admitted that many variables which substantially influence insurance costs were not cranked into the project models. Further, the study referred solely to expected changes in the average rate level which had the effect of concealing important variations regarding territory, class of victim, and class of vehicle. For example, the average rate projections failed to disclose whether S. 354, and H.R. 1900, would occasion a redistribution of premium costs which would be favorable to the high-risk motorist to the detriment of the low-risk motorist. The following excerpt from a *New York Times* article reporting on a New York insurance department study points out the significance of this distinction:

Since the inception a year ago of the states no-fault automobile insurance system, high-risk drivers rather than low-risk drivers have received the largest reductions in the amount they pay for personal injury liability insurance.

According to a report released by the State Insurance Department, the largest reductions—both in percentages and in dollar amounts—were realized by drivers who are considered prone to accidents. The smallest reductions went to drivers with good records who chose the largest amounts of coverages. (*New York Times*, Feb. 21, 1975)

Equally significant is M & R's failure to disclose the effect that federal no-fault would have on certain classes of victims such as the housewife and the elderly as a result of extensive tort limitations designed to reduce costs. The housewife's benefits are limited because she suffers no wage loss. The elderly, many of whom do not own cars, would be entitled to even fewer benefits since they also have no wage loss and since Medicare covers many of their medical bills.

A damaging blow to the projections of the M & R study was recently dealt by a similar study conducted by Allstate Insurance Company. Again the subject of the study was S. 354, but Allstate attempted to make its projections in such a manner so as to avoid many of the deficiencies of the M & R study. The Allstate study separated out the huge cost savings which will inure to the benefit of the commercial vehicle operators and reflected what the private passenger vehicle owner will pay. It utilized a more realistic survivors benefit and included an "induced cost" factor. Further, it utilized a more realistic relationship of special damages to general damages and took into effect the real world experiences in those few states where credible data has developed.

While we are certainly not actuarial experts, we can appreciate those instances in which the Allstate study was able to avoid the deficencies of the M & R study and accordingly, we feel that the results of the Allstate study reflect a higher degree of accuracy and reliability. These results led Allstate to conclude that S. 354 would increase costs for the vast majority of American automobile insurance buyers, and in some cases the increases would be fantastically large.

In our opinion, the most significant failing of the M & R study is that when compared to actual state experience the general conclusions of the study have not been confirmed. The overall contention of the study was inescapable; if S. 354 were enacted in the states substantial reductions in premium costs would result, while plans enacted with benefit levels similar to S. 354 but without limitation on tort lawsuits, would generally result in significant increases in premium costs.

The primary feature of S. 354 as far as benefits are concerned is the provision for unlimited medical expense coverage, a provision that the New Jersey plan also incorporates. Earlier this month it was reported that 250 automobile insurers in New Jersey have filed for an average 34.1% increase in automobile insurance rates. Many insurance observers have attributed this filing to the losses suffered by the companies as a result of the unlimited medical expense coverage.

On the other hand, the Oregon plan provides for substantial first-party benefits but does not limit the right to maintain tort lawsuits. While the benefits of the Oregon plan are not identical to that of S. 354 or H.R. 1900, they are sufficient to cover the economic losses of 98.5% of all Oregon accident victims. Despite a substantial increase in the level of these benefits since the plan was first enacted, the average private passenger automobile premium in Oregon has remained stable.

The Association adds its voice to those who have expressed concern for the regulation of any no-fault system by the federal government. Such federal regulation is specifically provided for by H.R. 1272. The authors of H.R. 1900 have attempted to provide for state regulation of the no-fault system within the framework of the minimum standards which it sets out. However, we agree with those who have pointed out that the provisions of H.R. 1900 would inevitably result in substantial regulation of the no-fault system by the federal government.

Certain provisions of H.R. 1900, such as Section 109(c), would impose upon state insurance commissioners requirements which presently exceed their existing authority. That Section would require them to establish and maintain, for automobile accident victims, medical and vocational rehabilitation programs. No state insurance commissioner has such authority today. Further, H.R. 1900 imposes requirements which overlap existing state insurance laws and which would require substantial state legislative action to conform to the dictates of H.R. 1900. For example, Section 105 sets forth specific standards for the operation of plans to make insurance coverages widely available. Today, each state has a plan through which any licensed automobile driver can obtain insurance, but because of local situations they vary substantially from state-to-state.

H.R. 1900 also imposes upon the states regulations which are in direct conflict with existing state automobile insurance regulatory laws. Consider Section 105(b) dealing with cancellation, refusal to renew, or termination of automobile insurance policies. While every state insurance law does restrict substantially the right to cancel such policies, not one state follows the detailed provisions contained in this Section.

In determining whether or not H.R. 1900 does in fact entail substantial federal regulation, we defer to the judgment of those who would be charged with administering that no-fault system, the state insurance commissioners. During recent hearings before the Senate Commerce Committee the witness representing NAIC stated:

"We submit that the impact of S. 354 on state insurance regulation would be substantial and fundamental rather than minimal, as suggested. The structure of the regulatory requirements imposed by S. 354 virtually assures that the federal government will be regulating automobiles insurance."

Our concern for federal regulation of the automobile accident reparations system stems from our observation of the many federal regulatory agencies that exist today. Federal regulation of matters which have as their objective consumer protection is repeatedly characterized as dilatory, inflexible, dependent, incompetent and unresponsive. Such regulation has often been demonstrated to be inefficient and overly expensive. We maintain that the present 51 state insurance regulators are in the best position to respond to consumer problems based on local needs. Such flexibility, inuring to the benefit of the consumer, would not exist under federal regulation of the system.

Early in 1974, H.R. 1900's counterpart, S. 354, became the subject of extensive constitutional scrutiny. Since most of the relevant features of S. 354 at that time are presently found in H.R. 1900, the concerns merit attention here. There is no general agreement regarding the validity of the constitutional challenges that have been leveled at the federal minimum standards no-fault bills, but it is essential to appreciate the inevitability of extensive litigation when considering their enactment.

Attorney General Levi recently described the primary constitutional infirmity of S. 354 before it was recently reported out of the Senate Commerce Committee. He stated the issue to be not whether Congress can enact legislation which would encourage states to adopt federally prescribed no-fault standards, but rather:

" . . . whether it is permissible or appropriate for the Congress to intrude upon such State sovereignty as is left by requiring State agencies and employees to perform as though they were Federal instruments or employees, or as though the Federal Congress were the state legislature and possessor of the state's sovereignty."

Evidently the arguments of the Attorney General were persuasive with the Senate Commerce Committee for the version of S. 354 that it reported out has eliminated this one particular pitfall.

Equally troubling to us is the substantial alteration in the relationship between our state and federal governments which would result from the approach of H.R. 1900. The possibility of such an alteration is deserving of careful and extensive consideration by those considering the enactment of such legislation. We have been most distressed by the manner in which this crucial matter has been so lightly dismissed by the proponents of federal no-fault.

A close examination of the existing automobile accident reparations system reveals that the hysteria for change which prompted the DOT study is greatly diminished and that today we confront a significantly changed system of automobile accident reparations. The availability of new types of insurance coverages, significant changes in insurance rating practices, more prompt payment to accident victims through advanced payment plans, walkaway releases, and expanded medical payment coverages are a few of the new developments. Also, a nationwide court reform movement has eased the congestion in our civil courts from that existing in 1971.

Current inflationary trends and the energy crisis are new considerations. Loss ratios have been influenced by lower speed limits and altered driving habits. The present level of inflation has added a new dimension to the cost of automobile insurance, as have safety campaigns and vehicle safety requirements. New coordination of benefits plans are being developed and utilized, and the use of arbitration has increased. Changes in the legal system, such as greater acceptance of the comparative negligence doctrine and the erosion of the various immunities, have reduced "gap" problems for the accident victim.

Finally, it appears that a basis for answering the common questions about the performance of the no-fault concept is developing, and is developing from the only source presently available, state action. Indications are that some of the answers might ultimately be contrary to what most theoreticians would have expected, a realization further emphasizing the crucial importance of continued experimentation at the state level. At this particular stage we do not need federal legislation which would establish a system plagued by the typical problems of federal regulation inherent in bills such as H.R. 1272 and H.R. 1900. We do need meaningful data and information from the states indicating the experiences of various types of no-fault plans, and we need a reasonable amount of time for that data to develop. These needs have been recognized and are being addressed by the National Association of Insurance Commissioners which has created a task force for the purpose of developing statistical data.

On behalf of the American Bar Association, I urge that the Subcommittee not approve H.R. 1272 or H.R. 1900 or any other legislation providing for the imposition of any federal plan or federal minimum standards for a no-fault automobile accident reparations system.

AMERICAN BAR ASSOCIATION SPECIAL COMMITTEE ON AUTOMOBILE INSURANCE LEGISLATION—RESOLUTION, ADOPTED BY THE HOUSE OF DELEGATES, FEBRUARY 5, 1975, CHICAGO, ILL.

Resolved, That the American Bar Association urges that those states not yet having done so immediately begin sincere consideration of their respective demographic, economic, geographic and attitudinal realities and enact, as expeditiously as possible, appropriate automobile accident reparations reform legislation.

Further resolved, That said legislation should encompass as minimum standards, but not necessarily be limited to, those substantive provisions of the present Association posture with regard to said legislation as previously adopted by the House of Delegates.

RECOMMENDATION

AMERICAN BAR ASSOCIATION, SPECIAL COMMITTEE ON AUTOMOBILE INSURANCE LEGISLATION—AUGUST 1972

1. That states which have not done so adopt laws which provide for required motor vehicle bodily injury and property damage liability with coverage limits of $15,000 for bodily injury to one person, $30,000 for all bodily injury associated with one accident and $5,000 for all property damage from one accident and that these laws be of a self-certification type.

2. That the laws which provide for required motor vehicle liability coverage also provide for required uninsured motorist coverage with limits of $15,000 for bodily injury to one person and $30,000 for all bodily injury from one accident.

3. That all states which have not done so adopt laws which require that minimum first party coverage of at least $2,000 be included in all motor vehicle liability insurance policies offering protection for economic loss to the named insured, members of his family residing in the same household as the named insured, guest passengers in the insured's vehicle and pedestrians struck by that vehicle. Those laws should give the innocent accident victim the option to seek indemnity for economic loss from his own insurer, or in an action in tort, but should avoid duplicate reimbursement for the same loss and should shift the ultimate burden for the loss to the tortfeasor or his insurer.

4. [THIS LANGUAGE WAS NOT ADOPTED BY HOUSE OF DELEGATES*] That in personal injury claims or actions arising out of motor vehicle accidents, general damages recoverable for pain, suffering, mental anguish, inconvenience and other similar loss should be limited to a multiple of one times the medical expenses unless they exceed $500 or unless the injury results in death, dismemberment, permanent total or permanent partial disability, temporary partial disability beyond 4 weeks duration, serious disfigurement, or loss or impairment of a bodily function.

5. That the American Bar Association reaffirm its support for the recommendations of the Special Committee on Automobile Accident Reparations, as modified by the foregoing proposals.

6. That persons designated by the President of the American Bar Association be authorized to support the adoption of legislation consistent with these resolutions and to oppose legislation inconsistent with these resolutions before appropriate legislative bodies and other groups.

7. That the Special Committee be continued.

REPORT

Since its creation in May, 1971, the Special Committee has met eight times. The Special Committee has reviewed existing and proposed legislation in the field of automobile insurance legislation in several states and on the national level. Members of the Special Committee, several of whom served on the Association's Special Committee on Automobile Reparations, have reviewed the extensive Report of that Committee.

During the spring of 1971, the U.S. Department of Transportation completed and published a twenty-four volume report on automobile accident reparations. Members of the Special Committee have reviewed that report. Based on its study, the Department of Transportation formulated proposed guidelines for no-fault automobile insurance legislation.

The Uniform Commissioners on State Laws has contracted with the Department of Transportation to draft a model no-fault automobile insurance law, consistent with the proposed Department guidelines. The Uniform Commissioners considered a tentative draft at their 1971 meeting and will consider a proposed final draft at their meeting August, 1972.

The Committee was charged with the responsibility of reexamining the recommendations of the Special Committee on Automobile Accident Reparations as approved, in principle, by the House of Delegates in August, 1969.[1] The re-

---

*Approved by the House of Delegates at the Association's Annual Meeting on Tuesday, August 15, 1972, with the following substitute for the Committee's Recommendation No. 4:
4. That the American Bar Association is opposed to any federal "no-fault" insurance legislation and believes that any changes which may be made in the so-called automobile accident reparations system should be by state action.

[1] Report of the American Bar Association Special Committee on Automobile Accident Reparations (June 1969) (Future references will be to Powers' Report, Powers' Committee or Powers' Recommendations. Recommendations of the Powers' Committee are contained in Appendix A, page 34 infra).

examination was to take place in light of developments which have occurred since that report was approved.

Developments which have taken place since the approval of the Powers' Report are numerous. Some of the most important ones include the completion of the study of automobile insurance and automobile accident reparations by the Department of Transportation;[2] the introduction of legislation in Congress to federalize automobile accident reparations if a state does not enact legislation which meets or exceeds motor vehicle insurance and accident reparation standards imposed by Congress;[3] and the enactment of legislation in a number of jurisdictions affecting the existing automobile accident reparations system.[4] As the Committee entered into its task of re-examining and re-evaluating the Powers' Report in light of developments since 1969, it became clear to the members of the committee that, even in light of changing circumstances, the Powers' Recommendations still serve as a viable blueprint for improvement of the present reparation system. This committee believes that if the Powers' Proposals were fully implemented the present system would be more efficient, more equitable and less costly.

We are unalterably opposed to legislation now pending in the United States Congress which would pre-empt state motor vehicle accident reparation reform by the establishment of a federal law governing the subject. We are similarly opposed to legislation developed by the Senate Commerce Committee which would coerce the states to meet or exceed certain motor vehicle insurance and reparation standards or face the imposition of a more stringent federal law. Rather, we are in accord with the view expressed by the Department of Transportation that state experimentation with diverse motor vehicle reparation plans offers the best solution to the development of meaningful reform in the public interest.[5] The legislation which has been enacted in ten states and Puerto Rico, in addition to studies underway and legislation being considered in other states, demonstrates that the states can and will act to meet the problems that are found to exist. We are unimpressed with arguments that legislation enacted to date is inadequate, or that the failure of certain states to enact "meaningful no-fault legislation" evidences disinterest with the problems facing their citizens. Those advancing these arguments support particular points of view or particular plans. Their dissatisfaction may be traced to the fact that the states have not adopted the type of plans which they are committed to support. We are convinced that a state legislature is in a much better position to judge the problems which exist within its borders, and the best means to correct them.

As lawyers we are subject to criticism if we caution against rapid change and seek evaluation and experimentation before a course of action becomes irreversible. We must face this criticism in the interest of the public unless we are convinced that change will promote the public welfare. On the other hand, where improvement and change are called for in the public interest we support it fully. The Powers' Report called for a retention of the adversary system and opposition to proposals that would severely reduce benefits to automobile accident victims or abolish the tort system. We reaffirm these principles but direct our attention to the 52 recommendations for improvement, particularly those that have an impact on the automobile reparation system. Some will say our recommendations have not gone far enough, others will say that we have gone too far. The committee believes it has recommended change where needed and provided a vehicle which can unify the Bar in its support of meaningful but responsible reform.

The committee is re-examining the Powers' Recommendations, determined that modification or change in the Powers' Recommendations are called for in areas of compulsory insurance, first party benefits and general damages.

DISCUSSION OF RECOMMENDATIONS

Recommendations 1 and 2

That states which have not done so adopt laws which provide for required motor vehicle bodily injury and property damage liability with coverage limits of

---

[2] Department of Transportation (DOT) Report, *Motor Vehicle Crash Losses and Their Compensation in the United States* (March 1971).
[3] *E.g., Committee Print Three of S. 945*, as amended and ordered reported by the Senate Commerce Committee (92nd Cong. 2d Sess., May 26. 1972); H.R. 10808 (92nd Cong. 1st Sess., July 29, 1971).
[4] Connecticut, Delaware, Florida, Illinois, Maryland, Massachusetts, Minnesota, New Jersey, Oregon and South Dakota.
[5] DOT Report, note 2 *supra* at 140; see also, statement of John T. Reardon on behalf of the American Bar Association before the Committee on Commerce of the United States Senate (May 5, 1971).

$15,000 for bodily injury to one person, $30,000 for all bodily injury associated with one accident and $5,000 for all property damages from one accident and that these laws be of a self-certification type.

That the laws which provide for required motor vehicle liability coverage also provide for required uninsured motorist coverage with limits of $15,000 for bodily injury to one person and $30,000 for all bodily injury from one accident.

The Powers' Committee recommended that states which have not done so should adopt compulsory automobile insurance laws applicable to both bodily injury and property damage and that such laws also require every policy issued to contain uninsured motorist coverage which includes insolvency protection.[6] The committee *unanimously* endorses this principle and recommends the foregoing for adoption by the Association.

With the adoption of the Powers' Recommendation in 1969, the American Bar Association committed itself to work for the preservation and improvement of the tort liability system, particularly as it relates to automobile accident reparations. If the tort system is to operate effectively as a reparation mechanism for innocent accident victims, as opposed to being merely a mechanism to fix legal responsibility for injury or damage, tortfeasors who cause accidents must be financially responsible.

At the present time, the states of Delaware, Florida, Massachusetts, New York and North Carolina require the purchase of liability insurance as a condition precedent to the operation of licensing of a motor vehicle.[7] Available information indicates that upwards to ninety percent of the motorists in compulsory insurance states comply with the laws.[8] The remaining states operate under so-called "Financial Responsibility" laws which compel the purchase of insurance only after accident involvement or a serious traffic law violation. The percentage of insured motorists in those states is reported to vary from a high of over eighty to a low of near fifty-five percent.[9] Based upon these realities, a person driving in a compulsory insurance state is faced with a probability of one in ten that he will be involved in an accident with an uninsured driver. Whereas, in states not having compulsory insurance the probabilities are much higher.

The widespread use of uninsured motorist coverage has taken some of the sting out of those probabilities. Certainly, even in compulsory insurance states, some motorists will attempt to avoid the law and drive without being insured. Uninsured motorists from other states will also cause accidents. However, if the choice of who is to pay for damages resulting from automobile accidents has to be made, as well it must, we conclude that it is preferable to assess the cost of accidents against those who are responsible for them through liability insurance premiums rather than to shift that cost to innocent accident victims through uninsured motorist coverage premiums.

Critics of required insurance assert that claim frequency will rise under such a system. While this is a factor, probably no small part of the claims frequency increase will be due to the fact that more persons will be insured and thus there will be more financially responsible persons against whom claims may be brought. Except for the question of limits, those persons who already insure their vehicles will be unaffected by the enactment of a required insurance law.

We are recommending a compulsory law only in the sense that automobile insurance would be required for all motorists. However, the law is based on the principle of self-certification and does not require that a motorist file a certificate from his insurer for his vehicle to be registered. This type of "required" insurance should not prove to be as costly to enforce as the "compulsory" type in effect in New York, Massachusetts and North Carolina. It should not add substantially to the cost of motor vehicle law enforcement in a state and is modeled after the Delaware Act.[10]

The Sample Statute which follows illustrates the type of required insurance law favored by this Committee. It provides for required bodily injury and property damage liability insurance with coverage limits of $15,000 for bodily injury to one person, $30,000 for all bodily injury associated with one accident and $5,000 for all property damage from one accident. The Powers' Committee recommended coverage limits of $10,000/20,000/5,000. Our recommendation increases those

---

[6] Powers' Report, note 1 *supra*, at 119-124 and at 125-126:
[7] *See* Ghiardi & Kircher, "Automobile Insurance Reparations Plans: An Analysis of Eight Existing Laws," 55 *Marq. L. Rev.* 1 (1972); legislation enacted in 1972 to become effective in 1973 in Connecticut, Maryland and New Jersey also provides for compulsory liability insurance, Conn. Public Act 273 (1972); Md. House Bill 444 (1972); N.J. Assembly Bill 667 (1972).
[8] DOT Report, *Driver Behavior and Accident Involvement* 212 (Oct. 1970).
[9] *Id.*
[10] Del. Code, ch. 21, tit. 21, § 2118 (1971).

limits to reflect economic changes since 1969. In addition, it has been reported that only forty percent of motorists carry bodily injury liability limits lower than $15,000/30,000 and that fifty-two percent carry limits higher than those figures.[11] It is also reported that only one and one-half percent of all auto claim payments for bodily injury are for sums in excess of $10,000 and that only three-tenths of one percent are over $25,000.[12] However, these payments represent over twenty-five percent of the total claim payment dollars.[13] At the present time, fifteen states have financial responsibility laws which require $15,000/30,000/5,000 or more in liability coverage.[14]

Our recommendation also calls for required uninsured motorist coverage with $15,000/30,000 limits. As noted previously, even under a required motor vehicle liability insurance law there will be those who operate in violation of the law and there will be uninsured motorists from other states. Uninsured motorist coverage provides a workable, inexpensive solution to the final financial responsibility gap. At the present time, fourteen states compel the inclusion of uninsured motorists coverage in all auto policies and in 34 states it must be included unless rejected by the insured.[15] A number of bills were introduced in various states this year to eliminate the right of rejection.[16] This portion of our recommendation should be read with our recommendation on minimum first party coverage which provides, in effect, that the insured must be given the option to extend the limits of his uninsured motorist coverage to the same values as his bodily injury liability coverage.[17]

The provisions of the Sample Statute define "uninsured motor vehicle" to include a vehicle with respect to which there is liability coverage at the time of the accident but the company writing the same is or becomes insolvent.[18]

Sample statute—Required motor vehicle insurance

(1) *Required Motor Vehicle Insurance.* No owner of a motor vehicle required to be registered in this state with the Department of Motor Vehicles pursuant to Section—, other than an authorized self-insurer pursuant to Section—, shall operate or authorize any person to operate and no person shall knowingly operate such vehicle unless the owner has insurance for such motor vehicle providing the following minimum coverages:

(a) *Liability Insurance.* Indemnity against loss from liability imposed by law for damages, including damages for care and loss of services, because of bodily injury to or death of any person and injury or destruction of property arising out of the ownership, operation, maintenance or use of a specified motor vehicle within this state, or elsewhere in the United States in North America or the Dominion of Canada, subject to a limit, exclusive of costs and interest, with respect to each such motor vehicle, of fifteen thousand dollars because of bodily injury to or death of one person in any one accident, to a limit of thirty thousand dollars because of bodily injury to or death of two or more persons in any one accident, and to a limit of five thousand dollars because of injury to or destruction of property of others in any one accident provided, however, that such policy need not be for a period coterminous with the registration period of the insured vehicle.

(b) *Uninsured Motorists Insurance.* Coverage in the amount of at least fifteen thousand dollars per person and thirty thousand dollars per accident for the protection of the insureds who are legally entitled to recover damages from owners or operators of uninsured motor vehicles because of bodily injury, sickness, or disease, including death resulting therefrom, occurring as the result of a motor vehicle accident. For the purpose of this coverage, the term "uninsured motor vehicles" shall include, but not be limited to, any motor vehicle with respect to which there is a bodily injury liability insurance policy applicable at the time of the accident but the company writing the same denies coverage thereunder or is or becomes insolvent.

(2) *Penalties for Non-Compliance.* Whoever violates any of the provisions of Section (1) shall be guilty of a misdemeanor and shall, upon conviction be fined. (The amount of fine to be fixed by state or local determination.)

---

[11] DOT Report, *Automobile Personal Injury Claims*, Vol. 1 at 99 (July 1970).
[12] *Id.*, at 49.
[13] *Id.*
[14] PF & M, Fire, *Casualty & Surety Analyses*, § 224.3.
[15] *Id.*
[16] *See e.g.*, Chapter 28 Wisconsin Laws of 1971, effective November 19, 1971.
[17] *See* page 14 *infra*.
[18] *Powers' Report*, note 1 *supra* at 125-126.

Recommendation 3
That all states which have not done so adopt laws which require that minimum first party coverage of at least $2,000 be included in all motor vehicle liability insurance policies offering protection for economic loss to the named insured, members of his family residing in the same household as the named insured, guest passengers in the insured's vehicle and pedestrians struck by that vehicle. Those laws should give the innocent accident victim the option to seek indemnity for economic loss from his own insurer, or in an action in tort, but should avoid duplicate reimbursement for the same loss and should shift the ultimate burden for the loss to the tortfeasor or his insurer.

A stage has been reached in the so-called "automobile accident reparation controversy" at which there appears to be little serious controversy over the question of whether all persons injured in auto accidents should have some form of first party insurance. The controversy now centers on the questions which concern the amount of loss which should be recoverable under the first party system and the extent to which tort liability should be abrogated, if at all, to finance the first party system.

In considering the question of first party coverage under auto insurance, the Powers' Committee recommended consideration of a so-called "Crossover Medical Plan" but only for the purpose of study and evaluation, and recommended opposition to compulsory first party coverage.[19] Since the Powers' Report was approved, little attention has been given to the Crossover plan. It has not been submitted as legislation in any state. Rather, laws which have been enacted in Connecticut, Delaware, Florida, Illinois, Maryland, Massachusetts, New Jersey and Oregon all follow along lines similar to this Committee's proposal. Motorists in those states who buy liability insurance are required to purchase first party coverage in specified amounts to protect themselves, their passengers and pedestrians. Our proposal would require the purchase of first party coverage.

It would not abrogate tort liability. This recommendation was approved *unanimously* but two members of the Committee would have preferred that a reasonable tort exemption be provided. The tortfeasor, or his insurer, will have ultimate responsibility for the damages caused. The innocent accident victim is given an option. He may seek full compensation under the tort system, or he may recover a portion of his damages from his own insurer and the balance from the tortfeasor. In the latter case, the insurer paying first party benefits will be able to seek reimbursement, to the extent of payment, from the tortfeasor or his insurer. The sample statute which follows this discussion illustrates the type of minimum first party coverage law favored by this Committee.

Section 1 of the sample statute requires that all motor vehicle [20] liability policies must provide a minimum of $2,000 in first party coverage for economic loss associated with personal injuries sustained in an auto accident. The $2,000 limit would be per insured and not per accident or occurrence. The named insured and members of his family residing in the same household as the named insured would be covered for any auto accident, whether riding in the insured vehicle or not. Other guest passengers and pedestrians would be covered if injured while riding in or when struck by the insured vehicle, subject to the provisions of Section 2. Economic loss which would be covered up to the $2,000 limit includes medical and related expenses and eighty-five percent of income loss. Also provided is up to $12 per day for expenses incurred to replace services the injured person would have performed had he not been injured—such as the hiring of a housekeeper while a housewife is disabled.

The $2,000 figure for minimum coverage is, at best, arbitrary. Some proposals would pay all medical and related expenses without time or dollar limits and wage loss without a limit as to time but up to a rather high monthly dollar limit.[21] These plans, however, would totally or almost totally eliminate tort liability. The $2,000

---

[19] *Id.* at 97 and 151.

[20] It should be noted that the first party insurance requirements in Connecticut, Florida, Illinois, New Jersey and Oregon apply only to "private passenger vehicles" as defined in those states' acts. In Grace v. Howlett N.E. 2d (Ill. 1972) the Illinois supreme court held that limiting the mandated coverage requirement to one class of vehicles to the exclusion of other classes amounted to "special" legislation contrary to the provisions of that state's constitution. The Sample Statute is therefore drawn broadly to apply to all motor vehicles. Those wishing to restrict this broad requirement should consider *Grace* in light of the provisions of their own state's constitution.

[21] *E.g.*, The American Insurance Association Plan; National Conference of Commissioners on Uniform State Laws, *Uniform Motor Vehicle Accident Reparations Act* (Ninth Tentative Draft, June 16-18, 1972); S. 945, note 3 *supra*, Title III, § 301(b)(1).

amount recommended was selected only after due consideration. It has been reported that over ninety-three percent of auto accident victims sustain economic loss under $1,500 and that another three percent sustain economic loss between $1,500 and $2,500.[22] Thus, a first party auto insurance system which would pay up to $2,000 to each person injured in an auto accident would cover the total economic losses sustained by nearly ninety-five percent of traffic accident victims.

It would not cover the total economic losses of all, but it must be remembered that the vast majority of Americans are protected by medical, hospital, and wage loss benefit plans collateral to auto insurance.[23] In addition, coverage for all economic loss under a first party auto insurance system would require a severe limitation of the tort right of recovery for general damages, so that the first party benefits can be financed.

Section 1 of the Sample Statute provides for coverage for the named insured and resident relatives in all auto accidents. Thus, they would be covered while they are guests in another's vehicle or while they are pedestrians. However, duplicate payment is to be avoided since it increases the cost of the system, therefore Section 3 was included. The net effect of Sections 1 and 3 is to have the first party coverage follow the person and not the vehicle. Guest passengers injured while in the insured vehicle and pedestrians struck by that vehicle would be afforded coverage under the vehicle's policy but only to the extent that they were not covered as a named or additional insured under another auto policy affording the same or similar first party coverage.

The coverage provided is primary and payment thereunder is not dependent upon the injured person's collateral sources of compensation. Thought was given to the possibility of having the coverage written so that the named insured could take deductibles, applicable to himself and his family members who occupy the same household as he does, up to the full amount of the coverage. This would allow an insured who had adequate collateral source to avoid duplicate coverage and additional premiums. However, it was recognized that the deductible feature would also be used by those who wished to have the cheapest form of auto insurance and who did not have adequate collateral source coverage. To prevent those persons from being unprotected, a decision was made to forego use of a deductible.

Section 4 is intended to avoid duplicate recovery for the same loss. This section is drafted to allow a person only one recovery for the damages covered by Section 1. It is also drafted so that the tortfeasor bears the ultimate responsibility for those damages.

In most instances, payments of first party benefits in accord with Section 1 would be made long before a tort settlement or judgment. However, it must be recognized that, at least in serious cases, liability insurers are making more use of the so-called "Advance Payment" technique. In a study of closed claims made by the Department of Transportation, nineteen percent of claimants who are eligible for the program were found to be receiving advance payments from liability insurers.[24] Subsection (a) of Section 4 was drafted so that a person receiving compensation for damages covered by Section 1 from a tortfeasor or a tortfeasor's liability insurer would not be entitled to recovery for the same loss from his own insurer.

Subsections (b) and (c) of Section 4 were drafted to shift the ultimate burden of paying for the losses covered by Section 1 to the tortfeasor. Subsection (b) gives the insurer paying first party benefits the right to reimbursement, to the extent of payment, from the tortfeasor's insurer when that insurer is also writing business in the same state. A system of intercompany arbitration is provided to determine liability and the amount of reimbursement. Subsection (c) gives the insurer paying first party benefits the right to reimbursement from a tortfeasor who is not insured by an insurer writing in the same state through a trust agreement system. The trust agreement system was used rather than contractual subrogation due to decisions in some states which have held that contractual subrogation under medical payments coverage violates the rule against splitting causes of action for personal injury.[25] Two members of the Committee opposed the use of subrogation and would have deleted parts of this section.

---

[22] Note 11 *supra*, Vol. 1 at 30 (those figures do not include property damage).
[23] At the end of 1970 it was estimated that 94 percent of the civilian population was covered by hospital insurance; 88 percent was covered by surgical insurance; 75 percent was covered by medical insurance; and 70 percent of the civilian labor force was covered by income continuation plans. *Source Book of Health Insurance Data*, 16, 25-6 (1971-72); *Statistical Abstract of the United States*, 210 (1971).
[24] Note 11 *supra*. Vol. 1 at 120.
[25] Pouros, Melendes & Craig. "Medical Payments Provision of the Automobile Insurance Policy: An Illustration of First Party Insurance Problems," 52 *Marq. L. Rev.* 445, 504 (1969).

Section 5 of the sample statute provides additional, optional benefits for the named insured and members of his family residing in his household. Subsection (a) would give the insured the right to extend the coverage limits of his required uninsured motorist coverage ($15,000/30,000) up to the amount of the limits of his own bodily injury liability coverage. It makes little sense for a man who buys very high liability coverage to be limited to low limit uninsured motorist coverage. He should be able to protect himself against financially irresponsible drivers with equally high limits. Section 5 was also drafted so that a person with high liability limits could protect himself against the eventuality that he will be injured through the fault of a person with only minimum liability limits. Thus, this section not only provides for extended uninsured motorists coverage but also for "underinsured motorists" coverage. However, a person's own bodily injury liability limits should be the upper limits of his extended uninsured motorist and underinsured motorist coverage. He should not be able to provide more protection for himself than he is willing to afford others.

Subsection 5(b) provides a death benefit which the named insured has the option of securing for himself and members of his family residing in the same household.

Section 6 of the sample statute is again an effort to avoid duplicate payment and therefore additional cost under the system. It prevents a guest passenger or pedestrian from recovering benefits under the first party coverages of the auto policy and then attempting to recover again for the same damages in a claim or suit under the liability or uninsured motorist coverage of the policy.

Section 7 is intended to allow an insurer to exclude an insured from recovering benefits when public policy would seem to militate against it. This could include persons who intentionally injure themselves, those injured because of alcohol or drug use, or those injured during the commission of a felony. To avoid the problems associated with defining the public policy for each State, the Committee has merely included a general provision in the sample statute so that each State may tailor the law in accord with its own needs.

Section 8 allows an insurer to offer broader benefits for appropriate premiums to those who wish coverage in excess of the mandated minimums.

Sample statute—Minimum first party coverage in automobile policies

Required first party coverages

(1) Every motor vehicle liability insurance policy issued or delivered in this State shall also provide a minimum of $2,000 per persons in Economic Loss Coverage payable, without regard to fault, to the named insured and members of his family residing in the same household as the named insured injured in any motor vehicle accident and to any other persons, except occupants of other motor vehicles injured while occupying or being struck by the insured motor vehicle. Benefits payable under Economic Loss Coverage shall include:

(a) *Medical and Hospital Benefits.* All reasonable expense necessarily incurred for medical, hospital, dental, surgical, ambulance and prosthetic services incurred within one year after the motor vehicle accident. Expenses for hospital room charges are to be limited to semi-private accommodations unless other accommodations are specifically prescribed for a necessary course of medical treatment.

(b) *Income Disability Benefits.* Eighty-five percent of the loss of income sustained by the injured person as a result of the accident and expenses, not to exceed $12 per day, which are reasonably incurred for essential services in lieu of those that the injured person would have performed, without income, for the benefit of himself or his family had he not been injured. As used in this Section, "income" includes but is not limited to salary, wages, tips, commissions, professional fees, and profits an individually owned business or farm.

(2) Authorized self-insurers, pursuant to Section — shall provide security for the payment of benefits equivalent to those specified in Section (1) hereof in accordance with requirements established by the Commissioner of Insurance.

(3) The policy shall provide that the coverages enumerated in Section (1) are not applicable to a person, other than the named insured or a member of his family residing in the same household as the named insured, injured while occupying or being struck by the insured vehicle to the extent that the same or similar coverages are afforded to said person either as the named insured or additional insured under the provisions of another valid motor vehicle insurance policy.

(4) A person injured in a motor vehicle accident who is entitled to benefits in accordance with the provisions of Section (1) shall be entitled to but one recovery,

in tort or under insurance, for the damages for which benefits are payable under Section (1). To carry out this purpose, the following provisions shall apply:

(a) The existence of a potential cause of action in tort by any recipient of the minimum benefits prescribed in Section (1) shall not obviate the insurer's obligation to pay such benefits promptly, provided, that if prior to the payment by the insurer of such benefits, payment in whole or in part of his loss is received by the recipient from the third person who is or may be liable in tort for such loss, or from his agent or insurer, either by way of advance payment or settlement of the potential liability of such third person, the recipient shall disclose such fact, and may not collect benefits hereunder to the extent that such benefits would produce a duplication of payment or reimbursement of the same loss.

(b) Every insurer licensed to write motor vehicle liability insurance in this state shall be deemed to have agreed as a condition to maintaining such license after the effective date of this Act that: (i) when its insured is or would be held legally liable for such damages for injuries sustained by any person to whom the minimum benefits provided in Section (1) have been paid by another insurer, it will reimburse such other insurer to the extent of such benefits, but not in excess of the amount of damages so recoverable for the types of loss covered by such benefits or in excess of the limits of its liability under its policy and (ii) that the issue of liability for such reimbursement and the amount thereof shall be decided by mandatory, binding, intercompany arbitration procedures approved by the Insurance Commissioner. In any event in which the insurer providing such benefits also has provided coverage to the same policyholder for collision or upset arising out of the same occurrence, such insurer shall also submit the issue of recovery of any payments thereunder to the same mandatory and binding arbitration proceeding as herein provided. Any evidence or decision in the arbitration proceedings shall be privileged and shall not be admissible in any action at law or in equity by any party or parties.

(c) If an insurer has paid benefits required by Section (1) to an insured who is injured by a person not covered by a motor vehicle liability policy issued by an insurer authorized to issue such policies in this state:

(i) The insurer shall be entitled, to the extent of such payment, to the proceeds of any settlement or judgment that may result from the exercise of any rights or recovery of the insured against such motorist legally responsible for the bodily injury because of which such payment is made;

(ii) The insured shall hold in trust, for the benefit of the insurer, all rights of recovery which he shall have against such person because of the damages which are the subject of claim made under this coverage, but only to the extent that such claim is made or paid herein;

(iii) The insured shall do whatever is proper to secure and shall do nothing after loss to prejudice such rights;

(iv) If requested in writing by the insurer, the insured shall take, through any representative not in conflict in interest with the insured, designated by insurer, such action as may be necessary or appropriate to recover such payment as damages from such another person, such action to be taken in the name of the insured, but only to the extent of the payment made hereunder. In the event of a recovery, the insurer shall be reimbursed out of such recovery for expenses, costs and attorney fees incurred by it in connection therewith; and

(v) The insured shall execute and deliver to the insurer such instruments and papers as may be appropriate to secure the rights and obligations of the claimant and the insurer established by this provision.

(5) In addition to the coverages enumerated in Section (1), the insurer shall offer the named insured the option of procuring the following coverages:

(a) *Extended Uninsured Motorist Coverage.* An endorsement which will extend the limits of liability of the uninsured motorist coverage of the insured's policy to the extent of the limits of liability of the insured's bodily injury liability coverage. Such endorsement shall provide that the uninsured motorist coverage, as extended, is not only applicable when the insured is entitled to recover damages from owners or operators of uninsured motor vehicles, but is also applicable when the limits of liability of the liability policy of the owner or operator of an insured motor vehicle are inadequate to provide full compensation for the damages sustained by the insured. -

(b) *Accidental Death Benefits.* An endorsement providing for a sum of at least $5,000 to be paid to the personal representative of the named insured or members of his family residing in his household should injury, sickness or disease resulting from an automobile accident result in death within one year of the accident causing the same.

(6) The amount an insurer is obligated to pay any insured under the policy's bodily injury liability or uninsured motorist coverage shall be reduced by the amount of benefits that insurer paid to said insured or his personal representative under the provision of Section (1) or Section (5)(b) of this statute.

(7) Any insurer may exclude benefits to any insured or his personal representative when the insured's conduct contributed to the injury he sustained in any of the following ways:

(To be determined locally)

(8) Nothing contained in this statute shall be construed as preventing an insurer from providing broader benefits than the minimum benefits enumerated in Sections (1) or (5).

Recommendation 4

That in personal injury claims or actions arising out of motor vehicle accidents, *general damages* should be limited to a multiple of one times the medical expense unless they exceed $500 or unless the injury results in death, dismemberment, permanent total or permanent partial disability, temporary partial disability beyond four weeks duration, serious disfigurement, or loss of impairment of a bodily function.

The position of the Powers' Committee, opposing any restriction on the right to recover general damages (except for its suggestion that a "Quick Settlement Option Plan" be studied and considered) must be reconsidered in light of present circumstances.[26] Plans have been enacted in Puerto Rico, Massachusetts, Florida, New Jersey and Connecticut which bar some innocent accident victims from the right to recover general damages.[27]

Proposals pending in the United States Congress would almost completely eliminate the right to recover general damages from a tortfeasor.[28] A draft of a Uniform Act being prepared for the Department of Transportation by a Special Committee of the National Conference of Commissioners on Uniform State Laws would allow recovery for general damages only in cases of death, permanent significant loss of body function, permanent serious disfigurement, or more than six months of complete inability to work in one's occupation.[29] A plan enacted in Illinois would have limited recovery for general damages, except in serious cases, to percentages of medical specials.[30]

To completely deny recovery for general damages or to allow recovery to some persons and deny it to others based on some arbitrarily selected special damage threshold is inequitable. In fact, a reading of all of the twenty-three preliminary reports and the final report of the Department of Transportation fails to reveal any sound reason for elimination of this element of damages. The arguments for its elimination stress pragmatic reasons—it is too hard to evaluate these damages and their payment costs too much money.

Although the approval of the Powers' Committee Report by the American Bar Association carried with it the strong expression of support for the preservation of the present reparation system it also carried with it support for improvement of the present system. The question which must be asked and answered is whether the system can be preserved and improved without finding a means of improving the process by which general damages are determined in the "smaller" cases.

The main problem cited by critics of the present system with relation to general damages centers around overpayment in the so-called "small case."[31] The "nuisance settlement" has become a fact of life for those insurers who believe it is less expensive in the long run to settle such cases for a little more than they are worth than to pay defense costs. One DOT report showed that claims payments for accident victims with special damages of $500 or less, averaged about four and one-half times the specials, whereas, those with specials of between $5 000 and $10,000 were paid an average of one and one-tenth times their specials.[32]

---

[26] Powers' Report, note 1 *supra*, 154–55.
[27] In Puerto Rico there is a tort exemption of the first $1,000 in general damages. Massachusetts has a $500 medical expense threshold. Florida employs a $1,000 medical expense threshold, New Jersey employs a $200 medical expense threshold but only in cases confined solely to "soft tissue" injury. Connecticut employs a $400 medical expense threshold.
[28] Note 3 *supra*.
[29] *Uniform Motor Vehicle Accident Reparations Act*, note 21 *supra*. § 5(a)(6).
[30] If medical specials are $500 or less no more than 50 percent of the amount of the specials could be recovered as general damages. It would allow recovery of an amount up to 100 percent of the specials over $500. Exceptions to the formula would be allowed if the injury resulted in conditions similar to those in this Committee's proposal. See discussion of constitutional implications of general damage limitations at page 23 *infra*.
[31] *See, e.g.,* O'Connell, *The Injury Industry and The Remedy of No-Fault insurance,* 34–35 (Commerce Clearing House 1971).
[32] DOT Report, Economic Consequences of Automobile Accident Injuries, Vol. 1 at 40 (April 1970).

Our recommendation seeks to control, not eliminate compensation for general damages in the small case. When medical specials are $500 or less, the claimant would not be able to recover more than a sum equal to this medical treatment cost as general damages. Above that amount, the present system would be unchanged. In addition, even if the amount of expenses were below $500, the limitation would not apply if the injury resulted in death, dismemberment, permanent total or permanent partial disability, temporary partial disability beyond four weeks duration, serious disfigurement, or loss or impairment of a bodily function.

It has been estimated that close to eighty percent of auto accident victims sustain economic loss (excluding property damage) of $500 or less.[33] This does not mean that all of those persons would be taken out of the tort system by our proposal. As to general damages all would remain under the tort system. However, for those whose medical specials do not exceed $500 or who do not meet the other "serious" injury exceptions, if fault can be established, their recovery for general damages would be limited.

A formula approach to pain and suffering damages is not perfect. There will be those who will over-utilize medical care in order to reach the $500 amount. This cannot be avoided. However, complete elimination of general damages or the use of thresholds in Massachusetts, Connecticut, New Jersey and Florida are harsh and inequitable alternatives. The Illinois plan's fifty percent limitation when specials are $500 or less is overly restrictive for the smaller case. Its imposition of a one hundred percent limitation when specials exceed $500 is not directed at the "smaller case" where regulation of general damages truly belongs. The other alternative, taking no action with regard to general damages, is unrealistic. Some limitation on the right to recover general damages seems inevitable. The method that is employed should be as equitable as possible. Our proposal presents the best possible alternative.

There are those who will raise a constitutional question as to the propriety of limiting general damages. It should be noted that the limitation found in the Sample Statute differs from the type employed in Illinois which was found unconstitutional by a state trial court.[34] First, the Sample Statute formula applies only to the so-called "small case" in which medical treatment expenses are $500 or less. The Illinois formula applied, across the board, to all cases except those involving death or very serious injury. Second, under the Illinois formula, as interpreted by the trial court, two accident victims with the same type of injuries could receive disproportionate amounts of general damages simply because one sought and was able to afford more expensive medical and hospital care.[35]

Under Subsection (4) of the Sample Statute, the amount actually paid for medical treatment expenses is not determinative of their reasonable value for the purpose of determining the amount of general damages which may be awarded. If a poor person were injured and received medical and hospital care without charge, or at some minimal charge, the reasonable value of the treatment received would be determinative of that person's right to general damages.

From a constitutional standpoint, it must be emphasized again that our proposal does not deny innocent accident victims the right to recover compensation for general damages. The threshold plans established in Connecticut, Florida and Massachusetts do deny recoveries to some accident victims. Although the Supreme Judicial Court of Massachusetts has upheld the constitutionality of that state's plan [36] that decision does not present clear authority for the premise that it is constitutional to deny some accident victims the right to recover general damages and to allow full recovery to others simply because of the amount of their

---

[33] DOT Report, *Automobile Personal injury Claims*, Vol. 1 at 30 (July 1970).
[34] Grace v. Howlett, 71 ch. 4737 (Cir. Ct. Cook Co. Ill., Ill. Co. Dept. Chancery Div. Dec. 29, 1971).
[35] The trial court found that because medical and hospital charges varied within the state and because accident victims with the same types of injuries would not be equally treated by the Illinois formula which, in the court's opinion, looked only to actual charges for the services, the formula ran afoul of the state and federal Equal Protection clauses. This issue, unfortunately, was not considered by the Illinois Supreme Court in affirming the unconstitutionality of the Act. Grace v. Howlett, ___ N.E. 2d ___ (Ill. 1972). For a discussion of the trial court and appellate court decisions, see Kircher, "Illinois No-Fault Issues Remain," 13 *For The Defense* 51 (May 1972).
[36] Pinnick v. Cleary, 271 N.E.2d 592 (Mass. 1971).

respective medical bills.[37] On the other hand, a noted jurist has stated that such an approach is not constitutionally permissible.[38]

We believe that the Sample Statute we have prepared to illustrate our proposal with respect to limitation of general damages for the "small case" will not be subject to the same constitutional problems found by the Illinois trial court. That court did not find fault with the concept of a general damage limitation, but only with the unequal application of the limitation, under the Illinois law.

Sample Statute—Regulation Of Awards For Pain And Suffering

Limitation on general damages

(1) In any action in tort for bodily injury, sickness or disease caused by accident occurring on or after the effective date hereof and arising out of the operation, ownership, maintenance or use of a motor vehicle within this state, the general damages recoverable for pain, suffering, mental anguish, inconvenience and other similar loss shall not exceed a sum equal to the amount of medical treatment expenses incurred by or on behalf of the person suffering the bodily injury, sickness or disease.

(2) The limitation described in (1) shall not apply:

(a) When the reasonable value of the incurred medical treatment expenses exceeds the sum of five hundred dollars, or

(b) When the bodily injury, sickness or disease results in death, dismemberment, permanent total or permanent partial disability, temporary partial disability beyond four weeks' duration, serious disfigurement, or loss or impairment of a bodily function.

(3) As used herein, the term "medical treatment expenses" includes charges for necessary medical, hospital, dental, surgical, ambulance and professional nursing services and prosthetic devices. The term shall also include expenses for any non-medical remedial treatment or care rendered in accordance with a recognized religious method of healing.

(4) Solely for the purpose of determinations under Subsections (1) and (2) (a) hereof, the charges actually made for medical treatment expenses shall not be conclusive as to their reasonable value. Evidence that reasonable value thereof was an amount different than that actually charged shall be admissible in all actions to which this section applies.

FUTURE CONSIDERATIONS

The Special Committee has been continued through the 1972-73 Association year. In the future, in addition to continuing to give consideration to developments in the automobile accident reparations field, the Committee will devote attention to the impact of property damage. It was the Committee's view that it should, at this time, concentrate on the personal injury liability aspect of the problem. In addition to property damage, the Committee will also give more thought to a limited tort exemption and the possible elimination of the principle of subrogation which is favored by two members of the Committee.

FURTHER RECOMMENDATIONS

So that the Committee can fulfill its additional responsibilities "to cooperate with interested sections and committees of the American Bar Association and with state and local bar associations to bring about enactment of legislation to improve automobile accident reparations procedures,"

We Further Recommend

(5) That the American Bar Association reaffirm its support for the recommendations of the special committee on automobile accident reparations, as modified by the foregoing proposals.

---

[37] For an analysis of the incomplete consideration given to the issues by the Massachusetts court see Kircher, note 35 *supra;* see also, "Insurance Law, Constitutionality of No-Fault in Massachusetts." 51 *Marq. L. Rev.* 198 (1971).

[38] Charles S. Desmond, former Chief Judge of the New York Court of Appeals prepared a memorandum under date of April 14, 1972, on the constitutionality of a bill then pending in the New York Senate (S8000) which provided for a $5,000 general damage threshold. Therein he states:

"It is conceivably possible that the state could forbid suits and recoveries for pain and suffering where the injury is so slight as to be considered 'de minimis' but to *forbid suit* unless the bill is $500 or $5,000 or any other amount is to take away from numerous injured persons a common law right of suit for pain and suffering without constitutional justification." (emphasis added)

(6) That persons designated by the president of the American Bar Association be authorized to support the adoption of legislation consistent with these resolutions and to oppose legislation inconsistent with these resolutions before appropriate legislative bodies and other groups.

(7) That the special committee be continued.

Respectfully submitted,

JOHN T. REARDON,
Chairman.
RICHARD W. GALIHER,
JAMES D. GHIARDI,
RAYMOND H. KIERR,
EDWARD W. KUHN,
RAOUL D. MAGANA,
J. DONALD REGNIER.

AUGUST 1972.

AMERICAN BAR ASSOCIATION SPECIAL COMMITTEE ON AUTOMOBILE INSURANCE LEGISLATION

MINORITY REPORT

The first three recommendations of the Special Committee, in which I fully concur, suggesting that

1. Every state have *compulsory liability insurance* in minimum limits for all motor vehicles;
2. *Uninsured motorist coverage* in like amounts be similarly required; and
3. Each of said insurance policies also cover at least two thousand dollars of *economic loss* on a *first-party basis*, constitute a plan that is presently feasible and probably adequate to compensate basically most vehicular accident victims. Adjustment would be primarily on a nonfault basis and the general tort law, thusly supplemented, would remain virtually unchanged.

This minority view is to record disagreement only with the Committee's fourth recommendation [1] that general damages be limited to an equivalent of the medicals unless a monetary medical expense threshold or other combination is met. Such an innovation is least premature, because meaningful statistics are not yet available on the so-called "no-fault plans" experimentally enacted by the legislatures of nine states.[2]

There are other criticisms, some perhaps answerable, concerning Recommendation No. 4.

One may argue tenably that to limit recovery of intangible damages (pain, suffering, anguish, inconvenience, etc.) to any extent at all, *e.g.*, where the medical expenses do not exceed a $500 threshold, is in fact an exclusion from, or at least diminishment of, the tort system and, therefore, is inconsistent with the Powers' Report, as approved in principle by the Association, recommending preservation of the present system with no restriction on the right to recover general damages.[3] The counterproposition is that this does not constitute a tort *exclusion* or a *restriction* on the extent of tort recovery but rather merely *controls* the amount of general damages in the "small" case. Aside from semantics, there seems good reason for apprehension as to whether this proposed modification of the present system would proliferate other exceptions to tort recovery, and whether this seemingly modest monetary threshold, once extant, may be increased readily severalfold by subsequent legislative enactments, first to the "moderate" and then to the "serious" case!

Another critique urged is that equating general damages with medical expense is unjustifiable either in law or in reason and merely constitutes an expedient, because there is no valid connection between the amount expended for medical care and the extent of the victim's pain and suffering. On the other hand, it may be said that this concept is no more offensive than the arbitrary limit now placed on recovery for wrongful death by several states.

---

[1] *Supra*, page 4.
[2] Connecticut, Delaware, Florida, Maryland, Massachusetts, Minnesota, New Jersey, Oregon and South Dakota. (Illinois' statutory plan was declared unconstitutional [see footnote 4, *infra*]; a Tennessee "no-fault" statute was vetoed.)
[3] The Section on Insurance, Negligence and Compensation Law, representing 13,000 of the Association's members, resolved through its Council to disapprove the limitation on general damages contemplated by Recommendation No. 4 (Minutes of Midwinter Meeting, New Orleans, Louisiana, February 5, 1972); this resolution, duly considered by the Special Committee pursuant to its mandate, was not implemented by the majority.

As to the cloud of illegality spawned by the unconstitutionality of Illinois' monetary threshold (keyed to the *actual* medical expenses),[4] Recommendation No. 4 may be salved by using "the reasonable *value* of . . . medical treatment expenses" as a yardstick for measuring general damages up to $500, a statutory distinction that may well make a constitutional difference, albeit a possible strain in logic through attempted correlation of the value of pain to medical costs.

The compelling criticisms of Recommendation No. 4 involve (I) the disadvantage of enacting now such a limiting threshold and abridgement without sufficient experimentation and (II) the inappropriateness of its universal application to all of the states without regard to their individual situations, both of which seem to be valid objections at this time for the following reasons:

I.

The Special Committee has quite properly concluded that a system assuring the motor vehicle accident victim compensation up to $2,000 on a first-party basis, for medical expenses, wage loss and other special damages, indeed would cover the total economic losses of the vast majority of all such claimants.[5] And, of course, such first-party insurance would pay a substantial portion of the economic losses of many of the remainder.

It is the considered judgment of many actuaries and other knowledgeable persons in the insurance industry, as well as of legislators who have studied and acted on the question, that for all practical purposes such payment via first-party economic loss insurance would take virtually 95% of all automobile injury claims out of the present tort system; this would be accomplished, they believe, without any limitation or diminution of the right to recover general damages. The underlying pragmatic reasons are simple: Most "small" claimants would not be motivated to sue for general damages if they had already recouped their economic losses; among the litigious few who would seek their day in court some may balk at paying cash retainers when counsel hesitates to accept contingent fee employment to handle a claim for pain and suffering alone without concomitant economic losses; or there may be disenchantment for potential plaintiffs at the prospect of a primary insurer claiming subrogation off the top of award.[6]

Persuaded that these projections are accurate, several experienced automobile insurance companies are currently offering first-party coverage for loss of wages at a low additional premium commensurate with that charged for medical payment coverage; in fact, recently one major insurance company voluntarily extended its medical payment coverage to include wage loss by like amount with no increase in premium. It would be well to wait and determine if the actuarial calculations are accurate, before making the initial gesture (small though it may be) contemplated by Recommendation No. 4 to abridge the extent of tort recovery for general damages. Could a first step in that direction lead to complete abrogation of the tort system for automobile accident reparations? If that is the issue, it deserves clear definition and confrontation.

The conservative course is to abide developments in the States of Maryland, Oregon, Delaware and South Dakota, where nonfault plans without limitation of general damages have been enacted.[7] These four states, out of nine with plans, may test prove that compulsory first-party insurance coverage for all economic losses in moderate limits will serve to alleviate court congestion and to remedy alleged overpayment and other problems attributed to the lesser cases, at least in some of the states. If this is so, then the Committee's first three recommendations should suffice, and Recommendation No. 4 may be overdesigning the plan.

---

[4] Grace v. Howlett. 71 Ch. 4737 (Cir. Ct. 1971); *aff'd*, —— N.E. 2d —— (Ill. S. Ct. 1972).

[5] "Department of Transportation study, 'Motor Vehicle Losses and Their Compensation in the United States,' published in March of 1971 . . . showed that 96 percent of paid personal injuries claimants suffered $2,500 or less in direct economic loss to the date of settlement." Report No. 92-891 of the Senate Committee on Commerce on S. 945, 92nd Congress, June 20, 1972, p. 89.

[6] The experience in Delaware during the first three months of its nonfault insurance program indicates that "without a base of tangible damages to support them a great many pain and suffering cases would probably not be brought at all." *Id.*, Report No. 92-891, p. 103. The projection for six months promises that claims frequency may be cut in half in Delaware.

[7] First-party nonfault insurance is not novel, having been available to the automobile owner in the forms of collision, medical payment, fire, theft, vandalism, glass breakage and comprehensive coverages. (Uninsured motorist liability coverage also has demonstrated the practicability of first-party indemnification.) The innovations have been: extension of one's own policy to cover economic losses; and making the entire program compulsory.

II.

Lastly, it is respectfully suggested that universal application of Recommendation No. 4 to every state may be neither necessary nor desirable. Thresholds, which create costing problems, may be palatable in a highly congested area and be totally inappropriate in a low-density rural state.

Uniformity, whether by state or by federal enactment, may be undesirable, if not unnecessary, at this time, thereby outweighing its usual advantages. Individual states have separate problems requiring different solutions. The impact of the automobile in Massachusetts is different than in Idaho.[8]

General application of the fourth recommendation should be deferred, for optimum benefit from the nonfault experiments underway.

RAYMOND H. KIERR.

Mr. VAN DEERLIN. Thank you. You very ably summarized your longer statement.

The thrust, I take it, is not opposition on principle to the Federal approach, but the caution that we need more information about what the States have done and are doing?

Mr. ALLEN. I think the chairman goes a little farther than I would care to go by saying that we are not opposed to Federal no-fault.

Mr. VAN DEERLIN. Well, I caught that proviso of yours; "at this time," you said.

Mr. ALLEN. Certainly at this time we do not have enough information to barely inform ourselves concerning whether Federal legislation would ever begin.

Mr. VAN DEERLIN. You do not at this time say that nor at any time in the future say that?

Mr. ALLEN. That would be beyond my place.

Mr. VAN DEERLIN. We have the inconvenience of conducting our hearings while the House is in session. I have to leave, and I will be as swift as possible if you will excuse me.

[Brief recess.]

Mr. VAN DEERLIN. Mr. Kinzler.

Mr. KINZLER. Thank you, Mr. Chairman.

Mr. Allen, on page 4 of your statement you say that California is debating no-fault now and will be debating it in the fall.

Mr. ALLEN. That is my understanding.

Mr. KINZLER. That is correct. I gather this comment is in support of your contention that States are actively considering no-fault?

Mr. ALLEN. That is one area.

Mr. KINZLER. Are you aware whether this is the first time that California considered no-fault?

Mr. ALLEN. I am confident that it is not.

Mr. VAN DEERLIN. Be careful what you say about California.

Mr. KINZLER. I have to handle this one gently. In fact, we have a chart which indicates to us that California first considered no-fault reform back in 1967. I wonder, since this is the ninth time we are going at it, whether this does not argue in favor of Federal standards no-fault?

---

[8] Concerning the results and validity thus far of the pioneer "no-fault" plan in Massachusetts, there is indeed a divergence of views. The Insurance Commissioner and some news media express accolades. But the state's ranking congressman is highly critical of the entire concept. (See *The National Underwriter*, June 9, 1972.) There is also marked polarization of opinion as to whether "no-fault" programs will result ultimately in increased premiums.

Mr. ALLEN. No, I think it argues in favor of the very real complexity of the problem and the difficulty in finding legislation which meets the requirements of the citizens of the several States.

Mr. KINZLER. In the same portion of your testimony, in connection with this point, you state you agree with Secretary Coleman's June 17 statement that a "reasonable time" has not yet run.

Do you also agree with the Secretary's statement that 2 to 5 years more would constitute a reasonable time? The basis for his statement was that the States would then have 6 to 10 years to consider no-fault.

Mr. ALLEN. I think perhaps any assessment of a period of time is arbitrary and I wouldn't necessarily agree with his 2 to 5.

Mr. KINZLER. Or 10 to 15?

Mr. ALLEN. It might be, or 6 months to 2 years; I don't know.

Mr. KINZLER. Thank you. On page 5 of your statement you cite ratemaking as an item which can more accurately be evaluated by individual States. Could you please tell the subcommittee how H.R. 1900 or H.R. 8441 would restrict State regulation of ratemaking?

Mr. ALLEN. I am not confident I can answer your question from analysis of the bill. I feel ratemaking will not be reflective of the individual State problems if a federally enacted legislation imposes certain types of insurance coverage upon the several States, their ability to be flexible in the ratemaking then being inhibited, in my judgment.

Mr. KINZLER. But they could still rate on the basis of frequency of accidents, and in the case of no-fault, on the amount of the potential loss as well. I don't understand how that would differ from traditional ratemaking.

Mr. ALLEN. Again, the type of—just to give an example, my daughter went to school in Colorado and I brought her an automobile—I put a down payment on it—and brought some insurance, and I was quite surprised to find the comprehensive portion of the coverage was quite high in Colorado compared to my own. The frequency of landslides and snowstorms in Illinois is substantially different from that in Colorado, I was told, and I don't—or that kind of ratemaking problem it seems to me is emphasized by a Federal requirement that you have thus and thus in the way of coverage.

Mr. KINZLER. Well, I don't see how a landslide would affect you if you have to have unlimited medical coverage.

Mr. ALLEN. Obviously I am making a corollary statement because unfortunately no one has yet to evolve a scheme which would cover the most difficult problem in automobile accidents, and that is the property damages, which is the highest portion of the coverage, the most difficult with which to wrestle from an insurance company's standpoint and from a consumer's standpoint certainly the most troublesome part of the automobile accident.

Mr. KINZLER. There does not seem to be too much of a ratemaking problem with respect to bodily injury as we are dealing with this legislation.

Mr. ALLEN. Again I will not concede your point because I am not fully informed concerning provisions of H.R. 1900.

Mr. KINZLER. On page 6 of your statement you say that a host of new questions now warrant investigation on the basis of State experience and you cite questions on jury attitude toward tort victims and the financing of third-party actions by first-party payments.

Aren't these problems arising in States with low medical thresholds and ones that would not apply in the H.R. 1900 situation where the thresholds are significantly higher?

Mr. ALLEN. I don't think so. I think the attitude respecting problems of limits of jury verdicts, for example, is engendered by a multitude of areas of concern, and I don't see H.R. 1900 as being any different from anything else, any other no-fault system, insofar as gaging what an individual juror will have as his attitude toward verdicts after he knows that the basic amounts have been paid.

Mr. KINZLER. Well, under H.R. 1900 the only residual tort in title II would be in death cases, 90 days of disability, permanent and serious injury or disfigurement. I can't quite understand how a jury would have a different attitude toward those particular items than they do presently as compared to the real problem you raise with respect to an area like Florida where you have a $1,000 medical threshold and maybe the jury thinks a person with $1,500 of loss is more deserving, but that is a different situation.

Mr. ALLEN. Well, again by analogy, in my own State we have a structural work act which entitles a victim of a certain type of accident to file suit even though he may be covered by workmen's compensation, The jurors are inclined to feel, from my analysis of their reporting to me, they are inclined to feel, I know he has his workmen's compensation I know his basic rights have been covered; he must have been horribly hurt and must have a lot of damages in order to be able to sue, therefore I must reward him with a high verdict.

Mr. KINZLER. The threshold of H.R. 1900 by definition is dealing only with the very seriously injured.

Mr. ALLEN. Well, of course, you are presuming that you can define the very seriously injured.

Mr. KINZLER. I don't have to.

Mr. ALLEN. I have not seen any definition which I would accept.

Mr. KINZLER. What would you object to in the definition I just stated to you?

Mr. ALLEN. I think any arbitrary definition of what constitutes a horrible injury is not feasible.

Mr. KINZLER. Let's go through them one-by-one. Death obviously is a horrible injury.

Mr. ALLEN. Maybe it is and maybe it is not. From an economic standpoint, the death of an 8-year-old child—it costs more to raise a child than you get in terms of economic benefits, therefore, there is a disparity there.

Mr. KINZLER. So you wouldn't argue under the existing tort system in favor of suits for the death of an 8-year-old girl, is that right?

Mr. ALLEN. I have argued with some success, I will immodestly state, that the benefits arising to the survivors from the death of an 8-year-old child, benefits—perhaps that is an improper or difficult choice of words, but I am sure you know what I mean.

Mr. KINZLER. This legislation in fact wouldn't affect, as I said, the tort remedy where your argument would be relevant, and all it would do would be to allow the States a reasonable amount of survivor's benefits, reasonable being as low as $1,000 worth of benefits, so you are not adding an awful lot more.

On page 10, you talk about the impact of bodily injury on today's amount of insurance and you cited a 1974 DOT study listing a number of other items having a much greater impact on the consumer's pocketbook. Are you making a de minimis argument here that bodily injury premiums don't mean that much?

Mr. ALLEN. I don't think I am making a de minimis argument so much as trying to put a proper connotation on just what it means to a buyer of automobile insurance to have no-fault benefits made available to him in terms of the reduction of premiums, the amount which he must pay for premiums.

I have an example. I just paid my automobile premium the other day. I think it was $442. Everything is cheaper in Peoria. But if they had given me all of the coverage which would be affected by no-fault insurance, premiums still would have been $278 or something like that, so it is a small part, about a third.

Mr. KINZLER. $150 or so reduction?

Mr. ALLEN. Yes, if they gave it to me, which they are certainly not.

Mr. KINZLER. The reason I question that is it is difficult to play with figures.

Mr. ALLEN. Of course it is.

Mr. KINZLER. Two cents a minute does not sound like very much by the minute, but it adds up over a lifetime. The bodily injury premiums for this country are somewhere over the $6 billion figure annually and I think that is a pretty high level of money we are dealing with.

Mr. ALLEN. Certainly it is, and we are also dealing with the rights which people have and for which they are willing to pay. It seems to me that it is difficult to separate one from the other.

Mr. KINZLER. I am not trying to separate them, but I want to make sure you are not arguing it is not a significant amount of money we are dealing with.

Mr. ALLEN. Of course it is a significant amount.

Mr. KINZLER. On page 12 of your statement you say that the average rate projections in S. 354 and H.R. 1900 would occasion a redistribution of premium costs which would be favorable to the high-risk motorist and a detriment to the low-risk motorist. Could you tell me exactly how it works, please?

Mr. ALLEN. Well, when you spread the risk in the fashion which these bills do, the high-risk motorist who has been paying a high premium is—or the experience in New York seems to indicate—is getting his premium reduced more in terms of percentages and more in terms of dollars than is the low-risk driver.

Mr. KINZLER. When you say "the poorest driver is the high risk," would you consider people in the assigned risk plan the highest risk or amongst the highest risks?

Mr. ALLEN. Well, one of the whole difficulties with the problem is the inability to reduce it to meaningful statistics or data outside of the abstract. Certainly many assigned risk pool members are high-risk drivers. When my son was 19 years old he was as careful a driver as I was. I don't think he was a high-risk driver, but the insurance pool treated him that way.

Mr. KINZLER. So even though he was a good driver, he had to pay more for insurance. Is this an equitable system that does that?

Mr. ALLEN. Not for him; it was not equitable.

Mr. KINZLER. You see, under a no-fault system your son at 19 would have to pay a premium based on only his potential wage loss and accident frequency rate and pay exactly what he deserves to pay. You can't do that now.

Mr. ALLEN. If he had a motorcycle?

Mr. KINZLER. The reason I asked about assigned risk plans is that 62 percent of the assigned risk applicants in the State of New York in 1969 enjoyed clean driving records, so I find it a little difficult to say that we are going to benefit the poor drivers.

Mr. ALLEN. Again, when you say that they have clean driving records, yes; but the 19-year-old, according to the insurance company statistics with which I am provided, is a high-risk driver, as is the 75-year-old.

Mr. KINZLER. But your son was not, and he paid for the average of everyone else.

Mr. ALLEN. Certainly, as I paid for many averages.

Mr. KINZLER. Would you prefer a system where if your son were a good driver he could pay less?

Mr. ALLEN. No.

Mr. KINZLER. And another kid who was a bad driver, he could pay more?

Mr. ALLEN. I don't think it necessarily follows.

Mr. KINZLER. What I am suggesting is under a no-fault system you would pay both for the potential wage loss and frequency of accidents. Under the existing system if a man is earning $50,000 he has to pay an insurance premium based upon the possibility of hitting the average driver in the area, with a potential work loss of $12,000, and the man with $5,000 income has to pay exactly the same premium as the man with the $50,000 income.

All we are saying is with no-fault we can bring those into line with the potential loss but we don't eliminate the difficulty with the bad driver, his premium could still be raised if he had a lot of accidents, that he causes.

Mr. ALLEN. Nothing you can do with no-fault or any type of no-fault I have seen would obviate the fact that the loss of a couple of fingers to Van Cliburn would mean a lot more to him than to me.

Mr. KINZLER. We are not talking about Mr. Van Cliburn but about everyone, and that is what we have to deal with.

Mr. ALLEN. Well, he is one that we have to deal with.

Mr. KINZLER. I gather from your statement you find Allstate's cost projections more reliable than State Farm's.

Mr. ALLEN. I find it difficult to accept either one of them because neither is based upon experience.

Mr. KINZLER. So you would not support any part of that?

Mr. ALLEN. I think it is important to realize that when—well, comparing State Farm and Allstate, my understanding is that the two companies had differing opinions respecting no-fault before the studies were done. I understand that the Milliman & Robertson study was commissioned by people who had ideas concerning no-fault.

I am not suggesting any one of the three as reasons for my conclusion, but I am saying that no one of the three is based upon experience.

Mr. KINZLER. All three, one an independent study, one by a supporter of Federal no-fault, and one by an opponent of Federal no-fault, all, if you bring those assumptions in line, come to within percentage points of one another.

Mr. ALLEN. I question the use of the word "independent."

Mr. KINZLER. Well, the National Association of Insurance Commissioners and the Department of Transportation were given a mandate to find an independent actuary and succeeded. Why are they not independent? They were not paid by an interested party.

Mr. ALLEN. I try law suits constantly. I have seen the bills which provide for independent medical examination and the minute the doctor makes an examination he becomes a protagonist for the patient he takes, therefore he loses his independence. I am only quarreling with the use of that word. I am suggesting to you that all three studies are projections, surmise, if you will, and no one of them is based upon any experience in the application of a no-fault concept to a particular State: which type of experience I should think the Congress would like to see before they engaged in this field.

Mr. KINZLER. One very minor methodological point: The other day we were told the way to determine the overall costs to the average consumer in this country, if given a particular cost projection State by State, would be to add up the plus 5 percent for one State, the minus 4 for another, and so forth, and divide by 50. Would you accept that methodology?

Mr. ALLEN. I am afraid I would not.

Mr. KINZLER. You would not, OK. That was the approach Mr. Spangenberg suggested to us the other day.

Mr. ALLEN. Mr. Spangenberg and I have many differences with respect to automobile accident injury cases and the like.

Mr. KINZLER. OK.

Mr. ALLEN. Don't misunderstand me. He is a fine lawyer and a splendid gentleman. But we are just on opposite sides of the table.

Mr. KINZLER. There is no question about his being a fine gentleman and lawyer.

With respect to the suggested tort reforms of the American Bar Association, you talked about such things as the change from contributory negligence to comparative negligence.

Mr. ALLEN. I think something like 25 or 26 States have made that change.

Mr. KINZLER. I think it is up to 32 now. They are making that change rather rapidly. You did not talk about abolition of guest statutes because in 1972 you indicated that would be too costly to the consumer, but it would leave passengers in guest statute States in pretty bad shape if they were hurt.

Mr. ALLEN. I might add with respect to your example of comparative negligence, there is comparative negligence and comparative negligence too; Wisconsin versus Mississippi, for example.

Mr. KINZLER. Again, you did not include abolition of guest statutes in your suggested reforms, did you?

Mr. ALLEN. I think that is correct. I did not review those, although I might add most States, if my understanding is correct, have already eliminated them.

Mr. KINZLER. Still not a majority, if I am correct.

Mr. ALLEN. Again, those things change so rapidly.

Mr. KINZLER. Third is removal of statutory limits on recovery for wrongful death.

Fourth is universal compulsory automobile liability insurance with mandatory uninsured coverage.

Fifth, you suggest an increase in minimum liability from 10 to 20 to 15 to 30. If we take the last one and change it from 15 to 30 to 50 and 100, and include the abolition of guest statutes, which I think would be a reasonable package for taking care of some of the problems, let me suggest to you I have some figures, which I will be delighted to supply you with, that show that the average increase in costs of such a plan as is described would be 53 percent in metropolitan areas and 58 percent on the average and 65 percent in the rural areas. Now my question from that is exactly this:

If we admit, or if you admit, and maybe you don't, there are some real serious problems with the existing system, we have to look toward some forms of reform, and I am suggesting that your tort reforms, which I would agree with within the existing systems, do not come for nothing. They are going to cost the consumer some money.

Mr. ALLEN. Well, I suppose it is an old argument, but we "don't throw the baby out with the bath water." We think that the existing tort system can be reformed to the effect that more people will benefit in more ways without the restrictions of rights and the increased costs of Federal no-fault.

I have trouble with the type of figures that you present because those again are somebody's estimate based upon what he thinks might happen if certain things took place.

Mr. KINZLER. That is the only way we can estimate, isn't it?

Mr. ALLEN. Well, that is one of the reasons why I quarrel with estimating, when we can have this available to us.

Mr. KINZLER. It is based also on actual experience of States who made those revisions.

Mr. ALLEN. I find it difficult to bring that into focus in the light of the fact that the increase from basic limits to more substantial limits to the average automobile driver is not very great.

Mr. KINZLER. It is not very great on an absolute level, but it is on a percentage level, and I will supply the figures for you.

Again, the point is that if we have a choice between a system which would cost about 50 percent more and still be slow in delivering benefits and an S. 354 approach which, according to the Senate staff for example, would cost 11 percent less in the State of Illinois, cover 26 percent more people and pay 39 percent more benefits, I suggest there is no comparison between the two systems.

Mr. ALLEN. Mr. Kinzler, your question presupposes a theory that the consuming public are dissatisfied with the methods of payments and the quickness of payments. I try law suits and I don't try many automobile cases any more because there are not many any more.

The insurance companies with their prepayments and the settlement arbitration systems and the like have obviated a lot of the tort litigation which was prevalent 25 years ago when I first started to practice.

The people whom I see as being victims of automobile accidents who are beneficiaries of the tort system in that they are filing suits almost always have their basic bills paid. I don't understand that there is the type of clamor which your question presupposes to exist.

Mr. KINZLER. Well, the Department of Transportation study still tells us that people with economic losses of $25,000 or more with the right to sue in tort only recover 30 percent of their economic losses. It seems to me that speaks for itself.

Mr. ALLEN. Well, again I have trouble in taking statistics of that kind. As we say in the country, "I don't know none of them people."

Mr. KINZLER. Thank you very much.

Mr. ALLEN. Thank you.

Mr. VAN DEERLIN. Mr. Scheuer of New York has just joined us. Mr. Scheuer, any questions?

Mr. SCHEUER. Mr. Allen, I was very much interested in your remarks. I am impressed with the consistent position that the American Bar Association has taken in support of the general concept of no-fault, and you make clear that they have on repeated occasions, both the special committee and the Bar Association itself, endorsed the principle of no-fault, the basic no-fault concept, as you say on page 2.

You go further than that and you have set up a special committee to monitor and evaluate new developments.

Mr. ALLEN. I have been a member of that committee and appeared in that connection.

Mr. SCHEUER. You cite that the ABA won't be satisfied until all States have taken appropriate action.

You go further and recommend some minimum standards for each of the States, right?

Mr. ALLEN. Yes, sir.

Mr. SCHEUER. And you are going to monitor what happens. You are four square on the principle of no-fault, you recommend it ought to be adopted by all States and you recommend minimum standards and you set up a monitoring capability.

Now why would you object if this committee and this Congress urged all States to set up some kind of no-fault, set some kind of minimum standard, perhaps very close to yours, and gave some encouragement in terms of cost sharing of the administration of the system; and then supposing this committee were to do more or less what you are doing; set up some kind of capability of monitoring the experience, you can exhort the States to pass no-fault but we can do a little better than that.

Mr. ALLEN. That is one of the problems, Mr. Scheuer.

Mr. SCHEUER. I am not sure we will want to require them, and maybe we will, maybe we will just head up some financial incentives to help relieve the pain of setting up the administrative mechanism.

But if you say all States should do it and if you are willing to set on paper minimum standards you would recommend, and then set up your own monitoring capabilities, how, consistent with that, can you object to the Congress requiring States to set up the same things that you are urging them to do, with the same kind of minimum standards more or less that you are urging them to adopt and with the same kind of monitoring capability you yourself are playing a lending role in carrying out in a very constructive and useful fashion?

What is wrong with the Government saying, "If this is what is going to be done, we are the logical body to do it"; and at the end of 4 or 5 or 6 years we can go through the same reevaluation process you are obviously going through in a very thoughtful and constructive way, and all together come to some conclusions as to how it works?

Mr. ALLEN. I find a major difference between the recommendations of associations such as ours and the imposition of a legislative fiat by the Congress. I do not think that the experience factor has been allowed to be a part of the consideration.

Mr. SCHEUER. Now, hold the phone, hold the phone. I am not saying how far we would go in detail. We might not go much further than you go, but you seem to have enough experience to give us some considerable rules of thumb as to what the minimum standard ought to be.

Mr. ALLEN. We are quite willing to admit we might be wrong.

Mr. SCHEUER. Sure.

Mr. ALLEN. But if you are wrong, it is not going to get changed as easily as it will if we say that "We admit we are wrong." Utah has adopted one law and South Carolina another, and it might be found to be more beneficial to adopt South Carolina's law. It would be far easier to change Utah's than to change an entire Federal structure with all of the cost factors that go into implementation of it.

Mr. SCHEUER. Well, the entire Federal structure might very well be not much different from the structure that the ABA is taking?

Mr. ALLEN. Again, we might both be wrong.

Mr. SCHEUER. It is possible, but, you know, we have been in business for 199 years and we are quite capable of seeing where changing conditions and insurance, changing circumstances, but the history of our legislation has indicated we restructure it and take a little different tack.

We are doing it every day in the week on hundreds and hundreds of laws. We are carrying on oversight about how the laws work, and we are in a constant process of evolving and changing laws to meet changing conditions and changing perceptions and changing needs. There is nothing new about that.

Mr. ALLEN. I find nothing in what I read and what I study and what the ABA has been able to put together, which would indicate a necessity for a uniform system of laws respecting automobile accidents throughout the States.

Mr. SCHEUER. Nobody is suggesting that.

Mr. ALLEN. I think the State problems ought to be for the States.

Mr. SCHEUER. You have suggested a uniform system to the extent you suggested certain minimum standards. What would be wrong with the Federal Government saying here, "We are going to encourage the States to set up no-fault. We are going to absorb a certain percent of their administrative costs and do other things to help them," and we think these are certain minimum standards more or less as the kind you indicated, up or down a little bit, no difference.

We want State administered maximum flexibility, and we are going to fund a constant review and reappraisal mechanism just as your ABA has funded apparently, and at the end of—well, to monitor and evaluate these developments, as you say here, and at the end of a stated period of time, we will have a comprehensive review and have hearings and call in Mr. Allen representing the ABA to get his perceptions as to how these 50 State plans have worked, also, to try to isolate the elements in the State plans that seem to be useful and constructive and other elements that do not seem to work so well, and maybe in 5 years we can put together a model piece of State no-fault legislation or Federal no-fault, for that matter. But what is wrong with us mandating what you say is desirable?

Mr. ALLEN. I can't find the necessity for Federal intervention in this field. I think that the States are accomplishing that which the ABA recommends, not that there is magic in our recommendation.

Mr. SCHEUER. Over half of them have not. What is wrong with our accelerating that process?

Mr. ALLEN. I think, within a very few years since the problem has been apparent, the fact that half of them have is more important than the fact that half of them have not.

Mr. SCHEUER. Well, I suppose it is based on whether the glass is half empty or half full. I think it is perfectly obvious that considerable progress has been made, but I don't know why we should not have a bigger experimental laboratory, let us say. Why should we not provide more incentive and more support for States to pass some kind of no-fault with minimum standards and then let's all sit back and evaluate what happens and have a period on which we can reflect on the experience that is taking place and then, as I say, isolate the elements that seem to be working very well and isolate the ones that do not seem to be meeting the needs of the times and say, 4 or 5 years from now, we can put together a comprehensive bill based upon 50 States' experience rather than 24.

It seems to me you lead us right up to the well. You want every State to participate. You believe fundamentally in the basic principles of no-fault. You, yourself, are willing to recommend certain minimum standards, and if all of those things are true, why should not Congress accept Mr. Allen's views and say, "OK, we accept the view of the bar association that all States should participate; we accept their view that no-fault is right; we accept their view that certain minimum standards are justified now, and here are some incentives and here are some supports, go ahead and do it and we will come back and talk to you in another 4 or 5 years and see where we have come out?"

You have taken us to the well, but you have not let us drink.

Mr. ALLEN. I am more fallible, perhaps, than the Congress, and the fact I recommend it does not mean necessarily I am right or the ABA is right.

I think we have a fundamental difference in accepting the question of whether or not this is a matter which necessitates the extremely high costs and legislative fiat of Federal intervention.

Mr. SCHEUER. What is the extremely high cost of Federal legislation?

Mr. ALLEN. Well, I think it was my friend from Missouri whose estimates—and, again, these are only estimates of the cost of implementation on these bills—is something like $10 million.

Mr. SCHEUER. Pardon?

Mr. ALLEN. Something like $10 million—you are going to have to hire people. You are going to have to print forms and hire people and send them out on the road to, say, fly to Oregon or California.

Mr. SCHEUER. How much is it going to cost?

Mr. ALLEN. I have no idea. I heard an estimate of $10 million, and I think it is a very conservative figure.

Mr. SCHEUER. We have a country with 210 million inhabitants. What are you talking about, one nickel a head?

I don't think 5 cents a head is too much for comprehensive—I mean, considering the moneys that we have really wasted in an egregiously foolish fashion.

Mr. ALLEN. I don't think wasting another nickel helps it.

Mr. VAN DEERLIN. As a spokesman for economy, I might point out, the bill principally under consideration authorizes $500,000. That might not be the last word, of course.

Mr. SCHEUER. I would think the ABA would not think a $10 million price tag on a useful national program is too high a price to pay, 5 cents a head.

I don't consider that a real answer to my question, frankly. You are leading us up to the well, but you won't let us take a drink. And I still don't understand why.

If we agree on the basic concept of no-fault as being a valid one and if you agree on certain minimum standards being valid and agree that all States should participate, how could you tell us that we should not act?

Mr. ALLEN. Because I believe the matter of automobile regulation, insurance regulation, to be a State matter and not a matter for the Federal Government.

Mr. SCHEUER. And we would agree with you. It is basically a State matter, but you would agree that certain mimimum standards are justifiable now with the present state of our knowledge.

I don't know why you would not like to see Congress apply the kind of structure that you have recommended, State action with minimum standards, uniformly carried out by all of the States and then a period of study and observation.

Mr. ALLEN. If you say we reached the water and have not got our feet wet, you and I have a basic difference on whether it is a matter for Federal legislation. And I think it is not.

Mr. SCHEUER. Thank you very much.

Mr. VAN DEERLIN. Ms. Nord tells me that, having been led to the well, she is going to refrain from drinking on this round.

Mr. ALLEN. Which is my misfortune.

Mr. VAN DEERLIN. Now, again, we have to answer the bells. I hope we can persuade Mr. Scheuer to rejoin the group after voting. We have an intersting witness from Texas coming up and several others.

Mr. SCHEUER. I came to do you homage on your birthday.

Mr. VAN DEERLIN. If I let you out, will you come back?

[Brief recess.]

Mr. VAN DEERLIN. Mr. Jeffers, who is representing the State Bar of Texas at all levels, I persume.

Will you proceed, Mr. Jeffers?

STATEMENT OF LEROY JEFFERS, PAST PRESIDENT, STATE BAR OF TEXAS, AND CHAIRMAN, COORDINATING COMMITTEE OF STATE BAR PRESIDENTS

Mr. JEFFERS. Mr. Chairman and gentlemen of the committee, I am Leroy Jeffers, the past-president of the State Bar of Texas, which is a statutory agency of the Judicial Department of the Government of the State of Texas, of which all of the more than 25,000 licensed lawyers in Texas are members.

I also appear as chairman of the Coordinating Committee of State Bar Presidents, which was formed in 1972, for the purpose of urging before the House of Delegates of the American Bar Association total opposition to Federal automobile no-fault legislation.

The State Bar of Texas, on four separate occasions during the past 4 years—in each year, by unanimous action of the 30-member board of directors, who are popularly elected by written mail ballot by the lawyers in their respective geographic districts—has gone on record officially as opposing totally and unremittingly Federal intervention in this field of tort law, which has traditionally belonged to the States.

The Coordinating Committee of State Bar Presidents, which was formed by 37 State Bars in the year 1972, takes that same position. I speak for them both here today in voicing that opposition, which we have previously expressed last year before this same committee and on several occasions before the Senate Commerce Committee and the Senate Judiciary Committee.

The opposition of the State Bar of Texas and the Coordinating Committee of State Bar Presidents to Federal intervention in this traditionally State law tort field is grounded upon the fact that it can only be viewed as the first great step towards the closing of the doors of the courthouses of this country to citizens to pursue full remedy for complete relief for wrongful injuries inflicted upon their person or upon their property. We know that with the enactment of a bill under which Federal authority would effectively preempt and displace State authority in the field of no-fault legislation that waiting in the wings as the next step is Federal malpractice no-fault, the next step is Federal products liability no-fault and the final step, as frankly envisioned by Professor Jeffrey O'Connell, who along with Professor Robert Keeton, conceived the Federal no-fault concept or idea, is enterprise no-fault, any injury to person or property resulting from any enterprise.

It is the first great step towards replacing, with a Federal administrative or bureaucratic procedure, the open doors of State courthouses to our citizens for the pursuit of full remedy, full relief, for injuries inflicted upon them.

Now, we further earnestly urge upon this committee that constitutional objection to this legislation cannot be swept under the rug, however distinguished the hand that seeks to sweep it there. When you have denied to this isolated, segregated group of our citizens, the innocent victims of automobile injuries, when you have denied to them any remedy, any reparations for physical pain and suffering of the bodies of these human beings, as the Federal no-fault bills, with the exception of the bill sponsored by the gentleman from Texas, Mr. Eckhardt, would uniformly do, you have denied them constitutional rights. H.R. 1900, as a counterpart of S. 354 in the Senate, except in the extreme circumstances of death, serious and permanent disability or disfigurement, or more than 90 days of continuous total disability, will say:

> There will be wiped out for automobile accident victims, the innocent victims of the drunken, doped up, or simply negligent driver, any recovery for the pain and suffering which a person may sustain bodily.

Now, you can't eliminate constitutional objections to segregating and isolating and invidiously discriminating against this group of citizens by saying to them that "you alone, out of the whole body of the negligently injured people, will be substantially denied any reparations, any remedy for pain and suffering."

Mr. SCHEUER. May I ask you a question?

Mr. JEFFERS. Surely, sir.

Mr. SCHEUER. What is your position on the 24 States that have passed State no-fault insurance laws?

Mr. JEFFERS. Generally speaking, those 24 States have not eliminated recovery for pain and suffering. Some of them have, but most of them have not.

My own State of Texas is included in that number. We enacted a mandatory offering of $2,500 minimum first party coverage. We abolished along with it contributory negligence and the guest statute and enacted comparative negligence. But there has been no abolition of recovery for pain and suffering.

Indeed, the position of the American Bar Association, which was taken by the House of Delegates, is against abolition of the recovery for pain and suffering.

Mr. SCHEUER. But you do have a no-fault law in Texas?

Mr. JEFFERS. We have a no-fault law in the sense that we have a mandatory offering provision that requires the offering of $2,500 for first party coverage, but it does not bar the recovery for nonecomomic damages.

Mr. SCHEUER. What was the position of the Texas Bar Association on that piece of legislation?

Mr. JEFFERS. The State bar of Texas sponsored that piece of legislation. It is, or it was enacted under the sponsorship of the State bar of Texas, as was, indeed, the repeal of contributory negligence and the guest statute and adoption of comparative negligence. It was all a part of the State bar legislative program.

Mr. SCHEUER. You have limited to a considerable extent the rights of citizens under the hallowed canons of Anglo-Saxon common law.

Mr. JEFFERS. We closed the court to no one. You can bring the same suits you could have brought before the statutes were enacted.

Mr. SCHEUER. You closed the door to the defendant to the extent he can't allege contributory negligence, and you have limited rights under the canons of Anglo-Saxon common law. You have certainly taken away their rights.

Mr. JEFFERS. It is a far cry, sir, to say you are going to change some of the rules of substantive law that govern recovery and saying we are going to bar you from any recovery.

Mr. SCHEUER. Has any member of the committee suggested that?

Mr. JEFFERS. Your bill, sir, bars any recovery for pain and suffering, except under the most extreme circumstances, and that is a provision of H.R. 1900 and it is a provision of S. 354 and it is a provision of all of the no-fault bills with the exception of that of the gentleman from Texas.

Mr. SCHEUER. While you are stating this, look, you are in favor of some kind of no-fault insurance; OK. You, yourself, from the State of Texas, with the support of the Texas Bar Association, have substantially interfered with the rights of parties, the rights that they held under the ancient canons of Anglo-Saxon law. You have already breached that, right?

Mr. JEFFERS. We have enlarged their rights, not diminished them.

Mr. SCHEUER. You have diminished the rights of defendants, if I remember right. You know, I went to law school, too, and if you say a defendant cannot plead contributory negligence on the part of the plaintiff, you sure as hell breached his rights and diminished his rights, is that true?

Mr. JEFFERS. I don't agree.

Mr. SCHEUER. Have you not diminished the rights of defendants when you take away a major plea in defense he can make under Anglo-Saxon law?

Mr. JEFFERS. It is not a right, this has at all times been subject to legislative control. There was no vested right in contributory negligence ever.

Mr. SCHEUER. There is legislative control in England, and for hundreds of years a defendant could plead contributory negligence and defeat a plaintiff's claim on those grounds.

Now, it is also subject to legislation, and that is what we are here to do, to legislate. The Texas Legislature breached the rights of the parties that they have had for hundreds and hundreds of years under Anglo-Saxon common law.

The girl is not a virgin any more, right?

Mr. JEFFERS. I totally disagree with there being any way to equate the abolition of contributory negligence as a defense with the total denial of any reparations or any remedy for pain and suffering.

Mr. SCHEUER. I am not saying that. I am simply saying you supported the Texas Legislature in a legislative intervention to change the rights of parties at common law, their rights at common law. You support that, and I support it, too. We are as one there.

The common law girl is no longer a virgin. Her virginity has been breached by the Texas Legislature and 23 other State legislatures.

Why are we getting into the great business of the problem of Congress now interfering with the rights of the parties under Anglo-Saxon, under the tenets rather, of Anglo-Saxon jurisprudence?

You and these other States have already done it. Isn't it now a question of degree, and if it is a question of degree, why don't you address yourselves to some of the specifics of this law, of the laws we have proposed? Tell us what is bad, and tell us how far you think we can go, or should go, legislatively in breaching the anciently hallowed rights of the English common law and let's get down to specifics.

I don't think it is logical for you to rest on this general opposition to legislative intervention to change these hallowed rights of common law, because you have already done it in Texas. And the Texas Bar Association supported it, for goodness sakes.

Now, we are getting down to specifics. I mean, as the old story goes, we have proven the lady's profession. Now, it is only a question of price. Now it is only a question of how far do we intervene legislatively, and why don't we address ourselves to that?

Mr. JEFFERS. If you please, sir, you can be no more specific than to say that neither this Congress nor any legislative body ought to repeal, eliminate, wipe out, or abolish recovery for pain and suffering, a real wrong. That is what this bill does. That is specific and that is, definite.

Mr. SCHEUER. Good.

Mr. JEFFERS. That is bad law. It ought not to be done.
Mr. SCHEUER. Very good.

I think it proper you address yourself to specifics. But I take it we have settled the question that legislative intervention is justifiable and it is only a question of degree?

Mr. JEFFERS. We have not settled the question at all, sir, that the Congress of the United States should not intervene in this field, which is a field that properly and historically has correctly been vested in the States. That is where it belongs. That is where it ought to stay.

There ought not be Federal interference with it, certainly not on the basis of holding a Federal gun at the head of each State legislature and saying "You pass a statute that contains these standards; if you don't we will impose them on you as a matter of Federal fiat anyhow."

That ought not to be done. There ought not be a Federal gun held, as title II and title III of S. 354 and these other bills do, at the head of a State, and calling it "State action," when it is under that kind of a Federal coercion and duress saying "You pass that bill with these standards in it or else."

The Senate bill S. 354, just reported, says to those who do not adopt the standards set out in title II—well, in title III, "We will not only impose it upon you by Federal law, but we will make it punitive. We will give less rights to the people in title III States, who are the injured victims of automobile accidents, than we give to the title II States that adopt the Federal standards, because, if you don't adopt them and we have to impose them, then there will be no tort recovery in those States, not for death, not for serious and permanent disfigurement, not for permanent disability. On no basis under title II of S. 354 as it came out of the Senate Commerce Committee, will there be any recovery in a tort action in a title III State, where we have to impose a Federal law."

Now, that is Federal coercion at its ultimate. That is Federal duress in the most gross form.

Mr. SCHEUER. It is not the ultimate, because the ultimate would be a Federal no-fault law that supersedes State laws and puts the State agencies out of business.

Mr. JEFFERS. That is exactly what title III does, just exactly. That is exactly what it does.

Mr. SCHEUER. Yes, OK.

Let me ask you, are there any minimum standards that you, as an individual, or that the Texas Bar Association, would be willing to recommend for other States?

Mr. JEFFERS. Not as something to be imposed by Federal law, definitely not.

Mr. SCHEUER. I didn't ask that question.

Mr. JEFFERS. Well, that is our basic position, sir.

I may individually think that it was good for my State and it would presumably be good for some other State to abolish contributory negligence and to adopt comparative negligence and have a mandatory $2,500 offering and to repeal the guest statute. I think that was good for Texas, but it is for the other sovereign 49 States to determine, on the basis of their individual needs and their individual situations, what are the standards that should be imposed by law in their State.

And it is not for the Congress. It is not for the American Bar Association. It is not for me to seek to impose by fiat upon all of the 50 sovereign States what their standards should be.

And certainly, to recommend the following of certain standards, as the American Bar Association witness, Mr. Allen, has just developed, is a far cry from saying, "If you don't adopt them we are going to ram them down your throats by force of a Federal law, whether you like it or not."

Mr. VAN DEERLIN. In his other subcommittee, Mr. Scheuer is helping to mark up a bill to impose Federal clean air standards on 50 States; are you not?

Mr. SCHEUER. Yes; indeed I am. In fact, I am due over there now. They are going to send the Clerk of the House to drag me out if I don't come voluntarily.

Do you think—and I hate to get into extraneous matter, but the chairman leads me there—does the Federal Government have a right to tell utilities they have to burn a certain amount of coal and put scrubbers on smokestacks to protect the people of Texas and the people surrounding Texas to prevent pollution from the smokestacks?

Mr. JEFFERS. Neither the State Bar of Texas nor the Coordinating Committee of State Bar Presidents has taken any position with reference to that legislation.

Mr. SCHEUER. Fair enough. Fair enough, but Mr. Leroy Jeffers has given me his perception of certain minimum characteristics he would like to see personally in a classic, typical State no-fault insurance legislation, and the State Bar of Texas has supported it. And the citizens of Texas, through their legislature, have spoken.

How about some of the other 26 States that may not have a spokesman of the integrity and credibility of a Leroy Jeffers, to lead them, to give them his professional perception—and I may sympathize with you, with your feeling that there are certain minimum standards that are desirable in no-fault insurance, and there are other States that do not have leaders of your capability. But they have people who are just as needful of the kind of protection you advocate.

If that is true, what is wrong with Congress seeing that there are 24 States that have enacted and 26 States that have not enacted, saying, "Well, there is a certain consensus on the minimum element that ought to be in a no-fault law, and we think we are going to encourage the 26 States that have not acted to do the kind of things that the leadership in the 24 States that have acted and have led those State legislatures to have effectuated?

Mr. JEFFERS. I would say, sir, that I am acquainted with the bar leadership in many if not most of those 26 States and I know the dedication and the seriousness with which they have approached their own State problems. I think it is quite outstanding that you have had 24 States act in the period of time that that has gone by and that indeed, in the face of that, there is less need, there is less justification for Federal intervention in this field today than there has been at any time in the modern automobile age.

There is a call here for Federal intervention at a time when there is less need for it, less justification for it, than at any time in the modern automobile age.

Mr. SCHEUER. Would you have justified our intervening before the States started passing no-fault insurance and there were not any States that had done it? That was not long ago, just a few years ago, and there were no States that had this no-fault. Would you have justified Federal intervention then?

Mr. JEFFERS. No; I would not have.

Mr. SCHEUER. You remind me a little bit of the "Arkansas Traveler." Do you know that famous song?

"He won't fix the the roof when it was sunny, but he certainly won't fix it when it is raining?" And when would you justify Federal intervention in the affairs of man, when the States have acted or have not acted?

Mr. JEFFERS. When you are dealing with a Federal problem and not when you are dealing with the local tort law on a local automobile collision and a local injury.

The Federal Government, indeed, has ample areas in which it has to operate to properly consume its time and money, without also undertaking to take over all of the tort law of the individual States and to preempt the States in that. I think the task of the Federal Government is quite enormous enough without its also shouldering the burdens of undertaking to reform all of the local tort laws of the 50 States. That is my view of it, sir.

Mr. SCHEUER. That is a very forceful and impressive statement of your views, and I thank you, Mr. Jeffers.

Mr. JEFFERS. Thank you ,sir.

Mr. VAN DEERLIN. Well, perhaps you feel that you were interrupted and you would like to proceed with your statement.

Mr. JEFFERS. Well, I do not object at all to the interruption, because I think that in that manner we can perhaps be most helpful in appearing before a committee, if we can appear, so I have no complaint about the interruption at all. I think it enabled us to focus on some of the important matters I did want to bring before the committee.

I had been developing the proposition there that constitutionally we still have a very grave constitutional issue when it is said that we are going to totally abolish any remedy, any relief, any reparations for pain and suffering as title III of S. 354 does—abolishes it in its entirety—and H.R. 1900 and some of these other bills abolish it, except in these extreme circumstances.

We say you just can't escape the grave constitutional question that arises under the due process clause and the equal protection of the law clause of the U.S. Constitution, when you say to just one isolated segregated group of people, when you say to them, "We are singling you out and you alone in the whole body of injured people, cannot recover for pain and suffering."

Furthermore, as titles II and III came out of the Senate Commerce Committee in S. 354, there, on the face of it, is the rankest discrimination, the vast and open and avowed discrimination against the citizens in those States whose legislatures do not enact the Federal standards by saying, We are going to punish you. We are going to penalize you. You are going to get something less than those who do adopt the Federal standards. You are not going to have any tort action at all for noneconomic damage, for economic damage; you are just not going to have a tort action.

Those that do adopt the standards, why you can still have a tort action for pain and suffering where you have death, permanent and serious disfigurement, permanent and serious injury, where you have continuous total disability for a period of 90 days. In those serious extreme instances, you can recover for pain and suffering in this group of States, but these States over here, you did not goosestep to the Federal tune, so you don't get anything. The door is closed to you.

How can that pass a constitutional muster?

How can it possibly, under the equal protection of the law clause, under the due process of law clause, regardless of whether it be a former dean of the Harvard Law School or former solicitor general that says it is constititional, or whether it be some other distinguished scholar, who says it is, just as a matter of lawyer commonsense, how can that, in its inequity and in its unfairness, ultimately pass constitutional muster?

I do not believe that it can, and I don't think that the committee can escape that proposition.

Certainly, the Senate Commerce Committee evidently ultimately faced up to the proposition that they could not by Federal law impose upon officials of the State as H.R. 1900 and some of these other bills would do the requirement that they carry out Federal functions and administer a Federal statute and that they become servants of the Federal Government, though they are State officers and State employees.

The Attorney General of the United States expressed the belief that that was unconstitutional under the 10th amendment, and under our Federal systems, if anything, was to remain of the sovereignty of the States. So, the bill was amended in the rewrite, and as it came out of committee, it says: "If the States do not want to administer the bill, if they don't adopt the standards and they don't want to administer the Federal bill that is imposed upon them, then the Secretary of Transportation will do it. The States won't have to do it."

But, then, they come along with this hooker and say, If you do that you are really going to pay for it, because we are going to impose upon you a burden. We are going to deny you a remedy that we grant in those States where they do adopt the standards.

These are not only grave constitutional questions, they are grave questions going to our system of jurisprudence, going to our concepts of good government in a Federal system.

There has been one other development since I last appeared before this subcommittee that I would like to refer to briefly, and then I will conclude, and that is that the Lyndon B. Johnson School of Public Affairs at the University of Texas, in Austin, on commission by the State insurance board, conducted a survey of no-fault legislation and of the tort system as applied to the State of Texas, which covered a period of 1 year's time from September 1973 to September 1974.

And this volume is the preliminary draft of the report that came out of the Lyndon B. Johnson School of Public Affairs. Its final conclusion was that it did not recommend the adoption of no-fault for Texas, but rather a modified tort system. It took serious issue with the elimination of recovery for pain and suffering, saying that pain and suffering was real and that where it existed, that under a humane and an advanced system of law, that it should be compensable, there should be reparations at law for pain and suffering wrongfully inflicted.

And they dealt, also, with the matter of costs, and they went into great depth in the various cost projections that have been made on the Federal no-fault proposal and came up with this:

"And the second problem encountered was the lack of reliable data upon which to base solid, unquestionable conclusions. The relative newness of the no-fault plans currently operating in other States, the demographic differences between these States and Texas and, most frustrating, the manipulation of statistics by both opponents and proponents of no-fault combine to make much of the available data either nontransferable or meaningless."

Then it dealt with the Milliman & Robertson survey, admitted the good faith and expertise of the people who did it, but concluded it was not sufficiently reliable upon which to base any recommendation of going to a no-fault system on the basis of cost savings alone, saying that it was chock full, not only with exceptions and caveats that appear from the face of the study itself, but, indeed, insofar as Texas is concerned, with the assumption of actuarial data that were contrary to the actual facts.

They came up in the instance of Texas with a projected cost savings of 17 percent on the model that they used to put into the computer. Well, this study says one of the things wrong with that is that they assumed that only 1.7 percent of the people injured in automobile accidents in Texas would die from the injuries. The truth of it is and the actual facts are that the actual statistics of the Department of Public Safety in Texas show that slightly over 3 percent of injuries in accidents result in death.

They say in another instance that it is assumed that some 92 percent of all of the medical expenses that are paid for personal injuries in Texas are paid to people who are injured in a private passenger automobile, as distinguished from a commercial vehicle. The truth is that the actual statistics of the State Board of Insurance show that it is only 67 percent instead of slightly more than 90 percent who are victims of private passenger automobiles who receive medical payments.

Both of these departures from the actual facts would tremendously reduce, if not wipe out, projected cost savings. More significantly, we know that in Texas, from the Board of Insurance Commissioners' records, that, in fact, the only kind of insurance that we are actually talking about here—supplanting personal injury liability insurance—that in each year in the past 8 years, through 1974, with the exception of 1 year in which no rate changes were made, that the average bodily injury liability insurance rates in Texas have gone down each year for the past 8 years with one exception of a year in which no rate changes were made. Those are the actual facts which are totally contrary to the data upon which the Milliman & Robertson study proceeded.

So that, we submit to the committee that all of the vaunted and highly publicized and propagandized cost savings that are going to result to the automobile owner from this great panacea of Federal no-fault are hallucinations, and they are a mirage and not based upon any reliable data or statistics. They only touch at the most one-third of the citizen's total automobile insurance package, because two-thirds of it goes to property damage, collision damage to vehicles, which is not covered at all by S. 354 or by H.R. 1900. It is covered, I believe, by the bill of the gentleman from Texas, Mr. Eckhardt, but generally, property damage is not dealt with. And indeed, the recent Senate committee report frankly admits that collision damage insurance, which is no-fault insurance, of course, voluntary no-fault insurance—the automobile owner is not compelled to take it—but it is no-fault paid without any reference to fault, that the rates on it have been going up, soaring in all of the States generally, that the same thing would be true under no-fault and is true in the States that have no-fault.

So, the idea that has been conveyed to the American public that there is going to be a great bounty, a great amount of Federal manna from the Washington heaven, falling into the laps of the automobile insurance buyer, the people are simply being misled by that idea being carried to them. When they go down to pay their renewal insurance premium and find that their total package, which they are looking at after Federal no-fault is enacted and it has not gone down, we are going to have an awful number of disillusioned folks in the country, because they have been led to believe by the propaganda we have had that—We are going to cut your insurance bill down to where it will really amount to something.

That can't be true, and there is no way it can be true. And there will be a lot of disappointed, disillusioned people knocking on the doors of the U.S. Congress and saying "Where is all of that panacea that we are going to get? Where is all of the relief we are going to get from our insurance premiums? It didn't appear on my bill when my renewal came up."

Mr. VAN DEERLIN. Mr. Kinzler, are you disillusioned?

Mr. KINZLER. I better not answer that question.

Mr. Jeffers, has the Federal Government ever interfered with the tort system, the common law tort system in transportation areas in the last 50 years?

Mr. JEFFERS. Insofar as tort law is concerned, not of which I am aware.

Mr. KINZLER. What about in the Federal Employers' Liability Act.

Mr. JEFFERS. Well, that is an area, of course, in which there has been Federal preemption. We have not had it in Workmen's Compensation, generally, but as to the Federal Employee's Liability Act, you are correct.

Mr. KINZLER. How about the Longshoremen and Harbor Workers' Compensation Act?

Mr. JEFFERS. Those are instances of the special statutes where you had it.

Mr. KINZLER. Both of those statutes deal with the transportation system, and they both were premised on the fact that these transportation systems were inherently dangerous and that recovery in the States was inadequate.

Mr. JEFFERS. And also premised, I think, on the proposition that you had interstate commerce primarily involved and that it was primarily Federal and not primarily local in nature.

Mr. KINZLER. Right. Do you have any idea about how much money the Federal Government has spent to help build the highway system in the country?

Mr. JEFFERS. All I know is that Federal grants for highway purposes through the years are enormous. I don't know the exact figure. I know they are quite enormous.

Mr. KINZLER. About $100 billion, close to that anyway.

Mr. JEFFERS. I would think that was true, but, of course, there are many other areas where you have had Federal grants of enormous sums of money where it has not been thought that there should go along with that total preemption of the field and Federal takeover regulations.

Mr. KINZLER. H.R. 1900 does not say total preemption; only H.R. 1272 talks about total preemption, is that correct?

Mr. JEFFERS. Well, that is true, except in essence it is the same. You hold the gun there with H.R. 1900 and say "You do it yourself like we tell you to do it, or we are going to preempt if you don't," so it is in substance the same thing.

Mr. KINZLER. One of the results of the highway system that we have developed is that approximately 20 percent of all fatal accidents involve an out-of-State driver, so we are not talking strictly about local, indigenous conditions when we talk about highway deaths and serious accidents?

Mr. JEFFERS. Yes, of course, his insurance follows him wherever he goes, such insurance he has.

Mr. KINZLER. If he happens to have an endorsement and if not it does not.

You indicate that under title III of S. 354 or H.R. 1900, the accident victim would lose more than he does under title II.

Are there any compensating benefits under title III he would get in? Would his wage loss be higher or his replacement services loss higher than under title II?

Mr. JEFFERS. No, not as I read it.

Mr. KINZLER. I would submit there is a significant difference. There are higher first party benefits under title III than under title II, so it is not a taking away a right in return for nothing.

The question—I think you put your finger on it, too—is whether what is given in return is adequate. It is very much the same question as under workmen's compensation, "Is there an adequate replacement for the existing system?" And would you agree that is the basis of the constitutional issue here—is it a reasonable and adequate replacement for a tort right?

Mr. JEFFERS. I think that is the constitutional question, yes.

Mr. KINZLER. OK.

The Senate report has indicated that under S. 354 there would be approximately 100 percent recovery of economic losses up to $25,000 and above that it would dip down to 90 percent, depending whether you had a tort remedy or not.

Under the existing system, as found by the Department of Transportation, at the bottom of the system, between $1 and $500 worth of loss, you get about 450 percent recovery, and at the top of the system, for losses in excess of $25,000, even with the right to sue for pain and suffering, the recovery is 30 percent of economic loss. Is that a fair rate? You obviously don't feel it is, but would you expand on that please?

Mr. JEFFERS. Insofar as the statistic itself is concerned, after repeated reading of it, I frankly have never been able to understand how it was arrived at or how it was constructed or how you would go about testing its validity.

Mr. KINZLER. It was a sampling. There are figures, national figures, with respect to overall recovery that showed that people with serious loss recovered about 50 percent of their loss from all systems, including tort and you would expect the higher the loss gets, obviously, the lower the recovery will be.

Mr. JEFFERS. There is no showing in any of those instances how you measure what is the total economic loss—if you measure it by what the plaintiff sues for, perhaps so, but all of us know as a practical matter that the suit is typically for a sum far exceeding actual loss.

Mr. KINZLER. Typically medical and wage loss, very identifiable kinds of things. At the bottom of the system, this 450 percent recovery for people with economic loss of less than $500, do you think it is pain and suffering recovery, or it is perhaps payment for the nuisance value to the insurance company?

Mr. JEFFERS. I think, of course, that there is some nuisance value that enters into the negotiated settlements of small claims, but that a substantial factor in it is the pain and suffering, and the pain and suffering is real. It is genuine, and under tort law, it is compensable. And it should be compensable, and the fact that economic loss may not be great does not alter the fact that the pain and suffering is genuine and real.

Mr. KINZLER. When you get down to less than $100, that average recovery goes up to something like 700-plus percent. Here we have a man with less than $100 of loss, who, also, for the most part, I would assume, would be less seriously injured than someone with $25,000 economic loss, and he recovers 700 percent. And the man at the top of the system, who would normally be the more serious loss, would be recovering only 30 percent, and if we have this kind of disparity in pain and suffering. All H.R. 1900 is attempting to do is reallocate the system so that more money goes to the seriously injured victim rather than the less seriously injured victim.

Mr. JEFFERS. I just think you are dealing in a hypothetical assumption there that you just can't set up a great Federal monolith and say we are going to correct all of these inequities that result in the present system: We are going to reach down and take some away from those with low economic loss and we will take away some of their reparations for noneconomic loss and put it up here at the top.

Well, there is no barrier under the existing law to the total recovery for pain and suffering for those whose economic loss is great.

Mr. KINZLER. There is no barrier, but it does not happen on the average.

If I were in an accident and I retained you as my attorney, I would expect a full recovery, but most people don't retain lawyers of your competence or don't even have a cause of action—single car collisions which will not give one a cause of action.

If you drive along the road and swerve to avoid a child and hit a tree and incur $25,000 worth of economic loss, you don't have a tort suit. You have other medical insurance, but not a tort suit, so you get nothing for pain and suffering. I don't see why you should be victimized in that situation.

Mr. JEFFERS. Well, of course, heretofore, we have not had voluntary coverage by insurance of the matter of pain and suffering. I notice that the Senate version came out of the Commerce Committee of S. 354 providing for an offering.

Mr. KINZLER. Mandatory offering.

Mr. JEFFERS. Mandatory offering—that is supposed to be exploring uncharted seas and sailing in unknown waters, just as I have commented as to my longtime and highly respected good friend from Texas—the gentleman from Texas, Mr. Eckhardt, that his bill, also, while intriguing, and, I think, in fairness and equity of concept, is the fairest and most equitable of all of the no-fault bills, still providing for paying of total reparations for economic and noneconomic loss alike and pain and suffering to both parties to an automobile collision, that we have no statistical data, we have no experience data upon which to make a cost estimate of that kind of coverage; that, on the face of it, it would appear that it would be so vast, that the costs would be so enormous—that it could not be borne by private insurance and probably would have to be carried by a government system or a government subsidy. And that is like having some new social security or medicare program rather than covering it by private insurance.

Mr. KINZLER. In the State of Texas, you have made some positive movement in reform of tort system such as repeal of the guest statute——

Mr. JEFFERS. Yes.

Mr. KINZLER [continuing]. And switching from contributory negligence to comparative negligence, and these are all attempts to overcome some of the inequities of the system.

All I suggest is, no-fault is exactly the same kind of attempt. It is not a perfect system, but if the present system is 30 percent perfect, then maybe a reform package of the nature you are talking about might be 40 percent and maybe no-fault would be 60 percent.

Mr. JEFFERS. Our answer to that is that, instead of no-fault being an idea whose time has come, that no-fault is an idea whose time has passed, because there is less need for it now than there has ever been by reason of the very substantial, affirmative action taken by so many States and the very progressive, affirmative action that we can reasonably anticipate will occur in other States that have it under active consideration.

There is just less justification and less need for intervention now than there has ever been.

Mr. KINZLER. Thank you, Mr. Jeffers.

Mr. VAN DEERLIN. Ms. Nord again informs me she will relinquish her role as designated hitter.

Mr. JEFFERS. Thank you so much for your time.

Mr. VAN DEERLIN. Thank you very much for being with us. It was excellent, and you are a most absorbing witness.

[Mr. Jeffers prepared statement follows:]

STATEMENT OF LEROY JEFFERS, PAST-PRESIDENT OF THE STATE BAR OF TEXAS AND CHAIRMAN OF THE COORDINATING COMMITTEE OF STATE BAR PRESIDENTS

Mr. Chairman and Gentlemen of the Committee: Through me today, the State Bar of Texas, a statutory agency of the Judicial Department of the Government of the State of Texas, of which all of the more than 25,000 lawyers licensed by the Supreme Court of Texas are members, joins with the Coordinating Committee of State Bar Presidents, of which I am currently the chairman, in stating total and unqualified opposition to the enactment of any federal automobile no-fault insurance bill, whether it be S. 354, or whether it be H.R. 1272 or H.R. 1900, or some other version of federal encroachment on this traditional area of tort law properly belonging to the states.

I am a Past-President of the State Bar of Texas, whose opposition to such federal interference has been officially declared in each of the past four years by unanimous action on four separate occasions by the Board of Directors of the State Bar of Texas, the statutory governing body of this state agency, composed of thirty directors elected by secret ballots by the lawyers of their respective geographic districts. This unretreating and mounting opposition has been previously stated before this Honorable Committee as well as before the Committees on Commerce and on the Judiciary of the United States Senate. At its meetings in April and July of this year, this Board of Directors again unanimously authorized me on its behalf to state its renewed and unrelenting opposition to federal no-fault insurance legislation in any form.

The opposition here spoken will also be on behalf of the Coordinating Committee of State Bar Presidents through me as its spokesman and current chairman. In 1972, the presidents of the organized bars of thirty-seven states formed the Coordinating Committee of State Bar Presidents and presented a petition to the House of Delegates of the American Bar Association meeting in San Francisco, urging American Bar Association forceful official opposition to any federal no-fault automobile insurance law. This action was overwhelmingly taken by the House of Delegates and became and continues to be the official position of the American Bar Association. The Coordinating Committee of State Bar Presidents has continued in existence, and in a meeting on April 6, 1975 authorized me as its chairman and spokesman to voice here today its continued opposition to federal intervention abolishing traditional tort remedies in state courthouses in the automobile accident field.

FEDERAL NO-FAULT BILLS GENERALLY CLOSE THE COURTHOUSE DOOR TO CITIZENS

The State Bar of Texas and the overwhelming majority of its sister state bars here condemn most federal no-fault bills, because their principal thrust is to padlock state courthouse doors to innocent injured citizens seeking a full remedy for a wrong done to them. This is true of H.R. 1900 and of its Senate counterpart, S. 354. I shall comment separately on H.R. 1272. H.R. 1900 and S. 354, by denying any courthouse relief for physical pain and suffering sustained at the hands of a drunken, doped or simply negligent driver, except in the most extreme and unusual situations, would erode and undermine the adversary system of justice under which the genius of American and English law has held open the door of free courts to free men for the full vindication of their rights. The state bars of the United States know that lurking in the Congressional wings and eager to follow in its wake are proposals to block court entry in medical malpractice and products liability cases. The ultimate goal is to wipe out the whole field of tort law developed by the English and American courts over the centuries as it applies to wrongful injuries to the individual bodies and minds of precious human beings born in the image of their Divine Creator. For the humanitarian concepts born of our hard-won common law, there would be substituted a monstrous soulless monolith of federally-compelled self-insurance to which alone the innocent injured citizen must look for compensation for his injuries.

This collectivist concept of the mass impersonal processing of money reparations for broken bones and disabled bodies is ecstatically envisioned by Professor Jeffrey O'Connell in his article captioned "Expanding No-Fault Beyond Auto Insurance: Some Proposals" published in the May 1973 issue of *Virginia Law Review*. 59 Virginia Law Review 749. The learned professor exuberantly unveiled his mind-boggling concept of extending the benign blessings of federal no-fault with its blight of any compensation for physical pain and suffering to its farthest reaches by covering any bodily injury resulting from any "enterprise." The united state bars will oppose this movement to the death because it moves toward the destruction, and H.R. 1900 or S. 354 is its opening step, of the adversary system of justice in a free and open court which is the best system yet devised for the defense of the rights and liberties of every man.

H.R. 1900 AND S. 354 ARE UNCONSTITUTIONAL

The State Bar of Texas and its sister state bars oppose H.R. 1900 and S. 354, because their denial of any legal remedy for physical pain and suffering and other non-economic losses constitutes an invidious discrimination against innocent automobile accident victims, and by segregating them in this denial from all other accident victims of every kind, thereby denies them that due process of law and that equal protection of the laws guaranteed to them by the Constitution of the United States. How can Congress look the courts and the people in the eye and say that it is fair, just and Constitutionally permissible to strip innocent automobile accident victims alone, out of the whole body of innocent accident victims from any and all causes, of any legal remedy or redress whatever against a wrongdoer for physical pain and suffering? Simple fair play will never ultimately permit H.R. 1900 or S. 354 to clear that Constitutional hurdle.

The state courts have already quickly perceived that state no-fault statutes which denied court access and legal recovery for negligent collision damage to vehicles below a certain threshold amount could not pass Constitutional muster. *Grace v. Howlett*, 283 N.E. 2d 474 (Ill. S. Ct., 1972); *Kluger v. White*, 281 So. 2d 1 (Fla. S. Ct., 1973). When a denial of court recovery for collision damage to an uninsured motorist who could have obtained his own separate collision insurance violates Constitutional guarantees, how can it be rationally contended that human pain and suffering which cannot be separately insured against and which will not be covered by federal compulsory no-fault self-insurance can, nevertheless, be denied court access and legal remedy with Constitutional impunity?

The Constitutional infirmities of H.R. 1900 and S. 354 simply cannot be swept under the rug, however distinguished and scholarly the hand that attempts it, by sole reliance on the Massachusetts decision in *Pinnick v. Cleary*, 271 N.E. 2d 592 (1971), as has been the sole recourse of the Constitution defenders of these bills up to now. The superficial reliance of the Massachusetts decision upon an inapropos analogy to the established Constitutionality of state workmen's compensation laws just cannot withstand grave and penetrating judicial scrutiny. The workmen's compensation statutes are Constitutional, because the employer must bear the total cost of premiums on insurance afforded for the protection of the employee in lieu of common law remedies; and this arrangement becomes a part of the employment contract by operation of law. Under all of the federal no-fault bills, the reverse is true, because the innocent victim, rather than the guilty offender, must bear the total premium cost of the federal no-fault compulsory self-insurance; and, certainly, the innocent injured victim enters no contract with the guilty wrongdoer that such shall be the case. The analogy is obviously lame and ludicrous, but it is the sole crutch upon which the Constitutionality of H.R. 1900 and S. 354 lean.

Again, the states generally, speaking through their Governors and their Attorneys General, oppose this unwanted and unwarranted intrusion into their affairs not only because it would outlaw traditional state remedies and cripple state courts, but because these federal standards bills, in a display of federal arrogance of unprecedented ugliness, propose by Congressional fiat to impose upon state officials the burden of discharging federal bureaucratic duties in the administration of these federal laws. After holding a federal gun at the head of each of the fifty sovereign states by provisions in which they are told the notes of the federal tune to which they are to goose step in the enactment of state statutes blindly imitating prescribed federal standards, the federal standards bills spell out the penalties which they shall pay in the absence of craven compliance to the federal demands in the form of a state no-fault motor vehicle insurance plan to be imposed by federal mandate. Not satisfied with this punitive action, these bills seek to impose the ultimate insult by making state insurance commissioners federal lackeys required to administer the federally-imposed plan. If this is still a federal union of sovereign states and if Amendment X ot the Constitution of the United States still retains any vitality, this proposal to reduce the states to federal administrative districts is obviously unconstitutional.

The Honorable John L. Hill, the brilliant trial lawyer and able statesman who is now Attorney General of Texas, has given fair notice in testimony before the Committee on the Judiciary of the United States Senate on S. 354 at the last session of Congress that Texas will not accept or abide by an unconstitutional federal statutory command that its state agencies and its state officers and employees discharge federal administrative duties. He made clear that any such attempt would be quickly challenged in the courts.

The soundness of the position taken by the Texas Attorney General was greatly fortified by the testimony of the distinguished and scholarly Attorney General of the United States, Honorable Edward H. Levi, when he testified before the Senate Commerce Committee on June 5, 1975, concerning the proposed National Standards No-Fault Motor Vehicle Insurance Act, that "in its present form, in my judgment, S. 354 does raise serious constitutional questions and does involve an impairment of constitutional Federalism." Attorney General Levi had previously pointed out the provisions of the Senate version of the federal standards bill which sought to impose federal duties upon recalcitrant states as follows:

"Section 104 generally would require each State to insure that the owners of any motor vehicles registered or present in that State obtain no-fault insurance. Section 105 would require a State to establish and administer an assigned risk plan; compel the State insurance commissioner to approve, among other arrangements, certain insurance company agreements relating to assigned risks; and establish favorable insurance rates for the economically disadvantaged. Section 108 would require a State to establish an assigned risk claims fund and an assigned claims bureau. Section 109 would require the State insurance commissioner to establish and maintain a program for the regular evaluation of medical and rehabilitation services. Section 111(d) can be interpreted to require a State to create a vocational rehabilitation agency if it lacks one."

Further in his discussion, Attorney General Levi referred to the Supreme Court's recent opinion in *Fry* v. *United States*, in twhich Justice Marshall referred to the Tenth Amendment as expressly declaring "the constitutional policy that Congress may not exercise power in a fashion that impairs the States' integrity or the ability to function effectively in a federal system." "The Court did not regard the Tenth Amendment as a mere truism without significance." Then Attorney General Levi made the telling comment: "The essence of the sovereignty of the States that remains is that State employees are not just Federal employees in disguise." Quoting further from this most significant and weighty testimony:

"If the failure of a uniform law to win acceptance among the States within three years is to be regarded as a reason for national enactment, I would suggest that the Commissioners on Uniform State Laws ought to go out of business right now. The whole basis of their endeavor was to win acceptance through reason, the example of experience, the possibility of diversity and change. Since 1972, when the National Conference of Commissioners voted approval of the Uniform Motor Vehicle Accident Reparations Act, fourteen States have adopted no-fault statutes, and four additional States have added no-fault features to existing statutes. To be sure there is great diversity among them."

A FEW OF THE FAULTS OF FEDERAL NO-FAULT

State governments and state bars generally oppose the federal standards bills not only because of the basic free-government principles and constitutional guarantees which they violate, but because of the numerous fatal faults and flaw which they embody. The State Bar of Texas, as a public profession with a duty to inform the public that it serves on matters of law affecting their daily lives, has undertaken to "lay it on the line" with the people of Texas on federal no-fault. One message which we have published to our people follows:

Federal No-fault Is No Good

The Federal No-Fault Automobile Insurance Act just passed by the United States Senate by a vote of 53 to 42 [referring to the predecessor of S. 354 which passed the Senate in the last session of Congress] is not a good bill. It is not in the interest of the people. The fact that its ultimate purpose is not to reduce automobile insurance premiums is probably best proved by the fact that its principal propagandist and supporter has been the American Insurance Alliance, composed of the major insurance companies of the United States.

The true facts about this bad bill are never told to the people. The true facts are that it gives the consumers nothing. On the contrary, it requires them on pain of fine or imprisonment to buy and pay the premium on their own compulsory self-insurance and to look to that and that alone for compensation for their injuries. It releases the driver of the other car from responsibility regardless of his negligence or fault.

Other true, unassailable facts about the federal no-fault fraud that the people are never told are as follows:

(1) The bill provides for nothing but compulsory self-insurance and releases the wrongdoer from any responsibility for his wrong. The drunken or doped-up driver who crashes into the back end of your car cannot be held responsible by you except in the most rare and unusual cases.

(2) The people can already buy *voluntarily* what the bill makes it *compulsory* for them to buy. A law now in effect sponsored by the State Bar of Texas requires that every automobile insurance policy contain a minimum of $2,500 personal injury insurance for the driver and occupants of the owner's car which will be paid to him for his injuries regardless of fault.

(3) Any recovery or compensation for pain and suffering will be wiped out except in the most extreme circumstances of death, total disability for some substantial continuous period or serious and permanent injury or disfigurement. The no-fault insurance will not pay for pain and suffering, and the injured party's own insurance will not cover it. This means that in every case of any kind of injury, except in an automobile accident, recovery of damages for pain and suffering may be had but that it is denied to the victim of the wild or drunken driver.

(4) The Federal No-Fault Bill does not cover damages to the owner's own automobile and he must buy his own separate insurance policy with its deductible to cover damage to his own automobile in a collision.

(5) The Federal No-Fault Bill is full of hidden hookers and gimmicks. It doesn't claim to pay for anything except lost wages and medical and hospital expenses. From lost wages, it deducts 15% as an income tax deduction on the theory that if the payment had been wages, it would have been subject to income tax. It deducts from the medical payment any payments received from Workmen's Compensation, Medicare or Social Security. It prorates any sums received by the injured party from his own group or individual hospitalization policy for the same injury. These hidden deductions are the only things that make possible the no-fault propagandist's claimed premium savings.

(6) In the first year of experience under no-fault in Massachusetts, 40% less people were paid 50% less money in automobile accidents than the year before. Premiums were reduced by paying fewer people less money.

(7) In Florida in the first year of no-fault experience, the cost of automobile insurance premiums has actually gone up.

(8) Under the Federal No-Fault Bill, the drunken or doped-up driver is paid the same amounts for the same injuries as the innocent, sober driver without any regard to fault. In fact, the premiums paid by the safe drivers go to help subsidize and underwrite the premiums on the wild and reckless drivers.

(9) The worst injustice is done to the older, retired citizens. They will receive no payments for income lost, because, being retired, they have no loss of income. Their injuries will already generally be covered by Medicare so that they will receive no medical payments. They will be required to pay premiums on their no-fault automobile policies, but it will only be in the extremely rare case that they are paid any no-fault benefits.

(10) Employed people in their 40's and 50's presently have the lowest insurance rates, because they are the best risks under actual experience. Unemployed persons in their teens or the 20's have the highest rates, because, under experience, they are the worst risks. No-fault will exactly reverse this situation. The employed people in their 40's and 50's will become the worst risk, because when fault is no factor, their loss of wages will be the greatest, and they will be more likely to be injured in a collision and will recover slower. The teenagers and 20-year-olds who are unemployed have no wage losses, are less prone to serious injury in an accident and will recover more speedily. Hence, when fault is no factor, they are the best risks and will receive the lowest rates.

(11) No-fault Found To Aid High-risk Drivers

In a news report under this headline, the *New York Times* of February 21, 1975, reported the result of actual experience under New York's new state no-fault law. The news story continues the report as follows:

"Since the inception a year ago of the state's no-fault automobile insurance system, high-risk drivers rather than low-risk drivers have received the largest reductions in the amount they pay for personal injury liability insurance.

"According to a report released by the State Insurance Department, the largest reductions—both in percentages and in dollar amounts—were realized by drivers who are considered prone to accidents. The smallest reductions went to drivers with good records who chose the largest amounts of coverage."

(12) S. 354 is a proposed system that would turn the handling of automobile insurance over to the Federal Government. Our experience has been that there are many things which the Federal Government does not do very well. This would undoubtedly be another in that long list.

CLAIMED COST SAVINGS UNDER THE FEDERAL STANDARDS BILLS ARE HALLUCINATORY

The only real justification that has ever been offered for the departure from traditional governmental and constitutional concepts proposed in H.R. 1900 or S. 354 is that it would pay people, guilty and innocent alike, more quickly for medical and hospital costs and lost wages resulting from an automobile accident at a lower insurance premium cost. The reasoning has been that it is worthwhile to give up almost all claims for physical pain and suffering and other non-economic losses in exchange for quicker payment of the out-of-pocket economic losses in medical and hospital bills and lost wages. It is argued that it is worth it to give up any legal claim against the wrongdoer causing the injury and for the innocent victim to look only to his own insurance which he will be compelled by law to buy and to pay the premium upon himself if that premium will be reduced, and he will get paid off quicker by his own insurance company. It becomes increasingly clear that these extravagant claims will inevitably prove to be a cruel mirage.

The proponents of these bills stake their cost-saving claim almost exclusively upon the Milliman and Robertson reports, although this firm wrote into its report numerous caveats against broad general claims of premium costs savings and in the celebrated *Washington Star-News* event, heatedly disclaimed the extravagant forecasts of premium cost savings falsely attributed to it. Milliman and Robertson have repeatedly emphasized that a major part of the increased premium costs in the average automobile insurance package has been in collision insurance on the insured's own automobile and property damage liability insurance on the vehicles of others, and that this major part of the insurance problem is not covered by the federal standards bills or by the study at all. We must, therefore, begin by removing the illusion that these bills and the Milliman and Robertson study relate to anything except personal injury protection with that confined strictly to medical and hospital costs, lost wages and a few other out-of-pocket economic losses.

Milliman and Robertson developed various computerized models of comparative insurance costs of hypothetical average insurance coverages predicated upon an array of factual assumptions. It constructed one of these hypothetical models related to the State of Texas which purported to show that on certain coverages and under certain assumptions, limited personal injury protection coverage would cost some 17% less than under the present system. Because of the hypothetical nature of the study, the tenuous nature of the assumptions upon which it was based and the caveats and uncertainties with which its conclusions were riddled, the State Board of Insurance in Texas could not accept the findings in the Milliman and Robertson survey related to Texas as the basis for decision and action without further inquiry. Accordingly, State Insurance Board Chairman Joe Christie asked the Lyndon B. Johnson School of Public Affairs at the University of Texas to make a comprehensive study of the feasibility of the no-fault insurance plan in Texas, including an examination of the Milliman and Robertson survey. After a one-year study extending from September 1973 to September 1974, the ultimate conclusion of the Lyndon B. Johnson School study was that it recommended at state modified tort liability plan rather than a no-fault plan as being in the best interests of the people of Texas. Turning to its conclusion on comparative costs studies, the L.B.J. School report initially observed that "most frustratingly, the manipulation of statistics by both opponents and proponents of no-fault all combined to make much of the available data either nontransferable or meaningless." It then immediately put the flamboyant claims of no-fault cost savings in focus under the following spotlight:

"It should be realized from the start, however, that even should the enactment of a no-fault law produce significant cost savings, they would apply only to one segment of the total automobile insurance premium. Typically, that part of the total premium paid for property damage coverages (i.e., property damage liability, collision, and comprehensive) remains unaffected by no-fault laws. *These coverages typically account for about ⅔ of the total premium.*" (emphasis mine). (p. 203).

The L.B.J. School study turned sharp scrutiny on the Milliman and Robertson Texas findings and thoroughly discredited them as follows:

"Milliman and Robertson used a death ratio (i.e., fatalities as a percent of total injuries in all automobile accidents) of 1.7% for Texas in 1969, while Department of Public Safety's statistics show that ratio to be nearly 3%. Use of the Department of Public Safety's statistics would significantly reduce the predicted costs savings of no-fault insurance for Texas." (p. 176). * * *

"* * * Milliman and Robertson assumed that first-party medical payments coverage in Texas totalled 24.1% of the payments under bodily injury liability coverage for private passenger cars. Statistics published later by the State Board of Insurance indicated that such medical payment losses are only 18.7% of private passenger bodily injury losses."* * *

"* * * the actual amount of medical payments shown in the model * * * would only be correct if private passenger bodily injury payments constituted 93.7% of all bodily injury payments, including commercial vehicles. The Texas publication (Board of Insurance Statistics) indicates that private passenger bodily injury payments constitute only about 68% of the total. Correction of the Milliman and Robertson Texas calculations for these two errors, according to Webb, would drop the projected savings from 17% to 9%." (pp. 177-178).

The final evaluation of the Milliman and Robertson findings as to Texas made by the Lyndon B. Johnson School of Public Affairs is as follows:

"Its reliability, however, is limited not only by the caveats that Milliman and Robertson cite but, further, by the vast array 'of actuarial judgments and data assumptions that are input into the model. For example, Milliman and Robertson data estimated the fatality ratio (the ratio of deaths per 100 injuries) in Texas for all drivers to be 1.7% in 1971. Department of Public Safety data, however, showed the actual 1971 fatality ratio to be approximately 3%. The difference in these two ratios alone, when input into the model, would significantly increase the personal injury premium projection over that produced by the Milliman and Robertson calculations. Many other estimates and assumptions affect Milliman and Robertson's cost estimations significantly. For these reasons, we conclude that we cannot justify recommending a switch to no-fault on the basis of premium reduction alone." (pp. 203-204).

This University study refused to accept the thesis that compensation for pain and suffering should be abolished, stating: "This study recognizes that real pain and suffering does exist and that recovery for pain and suffering where it does exist should be permitted." The study continued that: "It is probably true that severe restriction on this right to recovery for pain and suffering * * * would result in some cost savings, but it is doubtful that these modest savings justify surrendering the right to sue for pain and suffering where they legitimately exist." (p. 224).

If the L.B.J. Study finding of the total unreliability of the Milliman and Robertson projection of great premium costs savings in Texas from the federal standards bills needed further verification, the actual on-the-ground facts in Texas supply the clincher. The fact is that the only automobile insurance rates which have gone up in Texas are those on property damage, particularly on collision damage to the insured's own vehicle—the present no-fault portion of the automobile insurance package. These are rates that are totally unaffected by the federal standards bills. On the rates to which these bills have application—the bodily injury liability rates—the rates have gone down every year for the last seven years in which rate changes have been made, including 1974. The table of total rate changes compiled from the records of the Texas State Board of Insurance is as follows:

Texas State Board of Insurance bodily injury liability rate changes since 1966

Year:	Private passenger board of insurance rate change (statewide average) (percent)
1974	−0.2
1973	−7.4
1972	−.5
1971	−4.8
1970 (No rate change promulgated.)	
1969	−3.7
1968	−.9
1967	−1.0

From all of this emerges the one clear fact that the glowing prospect of automobile insurance rate reductions in Texas highly heralded by the proponents of H.R. 1900 and S. 354 is pure hallucination.

H.R. 1272 IS TOO VAST A FEDERAL UNDERTAKING

H.R. 1272, by the distinguished Gentleman from Texas, and my fellow Houstonian, Mr. Eckhardt, is the most intriguing and provocative of all of the federal no-fault approaches. The author of this bill readily recognized S. 354 and the various versions of its House counterparts as being totally unacceptable, because they deny recovery of substantial remedies and protection of precious rights now accorded by the tort law of the various states. The Eckhardt proposal refuses to accept the callous proposition of the federal standards approach that compensation for pain and suffering can simply be written off as an expendable intangible for the sake of expediency. As he stated it before the Insurance Information Institute on June 3, 1975:

"No system is fair and humane which considers a human being as a mere producing machine with compensation only for loss of work production potential. Though a person may be able to continue on the job with undiminished proficiency after an accident, it may only be with unabated pain. He or she may never again be able to play tennis or wade in a trout stream. They may never again sleep together. A law which fails to recognize that there are other aspects of 'personhood'—without which an individual is not the complete human being he or she once was—and which fails to provide compensation for these aspects is unacceptable."

With all of this, we totally agree. However, we cannot agree with his proposed remedy. He follows this magnificent statement immediately with the following description of H.R. 1272:

"Therefore, my bill provides that a person may bring suit against the first-party insurer to recover damages other than economical loss. The same method of measuring damages that is used in determining damages in tort suits should be available to the insured."

In addition to the basic objection that this provision totally displaces the traditional state tort system with a vast new federal preemption and constitutes, in effect, a basic change in our entire system of American and English jurisprudence, it constitutes a proposal to launch into a vast unknown and uncharted sea. We have totally no experience and no data on private insurance against claims for pain and suffering and other intangible injuries other than under automobile accident liability insurance policies. First-party insurance covering such claims is a total unknown. Such coverage has simply not been available. There is simply no way to calculate the cost of paying both parties, the guilty and innocent alike, to an automobile accident for pain and suffering and other intangible damages sustained by them along with their economic losses as the Eckhardt bill would do. We can only know that the cost must necessarily be vast, that the rate-making process for insurance affording such coverage must be highly speculative and that resulting rates for such total coverage of reparations for all losses now covered by the tort system as well as all losses sustained by the guilty party must, in all probability, be so staggering in total amount as to be beyond the reach of the average man. Yet under the proposal, he could not drive an automobile on the highways on pain of fine or imprisonment without buying and paying the premium upon such total no-fault insurance. Even if such a total federal displacement of the states in the area of automobile accident reparations did not violate basic constitutional and governmental principles, eventually, such a system would have to be underwritten by an enormous new federal program comparable to Social Security or Medicare.

The Eckhardt bill has many commendable and lofty philosophical concepts. It rejects out of hand the shabby sentiment that pain and suffering can be written off as inconsequential and automobile accident victims segregated and made the invidious victims of a discriminatory system which would deny to them alone total reparations through legal process for total damages against a wrongdoer. It is more fair and equitable in its concept than any of the other federal bills. It, at least, recognizes that if the state tort law system is to be replaced, that rights and remedies cannot be justly emasculated in the process and a mere pittance of reparations for total injury allowed. It recognizes that it would be not only futile and self-defeating, but totally inadequate to eliminate coverage of automobile property damage entirely as the other federal standards bills, including S. 354, do. It, therefore, would cover automobile property damage on a no-fault basis, paying both parties alike for damages to their vehicles, just as it would pay for pain and suffering and other general non-economic damages. Unlike the federal standards bills, it would also recognize the morality of the situation by denying recovery to one injured by reason of his own criminal misconduct. It would not treat the drunken or doped-up driver or the fleeing felon on the same basis and pay him for his injuries in the same manner as his innocent victim. Nevertheless, it would establish the most revolutionary change yet in our federal-state system of division of powers and would institute a radically new total reparations system of incalculable but necessarily staggering cost. It would be a giant step toward the total abolition of the tort system as we have known it and substitution therefor of a federal system of total reparations without reference to traditional concepts of fault and of remedies determined on the basis of right and wrong.

The Gentleman from Texas recognized, in his June 3, 1975 address to which I have referred concerning his bill, that:

"Ultimately, though, there are areas not subject to exact actuarial scrutiny in advance. I had always thought insurance companies are in the business of insuring *risk*. A gentleman, you know, never bets on a certainty."

We more nearly agree with his later statement:

"I am simply not willing to take away the authority of the states to continue a system of tort liability without accepting the federal responsibility of devising a system that will be afforded in its place. If no-fault remains experimental, let the states experiment on their own terms."

While H.R. 1272 may meet many of the Constitutional objections to which the federal standards bills are subject, such as denial of the equal protection and due process of law, and the violation of the Tenth Amendment, through imposition by federal fiat of federal duties on state employees, it nevertheless represents a total federal seizure of an area which rightfully and traditionally belongs to the states and with which they are progressively dealing. There is less justification for such a shattering proposal today than at any time in our history.

THE TIME FOR FEDERAL NO-FAULT HAS PASSED

Less showing can be made now of need for a federal no-fault law than at any time during the modern automobile age. If there was ever a time when the idea had a legitimate bid for credibility, that time has passed. The individual states, including the State of Texas under the leadership of the State Bar of Texas, have gone further in the enactment of progressive automobile accident reparations reform legislation than at any period in history. Any public fervor for this new federal intrusion into an area belonging to the states which the federal no-fault propagandists have feverishly fanned has long since ebbed and cooled. A survey conducted by the L.B.J. School of 1971 automobile accident victims which describes the tort system and the no-fault system without identifying either with labels reveals that more than one-half preferred the present system, about one-fourth preferred the no-fault system and one-fifth was undecided. (pp. 157-158). Even on this Capitol Hill the medical malpractice fury and the national health insurance fervor have long since rendered federal no-fault obsolete. Any thought that no-fault medical and hospital benefits can be legislated or their costs computed in isolation without any reference to the emerging proposals in these areas, and, particularly, to the impact of rising malpractice insurance costs and proposed malpractice legislation on medical and hospital costs, simply passeth all understanding.

Federal no-fault, at best, is an idea whose time has passed. Despite the liberal label sought to be attached to it by the strange alliance [1] that support them, S. 354 and H.R. 1900 stand exposed as reactionary, retrogressive legislation whose basic principle is to eliminate compensation for non-economic injuries and to impose ceilings on reparations for economic injuries growing out of automobile injuries to the bodies and minds of human beings. Federal no-fault is dead on the merits, and this Honorable Committee should give it Congressional burial and move on to better and brighter things.

Mr. VAN DEERLIN. I presume that people would like a luncheon break. What about coming back in at 1:30?

The hearing will recess until 1:30 p.m.

---

[1] The *Houston Chronicle* of June 15, 1975, quotes Leslie Cheeck, Vice President for Federal Affairs of AIA, principal propagandist organization for S. 354 and its counterparts, as saying with startling frankness to Newhouse News Service: "There is almost always a self-interest. Almost nobody is for no-fault for strictly altruistic reasons."

[Whereupon, at 12:30 p.m., the subcommittee recessed, to reconvene at 1:30 p.m., the same day.]

AFTER RECESS

[The subcommittee reconvened at 1:30 p.m., Hon. Lionel Van Deerlin presiding.]

Mr. VAN DEERLIN. The subcommittee will resume its hearing. The next witness is John Mackay, immediate past president of the Illinois State Bar Association.

STATEMENT OF JOHN R. MACKAY, IMMEDIATE PAST PRESIDENT, ILLINOIS STATE BAR ASSOCIATION

Mr. MACKAY. Mr. Chairman, my name is John R. Mackay. I am here as immediate past president of the Illinois State Bar Association. I would like to preface my statement by making a few observations.

First of all, I am here as an individual practicing lawyer from Wheaton, Ill. I am not a personal injury trial lawyer. As a matter of fact, only a relatively small number of the lawyers that are members of the Illinois State Bar Association are trial lawyers in the sense that they derive a substantial portion of their living from the trial of cases.

I cite this because in the past it has been said with some frequency that the opposition to no-fault has originated with and has substantially remained the burden or obligation of the trial lawyers, which I assert to you is not the case.

The Illinois State Bar Association has some 18,000 or 18,500 members out of the 23,000 to 24,000 practicing lawyers in the State of Illinois. The Association, through its 124-man assembly has voted to oppose no-fault insurance for the reasons which I will give hereafter.

Now, I would like to say at this juncture that we had participated in the hearings before the Senate committee. We realized then and we realize from our study of the documents which have been introduced before this committee that you have been supplied with a plethora of materials, statistics, and testimony from those that are more able than I and far better informed than I on those aspects of the subject.

I will confine my remarks today largely to the philosophical objections we have to it. So, if you and Mr. Kinzler are prepared to be philosophical I think we will get along famously.

The basic reasons for the opposition of the State of Illinois Bar Association to any scheme of national no-fault automobile insurance are threefold:

First and foremost: Because of the vast differences that exist between the States and among the regions of the United States, we urge that the subject of auto reparations is far better suited to resolution by the States as opposed to the Federal Government.

Second: The constitutional problems inherent in any Federal no-fault scheme must give concern to any citizens concerned about our constitutional Federalism and the rights of the American public.

Third: The more pragmatic but equally important issue of the ultimate cost of such a scheme to the American public must also be considered.

Because I am well aware that there has been considerable testimony offered to both the Senate committee on this question, I will not attempt to enlarge on testimony which has been previously given, but I will, however, touch upon what I believe to be the central or pivotal issues confronting this committee.

I would not be here today if the Illinois State Bar Association did not believe it of vital importance to add its voice to that of other groups opposing this legislation even though its opposition may very well be predicated upon the same objections.

In connection with our suggestion that automobile reparations reform is a subject peculiarly suited to resolution by the particular States, we say it is true that, while people may drive similar automobiles on similar highways in all of the 50 States involved and the District of Columbia, and are occasionally involved in accidents, the problems of New York are not those of Nevada; the problems of Illinois are not those of Maine.

Nevertheless, the attitudes of the public in various States toward the resolution of issues arising out of automobile accidents, the driving habits of citizens of different States, accident experience in various States, and premium structure in various States are only a few areas of distinct differences among the various States in the area of auto reparations.

The very multiplicity of State solutions to auto reparations problems is we believe irrefutable evidence that the citizens of different States will want to follow their own destiny as defined by them in determining whether or not to accept auto reparations as a method of approach which will adapt the legislation to their needs as they view them and understand them.

The pressure to impose a uniform plan on all the States is difficult to understand when we consider the vast diversities that exist within our society of over 200 million people.

Earlier in today's testimony it was observed that approximately half of the States have adopted no-fault or legislation corresponding or bearing the title of no-fault whereas approximately half have not.

The individual posing the question about the slowness of the States in responding to the issues indicated that the speed with which the issues were being resolved by the State were not responding quickly enough to the needs in question.

The one to whom the question was posed indicated it depended on how you looked at it. The pessimistic view would say the glass was half empty. The optimistic view would say the glass was half full.

In this subject matter today, we are departing from a method of solving problems which has existed time out of mind, to use a common law expression, and it is not the sort of problem which lends itself readily to solutions.

We think the mere fact that virtually more than half of the States have adopted auto reparations in differing forms is indicative of viability on the part of the States to handle this problem after their own fashion.

Auto reparations has had a relatively short history—so short that the experiences in the various States are difficult to analyze and synthesize at the present time. Yet, there are difinite indications that certain plans are well suited to certain States and the evidence on the various plans should be even more clear-cut within the next few years.

Contrasted to this empirical approach to the problem is the suggestion now presented to the subcommittee that, under the guise of minimum national standards, a Federal scheme for auto reparations be imposed uniformly and unilaterally in all 50 States. Commonsense dictates, we believe, that such a scheme not be adopted prior to the evaluation of the results of the individual efforts of the various States.

We suggest you have 50 different laboratories in which the experiments may be conducted, from which you may draw evidence after passage of a sufficient period of time to allow actuarial studies to be predicated on what has occurred and to accept actuarial studies as to what is likely to occur.

I am pleased that the position of the Illinois State Bar Association in this area is not confined to lawyers' organizations but, in addition, was articulated by the Honorable William T. Coleman, Jr., Secretary of Transportation, before the Senate Commerce Committee, which was at that time considering S. 354 in May of this year.

In addition to not being a personal injury trial lawyer, I concede that I am not a constitutional scholar. However, evidence presented both to the Senate committee regarding S. 354, as well as the testimony submitted to this committee regarding the two pending bills, raises the specter of the unconstitutionality of both approaches.

A scheme of the type embodied in S. 354 and H.R. 1900, in which the Congress invades States' sovereignty by requiring State agencies to act as though they were Federal instrumentalities certainly imperils the basic concept of constitutional Federalism.

A second constitutional issue which has somehow receded into the background in these discussions is the simple, yet fundamental, question of whether the deprivation of human rights in the interest of expediency can be justified. Depriving innocent auto accident victims in virtually every case from recovering damages from a negligent motorist strikes at the fundamentally simple but yet basic human right which our laws have consistently protected.

The third reason why the Illinois State Bar Association opposes the legislation is the anticipated economic impact of imposing such a scheme on all the citizens of all 50 States.

While it was originally suggested as a part of S. 354 and related legislation that cost saving of premiums was an important reason why such a bill should be passed, it seems that such an argument like others originally advanced in favor of such legislation has been abandoned.

As this subcommittee probably is aware, testimony was presented on behalf of the Allstate Insurance Co. to the Senate Committee that the effect of S. 354 would be to raise automobile insurance premium rates in virtually every State from 35 to 80 percent. Such testimony should not be ignored.

If the ultimate cost of S. 354 and H.R. 1900 is anywhere near this order of magnitude, the implication seems clear that the cost of such a scheme is too enormous to be desirable.

The second economic impact of H.R. 1900 would be to impose higher insurance premium rates on the suburban father who enjoys relatively low rates under the fault system, and a decrease in rates for the young single male driver who is currently a prime cause of auto accidents and pays auto insurance premiums accordingly.

A third economic impact of H.R. 1900 would be the possible destruction of many small insurance companies throughout the United States. I am advised of testimony before the Senate subcommittee to the effect that small insurance companies would find it difficult and perhaps impossible to obtain reinsurance for the writing of unlimited medical benefits such as proposed in S. 354 and H.R. 1900.

I mention this fact because Illinois is home for several of the largest automobile insurance carriers, among them State Farm and Allstate, but at the same time is also the domicile for many small independent insurance companies with a long history of good service to their local communities.

If the economic impact of H.R. 1900 were the only objection to the bill, I believe it should give the Congress serious cause for concern. When it is added to the other serious basic objections, the sum total of objections seems to far outweigh the benefits claimed by the supporters of such legislation.

I point to the fact that the studies made by two large responsible casualty insurance companies differ to such a substantial extent that it appears that they are not the results purely of the work of actuaries but reflect and incorporate many judgmental values which enter into it. Otherwise, the studies could not possibly vary to the degree that they do.

The Illinois State Bar Association has consistently supported fair and equitable auto reparation reform. Under its auspices, an auto reparations bill was drafted and supported in the Illinois Legislature in 1973. The bill was approved by both Houses of the legislature but subsequently vetoed by our Governor.

In 1971, Illinois adopted one of the first no-fault laws to be passed but our Supreme Court promptly declared it unconstitutional; indicating that one arm of our sovereign State disagreed with another regarding the public policy involved in that particular legislation; indicating further that no-fault insurance phrased along different lines embodying at least a slightly differing philosophy might very well meet with the approval of our Supreme Court.

I submit that our experience in Illinois whereby the legislature, the judiciary, and the executive had not yet agreed on any plan as appropriate for Illinois does not demonstrate any need for a Federal bill but, rather, indicates that the need for each State to work out its own destiny in this regard is essential.

Mr. VAN DEERLIN. At that point, could you bring us up to date on what happened this year? It was assumed that Illinois, like California, was going to move on it this year.

Mr. MACKAY. Yes, sir; there are two bills pending, sir, one which originated in the Senate and one which originated in the House.

The Senate bill has been amended in the House to eliminate the threshold. So, presently, we have two Oregon-type bills pending. It is anticipated that affirmative action will be taken on those bills or one of the bills this fall. Presently, we are operating under the fault system.

Mr. VAN DEERLIN. Is the Governor in a mood to sign it?

Mr. MACKAY. Neither bill has passed both Houses, Mr. Chairman.

Mr. VAN DEERLIN. Is there any indication of cooperation?

Mr. MACKAY. Yes; there is. It appears fairly certain that Illinois will adopt a no-fault bill. How it will fare in the courts, of course, I don't know. Usually litigation ensues to test the strength and the weaknesses of a bill of such importance. I would imagine that that will occur in this case, as well.

Now, I regard my appearance before this committee like arguing a case on appeal which I do more often than appearing before a legislative committee. This is not an opportunity to read a prepared statement to you necessarily but engage in a dialog as opposed to a monolog.

I welcome questions, if you have any.

[Mr. Mackay's prepared statement follows:]

STATEMENT OF JOHN R. MACKAY, IMMEDIATE PAST PRESIDENT, ILLINOIS BAR ASSOCIATION

Mr. Chairman and members of the committee: I make this statement to the Subcommittee on Consumer Protection and Finance on behalf of the Illinois State Bar Association of which I am the immediate past president.

The Illinois State Bar Association has approximately 18,000 members practicing in all areas of the law in the State of Illinois.

I am a practicing lawyer in Wheaton, Illinois. I am not a personal injury trial lawyer and do not engage in that type of practice. Only a relatively small number of the membership of the Illinois State Bar Association are trial lawyers. I cite these facts because in the past it has frequently been reported that opposition to federal no-fault automobile insurance by the legal profession has been undertaken by personal injury trial lawyers.

The Illinois State Bar Association, acting through its 124-person assembly elected from all parts of Illinois and representing a broad spectrum of the legal profession, has consistently supported auto reparations reform on the state level, but is opposed to any scheme of federal automobile no-fault legislation.

The basic reasons for the opposition of the Illinois State Bar Association to any scheme of national no-fault automobile insurance are three-fold. First, and foremost, is the reason that, because of the vast differences which exist among the states and among the regions of the United States, the subject of auto reparations is far better suited to resolution by the states and not the federal government. Second, the constitutional problems inherent in any federal no-fault scheme must give concern to any citizens concerned about our federal system and the rights of the American public. Third, the more pragmatic, but important issue of the ultimate cost of such a scheme to the American public must be considered.

I am well aware that there has been considerable testimony presented to the Congress as to each of these objections to a federal no-fault scheme. I will, therefore, make my observations very brief. However, I would not be present here today if the Illinois State Bar Association did not believe it of vital importance to add its voice to that of other groups opposing this legislation even though its opposition is predicated upon the same objections.

AUTOMOBILE REPARATIONS REFORM IS A SUBJECT PECULIARLY SUITED TO RESOLUTION BY THE INDIVIDUAL STATES

It is true that people drive similar automobiles on similar highways in all of the fifty states and are occasionally involved in accidents, but the problems of New York are not those of Nevada, nor are the problems of Illinois those of the State of Maine.

Nevertheless, the attitudes of the public in various states toward the resolution of issues arising out of automobile accidents, the driving habits of citizens of different states, accidents experience in various states, and premium structure in various states are only a few areas of distinct differences among the various states in the area of auto reparations.

The very multiplicity of state solutions to auto reparations problems is irrefutable evidence that the citizens of different states will approve different solutions to the subject of auto reparation reform.

The pressure to impose a uniform plan on all the states is difficult to understand when one considers the vast diversities that exist within our society of over 200 million persons.

As this Committee well knows, 24 states have passed some form of auto reparations legislation within the last few years and each of the remaining 26 states has considered the subject of auto reparation reforms during its 1975 legislative session.

Doubtless other states will eventually legislate in this area in a manner best suited to the needs of the citizens of those states. I might be so bold as to suggest that in a given state or states it might be determined that no auto reparations legislation is necessary.

Auto reparation reform has had a relatively short history. It is so short that the experiences in the various states are difficult to analyze and synthesize at the present time. Yet there are definite indications that certain plans are well suited to individual states and the evidence on the various plans should be even more clear cut within the next few years.

Contrasted to this empirical approach to the problem is the suggestion now presented to the Subcommittee that under the guise of minimum national standards, a federal scheme for auto reparations be imposed uniformly and unilaterally in all 50 states. Common sense dictates that such a scheme not be adopted prior to evaluation of the results of the individual efforts of the various states.

I am pleased that the position of the Illinois State Bar Association in this area is not peculiar to lawyers' organizations, but was articulated by the Honorable William T. Coleman, Jr., Secretary of Transportation, before the Senate Commerce Committee which was at that time considering S. 354, on May 5, 1975.

ISSUES OF CONSTITUTIONALITY

I have stated that I am not a personal injury trial lawyer and I am equally quick to concede that I am not a constitutional scholar.

Nevertheless, testimony presented to the Senate Committee regarding S. 354 clearly raises a specter of unconstitutionality as to S. 354 and H.R. 1900.

A scheme of the type embodied in S. 354 and H.R. 1900 in which the congress invades state sovereignty by requiring state agencies to act as though they were federal instrumentalities certainly imperils the basic concept of federalism.

A second constitutional issue, which has somehow receded into the background in these discussions, is the simple yet fundamental question of whether the deprivation of human rights in the interest of expediency can be justified. Depriving innocent auto accident victims in virtually every case from recovering damages from a negligent motorist strikes at a fundamentally simple, yet basic human right which our laws have consistently protected.

I respectfully suggest that the constitutional issues alone should militate against the approval of H.R. 1900.

THE ECONOMIC IMPACT OF H.R. 1900 IS ALSO A CAUSE FOR SERIOUS CONCERN

The third major reason why the Illinois State Bar Association opposes H.R. 1900 is the anticipated economic impact of imposing such a scheme on the citizens of all 50 states.

While it was originally suggested in support of S. 354 that cost saving of premium was an important reason why such a bill should be passed, it seems that such an argument, like many others originally advanced in favor of S. 354, has been abandoned.

As this Subcommittee probably is aware, testimony was presented on behalf of Allstate Insurance Company to the Senate Committee that the effect of S. 354 would be to raise automobile insurance premium rates in virtually every state from 35 to 80 percent. Such testimony cannot be ignored. If the ultimate cost of S. 354 and H.R. 1900 is any where near this order of magnitude, the implication seems clear that the cost of such a scheme is too enormous to be desirable.

The second economic impact of H.R. 1900 would be to impose higher insurance premium rates on the suburban father, (who enjoys relatively low rates under the fault system) and a decrease in rates for the young single male driver who is currently a prime cause of auto accidents and pays auto insurance premiums accordingly.

A third economic impact of H.R. 1900 would be the possible destruction of many small insurance companies throughout the United States. I am advised of testimony before the Senate Subcommittee to the effect that smaller insurance companies would find it difficult and perhaps impossible to obtain reinsurance for the writing of unlimited medical benefits, such as proposed in S. 354 and H.R. 1900. I mention this fact because Illinois is home for several of the largest automobile insurance carriers, but at the same time is also the domicile for many small independent insurance companies with a long history of good service to their local communities.

If the economic impact of H.R. 1900 were the only objection to the bill, I believe it should give the Congress serious cause for concern. When it is added to the other serious, basic objections, the sum total of objections seems to far outweigh the benefits claimed by supporters of S. 354 and H.R. 1900.

CONCLUSION

The Illinois State Bar Association has consistently supported fair and equitable auto reparation reform. Under its auspices an auto reparations bill was drafted and supported in the Illinois legislature in 1973. The bill was approved by both houses of the legislature and vetoed by our governor. In 1971 Illinois adopted one of the first no-fault laws to be passed. Our Supreme Court promptly declared it unconstitutional.

I submit that our experience in Illinois whereby the legislature, the judiciary and the executive have not yet agreed on which plan is appropriate for Illinois does not demonstrate any need for a federal bill, but rather indicates the need for each state to work out its own destiny in this regard.

At the present time there are two auto reparations bills pending before the Illinois legislature which should receive final consideration in the fall of this year. There exists strong sentiment in Illinois for auto reparations on a state level and I venture the opinion that Illinois will have an auto reparations plan in the near future. I respectfully request that you consider the wishes of the citizens of Illinois in this matter.

I wish to thank the Chairman and members of the Subcommittee for graciously granting me this opportunity to present the views of the Illinois State Bar Association.

Mr. VAN DEERLIN. Thank you.

Mr. KINZLER. Mr. Mackay, in the beginning of your statement you indicate that the Illinois State Bar Association acting through its 124-person assembly elected from all parts of Illinois voted in favor of this position. Can you supply the committee with the exact resolution and the vote on that resolution?

Mr. MACKAY. I cannot at the moment, but eventually I can; yes.

Mr. KINZLER. That would be useful to give some feeling as to what kind of split there was and what the resolution was.

[The following material was received for the record:]

EXTRACT FROM PROCEEDINGS OF ILLINOIS STATE BAR ASSOCIATION ASSEMBLY

AUTO ACCIDENT REPARATIONS

A report was received from the Chairman of this Committee concerning SB 945, "A bill to require no-fault motor vehicle insurance as a condition precedent to operating a motor vehicle on streets roads, and highways or other lands open to automobile use by the public in order to promote and regulate interstate commerce." Also considered was a resolution of the North Carolina Bar Association opposing SB 945, Part 3. Motion Sorensen/Jenkins that the Board of Governors of the Illinois State Bar Association oppose the adoption of the Hart-Magnuson Bill (SB 945). Carried unanimously.

Motion Corcoran/Weihl to adopt the following four resolutions:

(1) That the Illinois State Bar Association communicate this opposition to all Illinois Congressmen and to all members of the appropriate committees in the House of Representatives and Senate and the press, setting forth the reasons for the objection.

(2) That the Illinois State Bar Association take necessary steps to arrange for a delegation of Illinois attorneys to meet with Congressmen from Illinois to explain the objections of the Bar to this bill and that a specific memorandum in support of these objections be prepared.

(3) That attempts be made to arrange a meeting of a delegation of Illinois attorneys with the members of the committee or committees which will consider this bill in the US House and Senate.

(4) That the necessary expenditures be authorized to implement the above three resolutions.

Motion to adopt these four resolutions carried unanimously. [N.B.: President Allen appointed Messrs. Householter, Mullen, Weihl and Sorensen to draft the above referenced memorandum.]

Motion Decker/Mackay that the memorandum be distributed to the members of the Board of Governors by mail and objections, if any, to the report shall be made in writing within three days. Motion carried unanimously.

Motion Barnard/Jenkins that the President of the Association shall be the Chairman of such delegation meeting with legislative representatives. Carried unanimously.

[Telegram]

JULY 28, 1972.

Hon. CHARLES H. PERCY,
New Senate Office Building,
Washington, D.C.

The Board of Governors of the Illinois State Bar Association strongly urges referral of the Hart-Magnuson Bill (SB 945) be referred to the Senate Judiciary Committee for further study and consideration because of its impact upon the American motoring public.

Lyle W. Allen, President Illinois State Bar Association.

[This exact telegram was sent to Honorable Adlai E. Stevenson, Old Senate Office Building, Washington, D.C.]

Mr. KINZLER. What would you consider the basic objective of a reparations system?

Mr. MACKAY. I would imagine the basic objectives are the prompt payment of moneys to deserving injured parties.

Mr. KINZLER. Under the existing system, we were told yesterday, a clear-cut tort case—where there is no debate with respect to liability—can take 2 years to go through the courts to determine the damages. Is that still the case?

Mr. MACKAY. Is this typical?

Mr. KINZLER. This was a particular case. I am asking whether this is typical in your experience and knowledge?

Mr. MACKAY. In view of the fact I do not profess to be a personal-injury lawyer, I can hardly speak from experience. However, I have been active in the practice of law; I am in the courthouse daily; and I know this: In my county, Du Page County, Ill., immediately west of Chicago's Cook County, Ill., that the speed with which a case is tried is dependent, in large measure, on several factors:

One: The vigor with which counsel will push the case for trial, the difficulty and complexity of ascertaining the facts which would require, of course, discovery proceeding and availability of judge and jury for trial.

It is not typical in my county that it would take 2 years to try the average personal-injury case.

Mr. KINZLER. But it certainly would take at the very least a number of months?

Mr. MACKAY. Customarily, yes; that is correct.

Mr. KINZLER. The suggestion is that the no-fault type of proposal we have before us would pay people on receipt of their medical bills. In fact, one argument which has been made is that the present system discriminates against the poor because they don't have the economic wherewithal to wait out a long case or settlement, so they are forced to settle for a very much smaller percentage of their potential right in court than a rich person.

Do you feel that is an accurate statement?

Mr. MACKAY. There are two sides to that coin, Mr. Kinzler. Assuming that the injured person is not disabled from working, it would impose no particular——

Mr. KINZLER. No; but a more seriously injured person, a person who sustains $20,000 worth of economic loss, that is pretty serious.

Mr. MACKAY. Yes; I would agree that is a serious loss.

In the case of that, the Illinois Supreme Court rules make provision for advancing the case over cases which may have been filed before it under circumstances of that sort.

However, if that motion should be denied, I would concede that having to wait that period of time by a poor or deprived person would be unfair.

Mr. KINZLER. The difficulty we face is that there is no question that a low level of benefits, a $5,000 or $10,000-benefit package, with or without a tort threshold, will take care of 95 to 98 or even 99 percent of the people, but we have statistics before us, undisputed statistics, that 1 to 1½ percent of the people suffer 77 percent of the economic loss. Those are the people who have losses over $10,000.

What we are trying to devise is a system that can pay those people a greater percentage of their losses. The theory of no-fault is that in good part it cuts out the overpayment for nuisance claims and channels that money to the people with the most serious losses, who are now getting only 30 percent recovery of their economic losses.

Mr. MACKAY. I understand. I don't agree, however, that the approach you are taking is a proper approach from the point of view of society as a whole. You say a relatively small number of people sustain most of the economic loss.

Mr. KINZLER. Right.

Mr. MACKAY. Should the others, by that reasoning, be deprived of their right to litigate.

Mr. KINZLER. It becomes a question of why you buy insurance.

Mr. MACKAY. You have heard of the mythological highway robber, Procrustes?

Mr. KINZLER. I am about to hear about him.

Mr. MACKAY. Procrustes was a Greek mythological highway robber who had an iron bed. Every time he would rob somebody he would place him on the bed. If they were too long, he would cut them to shape the bed. If they were too short, he would stretch them to fit the bed.

I think, if you will pardon my observation, that this method of approach in some respects duplicates the efforts of Procrustes.

I don't think that by far the greater majority of people should suffer a substantial loss merely to facilitate the payment of moneys to a relatively small number of people.

Mr. KINZLER. You have put your finger on a number of things in addition to the bed. One is the question of substantial loss. I would submit that $500 is not a substantial loss for most people.

Mr. MACKAY. For most people.

Mr. KINZLER. Yet, the people who suffer those losses receive a distinctly disproportionate amount of money relative to their losses, not for pain and suffering, but for the nuisance value of their claim.

I don't think anybody would contend we should pay people much more than economic loss simply because it costs an insurance company more to litigate than what the economic loss is.

Why do we buy insurance? We certainly don't buy insurance to cover ourselves for a $500 or $1,000 loss. We buy it to cover us for a serious accident. That is why I buy insurance.

If, indeed, the subcommittee were to come to the conclusion that, for the same premium dollar, give or take 5 or 10 percent one way or the other, we could have a system that paid everybody 100 percent of their economic loss up to $25,000 or $30,000 or $40,000 compared to 450 percent for small economic losses, 260 percent for losses of approximately $7,000, down to about 100 percent for $10,000 but only 30 percent for economic losses of $25,000 or more. I would think it would be hard to stay with the tort approach.

Certainly people should have the right to recover for small losses. The question is, is it fair to give them more than their real losses when we can give their economic loss? Is it a more equitable system?

Mr. MACKAY. I think it is a more equitable system to give to each according to his needs.

I hope not to be accused of being a Communist because they say to each according to his need and from each according to his ability to pay. I think that this approach partakes of that philosophy slightly.

Now, the mere fact that somebody is deserving to a greater extent than the one sitting next to him does not mean that his case should take precedent or that the vindication of his rights should, of necessity, involve the invasion of diminution of the rights of a person sitting next to him.

It might very well be, Mr. Kinzler, that auto reparations or the form which apparently you visualize may ultimately be the way to go about it.

One of our objections is the way you go about it. We don't think you should start at the top. We don't think that you should start at the Federal level imposing a standard, abrogating, canceling, expurgating, whatever other participle I can think of, but, rather, I think you should relegate this problem to the States, allow the States to find their own destiny in this matter, profit by the mistakes which we make, and I am sure we will make some, perhaps many, profit by the mistakes which we make and then having had the benefit of knowing what mistakes we have made, what benefits we have conferred upon our peoples, then if you must have Federal legislation that would be the time to initiate it.

Mr. KINZLER. One final question——

Mr. MACKAY. If I may say this.

I do believe that the studies made by the Senate committee, as well as by this particular committee, have had a very beneficial catalytic effect upon American society in the sense it has brought us to think about and to do something about this particular subject possibly years before we might otherwise have been brought to do it.

I think that the greatest benefit which you can achieve would be to continue your studies, not recommend the adoption of the legislation, but adopt, I will say for want of a better word, a watchdog committee to see how the States fare in their efforts and the speed with which they accomplish things and, once having the benefit of that, then let us hear from you again.

In the meantime, we believe it is the sovereign function of the individual States to solve their own problems.

Mr. KINZLER. We have 1 or 2 minutes before the chairman has to leave again. Let me see if I can possibly fit in one more question.

If the subcommittee decided to go ahead with a minimum standards bill, could you talk to the question of what should be included in your viewpoing? In other words, what factors vary from State to State and what factors might be common to all States?

Stay with two specific elements, medical payment and wage loss.

Mr. MACKAY. I will begin by saying that I don't believe the Federal sovereign should impose a minimum standards bill.

Second, I would say in these experiments to be conducted by the States, and I don't mean a random or haphazard thing but a well thought out plan devised by the legislative bodies of each State, they should provide for prompt payments to deserving people and ideally without fault, if that is possible.

I believe that they should do it without having to pay expensive doctors, expensive experts, and sometimes expensive lawyers to represent them in that connection. I believe most of them would be satisfied with less delivered to them much quicker.

Mr. KINZLER. If I were to tell you that the difference between $50,000 medical coverage and unlimited coverage was one-tenth of 1 percent on a premium dollar, would you see any objection to giving everyone as a minimum standard unlimited medical coverage?

Mr. MACKAY. That sounds wonderful.

Mr. KINZLER. Thank you very much.

Mr. VAN DEERLIN. We will recess again for 10 minutes.

[Brief recess.]

Mr. VAN DEERLIN. Mr. Stoup of the Missouri Bar.

STATEMENT OF ARTHUR H. STOUP, PRESIDENT, THE MISSOURI BAR

Mr. STOUP. My name is Arthur H. Stoup. I am a practicing attorney in Missouri. I am the president of the Missouri Bar which is an integrated bar which means anyone desiring to practice law in the State of Missouri must be a member of that bar. We have approximately 8,000 members. Membership is represented, in turn, by a 35-member board of governors, which is elected. Any remarks I might make today I want the Chair to know are endorsed unanimously by our board of governors.

Before I get into the body of my remarks, I would hope that the chairman will excuse me a personal aside which illustrates two things:

One, the dedication of the Missouri Bar to the principles which we will speak to later, and the dedication of your speaker today to these principles; and, two, the concern that we have with the bills before this committee as to the scepter of bureaucracy which hangs over all of our heads.

The allusion I would like to make is this: For the first time yesterday in the 25 years I practiced law, I walked out of the courtroom and left a client to come here. The lawsuit only involves $10 million, which is one of the biggest lawsuits I have been involved in, and it has nothing to do with personal injuries; it is contract action. It involves a Government agency and the approval of a set-aside program where the Government was funding 80 percent of a building in Kansas City. The agency was UMTA, Urban Mass Transit Authority, an agency under DOT.

What had happened here was that the Government, in order to assure that there were minorities used in the erection of this building, set up what is known as a set-aside program whereby minorities had to be given the work in certain areas which encompasses some 55 percent of the total cost of this $10 million building.

DOT delegated to UMTA the responsibility to see that there was some compliance. UMTA delegated it to the director of human relations in Kansas City, who is a lady, and she made the determination that the two lowest bidders were not responsive; they did not address the set-aside areas. She, in turn, certified the third bidder who was a half million dollars higher.

It became apparent to some of those like myself who represented one of the lower bidding contractors that there might be things that did not quite meet the eye. So, I filed a lawsuit in Kansas City, Mo., in the courts there.

One of the other contractors decided that he was going to go through the plethora of bureaucracy and he filed an application for a review before the Comptroller General.

We all came up here to Washington 3½ months ago and we were going to get a quick remedy. We are now 3 months later and the Comptroller General has never ruled. We have demonstrated by sworn testimony to UMTA that their agent who certified the contractor, the third lowest bidder, did not follow even UMTA's guidelines and UMTA, rather than backing up and saying, look, we are going to decertify you, Mr. Contractor No. 3, they say, no, you let the courts in Missouri resolve it.

That is where we are. We have been in trial since Monday.

I did something I had to do yesterday and that was at 2:30, make up my mind whether my commitment was more to my client or more to my country. That is why I am here. I left that lawsuit, the biggest one I have handled, in the hands of one of my young associates because that is all I had left and I could not stop it. But I am terribly concerned over this pending legislation and that is why we are here.

I want to also say before I go any further that the views I express here are also the views of the South Dakota Bar, which is a small bar association, and their president, Frank Brady, says I can convey that to you today.

I want to make the record abundantly clear that the Missouri Bar and South Dakota Bar are in opposition to any legislation on the Federal level which would impose upon all of the people of the United States a system for automobile reparation.

So there is not any misunderstanding of my position and the position of the Missouri Bar, I want to again state to this committee that the Missouri Bar has for at least the last 3 years, if my memory is not incorrect, at each session of the legislature put into the hopper and actively and vigorously campaigned for a no-fault type of bill, what Mr. Kinzler would probly refer to as an add-on bill, but a bill, nonetheless, that would supply to the citizens of Missouri an ability to immediately get, (1) their medical costs paid; and (2) get some portion of their economic wage loss reimbursed to them. We can do this at not too great a cost, at no disruption of our basic system which has given us 200 years of freedom.

Now, in that regard, I have to report to you very sadly that it was not adopted at the last session of the legislature. The Senate takes one position and the House of Representatives takes another and they fought themselves to a standstill.

I can also say to you that within the last 2 months I have had extended conversations with the insurance carriers who are primarily interested in this in Missouri and I am confident, based on some things that we have worked out between ourselves and I will allude to these, that we will have a bill adopted next year.

The big problem we have in Missouri is very simply this: The carriers who have a powerful lobby in our legislature insisted on a floor, a threshold. They didn't care what it was but they wanted a threshold. It was a point of policy with them.

The constitution of Missouri, article I, section 14, says there shall be a remedy for every injury to person or property. That is literally the exact words. It does not say $200 or over $500 or $1,000. This is a nonnegotiable item. Even if we liked a threshold approach philosophically, we couldn't accept it, constitutionally.

The insurance carriers, the ones I have talked to, have now come to the realization that constitutionally what the bar has said for 4 years is accurate and correct and they are willing next year, so they have told me, to withdraw their objections to putting a bill through that doesn't have a threshold. I think with that out of the way we will have it passed.

The reason for not doing it this year, as they expressed it to me, is that, "We have spent too much time in educating this legislature on how great the threshold would be, and if we had to go back at this session we are going to lose face, we don't want to lose face. But, you put it in next year and we will stay out of your way."

Now, that may not be very binding on anybody, but I think it will work. These are all men of their word and they are gentlemen and I think they will live up to it.

So, I can report to you that I think Missouri next year will be a State with first-party benefits which addresses itself to probably any losses—98 or 99 percent of the people.

I am also concerned as was explained to other committees when Secretary Coleman referred to the problem of the significant watershed and traditional relationships between the Federal Government and State insurance regulations. I believe the enactment of any Federal bill on no-fault legislation would irreparably damage these valuable exploratory efforts that have been made in other areas or other States such as our sister State, Kansas.

In my opinion, the enactment of such sweeping Federal legislation should be premised on something more than a mere desired change of law. There should be a real compelling need for it. I don't think, parenthetically, that that need has been demonstrated. I am sure Mr. Kinzler is going to ask me some questions about that.

I think, to the best of my knowledge, three reasons have been put forth, or four reasons, why there should be a Federal no-fault bill: (1) to reduce the congestion in our courts; (2) to reduce the cost of insurance premiums; (3) to provide uniformity in a reparations system; and (4) to assure that all persons injured in automobile accidents are promptly and fairly paid their lost wages and expenses which they have incurred in securing medical, hospitalization, rehabilitation, and other services.

Taking first the question of the court congestion, I must confess, so to speak, that I am somewhat limited in that area because we don't have it in Missouri and I am a trial lawyer; I am not like John Mackay.

I try any kind of lawsuit that a person needs as long as it is on the civil side of the table, and I am over to that courthouse all the time.

So, I have very carefully watched what the statistics are, as well as having the gut reaction that I think any good lawyer has.

I have attached those statistics out of Jackson County, which is Kansas City, Mo., and a county of about 850,000 or more. The reason these statistics don't appear to be as clear as they might be is this, that, in Jackson County we get more litigation than most other counties get for the number of persons because our western boundary is the State line of Kansas. Kansas has a law which requires unanimous vote of all the jurors in a civil case. In Missouri, it only takes nine.

So, it is a more friendly forum in Missouri if you want to bring a plaintiff's case for personal injuries than you would find in Kansas because of this one problem, and other things. So, we get more litigation, so to speak, than most other areas do.

We are also very fortunate in Jackson County that we have computerized our caseloads. Amazing things come out. That is, if you look at our statistics, you will find that in 1970 something like 12.72 percent of all of the civil cases, and this is only civil cases, were people who were injured in vehicular automobile accidents. But between 1970 and 1974, which is the last full year of reporting, due to the fact that the lawyers and the insurance companies have worked together to try to get the people with the small claims paid, the companies are prepaying, paying benefits for doctors, voluntarily—we have no-fault, no State imposition at all—that our caseload has dropped from 12.72 percent in 1970 for people injured in automobile accidents, to 7.52 percent of the caseload in 1974.

That is a drop of 40 percent in 5 years without the help of the State or the Federal Government. It is amazing what you can do without enacting new laws.

I can get a trial in any civil case that I want to get it in, assuming it is all prepared and ready to go, in 6 months. This very matter I am trying right now I filed in the middle of March. We have been to the court of appeals because one of the parties didn't want to be dragged into court and he wanted to get the lower trial prohibited, and we have argued that out as well.

So, we have been to the court of appeals; we have been to the Comptroller General; and we are still at trial in 4 months. It is a very complex case and it involves 11 lawyers. It is difficult to even get that many bodies together at one time and we are still doing it. The system can work. It does work. So, court congestion is not a basis for a Federal no-fault bill.

I am not saying that there aren't cities or States with problems. But let them address the problem as we have in Missouri. Let them have their legislatures see to it that there are enough trial judges appointed to hear the cases if they have the problem.

As one of the witnesses said earlier, you don't throw the baby out with the bath water. I think that is very appropriate here. In any event, that is one of the problems, as I see it.

I don't think that we can do anything more, no matter what the system is, than to try to point out to people how they can solve some of their problems. Court congestion, in my opinion, is not one of the problems which will be solved by a Federal no-fault bill.

The second argument which has been advocated from time to time is that a Federal tort immunity law, Federal no-fault, automobile reparations is going to reduce the cost of automobile insurance. I am going to discuss this more fully in my written paper, but let me say this to you:

I don't think, and I have not seen anyone quote any figures that would prove to me, that this statement is anything more or less than a sham. In the first place, when we talk about auto insurance cost let us square something up.

Sixty-six percent of every insurance dollar in the automobile field goes to paying for property damage. It could be 65, but it is in excess of 60. This was verified to me by the insurance companies, MFA, one of the biggest carriers in the State of Missouri, right out of their records.

So, when we are talking about the thing addressed in H.R. 1900 or S. 354 on the Senate side or S. 72, when you are talking about a reduction of premium you are only addressing to the 30 or 33 percent of the problem side, the bodily injury premium.

If we accept the arguments of the proponents of Federal no-fault, the best they project is a 15 percent savings. This is the best. Let us take them at their word. Fifteen percent multiplied by 33 percent of the insurance dollar means you get a net savings of 4.5 percent of your total cost of insurance.

For 4.5 percent, you give up your right of trial, you give up the right to have your case heard before a fair court with a jury of peers and you subject yourself to another bureaucratic level and you put yourself at the mercy of those carriers who do not want to be fair for their own economic gain, and I am sure there must be one carrier someplace that would take that approach.

Now, this is what you give up, for a 4.5 percent savings.

I have discussed this at length in the few times that I can get my 4 children together to get their input because I may be all wet, and I get concerned about it at times. One of them came up with the best answer yet. He said, "Dad, do you know what it sounds to me like?"

"What is that?"

"It sounds like a rip-off."

And I like their expression. I think it is only too true. It is rip-off. I don't think this Congress is going to enact that kind of bill that shortchanges any significant portion of our citizens. I just don't believe it.

One of the other things that is concerning me, we have all seen the statistics where on the one hand Allstate, a reputable and certainly a substantial company, comes in and they say it is going to cost this if you put in something close to S. 354 in effect and then we get State Farm and they come along and come up with another set of figures.

Since there weren't any figures quoted from Missouri, I used our sister State, Kansas. If we listen to Allstate, and I find no quarrel with their figures, it is going to be 76 percent increase or something akin if S. 354 is adapted and imposed on them.

According to State Farm, I understand they say, "Well, you are going to save 3 percent," in Kansas based on the same bill.

So, the two companies are something on the order of 75 to 80 percent apart. This makes me concerned. I am concerned when the two of the biggest insurance companies in the United States can't get within 70 to 75 percent of each other in premiums and then for any group of people to say to this Congress you should mandate something that could have this kind of impact on our citizenry.

Now, I don't know who is right or who is wrong, but certainly we should not be so presumptuous as to jump into this hole and find out that the worst has happened, that maybe Allstate could be right. Let us find out about it even if we agree there should be something done in this area.

Another thing that has concerned me is the problem of the vehicular damage to automobiles that is caused by collision and the cost of repairing it. We all know that this jumps every day. In fact, I have tendered an exhibit, just the notice I received in the last couple of days from my carrier which happens to be Aetna. What they are doing is justifying why they raised my premium and there has never been an accident in my family; no claims have ever been made. They are justifying two things:

One, why they should raise my premium 14 percent, and it is not just 14 percent of my bodily injury part, they are raising it 14 percent of the property damage which is 66 percent of my entire cost of insurance. Yet, we know that the bodily injury side has not gone up any. Then they throw in a little gig that they support no-fault.

Well, no-fault legislation has nothing to do with 66 percent of this increase they are passing on to me but they don't tell that to their policy-holders.

I am just saying this is some of the unfair propaganda that is coming out. Automobile property damage has gone up daily. They say it is up 14 percent in the last year. I would not debate that with them at all. They are probably accurate in that regard.

Another thing is that certain of these bills that have been brought before this committee would, in my opinion, put claimants at the mercy, so to speak, of this one company who might be more interested in their own economic good than in the good of the policyholders. The way they would accomplish that is this:

The proponents of no fault would not be foolish enough to say, "Look, if we enact no-fault we are also going to enact the fact that no lawyer will represent you." They do it by indirection rather than by direction. They say no part of the basic benefits can be paid to any lawyer for any fee if the first party carrier does not pay the wage loss or the medical bill.

You not only can't assign any portion of that to a lawyer in return for his or her services; in addition to that, if a lawyer enters in an agreement for assignment which is not enforcible, that lawyer is deemed to have committed a crime.

Now, any lawyer that has any sense, and we have to assume they have a little sense or they wouldn't have a license, is not going to do something that would cost him or her a license. The average Joe comes to my office; he says, "Art, I was injured in an automobile wreck. They should have paid me for 3 weeks of compensation. They only paid me for 2. They only paid me for $200 of my medical bill and I had a $400 bill. So, I want to get my other $200 in wages and my other $200 that I have coming for my medical bill."

This poor fellow does not have the money or wherewithal under any of these "no-fault" bills to employ a lawyer. He is a working man. What does he say to me? He has to pay me a couple hundred dollars retainer fee. He says:

"I will give you a piece of the action. I think they call it a contingent fee."

"I can't accept it."
"I will see that you get paid. Don't worry about it."
"No; I can't enter into a contingent fee with you. If I get caught, which I am not going to do, I will lose my license. I can't do it. You will have to pay me in advance."

We have denied that man the right of counsel. I don't care what you say. I don't care if the cost is $200, $400, or $1,000, you still deny to the average general American the ability to hire a lawyer counsel because he cannot enter into the time old arrangement of contingent fees.

Now, this same thing happened back in the early days of social security. They had a limit. If you wanted to process a claim against social security, they turned you down at the administrative level; you could go to the courts but social security adopted a limit on attorneys' fees. It was something like $25. It did not make any difference whether you wound up in the Federal court or court of appeals, you got $25. There were not many cases you saw go up.

Then, about 1968, Senator Long and some other Senators got together and there was a new bill passed which allowed private individuals to contract with lawyers on a similar basis to what they would do in the private sector. Now all you have to do is pick up a Federal Reporter and you will find at least one or two cases in every volume where some Federal court has said: "We have reviewed your actions, Mr. Social Security Agency, now pay the man." Now, you never saw it before.

[Mr. Stoup's prepared statement follows:]

STATEMENT OF ARTHUR H. STOUP, PRESIDENT OF THE MISSOURI BAR

Mr. Chairman, my name is Arthur H. Stoup. I am a practicing attorney in Kansas City Missouri and the President of The Missouri Bar. I appear here today in opposition to the enactment of legislation which would establish federal regulation of the automobile accident reparations system.

So that there will be no misunderstanding of our position, let me say that The Missouri Bar supports meaningful reform of our automobile accident reparations system. We have supported efforts to pass no-fault legislation in Missouri, and we shall continue to work to obtain a no-fault law in Missouri. Likewise, we shall continue to oppose strenuously any proposed federal legislation in this area of the law which has been historically the sole domain of the states. In his statement before the Senate Commerce Committee on May 5, 1975, Secretary of Transportation Coleman suggested that enactment of S. 354, the Hart-Magnuson no-fault bill, "would constitute a significant watershed in the traditional relationship between the federal government and state insurance regulation." I believe that the enactment of *any* federal no-fault legislation would irreparably damage the valuable exploratory efforts of our several states in this new and sparsely-charted field of law reform.

The enactment of such sweeping federal legislation should be premised upon something more than a mere desire to change the law; there should be a compelling national *need* for such legislation. To the best of my knowledge, the arguments most frequently advanced to demonstrate a need for federal legislation are that such legislation is necessary to: (1) Reduce congestion in our courts, (2) Reduce the costs of insurance premiums; (3) Provide a uniformity in the reparations system, and (4) Assure that persons injured in automobile accidents are promptly, and fairly paid their lost wages and the expenses incurred in securing medical, hospitalization, rehabilitation and other services.

Taking first the matter of court congestion, I must confess that my experience with this subject is rather limited because court congestion is not a problem in Missouri. The absence of court congestion in Missouri is not because of the genius of our automobile accident reparations system—our no-fault bill has yet to be passed—but rather because our General Assembly has provided us with enough trial judges to do the job which must be done. According to the *National Survey of Court Organization*, published by the United States Department of Justice in

October, 1973, the ratio of major trial court judges to population in the United States is one judge for every 41,000 persons. In Missouri this ratio is one judge for every 44,000 persons. In Massachusetts by comparison the figure is one judge for every 123,000 persons. If court congestion exists in some parts of the country, the reason is obvious. Equally obvious is the fact that enactment of federal no-fault is not the panacea which is needed.

Of particular interest is the experience in Jackson County, Missouri, a typical urban county, in which Kansas City is situated. Because it borders and adjoins one of the largest metropolitan areas of Kansas, much litigation is filed in Jackson County which could be filed in either state because of Missouri's somewhat more liberal judicial system. (For example, Missouri requires only a nine-juror verdict in civil cases, while Kansas requires the agreement of all twelve jurors.) I have attached to this statement as Exhibit A an extract from the Jackson Circuit Court's Statistical Report for 1974. This report abundantly demonstrates that the impact personal injury actions have on the total case load in that jurisdiction is rather minimal. These statistics from our trial courts show that in 1970 there were 1,401 motor vehicle personal injury cases filed, accounting for 12.72% of all new civil cases. That number steadily decreased during the years 1971 through 1973 to the point in 1974 that only 835 new motor vehicle injury cases were filed, accounting for only 7.25% of all civil cases. During this five-year period, the filing of motor vehicle injury cases decreased by 40% without the assistance of *any* no-fault plan. Furthermore, as you will notice, only 165 personal injury suits of *all* types were tried in Jackson County in 1974. (This includes products liability, malpractice, and miscellaneous types of personal injuries).

It is clear that court congestion, if it exists, is not the result of the tort liability system. It is also clear that a reduction in the rate at which automobile injury suits are filed is not dependent upon the enactment of *any* no-fault bill, particularly a federal law. The reduction we have achieved is the product of action by the insurance industry and the Bar. The insurance companies, recognizing an obligation of fairness to victims of accidents and an economic pressure to reduce the cost of adjusting claims, have begun prompt reimbursement of the economic losses of accident victims, including medical expenses and lost income. Also, lawyers have assisted in eliminating the litigation of small claims by encouraging victims with comparatively small claims to settle directly with the insurance companies, pointing out that it doesn't make good economic sense, either for victim or for lawyer to pursue those claims in court. Lawyers and insurance companies have worked together to achieve the reduction in motor vehicle injury litigation which are obvious from our court statistics. This is how the system is supposed to work, and we've made it work in Missouri. If there are jurisdictions where court congestion is a problem, then I suggest the solution is for those jurisdictions to face up to their responsibilities and provide a judiciary adequate to the task and an atmosphere which encourages settlement of small claims between the claimant and the wrongdoer, or his insurance carrier. The solution is not, in my opinion, to penalize states such as Missouri by the imposition of arbitrary federal standards which will only damage an established system which is doing the job it is supposed to do. You will not improve the quality of justice available to Missourians by locking the doors to our courts.

The second argument for a federal tort immunity law is the need to reduce the cost of automobile insurance. I believe, and experience has proven, claims of lowered insurance costs are, at best, wishful thinking and, at worst, a shameful hoax being perpetrated on the American people.

On April 30th of this year, the Allstate Insurance Company furnished to the Senate Committee on Commerce a study of the cost implications of S. 354 (which I understand is essentially identical to HR 1900). That study, which was immediately attacked by proponents of federal no-fault legislation, predicted that the measure would result in increases in insurance costs in many states.

The study has recently been updated and even in its revised form it shows an appalling increase in the cost of insurance in many states—increases of up to 76.1% for our sister state of Kansas. The increase in premium costs nationwide would be 4.4%.

If a 4.4% increase seems unimportant or insignificant to you, let me point out that the April 30th report of Allstate makes clear that it is the common carriers that benefit from the lowering of insurance costs—not the owners of private passenger vehicles. The enormous uncertainty as to cost of federal no-fault should give pause to this committee. Consider the projected cost impact of S. 354 on the state of Kansas, as reported by an Associated Press story in the *Kansas City Times*, July 15, 1975. The story reported that the Allstate study, which I have already mentioned, predicted an increase of 76.1% in Kansas insurance premiums if S. 354 were enacted; another study by State Farm Insurance Company had predicted a decrease of 3%. The disparity between these estimates by two of the country's largest automobile insurance carriers produces a differential in projected cost of almost 80% for the state of Kansas alone! If such major automobile insurers, with a wealth of actuarial experience, are that far apart in their estimates, I think it would be hazardous for Congress to gamble on the effect of these bills.

It should be noted that in those instances in which the insurance buying public have been given the facts they have in each instance chosen to retain access to the courts and the right to payment for pain and suffering caused by another rather than sacrifice this for a *possible* savings in auto insurance premiums. I base this statement upon several things. First, upon the results of a methodologically sound survey of public attitude in Missouri by Research and Information, Inc., an independent survey organization. In its July, 1973 *Missouri Public Opinion Report*, the organization published responses to questions on the subject of automobile insurance. One question inquired as to the type of insurance each driver should be required to carry, and five alternatives or options were given. Of those polled, 2% favored requiring insurance which would afford injury protection to the driver and his passengers; 12.0% favored requiring insurance to cover injury and property damage caused to others; 2.4% thought insurance should not be required, and .2% had no opinion. But 82.5% responded that the driver should be required to carry insurance which would pay for injury to himself and his passengers *and* for injury and property damage to others. The message is very clear.

I also base my statement upon a very clear message by the citizens of Colorado. In 1972, an initiative drive was mounted in Colorado for the enactment by the people of a no-fault plan, and the issue was widely discussed and debated among the *public*, rather than in a legislative body. At the November election, the initiative proposal was overwhelmingly rejected by a vote of 216,163 for and 613,269 against the plan, which contained both type-of-injury and dollar amount thresholds.

My statement is also based upon an experience of mine. I had occasion to talk to a group of nineteen laymen on the subject of no-fault insurance. None of them had any real knowledge of no-fault insurance, particularly as to the total or partial abolition of tort liability through the use of a threshold limitation on the right to bring suit. I inquired at the outset how many present favored, or even understood, such proposals, and no one really did. I then explained what these proposals were about and how a threshold limitation worked—not my opinion of it, but what the proposals *themselves* provide. At the conclusion of my discussion, I again inquired how many present would favor a no-fault plan with a threshold, and the opposition to such a plan was unanimous!

Let's be realistic. Approximately two-thirds of every dollar paid out by insurance companies is used to pay for repair of damages vehicles. It should be noted that with the apparent exception of HR 1272, none of the bills being considered by this committee attempt to deal with higher repair costs, frequency and severity of accidents and so forth. The anticipated reductions can be applied only to the remaining one-third of the claim settlement dollar and if insurance costs should be lowered, a claim that I dispute, the savings can only be infinitesimal. Even if you assume a reduction of 15% in the personal injury portion of the premium dollar (as did Massachusetts and Florida when their no-fault plans were enacted), this means a saving of at most only 4.5% on the whole automobile insurance premium. And for such a miserly sum, victims of automobiles accidents are asked to give up their right to be made whole in an action for damages. In the words of my college-age children, this is a rip-off!

Within limits, experience has shown what no-fualt insurance will cost under several state plans. What experience has *not* shown, however, is the potential cost if a federal no-fault law is enacted. I refer here not merely to the cost of insurance, but to the total cost, since a federal no-fault law would necessarily involve considerable federal activity. I am advised that the Department of Transportation would require an initial, additional appropriation of $10,000,000 to carry out the tasks assigned to it under S 354, or HR 1900, should the bill become law. Not only would taxpayers face this expense, and others like it on a federal level, but there is every reason to suppose that the reporting requirements which would be imposed upon the states would result in increased state costs as well. To the extent that any additional burdens would be imposed upon insurance carriers, premiums would necessarily be raised. There is also the question of coordination of benefits and primary coverage—it is my understanding that the present form of these bills would leave to the states the determination whether no-fault policies or group health policies would be primary as to certain benefits.

If there is to be coordination of benefits and concomitant premium reductions on one type of policy or another, some rather extensive work will have to be done, and some enforcement procedures established. Someone will ultimately have to pay the administrative costs of achieving any premium reduction which may result from the coordination of benefits. The "savings" to be achieved by federal no-fault would be eroded considerably by administrative costs alone!

There is the problem of vehicular damage resulting from collision and the cost of repairing it. Almost the only certainty about any auto accident is that there will be damage to the vehicles involved—vehicular damage is almost a 100% certainty, much more likely to occur than personal injury. The impact of the cost of automobile repairs upon premium rates may be judged by referring to a pamphlet entitled, "The Increasing Costs of Automobile Insurance", published by The Aetna Casualty and Surety Company, to be mailed this month to all of Aetna's auto policyholders. The pamphlet reports that the cost of automobile repairs increased by 14.5% during the period December, 1973 through December, 1974, and that policyholders can expect rate increases because of this inflation. I attach a copy of the pamphlet as Exhibit B. Insurance loss payments for vehicle repairs have regularly exceeded loss payments for personal injuries. Yet this major cost item is not even included in any of the no-fault bills except H.R. 1272. A discussion of the "cost" of automobile insurance is meaningless without consideration of the cost of repairing the vehicles involved in a collision. A system which does not reduce this cost is not reaching the major element of cost in insurance loss payments.

The claim that uniformity is required among the states is only that—a claim. I recognize that in the testimony before the Senate Commerce and Judiciary Committees when S. 354 was being considered, some insurance industry spokesmen did contend that it was desirable to have a uniform system of automobile accident reparations.

This nation arose out of diversity and has thrived on difference. Even the common law of our states, which sprung from the common law of England, has grown in diverse directions reflecting the diversity of our people. The tort laws of our states may differ, yet they co-exist, and it is the genius of the American insurance industry that motorists have been able to travel from state to state, secure in the protection of automobile liability policies which are as good in Maine as in California.

Difference does not, and need not mean chaos or confusion. Beyond supposition, there is no evidence that fifty different automobile accident reparations laws cannot exist side by side, nor is there any evidence that insurance companies are or would be incapable of writing policies which would protect insureds under a variety of state laws, fault or no-fault. To the contrary, several industry spokesmen have testified that insurance companies can and do fashion policies to protect their insureds wherever they may travel. In the face of this accomplished fact, the claims of a "need" for federal legislation to assure "uniformity" becomes less credible.

It may be noted in passing that H.R. 1900 and S. 354 do not establish "uniformity"—they establish minimum standards. They thus leave open the very road they are supposed to close—a diversity among the no-fault laws of the fifty states. Title II of S. 354 sets out the minimum standards for acceptable no-fault insurance plans to be adopted by state legislatures by a certain deadline. If a state has not adopted an "acceptable" plan meeting the minimum standards of Title II, then Title III of the bill would impose a no-fault plan upon the offending state—using standards different from those contained in Title II. In fact, Titles II and III of S. 354 provide two inconsistent plans for "partial abolition" of tort liability, a remarkable thing in view of comments before Senate and House committees that a "uniform" national plan is needed to protect a motorist in interstate travel from the vagaries of local laws different from the laws of his own state which might inhibit his right to recover damages or increase his exposure to litigation, thus raising the cost of his insurance! These bills being considered by this committee would establish nationally the "evils" of inconsistency, the abolition of which inconsistency is offered as a justification for having federal no-fault legislation in the first place. For all these reasons, I believe H.R. 1900 and S. 354 fail to meet the preliminary test of "need" for federal intervention which is the only justification for such a radical intrusion by the federal government into an area of law which has been and sho ıld rightly be the sole concern of our states.

The provisions of HR 1272 and HR 285 would provide for a uniform system of federally administered no-fault automobile insurance, but this uniformity is achieved only by taking from the several states their historic right to regulate the insurance industry and by taking from an innocent victim of an automobile accident the right to be made whole in an action for damages, unless the person causing the accident was engaged in *criminal* conduct. Article I, Section 14 of our Missouri Constitution provides that: "(t)he courts of justice shall be open to every person, and certain remedy afforded for every injury to person, property or character, and that right and justice shall be administered without sale, denial or delay."

The tort immunity proposed by these bills would clearly violate Missouri's constitution, and is, I submit, the most manifestly unfair provision to be found in any proposed no-fault legislation I have studied.

It is argued that a Federal Act of this type is needed to assure "fair and prompt" payment for losses sustained by automobile accident victims.

What is "fair" about a system that allows the victim to recover "almost all his work loss"? As they are drawn, HR 1900 and S 354 would permit a state to limit the amount of lost wages which must be compensated to an injured party to a monthly amount not exceeding $1,000, times a fraction representing the ratio of the per capita income in the victim's home state divided by the national per capita income. The effect of this in states whose per capita income is below the national average would be to penalize anyone with a monthly income approaching $1,000. This would fall especially hard on the person holding down two jobs to cope with our soaring inflation. He could, of course, purchase income protection insurance, subject to such limitations as might be imposed by the "coordination of benefits" permitted by the no-fault law. He would not be able to recover his loss in court, except under very unusual circumstances. Any system which permits this result does not strike me as the sort of "low-cost, comprehensive and fair system" which should be imposed on the public. What is fair about a system that prohibits suits to recover for intangible losses unless the tort feasor was acting in a "criminal" fashion?

Also, because certain of these bills, at least, allow the insured to elect certain specified deductibles, they will operate to the serious disadvantage of those who suffer the greatest economic hardship as the result of an automobile accident—the poor. Everyone who has ever bought insurance knows that if you are willing to take a deductible, your premium cost is less because you agree to pay an initial sum yourself—commonly either $50 or $100 in the case of auto collision insurance—before the insurance company becomes liable. The motorist of limited means, faced with a no-fault plan which *requires* him to purchase insurance if he wants the privilege of using his automobile, will probably opt for all the deductibles which are available so as to save money on the insurance premium. Yet this is the very person who can least affort to pay a penny of his own out-of-pocket loss after an accident, let alone the first $100 of his medical expenses and his lost income. It is apparent that any plan which permits such deductibles will have the effect of denying the advantage of first party reimbursement to the very motorists who most desperately need it.

In addition, certain of these bills would place the public at the mercy of the insurance companies. This would be very effectively accomplished by the provision that none of the first party benefits can be assigned in return for legal services rendered. Under the traditional tort liability system, an insurance company confronted by a claimant with property damage expenses of $200 and medical bills of $100 will be encouraged to give serious attention to the claim, realizing that if the claimant is dissatisfied, he may go to see an attorney, and the attorney might consider the matter worth pursuing. Given those same bills in a no-fault situation, the carrier is in a different position. The property damage expenses can be ignored, since they have nothing to do with no-fault coverage. Under almost *any* no-fault injury threshold, the claimant is not likely to have the sort of injury which would permit him to maintain an action for damages. There is no premium to the company for fast settlement of the claim because there is little danger that the claimant will be able to obtain representation. The effect is to bar the public from finding advocates to challenge the unilateral decisions of the first party insurance carriers.

There is another aspect of these bills which is seriously objectionable: that is the skepticism of our legal process which permeates them. Their premise seems to be that an injured motorist should not be entitled to compensation for his medical expenses and lost wages unless his access to our courts is severely restricted. In my opinion, this assumption in unwarranted and unnecessary, and I believe it would be a grave error for Congress to enact a law establishing this premise as a national policy.

In the first place, the establishment of a no-fault system does not require the abolition of a citizen's right to have his day in court. The state legislatures of

Arkansas, Delaware, Maryland, Oregon, South Carolina, South Dakota, Texas and Virginia have seen fit to enact no-fault laws which preserve the tort liability system. It is safe to assume that other states which may subsequently enact no-fault laws will wish to preserve the tort liability system. The Missouri Bar had drafted and is working for the enactment of a no-fault bill in the Missouri General Assembly. This bill would provide for first party benefits, but it would preserve the tort liability system we enjoy. It is my firm expectation that this bill will be enacted by the next session of the Missouri General Assembly. In view of the action taken by the states I have mentioned to implement no-fault plans and in view of our efforts in Missouri, I believe this committee should reject any legislation which would take away the fundamental right of our citizens to have access to their courts, a right which has been reaffirmed by eight states which have enacted no-fault legislation.

Proposals to take away an individual's right to recover damages in a court of law often assume that our courts are so plagued with congestion and crowded dockets that claimants are denied expeditious hearing of their claims. This argument, as I have pointed out, has no application in Missouri.

In testimony before committees of the House and the Senate, The Missouri Bar has consistently maintained that no-fault legislation such as HR 1900 and S 354 is of dubious constitutionality at best. It is reassuring to discover that Attorney General Levi agrees. In testimony on June 5, 1975, before the Senate Commerce Committee, then considering S 354, Mr. Levi expressed concern about provisions of S 354 which would require state employees to act affirmatively in the administering of a federal law which might contravene the laws and constitution of the state.

The issue, as Mr. Levi perceived it, was: "whether it is permissible or appropriate for the Congress to intrude upon such State sovereignty as is left by requiring State agencies and employees to perform as though they were Federal instruments or employees, or as though the Federal Congress were the state legislature and possessor of the State's sovereignty."

Mr. Levi's conclusion was that such features as an assigned claims bureau, which is provided for in Section 7 of HR 1272, would violate the sovereignty of states and the principle of constitutional Federalism. He observed:

"The essence of the sovereignty of the States that remains is that State employees are not just Federal employees in disguise.

*   *   *   *   *   *   *

"Nor is the issue of constitutional Federalism a frivolous one. It is close to the protection of diversity, creativity and freedom within our system. The importance of protecting and promoting these values should be a compelling consideration in determining whether a Federal uniform automobile insurance law is desirable and particularly whether requiring State agencies to implement such a law is appropriate."

There is another aspect of these bills which I find disturbing. It seems incongruous to me that at a time when the Congress and the Bar are working diligently to increase the availability of legal services for all our citizens, Congress should also consider proposals which would deny legal representation to the overwhelming majority of automobile accident victims, as these no-fault bills would do. For example, HR 1272, which practically abolishes altogether an accident victim's right to sue a wrongdoer, also restricts effectively his right to counsel in a controversy with his insurer by its provisions as to how the accident victim may pay his attorney. Section 5(a)(5) of the bill not only prohibits the victim from contracting to pay an attorney our economic loss benefits recoverable under a policy, but also makes it an "unlawful act" for the attorney to enter into or "knowingly accept benefits" under such a contract. Section 8, relating to claimant's attorney fees, displays a similar cynicism as to representation for the claimant. Subsection (a) provides that the claimant may be awarded an attorney's fee if he has to sue the insurer to collect benefits, provided that the fee is reasonable, and based upon time actually spent, but no fee will be allowed if the court determines that the claim was "fraudulent, excessive, or frivolous". Subsection (b) appears to permit the claimant to retain a lawyer to sue for non-economic loss payable to him under a no-fault policy, but any contingent fee contract is limited to an amount not to exceed 25% of the amount of the non-economic loss recovery, and the 25% fee "may be further limited at the discretion of the court". From my reading of the bill, it appears that actions against another driver to recover for non-economic loss are limited to those situations in which the injury is caused by the "criminal conduct" of the other driver. It occurs to me that 25% of the non-economic loss recovery is 25% of nothing, because never in my experience since I began practicing law or in the experience of my firm have we represented a personal injury planitiff whose injuries were caused by the "criminal conduct" of another person.

The rather obvious effect of these provisions is to place in the hands of the court the decision whether or not claimant's counsel will be paid, particularly if the claimant is unable to bear the expense of attorney's fees out of his own pocket. No doubt these provisions are sincere efforts to prevent possible abuses in fee charges by lawyers. The effect of the provisions, however, is to discourage or preclude the claimant from obtaining competent counsel in disputes with his insurer.

During the first thirty years, approximately, of the Social Security Law, there was no provision in the act itself for the awarding of reasonable fees to attorneys in contested cases. I understand that fees were in fact severely restricted by the regulations then in force. During that period, very few decisions of the Social Security Administration were successfully challenged in court. However, the act was amended in 1968, and it is my recollection that the late Senator Edward V. Long of Missouri was one of the authors of the amendment, so as to provide for the allowing of a reasonable attorney's fee in contested cases. The pages of the Federal Reporter are now replete with cases finding against the Social Security Administration. If it is the intention of Congress to surrender the public to the mercy of bureaucrats, with all the problems that arise from making agencies omnipotent, then so be it. But if that is what is intended, then Congress should also consider the possibility of eliminating courts—even of eliminating elected representatives—so that all our citizens can equally share in the fruit of the bureaucratic vine.

I would also observe that the bills before this committee do nothing to eliminate or reduce the causes of accidents that take their heavy toll of human life and health. Automobile accidents cripple innocent victims. Let's not take fromthose victims their right to recover from the wrongdoers—let's do something truly worthwhile. Let us work to prevent the accident from occurring.

Finally, I submit that any bill that awards attorney's fees to a claimant filing a *fraudulent* or *excessive* claim (see Section 107(a) of S 354) could not have been drafted with the care and expertise that one would expect of legislation of such momentous import to the entire populace of the United States. Since such a glaring error does appear in Section 107(a) of S 354, one can only be suspect of the remainder of that and similar bills!

We have now begun the celebration of the 200th anniversary of the founding of this nation, and we are preparing to enter into a third century of freeeom. If passed into law, these measures you are considering today would take from our citizens basic rights we have enjoyed from our beginning as a nation. How ironic it is that we should now be called upon to surrender some of the very rights which our founding fathers struggled and died to secure for us. Almost 200 years ago, Thomas Paine observed, in *The American Crisis, No. 1*, that:

"What we obtain too cheap, we esteem too lightly; 'tis dearness only that gives everything its value. Heaven knows how to put a proper price upon its goods; and it would be strange indeed, if so celestial an article as *Freedom* should not be highly rated."

EXHIBIT A—EXTRACT FROM 1974 STATISTICAL REPORT OF THE 16TH JUDICIAL CIRCUIT (JACKSON COUNTY, MISSOURI TRIAL COURT)

"The following is the statistical report for the Circuit Court of Jackson County, Missouri (Sixteenth Judicial Circuit Court of Missouri) for the calendar year of 1974.

"The Court is a trial court of general jurisdiction that hears civil, criminal, domestic relations and juvenile cases. It's jurisdiction is co-extensive with Jackson County, which comprises 603 square miles and a population in excess of 650,000. Urban and major suburban areas served are Kansas City, Independence, Raytown, Grandview and Lee's Summit. The Court is composed of seventeen Judges and one Commissioner of the Juvenile Court. Thirteen Judges sit in the Kansas City Court House and four in the court house at Independence."

Cases disposed of during year	1974	1973	1972	1971	1970
Cases removed to Federal court	0	0	4	15	29
Personal injury with trial	165	142	188	195	225
Personal injury without trial	1,190	1,247	1,331	1,007	1,145
27.26 with hearing	21	23	40	23	21
27.26 without hearing	33	38	24	39	3
Other civil cases with trial	732	766	602	1,167	1,341
Other civil cases without trial	2,767	2,718	2,690	1,961	1,865
Total dispositions	4,908	4,934	4,879	4,407	4,629

Cases filed by nature of action

Nature of action	1974 Filed	1974 Percentage	1973 Filed	1973 Percentage	1972 Filed	1972 Percentage	1971 Filed	1971 Percentage	1970 Filed	1970 Percentage
8101—PI vehicular	835	7.52	873	8.31	1,131	10.63	1,209	11.01	1,401	12.72
8102—PI product liability	11	.10	19	.18	24	.23	19	.17	25	.23
8103—PI malpractice	25	.23	18	.17	19	.18	24	.22	25	.23
8104—PI other	174	1.57	177	1.69	207	1.95	205	1.87	190	1.73
8105—Property damage	62	.56	95	.90	103	.97	72	.65	55	.50
8106—Intentional tort	190	1.71	167	1.59	184	1.73	164	1.49	185	1.68
8107—Minor settlements	117	1.05	168	1.60	160	1.50	193	1.76	184	1.67
8108—Wrongful death	33	.30	40	.38	23	.22	39	.35	42	.38
8199—Other tort	11	.10	24	.23	35	.33	70	.63	45	.41
8201—Breach of contract	134	1.21	132	1.26	186	1.75	331	3.02	419	3.80
8202—Specific performance	34	.31	32	.30	20	.19	36	.33	30	.27
8203—Recission, reformation or cancellation	2	.02	2	.02	7	.07	4	.03	6	.05
8204—Promissory note	171	1.54	117	1.11	163	1.53	168	1.53	174	1.58
8205—Replevin	60	.54	55	.52	46	.43	37	.34	119	1.08
8299—Other contract	547	4.93	466	4.43	355	3.34	327	2.98	110	1.00
8301—Quiet title	13	.12	22	.21	31	.29	22	.20	23	.21
8302—Mechanics lien	122	1.10	56	.53	63	.59	73	.66	66	.60
8303—Ejectments	0	0	1	.01	0	0	0	0	0	0
8304—Partition	25	.23	44	.42	38	.36	32	.29	37	.34
8399—Other real estate	44	.40	44	.42	56	.53	56	.51	20	.18

EXHIBIT B—THE INCREASING COSTS OF AUTOMOBILE INSURANCE

1974 was a difficult year for automobile insurers, as it was for consumers. During most of the year, the rate of inflation was greater than at any other time since World War II. The increase in the Consumer Price Index during 1974 was the first since 1946 to exceed 10%.

Last year we increased our automobile rates in several states to compensate for the cost increases of medical care and car repairs in recent years. Unfortunately, continuing inflation has made it necessary to increase rates again in some areas. As shown by the list below, the average rise in the cost of automobile insurance last year was far outdistanced by cost increases in the goods and services your insurance pays for.

Item	Percentage increase [1]
Automobile repairs	14.5
Physicians' fees	14.0
Semi-private hospital rooms	16.5
Automobile insurance	3.0

[1] Percentages are based on the Consumer Price Index as reported by the Bureau of Labor Statistics, U.S. Dept. of Labor, covering the period from December 1973 through December 1974.

We are very concerned about rising costs and are trying to do everything we can to hold down the cost of automobile insurance, such as controlling our operating expenses and strongly supporting No-Fault legislation. However, there are times when we have no alternative but to adjust our rates if we are to continue providing the standards of service and fairness of claim payments on which you depend.

So if your automobile insurance costs more this year, this is one of the reasons why. If you have any questions about your policy or your premium, please call your agent. He will be pleased to go over it with you.

Mr. KINZLER. Mr. Stoup, if I might, we have two more witnesses. Unfortunately, we have a limitation of 4 o'clock.

So, if I might, let me ask you a couple of questions. I will try to keep the questions short if you will keep your answers short.

Mr. STOUP. I will do the best I can.

Mr. VAN DEERLIN. I am betting on neither of you.

Mr. KINZLER. You indicated that the proper damage portions of your automobile insurance other than bodily injury or medical is 66 percent. State Farm Mutual has indicated to me that their figures are 36 percent for bodily injury.

Mr. STOUP. MFA tells me 66 percent.

Mr. KINZLER. So, we are talking about a difference at most of 5 percent.

Mr. STOUP. I am sorry. What figures did you say?

Mr. KINZLER. I said for bodily injury.

Mr. STOUP. I am sorry.

Mr. KINZLER. We have gotten it reversed.

The national figures I have been able to derive from the Best figures indicate that bodily injury premiums run approximately $6 billion to $7 billion a year. Now, if we then take your 15 percent figures as an outside kind of figure for savings, which you don't have to agree to the validity of, but for argument's sake we are talking about a $900 million saving. I submit that is enough to talk about, not agree to, but talk about.

Mr. STOUP. I will talk to you about it but what price do you put on freedom? Is there a price tag on that?

Mr. KINZLER. My point is that you indicated the figures were almost de minimis. I am not admitting that. The cost of the figures within themselves make it worthwhile discussing. You seem to state that is 4½ percent of the average premium. I am saying that is a lot of money. Do you agree?

Mr. STOUP. No. If you could save 4½ percent of your total insurance premium, would you give up your right to go to the courthouse and have your case, if you had one, heard by a jury? I have yet to find one lay person who will accept that.

I can tell you a story about that. I addressed this question to 19 school teachers where I was giving a speech one day and asked them—and they were all social science teachers—with degrees from bachelors to doctors—"How many of you are in favor of the no-fault system from what you now know?" Eleven said yes; eight of them no. I then gave them the outlines of S. 354. "That is what you are going to get and what you are going to give up."

I took another vote. The proponents lost 19 to nothing. That is what lay people think of it.

Mr. KINZLER. I would be delighted to ask the same questions of lay people, but I don't have the time. I might frame the question somewhat differently than you did.

You submitted you are very concerned about the fact that Allstate and State Farm's figures were off by 79 percent for Kansas. Frankly, this subcommittee was very concerned about it, too. So, we asked Allstate, "Why are there differences in your figures from State Farm?"

They said, "The major difference is in our assumptions of survivors benefits. We also have the figure for increased utilization of benefits but we don't think that is terribly important after considering it."

I said, "What would happen if your survivors benefits were about the same level?" "Our figures would be almost the same, maybe a little lower than State Farm's." So, I don't think we have a cost dispute between State Farm and Allstate any more.

When we get figures from Allstate, which I would hope would be in the next 3 days, they will show a minus for Kansas, also, and a minus for every State except one or two.

Mr. STOUP. Even if we get involved in that, what will we do with people under these bills that will get their wage loss and their economic wage loss will be limited to $1,000 a month.

Mr. KINZLER. They have a right to take out more insurance if they choose.

Mr. STOUP. They can get made whole under the present system without even investing any more of their own dollars.

Mr. KINZLER. Under the existing system, with the right to recover an unlimited amount of money for pain and suffering, for wage loss and so forth, the average person with an economic loss of $25,000 or more recovers, with tort—this wonderful tort right—30 percent of economic loss. He could recover 450 percent but he doesn't. The average person recovers 30 percent. How does that reconcile itself with the right to go to court if it is an illusory right?

Mr. STOUP. It is not an illusory right. I am one of these fellows down in the pit and I try lawsuits. I have yet to see in my office in my practice a lawsuit involving $25,000 in economic loss to any one client. I am saying, whoever gave you that figure may be accurate but there is only one of those cases in every 250,000.

Mr. KINZLER. The Department of Transportation tells us there is one in every 100.

Mr. STOUP. Thousand?

Mr. KINZLER. One percent of all the cases.

Mr. STOUP. I don't believe that.

I can prove it to you out of Jackson County because we have our sheets. We get every week every verdict handed down. It tells what their economic loss was, medical loss, wage loss, and what the jury gave them.

I don't accept the validity of that figure. I think somebody gave you a spurious figure.

Mr. KINZLER. The Department of Transportation only spent $2 million to study it. I can't tell you any more.

Mr. STOUP. We also have somebody who certified a contractor in the law suit I am trying that had no right to do so, who worked for the Government. What I am saying is, just because it's a government figure doesn't make it accurate.

At a time when we are approaching our 200th anniversary, I am concerned about the fact that we are talking about giving our citizens something less than all the freedoms they are entitled to. I don't think we should start taking away from them in our 200th year.

As Thomas Paine said so eloquently, "'tis dearness only that gives everything its value . . . and it would be strange indeed, if so celestial an article as "Freedom" should not be highly rated."

Our system of justice is just as dear, Mr. Chairman.

Thank you for the opportunity to be here.

Mr. VAN DEERLIN. Thank you for the very impressive presentation.

Our next witness is Leland S. Sedberry, Jr., representing the New Mexico State Attorneys Association.

STATEMENT OF LELAND S. SEDBERRY, JR., NEW MEXICO STATE BAR ASSOCIATION

Mr. SEDBERRY. Thank you very much.

Mr. Chairman, I am here today to represent the New Mexico State Bar Association.

We have an integrated bar and therefore that represents all of the lawyers in New Mexico, the governing body of the bar association, which is the New Mexico Board of Bar Commissioners, the New Mexico Attorneys Association, and the Albuquerque Bar Association.

The views I express today are set forth in conclusion in a resolution passed by the bar commissioners, which is attached to my statement, unanimously opposing Federal no-fault legislation.

Because of the shortness of the time, Mr. Chairman, I won't read any portion of my prepared statement. I will just make a few comments for you, hoping that you and the other members of the committee will read my statement, and be ready to answer any questions.

First of all, I would like to say that when I arrived here yesterday on the airplane and met the heat and high humidity of Washington, I wondered why I came. You may be wondering why a country lawyer from New Mexico would come all the way to Washington to tell you his views on no-fault in such a distinguished group as has addressed you today.

I say that we come because we are concerned about the thought in Washington that they should pass a bill similar to S. 354 or the bills that you have before you.

We are concerned, Mr. Chairman, not because of what effect it might have on practicing lawyers, but we are concerned because of the effect it will have on the public, not only the people who pay premiums to insurance companies, but to people who are injured in automobile accidents.

We are concerned because we don't believe that it has been demonstrated to the degree necessary before the Congress passes a law such as this that this is the best law that can be passed.

We are concerned because the Congress is even thinking about taking away the rights of people to go to court for redress for their wrongs.

Mr. Chairman, the promises which have been made to the American people through the newspapers and through the statements of the proponents of no-fault cannot be carried out by Congress. Congress cannot fulfill these promises and that is promises of lower cost, promises of payments immediately, promises that this will be a better system.

Mr. Chairman, you have heard in this committee from people who say they represent consumers and unions and who say that they are for Federal no-fault insurance.

I say to you, Mr. Chairman, that our bar committee sent out speakers to talk to civic groups, to unions, to consumer groups, to old-age groups. Our purpose in talking to these people was not to try to influence them or to give them an inflammatory speech, but merely to tell them, 1, 2, 3, 4, the provisions of what are in the Federal no-fault bill and the provisions that were in the bill proposed in New Mexico. We had the same experience that Mr. Stoup had. When we went to the meeting, they were for no-fault because all they had read were the editorials, the promises, but when they found out the true facts as to what the no-fault bill would do to them, they voted against it unanimously.

So, I say that you should question further as to whether or not these groups are really for no-fault or whether just some of their lobbyists in Washington are for it.

Mr. Chairman, we are a relatively small State in population. We have a high unemployment rate; we have a lot of people on welfare benefits. These are poor people. We feel that no-fault insurance will not be fair to them, particularly if it is mandatory and if they can't drive their automobile without it. We think that this bill is discriminatory in many ways.

We ask you the question as to why motorcycles have been completely left out of the bill. If there is a great concern among the proponents of no-fault for the well-being of people who are injured in accidents, they cannot find any group who are injured with more frequency and more seriously than motorcycle riders. Therefore, I can see no reason why the Congress should not address itself to that question if it goes as far as to pass the Federal no-fault bills.

Motor vehicle transportation is a very important thing in New Mexico because of our widely scattered areas, and it is absolutely necessary for people to have the use of their automobiles.

Now, Mr, Chairman, in New Mexico, a no-fault bill was introduced and passed in a recent session of the legislature. In 1973, a $1,000 threshold bill was passed. It was passed at the last minute and was passed by an overwhelming majority of those voting on it.

However, the Governor took a look at it, he had the attorney general take a look at it, and a former judge who was working for the attorney general wrote an opinion that it was unconstitutional. The Governor vetoed it on that ground.

Following that, between 1973 and 1975, many of the legislators took a second look at the whole idea of no-fault and in 1975 turned down a similar threshold bill.

Now, the State Bar Association of New Mexico believes that add-on first party benefits are desirable. The evidence that we have seen to date is that it works in Oregon, it has worked in Delaware, in Arkansas and in other States. We introduced this similar type of legislation in 1973 and we had it introduced again in 1975, and we think that in the coming legislative session that serious consideration will be given to that type of program where the tort rights and liabilities are not abolished, they are not affected, but people have first party insurance to protect themselves if they are in an accident.

Mr. Chairman, without even having legislation in New Mexico, we do have a type of no-fault insurance.

On my own policy recently, I paid $8 additional premium and was given no-fault insurance first party benefits which will pay for economic and medical loss in the event I am injured, and no legislation was required for that.

Mr. Chairman, we believe, and certainly second the philosophy set forth here by the previous speakers today that the Federal Government has no business in the no-fault insurance field. We feel that this is not a Federal problem, that the States can handle it adequately, and that we can handle our own problems.

We have no court congestion in New Mexico and that is not a ro em. We can get to trial within a year or faster if we wish in any lawsuit.

The American public has been upset by premiums and premium rating methods of insurance companies. These aren't attacked by this Federal bill. These do not even approach the premium rating method. We have no assurance as to how rating will be done.

You have heard discussions already that the middle-class wage earner who earns a substantial living but has a high exposure to an insurance company, even though he may be a safe driver, may be the highest risk. We don't believe that that is a fair situation, Mr. Chairman.

Now, we, too, are greatly disturbed by the great variance in the anticipated rate increases that have been given out by various companies. We see Allstate at all times coming out with statements as to what they believe a specific bill will do as far as premiums are concerned. Their estimate in New Mexico is that premiums will increase for policyholders between 34 and 67 percent.

Mr. Chairman, I, personally, don't want to be a policyholder in a group such as this, where I have to pay that much additional insurance premium and where I don't have a right to a full recovery in the event I am injured by a negligent party.

I, too, Mr. Kinzler, asked Allstate why there was such a difference between Allstate and State Farm. Now, some thought was that there was a difference in the amount that the companies had put into their rating because of overutilization of the plan, as it was called. Now, I think that is a problem that this bill has not addressed and that is overutilization.

Would people tend to go and get overutilization of medical expenses? Would doctors tend to put people in the hospital and overutilize the hospitals when they are injured in accidents merely because the insurance company is there to pay all the bills? Do patients tend to keep going to doctors until they get a doctor to give them a permanent disability rating so that they can draw disability benefits?

There are no stopgaps for this in this bill and I don't believe any measures would prevent overutilization. Overutilization would result in higher payments by the companies and thus higher premiums and higher cost to the public.

Mr. Chairman, we submit that before the Federal Government abolishes a known system which is working well in our State, to adopt an experiment, in fact, I believe the Congressman from New York called it an experiment this morning, that more information should be developed, and we believe that the role of the Federal Government at this time should be to develop specific information as to what has gone on since the last DOT study. That study, incidentally, has been referred to several times today but it does not give us any aid and help in formulating a plan for automobile reparations in our State. The Federal Government's role could be helpful in that regard.

We believe that, instead of passing an experiment at this time, that it would be much better for the Federal Government to gather data and facts as to what the experience has been in those States that have made changes so that we can consider those changes, ourselves.

I would like to thank you for the opportunity, Mr. Chairman, to appear before you today.

[Mr. Sedberry's prepared statement and the resolution referred to. follow:]

STATEMENT OF LELAND S. SEDBERRY, JR., ON BEHALF OF NEW MEXICO STATE BAR ASSOCIATION, NEW MEXICO BOARD OF BAR COMMISSIONERS, NEW MEXICO ATTORNEYS ASSOCIATION, AND ALBUQUERQUE BAR ASSOCIATION

Mr. Chairman and gentlemen of the committee, I am here today to represent New Mexico State Bar Association, a state agency comprising all of the lawyers in New Mexico and its governing body, the New Mexico Board of Bar Commissioners. I also represent the New Mexico Attorneys Association, a voluntary association of lawyers throughout the state of New Mexico who are interested in good legislation, and the Albuquerque Bar Association, a voluntary association of lawyers in the City of Albuquerque, New Mexico. I wish to thank you for allowing me to appear. We are here to state that we are totally and unequivocally opposed to the enactment of H.R. 1272, H.R. 1900, Senate 354 and other similar National No-Fault Motor Vehicle Insurance Acts. At its meeting of June, 1975, the New Mexico State Bar Commission unanimously passed a resolution opposing Senate Bill 354 and National No-Fault Motor Vehicle Insurance. This was a reiteration of previous resolutions passed by this Commission. A copy of the resolution is attached to this statement.

Although New Mexico is a large state in terms of square miles, it is a relatively small state in terms of population. The total population is 1,122,500 (1974 census). Although there are 32 counties in New Mexico, Bernalillo County is the largest in terms of population, having a total population of 301,400 persons, and five of the 32 counties in New Mexico who have populations over 50,000 comprise 54.5% of the total population.

Thus, the vast majority of New Mexico is a rural community. There are 867,206 total vehicles in New Mexico and those are made up in part of 525,749 passenger vehicles, 214,378 trucks, and 33,521 motorcycles. Approximately 32.6% of the total vehicles are in Bernalillo County (283,301). Bernalillo County has New Mexico's largest city, which is Albuquerque. Unemployment continues to rise in New Mexico. As of March 1975, we had a total civilian labor force of 436,000 with 37,700 unemployed for 8.6% rate. This is up 41% from last year. Eight of the counties in New Mexico have an excess of 10% unemployment, with the highest being Mora County, a rural area, which has an unemployment rate of 37.7%. Many of these receive welfare and other government subsidies.

Government is the largest sector of the work force in the state and almost ⅓ of wage and salary jobs are held by persons in local, state, and federal agencies. Personal income in New Mexico, according to the Department of Commerce figures in 1974, was $4,642. In the nation, New Mexico ranks 49th in per capita income, with only Mississippi having a lower per capita income. This is compared to a per capita income in the United States of $5,434.

There are no actual figures on the number of autos with liability insurance, but the State Insurance Commissioner, Ralph Apodaca, estimates that approximately one-third of the drivers and automobiles in New Mexico are uninsured.

Automobile and pickup trucks are vital to transportation throughout the state and in most of the areas of the state are the only available means for transportation. Many of the residents live at great distances from their county seats, hospitals, schools and shops.

Many of the owners of vehicles are unable to afford high automobile insurance premiums and thus do not have liability insurance. The State Legislature has not required liability insurance as a prerequisite to driving a vehicle in New Mexico. They have, however, passed financial responsibility laws and those persons who are involved in accidents must show financial responsibility in order to continue driving.

We further have laws which require insurance companies to offer to sell uninsured motorist coverage to all purchasers of liability insurance. Thus, motorists can have the full protection afforded by liability insurance in the event of becoming involved in an accident with an uninsured motorist.

A No-Fault Bill was introduced into the New Mexico Legislature in 1973. It provided for a $1,000 threshhold No-Fault Plan, wherein injured parties must have $1,000 in special damages before they can file a tort suit. The Bill was written by the insurance industry and actively supported by the American Insurance Association and State Farm Insurance Company. The Bill was passed in the final day of the session of the legislature and sent to the Governor. Fortunately, the Governor read the Bill, and based upon an Attorney General's opinion that the Bill was unconstitutional, the Governor vetoed the Bill.

The reason the Bill was declared unconstitutional was because it could not be uniformly applied to all motorists in the State. The Attorney General's opinion is lengthy and I will not attempt to summarize it, but will be glad to furnish it to you if you so desire.

The New Mexico Legislature in 1975 turned down a No-Fault Bill during its regular session. The Bill provided for a $500 threshhold of medical expense before suit could be brought and provided for mandatory coverage of all motor vehicles before they could be registered in the state. The Bill provided for an appropriation of $750,000 to the Motor Vehicle Department for carrying out the provisions of the Act. There was testimony that the appropriation was insufficient to carry out the purposes of the Act and that estimates were as high as 37% that New Mexico motorists do not presently carry liability insurance. It is interesting to note that in 1975 the American Insurance Association and State Farm Insurance Company did not actively push this Bill, which is perhaps a reflection of their decision to support Federal Legislation.

The opinion of those involved was that the suggested appropriation would not be sufficient to adequately enforce mandatory No-Fault Insurance. This points up one of our objections to the Federal Bills which required that the states not only enact No-Fault bills, but to enforce them without additional funds which are required for such enforcement.

The New Mexico Bar Association has drafted and introduced legislation requiring that all insurance companies offer to motorists first party benefits without abolishing the present tort system, similar to the statutes enacted in Delaware, Oregon, and Arkansas. Prior to the meeting of the next legislature, we hope to have further studies as to the results in those states. If they are favorable, we hope to introduce such legislation in the next legislature.

We endorse a plan requiring the issuance of first party coverage on a voluntary basis to consumers for medical benefits, funeral and burial benefits, income continuation benefits, loss of service benefits, and survivor benefits. These plans are presently available through some insurers in New Mexico. On my own automobile insurance policy, I paid an additional premium for no-fault benefits. The bonus here is that the present system of giving me full relief against a wrongdoer who injures me or my family, is not abolished, and there is no need to do so.

Any person studying the variety of no-fault plans which have been entered both federally and statewide, will see that there are two essential aspects of no-fault automobile insurance.

1. No Fault refers to first party insurance (meaning one's own company), such as policy provisions for benefits payable for medical bills, incurred by someone injured in the insured car, regardless of whether anyone was at fault for the injury.

2. No-Fault also refers to a philosophy that persons should no longer be held at fault or responsible to compensate for injuries which they caused others by their negligence or carelessness in the operation of a motor vehicle.

First party insurance is already available and it appears that a great majority of Americans have first party coverage in one manner or another for their medical bills. A great number have first party coverage for loss of wages.

The second philosophy is necessary in order to support the first if you have mandatory no-fault which covers all persons under a system as the Federal Bills which are proposed. It is a strange incongruity that in an age of consumer protection and the influence of social direction and environmental concern brought about by individuals that there should be a clamor to deprive an individual of his right to receive full redress for disability, real misery and loss caused him by the negligence or carelessness of another person. We submit that such individual action is a measurable deterrent to other would be wrongdoers and that it is unnecessary to abolish the present system and go to an untried and unproven experiment with the lives and well being of all Americans. This is particularly true when an achievement of the first goal can be obtained without the necessity of abolishing the right of individuals for redress against the negligent party. We believe that when a member of our society has been injured and wronged by another, he should have access to the County Courthouse to determine his right for redress. When a man's health and happiness, his ability to engage in normal family, social and recreational activities have been taken from him through the negligence or carelessness of another or through wanton disregard for his safety, then he should be able to be compensated in the form of general damages. When there is a wrong in our society, there should be a remedy. The remedy should be determined based upon the individual circumstances of the case. We simply cannot accept the philosophy that one is going to be injured in an automobile accident in any event, and thus, is entitled only to medical expenses and a portion of his economic loss of wages.

Court congestion is cited as a reason for No-Fault Insurance. In New Mexico, we do not have any problem with Court congestion. Automobile accident cases involving claims of personal injury comprise less than 2 percent of the Court load. 25 percent of the filed cases are tried, with the best being settled, and of the cases tried, approximately two-thirds are non-jury cases. Only about 2 to 3 percent of the Court time is spent on such cases. The average time between filing and the trial in New Mexico is less than 10 months for jury cases and 6 months for non-jury cases. The cost of trying a personal injury case is no greater than the cost of trying workmen's compensation cases which are tried in the Courts of New Mexico and other cases involving administrative matters.

There will be litigation, of course, under any no-fault system, since it will be necessary for the insurance company and the injured to agree whether or not the alleged injuries are related to the accident, the extent of disability, when the injured person is able to return to work, the discontinuing of his no-fault income benefits, the payment of medical expenses and whether or not they are related to the accident. These are primarily the same issues which are litigated at the present time in personal injury cases with the additional issues, in some cases, of negligence of the parties.

Premiums and rating methods of insurance companies is one of the subjects which the public is most concerned with. Yet, under the proposed bills, the Federal Government has passed the "buck" to the State Commissioners. Yet, the safe driver, who is a higher risk medically and a higher risk for wage loss benefits, will now be the high risk for insurance companies while the unemployed young drivers will now be the low risks. The elderly person who is more easily injured and has the most difficulty recovering, will be the highest risk. These are generally the persons who can least afford higher insurance rates.

We also have many retired persons in New Mexico. In many cases, their income is limited and they are dependent upon social security for support. The Federal No-Fault bills are extremely unfair to these persons. They will be paying higher premiums, but the deductibles in the bill would deprive them of benefits.

The early proponents of No-Fault Insurance attempted to sell the idea to the public and the legislators by promising payment of benefits without fault and a lower insurance premium. Although cost may not be the most important consideration, it is one that should be closely considered. It is inconceivable to me that the Congress could spend two million dollars for a DOT study on the present system, could pay the Commissioner on Uniform Laws, $200,000 to write a Uniform No-Fault bill and not provide the public with a comprehensive and independent study of the premium costs.

The highly controversial study by Milliman and Robertson, Inc. was performed at the request of the National Association of Insurance Commissioners.

Allstate Insurance has used its computers to run various studies of No-Fault plans. Their most recent study of S. 354 shows that rates for their policy holders will increase between 34.7 and 67.0 percent.

The company claiming to be the largest insurer nationwide, State Farm Insurance Company, refuses to tell you either that rates will be decreased or how much they will cost.

The proponents of No-Fault, knowing that they cannot deliver lower rates, seem to have backed off the lower cost approach, but a great deal of controversy and uncertainty exists.

Because of the McClaren Act limiting the role of Federal Government in insurance ratings, the proposals simply establish the standards for the states to adopt and leave it up to the local insurance commissioners and agencies to control and regulate rates. The scheme is that a New Federal Agency will look over the states shoulders to require the states to adopt appropriate standards and to properly administer them.

Such Federal bureaucratic regulation will, by its own nature, grow, until eventually it will completely absorb the entire process.

We do not believe that this is in the public interest.

The idea of national standards for state laws is becoming more prevalent in legislation introduced in the Congress. Congress should not attempt to enact laws for states under the camouflage of national standards. If Congress feels that a national legislation is needed, it should introduce legislation to that effect without so called national standards. In the area of Federal No-Fault Insurance, we do not believe that National Standards are required or that a Federal bill is required in any form. The alleged ills of the present system can be cured by better ways than killing the system altogether. These determinations should be made upon a local basis because the needs of each state and its citizens are different. There is no correlation between the problems in New Mexico and the problems in the eastern populous states, such as Massachusetts, where automobile insurance legislation is concerned.

Because the proponents of No-Fault Insurance have found that they could not reduce premiums by having compulsory No-Fault Insurance, it was necessary to put into the legislation the introduction of deductibles, waiting periods, and exclusion of benefits where there are collateral sources. Even these have not brought the premiums lower than the present system, but there is a strong argument against the administrative mess which will be created and the unattainable-position which all but the most wealthy will be placed in. The Allstate studies have shown the rates in New Mexico would increase between 34.7% and 67.0%. This is an unnecessary burden to impose upon our citizens.

Attorneys fees have been limited and controlled by the provisions of the acts. I am not a member of the American Trail Lawyers Association. Although I have represented a few plaintiffs involved in automobile accident cases, the majority of my practice involves representing insurance companies and other corporations in litigation. I am a member of the International Association of Insurance Counsel and the Federation of Insurance Counsel. Automobile accident cases comprise a small percentage of my cases, and most of the cases involve death and serious permanent disability so that the Federal Acts would not affect whether these cases cases could be tried. I feel it is necessary to tell you this, Mr. Chairman, for two reasons:

1. I have no self interest as a practicing lawyer in the passage or non-passage of this Act. It will not affect my income.

2. There have been certain proponents of No-Fault insurance who have attacked the opinion of attorneys on this subject because of their self interest. I consider these attacks unwarranted and improper.

The opinion of insurance companies have been accepted without the same attacks, yet self interest and the profitable operation of the companies is apparent.

S. 354 abolishes the contingent fee and requires that the court award fees based upon the actual time expended to the plaintiff's attorney if the company is overdue in any no-fault benefits.

Payment for time involved may not be the best approach to the problem. Insurance Companies certainly will be back to you asking for further relief after they find out that, in many cases, plaintiff's attorneys spend more time preparing cases than defense attorneys do.

The trend toward having the losing side pay the winner's attorney's fees, may be one that you should thoroughly consider before adopting it. The contingent fee system, although criticized by many, has nevertheless, many redeeming aspects.

I seriously doubt that overall attorney's fees will be reduced, as the proponents predict.

Many proponents of Federal No-Fault Insurance do not consider the add-on type of plans adopted by Oregon and Delaware and other states, to be No-Fault. This apparently is because these states did not abolish the rights of its citizens to seek damages in tort, but merely added first party benefits to their insurance coverage. I fail to understand the opposition to such plans since apparently, in Oregon, the result has been excellent, as measured by reduced premiums, reduced small claims and litigation.

We submit that before the Federal Government abolishes a known system for yet another unknown and untried theory, that the citizens of this country be made aware of the facts and hard evidence.

One of the dangers of the Federal plan is that there may be over-utilization and excessive claims. The present studies are based upon claims under the present system. Excessive claims under No-Fault will drastically affect rates and drive up costs as it has been demonstrated under Medicare. We understand that Florida has experienced such abuses.

The proponents of Federal No-Fault cite the need for uniformity as an important factor supporting its enactment. I do not understand their argument. It seems that the experience being gained by the variations in approach in the 24 states which have adopted various no-fault plans, would be invaluable to an overall study as to the effectiveness of the various plans. We have many conflicting reports. The insurance commissioner of Massachusetts states that no-fault is working there to reduce rates. Yet, individuals state that the total insurance bill they pay is more. Since Massachusetts had some of the highest liability rates in the nation prior to No-Fault, which many think was caused by mandatory liability insurance, their experience may or may not be meaningful.

Yet, under S. 354 and H.R. 1900, many options are open to the states and many questions are unanswered, even to the definition of which vehicles are included. Thus, there will be *no* uniformity. If uniformity is so important, then perhaps Congress should consider uniform is so important, then perhaps Congress should consider uniform motor vehicle operating laws. This would certainly promote safety since all motorists would be operating under a set of uniform rules.

We find it completely unacceptable for Congress to set up a system involving 200 million people, untold billions of dollars, based upon theory, and then find out if it actually works. We submit that the Federal No-Fault plans will be unsatisfactory to the public resulting in demands for amendments and changes annually.

The most important role the Federal Government can undertake is to correlate and assemble factual information so that the states can determine the best plan for its residents. We need the information and facts.

This would enable the states to enact legislation beneficial to its residents depending upon the circumstances and needs of each state.

Accordingly, we suggest that you consider these and other arguments against enactment of the present legislation and instead, would request further study as to the no-fault bills and other enactments in various states which have been passed in order to cure problems in the present system.

Thank you for allowing me to appear today and express these views

RESOLUTION

The New Mexico State Bar Commission unanimously restates its position against Senate Bill 345, the National No-Fault Motor Vehicle Insurance Act.

The Bar Commission realizing that it represents a wide spectrum of attorneys throught the State of New Mexico and further realizing its obligation to represent the interests of the public and the advancement of the public welfare has examined the impact of National No-Fault Insurance on the public, and has concluded that such legislation is not in the best interest of the citizens of New Mexico.

The Commission commends the United States Senators from New Mexico for their stand and vote against Senate Bill 354 in 1974, and urges them to take a positive stand against Federal No-Fault Insurance in the Senate during the 1975 debate on the bill since the current version of Senate Bill 354 is substantially the same as the Bill considered in 1974.

The Commission commends Allstate Insurance Company for doing an actuarial study on the cost to the public for insurance under the National No-Fault Motor Vehicle Insurance Act, Senate Bill 354. The study disproves the often repeated misstatement that No-Fault Insurance would reduce premiums. The Commission feels strongly that the public should be informed of the study, and the fact that rates will increase in New Mexico between 34.7 and 67 percent over the present rates, while seriously limiting the benefits to those persons who are injured because of the negligent conduct of others. The Commission calls upon all of the news media, to fully inform the public of the actual provisions of National No-Fault Insurance, and the true impact upon the public, not only as to costs, but more importantly, as to the substantial and drastic change contemplated by the law.

The New Mexico State Bar Association stands ready to work with interested citizens and legislators in recommending reforce to make the present system in New Mexico more efficient in delivering benefits to the public, without substantially and unduly curtailing the basic traditional personal injury rights of the public to be compensated for losses. Such action should be local state action and not federal action.

Mr. VAN DEERLIN. Thank you for being here.
Mr. Kinzler.
Mr. KINZLER. In the light of the time and in an attempt to get to the last witness, I will ask only one thing.

I am sorry we don't have more time to get to your statement which is a very good one. You indicated there was some difference of opinion with respect to the Federal bill as far as protection against overutilization of medical benefits.

It would be to the benefit of the subcommittee if we do go ahead and consider Federal standards if we could have draft language, yours or anyone else's who is interested in finding a way to cope with this problem, if you would be so kind. Take a look at it and suggest some language.

Mr. SEDBERRY. Mr. Counsel, I would be happy to except for the fact that I can't live with the basic philosophy of your bill, to begin with. I don't believe any part of it is correct. I don't believe in abolishing the tort system, and you would have to do that to achieve the goals that you need.

Mr. KINZLER. We appreciate your position. It would not imply that you change your position at all. It would simply be a technical help to us if you wish to do so. If you don't, that is your decision.

Mr. SEDBERRY. I would like to comment to you about the fact that you have mentioned several times today the DOT study showing that a third of the people with economic losses over $25,000 do not get full recovery. I question that study. I question it severely. I question the group they included in the study, whether they are including people who are injured by the negligence of others or all people.

Mr. KINZLER. Let me give you some background on that one.

In that group, 42 percent of those people had a tort recovery and they recovered a little over 30 percent. Those without tort recovery recovered a little bit under 30 percent, the reason being that the economic loss was so high, and tort recovery—due to such things as the prevailing $10,000/$20,000 insurance—was so low it did not make much difference whether they had tort right or not. It is a figure supported by the Department of Transportation's subsequent study, as well.

Mr. SEDBERRY. I question that from the point of view of who they got the information from, who made the judgment as to whether they got adequate recovery.

Mr. KINZLER. There is a citation. If you wish to follow it up, I am sure DOT will give you the information.

Mr. SEDBERRY. I am sure they will but I still question it from my experience as a practicing lawyer.

Thank you, Mr. Chairman.

Mr. VAN DEERLIN. Thank you, sir.

One more 10-minute break.

[Brief recess.]

Mr. BRODHEAD [presiding]. I am sorry that things have been so hectic here. We are going to have to wind this up shortly.

I did want to give you a chance to make your concerns known. The chairman asked me to see that you did. Then we could, of course, have your full statement in the record.

Mr. Kinzler, our counsel, can prepare a summary of your statement and circulate it to members of the committee.

If you could, take a few minutes and make us aware for the record of what it is you would like to state.

STATEMENT OF PAUL W. BROCK, PRESIDENT, DEFENSE RESEARCH INSTITUTE, INC., MILWAUKEE, WIS.; ACCOMPANIED BY THEODORE P. SHIELD, PAST PRESIDENT, INTERNATIONAL ASSOCIATION OF INSURANCE COUNSEL, LOS ANGELES, CALIF.; AND PROF. JOHN J. KIRCHER, MARQUETTE UNIVERSITY SCHOOL OF LAW, RESEARCH DIRECTOR AND COUNSEL

Mr. BROCK. Something less than the hour and a half that I had planned will be acceptable, I guess.

Mr. BRODHEAD. Yes. I think we can get a consensus on it.

Mr. BROCK. I am Paul W. Brock. I am the president of the Defense Research Institute, Inc., which is a defense trial lawyers organization with something over 6,000 individual members and some 400 or 500 insurance and other corporate members.

Mr. BRODHEAD. I am a former defense trial lawyer, myself, so I think I can relate to that.

Mr. BROCK. To my right is Theodore P. Shield, past president of the International Association of Insurance Counsel, an insurance defense lawyers association, probably the largest in the world. All of its members are members of DRI.

To my left is John J. Kircher, a law professor at Marquette, and also the research director of DRI, and our lawyer at this hearing. If there were time for questions, and if we got asked specifically penetrating questions by Mr. Kinzler, we would probably refer them to Mr. Kircher.

We had with us earlier Mr. John D. Bauman, president of the Association of Insurance Attorneys, who had to make a plane.

We also had with us Phillip W. Knight, chairman of the board of the Federation of Insurance Counsel, an organization similar to Mr. Shield's. He, too, had to take a plane.

For all of us, I want to thank you for coming in here at the last moment and sort of jumping into this whirlpool and being with us. We shall try to be short.

Much of what we had planned to say has already been said very ably by many of the other witnesses before us.

DRI is an educational and research organization to aid defense trial lawyers. When Keeton and O'Connell wrote their first article in the mid-sixties we started looking into the question of what we call responsible reform. We have a paid staff in Milwaukee of some five full-time lawyers and other clerical, stenographic and lay help. We came up, after a period of years, with what we entitled "Responsible Reform," and then we did an update on it.

Essentially, it provides for two things: (1) It provides for the preservation of the fault system as we know it, which essentially is that a wrongdoer who injures someone or does damage to his property must bear the civil and moral responsibility for his fault, and then; (2) that if any changes are to be made in our present system, it ought to be done on a State-by-State basis.

We did have, and you do have in the record, our recommendations for improving the present tort system if changes need to be made on a State-by-State basis.

We recommend for consideration by the States mandatory liability insurance, mandatory first party insurance, conceivably arbitration of claims under $3,000, again on a State-by-State basis, regulation of the contingent fee system, elimination of the ad damnum clause in the complaint, modification of the collateral source rule and some other items which we think would probably improve the tort system as we have had it through the years.

However, we do not change the basic structure and we do not change the basic premise that a wrongdoer must bear the responsibility for what he does. He can insure against it by liability insurance if he wishes to do so. Obviously, if he wants to pay the small premium for first party coverage, for medical and for loss of earnings, he can do that. This is fine.

But our primary objection to an overwhelming no-fault plan like H.R. 1900 or H.R. 1272 is one of philosophy.

I want to express the caveat that, being defense trial lawyers who make our living in large part from the trial of cases, it would be obvious that our testimony in this regard would be suspect because we would have a vested interest in the continuation of litigation.

That is quite so; we do have a vested interest in it. But this particular type of litigation, the automobile skidmark or intersection case, is not of very much importance to us in a monetary way. It is probably the smallest segment of our practice; it is probably the least remunerative of our practice. I, myself, have not tried an automobile case for over a year. I cannot speak for my friend, Mr. Shield. I think that is generally true of what are termed defense lawyers, as a whole.

Our objection is based upon philosophy. It is this: At the moment, an individual in a State that has not adopted a complete no-fault plan has a right, if he is injured in an accident, to make a claim or not make a claim. That is his freedom of choice. If he makes a claim, he has the freedom to settle or go to court. If he goes to court, he has the freedom to have his case tried before a jury. If he tries it before a jury, he has the freedom to let it go to verdict and judgment or to settle before that is done.

These basic freedoms, in 95 percent of the present cases, in all except the most dramatic cases of injury that we have all discussed and know about, these freedoms would be taken away by these bills that you have under consideration. The right of an individual to enjoy the use of his life and his limb, his health, his mind, would be taken away from him in this regard. I say "would be taken away from him" because if you deprive him of the right to seek whatever redress his fellow citizens think he should have and you arbitrarily mandate what he is entitled to recover, you have taken away from him the freedom of choice that he had before.

Many of our freedoms of choice as citizens throughout the years have been taken from us. Included, I think, on the average is possibly the freedom of choice to spend roughly a third of our national income. I think there is some question as to how many freedoms of choice the citizens of this country can have taken from them before we are reduced to a sort of gray automated society without the freedoms that are the very cornerstone of this country.

I do not recall from my reading of the New Testament—and I am no Bible scholar; no one has ever accused me of being a great philosopher—I do not recall that Jesus of Nazareth ever preached or advocated a no-fault system. My recollection is that his teachings were that one who does wrong pays the price and is to be punished. I see nowhere in there where he said, "If you are robbed or stolen from or your property rights are impinged upon, don't worry about it. Look to your own resources, carry your own first party insurance.'

Mr. BRODHEAD. We do have a couple members of the subcommittee who are Jewish.

Could you advise us of Moses' position on this?

Mr. BROCK. Mr. Chairman, I have enough trouble with the New Testament in the King James version. I would not dare to say what Moses said or thought about that.

If you have this no-fault system that you talk about and that you have in these bills, I think it is reasonable to think that what you have is an accident and health system. I think it is reasonable that premiums would be based not upon the careless driving or the reckless driving or the injuries that are done to someone else but upon the driver's own propensity for being hurt.

I think if you have a man who is old, who is infirm, who has arteriosclerosis, heart trouble, has a predisposition to disease, so if there is an accident he is prone to be hurt, if he is driving a small car rather than a large one, I think he will pay more premiums than will someone else who is perhaps healthier or driving a bigger car, all of this without regard to his driving safety or driving record. I don't think this is a fair or reasonable sort of system to impose upon the public.

You have in your bill a wage formula. It is the per capita income in the State over the average of the per capita income of the country times $1,000 as the limitation on wage recovery.

In Alabama, a man making $15,000 a year would be limited to $757 per month under the formula. Alabama happens to be my home State, as California is Mr. Shield's, and Wisconsin is Professor Kircher's.

In Washington, D.C., he would get $1,375 a month. He loses the right to sue in tort for the difference. I don't think that is a reasonable or just or fair type of demarcation. I think that it is rather patently inequitable.

The arguments have been advanced that there should be a uniform system and that it should not be left to the States. I submit to you that there is no real merit in uniformity, as such. It is expedient but it does not satisfy anyone.

The testimony earlier which you missed and which I won't belabor everyone else with by repeating was about a bed in which the victims are cut to fit the bed if they are too long, or if they are too short, they are stretched to fit the bed. I think this is the kind of thing that the Federal no-fault bills would do.

In some States, perhaps in New York or New Jersey, where you have high industrial populations and heavy population concentrations, perhaps they have court congestion. We do not have it in Alabama. We get to trial there in 6 months or less.

The problems of the States are different. Half of them have adopted one plan or another. The other half, by and large, have plans under consideration and have seen fit not to adopt them yet. I do not know whether Alabama will ever need or want a no-fault system. If a State does want it, then that State legislature can tailor that bill to fit the needs of that State.

So, I would submit to you two things in this abbreviated statement of ours: First: Philosophically, a no-fault bill is morally wrong because it encourages moral irresponsibility and it takes away the civil fault that the law now places on a man and it makes him irresponsible for his misdeeds. Second: If there is to be any change in our tort system, then it should be on a State-by-State basis where it can be tailored to fit the needs of the citizens of that State.

Now, if I may, I don't know whether my friend, Mr. Shield, has anything to say, but, if I could yield the floor to him, I would like to. Thank you.

[Mr. Brock's prepared statement follows:]

STATEMENT OF PAUL W. BROCK, PRESIDENT, DEFENSE RESEARCH INSTITUTE

My name is Paul W. Brock. I am a practicing attorney from Mobile, Alabama. I am President of the Defense Research Institute. Joining me today are Theodore Shield of Los Angeles, immediate past president of the International Association of Insurance Counsel; Also accompanying us today is Professor John J. Kircher of the Marquette University School of Law who is the Research Director of the Defense Research Institute.

The Defense Research Institute is a national, non-profit organization with over 6,000 members. It is headquartered in Milwaukee, Wisconsin. Nearly all of our members are trial lawyers. They come from all 50 states, Puerto Rico and Canada. Our lawyer members are engaged in the defense of civil lawsuits. They are from law firms totalling over 20,000 attorneys. All of the lawyer members of the International Association of Insurance Counsel, Federation of Insurance Counsel and Association of Insurance Attorneys are members of DRI. However, each of those organizations is separate and autonomous.

The Defense Research Institute was organized in 1960 as a research and educational organization to promote improvements in the administration of justice and to improve the service of the legal profession to the public. Representatives of our organization have appeared before this and other Congressional committees in the past to present testimony on the subject of Federal involvement in automobile accident reparations reform. Our position here today is consistent with the position we have taken toward Federal legislation on this subject in the past.

We favor responsible reform; that is, reform which goes to the root causes of delay and inefficiency and at the same time preserves for the citizen long-recognized concepts of justice and fairness. As one part of our efforts to bring about responsible reform, we have supported meaningful state "no-fault" legislation. There are some practical advantages to "no-fault" automobile insurance reform. We recognize those advantages and have included them in our overall proposals for responsible reform. Our specific proposals are contained in a position paper, "Responsible Reform—An Update (1973)," which is a joint statement of the four defense lawyer organizations appearing today. We would be pleased to file copies of that position paper with this subcommittee if the chairman so wishes.

Meaningful reform, however, does not merely cater to the clamor of expediency, which standing alone can be, and has been, used to justify virtually anything. It seeks to preserve the sense of fairness and justice for both the individual citizen and society. To date, there is no groundswell of opinion which favors one method of reparation reform over another. The opinions, attitudes and beliefs of reasonable, knowledgeable persons differ significantly. The host of proposals, bills and amendments to bills relating to automobile accident reparations reform at both the state and federal level establish this beyond doubt. Likewise, there is no consensus of opinion as to the effect which any particular "no-fault" auto insurance proposal would have upon automobile insurance premium rates. Costs projections have differed sharply. The results from some of the statistical methods used have drawn severe criticism.

We are opposed to H.R. 1900, H.R. 1272, or any other Federal measure which would prevent the states from continuing to exercise their own independent judgments as to the type of automobile accident reparations reform which best serves the needs and interests of the citizens of the states. The extent of the disagreement concerning the proper mix of "no-fault" and fault systems, the speculative nature of the statistical projections concerning a Federal system, and the present success of the states in instituting meaningful reform, convinces us that freezing progress with an untested Federal system would be wholly unwarranted.

The issue is not whether reform is moving ahead. The fact is that meaningful reform is being accomplished at a rate which has surprised even the sceptics. The issue is not whether "no-fault" is being enacted in the states. The fact is that the states are acting. The issue is who is in the best position, within the context of particular needs and problems, to institute reform. We believe that the states are in the best position and are meeting their responsibilities.

THE UNIFORMITY MYTH

It has been argued that Federal automobile accident reparations reform legislation is necessary to create a uniform system within the country. When reduced to its simplest terms, the uniformity argument is that it is cheaper and more expedient to manage one system with one set of forms than to manage many systems. If that argument has validity, it should apply whenever two or more entities do the same task. Therefore it would be more expedient to have only one legislative house. It would be more expedient to have one giant state. There would be less duplication with one monopolistic business. However, uniformity demands unanimity and consensus. In the name of expediency divergent opinion or conflicting points of view cannot be tolerated. Individual needs blur into the average need, and no individual needs are met—but they are unfulfilled very expediently.

The proponents of Federal "no-fault" auto insurance reform appear to forget that divergent opinions spring from the very nature of a reparations system. The fault system has developed from basic beliefs that reach deep into our history. We have come to believe that in a civilized society citizens must be able to assume that their fellow men will act with due care toward them. Due care comes from the ordinary understanding and the moral sense of the community. The concept of liability is based on this justifiable reliance, and is part of the conditions of civilized society. The result has been a series of rules couched in terms of the duty of one citizen toward another. The whole modern law of negligence enforces the duty of citizens to observe an appropriate measure of prudence to avoid causing harm to one another. This element of Tort law has been referred to as the responsibility element. The moral and social tradition of this country has been that one is under a moral obligation not to inflict damage on his neighbor by an act which he could have avoided.

It was rationally followed that one who causes the harm wrongfully should be responsible to the injured person. The liability involved is an individual responsibility. Enforcing the right reinforces the duty owed to individual citizens and to society.

"No-fault," on the other hand, is merely a form of social insurance. Social insurance springs from the belief that in a complex, industrialized, heavily populated society, classes of people, or society as a whole, must bear the responsibility for loss. Responsibility is shifted from the wrongdoer to society through the mechanism of insurance or taxation. Under this system one necessarily pushes aside the concept of wrongdoing and focuses on the harm that is done. When the focus is exclusively on the harm done, the fault system becomes irrelevant. Predictably major efforts at social insurance will be accompanied by a clamor for abolition or radical modification of the tort system.

Not every section of this country in heavily industrialized, enormously complex or overly populated. There are areas in which individual responsibility and the duty one owes to his neighbor are of paramount importance. Each state must decide if, and to what extent, it wishes to rip any more of the threads of individualism out of the social and economic fabric than must be done in order to take adequate care of the basic human needs of the citizens. This is not a matter of mere regional difference based on geography or demography. Responsible reform of an institution such as automobile accident reparation is concerned with a balancing of needs. On the one hand, there is the need to preserve the strong-rooted belief that a person should be responsible for his actions. On the other hand, there is a need to efficiently and economically provide compensation to as many automobile accident victims as possible.

These needs can be met and are being met without having to select one to the exclusion of the other. To date, 24 states have enacted some type of automobile accident reparations reform legislation. Over 53 percent of the nation's population is now covered by some form of "no-fault" auto insurance plan. Each of the legislatures of the other 26 states have had legislation pending during the current legislative sessions and the momentum for action clearly continues in a number of states.

A predictable and highly desirable result of the state-by-state approach is evidenced in the diversity of plans which now exist. Conclusions as to the most appropriate balance between fault and "no-fault" can now be made by other states on the basis of the experience accumulating in those states having enacted plans. There is every reason to believe that as data indicating the experience of existing plans continues to accumulate, the pace of state "no-fault" action will quicken. Small claims are being taken out of the court system and more automobile accident victims are being promptly compensated for their economic loss. But, while H.R. 1900 for example, might affect desired reform in some of the states, experience to date would indicate that other plans incorporating different mixes of benefit levels and tort restrictions may achieve more success. The apparent successes of the Oregon and Delaware plans in achieving the basic "no-fault" objective while preserving the right to maintain tort remedies prove that there are many ways to achieve the desired results.

The experimentation in striking the proper balance continues with the use of first party add-on provisions, mandatory liability insurance and "no-fault" laws with various threshholds. At the same time the states enacting "no-fault" laws are discovering that the perfect statute has yet to be written. Inadequacies are being discovered. Ambiguities and conflicts of interpretation inevitably result. When the problems have been recognized the states have acted to correct the problems by amending their laws.

Quite separate from the issue of the need for a uniform reparations system is the question of whether H.R. 1900, or any similar Federal law, would achieve uniformity if enacted. We have concluded that uniformity would be a mere myth when the construction and interpretation of the law will be left to the courts and insurance departments of 50 states, the District of Columbia, Guam and the Virgin Islands.

If a Federal scheme is enacted, and it becomes apparent that, in a few states, inequities or ambiguities have arisen or cost protections were grossly in error, or a conflict of interpretation has surfaced, can we reasonably expect Congress to move promptly to correct the problems? Or is it more reasonable to assume that so long as the majority of states are unaffected, such truly national concerns as an energy policy, the economy, the defense, education, and the condition of our cities will take priority?

To supplant efforts by the states with an untested national system would be a major error. We would lose adaptability, experimentation and the responsiveness to effectively bring about responsible reform.

A concrete example of what we are talking about can be seen in the current medical malpractice dilemma. Some states are vitally affected. Others are experiencing few problems. The legislatures of the states most severely affected have moved quickly to effectuate solutions. While these state legislative solutions may not be perfect, they represent valid attempts by legislative bodies closest to the problems to cope with them. It would be utter nonsense to argue that the solution arrived at in Wisconsin, for example, should be imposed in other states having no problems or problems different from those experienced in Wisconsin. The value of the state legislative process lies in the fact that, being close to the problem, it is better able to act promptly and responsibly when a need for legislative action is found to exist.

It has been claimed that Federal legislation directed toward automobile accident reparations reform is necessary because of the possibility that a motorist driving through each of the 50 jurisdictions in the continental United States (including the District of Columbia but excluding Hawaii) may be exposed to 50 different state laws dealing with his rights and obligations in the event of an automobile accident. This, it is claimed, would hamper the free flow of interstate commerce.

It should be noted that claims of uncertainty and confusion on the part of motorists engaged in interstate travel in the face of differing state automobile accident reparation laws seem to be grounded upon the belief that most motorists are knowledgeable as to both the extent of their automobile insurance coverage and the laws applicable in their own states and are concerned with the possible differences in the laws in the other states in which they may travel. As lawyers with a good deal of experience in automobile accident cases, we find that this is hardly the case. Motorists do not curtail or alter their travels because of concern over differing state laws. In fact, in some 23 years of active automobile practice, I personally have never heard the matter mentioned by a motorist. Further, the insurance industry has responded to the problem. Policies are now written so that when a motorist from a state with a tort system drives into a "no-fault" state his policy is automatically changed to conform to the laws of the state in which he is operating his vehicle. This device is a remarkably simple answer to an alleged problem.

We do not presume to be able to judge what the best approach to automobile accident reparations reform should be in each jurisdiction of this country. We have studied this subject long enough, however, to realize that many gifted individuals from the legislative, academic, insurance and legal communities have drafted hundreds of different automobile reparations plans and proposals. While we are sure that each draftsman believes in the merits of his own work product, we are equally sure that state legislators, the persons closest to the motorists that these plans will serve, are in a better position to judge the type of plan which will be best for a particular jurisdiction. Labeling any plan as "genuine" or "phony" means nothing more than that the person who has chosen that label has made an evaluation of a plan based upon his own subjective beliefs as to the elements which a plan should contain.

The fact that twenty-four states have enacted differing auto reparations reform laws clearly demonstrates that the states which have acted are following the recommendations the Department of Transportation made when it closed its study of automobile accident reparations reform. As this subcommittee will recall, DOT recommended that the preferable procedure in automobile reparations reform was to have the states experiment with diverse plans to gain meaningful experiences as to the best course which should ultimately be followed. Federal legislation would not allow for this type of experimentation; in fact, it would tell the states that experimentation is unnecessary since Congress has devised the best possible approach to the problem. With all due respect to this subcommittee and the other members of Congress, we do not believe that anyone is now in a position to claim, with any degree of credibility, that the best practical automobile accident reparations reform plan has yet been found.

It is claimed that there is a need for Federal legislation in this area because the states are not moving quickly enough. We think that the determination of whether a state has moved quickly enough can only be made by those who are in a position to judge whether the problem in a given state is such that quick action is necessary. We again point to the current medical malpractice "crisis" which exists in some states to note that state legislative action has been prompt where a need for that action has been found. Interestingly enough, remedial medical malpractice legislation has been enacted in states such as Indiana and Wisconsin even though automobile reparations reform legislation has not been enacted there. We submit that states which have yet to enact such legislation should not be faulted for failing to act if their legislatures believe that their problems are of insufficient magnitude to warrant immediate action. In fact, the states which have yet to act are in the enviable position of being able to study the successes and failures of their sister states which have acted. They are thus in a position to shape the best possible legislation once there is an actual need for that legislation.

In summary, we oppose Federal automobile accident reparations reform legislation simply because it is grounded upon the false assumption that it presents the best alternative available and because of the further false assumption that the need for such a change in each and every jurisdiction in the country is essential now. We question whether a sound case for national uniformity has been presented. When the "no-fault" movement began several years ago, it was claimed that reform was necessary for the benefit of the persons served by the system—accident victims and insurance buyers. Rather than allowing each state to tailor its own laws to the needs of the individuals served by the system, the Federal approach to the problem would sacrifice those needs on the altar of uniformity.

SPECIFIC CRITICISMS OF THE HOUSE BILLS

We would like to call the subcommittee's attention, at this time, to specific criticisms we have of the provisions of the bills under consideration. We recognize that the subcommittee's time is limited and that other witnesses will deal with various problems of the bills from the frame of reference of their particular expertise. Therefore, since we are an organization of defense lawyers, we shall confine our observations to those specific provisions of the bills which affect the legal liability system.

H.R. 1900

As we understand the provisions of Section 204(b)(1) of HR1900, a state complying with the "minimum" requirements of Title II would establish a monthly limit for work loss benefits by multiplying $1,000 by a fraction whose numerator would be the average per capita income in the state and whose denominator would be the average per capita income in the United States. We further understand the provisions of Section 206(a)(4) of the bill to mean that an accident victim would be unable to recover, in tort, for the difference between his actual monthly wage loss and the amount of benefits received during any given month. Based upon this per capita income formula, we have computed the results in terms of monthly work loss benefit limits for certain selected states to show what the benefit limits in those states would be if they followed that formula:

Alabama, $757.
California, $1,141.
District of Columbia, $1,375.
Florida, $945.
Georgia, $863.
Illinois, $1,170.
Michigan, $1,106.
Mississippi, $701.

Nebraska, $981.
New Jersey, $1,171.
New York, $1,151.
Ohio, $1,019.
Texas, $882.
West Virginia, $778.
Wisconsin, $942.

It can be seen that, under the formula, if strictly followed, monthly work loss benefits could range from a high of $1375 in the District of Columbia to a low of $701 in Mississippi. Therefore, an employee of the Federal Government living in Washington, D.C. and earning $16,500 a year or $1375 a month would be entitled to full reimbursement for wage loss from his own insurer should he be injured in an automobile accident and suffer one month of disability. If that same government employee, at the same wage level, were transferred to Mississippi, and injured in an automobile accident resulting in one month of disability, $674 of his wage loss would be uncompensated. He would receive only $701 from his own insurer and, under the provisions of Section 206(a)(4) of the bill, would be prevented from seeking recovery for the uncompensated work loss from the person responsible for causing the automobile accident.

It strikes us as completely inequitable to have such an unfair work loss benefit schedule while barring the accident victim from seeking a tort remedy for the difference between the amount actually lost and the amount he is able to recover from his own insurer. The only way the accident victim with a high wage loss level (in comparison to the per capita income in his state) could protect himself would be to purchase additional insurance. This is taking away a remedy without providing any adequate substitute whatsoever. The ludicrous result is to ask a citizen to give up his right and then buy part of it back at his own expense.

Sections 103(2)(B) and 206(a)(4) effectively limit recovery for funeral and burial expenses to a maximum of $1,000. Any funeral and burial expenses over that limit would be uncompensated from any source, including the negligent motorist who caused the death. Information we have received leaves us to believe that, in most areas of the country, the $1,000 allowed by the bill, without any right in tort to seek compensation for funeral and burial expenses above that sum, would be grossly inadequate.

As we understand the provisions of Section 206(a)(5) of the bill, states complying with the provisions of Title II would be allowed to preserve tort liability for "noneconomic detriment" only in cases involving accidents resulting in death, serious and permanent disfigurement, other serious and permanent injury, or more than 90 continuous days of total disability.

That which the bill refers to as "noneconomic detriment" has also been called "pain and suffering" or "general damages." Labels or titles do not adequately describe the type of damage for which this section of the bill would attempt to limit recovery. Affected would be more than physical hurt associated with an injury. Also included within that definition would be mental anguish; aggravation of a pre-existing disease; aggravation of a pre-existing physical condition; impairment of physical or mental abilities; disfigurement, scarring and dismemberment; loss of body functions; inconvenience and discomfort; fright and shock; humiliation, indignity and insult; loss of enjoyment of life; loss of society and companionship of a loved one; worry about future consequences of injury; loss of earning capacity; and various forms of disability.

From statistics developed by the Department of Transportation it may be safely assumed that the application of these tort restrictions would effectively preclude over 95% of all automotibile accident victims from recovering for their general damages. Using 1973 statistics, this would mean that 4,985,410 of the persons injured in automobile accidents would have no right to seek a tort remedy.

It has been claimed that some limitations on the right to seek a tort recovery for "noneconomic loss" or "general damages" are necessary. The necessity for such a restriction is premised on the belief that there is over-compensation of general damages in cases of minor injury and that limiting this over-compensation is necessary to keep the costs of added first-party benefits under a "no-fault" system affordable. Based upon our study of the subject, we would not object to state restrictions on recoveries for general damages in cases involving minor injuries where the pain is transitory and soon forgotten. However, the provisions of this bill go much too far in limiting the right of recovery and, indeed, go farther than almost any state plan which has been enacted to date.

As we interpret the provisions of Section 111 of the bill, state plans complying with Title II would allow almost all losses from automobile accidents to lie where they fall. That is, insurers paying first-party benefits to their insureds could not by means of subrogation, seek recovery for the benefits paid from the insurer of the person responsible for causing the accident. Compliance with Title II would change the automobile accident reparations system from a liability insurance system to what is basically an accident and health insurance system. In other words, a motorist's insurance record, and ultimately his insurance premiums, would reflect the losses he has suffered and not the losses he has caused. It would appear to us that auto insurers without the ability to shift losses back to tortfeasors will be more concerned with their insured's potential for sustaining loss than with their potential for causing loss to others. If so, auto insurers will become extremely interested in those matters affecting their insureds which would indicate a potential for large benefit payments in the event of an automobile accident. Persons with pre-existing diseases or physical conditions may well find their auto insurance extremely expensive, regardless of their driving records, since, in the event of an accident, their insurers would probably be liable for the payment of substantial sums of benefits far in excess of the norm. Similarly, drivers of oversized, heavy road equipment could expect to pay less because of their obvious physical advantages in the event of a wreck.

No-fault automobile insurance systems do exist under which loss reallocation is still available based upon fault. This process would not result in a delay of payments from an insurer to his own insured since, as presently operated in most states, loss reallocation would be based upon insurance company arbitration. The net result is that the states are developing systems which would be fairer than those contemplated by federal bills since the persons responsible for causing accidents would not be rendered anonymous. They would bear the burden of the irresponsible driving

H.R. 1272

As we understand the provisions of H.R. 1272, tort liability for vehicular accidents would be completely eliminated (except in cases of "criminal conduct") and would be replaced by first party, "no-fault" insurance system.

We must admit that H.R. 1272 clearly places the choice between a "fault" and "no-fault" system at issue. Unlike other Federal bills, it does not contain a mix of "fault" and "no-fault," but presents the choice of the latter over the former. While we are opposed to H.R. 1272 because of our general opposition to a Federal approach to automobile accident reparations reform, there are two central problems which this bill presents which also make it completely unacceptable to us.

First, we are opposed to the bill's total "no-fault" approach. We are not generally opposed to the concept of "no-fault" or first-party insurance itself. We all have have accident and health insurance, fire insurance and other forms of first-party coverage. What concerns us about this bill is its lack of a loss real location mechanism. This prevents the losses which are generated and which are paid by a first-party system from being shifted back to the persons whose careless driving produced the losses in the first instance. Each motorist would be forced to protect himself against the reckless and irresponsible conduct of his fellow motorists. Each motorist's auto insurance premium will reflect his potential for sustaining loss, not causing loss. To us this is completely inequitable.

Second, if we understand the bill's provision respecting insurance coverage correctly, especially Section 5(b)(1), each accident victim, regardless of his fault in causing an accident, will be able to recover *all* of his out-of-pocket losses, as well as damages for pain and suffering, from his own insurer. There would be no dollar or time limits on the coverage. Although we are not insurance actuaries, we cannot help but believe that this must greatly increase the cost of auto insurance. The bill would present no built-in feature that would result in cost savings. Essentially, it would substitute an accident victim's own insurer for the insurer of a third party. However, the insured's fault would be immaterial and there would be no dollar limit on the insurer's responsibility to respond in damages. Not only would this add to the cost of the system in terms of benefit payments, but it would surely increase litigation. The accident victim would stand to lose nothing by suing his own insurer to obtain the highest damage award possible.

CONSTITUTIONAL PROBLEMS

As the members of this Subcommittee are now aware, serious questions have been raised as to the constitutionality of various proposals for Federal automobile accident reparations reform. We shall not burden the members of the Subcommittee with a detailed exposition on the subject. Suffice it to say, there is a difference of opinion among knowledgeable experts as to the constitutionality of Federal "no-fault." The plethora of constitutional problems do not center on the issue of the Federal regulation of insurance. That subject was resolved a long time ago by the case of *United States* v. *South-Eastern Underwriters Assoc.* [322 U.S. 533 (1944)]. We fully understand the power of Congress to repeal or revise the McCarran-Ferguson Act [Public Law 15 of 1945]. The basic question, rather, is whether the Congress has the power to revise or eliminate state tort law and require state government to abide by its decision in that regard. Our own view is that, while the powers of Congress under the Commerce Clause are broad, they are not broad enough to override the constitutional protections afforded to the citizens of this country under the Ninth Amendment, especially as that provision of the Constitution has been interpreted by the Court in *Griswold* v. *Connecticut* [38] U.S. 479 (1965)].

The doubtful constitutionality of such Federal legislation presents another problem for the motorists of the United States. It is one thing for a state "no-fault" law to be found unconstitutional, resulting in problems for the citizens of that state. It is yet another thing for a Federal law, affecting all 50 states, to be found unconstitutional. The problems would be magnified 50 fold, and the solution would be infinitely more difficult.

CONCLUSION

To summarize, our opposition to HR1900, HR1272, or any other bill offering a Federal approach to the reform of the automobile accident reparations system is not grounded upon the Defense Bar's opposition to meaningful "no-fault" legislation. We favor such legislation, but are of the firm belief that the individual state legislatures, and not the Congress, are in the best position to balance all of the factors which must be considered to achieve fairness and efficiency. We do not claim, as individuals or as national defense lawyer organizations, to be in the position to determine what is needed in each jurisdiction. We firmly believe, however, that to the extent that first-party benefits are not provided under a state plan for certain losses, the accident victim's right to pursue a tort remedy should be preserved.

We ask that this Subcommittee recommend to the House that Federal legislation on this subject not be enacted. We recognize that this and other committees of the Congress have expended a great deal of time and effort in the development of this legislation, which time and effort are to be commended. However, we are satisfied that the abatement of Federal legislation is fully justified and is in the best interest of the persons that the automobile accident reparations system is intended to serve—the citizens of these United States.

Mr. BRODHEAD. Yes, sir.

Mr. SHIELD. Thank you, Mr. Broadhead, and Mr. Kinzler.

I know you are waiting with bated breath to hear me say that I adopt the statements of Mr. Brock and I have nothing further to say.

I will just take a minute, though, if I may.

I am Theodore P. Shield from Los Angeles, Calif. I am a practicing lawyer, a trial lawyer. I am appearing as immediate past president of the International Association of Insurance Counsel in place of Jerry V. Walker of Houston, who was unable to be here. He is the current president.

I have been here before and I have been before the Senate committee and, after listening to the witnesses who testified today, I wonder why I am here today because they have said everything that can be said in favor of our position.

Our organization is composed of lawyers who represent insurance companies in defending personal injury cases of all kinds, not only automobile accidents but those are part of them. We are not employees of insurance companies.

I am glad that Mr. Brodhead came in and indicated that he had been a defense lawyer at one time. I don't have to explain to him that trial lawyers come in all sizes and shapes, and charge accordingly, and that all trial lawyers such as the ones who represent plaintiffs in personal injury cases cannot be lumped together.

Mr. Brodhead, I am sure, is familiar with the fact that the defense lawyer is not paid on the same basis as the plaintiff's lawyer in a personal injury case. Therefore, I think that our voice as lawyers who represent insurance companies is an important voice to be heard in this matter because we do not have that alleged economic self-interest that the plaintiff's lawyers are charged with.

I am not so cynical as to believe that plaintiffs' attorneys are opposed to no-fault simply because of their economic self-interest, although I am frank to admit that that is part of it, must be part of it.

In any event, we, as lawyers representing insurance companies, not only are not advancing our self-interest by being opposed to Federal no-fault, but we are hurting ourselves in certain respects because some of the large insurance companies that we represent are in favor of Federal no-fault legislation, and, to their credit, as far as I know, they have not tried to influence us as independent lawyers to abide by their view of what should be done in this field.

For that reason, and with that background about our identity, I think it is who we are that is important to be known by this committee rather than what we say because we do adopt all of the things that have been said by the witnesses that have appeared today.

I think that I speak for all of our members in saying that we are not opposed to reform of the auto reparations system; we are not opposed to no-fault insurance of some type or another; but we do not feel that the Federal legislation is the answer to it. We think that the States can decide for themselves what their problems are.

It has been pointed out the differences between various States and numbers of people, numbers of cars, types of accidents, and the general differences demographically in the States. The fact that California does not have a no-fault bill at this time does not seem to me to be an argument in favor of Federal legislation forcing California to have a bill. It is evidence that California is trying to decide what kind of bill they want.

I called Sacramento Wednesday before I came back here and found that the assembly bill, a no-fault bill, was passed in June and is now before the Senate Judiciary Committee for consideration. Hearings have not been set for that bill but, although we don't have Mr. Jeffers in California, we have plenty of people in our bar and in our legislature who are familiar with all the problems and all the considerations that have to go into the making of a no-fault bill. When our people are ready for one, our legislature will respond to it and pass it. It will be one that will fit the people of California.

I don't think there has been any wave of sentiment from the public that threatens to engulf this Congress if it doesn't enact a Federal no-fault bill. I think the Congress should reflect the will of the people. If the people want it badly enough, they will let their local legislators know what they want and the legislators will respond to that will.

Thank you very much for allowing us to be heard.

Mr. BRODHEAD. Thank you.

Do you have anything to add, Professor?

Mr. KIRCHER. Mr. Brodhead, about the only question that was posed concerned the question of the Jewish approach to the situation.

Working for the good Jesuit fathers, in addition to DRI, I don't think I can respond.

Thank you very much for allowing me to be here.

Mr. BRODHEAD. We thank all you gentlemen for coming a long way to be with us. I can assure you that a transcript will be made of your remarks and that your full statements will be available. We will be discussing your testimony with Mr. Kinzler and Mr. Van Deerlin.

Thank you very much.

Mr. BROCK. Thank you, sir.

[The following statements and letters were received for the record:]

STATEMENT OF THE CAR AND TRUCK RENTING AND LEASING ASSOCIATION

Mr. Chairman and members of the committee, my name is J. Michael Payne. I am the Executive Director of the Car and Truck Renting and Leasing Association (CATRALA). CATRALA is a voluntary trade association with a membership in excess of 3,000 firms and persons engaged in the rental and leasing of motor vehicles in the United States. Services offered by our members range from the familiar rental cars and trucks to the long term leasing of trucks and automobiles.

CATRALA, as an association on behalf of its members, has supported what has come to be known as no-fault reform in our existing vehicle accident reparations system for many years. The massive Department of Transportation study in 1971 pointed out to us, as I think it did for many consumers, the costly and tragic deficiencies in the fault system of reparations and led us to support the no-fault principle suggested in a comprehensive way by Professors Keeton and O'Connell some years ago.

In May of 1971, when spokesmen from our Association first testified before Senator Hart and Congressman Moss, the rallying cry was "No-Fault is an idea whose time has come." Now, four years later, it is becoming increasingly obvious that no-fault is an idea, the implementation of which is long overdue.

Our Association has, as a matter of policy, supported all efforts to pass meaningful no-fault laws on both the federal and state levels and shall continue to do so.

Because of the failure of many states to enact no-fault legislation, and because of the absence of any real uniformity among the few existing state no-fault plans, there is considerable chaos in the administration of the various no-fault programs.

Because of the failure of the states to understand the basic nature of no-fault, several laws have been enacted that are illegitimately called "No-Fault" that have no limitation on the right to sue, thus only increasing costs to an unwieldy and wasteful tort system.

Because of the failure of the states to draft proper legislation we have seen no-fault laws being declared unconstitutional in New York, Illinois and Florida after a year of operation this adding even more confusion.

Because of the above listed failures it is the opinion of our Association that the only answer to uniformity, legitimacy and constitutionality can be found in federally legislated minimum standards to be met by the states.

Professor Keeton has been quoted as saying that the inadequate no-fault laws enacted, though steps in the right direction, are "enemies of the better." We concur in this view.

We believe that approaches such as H.R. 1900 or S. 354 as reported from the Senate Commerce Committee will provide:

(1) Uniformity in that the states for the first time will share a common philosophy and language;
(2) Benefits to the consumer by the elimination of waste;
(3) The elimination of delay in receiving payments;
(4) The reduction of costs while increasing benefits.

For these reasons CATRALA strongly supports and urges Congress to adopt no-fault legislation such as H.R. 1900 or S. 354.

The companies who are members of CATRALA are, like you, purchasers of automobile liability insurance. The one major difference is in the amount of insurance they purchase. As consumers of insurance, we are interested in seeing that we get the best possible coverage for the premium dollar. Our present system, where less than half of the premium dollar is returned to the consumer, is simply not a very good buy. We know that we receive a better return on our dollar from almost any other type of insurance.

We need a system which provides uniformity. We do not believe that the peculiarities of each state provide the basis for elaborately different conceptions in this regard. It is an old story that we are a mobile people. People who live or visit in the Washington, D.C., area for example, routinely travel in or through three separate jurisdictions. It seems inconceivable that they might or ought to be subject to three differing liability arrangements. For an industry such as ours, passage across state lines is an ordinary occurrence. People who have business in Cincinnati, Ohio make use of car rental service from that city's airport which is located in Kentucky. Why should the standard of liability for them be measured by sharp differences in the 14 or 15 miles they travel? The answer to where you are from really doesn't answer automatically the question of where you may have an automobile accident. Nor is the problem merely one of equity for a mobile public. The problem is also one of narrowing the complexity and the cost in the administration of the insurance system. We believe that complexity can be avoided and the differences significantly narrowed by federally legislated minimum standards. Many of the bills you are considering go a long way toward the objectives we have in mind.

Now is not the time to beg the issue by saying we support no-fault, but "the change should take place at the state level, where useful, *instructive experimentation* (emphasis added) with different types of no-fault systems should be undertaken." [1] Nor is it the time to say "There is much to be gained, . . ., from allowing the states to continue experimenting with different plans and approaches." [2] What experimentation is needed? H.R. 1900 allows those states which have already enacted no-fault legislation four more years to experiment and bring their laws in line with the minimum standards set in H.R. 1900. With the passage of H.R. 1900, all states continue to be free to experiment in a wide variety of areas. They include: (1) Property loss, (2) the limits on work loss benefits, (3) deductibles and waiting periods, (4) replacement services loss benefits, (5) survivor's loss, (6) restrictions on tort lawsuits, (7) plans to assure availability of required coverages, (8) supplemental liability insurance, (9) no-fault pain and suffering insurance, (10) procedures for qualifying as a self-insurer, (11) cancellation and non-renewal of insurance, (12) exemption of no-fault benefits from garnishment, etc., and (13) non-reimbursable tort fines.

When considering meaningful and viable no-fault legislation, the concept of "instructive experimentation" provokes great concern among those who support such a plan in three specific areas. These are: (1) Allowable expense, (2) work loss, and (3) tort liability.

Since the first state no-fault law was passed in Massachusetts in 1970, it has become clear that in order to best restore one to the physical status one had prior to an accident, unlimited medical and rehabilitation benefits are required. Without an unlimited allowable expense, those people who are catastrophically injured will continue to be uncompensated. In the absence of unlimited allowable expenses, the severely injured person will not only continue to be denied proper compensation for his economic loss, but he will not be given the best opportunity for his economic loss, but he will not be given the best opportunity to make a full physical recovery. The price which has been paid to date for "instructive experimentation" has already clearly demonstrated the inadequacy of limited no-fault in terms of tragic human suffering.

---

[1] P. 9, testimony of Secretary William T. Coleman, Jr., before the Senate Commerce Committee, May 5, 1975.
[2] P. 2, testimony of Secretary William T. Coleman, Jr., before the House Subcommittee on Consumer Protection and Finance, June 17, 1975.

In today's inflationary society a minimum of $15,000 for wage loss is not an exorbitant dollar figure. In H.R. 1900 the states are allowed to increase this amount upwards if they desire, or an individual may further protect one's wage loss by buying optional insurance. Is there a need for "instructive experimentation" in this area? We say no!

Finally, it has been show in unmistakable terms that the less restrictive the tort liability threshold the more one should be concerned with increasing costs in a no-fault system. As can be seen from expert testimony presented by interested parties, a tight tort threshold is an absolute necessity when one desires cost savings to the customer. In states where access to the courts is only slightly restricted, people are continuing to abuse the system with costly court action. Thus, the system is not working to the full benefit of the consumer. If one agrees that the goal of H.R. 1900, and no-fault, is to provide real and substantial benefits at reduced costs, then further "instructive experimentation" with tort liability is surely not needed.

Now is the time to enact legislation such as H.R. 1900. State inactivity (it appears that in 1975 only North Dakota will have enacted no-fault reform legislation) in passing meaningful no-fault legislation will continue without leadership action by the Congress. "Instructive experimentation" has shown us what is needed today in a minimum standards bill. H.R. 1900 meets these minimum requirements while still allowing proper and appropriate experimentation at the state level.

We support no-fault reform such as H.R. 1900 and thank you for the opportunity to present our views.

STATEMENT ON BEHALF OF THE COMBINED INSURANCE COMPANY OF AMERICA ON H.R. 1900 AND SIMILAR BILLS

(Submitted by Earl W. Kintner, Jack L. Lahr, Jerry R. Selinger, Arent, Fox, Kintner, Plotkin & Kahn) Washington, D.C.

Mr. Chairman and members of the subcommittee, we are exceedingly grateful for the opportunity so submit this statement on behalf of the Combined Insurance Company of America, a Chicago, Illinois life and health insurance company which is licensed to do business in 49 states. We urge that federal no-fault insurance legislation clearly provide that individuals may have the opportunity to supplement their required no-fault benefits with additional insurance protection of their choice. H.R. 1900 incidentally contains such provisions and we simply seek to ensure that revisions in Subcommittee continue to provide expressly for this individual opportunity.

I. INDIVIDUALS SHOULD BE ALLOWED TO SUPPLEMENT THE BASIC PROTECTION AFFORDED BY NO-FAULT INSURANCE

According to the Declaration of Policy of the no-fault bill under consideration by this Subcommittee, the legislation has as its paramount objectives the rehabilitation of individuals who are injured in automobile accidents and the recompensation of such individuals for their economic losses. To this end the bill, which sets minimum standards with which state no-fault plans must comply provides that all automobile accident victims must be compensated for "reasonable" charges incurred for medical treatment and vocational rehabilitation services. Furthermore, such victims must receive a measure of compensation for their loss of income and must be reimbursed for replacement services engaged during their incapacity. Finally, in the event that death results, the victims' survivors are entitled to be compensated for funeral costs and the like.

The no-fault plan presently before you intentionally does not mandate full restitution to automobile accident victims for their economic losses. For example, the bill does not demand that the state programs require complete reimbursement for non-medical economic losses, nor does it allow full compensation for all medical costs, such as the cost of a private hospital room, absent a medical justification therefor. Similarly, it does not provide for the recovery of non-economic injury such as pain, suffering, inconvenience and physical impairment and it substantially limits the right of individuals to institute tort litigation to recover for such non-economic losses.

This is not to imply, however, that the no-fault plan precludes recovery by victims for all such losses. On the contrary, the proposed legislation encourages the procurement by individuals of additional insurance coverage for the purpose of ensuring their comprehensive protection in the event of an automobile accident.

Thus, section 103(37) of H.R. 1900 encourages the purchase of life insurance by defining "survivors loss" in such a way that compensation owed to a deceased victim's survivors is not downwardly adjusted to reflect life insurance proceeds received by the survivors. Section 208(a) explicitly excludes insurance proceeds from a litany of government benefits which must be subtracted from loss in calculating net loss. Moreover, section 209 provides that no-fault insurers may sell insurance to supplement the minimum coverage mandated by this legislation. Accordingly, it seems accurate to state that the proposed no-fault legislation is not intended to preclude individuals from obtaining additional death benefit coverage (e.g., life insurance in its many forms), and other supplemental coverage to ensure that they may be fully compensated for their injuries, without regard to fault.

II. COORDINATION OF BENEFITS, IF REQUIRED, SHOULD APPLY TO GROUP PLANS PROVIDING BENEFITS TO VICTIMS SIMILAR TO THE COMPULSORY NO-FAULT BENEFITS

To minimize the cost of comprehensive automobile accident coverage to the consumer, the 93d Congress initially adopted the marketplace approach to coordination of benefits that was articulated by the National Conference of Commissioners on Uniform State Laws in the Uniform Motor Vehicle Accident Reparations Act (UMVARA). This approach is reflected in section 204(f) of H.R. 1900, which provides that a state no-fault plan:

"Shall permit any legally constituted entity, which is providing benefits other than no-fault benefits on account of an injury, to coordinate such benefits payable by any restoration obligor on account fo the same injury. In order for such coordination to occur, there must be an equitable reduction or savings in the direct or indirect cost to the purchasers of benefits other than no-fault benefits. . . ."

In effect, this means that insurance companies *may* coordinate benefits payable on account of an automobile injury provided that a concomitant saving is passed on to the insured. Whether such coordination does, in fact, become a reality would seemingly depend upon competition among insurance companies in the marketplace and the cost effectiveness of coordination.

This marketplace approach was abrogated to a large extent by section 208(c), which comprises a last minute amendment to the no-fault bill passed by the Senate in the 93d Congress. This provision provides that, subject to certain conditions, employee group insurance programs other than no-fault insurance are to be the primary source of no-fault recovery unless a state determines that this would discriminate against the interests of persons required to provide no-fault insurance. Coordination of individual policies, though, is not affected by section 208(c) and remains under the auspices of the section 204(f) marketplace approach.

A great deal of controversy was generated in the Senate when Senator Mondale introduced section 208(c) and the bill presently being considered in the Senate, S. 354, contains a compromise coordination provision. Specifically, the Senate version now provides that:

"A no-fault plan for motor vehicle insurance in accordance with national standards or title III shall include a program for coordination between—
(1) security covering a motor vehicle; and
(2) sources other than such security that provide benefits to victims; in order to minimize duplication of benefits and to produce cost savings."

According to the accompanying Senate committee report, S. Rep. No. 283, 94th Cong., 1st Sess. 86 (1975),

"[t]he contents and application of the program are matters for each State to determine. . . . A State may merely encourage, through programs of public education with industry participation, owners of motor vehicles to coordinate their health, wage continuation, and life insurance coverages with their no-fault insurance coverages by purchasing health, wage continuation, and life policies which do not provide benefits for auto accidents."

Unfortunately, the wording of the Senate compromise provision is rather ambiguous and recourse to the accompanying committee report is necessary to evince the point that regardless of whether automobile insurance or other insurance is the primary source of no-fault recovery, coordination is only required of insurance programs that provide benefits equivalent to the required no-fault benefits. Moreover, the Senate compromise eliminates, apparently inadvertently, the distinction between group and individual insurance policies insofar as the requirement of coordination is concerned. But this distinction is material and should be preserved in a no-fault law for the ultimate benefit of the consumer.

There are a number of reasons why this distinction is important. For example, the mechanics of coordinating these individual insurance policies may substantially impair the administrative cost-effectiveness of such policies, as well as the willingness of the insurance companies to enter the supplemental insurance market, contrary to the purport of this no-fault legislation and against the interests of the consuming public.

A further reason for making a distinction between groups and individually obtained insurance is that employee group insurance programs are often a negotiated fringe benefit and individual members of such a group most often have minimal control over the scope of insurance coverage. In contrast, other insurance plans are specifically chosen by individuals to fill what they believe to be a gap in their basic insurance protection. Competition is a key factor in shaping these other policies; insurance companies strive to offer what the public wishes to purchase. To the extent, then, that there may be some duplication of benefits, the duplication obtains because consumers want the additional benefits and are willing to pay for them.

In view of the above, if this Subcommittee chooses to follow the Senate Commerce Committee's approach to the no-fault legislation, the following language is suggested as a substitute for the coordination provision of S. 354.

Coordination and cost savings

A no-fault plan for motor vehicle insurance in accordance with national standards or title III shall include a program for coordination between—
  (1) required no-fault coverage; and
  (2) sources other than such coverage that pay benefits for the same purposes to victims on a group basis; in order to minimize duplication of benefits and to produce cost savings.

This proposed language accords with the substance of the Senate bill and leaves to the states the question of primacy, while clearly establishing the minimum federal standards for coordination. It also reinserts an express provision outlining the extent of required coordination.

III. THE ALTERNATE DRAFT BILL CONTAINS AN ANTICONSUMER COORDINATION PROVISION AND SHOULD BE REJECTED

This Subcommittee also has before it a draft of a no-fault bill which differs in many respects from the bills heretofore considered by Congress. Of particular concern, the draft includes the following rather inflexible coordination of benefits provision which, in fact, will adversely affect both the consumer and the insurance industry:

"SEC. 210. (a) GENERAL—An approved State plan shall provide for a program for coordination between—
  (1) compulsory coverage; and
  (2) sources other than such coverage that pay benefits to victims;
in order to minimize duplication of benefits and to produce cost savings. Such program shall include the following provision together withone of the three subparagraphs succeeding such provision: Whenever a source other than compulsory coverage that pays benefits to victims is available to pay or provide benefits in whole or in part *for any item or loss for which basic no-fault benefits are available*, then—
  (A) such other specified source pays such benefits and the amount thereof is subtracted from loss in calculating net loss, pursuant to subsection (b);
  (B) such other sources shall not pay such benefits, and the victim shall receive, directly or indirectly, pursuant to State law, an appropriate adjustment in premiums paid therefor; or
  (C) both compulsory coverage and such other source pay the benefits which each is obligated to provide, except that if this alternative is included such program shall further provide for voluntary coordination with each named insured authorized to elect which, if any, of these sources shall be primary and which shall be excess or secondary." (emphasis added)

Thus, this provision mandates coordination and, indeed, forces the states to choose their coordination programs from among three particular options, rather than allowing the states to tailor their coordination programs to the particular conditions existing in each locality.

But this is not the major defect of this provision. The full extent of the unfairness engendered by this language is not apparent on its face and becomes obvious only when we consider the interaction between this draft provision and the added no-fault benefit (supplemental insurance) provisions which are contained in all of the pending no-fault bills. For example, section 202(g) of the draft provides that:

"An approved State plan shall require that each insurer (other than a self-insurer) offer coverages which will provide the following added no-fault benefits:

* * * * * * *

(2) Benefits for work loss sustained by a victim *in excess of any limitation* on benefits for work loss under subsection (b)[required no-fault benefits];

(3) Benefits for loss due to death *in excess of any limitation* on death benefits under subsection (d) [required no-fault benefits] . . ." (emphasis added)

To understand the problems inherent to these provisions, we must first recognize that no-fault insurers (automobile insurance companies) are required by this added no-fault benefits provision to offer consumers supplemental insurance benefits as well as the basic no-fault benefits. Quite logically, the coordination requirement has no effect on such added no-fault benefits when they are paid by a no-fault insurer, because the benefits are not "for any item of loss for which no-fault benefits are available."

In contrast, the draft coordination provision does encompass analogous supplemental benefits which happen to be purchased from an insurer who does not sell automobile insurance. A substantial number of insurance companies are not active in the field of automobile insurance, but instead specialize in the areas of accidental death, dismemberment, and income continuation insurance. In the event national no-fault insurance becomes a reality, these insurance companies will be selling coverage which is equivalent to added no-fault protection, because the no-fault insurers will be providing the basic no-fault protection policies. In this situation, consumers will pruchase supplemental coverage from the specialized companies merely as an alternative to purchasing added no-fault benefits from the no-fault insurers.

Nevertheless, supplemental income continuation benefits will be coordinated against and reduce an insureds' no-fault benefits if they are purchased from the specialized carriers, but not if the additional coverage is procured from a no-fault insurer. And this built-in bias against such specialized companies has both anticompetitive and anticonsumer ramifications.

Thus, the additional cost that specialized carriers incur because only they must coordinate additional benefits will quite likely be passed on to consumers in the form of higher prices and decreased service. Furthermore, by placing such carriers at a clear competitive disadvantage, the large no-fault insurers will become even more dominant.

This, however, is not the full extent of the injustice wrought by the draft coordination provision. Indeed, this inauspicious provision, by positing a mandatory reduction of benefits to compensate for benefits generated by insurance policies which are inteneded to be equivalent to added no-fault benefits but which are purchased from the "wrong" company, will actually deprive consumers of insurance benefits that they have paid for. The short term result of this will be disquieting to the insured, who will be deprived of funds which he has counted upon to tide him over during his incapacity. The long range effect might well be to force consumers into purchasing added no-fault benefits only from no-fault insurers and regardless of price. Such a loss of business would, in turn, cause many accident and health insurers to abandon this field of insurance to the no-fault insurers and a decrease in competition would be the end result.

This situation seems clearly undesirable and quite inconsistent with the stated purpose of the federal no-fault legislation, In order to ensure that consumers have the opportunity to purchase as much insurance as they deem necessary to provide adequate compensation for work loss and the like at the lowest possible cost, this Subcommittee is urged to reject the draft coordination provision in favor of the alternatives described in previous sections.

IV. CONCLUSION

In conclusion, it is respectfully urged that any no-fault bill given your favorable consideration include provisions which preserve for individuals the opportunity to supplement the basic no-fault benefits provided in such a bill. In order to ensure that the consumer receives full insurance coverage at minimum cost and without regard to the question of primacy, it is also urged that any coordination of benefits requirement be applied only to employee group plans providing benefits to victims similar to the compulsory no-fault benefits.

Statement of the Continental Association of Funeral and Memorial Societies, Inc.

The Continental Association of Funeral and Memorial Societies, Inc. consists of 130 non-profit cooperative funeral and memorial societies active in 42 states and the District of Columbia and representing more than a half million individuals. The purpose of these societies is to obtain for their members economy, dignity and simplicity in funeral arrangements by advance planning and by negotiating group agreements with funeral directors.

We are alarmed by the provision in No-Fault legislation for funds specifically allocated to cover funeral expenses—in H.R. 1900 the maximum is $1,000 and in H.R. 1272 the allowance is unlimited.

We oppose the inclusion of a funeral allowance on the following grounds:

(1) A funeral allowance constitutes a subsidy to the funeral industry. Even when a ceiling is imposed on the funeral allowance, that ceiling will soon become the base price charged the victims of automobile accidents and ultimately, we fear, all consumers of funeral industry products and services.

Commercial insurance companies have long been aware that the death benefits written into their policies are absorbed by the funeral industry and that morticians often tailor their bills to fit the assets of the deceased.

This conclusion was reached in independent studies by the Metropolitan Life Insurance Company, the Attorney General of New York, the Retail, Wholesale and Department Store Union Local 65 in New York and the International Ladies Garment Worker's Union whose Director of Death Benefits, Harry Hakeel, testified before the United States Senate in 1964. He reported that a five year survey revealed that,

"Each successive increase in the death benefit paid by our Union was invariably followed by increases in funeral charges which have now practically absorbed the entire death benefit. . . .

"It is common knowledge that some funeral directors ascertain the benefits accruing to the family of a member before making funeral arrangements. This enables them to determine 'what the traffic will bear'; namely, how expensive a funeral can be sold to the family."

(2) The Social Security Administration and the Veterans Administration already provide for funeral allowances on scale that is consistent with the going prices for modest funerals and cremations.

Inexpensive funerals are available for those who choose them and religious leaders, union officials and consumer groups are urging their followers to insist upon inexpensive, simple, meaningful funeral arrangements. Memorial societies across the country make inexpensive funerals or cremations available to their members for prices ranging from $150 to $400. Commercial cremation services which typically charge $250 are proliferating. The Federal Trade Commission found in a survey of funeral prices in the District of Columbia that minimum priced funerals are available for $210 to $395, and that minimum priced cremations range from $80 to $170 in that city.

We realize that the average price paid for what the industry calls the "complete adult funeral" is higher than these prices and exceeds $1,000. However, the high prices paid are not always because the consumer chooses to pay this much. Funerals are typically purchased in an atmosphere of consumer ignorance and irrationality and under extreme time pressure—a situation which works to the benefit of the salesman. In evaluating the results of its survey in the District of Columbia, the Federal Trade Commission staff emphasized the absence of price competition and suggested that one reason the less expensive funerals are rarely purchased is that the mortician does not mention their availability. If he knew in advance that the deceased was a carrier of a No-Fault insurance policy allowing $1,000 in funeral expenses in addition to social security and VA benefits plus life insurance and other assets, the funeral director would be expected to push for the highest price he can get.

Further, there is a peculiarity with billing practices in funeral establishments which means that a customer often pays for goods and services that he does not in fact use. This is because funerals typically have a package price, pegged to the price of the casket, which includes a number of things such as embalming, viewing, use of funeral home facilities, etc., which a customer, choosing simplicity, may not use, but, since it is a package price, will pay for anyway.

By including a funeral allowance in No-Fault, the Congress will underwrite high average funeral prices, encourage the described billing practices and, ominously, threaten the very availability of low priced alternatives. The Federal

Trade Commission has proposed a trade practice rule designed to eliminate known abuses in the funeral industry, encourage price competition and result in savings to consumers. Funeral benefits of unreasonable magnitude would simply frustrate the intentions of this FTC action and similar efforts in several states to bring fair competition into the industry.

(4) A funeral allowance would result in inequitable insurance rates. Enactment of a funeral allowance, even with an imposed maximum limit, would result in a rate structure situation in which individuals, such as memorial society members, who deliberately choose modest funeral arrangements, will subsidize through their insurance payments those individuals who, either by choice of by default, use the entire funeral allowance.

Those individuals who choose to spend money on elaborate funerals have every right to do so. But, those of us who choose, for reasons of economy, taste, religious belief or humanitarian conviction, to have simple and dignified funerals should not be required by the government to subsidize other people's expensive funerals both through our insurance rates and because high subsidies to the industry jeopardize the existence of our lower priced alternatives.

Having posed some of the dilemmas involved in setting a funeral allowance we now propose a solution: eliminate all mention of funeral allowances in No-Fault, and provide simply for a cash benefit under the survivor's loss section of the Bill. This cash benefit could be spent however the survivor sees fit. Those who choose to spend it on a funeral would be free to do so. Those who choose to spend it in some other way would be able to, confident that the insurance payments are yielding full value. Surely most holders of No-Fault insurance would prefer that the beneficiaries of their policies be their families rather than the local funeral director.

Whereas we oppose the inclusion of a funeral allowance in this legislation, we recognize that your subcommittee may nevertheless decide to include one. We are aware also that the Senate passed No-Fault Bill includes a funeral benefit. In S. 354, the funeral allowance has been termed a "survivor's loss" rather than an "allowable expense" and the option to impose a limit on the allowance has been left to the states.

We do not object to calling funeral expenses a "survivor's loss" if they do appear in the legislation. However, we believe it is imperative that any funeral allowance included in this Bill carry a federally mandated maximum of no more than $500 including Social Security and VA benefits. Our objections to an allowance any greater than that have already been stated.

If the determination of a ceiling is left to the states, some can be expected to impose no ceiling and others to impose a low ceiling. Such a situation invites enormously complicated inequities in the setting of insurance rates and the awarding of benefits. From both the consumer's and the industry's points of view, permitting each state to set its own standards plays into the hands of the more powerful of the state funeral directors associations. From the consumer's point of view, it would add yet another dimension to the already arbitrary and inconsistent price-setting patterns in the industry and further remove the funeral trade from the normal competitive forces in the marketplace.

Therefore, should you decide to include a specified funeral allowance in this legislation, we urge you to phrase it as follows: "expenses directly related to the funeral, burial, cremation or other form of disposition of the remains of a deceased victim, not to exceed $500 including Social Security and/or Veterans Administration burial benefits."

Respectfully submitted.

REBECCA COHEN,
Executive Secretary.

STATEMENT OF ROBERT E. J. WISEMAN, EXECUTIVE VICE PRESIDENT, FARM BUREAU MUTUAL INSURANCE COMPANY OF MICHIGAN AND COMMUNITY SERVICE INSURANCE COMPANY

The following statement is offered for inclusion in the Record of the hearings on No-Fault Automobile Insurance held by the Subcommittee on Consumer Protection and Finance of the House Interstate and Foreign Commerce Committee. It is submitted by Robert E. J. Wiseman, Executive Vice President of

Farm Bureau Mutual Insurance Company of Michigan and Community Service Insurance Company. These companies, licensed to write Property and Casualty coverages only in the State of Michigan, have combined assets of $62 million as of June 30, 1975. Combined direct written premiums for 1974 exceeded $45 million. Farm Bureau Mutual has an A+AAAA+A.M. Best rating.

We have followed with keen interest the evolution of No-Fault Automobile Insurance concepts as they have developed throughout the United States. Now, as you consider legislation to provide so-called Federal Minimum Standards to which state legislation must conform, we offer the following information which we trust will be helpful. The "Unlimited Medical" provisions of H.R. 1900, as is well known, closely parallels those of Michigan Public Act 294 which effected No-Fault in our State on October 1, 1973. Michigan's No-Fault Medical coverage extends payment for "all reasonable charges incurred for reasonably necessary products, services and accommodations for an injured person's care, recovery or rehabilitation."

We understand you have heard testimony and data regarding the cost of such "Unlimited Medical" coverage, which, of course, must be borne by the consumer. This is of special concern to us because our auto insurance writings are predominately in the rural and suburban areas, where, because of greater accident severity, premium rates can be expected to rise disproportionately.

We will, however, confine our statement to what we consider to be a problem of more immediate concern. It is our judgment that "Unlimited Medical" coverage is potentially devastating to the financial stability of small and medium sized insurance companies. We understand that in the main, testimony in this area has been in the nature of speculation and judgment with very little actual cost or experience information. This, we presume, is simply because there is, in fact, little or no such experience as yet developed. For that reason we present herewith an outline of our experience, as a small company.

Since October 1, 1973, our companies have experienced six (6) claims under the "Unlimited Medical" provision which can be described as catastrophic in nature. Loss reserves on these cases now exceed $800,000. Actual payments to date are approaching $230,000.

These losses were reinsured. Even though we have only an average $30,000 retention on each of these individual losses, they will have a serious effect on our future financial results.

To illustrate, prior to No-Fault we purchased reinsurance for 3 percent of our Bodily Injury and Property Damage premium, with a retention of $30,000. In January, 1974, our rate went to 5.6 percent with the same $30,000 retention. In April of 1974, we increased our retention to $50,000 and still had to pay a rate of 4 percent. The reinsurer now is requesting an increase to 5.3 percent in midterm—plus an increase in our retention from $50,000 to $55,000.

This amounts to a 50 percent increase in our reinsurance costs during the past 21 months. The reinsurer has ample justification for seeking rate increases, we agree, due to adverse claim development. Our development through April 15, 1974, indicates that we ceded $127,000 of auto premium to the reinsurer who has incurred $922,000 in losses.

Our companies, as the attached information would indicate, are presently in a most stable financial position. The combined surplus to premium ratio was 41.5 percent at 6/30/75. However, if the catastrophic loss incidence under "Unlimited Medical" continues, this position will surely be weakened.

The point is this. There are hundreds of small and medium sized companies like ours throughout the United States—many of which traditionally and/or currently are in a much less secure position than we enjoy. Subjecting these organizations to loss exposure inherent in "Unlimited Medical" coverage could quickly threaten their solvency.

The problems are compounded by the unknowns associated with "Unlimited Medical" coverage. Prior to Michigan's No-Fault law, catastrophic losses were generally dealt with under liability coverage. A maximum coverage amount was available for use in determining ultimate exposure. Proper loss reserves could be readily established for protection of the policyholder and the company.

With "Unlimited Medical", loss reserving has become cumbersome, demanding and, at best, most unscientific. There are no guidelines to follow. Our files indicate the most generous estimates of future costs are soon rendered inadequate due to the unknowns and inflation. Our current loss reserves may be wholly inadequate.

It would be inappropriate, however, to leave you with the impression that we are basically dissatisfied with Michigan's No-Fault law. On the contrary, it has many characteristics which have proven favorable to the insuring public and insurance companies. Expanded first-party Medical coverage, for example, has been accepted very well by the consumer. We are certain, however, that our "Unlimited Medical" poses a serious threat to all but the larger insurance companies. This feature of No-Fault theory if forced upon the country by virtue of Federal No-Fault legislation, can very well spell the demise of small and medium sized insurers.

This is a matter to which the Subcommittee should give the most thoughtful and careful consideration. It is an area in which there is far too little experience yet, or in which hard evidence is available. The analogy of Workmen's Compensation which is so easily offered by some should not and does not apply, and hopefully will not mislead the committee.

We appreciate the opportunity of presenting this material. We will gladly furnish any further information. Thank you.

STATEMENT OF HERBERT R. WELLS, CPCU, CLU, CHIEF PRODUCT RESEARCH SPECIALIST, FARMERS INSURANCE GROUP—LOS ANGELES, CALIF.

Farmers Group, Inc., is the attorney-in-fact for the Farmers Insurance Exchange, the Truck Insurance Exchange, and the Fire Insurance Exchange; and also manages the Mid-Century Insurance Company, 3 life insurance companies, and related operations under the title of "Farmers Insurance Group." Farmers is among the 25 largest insurance groups, it is the third largest writer of private passenger automobile insurance in the United States, and a large writer of Truck, Commercial, and Property insurance. Farmers Group of companies operate principally in 25 Mid-Western and Western states, and have over 3 million automobile policies in force, and over 5 million policies of all kinds.

Farmers Group of companies are independently acting, and our position is different than companies belonging to the American Insurance Association, the National Association of Independent Insurers, or the American Mutual Alliance. Farmers pioneered Uninsured Motorist coverage, we have been a leader in low cost insurance through direct billing, a continuous policy, an exclusive agency force, and automation. We have been researching the no fault concept since 1962.

Farmers is not opposed to evolutionary reform, or the first party, no fault concept. Our position, has been stated in previous testimony before the Senate Judiciary Committee, the House Subcommittee on Commerce and Finance of the Interstate and Foreign Commerce Committee, and before the Senate Commerce Committee. No Fault reform should be evolutionary, it should lower insurance costs to the public without a corresponding reduction in benefits, there should be a better utilization of resources, rates for losses should be based on driving experience, and there should be some improvement in the litigation process to control claims costs and abuse. None of the no fault bills before Congress, and those enacted in the various states, meet these criteria.

In previous testimony, the following points were established:

1. The cost of no fault will increase in spite of the fact that benefits have been reduced.

2. Innocent drivers will lose tort benefits in excess of 1.4 billion dollars, and the innocent poor will not be able to afford the no fault alternative to tort recovery.

3. Commercial operators will gain a "windfall" of about 1.5 billion dollars because of tort "threshold" concept.

4. No Fault completely re-defines the law of reparations, as new and untested and controversial laws replace rights that have taken centuries to develop.

5. No-Fault creates a system of "phantom benefits", recoveries under other financial protection systems are used to offset no fault costs.

6. No Fault results in over-utilization as excessive and costly wage and replacement service benefits are provided without third party verification of loss.

In addition, at other hearings, Farmers submitted testimony to show the inaccuracy of the consulting actuaries costing of no fault, the added cost and fragmentation of the system if group accident and health is made primary in automobile reparations, the problems of Federal regulation of automobile insurance, and the undesirable erosion of personal responsibility arising from tort restrictions.

The testimony now submitted to the Consumer Protection and Finance Subcommittee of the House Interstate Foreign and Commerce Committee is not a reiteration of previous testimony and exhibits; instead the testimony and exhibits will show some results of no fault that indicate the original premise, that no fault would reduce costs, is fallacious.

Evidence and opinion will also show that no fault is not a ground swell wish of the people, but forced social reform to bring about the socialization of injuries. The proof of these contentions will be offered by showing that the proponents of no fault have used reprehensible consumer practices—"bait and switch," "false advertising," and "false packaging"—to institute their reforms.

The root causes of automobile accidents have been ignored in the six or seven-year Congressional and Government quest to find a solution to the automobile reparations, and the automobile insurance problem. Less than 1% of the testimony and exhibits submitted to the Senate and House Committees conducting hearings on no fault (about 4 pages of testimony out of 4,367 in 1973, 1974 and 1975) are directed to the causes of automobile accidents: high powered, cosmetically designed vehicles; habitual drunken and drugged drivers; lack of uniform licensing standards; the failure to use vehicle safety equipment; defective road systems; insufficient driver education; inadequate and inefficient highway law enforcement; lack of periodic vehicle inspection; and the failure to remove unsafe vehicles from the highways.

Finally, the testimony submitted today will state the reason why government solutions to insurance problems are unworkable. Although both have the same objective, the protection of the people from unbearable burdens, the government solution is tax funded, deficit spending on a non-qualified basis. The insurance method is the contractual funding of future losses on an actuarial basis, with a guaranteed right of payment. The guarantee is *insured;* solvency is the sine qua non of insurance.

1. INSURANCE COSTS NO MORE IN 1975 THAN IT DID IN 1940, OR 1950

In 1940, for example, Farmers' San Diego Territory 7 5/10/5 liability insurance (the equivalent of $15,000 in coverage) cost $15.80 a year, or $1.05 per $1,000 of liability. In 1975, the equivalent coverage, 15/30/10—roughly $40,000—costs $66.60 a year, or $1.67 per $1,000 of liability. Although this analysis shows the costs as 60 percent higher per $1,000, the coverage is easily twice as broad, because of innovations in the law since then—the abolishment of traditional defenses, and the creation of new causes of action. Traditional defenses have eroded—the imputation of negligence between spouses, the guest law, and now contributory negligence. The 1975 policy provides broad form, omnibus, driver-other-car coverage, financial responsibility protection, insolvency protection, and the like. There is a spirit of litigation in the land—claims consciousness—that has mushroomed to alarming proportions with the development of demonstrative evidence, litigation workshops, the acceptance of non-medical terminology such as "whiplash" to heighten damage awards, and the current fetish—punitive damages for employee errors.

A better gauge to determine the frequency and severity of accidents is the physical damage statistics, as they are not subject to as many emotional, or inflationary abstractions. The premium in 1940 for $50 deductible Collision insurance in San Diego for a new automobile costing $1,000 was $14.80 a year, or $1.48 per $100 of value. Collision insurance now on a new 1975 automobile costing $4,500 is $66.80 a year, or $1.48 per $100 of value. *See Exhibit 1.*

EXHIBIT 1. Auto insurance premiums.

FARMERS AUTOMOBILE INTER-INSURANCE EXCHANGE — **LEVEL PREMIUM—SEMI-ANNUAL RATES**

PASSENGER CARS		FARM TRUCKS		THRIFT POLICY			PARAGON POLICY		
B.I. & P.D.—$10/20—5	B.I. & P.D.—$10/20—5	FIRE & THEFT and COLL.					Age: Min. 16 Yrs. Max. 67 Yrs. Membership $3.00 Premium $2.50		
8.80	Not exceeding 1½-ton load carrying capacity. 12.60	Determine Class from Manual and Apply Passenger Car Rates.		See Rules Section of Rate Table for Method of Determining Thrift Policy Rates.					
	Age Group	AA	A	B	C	D	E	F	G	H	J
FIRE & THEFT	1 2 3	1.70 1.50 1.20	1.80 1.60 1.30	2.10 1.70 1.40	2.30 1.80 1.40	2.60 1.90 1.50	2.80 2.00 1.50	3.40 2.10 1.50	3.80 2.40 1.50	4.30 2.70 1.80	5.20 3.20 1.80
COMPREHENSIVE SUPPLT.	1, 2 & 3	1.00	1.00	1.00	1.25	1.25	1.50	1.50	2.00	2.00	2.00
COLLISION 80% Standard Insured's Limit $50	1 2 3	9.80 7.60 6.10	10.60 8.20 6.60	12.40 9.60 7.70	15.40 11.80 9.40	17.20 13.20 10.60	18.80 14.40 11.50	20.00 15.40 12.30	21.80 16.80 13.40	23.60 18.20 14.60	25.60 19.80 15.80
20% Deductible with $25 Limit	1 2 3	11.80 8.60 6.90	12.00 9.20 7.40	14.00 10.80 8.60	17.40 13.20 10.60	19.40 14.80 11.80	21.20 16.20 13.00	22.60 17.40 13.90	24.60 18.80 15.00	26.60 20.40 16.30	28.80 22.20 17.80
$25 Deductible	1 2 3	6.60 4.60 2.70	7.20 5.00 3.30	8.20 5.40 3.60	9.20 6.40 4.20	11.20 6.80 4.50	12.80 7.80 5.10	14.40 8.20 5.40	15.80 9.20 6.00	17.20 10.00 6.60	18.80 10.40 6.90
$50 Deductible	1 2 3	4.20 3.00 2.00	4.60 3.20 2.20	5.60 3.60 2.40	6.20 4.60 3.00	7.40 5.40 3.00	9.40 5.60 3.60	11.40 6.00 3.90	12.80 6.40 4.20	14.20 7.80 5.10	15.40 8.20 5.40
100% Full Coverage	1 2 3	17.40 13.40 12.10	20.20 14.60 13.10	23.20 18.00 16.20	28.60 20.60 18.50	29.80 21.60 19.40	32.40 23.80 21.40	34.80 25.40 22.90	38.20 26.40 23.80	41.00 28.20 25.40	44.40 28.40 25.60
80% Limited		Deduct 40% from 80% STANDARD Premium Coll Rates.									

STATE: CALIFORNIA   TERRITORY 7   Effective: N.B. July 20, 1940

1-8—E.20—3500—7-40

FARMERS INSURANCE GROUP
Farmers and Truck

SEMI ANNUAL RATES

Effective date: N 3 JUN 01, 1975   206 REN state CALIFORNIA   territory 01   1A

COVERAGE		SINGLE CAR			TWO OR MORE CARS			
		Accident Free		Standard		Accident Free		Standard	
BI/PD		100 DED	200 DED	100 DED	200 DED		200 DED	100 DED	200 DED
10/20/10		39.20		49.00		31.40	14.00	39.20	17.40
15/30/10		41.60		52.00		33.30	16.30	41.60	20.40
25/50/10		43.90		54.90		35.10	20.90	43.90	26.20
50/100/10		46.70		58.30		37.30	26.20	46.70	32.80
100/300/10		49.00		61.30		39.20	32.00	49.00	39.90
COLLISION							37.10		47.10
AGE GROUP 1	G	21.70	15.50	27.10	19.40	19.50	11.70	24.40	14.60
	H	24.70	18.10	30.90	22.70	22.30	13.70	27.30	17.10
	K	31.00	23.30	38.80	29.10	27.90	17.60	34.90	21.90
	L	37.10	29.10	46.40	36.40	33.40	22.00	41.80	27.50
	M	43.40	35.50	54.30	44.40	39.10	26.80	48.80	33.50
		49.90	41.90	62.40	52.30	44.90	31.60	56.20	39.50
COLLISION							37.10		
AGE GROUP 2	G	18.20	13.00	22.80	16.30	16.40	11.70	20.50	14.60
	H	20.80	15.20	25.90	19.00	18.70	13.70	23.40	17.10
	J	26.00	19.50	32.50	24.40	23.40	17.60	29.30	21.90
	K	31.10	24.40	38.90	30.60	28.00	22.00	35.00	27.50
	L	36.40	29.80	45.50	37.20	32.80	26.80	41.00	33.50
	M	41.90	35.10	52.30	43.90	37.70	31.60	47.10	39.50
COLLISION									
AGE GROUP 3	G	14.00	10.00	17.50	12.50	12.60	9.00	15.80	11.30
	H	16.00	11.70	20.00	14.60	14.40	10.50	18.00	13.20
	J	20.00	15.00	25.00	18.80	18.00	13.50	22.50	16.90
	K	23.90	18.80	29.90	23.50	21.60	16.90	26.90	21.20
	L	28.00	22.90	35.00	28.60	25.20	20.60	31.50	25.80
	M	32.20	27.00	40.30	33.80	29.00	24.30	36.20	30.40

TOWING 1.20   DEATH–DISMEM 1.30   DISABILITY 1.50   COLLISION PLUS 3.30

GUAR. BENEFITS 12.60   14.90   11.20   13.20

Automobile insurance cost less in weekly wages now, than it did in 1940

In 1940, the average gross weekly earnings in manufacturing industries was $25.20, and insurance coverage for Bodily Injury and Property Damage, comprehensive, fire and theft, and collision insurance, cost $38.30 a year, or 1.5 weeks' of wages. In April 1974 average gross weekly earnings—manufacturings—was $166.00 a week, and the same coverage cost $156.80 a year, or 9/10 of a week's wages. In 1940, a man had to work 10 days to pay his insurance, but in 1974 he only had to work 6½ days. The savings of 3½ days work, is equivalent to a 35 percent savings.

Exhibit number 2 is a chart of pertinent statistics taken from the 1974 and 1950 statistical abstract. On line 14 the wholesale price of private passenger motor vehicles is shown for the years 1940, 1950 and 1973. The next line below is the cost of $50 deductible Collision insurance for those same years. The cost of insurance per $100 of wholesale value, ranges from 2.3 to 2.8 percent. Between 1940 and 1973—a period of 33 years, the increase was only 5.62 percent—about two-tenths of 1 percent a year.

EXHIBIT 2

CONSUMER STATISTICS

Item	1940	1950	1972–75	Percent change 1940–75	Percent change 1950–75	Reference
1. Population	131,699,000	151,326,000	211,782,000	60.8	40.0	Statistical Abstract, 1950–74.
2. Automobiles	27,372,000	49,300,000	101,004,000	269.0	104.9	
3. Ratio	1:5	1:3	1:2			(Line 1÷2).
4. Autos per family	½:1	1:1	1:1½			(Line 2÷(line 1÷3)).
5. Liquor consumption (gallons per capita).	14.26	26.70	34.95	145.1	30.9	S.A. 1950 p. 787; 1974 p. 737.
6. Total horsepower (autos in millions).	2,511	4,404	23,029	817.1	422.9	S.A. 1974 p. 514.
7. Average horsepower per car.	91	89	228	150.5	156.2	Line 6÷2.
8. Percent urban travel	51.7	50.2	56.5			
9. Average speeds	NA	48.7	61.6			P. 284 (1974).
10. Percent exceeding 55 mph.	NA	20.0	70.0			P. 227 (1974).
11. Average income	$2,495	$3,416	$9,612	285.3	181.4	S.A. 1950 and 1974.
12. Average income tax	$102	$349	$1,202	1,078.4	244.4	S.A. 1950 and 1974.
13. Social Security tax	$30	$45	$824	2,646.7	1,731.1	S.A. 1950 and 1974.
14. Wholesale price—autos	$639.00	$1,270.00	$2,728.00	326.9	114.8	1974, p. 556.
15. $50 deductible	$14.80	$36.00	$66.80	351.4	85.6	Farmers rate books.
16. Cost per $100	$2.34	$2.83	$2.45			(15÷14).
17. Average weekly wage (Mgft.).	$25.20	$56.20	$166.60	561.1	196.4	S.A. 1950, p. 203.
18. Annual insurance cost	$28.30	$68.80	$151.62	295.9	120.7	Farmers rate books.
19. Cost in days worked	7.7	6.1	4.5	−41.6	−26.2	(17÷18).

EMPLOYMENT STATISTICS	1950	1960	1973	Percent change 1950–75	Percent change 1960–75	Reference
20. Civilian employment	43,765,000	65,800,000	88,700,000	102.7	34.8	1950, p. 176, (1974).
21. Government (Federal)	2,275,000	2,400,000	2,800,000	23.1	16.7	1950, p. 195 (S.A.).
22. Government (State and local).	3,912,000	6,400,000	11,400,000	191.4	78.1	1950, p. 201 (supplement)
23. Old age assistance	2,736,000	2,300,000	1,800,000	−34.2	−21.7	1950, p. 251 (1974).
24. Aid to dependent children (families).	599,000	3,100,000	10,800,000	1,703.0	248.4	1950, p. 251 (S.A.).
25. Social welfare expenditures (billions).	$2.2	$52.3	$215.2	9,681.8	311.5	1950, p. 251 (supplement).

CRIMINAL STATISTICS	1950	1960	1972–75	Percent change 1950–75	Percent change 1960–75	Reference
26. Crimes against persons	290,496	286,000	869,000	199.7	203.8	1950, p. 137.
27. Rate per 100,000	192	160	414			S.A. 1974.
28. Crimes against property	2,068,270	3,067,000	7,769,000	275.7	153.3	S.A. 1974.
29. Rates per 100,000	2,367	1,710	3,702			S.A. 1974.
30. Public expenditure (millions).	NA	$3,349	[1] $11,271		226.5	S.A. 1974.
31. Federal deficit (billions)	−$1.8	$0.3	−$70.0	3,788.9	23,333.4	1974 S.A. supplement.

[1] 1972.

In 1940, coffee was a nickel a cup; gasoline, about 10 cents a gallon; steak, about 35 cents a pound; and collision insurance, about $2.50 per $100. In 19715, coffee is 25 cents a cup, gasoline 70 cents a gallon, steak $2.50 a pound, and colision insurance, still $2.50 per $100 of wholesale value. In 1940 the mythical average family owned one-half of an automobile, worth about $320, which cost $28.30 a year to insure. In 1973, the average family owned 1½ automobiles worth $4,092, costing $227.40 to insure. The exposure and value is twelve times as high but the cost is only 8 times as much. The average cost of insurance decreased from $8.80 per $100 of value to $5.45 per $100. That's a 38 percent reduction?

In 1940 there were 27 million autos with an average horsepower of about 90, capable of maintaining an average speed of about 40 mph. In 1973, there were 101 million cars with an average horsepower of 228, capable of average speeds of 60 mph. In 1950, at certain designed testing areas, 20 percent of the vehicles exceed 55 miles per hour, but in 1974 it was 70 percent.

In addition to a greater concentration of higher horsepower cars in urban areas, public attitudes have changed. In one of its studies, the DOT found that about half of the accidents in which people were killed or injured, involved alcohol consumption. Significantly, since 1940 the consumption of alcoholic beverages has increased from 14.26 gallons per capita to 34.95 gallons per capita in 1972, an increase of 145 percent.

In spite of what the no fault proponents allege, the insurance claims system is not the cause of high insurance premiums. The cause is pure and simple—too many accidents. The formula for accidents is careless or inattentive drivers + high powered cars × speed × booze.

2. THE RESULTS OF STATE NO FAULT TO DATE

In January, 1974 the Milliman and Robertson consulting actuaries, along with proponents of Federal No Fault, testified that savings under S-354 would be 20 to 30 percent. Farmers testified that costs would increase 15 to 30 percent, or more.

In the year and a half since then, No Fault experience and statistics are beginning to accumulate.

In 1975, for the first time, the Farmers Exchange and Mid-Century Company Report 1A, Comparison of Premiums Earned to Losses Incurred, includes No Fault as a statistical item. The January to June figures in our six No Fault states show a loss ratio of 119.6 percent, for a deficit of $7,583,389. On an annualized basis, assuming no rate relief, Farmers Group will have a deficit of $15,166,778. (See below.)

FARMERS AND MIDCENTURY

State	No-fault premium	Losses	Loss ratio percent	Premium deficit dollars
Nevada	$720,859	$809,566	112.4	−$487,448
Kansas	1,296,266	828,566	63.9	+60,356
Colorado	1,913,880	2,305,292	120.5	−1,526,850
Minnesota	771,681	1,601,979	207.6	−1,619,332
Michigan	3,959,985	4,486,747	113.3	−2,736,652
Utah	1,002,653	1,526,338	152.0	−1,275,463
6 States	9,665,324	11,557,882	119.6	−7,583,389
Annual basis				15,166,778

The total liability, uninsured motorist, medical and no-fault premium in these six states show no corresponding offset of savings in other areas. (January to June, 1975)

State	BI/UM MED/NF premium	Losses	Loss ratio (percent)	Premium deficit
Nevada	$2,031,318	$1,859,678	91.6	−$744,320
Kansas	2,840,146	2,471,725	87.0	−848,995
Colorado	4,704,806	3,523,462	74.8	−554,092
Minnesota	5,783,823	4,800,226	83.0	−1,380,693
Michigan	7,161,039	7,232,984	101.0	−3,634,459
Utah	2,871,099	2,593,527	90.3	−999,836
6 States	25,392,231	22,481,602	88.5	−8,162,395
Annual basis				−16,324,709

Comparison

The bodily injury, uninsured motorist, and medical premium and losses for six comparison states have more favorable loss ratios, and show a slight profit.

State	BI/UM/MED premium	Losses	Loss ratio percent	Gain
Arizona	$6,161,469	$4,811,340	78.1	—$1,019,635
Oklahoma	3,727,499	2,022,133	54.2	+475,291
New Mexico	1,456,021	690,655	47.4	+284,879
Wisconsin	1,612,198	1,094,478	67.9	—14,306
Illinois	2,880,143	1,972,193	68.5	—42,498
Idaho	1,823,030	712,778	39.1	+508,652
6 comparison States	17,660,360	11,303,577	64.0	+192,383

Projection

The Farmers Group is looking at a 16 million dollar deficit in our six no-fault states for 1975.

Farmers Group writes 8.8 percent of the private passenger auto liability insurance in these six states. Assuming other companies and groups have the same or similar experience, the industry year-end deficit from no-fault in these states will be in the neighborhood of 180 million dollars.

Seventy-five percent of the no fault premium is written outside of Farmers Group operating territory. If the industry experience tracks Farmers'—and it will be as bad or worse—the 1975 industry deficit resulting from no fault will approximate 800 million dollars.

Projected Deficits Under S-354 (or Michigan type) No Fault Law

Michigan liability, uninsured motorist, and no fault premium constitute 4.4 percent of the Farmers and Mid-Century premium in force. If an S-354 type of no fault (or a Michigan type) were in force in our 25 operating states, the No-Fault loss to Farmers, assuming no rate or policy corrections, would be 82 million dollars. The industry loss in these 25 states would be over 900 million dollars. If S-354 or similar law applies to the entire United States, the premium deficit for 1975 would be 3.6 billion dollars.

3. THE HISTORICAL DEVELOPMENT OF NO-FAULT

In 1870, Prince Otto von Bismarck instituted social security and Workmen's Compensation reforms to difuse the social protests of German workers. This system was studied by John Graham Brooks, a Harvard Law School graduate, and later a syndicalist, who in 1895 recommended a Workmen's Compensation system in the U.S. In 1908 the Federal Government enacted a Federal Workmen's Compensation Act, and within 25 years, Workmen's Compensation was almost universal throughout the United States.

No Fault was first proposed for automobile accidents in 1919, based on the Workmen's Compensation concept, notwithstanding the essential differences. Workmen's Compensation arises out of a contractual relationship in which the employer has control of the work environment, not out of a chance accident. In addition, unlike automobile no fault, in which the victim pays his own medical wage loss damages, the employer pays the benefit.

Automobile compensation was academically considered in studies conducted at Columbia University in 1932, but the concept was repeatedly rejected by state legislatures and study commissions in the years that followed. Its only acceptance was in the socialistic province of Saskatchewan in 1947, a remote and rural area, snowbound a large part of the year, with fewer automobiles than San Diego County. (Incidentally, the Government Insurance Office in Saskatchewan is now the largest insurer in the province, a multiple line, bureaucratic, anti-competitive, non tax-paying concern.) How then did Automobile No Fault, an idea repeatedly rejected by State Legislators and study commissions from 1932 to 1962, become "an idea whose time has come in 1972–1975"?

Automobile no fault was hammered out by legal activists, and others entrenched in the government, espousing forced social reform at whatever cost. The resurrection began in 1963 with the publication of Ralph Nader's book, "Unsafe At Any Speed" which put the blame for the countless auto deaths and injuries at the door of the automobile industry. The public became aware of the high, and somewhat foolish, cost of automobiles, and the wastage in our society caused by planned obsolescence, conspicuous consumption, unnecessarily high horsepower, speed, and automobile accidents.

In 1963, the Conard Study published by the University of Michigan Law School, financed by the Walter Cook Foundation, and the Walter F. Meyer Foundation for Legal Research, brought attention to the plight of automobile accident victims, to the cost of their treatment, and to the compensation they received.

Again in 1963, studies of the automobile claims system by Harvard Law School, financed by Harvard, and the Walter F. Meyer Foundation for Legal Research, culminated in the Keeton-O'Connell Basic Protection Plan, published in 1965. This was the old Columbia University plan of 1932—warmed over.

The public, smouldering with resentment over the inflation caused by the Vietnam War and welfare expenditures, their anger fueled by Nader's book and the Conard Study, became inflamed over the high automobile accident costs, reflected in automobile insurance premiums. Continued studies by the Senate Judiciary and Commerce Committee from 1963 to 1967—touching on every facet of automobile insurance, kept the heat on the automobile insurance industry—and off the automobile manufacturing industry—culminating in the Department of Transportation's 2-year, 2-million dollar automobile reparations study.

The Director of the DOT reparations study came from the Senate staff committee to No Fault reform. Some of his staff and advisors were the law school, research-oriented professors who authored the publications calling for reforms. The Conard Study was the progenitor of the DOT study; the Keeton-O'Connell Plan, the basis of UMVARA. The Walter F. Meyer Research Institute of Law said, "The Meyer-sponsored studies have been happily received by the staff of the new (DOT) Commission." (The conclusion was in before the evidence and findings!) These men helped write the DOT sponsored Federal No Fault Law, and DOT funded the Uniform Motor Vehicle Reparations Act, the NAIC actuarial study, and the Milliman and Robertson Consulting Actuaries costing of Federal No-Fault.

The Hon. Erwin Griswold, the former Solicitor-General of the United States, and Harvard Law School Dean, testified on the constitutionality of Federal No-Fault, by the grace of the Clean Air Act of 1970. He was a member of the Walter F. Meyer Research Institute of Law, which, while he was Dean, gave grants of $563,-000 to Harvard. Time says of him (Griswold)—October 6, 1967—"Legal realism—the sociological observation that judges make the law rather than find it—was nurtured at Columbia and Yale in the '30s. Though Harvard Law Dean Roscoe Pound was leading sociological scholar, his colleagues did not follow. Griswold, ("The Griz"), who has been in the dean's chair since 1946, has made a determined effort to press once again into the vanguard."

Academic Influence

In testimony submitted by Leonard M. Ring to the Hon. John Moss, the following quotation is taken:

"As often noted, most of the proposal for change in the tort system comes from Law School Professors, that is from the 'intellectuals' rather than from those actually working in the day to day conduct of the system. Indeed the past several years have been marked by a great upsurge in the influence of the intellectual in many aspects of American political and economic life.

"I do not deplore this emergence.

"But with this new power should come a deeper responsibility. A college or law school professor, who has no direct participation in the final decisions that must be made, is expected to challenge, to question, to dissent, to raise questions about the validity of conventional wisdom. But when the influence of the professors moves from the classroom to the legislative, or to the executive or the judicial branch of our government, some changes occur. In the new context there are new responsibilities. Sometimes in the past this new responsibility has served to change a radical professor into a conservative judge. But this is because the judge has a direct responsibility. This direct responsibility is lacking when the proposals originating with the intellectuals result in legislative or executive action.

"When academic scholarship becomes the source of action proposals something important happens.

"Suddenly the criteria of excellence takes on some new dimensions. When scholarship alone is involved, originality is important. The scholar is in the natural role when he is directing minds toward new patterns of thought, and when truth is sought for its own sake. The price for being wrong need not be paid at once or may be avoided entirely as the continued search produces revisions of the concepts.

"But being in the role of the harbinger of change is not the same thing as being actually involved in the political maneuvering that is so often associated with the accomplishment of change. When the intellectual becomes the man of political action, or the zealous advocate of 'a cause', he takes on some attributes that do not coincide very well with those of a scholar, and he is apt to find himself involved in the sort of rough and tumble debate that is apt to produce overstatements and distortions and, as in Massachusetts, we are apt to find Professors on both sides of the argument.

"The political man appreciates that there should be some pauses along the road to consensus so that the concepts may be learned, understood and accommodated to the needs of the various elements in the body politic. Even the most unassailable logic needs to be imposed, if it is to be imposed at all, at a pace measured by the ability of the people to comprehend what the leaders are doing.

"There is something incongruous, perhaps even damaging to both the scholars and to the rest of the population, when the scholars become drawn into the political machine rather than remaining as members of the general community of scholars. Whether both roles can be successfully occupied simultaneously is, I suggest, at least open to doubt."

The source of the law should be the will of the people, as expressed through their legislators, and interpreted by the courts in an adversary proceeding. The purpose and function of the law schools is to teach the law as the courts find it; but it now appears that "legal activism" has reversed the process. The source of the law seems to be the heavily financed research products of law schools working with dedicated and committed legislative and administrative staff members to propagate their reform doctrines. The Hon. John W. Barnum, Acting Secretary of Transportation, testified on June 7, 1973 before Sen. Magnuson, "In summary, over the past 2 years we have been actively and vigorously working for, not simply talking about first party, no fault automobile insurance reform."

4. WHY FEDERAL NO-FAULT IS BAD FOR CONSUMERS

Three times Farmers Group has presented testimony to Senate and House Committees that Federal No-Fault will increase the real costs of insurance while reducing benefits, that the poor and uninsured will be penalized, and that commercial operators—big business—will reap a bonanza at the expense of private passenger automobile owners. Under S-354, a 70-page law with 9 pages of definitions—there will be an explosion of litigation, a switching and substitution of benefits, and an over-utilization that will create a system of auto welfare. The primacy of group accident and health insurance will fragment the reparations system; Federal involvement will have an inflationary impact, and bring about an undesirable erosion of personal responsibility.

No-Fault Consumer Practices

"*Bait and Switch.*"—The proponents of no fault have consistently used the "bait" that no fault would reduce insurance costs as much as 57 percent, but since testimony, and the results of state no fault, indicate costs will be 50 percent higher or more, they have "switched" to a better cost/benefit ratio.

"*False Advertising.*"—No-Fault proponents have also used the reprehensible consumer practice of "false advertising" to sell their product. The Department of Transportation, in their biased and structured indictment of the automobile insurance industry, ignored the grave warnings of the speculative nature of the findings, and the substantial errors in classifying various individuals, and the arbitrary criteria used for defining "seriously injured."

Critic after critic has complained that the DOT broadcast and circulated the study as 513,000 seriously injured traffic victims, but actually the number was 1,376 victims adversely selected from a sample of 15,081. The DOT Study alleged that only 20 percent of the costs of automobile injuries were paid by insurance, but three-fifths of the costs (5.1 billion) was based on speculative lifetime societal losses suffered by 167 victims (6 percent of the sample) interviewed 18 to 30 months after the accident.

"*False Packaging.*"—In addition to "bait and switch" and "false advertising" tactics, the proponents of Federal No-Fault have "falsely packaged" the No-Fault benefits. There is *no deduction* of benefits under the present system for social security, workmen's compensation, state disability, medicare, income tax, etc., which account for 35 percent to 50 percent of the no-fault premium savings. The $1,000 wage loss promised in the "big print" of the no fault law is reduced to $550 when these "offsets" reduce the no fault recovery.

"*The DOT Gospel.*"—Although the DOT Economic Consequences report, and some of the other studies, have been accepted as "gospel," much of it is erroneous.

The preconceived bias of many of the progenitors of the "study" discredits the findings and conclusions.

Federal No Fault is poor consumer legislation. It will increase the cost of insurance to poor people, and deprive the innocent poor of free benefits they receive under tort. Approximately 600,000 poor lose about 1.6 billion dollars under the "threshold" feature which inures to the benefit of commercial operators, who save that much—about 40 percent of their pre-no fault insurance costs.

Litigation will increase as the present, well known and understood system is replaced by controversial, unknown, and untried reforms contained in a 70-page law, with 9 or 10 pages of definitions, and guaranteed attorney fees. There will be a proliferation of claims as the over-generous wage loss and replacement service benefits serve as income replacement from whatever cause, as there are no "third party" or adversary verifications of loss, to protest the filing of unwarranted claims.

5. THE INEVITABLE CONFLICT BETWEEN GOVERNMENT AND INSURANCE

Government and Insurance have the same basic objective, protection of the people from unbearable burdens. Death, disaster, flood, sickness, unemployment, etc. create the need, and trigger the response.

At one time in society, personal and social disasters were without recompense. The individual lived and died within the family unit, which provided for his needs and wants under all circumstances. The early Christians began to look after the spiritual and physical needs of the community on a charitable basis, as evidenced by the spiritual works of mercy: to pray for the living, the sick, and the dead; and the corporeal works of mercy: to feed the hungry, clothe the naked, visit the sick, and bury the dead.

For centuries personal and social needs, both spiritual and physical, were performed by the institutionalized church—but with the Reformation, urbanization, and the gradual industrialization of society, the church was fragmented, and the family unit splintered.

In England, the Government became involved in social needs, as evidenced by the Elizabethan "poor laws". About the same time, the fledging insurance industry provided the economic tools, the law of large numbers, and the sharing of risks, to make the Christian ideal "To bear one another's burdens" financially possible.

In 1870 in Germany (somewhat later in Great Britain and the United States) the concept of social responsibility developed, and laws to compensate workers from the financial loss of industrial accidents and from sickness and death, were enacted, on the principle of insurance—sharing costs and losses.

Basic qualifications for recovery were established: periodic contributions to the insurance fund on a actuarial basis, and a fund with sufficient reserves to guarantee payment.

Under private insurance, the qualifications for recovery require a premium payment based on predicted losses. The insurance fund must be maintained at a sufficient level to guarantee solvency. When the surplus of the insurer diminishes, the issuance of policies must be restricted.

The Socialization of Protection

The recent enactment of social reforms establishes need, the sharing of losses but not costs, as the basis of recovery. Recovery is a legal right based on existence, or necessity, not on contribution to the fund. The result is that there are no limitations to need, and there are no methods to predict what the needs will be. Since there are no actuarial methods to obtain contributions, the required solvency is not obtainable, or maintainable, and the fund becomes deficit.

Government has the power, up to a point, to maintain programs on the basis of deficit spending, but the insurance industry does not. When the Congress or the Legislatures enact laws which require actuarially unsound insurance, or which permit recovery without qualified contributions, the government's power to mandate benefits conflicts with the insurance requirement to maintain solvency.

The government's mandates to insure the uninsurable, or to insure on the basis of need, not contribution, will bankrupt the insurance industry, just as similar U.S. government legislation has almost bankrupted Social Security, and unfunded social legislation has almost bankrupted New York City, and endangers the solvency of other cities, and states.

Financial soundness, as a principle of insurance, has given way to political expediency—promises that raise expectations, but cannot deliver the protection that people demand at a price they can afford.

STATEMENT OF MEMORIAL SOCIETY OF METROPOLITAN WASHINGTON

This statement is filed by Edward M. Knapp, President of the Memorial Society of Metropolitan Washington, on behalf of six memorial societies of the Washington area. We urge the Committee to amend both H.R. 1272 and H.R. 1900, both bills cited as "The National No-Fault Motor Vehicle Insurance Act", insofar as "funeral, cremation, and burial expense" is listed as a Basic Restoration Benefit under the act. As S-354 was introduced in the U.S. Senate it was identical with H.R. 1900 with respect to the inclusion of $1,000 as insurance required for funeral expense. This bill has now been amended by the Commerce Committee of the U.S. Senate.

We urge the Committee (1) to strike from H.R. 1272 the words "(ii) funeral expense" appearing on page 5, lines 3 and 4, (2) to strike from H.R. 1900 section 103 (2)(D) appearing on page 8, lines 7, 8, and 9 (both from the committee prints). In the last paragraph of this statement we will propose substitute language for a bill to be reported by this Committee. H.R. 1900 raises the national average price of a funeral from $1,395 (1974) to $2,140 immediately on the effective date of the act. H.R. 1272 puts no limits whatsoever on the prices of funerals and provides that they all be paid by insurance.

We argue as follows: 1. All prices in the United States for minimal funeral service are based on the Social Security Benefit of $255 as the amount available regardless of the service rendered. 2. All prices in the United States for funeral service above the minimal are derived by adding to the Social Security Benefit figure itemized charges for a number of particular services, the details of which are kept secret by most funeral directors with the customer receiving a flat package price without discount for services declined. Many, but not all, funeral directors ask survivors the amount of insurance carried by the deceased over and above the Social Security Benefit and *then* adjust the price to be quoted to the customer upward to absorb all but a few dollars of the amount of insurance available.

On Point 1—In 1974, Mr. James Sears of Santa Barbara, California, conducted a survey of the minimal funeral prices quoted memorial societies across the country. His results are shown in Exhibit 1 attached, with an average price of $271 and a median of $265. Since these prices have no relationship to the costs of providing this service, it is noteworthy and persuasive that both average and median are so close to the Social Security Benefit figure.

On Point 2—Details of typical itemized charges now in use by funeral directors are given in Exhibit 2 attached. We got this data from funeral directors in Washington, D.C. during our own negotiations with them to arrange for service to our own members. A number of bills given customers from other areas of the country were introduced at hearings by the House District of Columbia committee on a bill to require itemization. They show that such itemized charges were used in the computation of the bills by adding them to the basic Social Security Benefit. They also show that the details were not given to the customer.

On Point 3—We cannot prove specific cases in court. This Memorial Society and other memorial societies constantly hear of cases where the circumstantial evidence is persuasive but where there are not enough witnesses to prove the act or the willful intent. We find that the service was priced higher than at standard rates, the total is close to the total amount of insurance financing available, and we hear that the total was changed upward during the discussion between the survivors and the funeral director. Earlier, the Federal Trade Commission had received enough complaints on the practice to justify the Commission in asking memorial societies to report to it cases of the abuse that the societies knew about.

The benefit in H.R. 1900 (or H.R. 1272) would apply only to the 60,000 deaths per year from automotive accidents, discriminating in theory in favor of those 60,000 (they can fund the fancy funeral) but in reality discriminating against the entire rest of the population by raising the price without providing the benefit to pay for the higher cost. Funeral directors will not set two prices, a higher one for those who die in an automobile accident and a lower one for those who don't. It will be one price, as high as the assumed amount of funding will permit.

Funeral Directors are professionals, with generally high ethics, but they are also businessmen trying to keep their doors open, and many are trapped into improper practices by the structure of the industry, its economics, and its leadership. No person is being buried indecently, just because of a lack of funds (there are other causes). Funeral directors generously provide service for the absolutely penniless at a loss. This is to their credit, but there is no reason for an extreme increase in the prices of funerals in general, the increase provided for by Congressional edict.

We submit the following language to be included in any bill pertaining to National No Fault Motor Vehicle Insurance to be reported to the House by the Interstate and Foreign Commerce Committee. The proposed language combines an amendment to S-354 as it appears in the bill reported to the Senate with some additional language which we propose. The text from S-354 is in capital letters and our language is italic.

"EXPENSES DIRECTLY RELATED TO THE FUNERAL AND BURIAL, CREMATION, OR OTHER FORM OF DISPOSITION OF THE REMAINS OF A DECEASED VICTIM, *not to exceed the amount of the lump sum death benefit stated in Section 202 (i) of the Social Security Act, as amended and in force at the time of death of the beneficiary.*"

Reference to S-354—[Sec. 103 (37)(B)]

The language of the Senate bill is inadequate in that it states no limit for the incurring of funeral expenses to be paid by the Social Security System. We do not want all funeral costs to be paid by Social Security. The additional financial burden on Social Security would run from more than one billion dollars per year for the formula in H.R. 1900 to close to three billion dollars for the language of H.R. 1272. Most of the deaths in the country each year are now covered by the Social Security Benefit, including most of those who would die of automotive accidents. States can go beyond the benefits provided in the National Act, and precise dollar figures set as maximums in any national act will tend to become floors.

MEMORIAL SOCIETY OF METROPOLITAN WASHINGTON

EXHIBIT 1.—*Table of minimal funeral prices*

Area	Price	Area	Price
Arizona:		Indiana:	
Scottsdale	$273	Bloomington	$380
Prescott	298	Fort Wayne	390
Tucson	360	Indianapolis	350
California:		Lafayette	296
Arcata	325	Iowa: Davenport	255
Berkeley	225	Kentucky:	
Los Angeles	200	Lexington	325
Midway City	215	Louisville	175
Modesto	175	Louisiana: Baton Rouge	500
Palo Alto	187	Maryland:	
Sacramento	225	Baltimore	300
San Diego	200	Columbia	195
San Luis Obispo	320	Rossmoor	240
Santa Barbara	200	Silver Spring	255
Colorado: Denver	275	Massachusetts: Brookline	375
Connecticut:		Michigan:	
Hamden	325	Ann Arbor	300
Westport	500	Detroit	350
District of Columbia: Washington	250	East Lansing	250
		Minnesota: Minneapolis	250
Florida:		Missouri:	
Fort Myers	350	Kansas City	375
Gainesville	350	St. Louis	375
Jacksonville	325	Nebraska: Omaha	275
Land o' Lakes	275	Nevada: Reno	265
Miami	250	New Jersey:	
Orlando	395	East Brunswick	235
Sarasota	325	Maplewood	200
St. Petersburg	275	Montclair	295
Tallahassee	295	Morristown	300
West Palm Beach	250	Paramus	250
Georgia: Riverdale	265	Plainfield	210
Hawaii, Honolulu	175	Princeton	250
Illinois:		New Mexico:	
Chicago	290	Albuquerque	300
Urbana	125	Los Alamos	350

EXHIBIT 1.—*Table of minimal funeral prices*—Continued

Area	Price	Area	Price
New York:		Oregon: Portland	$250
Albany	$300	Pennsylvania:	
Brooklyn	200	Erie	330
Flushing	284	Harrisburg	290
Ithaca	375	Philadelphia	200
New York City 10002	250	Pittsburgh	250
New York City 10016	265	Tennessee:	
New York City 10027	367	Knoxville	100
Pomona	350	Nashville	350
Port Washington	284	Texas:	
Rochester	335	Austin	500
Syracuse	305	Dallas	295
White Plains	200	Utah: Salt Lake City	199
North Carolina:		Virginia:	
Asheville	300	Alexandria	240
Chapel Hill	175	Arlington	260
Greensboro	190	Charlottesville	350
Ohio:		Fairfax	260
Akron	250	Washington:	
Cincinnati	412	Seattle	159
Cleveland	250	Spokane	236
Columbus	235	Wisconsin:	
Dayton	400	Madison	350
Toledo	175	Milwaukee	250
Wilmington	200	Racine	220
Yellow Springs	185		

Source: Survey by Mr. James F. Sears of prices quoted to Memorial Societies. Coverage: 103 societies from 44 states, with a population of 190,000,000. Average price $271; median price $265.

EXHIBIT 2.—*Itemized charges included in an average complete funeral*

Embalming $175, Dressing the Body $30, Barber or Beautician $35, Restoration $75, Limousine $55 each per use, Hearse $55, Professional Services $350, Use of Funeral Home Chapel $100, Reposing Room $75 per night, Burial Clothes $100, Vault (if sold by the Funeral Director) $410, Casket $250 (this can go as high as $5500), Newspaper Notices $35, Telephone $17, Pall Bearer's Car $35, Flower Car $50.

STATEMENT OF A. D. SAPPINGTON, PRESIDENT, MFA MUTUAL INSURANCE CO.

Mr. Chairman and members of the committee, my name is A. D. Sappington. I am president of the MFA Mutual Insurance Company of Columbia, Missouri. Our company was organized and began business January 1, 1946. We are now actively doing business in 15 states in Mid-America extending from Indiana to Colorado and from Louisiana to Minnesota. While our company was sponsored by the Missouri Farmers Association, we have never restricted our writing of insurance to members of that organization nor to farmers. Today, approximately one-half of our business is in urban areas and one-half is in small towns or rural areas. About 40% of our business is in Missouri, and the remainder is in the other 14 states in which we actively do business. We write practically all lines of casualty insurance but automobile insurace accounts for 80% of our total volume. Our total premium in 1974 was $125,000,000 with $96,500,000 representing premium on automobile insurance. As of the end of 1974, in MFA Mutual we had 752,000 automobile policies in force insuring more than two and a quarter million owners and drivers of motor vehicles.

This statement is submitted in opposition to HR-1272 and HR-1900. While the approach to no-fault differs in these two bills, the specific provisions of the bills themselves will be or have been ably explained by others. Our opposition to the enactment of a federal no-fault bill is more fundamental and basic than a mere disagreement with the technical terms and provisions of the bills themselves.

We oppose enactment of H.R. 1272, H.R. 1900 or any of the other pending federal no-fault proposals because they constitute an intrusion by the federal government into the regulation of the automobile insurance business. The regulation of the business of insurance has been and largely remains the responsibility of state government rather than the federal government. No valid compelling reason has been advanced for the regulation of the automobile insurance business by the federal government which we contend obviously means regulation by the federal bureaucracy. H.R. 1900 which provides for a national no-fault program administered by the Department of Transportation is an open takeover of insurance regulation by the federal government. There are those who may contend that H.R. 1272 leaves the regulation of the insurance business to the states. We submit that if that principle is true and is a desirable end, then why is there a federal bill such as H.R. 1272 is the first place? If we are going to leave change in the automobile reparations system to state legislatures and the regulation of the insurance business to states, where it properly belongs, then there is absolutely no need to enact a federal law of any kind. I submit that when a federal law is enacted requiring the monumental changes either H.R. 1272 or H.R. 1900 would require in the automobile insurance business, then there can be no question but that the federal government is boldly and openly entering into the regulation of the automobile insurance business.

Furthermore, I submit that if either of these bills are enacted, the next logical step which follows, surely as night follows the day, is that the federal government will decree uniformity in policy provisions as well as engage in price fixing of insurance. The passage of a federal no-fault law will bring into being, in a short time, yet another large federal bureaucracy uncontrollable by the people through our elected officials, including the members of Congress.

Perhaps, if we assume the most optimistic result, we shall continue to have state regulation of the business of insurance, but superimposed upon that will be the ever-watching eye of Big Brother in the form of federal controls. Perhaps the giants of the insurance industry can survive under such a system of regulation, but the small insurance companies, and even the small to middle-size companies such as ours, may well fall by the wayside. The smaller companies will not be able to effectively compete with the rigidity that will likely be imposed on a federally regulated insurance industry. Rather than a regulatory system which will promote and encourage a free enterprise insurance industry, we will have a regulatory system which will breed and nurture the growth of monopolistic giants.

We believe our form of democracy, while not perfect, is the best ever devised by man. But even so, we do not believe that all government and all power and all authority should be vested in the federal government. As much as possible, government should be as close to the people as possible, and state government is unquestionably closer to the people than is federal government. When a real and pressing need is demonstrated for change or reform and local or state governments fail to respond, then it is time for the federal government to respond with appropriate action. In the case of no-fault insurance, we submit that no real and pressing need has been demonstrated for the violent, radical and abrupt change in our basic laws as is proposed by H.R. 1272, H.R. 1900 and the other federal no-fault proposals.

We in the everyday world of actually conducting an insurance business are closer than anyone else to the needs and desires of the people we insure, as well as to the other people to whom we pay benefits. Our company, in an effort to best serve our customers, actively encourages policyholders and claimants to write to or get in touch with us with reference to service, coverage, claims, and all other matters with respect to our business. As a result of our efforts, we get addressed to my office, by letter or telephone, 30 to 50 inquiries per week. Some are routine such as they have not received their policy, or they did not receive the type of service that they expected from an agent or claims adjuster. Some complain that the amount offered in payment of the damages to their car was inadequate, or that the body shop did not do a good job in repairing their car. My office also receives letters from policyholders inquiring as to why we refuse to renew a policy or why we decline to insure a person in the first place. And many, believe it or not, write or call to say thanks for the help and service we provided.

But of all the letters, telephone calls and communications we have received in the 29 years I have been connected with this company, no injured policyholder and no injured claimant has complained that he has not been paid enough money when he was at fault in an accident. As a matter of fact, out of the thousands of letters I have received over the years, no injured person, whether at fault or not, has complained about the reimbursement or payment made to him by our company.

I have found only one letter which made a voluntary inquiry about no-fault insurance. The writer inquired as to the effect no-fault insurance would have on reducing insurance rates. I submit that the only interest of the American public in no-fault insurance has resulted from the widespread false propaganda that no-fault insurance will substantially reduce the price of insurance.

It is my firm conviction that the automobile insurance Industry has done a magnificent job of meeting the needs and desires of the American people through the competitive free enterprise system. No-fault insurance in the form of medical pay coverage, disability income and accidental death coverage has been available to automobile policyholders from their insurance companies for many years. These coverages were made available by innovative insurance companies without compulsion by the federal government and are today carried by many policyholders. The broadening of these no-fault coverages should logically come through an evolutionary process by competitive insurance companies acting under state laws not federal laws. We should not and must not violently overturn a reparations system which has been hundreds of years in the making. Changes to be made should be made through a deliberate and careful evolutionary process such as is now being carried out under various state laws by our competitive free enterprise insurance industry. The enactment of H.R. 1272, H.R. 1900 or any of the other pending federal no-fault proposals would bring chaos into what is now an orderly evolution of the reparations system to meet the desires and needs of the American people.

STATEMENT OF THE NATIONAL ASSOCIATION OF CASUALTY AND SURETY AGENTS

The National Association of Casualty and Surety Agents (NACSA) is an organization comprised of the larger independent property and liability insurance agencies and brokerages located throughout the United States. Our members' annual volume of business is over two billion dollars in premiums with ensuing insurance coverage of over 400 billion dollars. NACSA members serve a majority of the nation's commercial, industrial and institutional entities and provide much of the workmen's compensation and public liability insurance written in the United States.

Since 1971, we have lent our full support to the concept of no-fault automobile insurance attained through legislation enacted, hopefully, by the individual states.

However, by 1974, it was clear that pressures exerted in the state legislatures by the Trial Bar and others have effectively blocked passage of meaningful no-fault legislation in a majority of the states. Therefore, in 1974, we reevaluated our position, and decided it had become necessary to support federal legislation which would establish minimum standards for no-fault auto insurance, such insurance continuing to be regulated and supervised by the individual states, and *not* by the federal government.

We believe that no-fault legislation, to be truly effective, and to adequately serve the needs of the insurance-buying public, must contain certain fundamental features, including:

(1) Primacy of no-fault auto insurance benefits over other benefit sources, except for benefits paid under state workmen's compensation laws;

(2) Unlimited "first-party" medical, hospital, and rehabilitation benefits; adequate wage reimbursement and reasonable household services coverage;

(3) Prohibition of tort action for recovery of economic loss covered by no-fault benefits, and restriction of lawsuits for non-economic loss to cases involving death, serious injury or disfigurement, or to cases involving more than 90 days of total disability;

(4) Elimination of any transfer of loss among no-fault insurers based on fault except in cases of accidents involving both private passenger and commercial vehicles.

PRIMACY

Of the bills being considered by your Subcommittee, only H.R. 8441 specifically provides for the primacy of no-fault auto insurance over other benefit sources. H.R. 1272 makes no-fault auto insurance benefits secondary to virtually all other benefit sources, and H.R. 1900 calls for the primacy of group health insurance which meets certain requirements.

We strongly believe auto insurance should be made the primary source of payment to accident victims for the following reasons:

(1) A single, no-fault auto insurance PIP benefit source, compulsory for all vehicle owners, would make it possible to minimize or eliminate duplication of coverage. Permitting health carriers to pay first party benefits would result in *expensive* duplication of benefits, wasteful duplication in claims handling and

duplication in money expended for administration of claims, all of which could obviously tend toward driving up the total cost of no-fault insurance.

(2) If health insurance were made primary, non-drivers participating in group health plans would be forced to subsidize, by their premiums, those in the plan who are drivers. Since less than one-half of the population drives, eliminating this subsidy would result in health insurance cost savings to those who do not drive.

(3) If auto insurance is primary, health benefit programs would be fully available for non-auto accident related loss. Since most health benefit programs limit the total amount of benefits, it is now possible to use up health benefits for auto accident expenses and to be left without coverage for medical expenses resulting from other accidents or illnesses.

(4) Members of the motoring public would have no option of choice in deciding whether to have their automobile insurance cover them for all their auto accident related losses should health insurance be made primary.

(5) The health carrier does not have the capacity to conduct expeditious investigations and apply the necessary controls needed for efficient administration of auto accident insurance benefits.

(6) Auto insurance coverage should not be split into two or more parts. It does not make good economic sense to parcel out coverage for each element of auto accident loss among several different sources of insurance benefits.

(7) If health insurance is made primary, the affluent driver with many employer-paid fringe benefits, including group health insurance, would pay proportionately less for his auto insurance than an individual with few, if any, employer-paid benefits, including health insurance.

(8) Health care plans vary greatly from state to state, and in many out-of-state cases, the insured would have to pay medical bills and seek reimbursement, and on a non-uniform basis if health insurance were the primary source of benefits for auto accidents. All automobile insurance is good anywhere in the United States and its possessions.

(9) If health care plans were to be made primary, it would result in huge losses of tax revenues to state and federal governments. The majority of health care plans, other than those provided by an insurance company, are designated nonprofit corporations. As such they do not pay state premium taxes nor state or federal income taxes. This revenue would have to be replaced by other taxes, making the general public pay a portion of the motorists' costs. In addition, the huge automobile insurance segment of the private insurance industry would suffer substantial unemployment if health insurance were made primary.

BENEFIT LEVELS

Two of the bills under consideration—H.R. 1272 and H.R. 1900—meet the criteria of high first-party benefits, H.R. 8441 calls for a combined medical, wage and other benefit limit of $50,000.

While statistics indicate that a $50,000 limit would compensate some 99 percent of all persons injured in auto accidents, what is the point of establishing this limitation and thereby penalizing the 1% of accident victims incurring expenses in excess of $50,000?

If the basic objective of a no-fault reparation systems is the timely restoration of *all* persons injured in auto accidents, then it follows that providing for unlimited medical, hospital, and rehabilitation benefits is a necessary feature of such a system.

Regarding the cost to the consumer of unlimited medical benefits coverage, a 1974 report on the subject pointed out that the frequency of large medical, hospital and rehabilitation expenses in auto accidents cases is so low that unlimited medical benefits can be provided for 0.1 percent more than the premium for $50,000 of such coverage. Further, there is no evidence, to our knowledge, to show that the requirement of unlimited medical, hospital and rehabilitation benefits will so increase reinsurance costs for smaller insurance companies that it may put some of them out of business.

This certainly has not been the case with workers' compensation laws in the 47 states which place no limit on workmen's compensation medical benefits.

H.R. 1272 alone provides not only high first-party benefits for economic loss, but also unlimited non-economic loss benefits. The costs of this approach, however, make it impractical, in our view. It certainly would not be possible to pay all accident victims not only all of their economic loss but also their non-economic losses, without substatially increasing the cost of auto insurance.

While there is little debate over the high premium costs of no-fault auto insurance if it were to provide unlimited non-economic loss benefits, there seem to be differences of opinion regarding premium cost savings or increases which would result from the more limited no-fault system offering only economic loss benefits. In our view, such debate clouds the real issue of much needed reform of the auto insurance reparations system. The merits of a no-fault auto reparations system should not rest on any alleged cost savings, which, at best are based on educated estimates. Nor should the no-fault concept be rejected if it is shown to cost consumers somewhat more than the present tort system. A consumer advocate recently testified that she would welcome an effective no-fault auto insurance system even if it cost slightly more than the present system. The fact is, that until a uniform no-fault system is actually working in a majority of the states, we will not know whether actual experience will effect some premium cost savings or whether rates will be higher than in the present tort system.

RESTRICTING LAWSUITS

H.R. 1272 and H.R. 1900 also meet our criteria for restrictions on tort remedy. H.R. 1272 entirely eliminates tort liability for bodily injury, while H.R. 1900 provides for a 90-day disability threshold for non-economic loss claims. H.R. 8441, however, allows tort action for non-economic losses when the victim's medical expenses exceed $2,000. We disagree with this approach.

We believe that the severe restriction of tort remedies is at the very heart of an effective no-fault system. The almost 32 cents of every auto bodily injury insurance premium dollar now devoted to the legal process of fault-finding cannot be turned into first-party benefits unless it becomes unnecessary to determine fault in the great majority of cases.

PROHIBITING REIMBURSEMENT

H.R. 1272 and H.R. 1900 meet our criteria with respect to prohibitions on subrogation or loss cost transfer based on policyholder fault where private passenger vehicles only are involved. H.R. 8441, however, permits such loss cost transfer in cases where loss exceeds $2,000.

We are opposed to allowing private passenger vehicle insurers to shift no-fault loss costs among each other on the basis of policyholder fault because such loss shifting would turn the no-fault system back into a "behind-the-scene" fault system and would frustrate no-fault's potential for changing the way in which auto insurance premium costs are assessed.

We recommend, however, that loss cost transfer be permitted among private passenger and commercial vehicle no-fault insurers in accidents involving both type of vehicles, since the greater weight of commercial vehicles such as trucks virtually guarantees that they will inflict far more damage than they will sustain. Unless loss cost transfer is permitted in private passenger-commercial vehicle accidents, private passenger no-fault policy holders will have to bear a disproportionate share of the losses created by such accidents.

H.R. 1900 and H.R. 8441 allow such transfer, but only when losses exceed $5,000. We believe that legislation should permit reimbursement for losses sustained in private passenger-commercial vehicle accidents which exceed $100.

We estimate that a loss transfer system with a deductible of $5,000 as called for in H.R. 8441 and H.R. 1900 would cause an *increase* in private passenger auto insurance rates of from 43 percent to 62 percent, or some $2 billion per year, over the cost of private passenger auto insurance that would otherwise be possible if this threshold were $100. Such an additional burden of cost on the private passenger auto owner cannot be justified.

We respectfully point out that Section 208(a) of H.R. 1900, and H.R. 8441 already provide the trucking industry with substantial savings in auto insurance costs because workmen's compensation is made a primary source of benefits under the terms of this Section.

We believe firmly that the further advantage granted in H.R. 8441 and H.R. 1900 to operators of commercial vehicles by loss shifting among restoration obligors, based on fault, with respect to benefits paid for loss in excess of $5,000, is unwarranted, and would create an undeserved windfull for commercial vehicle operators at the expense of no-fault auto insurance premium savings to owners of private passenger autos.

FEDERAL STANDARDS—STATE REGULATION

H.R. 1900 and H.R. 8441 substantiate our belief that reform of the auto accident reparations system can be achieved through federal minimum standards which leave the traditional insurance regulatory and supervisory functions to the states. H.R. 1272, however, would totally preempt reparations reform by the states as well as state auto insurance regulatory activity, a step we think unwarranted in the achievement of reform.

Since 1948, all states have had professionally-staffed departments of insurance. Thus, the states are equipped to regulate insurers under federal no-fault legislation, and it makes sense, we believe to promulgate a federal bill so as to allow the states to continue to do under the no-fault system what they have long been doing under the fault system. We believe it is important to give recognition to the role of the states under our federal system, while at the same time establishing the basic criteria for a countrywide system of reasonably uniform no-fault compensation laws for the victims of auto accidents.

CONCLUSION

In our view, the language contained in Section 208(c) of H.R. 8441 which states unequivocally that no-fault auto insurance benefits are to be primary (other than workers' compensation) to other benefit sources is ideal. However, as we have stated in our consideration of benefit levels, we would not favor the $50,000 limit on medical benefits as provided for in H.R. 8441, but would prefer that no-fault auto insurance be primary for *unlimited* medical benefits.

If, in addition, H.R. 8441 could be modified to provide for the elimination of tort action except for death, serious injury or disability of over 90 days, and the prohibition of reimbursement or lost cost transfer between insurers of private passenger autos while allowing reimbursement between insurers of private passenger and commercial vehicles, we feel that H.R. 8441 would provide for a sound minimum standards no-fault auto reparations system.

We appreciate this opportunity to present our views and hope that the Subcommittee will consider them in their deliberations on this important legislation.

Respectfully submitted.

EDWARD W. SUNDER, Jr.,
President.

STATEMENT OF REINSURANCE ASSOCIATION OF AMERICA

During the Subcommittee's hearings on pending no-fault automobile insurance legislation, the impact of unlimited medical and rehabilitation benefits on the reinsurance premiums of small insurers was discussed by both proponents and opponents of the unlimited benefits concept. Because of the significance of this issue, the Reinsurance Association of America had requested an opportunity to appear. Since the hearings now have been terminated without an opportunity to testify before the Subcommittee, this written statement is being submitted for the consideration of the Subcommittee and for the record.

The Reinsurance Association of American is a trade association which represents a majority of the professional reinsurers in the United States. Professional reinsurers are those insurance companies which are principally and substantially engaged in writing property and casualty reinsurance (nonlife) in contrast to departments and divisions of direct writing primary companies which also may write reinsurance. The Reinsurance Association's fifteen member companies in 1974 had combined assets of over 3.1 billion dollars and assumed in excess of 1.7 billion dollars of gross reinsurance premiums.

By way of further introduction, the business of reinsurance, as it relates to the legislation before the Subcommittee, is essentially the insuring of insurance companies. Our companies' clients are not the insurance buying public, but instead, the direct or primary insurance companies.

Of particular significance to the insurance business is the protection provided by reinsurers to most primary companies against excessive automobile liability or first party medical and related benefits liability. This reinsurance protection is afforded in several ways, but the basic principle is that in exchange for a premium, the reinsurer agrees to indemnify the primary insurer against loss in accordance with an agreement that provides for the reinsurer to pay a proportion of every loss (pro rata reinsurance) or all losses above a fixed retention up to a fixed amount (excess of loss reinsurance).

There are approximately 1,200 property and casualty insurers listed in Best's Key Rating Guide. In addition there are several hundred more small local insurers who are not listed in Best's. Most of these primary insurers have and need some reinsurance. Reinsurance protects them against shock losses, serves to stabilize their results and enables them to plan for orderly growth and expended service to their insureds.

During earlier consideration of no-fault legislation, the Association took no position with respect to the advisability of mandating unlimited medical and rehabilitation services as part of first party no-fault insurance. It was, and continues to be, our belief that there is adequate reinsurance capacity available in the American market to provide these unlimited benefits. However, there are a a number of caveats to this conclusion.

First, reinsurance, as always, will be available at a cost commensurate with the experience and exposure of the particular primary company. For a large company this will involve increments based upon the general average of its experience. For a smaller company that specializes in particular forms of automobile insurance, this will involve a reinsurance cost based upon additional factors, including that particular insurer's book of business, experience and market distribution. For a smaller insurer, with a limited number of insureds, it is far more difficult to use past experience as a basis for predicting future results.

Second, to the extent that pending bills would require primary companies to provide coverages they do not now offer and for which they would want reinsurance, these bills will result in a new expense. For example, several specialty companies offering only minimum limits presently may have no reinsurance requirements.

Third, reinsurance coverages, as in the case of workers' compensation, will continue to be provided at high, established levels. The upper limits of available reinsurance coverage will undoubtedly accommodate every conceivable occurrence, but it is not written on an "unlimited" basis.

EXPERIENCE UNDER STATE "UNLIMITED MEDICAL BENEFITS" NO-FAULT LAWS

In addition to the foregoing caveats, we are now in a position to better assess the impact of a no-fault requirement to provide unlimited medical benefits. With the experience of another year to observe the results of the provisions for unlimited medical and rehabilitation expenses found in the New Jersey and Michigan no-fault laws, the Association has concluded that the federal bills, as they set minimum national standards, should be amended to provide for some reasonable limit on these expenses. We do not have an agreed upon limit to propose, but we submit that the minimum standard should be high enough to cover all the medical and rehabilitation expenses in most cases and the all-important early expenses for even the most serious injury. A figure in the area of $100,000 would achieve these goals.

With unlimited medical as a minimum requirement, primary companies will be forced to buy high reinsurance limits. Large primary companies, because of their spread of risk, may be able to afford it, but the smaller ones cannot. An alternative for them is to take a very high retention for each accident, but they cannot afford that if it threatens their solvency. Another alternative for the small company would be to leave the automobile insurance market altogether if unlimited medical becomes a federal minimum standard. Market constriction has not happened yet, but judging from the frequency and severity of losses being reported in Michigan and New Jersey, the time is fast approaching when it will.

New Jersey and Michigan experience has already resulted in large increases in reinsurance costs to some companies who have had large first party medical expense cases. As examples of losses leading to reinsurance cost increases, one member company of the Reinsurance Association of America has already had reported to it first party medical expense losses in excess of $6 million for only thirty-two cases in Michigan. Another large reinsurer has thirty-one New Jersey and seventeen Michigan first party medical expense cases with ground-up reserves of approximately $3.3 million. Finally, another reinsurer has reported twelve losses from three primary companies totaling in excess of $2.8 million. These reports, which are by no means the last word, are the cause of increased reinsurance rates and are the source for the alarm and concern on the part of smaller insurers who are not now doing business in Michigan or New Jersey. Comparable facts were cited recently in a series of requests for primary rate increases in New Jersey.

INAPPROPRIATE ANALOGY TO WORKERS' COMPENSATION

Proponents of unlimited benefits have argued that insurers have covered unlimited services under workers' compensation laws for some time and that there have been no difficulties. However, experience under the New Jersey and Michigan laws has already shown that the analogy to the unlimited medical benefits under workers' compensation statutes is not completely appropriate. We are experiencing far more serious automobile injuries suffered by younger individuals with greater life expectancies than were anticipated. Accurate statistics were simply not available for single car accidents. Still, we do know that last year approximately 41,000 people were killed in automobile accidents, but fewer than 15,000 were killed in industrial accidents. It appears that a comparable difference would exist for serious injuries. Two other relevant differences between automobile and workers' compensation injuries are the number and size of most companies engaged in workers' compensation—an estimate would be that only 10 percent of the automobile insurers are engaged in workers' compensation and usually they are the larger companies. Very few of the smaller insurers write workers' compensation. Also relevant is the fact that primary premiums attributable to automobile no-fault coverages have not been adequate and the laws have lacked comparable controls as to the selection and utilization of doctors, medical services and rehabilitation. Although reinsurers have already seen that the seriousness and frequency of injuries requiring extensive medical expenses under no-fault coverages have been greater than anticipated, we know that the normal delay in reporting such losses suggests that we can expect even more such information as the year progresses.

PRESENT COST EXAMPLES OF "UNLIMITED BENEFITS"

In order to provide some understanding of the problem faced by companies in providing unlimited medical benefits, it might be helpful to relate some relatively current data regarding the life expectancy and annual medical cost for certain catastrophic disabling infirmities. These statistics are drawn from the *Medical Rehabilitation Guide* prepared by General Reinsurance Corporation, the country's largest reinsurer and a member of the Reinsurance Association.

With respect to life expectancy, the most significant factor so far as the purchaser of long-term maintenance is concerned is the rapidly changing and greatly extended life expectancy of severely handicapped persons in the past several decades. Medical science has developed the means to treat successfully complications that were formerly fatal to such persons.

A 1968 Canadian study of spinal cord injury cases from 1945 to 1966 has led to the development of the following table of the approximate expectancy of an injured person expressed in additional years of life:

Age	Partial paraplegic	Partial quadriplegic	Complete paraplegic	Complete quadriplegic
20	48	40	33	21
30	38	33	26	16
40	30	24	19	11
50	22	17	13	6

This study is now several years old and the life expectancies in each class probably should be increased.

In developing expected medical costs, an approximation of current average costs can be given. Individual cases may vary widely from these figures and inflation in medical costs can make them obsolete very quickly.

Injury:

	Medical cost
Paraplegic (complete):	
1st year cost	$25,000
2nd year cost	15,000
Thereafter	8,000
Quadriplegic (complete):	
1st year cost	35,000
2nd year cost	25,000
Thereafter	15,000
Brain Damage (comatose):	
1st year cost	40,000
Thereafter	15,000
Burns (over 40 percent—some 3d degree):	
1st year cost	30,000
Thereafter	2,000

As an example then, we can assume that a complete paraplegic aged 20 may live 30 years and his lifetime medical expenses can be computed as:

1st year cost	$25,000
2d year cost	15,000
Remainder (28 years) cost	224,000
Total	264,000

As a further example, a complete quadriplegic aged 30 may live 21 years. His expenses might accrue to:

1st year cost	$35,000
2d year cost	25,000
Remainder (19 yr cost)	285,000
Total	345,000

It should be reemphasized that these are only examples and many factors must be considered by an insurer in establishing the appropriate reserve for a particular injury.

REINSURANCE COSTS

Having noted the potential expenses on a hypothetical basis, to understand the problems on a practical basis, we must turn to the role of reinsurance in the system. As noted previously, most insurers will purchase reinsurance at some level to provide protection against shock or unusually large losses. A smaller insurer may purchase protection in excess of $25,000 or $50,000, while a larger insurer might retain losses up to $250,000 before buying reinsurance protection. The lower the retention the higher the per insured cost must be. Furthermore, the reinsurance costs for a small insurer will be higher when the insurer experiences a greater than actuarially anticipated number of large losses. For example, if a smaller insurer with 50,000 insured automobiles is forced to reserve for even $1 million of unlimited medical expenses, this is equivalent to a charge of $20 per policy. Such a per policy loading would be difficult to obtain in a competitive market.

Reinsurance rate arrangements are individually negotiated and will vary due to factors as retention, experience, the underwriting philosophy of the primary insurer, and the size of the primary insurer. The reinsurance market is very competitive and while a reinsurer may increase the charge to a primary company to reflect adverse experience, if the increase is inordinate, the primary company will probably locate a new reinsurer. In some instances the reinsurance agreement may provide coverage at a fixed rate for a one-year period. In other cases, the agreement will contain a rate which will vary within limits depending upon experience. Thus, since loss experience is the most significant influence on cost, if the accident rate and losses are worse than anticipated, the rate would be the maximum stated in the agreement. In the succeeding year there would probably be an increase in the rate range.

In this regard, the adverse experience under unlimited benefits in New Jersey and Michigan has been mentioned earlier. We also are aware that a number of regional insurers have experienced very large increases in their reinsurance premiums. As for contrary statements from representatives of very large insurers, we can only say that they would have no reason to know otherwise.

It is unfortunate that many proponents of no-fault have attempted to sell the concept to the public and legislative bodies on the basis of cost. In almost every state where no-fault legislation has been enacted, and in Congress as well, it has been advocated as a means to achieve rate reductions, and some jurisdictions have even mandated rate reductions as a part of the no-fault law. Only recently has it generally been acknowledged by proponents of no-fault that whatever cost savings may accrue will be only temporary and that inflation will continue to cause insurance rates to increase.

Less recognized is the fact that in the real competitive world of insurance costs and marketing actuarially projected cost savings from reduced claim and litigation expenses under no-fault on a system-wide basis will not be directly transferred to the payment of all medical and rehabilitation expenses. Small insurers suffering shock losses covered by experience-rated reinsurance treaties usually cannot rely on reduced litigation expenses to balance substantially increased reinsurance costs. When primary insurance rates are already inadequate, the eventual result may well be reduced competition and the elimination of smaller insurers from the automobile insurance marketplace.

CONCLUSION

In summary, the Association believes that experience with unlimited medical and rehabilitation expenses in Michigan and New Jersey shows the advisability of a reasonable base limit on these expenses which must be covered in any federal minimum standards bill. Just as the pending legislation would establish a limit on wage loss, we believe it is appropriate to apply a reasonable but high limit on medical and rehabilitation benefits for this new program whose effects would be felt immediately in every state without closely defined controls or limits to avoid abuses of unnecessary or improper utilization. We submit that a ceiling of $100,000 for medical and rehabilitation expenses would be an appropriate and responsible first level for such a revolutionary program. The present problems now surfacing in Michigan and New Jersey suggest the appropriateness of this action.

STATEMENT OF BOARD OF CHURCH AND SOCIETY OF THE UNITED METHODIST CHURCH

NO-FAULT AUTOMOBILE INSURANCE

A. The Situation Which Makes This Statement Timely and Advisable:

The issue has recently been before the United States Congress for action. At this writing, the Senate bill (S. 354) has passed the Senate and the question is pending in the House. Senator Warren Magnuson, chief sponsor of the bill, has said that there is something wrong with the present system when premiums paid into the system annually total $16 billion and the claims paid out total $8.4 billion.

An independent study of five states by the actuarial firm of Milliman and Robertson, Inc. has shown a decrease in premium rates in almost every instance in which no-fault insurance was adopted.

B. The Biblical-Theological-Ethical Basis of This Statement:

Even the most literal noninterpretative application of the Good Samaritan story would say that persons injured along the road should be helped. No-fault is an attempt to provide more help for those involved in automobile accidents. It is also an attempt to provide that help more quickly, For "justice delayed is justice denied."

Consumers of auto insurance protection form a class represented by the general public. Their plight, if adversely affected, is of concern to the Christian—more so than that of any special interest group. The government has a particular responsibility to see to it that the welfare of the unorganized weak is secured.

The Board of Church and Society affirms its support for a national no-fault auto insurance system.

Under such a law the federal government should require each state to enact a no-fault law that meets minimum federal standards. If a state fails to take action during the first legislative session after passage of the national law, then reasonable federal standards should be imposed.

Minimum standards in the law should assure that:

    the victim of an automobile accident be entitled to unlimited benefits for all appropriate medical expenses.

    reasonable benefits be payable for work loss, replacement services, and survivor's loss.

The right to sue should be retained at least in accident cases such as the following:

    (1) an uninsured motorist;

    (2) a car which was involved in an accident because it had not been properly designed, manufactured, repaired or services;

    (3) intentional injury;

    (4) tangible losses that exceed state limitations on total work loss, replacement services and survivor's loss benefits; and

    (5) intangible damages (pain and suffering) in excess of $2,500 if the accident caused death, serious and permanent disfigurement, other serious and permanent injury or more than six continuous months of total disability.

In an inflationary society, it is imperative that the nation give full attention to a no-fault auto insurance system which could not only provide improved services for the public, but also—according to independent studies—reduce the costs of auto insurance premiums.

STATEMENT OF JAMES R. SNYDER, NATIONAL LEGISLATIVE DIRECTOR, UNITED TRANSPORTATION UNION

My name is James R. Snyder. I am National Legislative Director of the United Transportation Union, a railroad labor organization representing the vast majority of railroad operating employees, and wish to express to you and the Committee our thoughts on needed improvements in H.R. 1272, H.R. 1900 and other related bills, requiring no-fault motor vehicle insurance as a condition precedent to using a motor vehicle on public roadways.

Our union represents some 280,000 members who, with their families, live wherever railroads operate in this country. All of them own one or more automobiles and in addition to their own cars, are often involved in transportation over highways by carrier-owned vehicles and other carrier-ordered transportation such as taxis.

We understand that a good "no-fault" law would establish a nationwide system of no-fault automobile insurance. Under it, a policyholder would be compensated—immediately and fairly—by his insurance company without lengthy and expensive court proceedings to determine who was at fault. This process would mean reduced insurance costs which would then be passed on to the policyholder as lower premiums, improved insurance coverage, and more equitable benefits payments. Additionally, no insurance company could cancel a policy unless the policyholder lost his operator's license or failed to pay his premium.

The United Transportation Union has some serious reservations in regard to these bills. These objections are as follows:

1. No-fault could interfere with sick benefits under railroad retirement or carrier plan.

2. No-fault requires exhausting of benefits under Travelers Health and Welfare before receiving benefits from automobile insurance plan.

3. No-fault could have serious effects on "deadhead insurance" while riding on carrier off-track vehicles.

4. One major concern of the union centers upon the effect of no-fault insurance upon the previously negotiated accident and health plans included in labor contracts. If the no-fault benefits were secondary to the accident and health benefits, then the worker would be paying for automobile insurance which he could never collect. If the no-fault benefits were primary, then the worker would suffer a payroll deduction with no benefit. This problem will have to be resolved.

My other comments are quite similar to those of the AFL-CIO whose testimony was presented to the Committee by Mr. Andrew J. Biemiller, Director of Legislation for the AFL-CIO, of which the United Transportation Union is a member.

We agree that *all* drivers must carry adequate insurance to cover themselves and uninsured passengers and pedestrians and that there be full compensation on a "no-fault" basis of all reasonable medical expenses and related rehabilitation costs.

The requirement for payment of claims within a 30-day period is absolutely necessary and a penalty for interest and legal fees if court action is required to obtain payment is likewise necessary. Provisions prohibiting subrogation are also necessary.

In our opinion, the bills should have the following improvements placed in them by the Committee:

 A wage replacement formula adopted to fit the wage replacement section of an individual's auto insurance policy to his exact salary or annual earnings with no time or dollar limitations. A low income worker must not be forced to carry sufficient liability insurance to replace the wage loss of a highly paid executive or professional person.

 Stationary property losses should be included as part of basic reparations benefits.

 Pain and suffering losses should not be subject to court suits but be covered by an option in the policy of the individual.

 These bills should permit cancellation or non-renewal only if the holder loses his driver's license or fails to pay the premiums.

 States should be permitted to assess insurance companies operating within their jurisdiction a percentage of their premiums to insure improved rehabilitation of services and improved emergency response systems.

 A time limit of ten working days should be set for giving written notice of claim rejections. We also believe that lump sum benefits in excess of $2,500 should either be banned or provision made for payment of claimant's legal fees if claimant is required to go to court to seek a higher justified payment.

 Clarifying language requiring that insurance companies offer reduced premiums to those policyholders who have health, life or disability income insurance, or wage replacement coverage and who elect to look first to these policies for such benefits must be included. 30 State laws now prohibiting group auto insurance should be eliminated.

It is my hope that the Committee will report out a bill which will be entirely beneficial to all automobile drivers and passengers which and will correct those items which, in our view, must be corrected.

STATEMENT OF BERNARD L. WEBB, CPCU, FCAS, PROFESSOR OF ACTUARIAL SCIENCE AND INSURANCE, GEORGIA STATE UNIVERSITY

THE COST OF NO-FAULT AUTOMOBILE INSURANCE

This statement will concentrate on the cost implications of no-fault automobile insurance, and specifically the cost implications of S. 354 and H.R. 1900. I recognize that cost is not the only consideration in the decision to adopt or not to adopt a no-fault law. However, I will emphasize the cost implications for two reasons. First, cost is the facet of the no-fault controversy which has been of greatest interest to the public. Second, the cost implications have been misrepresented consistently, due either to unintentional miscalculations or to intentional misrepresentations by those who have a financial or political stake in the adoption of no-fault laws.

During the past ten years, the public has been subjected to a barrage of claims regarding the miraculous savings in insurance premiums which will result from the adoption of no-fault automobile insurance laws. It now is becoming obvious to any careful observer of the automobile insurance market that no premium reductions will result from the adoption of any no-fault law providing benefit levels acceptable to the public, except possibly under very unusual circumstances.

Of the states which have had no-fault laws long enough to develop reasonable experience data, only Massachusetts can lay any claim to insurance rate reductions. The savings there may be more apparent than real. In any case, Massachusetts was and is an exceptional situation, totally different from any other state in the country.

The unique nature of the automobile insurance situation in Massachusetts is clearly indicated by the fact that fewer people have been paid for bodily injury claims under the no-fault law than were paid under the preceding tort liability system, although the payment of a larger percentage of traffic victims is one of the major advantages claimed for no-fault laws. To be more precise, about one-third fewer people have been paid for bodily injury under the no-fault law than were paid during a comparable time period under tort liability.

There are several logical explanations for this anomaly, all traceable to the unique situation which existed in Massachusetts but does not exist to anywhere near the same degree elsewhere in the United States. First, Massachusetts had required all motorists to carry bodily injury liability coverage, but not property damage liability coverage, for many years. It was common practice for persons who had sustained property damage to feign bodily injury in order to recover for their property damage, whether or not the offending vehicle was insured for property damage liability. The adoption of the no-fault law, with its $500 medical threshold on tort claims, closed the door to this tactic. Consequently, bodily injury insurance costs decreased an average of 38% for Massachusetts motorists. However, this was more than offset by a 40% increase in property damage liability, collision and comprehensive insurance rates, as motorists began to collect more of their property damage claims under those coverages.

A second reason for the reduction in bodily injury insurance costs in Massachusetts was the very large number of fradulent claims prior to the adoption of the no-fault law. Fraudulent claims were so common that the state found it necessary to establish a special law enforcement agency solely to detect and prosecute perpetrators of fraudulent automobile insurance claims. For a period of years in the 1950s there were more people who collected bodily injury liability claims than there were who reported injuries to the Massachusetts Motor Vehicle Registry,[1] an extremely unusual situation. In fact, to the best of my knowledge, it has never occurred in any other state. The no-fault law appears to have reduced the number of fraudulent claims at least temporarily.

However, it appears that the improvement, if any, in Massachusetts may have been temporary. Automobile insurers in that state have now requested rate increases averaging 46 percent, or about $100 per vehicle. They reported that the number of claims during 1974 was 21 percent greater than during 1973, and that they now are paying one claim for every three insured vehicles, an amazingly high frequency. They also report that the claims frequency for the first six months of 1975 was even higher than for 1974, foreshadowing even more increases in the future.[2]

The experience in Florida has been even worse than in Massachusetts, and is likely to be more typical of the experience to be expected in the rest of the country. During 1974 all, or virtually all, automobile insurers operating in Florida implemented substantial rate increases, ranging upward to 30 percent or more.[3] The Allstate Insurance Company, which started the first wave of Florida rate increases, has already implemented a second increase of 20 percent.[4] It seems likely that other insurers will follow their lead.

The Chairman of the Insurance Committee of the Florida House of Representatives was quoted recently as saying the Florida no-fault law "has just really been a bomb." He continued to say that:

"A great deal of your no-fault states lead the nation in loss ratios with the insurance companies. It's worse than under the old tort system. Under no-fault, everybody collects—the good and the bad. It doubles the chance of abuse." [5]

He advocated drastic changes in the Florida no-fault law in an effort to reduce fraud and slow rapidly rising insurance costs.

A recent report of the Florida Association of Insurance Agents showed that the private passenger automobile insurance loss ratios (the ratio of claims incurred to premiums earned) in Florida for 1974 was 85.4 percent, as opposed to a national loss ratio of 69.2 percent. A telephone survey of insurers by that organization indicated that Florida loss ratios for the first six months of 1975 were substantially higher than they were for 1974.[6] It is clear, therefore, that Florida can expect substantial additional rate increases. It seems clear that the Florida no-fault law is a major cause of these increases. Some state officials have attempted to blame the increases on inflation. However, the adjoining states of Georgia

---

[1] Casualty Insurance Companies Serving Massachusetts, *The First Thirty Years,* (Boston: Casualty Insurance Companies Serving Massachusetts, 1957), pp. 23, 33, 43.
[2] "With 1 Damage Claim For Every 3 Insured Cars, Massachusetts Asked For 46 Percent Hike In Auto Rates," *National Underwriter,* (Property and Casualty Insurance Edition), August 22, 1975, p. 1.
[3] Charles F. Hesser, "Auto Insurance Soars In Florida," *The Atlanta Journal and Constitution,* December 15, 1975, p. 2-C, see also "Justify Rate Hike State Farm Told," *Journal of Commerce,* January 12, 1975, p. 4-E.
[4] "Florida Sends Team to Probe Allstate Figures," *The Journal of Commerce,* August 25, 1975, p. 12.
[5] "Florida Seeks to Curb No-Fault Auto Frauds," *The Atlanta Journal,* August 28, 1975, p. 15-D.
[6] Florida Association of Insurance Agents, *Agents Confidential,* August 19, 1975, p. 2.

and Alabama, which should be equally affected by inflationary forces, have not experienced such increases.

The experience in New Jersey has been similar to that in Florida.[7] One major insurer, a member of a trade association which has been telling Congress about the savings from no-fault insurance, filed for a 50 percent rate increase in New Jersey one day after the insurance commissioner had approved a previously filed increase of 6.4 percent.[8]

Meaningful statistics are not yet available publicly for other states. However, the insurance commissioner for Connecticut has indicated that no-fault has brought rate increases in that state.[9] A news release by State Farm indicates with regard to the Michigan law that "State Farm estimates that premiums under the new law will be 20 to 30 percent higher than" the rates that existed in Michigan under the tort system.

In spite of the almost disastrous experience in the several no-fault states, efforts are still being made by no-fault proponents to picture no-fault as a means of reducing the cost of automobile insurance. The only evidence they can produce to support this claim consists of (1) the early Massachusetts no-fault experience, (2) the theoretical study of probable no-fault costs conducted by the actuarial consulting firm of Milliman and Robertson, and (3) the more recent theoretical study conducted by the State Farm insurance companies.

As indicated above the Massachusetts experience cannot be relied upon as an indication of the results to be expected in other states for three reasons. First, the situation in Massachusetts was and is simply too different from the situation in the rest of the country. Second, the actual amount of reduction, if any, in Massachusetts cannot be ascertained because of tradeoffs between bodily injury premiums and property damage and physical damage premiums. Finally, recent developments in Massachusetts strongly suggest that any reductions that may have occurred were temporary. It appears that the same fraudulent practices that gave Massachusetts by far the highest automobile insurance rates under the tort system will now result in even higher rates under the no-fault system.

The theoretical studies conducted by Milliman and Robertson and State Farm suffer from at least two very serious problems: (1) A lack of statistical information derived from the operation of no-fault systems, and (2) inadequate understanding of the operation of no-fault systems. These weaknesses can be corrected only by several years of observation of no-fault systems. Fortunately, the existing state no-fault laws offer a wide variety of no-fault systems in a wide variety of environments. Careful observation of the existing laws over the next four or five years should provide adequate statistical information to permit the accurate forecasting of no-fault insurance costs.

The weakness of the Milliman and Robertson model is best indicated by comparing its projected costs in Florida and Massachusetts with the actual results in those states.

Milliman and Robertson projected a 15 percent reduction in insurance rates in Florida under the no-fault law.[10] It is now abundantly clear that the actual result in Florida has been a very substantial increase in cost.

---

[7] "Five Majors: NJ Rates Hikes Filed," *Journal of Commerce*, October 8, 1974, p. 2.
"Inadequate NJ Auto Rates Seen Resulting in Losses," *Journal of Commerce*, May 23, 1975, p. 2.
Vincent R. Zarate, "11 Firms in NJ Seek Auto Rate Increases," *Journal of Commerce*, May 29, 1975, p. 2. (State Farm was one of these companies with an increase of 16.2%.)
"ISO Files: NJ Auto Rate Hike Sought," *Journal of Commerce*, July 15, 1975, p. 10.
Vincent J. Zarate, "New Jersey No-Fault Fails to Halt Rate Increases," *Journal of Commerce*, July 15, 1975, p. 10.
Tom Herman, "Major Auto Insurers in New Jersey Renew Old Battle to Win Sharp Rate Increases," *Wall Street Journal*, July 16, 1975, p. 10. (Quotes the president of State Farm as saying that State Farm is "losing its shirt" in New Jersey).
Vincent R. Zarate, "No-Fault in NJ Termed Successful Despite Miscalculations on Cost," *Journal of Commerce*, July 23, 1975, p. 2.
Vincent R. Zarate, "Three NJ Insurers File Auto Rate Hikes," *Journal of Commerce*, July 28, 1975, p. 8.
"GEICO Halts New Business in NJ," *Journal of Commerce*, August 18, 1975, p. 2.
"Record Number Reached: NJ Auto Rate Hike Requests Up," *Journal of Commerce*, August 21, 1975, p. 2.
[8] Vincent R. Zarate, "Three NJ Insurers File Auto Rate Hikes," *Journal of Commerce*, July 28, 1975, p. 8.
[9] "Auto No-Fault Praised by Senator Scored by Commissioner in Conn.," *Journal of Commerce*, August 19, 1975, p. 2.
[10] *Milliman and Robertson, Inc., Final Report Concerning the Cost Estimating System for No-Fault Automobile Insurance*, (Milwaukee: The National Association of Insurance Commissioners, 1973), pp. 10, 11.

Milliman and Robertson projected a 24 percent cost reduction in Massachusetts. The initial experience resulted in a reduction of 38 percent. However, more recent statistics indicate that the eventual result will be a large increase there as well.

The results of the State Farm study show equally inconsistent conclusions. The State Farm study concluded that S. 354 or H.R. 1900 would reduce automobile insurance costs in all states except Florida, Massachusetts, New Jersey and New York. The increases projected for those states are: Florida, +8 percent; Massachusetts, +15 percent; New Jersey, +3 percent; and New York, +4 percent.

A State Farm actuary, in testimony before the Senate Committee on Commerce, stated that:

"In all four cases they have this no-fault plan, and the basic reason is that the benefit package envisioned under S. 354 more than offsets the savings that might accrue because of the tighter tort threshold."

Yet, as already shown herein, the no-fault laws of Florida and New Jersey have already brought substantial cost increases in those states, and increases appear to be on the way for Massachusetts. If H.R. 1900–S. 354 will bring further increases to states whose insurance costs have already been increased by state no-fault laws, how can it bring reductions to states which have not yet had such increases?

It should be noted also that the states of New York and New Jersey, where increases are projected, are highly urbanized states, while the largely rural state of Texas is projected to receive the largest reduction. Such results are contrary to logic. The rural states have more single car accidents, which cost little under tort law but will be very expensive under no-fault laws. Urban states, on the other hand, have more low speed, multi-vehicle accidents. These accidents are expensive in the aggregate under tort law, but should cost less under no-fault because the tort threshold should eliminate general damages in most cases.

In addition, New York and New Jersey, for which State Farm projects increases, already have automobile insurance rates which are among the nation's highest. On the other hand, the rates in Texas, which are projected to drop by 26 percent, are among the nation's lowest.

I should add that State Farm estimates that H.R. 1900 would result in a cost reduction of 7 percent in Michigan, which now has a no-fault law. If this is combined with their estimate that the existing Michigan no-fault law will result in cost increases of from 20 to 30 percent above the cost of tort liability insurance, it would seem to indicate that H.R. 1900 would cost 12 to 21 percent more than the tort system in Michigan. However, the Michigan automobile insurance market is dominated by the Detroit metropolitan area. Consequently, one would expect no-fault to produce a cost reduction in Michigan if it does so in most of the other states.

These various inconsistencies show clearly that the State Farm cost projections are not reliable indications of the relative cost of no-fault automobile insurance.

CONCLUSIONS

I have shown that (1) we cannot accurately predict the cost of no-fault insurance on the basis of present knowledge, and (2) the probability that no-fault insurance will cost more than tort liability insurance is at least as great as the probability that it will cost less.

It is clear that the potential additional cost of no-fault insurance is more than the public wants to assume at this time. It also is extremely doubtful that some of the other claimed advantages of no-fault will materialize. The only exception is the advantage of paying more people. That advantage has materialized in several states, but at the cost of much higher insurance premiums.

Fortunately, our ignorance of the results of no-fault laws will be corrected over the next four or five years. Some twenty states have adopted no-fault laws. Their experience with a wide variety of laws in a wide variety of environments should enable us to estimate costs and other results of no-fault laws in the remaining states.

I strongly urge that Congress withhold any action on a national no-fault law or national standards for state no-fault laws until the operation of such laws is better understood. I hope that Congress will resist the urgings of those who have a profit interest in the adoption of no-fault laws. I hope that Congress will turn a deaf ear to those state officials who see a national no-fault law as a means of protecting their political futures from the wrath of constituents who have been a e with sharply higher insurance costs because of unwise state no-fault laddl d

While the tort law system may not be perfect, it is functioning well enough so that we need not launch the nation into a poorly understood insurance system which very likely will saddle the majority of motorists with sharply higher insurance costs.

AMERICAN AUTOMOBILE ASSOCIATION,
September 11, 1975.
Re No-fault automobile insurance (H.R. 1272, H.R. 1900, H.R. 7985, et al.).
Hon. LIONEL VAN DEERLIN,
Chairman, Subcommittee on Consumer Protection and Finance, U.S. House of Representatives, Rayburn House Office Building, Washington, D.C.

DEAR CHAIRMAN VAN DEERLIN: The American Automobile Association (AAA) continues its support for the concept of no-fault automobile insurance. Likewise, we continue in the firm belief that the most appropriate forum for the consideration of such legislation is the state legislatures.

Official AAA Policy on no-fault automobile insurance, as approved by the Delegates at our last Annual Meeting, is attached as Exhibit "A".

The most significant and important part of the AAA policy position is that it supports continued state regulation of automobile insurance to insure maintenance of a system which is responsive to local needs. In this regard, we would emphasize that the new policy calls for limitations on tort recoveries through the enactment of modified no-fault laws to be implemented on a state by state basis.

The high cost of insurance premiums remains the major source of dissatisfaction to the consumer. One method of reducing costs is to eliminate duplicate payments and general damages for minor injuries. However, this must be carefully balanced against the need to promptly provide medical and income loss benefits to all automobile injury victims.

AAA is deeply concerned about the cost reduction question. Figures from opponents and proponents alike change from day to day. Some of the strongest no-fault supporters are now retreating from their claims of premium reductions which would result from enactment of no-fault legislation, while much of the media still continues to "sell" the program on the basis of alleged great savings to the consumer. It seems to us to be the height of folly to even consider legislation which has any possibility of increasing the cost of insurance premiums during an inflationary period such as this.

Among the various states there are wide differences in accident frequencies, wages and cost of medical care. Such variations demonstrate a need for differing state laws based on those ranges. In this regard, levels for specific basic benefits and tort threshold limitations are suggested below:

	States with—[1]	
	Lower costs	Higher costs
Medical limit [2]	$2,500 to $5,000	$5,000 to $10,000.
Income limits:		
Wage percentage	60 to 85	60 to 85.
Monthly maximum	$500 to $750	$600 to $900.
Duration of benefits	1 to 3 yr	1 to 3 yrs.
Extra expenses [3]	$8 to $12 per day	$10 to $15 per day.
Tort threshold	$500 to $1,000	$750 to $1,500.

[1] For specific State, see attached "Exhibit B".
[2] Higher medical limits can be considered when estimated additional insurance cost is not prohibitive.
[3] Extra expenses means reimbursement for necessary miscellaneous household expenses incurred resulting from the disability of nonemployed spouses.

The AAA policy calls for elimination of claims between injured parties which do not exceed a specified level. However, it does not propose elimination of claims involving serious and permanent disfigurement or disability, or death. The policy would have the effect of controlling damages for pain and suffering by limiting recovery to actual economic loss.

At present, there is considerable duplication of payments for hospital and medical costs and lost wages. The policy calls on accident and health companies to write their policies so as to cover only those losses not fully covered by the automobile policy. The resultant savings should be reflected in reduced premiums for accident and health insurance.

In the area of collateral sources, Workmen's Compensation, and other government mandated programs should be the primary source of benefits. Automobile insurance coverage would be used only when the loss exceeds payments. For those not covered in this manner, the automobile insurance would be the source of payment.

The policy also calls for the penalizing of those companies which delay basic benefit claims payments, except where the claim is unreasonable, or fraudulent. Disputed claims would be arbitrated at no cost to the policyholder.

AAA Objection to Federal No-Fault Legislation

1. The states *are* taking action on the subject of motor vehicle accident reparations reform. Naturally, the degree and type varies from state to state. The record is clear, however, with twenty four states having enacted some version of reparations reform. While not all of these new laws constitute true "no-fault insurance", we feel they constitute sufficient state action so as to warrant a delay in any action on the Federal level at this time. The state action to date, coupled with the absence of any bona fide crisis in this area is adequate justification for delaying action on the Federal level.

2. Provisions which permit employer provided group accident and health insurance to be made primary over automobile insurance will serve to increase "red tape" for claimants, rather than reducing it as no-fault proponents claim. Claimants will have to deal with two insurance companies causing them much inconvenience, so this provision will increase the overall costs. In addition it is arguable that it is better to have all costs of an automobile related accident charged to the automobile insurance so that those who use motor vehicles are the ones who pay for the full costs of using motor vehicles.

3. The proponents of H.R. 1900 and similar no-fault legislation have led the public to believe that enactment of such legislation would reduce their insurance premiums overnight. We believe that case to be overstated.

Now we have considerable company as indicated by statements such as the following made before your Committee by State Farm Insurance Company, one of the major supporters of Federal no-fault legislation:

"We believe the importance of cost projections has been overemphasized. Although cost projections are necessary as *general background* so as to give decision-makers information to determine whether they are creating a reparations system beyond reasonably affordable cost for consumers, by far the most important test, as we previously stated, is one of *value*. Fortunately, in our judgment, we believe, conversion to no-fault programs meeting the standards established by a S. 354 type law would *generally introduce a cost-reducing element* into the total rate making picture." (Emphasis added.)

Coupled with statements such as this we see a pattern developing in no-fault states where there is a legislatively mandated reduction in premiums in the area of 15 percent accompanying the original enactment. The following year the carriers go back and plead with the Insurance Commissioner for rate increases of 25 to 30 percent. Massachusetts residents, about to be hit with a still further increase in premiums, will be surprised to learn that their no-fault law doesn't meet the requirements of H.R. 1900. There is a requested rate increase of 46 percent now pending in Massachusetts. New Jersey insurers have asked for increases ranging as high as 50 percent. Last year Florida motorists were socked with increases of 30 percent, and even higher in some cases.

Another disturbing factor on this whole question of cost relates to the claims of the extent of the reduction claimed by proponents. (This ignores for the moment the opposing view that no-fault will force *increases* in premiums). Proponents admit their figures are derived from averages. In fact, it was noted during your hearings that "we have to deal in averages". But to come up with the *average* decrease of 10 percent claimed by State Farm, there obviously will be some increase in somebody's premium. And woe be to the poor motorist who is forced to balance out that "average"!

All of this convinces us that there is a clear need for much more state experience and accumulation of acturial data before we even consider enactment of Federal no- ault.

4. It has been estimated that large, heavy commercial vehicles will enjoy a $2.66 billion dollar reduction in costs under the provisions of H.R. 1900. What possible justification can there be for shifting this huge cost from these vehicles to the individual automobile owner?

5. Proponents of H.R. 1900 urge its enactment so that *all* victims of motor vehicle accidents may be fully, promptly, and professionally treated for their injuries. Who is more likely to suffer serious injury in an accident than a motorcyclist? Yet, the bill permits states to exclude him from no-fault coverage.

6. A tort threshold of 90 days is unrealistically low.

7. There are several serious constitutional problems with Federal no-foult insurance, especially H.R. 1900. The constitutions of several states would appear to bar no-fault insurance of the type required by bills such as H.R. 1900. This presents still another reason for state by state legislation in this area, and state by

state determination, where appropriate, of the constitutional issues involved. In addition, there are several serious questions as to the legality of this type of legislation under the U.S. Constitution. To enact such legislation without prior resolution of these questions would throw the insurance industry into chaos.

At one point it was suggested that a potential Constitutional defect could be cured by using a cutoff of Federal Aid Highway Funds as the "threat" to force state enactment of no-fault laws. We submit that the Highway Trust Fund has already been stretched so far beyond its original purpose that it is hardly recognizable, and to further distort its function with such a provision would be disastrous. AAA urges rejection of any such proposals.

8. Provisions authorizing an on-going review of no-fault insurance by the Department of Transportation (DOT) appear to be a further step in the direction of Federal control and regulation of insurance. It is all the more ridiculous in the face of DOT's admission that not only does it lack staff to conduct such a study, that few qualified people are available to conduct such studies.

9. The unlimited medical and rehabilitation provisions cause us concern. They could well drive the cost of motor vehicle insurance out of reach for many motorists. We have received some indications that these provisions in one state's no-fault law are causing more of the very lawsuits which no-fault insurance is supposed to eliminate. There, insurance carriers are being sued for punitive damages, as well as resumption of medical and rehabilitational benefits, in cases where the carrier terminated the benefits after what appeared to be a thorough review by a medical review committee.

These same unlimited medical and rehabilitation provisions could drive many small insurance companies out of business. With unlimited coverages such as provided in some of the bills under consideration the cost of reinsurance would become prohibitive in many cases, if available at all. The experience under Michigan and New Jersey no-fault laws appear to be a serious warning sign in this regard.

For these reasons we feel that H.R. 1900 and similar bills have too many flaws, and that it is not in the public interest to enact them at this time.

We request that this statement be made a part of the printed record on this egislation.

Sincerely yours,

JOHN DE LORENZI,
*Managing Director,
Public Policy Division.*

EXHIBIT A

POLICIES AND RESOLUTIONS

(For the Year Ending September, 1975)

F-2. Automobile insurance and accident compensation

The American Automobile Association has a profound and continuing interest in the general availability of auto insurance that provides fair and equitable protection against economic loss and suffering resulting from motor vehicle accidents.

The AAA analysis of the study findings of the Department of Transportation confirms the immediate need for positive action to correct the present automobile accident compensation system.

The AAA believes that private enterprise in a competitive market can best provide the quality of insurance protection required by the public. The AAA also supports continued state regulation of auto insurance to insure maintenance of a system which is responsive to local needs.

The AAA advocates and calls upon the state legislatures to enact an auto insurance compensation system which embraces the following principles:

1. Basic benefits, within limits prescribed, should be payable to the injured person by his own insurance company without regard to fault.

2. Such basic benefits should provide coverage for the insured, resident, relatives of his household, his guest passengers, and pedestrians struck by the insured automobile.

3. Such basic benefits should provide compensation for economic loss without regard to fault, subject to reasonable deductibles and limits, including the costs of medical care, hospitalization and wage losses. Insurance companies making such payments should be entitled to reimbursement by the responsible party or his insurer, with the requirement of inter-company arbitration between insurers in appropriate cases.

4. The owner or registrant of a motor vehicle required to be registered shall maintain insurance or other acceptable security for basic benefits which shall be in effect continuously during the period of registration of the motor vehicle.

5. An assigned claims plan should be available to provide basic benefits for persons who otherwise would not be covered.

6. Limitations should be placed on the rights of individuals with minor injuries to pursue damages in excess of their actual economic losses. An individual incurring medical expenses below a specified level should be limited to recovery of basic benefits to compensate him for his actual economic losses. This limitation should not apply in the case of the death of the victim or in the event of his serious and permanent disfigurement or disability.

7. Auto insurance should be the primary source of basic benefits with the exception of Workmen's Compensation and other government mandated indemnity programs.

8. To prevent duplicate premium costs and loss payments, benefits other than Workmen's Compensation and other government mandated indemnity payments should be excess over the automobile insurance basic benefits.

9. Insurance companies paying basic benefits for economic loss should be required to do so promptly, with specific penalties for failure of prompt payment except where the claim can be demonstrated to be unreasonable or without merit. In such cases of controversy, provision should be made for arbitration at no cost to the consumer.

Exhibit B

	Average hospital cost per day, 1972	Median family income	Type of State
Alabama	$81	$7,266	Low.
Alaska	149	12,433	High.
Arizona	123	9,187	High.
Arkansas	71	6,273	Low.
California	149	10,732	High.
Colorado	103	9,555	High.
Connecticut	135	11,811	High.
Delaware	115	10,211	High.
Florida	98	8,267	High.
Georgia	91	8,167	Low.
Hawaii	105	11,554	High.
Idaho	88	8,381	Low.
Illinois	110	10,959	High.
Indiana	90	9,970	Low.
Iowa	80	9,018	Low.
Kansas	81	8,693	Low.
Kentucky	78	7,441	Low.
Louisiana	101	7,530	High.
Maine	91	8,205	Low.
Maryland	126	11,063	High.
Massachusetts	140	10,835	High.
Michigan	117	11,032	High.
Minnesota	89	9,931	Low.
Mississippi	70	6,071	Low.
Missouri	88	8,914	Low.
Montana	76	8,512	Low.
Nebraska	81	8,564	Low.
Nevada	120	10,692	High.
New Hampshire	90	9,698	Low.
New Jersey	99	11,407	High.
New Mexico	104	7,849	High.
New York	134	10,617	High.
North Carolina	80	7,774	Low.
North Dakota	77	7,838	Low.
Ohio	100	10,313	High.
Oklahoma	85	7,725	Low.
Oregon	104	9,489	High.
Pennsylvania	127	9,558	High.
Rhode Island	74	9,736	Low.
South Carolina	89	7,261	Low.
South Dakota	69	7,494	Low.
Tennessee	81	7,447	Low.
Texas	89	8,490	Low.
Utah	102	9,320	High.
Vermont	95	8,929	High.
Virginia	83	9,049	Low.
Washington	117	10,407	High.
West Virginia	73	7,415	Low.
Wisconsin	91	10,068	Low.
Wyoming	71	8,943	Low.
District of Columbia	143	9,583	High.

Sources: Hospital costs, U.S. Department of Health, Education, and Welfare, 1974; Family income, U.S. Statistical Abstract 1971.

AMERICAN TRUCKING ASSOCIATIONS, INC.
Washington, D.C., August 27, 1975.

Hon. LIONEL VAN DEERLIN,
Chairman, Subcommittee on Consumer Protection and Finance, Committee on Interstate and Foreign Commerce, U.S. House of Representatives, Rayburn House Office Building, Washington, D.C.

MY DEAR MR. CHAIRMAN: This will refer to H.R. 1272 and H.R. 1900 which your Committee is considering to establish a nationwide system of "no-fault" motor vehicle insurance.

This association has endorsed the principle of federal no-fault insurance, conditioned on the understanding that any such proposal not discriminate against trucks. One virulent form of such discrimination is contained in the so-called Uniform Vehicle Accident Reparations Act (UMVARA), which would require owners and operators of large vehicles to assume almost the entire cost of any and all accidents involving their vehicles and passenger cars regardless of fault.

The accident involvement record of vehicles operated by Class I and Class II for-hire motor carriers regulated by the Interstate Commerce Commission is far superior to that of passenger cars. Therefore, there is no basis for preferential treatment of passenger cars. Any distinction between vehicles is repugnant to the basic tenets of no-fault insurance. No-fault supposedly means just that—namely, that the vehicle owner is reimbursed for his accident loss by his own insurance company irrespective of negligence or fault in the accident.

H.R. 1272 contains no preferential treatment of passenger cars. We would caution, however, that since there are no limits on payments for economic or non-economic loss by insurers (other than, presumably, life expectancy), premiums could be very steep, which may or may not be off-set by protection against tort suits.

H.R. 1900, on the other hand, would allow "a right of reimbursement among and between restoration obligors based upon a determination of fault" where an accident involves a motor vehicle other than a passenger car. Such reimbursement is limited to benefits paid for loss in excess of $5,000. (See Sec. 111(a)(3))

H.R. 1900 is similar to S. 354 presently under consideration of the Senate Committee on Commerce. In a letter to Chairman Magnuson of that Committee, we noted that, while we favor a bill which allows no reimbursement whatever among insurers, "this provision (Sec. 111(a)(3)) is better than any other reimbursement proposal which has been seriously advanced, and is acceptable to the trucking industry."

For these reasons, we prefer H.R. 1272, which contains no preferential treatment of passenger cars, if reasonable limits are placed on what constitutes "economic" and "non-economic loss". However, H.R. 1900 is acceptable to our industry since reimbursement is limited on a fault basis, rather than on some basis other than fault.

Sincerely yours,

W. A. BRESNAHAN, *President.*

BLUE CROSS ASSOCIATION AND
NATIONAL ASSOCIATION OF BLUE SHIELD PLANS,
Chicago, Ill., September 8, 1975.

Re Federal no-fault automobile insurance legislation.

Hon. LIONEL VAN DEERLIN,
Chairman, Subcommittee on Consumer Protection and Finance, Committee on Interstate and Foreign Commerce, U.S. House of Representatives, Washington, D.C.

DEAR MR. CHAIRMAN: The Blue Cross Association and the National Association of Blue Shield Plans represent 146 locally based, not-for-profit health care prepayment Plans employing 75,000 persons. Collectively, we provide comprehensive health care protection to nearly 86 million subscribers in our private business.

We would like to comment briefly on the relationship of health care benefits to no-fault health care coverage under the proposed legislation before your Committee.

Specifically, our major interest in federal no-fault legislation is to assure that the consumer receives benefits for health care services in the most efficient and economic manner regardless of the cause of his illness or injury.

As specialists in the health care prepayment field, we support the concept of minimum federal standards for no-fault automobile insurance. We agree that persons injured in traffic accidents should have full coverage for health care and rehabilitation expenses at the lowest cost possible. Further, we agree with the principle that no-fault coverage should follow the insured person rather than the automobile.

One of the keys to designing a no-fault program that offers maximum protection at an affordable cost is "coordination of benefits" (COB). In situations where a person has more than one source of health care benefits, COB gets his insurers together to see that his loss is covered 100 percent, but that he does not make a profit from duplicate payments. Without COB, the whole community loses when a person is over-insured because everyone, then, has to pay higher premiums to make up for his profit. In their regular business, Blue Cross Plans, Blue Shield Plans, and health insurance companies have developed efficient coordination of benefits programs that are in place and are today achieving substantial savings to the benefit of our subscribers. These same programs can be used to coordinate benefits between health insurance and auto insurance. If used properly, COB will yield substantial savings for purchasers of no-fault automobile coverage.

The best and least expensive way to produce those savings is to make health insurance a deductible collateral source for auto accident-related personal injury under no-fault auto legislation. Auto insurers would provide "wrap-around" coverage that would pay all health care expenses not covered by this or any other collateral source. We would like to discuss briefly a few of the more important reasons why we believe that existing health insurance should be a deductible collateral source.

Perhaps the major economic factor to be considered is the disparity in payout ratios between automobile insurance companies and health care prepayment plans such as Blue Cross and Blue Shield Plans. Our average combined operating expense is only 7 percent of premium income. The other 93 percent is paid out in benefits. Commercial health insurers, combining their group and non-group premium income, pack back an average of 80 percent of premiums in benefits, with many of their group plans near the combined Blue Cross and Blue Shield Plan average. Compare these figures with the present 45 percent administrative expense of the automobile insurance industry—a return of only 55 percent of premium in the form of benefits. In terms of average costs to individuals, the current difference in operating costs means that Blue Cross and Blue Shield Plan subscribers would continue to pay $107.53 and receive back $100 in auto accident-related health care benefits, whereas, if automobile insurance pays first, they will have to pay the automobile insurance companies $181.82 for that same $100 in benefits. We recognize that the auto insurers return to the customer may improve under no-fault auto insurance; however, we are confident that the record of health insurance carriers in this regard will remain significantly superior.

According to the National Safety Council, in 1972, automobile accidents caused $1.4 billion in medical care costs. In Puerto Rico, where the no-fault program requires that whatever health insurance a person has must pay first, automobile insurance personal injury premiums were lowered 30 percent in 1970 and 20 percent in 1972. Nationwide, the savings created by having lower cost health carriers pay automobile accident-related health care benefits could amount to hundreds of millions of dollars. Such savings would make mandatory no-fault automobile coverages more affordable for the consumer. Further, such savings would enhance the possibility that the consumer would be able to purchase additional, optional coverages.

Traditionally, the major responsibility of automobile insurance carriers has been to determine eligibility and liability. In paying claims for personal injury, automobile insurance carriers reimburse the consumer for expenses he has already incurred. We in the health care prepayment field are well aware of the need for the payment mechanism to be more than a conduit for funds which cannot apply the economic incentives that are needed in the interest of reducing the cost of actually providing health care.

Health benefit carriers such as Blue Cross and Blue Shield Plans deal with health care financing and delivery in a manner designed to help control the cost of health care to the American people. This not only can but does influence the cost of care on behalf of their subscribers. Further, health benefit carriers are able to do this while at the same time minimizing administrative costs and assuring subscriber satisfaction with the simplicity and the predictability of the process. In all, health benefit carriers have a specialized system with many attendant advantages.

We believe that consumers benefit considerably from these cost control advantages which have been developed and are being employed by health benefit carriers. We believe, further, that these cost containment efforts should be supported, not weakened, by a no-fault automobile insurance program, the basic thrust of which is to reduce costs to the consumer.

Each of program administration has important implications for both costs and consumer satisfaction. In this regard, we would underscore a very basic point: Non-duplication of auto accident health care expense benefits will be accomplished only when the secondary insurer—health or casualty—examines its claims to identify deductible collateral sources of payment. We submit that in view of the much greater volume of health insurance claims, it will be less costly and more efficient, with corresponding advantages to the consumer for the no-fault auto insurers to examine their lesser volume of auto claims for the existence of deductible health insurance and then pay for any residual uncovered expenses.

The consumer's health care coverage should not be fragmented by mandating that automobile insurance carriers cover one specific area of his health care. In all, we seek to assure the consumer that the integrity of his health coverage provided by health benefit carriers is preserved and to assure the consumer that he will receive benefits for health care services in the most efficient and economic manner regardless of the cause of his illness or injury.

To realize these advantages to the consumer, health insurance should pay accident-related health benefits under all no-fault automobile insurance policies as a mandated collateral source deductible. In fact, most no-fault bills provide that collateral sources—such as workmen's compensation, social security, state disability plans, and other government health benefit programs—should pay benefits before no-fault automobile insurance pays. The effect of the use of these other sources of benefits is lower no-fault auto insurance premiums.

In a recent study of a proposed state no-fault law, the actuarial firm of Milliman and Robertson indicated that if most collateral sources—including private health plans—paid first, medical benefits payable under no-fault would be reduced 57 percent and wage loss benefits would be lowered by 35 percent. Again, these figures translate into lower automobile insurance premiums.

To accomplish this, we suggest that the language in H.R. 1900, for example, be modified as follows: (1) delete Section 209, and (2) modify Section 208(a) to read as follows:

"Except as provided in paragraph (3) of subsection (a) of section 108 of this Act, all benefits or advantages (less reasonably incurred collection cost) that an individual receives or is entitled to receive from social security (except those benefits provided under Title XIX of the Social Security Act), health insurance, workmen's compensation, any state-required temporary, nonoccupational disability insurance, and all other benefits (except the proceeds of life insurance) received by or available to an individual because of the injury from any government, unless the law authorizing or providing for such benefits or advantages makes them excess or secondary to the benefits in accordance with this Act, shall be subtracted from loss in calculating net loss."

If an alternative is necessary, despite the considerable merit of the position we have outlined, we urge that the bill at least guarantee to consumers the right to choose between health insurance and auto insurance for auto accident health benefits. This could be accomplished by modifying Section 208(c) of H.R. 1900, for example, to mandate at least such consumer freedom of choice. Further, we recommend that, for those who choose to have their health insurance pay first, health insurers be required to provide auto accident health care benefits at least equal to those provided for other types of injury within the scope and limits of their existing contracts. Under this alternative, unlimited coverage would also be available to the consumer by the "wrap-around" coverage provided by his no-fault auto insurance policy. Those consumers who made this choice would receive an appropriate reduction in auto insurance premiums.

Two states, Michigan and Pennsylvania, have enacted no-fault insurance laws similar to this. The Pennsylvania law has just been implemented; the Michigan program has been in effect for over a year and the results are promising. It is expected that, for those individuals who elect to have their health insurance and wage loss coverages pay first, auto insurance personal injury premiums will prove to have been reduced 40 percent to 50 percent. This reduction may mean a 10 to 25 percent reduction in the total cost of auto insurance. As a minimum, we urge that this cost savings be available to all consumers.

One hundred eighty-two million Americans are covered by private health plans. Three-quarters of them have group coverage. Group health plans, as well as many individual coverages, have administrative costs far lower than the automobile insurance industry. By channeling appropriate no-fault personal injury benefits through these health plans rather than auto insurance plans, hundreds of millions of dollars in administrative expense and duplicate benefit cost can be saved. That money can remain in the consumer's pocket or it can be used to finance greater benefits.

We all share a concern with the high cost of health care coverage and automobile insurance premiums. Under Federal minimum standard no-fault legislation, you have the opportunity to help coordinate health and automobile insurance benefits and thus keep the cost of required coverages within the reach of everyone.

The enactment of no-fault legislation presents an opportunity to establish a proper interface between the two insurance systems that cover the cost of health care services which result from automobile accidents. This opportunity should not be ignored. Failure to incorporate rational cost saving features will be a disservice to the consumer.

The mechanisms we have proposed are responsible to the present opportunity and offer distinct advantages to the consumer.

We greatly appreciate this opportunity to comment for the record. As you proceed in your consideration of this matter, we will be available to provide any additional information you may desire.

Sincerely,

WALTER J. MCNERNEY,
President, Blue Cross Association.
NED F. PARISH,
President, National Association of Blue Shield Plans.

KAISER FOUNDATION,
HEALTH PLAN, INC.,
Oakland, Calif., August 7, 1975.

Representative LIONEL VAN DEERLIN,
Chairman, Subcommittee on Consumer Protection and Finance, Committee on Interstate and Foreign Commerce, Rayburn House Office Building, Washington, D.C.

DEAR MR. VAN DEERLIN: The Subcommittee which you chair has been considering bills which would establish a Federal no-fault motor vehicle insurance program. Kaiser Foundation Health Plan presents these comments for inclusion in the record on this subject.

The concern of our program is to assure the proper care of members who are injured by motor vehicles and further to assure equal treatment of health benefits carriers.

In cases where an accident victim enrolled in a direct-service group-practice prepayment plan is treated by the physicians or hospitals associated with the plan, the plan or the associated providers should be reimbursed for the value of the direct health care services rendered. In addition, when health care services are rendered on a prepaid basis by a direct-service group-practice prepayment plan, the value of the services should be fully credited, for no-fault purposes, to the provider or the beneficiary of the no-fault policy. This is done in Section 103(2) of both S. 354 and H.R. 1900. H.R. 1272 is deficient in that it would credit only "expenses incurred" for medical, hospital, and related health care. Any direct services obtained through a plan should be considered as "expenses incurred" for purposes of the legislation. To do otherwise would penalize those who have chosen a direct-service health care plan rather than an indemnity plan.

These three bills should be amended to permit direct payments by no-fault carriers to providers of health care services to persons covered by no-fault insurance. The provider should not be required to pursue the patient for payment. This is the situation prevailing if the no-fault carrier is permitted to pay the patient rather than the provider. The patient should be paid directly by the no-fault carrier for health care services only when he has actually paid the provider for those particular services. The intent of this paragraph can be partially accomplished through an assignment procedure as provided in Section 106(d) of S. 354 and H.R. 100. H.R. 1272 should be amended to include a similar provision. All three should have additional language calling for direct payment by carriers to providers.

Some state no-fault insurance programs permit the sale of policies with deductible features. Where these deductibles are applicable to the health care offered to a no-fault beneficiary, they may discourage delivery of prompt services by health care providers for fear that because of the deductible they may not be adequately compensated. To remedy this potential problem, we recommend that the Federal legislation specifically forbid any deductibles applicable to health care benefits of no-fault policies.

In S. 354 and H.R. 1900, certain provisions of Section 208(d) apparently do not apply to prepaid group practice plans; at least, we hope that they do not. They seem to apply only to health care programs that are classified as insurance, use group experience rating mechanisms, offer vocational rehabilitation coverage and referral services, and are required to share in the cost of state no-fault and assigned claims operations. It would be desirable to clarify this section to make certain that prepaid group practice plans and health maintenance organizations are excluded from Section 208(c) and thus participate fully and equally in receiving compensation from no-fault carriers for the value of health care services provided to victims of automobile accidents. Otherwise, these health care plans would be required to subsidize no-fault carriers and relieve them of part of the burden of health care costs arising from the use of motor vehicles.

Thank you for this opportunity to express our views to your Subcommittee.

Sincerely,

ARTHUR H. BERNSTEIN, *Counsel.*

NEW YORK UNIVERSITY,
SCHOOL OF LAW,
New York, N.Y., August 7, 1975.

PETER KINZLER, Esq.,
Counsel, Subcommittee on Consumer Protection and Finance, House of Representatives, Rayburn House Office Building, Washington, D.C.

DEAR MR. KINZLER: This is in reply to your letter of July 1st in which you solicit my views on the constitutionality of H.R. 1272 and H.R. 1900, which would require no-fault motor vehicle insurance. I have reviewed these bills from the standpoint of the issues I discussed in my testimony before the Senate Judiciary and Commerce Committees, and the article I wrote, based on this testimony, The National No-Fault Motor Vehicle Insurance Act: A Problem in Federalism, 49 N.Y.U. L. Rev. 45 (1974).

I believe that H.R. 1272, which would involve a complete federal takeover of automobile insurance, is supported by the commerce power. See 49 N.Y.U. L. Rev. at 47–48.

I also believe that the amendment to H.R. 1900, set out in your letter, avoids the Tenth Amendment problems that concerned me about S. 354, and therefore the particular objections I offered in my earlier testimony and article no longer are applicable.

In expressing these views, I would like to emphasize that I am not commenting on other constitutional issues that may be presented by the bills—for example, the withdrawal of the traditional tort compensation for injuries sustained in an automobile accident. Nor am I commenting on the wisdom of enacting these bills, including the compensation approach they take or the appropriate relationship between the Federal Government and the states in regard to compensation for motor vehicle accidents. These are questions that should obviously be given close attention.

Thank you for soliciting my views, which I hope will be helpful to the subcommittee.

Sincerely,

NORMAN DORSEN,
Professor of Law.

TRANSPORTATION ASSOCIATION OF AMERICA,
Washington, D.C., June 18, 1975.

Hon. LIONEL VAN DEERLIN,
Chairman, Subcommittee on Consumer Protection and Finance, Interstate and Foreign Commerce Committee, U.S. House of Representatives, Washington, D.C.

DEAR MR. CHAIRMAN: I understand that your Committee is currently considering H.R. 1272 and related bills, which would establish a nationwide system of no-fault motor vehicle insurance.

The Transportation Association of America (TAA) has adopted a policy in support of such a system, provided that it does not discriminate among vehicles on the basis of size, weight, operating characteristics or other grounds. TAA therefore supports these bills provided that the legislation does not incorporate any such discriminatory provisions.

The Transportation Association of America is a national non-profit organization whose members include not only carriers of all modes of transportation, but also users of the services of those carriers and investors in the transportation industry. TAA is the forum wherein the divergent views of these various interests may be reconciled on issues of major transportation importance for the good of the industry as a whole. A list of the Board of Directors is enclosed for your information.

We are concerned that the various versions of no-fault legislation that have thus far received consideration by the Congress, including the present bill pending before your Committee, either explicitly or implicitly permit or encourage discrimination against certain types of vehicles—in particular, against large and heavy commercial trucks and buses. In view of the public discussions and debate that have taken place on this question, as represented in some of the testimony previously submitted before Congress, we are concerned that operators of large and heavy commercial vehicles may be asked to bear a disproportionately large share of damages resulting from highway accidents, through legislative language assigning added tort liability to these—but not other—types of vehicles.

We believe, on the basis of a substantial body of evidence, that such discrimination would be both unfair and unreasonable. We believe, accordingly, that any no-fault legislation approved by your Subcommittee should be drafted so as to specifically preclude the exercise of such discrimination in development of a standardized national no-fault insurance system.

I am attaching for your information a copy of an extensive research study conducted by TAA dealing with the relative propensity of passenger cars and commercial vehicles for causing or culpably contributing to the causes of highway accidents which result in property damage, personal injury or loss of life. We believe that no-fault automotive insurance should not seek to burden any one class of vehicles with added cost of liability unless historical evidence clearly provides a basis for such discrimination. This study, we believe, demonstrates clearly that no such basis for discrimination exists in connection with commercial vehicles as compared with private automobiles. We therefore believe these two types of vehicles, on the basis of the evidence, are entitled to equal treatment under any no-fault insurance system.

Thank you very much for your attention and consideration. I would like to request that this letter and its attachment be made part of the official record on this legislation.

Sincerely,

PAUL J. TIERNEY, *President.*

Enclosure.

TRANSPORTATION ASSOCIATION OF AMERICA

WHOSE FAULT UNDER NO-FAULT?

Should any one class of Americans bear an unequal share of the economic burden under no-fault automotive insurance?

Only—and this is the only fair answer—if those individuals are also responsible for an unequal share of the economic damage resulting from highway accidents. After all, the purpose of no-fault insurance is to correct the ills of the present system, not cause new ones.

Nevertheless, present proposals for federal no-fault legislation, as well as many existing state laws, discriminate severely against the operators of commercial vehicles. If anything, trucks and buses are responsible for *less* than their proportionate share of accident-related economic damage; yet the operators of these vehicles would be forced to pay *more* than their proportionate share of the national highway insurance bill.

This is a matter for serious national concern. America depends on its national transportation system. Virtually all goods and products consumed in the United States receive truck transportation at some stage. A substantial segment of the population rides local or long-distance buses. Americans have a major stake in the transportation system.

If the operators of these vehicles must pay unfairly high costs for their insurance, it is inevitable that at least some of these costs will have to be "passed through" to their customers. That could mean higher freight rates, which will eventually be translated into higher consumer prices. It could mean higher passenger fares.

In the end, almost every American would in one way or another be victimized by the inequitable burden of this type of discriminatory no-fault insurance.

How does this discrimination work?

Basically, no-fault insurance is intended to eliminate the problems of our present approach to highway insurance by making everyone pay for his own damage, no matter who's at fault in a particular accident. If your car and another person's are in an accident, your insurance company pays to repair your car (and, up to a point, pays for any injuries to your car's occupants), and the other person's insurance company likewise pays his damages.

Thus, no-fault laws specifically prohibit "reallocation" of the economic burden among insurers based on who was at fault. Even if the other person was clearly and unquestionably at fault, your insurance company can't claim reimbursement from him or his insurer.

But, although the laws, both present (state) and proposed (federal), prevent re-allocation on the basis of fault, they do *not* prevent re-allocation on some other basis. Some laws specifically encourage insurers to re-allocate on grounds such as different vehicle size and weight; other laws simply allow this without specifically mentioning it.

In practice, here's what this means when, for example, a car and a truck are involved in an accident. The truck's insurance company (or, since many commercial carriers are self-insured, the truck operator himself) must pay for all damage to the truck and injuries to its occupants; that's normal under no-fault. But then he must *also* pay for part of the damage to the car and injuries to *its* occupants. And it doesn't matter whether the car or truck was at fault; either way, the truck operator still must pay the lion's share of the costs.

For example, a truck driver could park his vehicle and walk away, only to find when he came back that a car had run into his parked truck—and he, the trucker, would be automatically responsible for paying part of the cost of repairing the car, as well as the cost of fixing his own truck. In effect, no-fault insurance under these conditions would pre-judge the truck or bus operator's responsibility in every highway accident, no matter what the facts were.

Despite obvious inequities on a case-by-case basis, this approach to no-fault might at least be defensible if commercial vehicles were responsible for a disproportionately high percentage of accident-caused damage. Under the present law in most jurisdictions, the party at fault in an accident pays all the damages, both his own and the other pary's. If experience showed, for instance, that truck and bus operators were most frequently at fault in car/truck accidents—and consequently usually paid the damages—no-fault re-allocation could be justified as simply "averaging out" this result.[1]

But that's not the case. Data compiled by such impartial and reputable organizations as the U.S. Department of Transportation and the National Technical Information Service, among others, prove:

> In car/truck accidents, trucks are at fault in at most 47.6 percent—less than half.

> The more serious the accident, the less probable it is that the truck was at fault.

> Overall, trucks and buses are considered better actuarial risks by insurance companies than are private cars. They pay lower premiums, and are responsible for lower insurance pay-outs.

The most statistically broad information concerning car/truck highway accidents is available in data collected by the Department of Transportation covering

---

[1] This is just what those who support this approach to no-fault do claim. For example, the following is quoted from the so-called UMVARA (Uniform Motor Vehicle Accident Reparations Act) draft prepared under the auspices of the National Conference of Commissioners on Uniform State Laws (NCCUSL), Nov. 1, 1972, pp. 77–78:

"Under the tort liability insurance system, ordinarily the payment to an occupant of a car . . . arising from a car/truck collision, is made by the liability insurer carrying coverage on the truck. . . . [I]t has been estimated that over 90 percent of the total payment by liability insurers and self-insurers on claims for injuries sustained in car/truck collisions is paid by liability insurers for trucks, or by self-insuring truck lines, and less than 10 percent by liability insureirs for cars. Whether or not this estimate is correct, it is clear that the fraction of these costs now borne by truckers is very great, and that borne by car owners very small."

As shown herein, this is simply contrary to the established facts. The NCCUSL submitted no factual evidence in support of its statement, and NCCUSL members describe it as merely an "extrapolation" made without specific factual basis.

the period 1969–72.[2] A total of 87,265 car/truck accidents are categorized in this data according to what the Department considers the "proximate cause" of the accident; these accidents involved 49,531 personal injuries, and 3,780 deaths.

Although the Department does not specifically identify which vehicle was considered "at fault" in any particular accident, it is possible to make reasonable assumptions about the question of fault from the proximate-cause information reported by the DOT. For example, if one vehicle is reported as having side-swiped another, or as having struck another headon in the opposite lane of traffic, it is reasonable to infer that the first vehicle was probably at fault in the accident.[3]

Based on this information, the DOT reports indicate that trucks might be considered at fault in, *at most*, 47.6 percent of the accidents. The data further indicates that more serious accidents (i.e., those which involved personal injury or death) were less frequently the presumed fault of the truck. At a maximum, only 41.6 percent of the personal injuries, and 24.1 percent of the deaths, might be said to have resulted from accidents in which the truck was at fault.[4]

Since, under present law in most jurisdictions, the party at fault pays the damages, this clearly indicates that commercial vehicle operators are not presently responsible for any disproportionate share of accident-related damages. There is, thus, no experiential basis for legislation which would make them liable for a disproportionate share of damages under a no-fault system.

This result is confirmed by a smaller study performed by the Department of Safety of the American Trucking Associations, Inc. Disregarding the question of fault, the survey sought to determine who actually paid damages in 4,504 accidents involving trucks and private cars.

The truck operators reported that they paid the damages in about 55 percent of the cases. This figure, although slightly higher than might be expected based on the DOT accident data, is close enough to confirm the view that there is no basis in experience for major economic discrimination under no-fault insurance systems.[5] Further, there are complicating factors which tend to force truck operators to pay damages in more instances than might normally result if fault alone were the question:

> In many instances trucking companies will pay accident-related claims even when they believe they are not legally liable, rather than bear the high costs of litigating the question. (Significantly, one major goal of no-fault insurance is to eliminate this costly aspect of the fault-based system, which frequently forces accident victims to accept injustice because it is too expensive to fight for justice.)
>
> Both insurance and transportation experts acknowledge that a significant bias exists against transportation companies, so that juries tend to resolve any doubts against the carriers. Knowing this, truck and bus operators will sometimes accept unfavorable out-of-court settlements rather than risk a jury trial in disputed cases, too.

The purpose of no-fault insurance is to help remove such inequities and prejudices from the highway accident question—not to institutionalize them as part of the system itself. Discriminatory no-fault laws would simply perpetuate inequities, not remedy them.

The insurance industry is perhaps best situated to judge whether commercial vehicles or private cars are better risks. If experience showed that operators of commercial vehicles paid a disproportionate share of the damages in highway accidents, this would inevitably be reflected in insurance statistics.

Yet, on a vehicle-mile basis (i.e., the number of miles traveled by each vehicle), insurance premiums are lower for commercial vehicles than for private cars. And insurance companies pay out less in claims on commercial vehicle policies than on private auto policies.[6]

Thus, from every available source of information, the facts indicate clearly that there is *no reasonable basis* for discrimination against commercial vehicles in no-fault insurance systems.

---

[2] In 1973 the DOT changed its data compilation methods, introducing a number of reporting errors which make it impossible to use more recent figures.
[3] For study purposes, where any doubt existed as to which vehicle was at fault, that doubt was resolved in favor of the private car. Thus, any questionable accident category was always presumed the fault of the truck.
[4] A detailed presentation of the DOT accident statistics is in app. I.
[5] See the specific figures in app. II.
[6] See the specific information set forth in app. III.

No-fault insurance should be, if it is to achieve the purposes for which it is intended, truly no-fault in character. Once unjust discrimination is allowed to creep in, the essential fairness so necessary to any highway insurance system is destroyed. And the result will be, not a better system, but a worse one—to the ultimate disadvantage of the U.S. transportation system, of the nation, and of its citizens.

APPENDIX I

AUTO/TRUCK ACCIDENTS PRESUMED RESPONSIBILITY OF THE TRUCK

	Killed	Injured	Total accidents
1969:			
Total	966	12,194	19,244
Number presumed responsibility of truck	216	5,196	9,244
Percentage presumed responsibility of truck	22.4	42.6	47.9
1970:			
Total	930	11,700	20,167
Number presumed responsibility of truck	198	4,789	9,569
Percentage presumed responsibility of truck	21.3	40.9	47.4
1971:			
Total	931	12,459	22,578
Number presumed responsibility of truck	259	5,209	10,722
Percentage presumed responsibility of truck	27.8	41.8	47.5
1972:			
Total	953	13,178	25,276
Number presumed responsibility of truck	238	5,428	12,035
Percentage presumed responsibility of truck	25.0	41.2	47.6
Cumulative 1969–72:			
Total	3,780	49,531	87,265
Number presumed responsibility of truck	911	20,622	41,550
Percentage presumed responsibility of truck	24.1	41.6	47.6

EMPIRICAL BREAKDOWN OF TRUCK/AUTO ACCIDENTS BY CATEGORY, 1969-72

	1969			1970			1971			1972		
	Killed	Injured	Number	Killed	Injured	Number	Killed	Injured	Number	Killed	Injured	Number
Backing truck into auto	1	120	677	4	88	795	3	113	944	2	143	1,255
Backing auto into truck	5	44	159	4	45	153	2	54	190	2	57	207
Head-on, truck left of center	20	81	73	14	77	50	20	74	56	17	47	51
Head-on, auto left of center	166	520	474	129	337	312	159	441	437	136	363	400
Rear end, truck into auto	43	2,428	3,079	46	2,198	3,028	37	2,294	3,378	33	2,044	2,908
Rear end, auto into truck	134	2,017	2,628	121	1,754	2,414	115	1,854	2,721	105	1,574	2,406
Passing, truck into auto	18	406	960	13	304	761	64	1,029	2,821	67	1,496	3,554
Passing, auto into truck	51	625	1,305	22	531	1,137	78	1,277	2,846	104	1,615	3,867
Sideswipe opposite direction by truck	7	152	388	19	330	1,032	7	115	248	20	92	126
Sideswipe opposite direction by auto	43	370	569	42	597	1,186	45	251	454	66	312	460
Skid, truck into auto	23	275	464	15	277	426	11	245	401	15	294	498
Skid, auto into truck	39	423	725	29	311	612	19	352	625	17	333	629
Intersection, truck into auto	22	525	722	20	467	607	53	459	618	34	336	543
Intersection, auto into truck	199	1,345	1,832	148	1,449	1,994	73	1,013	1,470	90	946	1,388
Stop in traffic, auto into truck	6	44	86	1	32	45	11	354	508	15	627	786
Stop in traffic, truck into auto	1	59	78	5	48	80	14	210	285	9	206	361
Controlled railroad crossing	0	1	3			2	0	0	0	0	1	1
Uncontrolled railroad crossing				1	1	2	0	0	1	0	0	0
Left turn, truck into auto	14	271	621	0	164	450	10	258	569	14	333	949
Right turn, truck into auto	1	184	919	6	130	906	0	160	863	0	213	1,348
Rollaway, truck into auto	2	4	25	1	6	23	1	0	35	1	6	48
Rollaway, auto into truck	1	6	23	0	2	25	0	5	32	0	3	24
Truck pushed or towed	0	2	2	0	4	2	0	4	1	1	0	0
Cargo shift on truck	0	10	28	0	0	14	0	0	8	0	3	7
Other	59	633	1,120	55	640	1,331	38	206	418	19	143	290
U-turn, truck into auto	5	45	65	0	55	62	41	41	76	9	71	96
Adverse vehicle out of control	124	821	996	173	1,039	1,376	111	903	1,229	105	1,202	1,648
Right turn, auto into truck	2	58	159	1	56	155	0	67	180	1	60	219
Left turn, auto into truck	19	334	482	23	338	498	12	220	407	21	254	502
Auto pulled in front of truck	42	391	582	39	420	691	46	459	757	52	404	705
Total	966	12,194	19,244	930	11,700	20,167	931	12,459	22,578	953	13,178	25,276

Source: Reports of Bureau of Motor Carrier Safety, U.S. Department of Transportation, entitled "Accidents of Large Motor Carriers of Property" ("large motor carriers" being defined as those with annual operating revenues of $300,000 or more) for the years 1969, 1970, 1971, and 1972.

Categories of accidents shown by Department of Transportation

Category	Presumed responsibility [1]
Backing truck into auto	Truck.
Backing auto into truck	Auto.
Head-on, truck left of center	Truck.
Head-on, auto left of center	Auto.
Rear-end, truck into auto	Truck.
Rear-end, auto into truck	Auto.
Passing, truck into auto	Truck.
Passing, auto into truck	Auto.
Side-swipe opposite direction by truck	Truck.
Side-swipe opposite direction by auto	Auto.
Skid, truck into auto	Truck.
Skid, auto into truck	Auto.
Intersection, truck into auto	Truck.
Intersection, auto into truck	Auto.
Stop in traffic, auto into truck	Do.
Stop in traffic, truck into auto	Truck.[3]
Controlled railroad crossing [2]	Truck.
Uncontrolled railroad crossing [2]	Do.
Left turn, truck into auto	Truck.
Right turn, truck into auto	Do.
Roll-away, truck into auto	Do.
Roll-away, auto into truck	Auto.
Truck pushed or towed	Truck.[2]
Cargo shift on truck	Truck.
Other	Truck.[4]
U-turn, truck into auto	Truck.
Adverse vehicle [5] out of control	Auto.
Right turn, auto into truck	Do.
Left turn, auto into truck	Do.
Auto pulled in front of truck	Do.

[1] Based on consultation with officials of DOT's Bureau of Motor Carrier Safety. It is recognized that the DOT accident categories are concerned with what took place, rather than with affixing blame or responsibility. However, in the normal event the vehicle which struck the other vehicle, or which otherwise experienced some abnormality in operation leading to the accident, would be regarded as the vehicle most responsible for having caused the accident. It may reasonably be anticipated that any deviations from this norm will, over the 87,265 accidents reviewed, even out; thus, any such variances may be disregarded without distortion to the overall statistics.

[2] The category of "controlled railroad crossing" was shown only for the years 1969, 1971 and 1972; the category of "uncontrolled railroad crossing" was shown only for the years 1970, 1971 and 1972.

[3] In several cases where it was difficult to base a presumption of responsibility on the DOT category description, an arbitrary assumption was made to affix responsibility to the truck, thus avoiding any responsibility of weighting the statistics in favor of the truck.

[4] In the statistical studies, it has been presumed that all accidents falling in the category "other" resulted from the fault of the truck operator. In all likelihood, this is not correct; the statistics are thus somewhat weighted against the truck.

[5] "Adverse vehicle" is defined by DOT personnel as the vehicle *other than* the truck— i.e., as here pertinent, the auto. Therefore, for purposes of this study, the category "adverse vehicle out of control" is concerned only with accidents arising when the automobile was out of control.

APPENDIX II

18-CARRIER STUDY OF CLAIMS PAYOUTS RELATIVE TO TRUCK/AUTO HIGHWAY ACCIDENTS UNDER TORT LIABILITY SYSTEM—1973

	Total number [1]	Percentage [1]
Total number of accidents involving a collision between your truck and a passenger car	4,504	
Total number of car-truck accidents resulting in fatalities and/or injuries	569	
(a) Number of above accidents paid by your fleet	312	55.61
(b) Number of above accidents paid by other parties	249	44.39
Total number of car-truck accidents involving property damage only	3,935	
(a) Number of above accidents paid by your fleet	2,104	54.78
(b) Number of above accidents paid by other parties	1,737	45.22

[1] In some instances litigation was still pending, or for some other reason settlement had not yet been made, at the time the questionnaires were completed. Therefore, number of accidents "paid" do not include all accidents which occurred. Percentages are drawn based solely on settled claims, disregarding all cases in which settlement has not yet been made.

Note: Data presented in this study derived from questionnaires transmitted by the Department of Safety of the American Trucking Associations, Inc., to national and regional officers of the ATA's Council of Safety Supervisors and members of the Council's Insurance Committee. Responses were received from 18 carriers, with aggregate 1973 operating revenues of $1,232,153,661. Data are presented below using the precise wording of the questionnaires transmitted to the carrier.

APPENDIX III

NATIONWIDE ACTUARIAL EXPERIENCE OF HIGHWAY ACCIDENT LIABILITY, 1973

[In millions]

	Private cars	Commercial vehicles
Vehicle-miles operated [1]	1,034,600	[2] 273,400
Insurance premiums paid [3]	$9,354	$2,260
Insurance losses [3]	$5,784	$1,505
Insurance premiums per vehicle-mile (cents)	0.904	0.827
Insurance losses per vehicle-mile (cents)	0.559	0.550

[1] Source: National Technical Information Service, Springfield, Va.
[2] Aggregate of vehicle-miles operated by property-carrying vehicles (268,200,000,000) and passenger-carrying vehicles (5,200,000,000).
[3] Source: "Best's Executive Data Service," published by A. M. Best & Co., Morristown, N.J.

[Whereupon, at 4:23 p.m., the hearings were adjourned.]

O

Lightning Source UK Ltd.
Milton Keynes UK
UKHW022228081218
333475UK00009B/1164/P